THE INTERNATIONAL LAW OF HUMAN RIGHTS

ADAM McBETH · JUSTINE NOLAN · SIMON RICE

OXFORD
UNIVERSITY PRESS
AUSTRALIA & NEW ZEALAND

OXFORD
UNIVERSITY PRESS

Oxford University Press is a department of the University of Oxford. It furthers the University's objective of excellence in research, scholarship, and education by publishing worldwide. Oxford is a registered trademark of Oxford University Press in the UK and in certain other countries.

Published in Australia by
Oxford University Press
253 Normanby Road, South Melbourne, Victoria 3205, Australia

Published 2011

National Library of Australia Cataloguing-in-Publication entry

Author: McBeth, Adam.

Title: The International Law of Human Rights / Adam McBeth, Justine Nolan, Simon Rice.

ISBN: 9780195568806 (pbk.)

Notes: Includes index.

Subjects: Human rights.

Other Authors/Contributors: Nolan, Justine, Rice, Simon.

Dewey Number: 323

Edited by Valina Rainer
Typeset by diacriTech, Chennai, India
Proofread by Puddingburn Publishing Services
Indexed by Puddingburn Publishing Services
Printed by Sheck Wah Tong Printing Press Ltd

FOREWORD

The Hon Michael Kirby AC CMG
One time Justice of the High Court of Australia

This book concerns a subject of great importance, and much interest, for judges, practising lawyers, law students and citizens. The international law of human rights, once the Cinderella of the law, is suddenly becoming a star. She is on everyone's lips. And it is increasingly becoming impossible to envisage a world of law and legal practice without her.

There are five special features of this book that I especially appreciate and for which I praise the authors.

First, they have written this text in an historical way, tracing the relatively sudden advent of universal human rights law from the moment when the *Charter* of the United Nations was adopted. That event occurred at San Francisco in 1945. It marked the end of the Second World War, the creation of a new world order, the beginning of the conclusion of the era of colonial imperialism and white hegemony and the response of the world community to the shocking revelations of genocide (including the Holocaust) that preceded and followed the end of the conflict. The new order also responded to the frightening danger of nuclear proliferation and its potential for global and existential catastrophe. It was soon after that time that steps were taken to develop the *Universal Declaration of Human Rights*. That instrument was brought into operation by a vote of the General Assembly of the United Nations on 10 December 1948, over which an Australian, and past Justice of the High Court of Australia, Dr H V Evatt, presided. As the authors show, the developments of international human rights law can substantially be traced back to these historic events and to the institutional and doctrinal consequences that have flowed from them. The institutions and the doctrines, as well as the machinery for further development, are accurately and incisively described.

Secondly, the authors recognise that, of its nature, international human rights law is in a constant state of evolution. However, its foundations lies in 'black letter' provisions expressed in the successive declarations, covenants, conventions and treaties that have proliferated since 1945 and that continue to evolve from the 'soft law' that ordinarily precedes the emergence of binding rules of international law. In my experience, the most accomplished and successful human rights lawyers are those who appreciate the need to refine their legal skills and not simply to treat human rights law as aspirational or as comprising moral generalities. This is a new body of *law*. However, it is *law* nonetheless. It is therefore a worthy, and I believe essential, part of the equipment of a contemporary lawyer, especially one facing the prospect of a lifetime's service to the law as it is now shaping up for the future.

Thirdly, the authors describe, fairly I believe, the responses of the traditional common law 'dualist' system to contemporary international human rights law. They reveal the sometimes hostile and occasionally welcoming approach of the judges to the interaction of the domestic and international legal systems. Hostility cannot endure as a permanent approach, simply because of the very rapid and pervasive expansion of international law, including the international law of human rights. In one of the most important decisions of the High Court of Australia, one that re-expressed a basic principle of land law in the context of native title rights in *Mabo v Queensland [No 2]* (1992) 175 CLR 1 at 44, Justice Brennan (for the majority) reached out to a principle of universal human rights law in order to rectify a great legal wrong that the courts and legislatures of Australia had not to that time corrected. Interactions of this kind between conventional approaches to finding and declaring the law and a more modern dialogue between the systems of domestic and international law are bound to expand despite occasional rear-guard resistance by local formalists. A great merit of this book is that it demonstrates how such changes are already happening on many fronts. And it suggests ways in which, in the future, more such changes will happen.

Fourthly, the 'snapshots' (as they are called) which appear throughout the book give short and interesting instances of real life decisions and circumstances where international human rights law has been invoked, and sometimes applied with varying success. Through a set of curious chances, I have enjoyed a number of opportunities to witness the creation, application and refinement of international human rights law in practice. This can sometimes leave one with a sense of frustration and even occasionally disillusionment. However, more usually, the result is encouraging, causing optimism as human beings in many countries, despite differing legal, cultural and other traditions, seek to find basic principles that they hold in common, simply because they are human. As a participant in the special procedures of the United Nations human rights machinery, I saw this when I was Special Representative of the Secretary-General for Human Rights in Cambodia. But I also witnessed it as a member of the UNESCO International Bioethics Committee, drafting the *Universal Declaration on Bioethics and Human Rights* (2005). And currently, I can see the same forces at work in the activities of the UNDP Global Commission on HIV and the Law. Human beings increasingly realise the need to work together and to seek common ground in the practical challenges to universal human rights. By their 'snapshots', the authors illustrate instances, local and international, where this is actually happening.

Fifthly, the authors look to the future. They make it clear that the institutions which they describe, and the doctrines that they analyse will continue to evolve and to enter entirely new fields that will need to be included in later editions of this work. For example, I have no doubt that, in future editions there will be added chapters in Part 6 on 'Vulnerable People' for whom the international law of human rights already has important lessons to teach. One such category that might now or soon be added is *data subjects*, drawing on the OECD *Guidelines on Protection of Privacy and Transborder Data Flows*, in which I was involved in 1978–80. In the world of the internet, of social networks, of Wikileaks, and attempted censorship and regulation, the data profiles of human beings will assume an importance that could scarcely have been imagined back in the 1970s. Another 'vulnerable' group of people are the *sexual minorities* such as homosexuals, bisexuals, transsexuals, intersex and 'queer' people. Already in the decision of the Human Rights Committee in *Toonen v Australia* (1994) 1 *Int Hum Rts Reports* 97 and in the *Jogjakarta Principles*, relevant rules of international law have begun to emerge.

The continued oppression of sexual minorities, which is such a special feature of countries that derive their domestic legal systems from Britain, should secure attention in the next edition of this book. Relevant legal changes, including international developments in human rights law, are happening apace. So that category should not be omitted. Likewise, perhaps, should the category of people living with HIV and AIDS (PLWHAs) upon whom international human rights law has begun to have a voice. Nor should the debates concerning *endemic poverty* as a serious human rights issue (and one akin to the slavery of earlier times) be neglected, about which Professor Thomas Pogge has written so powerfully. And just around the corner are entirely fresh developments that may not be human rights as such, but may require a re-conceptualisation of the integrated field of rights in the world. I refer here to the needs for protection of the biosphere to nourish and safeguard all the species that depend upon it for their existence. And the growing debates about animal welfare and rights that surfaced recently in Australia with the shocking television images of cruelty to sentient animals from Australia in slaughter houses beyond our shores to which those animals had been shipped, placing them outside the humane protection of our laws. As human beings reflect upon moral questions, they will increasingly recognise their duties to other creatures that feel joy, pain and fear, as we ourselves do. All of which is simply to demonstrate that the subject matters of this book continue to expand and to change quite radically.

The debates for the present and the future are, in part, moral and philosophical in character. But they also have a hard edge when the conscience of humanity produces legal norms and institutions that give effect to them: both in domestic law and in international law. This is a most exciting time in which to be observing the important changes that are happening in the fields of law described in this book. Little could Herbert Vere Evatt have imagined the growth, speed and commonality with which the *Universal Declaration of Human Rights* would expand in the six decades that followed his pronouncement in 1948 that the global community had started the journey that is now described in this book. At that moment, Evatt observed that this was:

> [T]he first occasion on which the organised community of nations had made a declaration of human rights and fundamental freedoms. That document was backed by the body of opinion of the United Nations as a whole and millions of people, men, women and children all over the world, would turn to it for help, guidance and inspiration. (UN *General Assembly Record*, 10 December 1948, 934).

As human beings, we can share a measure of satisfaction over to the achievements that are recorded by the authors. Yet much remains to be done. And the most important challenges for humanity and its precious environment still lie ahead.

Michael Kirby
Sydney
1 October 2011

CONTENTS

TABLE OF CASES

TABLE OF STATUTES

Western Australia

International

Canada

India

Philippines

Republic of Congo

Slovenia

South Korea

Uganda

Zambia

Zimbabwe

ACRONYMS

AAA	American Anthropological Association
AALCO	Asian-African Legal Consultative Committee
ACAN	Australian Corporate Accountability Network
ACFTU	All China Federation of Trade Unions
ACHPR	African Charter on Human and People's Rights
ACHR	American Convention on Human Rights
ACOSS	Australian Council of Social Service
ACSJC	Australian Catholic Social Justice Council
ACT	Australian Capital Territory
ADA	*Age Discrimination Act 2004* (Cth)
AFP	Australian Federal Police
AHRC	Australian Human Rights Commission
AI	Amnesty International
AICHR	ASEAN Intergovernmental Commission on Human Rights
ALRC	Australian Law Reform Commission
ANC	African National Congress [South Africa]
ANCP	Australian National Contact Point (*for the OECD Guidelines for Multinational Enterprises*); *see also* NCP
APEC	Asia-Pacific Economic Cooperation Council
ASEAN	Association of South-East Asian Nations
ASIO	Australian Secret Intelligence Organisation
ATCA	*Alien Tort Claims Act* 1789 (US)
AU	African Union
BCE	before Christian era
BPFA	Beijing Platform for Action [*from* Fourth UN Conference on Women's Human Rights, Beijing, 1995]
BONGO	business-organised NGO
CANZUS Group	Canada, Australia, New Zealand and the United States
CAT	Convention Against Torture and Other Cruel, Inhuman or Degrading Treatment or Punishment
CE	Christian era
CEACR	ILO Committee of Experts on the Application of Conventions and Recommendations
CEDAW	Convention on the Elimination of All Forms of Discrimination against Women
CEO	Chief Executive Officer
CERD	UN Committee on the Elimination of All Forms of Racial Discrimination

CESCR	UN Committee on Economic, Social and Cultural Rights
CFA	ILO Committee on Freedom of Association
CIDSE	Coopération Internationale pour le Développement et la Solidarité
CoNGO	Conference of NGOs in Consultative Relationship with the United Nations
CRC	UN Committee on the Rights of the Child
CROC	Convention on the Rights of the Child
CROC-OPAC	*See* OP-CRC-AC
CROC-OPSC	*See* OP-CRC-SC
CRPD	Convention on the Rights of Persons with Disabilities
CRPD Committee	UN Committee on the Rights of Persons with Disabilities
CRPD-OP	*See* OP-CRPD
CSO	civil society organisation
CSO-Net	Civil Society Network [web portal of DESA]
CSW	UN Commission on the Status of Women
DAW	UN Division for the Advancement of Women (replaced by UN Entity for Gender Equality and the Empowerment of Women *aka* UN Women)
DDA	*Disability Discrimination Act 1992* (Cth)
DESA	UN Department of Economic and Social Affairs
DPCS Act	*Drugs, Poisons and Controlled Substances Act 1981* (Vic)
DPSP	Directive Principles of State Policy [India]
DRC	Democratic Republic of the Congo
DPRK	Democratic People's Republic of Korea [North Korea]
ECA	UN Economic Commission of Africa
ECCC	Extraordinary Chambers in the Courts of Cambodia
ECHR	European Convention on Human Rights; *aka* European Convention for the Protection of Human Rights and Fundamental Freedoms
ECJ	European Court of Justice
ECOSOC	UN Economic and Social Council
EOWA	Equal Opportunity for Women in the Workplace Agency [Australia]
ESC	economic, social and cultural
ESCAP	UN Economic and Social Commission for Asia and the Pacific
ESCR	economic, social and cultural rights
ESCR-Net	International Network for Economic, Social & Cultural Rights
EU	European Union
FAO	UN Food and Agricultural Organisation
FIDH	International Federation for Human Rights
FLA	Fair Labor Association [US]
FPLC	Forces patriotique pour la libération du Congo
GAPWUZ	General Agricultural and Plantation Workers' Union (*an affiliate union of ZCTU, which see*) [Zimbabwe]
GONGO	government operated NGO
G3ict	Global Initiative for Inclusive Information and Communication Technologies (*an initiative of* UN-GAID)

HRA	*Human Rights Act 2004* (ACT)
HRC	UN Human Rights Committee
HREOC	Human Rights and Equal Opportunity Commission (*replaced by* AHRC)
ICC	International Criminal Court
ICCPR	International Covenant on Civil and Political Rights
ICCPR-OP1	(First) Optional Protocol to the International Covenant on Civil and Political Rights (to establish a complaint mechanism for individuals)
ICCPR-OP2	Second Optional Protocol to the International Covenant on Civil and Political Rights (Aiming at the abolition of the Death Penalty)
ICERD	International Convention on the Elimination of All Forms of Racial Discrimination
ICESCR	International Covenant on Economic, Social and Cultural Rights
ICESCR-OP	Optional Protocol of the International Covenant on Economic, Social and Cultural Rights (to establish a complaint mechanism for individuals and groups)
ICHRP	International Council on Human Rights Policy
ICJ	International Court of Justice
ICPED	International Convention for the Protection of All Persons from Enforced Disappearance
ICRC	International Committee of the Red Cross
ICRMW	International Convention on the Protection of the Rights of All Migrant Workers and Members of Their Families
ICSID	International Centre for Settlement of Investment Disputes
iCSO	integrated Civil Society Organizations System [within the NGO Branch of UN Department of Economics and Social Affairs]
ICTR	International Criminal Tribunal for Rwanda
ICTY	International Criminal Tribunal for the Former Yugoslavia
IDPs	internally displaced persons
IFAD	International Fund for Agricultural Development
IFRC	International Federation of the Red Cross and Red Crescent Societies
IGO	intergovernmental organisation
ILC	International Labour Conference
ILO	International Labour Organisation
ILO MNE Declaration	ILO Tripartite Declaration of Principles Concerning Multinational Enterprises and Social Policy
ILRF	International Labor Rights Fund [United States]
IMT	International Military Tribunal (*aka* Nuremberg Tribunal)
INGO	international non-governmental organisation
INSTRAW	International Research and Training Institute for the Advancement of Women (*replaced by* UN Entity for Gender Equality and the Empowerment of Women *aka* UN Women)
IOE	International Organisation of Employers
IOM	International Organization for Migration
IPEC	International Programme on the Elimination of Child Labour
JSCOT	Joint Standing Committee on Treaties [Australia]
LICADHO	Cambodian League for the Promotion and Defense of Human Rights

LRA	The Lord's Resistance Army [Uganda]
MDG	Millennium Development Goals
MNE	multinational enterprise
MONUC	UN Organisation Mission in the Democratic Republic of the Congo
NAP	national (human rights) action plan
NATO	North Atlantic Treaty Organisation
NCP	National Contact Point (*for the OECD Guidelines for Multinational Enterprises*)
NGO	non-governmental organisation
NHRI	national human rights institution
NIA	National Interest Analysis [Australia]
NT	Northern Territory [Australia]
NTER	Northern Territory Emergency Response
OAS	Organization of American States
OAU	Organisation of African Unity (*now replaced* by AU)
OECD	Organisation for Economic Cooperation and Development
OHCHR	Office of the UN High Commissioner for Human Rights
OIC	Organisation of the Islamic Conference
OP-CAT	Optional Protocol to the Convention against Torture and Other Cruel, Inhuman or Degrading Treatment or Punishment (to establish a Subcommittee on Prevention of Torture and Other Cruel, Inhuman or Degrading Treatment, to conduct regular inspections of places of detention)
OP-CEDAW	Optional Protocol to the Convention on the Elimination of All Forms of Discrimination against Women (to establish a complaint mechanism for individuals)
OP-CRC-AC	Optional Protocol to the Convention on the Rights of the Child on the involvement of children in armed conflict
OP-CRC-SC	Optional Protocol to the Convention on the Rights of the Child on the sale of children, child prostitution and child pornography
OP-CRPD	Optional Protocol to the Convention on the Rights of Persons with Disabilities (to establish a complaint mechanism for individuals and groups)
OP-ICESCR	Optional Protocol to the International Covenant on Economic, Social and Cultural Rights
OSAGI	Office of the Special Adviser on Gender Issues and Advancement of Women (*replaced by* UN Entity for Gender Equality and the Empowerment of Women *aka* UN Women)
PCIJ	Permanent Court of International Justice
PIF	Pacific Islands Forum
POSA	Public Order and Security Act [Zimbabwe]
QUANGO	quasi-NGO
RAID	Rights and Accountability in Development (UK NGO)
RDA	*Racial Discrimination Act 1975* (Cth)

RQD	Refugee Qualification Directive [European Union]
SAARC	South Asian Association on Regional Cooperation
SDA	*Sex Discrimination Act 1984* (Cth)
SIS	Security Intelligence Service [New Zealand]
SPT	UN Subcommittee on Prevention of Torture and other Cruel, Inhuman or Degrading Treatment or Punishment
TAC	Treatment Action Campaign
TNC	transnational corporation
UDHR	Universal Declaration of Human Rights
UN	United Nations
UN ESCOR	UN Economic and Social Council Official Records
UN GAOR	UN General Assembly Official Records
UN SCOR	UN Security Council Official Records
UN Women	UN Entity for Gender Equality and the Empowerment of Women
UNCHR	UN Commission on Human Rights
UNCTAD	UN Conference on Trade and Development
UNDG	UN Development Group
UNDP	UN Development Programme
UNDPI	UN Department of Public Information
UNESCO	UN Educational, Scientific and Cultural Organization
UN-GAID	UN Global Alliance for ICT and Development
UNHCR	UN High Commission for Refugees
UNICEF	UN Children's Fund (*formerly* UN International Children's Emergency Fund)
UNIFEM	UN Development Fund for Women (*replaced by* UN Entity for Gender Equality and the Empowerment of Women *aka* UN Women)
UN-NGLS	UN Non-Governmental Liaison Service
UN-NGO-IRENE	UN-sponsored NGO Informal Regional Network
UNPFII	UN Permanent Forum on Indigenous Issues
UNRWA	UN Relief and Works Agency for Palestine Refugees in the Near East
UPC	Union of Congolese Patriots
UPR	Universal Periodic Review
WANGO	World Association of Non-Governmental Organisations
WGIP	Working Group on Indigenous Populations
WHO	World Health Organisation
WPA	World Programme of Action concerning Disabled Persons
WTO	World Trade Organization
ZCTU	Zimbabwe Congress of Trade Unions

PREFACE

Each of the authors has worked in and taught human rights law over many years. We have been lawyers, advocates, campaigners, commentators, trainers, writers and teachers. In doing this we have adapted materials on human rights law to a wide range of purposes, and have gained a good understanding of the central issues in the philosophy and practice of human rights law. This understanding has informed us in writing a book that explains the fundamentals of human rights law in a coherent and connected way, and examines some of the difficult and challenging contemporary issues.

Dealing with human rights law, in discussion or in practice, means dealing with both its origins and its explication in international and regional forums. International documents, institutions and jurisprudence have established, and continue to explore, a new understanding of humanity, premised on a fundamental commitment to peace through respect. This commitment is detailed in a chain of instruments which starts with the Charter of the United Nations and the Universal Declaration of Human Rights, and continues today with the possibility of, for example, a treaty to recognise the human rights of the world's indigenous peoples.

Although the idea of human rights is not dependent on these international instruments, the existence of international human rights law is. The practical enjoyment of human rights, and the enforcement of reciprocal responsibilities, are dependent on the terms and operation of the institutions of human rights law, which in turn gain their legitimacy from agreement among states, both internationally and regionally. As a result, we have structured the book on the premise that human rights law is what is found in the Universal Declaration of Human Rights, the consequent covenants and conventions, and the related jurisprudence. Our positivist approach to human rights law is conscious, and follows from the positivism of the international law regime. It has, for example, led to our illustrating many aspects of international human rights with 'snapshots' of current practice and issues.

The book is in two related sections. First, Parts 1 to 4 describe in detail the system of international human rights law—internationally, in regions, and in Australia. In the context of that account, Parts 5–7 then focus on current issues in human rights, with particular attention to dealing with human rights abuses, the situation of vulnerable and marginalised people, and contemporary challenges to human rights law.

In Part 1 we introduce human rights law by reference to the developments in international cooperation after the Second World War, and we describe the history of rights discourse which informed the 20th century formulation of human rights. Part 2 provides a detailed account of those rights, following an established but debatable distinction between civil and political rights on the one hand, and economic, social and cultural rights on the other. In Part 3 we give an account of the international system for protection and promotion of human rights, principally through the United Nations, as well as through regional arrangements and the activity of non-government organisations. In Part 4 we give an account of the arrangements in Australia for complying with and implementing international human rights law, and of Australia's attitude to its human rights treaty obligations.

Part 5 focuses on initiatives to achieve a system of accountability for gross violations of human rights, from the Nuremberg trials to the International Criminal Court, and discusses the role and operation international humanitarian law. In outlining the human rights of vulnerable and marginalised people in Part 6, we have concentrated on the situation of children, indigenous peoples, people with disabilities, refugees, women and workers. Finally, in Part 7, we give an overview of some of the contemporary challenges for the international human rights regime posed by terrorism, transnational corporations, and the place of extra-territorial obligations and non-state actors.

It is our hope that the book's narrative arc—from origins to current issues—will give readers a sound understanding of the story of international human rights, a story not yet 70 years old. At the same time, the book's seven parts, divided into 20 chapters, will enable readers to use the book as a reference on particular topics.

We have found writing this book to be difficult and rewarding. Difficult because we have, at the same time, been busy with teaching, administration and research as academics, and with the lives of our young families. Rewarding because we have shared each other's support, enthusiasm and knowledge, and have had the support and counsel of our colleagues, friends and families. Adam particularly wishes to thank Belinda, Jamie, Xavier and Micah, who only arrived during the editing phase of this book, for their support and accommodation. Justine is thankful for the unwavering support of Mike, Jack, Lucy and Sara. Simon is forever grateful to Elizabeth, and Michael, Emily, Daniel and Nicholas, for their patience and understanding.

We did not write this book alone. We were encouraged and guided by our editors at Oxford University Press, Katie Ridsdale and Michelle Head. Lynne Spender and John Warburton were meticulous editorial assistants at different stages. Our respective law schools gave us time and funds to research and write, and our colleagues gave us advice, direction and encouragement. We received invaluable research assistance on different topics from Zoe Adams-Lau, James Anderson, Clare Brennan, Ji-Shen Loong, Jessica Roth and Sephora Sultana. We are grateful to our colleagues Andrew Byrnes, Andrea Durbach, Beth Goldblatt, Sarah Joseph, Andrew Lynch, Chris Michealsen, Kerry Murphy, Tania Penovic, and Molly Townes O'Brien for their comments and suggestions, and to officers in a number of non-government organisations and Commonwealth, State and Territory agencies for information and assistance.

Developments in human rights law can be rapid or glacial, but there is always a treaty or a case or a report pending. The text reflects our best knowledge of the state of affairs as at 30 June 2011, with reference as well to the Australian High Court cases of *Plaintiff M70* and *Momcilovic*.

Adam McBeth, Senior Lecturer, and Deputy Director of the Castan Centre for Human Rights Law in the Faculty of Law at Monash University.

Justine Nolan, Senior Lecturer, and Deputy Director of the Australian Human Rights Centre in the Faculty of Law at the University of New South Wales.

Simon Rice, OAM, Associate Professor, and Director of Law Reform and Social Justice in the ANU College of Law at Australian National University.

September 2011

ACKNOWLEDGMENTS

The author and the publisher wish to thank the copyright holders for permission to reproduce their material. Every effort has been made to trace the original source of copyright material contained in this book. The publisher would be pleased to hear from copyright holders to rectify any errors or omissions.

PART ONE

INTRODUCING HUMAN RIGHTS

1 THE INTERNATIONAL BILL OF HUMAN RIGHTS

CONTENTS

1.1 INTRODUCTION

Three United Nations (UN) documents—the *Universal Declaration of Human Rights* (UDHR), the *International Covenant on Civil and Political Rights* (ICCPR) and the *International Covenant on Economic, Social and Cultural Rights* (ICESCR)—are commonly referred to as the International Bill of Rights, and are seen as constituting the definitive contemporary statement of human rights.[1] Those documents, supplemented by others such as treaties, comments and views,[2] set out the rights, freedoms and responsibilities which together comprise 'human rights law', but they offer only a limited explanation of what, conceptually, human rights are.

Anyone working with human rights must be able to explain the idea of a 'human right', beyond merely relying on the fact that such rights are set out in the UN documents. A clear understanding of the conceptual basis for human rights is necessary to defend the claim that human rights have universal value, or to assert that human rights can take priority over other rights, or to explain why some claims are not recognised as human rights.

The widespread adoption of the International Bill of Rights by countries of diverse cultures, histories and politics gives a deceptive appearance of substance, suggesting that precisely because they have been so widely recognised, human rights are what they say they are: fundamental, universal and integral to the dignity and worth of the human person.[3] When someone asks—as many do—'*why* are human rights fundamental, universal and integral to the dignity and worth of the human person?' it is not enough to reply, 'because the UN says so'. A defensible answer must be able to explain the rationale that lies behind these claims about human rights.

As is discussed below, the mid-twentieth century articulation of human rights was in response to the inhuman conduct of the immediately preceding years: it did not continue an established tradition of human rights or invoke previously described human rights. Rather, it was a new articulation of an idea which was familiar from centuries of politics, philosophy and religion: the idea that there is an essential moral value in our being human. While the history of contemporary human rights starts with the post-war peace processes of the mid-1940s, that history has been possible only because of a much longer history of ideas of personal freedom and states' obligations.

The focal point of this chapter is the UDHR: what led up to it, how it was formulated, and how it has evolved. As background to the process of formulating contemporary human rights, the chapter outlines the various cultural, political, philosophic and religious sources which were brought together—'institutionalised'[4]—in the Universal Declaration.

1 See the detailed discussion of the *International Covenant on Civil and Political Rights* (ICCPR), opened for signature 16 December 1966, 999 UNTS 171 (entered into force 23 March 1976), in Chapter 3 and the *International Covenant on Economic, Social and Cultural Rights* (ICESCR), opened for signature 16 December 1966, 993 UNTS 3 (entered into force 3 January 1976), in Chapter 4.

2 Discussed in detail in Chapter 7.

3 *Universal Declaration of Human Rights* (UDHR), GA Res 217A (III), UN GAOR, 3rd sess, 183rd mtg, Preamble, UN Doc A/810 (1948).

4 M Ishay, *The History of Human Rights: From Ancient Times to the Globalization Era*, 2nd edn, University of California Press, Berkeley, 2008, Chapter 4.

1.2 BACKGROUND TO THE UNIVERSAL DECLARATION

The contemporary conception of human rights, set out in the the International Bill of Rights, can be traced directly to the political aftermath of the Second World War, in the mid to late 1940s. The Second World War was a major catalyst for reorganisation of the international legal system, perhaps most of all in the area of human rights. The horrors and sheer scale of the war prompted reorganisation of international relations in an attempt to prevent such a world war from ever occurring again, trying to succeed where the League of Nations had failed after the First World War.

1.2.1 From the First to the Second World War

The League of Nations

In the aftermath of the First World War, the League of Nations was established in 1920 as an outcome of the 1919 Paris Peace Conference; Australia was among the 20 founding member countries.[5] Many of the League's activities can be seen in hindsight as important steps towards the new international legal framework of human rights which would emerge after the Second World War.

The League, for example, oversaw distribution of former German colonies, with an approach that was characterised by a sense of duty to accord minimum entitlements to all. The League created a system of mandates under which the former colonies were governed as trust territories, on the principle 'that the well-being and development of such peoples form a sacred trust of civilisation and that securities for the performance of this trust should be embodied in this Covenant'.[6] More broadly, members of the League covenanted to address issues which would now be recognised as human rights concerns, such as securing 'fair and humane conditions of labour', ensuring 'just treatment of the native inhabitants of territories under [members'] control', and supervising traffic in women, children and drugs.[7]

Another contribution of the League of Nations to international responsibility for human rights was a series of bilateral treaties among European states to protect the rights of minorities, including protection of life, liberty and equality before the law. Although they were specific to certain states and formed part of the post-war settlement, these treaties were an important step towards states' accepting that international law can protect human rights within a state, even when to do is to challenge a state's sovereignty:

> For the first time, international law imposed on the sovereign states concerned certain obligations to treat their inhabitants in certain ways—a stark contrast to the 'blank canvas' position [that prevailed before the First World War]. Equally radical for its time was the idea of institutionalized oversight of such obligations,

---

5 On the League of Nations see generally, E Bendiner, *A Time For Angels: The Tragicomic History of the League of Nations*, Knopf, New York, 1975; D S Birn, *The League of Nations Union, 1918–1945*, Clarendon Press, Oxford, 1981.

6 *Covenant of the League of Nations* art 22; see also J F Engers, 'From Sacred Trust to Self-Determination' (1977) 24 *Netherlands International Law Review* 85.

7 *Covenant of the League of Nations* art 23(c). Three other areas were also specified in paragraphs (d)–(f) of that article: trade in arms and ammunition, freedom of communications and commerce, and the prevention and control of disease.

> especially the notion that individuals could petition international organs, potentially challenging the actions of their own national authorities. In this way the treaties started to challenge the orthodox view that individuals simply could not be the subjects of international law.[8]

Despite its respect for the rights of indigenous peoples, the universal aims of the League were compromised at the outset by the refusal of some founding members, including Australia, to include in its Covenant a commitment to non-discrimination on the basis of race; a significant factor in the development of contemporary human rights was the brutal discrimination of people on the basis of race in the Second World War.

The International Labour Organisation

Another outcome of the 1919 Paris Peace Conference was the International Labour Organisation (ILO). In light of the Russian Revolution in 1917, the establishment of the ILO reflected a desire to improve living standards of workers, but perhaps as well a desire to avoid similar anti-bourgeois revolutions elsewhere. Whatever the motivations of the founding member states may have been, the formation of the ILO was significant in the development of international human rights law and, looking ahead to developments later in the 20th century, it emphasised the importance of economic rights such as labour rights to the maintenance of long-term peace and stability.

By ratifying the standards promulgated by the ILO, states agree to subject their sovereignty in the area of labour rights to those standards, not as part of any inter-state bargain, but because it is the right thing to do. The system of ILO conventions was the first comprehensive system in which states assume obligations towards the treatment of their own people, accountable to the international community under international law. The structure of the ILO and some of its key conventions are discussed in more detail in Chapter 17.

1.2.2 The Charter of the United Nations

It is unsurprising that during the Second World War talk of peace was accompanied by a call for formally recognising 'human rights'. The particular feature of the Second World War that galvanised the world to respond in terms that sought not only peace, but respect for 'human rights', was the systematic targeting by the state of minority groups: citizens were humiliated, brutalised and murdered, not as the incidental victims of war, but as explicit state policy. The dehumanising nature of the Holocaust atrocities—which the UDHR later declared 'outraged the conscience of mankind'[9]—was undoubtedly influential in convincing states that a sovereignty-dominated model of international law needed to be reconsidered.

A system in which states were largely free to do as they saw fit within their own territory, as long as they did not violate the interests of other states, could no longer be tolerated now that the potential

8 E Bates, 'History' in D Moeckli, S Shah and S Sivakumaran (eds), *International Human Rights Law*, Oxford University Press, Oxford, 2010, 31.

9 UDHR, see above, n 3.

for human harm had been so shockingly demonstrated. The protection of people against mistreatment by the state became a legitimate concern of international law, even when it concerns a state's intra territorial treatment of its own people. The new thinking was that, if necessary, state sovereignty would need to yield to international standards.

The *UN Charter* was the culmination of a relatively brief and very intense period of negotiation among nation states—principally the world powers at the time—during and at the end of the Second World War, and it was then that the contemporary idea of fundamental and universal human rights was developed.

The Atlantic Charter

It was US President Franklin D Roosevelt who began the wartime momentum towards universal personal freedoms which are now recognised as human rights. In an address to the US Congress on 6 January 1941, Roosevelt stated his vision of a world 'founded upon four essential human freedoms': freedom of speech, freedom to worship, freedom from want and freedom from fear. In his 1944 State of the Union address, Roosevelt took the idea of 'freedom from want' further, proposing an 'Economic Bill of Rights', discussed further in Chapter 4.

In August 1941 Roosevelt met with British Prime Minister Winston Churchill on board British and US naval ships in the Atlantic Ocean to discuss the progress of the war. They issued a statement which gave a preliminary description of their talks and then set out a 'joint declaration' that has since become known as the *Atlantic Charter*.[10]

ATLANTIC CHARTER

The President of the United States of America and the Prime Minister, Mr Churchill, representing His Majesty's Government in the United Kingdom, being met together, deem it right to make known certain common principles in the national policies of their respective countries on which they base their hopes for a better future for the world.

- First, their countries seek no aggrandizement, territorial or other;
- Second, they desire to see no territorial changes that do not accord with the freely expressed wishes of the peoples concerned;
- Third, they respect the right of all peoples to choose the form of government under which they will live; and they wish to see sovereign rights and self government restored to those who have been forcibly deprived of them;
- Fourth, they will endeavour, with due respect for their existing obligations, to further the enjoyment by all States, great or small, victor or vanquished, of access, on equal terms, to the trade and to the raw materials of the world which are needed for their economic prosperity;
- Fifth, they desire to bring about the fullest collaboration between all nations in the economic field with the object of securing, for all, improved labour standards, economic advancement and social security;
- Sixth, after the final destruction of the Nazi tyranny, they hope to see established a peace which will afford to all nations the means of dwelling in safety within their own boundaries, and which will afford assurance that all the men in all the lands may live out their lives in freedom from fear and want;

10 *The Atlantic Charter* (1941), North Atlantic Treaty Organisation <www.nato.int/cps/en/SID-2788FECD-8FACF71E/natolive/official_texts_16912.htm>.

- Seventh, such a peace should enable all men to traverse the high seas and oceans without hindrance;
- Eighth, they believe that all of the nations of the world, for realistic as well as spiritual reasons must come to the abandonment of the use of force. Since no future peace can be maintained if land, sea or air armaments continue to be employed by nations which threaten, or may threaten, aggression outside of their frontiers, they believe, pending the establishment of a wider and permanent system of general security, that the disarmament of such nations is essential. They will likewise aid and encourage all other practicable measures which will lighten for peace-loving peoples the crushing burden of armaments.

The *Atlantic Charter* refers in the sixth point to only two of Roosevelt's four freedoms: freedom from fear and freedom from want. Whether this was due to political negotiations or oversight is not known, but Roosevelt attempted to clear up any confusion over the status of all four freedoms when he reported back to the US Congress: 'the [*Atlantic Charter*] declaration of principles includes of necessity the world need for freedom of religion and freedom of information ... which are a part of the whole freedom for which we strive'.[11] Later the same year, H V (Doc) Evatt 'quoted [the four freedoms] in the Australian Parliament as one of the guiding principles for post-war redevelopment'.[12]

Despite its almost passing reference to human rights, the *Atlantic Charter* exerted remarkable influence: its simple effect was to make human rights a legitimate part of international discussions about peace and post-war institutional arrangements.

Roosevelt referred explicitly to human rights when, on its first anniversary, he promoted the *Atlantic Charter* as a 'common programme of purposes and principles' which 'nations and groups of nations in all the continents of the earth' were united in realising. These nations, he said, had 'faith in life, liberty, independence, and religious freedom, and in the preservation of human rights and justice in their own as well as in other lands'.[13] After Roosevelt's death in April 1945 the idea of 'human rights' was developed and ultimately adopted in the new international organisation, the United Nations, and its documents and institutions.

The *Dumbarton Oaks Proposals*

After the *Atlantic Charter*, important steps were taken towards establishing a basis for the international co-operation which underpinned the formulation of international human rights law.

Between 1941 and 1944, 26 allied nations signed a *Declaration by United Nations* which explicitly evoked the *Atlantic Charter*, and stated the signatories' conviction that victory in the war was 'essential to defend life, liberty, independence and religious freedom, and to preserve human rights and justice in their own lands as well as in other lands'.[14] In October 1943 the USA, Soviet Union, United Kingdom and China signed the *Moscow Declaration on General Security*, in which they recognised

11 R Russell, *A History of the United Nations Charter: The Role of the United States 1940–1945*, The Brookings Institution, Washington, 1958, 41–2, quoting F D Roosevelt, *Public Papers and Addresses of Franklin D Roosevelt; 1941: Call to Battle Stations*, Harper, New York,1950, 334.

12 A Devereux, *Australia and the Birth of the International Bill of Human Rights 1946–1966*, The Federation Press, Sydney, 2005, 14, citing Australia, *Hansard*, House of Representatives, 27 November 1941, 978. Note that at the time of the debate Evatt was Attorney-General and Minister for External Affairs.

13 See above, n 10.

14 *Yearbook of the United Nations 1946–47*, 1.

'the necessity of establishing at the earliest practicable date a general international organisation ... for the maintenance of international peace and security'.[15] At the Bretton Woods (USA) conference of July 1944, 44 allied states planned for post-war global economic relations, resolving to establish the International Monetary Fund (IMF) and the International Bank for Reconstruction and Development (IBRD), which is now part of the World Bank. But it was the Dumbarton Oaks Conversations in 1944 that represented '[t]he first concrete step toward the creation of a general international organisation'.[16]

The Dumbarton Oaks Conversations, which took place in Washington DC, USA between August and October 1944, resulted in the *Dumbarton Oaks Proposals*, in which the USA, the UK, the USSR and China agreed on establishing 'an international organisation under the title of the United Nations'. They agreed that there would be a General Assembly of the organisation which, among many other things, would establish an Economic and Social Council to 'facilitate solutions of international economic, social and other humanitarian problems and promote respect for human rights and fundamental freedoms'.[17]

The last clause, referring to human rights and fundamental freedoms, was the subject of dispute and debate. It was proposed by the USA but was opposed by the UK because of concerns about international intervention in the internal affairs of states, and by the USSR because the proposed organisation was concerned not with human rights but with international security. They agreed with the final wording as it did no more than authorise the promotion of respect for human rights.[18]

Early the following year Roosevelt, Churchill and the Soviet leader Joseph Stalin met at Yalta in Crimea and announced that a conference would be held in San Francisco 'to prepare the charter' of the proposed 'general international organisation'.[19] At the 1945 San Francisco conference—officially the United Nations Conference on International Organisation—the states that had signed the *Declaration by United Nations* were invited, along with non-governmental organisations (NGOs),[20] to meet to finalise the details of the new organisation.

The San Francisco Conference

The San Francisco Conference took place between April and June 1945. The Australian delegation to the San Francisco conference was led by the Deputy Prime Minister, Frank Forde, and H V Evatt, and included one woman, Jessie Street.

15 *Moscow Declaration on General Security* art 4; cf ibid 3.

16 *Dumbarton Oaks Proposals*, Chapter IX, para 1 cited in *Yearbook of the United Nations 1946–47*, 4.

17 See above, n 14, 4.

18 R Russell, see above, n 11, 423–4.

19 See above, n 14, 9.

20 The presence of non-governmental organisations was significant, and led to their being recognised in the UN Charter as integral to addressing and resolving international issues. See generally C J Snider, 'The Influence of Transnational Peace Groups on US Foreign Policy Decision-Makers During the 1930s: Incorporating NGOs into the UN' (2003) 27 (3) *Diplomatic History* 377; the detailed discussion of non-governmental organisations in Chapter 9.

The text of the *Dumbarton Oaks Proposals* was the basis of discussions at the Conference, but NGOs and states other than the major powers called for stronger recognition of human rights in the text.[21] The San Francisco Conference established a number of technical committees to make recommendations on different parts of the text for what would become the *UN Charter*. It was the work of the smaller states and NGOs in these committees[22] that succeeded in including in the Preamble to the Charter a statement that 'reaffirm[s] faith in fundamental human rights, in the dignity and worth of the human person, in the equal rights of men and women and of nations large and small'.

Recommendations from the technical committees[23] resulted in the purpose of the proposed international organisation being revised to include 'international cooperation in the ... promotion and encouragement of respect for human rights and for fundamental freedoms without distinction as to race, language, religion or sex', and the functions and powers of the proposed UN General Assembly being revised to include the power to 'initiate studies and make recommendations ... to assist in the realisation of human rights and basic freedoms for all, without distinction as to race, language, religion or sex.' Similarly, the powers of the proposed Economic and Social Council were extended to include making 'recommendations for promoting respect for human rights and fundamental freedoms'.

These references were inserted, however, only after diplomatic debate about the implications of using different terms such as 'assure', 'protect', 'promote' and 'encourage respect for', and about whether 'cultural' issues included 'educational' issues (it was decided that they did).[24] In article 55 of the *UN Charter*, when describing the UN's role in relation to economic and social cooperation, the reference to human rights is different from, and arguably stronger than, the usual formulation of 'promoting' human rights, saying instead that the UN 'shall promote ... universal respect for, and the observance of, human rights and fundamental freedoms ...'[25]

Russell attributes this wording to a proposal by the Australian delegation,[26] whose principal advocate was H V Evatt; Evatt is credited with significant influence over the terms of the *UN Charter*.[27] Australia was responsible, too, for article 56, in which UN member states 'pledge themselves to take joint and separate action' to achieve the UN's economic and social purposes, including those relating to human rights. The wording reflects 'the Australian Pledge', a demand that the Australian delegation

---

21 The smaller states included Latin American countries, particularly Chile, Cuba and Panama, as well as Australia, New Zealand, India and the Philippines; NGOs included the American Jewish Committee, the World Trade Union Congress, the Provisional World Council of Dominated Nations, the West Indies National Council, the Sino-Korean People's League, the Council of Christians and the National Association of the Advancement of Colored People.

22 M Ishay, see above, n 4, 215.

23 See above, n 14, 14.

24 R Russell, see above, n 11, 780–1.

25 *Charter of the United Nations* art 55(c).

26 R Russell, see above, n 11, 783.

27 See M Dee, 'Dr H V Evatt and the Negotiation of the United Nations Charter' in G Robin (ed) *8e Conférence Internationale des Éditeurs de Documents Diplomatiques: des états et de l'ONU*, Peter Lang, Brussels, 2008, 137; K Buckley, B Dale & W Reynolds, *Doc Evatt: Patriot, Internationalist, Fighter & Scholar*, Longman Cheshire, Melbourne, 1994; A Devereux, see above, n 12, 206–9.

had made for a strong commitment to achieving economic and social goals, which bound a state not only to co-operate internationally but to commit to act domestically.[28]

The *UN Charter* and Human Rights

The *UN Charter* was approved unanimously on 26 June 1945 by the 50 states at the San Francisco Conference, and came into effect on 24 October 1945.[29]

UN CHARTER

WE THE PEOPLES OF THE UNITED NATIONS DETERMINED

to save succeeding generations from the scourge of war, which twice in our lifetime has brought untold sorrow to mankind, and
to reaffirm faith in fundamental human rights, in the dignity and worth of the human person, in the equal rights of men and women and of nations large and small, and
to establish conditions under which justice and respect for the obligations arising from treaties and other sources of international law can be maintained, and
to promote social progress and better standards of life in larger freedom,

AND FOR THESE ENDS

to practise tolerance and live together in peace with one another as good neighbours, and
to unite our strength to maintain international peace and security, and
to ensure by the acceptance of principles and the institution of methods, that armed force shall not be used, save in the common interest, and
to employ international machinery for the promotion of the economic and social advancement of all peoples,

HAVE RESOLVED TO COMBINE OUR EFFORTS TO ACCOMPLISH THESE AIMS

Accordingly, our respective Governments, through representatives assembled in the city of San Francisco, who have exhibited their full powers found to be in good and due form, have agreed to the present Charter of the United Nations and do hereby establish an international organization to be known as the United Nations.

CHAPTER 1

PURPOSES AND PRINCIPLES

ARTICLE 1

The Purposes of the United Nations are:

1 To maintain international peace and security, and to that end: to take effective collective measures for the prevention and removal of threats to the peace, and for the suppression of acts of aggression or other breaches

28 R Russell, see above, n 11, 786–8.

29 See above, n 14, 33.

of the peace, and to bring about by peaceful means, and in conformity with the principles of justice and international law, adjustment or settlement of international disputes or situations which might lead to a breach of the peace;

2 To develop friendly relations among nations based on respect for the principle of equal rights and self-determination of peoples, and to take other appropriate measures to strengthen universal peace;

3 To achieve international cooperation in solving international problems of an economic, social, cultural, or humanitarian character, and in promoting and encouraging respect for human rights and for fundamental freedoms for all without distinction as to race, sex, language, or religion; and

4 To be a centre for harmonizing the actions of nations in the attainment of these common ends.

It is significant that the *Charter of the United Nations* recognises and promotes protection of human rights. Without that base, it is uncertain that the UN would have gone on to develop our contemporary conception of human rights. The phrase 'human rights' appears seven times in the *UN Charter*, usually in the phrase 'human rights and fundamental freedoms' and in terms that assert that such rights are held by 'all', that is, are universal. Beyond these references to human rights, there was an opportunity to include in the *UN Charter* an international statement of rights which had been under development for some years in the US State Department.[30] The US State Department's draft *Declaration of Human Rights* was appended to the draft *UN Charter*, but the inclusion of such a statement was seen as a possible barrier to acceptance of the *UN Charter* itself.[31]

That the *UN Charter* addresses the issue of human rights at all is credited to the NGOs that were present; in the face of opposition by the United Kingdom, the United States and the USSR, it was NGOs' 'persistent pressure [which] led the governments to incorporate the promotion of human rights into the Charter'.[32] Instead, the San Francisco Conference agreed to insert throughout the *UN Charter* reference not only to the UN's promoting respect for human rights and fundamental freedoms, but also to its doing so 'for all without distinction as to race, sex, language, or religion'.[33]

The *UN Charter* today plays a quasi-constitutional role in international law, in part because article 103 of the Charter provides that the Charter obligations of UN member states (membership which today is almost universal) prevail over obligations deriving from any other international agreement. In part it is also due to the character of the Charter as an instrument laying out the framework for the conduct of international relations in the envisaged post-war world order, including not only the mechanics of how such relations would work, but also the purposes that should be served by such interaction.

30 E A Lang, 'The Contribution of the Atlantic Charter to Human Rights Law and Humanitarian Universalism', (1989–90) 26 *Williamette Law Review* 113, 124–8; R Russell, see above, n 11, 323–7.

31 R Russell, see above, n 11, 327–9.

32 Z F K Arat, *Human Rights Worldwide: A Reference Handbook*, ABC-CLIO, Santa Barbara, 2006, 13, citing W Korey, *NGOS and the Universal Declaration of Human Rights: 'A Curious Grapevine'*, St Martin's Press, New York, 1998, 29–41.

33 *Charter of the United Nations* arts 1(3), 13(1)(b), 55(c).

By its terms the *UN Charter* treats human rights as a concept which was pre-existing and understood. The Charter does not purport to create a concept of human rights: the preamble to the Charter speaks of the determination 'to *reaffirm* faith in fundamental human rights',[34] indicating that member states both understood the concept and agreed to subject themselves to its standards as rules of international law.

In a 1948 report to the International Law Association, Hersch Lauterpacht was of the view that the *UN Charter* itself imposed binding human rights obligations on the UN Member States.[35] This view, however, has to be reconciled with the apparently contradictory preservation in the Charter of state sovereignty over domestic matters in article 2(7) of the Charter, which provides:

> Nothing contained in the present Charter shall authorize the United Nations to intervene in matters which are essentially within the domestic jurisdiction of any State or shall require Members to submit such matters to settlement under the present Charter; but this principle shall not prejudice the application of enforcement measures under Chapter VII.

Lauterpacht's explanation is that 'by having been included among the principal purposes of the United Nations and by having become a persistent theme of the Charter, [the question of respect for and observance of human rights and fundamental freedoms] has become one which, far from being essentially within the domestic jurisdiction of States, is essentially of international concern'.[36] He concludes that '[t]he legal character of [the Charter's] authority and obligations is not decisively affected' by article 2(7). He says as well that 'questions bearing upon the respect for and observance of human rights and fundamental freedoms are not 'solely within the domestic jurisdiction of any State' inasmuch as, by virtue of the Charter, they have become matters essentially of international concern', and that article 2(7)

> does not in any case affect the right and the obligation of the United Nations to implement the provisions of the Charter in the matter of human rights and fundamental freedoms by means falling short of intervention as understood in international law. These means include study, enquiry, investigation, and recommendation either of a general character or addressed specifically to individual Members of the United Nations.[37]

Despite the many international human rights agreements which have followed, the Charter's recognition of human rights remains important because of the binding nature of the Charter on all UN member states. The Charter-based authority enables the operation of the many established universal human rights mechanisms, discussed in detail in Chapter 5. Even if a state had not ratified a single human rights treaty (which is not actually the case for any state) it would nevertheless be bound by the general obligation to respect human rights that arises from the *UN Charter*.

---

34 Ibid Preamble, para 2 (emphasis added).

35 H Lauterpacht, *Report to the International Law Association: Human Rights, the Charter of the United Nations and the International Bill of the Rights of Man*, para 6, UN Doc E/CN.4/89 (1948). In 1993 the World Conference on Human Rights *Vienna Declaration and Programme of Action*, GA Res 421(v) pt 1, UN Doc.A/CONF.157/23 (1993), recognised that the UN Charter contained legally binding obligations for states to protect and promote human rights.

36 H Lauterpacht, ibid para 9, UN Doc.A/CONF.157/23.

37 H Lauterpacht, ibid para 16.

1.2.3 The International Military Tribunal at Nuremberg

In August 1945, as the Second World War came to a close and just a few weeks after the signing of the *UN Charter*, the *London Charter of the International Military Tribunal* was concluded by the four major allies—the United Kingdom, United States, France and the USSR. The categories of crime provided for under the *London Charter* were crimes against peace; war crimes; and crimes against humanity.[38] The formation of the Tribunal and its proceedings, as well as subsequent international criminal tribunals, are discussed in detail in Chapter 11.

The creation of an international criminal tribunal was significant in international law because it provided an avenue for the direct accountability of individuals for violations of international law, as opposed to placing responsibility solely on states. For the development of international human rights law, the creation of the category of crimes against humanity ahead of the Nuremberg trials was a significant advance. After the trials it was clear that state conduct causing serious harm to people is the legitimate concern of international law, even when occurring within a state's own borders. The balance between state sovereignty and international concern for the protection of people had shifted irrevocably, and the stage was set for the development of a new statement of the rights of people.

1.3 THE *UNIVERSAL DECLARATION OF HUMAN RIGHTS*

At the time of the *UN Charter*, the term 'human rights' had strong rhetorical power but no clearly defined scope. In light of the state-sanctioned brutality and discrimination in the recent war, a call for human rights was a call generally for respect for minority communities and a constraint on state power. It was in the three years after the *UN Charter* that the UN developed its *Universal Declaration of Human Rights* (UDHR) and gave defined meaning to 'human rights'. The history of our contemporary conception of human rights is primarily the history of the development of the UDHR in the period 1945–48.

1.3.1 Drafting by the UN Commission on Human Rights

The signatories to the *UN Charter* in 1945 agreed to interim arrangements that established a Preparatory Commission of the United Nations, the Executive Committee of which recommended that the Economic and Social Council (ECOSOC) establish a Commission on Human Rights at its first meeting.[39] Under article 68 of the *UN Charter*, which empowered the UN to set up 'commissions in economic and social fields and for the promotion of human rights', ECOSOC established a Commission on Human Rights at its first session in 1946. The Commission, at its first meeting in February 1947, immediately set about drafting what it called an International Bill of Rights.[40]

38 *London Agreement* (1945), Annex, art 6.

39 See above, n 14, 38.

40 E A Lang, see above, n 30, 141.

The Drafting Committee

The Commission appointed a drafting committee, initially comprising Eleanor Roosevelt, wife of the President of the USA and the only woman on the committee; Habib Charles Malik, a Lebanese philosopher and diplomat; and Peng-Chun Chang, a diplomat, writer and philosopher representing the Chinese Nationalist Government.[41] The committee was later expanded to include Colonel William Hodgson, an Australian soldier and diplomat; Hernán Santa Cruz, a Chilean judge; René Cassin, a French judge; Alexander Bogomolov, a Russian diplomat; English civil servant Geoffrey Wilson and Charles Dukes, an English trade unionist; and John Humphrey, a Canadian lawyer.[42]

There is no doubt that the horrors of the Second World War loomed large in the minds of the drafting committee. Geoffrey Wilson is reported to have said at the first session of the drafting committee that 'Germany and other enemy countries during the war had completely ignored what mankind had regarded as fundamental human rights and freedoms.'[43] The committee met, he said, 'as a first step toward providing the maximum possible safeguard against that sort of thing in the future.'[44]

The committee delegated the task of drafting a declaration to John Humphrey, director of the Human Rights Division of the UN Secretariat. The drafting committee was divided on the approach to take in formulating human rights. Humphrey wrote that, 'Chang and Malik were too far apart in their philosophical approaches to be able to work together on text';[45] Malik, a devout Christian, took a natural law approach while Chang was a pragmatist and pluralist, opposed to basing human rights on natural law.[46] During March 1947 Humphrey worked on a draft declaration, based primarily on the 20 or so drafts that had been submitted; he later wrote that 'with two exceptions, all these texts came from English-speaking sources, and all of [those texts] came from the Democratic West'.[47]

The Humphrey-Cassin Draft

Humphrey's draft, which set the course of contemporary human rights, was a carefully constructed and pragmatic attempt to reconcile a range of different approaches, principally, as he said himself, 'to combine humanitarian liberalism with social democracy'.[48] It was referred by the drafting committee to a working group

41 Chang's presence was 'repeatedly protested' by the USSR, who supported the communists who would come to take power in China in 1949. A Devereux, see above, n 12, 17.

42 See, eg, *The Universal Declaration of Human Rights: An Historical Record of the Drafting Process*, United Nations <http://www.un.org/Depts/dhl/udhr/members_eroos.shtml>; Celebrating Eleanor Roosevelt & the Universal Declaration of Human Rights, United Nations <http://www.erooseveltudhr.org/index.php?option=com_content&task=view&id=23&Itemid=80>.

43 J Morsink, *The Universal Declaration of Human Rights: Origins, Drafting and Intent*, University of Pennsylvania Press, Philadelphia, 1999, 36, quoting G Wilson from the record of the first session of the UDHR Drafting Committee of the Commission on Human Rights, UN Doc E/CN.4/AC.1/SR.7 (1947).

44 Ibid.

45 J Humphrey cited in A Danilovic, *Pragmatism, Philosophy and International Politics: The UNESCO Committee on the Philosophic Principles of the Rights of Man and the Drafting of the Universal Declaration of Human Rights* (Masters Thesis, University of British Columbia, 2002, 9 <http://hdl.handle.net/2429/12439>.

46 Ibid.

47 Ibid 11.

48 Ibid 19.

made up of Malik, Cassin and Wilson, and it was Cassin who took on the task of redrafting the text 'in light of the Committee's discussions' and proposing 'a logical re-arrangement of the articles'.[49] Cassin's redraft relied substantially on Humphrey's but gave it a new structure and an explicit philosophy.

The structure of Cassin's draft had the symbolism of classical architecture, built on four pillars: dignity, liberty, equality and brotherhood. Cassin subsequently said that 'for learning purposes, the structure of human rights can be visualised as a temple (or Asian pagoda, or African meeting hut) founded on four pillars'.[50] Ishay describes the design, which was maintained in the final declaration, in this way:

> [A] first pillar, constructed out of the first two articles [of the Declaration], stands for human dignity, which is shared by all peoples regardless of race, religion, creed, nationality, social origin, or sex; a second pillar, composed of articles 3–19 of the declaration, invokes the first generation of civil liberties and other rights that were fought for during the Enlightenment; a third pillar, consisting of articles 20–26, addresses the second generation of rights, those related to political, social and economic equity and championed during the industrial revolution; the fourth, representing articles 27–28, focuses on the third generation of rights, those associated with communal and national solidarity and advocated during the late nineteenth century and early twentieth century and throughout the post-colonial era.[51]

Cassin saw the three remaining articles, 28-30, as the 'pediment of the temple', which are 'harmonising provisions designed to hold the structure together and calling upon governments to make arrangements in support of human rights'.[52]

The explicit philosophical basis that Cassin gave to human rights was human dignity, discussed in greater detail below at Chapter 2.4. For example, the terms of article 1 of the final Declaration—'*All human beings are born free and equal in dignity and rights. They … should act towards one another in a spirit of brotherhood*'—essentially reflects Cassin's draft, which read: 'All men, being members of one family, are free, possess equal dignity and rights, and shall regard each other as brothers'.[53]

Humphrey and Cassin shared a view that acceptance of declared human rights as a new international norm would require very careful phrasing, but they differed in their approach. Humphrey aimed for a straightforward statement of what human rights are, avoiding what he thought would be distracting references to philosophical justifications that would invite dispute. In taking this approach Humphrey showed both his diplomatic pragmatism and a positivist legal philosophy where the authoritatively stated word was itself 'law', without the need for reference to an external rationale.

49 Ibid 19–20.

50 R Cassin, 'Historique de la Déclaration Universelle de 1948' in *La Pensée et l'Action*, Centre Nationale de la Recherche Scientifique, Paris, 1981, 109–21, 114, quoted in R P Claude & B H Weston, *Human Rights in the World Community: Issues and Action*, 2nd edn, University of Pennsylvania Press, Philadelphia, 1992, 62.

51 See above, n 4, 3–4.

52 R P Claude & B H Weston, *Human Rights in the World Community: Issues and Action*, 2nd edn, University of Pennsylvania Press, Philadelphia, 1992, 162.

53 M A Glendon, *A World Made New: Eleanor Roosevelt and the Universal Declaration of Human Rights*, Random House, New York, 2001, cited in A Danilovic, above, n 45.

Cassin, on the other hand, felt it was necessary not only to declare a norm, but to offer a reason for it beyond the authority of the declaration. Mindful of the political need to negotiate wide acceptance of a declaration, Cassin's 'dignitarian' philosophy[54] was a 'synthesis [that] was bringing something new into the world', one which avoided 'the extremes of [both] capitalist individualism and socialist collectivism'.[55]

The UNESCO Survey

In March 1947, while Humphrey was involved in his drafting, the United Nations Educational, Scientific and Cultural Organization (UNESCO) surveyed about 150 'individual thinkers', asking them for a 'statement on the subject [of human rights] or a particular aspect of it'.[56] The UNESCO Committee on the Philosophic Principles of the Rights of Man which oversaw the survey comprised principally 'intellectuals from the Western Democracies because of their proximity to UNESCO headquarters in Paris ... [and] on the basis that consistency of philosophy was required if agreement on a coherent solution to the philosophical problems in issue was to be achieved expeditiously'.[57]

The UNESCO Committee 'decided that its task was to explore the philosophic bases of human rights for the purpose of clarifying grounds of possible agreement underlying divergent philosophical approaches and ... facilitating the removal of differences due to the variety of possible philosophic interpretations'.[58] It was not actually the case, as Ishay claims, that the modern conception of human rights 'look[ed] to all the world's great religions and cultures for ... universal notions of the common good'.[59] Rather, the Committee drew together those arguments that would 'secure agreement concerning fundamental human rights',[60] and those arguments were from the Western philosophical tradition.

54 A Danilovic, see above, n 45.

55 M A Glendon, see above, n 53, 22.

56 *Memorandum on Human Rights*, UN Doc UNESCO/Phil./1/1947 (1947) quoted in A Danilovic, above, n 45.

57 A Danilovic, see above, n 45, 24. Huxley is quoted as saying 'all of them should be from Western Europe as the matter is urgent'.

58 *Report of the Meeting of the UNESCO Committee on the Philosophic Principles of the Rights of Man*, p 1, UN Doc UNESCO/Phil./9/1947 (1947).

59 See above, n 4, 17.

60 *The Grounds of an International Declaration of Human Rights: Report of the UNESCO Committee on the Philosophic Principles of the Rights of Man to the Commission on Human Rights of the United Nations*, UN Doc UNESCO/Phil./10/1947 (1947) quoted in A Danilovic, above, n 45.

Many of the survey replies rejected the possibility of synthesising philosophical views. A socialist perspective, expressed not only by a Russian expert but also by Western socialists, insisted that achieving human rights was impossible under liberal capitalism; at the same time liberal democratic experts rejected the possibility of reconciling a natural law approach of inalienable rights with a historical view that rights accrue according to class and power.[61]

One of the survey respondents, Jacques Maritain, anticipated this impasse. He thought 'it would be possible to establish a common formulation of ... the different rights recognised as pertaining to the human being in his personal and social existence', but that it 'it would be quite hopeless to look for a *rational justification* ... of those rights'.[62] He proposed leaving 'on one side as far as possible ... pre-occupation with theoretical justifications', and proceeding[63]

> by consultation and co-operation between representatives of the different schools of thought and ways of civilisation into which men today are grouped, who should first of all be asked, each in turn, to formulate the articles of a Declaration of rights, as each conceives it. The practical conclusions of the disciples of Locke, Rousseau or Tom Paine, Roman Catholicism, Marx-Leninism, Humanitarian Socialism, Existentialism, Rationalism, Greek orthodoxy, Calvinism, Ghandism, Confucianism, etc, would thus be formulated (without their ideological context). They would then be compared with each other, and the formulae would be recast and perfected by common effort, so as to make them acceptable to all as embodying a practical convergence of views, whatever the differences of theoretical perspectives.
>
> I think that ... we could thus arrive at a new and enlarged Declaration of the Rights of Man ... In particular, the conception which holds the field of classic individualism, of human rights and liberties as being concerned with man's personal destiny, and the conception which holds the field of Marxist perspectives, of his rights and liberties as being involved in the historical mission of the communities to which he belongs, would as the [memorandum prepared by the Philosophy Sub-Section of UNESCO] rightly suggests, end by completing and co-ordinating with each other—within ... the sphere of practical assertions and conclusions formulated in the articles of the Charter ... But I do not think it is reasonable to hope for more than this practical convergence. If a reconciliation of theories and an ideological synthesis are to be aimed at, this could only come about as a result of vast philosophical labour of investigation and purification which would involve superior institutions, a new process of systematisation and the radical criticism of a large number of errors—a labour which ... would remain one doctrine among many accepted by some and rejected by others, and could not claim to establish, in actual fact, universal ascendency over men's minds.

The UNESCO Committee's final report, *The Grounds of an International Declaration of Human Rights*,[64] observed that '[t]he history of the philosophic discussion of human rights, of the dignity and

61 UNESCO (ed), *Human Rights: Comments and Interpretation*, Alan Wingate, London, 1949, cited in A Danilovic, above, n 45.

62 *Communication with Regard to the Draft World Declaration on the Rights of Man*, 1, UN Doc UNESCO /Phil./5/1947 (1947), <http://unesdoc.unesco.org/images/0012/001243/124341eb.pdf> (emphasis original).

63 Ibid 2.

64 *The Grounds of an International Declaration of Human Rights: Report of the UNESCO Committee on the Philosophic Principles of the Rights of Man to the Commission on Human Rights of the United Nations*, UN Doc UNESCO/ Phil./10/1947 (1947), <http://unesdoc.unesco.org/images/0012/001243/124350eb.pdf>.

brotherhood of man, and of his common citizenship in the great society is long; it extends beyond the narrow limits of the western tradition, and its beginnings in the West as well as in the East coincide with the beginnings of philosophy'.[65] Reflecting Maritain's view, the Committee avoided trying to reconcile those philosophies, and in fact avoided even giving an account of them. Instead it relied on the various ways those philosophies had been implemented, the practical realisation of the theorised rights, to justify its identification of contemporary human rights.

An international declaration of human rights was seen as 'a foundation for convictions universally shared by men, however great the difference of the circumstances and their manner of formulating human rights'.[66] The UNESCO Committee was 'convinced that the philosophic problem involved in a declaration of human rights is not to achieve doctrinal consensus but rather to achieve agreement concerning rights ... which may be justified on highly divergent doctrinal grounds.'[67] The Committee's intention was 'not to set up an intellectual structure to reduce [the theories] to a single formulation, but rather to discover the intellectual means to secure agreement concerning fundamental rights and to remove difficulties in their implementation such as might stem from intellectual differences'.[68]

1.3.2 The Final Draft of the UDHR

The UN Commission on Human Rights was immediately highly critical of the UNESCO Committee's report,[69] although it seems that the report's 'feasible and practicable' approach to human rights did influence the Commission's formulation of the final Declaration.[70] The UN Commission on Human Rights, ostensibly basing its work on the Humphrey-Cassin document produced by the drafting committee, completed the declaration and unanimously adopted it.[71] The Commission then reported the draft to the Economic and Social Council, which transmitted it to the UN General Assembly. The UN General Assembly referred it to the Third Committee which, at 81 meetings between September and December 1948,[72] considered

65 Ibid 2.

66 Ibid 1.

67 Ibid 4.

68 Ibid 5.

69 *Commission of Human Rights*, UN Doc E/CN.4/SR.26 cited in A Danilovic, above, n 45.

70 Danilovic offers various examples of how the Commission's own debates were resolved by reference to the pragmatic approach of the UNESCO Committee's report, A Danilovic, see above, n 45, 44–7. See also J Morsink, see above, n 43, 318.

71 A Trindade, *Universal Declaration of Human Rights: Paris, 10 December 1948* (2008) United Nations, Audovisual Library of International Law <http://untreaty.un.org/cod/avl/ha/udhr/udhr.html>.

72 Ibid.

168 resolutions for amendments to the draft. The Third Committee finally adopted the draft Declaration by a vote of 29 to none, with seven abstentions, and reported to the UN General Assembly.

The Text of the UDHR

Resolution 217 (III), 'International Bill of Human Rights', was adopted by the UN General Assembly on 10 December 1948, by a vote of 48 to none, with 8 abstentions.[73] Australian H V Evatt, who was President of the UN General Assembly at the time, welcomed the Declaration as a 'step forward in a great evolutionary process'.[74]

UNIVERSAL DECLARATION OF HUMAN RIGHTS

PREAMBLE

Whereas recognition of the inherent dignity and of the equal and inalienable rights of all members of the human family is the foundation of freedom, justice and peace in the world,

Whereas disregard and contempt for human rights have resulted in barbarous acts which have outraged the conscience of mankind, and the advent of a world in which human beings shall enjoy freedom of speech and belief and freedom from fear and want has been proclaimed as the highest aspiration of the common people,

Whereas it is essential, if man is not to be compelled to have recourse, as a last resort, to rebellion against tyranny and oppression, that human rights should be protected by the rule of law,

Whereas it is essential to promote the development of friendly relations between nations,

Whereas the peoples of the United Nations have in the Charter reaffirmed their faith in fundamental human rights, in the dignity and worth of the human person and in the equal rights of men and women and have determined to promote social progress and better standards of life in larger freedom,

Whereas Member States have pledged themselves to achieve, in co-operation with the United Nations, the promotion of universal respect for and observance of human rights and fundamental freedoms,

Whereas a common understanding of these rights and freedoms is of the greatest importance for the full realization of this pledge,

Now, Therefore THE GENERAL ASSEMBLY proclaims THIS UNIVERSAL DECLARATION OF HUMAN RIGHTS as a common standard of achievement for all peoples and all nations, to the end that every individual and every organ of society, keeping this Declaration constantly in mind, shall strive by teaching and education to promote respect for these rights and freedoms and by progressive measures, national and international, to secure their universal and effective recognition and observance, both among the peoples of Member States themselves and among the peoples of territories under their jurisdiction.

---

73 UDHR, see above, n 3.

74 A Devereux, see above, n 12, 1, quoting the UN text quoted in N Harper & D Sissons, *Australia and the United Nations*, Manhattan Publishing Co, New York, 1955, 289.

After the Preamble, the UDHR sets out 30 articles which enumerate substantive rights. Article 1 declares that 'All human beings are born free and equal in dignity and rights. They are endowed with reason and conscience and should act towards one another in a spirit of brotherhood.' Article 2 then declares that everyone is entitled to all the rights set out in the Declaration 'without distinction of any kind such as race, colour, sex, language, religion, political or other opinion, national or social origin, property, birth or other status ... [or] on the basis of the political, jurisdictional or international status of the country or territory to which a person belongs'. The list of substantive rights then follows:

Article 3	Right to life, liberty and security of person
Article 4	Freedom from slavery and servitude
Article 5	Freedom from torture and cruel, inhuman or degrading treatment or punishment
Article 6	Right to recognition as a person before the law
Article 7	Freedom from discrimination under law
Article 8	Right to effective remedy for violation of human rights
Article 9	Freedom from arbitrary arrest, detention or exile
Article 10	Right to a fair trial
Article 11	Presumption of innocence and prohibition on retroactive criminal law
Article 12	Right to privacy
Article 13	Freedom of movement and the right to leave any country and return to one's own country
Article 14	Right to asylum
Article 15	Right to a nationality
Article 16	Right to marry and found a family, including equal rights in marriage, and to protection of the family.
Article 17	Right to own property
Article 18	Freedom of thought, conscience and religion
Article 19	Freedom of opinion and expression
Article 20	Freedom of assembly and association
Article 21	Right to political participation
Article 22	Right to social security
Article 23	Right to work, fair conditions of work and the right to join a trade union
Article 24	Right to rest and leisure
Article 25	Right to an adequate standard of living including rights to food, clothing, housing, medical care, social services and social security and special protection for mothers and children
Article 26	Right to education
Article 27	Right to participate in cultural life, and balance between public benefit and authors' rights of intellectual property.

Articles 28–30 stipulate the right to a society and community in which these individual rights are to be enjoyed, and set out corresponding duties to the community, and permissible limitations on the rights.

The UDHR was not intended to be binding, but rather to provide the standards against which the obligations contained elsewhere could be applied. The 30 substantive articles in the UDHR both expand on the human rights provisions of the *UN Charter* and the customary international law which preceded it, and pave the way for the binding human rights treaties that were to follow. In Morsink's view, '[t]he fact that the Declaration is itself not intertwined with any piece of ... machinery of implementation gave it from the start an independent moral status in world affairs and law'.[75]

A Convergence of Perspectives

The UDHR was a statement of new principle which asserted universally held truths without necessarily being tied to a particular philosophical source: 'a composite synthesis, the like of which has never before occurred in history ... While fully allowing for man's material requirements and for his duties to society, the balance in the present synthesis is decidedly in favour of man's inner freedom, and his natural and inalienable rights.'[76]

Although the UDHR was a new statement of human rights, it represented Maritain's 'practical convergence of views, whatever the differences of theoretical perspectives'. The two principal theoretical perspectives which converged to become the practical synthesis of the UDHR follow from the two principal Western political traditions that informed the post-war formulation of human rights. One was a liberal tradition, whose history is traced back through centuries of European politics and philosophy, and whose essential feature is the recognition and defence of the rights of an individual against the oppressive exercise of state power; these are the rights called 'civil and political rights'. The other was a socialist tradition, whose history is in the struggle of organised labour against capital, and which recognises the right of a community to the protection of the state, rights called 'economic, social and cultural rights'.

In the second half of the twentieth century, these two groups of rights were set up in contrast with each other, a consequence of the extensive political and military hostility between democratic and socialist states. But at the time of the post-war formulation of human rights, these two groups of rights were seen as together forming the whole of the collection of human rights. Although the dominant Western liberal powers more readily recognised civil and political rights, and the powerful Western socialist powers promoted economic, social and cultural rights, there was strong sympathy for the latter group of rights from some western liberal states.

As is described in more detail in Chapter 2, there had been statements of the 'rights of man' well before the UDHR. The novel claim made for such rights in the UDHR and the documents and debates that preceded it was that those rights were enjoyed equally, by all, regardless of race, language, religion or sex. Both this claim to universality and the philosophical basis of human rights remain

75 J Morsink, see above, n 43, 20.

76 H C Malik, *The Challenge of Human Rights: Charles Malik and the Universal Declaration*, Charles Malik Foundation and Centre for Lebanese Studies, Oxford, 2000, 132, quoted in A Danilovic, above, n 45.

contested. A positive characterisation of this genesis of contemporary human rights is that they are 'the result of a cumulative historical process that takes on a life of its own, *sui generis*, beyond the speeches and writing of progressive thinkers, beyond the documents and main events that compose a particular epoch'.[77]

There are many ways of explaining the claim for universality, and whether some or any of them are accepted is a matter of preference and belief. There was no single or comprehensive philosophical basis for human rights at the time they were articulated in the 1940s—their formulation was an avowedly pragmatic exercise, drawing on different philosophies. Whether and how human rights can be given philosophical coherency is a continuing debate.

The Legal Status of the UDHR

As a UN General Assembly resolution, the UDHR is not, prima facie, legally binding. However, if it could be considered a restatement of customary international law in whole or part, or an elaboration on the obligations set out in the *UN Charter*, its terms would be considered legally binding.

At the time it was adopted by the UN General Assembly, Eleanor Roosevelt, then the chair of the UN Commission on Human Rights, famously proclaimed that the UDHR 'is not a treaty; it is not an international agreement. It is not and does not purport to be a statement of law or of legal obligation. It is a declaration of basic principles of human rights and freedoms ... to serve as a common standard of achievement for all peoples of all nations.'[78]

René Cassin did, however, insist that the UDHR would be 'an authoritative interpretation of the Charter of the United Nations,' even though it would not directly have 'coercive legal force.'[79] Indeed, Sohn relies on Cassin in concluding that not only the UDHR, but also subsequent treaties such as the *Convention on the Elimination of All Forms of Racial Discrimination*, constitute a restatement and refinement of the principles contained in the *UN Charter*.[80]

Egon Schwelb, who was the Deputy Director of the UN Division of Human Rights when the UDHR was drafted, has said that it 'would have been a rather daring statement to assert then [in 1948] that the Declaration was a legally binding instrument.'[81] He observed, however, that at the time he was writing, in 1963, states were treating the UDHR as legally binding, despite its origins as a declaration of the UN General Assembly and the mixed intentions of its drafters. He notes that it was 'used as a yardstick to

77 M Ishay, see above, n 4, 2.

78 H Hannum, 'The Status of the Universal Declaration of Human Rights in National and International Law' (1995) 25 *Georgia Journal of International and Comparative Law*, 287, 318.

79 R Cassin at the deliberations of the third session of the Commission of Human Rights in May–June 1948, quoted in J Morsink, above, n 43, 295.

80 L Sohn, 'The Human Rights Law of the Charter' (1977) 12 *Texas International Law Journal*, 12; L Sohn, 'The New International Law: Protection of the Rights of Individuals Rather than States' (1982) 32 *American University Law Review* 1, 16.

81 E Schwelb, *Human Rights and the International Community: The Roots and Growth of the Universal Declaration of Human Rights 1948–1963*, Quadrangle Books, Chicago, 1964, 36–7.

measure the compliance by Governments with the international standards of human rights.'[82] He cites as examples the invocation of the UDHR by the UN General Assembly in 1949 in its response to a complaint about the Soviet Union's preventing Soviet wives and children of foreign nationals from leaving the country, and its response to incidents involving Tibet, southwest Africa, forced labour and 'customs and practices inconsistent with the physical integrity and dignity of women.'[83]

Schwelb observes that by 1960 the *Declaration on the Granting of Independence to Colonial Countries and Peoples* indicated that the binding nature of the UDHR was taken for granted,[84] as it provided that '[a]ll states shall observe faithfully and strictly the provisions of the *Charter of the United Nations*, the Universal Declaration of Human Rights and the present Declaration.'[85] Noting the same approach in the ILO *Abolition of Forced Labour Convention of 1957*, which invokes 'the rights of man referred to in the Charter of the United Nations and enunciated by the Universal Declaration of Human Rights,'[86] Schwelb concludes that as at 1963, 'it can no longer be maintained, whatever the position may have been in 1948, that the Declaration has 'only moral force".[87]

In a comprehensive survey of scholarly opinion, national and international judicial decisions and government pronouncements on the legal status of the UDHR,[88] Hannum points to a consensus that, 'under whatever list of criteria one adopts, the Universal Declaration constitutes at least significant evidence of customary international law,'[89] although he notes the difficulties of applying traditional criteria for identifying norms of customary international law to a human rights instrument which is focused on human rights rather than on reciprocal state obligations. The opinions Hannum canvassed run the spectrum, from the entire UDHR's constituting norms of *jus cogens*[90] to its having no more than moral force, with an intermediate position that some or all of its norms are customary norms.

Simma and Alston reject the characterisation of the UDHR as customary international law on the ground that the prerequisite of consistent state practice is not evident for many of the rights it sets out.[91] Indeed, evidence of states acting in violation of the human rights set out in the

82 Ibid 38.

83 Ibid 38–9.

84 Ibid 37–8.

85 *Declaration on the Granting of Independence to Colonial Countries and Peoples*, GA Res 1514 (XV), UN GAOR, 15th sess, supp no 16, art 7, UN Doc A/4684 (1961).

86 *Convention Concerning the Abolition of Forced Labour* (ILO Convention 105), opened for signature 25 June 1957, 320 UNTS 291, (entered into force 17 January, 1959) Preamble, para 6.

87 See above, n 81, 47.

88 See above, n 78, 287.

89 See above, n 78, 322.

90 A norm of *jus cogens* is a peremptory norm of international law 'accepted and recognized by the international community of States as a whole as a norm from which no derogation is permitted and which can be modified only by a subsequent norm of general international law having the same character': *Vienna Convention on the Law of Treaties* (1969) art 53.

91 B Simma & P Alston, 'The Sources of Human Rights Law: Custom, *Jus Cogens*, and General Principles' (1992) 12 *Australian Yearbook of International Law*, 82, 96–100.

UDHR—thereby evidencing a lack of customary status—is all too easy to come by. However, their alternative characterisation of the rights in the UDHR as 'general principles of law recognized by civilized nations,'[92] within the meaning of the Statute of the International Court of Justice,[93] still leads to the result that the UDHR constitutes a source of binding international law.

Today, the UDHR is clearly treated by states, international institutions and NGOs with a degree of reverence that belies its legal origins as a UN General Assembly resolution. For example, the Human Rights Council's Universal Periodic Review of the human rights performance of states, discussed in detail in Chapter 6, requires states to report not only against the human rights obligations they have consented to by ratifying treaties, but also against those contained in both the *UN Charter* and the UDHR. States clearly treat the UDHR as the source of standards with which they need to comply, whatever the legal theory for invoking it might be.

1.4 THE INTERNATIONAL COVENANTS

1.4.1 The Debate over Categorising Rights

The legally binding treaties that were intended to follow the UDHR—detailing the list of declared human rights into obligations for states—were not as quick to eventuate as originally hoped. The delay was due in large part to the significant and continuing debate about the differences—if any—between political rights on the one hand and economic, social and cultural rights on the other.

As is detailed in Chapter 3, the rights that are generally designated civil or political rights protect a broad range of aspects of life. Generally speaking, they tend to be directed towards the protection of the physical integrity of a person (such as the right to life and freedom from torture), a person's characteristics or beliefs (including non-discrimination, freedom of speech, freedom of religion) and the equal protection of individuals under the law (including freedom from arbitrary arrest and detention and the right to a fair trial). The 'physical integrity' nature of these rights can be contrasted with economic, social and cultural rights, described in Chapter 4, which address mainly a person's standard of living and economic well-being, including the rights to health, education and labour rights. Of course, there is considerable overlap between many of these rights, and there are many other ways one could categorise them. Indeed, this is one reason why the stark division between civil and political rights on the one hand and economic, social and cultural rights on the other is artificial.

Although the UN has maintained the rhetoric of the 'interdependence and indivisibility'[94] of all rights, as the following account shows, recognition of and accountability for human rights have tended to favour civil and political rights over economic, social and cultural rights. Violations of the former set are treated as both justiciable and capable of immediate enforcement, while violations of the latter are more often viewed as social injustices rather than rights violations.

92 Ibid 104.

93 *Statute of the International Court of Justice*, art 38(1)(c).

94 World Conference on Human Rights, *Vienna Declaration and Programme of Action*, GA Res 421(v) pt 1, para 5, UN Doc.A/CONF.157/23 (1993).

1.4.2 Drafting the International Covenants

After the adoption by the UN of the UDHR in 1948, the UN Commission on Human Rights had the task of drafting a treaty that would detail the human rights that had been declared. The drafting of these treaties was slow, partly because of a decision by the Commission to split the rights into two separate covenants which would be developed and presented to the UN General Assembly simultaneously.[95] Eide explains:

> Underlying this decision were several assumptions, not all of them well founded. It was argued and subsequently often repeated that the two sets of rights were of a different nature and therefore needed different instruments. Civil and political rights were considered to be 'absolute' and 'immediate', whereas economic, social and cultural rights were held to be programmatic, to be realized gradually, and therefore not a matter of rights. A related assumption was that civil and political rights were 'justiciable' in the sense that they could easily be applied by courts and similar judicial bodies, whereas economic, social and cultural rights were more of a political nature. It was further believed that civil and political rights were 'free' in the sense that they did not cost much. Their main contents were assumed to be obligations of states not to interfere with the integrity and freedom of the individual. The implementation of economic, social and cultural rights, in contrast, was held to be costly since they were understood as obliging the state to provide welfare to the individual. Thus, the arguments centred around the issue of the differences in state obligations arising from the two sets of rights. For this reason, it was expected that states who did not want to undertake the obligations arising from economic, social and cultural rights would be willing to ratify an instrument which contained only civil and political rights.[96]

Henkin notes that in the international negotiation of the Covenants, 'it was necessary to accommodate, bridge, submerge, and conceal deep divisions and differences, especially between democratic-libertarian and socialist-revolutionary states—differences in fundamental conceptions about the relation of society to the individual, about his (sic) rights and duties, about priorities and preferences among them'.[97]

Western countries favoured civil and political rights but were loath to recognise binding legal obligations for economic, social and cultural rights, and communist states of the former Soviet bloc, along with most developing countries in other parts of the world, prioritised economic, social and cultural rights. The Cold War context in which these discussions occurred exacerbated the divide. If it had been decided that the full range of rights be included in a single covenant, it is likely that the level of specificity of the rights in both covenants, and the inclusion of the immediate, unqualified obligation to realise civil and political rights, would have been significantly diluted as a precondition to Western agreement to the coverage of economic, social and cultural rights.

The result of these differences was the creation of separate treaties: for civil and political rights, the *International Covenant on Civil and Political Rights* (ICCPR); and for economic, social and cultural

95 V Pechota, 'Development of the Covenant', in Louis Henkin (ed), *The International Bill of Rights: The Covenant on Civil and Political Rights*, Columbia University Press, New York, 1981, 39.

96 A Eide, 'Economic, Social and Cultural Rights as Human Rights' in A Eide, C Krause & A Rosas (eds), *Economic, Social and Cultural Rights*, 2nd edn, Martinus Nijhoff Publishers, Dordrecht, 2001, 9–28, 10.

97 L Henkin, 'Introduction', in Louis Henkin (ed), *The International Bill of Rights: The Covenant on Civil and Political Rights*, Columbia University Press, New York, 1981, 9.

rights the *International Covenant on Economic, Social and Cultural Rights* (ICESCR). Pechota sees that '[i]n practical terms, the decision to prepare two instruments had both advantages and disadvantages', and says that:

> On the positive side, the separation made it possible to maintain the absolute character of civil and political rights and to strengthen their international implementation while encouraging a bolder approach than might otherwise have been feasible toward the formulation of economic, social, and cultural rights, notably by omitting that they could be implemented progressively. On the negative side, the division created uncertainty about the equal standing of the two categories of rights and led to duplication of a number of provisions in the covenants, raising problems of interpretation. However, the common ground and the identity of purpose, as well as the similarity of many provisions in the final drafts, make the covenants complementary and mutually reinforcing.[98]

The ICCPR and ICESCR were finally completed, presented to the UN General Assembly and opened for signature in December 1966.[99] The ICESCR came into force on 3 January 1976, with Australia, the United Kingdom, Germany and four Scandinavian countries the only original Western states parties. Today this ostensible ideological divide has disappeared: the United States is the only significant Western state not to have ratified it.[100] The ICCPR came into force on 23 March 1976, with the Soviet Union and several Eastern bloc countries among the original states parties. Despite the expectation that states would choose between ratifying a treaty on economic, social and cultural rights and one which contained only civil and political rights,[101] the overwhelming majority of states have ratified both.[102]

Drafting Differences Between the International Covenants

Even though most states are party to both treaties, the history of their drafting led to there being distinct differences between them, resulting in a perceived hierarchy of rights that continues to affect the human rights system today.

Among the differences, contrasting phrasing is used in the two treaties: the ICCPR employs classic and more rigid rights terminology focused on individual rights, such as 'Every human being has the inherent right to life' (article 6) or 'No one shall be held in slavery' (article 8), while the more flexible language of the ICESCR focuses on the obligations of the state, such as 'The States Parties to the present Covenant recognise the right to work' (article 6) or 'The States Parties to the present Covenant recognise the right of everyone to education' (article 13). Beyond their phrasing, the actual operation

98 V Pechota, see above, n 95, 43.

99 ICCPR, GA Res 2200 A (XXI), UN GAOR supp no 16, para 52, UN Doc A/6316 (1966); *International Covenenant on Economic, Social and Cultural Rights*, GA Res 2200 A (XXI), UN GAOR supp no 16, para 49, UN Doc A/6316 (1966).

100 The United States signed the ICESCR in 1977, but as at January 2011, has not ratified it. See United Nations Treaty Series, <http://treaties.un.org/pages/ViewDetails.aspx?src=UNTSONLINE&tabid=2&mtdsg_no=IV-3&chapter=4&lang=en#Participants>.

101 A Eide, see above, n 96.

102 As at July 2011, the ICESCR has 160 states parties while the ICCPR has 167.

of the treaties differs: while the ICCPR states in article 2(1) the scope of that treaty is limited to the territory and jurisdiction of the state party, the ICESCR does not contain any express limitations. In addition, the ICESCR does not provide for a monitoring body to ensure state compliance,[103] nor (until recently) was there a mechanism (such as the *First Optional Protocol* to the ICCPR) for reviewing individual complaints. Another important difference is that while the ICCPR article 2(3) requires states to provide effective remedies for violations of rights, the ICESCR has no such requirement; rather, the ICESCR requires states only to achieve full realisation of rights 'progressively' (article 2).

The division between civil and political rights and economic, social and cultural rights has waned in the decades since the adoption of the two covenants. More recent treaties, such as the *Convention on the Rights of the Child* (CROC), the *Convention on the Elimination of All Forms of Discrimination against Women* (CEDAW), *the Convention on the Rights of Persons with Disabilities* (CRPD) and the *International Convention on the Protection of the Rights of All Migrant Workers and Members of Their Families* (ICRMW) have returned to the vision of the UDHR and have incorporated economic, social and cultural rights alongside civil and political rights. *The African Charter on Human and Peoples' Rights* is the first regional human rights treaty to incorporate certain economic, social and cultural rights alongside civil and political rights in a single document. Also, significantly, western human rights NGOs,[104] which have been more likely to focus primarily on civil and political rights, have recognised a growing need to draw economic, social and cultural rights within their ambit, even though some of them are still struggling with what they claim is a lack of clarity around violations of such rights and possible remedies, which can pose difficulties in advocating on behalf of victims.[105]

International expert bodies, particularly the treaty bodies, have also helped to define the content of rights. The efforts of the Human Rights Committee (in relation to the ICCPR) and the Committee on Economic Social and Cultural Rights (with respect to the ICESCR)[106] have been considerable in terms of further defining these treaty rights. The development of the *Optional Protocol* to the ICESCR[107] will also help identify the scope and content of economic, social and cultural rights.

However, while it is obvious that domestic case law that pertains to economic, social and cultural rights is far more limited than that pertaining to civil and political rights, a burgeoning body of domestic cases (of which examples are discussed below in Chapter 4) relating to issues such as the right to housing, health and food is fostering litigation that was simply unknown decades ago. Such decisions are helping change the perception of economic, social and cultural rights, from aspirational and vague to real and enforceable.

103 Note, however, that the Economic and Social Council (ECOSOC) carries out this task, see Chapter 7.3.

104 See further Chapter 9.

105 See K Roth, 'Defending Economic, Social and Cultural Rights: Practical Issues Faced by an International Human Rights Organization' (2004) 26(1) *Human Rights Quarterly* 63; L S Rubenstein, 'How International Human Rights Organizations Can Advance Economic, Social and Cultural Rights: A Response to Kenneth Roth' (2004) 26(4) *Human Rights Quarterly* 845.

106 See Chapter 7 for a discussion of these committees.

107 See Chapter 4.4.

Conceptual Differences Between the Two Types of Rights

The formal position under international law is that civil and political rights, and economic, social and cultural rights, all form part of the same indivisible body of international human rights law and cannot be given effect to selectively. In 1993 the *Vienna Declaration and Programme of Action* declared: 'All human rights are universal, indivisible and interdependent and interrelated',[108] and in 2006 the UN General Assembly resolution establishing the Human Rights Council reaffirmed 'that all human rights are universal, indivisible, interrelated, interdependent and mutually reinforcing, and that all human rights must be treated in a fair and equal manner, on the same footing and with the same emphasis'.[109] The Universal Periodic Review process, which commenced in 2008 and is described in Chapter 6.7, made a concrete step towards ensuring that human rights are treated as indivisible, by subjecting states to review of all their obligations under all treaties to which they are a party, as well as the *UN Charter* and the UDHR, in a single process.

Nevertheless, civil and political rights continue to enjoy something of a privileged position in practice compared with economic, social and cultural rights. This is particularly true at the domestic level. Of those states with some sort of constitutional or other entrenched protection of human rights in their law, virtually all cover at least a core group of civil and political rights. Provisions to recognise and protect economic, social and cultural rights, by comparison, are significantly less common in domestic constitutions. One of the main reasons for that is the difficulty that economic, social and cultural rights are sometimes said to pose for the allocation of resources and for the justiciability of complaints.

The allegedly prescriptive nature of economic, social and cultural rights (which carries with it the binary assumption that civil and political rights are proscriptive) is one of the more durable objections to their recognition and enforcement. It is said that

> because economic, social and cultural rights cast positive duties on states ... they require active steps for their realisation and, therefore, fulfilment is fundamentally a matter of social and government policy and ought not to be considered the domain of the court ... On the other hand, civil and political rights are viewed as proscriptive in the sense of constituting negative commandments prohibiting infringements of, for instance, the right to life and freedom of conscience and religion. In this respect, they are seen as amenable to judicial supervision and enforcement because their contravention involves actions readily conceivable as 'wrongs'.[110]

All rights have social policy implications, and the duty to respect economic, social and cultural rights and civil and political rights extends not only to refraining from actions infringing rights,

108 See above, n 94.

109 *Human Rights Council*, GA Res 60/251, UN GAOR, 60th sess, 72nd plen mtg, Preamble, para 3, UN Doc A/Res/60/251 (2006).

110 J Nolan & L Taylor, 'Corporate Responsibility for Economic, Social and Cultural Rights: Rights in Search of a Remedy?' *Journal of Business Ethics*, Volume 87, Supplement 2 (2009), 433–436.

but also to positive actions to uphold rights.[111] Every human right is capable of imposing an array of positive and negative obligations, not dependent on whether it is classified as civil, political, economic, social or cultural.

1.4.3 Justiciability

Questions about the vague nature of economic, social and cultural rights stem in part from the perception that they are not 'real' rights; rather, they are mere moral claims or aspirations which, unlike civil and political rights (it is said), are incapable of judicial enforcement. A lack of specificity can impede judicial enforcement of rights, and while the allegation of vagueness has some substance, it is equally applicable to many civil and political rights. Going from broadly framed principles to more clearly defined obligations is not a new challenge for lawyers, or for international human rights law in particular. Classic rights, such as the right to be free from torture or the right to life, as very simply defined in the ICCPR, raise more questions than answers, but their content and scope have been refined over time through a variety of mechanisms including domestic and international case law.

The *Vienna Declaration and Programme of Action* stresses the 'universal, indivisible and interdependent and interrelated' nature of human rights,[112] but a historical (and lingering) ambivalence continues towards the justiciability of economic, social and cultural rights. Many arguments have been raised to dispute their justiciability, including those mentioned above relating to the alleged 'vagueness' of the rights themselves, and the view that economic, social and cultural rights are necessarily (and solely) prescriptive. Arguments against their justiciable nature also stress that the adjudication of such rights would require courts to make policy judgments, would assume governmental roles regarding the allocation of resources that may then breach the doctrine of separation of powers,[113] and would potentially jeopardise the rule of law.[114] Justiciability is not the only means of enforcing economic, social and cultural rights, but denying judicial intervention weakens both the remedies available to victims and the accountability of the state for upholding economic, social and cultural rights.[115]

Following the passage of the UDHR, some in the West 'went so far as to deny the very legitimacy of ESC issues as rights'.[116] As discussed above, concerns about issues such as the justiciability (which may

111 Ibid 436 and more generally S Liebenberg, 'The Value of Human Dignity in Interpreting Socio-Economic Rights', (2005) *South African Journal on Human Rights*, 21, 1–31.

112 World Conference on Human Rights, *Vienna Declaration and Programme of Action*, GA Res 421(v) pt 1, para 5, UN Doc.A/CONF.157/23 (1950).

113 The doctrine of the separation of powers divides the institutions of government into three branches: legislative, executive and judicial, where each of the three branches acts as a check and balance on the others.

114 See for example the discussion of *Soobramoney v Minister of Health (KwaZulu-Natal)* [1998] 1 SA 765, [43] (Constitutional Court) and *Purohit and Moore v Gambia*, Communication 241/2001 (2003) AHRLR 96 (ACHPR 2003) in Chapter 4.

115 See generally International Commission of Jurists, *Courts and the Legal Enforcement of Economic, Social and Cultural Rights: Comparative Experiences of Justiciability* (2008) <http://www.icj.org/dwn/database/ESCR.pdf>.

116 K Roth, 'Defending Economic, Social and Cultural Rights: Practical Issues Faced by an International Human Rights Organization' (2004) 26(1) *Human Rights Quarterly* 63, 64. See generally M Cranston, *What Are Human Rights*, 2nd edn, Bodley Head, London, 1973.

include judicial, quasi-judicial and administrative remedies) of economic, social and cultural rights led to the eventual splitting of a single proposed covenant into two, the ICCPR and the ICESCR.

There is no inherent jurisprudential reason for denying the justiciability of any human right. A decision that certain rights ought not be subject to judicial oversight and intervention is a political decision; this is recognised by article 8 of the UDHR, which provides that everyone has the right to an effective remedy.[117] Both the Limburg Principles[118] and the Maastricht Guidelines[119] argue that judicial remedies should be available for economic, social and cultural rights. The UN Committee on Economic, Social and Cultural Rights (CESCR) has also stressed the justiciability of economic, social and cultural rights. Despite (or because of) the discrepancy in phrasing between articles 2 of the ICESCR and ICCPR (article 2(3) of ICCPR explicitly states the need to provide a judicial remedy for civil and political rights), the CESCR has confirmed the justiciable nature of economic, social and cultural rights. General Comment 3 (1990) notes that '[a]mong the measures which might be considered appropriate, in addition to legislation, is the provision of judicial remedies with respect to rights which may, in accordance with the national legal system, be considered justiciable'.[120] In General Comment 9 (1998), the CESCR dealt with arguments distinguishing civil and political rights and economic, social and cultural rights on the basis of justiciability.

CESCR GENERAL COMMENT 9[121]

In relation to civil and political rights, it is generally taken for granted that judicial remedies for violations are essential. Regrettably, the contrary assumption is too often made in relation to economic, social and cultural rights. This discrepancy is not warranted either by the nature of the rights or by the relevant Covenant provisions. The Committee has already made clear that it considers many of the provisions in the Covenant to be capable of immediate implementation ... It is important in this regard to distinguish between justiciability (which refers to those matters which are appropriately resolved by the courts) and norms which are self-executing (capable of being applied by courts without further elaboration). While the general approach of each legal system needs to be taken into account, there is no Covenant right which could not, in the great majority of systems, be considered to possess at least some significant justiciable dimensions. It is sometimes suggested that matters involving the allocation of resources should be left to the political authorities rather than the courts. While the respective competences of the various branches of government must be respected, it is appropriate to acknowledge that courts are generally already involved in a considerable range of matters which have important resource implications. The adoption of a

117 J Nolan & L Taylor, see above, n 110.

118 UN Commission on Human Rights, *The Limburg Principles on the Implementation of the International Covenant on Economic, Social and Cultural Rights*, 43rd sess, Provisional Agenda Items 8 and 18, UN Doc E/CN.4/1987/17 (8 January 1987) Annex, para 8. See the discussion in Chapter 4.

119 '*The Maastricht Guidelines on Violations of Economic, Social and Cultural Rights*, Maastricht,' (1998) 20 *Human Rights Quarterly* 691, [22].

120 Committee on Economic, Social and Cultural Rights, *General Comment 3: The Nature of States Parties Obligations* (art 2, para 1), 50th sess, para 5, UN Doc E/1991/23 (1990).

121 (1998) para 10.

rigid classification of economic, social and cultural rights which puts them, by definition, beyond the reach of the courts would thus be arbitrary and incompatible with the principle that the two sets of human rights are indivisible and interdependent. It would also drastically curtail the capacity of the courts to protect the rights of the most vulnerable and disadvantaged groups in society.

Decisions of courts in various national and regional forums[122] counter the fallacy that only civil and political rights are, or ought to be, justiciable. Decisions in South Africa since the passage of the *Constitution of the Republic of South Africa*, 1996, have perhaps contributed most to a growing international awareness of the way economic, social and cultural rights can be rendered justiciable. In *Grootboom*, Yacoob J, speaking for the Constitutional Court, emphasised the inextricability of the interrelationship between economic, social and cultural rights and civil and political rights:

> Our Constitution entrenches both civil and political rights and social and economic rights. All the rights in our Bill of Rights are inter-related and mutually supporting. There can be no doubt that human dignity, freedom and equality, the foundational values of our society, are denied those who have no food, clothing or shelter. Affording socio-economic rights to all people therefore enables them to enjoy the other rights enshrined in Chapter 2. The realisation of these rights is also key to the advancement of race and gender equality and the evolution of a society in which men and women are equally able to achieve their full potential.[123]

In the first decision of Constitutional Court of South Africa, the Court acknowledged some of the arguments against allowing judicial remedies for economic, social and cultural rights, particularly those that argued courts should not be involved in resource allocation, but ultimately the Court determined that such rights, along with civil and political rights, are capable of judicial determination by courts without any breach of the separation of powers doctrine.

122 See especially *Purohit and Moore v Gambia* (Communication 241/200), decided at 33rd Ordinary Session of the African Commission, 15–29 May 2003 (dealing with the right to health of mental health patients); *SERAC and CESR v Nigeria*, African Commission on Human Rights, Case No 155/96, decision made at 30th Ordinary Session, Banjul, The Gambia, 13–27 October 2001 (dealing with the right to health and the implied rights to food and housing); Argentina: *Jehovah's Witnesses*, Case 2137, Inter-Am. CHR 43, OEA/Ser.L/V/II.47, doc 13 rev 1 (1979) (Annual Report 1978) (dealing with the right to education); *Jorge Odir Miranda Cortez et al v El Salvador*, Inter-American Commission on Human Rights, Case 12.249, Report No 29/01, OEA/Ser.L/V/II.111 doc 20 rev at 284 (2000) (admissibility decision dealing with the economic, social and cultural standards enshrined in the OAS Charter); *Comunidad Mayagna (Sumo) Awas Tingni v Nicaragua*, Inter-American Court of Human Rights Series C, No 79, 31 August 2001 (involving the right to property); *Dilcia Yean and Violeta Bosica v Dominican Republic*, 7 December 2005 (involving education rights and rights of the child). See *Autisme-Europe v France*, Complaint No 13/2002, 7 November 2003 (dealing with the education rights of persons with autism); *FIDH v France*, Complaint No 14/2003, 8 September 2004 (involving, inter alia, the right to medical assistance of non-nationals); and most recently *European Federation of National Organisations Working with the Homeless (FEANTSA) v France*, Complaint No 39/2006 (dealing with the right to adequate housing and failure to make sufficient progress in addressing homelessness). See generally M Langford (ed), *Social Rights Jurisprudence: Emerging Trends in International and Comparative Law*, Cambridge University Press, Cambridge, 2008; ESCR-Net Case Law Database, International Network for Economic, Social and Cultural Rights <http://www.escr-net.org/caselaw/>.

123 *Government of the Republic of South Africa v Grootboom and others* 2000 (11) BCLR 1169 (CC); 2001 (1) SA 46 (CC), para 23.

> It is true that the inclusion of socio-economic rights may result in courts making orders which have direct implications for budgetary matters. However, even when a court enforces civil and political rights such as equality, freedom of speech and the right to a fair trial, the order it makes will often have such implications. A court may require the provision of legal aid, or the extension of state benefits to a class of people who formerly were not beneficiaries of such benefits. In our view it cannot be said that by including socio-economic rights within a bill of rights, a task is conferred upon the courts so different from that ordinarily conferred upon them by a bill of rights that it results in a breach of the separation of powers.[124]

The recognition and enforcement of economic, social and cultural rights remains more difficult in countries where, unlike South Africa, the rights are not enshrined in their constitution or laws or where international law is not automatically incorporated in the domestic law. Chapter 4 outlines the differing approaches to economic, social and cultural rights in South Africa and India and Chapter 10 discusses how economic, social and cultural rights are approached in Australia.

It is worth emphasising the point made by the CESCR that no principled reason exists for upholding the justiciability of civil and political rights over economic, social and cultural rights, as all rights are based on the fundamental principles of equality, freedom and respect among human beings. While the nature of certain economic, social and cultural rights might require a nuanced approach when brought before a court, it is possible that the emerging recognition of the justiciability of economic, social and cultural rights will in time engender a commensurate body of referable jurisprudence that will ultimately close this debate and recognise the universal, indivisible and interdependent and interrelated nature of all human rights, both in terms of their content and available remedies.

1.5 CHANGING APPROACHES TO INTERNATIONAL HUMAN RIGHTS

The UDHR is the foundation of contemporary international human rights law. The rights it declares described in more detail in the subsequent ICCPR, (discussed in Chapter 3) and the ICESCR (discussed in Chapter 4).

In a remarkably short time—a little over 60 years since the UDHR and not yet 40 years since the covenants came into force—the system of international human rights law has become not merely established, but pervasive in global and national life. The rights in the UDHR were agreed on and declared with remarkable speed and consensus, so it is unsurprising that their full meaning and potential continue to be explored.

1.5.1 Post-Colonialism and the Influence of Newly Independent States

The changing complexion of the international community and membership of the United Nations was a significant influence on the development of international human rights law after the adoption of the UDHR. The process of decolonisation, particularly in Asia and Africa, which accelerated through the 1950s and 60s, resulted in a large number of newly independent states becoming UN members within a short time. From 1956 to 1968, 49 new states became members of the UN, all but Japan being the result

124 *Ex Parte Chairperson of the Constitutional Assembly: In Re Certification of the Constitution of the Republic of South Africa*, 1996 (4) SA 744; 1996 (10) BCLR 1253 (CC), para 77.

of decolonisation. Total UN membership at the time of adoption of the UDHR in 1948 was 56, but within 20 years the number had more than doubled, to 123.

The newly independent states often shared the priorities of pre-existing developing countries such as those in Latin America, and on ideological issues they were often supported by established Socialist states. Their emerging weight of numbers culminated in the formation among developing countries of the Non-Aligned Movement in 1961, an alternative to allegiance with one of the two Cold War blocs. It enabled newly independent and developing states to assert their priorities within the UN, including in the development of human rights; it continues to exist, and now commands a majority of the UN General Assembly.

The changing balance of colonial and post-colonial states raises challenging issues for the international community. The colonial/post-colonial split can be characterised in terms of developed/developing states, and West/East political cultures. This has precipitated international debate about whether human rights are truly universal or are in some way 'relative', discussed in Chapter 2, about whether civil and political rights are of greater relevance and are more valued in Western and developed states than in Eastern and developing states, and about whether the converse is true of economic, social and cultural rights.

A Right to Self-Determination

Chief among the priorities of the Non-Aligned Movement was support for decolonisation of countries which remained under colonial rule, as well as legal recognition of the independence of the new states, including not only territorial sovereignty but also sovereignty over resources. This emphasis of the newly independent states was the driving force behind the inclusion in both the ICCPR and the ICESCR of the right to self-determination, a right which had not been included in the UDHR.

Western states, particularly those such as the United Kingdom, France and Belgium which still had colonial possessions at the time, opposed the inclusion of the right to self-determination.[125] As Henkin observes, 'Western states resisted [a right of self-determination], arguing that both [covenants] are at best rights of a "people", not of any individual, and surely not—like human rights generally—rights of individuals against their own society. They argued, too, that content of these norms was highly uncertain and controversial. ... But the arguments of the Western states did not prevail, and identical provisions on self-determination now head both covenants'.[126]

Article 1 of both covenants includes identical language which recognises the right of all peoples to self-determination, including the right to 'freely determine their political status and freely pursue their economic, social and cultural development.'[127] It also includes a right for all peoples, 'for their own

125 At the Commission stage, the article on self-determination in the draft ICCPR was adopted by a vote of 13:4, with Australia, the United Kingdom, France and Belgium the only states to oppose it.

126 See above, n 97, 9–11. Extending the right to control over natural resources was particularly objectionable to some Western states as a potential obstacle to foreign investment: see A Cassese, 'The Self-Determination of Peoples', in Louis Henkin (ed), *The International Bill of Rights: The Covenant on Civil and Political Rights*, Columbia University Press, New York, 1981, 93.

127 ICCPR, see above, n 1, art 1(1); ICESCR, see above, n 1, art 1(1).

ends, [to] freely dispose of their natural wealth and resources'.[128] The right was recognised by the Vienna World Conference on Human Rights, and is today considered a primary rule of international law.[129] Some Western states revisited their opposition to a right of self-determination during the negotiation of *Declaration on the Rights of Indigenous Peoples* in the early twenty-first century, discussed in Chapter 13 and there remains a question of the extent to which a people's right to self-determination poses a challenge to the social and political integrity of the state of which they are a part.

A Right to Development

A further influence of the group of developing countries in the post-colonial era has been the emergence of the right to development as a human right. The *Declaration on the Right to Development*, adopted by the UN in 1986,[130] sought to include the process of development as a human right. Article 1 declared the right to development as both an individual's right, and a collective right of peoples:

> The right to development is an inalienable human right by virtue of which every human person and all peoples are entitled to participate in, contribute to, and enjoy economic, social, cultural and political development, in which all human rights and fundamental freedoms can be fully realized.

The right to development has in its various iterations been expressed as a right in itself as well as an approach to development and a process for approaching all the other human rights in the context of development.[131] As a result, it has been criticised as incoherent.[132] Nevertheless, its recognition by the Vienna World Conference on Human Rights, and its persistence in statements of international human rights law, clearly reflect the priorities of developing countries and their influence in the formation of human rights norms since the period of rapid decolonisation. In particular, the right focuses on outcomes, processes and the availability of the means for the realisation of rights, rather than on the traditional Western concern with the prohibitions against oppression and infringements of liberty.

Even though the right to development has attained general acceptance as a human right at the rhetorical level,[133] there are continuing questions as to its precise content, and consequently, questions as to precisely what states are required to do to comply.

---

128 ICCPR, see above, n 1, art 1(2); ICESCR, see above, n 1, art 1(2). For further discussion of the right to self-determination, see Chapter 3.2.1.

129 *Case Concerning East Timor* (*Portugal v Australia*) [1995] ICJ Rep 90 [29]; *Legal Consequences of the Construction of a Wall in the Occupied Palestinian Territory* (Advisory Opinion) [2004] ICJ Rep 136 [88], [155–6].

130 *Declaration on the Right to Development*, GA Res 41/128, art 1, UN doc no A/RES/41/128 (1986).

131 See World Conference on Human Rights, above, n 94, paras 10–12, for an example of the right to development expressed in terms of a process for fulfilling other human rights.

132 See, eg, C Tomuschat, *Human Rights: Between Idealism and Realism*, 2nd edn, Oxford University Press, Oxford, 2008, 55.

133 See, eg, the resolution establishing the Human Rights Council, which makes repeated reference to 'all human rights, civil, political, economic, social and cultural rights, including the right to development', Human Rights Council, GA Res 60/251, UN GAOR, 60th sess, Preamble and para 4, UN Doc A/RES/60/251 (2006).

1.5.2 Emergence of Human Rights as a Mainstream Legal, Social and Political Issue

In 1993, the World Conference on Human Rights was convened in Vienna in an attempt to achieve and record a consensus on the state of international human rights law in the post-Cold-War era. The conference was attended by 171 states and hundreds of NGOs, and the resulting document, the *Vienna Declaration and Programme of Action*, provides an excellent snapshot of the perception of the international community of the status and content of international human rights law at that time.

Among the key statements in the Vienna Declaration were a reaffirmation of human dignity, inherent in the birth of every human being, as the source of human rights, recognition that the *UN Charter* contained legally binding obligations for states to protect and promote human rights, the recognition of the universal nature of human rights and the interdependence and inseparability of civil and political and economic, social and cultural rights, and the reaffirmation of the rights to self-determination and to development.

Further attempts to strengthen the human rights framework of the UN followed, with the creation of the Office of the High Commissioner for Human Rights and, through UN Secretary-General Kofi Annan's blueprint for UN reform, *In Larger Freedom*, the creation of the Human Rights Council and the Universal Periodic Review.[134] Meanwhile, regional systems developed in Europe, the Americas and Africa have added another layer of accountability for human rights.[135]

Forty-five years after the UDHR, the Vienna Conference demonstrated that the legitimacy of human rights as a mainstream concern for the international community and the status of human rights as legal rights with corresponding international obligations were beyond question. The continuing questions for contemporary debate thus relate not to the existence of human rights or their status as law, but to the scope of human rights and obligations—for example, questions about the extra-territorial reach of human rights obligations and the conditions in which they may be invoked, discussed in Chapter 20—and questions about the actors to which those obligations might apply—for example, non-state actors such as multinational corporations, discussed in Chapter 19.

134 See Chapter 6.1.5 for greater discussion of *In Larger Freedom* and the formation of the Human Rights Council.

135 See Chapter 8.

2 EARLIER CONCEPTIONS OF 'HUMAN RIGHTS'

CONTENTS

2.1 INTRODUCTION

Chapter 1 discussed the origins of the *Universal Declaration of Human Rights* (UDHR) in the aftermath of the Second World War, where the UN drafting committee achieved a practical synthesis of two principal theoretical perspectives: the liberal tradition which emphasises defending the rights of an individual against the oppressive exercise of state power, and the socialist tradition, based in the struggle of organised labour against capital, which emphasises the right of a community to protection of and support by the state. In the absence of a single or comprehensive philosophical basis for the UDHR, two defining claims are made for contemporary human rights: that they are derived from the idea of human dignity, and that they are universal.

This chapter outlines the liberal and socialist traditions, illustrating how they provided the essential basis for the rights articulated in the UDHR. It goes on to discuss the continuing debate about whether and how dignity and universality are plausible claims to make for human rights, and the extent to which they have a basis in established philosophical traditions. The chapter concludes by noting a range of critiques of the conventional idea of human rights that explore the possibility of their being relative, rather than absolute, in their origin and application.

2.2 INDIVIDUAL RIGHTS

In its final report (discussed in Chapter 1), the UNESCO Committee discussed the two dominant traditions of Western political thought regarding human rights, which it labelled 'civil and political rights', and 'economic social and cultural rights' respectively. The civil and political rights in the UDHR were derived from, but are not the same as, the 'natural rights' which had been at the heart of western European and North American politics for about 400 years; natural rights discourse constituted a significant philosophical tradition that contributed to the contemporary human rights articulated in the UDHR.

Without explicitly referring to natural rights, section 1 of the UNESCO Committee's report outlined a history of civil and political rights:[1]

REPORT OF THE UNESCO COMMITTEE ON THE PHILOSOPHIC PRINCIPLES OF THE RIGHTS OF MAN

The fundamental human rights which were specified first and proclaimed widely at the beginnings of the modern period were rights which regulated man's relations to political and social groups and which are therefore usually referred to as Civil and Political Rights. They had as purpose to protect man in actions which do not derogate from the freedom or well-being of others and to assign to him the exercise of functions by which he might exert a proper influence on the institutions and laws of the state.

As a result of religious movements and the development of nation states, a series of freedoms were formulated more and more precisely and insistently from the Renaissance to the eighteenth century: to free men from unwarranted interference in his thought and expression, the freedom of conscience, worship, speech, assembly, association and the press. During the seventeenth century, each of these freedoms received eloquent defense of the grounds, not only that they may be granted without danger to the peace of the state, but also that they may not withheld without danger. Legal implementation for their protection was step by step provided by the institution of courts to the extension of the jurisdiction of existing courts, and these rights may, therefore be associated with respect to the means of securing them, with other personal rights and with the right to justice, by which it was recognised that all men have an equal right to seek justice by appeal to law, and in that appeal to be protected from summary arrest, cruel treatment and unjust punishment.

As civil rights, moreover, they are closely related to the right to political action by which the function of citizens in states is defined, and the growth of the democratic institutions during this period is largely an expression of the conviction men can achieve justice and the defence of their rights only by participation direct or indirect in the

1 *The Grounds of an International Declaration of Human Rights: Report of the UNESCO Committee on the Philosophic Principles of the Rights of Man to the Commission on Human Rights of the United Nations*, 5–6, UN Doc UNESCO/Phil./10/1947 (1947).

governments by which they are ruled. Political rights were therefore written into instruments and institutions of government, whereas civil rights, protected from interference by governments by recourse to courts, were written into bills of rights. The right to political action within a state discussed during this period, moreover, in close conjunction with the right to rebellion or revolution by which men might set up a government in conformity with justice if the fundamental principles of justice and the basic human rights are violated in such fashion as to permit no redress by recourse to peaceful means, and also in conjunction with the right to citizenship by which men may abandon their existing citizenships and assume citizenship of an country which is prepared to accept them as citizens.

Finally, during the nineteenth century, the discussion of the right to political action made increasingly clear that it is a right which can be exercised wisely only in conjunction with the right to information by which the citizen may equip himself for the proper exercise of his political functions.

2.2.1 Natural Law (Not Natural Rights)

When the UNESCO report above refers to 'a series of freedoms [which] were formulated more and more precisely and insistently', it is referring to natural rights, the origins of which are in natural law. Natural rights were conceived in European political philosophy on the basis of classical Greek, Roman and Christian thinking about natural law; their precise history is complex and debateable,[2] but 'it is clear that a crucial influence in the formative stages of human rights has been that of natural law as developed by European thinkers such as John Locke and Thomas Hobbes during the Enlightenment period'.[3] The following account is an overview of the principal and better-known origins of natural rights at the generalised level at which they were understood by, and influential on, the drafters of the UDHR. When reading this account it is important to follow the use of the terms 'natural law' and 'natural rights', and the transition from one to the other in the seventeenth century.

The essential contribution of natural law to the contemporary formulation of human rights is that of universality: application to all people and at all times, because of the essential nature of being human. Natural law was concerned not with individual rights, but broad social responsibility; it was articulated as a basis for moral conduct, enabling people to comply with a natural order of what was good, as the basis for a just society. It was not until the seventeenth century—more than 2000 years after its origins—that natural law developed into the idea of an individual's natural rights.

The origins of natural law are in the work of the Greek philosophers Plato, Socrates and Aristotle in the sixth to the fourth centuries BCE. They developed an argument for the existence of the common good, and for each person's ethical responsibility to act in the best interests of society. The responsibility was perhaps due only to people in the same community, and perhaps only to people within the same social class, but their identification of the rational being's responsibility to the common good was the basis of the philosophy of citizenship developed in the first century BCE by the Roman lawyer Cicero.

Based on the Stoics' view that human nature was characterised by reason, distinguishing man from animals, Cicero argued for a 'natural law': the law of 'right reason which is in accordance with nature,

2 See B Tierney, *The Idea of Natural Rights*, Scholars Press, Atlanta, 1997, 1–2.

3 E Brems, *Human Rights: Universality and Diversity*, Martinus Nijhof, The Hague, 2001, 17.

applies to all men, and is unchangeable and eternal'.[4] Such a law is to be contrasted with the variable and arbitrary laws of custom or governments. For Cicero, the capacity for reason was common to all people, and so natural law is law that all people can recognise. This theory of natural law survived the fall of the Roman Empire in the theology of the Roman Catholic Church, which succeeded the Roman Empire as the dominant social and political force in Europe.

Christian belief similarly identified a law which was common to all and which transcended the laws of custom or governments; such a natural law was referable, however, not to universal reason but to an omniscient God. Augustine of Hippo had articulated this view in the early fifth century CE, synthesising 'Stoicism, Neoplatonism and elements suggested by Christian Scriptures',[5] and in the thirteenth century Thomas Aquinas wrote *The Summa Theologica*,[6] in which he set out his Treatise on Law,[7] the Christian theological statement of natural law. Aquinas combined the classical Greek and Roman idea of people's universal capacity for 'reason' with a Christian idea of the universal authority of God, saying that 'natural law, though of divine origin, could be ascertained through reason'.[8]

THOMAS AQUINAS, *THE SUMMA THEOLOGICA*[9]

[On 'law and reason']

A law, properly speaking, regards first and foremost the order to the common good. Now to order anything to the common good, belongs either to the whole people, or to someone who is the vice-regent of the whole people. And therefore the making of a law belongs either to the whole people or to a public personage who has care of the whole people …

[On 'eternal law']

[A] law is nothing else but a dictate of practical reason emanating from the ruler who governs a perfect community. Now it is evident, granted that the world is ruled by Divine Providence … that the whole community of the universe is governed by Divine Reason. Wherefore the very Idea of the government of things in God the Ruler of the universe, has the nature of a law …

4 Cicero, *On the Commonwealth*, bk 3, 22, 215, cited in M Ishay, *The History of Human Rights: From Ancient Times to the Globalization Era*, 2nd edn, University of California Press, Berkeley, 2008, 25.

5 R W Dyson & P M R Stirk, *Natural law and Political Realism in the History of Political Thought*, vol 2, Peter Lang, New York, 2007, 147. On Augustine of Hippo see generally, R W Dyson & P M R Stirk, n 5, 146–208; P Brown, *Augustine of Hippo: A Biography*, University of California Press, Berkeley, first published 1967, 2000.

6 T Aquinas, *The Summa Theologica*, Benziger Bros edn, 1947 <www.ccel.org/a/aquinas/summa/FS.html>, q 91.

7 Ibid 'Treatise on Law'.

8 N O'Neill, S Rice & R Douglas, *Retreat from Injustice: Human Rights Law in Australia*, The Federation Press, Sydney, 2004, 3.

9 See above, n 6, questions 91(1)–(3).

[On 'natural law']

[A]mong all others, the rational creature is subject to Divine providence ... [w]herefore it has a share of the Eternal Reason, whereby it has a natural inclination to its proper act and end: and this participation of the eternal law in the rational creature is called the natural law ... [That] we discern what is good and what is evil, which is the function of the natural law, is nothing else than an imprint on us of the Divine light. It is therefore evident that the natural law is nothing else than the rational creature's participation of the eternal law.

[On 'human law']

[A] law is a dictate of the practical reason. Now it is to be observed that the same procedure takes place in the practical and in the speculative reason: for each proceeds from principles to conclusions, as stated above (De Lib. Arb. i, 6). Accordingly we conclude that just as, in the speculative reason, from naturally known indemonstrable principles, we draw the conclusions of the various sciences, the knowledge of which is not imparted to us by nature, but acquired by the efforts of reason, so too it is from the precepts of the natural law, as from general and indemonstrable principles, that the human reason needs to proceed to the more particular determination of certain matters. These particular determinations, devised by human reason, are called human laws, provided the other essential conditions of law be observed, as stated above (Question [90], Articles [2],3,4). Wherefore Tully says in his Rhetoric (De Invent. Rhet. ii) that 'justice has its source in nature; thence certain things came into custom by reason of their utility; afterwards these things which emanated from nature and were approved by custom, were sanctioned by fear and reverence for the law'.

The consistent theme of natural law in the 2000 years from Plato to Aquinas was its recognition of the human capacity to reason, and so to comprehend some higher sense of right that transcends temporal laws: 'Man is celebrated as a rational being and is given a pre-eminent position above the rest of nature ... Following [reason's] commands is to follow our nature'.[10] This idea of natural law was a moral code which both enabled and obliged people to be 'good' and 'just' in their conduct by reference to something other than custom and the laws of the state.

Aquinas's writing was the high point of natural law, and in its own terms suggests the reason for the decline of natural law that followed. In his account of 'law and reason', Aquinas attributed natural law ('the order to the common good') to *either* the people *or* to a ruler of the people. Recognition of the authority of the people soon gave way to recognition of the exclusive authority of the ruler, and until the late sixteenth century the classical connection between natural law and human reason was wholly supplanted by a connection between natural law and a ruling authority. The power to identify the rational natural law on behalf of all people was claimed by the absolute monarch and, over time, by the Christian Churches. Competing claims to being the authoritative source of natural law were often resolved by recognising in a monarch a divine right to rule, thus conflating the monarch and God as the source of universal law. What the ruler/Church said was law, without reference to external ideas of morality, and so ideas of justice 'gradually descended into positivism'.[11]

---

10 C Douzinas, *The End of Human Rights: Critical Legal Thought at the Turn of the Century*, Hart Publishing, Oxford, 2000, 52.

11 Ibid 50.

2.2.2 Natural Rights

The rise of the nation state in Europe in the seventeenth century redefined the relationship between the state and its people and precipitated the emergence from natural law of the idea of natural rights.

In the early seventeenth century the Dutch statesman Hugo Grotius reasserted the place of human reason in identifying natural law, proposing that people have the capacity to know what is good, and that the teachings of the organised Christian Church are not the sole source of what is right.[12] Grotius recognised the existence of God's laws as natural law, but asserted the existence as well of secondary laws of nature, which derive from human reason. Grotius applied his theory of laws to international law, and to trade and war, with revolutionary and lasting effect. At the same time, his restatement of the rational and secular basis of natural law had implications for the emerging relationship between state and citizen. This was the beginning of 'the rebellion of reason against the theocratic organisation of authority',[13] and was a platform for the transition from natural law to natural rights later in the seventeenth century.

The development of natural rights was not necessarily a rejection of natural law's concern with the conduct that was required for a just society. Rather, it addressed an additional concern, the place of an individual in relation to the state. Douzinas argues, however, that the shift to a focus on the place of the citizen was in fact at the expense of broader concerns for a just society, and suggests that Thomas Hobbes was, in his work *Leviathan*, 'the first philosopher to replace fully the concept of justice with the idea of rights'.[14]

In the course of developing a political thesis concerning the power of the state, Hobbes sets out a conception of law and the individual that clearly anticipates the emergence of the individual as a rights-holder, for example in this text from *Leviathan*:[15]

THOMAS HOBBES, *LEVIATHAN* [16]

The *right of nature*, which writers commonly call *jus naturale*, is the liberty each man hath to use his own power as he will himself for the preservation of his own nature; that is to say, of his own life; and consequently, of doing anything which, in his own judgement and reason, he shall conceive to be the aptest means thereunto.

By *liberty* is understood, according to the proper signification of the word, the absence of external impediments; which impediments may oft take away part of a man's power to do what he would, but cannot hinder him from using the power left him according as his judgement and reason shall dictate to him.

12 Hugo Grotius, *De Jure Belli et Pacis Libri Tres* [*The Rights of War and Peace*], 1625. See generally, B Tierney, above, n 2, 316–42.

13 See above, n 10, 64.

14 See above, n 10, 69.

15 T Hobbes, *Leviathan*, M Oakeshott (ed), Touchstone, New York, 1997.

16 Ibid Chapter 14: 'Of the First and Second Natural Laws, and of Contracts', M Oakeshott (ed), Touchstone, New York, 1997, 103.

A *law of nature, lex naturalis*, is a precept, or general rule, found out by reason, by which a man is forbidden to do that which is destructive of his life, or taketh away the means of preserving the same, and to omit that by which he thinketh it may be best preserved. For though they that speak of this subject use to confound *jus* and *lex, right* and *law*, yet they ought to be distinguished, because right consisteth in liberty to do, or to forbear; whereas law determineth and bindeth to one of them: so that law and right differ as much as obligation and liberty, which in one and the same matter are inconsistent.

This 'concise and epigrammatic statement', says Douzinas,

> is a clear declaration and definition of the modern rights of man ... It is still in conversation with the Aristotelian tradition which distinguished between right ... and law ... and attribute the dignity of nature to the former. But ... [n]atural right is not the just resolution of a dispute offered by a harmonious cosmos or God's commands. It derives exclusively from the nature of 'each man'. The course or basis of right is no longer the observation of natural relations, philosophical speculation about the 'best polity', or the interpretation of divine commandments, but human nature.[17]

Hobbes is credited with 'having transposed the idea of natural law into individualist terms' and with being 'the first to produce a genuinely philosophical account of something called "natural right"',[18] but he was only a remote ancestor of the type of natural right later developed by John Locke. Hobbes did focus on the nature of the individual and did distinguish each person by their capacity to reason, but he did so not to promote natural rights flowing from that status but to identify what it is that a subject surrenders to a sovereign.

Whether modern thinking of rights began about this time—and principally with the work of Locke described below—is debated by legal historians. Tierney says, for example, that Michel Villey's view[19] of the fourteenth century theologian William of Ockham as the originator of rights theories 'is widely accepted in current American studies',[20] but Tierney's own thesis is that '[t]he history of natural rights theories can best be seen as a series of creative responses to a variety of past experiences ... at the end of the [fifteenth century] the process of development was by no means completed'. Whatever the argument among historians, for the purpose of surveying the ideas that informed the drafters of the UDHR, it is clear that the idea of natural rights became widely written about, discussed and influential during the seventeenth century as a result of the work of Grotius and then, most importantly, Locke.

The English philosopher John Locke, 'a disciple of the Stoics',[21] had studied the works of Grotius and Samuel von Pufendorf[22] and spent some years in Europe. While Locke did not follow Hobbes's thesis of

---

17 C Douzinas, see above, n 10, 70.

18 K Minogue, 'The History of the Idea of Human Rights', in W Laqueur & B Rubin (eds), *The Human Rights Reader*, Temple University Press, Philadelphia, 1979, 3–16, 7.

19 M Villey, *La Formation de la Pensée Juridique Moderne*, 4th edn, Montchrétien, Paris, 1975.

20 B Tierney, see above, n 2, 14, n 5. On Ockham, see above, n 2, 97–103.

21 M Cranston, *What are Human Rights?*, Bodley Head, London, 1973, 1.

22 See S von Pufendorf, *De Officio Hominis et Civis Iuxta Legem Naturalem* [*On the Duty of Man and Citizen According to Natural Law*], 1682.

political power,[23] he took up Hobbes's view of the 'right of nature' that each person has the liberty to do what their reason dictates. In similar vein, Locke wrote that 'all Men are naturally in ... a *State of Perfect Freedom* to order their Actions, and dispose of their Possessions and persons, as they think fit, within the bounds of the Law of Nature, without asking leave, or depending upon the Will of any other Man'.[24] This 'perfect freedom' is a natural right, derived from natural law, and is a forerunner of the freedoms from state intervention that are described in contemporary human rights.

But this freedom is not 'a state of licence'. Rather, it 'has a Law of Nature to govern it, which obliges every one: And Reason, which is that Law, teaches all Mankind, who will but consult it, that being all equal and independent, no one ought to harm another in his Life, Health, Liberty, or Possessions'[25] Locke limits the exercise of freedom by reference to each person's 'equality and independence'—qualities that, Locke says, are apparent from simple reason.

Fifty years after Locke, the French Enlightenment philosopher Baron de Montesquieu (Charles-Louis de Secondat) published *The Spirit of Laws* in 1748. Montesquieu too promoted individual liberty, but saw the need to set limits on it. He admired the English constitutional arrangements, which separated the executive and the legislature and created a balance between individual freedoms and sovereign power, and promoted a theory of separation of powers that was influential on the drafters of the US Constitution.[26]

This new political philosophy of natural rights derived its claim to universality from natural law, and the idea that people held a universal right to their own freedom fitted the times in Western Europe. The period during which Locke and Montesquieu were writing was one of dramatic expansion in trade and commerce, carrying with it the need for individual freedoms of movement and expression: 'The great discoveries, the marvellous inventions and the triumph of the mercantile and urban economies, aided by the levelling exchange-value of money, combined to increase the cachet of the universal.'[27]

The natural rights were essentially freedoms: freedom from arbitrary power and freedom of expression, movement, property ownership and civil participation. The effect of the popular revolutions in England, France and the United States (discussed below) was to establish a political compromise between a newly assertive people who claimed these freedoms, and a state that deferred to the rule of law rather than the rule of a sovereign. Although it took different forms—a constitutional monarchy in England and forms of a republic in France and the United States—the new political order was a social contract,[28] and the state's respect for people's natural rights were integral to it.

23 P Laslett in his 'Introduction' to Locke's *Two Treatises of Government*, rev edn, Cambridge University Press, New York, 1963, 87–8, tells how Locke, though fascinated by *Leviathan* and influenced by Hobbes, ultimately rejected Hobbes's thinking; noted in N O'Neill, S Rice & R Douglas, see above, n 8, 5, n 19.

24 J Locke, *The Second Treatise of Government: An Essay Concerning the True Original Extent and End of Civil Government*, rev edn, Cambridge University Press, Mentor, 1960, 309.

25 Ibid 311.

26 See S Krause, 'The Spirit of Separate Powers in Montesquieu' (2000) 62 (2) *The Review of Politics*, 231.

27 C Douzinas, see above, n 10, 67.

28 See J-J Rousseau, *Du Contrat Social ou Principes du Droit Politique* [*Of the Social Contract, or Principles of Political Right*], 1762.

At this point it is worth recalling the historical trajectory from the natural law of Plato to the natural rights of the eighteenth century. The common thread is the conception of a rational being, one 'with the capacity to reason critically and a capacity for inner goodness, an ability to search for just courses of action and develop good governments.'[29] A person exercising this rational capacity contributes to the common good: for the Greeks and Romans the person thereby fulfilled their destiny as a good citizen; while for Christians the person thereby fulfilled their destiny as a servant of God, or of a sovereign who rules by divine right.

The promise that rationality had 'for challenging oppressive regimes'[30] was not apparent until the philosophers of the sixteenth and seventeenth centuries developed from *natural law* the idea of *natural rights*; human rationality then became not merely a means of contributing to a common good, but a means of asserting claims of personal freedom against the state.

> Classic natural law contained a passion for justice but did not coincide with it. Natural rights enters the historical agenda ... every time people struggle to 'overthrow all relations in which man is a degraded, enslaved, abandoned or despised being'.[31] In that way the Graeco-Roman idea of natural law can be seen as laying the foundation for human rights activism.[32]

2.2.3 Similar Traditions

The idea of a rational person acting for the common good is not unique to the Western philosophical tradition: 'most religious texts incorporate a notion of universalism containing altruistic guidelines that could apply if not to all individuals, as a contemporary definition would require, then to a substantial proportion of humanity ... [for example] Micah (the Hebrew Bible), Paul (the New Testament), the Buddha and others'.[33] Ishay surveys a wide range of cultures to identify a similar theme, cautioning that

> it would be excessive to claim that what we understand today as liberty is [easily] traceable to the pre-Enlightenment period. Nonetheless, it is worth drawing attention to some of the inklings of these notions within various traditions, if only to show that the idea of liberty was not born *ex nihilo* [out of nothing] during the Enlightenment ... conceptions one may associate with liberty or freedom were not unknown in ancient religious and secular texts.[34]

29 M Ishay, see above, n 4, 58.

30 M Ishay, see above, n 4, 58.

31 C Douzinas, see above, n 10, 68, citing E Bloch, *Natural Law and Human Dignity* (DJ Schmidt trans), MIT Press, Cambridge, 1998, xxviii–ix.

32 M Ishay, see above, n 4, 58.

33 M Ishay, see above, n 4, 18–19.

34 M Ishay, see above, n 4, 27–8.

In a list that is reminiscent of Maritain's in his response to the UNESCO Committee's survey,[35] Ishay's account starts with the Hammurabi Code of Babylon from the eighteenth century BCE and traverses the Hebrew Bible, the teachings of Buddha and Confucius in the sixth and fifth centuries BCE, the Hindu text *Arthashastra* from around 300 BCE, the Greeks and Romans, early Christianity, and Islam.[36] She concludes that 'all of the aforementioned traditions ... share basic views of a common good, thereby reinforcing the Socratic argument for universal goodness'.[37]

Ishay's account illustrates the plausibility of Maritain's call for 'a practical convergence of views, whatever the differences of theoretical perspectives',[38] and it is significant that it is possible now to identify across many cultures the common heritage of the essential features of the human rights set out in the UDHR. While the drafting of the UDHR was built substantially on the Western liberal tradition, its terms were accepted at the time by nations of all cultures. Clearly the principles that were articulated were not foreign or objectionable, and the drafting of the UDHR did succeed in arriving at Maritain's practical convergence of views. Tierney points out that the

> one necessary basis for a theory of human rights is a belief in the value and dignity of human life ... all the great world religions have taught respect and compassion for the human person. And the human needs to which human rights respond are not characteristic only of Western people. Surely in all societies, humans have preferred life to death, freedom to servitude, sufficiency of food to starvation, dignity to humiliation. The rights language that grew up in Western culture was one way of addressing such universal concerns.[39]

2.2.4 Natural Rights in Politics

The idea of natural rights was the theoretical basis for the popular revolutions in England, France and the United States in the seventeenth and eighteenth centuries while, at the same time, the unfolding of those revolutions contributed to the refinements of natural rights and the relationship between the state and rights-holding citizens.

Differently from natural law, which was a social and religious philosophy about the way people ought to engage with and participate in society, natural rights were a secular and political claim about the way people ought be treated by the state. Recognition by the state of an individual's rights was, at the same time, a concession by the state of the extent of its sovereignty. As a result, the rise of natural rights can be tracked through the interactions between individuals and the state that characterised Western politics from the thirteenth to the eighteenth centuries.

---

35 See Chapter 1.3.1.

36 M Ishay, see above, n 4, 28–59.

37 M Ishay, see above, n 4, 60.

38 J Maritain, *Communication with Regard to the Draft World Declaration on the Rights of Man*, p 2, UN Doc UNESCO/Phil./5/1947 (1947); see Chapter 1.3.1.

39 B Tierney, see above, n 2, 347.

Magna Carta

In light of the account given above, the thirteenth century is an early point in time at which to identify a political realisation of natural rights: a sovereign's divine right to rule was asserted by English and French monarchs until the seventeenth century, at about the same time that Grotius was laying the intellectual foundation for natural rights. But it was in 1215,[40] in *Magna Carta*, that a sovereign conceded to popular demands for recognition of what can, in hindsight, be seen as individual rights.

Most of the concessions made by King John in *Magna Carta* were particular to the times and to his dispute with the barons, and few of them are of lasting import. But those few have survived as fundamental rights in English common law and were influential in informing the content of contemporary human rights: the right not to be detained arbitrarily,[41] the right to freedom of movement[42] and the right to legal process.[43]

Magna Carta did not precipitate a popular assertion of individual rights. Indeed, it could not, as the 'liberties' that it recognised were only those of 'freemen of [the] realm',[44] not of the serfs and peasants—much greater in number—who were uneducated, under the controlling influence of the Christian Church and had no political sensibilities, let alone organisation. It was another 400 years before revolutionary thinking within the Church and among philosophers, combined with the devastating effect of wars waged by power-hungry monarchs, led to a widespread popular assertion of individual rights. When the time came, *Magna Carta* was invoked as the founding statement of individual rights in English law, taking on a symbolic role much larger than its actual terms warrant.

In truth, the concessions made in *Magna Carta* could actually be seen as a 'triumph of the King's Courts over all rivals [by] undertaking to correct the worst abuses in order to maintain the pre-eminence of royal justice'.[45] Justice Samuels quotes McKechnie[46] to say that *Magna Carta* 'has had much read into it that would have astonished its framers: application of modern standards to ancient practice has resulted in complete misapprehension'. The 'misapprehension' is blamed in part on the eminent seventeenth century lawyer Sir Edward Coke, who reinstated the *Magna Carta* 'as a document of political importance' and misled subsequent generations by 'assuming the existence, in *Magna Carta*, of a warrant for every legal principle of [the] day'.[47]

40 References to provisions of *Magna Carta* are to the version of *Magna Carta* that continues in effect today, enacted as a statute by the English Parliament under Edward I in 1297. See H Evans, 'Bad King John and the Australian Constitution' (Speech delivered as an 'Occasional Lecture' commemorating the 700th anniversary of the 1297 issue of *Magna Carta*, Canberra, 17 October 1997).

41 *Magna Carta*, 1297, cl 29.

42 Ibid cl 30.

43 Ibid cl 28 & 29.

44 Ibid 1297, cl 1.

45 *Jago v The District Court of New South Wales* (1988) 12 NSWLR 558, 573 (Samuels JA).

46 W S McKechnie, *Magna Carta: A Commentary on the Great Charter of King John*, 2nd edn, J Maclehose and Sons, Glasgow, 1914, 395.

47 See above, n 45, 574 (Samuels JA) quoting W S McKechnie, ibid 385.

It probably does not matter now that *Magna Carta* was not at the time the declaration of individual rights for which it has since been revered. It has a symbolic status, which was influential in the drafting of the US Bill of Rights, and which continues to be invoked by citizens in their battles with the state.[48]

The English Bill of Rights

More than 400 years after *Magna Carta*, the next significant political recognition of individual rights was the English *Bill of Rights* in 1688,[49] the background to which were the religious upheavals precipitated by Martin Luther's revolutionary Protestantism.

In the early sixteenth century Luther's teachings were a clear challenge to the authority of the established Church: 'Luther's views, as espoused, or revised, by supporters like Jean Calvin ... had far-reaching political repercussions: they not only undercut the power structure cemented by the feudal church, but also the system of privileges granted by divine grace'.[50] The period from the mid-sixteenth to the mid-seventeenth century was characterised in Europe by almost continuous Protestant–Catholic wars, until the Treaty of Westphalia in 1648.

The religious wars resulted in increasingly strident rejection of the power of the state to dictate religious belief and to subject the population to the brutality of war in the name of religion. This was the environment in which Grotius asserted individual reason independently of God's will, Hobbes recognised individual liberty and Locke articulated natural rights. The fleeing to North America by persecuted religious minorities illustrated that this call for religious freedom was at the heart of the religious wars.

The *Bill of Rights* was the culmination of a tumultuous period in England, during which Charles I, Charles II and James II asserted a divine right to rule. Charles I had assented in 1628 to the *Petition of Right*, which substantially restated the liberties of *Magna Carta* but was in effect merely a declaration, without any real means of constraining sovereign power. Resentment of the 'divine right' was one of the many domestic pressures that finally forced James II to abandon the throne, which was offered to his daughter Princess Mary and her husband Prince William of Orange in 1689, subject to their accepting the *Bill of Rights*.[51] The *Bill of Rights* rejected the divine right of the monarch to rule, and made a declaration 'for the vindicating and asserting ... ancient rights and liberties'. It

> ensured that the King governed through Parliament, subject to the law. Of special interest is the fact that the *Bill of Rights* bears the long title 'An Act Declaring the Rights and Liberties of the Subject ...'. Before the seventeenth century, the word 'right' or 'rights' was not in common usage and where used it was to describe the authority

48 See, eg, *Fyffe v Victoria* [2000] HCA 31; (2000) 172 ALR 336.

49 N O'Neill, S Rice & R Douglas, see above, n 8, 5–8, and references cited there.

50 M Ishay, see above, n 4, 77.

51 *An Act Declaring the Rights and Liberties of the Subject and Settling the Succession of the Crown* I Will and Mary, st 2, c 2 (1688). 'The Bill of Rights is sometimes given the date 1688 because the Declaration of Rights was passed on 13 February 1689 and at that time and until the *Calendar (New Style) Act 1750*, the new calendar year began on 25 March rather than 1 January. However, the *Declaration* was not enacted in statutory form, as the *Bill of Rights*, until 25 October 1689', N O'Neill, S Rice & R Douglas, see above, n 8, 7, n 40.

> or title of a ruler over his subject, or of a lord over his vassal, rather than the claims of the citizen. In the [*Bill of Rights*] the word 'right' bears neither of these meanings: it is used in the sense of what is fair or just. While the word 'liberty' was used before the seventeenth century to mean the state of being free, the plural 'liberties' had not then been conceived as meaning the rights and freedoms of individual citizens. Thus, the use of the words 'rights and liberties of the subject' in the *Bill of Rights* must be an indication of the new perception of natural rights brought about through the writing of philosophers like Hobbes and Locke.[52]

As with *Magna Carta*, many of the matters declared in the *Bill of Rights* were particular to the times and not all are of lasting import. But many do survive as fundamental rights in English law, and three in particular are echoed in contemporary human rights: freedom of speech (although limited at the time to parliamentary speech), free elections and freedom from cruel and unusual punishment.

AN ACT DECLARING THE RIGHTS AND LIBERTIES OF THE SUBJECT AND SETTLING THE SUCCESSION OF THE CROWN

...

Whereas the late King James the Second, by the assistance of divers evil counsellors, judges and ministers employed by him, did endeavour to subvert and extirpate the Protestant religion and the laws and liberties of this kingdom;

...

... the said Lords Spiritual and Temporal and Commons, pursuant to their respective letters and elections, being now assembled in a full and free representative of this nation, taking into their most serious consideration the best means for attaining the ends aforesaid, do in the first place (as their ancestors in like case have usually done) for the vindicating and asserting their ancient rights and liberties declare

...

That election of members of Parliament ought to be free;

...

That the freedom of speech and debates or proceedings in Parliament ought not to be impeached or questioned in any court or place out of Parliament;

...

That excessive bail ought not to be required, nor excessive fines imposed, nor cruel and unusual punishments inflicted ...

One of the freedoms recognised by the *Bill of Rights* was the right of Protestants 'to have arms for their own defence', a right that lives on in the US *Bill of Rights*,[53] extended to all citizens.

Magna Carta, the *Petition of Rights* and the *Bill of Rights* are together the great historical statements in English law of individual rights. They can be viewed as signs of a growing awareness and assertion of

52 N O'Neill, S Rice & R Douglas, see above, n 8, 7–8, citing J H Burns, 'The Rights of Man Since the Reformation: An Historical Survey' in Sir F Vallat (ed), *An Introduction to the Study of Human Rights*, Europa Publications, London, 1971, 19–30, 19–21.

53 United States Constitution amend II.

individual rights and, arguably, as having inspired the later and more comprehensive US *Bill of Rights*.[54] But as precursors to contemporary human rights they were limited, principally because the rights that were enumerated were not claimed by, or asserted for, all people equally: 'These historical texts ... did not constitute general declarations about the relations between subjects and political power. Instead, they had established remedies and procedures for the protection of predominantly feudal and private rights.'[55] In debating the proposed Bill of Rights in the US Constitution, Alexander Hamilton and John Jay had made the same point: 'bills of rights are, in their origins, stipulations between kings and their subjects, abridgements of prerogative in favour of privilege, reservations of rights not surrendered to the prince. Such was the *Magna Carta* ... Such was the *Petition of Rights* ... [and] the *Bill of Rights*.'[56]

The American and French Declarations

The rights recognised in the English declarations, while they were informed by a growing rights consciousness, were claimed by and for classes of people—male and propertied—with no suggestion that they would be enjoyed equally by all citizens; the 'rights' were privileged, not universal. Locke's philosophy of natural rights was not influential in England's seventeenth century political revolution; it was 'not typical of the time, nor did it set the tone for English political discussion in the century that followed ... [N]atural rights ... were strictly a commodity for export, particularly to France and to the American colonies'.[57] Locke's thesis of natural rights did find its place in continental Europe, embraced by the Italian intellectual Cesare Beccaria,[58] and the French philosopher Voltaire.[59] The American and French revolutions took place just a few years later.

The taxation demands that George III made of his North American colonies to fund Britain's involvement in the Seven Years' War led to a revolt, a war of independence, and the consequent *United States Declaration of Independence*. The events followed the pattern of a century earlier, when Charles I's excessive taxation demands to fund a war against Spain led to political upheaval, civil war and, eventually, the English *Bill of Rights*.

One of the great pamphleteers of the North American colonies at the time was Thomas Paine, whose *Common Sense* inspired revolutionary fervour in its passionate attack on the failure of the British state to respect and protect its people in the colonies.[60] Paine's rhetoric of individual rights and freedoms was

54 C Douzinas, see above, n 10, 87, citing G Jellinek, *La Déclaration des Droits de l'Homme et du Citoyen*, (G Fardis, trans) Paris, 1902.

55 C Douzinas, see above, n 10, 87.

56 A Hamilton & J Jay, 'The Federalist Papers 84' (1788), in W Laqueur and B Rubin (eds), *The Human Rights Reader*, Temple University Press, Philadelphia, 1979, 111–15, 113.

57 K Minogue, see above, n 18, 3–16, 6.

58 C Beccaria, 'Essay on Crimes and Punishments' (1764), in W Laqueur and B Rubin (eds), *The Human Rights Reader*, Temple University Press, Philadelphia, 1979, 75–8, 75.

59 F Voltaire, 'Philosophical Dictionary' (1764), in W Laqueur and B Rubin (eds), *The Human Rights Reader*, Temple University Press, Philadelphia, 1979, 79–82, 79.

60 Cf J Keane, *Tom Paine: A Political Life*, Bloomsbury, London, 1995, 108–14.

the political expression of the natural rights philosophy of John Locke, who had collaborated in drafting the Constitution of the new colony of Carolina in 1669[61] and whose work had been influential in the drafting in 1776 of the *Virginia Declaration of Rights*. The revolutionary potential of natural rights, as a philosophy for resisting autocracy, was well received by the European settlers of North America, many of whom were traders and religious refugees. The traders were entrepreneurial and engaged in accumulating personal wealth through their own labour and initiative; they were sympathetic to claims of individual rights against an autocratic state. Although socially conservative, the religious refugees were committed to freedom of religion and thought, at least as far as state interference was concerned.[62]

Paine's advocacy of natural rights philosophy influenced his friend and patron Thomas Jefferson, who in 1776 drafted the *United States Declaration of Independence*. The Preamble of the *Declaration* famously declares, 'We hold these truths to be self-evident, that all men are created equal; that they are endowed by their Creator with certain unalienable rights; that among these are life, liberty and the pursuit of happiness'. Just as the English *Bill of Rights* in 1689 had recounted a litany of acts by the King that limited life, liberty and the pursuit of happiness, so the *United States Declaration of Independence* listed George III's 'history of repeated injuries and usurpations'.

The French Revolution in 1789 was led by an educated middle class who were deeply resentful of feudal dues, and of taxes levied by the state, from which the Church and nobles were exempt. This middle class knew enough of what was happening in the world, principally the submission of the British Crown to Parliament and the American War of Independence, to demand freedom and equality. The desperate poverty and hunger of the common people in France moved them to support the revolution. The revolution initially resulted in King Louis XVI conceding sovereignty to an elected legislature while maintaining his Crown; later, in 1792 the monarchy was abolished and a republic was declared. It was in 1791, during the brief constitutional monarchy, that the *Declaration of the Rights of Man and Citizen (La Déclaration des Droits de l'Homme et du Citoyen*) was adopted.

In the same way that the *United States Declaration of Independence* declared that 'all men are created equal ... endowed ... with certain unalienable rights [of] life, liberty and the pursuit of happiness', so did the French *Declaration of the Rights of Man and Citizen* declare 'that 'the natural inalienable, and sacred rights of man' are 'liberty, property, security and resistance to oppression', enjoyed by men who are 'born and remain free and equal in rights'.[63] The drafting of the *Declaration of the Rights of Man and Citizen* was influenced by Jefferson, who was America's representative to France, by Paine who visited Paris regularly, and by the Marquis de La Fayette, 'a deputy of the First French National Assembly, who had commanded an American division in the War of Independence, and who submitted to the drafting committee for the French Declaration, a text based on the *Virginia Declaration of Rights* 1776 and the

61 N O'Neill, S Rice & R Douglas, see above, n 8, 8, n 42.

62 The assertion of the rights of the American colonists foreshadows a similar assertion of rights by the colonies of the Western powers in the aftermath of the Second World War.

63 Trans in W Laqueur & B Rubin (eds), *The Human Rights Reader*, Temple University Press, Philadelphia, 1979, 118–120, 118.

American *Declaration of Independence*.'[64] The French *Declaration of the Rights of Man and Citizen* was the model, 'in substance and form',[65] for the UDHR.

2.2.5 The Decline of Natural Rights

The American and French declarations were the high-water mark of the political influence of natural rights. Although 'the idea of natural rights was the vocabulary in which [the American and French] revolutions were conducted',[66] the idea fell out of favour during the eighteenth and nineteenth centuries as new political philosophies responded to the changing nature of state–citizen relations in the industrial revolution and emerging capitalism. Jean-Jacques Rousseau, for example, refined natural rights by reasserting a role for the state. He recognised that the new state was a different form of sovereignty from the regal autocracy to which Locke's thesis of an individual's natural rights had been a reaction, and maintained that in the new society, 'individuals were not merely securing the rights they acquired in the state of nature but were creating a new entity, one committed to the common welfare'.[67]

But the scientific rationalism of the Enlightenment was impatient with the abstract and almost mystical nature of natural rights. It sought a more reasoned basis for the relationship between a state and its subjects, one that was scientific and based on experience rather than on an assertion—even a 'rational' one—of the natural order. Because it was derived from 'natural law', the actual content of natural rights was unclear, and the practical articulation of natural rights was a matter of politics. The United States *Declaration*, for example, identified only '*certain* unalienable rights' and said that '*among these* are life, liberty and the pursuit of happiness', while the French *Declaration* identified 'the final end of every political institution is the preservation of the natural and *imprescriptable* rights of man'.[68] This vagueness in the content of natural rights was famously attacked by Jeremy Bentham: '[n]atural rights is simple nonsense: natural and imprescriptable rights, nonsense upon stilts ... They know not of what they are talking under the name of natural rights, and yet they would have them imprescriptable'.[69]

Bentham, and after him John Stuart Mill, promoted a radical alternative to natural rights, utilitarianism, which proposed that society's goal was not to enable each individual to pursue their

64 N O'Neill, S Rice & R Douglas, see above, n 8, 9, citing A H Robertson, *Human Rights in the World*, 2nd edn, Manchester University Press, Manchester, 1982, 3.

65 M Ishay, see above, n 4, 3; S P Marks, 'From the "Single Confused Page" to the "Decalogue of Six Billion Persons": The Roots of the Universal Declaration of Human Rights in the French Revolution' (1998) 20(3) *Human Rights Quarterly* 459; C Douzinas, 'The End(s) of Human Rights' (2002) 26 (2) *Melbourne University Law Review* 445, 448–9.

66 K Minogue, see above, n 18, 3–16, 10.

67 M Ishay, see above, n 4, 103.

68 (Emphasis added).

69 J Bentham, 'Anarchical Fantasies' in A Melden (ed), *Human Rights*, Wadsworth, Belmont, 1970, 28–60, 30–4; J Bowring (ed), *The Works of Jeremy Bentham*, Vol II, W Tait, Edinburgh, 1843, 501; B Parekh (ed), *Bentham's Political Thought*, Croom Helm, London, 1973, 269.

own natural rights but to achieve 'the greatest happiness of the greatest number'.[70] This was seen as a measureable basis for society's operation, rather than the rhetorical and 'nonsensical' claims of natural rights. Utilitarianism's conflict with natural rights suggests that it is fundamentally at odds with human rights: a calculation of what should be done to secure the greatest happiness for the greatest number cannot be reconciled with a principle that demands a minimum standard of conduct towards every human being. A criticism of utilitarianism is that such a calculation is never possible, as there is no absolute measure of what will constitute the 'best' result' in a situation; indeed, it may be that ensuring protection to a minimum standard is itself the best result for most people.[71]

With a similar desire for scientific certainty, Mill advocated for a positivist approach to law. Natural rights were seen as moral claims, but did not have the status of binding law, which could be only the actual law prescribed by a sovereign power. In a positivist view, law has authority only if it derives from a sovereign power and is posited in stated terms by that power; consequently, a moral assertion of how a person 'ought' to behave has no authority. This impatience with claims that are not positively stated as law is Bentham's impatience with the 'imprescriptable rights of man'. The result is that positivism rejects claims to natural rights and, by extension, '[i]n its essence positivism negates the moral philosophic basis of human rights'.[72] The response made for natural rights, and in the same way for human rights, is that positivism is itself an insufficient explanation for moral conduct, and a mere posited statement of law by a sovereign power is insufficient to constitute a law that will command respect and obedience by moral beings. A contemporary positivist argument is that to found rights in something other than a statement of law is undemocratic, depriving people of a say in the existence of rights.[73] On the other hand, the majoritarian nature of this 'democratic' argument for positivism would permit the oppression of minorities without any guarantee of basic protection, provided that such oppression could be characterised as the will of the majority.

An aspect of natural rights which distinguishes them from the human rights articulated in the UDHR is that natural rights did not claim to be 'universally' held. To say that natural rights were enjoyed by 'all' people meant that they were enjoyed by all *rational* people, and not all people were considered rational. The natural law from which natural rights developed was founded on the Graeco-Roman idea of the 'rational person', and that rationality was not ascribed universally. It was possible therefore to promote natural rights without attributing them to, for example, slaves or women, on the basis that slaves and women had not attained the same level of rationality. On this basis, the human rights of the UDHR are significantly different from natural rights: the UDHR recognises the human rights of all people equally.

The non-universal nature of natural rights has long been the subject of criticism, and in terms that foreshadowed contemporary relativist critiques discussed below. In relation to the exclusion of women, Mary Wollstonecraft, author of *Vindication of the Rights of Woman* in 1792 said: 'If the abstract rights of man will

70 J Bentham, *An Introduction to the Principles of Morals and Legislation*, 1781, Chapter 1, part xiii.

71 See I Law, 'Utilitariansim and Human Rights' in R Smith & C van den Anker (eds), *The Essentials of Human Rights*, Hodder Arnold, London, 2005, 356–8; see also J J Shestack, 'The Philosophic Foundations of Human Rights' (1998) 20(2) *Human Rights Quarterly* 201, 213–15; A Gibbard, 'Utilitarianism and Human Rights' (1984) 1 *Social Philosophy and Policy* 92.

72 J J Shestack, ibid 209.

73 See T Campbell, 'Democracy, Human Rights and Positive law', (1994) 16 *Sydney Law Review*, 195; T Campbell, *Prescriptive Legal Positivism: Law, Rights and Democracy*, Routledge, 2004, Chapter 9.

bear discussion and explanation, those of woman, by a parity of reasoning, will not shrink from the same test ... if women are not permitted to enjoy legitimate rights, they will render both men and themselves vicious to obtain illicit privileges'.[74] A year before, Olympe de Gouge had published *The Declaration of the Rights of Woman*, declaring that '[w]oman is born free and lives equal to man in her rights'.[75]

The position of slaves illustrates the varying extent of natural rights according to political circumstance. Although advocacy against slavery in France resulted in its abolition in 1794, slavery continued in Britain until 1807, and in the United States until the time of its civil war in 1863.[76]

Many who were not explicitly excluded from the declarations of 'natural rights' were effectively denied such rights because of the failure of the state to act to recognise or protect them. Natural rights were merely a constraint on state conduct that curtailed freedoms, not an obligation on the state to ensure and protect freedoms, so those without property or political power (much the same thing at the time) enjoyed few of the declared liberties. Ishay recounts the 'ascendency of men of property' and the exclusion of those without property, in England, America and France.[77]

The selectiveness of natural rights clearly distinguishes natural rights from the human rights of the UDHR. The claim that the UDHR makes for universality is unequivocal and unqualified.

2.2.6 The Significance of Natural Rights to the UDHR

By 1945 natural rights were characterised by vagueness, lack of universality and loss of political favour, and had been the subject of a powerful Marxist critique described below. Nevertheless, the legacy of natural rights theory is clear in the terms of the UDHR. The most significant contribution that natural rights made to Western political thinking that influenced the drafting of the UDHR was the recognition of individual liberties in relation to the state. As noted above, the importance of individual freedoms was recognised in other philosophical traditions, so Maritain's pragmatism was able to identify broadly agreed views without having to try too hard to reconcile the detail. It happened that, in relation to individual freedoms, the dominant philosophical tradition at the drafting of the UDHR was that of natural rights, so much so that 'while fully allowing for man's material requirements and for his duties to society, the balance ... is decidedly in favour of man's inner freedom, and his natural and inalienable rights'.[78]

But it must be kept in mind that natural rights were only an influence on what Malik called 'a composite synthesis, the like of which has never before occurred in history'.[79] It is an oversimplification

74 k Minogue, see above, n 18, 3–16, 15.

75 M Ishay, see above, n 4, 112.

76 M Ishay, see above, n 4, 111–16.

77 M Ishay, see above, n 4, 108–9.

78 H C Malik, *The Challenge of Human Rights; Charles Malik and the Universal Declaration*, Charles Malik Foundation and Centre for Lebanese Studies, Oxford, 2000, 132, cited in A Danilovic, *Pragmatism, Philosophy and International Politics: The UNESCO Committee on the Philosophic Principles of the Rights of Man and the Drafting of the Universal Declaration of Human Rights* (Masters Thesis, University of British Columbia, 2002, 47 <http://hdl.handle.net/2429/12439> at 11 March 2011, 47.

79 Ibid 47 <http://hdl.handle.net/2429/12439>.

to say that '[w]hat are nowadays called 'human rights' ... were once called 'natural rights'.[80] For the drafters of the UDHR there was no direct evolutionary line from natural rights to human rights. Rather, there were the echoes of an old idea in the development of a new and significantly different one. That an individual has a claim against the state, as an individual, is common to natural rights and to many, though not all, the human rights of the UDHR.

The civil and political rights of the UDHR are significantly different from natural rights in three ways: they are specific, not unspecified; they are universal, not limited to some; and they derive from human dignity, not from human reason.

2.2.7 Common Law Rights

In the Australian debate about a legislative guarantee of human rights,[81] opponents of such legislation invoke the Australian common law (of English heritage) as a sufficient, if not superior, means of protecting human rights.[82] Against this, it has been said that, '[i]n fact, the common law is the least significant source of human rights law'.[83] Certainly the common law recognises fewer rights than are known as human rights and, of necessity because it is the law of the courts and not of the parliament, the common law offers no guarantees of recognition or protection of human rights.

The first observation to make about common law rights is that they are different from human rights. English common law rights are essentially the natural law rights and freedoms which were developed in England between the thirteenth and eighteenth centuries. The common law recognises, for example, rights to liberty and security of the person (such as *habeas corpus*),[84] a right to a fair trial,[85] freedom of assembly (short of breaching the peace),[86] freedom of association,[87] and freedom of expression (short of defamation, sedition and blasphemy).[88] The English courts recognised these rights and freedoms as deriving from *Magna Carta* or the *Bill of Rights*, or simply as part of the unwritten constitutional arrangements between state and citizen, which developed in and after the seventeenth century. As noted above, these rights and freedoms were precursors of, but not the same as, human rights. They continue to operate in common law, quite separately from human rights.

A more important observation about common law rights is that their content and status are as uncertain as the natural rights they reflect. The common law has no single authoritative source but is a collection of court decisions—'a wilderness of single instances'.[89] It has a strand of commonality

80 M Cranston, 'What are Human Rights', in W Laqueur & B Rubin (eds), *The Human Rights Reader*, Temple University Press, Philadelphia, 1979, 17–25, 17.

81 See Chapter 10.3.3.

82 See J Leeser & R Haddrick (eds), *Don't Leave Us With the Bill: The Case Against an Australian Bill of Rights*, Menzies Research Centre, Barton, 2009.

83 N O'Neill, S Rice & R Douglas, see above, n 8, 106.

84 Discussed in N O'Neill, S Rice & R Douglas, see above, n 8, 213–18.

85 N O'Neill, S Rice & R Douglas, see above, n 8, 225–38.

86 N O'Neill, S Rice & R Douglas, see above, n 8, 282 & 288–95.

87 N O'Neill, S Rice & R Douglas, see above, n 8, 326–67.

88 N O'Neill, S Rice & R Douglas, see above, n 8, 369–97.

89 Lord A Tennyson, *Alymer's Field* (1864), quoted in in N O'Neill, S Rice & R Douglas, see above, n 8, 107.

running through decisions which, over time, are made consistently in similar circumstances: a person before a court can be confident that their circumstances will be dealt with according to the precedent set by earlier decisions in similar circumstances. In this way there will be some sense of 'right', in that a person before a court is entitled to expect a decision that accords with precedent. So it is difficult to find any clear source in the common law for individual rights.

A right must be found in the history of the common law; judges cannot 'make' new rights.[90] The furthest that the courts are prepared to go in developing the common law is to expand or modify an existing rule for the sake of fairness or efficiency, or change a rule to avoid manifest injustice, an approach that is well short of creating rights. This leaves very little room for judicial creativity and confines common law rights to those that can be found in common law history, although the historical inquiry is a complex and uncertain exercise.[91] Even if a common law right is found or recognised, it is always vulnerable to modification or repeal by the legislature.

2.3 SOCIAL RIGHTS

As noted in Chapter 1, at the time of the drafting of the UDHR the groups of rights called 'civil and political' were not sharply distinguished from 'economic, social and cultural' rights. Although there was debate at the time about their relative status,[92] the real separation came later when, in the international political context of the Cold War, they were grouped into separate treaties, the *International Covenant on Civil and Political Rights* and the *International Covenant on Economic, Social and Cultural Rights*. Nevertheless, these two broad groups of rights do have different origins.

In the nineteenth century, natural rights, and the new political order in Europe which they underpinned, were subject to powerful attack by Marx and Engels's social critique. Their socialism was a clear alternative to Western liberal politics, and became the other significant influence on the drafting of the UDHR. In discussing the two dominant traditions of Western political thought regarding human rights, the UNESCO Committee's final report[93] outlined a history of economic social and cultural rights:

UNESCO THE GROUNDS OF AN INTERNATIONAL DECLARATION OF HUMAN RIGHTS

During the nineteenth century there were added to these rights another set of fundamental human rights which grew out of the recognition that to live well and freely men must have at least the means requisite for living and which was made increasingly practicable by the advances in technology and industrialisation in making the means

90 See *Mabo and Others v Queensland (No 2)* [1992] HCA 23; 175 CLR 1, 29–30 (Brennan J) (citations omited). See also Brennan J's later similar comments in *Dietrich v The Queen* [1992] HCA 57; (1992) 177 CLR 292, 319–21.

91 See, eg, *Jago v The District Court of New South Wales* (1988) 12 NSWLR 558, 572–7 (Samuels JA); 569 (Kirby P); *Jago v The District Court of New South Wales* [1989] HCA 46; (1989) 168 CLR 23.

92 See, eg, A Devereux, *Australia and the Birth of the International Bill of Human Rights 1946–1966*, The Federation Press, Sydney, 2005, 28–9; M Craven, *The International Covenant on Economic, Social and Cultural Rights: A Perspective on its Development*, Clarendon Press, Oxford, 1998, 9–12.

93 See above, n 1, 6.

of livelihood potentially accessible to all men. These have come to be called Economic and Social Rights. They were first treated as sub-divisions or extensions of civil and political rights, but in the course of the last hundred years it has become apparent that they are different in kind from the older rights and that they therefore require different implementation. In their earliest form they are associated with the right to property, which in the eighteenth century was conceived by many philosophers to be the basic human rights from which the others are derived, in such fashion that even liberty and the pursuit of happiness are often treated as property rights of men.

The evolution of social and economic rights depended on the discussion of the relation of the ownership and the use of property, of private and common ownership, and of private rights and public responsibility. Similarly, the right to education was early conceived to belong to all men, and the institution of public systems of education was designed to effect the realisation of that right. Likewise, the right to work was trusted first as a freedom consequent on the right to property and was only later implemented with legal provisions for bargaining and arbitration concerning the conditions and the rewards of work. The right to protection of health usually started in the various states from modest beginnings in pure food and drugs legislation under the provisions on police power, and slowly extended to the provision of minimum medical and dietetic services, while the end of the nineteenth century and the beginning of the twentieth century saw the growth of various forms of social security designed to embody the right to maintenance during infancy, old age, sickness and other forms of incapacity, and involuntary unemployment.

Finally, there are few to deny, in the retrospect of technological advances today, the right of all to share in the advancing gains of civilisation and to have full access to the enjoyment of cultural opportunities and material improvements.

2.3.1 Private Property and Marxism

Locke had developed his theory of natural rights in reaction to the oppressive conduct of the British monarchy, which appropriated people's freedoms—and property—under a claimed 'divine right'. Consequently, the idea of an individual's right to private property was central to Locke's conception of natural rights. The French *Declaration,* for example, identified property as one of the 'the natural inalienable, and sacred rights of man'. The individual's right to private property propelled the rise of capitalism during the industrial revolution of the eighteenth and nineteenth centuries, and so was a focus of Marx's socialist critique.

In Marx's view, the rights of liberal capitalism were 'merely egotistical', 'the rights of the restricted individual withdrawn into himself'.[94] Marx rejected the (deontological) proposition that each person's rights are predetermined for them by nature—he saw this as separating a person from society and giving them life without context. Instead, Marx maintained that a person's identity—and their rights—are determined by their social circumstances, and he believed that capitalism constrained the communal life necessary for happiness.

2.3.2 The Russian Revolution

The idea of natural rights had supported revolutions against royal autocracy in England, America and France, and the flourishing of capitalism throughout the eighteenth and nineteenth centuries.

94 B Tierney, see above, n 2, 345, quoting Marx, unsourced.

The new liberalism gave constitutional recognition to individual freedoms and imposed constitutional restraint on sovereign power, establishing a 'Western' model of the state which spread throughout Europe. But Russia remained untouched by the political transformation of Europe.

The Romanov dynasty in Russia relied on a powerful and loyal army to keep control of a feudal state, and an uneducated and impoverished peasant population. The tsars had managed until the late nineteenth century to maintain their claims to ownership of all Russia, to a divine right to rule and to a paternal concern for the Russian people.[95] Russian royalty and nobility were keenly aware of political developments in Europe, and it suited them to keep the people of the vast Russian empire in ignorance. Serious expression of popular resentment did not emerge until the late nineteenth century, generations after the natural rights-inspired revolutions of England, America and France. The emancipation of the serfs in 1861 and the reformist rule of Alexander II was perhaps the beginning of the fraying of the fabric of feudal Russia, but the oppressive reassertion of old-style tsardom by Nicholas III in the 1890s brought reaction to the surface at a time when rapid industrialisation was bringing peasants to the cities, exposing them to new ideas and creating opportunities for organisation.

As the momentum for reforms in Russia built in the early twentieth century, there was strong support among reformist nobles for Western-style capitalist reforms and a constitutional monarchy. But their reform proposals were swept away by the Bolshevik revolutionaries' organisation of the mass of Russian urban factory workers, and their commitment to Vladimir Lenin's interpretation of the socialism of Marx and Engels.[96] Marxism spoke to a communal society of workers in a way that the individualised ethos of natural rights did not: 'The special attraction of Marxism stemmed from the importance it gave to the role of the working class and to the idea of progress'.[97] Marxism saw in the individual ownership of property the necessary exercise of individual power, at odds with communal interests.

In promoting Marxism as the appropriate revolutionary philosophy for Russia, Lenin was able to point to the unequal access to 'natural rights' among the post-revolutionary societies of the West:

> even in the most democratic bourgeois republic 'freedom of assembly' is a hollow phrase, for the rich have the best public and private buildings at their disposal, and enough leisure to assemble at meetings ... The rural and urban workers and the small peasants—the overwhelming majority of the population—are denied all these things ...
>
> 'Freedom of the press' is another of the principal slogans of 'pure democracy'. And here too the workers know ... that this freedom is a deception while the best printing presses and the biggest stocks of paper are appropriated by the capitalists, and while capitalist rule over the press remains—a rule that is manifested throughout the world all the more strikingly, sharply and cynically the more democracy and the republican system are developed, as in America for example.[98]

95 O Figes, *A People's Tragedy: The Russian Revolution 1891–1924*, London, Pimlico, 1996, 6–7.

96 See, eg, V I Lenin, *Karl Marx: A Brief Biographical Sketch with an Exposition of Marxism*, Foreign Languages Press, Peking, 1967.

97 See above, n 95, 119.

98 V Lenin, 'Report to the First Congress of the Third International' (1919), quoted in W Laqueur & B Rubin (eds), *The Human Rights Reader*, Temple University Press, Philadelphia, 1979, 183–8, 184.

As was the case with England, the United States and France, the Russian state that emerged from political revolution was modelled along the lines of the philosophy that had underpinned the revolt. In the case of the new Russia—the Union of Soviet Socialist Republics (USSR)—the philosophy was Marxist socialism, which was not only distinctive but also antithetical to the individual liberalism of the West.

2.3.3 Western Socialism

There was a strong socialist history in Europe quite apart from the emergence of the new Russia after the Bolshevik revolution of 1917. The property-based critique of liberalism was not unique to Marx, and Russia was not the first place in which it became politically relevant. Ishay elaborates on her account of the political exclusion of people without property in England, America and France, describing the many eighteenth- and nineteenth-century socialist movements against the institutional power of the wealthy.[99] First in England and France, and then more broadly across Europe, industrialisation was urbanising workers, and promoting opportunities for education, social awareness and mass organisation. The individual rights which originated in natural law were concerned with civic freedoms and political participation; social rights developed as a reaction to the practical exclusivity of these civil and political rights. Social rights focused on the shared needs of an emerging class of workers—for example, for education, work and housing—and were campaigned for by socialists throughout Europe.

Socialists focused on the power wielded by individuals who had both private property and guaranteed freedoms. They saw that this power enabled some people to profit at the expense of others, and what they saw fitted Marx and Engels's theory of the exploitation of workers by the owners of agricultural and industrial property. They demanded a genuine equality, where rights were enjoyed collectively, without distinction. Socialism suggested a degree of universalism that was absent in the reality of liberal states at the time; socialists 'broadened the narrow definition of universalism they inherited from the Enlightenment, articulating a broad commitment to enhance simultaneously, rather than selectively, the rights of slaves, children, women, homosexuals and Jews'.[100]

Of Roosevelt's four freedoms,[101] the 'freedom from want' in particular invokes ideas familiar to socialism: guarantees of 'employment opportunities, social security, education and health care'.[102] However '[i]t was not intended to have such a wide import but to incorporate the United States' faith in international free trade as the means of guaranteeing economic security'.[103] Nor was his proposed 'Economic Bill of Rights'[104] a call for state-sponsored social support, but rather an aspiration of what a healthy capitalist economy could enable individuals to achieve for themselves.

99 M Ishay, see above, n 4, 135–55.

100 M Ishay, see above, n 4, 155.

101 See Chapter 1.2 for a discussion of Roosevelt's four freedoms and the context in which they arose.

102 A Devereux, see above, n 92, 13.

103 A Devereux, see above, n 92, 13, citing M G Johnson, 'The Contributions of Eleanor and Franklin Roosevelt to the Development of International Protection for Human rights' (1987) 9(1) *Human Rights Quarterly* 19, 21.

104 F Roosevelt, *State of the Union Address, Congress of the United States of America*, 11 January 1944.

Australia, on the other hand, has strong traditions of collective politics and policies, and Roosevelt's 'freedom from want' was understood at the time to be a call for state action to provide for those in need:

> In post-war Australia, there was an intense expectation of a new era bringing if not immediate prosperity, then at least an end to war-time privation and the hope of a better economic future. Politicians on both sides of the divide tapped into this desire. [H V] Evatt, for instance, declared that peace would be meaningful only if it were based on 'social justice and economic betterment'. [Robert] Menzies supported the establishment of a Joint Parliamentary Committee on Social Security to report on means of improving social and living conditions in Australia. 'Full employment ' was taken up as an objective of many governments, including the United Kingdom and Australia. Internationally, Australia saw collective efforts with respect to social and economic problems as necessary in order to provide for durable peace.[105]

Devereux notes that the Australia delegation led by H V Evatt was influential in aspects of the *UN Charter*, and gave 'unstinting support' to the international recognition of economic, social and cultural rights.[106]

Differently, therefore, from the political Marxism of the USSR, socialism had wide support in the West, where there was a concurrent commitment to broad social standards and individual liberties. An early and persistent example of Western acceptance of social rights is the International Labour Organisation (ILO) and its many conventions to protect and promote workers' rights. Although its initial remit in 1919 was protecting 'workers against a loss of earning capacity', the 1944 *Declaration of Philadelphia* considerably expanded the ILO's vision, aspiring to establish 'social security systems of a universal rather than categorical nature throughout the world'.[107] That goal was enshrined as a human right in article 22 of the UDHR.

2.4 DIGNITY AND UNIVERSALITY

The preceding account strongly suggests that contemporary human rights are effectively a novel creation, based on a history of religious and political philosophies that came together in a pragmatic, international political exercise in the mid-twentieth century in the shadow of the unprecedented death, cruelty and oppression of the Second World War. Since then, the idea of human rights has been vulnerable to just the sort of deep analysis that Maritain's pragmatism succeeded in avoiding in the debates leading up to the *Universal Declaration*. While people and states did—and continue to—accept the broad idea of human rights, its theoretical rationale has been under consistent scrutiny.

Jerome Shestack, a former US Ambassador to the UN Commission on Human Rights, notes the substantial body of international human rights law that has been built on the UDHR and asks, '[h]aving

105 A Devereux, see above, n 92, 27 (citations omitted).

106 A Devereux, see above, n 92, 30–1.

107 A Supiot, 'The Position of Social Security in the System of International Labour Standards' (2005–2006) 27(2) *Comparative Labor Law and Policy Journal*, 113, 113. See Chapter 17.2.

come this far legally, why then should one still be concerned with [its] philosophic foundations'?'[108] Answering his own question, he suggests that not only is there merit simply in pursuing deeper understanding for its own sake, but that knowing the philosophic foundations of human rights will both strengthen international law and promote the university of human rights.[109] Human rights must make not only a pragmatic but a moral claim if they are to achieve respect and willing compliance. This calls for a clear and defensible theoretical rationale which can sustain the idea of human rights beyond their pragmatic articulation in international documents.

The most persistent claims made in theoretical support of human rights is that they follow from the fact of inherent human dignity, and that human rights are therefore universal. These two claims—dignity and universality—are both essential features of contemporary human rights. At the same time they are claims that are disputed, and acceptance of their legitimacy turns on differing views of dignity and universality.

2.4.1 Dignity

The Idea of Dignity at the United Nations

Human dignity is not the only basis on which an argument can be made for human rights. Referring to a range of commentators, Brooke Ackerly argues that human rights are immanent in political and practical experience, and lists as other possible sources of human rights 'the individual moral standing of a person, individual autonomy, human agency ... equal creation by a divinity, membership in the human family, membership in political society, well-being, and human functioning'.[110]

There are also commentators who challenge the idea of human dignity, or say that it cannot be a basis for human rights:[111]

> Objections raised by critics centre on the perceived indeterminacy of the concept of human dignity and what some theorists consider to be its excessive individualism. As a result, sceptics argue, dignity provides an insecure basis for the transformation required to realise the promise of substantive equality. Commenting on the role of dignity in constitutional jurisprudence, Feldman, for example, asserts that 'the legitimacy of judicial action on the basis of a notion as malleable as dignity is not self-evident'.

But whatever the philosophical arguments that are now made for (and against) human rights, inherent human dignity is recognised at the UN to be the source of human rights. Practically and politically, it is the rhetoric of 'inherent human dignity' that states invoke when they debate their recognition, observation and violation of international human rights.

---

108 J J Shestack, see above, n 71, 201.

109 J J Shestack, see above, n 71, 201–2.

110 B A Ackerly, *Universal Human Rights in a World of Difference*, Cambridge University Press, Cambridge, 2008, 73 (citations omitted).

111 E Grant, 'Dignity and Equality' (2007) 7(2) *Human Rights Law Review* 299, 301. Grant cites C Albertyn & B Goldblatt, 'Facing the Challenge of Transformation: Difficulties in the Development of an Indigenous Jurisprudence of Equality' (1998) 14 *South African Journal on Human Rights*, 248, 257–8 & 272; E Grabham, '*Law v Canada*: New Directions for Equality under the Canadian Charter?' (2002) 22(4) *Oxford Journal of Legal Studies* 641, 653; C M Bredt & A M Dodek, 'Breaking the Law's Grip on Equality: A New Paradigm for section 15' (2003) 20 *Supreme Court Law Review*, 33, 46; D M Davis, 'Equality: The Majesty of Legoland Jurisprudence' (1999) 116 *South African Law Journal*, 398, 413; D Feldman, 'Human Dignity as a Legal Value—Part 1' (1999) (Winter) *Public Law*, 682, 697.

The idea of inherent human dignity as the foundation of human rights is pervasive in the history of the UN. It was asserted in 1945 as an established and accepted phenomenon in the Preamble to the *Charter of the United Nations*, which states that the peoples of the United Nations 'reaffirm faith ... in the dignity and worth of the human person ...' Similarly, the Preamble to the UDHR recognises 'the inherent dignity and ... the equal and inalienable rights of all members of the human family'. Article 1 of the UDHR states simply, 'All human beings are born free and equal in dignity and rights.' Article 22 states that 'economic, social and cultural rights [are] indispensable for ... dignity', and article 23 that a worker has a 'right to just and favourable remuneration ensuring for himself and his family an existence worthy of human dignity'.

Every subsequent UN statement of human rights relies on the idea of inherent human dignity, an idea which has become 'commonplace in new international human rights and humanitarian law instruments'.[112] Numerous international human rights treaties, some International Labour Conventions and some international agreements,[113] refer to human dignity in their Preambles and many rely on the idea of human dignity in various provisions that articulate specific rights.[114] As one commentator observes, '[b]y 1986 dignity had become so central to United Nations' conceptions of human rights that the UN General Assembly provided, in its guidelines for new human rights instruments, that such instruments should be 'of fundamental character and derive from the inherent dignity and worth of the human person'.[115] The concept of human dignity was adopted as 'the central organising principle' of the 1993 Vienna World Conference on Human Rights, which in turn adopted it as 'foundational ... to human rights in general'.[116] The same idea of dignity has been adopted very widely in regional (inter-American, Arab, African and European) human rights instruments,[117] in international treaties[118] and in national constitutions, particularly in post-communist states in the 1990s.[119]

The pervasiveness of the idea of inherent human dignity seems to make its centrality to human rights self-evident: it is hard to doubt such a widely accepted concept as the source of human rights. But the persistent restatement of its existence does not explain how it came to be so, nor what it actually means. Both questions need to be answered if the idea of human rights is to be defended as having

112 C McCrudden, 'Human Dignity and Judicial Interpretation of Human Rights' (2008) 19(4) *European Journal of International Law*, 655, 668.

113 As an example, the inter-governmental agreement to establish IFAD, the International Fund for Agricultural Development, adopted in Rome by the United Nations Conference on the Establishment of an International Fund for Agricultural Development on 13 June 1976.

114 See above, n 112, 669–70.

115 See above, n 112, 669, referring to *Setting International Standards in the Field of Human Rights*, GA Res. 41/120, UN GA, 41st sess, 97th plen mtg, UN Doc A/Res/41/120 (1986), quoted in A Clapham, *Human Rights Obligations of Non-State Actors*, Oxford University Press, New York, 2006, 538.

116 See above, n 112, 670.

117 See Chapter 8 below.

118 See Chapter 7.3 below.

119 See above, n 112, 671–3.

theoretical substance rather than mere political utility. The German philosopher Jürgen Habermas captures the importance of the philosophical question concerning the idea of human dignity when he asks:[120]

> whether human dignity signifies a substantive normative account from which human rights can be deduced by specifying the conditions under which human dignity is violated. Or does the expression merely provide an empty formula that summarises a catalogue of individual unrelated rights?

Although the Preamble to the *Charter of the United Nations* 'reaffirms faith in the dignity and worth of the human person', few references to such faith pre-date the Charter. There had been 'scattered references' to dignity in humanitarian documents in the nineteenth and early twentieth centuries,[121] and '[s]everal countries in Europe and the Americas incorporated the concept of dignity in their constitutions' in the early twentieth century: Mexico, Weimar Germany, Finland, Portugal, Ireland and Cuba. But 'this constitutional use of dignity remained pretty marginal ... until the end of the Second World War'.[122] The constitutional use of dignity reflected aspects of political philosophy of the eighteenth and nineteenth centuries, but the notion had a very modest place in law and politics before it was 'reaffirmed' by the *UN Charter* in 1945 and became the source of human rights in the UDHR in 1948.

It is unclear how 'dignity' came to be referred to, let alone 'reaffirmed', in the Preamble of the *UN Charter of the United Nations*. It may have been proposed by the South African drafter of the preamble, Jan Christian Smuts, although the term was in 'common use in the circles devising the new United Nations global architecture'.[123]

When Cassin reworked Humphrey's draft of the UDHR he added the idea of human dignity.[124] Cassin's dignitarian philosophy[125] was a practical solution to the problem of gaining consensus: 'human dignity was a rallying cry in intellectual debate across the political and philosophical spectrum'.[126] As a simple and very effective means of achieving consensus, the idea of human dignity was 'included in that part of any discussion or text where the absence of a theory of human rights would have been embarrassing.'[127] Eleanor Roosevelt was able to argue in the drafting committee that the reference to dignity was 'to emphasise that every human being is worthy of respect ... to explain why human beings have rights to

120 J Habermas, 'The Concept of Human Dignity and the Realistic Utopia of Human Rights' (2010) 41(4) *Metaphilosophy*, 464, 466.

121 C McCrudden, see above, n 112, 667.

122 C McCrudden, see above, n 112, 664.

123 C McCrudden, see above, n 112, 675–6.

124 C McCrudden, see above, n 112, 677.

125 M Glendon, *A World Made New: Eleanor Roosevelt and the Universal Declaration of Human Rights*, Random House, New York, 2001, 217.

126 C McCrudden, see above, n 112, 677.

127 C McCrudden, see above, n 112, 677.

begin with'.[128] In an exercise that was designed to articulate human rights, such self-referential reasoning was hard to argue with: human beings have rights because, as human beings, they are worthy of respect.

It has become a truism that human dignity gives rise to human rights. The question that no one particularly wanted or needed to answer in 1948, but that has been asked (and answered) since, is what is it about humans that makes them worthy of respect: what *is* the idea of human dignity that underpins human rights?

Historical Meanings of Dignity

Clearly the idea of human dignity had sufficient meaning 'across the political and philosophical spectrum' to enable agreement on the terms of the UDHR in 1948: 'appealing to the concept of human dignity undoubtedly made it easier to reach an overlapping consensus'[129] and deliberately avoided debate about the theoretical foundations of human rights.[130]

Precisely because the UDHR avoided referring to any specific traditions of thought or practice, it is not possible to say that its reference to dignity was based on any particular understanding of its meaning: dignity was a term which embraced a wide range of meanings, all of them related in some way with the state of being human. Its strength was that 'it carried an enormous amount of content, but different content for different people'.[131] The political pragmatism behind the UDHR's statement of human rights led to its taking a declaratory approach: it stated a new truth, based on established ideas.

Whatever the idea of human dignity stood for, it was far from a new idea—the participants in the UDHR debates all seemed to recognise something in it. Indeed, the idea of human dignity was familiar at the time from a wide range of sources, religious, social, political and philosophical.

Of the many different ways of thinking of human dignity, the one that most closely aligns with human rights is on based on the philosophy of Immanuel Kant: the idea that fundamental or integral dignity derives from rational agency; rationality is said to be 'the foundation of our essential dignity, explaining why certain of our rights are inherently inalienable'.[132] Maritain, one of the architects of the UDHR, endorsed precisely this view in his own writing.[133]

Kant's idea of inherent dignity should be distinguished from other commonly understood ideas of human dignity, such as onto-theological dignity (man created in the image of God),[134] 'aristocratic

128 C McCrudden, see above, n 112, 677, quoting M Glendon, see above, n 125, 146.

129 See above, n 120, 467.

130 P Carozza, 'Human Dignity and Judicial Interpretation of Human Rights: A Reply' (2008) 19(5) *European Journal of International Law*, 931, 941.

131 C McCrudden, see above, n 112, 677.

132 E Engle, 'Universal Human Rights: A Generational History' (2006) 12 *Annual Survey of International and Comparative Law*, 219, 253.

133 M Cranston, see above, n 21, 21.

134 K Dicke, 'The Founding Function of Human Dignity in the Universal Declaration of Human Rights', in D Kretzmer & E Klein (eds), *The Concept of Human Dignity in Human Rights Discourse*, Kluwer Law International, The Hague, 2002, 111–20, 113. See also, N Jacobson, 'A Taxonomy of Dignity: A Grounded Theory of Study' (2009) 9(3) *BMC International Health and Human Rights*, 3, 4, citing, among others, R C Dales, 'A Mediaeval View of Human Dignity' (1977) 38(4) *Journal of the History of Ideas*, 557.

dignity (associated with rank), comportment dignity (compliance with social norms), and meritorious dignity (virtue in adversity)'.[135] Each of these in different ways is concerned with aspects of being human, and each confers on a person the attribute of dignity, which defines their identity in a positive or affirming way. Aristocratic dignity, for example, can be traced back through European institutions, such as royalty, to the concept of *dignitas hominis*, which in Roman times indicated a status (of a person or institution) that was deserving of honour and respect.[136] Dignity in this sense can never be accorded to people who are not of an appropriate social status; it is conferred only on certain people, and only in certain circumstances: these types of dignity are not true of all people at all times. The significant dimension of the type of dignity that underpins human rights, however, is that it is said to be true of all people at all times—leading to the 'universality' of human rights discussed below—hence the reference to dignity's being 'fundamental to' or 'inherent in' humans.

The idea that being human carries with it an inherent dignity is ancient: '[i]t was the Stoics who first made the connection between the idea that individuals were reasonable beings who should be respected and the notion of a universal system of rules or law of nature. Human nature, in Stoic terms, was characterised by reason. It was this quality that distinguished man from animals. Because all men had reason, they were all equal and worthy of respect. This is the basis of human dignity'.[137] For the Roman thinker Cicero, the idea of dignity 'referred also to the dignity of human beings as human beings, not dependent on any particular status'.[138] He observed that while animals are concerned only with 'bodily satisfactions ... Man's mind ... is developed by study and reflection ... From this we may learn that sensual pleasure is wholly unworthy of the dignity of the human race'.[139] Cicero's reference to the distinctive human capacity for reflective thought anticipated by 1800 years Kant's identifying the human capacity for pure reason.

In the centuries between Cicero and Kant in Western thought, the idea of dignity was most commonly found in Christian theology. The onto-theological idea of dignity[140] was that humans ('man') have dignity (or 'worth') simply because they are created in the image of God:[141] the dignity is effectively the dignity of

135 S Killmister, 'Dignity: Not Such a Useless Concept' (2010) 36(3) *Journal of Medical Ethics*, 160, 160–1, citing D Schroder, 'Dignity: Two Riddles and Four Concepts' (2008) 17(2) *Cambridge Quarterly on Healthcare Ethics*, 230.

136 C McCrudden, see above, n 112, 656–7.

137 E Grant, see above, n 111, 304, citing H Cancik, ''Dignity of Man' and 'Persona' in *Stoic Anthropology: Some Remarks on Cicero, De Officiis*, I, 105–7', in D Kretzmer & E Klein (eds), *The Concept of Human Dignity in Human Rights Discourse*, Kluwer Law International, The Hague, 2002, 19–39, 21.

138 C McCrudden, see above, n 112, 657.

139 Cicero, *De Officiis*, I, 30 quoted in C McCrudden, see above, n 112, 657.

140 K Dicke, see above, n 134. See also N Jacobson, see above, n 134.

141 *The Bible, Book of Genesis*, Chapter 1, verses 26–7.

being God's creature, not derived from anything integral to being human. The idea of 'man in the image of God' is not unique to the Christian Bible but is found as well in the Quran, the Talmud, the Bhagavad-Gita and 'other religions with a deistic base'.[142] Nor is it novel to see 'that there is a humanity behind or beneath the roles and norms imposed by society'; it was recognised in ancient sources such as the stories of the Hebrew Bible, the plays of Sophocles and the parables of the Confucian philosopher Mencius.[143]

The Christian philosopher Thomas Aquinas was one of the earliest scholars to look past God-creation as the basis of human dignity and to identify—as Cicero had and Kant would—the human capacity to reason as the source of human dignity. Although the capacity to reason was itself attributed to the God-creator, with this conceptual development the idea of dignity became 'divorced from office and hierarchy'.[144] The resulting idea of human dignity—that a person had recognition and respect *simply for being human*—became widely used in political debate in the eighteenth and nineteenth centuries; it 'became closely connected with the growth of republicanism', particularly in France, and 'came to be used as a rallying cry for a variety of other social and political movements advocating specific types of social reform during the nineteenth century', from women's emancipationists to anti-slavery activists and social welfare campaigners.[145]

The French *Declaration of the Rights of Man and of the Citizen* was arguably the single most influential statement of rights for the drafting of the UDHR,[146] and it was 'predicated on legitimate claims the individual has by virtue of being a human and ... not dependent on society conferring rights on its members'.[147] While true, this glosses over the limited range of people who were accepted at the time as in fact having 'claims by virtue of being a human': dignity was inherent only for those who were recognised, socially and politically, as having the status.

Throughout this period there was no clear articulation of a theoretical basis for asserting human dignity and the resulting claims that were made. The capacity to reason, which encompassed the capacity to choose, was the essential thesis, usually underpinned by the persistent attribution to a Christian God. As a result, the idea of human dignity was contested: groups of people had to make a case for having the status that gave them human dignity (eg women), and groups of people were presumptively denied the status and so were denied human dignity (eg children, serfs, slaves, non-Europeans etc). In politics and society, as recently as the early twentieth century, the idea of human dignity had not reached a stage that recognised the idea that '[a]ll humans, not merely rich white males, have an essential dignity and beauty as humans because of the capacity to think'.[148]

142 J J Shestack, see above, n 71, 205.

143 P Berger, 'On the Obsolescence of the Concept of Honour' in M J Sandel (ed), *Liberalism and Its Critics*, NYU Press, New York, 1984, 153.

144 C McCrudden, see above, n 112, 659.

145 C McCrudden, see above, n 112, 660–1.

146 S P Marks, see above, n 65.

147 S P Marks, see above, n 65, 473.

148 E Engle, see above, n 132.

Separately from the politics of the time, a philosophical 'essentialist' view of human dignity was developed by Immanuel Kant, whose theory was the 'first modern definition of human dignity'.[149] It is 'probably the most often cited non-religiously-based conception of dignity'[150] and 'is perhaps the best account of what is now going on, at least among moral philosophers and philosophically literate rights advocates'.[151]

Kant's Conception of Dignity ('Würde')

Kant explored the idea of social contract and the relationship of human beings with the state and with each other. The sources of his idea of human dignity are his *Groundwork of the Metaphysics of Morals* (*Grundlegung zur Metaphysik der Sitten*), which he published in 1785, and his *Metaphysics of Morals* (*Die Metaphysik der Sitten*), which he published in 1797.[152]

In *Metaphysics* Kant identifies three aspects of being human: as a sentient being, as a rational being and as an intelligible being. The first of these is simply human-as-animal, as a being. The second is human-as-rational-animal, a creature that can reason. Such reasoning can extend to mathematics and logic, and can help determine the best way to act to achieve desired ends, but it distinguishes humans 'only quantitatively ... from other animals which act intelligently'. The desired ends are animal-like, 'determined by ... physical drives and desires'. The third aspect of being human is human-as-moral-personality, characterised by having freedom in two senses: freedom for being driven by sensual desire, and freedom to engage in pure reason as an end in itself. This freedom is autonomy. An autonomous human has a capacity for 'personality independent from physical determinants' and for being able to act according to principle, independently from ends determined by animal nature. Kant is clear that:[153]

> The human being is a person by virtue of [their] trait for moral personality. A person is a 'being endowed with freedom'. A physical person is a living corporeal entity being endowed with freedom. Freedom, like conscience and moral sentiment, is also a 'human capacity'. Conscience and moral sentiment are constitutive of this freedom ... [and] are those human traits that make someone human.

The 'intelligible' aspect of being human—human-as-moral-personality—enables a person to comprehend the nature of their freedom. That freedom does not derive from anything that can be established empirically: it does not follow from physical or psychological causes. Rather, a person is aware of their autonomy when they are aware of a reason for being that transcends natural necessity; Kant calls that 'reason for being' the 'categorical imperative', or 'moral imperative'. Rather than merely describing what a person must do, as a natural imperative would, the categorical imperative prescribes

---

149 M Iovane, 'The Universality of Human Rights and the International Protection of Cultural Diversity: Some Theoretical and Practical Considerations' (2007) 14 *International Journal of Minority and Group Rights* 231, 232.

150 C McCrudden, see above, n 112, 659.

151 J Waldron, 'Dignity and Rank' (2008) 48(2) *European Journal of Sociology*, 201, 209–14 & 235.

152 In this and the following paragraph the text is based on, and the quotes are from, J Hruschka, 'Kant and Human Dignity', in B S Byrd & J Hruschka (eds), *Kant and Law*, Ashgate, Burlington, 2006, 69–86, 69.

153 J Hruschka, ibid 80, quoting Kant's *Metaphysics of Morals*.

what must be done. Mere ends-oriented animal reasoning will not recognise the categorical imperative; rather, it is known through the pure reasoning that an intelligible human is capable of.

Kant formulated the categorical imperative—the transcendent morality that humans understand—in different ways. The second formulation (in *Groundwork of the Metaphysics of Morals*) is that a person shall act in such a way that they treat themselves and other people always as an end, and never simply as a means. This moral imperative illustrates Kant's idea of human dignity; Habermas observes that 'Kant defines the concept of dignity in the context of the moral injunction to treat every person as an end in himself'.[154]

Kant's thesis is that a person has dignity because of the human capacity to engage in moral reasoning. Dignity is not limited only to those who actually can or do engage in such reasoning: it is the capacity of *humanity* for moral reasoning which endows each person with dignity, 'even those who are depraved'; Kant stipulates that there is intrinsic worth which inheres in every human being.

Kantian dignity has been criticised as 'contentless',[155] and Waldron has argued that the Kantian idea of human dignity is merely a stipulation—a synthetic proposition[156]—rather than a substantial description of what dignity actually is.[157] He suggests that Kant's idea of dignity is perhaps more evaluative than descriptive',[158] explaining that dignity is *what people have*, but not saying *what dignity is*. In fact the content of Kantian dignity comes from the reasoning that gives rise to it: dignity is the individual autonomy that follows from human rationality. Dignity gives a person the right to be respected for having personal autonomy and, consequently, the right to not be used as a means but only ever to be respected in their own right.

In his survey of dignity Habermas argues that 'changing historical conditions have made us aware of something that was inscribed in human rights implicitly from the outset—the normative substance of the equal dignity of every human being that human rights only spell out'.[159] He claims that the use of dignity as a device to reach consensus over the drafting of the UDHR was *not* actually a 'smokescreen for disguising ... profound differences', but was the realisation of a 'background intuition of humiliation'. The sense of violation of human dignity is present in human history and experience:

> be it in view of the unbearable social conditions and the marginalization of impoverished social classes; or in view of the unequal treatment of women and men in the workplace, and of discrimination against foreigners and against cultural, linguistic, religious, and racial minorities; or in view of the ordeal of young women from immigrant families who have to liberate themselves from the violence of a traditional code of honor; or finally, in view of the brutal expulsion of illegal immigrants and asylum seekers.

154 J Habermas, see above, n 120, 465; see also J Hruschka, ibid 80–2 quoting Kant's *Metaphysics of Morals*.

155 C McCrudden, see above, n 112, 661 quoting A Schopenhauer; McCrudden notes that it was criticised as well for being a 'refuge from history in morality' (K Marx) and 'sentimental egalitarianism' (F Nietzsche).

156 A synthetic proposition is a claim that can be made, based on a premise, but does not necessarily follow from that premise without further argument

157 See above, n 151, 235.

158 See above, n 151, 209–14.

159 J Habermas, see above, n 120, 467.

Habermas argues that it is 'from the plethora of what it means to be humiliated and deeply hurt', that we understand the 'different aspects of the meaning of human dignity'.[160] In this way, the idea of human dignity is 'the key to the logical interconnectedness' of the various human rights.[161] Habermas's description of the many humiliations that explain our sense of dignity is, at the same time, an account of violations of Kant's moral imperative—when humans have been used as a means and have not been respected as ends in themselves.

The Idea of Dignity in Human Rights

Kant's idea of human dignity comes closest to the idea of human dignity that is invoked in the UDHR. The declaration in article 1 that 'All human beings are born free and equal in dignity and rights' is followed by the statement that all human beings 'are endowed with reason and conscience and should act towards each other in a spirit of brotherhood'. The reference to humans' reason and conscience connects directly with Kant's statement of human freedom in *Metaphysics of Morals*, and the injunction to 'act towards each other in a spirit of brotherhood' connects directly with Kant's moral imperative of means and ends.

Even though 'there was no systematic reference to human dignity in legal language until the 1940s',[162] the influence of the Kantian conception of dignity is quite clear. At the same time, proposals to the drafting committee of the UDHR invoked ideas of dignity based on each of Christian theology, Jewish traditions and natural law theory.[163] The convergence of these calls to recognise and respect dignity seems remarkable, but is readily explained by the context: the United Nations human rights project was born out of the enormous human cruelty and suffering of the Second World War, the source of most accounts of contemporary human rights.[164] In the Second World War the world saw, for the first time, graphic images of—in Habermas's terms—'what it means to be humiliated and deeply hurt', and it is from that experience that the world understood the meaning of human dignity.

The idea of dignity that underpins human rights seems to be just that—an idea, but one that is recognisable to all people, whether as an expression of their reason, their autonomy, their suffering, their status or their having been created by God or in God's image. It is a remarkably evocative idea, with remarkably wide appeal, which gives it its 'legitimising function' for human rights.[165] It is too a powerful idea; Schachter points out:

> The general idea that human rights are derived from the dignity of the person is neither truistic nor neutral. It has two corollaries that challenge conceptions prevalent in some societies an ideologies. The first corollary is the idea that basic rights are not given by authority and therefore may not be taken away; the second is

160 J Habermas, see above, n 120, 467–8.

161 J Habermas, see above, n 120, 468.

162 K Dicke, see above, n 134, 112.

163 K Dicke, see above, n 134, 113.

164 B A Ackerly, see above, n 110, 32.

165 K Dicke, see above, n 134, 118.

> that they are rights of the person, every person. It is not unrealistic to assume that ideas of this kind will have a role in challenging existing attitudes. When they are found in official declarations, they become part of the instruments of change, sometimes loudly proclaimed, at other times almost imperceptibly affecting ideas of legitimacy.[166]

The incidents and implications of the idea of human dignity will play out differently at different times and in different places, raising the most important current issue of human rights theory: the claim to universality of the rights that are said to flow from human dignity.

2.4.2 Universality

There are technical discussions about the universal application of human rights principles in international law, both as positive law (such as treaties) and as customary law (*jus cogens*).[167] But importantly in a discussion about popular acceptance of the idea of human rights, '[a] third form of human rights universalism refers to [human rights] generally ... in that they apply and are available to all'.[168]

The claim to universality of application has been made for contemporary human rights since they were first declared in the UDHR in 1948, and has been repeated consistently since. But as with the idea of human dignity, mere repetition of what was, at the time, a pragmatic, persuasive and widely supported idea is not enough to give it validity in the face of the scrutiny that has taken place since. The claim of universality must have a clear and defensible theoretical rationale—there must be an answer to 'why is it so?'—if the idea of human rights is to be sustained beyond its pragmatic declaration.

Human Dignity

The initial claim to universality, although it was contested, was largely accepted as unremarkable at the time: it was a self-evidently true claim that followed from the assertion of human dignity: all people have human dignity (human dignity is universal), therefore all people have human rights (human rights are universal). This is a commonly made argument,[169] which depends on acceptance of the idea of inherent human dignity: '[d]enial of that principle ... shatters universalism'.[170] Claiming universality on the basis of human dignity has the 'advantage [of being] unproblematic'[171] only if the idea of human dignity is accepted. It is what Donnelly calls a 'conceptual', approach to establishing the universality of human rights, failing to answer 'substantive' questions about whether human rights can actually be shown to be universal.

166 O Schachter, 'Editorial Comment: Human Dignity as a Normative Concept' (1983) 77(4) *American Journal of International Law*, 848, 853.

167 See M Goodhart, 'Universalism', in R Smith & C van den Anker (eds), *The Essentials of Human Rights*, Hodder Arnold, London, 2005, 353–6, 354–5.

168 Ibid 355. Donnelly refers to this as 'international legal universality', J Donnelly, 'The Relative Universality of Human Rights' (2007) 29(2) *Human Rights Quarterly*, 281, 288–9.

169 E Brems, see above, n 3, 5, n 7 and the references there.

170 H Steiner, P Alston & R Goodman, *International Human Rights in Context: Law, Politics and Morals*, 3rd edn, Oxford university Press, Oxford, 2007, 519.

171 E Brems, see above, n 3, 5.

Cultural Relativism, or 'Particularism'

The principal attack on the universality of human rights comes from 'cultural relativism', and it continues to be 'the most discussed issue in the theory of human rights'.[172] Other critiques—all of them in some way developing a relativist perspective—are discussed in the following part of this chapter. The 'cultural relativism' critique is the most widely expressed and popularly understood of them.

An argument for the relative nature of conceptions of rights was argued for as long ago as the eighteenth century, when Edmund Burke disputed the acceptability in other cultures of the universal claims made in the French *Declaration of the Rights of Man*, saying that 'the liberties and the restrictions vary with times and circumstances, and admit of infinite modifications, that cannot be settled upon any abstract rule'.[173]

As is discussed above, the formulation of contemporary human rights was largely an exercise in pragmatism, intended to find a widely encompassing conception. Donnelly points out that while '[t]here may be considerable historical/anthropological universality of values across time and culture [no] society, civilization, or culture prior to the seventeenth century ... had a widely endorsed practice, or even vision, of equal and inalienable individual human rights.'[174] Similarly, Kennedy observes that '[a]lthough there are lots of interesting analogies to human rights ideas in various cultural traditions, the particular form these ideas are given in the human rights movement is the product of a particular moment and place'.[175]

The contemporary human rights promulgated under the UDHR have been consistently attacked as being 'Western' in origin, unrecognised by, or at least not well-understood in, traditions of thought outside those of Britain, Western Europe and North America. The diverse backgrounds of the drafters, and the wide range of states that have made the political decision to adopt the UDHR, is not a sufficient answer to those who feel that international human rights do not address or allow for their own cultural practices.

The 'cultural relativism' debate began even before the UDHR was adopted, when the American Anthropological Association (AAA) made a submission to the drafting committee, which asked 'How can the proposed Declaration be applicable to all human beings, and not be statement of rights conceived only in terms of the values prevalent in the countries of Western Europe and America?'.[176] That is a fair question, but it was undermined in that instance by the AAA's own stance that 'culture [is] a static and homogenous "thing" rather than the dynamic and contested process that anthropologists

172 J Donnelly, see above, n 168, 282.

173 A Sen, 'Elements of a Theory of Human Rights' (2004) 32(4) *Philosophy and Public Affairs* 315, 350, citing the quotation in S Lukes, 'Five Fables about Human Rights' in M Ishay (ed), *The Human Rights Reader*, Routledge, London, 1997, 233–46, 238.

174 J Donnelly, see above, n 168, 284–5.

175 D Kennedy, 'The International Human Rights Movement: Part of the Problem? Boundaries in the Field on Human Rights' (2002) 15 *Harvard Human Rights Journal*, 101, 114.

176 'Statement on Human Rights' (1947) 49 *American Anthropologist*, 539, cited in M Dembour, 'Critiques', in D Moeckli, S Shah & S Sivakumaran (eds), *International Human Rights Law*, Oxford University Press, Oxford, 2010, 64–86, 75. Parts of the Statement are extracted in H Steiner, P Alston & R Goodman, see above, n 170, 528–9.

have now demonstrated culture always is'.[177] In 1999 the AAA declared a position that supports the contemporary idea of human rights, while reserving room to contest the nature and type of human rights in particular circumstances:[178]

> [T]he AAA founds its approach on anthropological principles of respect for concrete human differences, both collective and individual, rather than the abstract legal uniformity of Western tradition. In practical terms, however, its working definition builds on the Universal Declaration of Human Rights (UDHR), the International Covenants on Civil and Political Rights, and on Social, Economic, and Cultural Rights, the Conventions on Torture, Genocide, and Elimination of All Forms of Discrimination Against Women, and other treaties which bring basic human rights within the parameters of international written and customary law and practice. The AAA definition thus reflects a commitment to human rights consistent with international principles but not limited by them. Human rights is not a static concept. Our understanding of human rights is constantly evolving as we come to know more about the human condition. It is therefore incumbent on anthropologists to be involved in the debate on enlarging our understanding of human rights on the basis of anthropological knowledge and research.

The AAA defines territory where, although anthropology has a 'commitment to human rights consistent with international principles', it is not limited by those principles in 'enlarging ... understanding of human rights on the basis of anthropological knowledge and research'. This leaves the door open for a closer analysis of human rights in their local context, which, as is discussed below, may be the best way of resolving the universalism/relativism debate.

An absolutist position on cultural relativism, such as that originally adopted by the AAA, simply sets up an irresolvable dispute between competing cultural claims. In those circumstances, cultural relativism can be an excuse for values and practices that are merely politically expedient for the proponent, or that are indeed held to be universally abhorrent.

> Recognising that different societies hold different values need not logically lead to the conclusion that all these different values and practices must be tolerated. The observation that cultures produce different moral norms does not say anything about the respective value of these norms. Despite this ... cultural relativism came to be denigrated for demanding that the intolerable be tolerated ... It has also been criticised for lending itself to abuse, allowing those in power to make spurious or disingenuous cultural arguments in pursuit of their own political ends.[179]

Nevertheless, the idea of cultural relativism reminds us of 'the difficulty of establishing reasonable and general grounds for making moral judgements about the actions of others'.[180] The constructive aspect of a cultural relativist critique is that it alerts us to the risk that '[m]oral egoism easily leads to arrogance, and universalism to imperialism'.[181]

177 M Dembour, ibid 75–6, citing J Cowan, M Dembour & R Wilson (eds), *Culture and Rights: Anthropological Perspectives*, Cambridge University Press, Cambridge, 2001.

178 *Declaration on Anthropology and Human Rights*, American Anthropological Association, 1999, <http://www.aaanet.org/stmts/humanrts.htm>.

179 M Dembour, see above, n 176, 76.

180 E Hatch, 'The Good Side of Relativism', (1997) 53(3) *Journal of Anthropological Research* 371, 372.

181 C Douzinas, see above, n 65, 453–4.

Cultural reservations about the universality of human rights stem from a focus on the particular, where a purportedly universal human rights standard may seem to be irrelevant, or unrealistic, or ignorant of local considerations.[182] It would seem that resistance to the universality of human rights is not based on a concern about the 'relative' merits of Western and other cultures as much as it is on a concern that human rights do not appear to acknowledge aspects of a particular culture. This is suggested, for example, by a description of the 'cultural relativists' as those who 'assert that moral truth or validity is an expression of the values and beliefs of a particular culture'.[183]

It is consistent with this to identify the challenge to universalism not as cultural relativism but as 'particularism', a term that has the advantage of 'avoiding both the possibly reifying tone of the reference to culture and the embarrassment of the faint moral position commonly associated with 'cultural relativism'."[184] The term 'particularism' is indeed a more accurate and less emotive term than 'cultural relativism', but widespread common usage dictates that the latter term is used in this discussion.

Culture

The idea of 'culture', whether relative or particular, remains at the heart of widespread reservations about human rights' claim to universality. But culture is an elusive idea. It 'has many meanings in the contemporary world. It is often seen as the basis of national, ethnic, or religious identities ... In international human rights meetings, culture often refers to traditions and customs: ways of doing things that are justified by their roots in the past'.[185]

Noting that 'human rights relies on an essentialised model of culture', Merry describes two of the 'myriad ways culture is imagined in transnational human rights discussions'.[186] First, she describes culture as a synonym for tradition, saying that '[c]ulture used in this sense is not used to describe the affluent countries of the global North but the poor countries of the global South'.[187] Merry describes another use of culture as 'national essence or identity', which she says is 'fundamental to claims to indigenous sovereignty and ethnonationalism, often in resistance to human rights', giving as an example the claim made for 'Asian values'.[188]

182 C Douzinas, see above, n 65, 457.

183 M Goodhart, see above, n 167, 353.

184 M Dembour, see above, n 176, 78.

185 S Engle Merry, *Human Rights and Gender Violence: Translating International Law into Local Justice*, The University of Chicago Press, Chicago, 2006, quoted in H Steiner, P Alston & R Goodman, see above, n 170, 525.

186 H Steiner, P Alston & R Goodman, see above, n 170, 526.

187 H Steiner, P Alston & R Goodman, see above, n 170, 526.

188 H Steiner, P Alston & R Goodman, see above, n 170, 526–7.

'Asian values'

The 'Asian values' debate can be seen as an assertion by emerging Asian countries of their distinctive identity, in the face of pressures exerted by a globalised market driven by Western capital and consumers. Few of the objections taken to the universality of human rights in the Asian values' debate are peculiar to Asia, and could be made by most states in most regions. Although politicians in China and Malaysia, for example, have rejected the universality of human rights as a threat to sovereignty and as interference in a sovereign state's internal affairs,[189] Donnelly points out 'there is nothing distinctively Asian about a commitment to sovereignty'.[190] More to the point, the argument does not address the nature of the claim to universality made for human rights. The argument is a political one, concerned with the power of a state to manage its own affairs, and on that score the tension between sovereignty and human rights standards is merely a feature of the contemporary world, the same as that between sovereignty and international standards relating to, for example, trade and intellectual property. This political argument does not address the claim made for human rights that their universality derives from their basis in inherent human dignity, transcending political boundaries.

Another objection to the universality of human rights in the 'Asian values' debate is made on the basis that states are at different stages of development, meaning they have different capacities to respect human rights. Again, 'there is nothing distinctively Asian to such arguments'[191] and again, the argument is one of practice and politics, not principle. It is the case that developing states—and not only in Asia—often do not have the resources to extend to their citizens the same degree of enjoyment of human rights that developed states have. That is not to say that the people do not have those human rights, only that they do not yet enjoy them. Nor does the argument suggest a reason why, in principle, a developing state should not respect those human rights, quite apart from the pragmatic question of its capacity to give full effect to them.

Sen's response to the claim for distinctive 'Asian values' that is set up against the universalist claim of human rights is that '[n]ot only are the differences on the subject of freedoms and rights that actually exist between different societies often much exaggerated, but also there is, typically, little note taken of substantial variations *within* each local culture—over time and even at a point of time (in particular, right now)'.[192]

The 'Asian values' debate—and cultural relativism generally—suffers from an overly simple, and often rhetorically attractive, tendency to dualism. The dualistic terms pervade the universalism debate: North/South, developed/developing, capitalist/socialist, Western/Asian, individual/collective and so on. Otto's extensive analysis of these dualisms[193] demonstrates Sen's point that the differences

189 J Donnelly, *Universal Human Rights in Theory and Practice*, Cornell University Press, 2003, 108–9.

190 Ibid 108.

191 See above, n 189, 109.

192 A Sen, see above, n 173, 353.

193 D Otto, 'Rethinking the "Universality" of Human Rights Law' (1997–1998) 29 (1) *Columbia Human Rights Law Review*, 1.

are often exaggerated, and identifies considerable common ground. The Bangkok Declaration,[194] for example, 'does not ... depart from the underlying normative framework and principles of the *UN Charter* and the UDHR',[195] and is 'only describ[ing] what is obvious—that all human rights are in a constant state of evolution which relies on debate and contending claims'.[196] It does, however, promote a way of seeing those principles which reflects the particular perspectives of states that, for example, have been subject to colonialism, and that do not have traditions of recognising individual rights as readily as is the case in, say, Western Europe.

Reconciling Universalism and Relativism

Advocates for human rights plead for a view that transcends the particular, and that finds the universal in every person's lived experience. Invoking Adam Smith, Sen describes this as 'the necessity of viewing actions and practices from a 'certain distance' ... important for the understanding of ... human rights'.[197] The distance is necessary because '[w]hat are taken to be perfectly 'normal' and 'sensible' in an insulated society may not be able to survive a broad-based and less limited examination once the parochial gut reactions are replaced by critical scrutiny, including an awareness of variations of practices and norms across the world'.[198] Thus Higgins, from a distance, asserts that:

> Individuals everywhere want the same essential things: to have sufficient food and shelter; to be able to speak freely; to practise their own religion or abstain from religious belief; to feel that their person is not threatened by the state; to know that they will not be tortured, or detained without charge, and that, if charged, the will have a fair trial.[199]

Higgins believes that 'there is nothing in these aspirations that is dependent upon culture, or religion, or state of development. They are as keenly felt by the African tribesman as by the European city-dweller'.[200] In saying this, Higgins refers to the 'universality of the human spirit',[201] which may be another way of describing the idea of human dignity, or may be an appeal to a subtly different sense in which all humans can be said to share fundamental 'aspirations'.

The question then is how are these aspirations realised? What is the actual translation from the universal principle to the particular circumstance? Sen argues for 'using basic universalist principles in general, while taking note of ... the relevance of local circumstances and regional conditions in

194 *The Bangkok Declaration on Human Rights*: see *Final Declaration of the Regional Meeting for Asia of the World Conference on Human Rights*, UN GAOR, UN Doc A/CONF.157/ASRM/8 (7 April 1993) para 8. See Chapter 8.6.

195 D Otto, see above, n 193, 9.

196 D Otto, see above, n 193, 10 citing B Kausikan, 'An Asian Approach to Human Rights' (1995) 89 *American Society of International Law Proceedings*, 146, 148.

197 A Sen, see above, n 173, 354.

198 A Sen, see above, n 173, 355.

199 R Higgins, *Problems and Process: International Law and How We Use It*, Clarendon Press, New York, 1994, 96, quoted in H Steiner, P Alston & R Goodman, see above, n 170, 539.

200 H Steiner, P Alston & R Goodman, see above, n 170, 539–40.

201 H Steiner, P Alston & R Goodman,, see above, n 170, 539.

appropriately contingent, or parametric, specification of the exact demands of human rights'.[202] The universal is found in the particular: '[w]hen a state adopts 'universal' human rights, it will interpret them and apply them, if at all, according to local legal procedures and moral principles, making the universal the handmaiden of the particular'.[203] Donnelly uses the term 'relative universalities', describing human rights as '(relatively) universal at the level of the *concept*, broad formulations such as the claims in [the UDHR]. Particular rights concepts, however, have multiple defensible *conceptions*. Any particular conception, in turn, will have many defensible *implementations*'.[204]

So while all people, as a matter of fundamental principle, have human rights because of the inherent dignity of being human—rights to, for example food, shelter, work, and freedom—most people do not have the opportunity to *enjoy* their human rights because of politics, practice, resources and circumstances. Human rights, though universally held, are far from universally realised. Universalism and relativism are reconciled by appreciating that human rights operate at levels of principle and context, and that the particular realisation of a human right will differ according to local conditions. Human rights principles guarantee, for example, a fair trial, but do not prescribe what constitutes a fair trial.[205]

Universal human rights will therefore find their expression differently according to people's circumstances. It will be a matter of judgment and debate—and perhaps dissent and political protest—as to whether the extent and nature of the local enjoyment of a human right is sufficiently close to the essential extent and nature of that right in principle.

2.5 FUTURE CHALLENGES FOR THE IDEA OF HUMAN RIGHTS

This chapter extends the discussion in Chapter 1, giving an account of the principal philosophical traditions that informed the formulation of the UDHR, and illustrating how 'the concept of human rights has slowly been determined over the course of centuries',[206] both through philosophical reasoning and 'socio-political upheavals',[207] and describes the claims of dignity and universality which are integral to the contemporary conception of human rights. The account is, however, what could be called a conventional one, and the chapter ends where current debates begin. The next stage of inquiry is to subject the idea of human rights to contemporary theoretical critiques.

The law of international human rights, with which this book is concerned, will continue to develop, and to be secure, within its international and domestic legal intuitions. But the law of human rights is merely a formal expression of an idea that will continue to be tested from a range of critical perspectives. The perceived legitimacy of human rights law—and the extent of peoples' and states' compliance with the law—will turn on the persuasiveness of those critiques. The 'particularism' critique discussed

202 A Sen, see above, n 173, 351.

203 C Douzinas, see above, n 65, 459.

204 J Donnelly, see above, n 168, 299 (emphasis in original).

205 See Chapter 3.2.10.

206 J Derrida, 'Spectres of Marx', (1994) 205 *New Left Review* 31, 52.

207 Ibid 52.

above in relation to universalism is only an example of the many current critical perspectives on human rights. Not all critiques necessarily undermine the contemporary idea of human rights, or are intended to; many are intended to explore a deeper and more complex understanding of human rights. They offer rich material for continuing discussion and debate about the idea of human rights.

The critical perspective with the greatest capacity to undermine contemporary human rights is post-modernism, a social philosophy which is essentially relativist, and so is anti-universalist.[208] The contest is illustrated, for example, in Michel Foucault's critique of Habermas, whose development of Kantian dignity is discussed above. Foucault's focus on the reality of power in any given social context leads him to challenge Habermas's reliance on universal, Kantian truths.[209] Foucault's contextual approach is a particular form of relativism, a distinguishing feature of post-modern thought:[210]

> In postmodernity, the eternal becomes contingent; universalism a delusion ... Everything becomes relative, localised, ephemeral ... Facing such conditions, how can one still uphold the validity of the Universal Declaration of Human Rights, grounded on the rational and humanistic foundations of the Enlightenment with inputs from its liberal and socialist current? How can one defend the idea that 'the equal and inalienable rights of all members of the human family [are] the foundation of freedom, justice and peace in the world'? How can one insist on the assertion that all human beings 'are endowed with reason and conscience and should act towards one another in a spirit of brotherhood'? How can those rights historically built on the Western tradition be made universal without adopting an imperialist stance?

As Alves observes, none of these questions has an easy answer. His answer lies in recognising the UDHR as a statement of 'commanding importance', which has been voluntarily adopted—and therefore universalised—by states of all cultures and histories.[211] Whether this is a sufficient defence against post-modernism is a matter for debate.

A phenomenological critique of human rights similarly focuses on the rational Enlightenment origins of contemporary human rights. It challenges the idea of human rights for being based on reason rather than on intuition, and proposes a 'more radical, more private, less public, and less Rationalist awareness of the world'.[212] This awareness draws on not only the asserted truth of how people ought behave—the normative demand of human rights—but also on how people feel in any particular circumstance they ought behave.

Hannah Arendt's ability to ground a claim for human rights in people's lived experience[213] is an example of a phenomenological approach, which 'allowed Arendt to avoid unnecessary attempts to ground human rights in an understanding of human nature and to seek prematurely pragmatic

208 See generally M Salter, 'The Impossibility of Human Rights within a Postmodern Account of Law and Justice' [1996] *Journal of Civil Liberties* 29.

209 See B Flyvbjerg, 'Ideal Theory, Real Rationality: Habermas Versus Foucault and Nietzsche', Paper for the Political Studies Association's 50th Annual Conference, *The Challenges for Democracy in the 21st Century*, London School of Economics and Political Science, 2000.

210 J L A Alves, 'The Declaration of Human Rights in Postmodernity' (2000) 22 *Human Rights Quarterly* 478, 491; omitting references to provisions of the UDHR.

211 Ibid 496–500.

212 R Pettman, 'The Phenomenology of Human Rights' (2004) *Human Rights Research Journal* [8] (online) 7.

213 See eg H Arendt, *Eichmann in Jerusalem: A Report on the Banality of Evil*, (1963).

justifications for human rights'.[214] Arendt goes beyond the rational posited idea of human rights, and says that 'they are they are made real only through human involvement and commitment, which can only occur within a political community'.[215] This situated approach can, however, be criticised for ignoring the political dimension of human rights, grounding them in 'mere' human experience;[216] whether human rights are necessarily understood best, or only, with a phenomenological insight is, again, a matter for debate.

A common thread running through the critiques noted above is that they attack the essentialist nature of the conventional arguments in support of human rights. It is arguable that these conventional arguments—those set out in this chapter and Chapter 1—'assume that we can know either the nature, essence of the human being, or the nature of morality, and further that all can agree on this [but] both of these assumptions are highly questionable and particularly problematic in a post-metaphysical intellectual climate. That is, one can no longer take for granted universal metaphysical claims about nature ... human rights run the risk of only being applicable to those who share ... assumptions about human beings or morality'.[217] A similar sensibility characterises other critiques, such as feminism, and a postcolonial analysis, which challenges the inclusionary claims that are implicit in the conventional arguments for human rights.[218] The positivist-based democratic critique of human rights, and the related utilitarian critique do not clearly share this non-essentialist theme, but continue to be relevant contemporary perspectives on human rights.

Thinkers such as Foucault, Derrida and Arendt (themselves all quite different in their approach) do not necessarily reject the idea of human rights, but pursue it in a way that is not dependent on asserted universal human attributes. The various aspects of a non-essentialist critique will continue to be one of the great debates on human rights.

214 C Lawson, 'Review of Serena Parekh, "Hannah Arendt and the Challenge of Modernity: A Phenomenology of Human Rights"', *H-Human-Rights*, September, 2010, <www.h-net.org/reviews/showrev.php?id=29593>.

215 S Parekh, 'Resisting "Dull and Torpid" Assent: Returning to the Debate Over the Foundations of Human Rights' (2007) 29 *Human Rights Quarterly*, 754, 757; and see S Parekh, *Hannah Arendt and the Challenge of Modernity: A Phenomenology of Human Rights*, (2008); L Hinchman and S Hinchman, 'In Heidegger's Shadow: Hannah Arendt's Phenomenological Humanism' (1984) 46(2) *The Review of Politics* 183.

216 See A Schaap, 'Enacting the Right to Have Rights: Jacques Rancière's Critique of Hannah Arendt', (2011)10(1) *European Journal of Political Theory* 22.

217 S Parekh, 'Resisting "Dull and Torpid" Assent, see above, n 215, 769.

218 See M Dembour, see above, n 176, 81–4.

PART TWO

THE SUBSTANTIVE RIGHTS

3
CIVIL AND POLITICAL RIGHTS

CONTENTS

3.1 INTRODUCTION

The body of human rights recognised under international law is not limited to the list of rights enunciated in the *Universal Declaration of Human Rights* (UDHR) and the two covenants that followed it, the *International Covenant on Civil and Political Rights* (ICCPR) and the *International Covenant on Economic, Social and Cultural Rights* (ICESCR). Other treaties have emerged with a more specific thematic focus, such as the rights of children (*Convention on the Rights of the Child* [CROC]) or persons with disabilities (*Convention on the Rights of persons with Disabilities* [CRPD]) and therefore provide greater elaboration on the scope of human rights in those contexts. Similarly, different regional treaties may express similar concepts with a different scope or emphasis from that found in the ICCPR. Indeed, the ICCPR itself notes that other treaties or bodies of customary law, as well as municipal or regional law, may contain human rights guarantees that extend beyond the terms of the ICCPR.[1] It would therefore be wrong to equate the list of rights in the ICCPR with a definitive list of civil and political rights under international law. Nevertheless, the intended universal application of the ICCPR and its near-universal ratification make it the best starting point for canvassing the content of civil and political rights.

The following sections give a very brief summary of each of the rights guaranteed in the ICCPR in order to give a picture of the breadth of civil and political rights. The content of each of those rights is, of course, far more complex than space permits in this book. To appreciate the depth of human rights, one right has been chosen for a more detailed case study later in this chapter: the right to life. While some of the nuances, case law and commentary on the different aspects of that right will be discussed in the case study, comparable layers of complexity lie beneath each of the brief summaries of civil and political rights that follow.

3.2 THE SUBSTANTIVE RIGHTS

3.2.1 The Right to Self-Determination: Article 1

The first article of both the ICCPR and ICESCR contain identical text setting out the right to self-determination. As such, self-determination, more than any other, is a right that defies categorisation:

1 *International Covenant on Civil and Political Rights* (ICCPR), opened for signature 16 December 1966, 999 UNTS 171 (entered into force 23 March 1976), art 5(2).

it is a right that has simultaneously civil, political, economic, social and cultural aspects. Crucially, unlike the civil and political rights examined below, the right to self-determination is not vested in individuals, but in the collective entity of the 'people'. The first sentence of article 1 in the ICCPR and ICESCR is therefore: 'All *peoples* have the right of self-determination.'[2]

A definition of a 'people' is not provided in either covenant, but the term is generally understood to mean a group that is bound together by a common identity, such as a distinct ethnicity, language, religion or culture, and that lives in a distinct area. The lack of a precise definition is likely to be deliberate, to ensure that it is adaptable to the very different circumstances that exist in different parts of the world, without excluding any relevant group.

The political element of the right to self-determination entitles a people to 'freely determine their political status'.[3] There is a strong historical link between the emergence of the right to self-determination in international human rights instruments and the movement for decolonisation, which gathered momentum from around 1960.[4] The inclusion of the right to self-determination and the reference to a people determining their political status as the very first article of both the Covenants therefore need to be interpreted as motivated by the colonial context and as including the right of a distinct and identifiable people to be free from colonial domination, if the people expressed such a wish. The Committee on the Elimination of Racial Discrimination described this element as 'external self-determination', which it distinguished from 'internal self-determination'; the latter ensuring that a distinct people has the right to pursue its own political and economic interests within a state without interference.[5] The political element of the right to self-determination is therefore far more nuanced than simply a right to secede or declare independence and will depend on the particular situation.

While the right to self-determination is not formulated in a manner that limits its application to post-colonial situations—indeed, the right is guaranteed to *all peoples*, not only those living under a particular political arrangement—there is no doubt that it has been most commonly invoked in a colonial context. Accordingly, some writers maintain that its relevance is limited to decolonisation. The better view is that offered by Robert McCorquodale:

> the right of self-determination applies to any peoples in any territory (including non-colonial territories) who are subjected to 'alien subjugation, domination and exploitation'.[6] Indeed, it would be contrary to the concept of a human right if the right of self-determination could only be exercised once (such as by a colonial territory) and then not again. So, all peoples in all states have the right of self-determination.[7]

---

2 ICCPR, see above, n 1, art 1(1) and *International Covenant on Economic, Social and Cultural Rights* (ICESCR), opened for signature 16 December 1966, 993 UNTS 3 (entered into force 3 January 1976), art 1(1) (emphasis added).

3 Ibid.

4 See for example the *Declaration on Independence for Colonial Countries and Peoples*, GA Res 1514 (XV), 14 December 1960, para 2, from which the wording of art 1(1) of the ICCPR and ICESCR is taken.

5 Committee on the Elimination of Racial Discrimination, *General Recommendation XXI: The Right to Self-Determination* (1996), para 4.

6 McCorquodale is quoting here from the *Declaration on Independence for Colonial Countries and Peoples*, see above, n 4, para 1.

7 R McCorquodale, 'Rights of Peoples and Minorities', in D Moeckli, S Shah & S Sivakumaran (eds), *International Human Rights Law*, Oxford University Press, Oxford, 2010, 374.

The right to self-determination also includes an economic element. The ICCPR and ICESCR stipulate: 'All peoples may, for their own ends, freely dispose of their natural wealth and resources. ... In no case may a people be deprived of its own means of subsistence.'[8] The inclusion of the economic element of the right in a separate paragraph clarifies that it is intended to have an independent existence, such that a people's control over their own wealth and resources and access to the means for their own subsistence is not dependent on their exercising formal political independence.

A peculiar consequence of the collective nature of the right to self-determination is that the Human Rights Committee has held it to be non-justiciable, since the communications system under the *First Optional Protocol* to the ICCPR only permits complaints by individuals.[9] The International Court of Justice, however, has held the right of self-determination to be 'one of the essential principles of contemporary international law' and a principle of customary international law with *erga omnes* character.[10]

3.2.2 The Right to Life: Article 6

This section provides a brief overview of the right to life. There is a more detailed case study of this right in Chapter 3.5.

Article 6(1)of the ICCPR provides: 'Every human being has the inherent right to life. This right shall be protected by law. No one shall be arbitrarily deprived of his life.'

At its core, the right to life is really a right not to be arbitrarily deprived of life. Not every action that results in death will be arbitrary, and therefore not every death will be a violation of the right to life. The bulk of the jurisprudence surrounding the right to life therefore concerns whether a given death was arbitrary.

Much of the text of article 6 is devoted to the death penalty, seeking to limit the circumstances in which it is used by states that have retained it so as not to render executions arbitrary. Extrajudicial executions, on the other hand, are by their nature arbitrary and will violate the right to life. The state's failure to investigate such killings adequately or to punish the offenders can also amount to a violation of the state's obligations under the right to life.

Some controversial aspects of the right to life include the questions of abortion and euthanasia. In both cases, the central question is the same as for other elements of the right to life, namely: Does the practice in question result in the arbitrary deprivation of life? However, answering that question requires one to define 'life' in a way that necessarily draws upon one's moral beliefs, as well as balancing life (or potential life) against other interests such as the life, health or personal autonomy of the mother in the case of abortion, or the quality of life or the wishes of the patient in the case of euthanasia. The Human Rights Committee has tended to support access to safe abortions, emphasising the risks to the life of the mother that tend to result when abortions are prohibited and conducted underground. Euthanasia laws generally seem to clear the hurdle of not being arbitrary and

8 ICCPR, see above, n 1, art 1(2) and ICESCR, see above, n 2, art 1(2).

9 *Ominayak and the Lubicon Lake Band v Canada*, CCPR/C/38/D/167/1984(1990) para 32.1. For an explanation of the individual communication system under the UN Treaty Monitoring Committee system, see Chapter 7.4.7.

10 *Case Concerning East Timor (Portugal v Australia)* [1995] ICJ Rep 90, para 29. An *erga omnes* obligation is one owed by every state to the international community as a whole.

therefore not violating the right to life, although the Human Rights Committee has expressed fears about ensuring adequate safeguards are in place to prevent such systems crossing the line into the arbitrary deprivation of life.

The right to life also carries proactive obligations for states. The Human Rights Committee has noted that '[t]he expression 'inherent right to life' cannot properly be understood in a restrictive manner, and the protection of this right requires that States adopt positive measures ... it would be desirable for States parties to take all possible measures to reduce infant mortality and to increase life expectancy, especially in adopting measures to eliminate malnutrition and epidemics.'[11]

3.2.3 Freedom from Torture and Cruel, Inhuman or Degrading Treatment or Punishment: Article 7

The prohibition of torture is generally accepted as binding on all states under customary international law regardless of treaty ratification. It is one of the rare 'absolute' rights in the sense that international law permits no exceptions or limitations to the prohibition.

The ICCPR prohibits torture without explicitly defining the term. The *Convention Against Torture* (CAT) defines torture as:

> any act by which severe pain or suffering, whether physical or mental, is intentionally inflicted on a person for such purposes as obtaining from him or a third person information or a confession, punishing him for an act he or a third person has committed or is suspected of having committed, or intimidating or coercing him or a third person, or for any reason based on discrimination of any kind, when such pain or suffering is inflicted by or at the instigation of or with the consent of or acquiescence of a public official or other person acting in an official capacity.[12]

Thus, torture requires the deliberate infliction of severe suffering on the victim for some ulterior motive, and there must be some involvement or acquiescence of the state.

The CAT goes on to make clear that '[n]o exceptional circumstances whatsoever, whether a state of war or a threat of war, internal political instability or any other public emergency, may be invoked as a justification of torture.'[13] Similarly, the ICCPR permits no derogation from the prohibition on torture or cruel, inhuman or degrading treatment or punishment in times of public emergency.[14]

In practice, however, states often attempt to justify their actions by defining them as something less than torture, and therefore permissible in certain circumstances.

SNAPSHOT: THE US 'TORTURE MEMOS'

A series of legal memoranda written by senior officials in the US Attorney-General's office between 2002 and 2004 sought to establish which interrogation methods would amount to torture and which would not,

11 Human Rights Committee, *General Comment No 6: The Right to Life*, 30 April 1982, para 5.

12 *Convention Against Torture and Other Cruel, Inhuman or Degrading Treatment or Punishment* (CAT), opened for signature 10 December 1984, 1465 UNTS 85 (entered into force 26 June 1987), art 1(1).

13 Ibid art 2(2).

14 ICCPR, see above, n 1, art 4. See 3.2 below for discussion of derogation in a case of emergency.

and would therefore be permissible to use in the so-called 'war on terror' (although the fact that methods not reaching the threshold of torture would still violate international law as cruel, inhuman or degrading treatment is glossed over). Those memoranda are commonly referred to collectively as the 'torture memos'.

The torture memos each focused on a definition of torture that required 'severe pain or suffering'. In a memorandum from the Assistant Attorney-General to the Central Intelligence Agency (CIA) in August 2002 regarding the interrogation of alleged Al Qaeda operative Abu Zubaydah, the following comments were made regarding the process of waterboarding:

> In this procedure, the individual is bound securely on an inclined bench, which is approximately four feet by seven feet. The individual's feet are generally elevated. A cloth is placed over the forehead and eyes. Water is then applied to the cloth in a controlled manner. As this is done, the cloth is lowered until it covers both the nose and mouth. Once the cloth is saturated and completely covers the mouth and nose, air now is slightly restricted for 20 to 40 seconds due to the presence of the cloth. This causes an increase in carbon dioxide level in the individual's blood. This increase in the carbon dioxide level stimulates increased effort to breathe. This effort plus the cloth produces the perception of 'suffocation and incipient panic,' ie, the perception of drowning. The individual does not breathe any water into his lungs. During those 20 to 40 seconds, water is continuously applied from a height of twelve to twenty-four inches. After this period, the cloth is lifted, and the individual is allowed to breathe unimpeded for three or four full breaths. The sensation of drowning is immediately relieved by the removal of the cloth. The procedure may then be repeated. The water is usually applied from a canteen cup or small watering can with a spout. You have orally informed us that this procedure triggers an automatic physiological sensation of drowning that the individual cannot control even though he may be aware that he is in fact not drowning. You have also orally informed us that it is likely that this procedure would not last more than 20 minutes in any one application.[15]
>
> ...
>
> In order for pain or suffering to rise to the level of torture, the statute requires that it be severe. As we have previously explained, this reaches only extreme acts.[16]
>
> ...
>
> As we understand it, when the waterboard is used, the subject's body responds as if the subject were drowning even though the subject may be well aware that he is in fact not drowning. You have informed us that this procedure does not inflict actual physical harm. Thus, although the subject may experience the fear or panic associated with the feeling of drowning, the waterboard does not inflict physical pain. As we explained in the Section 2340A Memorandum, 'pain and suffering' as used in Section 2340 [a US statutory provision prohibiting torture][17] is best understood as a single concept, not distinct concepts of 'pain' as distinguished from 'suffering'.

15 Jay Bybee, Assistant Attorney-General, Interrogation of al Qaeda Operative, memorandum to John Rizzo, Acting General Counsel for the Central Intelligence Agency, 1 August 2002, 3–4.

16 Ibid 9.

17 18 USC 2340A prohibits torture under US law. Torture is defined in the previous paragraph as 'an act committed by a person acting under the color of law specifically intended to inflict severe physical or mental pain or suffering (other than pain or suffering incidental to lawful sanctions) upon another person within his custody or physical control'. The definition is therefore based on the definition in the *Convention Against Torture,* although it could be considered slightly narrower in some respects, particularly in regard to the requirement of 'specific' intent.

> ... The waterboard, which inflicts no pain or actual harm whatsoever, does not, in our view inflict 'severe pain or suffering.' Even if one were to parse the statute more finely to attempt to treat 'suffering' as a distinct concept, the waterboard could not be said to inflict severe suffering. The waterboard is simply a controlled acute episode, lacking the connotation of a protracted period of time generally given to suffering.[18]

The practice of waterboarding, along with other practices described as attention grasp, walling, facial hold, facial slap, cramped confinement, wall standing, stress positions, sleep deprivation and insects placed in a confinement box, were all considered by the memorandum's author not to constitute torture.

Freedom from torture in the context of anti-terrorism measures is discussed in more detail in Chapter 18.4.3.

The prohibition in the ICCPR extends to inhuman and degrading treatment or punishment and is therefore broader than the definition of torture given in the CAT. The jurisprudence of the European Court of Human Rights has found that conduct that was not carried out for a specific ulterior purpose or was less severe than that required for torture could amount to inhuman or degrading treatment or punishment.[19]

3.2.4 Freedom from Slavery and Compulsory Labour: Article 8

Freedom from slavery and the prohibition of the slave trade refer to the practice of treating human beings as property. While compulsory labour is commonly demanded of slaves and was historically a key factor driving the slave trade, hence the inclusion of these two rights in the same article of the ICCPR, it is possible to hold a person in slavery or engage in the slave trade without requiring the slave to engage in labour, and vice versa. Freedom from slavery is universally considered to be a norm of customary international law. Derogation from the ban is not permitted in times of public emergency.[20]

SNAPSHOT: HUMAN TRAFFICKING IN AUSTRALIA—*R v WEI TANG*[21]

Slavery and the trade in slaves, including possessing a slave and entering into a commercial transaction involving a slave, are crimes in Australia under the Commonwealth Criminal Code.[22]

Wei Tang owned a licensed brothel in Melbourne. She paid 'recruiters' in Thailand $20 000 each for five women to come to Australia to work in the brothel. Each woman was then said to have a debt of approximately $45 000, including the initial payment and accumulated costs such as living expenses. The debt was to be worked off at Wei Tang's brothel, with the proceeds from each client being split between Wei Tang and other

18 Jay Bybee, see above, n 15, 11.

19 See for example *Ireland v United Kingdom* (Application No 5310/71, Judgment of 18 January 1978); *Kaya v Turkey* (Application No 22729/93, Judgment of 19 February 1998).

20 ICCPR, see above, n 1.

21 [2008] HCA 39; (2008) 237 CLR 1.

22 *Criminal Code Act 1995* (Cth), s 270.3(1).

investors who had bought into the syndicate. The women received nothing from their work as sex workers, except the one 'free day' per week, when they were allowed to keep $50 per client, with the balance going to Wei Tang and the syndicate. All of the women had consented to come to Australia to work as sex workers and to work off their debts before they could be paid for their work. Two of the five women ultimately worked off their debt and were subsequently paid for their services.

The women were housed and fed at premises provided by Wei Tang and she provided their medical services. They were not locked up, but Wei Tang held their passports.

Wei Tang was convicted in the Victorian County Court of five counts of possessing a slave and five counts of using a slave as an indicator of ownership. She was sentenced to ten years in prison.

On appeal, the High Court held that the slavery provisions in the Criminal Code were constitutionally valid under the external affairs power as implementation of the 1926 Slavery Convention and the *Rome Statute of the International Criminal Court*.[23] The High Court cited decisions of the European Court of Human Rights and the International Criminal Tribunal for the Former Yugoslavia in reaching that conclusion.

Slavery is defined in the Criminal Code as 'the condition of a person over whom any or all of the powers attaching to the right of ownership are exercised, including where such a condition results from a debt or contract made by the person.'[24] The additional reference to debt or contract-based slavery, which does not appear in the Slavery Convention, was held not to be an extension of the international legal definition of slavery (which could have rendered the provision unconstitutional).

The majority of the High Court held that Wei Tang was exercising the powers of ownership over the women and her conviction was upheld.

Forced or compulsory labour is also prohibited under article 8 of the ICCPR, although it is subject to exceptions. Performance of labour as part of a prison sentence will not breach a state's obligations.[25] Likewise, compulsory military service or work that forms part of 'normal civil obligations' will not be considered forced labour.[26] In that respect, Australia's Work for the Dole scheme was held by the Human Rights Committee not to violate the prohibition on forced labour.[27] Slavery and forced labour is discussed in more detail in Chapter 17.2.3.

3.2.5 Freedom from Arbitrary Arrest and Detention: Article 9

The freedom from arbitrary arrest and detention is sometimes referred to as the right to liberty, as it is the requirement that no person be detained except in accordance with the law of the relevant jurisdiction. It is therefore a right requiring that the rule of law or 'due process' be followed when state

23 See Chapter 10.2.

24 See above, n 22, s 270.1.

25 ICCPR, see above, n 1, art 8(3)(b).

26 Ibid art 8(3)(c).

27 *Faure v Australia, Human Rights Committee*, communication no 1036/2001, UN doc no CCPR/C/85/D/1036/2001, 3 November 2005.

authorities exercise their powers of arrest. Article 9 of the ICCPR requires the arresting authority to notify the person being arrested of the reasons for the arrest, to inform the person promptly of any charges against him or her, and to bring the person promptly before a court or otherwise release him or her. The right of habeas corpus, which enables a detained person to challenge the lawfulness of his or her detention, is also guaranteed under article 9(4) as an essential guarantee against arbitrary detention. The Human Rights Committee has held that laws that permit continued detention after a person has completed his or her sentence, for instance to protect the community from the perceived risk of recidivism from a child sex offender, to be necessarily arbitrary, because the detention relates to predicted future behaviour rather than punishment of previous behaviour for which a sentence has already been passed.[28]

Article 9 applies not only to situations where people are detained under the criminal justice system, but also to detention for administrative purposes, such as the detention of immigrants while they await processing.

SNAPSHOT: MANDATORY DETENTION OF ASYLUM SEEKERS AS ARBITRARY DETENTION

Australia's system of mandatory detention of certain types of asylum seekers, introduced by the Keating Labor Government in 1992 and amended by successive governments since then, has been challenged numerous times before the Human Rights Committee on the grounds that such detention was arbitrary.[29]

A v Australia (communication no 560/1993, decided 3 April 1997)[30]: The author was a Cambodian national who arrived in Australia by boat and was detained for four years before ultimately receiving a visa. The Committee rejected the argument that immigration detention *per se* is arbitrary within the meaning of article 9 of the ICCPR, but found that the blanket policy of detention, without any consideration of the requirements of the specific case, amounted to arbitrary detention. Australia was therefore found to have violated article 9.

C v Australia (communication no 900/1999, decided 28 October 2002): The author was an Iranian national who was detained after arriving by air without a return ticket and subsequently made an asylum claim. The author applied to the Federal Court to be released pending determination of his refugee claim and presented evidence indicating that his mental health had been severely affected by the detention. The Federal Court rejected the application, as the migration legislation made no provision for release until a final determination had been made, regardless of the circumstances. The author was granted refugee status after three years of detention, during which time he became seriously mentally ill. He later broke into a relative's home on two occasions and made a phone call threatening to kill her. He was sentenced to three and half years in prison and the immigration minister subsequently ordered his deportation. The Human Rights Committee held that the legislation's prohibition against taking into account specific circumstances, including the inability of the Federal Court to order release from detention, made the initial detention arbitrary. It further found that the

28 *Fardon v Australia*, Human Rights Committee, communication no 1629/2007, UN document no CCPR/C/98/D/1629/2007, 10 May 2010, para 7.4; *Tillman v Australia*, Human Rights Committee, communication no 1635/2007, UN document no CCPR/C/98/D/1635/2007, 10 May 2010, para 7.4.

29 See also Chapter 10.5.4.

30 The term 'communication' refers to a written complaint about a violation of a human rights treaty. See Chapter 7.4.7.

continuing detention once authorities were aware of the effect on the author's mental health amounted to cruel, inhuman or degrading treatment in violation of article 7.[31]

Bakhtiyari v Australia (communication no 1069/2002, decided 29 October 2003): The authors were a husband and wife who claimed to be nationals of Afghanistan. Mr Bakhtiyari arrived in Australia by boat in 1999 and was recognised as a refugee and granted a protection visa the following year. Mrs Bakhtiyari and her 5 children then arrived in Australia by boat in 2001, but were denied protection visas because immigration officials did not believe that they were fleeing Afghanistan as claimed, but believed them to be Pakistani nationals. Mrs Bakhtiyari and her children were then held in immigration detention, while Mr Bakhtiyari's visa was subsequently cancelled on the basis of fraud. The three youngest children had been held in detention for nearly three years when the Family Court ordered their release in 2003. The Human Rights Committee found that the detention of Mrs Bakhtiyari and her children was arbitrary, because it had not been justified by reference to their individual circumstances. The right of children to protection under article 24 of the ICCPR was also held to have been breached. After the Human Rights Committee's decision, the High Court of Australia ruled that the Family Court had no jurisdiction to order the children's release from detention.[32] The family was deported to Pakistan in December 2004.

3.2.6 Right to Humane Treatment in Detention: Article 10

While article 9 of the ICCPR provides that no person should be arbitrarily deprived of his or her liberty, it is still permissible for authorities to detain individuals either as a punishment, following proper judicial process, or as an administrative process where the circumstances of the case require that the person be detained. Examples of lawful administrative detention include immigration detention, remand awaiting trial, or detention in a psychiatric hospital.

In addition to requiring that the detention itself not be arbitrary, international human rights law requires that certain minimum standards of treatment are accorded to those who are deprived of their liberty. Article 10(1) of the ICCPR provides that 'All persons deprived of their liberty shall be treated with humanity and with respect for the inherent dignity of the human person.' The underlying principle of treating a person with dignity while deprived of his or her liberty requires that the person's rights should only be curtailed to the extent necessary due to the confinement;[33] all other rights are to be guaranteed to the same extent to detained persons as they would be to anybody else. This is a clear repudiation of the notion that convicted criminals should have no rights. The punishment, according to international human rights law, is intended to be limited to the deprivation of liberty, and only those other rights that necessarily cannot be fulfilled in the context of detention can lawfully be denied. The Supreme Court of Victoria in *Castles v Secretary to the Department of Justice*, interpreting a provision of the Victorian *Charter of Human Rights and Responsibilities* that was based on article 10 of the ICCPR, recently approved that

31 In the later case of *Shafiq v Australia*, Human Rights Committee, communication no 1324/2004, UN Doc CCPR/C/88/D/1324/2004, 13 November 2006, Australia was similarly held to have violated the freedom from arbitrary detention in art 9 in relation to the mandatory detention of a Bangladeshi asylum seeker who was detained for over six years and who developed a mental illness as a result of his incarceration.

32 *Minister for Immigration and Multicultural Affairs v B* (2004) 219 CLR 365.

33 Human Rights Committee, *General Comment 21: Humane Treatment of Persons Deprived of Liberty*, (1992) para 3.

approach, with Emerton J accepting that 'the starting point should be that prisoners not be subjected to hardship or constraint other than the hardship or constraint that results from the deprivation of liberty.'[34]

Article 10 of the ICCPR requires that individuals held on remand awaiting trial be separated from those who have been convicted.[35] It further requires separation of adults and juvenile persons, both at the pre-trial[36] and post-sentence stage.[37] Australia has entered reservations to the elements of article 10 that require segregation,[38] on the basis that Australia's geography and stretched resources sometimes makes such separation impracticable and segregation therefore ought to be achieved progressively.

The obligations of humane treatment are in recognition of the especially vulnerable position of individuals who are detained by the state. Detailed standards of treatment for detained persons have been developed, such as those contained in the UN Standard Minimum Rules for the Treatment of Prisoners,[39] which detail the 'minimum conditions that are accepted as suitable by the United Nations' on such matters as sleeping arrangements, hygiene, bedding, exercise, work, medical treatment, discipline and communication with the outside world, with separate provisions for prisoners under sentence, insane prisoners, prisoners awaiting trial, civil prisoners and persons detained without charge.

3.2.7 Freedom from Imprisonment for Debt: Article 11

Article 11 of the ICCPR prohibits the imprisonment of any person 'merely on the ground of inability to fulfil a contractual obligation'. The intention of this provision is to repudiate the historical phenomenon of debtors' prisons. It is therefore closely linked to the requirement that detention not be arbitrary.

3.2.8 Freedom of Movement: Article 12

The freedom to move within a country and to leave a country are guaranteed under international human rights law.[40] However, the freedom to leave one country does not necessarily extend to the freedom to enter another. States therefore retain the ability to restrict immigration, require entry permits and the like without infringing freedom of movement.

Article 12(3) of the ICCPR permits states to restrict free movement when such a restriction is provided by the state's law and is 'necessary to protect national security, public order (*ordre public*), public health or morals or the rights and freedoms of others'. Targeted or temporary restrictions on

34 *Castles v Secretary to the Department of Justice*, [2010] VSC 310 (9 July 2010), para 108.

35 ICCPR, see above, n 1, art 10(2)(a).

36 Ibid art 10(2)(b).

37 Ibid art 10(3).

38 See further Chapter 10.2.4.

39 Adopted by the First United Nations Congress on the Prevention of Crime and the Treatment of Offenders in 1955: ESC Res 663C, UN ESCOR, Annex, Supp 1, [11], UN Doc A/CONF/611 (1955); amended by ESC Res 2076, UN ESCOR, Supp 1, [35], UN Doc E/5988 (1997).

40 ICCPR, see above, n 1, art 12.

movement, such as restricting movement to a dangerous area during a natural disaster, or a curfew in a time of civil disturbance, or a quarantine of certain population to prevent the spread of an epidemic, will therefore be permissible. Such restrictions must also be consistent with other human rights. Therefore, for example, any person deprived of his or her liberty must be accorded the safeguards against arbitrariness and the levels of humane treatment discussed above.

SNAPSHOT: SECURITY WALL IN THE OCCUPIED PALESTINIAN TERRITORY

The territory of the West Bank has been under effective Israeli occupation since the conclusion of the 1967 Six Day War. In recent years, terrorism concerns have led Israel to take a number of drastic security measures, including the construction of a barrier, commencing in 2003, which ran partly along the 'green line', demarcating the territory of Israel from the Palestinian territories agreed in the 1949 armistice, but partly diverging from the green line into Palestinian territory. The wall was designed to prevent free movement from the West Bank into Israel by potential terrorists. Consequently, anyone wishing to pass from one side of the wall to the other must pass through security checkpoints, often involving a significant detour and often taking a long time. Palestinians are only permitted to cross the barrier if they hold a permit, while Israelis are prohibited from crossing into the Palestinian Territory.

The International Court of Justice gave an advisory opinion on the status of the wall under international law in 2004.

> That construction, the establishment of a closed area between the Green Line and the wall itself and the creation of enclaves have moreover imposed substantial restrictions on the freedom of movement of the inhabitants of the Occupied Palestinian Territory (with the exception of Israeli citizens and those assimilated thereto). Such restrictions are most marked in urban areas, such as the Qalqiliya enclave or the City of Jerusalem and its suburbs. They are aggravated by the fact that the access gates are few in number in certain sectors and opening hours appear to be restricted and unpredictably applied. For example, according to the Special Rapporteur of the UN Commission on Human Rights on the situation of human rights in the Palestinian territories occupied by Israel since 1967, 'Qalqiliya, a city with a population of 40 000, is completely surrounded by the Wall and residents can only enter and leave through a single military checkpoint open from 7 am to 7 pm.'
>
> ...
>
> It has further led to increasing difficulties for the population concerned regarding access to health services, educational establishments and primary sources of water.
>
> ...
>
> The Special Rapporteur on the Right to Food of the United Nations Commission on Human Rights has also observed that 'With the fence/wall cutting communities off from their land and water without other means of subsistence, many of the Palestinians living in these areas will be forced to leave.' In this respect also the construction of the wall would effectively deprive a significant number of Palestinians of the 'freedom to choose [their] residence'. In addition, however, in the view of the Court, since a significant number of Palestinians have already been compelled by the construction of the wall and its associated regime to depart from certain areas, a process that will continue as more of the wall is built, that construction, coupled with the establishment of the Israeli settlements ..., is tending to alter the demographic composition of the Occupied Palestinian Territory.

To sum up, the Court is of the opinion that the construction of the wall and its associated regime impede the liberty of movement of the inhabitants of the Occupied Palestinian Territory (with the exception of Israeli citizens and those assimilated thereto) as guaranteed under Article 12, paragraph 1, of the International Covenant on Civil and Political Rights. They also impede the exercise by the persons concerned of the right to work, to health, to education and to an adequate standard of living as proclaimed in the International Covenant on Economic, Social and Cultural Rights and in the United Nations Convention on the Rights of the Child.[41]

With regard to the question of whether the interference with freedom of movement was justified for reasons of national security or public order, the Court held:

The Court would observe that the restrictions provided for under Article 12, paragraph 3, of the International Covenant on Civil and Political Rights are, by the very terms of that provision, exceptions to the right of freedom of movement contained in paragraph 1. In addition, it is not sufficient that such restrictions be directed to the ends authorized; they must also be necessary for the attainment of those ends. As the Human Rights Committee put it, they 'must conform to the principle of proportionality' and 'must be the least intrusive instrument amongst those which might achieve the desired result'. On the basis of the information available to it, the Court finds that these conditions are not met in the present instance.

...

To sum up, the Court, from the material available to it, is not convinced that the specific course Israel has chosen for the wall was necessary to attain its security objectives. The wall, along the route chosen, and its associated régime gravely infringe a number of rights of Palestinians residing in the territory occupied by Israel, and the infringements resulting from that route cannot be justified by military exigencies or by the requirements of national security or public order. The construction of such a wall accordingly constitutes breaches by Israel of various of its obligations under the applicable international humanitarian law and human rights instruments.[42]

3.2.9 Procedural Rights of Aliens: Article 13

Human rights in general are guaranteed not only to citizens, but to any person within the territory or jurisdiction of the relevant state.[43] However, there are certain rights in relation to which states are permitted to differentiate between citizens and non-citizens (or 'aliens'). Among these is the right to participate in the political system, which is reserved to citizens.[44] The state also retains the right to expel aliens from the state's territory. However, article 13 of the ICCPR requires that such expulsion must be accompanied by procedural fairness, in the sense that the decision to expel must be made according to law, and that the alien be given an opportunity 'to submit the reasons against his expulsion and to have his case reviewed by' the relevant authority. That right to be heard includes a right to representation. However, these procedural rights may be excluded 'where compelling reasons of national security otherwise require.'[45]

41 *Legal Consequences of the Construction of a Wall in the Occupied Palestinian Territory*, ICJ 2004, paras 133–4.

42 Ibid paras 136–7.

43 See for example ICCPR, art 2(1). See Chapter 20.2 for further discussion on the scope of state obligations within territory and jurisdiction.

44 ICCPR, see above, n 1, art 25.

45 Ibid art 13.

3.2.10 Right to a Fair Trial and Related Rights in the Judicial System: Article 14

The right to a fair trial and related rights of fair treatment within the judicial system are set out in the longest and most complex article of the ICCPR, article 14. The fair trial guarantees are designed to ensure a fair process and to remove the scope for arbitrariness and abuse in the justice system, consistently with the theme of much of international human rights law, while still recognising that states operate very different legal systems developing out of different legal traditions. International human rights law therefore does not prescribe a specific legal system (for instance, the absence of any reference to juries will be notable to readers from the Anglo-American legal tradition); rather, it sets down a series of key guarantees considered essential for the fairness of any judicial process and leaves it to the state as to the method of incorporating those guarantees within its particular legal system. The guarantees expressly provided in article 14 of the ICCPR are:

- Equality before courts and tribunals
- Entitlement to a fair hearing by a competent, independent and impartial tribunal established by law
- Open courts, except where reasons of morals, public order (*ordre public*) or national security in a democratic society, or the privacy of the parties or the interests of justice justify the exclusion of the press or the public[46]
- Presumption of innocence in criminal cases
- Right to be informed fully and promptly of charges and to prepare one's defence
- Right to be tried without undue delay
- Right of a defendant to be present during a criminal trial (not to be tried *in absentia*)
- Right to defend oneself or to be represented by defence counsel, including a right to have defence counsel appointed if the defendant cannot afford to pay
- Right to examine witnesses on equal terms with the prosecution
- Right to an interpreter where necessary
- Privilege against self-incrimination
- Appropriately adapted process for juvenile offenders
- Right to appeal against conviction and sentence according to law
- Right to compensation in the event of miscarriage of justice being revealed
- Double jeopardy (*ne bis in idem*)

The right to a fair trial applies not only to criminal trials, but also to civil proceedings and to other quasi-judicial hearings, such as those before administrative tribunals,[47] although some of the listed guarantees are specific to criminal trials.

46 Human Rights Committee, *General Comment No 32: Right to Equality Before Courts and Tribunals and to a Fair Trial*, (2007) paragraphs 3 and 29, clarifies that art 14(1) of the ICCPR establishes a presumption that courts are to be open, and that media and the public are to be excluded 'only' in the circumstances listed in the text of art 14(1), which the General Comment describes as 'exceptional circumstances'.

47 Ibid para 16.

The Human Rights Committee has emphasised the important role that the right to a fair trial plays in securing many of the other substantive rights,[48] since the legal system is often engaged either by the individual seeking cessation and/or a remedy for a breach of another right, or by authorities in seeking to curtail a person's rights, for example by way of imprisonment, deportation, or denial of some form of civic entitlement through administrative processes. The need to ensure that the process invoked in such a scenario is fair can therefore affect the realisation of other rights.

SNAPSHOT: THE JUDICIAL SYSTEM IN CAMBODIA

Cambodian courts are frequently criticised for lacking independence from the government and being prone to corruption. That is due in part to the structural organisation of the courts, which lends itself to interference by the executive; in part to the lack of funding and protection of legal tenure of judges, which leads to corruption; in part to the lack of training and of a tradition of a competent and independent legal profession and judiciary; and in part to historical and other factors. Accusations commonly made against Cambodian courts include politically motivated prosecutions and politically influenced trials;[49] the inability of poor people to access the courts;[50] corruption; long delays; and the inability of prisoners to seek a timely appeal of their conviction or sentence.[51]

The Special Rapporteur on the Situation on Human Rights in Cambodia reported in 2010 on the impact of inadequacies in the judicial system on two other rights: housing and land-related rights[52] and freedom of expression. As the right to a fair trial and respect for the rule of law are essential to the ability to enforce one's rights, the examples of problems in the judicial system cited by the Special Rapporteur demonstrate how practically the full range of human rights can be undermined when the right to a fair trial is lacking.

SPECIAL RAPPORTEUR ON THE SITUATION ON HUMAN RIGHTS IN CAMBODIA, *REPORT TO THE HUMAN RIGHTS COUNCIL*, SEPTEMBER 2010[53]

42 The courts are not trusted by the people to provide impartial justice. As a consequence, citizens seek alternative methods of remedy which tend to undermine further the rule of law. In land disputes, communities tend to bypass the court system, petitioning top leaders to intervene on their behalf, reinforcing the already overwhelming executive authority. Prior to the war, [King] Norodom Sihanouk was the focus of these petitions. Nowadays, groups of villagers are almost permanently encamped outside the gates of the Prime Minister's residences in Kandal province and in Phnom Penh. Interventions by the Prime Minister are frequent in response to direct petitions by private citizens.

48 Ibid paras 58–65.

49 See for example Cambodian League for the Promotion and Defense of Human Rights (LICADHO), *The Role of the Cambodian Judiciary in Political Cases*, July 2010, <http://www.licadho-cambodia.org/reports/files/144ChoeunSummary-ENG.pdf>.

50 Special Rapporteur on the Situation of Human Rights in Cambodia, *Report to Human Rights Council*, 16 September 2010, UN document A/HRC/15/46, para 7.

51 See for example Cambodian League for the Promotion and Defense of Human Rights (LICADHO), *In Absentia: The Right of Appeal and Cambodia's Inmate Transportation Crisis*, February 2010, <http://www.licadho-cambodia.org/reports/files/140LICADHOInAbsentiaBP-Eng.pdf>.

52 See discussion of the right to housing in Chapter 4.

53 See above, n 50.

43 The quality of legal argumentation in the courtroom is disappointing and often nonexistent. Until recent reforms made it a requirement for reasoned arguments to be included in judgments, judges rarely supported their verdicts with a sound analysis of the law. The line of logic running through some legal arguments is often difficult to follow. …

44 In the absence of the law on the status of judges and prosecutors guaranteeing their security of tenure and independence, the judges seem to be operating to a greater or lesser extent in a climate of fear in which they are careful not to take steps which might attract criticism from people in power and in prominent positions. The ways in which they respond to this climate is clear from their behaviour in politically sensitive cases progressing through the courts. … Prosecutors tend to accept criminal complaints from prominent political figures without question—this is particularly the case with charges of criminal defamation and disinformation—and such cases invariably result in convictions, even when culpatory evidence is lacking and exculpatory evidence is abundant. Judges in lower courts tend to be more fearful of taking independent action than those in the higher courts. As a consequence there is a high rate of appeals all the way to the Supreme Court.

45 A recent illustration was the decision of the Supreme Court in December 2008 to release the men convicted of the murder of a trade union leader, Chea Vichea, and to request the Appeal Court to re-examine the case. The case against the two men had become a cause célèbre because there was almost no evidence against them but an abundance of exculpatory evidence. The original trial had failed to meet basic procedural standards and the Appeal Court had attracted international criticism in failing to correct these errors. Yet in reality the case was of such political significance that it is inconceivable that a lower court could have acquitted the men, despite the lack of evidence against them, without a clear indication from the Government that such a decision was acceptable. The original investigating judge courageously dismissed the case. Within weeks he was reassigned to a remote provincial court and the case was forced back to trial.

The right to a fair trial in the context of anti-terrorism measures is discussed in more detail in Chapter 18.4.3.

3.2.11 Prohibition on Retrospective Criminal Laws: Article 15

Closely related to the fair trial rights noted above is the prohibition on finding a person guilty of an offence that was not criminalised under municipal or international law at the time of the relevant conduct.[54] The familiar themes of the rule of law and ensuring that restrictions on liberty are not arbitrary are evident here once more. The prohibition on retrospective criminal laws is a well-established principle in international criminal law, often referred to by the maxim *nullem crimen sine lege*.[55]

However, article 15(2) of the ICCPR clarifies that a person can still be punished for something that 'was criminal according to the general principles of law recognised by the community of nations' at the time it was committed, even if not specifically criminalised in the municipal law of the relevant

54 ICCPR, see above, n 1, art 15.

55 See for example the *Rome Statute of the International Criminal Court*, art 22, and see Chapter 7, for further discussion.

state. That provision affirms the approach of the International Military Tribunal at Nuremberg, which held that the trial of individuals on charges that were criminal under customary international law at the time they were committed, such as war crimes and crimes against humanity, did not violate the rule against retrospectivity, even though the crimes were not specifically provided for in the municipal law of the states where they were committed.[56] While there has been significant debate about the robustness of the claim that those crimes enjoyed customary international law status before 1945, the general principle remains that customary international law will suffice as a source of criminality for the purposes of the prohibition on retrospectivity.

3.2.12 Right to Personal Standing Before the Law: Article 16

Article 16 of the ICCPR provides: 'Everyone shall have the right to recognition everywhere as a person before the law.' The essence of this right is to prohibit states from treating any class of people as non-people or lesser people under their law. This right is therefore closely linked to the philosophical roots of human rights in ensuring the essential dignity of every human being, regardless of any characteristics or classification that might be assigned to them.[57] It is also closely related to the principle of non-discrimination.

The Human Rights Committee has commented on the significance of the link between the right to recognition as a person before the law and discrimination against women:

> The right of everyone under article 16 to be recognized everywhere as a person before the law is particularly pertinent for women, who often see it curtailed by reason of sex or marital status. This right implies that the capacity of women to own property, to enter into a contract or to exercise other civil rights may not be restricted on the basis of marital status or any other discriminatory ground. It also implies that women may not be treated as objects to be given, together with the property of the deceased husband, to his family.[58]

Without protection of one's legal personality, the ability to realise the other substantive human rights would be greatly diminished. It also forms an important threshold point from which the principles in the right to a fair trial, discussed above, can proceed.

3.2.13 Right to Privacy: Article 17

The right to privacy protects individuals from 'arbitrary or unlawful interference with his privacy, family, home or correspondence', as well as from 'unlawful attacks on his honour and reputation'.[59] The scope of interests thus protected is potentially very broad. It covers privacy in the narrow sense of data, personal information or correspondence, requiring states to regulate who may lawfully access such information and to protect individuals from unauthorised access. However, interference with

56 Judgment of the International Military Tribunal, (1947) 41 *American Journal of International Law*, 172, 249. See Chapter 7.2, and 7.3, for further discussion of this issue and Chapter 11.2 and 11.3 for further discussion with regard to the Nuremberg trials.

57 See Chapter 2.4.

58 Human Rights Committee, *General Comment No 28: Article 3 (The Equality of Rights Between Men and Women)*, (29 March 2000), para 19.

59 ICCPR, see above, n 1, art 17.

privacy, family and home has been held to extend to protect individuals from unwarranted incursions by the state into the private sphere. Arbitrary or unreasonable searches must therefore be prohibited by municipal law.[60]

The right to privacy has also been used to challenge the criminalisation of consensual homosexual sex. The European Court of Human Rights, interpreting a right to privacy under the European Convention on Human Rights, which ensures that 'everyone has the right to respect for his private and family life, his home and his correspondence', held in *Dudgeon v United Kingdom* that such a law breached the right to privacy.[61] The European Court went further in the later case of *Norris v Ireland*, finding that the existence of a law criminalising homosexual sex was a continuing threat against a person's private life, even if the victim had not been charged or interrogated under it.[62] The Human Rights Committee reached the same conclusion in *Toonen v Australia*, finding the Tasmanian laws criminalising homosexual sex between consenting males, which were not being enforced at the time, to be in breach of article 17 of the ICCPR.[63] In each of those cases, the European Court and the Human Rights Committee rejected the respective states' arguments that the laws were justified for the protection of public morality.

The treaty monitoring committees have noted a number of areas where the right to privacy is engaged in connection with other rights. The Committee on Economic, Social and Cultural Rights has pointed to the reference to unlawful or arbitrary interference with one's home, and has read that provision together with the right to an adequate standard of housing in the ICESCR.[64] The Committee on Economic, Social and Cultural Rights (CESCR) has concluded that these two rights read together amount to a right not to be forcibly evicted from one's home without lawful justification and without compensation or adequate support to establish a new home.[65]

Elements of the right to privacy that particularly affect women include practices 'where the sexual life of a woman is taken into consideration in deciding the extent of her legal rights and protections, including protection against rape'.[66] Laws that require the consent of husbands or male family members for reproductive procedures and laws that require abortions to be reported also potentially infringe a woman's privacy.[67] Laws requiring women to wear specific items of clothing in public can also be considered an unjustified incursion into the private sphere.[68] There is a clear relationship in those cases with non-discrimination, discussed below at Chapter 3.2.22.

60 Human Rights Committee, *General Comment No 16: Article 17 (Right to Privacy)*, (1988), para 8.

61 *Dudgeon v United Kingdom* (1981) 4 EHRR 149, Ser A, no 45, para 40.

62 *Norris v Ireland* (1989) 13 EHRR 186, Ser A, no 142, para 36.

63 *Toonen v Australia*, Human Rights Committee, Communication no 488/1992, para 8.2.

64 ICESCR, see above, n 2, art 11(1).

65 Committee on Economic, Social and Cultural Rights, *General Comment No 7: The Right to Adequate Housing, (art 11(1) of the Covenant): Forced Evictions*, (1997), para 8.

66 See above, n 58, para 20.

67 See above, n 58.

68 See above, n 58, para 13.

While the right to privacy has a very broad scope, it is a right that is often required to be balanced against competing rights, particularly freedom of opinion and expression. If exercised to its fullest possible extent, the right to privacy would place a considerable constraint on the things that could be said or published about a person, if they were considered to impinge upon that person's private sphere, thereby curtailing the right to freedom of expression. In contrast, a liberal approach to freedom of expression would permit disclosure of information harmful to a person's privacy, reputation and potentially safety. The balance struck by the ICCPR is to require states parties to protect individuals from 'unlawful attacks on [their] honour and reputation', which can be achieved through defamation laws, among other means. However, the ICCPR is not restrictive as to precisely how the balance ought to be resolved; states are given a margin of discretion in finding the appropriate balance between the protection of privacy, honour and reputation and the protection of speech. The very different approaches to defamation in different states are a testament to the different views that persist as to the appropriate balance.

3.2.14 Freedom of Thought, Conscience and Religion: Article 18

The Human Rights Committee has described the freedom of thought, conscience and religion as 'far-reaching and profound; it encompasses freedom of thought on all matters, personal conviction and the commitment to religion or belief, whether manifested individually or in community with others.'[69] It applies to religious beliefs, atheistic beliefs and non-religious beliefs. The right therefore encompasses both a right to non-discrimination on the basis of one's beliefs and a right to conscientious objection from the dominant ideology, whether that be religious or political.

The freedom to hold particular beliefs, as distinct from the expression and manifestation of those beliefs, is effectively absolute. No derogation is permitted from the right, even in times of public emergency,[70] and there is no reason why holding a belief should ever be limited by inconsistency with another right. The ability to manifest one's religion or belief, however, is able to be limited to the extent necessary to protect public safety, order, health or morals or the fundamental rights and freedoms of others.

> The freedom to manifest religion or belief may be exercised 'either individually or in community with others and in public or private'. The freedom to manifest religion or belief in worship, observance, practice and teaching encompasses a broad range of acts. The concept of worship extends to ritual and ceremonial acts giving direct expression to belief, as well as various practices integral to such acts, including the building of places of worship, the use of ritual formulae and objects, the display of symbols, and the observance of holidays and days of rest. The observance and practice of religion or belief may include not only ceremonial acts but also such customs as the observance of dietary regulations, the wearing of distinctive clothing or head coverings, participation in rituals associated with certain stages of life, and the use of a particular language customarily spoken by a group.[71]

69 Human Rights Committee, *General Comment No 22: Article 18 (Freedom of Thought, Conscience and Religion)*, (1993), para 1.

70 ICCPR, see above, n 1, art 4(2).

71 See above, n 69, para 4.

SNAPSHOT: BANNING RELIGIOUS DRESS

HUDOYBERGANOVA V UZBEKISTAN, HUMAN RIGHTS COMMITTEE

Uzbekistan banned the wearing of religious dress in public places in 1998. Raihon Hudoyberganova was expelled from her tertiary education institution shortly after the law was passed for wearing the Islamic headscarf known as the hijab. The Human Rights Committee found that there had been a violation of the right to freedom of religious expression, given that the Uzbek government had not invoked any justification for the ban. However, the Committee noted that the right to religious expression can legitimately be limited in certain circumstances, leaving open the possibility that a ban on religious dress could be lawful if properly justified.

> The Committee has noted the author's claim that her right to freedom of thought, conscience and religion was violated as she was excluded from University because she refused to remove the headscarf that she wore in accordance with her beliefs. The Committee considers that the freedom to manifest one's religion encompasses the right to wear clothes or attire in public which is in conformity with the individual's faith or religion. Furthermore, it considers that to prevent a person from wearing religious clothing in public or private may constitute a violation of article 18, paragraph 2, which prohibits any coercion that would impair the individual's freedom to have or adopt a religion. ... It recalls, however, that the freedom to manifest one's religion or beliefs is not absolute and may be subject to limitations, which are prescribed by law and are necessary to protect public safety, order, health, or morals, or the fundamental rights and freedoms of others (article 18, paragraph 3, of the Covenant). In the present case, the author's exclusion took place on 15 March 1998, and was based on the provisions of the Institute's new regulations. The Committee notes that the State party has not invoked any specific ground for which the restriction imposed on the author would in its view be necessary in the meaning of article 18, paragraph 3. Instead, the State party has sought to justify the expulsion of the author from University because of her refusal to comply with the ban. Neither the author nor the State party have specified what precise kind of attire the author wore and which was referred to as 'hijab' by both parties. In the particular circumstances of the present case, and without either prejudging the right of a State party to limit expressions of religion and belief in the context of article 18 of the Covenant and duly taking into account the specifics of the context, or prejudging the right of academic institutions to adopt specific regulations relating to their own functioning, the Committee is led to conclude, in the absence of any justification provided by the State party, that there has been a violation of article 18, paragraph 2.[72]

ŞAHIN V TURKEY, EUROPEAN COURT OF HUMAN RIGHTS

The Turkish constitution proclaims that Turkey is 'a democratic, secular and social State based on the rule of law that is respectful of human rights in a spirit of social peace, national solidarity and justice...' Throughout the history of modern Turkey, various laws have restricted the wearing of religious dress in public in order to protect the secular values of the society against the perceived threat of religious sectarianism. The Turkish Constitutional Court upheld such bans by distinguishing between the right to hold religious beliefs and practise one's religion in private or in a place of worship, and the way one dressed in public, which could be

72 *Hudoyberganova v Uzbekistan*, Human Rights Committee, communication no 931/2000, 18 January 2005, UN document no CCPR/C/82/D/931/2000, para 6.2.

construed as political or provocative.[73] In 1998, Istanbul University issued a directive banning students wearing headscarves or with beards from participating in academic studies:

> students whose 'heads are covered' (who wear the Islamic headscarf) and students (including overseas students) with beards must not be admitted to lectures, courses or tutorials. Consequently, the name and number of any student with a beard or wearing the Islamic headscarf must not be added to the lists of registered students.[74]

Leyla Şahin was barred from classes and exams in the medical faculty on that basis for wearing a headscarf. The Grand Chamber of the European Court of Human Rights observed:

> Having regard to the above background, it is the principle of secularism, as elucidated by the Constitutional Court, which is the paramount consideration underlying the ban on the wearing of religious symbols in universities. In such a context, where the values of pluralism, respect for the rights of others and, in particular, equality before the law of men and women are being taught and applied in practice, it is understandable that the relevant authorities should wish to preserve the secular nature of the institution concerned and so consider it contrary to such values to allow religious attire, including, as in the present case, the Islamic headscarf, to be worn.[75]

The Court went on to find that the limitation of the right of religious expression in this case was justifiable within the state's margin of appreciation and was therefore not a breach.[76]

In her critique of the *Şahin* case, Carolyn Evans argued:

> The Court sided with the state against a student who was denied access to education and forced out of university. Such judgments, justified on the basis of equality, tolerance and human rights, do harm to the very notion of neutrality that the Court claims to be central to proper adjudication in these areas. When those who are not Christians but whose rights have been violated can gain no relief from the Court because the Court employs stereotypes and refuses to engage with the complexity of modern religious pluralism, then religious freedom and pluralism are undermined and the notion of human rights degraded.[77]

FRENCH BANS ON FACE COVERINGS AND ON RELIGIOUS SYMBOLS IN SCHOOLS

In April 2011, a French law banning anyone from covering their face in public came into effect. While the law does not specify any particular item of dress, it is clearly targeted at the burqa. Women defying the ban can be fined €150, while men found to have forced a woman to wear a face covering can be fined €30,000 or be imprisoned for one year. The French Constitutional Council ruled that the ban would not be enforceable in public places of worship, due to conflict with the right to freedom of religion, but was constitutional as regards all other public places.[78]

73 *Şahin v Turkey*, European Court of Human Rights, application no 4474/98, Grand Chamber judgment, 10 November 2005, para 39.

74 Ibid para 16.

75 Ibid para 116.

76 Ibid paras 122–3.

77 C Evans, 'The "Islamic Scarf" in the European Court of Human Rights' (2006) 7 *Melbourne Journal of International Law*, 52, 72.

78 'French "burqa" ban passes last legal hurdle' *Agence France Press*, 7 October 2010.

In 2004, the French Parliament enacted a law that banned students from wearing 'conspicuous' or 'ostensible' religious symbols in French government primary and secondary schools.[79] The ban was in pursuit of the principle of secularism and was seemingly aimed at safeguarding public order. While the ban was broad enough to account for all students wearing a head covering, such as a Jewish skullcap (kippah) or a Sikh turban, the impact of the ban fell disproportionately on Muslim girls. For some of France's Muslim population, the wearing of the Islamic headscarf is considered a religious obligation, thus potentially affecting the attendance of Muslim girls at school. Several UN treaty bodies have since made recommendations calling on France to closely monitor the impact of the ban, and in 2008 the UN Human Rights Committee recommended that France re-examine the ban.[80] The introduction of the 2011 French law stands in defiance of this recommendation.

Freedom of opinion and expression and freedom of assembly also protect the ways in which thoughts, beliefs and religions are given expression, as does freedom from discrimination.

3.2.15 Freedom of Opinion and Expression: Article 19

Freedom of opinion and expression covers both the right to express an opinion, through speech, writing, art, or any other form, and the right to seek out and receive the expressions of others. The ability to engage in that exchange of ideas without interference is necessary for the fulfilment of many other rights, as the means through which one's cultural identity, religious or political beliefs and political participation can be manifested, as well as being an important end in its own right.

However, if expression were left absolutely unfettered and carried no consequences, it is easy to see how certain forms of expression could infringe the rights of others, for instance by inciting racial or religious hatred, infringing a person's privacy or harming his or her reputation, or posing a threat to his or her physical safety. The text of article 19 of the ICCPR, as well as equivalent provisions in other human rights instruments guaranteeing freedom of expression,[81] therefore stipulates that the exercise of this freedom 'carries with it special duties and responsibilities' and may therefore be subject to certain restrictions provided for by law.[82] Such restrictions must be shown to be necessary for respect of the rights or reputations of others, or for the protection of national security or public order, or of public health or morals.[83]

States are given considerable leeway in determining an appropriate balance between freedom of expression and the protection of other rights by partially restricting speech. The United States, for example, has a notoriously strident adherence to the freedom of speech guaranteed in the US Constitution to the exclusion of various attempts to restrict certain types of communication; in contrast, several European countries place a higher value on the protection of other rights and have laws in place restricting

79 Law No 2004–228 of 15 March 2004.

80 Human Rights Committee, *Concluding Observations on France*, UN Doc CCPR/C/FRA/CO/4 (31 July 2008), para 23.

81 See for example ECHR, art 10; *American Convention on Human Rights*, art 13.

82 ICCPR, see above, n 1, art 19(3).

83 Ibid. See further the discussion of limitations in Chapter 3.3, for the manner in which these restrictions are applied.

communications and the release of information in certain circumstances. In order for such restrictions to be legitimate under international human rights law, they must not only be prescribed by the law of the relevant state, but must also be *necessary* to achieve the protection of one of the permitted interests.

SNAPSHOT: INTERNET CENSORSHIP IN CHINA

Recent cases of cooperation by multinational internet companies with efforts by the Chinese government to censor the internet and punish dissidents for their online communications have raised questions regarding the scope of freedom of expression in the internet age and the responsibility of companies in assisting or resisting governments intent on limiting such expression.[84] The following extract from an Amnesty International report summarises the issues in relation to three large US-based companies: Yahoo!, Microsoft and Google.

> All three companies have, in one way or another, facilitated or colluded in the practice of censorship in China. Yahoo! has provided the Chinese authorities with private and confidential information about its users. This included personal data that has been used to convict at least two journalists, considered by Amnesty International to be prisoners of conscience. Microsoft has admitted to shutting down a blog on the basis of a government request. Google has launched a censored version of its international search engine in China. All three companies have demonstrated a disregard for their own internally driven and proclaimed policies ...
>
> While each of Yahoo!, Microsoft and Google may be considered to be complicit in the Chinese government's denial of freedom of information, Yahoo!'s actions have, in particular, assisted the suppression of dissent with severe consequences for those affected. The company allowed its Chinese partner to pass evidence to the authorities that was subsequently used to convict individuals, at least two of whom received long prison sentences for peacefully exercising their legitimate right to freedom of expression. Thus Yahoo! appears to have failed to honour its responsibility to ensure that its own operations and those of its partners are not complicit in human rights abuses. This is in breach of widely recognised international human rights principles for companies.
>
> In defending their actions in China, Yahoo!, Microsoft and Google maintain they are under an obligation to comply with local law. They argue that although it is not an ideal situation, their presence in China is a force for good. They assert that without their input, censorship would still take place and that censored information is better than no information at all.[85]

3.2.16 Prohibition on Propaganda for War and Advocacy of National, Racial or Religious Hatred: Article 20

One limitation on freedom of expression that is expressly prescribed in the ICCPR is the requirement in article 20 that states parties prohibit propaganda for war and 'any advocacy of national, racial or religious hatred that constitutes incitement to discrimination, hostility or violence'.

84 See Chapter 19, for more detailed discussion of the responsibility of corporations for human rights.

85 Amnesty International, *Undermining Freedom of Expression in China: The Role of Yahoo!, Microsoft and Google*, 2006, Amnesty International UK, London, available at <http://www.amnestyusa.org/business/Undermining_Freedom_of_Expression_in_China.pdf>, 5–6.

An equivalent provision containing stronger language and more detail about the types of expression to be prohibited is contained in the *International Convention on the Elimination of All Forms of Racial Discrimination* (ICERD):

> States Parties condemn all propaganda and all organizations which are based on ideas or theories of superiority of one race or group of persons of one colour or ethnic origin, or which attempt to justify or promote racial hatred and discrimination in any form, and undertake to adopt immediate and positive measures designed to eradicate all incitement to, or acts of, such discrimination and, to this end, with due regard to the principles embodied in the Universal Declaration of Human Rights and the rights expressly set forth in article 5 of this Convention, inter alia:
>
> [a] Shall declare an offence punishable by law all dissemination of ideas based on racial superiority or hatred, incitement to racial discrimination, as well as all acts of violence or incitement to such acts against any race or group of persons of another colour or ethnic origin, and also the provision of any assistance to racist activities, including the financing thereof;
>
> [b] Shall declare illegal and prohibit organizations, and also organized and all other propaganda activities, which promote and incite racial discrimination, and shall recognize participation in such organizations or activities as an offence punishable by law;
>
> [c] Shall not permit public authorities or public institutions, national or local, to promote or incite racial discrimination.[86]

Given differing attitudes relating to the value of free speech and its restriction for the protection of the rights of others in different states, this provision has been the subject of a significant number of reservations and interpretative declarations in both its ICCPR and ICERD iterations.[87] For instance, the United States entered a reservation to the ICCPR: 'That article 20 does not authorize or require legislation or other action by the United States that would restrict the right of free speech and association protected by the Constitution and laws of the United States.' Denmark, Finland and Iceland all entered reservations against the requirement in article 20 of the ICCPR to prohibit propaganda for war, on the ground that they had all voted against the inclusion of that provision in the UN General Assembly in 1961 and continued to oppose it as an inappropriate restriction on free speech.[88]

3.2.17 Freedom of Assembly: Article 21

Freedom of assembly protects the right to gather peacefully, subject only to restrictions 'which are necessary in a democratic society in the interests of national security or public safety, public order (*ordre public*), the protection of public health or morals or the protection of the rights and freedoms of others'.[89] It is closely related to the rights of freedom of association, freedom of expression and the right to political participation, as the realisation of each of those rights would be severely curtailed if

86 *International Convention on the Elimination of All Forms of Racial Discrimination* (ICERD), opened for signature 7 March 1966, 660 UNTS 195 (entered into force 4 January 1969), art 4.

87 See Chapter 7.2.4.

88 Australia, Belgium, France, Ireland, Luxembourg, Malta, the Netherlands, New Zealand, Norway, Sweden, Switzerland and the United Kingdom have also entered reservations or declarations to art 20 of the ICCPR.

89 ICCPR, see above, n 1, art 21.

people were prevented from gathering together to meet, exchange ideas, express political solidarity, or indeed for some more mundane purposes. The state will therefore be permitted to restrict public gatherings by requiring advance notice, permits and the like, and will be permitted to take action to disperse a gathering that is becoming violent, but such restrictions cannot be a cloak for the unreasonable restriction of political opposition.

SNAPSHOT: CRACKDOWN ON PROTESTERS IN MYANMAR

REPORT OF THE SPECIAL RAPPORTEUR ON THE SITUATION OF HUMAN RIGHTS IN MYANMAR, PAULO SÉRGIO PINHEIRO, 7 DECEMBER 2007[90]

1 On 15 August 2007, the Government of Myanmar increased the retail price of fuel by up to 500 per cent. This decision has drastically affected the livelihoods of the people of Myanmar. The population, which has seen its standards of living severely curtailed over the last few years, reacted strongly to this decision and started small peaceful demonstrations throughout August and into early September. On 5 September during a demonstration in Pakokku a number of monks were beaten up. The population and the monks, dissatisfied with this action, continued expressing their discontent over economic living conditions and undertook large peaceful demonstrations from 18 to 26 September across the country including in Yangon, Mandalay, Pakokku and Sittwe.

...

37. The use of lethal force by law enforcement officials from 26 to 29 September 2007 in Myanmar was inconsistent with the fundamental principles reflected in the basic international norms deriving from international customary law. They ignored the principles of necessity and proportionality ... Whereas the Myanmar Code of Criminal Procedure provides for the use of civil force (art 128) and military force (art 129) to disperse an assembly, it also provides for the use of as little force as is consistent with dispersing an assembly, in order to avoid 'injury to person and property' (art 130). From 26 to 29 September, the security forces without doubt exceeded the limits of the power conferred on them by the law.

...

58 ... The events of September and October 2007 represent another manifestation of the severe methods of persecution and harassment that prevail in Myanmar. From 26 September to 20 October, the ban on gatherings (five people or more) enshrined in the Myanmar law was strictly applied and a curfew severely restricted the freedom of movement of people, lending a hand to the security forces for the conduct of night raids.

...

60 From 26 September to 6 October, the security forces reportedly raided 52 monasteries across the country, looting the possessions of monks and beating and arresting them in large numbers. Allegations of killings were also received. Early on Thursday 27 September at 12.30 am, security forces raided the Ngwe Kyar Yan monastery, a famous Buddhist teaching centre in Yangon (South Okkalapa Township),

90 *Report of the Special Rapporteur on the Situation of Human Rights in Myanmar, Paulo Sérgio Pinheiro*, UN document no A/HRC/6/14, 7 December 2007.

where they allegedly opened fire, physically assaulted and arrested an estimated 70 monks. Pictures taken at the scene after the curfew show blood spattering at different locations in the monastery and destruction of property, including gates, windows and other furniture.

...

64 Whereas it is difficult to clearly identify at this stage of the inquiry the chain of command that led to the tragic events of September and October 2007, the Special Rapporteur found that the Government had knowledge that severe human rights abuses would be likely to take place and failed to prevent these abuses by not using all available options and not exercising restraint in policing the demonstrations. He further found that the crackdown on demonstrations was not a policing but a military response. The Special Rapporteur noted that the excessive use of force, including lethal force was unnecessary and disproportionate. He also found that a ruthless campaign of reprisals took place, targeting monks, nuns, political activists, human rights defenders and other individuals who organized or participated in the peaceful demonstrations, as well as their family members.

...

71 The incidents reported demonstrate the vulnerability of the economic and social foundations of Myanmar's society. It shows that the right to freedom of expression and the right to peaceful assembly have yet to be fully guaranteed and the tremendous challenges faced by Myanmar in ensuring the rule of law by holding accountable the perpetrators of serious criminal acts documented in this report. It further reveals the urgent need to repeal or amend old laws and regulations in accordance with international human rights standards, and to reconsider the participation of the army and non law enforcement officials in policing demonstrations.

72 Moreover, the events represent a compelling example of the indivisibility of human rights. Decades of denial of basic civil and political rights have compromised the standard of living of the population. By severely restricting the right to freedom of expression and the right to peaceful assembly, the Government has prevented over many years the emergence of a platform for genuine public dialogue, where people could share their concerns over their increasing lack of access to job opportunities and basic social services, including health and food.

3.2.18 Freedom of Association: Article 22

Freedom of association is closely related to freedom of assembly, but protects not only the right to meet, but also the right to form a group with like-minded people. This right is particularly pertinent in the context of trade unions and political parties, although it extends to all forms of 'association with others'.[91] Because of its importance to trade unions and the protection of labour rights, freedom of association features extensively in the conventions of the International Labour Organisation. It is discussed in more detail in Chapter 17.

91 ICCPR, see above, n 1, art 22.

3.2.19 Freedom to Marry and Found a Family and Protection of the Family: Article 23

Article 23 of the ICCPR contains a collection of rights relating to marriage and the family. First, the family is declared to be 'the natural and fundamental group unit of society and is entitled to protection by society and the State.'[92] The Human Rights Committee has clarified that the definition of what constitutes a family may differ from state to state, for instance extending to de facto partnerships or extended families in some countries, but that whatever definition is applied in a state's laws and practices must be afforded protection.[93]

Second, the right of 'men and women of marriageable age' to marry is recognised. In the same sentence is the protection of the right 'to found a family', meaning that couples should be allowed to procreate (at least where it is physically possible to do so) and to live together.[94] State policies prohibiting intermarriage of people from certain ethnic backgrounds, enforcing sterilisation, or resulting in the separation of family members against their will, are all examples of policies that would violate this right.

SNAPSHOT: CHINA'S ONE CHILD POLICY

China's family planning policy (commonly referred to as the 'one child policy'), which has applied in mainland China since 1979, prohibits couples from having more than one child, subject to certain categories of exemption. The one child policy has been implicated in forced abortions and sterilisations, as well as a high rate of infanticide and 'voluntary' abortions by parents who are determined that their one child be a boy.

China is not a party to the ICCPR. The effect of the one child policy on the protection of the family and the right to found a family therefore cannot be analysed in terms of a breach of the ICCPR. However, the treaty-monitoring committees of other treaties to which China is a party have expressed grave concerns about the policy and the human rights consequences, demonstrating that policies that impact on human rights frequently transcend the somewhat arbitrary boundaries between civil/political and economic/social/cultural. The Committee on Economic, Social and Cultural Rights made the following observations in relation to the effects of the one child policy on article 10 of the ICESCR, which, like article 23 of the ICCPR, provides for protection of the family, as well as special protection for mothers and children.

> 36 The Committee is deeply concerned about reports of forced abortions and forced sterilizations imposed on women, including those belonging to ethnic minority groups, by local officials in the context of the one-child policy, and about the high maternal mortality rate as a result of unsafe abortions.
>
> ...
>
> 65 The Committee urges the State party to undertake effective measures to ensure that abortions are carried out voluntarily and under adequate medical and sanitary conditions and to ensure that the

92 ICCPR, see above, n 1, art 23(1).

93 Human Rights Committee, *General Comment No 19: Article 23 (The Family)*, (1990), para 2.

94 Ibid para 5.

existing legislation governing the one-child policy does not violate the rights enshrined in article 10 of the Covenant. The Committee requests the State party to provide information in its next periodic report in this regard, including information on women belonging to ethnic minority groups.[95]

In 2006, the Committee on the Elimination of Discrimination Against Women highlighted the human rights ramifications of practices by government agencies and private individuals that commonly occur despite the presence of protective laws on the books.

31 While noting that legal measures prohibiting sex-selective abortions and female infanticide and other measures are in place, such as the nationwide campaign, 'Operation Caring for Girls', launched in 2006 and a system of incentives, the Committee remains concerned at the persistence of illegal practices of sex-selective abortion, female infanticide and the non-registration and abandonment of female children, and about forced abortions. The Committee is concerned about the impact of the adverse sex ratio, which may contribute to the increase in trafficking in women and girls.

32 The Committee urges the State party to strengthen its monitoring of the implementation of existing laws against selective abortion and female infanticide and to enforce them through fair legal procedures that sanction officials acting in excess of their authority. It also urges the State party to investigate and prosecute the reports of abuse and violence against ethnic minority women by local family planning officials, including forced sterilization and forced abortion. The Committee recommends that the State party introduce mandatory gender-sensitivity training for family planning officials. It encourages the State party to continue to strengthen efforts to ensure that all girls are registered at birth, in particular in rural areas. It further recommends that the State party vigorously address the causes of son-preference, which remain strong in rural areas, and of the negative consequences of the one-child policy as regards the adverse sex ratio by expanding insurance systems and old age pensions to the population at large, in particular in rural areas.[96]

In more general terms, the Human Rights Committee said in its General Comment on the protection of the family:

> When States parties adopt family planning policies, they should be compatible with the provisions of the Covenant and should, in particular, not be discriminatory or compulsory.[97]

The reference to 'men and women of marriageable age' does not extend to a right of same sex couples to marry or to found a family. In the case of *Joslin v New Zealand*, the authors, who were in a lesbian relationship and caring for the children of previous marriages, claimed that the refusal of New Zealand authorities to issue them a marriage licence was discriminatory. The authors submitted that the phrase 'men and women' in article 23(2) 'does not mean that only men may

95 Committee on Economic, Social and Cultural Rights, *Concluding Observations on the People's Republic of China 2005*, UN document E/C.12/1/Add.107, 13 May 2005.

96 Committee on the Elimination of Discrimination Against Women, *Concluding Comments of the Committee on the Elimination of Discrimination Against Women: China*, UN document CEDAW/C/CHN/CO/6, 25 August 2006.

97 See above, n 93, para 5.

marry women, but rather that men as a group and women as a group may marry'.[98] The Human Rights Committee rejected that interpretation, finding that New Zealand's failure to provide for same sex marriage was not a violation of the ICCPR.[99] The same interpretation has been applied to the equivalent provision in the European Convention on Human Rights.[100] However, in light of the Human Rights Committee's General Comment regarding protection of the family in its various forms,[101] in a country where the state's practice recognises a same sex couple as a de facto family, it may be reasonable to expect the state to accord the same legal protection to such families as it does to other families, other than the right to marry.

The third paragraph of article 23 prohibits forced marriage. The final paragraph requires states to ensure equality of spouses within a marriage and also in the event of the dissolution of a marriage, while also requiring states to provide for the necessary protection of any children upon dissolution of a marriage.

3.2.20 Protection of Children: Article 24

Special protection is accorded to children on the basis of their particular vulnerability as minors. Article 24 of the ICCPR provides that every child shall be registered immediately after birth, shall have a name and shall have the right to acquire a nationality,[102] all of which are aspects of recognition as a person before the law.[103] It is therefore put beyond doubt that children are to be treated as having legal entitlements in their own right, even though they may not have legal capacity for certain purposes. It also requires that 'such measures of protection as are required' be accorded to the child by the child's family, society and the state without discrimination.[104]

The non-specific, broadly defined protection for children in the ICCPR has been elaborated upon in a separate treaty directed specifically at the rights of children: the *Convention on the Rights of the Child* (CROC). The underlying principle in CROC is that in all actions concerning children, 'the best interests of the child shall be a primary consideration.'[105] A range of specific issues relevant to the particular vulnerability of children are addressed in CROC, including identity, separation from parents and protection from exploitation, as well as reiterating the range of civil and political rights discussed here and many of the economic, social and cultural rights discussed in the next chapter as being applicable to children.

The protection of the rights of children is discussed separately in Chapter 12.

---

98 *Joslin v New Zealand*, Human Rights Committee, *Communication No 902/1999*, UN Document No CCPR/C/75/D/902/1999, para 3.8.

99 Ibid paras 8.2–8.3.

100 *Sheffield & Horsham v United Kingdom*, ECtHR, (31-32/1997/815-816/1018/1019) 30 July 1998.

101 See above, n 93.

102 ICCPR, see above, n 1, art 24(2) and (3).

103 See section (m) above and ICCPR, see above, n 1, art 16.

104 ICCPR, see above, n 1, art 24(1).

105 *Convention on the Rights of the Child* (CROC), opened for signature 20 November 1989, 1577 UNTS 3 (entered into force 2 September 1990), art 3(1).

3.2.21 Right to Political Participation: Article 25

Despite the traditional insistence of a sovereignty-based system of international law not to impose any particular system of law on any state, the right to political participation effectively confers a right to a democratic system—or at least a system containing fundamental democratic elements—by conferring a right to vote. Article 25 of the ICCPR grants all citizens a right to vote and to stand for election 'at genuine periodic elections'.[106] Furthermore, 'universal and equal suffrage' is prescribed, ensuring that a vote is truly democratic and not subject to discrimination in terms of who is allowed to vote. The vote is also required to be held by secret ballot.

DECLARATIONS AND RESERVATIONS TO ARTICLE 25(b) OF THE INTERNATIONAL COVENANT ON CIVIL AND POLITICAL RIGHTS

KUWAIT

The Government of Kuwait wishes to formulate a reservation with regard to article 25(b). The provisions of this paragraph conflict with the Kuwaiti electoral law, which restricts the right to stand and vote in elections to males.

An equivalent reservation was entered by Kuwait to article 7 of CEDAW, and was subjected to an objection by Denmark supported by other European states. The reservation to CEDAW was withdrawn on 9 December 2005, following an amendment to the Kuwaiti electoral law in 2005 granting women the vote. The reservation to article 25(b) of the ICCPR remains in force at the time of writing, and is the subject of an objection by Finland, but the amendment of Kuwaiti electoral law in 2005 means that the substance of the reservation is not currently operative.

SWITZERLAND

The present provision shall be applied without prejudice to the cantonal and communal laws, which provide for or permit elections within assemblies to be held by a means other than secret ballot.

The Swiss reservation was designed to permit the traditional practice of conducting local elections in open air by a show of hands to continue in the two cantons that still conduct elections in that manner. No state has objected to the Swiss reservation.

The right to political participation is unusual in that it is limited to citizens, as distinct from the usual formulation whereby a state is obliged to respect, protect and promote the rights of 'all individuals within its territory and subject to its jurisdiction'.[107] States are permitted to determine who is eligible to be a citizen by their own methods, provided they comply with their other international obligations when doing so; for instance, it would not be permissible to disqualify certain groups from citizenship on the basis of their race or religion, since that would violate the prohibition on racial and religious discrimination.

The text of the ICCPR does not permit a state to restrict voting rights or rights of political participation to certain classes of people once they have been deemed 'citizens'. However, state practice limiting the

106 ICCPR, see above, n 1, art 25(b).

107 See for example ICCPR art 2.

franchise in certain circumstances, such as denying the vote to people serving a prison sentence, is common.

SNAPSHOT: RESTRICTION OF VOTING RIGHTS FOR PRISONERS

EUROPE

The European Court of Human Rights in *Hirst v United Kingdom*[108] held that a blanket ban on prisoners voting violated the 'right to free elections' under article 3 of the *First Protocol to the European Convention on Human Rights*. The majority suggested that a more limited ban on certain types of prisoners might be appropriate if it was proportionate to the aim of 'enhancing civic responsibility and respect for the rule of law', however it should be noted that the text of the *Protocol to the European Convention* does not contain the same guarantee of universal and equal suffrage contained in the ICCPR.

CANADA

In *Sauvé v Canada*,[109] a 5:4 majority of the Supreme Court of Canada held that legislation disenfranchising prisoners serving a term of two years or more violated section 3 of the *Canadian Charter of Rights and Freedoms*, which guarantees every citizen the right to vote. The legislation had been amended to introduce the two year sentence qualification after an earlier ruling of the Supreme Court found that a blanket disenfranchisement of all prisoners violated the right to vote in the *Canadian Charter*.[110] Section 1 of the *Canadian Charter* permits 'such reasonable limits [on the rights in the *Charter*] prescribed by law as can be demonstrably justified in a free and democratic society'. The minority in *Sauvé* considered that test to have been met.

AUSTRALIA

As Australia has no comprehensive federal protection of human rights and no applicable regional system, the protection of the right to vote as a human right must rely on rights implied from the constitution.[111] In *Roach v Electoral Commissioner*,[112] the majority of the High Court of Australia held that a blanket disenfranchisement of prisoners was unconstitutional, however the ban on prisoners serving a sentence of three years or longer from voting, which applied before the *Commonwealth Electoral Act* was amended in 2006, was constitutionally sound. No reference was made to international human rights law in making that decision.

The right to political participation extends beyond the right to participate in elections and includes the right 'to take part in the conduct of public affairs'[113] and 'to have access, on general terms of equality, to public service' in one's country.[114] As such, this right is closely linked to the rights of

108 *Hirst v United Kingdom (No 2)* (2006) 42 EHRR 41.

109 *Sauvé v Canada (Chief Electoral Officer)* [2002] 3 SCR 519.

110 *Sauvé v Canada (Attorney General)* [1993] 2 SCR 438.

111 See Chapter 10.3.3.

112 *Roach v Electoral Commissioner* (2007) 233 CLR 162

113 ICCPR, see above, n 1, art 25(a).

114 Ibid art 25(c).

freedom of opinion and expression, freedom of association, freedom of assembly and freedom from discrimination.

3.2.22 Freedom from Discrimination: Article 26

Non-discrimination is both a free-standing substantive right, which appears in article 26 of the ICCPR, and a standard for the realisation of all other human rights. The principle of non-discrimination reflects the very essence of human rights, in that every person holds the same rights by virtue of being born human and not by virtue of some particular characteristic or membership of some particular social group.

In taking measures to ensure the respect, protection and promotion of human rights, states are not permitted to discriminate between different groups. Article 2 of the ICCPR expressly lists 'race, colour, sex, language, religion, political or other opinion, national or social origin, property, birth or other status' in the inclusive list of grounds upon which discrimination in the fulfilment of human rights is prohibited.[115]

That is not to say that differential treatment for a particular group will necessarily constitute prohibited discrimination. In guaranteeing the 'equal and effective protection of the law' for all persons, international human rights law recognises that some groups may be particularly vulnerable and may require differential treatment in order to receive the protection of the law and the fulfilment of human rights on the same effective basis as other groups.

HUMAN RIGHTS COMMITTEE, *GENERAL COMMENT NO 18: NON-DISCRIMINATION*

The Committee also wishes to point out that the principle of equality sometimes requires States parties to take affirmative action in order to diminish or eliminate conditions which cause or help to perpetuate discrimination prohibited by the Covenant. For example, in a State where the general conditions of a certain part of the population prevent or impair their enjoyment of human rights, the State should take specific action to correct those conditions. Such action may involve granting for a time to the part of the population concerned certain preferential treatment in specific matters as compared with the rest of the population. However, as long as such action is needed to correct discrimination in fact, it is a case of legitimate differentiation under the Covenant.[116]

Chapters 13, 14 and 16 provide a detailed examination of three particularly vulnerable groups, namely indigenous peoples, persons with disabilities and women, and consider the approaches taken under international human rights law in addressing the needs of those groups.

3.2.23 Minority Rights: Article 27

Ethnic, religious and linguistic minority groups are recognised as holding special rights as a group under article 27 of the ICCPR. As such, members of such minority groups have the right to enjoy their

115 Ibid art 2(1).

116 Human Rights Committee, *General Comment No 18: Non-Discrimination*, (1989), para 10.

own culture, to profess and practise their own religion, or to use their own language, 'in community with the other members of their group'.[117] This category of rights therefore differs from rights such as freedom of opinion and belief, freedom of expression and freedom of assembly because it is not just the individual practice or expression that is being protected, but the cultural heritage of which that practice or expression is a part. Although minority rights are vested in individuals—unlike the right to self-determination, which is vested in a people[118]—it is the communal nature of the exercise of those rights that gives rise to their protection.

The Human Rights Committee has noted that 'culture' in the context of article 27 of the ICCPR 'manifests itself in many forms' and can extend to carrying on a particular way of life, including fishing, hunting and maintaining a connection with traditional lands, particularly in the case of indigenous peoples.[119]

3.3 NATURE OF OBLIGATIONS UNDER THE ICCPR

3.3.1 Immediate Nature of Obligations

One of the reasons sometimes proffered for the separation of civil and political rights from economic, social and cultural rights at the time of drafting the ICCPR and ICESCR was the desire to give full, immediate effect to those rights that were thought amenable to immediate implementation—namely civil and political rights—without having them diluted by the more progressive implementation obligations attached to economic, social and cultural rights. Whatever the merits of that reasoning (the debates regarding the separation of the two sets of rights are discussed in Chapter 1), the ICCPR imposes immediate obligations on states to implement the rights fully from the moment they ratify the covenant,[120] subject only to the limitations in the text of various articles and the inherent balancing exercises between rights. Unlike the ICESCR, there is no qualification that the expectations regarding measures taken towards the realisation of human rights are relative to a state's resources, nor is the realisation of the rights intended to be progressive or gradual.[121]

The Human Rights Committee confirmed the immediate nature of state obligations in a General Comment, in response to a perception that the obligation to 'take steps' implied progressive realisation:

> The requirement under article 2, paragraph 2, to take steps to give effect to the Covenant rights is unqualified and of immediate effect. A failure to comply with this obligation cannot be justified by reference to political, social, cultural or economic considerations within the State.[122]

---

117 ICCPR, see above, n 1, art 27.

118 See the distinction drawn by the Human Rights Committee, *General Comment No 23: Article 27 (Rights of Minorities)*, (1994) para 3.1. See also the discussion of the right to self-determination in section (b) above.

119 Human Rights Committee, ibid para 7; and see the discussion at Chapter 13.3.2.

120 ICCPR, see above, n 1, art 2.

121 Compare ICESCR, see above, n 2, art 2(1). See discussion Chapter 4.3, regarding the nature of state obligations regarding economic, social and cultural rights.

122 Human Rights Committee, *General Comment No 31: The Nature of the General Legal Obligation Imposed on States Parties to the Covenant*, 29 March 2004, para 14.

The immediate and generally unqualified nature of state obligations regarding the realisation of civil and political rights compared with economic, social and cultural rights is typically replicated in regional treaties and domestic human rights systems.[123]

3.3.2 Duties to Respect, Protect and Ensure Human Rights

The wording in article 2(1) of the ICCPR requires states parties 'to *respect* and to *ensure* to all individuals within its territory and subject to its jurisdiction' the rights listed in the Covenant, without discrimination.[124] The state's duty to *respect* human rights is essentially a duty of non-interference, meaning that the state must refrain from actions that would interfere with the enjoyment of any of the rights listed in the Covenant. The duty to respect is therefore sometimes referred to as the 'negative' aspect of a state's human rights obligations. The Human Rights Committee explains the duty to respect in the following way:

> The legal obligation under article 2, paragraph 1, is both negative and positive in nature. States parties must refrain from violation of the rights recognized by the Covenant, and any restrictions on any of those rights must be permissible under the relevant provisions of the Covenant. Where such restrictions are made, States must demonstrate their necessity and only take such measures as are proportionate to the pursuance of legitimate aims in order to ensure continuous and effective protection of Covenant rights. In no case may the restrictions be applied or invoked in a manner that would impair the essence of a Covenant right.[125]

The duty to *ensure* human rights is the positive aspect of a state's human rights obligations. States are obliged to take positive measures, including through legislation, judicial or administrative action and education, to give effect to civil and political rights.[126] Therefore, while simply refraining from causing harm will satisfy the state's duty to respect human rights, doing nothing will not be sufficient to satisfy the duty to ensure human rights. For example, if the state's agents commit an extrajudicial killing, the state will have breached the duty to respect the right to life. However, if a murder is carried out by a person with no connection to the state, the state's duty to ensure the right to life would require positive actions, such as a genuine investigation, a prosecution if appropriate before an impartial court, and indeed the provision of adequate criminal laws. In many instances, including this example, such positive actions will require the expenditure of resources. It is therefore false to distinguish between civil and political rights on the one hand and economic, social and cultural on the other on the basis that the latter requires the expenditure of resources while the former is resource-neutral.

---

123 Compare for example the qualified language in the *European Social Charter* (containing economic, social and cultural rights) with the *European Convention on Human Rights* (which contains predominantly civil and political rights).

124 ICCPR, see above, n 1, art 2 (emphasis added).

125 See above, n 122, para 6.

126 ICCPR, see above, n 1, art 2(1) and (2); Human Rights Committee, see above, n 122, para 7.

International human rights law works by enunciating rights and imposing obligations at the international level, while relying on states to give practical effect to those rights and obligations at the domestic level. Accordingly, states are responsible for ensuring that their legal system and their administrative practices actually respect and ensure the fulfilment of human rights in the manner envisaged in treaties such as the ICCPR. Depending on the state's constitutional arrangements, the treaty obligations might automatically form part of the state's municipal law (so-called monist states), or they might require specific domestic legislation to be incorporated (so-called dualist states).[127] In both cases, the onus is on the state to make appropriate changes to its laws and practices.

> Article 2, paragraph 2, requires that States parties take the necessary steps to give effect to the Covenant rights in the domestic order. It follows that, unless the Covenant's rights are already protected by their domestic laws or practices, States parties are required on ratification to make such changes to domestic laws and practices as are necessary to ensure their conformity with the Covenant. Where there are inconsistencies between domestic law and the Covenant, article 2 requires that the domestic law or practice be changed to meet the standards imposed by the Covenant's substantive guarantees. Article 2 allows a State party to pursue this in accordance with its own domestic constitutional structure and accordingly does not require that the Covenant be directly applicable in the courts, by incorporation of the Covenant into national law. The Committee takes the view, however, that Covenant guarantees may receive enhanced protection in those States where the Covenant is automatically or through specific incorporation part of the domestic legal order. The Committee invites those States parties in which the Covenant does not form part of the domestic legal order to consider incorporation of the Covenant to render it part of domestic law to facilitate full realization of Covenant rights as required by article 2.[128]

A significant part of the process of domestic implementation is the obligation for states to provide access to an effective remedy for those who wish to complain of a violation of their rights.[129] What constitutes an effective remedy will depend on the specific circumstances that gave rise to the violation. It will often be appropriate for the government to change a particular law or a particular practice to ensure that the violation is not repeated in similar circumstances, for example where a particular law or practice is found to be discriminatory.[130] If the violation is ongoing, it will be appropriate to cease the offending action, for example releasing a person from detention that was found to be arbitrary. Where the violation has ceased and cannot be reversed, for example if a person has been arbitrarily killed, reparation to the victim or the victim's family may be appropriate. It is important to note that it is not only the remedy that is important, but also the ability of individuals to have access to a process to hear their claims of human rights violations and to decide the applicable remedy, if any.

127 See Chapter 7.2.7.

128 See above, n 122, para 13.

129 For example, ICCPR, see above, n 1, art 2(3).

130 See the discussion of Australia's response to adverse human rights findings, Chapter 10.5.5.

SNAPSHOT: RIGHT TO A REMEDY—*FAURE v AUSTRALIA*[131]

The purported victim complained that Australia's 'Work for the Dole' program amounted to forced or compulsory labour in contravention of article 8 of the ICCPR. She attempted to challenge the policy on that basis before Australia's Human Rights and Equal Opportunity Commission,[132] which determined that it had no jurisdiction to hear the complaint. The Human Rights Committee in considering Ms Faure's claim concluded that Work for the Dole did not constitute forced labour and that there was therefore no substantive human rights violation in this case.[133] However, the Committee found that the obligation to provide an accessible, effective and enforceable remedy meant that where an individual has an arguable case that his or her human rights have been violated, there should be an avenue for an individual to make such a claim and seek a remedy in the state's legal system.

> Applying this reasoning to the present claim that the State party did not provide an effective remedy for the alleged breach of article 8 of the Covenant, the Committee observes, with reference to its admissibility considerations identified above in the context of exhaustion of domestic remedies, that, in the State party's legal system, it was and remains impossible for a person such as the author to challenge the substantive elements of the Work for Dole program, that is, the obligation imposed by law on persons such as the author, who satisfy the pre-conditions for access to the program, to perform labour in exchange for receipt of unemployment benefits. The Committee recalls that the State party's proposed remedies address the question of whether or not an individual in fact satisfies the requirements for access to the program, but no remedy is available to challenge the substantive scheme for those who are by law subject to it.[134]

The Committee therefore found no breach of article 8 of the ICCPR, as it concluded that the Work for the Dole scheme did not constitute forced labour, but nevertheless found Australia in breach of its obligations under article 2(3) of the ICCPR for its failure to provide a mechanism for Ms Faure to argue her case.[135]

Logically, if there is no capacity to seek a remedy in an arguable case, the right to a remedy is meaningless, as it would provide no independent mechanism for determining whether a violation had in fact taken place.

131 See above, n 27.

132 The Human Rights and Equal Opportunity Commission (HREOC) has since be renamed the Australian Human Rights Commission (AHRC). See Chapter 10.4.2 for discussion of the mandate and work of the AHRC and its predecessor.

133 See above, n 27, para 7.5.

134 See above, n 27 para 7.3.

135 See above, n 27 para 8. Note also that Human Rights Committee member Ruth Wedgwood issued a scathing individual opinion, writing that a case as trivial as Ms Faure's 'demeans the significance' of the ICCPR. Ms Wedgwood disagreed that Ms Faure had an arguable case and therefore found no violation of art 2(3).

3.3.3 Limitations and Derogations

There are very few circumstances in which human rights can be considered absolute. There are a number of ways in which the exercise of a person's human rights can be limited, and accordingly the state's human rights obligations limited. These include: limitations included in the text of a provision setting out the scope of the right; an implied limitation that the exercise of one right should not unduly impede the exercise of rights by others; a state's ability to enter a reservation to a human rights treaty; and the state's ability to derogate from specific human rights obligations in a state of emergency.

Limitations Inherent in Text

The scope of many rights set out in the ICCPR is limited by the language of the provision. For example, several rights prohibit only 'arbitrary' actions, meaning that actions carried out according to the rule of law and which are justifiable and non-discriminatory will not amount to a breach of those rights. Thus a person's right to life is expressed as a right not to be 'arbitrarily deprived of his life';[136] death, even directly at the hands of the state, will therefore only amount to a violation if it is arbitrary.[137] Similar limitations are inherent in a person's right not to be 'subjected to arbitrary arrest or detention',[138] 'arbitrarily deprived of the right to enter [his] own country',[139] or 'subjected to arbitrary or unlawful interference with [his] privacy, home or correspondence'.[140]

In other cases, the right is subject to specific exceptions. For example, freedom of expression can be subject to restrictions

> 'provided by law and [that] are necessary:
>
> (a) For respect of the rights or reputations of others;
> (b) For the protection of national security or of public order (*ordre public*), or of public health or morals.'[141]

An equivalent formulation is used in stipulating the permitted restrictions to the rights to freedom of movement,[142] a public hearing,[143] freedom of religion,[144] freedom of assembly[145] and freedom of association.[146] A common condition is that the state has entrenched the limitation in its law (whether

136 ICCPR, see above, n 1, art 6(1).

137 See further the discussion of the right to life in Chapter 3.5.

138 ICCPR, see above, n 1, art 9(1).

139 Ibid art 12(4).

140 Ibid art 17(1).

141 Ibid art 19(3).

142 Ibid art 12(3).

143 Ibid art 14(1).

144 Ibid art 18(3).

145 Ibid art 21.

146 ICCPR, see above, n 1, art 22(2).

by statute or through the common law or an equivalent non-written law), as opposed to permitting state agents to curtail human rights on their own whim. Legal prescription on its own, however, is not enough for a limitation to be valid. It must also be designed to achieve a legitimate purpose under international law, such as the protection of the rights of others, or the pursuit of one of the objectives set out in the text of the relevant article: for example, national security, public order, public health or public morals in the case of freedom of expression.

Furthermore, there is an element of proportionality. The limitations to freedom of expression in article 19(3) of the ICCPR, set out above, use the word 'necessary' to convey the requirement that a limitation of that particular right must be proportionate to achieve the legitimate goal. For example, some limited degree of filtering of the internet might be justifiable (leaving aside questions of the technical feasibility of such proposals) to protect the public from images of child pornography and the like; that is, protecting the rights of children from abuse and protecting public morals. Creating criminal offences for creating and transmitting such images would also clearly be justifiable, notwithstanding that they constitute a form of communication that would prima facie be protected. However, a complete ban on the internet to achieve those legitimate purposes would clearly be disproportionate, and could therefore not be considered 'necessary' within the meaning of article 19.

Reservations

As noted in Chapter 7.2.4, reservations to human rights treaties create technical difficulties that do not arise for treaties on other topics, given that the intended beneficiaries of obligations in human rights treaties are the people in each state, rather than the other states parties to the treaty. It is therefore more problematic to allow states to enter reservations to a human rights treaty, which allows states to modify the extent of their obligations, than it would be for an ordinary treaty concluded on a reciprocal basis. The Human Rights Committee has issued a General Comment on the question of reservations, which is extracted in Chapter 7.2.4, explaining when a reservation to the ICCPR will be impermissible. In summary, reservations must not contradict peremptory norms of international law and must be compatible with the object and purpose of the treaty.

SNAPSHOT: EXAMPLES OF RESERVATIONS TO THE ICCPR[147]

UNITED STATES—ARTICLE 6 (RIGHT TO LIFE)

That the United States reserves the right, subject to its Constitutional constraints, to impose capital punishment on any person (other than a pregnant woman) duly convicted under existing or future laws permitting the imposition of capital punishment, including such punishment for crimes committed by persons below eighteen years of age.

CONGO—ARTICLE 11 (PROHIBITION ON IMPRISONMENT FOR DEBTS)

The Government of the People's Republic of Congo declares that it does not consider itself bound by the provisions of article 11. Article 11 of the *International Covenant on Civil and Political Rights* is quite

147 For discussion of reservations entered by Australia, see Chapter 10.2.4.

incompatible with ... *Congolese Code of Civil, Commercial, Administrative and Financial Procedure* ... Under those provisions, in matters of private law, decisions or orders emanating from conciliation proceedings may be enforced through imprisonment for debt when other means of enforcement have failed, when the amount due exceeds 20 000 CFA francs and when the debtor, between 18 and 60 years of age, makes himself insolvent in bad faith.

[BANGLADESH—ARTICLE 14 (RIGHT TO A FAIR TRIAL)]

The Government of the People's Republic of Bangladesh reserves the right to apply paragraph 3 (d) of article 14 in view of the fact, that, while the existing laws of Bangladesh provide that, in the ordinary course a person, shall be entitled to be tried in his presence, it also provides for a trial to be held in his absence if he is a fugitive offender, or is a person, who being required to appear before a court, fails to present himself or to explain the reasons for non-appearance to the satisfaction of the court.

[DENMARK—ARTICLE 14 (RIGHT TO A FAIR TRIAL)]

Article 14, paragraph 1, shall not be binding on Denmark in respect of public hearings. In Danish law, the right to exclude the press and the public from trials may go beyond what is permissible under this Covenant, and the Government of Denmark finds that this right should not be restricted.

[GAMBIA—ARTICLE 14 (RIGHT TO A FAIR TRIAL)]

For financial reasons free legal assistance for accused persons is limited in our constitution to persons charged with capital offences only. The Government of the Gambia therefore wishes to enter a reservation in respect of article 14 (3) (d) of the Covenant in question.

[MAURITANIA—ARTICLE 18 (FREEDOM OF THOUGHT, CONSCIENCE AND RELIGION)]

The Mauritanian Government, while accepting the provisions set out in article 18 concerning freedom of thought, conscience and religion, declares that their application shall be without prejudice to the Islamic Shariah.

[ISRAEL—ARTICLE 23 (RIGHT TO MARRY AND FOUND A FAMILY AND PROTECTION OF THE FAMILY)]

With reference to article 23 of the Covenant, and any other provision thereof to which the present reservation may be relevant, matters of personal status are governed in Israel by the religious law of the parties concerned. To the extent that such law is inconsistent with its obligations under the Covenant, Israel reserves the right to apply that law.

[KUWAIT—ARTICLE 25 (RIGHT TO POLITICAL PARTICIPATION)]

The Government of Kuwait wishes to formulate a reservation with regard to article 25(b). The provisions of this paragraph conflict with the Kuwaiti electoral law, which restricts the right to stand and vote in elections to males. It further declares that the provisions of the article shall not apply to members of the armed forces or the police.

[MEXICO—ARTICLE 25 (RIGHT TO POLITICAL PARTICIPATION)]

The Government of Mexico also makes a reservation to this provision, since article 130 of the Political Constitution of the United Mexican States provides that ministers of religion shall have neither a passive vote nor the right to form associations for political purposes.

Derogations During a State of Emergency

The ICCPR permits states to opt out of certain obligations temporarily in order to address a state of emergency by a process known as derogation. Article 4 of the ICCPR permits states to take measures derogating from their obligations '[i]n time of public emergency which threatens the life of the nation and the existence of which is officially proclaimed,' provided that the derogating measures are 'strictly required by the exigencies of the situation', are not inconsistent with the state's other obligations under international law and do not discriminate on the grounds of race, colour, sex, language, religion or social origin.[148] The intention is to allow a state to take emergency measures on a temporary basis to deal with a crisis. For example, measures such as imposing a curfew or limiting freedom of movement, or conscription into a work gang, might be reasonable steps to take to deal with a state of emergency (depending on the type of emergency), even though they are inconsistent with the rights contained in the ICCPR.

However, not all rights can be derogated from. Article 4 of the ICCPR expressly prohibits derogation from the right to life, freedom from torture, freedom from slavery and servitude, the prohibitions on imprisonment for contractual obligations and criminal retrospectivity, the right to recognition as a person before the law and freedom of thought, conscience and religion.[149] Some of the rights on that list are included because of their fundamental nature, such as the right to life and freedom from torture, while others are included because it is inconceivable that their suspension could ever be necessary to address a public emergency, as in the case of the prohibition on imprisonment for contractual obligations. Further discussion of when derogation is permitted in the context of terrorism is contained in Chapter 18.4.

In 1984, a group of 31 experts in international law, convened by the International Commission of Jurists, the International Association of Penal Law, the American Association for the International Commission of Jurists, the Urban Morgan Institute for Human Rights and the International Institute of Higher Studies in Criminal Sciences, met in Siracusa, Italy, to consider article 4, and developed the 'Siracusa Principles on the Limitation and Derogation Provisions in the International Covenant on Civil and Political Rights',[150] which assist in understanding and interpreting article 4.

THE SIRACUSA PRINCIPLES DECLARE:

Public Emergency which Threatens the Life of the Nation

39 A state party may take measures derogating from its obligations under the International Covenant on Civil and Political Rights pursuant to Article 4 (hereinafter called 'derogation measures') only when faced with a situation of exceptional and actual or imminent danger which threatens the life of the nation.

148 ICCPR, see above, n 1, art 4(1).

149 Ibid art 4(2).

150 Commision on Human Rights, *Siracusa Principles on the Limitation and Derogation Provisions in the International Covenant on Civil and Political Rights*, 41st sess, Provisional Agenda Item 18, UN Doc E/CN.4/1985/4 (28 September 1984).

A threat to the life of the nation is one that:

a. affects the whole of the population and either the whole or part of the territory of the State, and
b. threatens the physical integrity of the population, the political independence or the territorial integrity of the State or the existence or basic functioning of institutions indispensable to ensure and protect the rights recognised in the Covenant.

40 Internal conflict and unrest that do not constitute a grave and imminent threat to the life of the nation cannot justify derogations under Article 4 …

54 The principle of strict necessity shall be applied in an objective manner. Each measure shall be directed to an actual, clear, present, or imminent danger and may not be imposed merely because of an apprehension of potential danger.

The UN Human Rights Committee, in *General Comment No 29 on Article 4 of the ICCPR*, observed that '[m]easures derogating from the provisions of the Covenant must be of an exceptional and temporary nature.'[151]

HUMAN RIGHTS COMMITTEE: *GENERAL COMMENT 29: STATES OF EMERGENCY*[152]

2 Measures derogating from the provisions of the Covenant must be of an exceptional and temporary nature. Before a State moves to invoke article 4, two fundamental conditions must be met: the situation must amount to a public emergency which threatens the life of the nation, and the State party must have officially proclaimed a state of emergency. The latter requirement is essential for the maintenance of the principles of legality and rule of law at times when they are most needed. …

3 Not every disturbance or catastrophe qualifies as a public emergency which threatens the life of the nation, as required by article 4, paragraph 1. During armed conflict, whether international or non-international, rules of international humanitarian law become applicable and help … to prevent the abuse of a State's emergency powers. The Covenant requires that even during an armed conflict measures derogating from the Covenant are allowed only if and to the extent that the situation constitutes a threat to the life of the nation. If States parties consider invoking article 4 in other situations than an armed conflict, they should carefully consider the justification and why such a measure is necessary and legitimate in the circumstances. On a number of occasions the Committee has expressed its concern over States parties that appear to have derogated from rights protected by the Covenant, or whose domestic law appears to allow such derogation in situations not covered by article 4.

4 A fundamental requirement for any measures derogating from the Covenant, as set forth in article 4, paragraph 1, is that such measures are limited to the extent strictly required by the exigencies of the situation. This requirement relates to the duration, geographical coverage and material scope of the state of emergency and any measures of derogation resorted to because of the emergency. Derogation from some Covenant obligations in emergency situations is clearly distinct from restrictions or limitations allowed even in normal times under

151 Human Rights Committee, *General Comment No 29: States of Emergency*, (article 4), 72nd sess, 1950th mtg, UN Doc CCPR/C/21/Rev.1/Add.11 (31 August 2001) para 2.

152 Ibid.

several provisions of the Covenant. Nevertheless, the obligation to limit any derogations to those strictly required by the exigencies of the situation reflects the principle of proportionality which is common to derogation and limitation powers. Moreover, the mere fact that a permissible derogation from a specific provision may, of itself, be justified by the exigencies of the situation does not obviate the requirement that specific measures taken pursuant to the derogation must also be shown to be required by the exigencies of the situation. In practice, this will ensure that no provision of the Covenant, however validly derogated from will be entirely inapplicable to the behaviour of a State party.

3.4 OPTIONAL PROTOCOLS

In addition to the obligations contained in the ICCPR, states parties are able to consent to additional obligations by ratifying an optional protocol. There are two optional protocols to the ICCPR. The first optional protocol recognises the competence of the Human Rights Committee to consider complaints of violations of the ICCPR by an individual subject to that state's jurisdiction who claims to be a victim of those violations. The role of the Human Rights Committee under the optional protocol is discussed in detail in Chapter 7.3. The *First Optional Protocol* was opened for signature at the same time as the ICCPR in 1966.

The *Second Optional Protocol* concerns the abolition of the death penalty and was opened for signature in 1989. The crucial elements of the *Second Optional Protocol* are that its parties agree to abolish the death penalty within their jurisdictions and that no person within their jurisdictions may be executed.[153] As at July 2011, 114 of the 167 states parties to the ICCPR are also parties to the *First Optional Protocol* and 73 are parties to the *Second Optional Protocol*. Australia is a party to both optional protocols.

3.5 CASE STUDY: THE RIGHT TO LIFE

All human rights and their corresponding obligations carry more depth and nuance than is evident simply from reading the text of a provision in a treaty protecting a particular right. The manner in which a right is applied, the limitations to the right and the types of balancing exercises that might be involved are all complex questions that will vary from one right to another and from one scenario to another. It would be impossible here to set out in full all of those issues as they pertain to each substantive right. Instead, there is a brief summary above for each of the civil and political rights, with a few illustrative examples. One right is explored in greater depth in order to give an idea of the degree of complexity that the application of human rights entails. This case study examines the right to life.

153 *Second Optional Protocol to the International Covenant on Civil and Political Rights, Aiming at the Abolition of the Death Penalty*, opened for signature 15 December 1989 (entered into force 11 July 1991), art 1.

3.5.1 Text of Article 6 of the ICCPR

ARTICLE 6 OF THE ICCPR

1. Every human being has the inherent right to life. This right shall be protected by law. No one shall be arbitrarily deprived of his life.
2. In countries which have not abolished the death penalty, sentence of death may be imposed only for the most serious crimes in accordance with the law in force at the time of the commission of the crime and not contrary to the provisions of the present Covenant and to the Convention on the Prevention and Punishment of the Crime of Genocide. This penalty can only be carried out pursuant to a final judgement rendered by a competent court.
3. When deprivation of life constitutes the crime of genocide, it is understood that nothing in this article shall authorize any State Party to the present Covenant to derogate in any way from any obligation assumed under the provisions of the Convention on the Prevention and Punishment of the Crime of Genocide.
4. Anyone sentenced to death shall have the right to seek pardon or commutation of the sentence. Amnesty, pardon or commutation of the sentence of death may be granted in all cases.
5. Sentence of death shall not be imposed for crimes committed by persons below eighteen years of age and shall not be carried out on pregnant women.
6. Nothing in this article shall be invoked to delay or to prevent the abolition of capital punishment by any State Party to the present Covenant.

3.5.2 Scope of Prohibition: Arbitrary Deprivation of Life

The right to life has been described as 'the supreme right from which no derogation is permitted, even in times of public emergency ... It is basic to all human rights.'[154] Nevertheless, the right to life is not absolute. Accordingly, not every death will necessarily be a violation of the right to life. In order for a death to violate the right to life, the deprivation of life must be arbitrary. A killing by a state's armed forces during a war, for example, will not be arbitrary. A person shot dead by police to prevent him killing the police officer or another person will likewise not be arbitrary, as the killing was in response to a direct threat and took place to preserve the rights (in this case the life) of another person. Even though both examples are deprivations of life caused by the direct act of a state agent, neither violates the state's obligations under the right to life.

On the other hand, summary executions clearly violate the right to life. The forced disappearance of individuals—a phenomenon that emerged under the military regimes in South America in 1970s–1980s[155] and more recently spawned its own treaty[156]—is also a violation of the right to life, because disappearance was generally assumed to lead to death.[157] Common factors among those types

154 Human Rights Committee, see above, n 11, para 1.

155 See Chapter 8.3.6.

156 *International Convention for the Protection of All Persons from Enforced Disappearance*, (opened for signature 20 December 2006), not yet in force.

157 Human Rights Committee, see above, n 11, para 4.

of killings are that they usurp the judicial process (ie victims are executed or 'disappeared' by state agents rather than being arrested, charged and tried), and there is no pressing urgency for killing the victim, unlike the situations of war or defence of another person.

Once a deprivation of life has been identified, the key question is whether the killing was arbitrary, or whether there were circumstances that might render the killing justifiable under international law.

The right to life is significantly broader than simply a prohibition on extrajudicial killing by state agents. While the duty to respect the right to life undoubtedly means that states should ensure that their agents do not engage in such killing, the duty to ensure the right to life includes obligations to take positive steps to protect the lives of individuals, including through a criminal justice system that prohibits arbitrary killing (for example through murder and manslaughter laws) and investigates and prosecutes offenders. It also extends to taking measures to prevent unnecessary deaths, including through malnutrition and disease.

> Moreover, the Committee has noted that the right to life has been too often narrowly interpreted. The expression 'inherent right to life' cannot properly be understood in a restrictive manner, and the protection of this right requires that States adopt positive measures. In this connection, the Committee considers that it would be desirable for States parties to take all possible measures to reduce infant mortality and to increase life expectancy, especially in adopting measures to eliminate malnutrition and epidemics.[158]

3.5.3 State Killing

While an arbitrary killing carried out by a state agent will violate the right to life, it is not always clear when a killing will be arbitrary. One such case is where the killing was lawful under the municipal law of the state where it occurred. However, lawfulness under municipal law will not automatically prevent a killing from being arbitrary. If there were not an independent meaning of 'arbitrary' over and above municipal lawfulness, it would be possible for a repressive regime to pass laws permitting it to execute its political detractors summarily, without those executions violating the right to life. In less extreme cases, authorisation by municipal law will be a useful indicator, as it is a necessary precondition before a killing will be deemed not to be arbitrary, but it is not sufficient in itself.

ARBITRARINESS AND MUNICIPAL LAW: *SUAREZ DE GUERRERO v COLOMBIA* (HUMAN RIGHTS COMMITTEE, 1979)

Police in Colombia raided a house where they suspected a kidnapped former ambassador was being held, but found no one home and did not find the ambassador. The police stayed at the house and lay in wait for the occupants. Seven people, arriving back at the house at intervals, were shot by the police at point-blank range upon entering the house.

Colombian law at the time had a number of provisions designed to deal with widespread crime. Among them was a provision that police officers had a defence if they killed anyone in the course of operations to crack down on kidnapping, extortion or drug trafficking. The killings of the seven people were therefore

158 Human Rights Committee, see above, n 11, para 5.

legal under Colombian law. The question for the Human Rights Committee was whether 'not arbitrary' simply means 'according to municipal law', or whether there is a broader meaning that municipal law cannot displace.

The Committee held that arbitrary means more than just 'lawful'. The Committee's view was that it is legitimate for a state to authorise the use of lethal force in some circumstances. However, the killing of any given person must still be proportionate to the circumstances if it is not to be arbitrary. If the police had found kidnappers with a hostage, it might have been reasonable to have killed some of them in order to rescue the hostage and use the defence provided by Colombian law for that purpose. However, in this case, the evidence suggested the victims were ambushed and shot execution-style. The police could easily have arrested them and commenced criminal trials on kidnapping charges (if they really were kidnappers) without killing them. The Committee therefore said there was no proportionality and these killings were arbitrary, violating Colombia's obligations under article 6 of the ICCPR.

States have a further obligation to investigate killings and to punish the perpetrator where appropriate. Failure to do so will breach the state's obligations under the right to life. In *Baboeram v Suriname*,[159] the Human Rights Committee found that the state's failure to investigate the circumstances of the killing of 15 people by the military breached the state's human rights obligations. In that case, 15 detainees, who had been arrested the previous day when authorities in Suriname allegedly foiled a coup attempt, were shot dead. The military had claimed that the victims had been shot while trying to escape, although the markings on the bodies were inconsistent with that explanation and also suggested that the victims had been tortured. The Human Rights Committee concluded that the state had an obligation to investigate the circumstances of the killings to ensure that they were not arbitrary. Such an investigation must be bona fide, not merely a formality.[160] If it discovered that the killings were arbitrary, the state would have the further obligation to bring the perpetrators to justice and provide compensation to the surviving families.

3.5.4 Capital Punishment

Five of the six paragraphs in article 6 of the ICCPR address the issue of capital punishment. While capital punishment obviously involves the deprivation of life at the hands of the state, it is not necessarily an arbitrary deprivation, provided it is carried out after a fair trial in which the death sentence was passed, and provided that the death penalty is prescribed by the law of the relevant state for the offence in question. Capital punishment is therefore not prohibited per se by the right to life as it appears in the ICCPR.

A series of qualifications appear in the ICCPR for 'countries which have not abolished the death penalty', setting out the circumstances in which the death penalty will be permissible. In

159 *Baboeram v Suriname, Human Rights Committee, Communication No 146/1983*, UN doc no CCPR/C/24/D/146/1983 (4 April 1985).

160 The Human Rights Committee found in *Herrera Rubio v Colombia* that an investigation into a forced disappearance, which found no evidence that the military was responsible as alleged and therefore closed the investigation, was inadequate and therefore breached the state's positive obligations under the right to life. *Herrera Rubio v Colombia*, Human Rights Committee, *Communication No 161/1983* (2 November 1987), para 10.5.

Rolando v the Philippines,[161] the Human Rights Committee was called upon to consider the situation where the Philippines had abolished the death penalty, then reintroduced it. Three of the Committee members considered that the reintroduction of the death penalty once it had been abolished was itself a violation of article 6 of the ICCPR, since the Philippines was not a country that had 'not abolished the death penalty' within the meaning of article 6(2). The other members of the Committee did not consider that issue. It therefore seems that abolition of the death penalty may have a ratchet effect, in that once it is abolished, it would violate a state's obligations under the right to life if it were reintroduced.

There has been movement in the jurisprudence of the Human Rights Committee on the question of whether a mandatory death penalty is permissible. While earlier cases found that a mandatory death penalty could still be permissible provided the other qualifications were complied with,[162] the current position appears to be a consensus that a mandatory penalty is itself arbitrary and therefore violates the right to life.[163]

In summary, the qualifications on the imposition of the death penalty set out in article 6 of the ICCPR are that it must:

- only apply for the most serious crimes;
- be provided by law at the time of the offence;
- be carried out only after a final sentence by a competent court;
- be subject to a right to seek and be considered for pardon or commutation;
- not apply for crimes committed by persons under 18; and
- not be carried out on pregnant women.

The Human Rights Committee has declared that 'the expression 'most serious crimes' must be read restrictively to mean that the death penalty should be a quite exceptional measure.'[164] However, guidance on which specific crimes meet that threshold can only be determined by induction from the Committee's views and concluding observations in various cases. According to Joseph, Schultz and Castan, the Human Rights Committee has held that treason, piracy, robbery, aggravated robbery, traffic in toxic or dangerous waste, abetting suicide, drug-related offences, property offences, repeated evasion of military service, apostasy, consensual homosexual acts, adultery, embezzlement, corruption, economic crimes and abduction not resulting in death are not 'most serious crimes'.[165] They conclude, 'In summary, it appears that only intentional killings or attempted killings, and *perhaps* the intentional infliction of grievous bodily harm, may attract the death penalty under article 6(2).'[166]

A related issue to the imposition of the death penalty is whether a state that does not have it should cooperate with states that do, by extraditing defendants facing capital charges. The issue is whether the extraditing state would be subjecting a person to death, in violation of its own commitments under

161 *Rolando v the Philippines,* Human Rights Committee, communication no 1110/2002 (2004).

162 *Brown v Jamaica,* Human Rights Committee, communication no 775/1997 (1999).

163 *Kennedy v Trinidad & Tobago,* Human Rights Committee, communication no 845/1998 (2002). The question was treated as settled law by the Committee in *Rolando v the Philippines,* Human Rights Committee (2005).

164 Human Rights Committee, *General Comment 6: The Right to Life,* 30 April 1982, para 7.

165 S Joseph, J Schultz & M Castan, *The International Covenant on Civil and Political Rights: Cases, Materials, and Commentary,* 2nd edn, Oxford University Press, Oxford, 2004, 167.

166 Ibid 167 (original emphasis).

the ICCPR. This is also an issue where the jurisprudence of the Human Rights Committee has evolved to take an increasingly strict stance against the death penalty.

In *Judge v Canada*,[167] the majority of the Human Rights Committee noted a growing international consensus against the use of the death penalty in the previous decade (1993–2003) and decided that the obligation ought now to be read more broadly than had previously been the case. It decided that states that have abolished the death penalty have an obligation not to expose a person to execution. It follows that such states are obliged to seek assurances that a defendant will not be executed before it agrees to his or her extradition. That decision directly departed from a decision ten years earlier—*Kindler v Canada*—with almost identical facts, in which extradition to the USA to face the death penalty was held not to be a violation by the extraditing state.[168]

The restrictions on extraditing from a country that does not have capital punishment to one that does creates a paradox in international human rights law, where different states have different obligations. Given that the convictions in *Kindler and Judge* were for premeditated murder—on any measure a 'most serious crime'—the USA would probably not be in violation of article 6 of the ICCPR for executing them, even though Canada was held in violation in *Judge* for extraditing him to the US. Thus the imposition of the death penalty by one state under its domestic law might breach international human rights law, when the death penalty by another state for exactly the same crime would not, depending on whether capital punishment had previously been abolished at some point.

SNAPSHOT: THE 'BALI NINE' CASE

In April 2005, five Australian nationals carrying heroin were arrested by Indonesian police at the airport in Bali as they prepared to board a flight to Australia, and a further four Australian nationals allegedly linked to the group were arrested in their hotel. The nine Australians were subsequently charged with offences relating to trafficking heroin under Indonesian law, which potentially carried the death penalty. Following trials in Indonesian courts and a series of appeals, six of the nine were sentenced to death.[169]

Indonesian police had been alerted to the trafficking operation by the Australian Federal Police (AFP). The father of one of the nine, Scott Rush, had contacted the AFP to share his suspicion that his son may be preparing to act as a drug mule, in the hope that he could be stopped before leaving Australia, thereby preventing a crime from occurring and preventing him from being exposed to the death penalty in Indonesia. Instead, the AFP passed detailed information to Indonesian police, asking them to keep the group under surveillance, and 'should they suspect that Chan [one of the suspected ringleaders] and/or the couriers are in possession of the drugs at the time of their departure, that they take what action they deem appropriate.'[170]

167 *Judge v Canada*, Human Rights Committee, communication no 829/1998 (2003).

168 *Kindler v Canada*, Human Rights Committee, communication no 471/1991 (1993).

169 By July 2011, appeals against the death sentence by four of the six condemned defendants had succeeded in reducing their death sentence to life imprisonment, while the appeals of Andrew Chan and Myuran Sukumaran were refused, leaving two of the nine on death row.

170 S Neighbour, 'How the AFP trapped the Bali Nine', *The Australian*, 27 August 2010, quoting correspondence from the AFP to the Indonesian National Police dated 8 April 2005 headed 'Subject: Heroin couriers from Bali to Australia.'

As Australia is a state that has abolished the death penalty, while Indonesia retains the death penalty for various crimes including drug trafficking, it is clear that Australia has an obligation not to extradite suspects from Australia to Indonesia without obtaining an assurance that those suspects would not face the death penalty if convicted. The Bali Nine case was not a case of extradition, but a case in which information was provided by Australian authorities that set in chain a series of events exposing Australian nationals to the death penalty—an outcome that was clearly foreseeable. The nine suspects were all outside the territory of Australia and the physical control of Australian authorities at the time of AFP intervention, distinguishing this case from a case of extradition, in which the suspect is necessarily in the custody of the extraditing state. The actions of the AFP could therefore only be considered a violation of Australia's obligations under the right to life if they could be construed as within Australia's jurisdiction, or if the right to life is considered to give rise to extra-territorial obligations with regard to exposure to the death penalty in another state.

The Human Rights Committee in its 2009 Concluding Observations on Australia's periodic report under the ICCPR[171] concluded that the provision of assistance of the kind provided in the Bali Nine case (although the case was not specifically mentioned) violates the obligations of abolitionist states under the right to life and the Second Optional Protocol to the ICCPR, aiming at the abolition of the death penalty, to which Australia is a party. The fact that the Committee addressed law enforcement cooperation in the same paragraph as extradition to states retaining the death penalty suggests that the Committee considers the two situations analogous, despite the difference on the point of presence in the territory. The relevant paragraph of the Concluding Observations is reproduced below.

> The Committee notes with concern the residual power of the Attorney-General, in ill-defined circumstances, to allow the extradition of a person to a State where he or she may face the death penalty, as well as the lack of a comprehensive prohibition on the providing of international police assistance for the investigation of crimes that may lead to the imposition of the death penalty in another state, in violation of the State party's obligation under the Second Optional Protocol.
>
> The State party should take the necessary legislative and other steps to ensure that no person is extradited to a State where he or she may face the death penalty, as well as whereby it does not provide assistance in the investigation of crimes that may result in the imposition of the death penalty in another State, and revoke the residual power of the Attorney-General in this regard.[172]

3.5.5 Abortion and Euthanasia

Abortion and euthanasia have been difficult issues to reconcile with the standard of international human rights law that everyone has the right to life and that no one shall be arbitrarily deprived of his or her life. In both instances, there are important definitional issues involved, although it is impossible to disentangle them entirely from the moral or religious perspective from which both issues are commonly viewed.

In the case of abortion, the key definitional issues in terms of the right to life include the definition of life itself, in terms of when life is said to begin—whether from the moment of conception, the

171 See Chapter 10.5.2.

172 Human Rights Committee, *Concluding Observations on Australia*, UN document no CCPR/C/AUS/CO/5, 7 May 2009, para 20 (emphasis in original, indicating a recommendation of the Committee).

moment of birth, or some interim phase of gestation, such as the point at which a foetus would be viable outside the womb. The declaration in article 1 of the UDHR that '[a]ll human beings are *born* free and equal in dignity and rights'[173] suggests that human rights crystallise at birth. As has been pointed out in the context of the abortion debate, an attempt during the drafting of the UDHR to remove the word 'born' from article 1 expressly canvassed the question of whether human rights protection should be expressed to cover a period before birth, but states voted to retain the word 'born' over those objections.[174] Nevertheless, the sensitivities of certain states that regard abortion as an arbitrary deprivation of life have been a constant feature of the international human rights landscape.

The treaty monitoring committees have avoided squarely addressing the question of whether a foetus is a life and whether an abortion is an arbitrary deprivation of life; the Human Rights Committee's General Comments on the right to life are conspicuously silent on that question. Instead, the committees have emphasised the danger to women's health and lives that can result from a blanket ban on abortions in all circumstances. For instance, in its 2007 Concluding Observations on Chile, the Human Rights Committee concluded: 'The Committee reiterates its concern about Chile's unduly restrictive abortion laws, particularly in cases where the mother's life is in danger. ... The State party should amend its abortion laws to help women avoid unwanted pregnancies and not have to resort to illegal abortions that could put their lives at risk.'[175]

In *Llantoy Huamán v Peru*, the Human Rights Committee considered an individual communication from a woman who at 17 years of age was denied access to an abortion of a foetus with serious diagnosed health defects, and who was then forced to carry the baby to term, give birth and breastfeed until the baby died four days later, at which time the mother fell into a state of deep depression. The committee found that the mental anguish caused by refusing to allow an abortion in those circumstances amounted to cruel and inhuman treatment and an arbitrary interference in the woman's private life.[176] One member of the committee gave a dissenting opinion, concluding that the author's right to life had also been violated, as the refusal to perform the abortion had put her life in grave danger.[177]

The Committee for the Elimination of Discrimination against Women and the Committee on Economic, Social and Cultural Rights have also emphasised the health care aspect of access to safe abortions and the risk to the life and health of the mother if safe abortion is not an available option.[178]

173 *Universal Declaration of Human Rights* (UDHR), GA Res. 217A (III), art 1 (emphasis added).

174 J Morsink, *The Universal Declaration of Human Rights: Origins, Drafting and Intent*, University of Pennsylvania Press, Philadelphia, 1999, 291; Tania Penovic, 'Rita Joseph: Human Rights and the Unborn Child' (2011) 33 *Human Rights Quarterly* 229, noting that the proposal to remove the word 'born' was defeated by 20 votes to 12, with 5 abstentions.

175 Human Rights Committee, *Concluding Observations on Chile*, 18 May 2007, UN doc no CCPR/C/CHL/CO/5, para 8.

176 *Karen Noelia Llantoy Huamán v Peru*, Human Rights Committee, 3 November 2005, Communication no 1153/2003, UN doc no CCPR/C/85/D/1153/2003, paras 3.4, 3.6 and 6.2—6.4. The committee therefore found violations of arts 7 and 17 of the ICCPR. A violation of art 24, requiring special protection for children, was also found on the basis that the author was 17 years old at the time of seeking the abortion.

177 Ibid dissenting opinion of Hipólito Solari-Yrigoyen.

178 See for example Committee on the Elimination of Discrimination Against Women, *Concluding Comments on Ghana*, 25 August 2005, UN doc no CEDAW/C/GHA/CO/5, paras 10, 31 and 32.

However, in some cases, treaty monitoring committees have expressed concern when abortion rates have seemed particularly high and have urged states to take measures to reduce the instances of abortion,[179] albeit without linking such expressions of concern to a potentially arbitrary deprivation of life.

The pragmatic approach of international human rights law therefore seems to be to avoid a direct stance on whether a foetus can be a life or is entitled to any human rights protection before the moment of birth. Such a pragmatic stance is possible because it can be said that even if terminating a pregnancy is a deprivation of life, then it is not arbitrary, particularly when balanced against the woman's rights to life and health. A woman's choice to terminate her pregnancy will therefore not be considered to violate the right to life under international human rights law (despite the use of the 'right to life' terminology by anti-abortion activists), although forced abortions or sterilisations will violate other human rights, such as freedom from torture, cruel, inhuman and degrading treatment and the right to found a family.[180]

In contrast, euthanasia unequivocally involves the ending of a life. The only justification for euthanasia consistent with the right to life would therefore be that such a deprivation is not arbitrary. In 2001, the Netherlands passed legislation permitting euthanasia of a terminally ill patient by a physician when certain conditions were met. The Human Rights Committee considered the new laws as part of the periodic report of the Netherlands under the ICCPR in 2001. The Committee made no explicit statement on whether the deprivation of life under the Dutch legislation would be arbitrary within the meaning of the right to life, but did express serious concerns about the degree of oversight to be exercised by Dutch authorities to ensure that the conditions for lawful euthanasia were in fact met, as well as expressing concerns about the potential application of the legislation to children as young as 12 at the child's request with parental consent.[181] The implication, though, was that euthanasia that was truly voluntary on the part of the patient and not for any ulterior motive on the part of the person administering the death would not violate the right to life. However, in the Human Rights Committee's consideration of the next report of the Netherlands in 2009, the Committee noted that it 'remains concerned at the *extent* of euthanasia and assisted suicides in the State party.'[182] While the Committee went on to criticise the potential for 'undue influence or misapprehension' to prevail under the amended Dutch laws,[183] the earlier criticism of the extent of euthanasia per se suggests a level of unease with the practice among at least some members of the Committee. In summary though, it

179 See for example Human Rights Committee, *Concluding Observations on Albania*, 2 December 2004, UN doc no CCPR/CO/82/ALB, para 14.

180 See the discussion of measures to enforce China's one child policy under the right to marry and found a family in Chapter 3.2.19.

181 Human Rights Committee, *Concluding Observations on the Netherlands*, 27 August 2001, UN doc no CCPR/CO/72/NET, para 5. For additional comment on the issue of the application of the euthanasia law to children, see the Committee on the Rights of the Child, *Concluding Observations on the Netherlands*, 26 February 2004, UN doc CRC/C/15/Add.227, para 33, and Committee on the Rights of the Child, Concluding Observations on the Netherlands, 27 March 2009, UN doc CRC/C/NLD/CO/3, paras 30 and 31.

182 Human Rights Committee, *Concluding Observations on the Netherlands*, 25 August 2009, UN doc no CCPR/CO/4/NLD, para 7 (emphasis added).

183 Ibid para 7.

would seem that euthanasia of a terminally ill patient, who has communicated his or her wish to die, when there is no ulterior motive on the part of anyone involved with the death, does not amount to an arbitrary killing and will not violate the right to life. The Committee has, however, urged a very high standard of vigilance on states to ensure that those preconditions are met.

The European Court of Human Rights refused to imply a right to die as a corollary of the right to life in *Pretty v United Kingdom*.[184] In that case, Diane Pretty, who was suffering from motor neuron disease, sought an undertaking from the English Director of Public Prosecutions that her husband would not be prosecuted for assisting her to end her life. When the DPP refused and the refusal was upheld by the House of Lords, Mrs Pretty claimed that her right to life included 'a right to die to avoid inevitable suffering and indignity,'[185] and that the potential prosecution of her husband for assisting her to die constituted an interference with that right. The European Court of Human Rights rejected that argument, finding that there had been no breach of Mrs Pretty's human rights by the English authorities.[186] Therefore, while the approach of the Human Rights Committee indicates that laws permitting euthanasia with appropriate safeguards will not violate the right to life, the European Court of Human Rights in *Pretty* suggests that there is no entitlement in human rights law to be assisted to end one's life.

3.5.6 Socio-Economic and Environmental Issues

It was noted above that the right to life encompasses not only negative obligations (preventing arbitrary killing), but also positive obligations. The Human Rights Committee in its General Comment 6 on the right to life highlighted 'measures to reduce infant mortality and to increase life expectancy, especially in adopting measures to eliminate malnutrition and epidemics' as part of the right to life.[187]

It has also been observed, in the context of explaining the link between the right to development and the right to life, that 'the essence of the right to development is the principle that the human person is the central subject of development and that the right to life includes within it existence in human dignity with the minimum necessities of life.'[188]

To the extent that life expectancy is greatly improved by lifting people out of poverty, an obligation on the state to reduce poverty is intrinsically linked to the right to life. The close link to the right to health and the rights to adequate food and water is also clear. However, for those positive aspects of the right to life involving the incremental improvement of conditions of life so as to safeguard life itself, the dependence on available state resources cannot be disregarded. The progressive improvement of such essentials of life may be considered part of the state's obligation to promote the right to life, while the same measures may also be classified as the realisation of various relevant economic, social and cultural rights. The interrelated, indivisible nature of all human rights is therefore evident in the realisation

184 *Pretty v United Kingdom*, [2002] European Court of Human Rights (app no 2346/02).

185 Ibid para 35.

186 Ibid paras 39–42.

187 Human Rights Committee, see above, n 11, para 5.

188 *The Right to Development*, GA Res 55/108, UN Doc A/RES/55/108 (13 March 2001) art 3(a).

of the various rights connected to the sustenance of life itself. However, the fact that the obligations contained in the ICCPR, including the right to life, are intended to be immediate and not relative to a state's resources, suggests that the failure to take proactive measures involving the allocation of resources, such as the provision of health care, might be more appropriately addressed through the ICESCR framework.

Serious environmental threats to health, and therefore to life, have occasionally invoked the right to life, demonstrating a connection between a healthy environment, human health and protecting against the arbitrary deprivation of life due to environmental harm. In *EHP v Canada*, the author of the communication submitted that the right to life of both current and future generations of people living in an area where nuclear waste had been dumped in the 1940s and 50s, and which was planned for intensive development by the time of the communication in 1980, was imperilled by the exposure to radioactivity, causing cancer and genetic defects.[189] The Human Rights Committee ultimately found the communication inadmissible for failure to exhaust domestic remedies, but observed that the communication raised 'serious issues, with regard to the obligation of States parties to protect human life'.[190] The question of whether the state was obliged to protect the lives of 'future generations', which would imply human rights for those who are yet to be born and would be problematic for the reasons discussed above in the context of abortion, was evaded by the Committee. Instead, the Committee decided to 'treat the author's reference to 'future generations' as an expression of concern purporting to put into due perspective the importance of the matter raised in the communication.'[191]

In *Yanomami Indians v Brazil*, the Inter-American Commission on Human Rights found that the destruction of the traditional habitat of indigenous people to build a highway,[192] combined with the encouragement of mining exploration in the area, constituted a violation of the right to life, liberty and security under the American *Declaration of the Rights and Duties of Man*.[193] The influx of outsiders to a previously isolated community brought diseases to which the community was not immune, causing epidemics that led to numerous deaths.[194]

The link between environmental protection, development and the impact on the right to life was recognised by Vice President Weeramantry of the International Court of Justice in his separate opinion in the *Gabčíkovo-Nagymoros Project* case.[195] In the context of explaining the content and legal basis for the principle of sustainable development in international law, Weeramantry VP acknowledged the right to development as an inalienable human right, then continued:

> The protection of the environment is likewise a vital part of contemporary human rights doctrine, for it is a *sine qua non* for numerous human rights such as the right to health and the right to life itself. It is scarcely

189 *EHP v Canada*, Human Rights Committee, Communication no 67/1980, 27 October 1982, paras 1.2–1.3.

190 Ibid para 8.

191 Ibid para 8(a).

192 See Chapter 8.3.5.

193 *Yanomami Indians v Brazil*, Inter-American Commission on Human Rights, case 7615, 5 March 1985, resolutions, para 1. Violations of the rights to residence and movement and to the preservation of health and well-being were also found.

194 Ibid para 3(a).

195 *Case Concerning the Gabčíkovo-Nagymoros Project* (*Hungary v Slovakia*), [1997] ICJ Rep 7.

> necessary to elaborate on this, as damage to the environment can impair and undermine all the human rights spoken of in the Universal Declaration and other human rights instruments.[196]

More recently, the effects of global warming have been associated with a threat to the right to life. In a petition to the Inter-American Commission on Human Rights, which the Commission ultimately declined to hear, the right to life (among other rights) was invoked by representatives of the Inuit community of Canada and the United States. The petition argued: 'Changes in ice and snow jeopardize individual Inuit lives, critical food sources are threatened, and unpredictable weather makes travel more dangerous at all times of the year'.[197] Interference with food sources in a subsistence culture was alleged to threaten the right to life.[198]

3.5.7 Concluding Remarks on the Right to Life

The right not to be arbitrarily deprived of life is much broader than the obligation of a state merely to refrain from extrajudicial killing that is suggested by a straight and narrow reading of article 6(1) of the ICCPR. There is a clear trend for the right to be interpreted ever more broadly, particularly as regards the necessities for sustaining life. In that way, there is clear evidence in the right to life of the interrelated nature of the different categories of human rights. Like all human rights, there is a significant amount of nuance related to the application of the right to life, much of which manifests itself in the determination of when a death can be said to be arbitrary. A similar degree of depth and nuance can be found in the jurisprudence associated with most of the other human rights listed earlier in this chapter; this case study of the right to life sought to illustrate the degree of that depth and the types of issues that are commonly addressed.

3.6 CONCLUSION AND ISSUES

Civil and political rights have enjoyed a significant head start over their counterparts, economic, social and cultural rights, particularly in terms of enforcement. The longstanding rhetoric of international law that holds all human rights to be indivisible and interdependent is finally gaining some traction, with civil and political rights being considered alongside all other rights in the Universal Periodic Review[199] and with the conclusion of an optional protocol to the ICESCR,[200] bringing practice for monitoring compliance with that treaty into line with that for the ICCPR.

Certain inconsistencies are apparent in the implementation of civil and political rights. The formal double standard between death penalty states and abolitionist states built into the right to life was

196 Ibid separate opinion of Weeramantry VP at 91–2.

197 *Watt-Cloutier et al v United States*, petition to Inter-American Commission on Human Rights, 7 December 2005, 90.

198 Ibid 91.

199 See Chapter 6.7.

200 See Chapter 4.4.

noted above as one example. Other inconsistencies involve the way states interpret and apply the rights, especially when resolving potential clashes between different rights.

The approach to civil and political rights, like all human rights, is not static. Some of the challenges ahead for their implementation, such as the available enforcement mechanisms, the question of the territorial or extra-territorial scope of obligations, the extension of obligations to non-state actors, the tensions between prosecution for gross atrocities and peace and reconciliation, and the application of human rights in an anti-terrorism context, among many others, are examined in the coming chapters, particularly Chapter 20.

4 ECONOMIC, SOCIAL AND CULTURAL RIGHTS

CONTENTS

4.1 INTRODUCTION

4.1.1 From Theory to Practice

The international catalogue of rights set out in the *Universal Declaration of Human Rights* (UDHR) includes both civil and political rights and economic, social and cultural rights, but '[i]n the years that have since gone by, civil and political rights have attracted much attention in theory and practice, while economic, social and cultural rights have often been neglected'.[1] Chapter 1 discusses the 'modern' (i.e. post World War II) developments of human rights and the formation of two separate, and in some ways quite distinct treaties dividing civil and political rights from the category of economic, social and cultural rights.

Interestingly, prior to the developments initiated within the UN, economic, social and cultural rights were more prominent than civil and political rights on the international agenda in the late nineteenth and early twentieth centuries in the lead-up to the establishment of the League of Nations and, later, the United Nations. After his 'Four Freedoms' speech in 1941,[2] President Franklin D Roosevelt in his 1944 State of the Union address spoke out in favour of an 'Economic Bill of Rights' saying that:

> We have come to the clear realization of the fact that true individual freedom cannot exist without economic security and independence. 'Necessitous men are not free men.' People who are hungry and out of jobs are the stuff of which dictatorships are made.[3]

This notion of freedom explicitly included economic and social rights, and in elaborating on the entitlements associated with the freedom from want, Roosevelt urged the recognition of 'the right of every family to a decent home; the right to adequate medical care and the opportunity to achieve and enjoy good health; the right to adequate protection from the economic fears of old age, sickness, accident, and unemployment; [and] the right to a good education'.[4]

As discussed in Chapter 1, the 'Australian pledge' that was promoted by H V Evatt during the drafting of the *UN Charter* emphasised the importance of incorporating economic, social and cultural rights as an essential element of any rights framework, urging the UN to commit to promote 'higher standards of living, full employment and conditions of economic and social progress and development'. Despite the declaration at the World Conference on Human Rights in Vienna in 1993 that '[a]ll human rights are universal, indivisible and interdependent and interrelated [and that] [t]he international community must treat human rights globally in a fair and equal manner, on the same footing, and with the same emphasis'[5]

1 A Eide & A Rosas, 'Economic, Social and Cultural Rights: A Universal Challenge' in A Eide, C Krause and A Rosas (eds), *Economic, Social and Cultural Rights*, 2nd edn, Martinus Nijhoff, The Hague, 2001, 3.

2 See Chapter 1.2.

3 Quoted in P Alston, 'US Ratification of the Covenant on Economic, Social and Cultural Rights: The Need for an Entirely New Strategy' (1990) 84 *American Journal of International Law* 365, 387.

4 F D Roosevelt, 'Eleventh Annual Message to Congress (January 11, 1944)' in F L Israel (ed), *The State of the Union Messages of the Presidents, 1790–1966*, Vol 3, Chelsea House, 1967, 2881.

5 World Conference on Human Rights, *Vienna Declaration and Programme of Action* (14–25 June 1993) [5].

there does continue to exist (in some not all jurisdictions) a perceived hierarchy of rights that affects how economic, social and cultural rights are both interpreted and enforced.

4.1.2 The US and Economic, Social and Cultural Rights

The US is most commonly seen as having a largely negative role in the development of economic, social and cultural rights. However, the role played by the US with respect to economic, social and cultural rights is complex. Starting with President Roosevelt and his 'Four Freedoms',[6] subsequent administrations have waxed and waned in their support for these rights. Alston, in his chronological survey of the approach of US administrations to economic, social and cultural rights, notes the variance in attitudes of subsequent US Presidents to economic, social and cultural rights.

SNAPSHOT: PHILIP ALSTON, 'PUTTING ECONOMIC, SOCIAL AND CULTURAL RIGHTS BACK ON THE AGENDA OF THE UNITED STATES'[7]

President Harry Truman supported including economic, social and cultural rights in the Universal Declaration and it was under his auspices that Eleanor Roosevelt participated in the early and crucial phases of the drafting of the *International Covenant on Economic, Social, and Cultural Rights* (ICESCR). President Dwight Eisenhower ... repudiated both the draft covenant and the draft of the *International Covenant on Civil and Political Rights* (ICCPR) but neither he nor other opponents of the UN's human rights aspirations expressed special animus toward the covenant that dealt with economic, social and cultural rights.

The administration of President Lyndon Johnson not only participated in the resumed drafting of the ICESCR but also voted in favor of its adoption in 1966 by the UN General Assembly. And the same administration supported the inclusion of economic and social rights provisions in the *International Convention on the Elimination of All Forms of Racial Discrimination*.

In 1975, President Gerald Ford signed the *Helsinki Accords*, which proclaimed that the participating states would 'promote and encourage the effective exercise of civil, political, economic, social, cultural and other rights and freedoms all of which derive from the inherent dignity of the human person and are essential for his free and full development.' By agreeing to a follow-up declaration, adopted in Vienna in January 1989 by the Conference on Security and Cooperation in Europe, the United States joined other countries in recognizing that the promotion of economic, social and cultural rights 'is of paramount importance for human dignity and for the attainment of the legitimate aspirations of every individual.' Accordingly the United States said it would guarantee the 'effective exercise' of economic, social, and cultural rights and to consider acceding to the ICESCR.

The administration of President Jimmy Carter embraced economic, social and cultural rights as a central part of its human rights policy; Carter signed the ICESCR in 1978 and transmitted to the Senate for its advice and consent. Although hearings were held which included coverage of the ICESCR, the Senate took no action in relation to it.

One of the first acts of President Ronald Reagan's administration in the human rights field was to signal a clear and straightforward policy of opposition to economic and social rights. The earliest and best known

---

6 See Chapter 1.2.

7 *New York University School of Law, Center for Human Rights and Global Justice Working Paper No 22*, 1 May 2009 <http://www.chrgj.org/publications/docs/wp/Alston%20Spring%2009.pdf>.

statement of policy was included in the introduction written in 1982 by the new assistant secretary of state for human rights and humanitarian affairs, Elliott Abrams, and published in the State Department's annual review of human rights practices around the world. This report explicitly removed the treatment of economic and social rights, which had previously been included in the reports. Abrams subsequently offered several justifications for the policy change. The most significant was that the inclusion of these rights blurred 'the vital core of human rights.' The distinction he drew was between economic and social rights, which he portrayed as 'goods [that] the government ought to encourage over the long term,' and civil and political rights, which are 'rights [that] the government has an absolute duty to respect at any time.' The second reason given was that economic and social rights are easily exploited for propaganda purposes by unscrupulous governments whose real aim is to avoid respect for civil and political rights. Because such abuses have occurred, the more prudent path was seen to be to deny the very existence of economic and social rights.

The administration of George H W Bush was considerably less ideologically engaged, at least overtly, in its opposition to these rights but, when it advanced (and achieved) the ratification of the [ICCPR] in 1992, no thought was given to advocating concurrent action on the "other" covenant.

More recent US administrations have also continued their inconsistent approach to economic, social and cultural rights. President Clinton's administration supported the proclamation of the 1993 Vienna World Conference on Human Rights, that 'the international community must treat human rights globally in a fair and equal manner, on the same footing, and with the same emphasis'[8] but Alston argues that the administration later 'began to distance itself from its original embrace of economic, social and cultural rights and adopted a number of policies effectively designed to marginalize them.'[9]

President George W Bush pursued the agenda of treating the two sets of rights as being fundamentally different: 'At best, economic, social and cultural rights are goals that can only be achieved progressively, not guarantees.'[10] This view perpetuates the notion that economic, social and cultural rights are only aspirational while civil and political rights are inalienable and immediately enforceable. Alston summarises the principal concerns of the Bush administration regarding economic, social and cultural rights as focusing on '1) a belief in the chronological priority of civil and political rights; 2) an objection to the terminological equivalence of the different sets of rights; 3) a concern over what might be termed the "internationalization of responsibility" for failures to meet economic and social rights; and 4) a concern about the justiciability of economic and social rights.'[11]

The early emphasis given to the reform of the US health care system by President Obama and the passage of health care reform legislation in 2010 by the US Congress indicates at least acceptance of the need to financially support the right to health, even if that support has not been considered (in this context) to explicitly address an international human right.

8 See above, n 5.

9 P Alston, 'The U.S. and the Right to Housing: A Funny Thing Happened on the Way to the Forum,' (1996) 1 *European Human Rights Law Review* 120.

10 Commission on Human Rights, *Report of the Open-Ended Working Group on the Right to Development*, UN ESCOR, Commission on Human Rights, 57th sess, Provisional Agenda Item 7, UN Doc E/CN4/2001/26 (20 March 2001) para 8.

11 P Alston, 'Putting Economic, Social and Cultural Rights Back on the Agenda of the United States' (*New York University School of Law, Center for Human Rights and Global Justice Working Paper No 22*, 2 August 2011) 6.

The domestic demystification and clarification of the scope of economic, social and cultural rights may be beneficial to garnering support for a state's ratification of the ICESCR and its *Optional Protocol*. Simple reliance on the assumption that economic, social and cultural rights will necessarily flow from the establishment of civil and political rights, and more broadly from democratic political systems, appears to have fallen flat.[12] As a result, the failure by a succession of US administrations to support economic, social and cultural rights has come at the cost of actually realising those rights.

4.2 THE SUBSTANTIVE RIGHTS

4.2.1 Overview of ICESCR

The Preamble of the *International Covenant on Economic, Social and Cultural Rights* (ICESCR) recognises, *inter alia*, that economic, social and cultural rights derive from the 'inherent dignity of the human person' and that 'the ideal of free human beings enjoying freedom of fear and want can only be achieved if conditions are created whereby everyone may enjoy his economic, social and cultural rights, as well as civil and political rights.' As in its counterpart, the *International Covenant on Civil and Political Rights* (ICCPR), one of the overarching principles of the Covenant is in ensuring equality and non-discrimination in regard to the enjoyment of all the rights set forth in the treaty.

The ICESCR is divided into five parts. Part I (article 1) recognises the right of all peoples to self-determination, including the right to 'freely determine their political status', pursue their economic, social and cultural development, and manage and dispose of their own resources. Of particular relevance at the time of the formation of the UN was the status and future governance of non-self-governing and trust territories (colonies), and as such it emphasises respect for their self-determination. The right to self-determination is discussed in more detail in Chapter 3.2.1.

Part II (articles 2–5) establishes the general nature of states parties' obligations under the Covenant, including article 2(1), which establishes the principle of 'progressive realisation', and article 2(2), which requires the rights be recognised 'without discrimination of any kind as to race, colour, sex, language, religion, political or other opinion, national or social origin, property, birth or other status'. Article 3 confirms the equal rights of men and women, and articles 4 and 5 discuss the general limitations of the Covenant.

The substantive rights of the ICESCR are set out in Part III (articles 6–15) and are discussed below. Part IV (articles 16–25) discusses the international implementation and system of supervision of the ICESCR, including the progressive reporting requirements imposed on states parties (article 17). Part V (articles 26–31) focuses on the regular provisions of treaties relating to ratification, entry into force and amendments.

12 See the examples quoted by P Alston, ibid 18, which include the example of North Korea and Zimbabwe where civil and political were focused on to the exclusion of the major economic, social and cultural rights violations occurring in those countries.

There is no clear distinction between 'social', 'economic' and 'cultural' rights, and there appears to be no obvious advantage in seeking one. For example, the monitoring committee for the ICESCR, the Committee on Economic, Social and Cultural Rights (CESCR),[13] has acknowledged that the right to education 'has been variously classified as an economic right, a social right and a cultural right. It is all of these. It is also, in many ways, a civil and political right, since it is central to the full and effective realisation of those rights as well.'[14] The right to health is also illustrative of the difficulty of classifying a right as definitively social, economic or cultural. For example, the right to health deals with elements of health care and the underlying preconditions for health, such as the provision of safe drinking water and adequate housing, but also may offer protection against harmful traditional practices and as such crosses all three classifications of these rights.

The following sections give a brief summary of the rights set out in the ICESCR. As was discussed when summarising civil and political rights in Chapter 3, the manner in which a right is interpreted and applied, and the types of balancing exercises that might be involved are all complex issues that will vary from right to right and from one scenario to another. This section provides a summary of some of these issues with a few illustrative examples. The right to water is used as a case study to provide a more in depth analysis of some of these questions. Article 1 of the ICESCR sets out the right to self-determination and is identical to the text in the ICCPR.[15]

4.2.2 The Rights to Equality and Non-Discrimination: Articles 2 and 3

While the concept of progressive realisation applies to all rights under the ICESCR,[16] some obligations are of immediate effect; in particular, the undertaking to guarantee that all rights are exercised on the basis of non-discrimination. Non-discrimination is a fundamental component of human rights and, as it is for the ICCPR,[17] it is an immediate obligation in the ICESCR. Article 2(2) requires states parties to guarantee that the rights set out in the Covenant 'will be exercised without discrimination of any kind as to race, colour, sex, language, religion, political or other opinion, national or social origin, property, birth or other status'. The prohibition on discrimination and equality rights are discussed in more detail below in relation to particular groups (indigenous peoples, people with disabilities and women).[18] But generally discrimination constitutes any distinction, exclusion, restriction or preference or other differential treatment that is directly or indirectly based on the prohibited grounds of discrimination, and that has the intention or effect of nullifying or impairing the recognition, enjoyment or exercise, on an equal footing, of economic, social and cultural rights.[19] The CESCR's General Comment 20 discusses the express grounds of discrimination

13 See Chapter 7.3.5.

14 CESCR, *General Comment No 11: Plans of Action for Primary Education*, 20th sess, UN Doc E/C.12/1999/4 (10 May 1999) para 2.

15 See Chapter 3.2.1.

16 See discussion below at Chapter 4.3.3.

17 See Chapter 3.2.22.

18 Chapters 13, 14 and 16.

19 CESCR, *General Comment No 20: Non-Discrimination in Economic, Social and Cultural Rights (art 2, para 2, of the International Covenant on Economic, Social and Cultural Rights)*, UN ESCOR, 42nd sess, UN Doc E/C.12/GC/20 (2 July 2009) para 7.

set out in article 2(2) but also notes that the nature of discrimination may vary over time and additional grounds of discrimination have emerged or will continue to emerge. Other grounds of discrimination may include: disability, age, nationality, marital and family status, sexual orientation[20] and gender identity, health status, place of residence and/or economic and social situation.[21]

4.2.3 The Right to Work: Articles 6, 7 and 8

The right to work, that is 'the right of everyone to the opportunity to gain his living by work', is recognised by Article 6 of the ICESCR. Articles 7 and 8 also provide (respectively) for the enjoyment of just and favourable conditions of work and the rights of workers to form and join trade unions. These rights are discussed in detail in Chapter 17.

4.2.4 The Right to Social Security: Article 9

Article 9 of the ICESCR is succinct and simply states that 'the States Parties to the present Covenant recognise the right of everyone to social security, including social insurance'. Elaboration of the meaning of this right can be found in the CESCR's General Comment 19, which acknowledges that the right encompasses:

> the right to access and maintain benefits, whether in cash or in kind, without discrimination in order to secure protection, inter alia, from
>
> (a) lack of work-related income caused by sickness, disability, maternity, employment injury, unemployment, old age, or death of a family member;
> (b) unaffordable access to health care;
> (c) insufficient family support, particularly for children and adult dependents.[22]

As with all economic, social and cultural rights, states parties undertake to implement the right to the maximum of their available resources.[23] While recognising that elements of the right to social security may vary according to different conditions, the CESCR in General Comment 19 stipulates that there are a number of essential factors that apply in all circumstances. The core elements of a social security system should provide for the coverage of the following nine areas: health care, sickness, old age, unemployment, employment injury, family and child support, maternity, disability and provision for survivors and orphans.[24]

---

20 In June 2011, the UN Human Rights Council passed a resolution on human rights violations based on sexual orientation and gender identity (A/HRC/17/L.9/Rev.1). The resolution, presented by South Africa along with Brazil and 39 additional co-sponsors from all regions of the world, was passed by a vote of 23 in favour, 19 against, and 3 abstentions. This is the first UN resolution ever to bring specific focus to human rights violations based on sexual orientation and gender identity. It requests the High Commissioner for Human Rights to prepare a study on violence and discrimination on the basis of sexual orientation and gender identity, and calls for a panel discussion to be held at the Human Rights Council to discuss the findings of the study in a constructive and transparent manner, and to consider appropriate follow-up.

21 CESCR, see above, n 19, paras 27–35.

22 CESCR, *General Comment No 19: The Right to Social Security (art 9 of the Covenant)*, UN ESCOR, 39th sess, UN Doc E/C.12/GC/19 (4 February 2008) para 2.

23 See discussion at Chapter 4.3.4.

24 CESCR, see above, n 22, paras 12–21.

SNAPSHOT: THE EXTENSION OF SOCIAL SECURITY RIGHTS TO IMMIGRANTS

Two cases, one from the Constitutional Court of South Africa and the other from the Argentinean Supreme Court, illustrate the application of the rights to social security in two particular scenarios. In *Khosa v Minister of Social Development*[25] the South African court examined the interrelationship between equality rights and economic, social and cultural rights and the applicability of social security rights to non-citizens. The applicants were Mozambican citizens living in South Africa as permanent residents. If they had been South African citizens, all of them would have qualified to receive social security under the *Social Assistance Act 59 of 1992*, but as permanent residents they did not. They brought the application in their own names, and on behalf of their minor children, of other people who had joined the application but could not litigate personally, of the class of permanent residents as a whole, and in the general public interest. The Court held, among other things, that the Constitution gave 'everyone' the right to have access to social security—not merely citizens—and that 'everyone' would include those residing in the country legally. The Court found the scheme's exclusion of permanent residents to be unreasonable, stating that the importance of providing access to social assistance to all who live permanently in South Africa, as well as the impact upon life and dignity that a denial of such access would have, far outweighed the financial and immigration considerations on which the state relied. The Court also held that the exclusion of children from access to social security on the basis of their parents' nationality amounted to unfair discrimination. The effect of the Court's finding was that the government's social security budgetary allocations were subsequently expanded to include this previously excluded group of non-citizens.[26]

The concerns of some human rights activists in Argentina about the progressive degradation of the right to social security in that country were given prominence in a case in 2007. In *Reyes Aguilera, Daniela v Argentina,*[27] the Supreme Court of Argentina held it was unconstitutional and discriminatory to link residence requirements to the availability of a disability pension. Representatives of Daniela Reyes Aguilera, a Bolivian girl with a disability, initiated the case, questioning the constitutionality of a requirement that immigrants prove 20 years' residence in Argentina to qualify for a disability pension. When the case was filed, Daniela was 12 years old and had been a permanent resident for two years and a de facto resident for four years. The Supreme Court declared the residence requirement unconstitutional by a majority vote, but the decision was based on varied reasoning. Some justices held the requirement implied an unreasonable and disproportionate limitation to the human right to social security, whereas other justices based their decision on the prohibition against discrimination based on prohibited grounds.

4.2.5 The Right to Protection and Assistance for the Family and the Prohibition of Child Labour: Article 10

Article 10(1) requires that states parties recognise that 'the widest possible protection and assistance should be accorded to the family', and that 'marriage must be entered into with the free consent of

25 *Khosa v Minister of Social Development* [2004] 6 SA 505 (Constitutional Court).

26 In a subsequent decision, *Union of Refugee Women v Director, Public Security Industry Regulatory Authority* [2007] 4 SA 395 (Constitutional Court), the Constitutional Court adopted a more restrictive approach to extending socio-economic entititlements to another category of non-nationals—refugees.

27 Reyes Aguilera, *Daniela v Argentina* (4 September 2007, Supreme Court of Argentina) R 350 XLI.

the intending spouses'. Articles 10(2) and (3) recognise that 'special protection should be provided to mothers during a reasonable period before and after childbirth' and that 'special measures of protection and assistance should be taken on behalf of all children', in particular to prevent the economic and social exploitation of children. Article 10(3) asks states to set 'age limits below which the paid employment of child labour should be prohibited and punishable by law'.

As noted when discussing the equivalent provision in the ICCPR, article 23,[28] the concept of 'family' has changed over the years and may vary according to social, cultural, economic or religious backgrounds. Issues arising under article 10 are likely to closely interact with the general non-discriminatory provisions of article 2(2) and those of Article 3 ensuring the equality of men and women to enjoy all economic, social and cultural rights.[29] The rights of women and children have, of course, been developed in far greater detail in subsequent treaties such as the CEDAW and the CROC, discussed in more detail in Chapters 13 and 17.

4.2.6 The Right to an Adequate Standard of Living: Article 11

The right to an adequate standard of living is defined in article 11 of the ICESCR, which first sets out a general statement of the right (including reference to the rights to food, clothing and housing) and then discusses in more detail the particular right to freedom from hunger. The right to water is not explicitly recognised in article 11 but it is now generally agreed that it is implied (see the case study below in Chapter 4.6).

Article 11(1) notes that the 'States Parties . . . recognize the right of everyone to an adequate standard of living for himself and his family, including adequate food, clothing and housing, and to the continuous improvement of living conditions'. Article 11(2) goes on to recognise the 'fundamental right of everyone to be free from hunger'.

The right to an adequate standard of living is arguably one of the most important rights recognised in the ICESCR, in the same way as the right to life is to the ICCPR. As Bailey notes, '[t]he centrality arises because the other rights listed in the Covenants all appear to be in some sense derivative from these core rights. For example, freedom of religion can reasonably be regarded as detailing aspects inherent in the rights to life and privacy. Likewise, the rights to social security or to work can be regarded as detailing aspects of the right to an adequate standard of living. Putting it the other way round, without some realisation of the right to an adequate standard of living, other economic and social ... as well as civil and political ... rights would have little meaning'.[30]

The Right to Adequate Food

In General Comment 12, the CESCR affirms the centrality of this right by noting that the right is 'indivisibly linked to the inherent dignity of the human person and is indispensable for the fulfilment of other human

28 See Chapter 3.

29 CESCR, *General Comment No 16: The Equal Right of Men and Women to the Enjoyment of All Economic, Social and Cultural Rights (art 3 of the International Covenant on Economic, Social and Cultural Rights)*, UN ESCOR, 34th sess, Agenda Item 5, UN Doc E/C.12/2005/4 (11 August 2005) para 27. Also see CESCR, above, n 19, para 26.

30 P Bailey, 'The Right to an Adequate Standard of Living: New Issues for Australian Law' (1997) 4(1) *Australian Journal of Human Rights* 25.

rights …'[31] General Comment 12 also provides guidance on the normative content of the right to food and notes that 'the right is realized when every man, woman and child, alone or in community with others, has physical and economic access at all times to adequate food or means for its procurement. The right to adequate food should not be interpreted in a narrow sense, for example by equating it simply with a minimum package of nutrients. States have a core obligation to take the necessary action to mitigate and alleviate hunger … even in times of natural or other disasters'.[32] General Comment 12 also recommends states parties might take into account several factors in progressively realising this right including:[33]

- *availability* of food in a quantity and quality sufficient to satisfy the dietary needs of individuals, free from adverse substances and acceptable within a given culture (paragraph 8);
- *economic accessibility*: financial costs to acquire food for an adequate diet should be at a level such that other basic needs are not threatened or compromised (paragraph 13);
- *physical accessibility:* adequate food must be accessible to everyone, including physically vulnerable individuals, such as children, elderly and the physically disabled (paragraph 13).

SNAPSHOT: NIGERIA AND THE RIGHT TO ADEQUATE FOOD

In 2001 the African Commission on Human and Peoples' Rights held that the destruction of crops by government and non-state actors (in this case corporations) violated the Nigerian government's duties to protect existing food sources and ensure access to adequate food for all its citizens.[34] The communication, brought by two NGOs, alleged that the Nigerian government had destroyed and threatened food sources of the Ogoni (indigenous peoples in the Niger Delta region of southeast Nigeria) through a variety of means including approving and participating in reckless oil development that polluted the Ogoni soil and water used for farming and fishing. The Nigerian security forces were also alleged to have destroyed farmland and animals, and more generally to have created a state of terror and insecurity that made it impossible for many Ogoni villagers to return to their fields.

Although the right to adequate food is not explicitly stated in the *African Charter*,[35] the Commission argued that the right was implicitly guaranteed. The Commission held that the *African Charter* and the ICESCR bound Nigeria with regard to the right to food, and that complying with the right required the Nigerian government to not destroy or contaminate food sources, or allow private parties to do, and to not prevent peoples' efforts to feed themselves.[36]

31 CESCR, *General Comment 12: The Right to Adequate Food (Art 11)*, UN ESCOR, 20th sess, Agenda Item 7, UN Doc E/C.12/1999/5 (12 May 1999) para 4.

32 Ibid para 6.

33 Ibid paras 6–13.

34 *Social and Economic Rights Action Center and the Center for Economic and Social Rights v Nigeria*, Communication No 155/96 (2001) AHRLR 60 (ACHPR 2001).

35 *African [Banjul] Charter on Human and People's Rights*, 21 ILM 58 (adopted 27 June 1981, entered into force 21 October 1986).

36 See above, n 34, paras 64–6. Also see: Christine Kaufmann and Simone Heri, 'Liberalizing Trade in Agriculture and Food Security—Mission Impossible?' [2007] *Vanderbilt Journal of Transnational Law* 1039.

The Right to Adequate Housing[37]

The right to adequate housing is a vital component of the right to an adequate standard of living in article 11. The core elements of the right to adequate housing are set out the CESCR's General Comment 4,[38] which notes that the right applies to everyone and should be interpreted in a broad and inclusive sense. While the definition of 'adequacy' with regard to housing may be affected by particular social, economic, cultural and geographic factors (among others), certain aspects of the right are applicable in any context. These are:

(a) Legal security of tenure. ... all persons should possess a degree of security of tenure which guarantees legal protection against forced eviction, harassment and other threats.

(b) Availability of services, materials, facilities and infrastructure. ... All beneficiaries of the right to adequate housing should have sustainable access to natural and common resources, safe drinking water, energy for cooking, heating and lighting, sanitation and washing facilities, means of food storage, refuse disposal, site drainage and emergency services.

(c) Affordability. Personal or household financial costs associated with housing should be at such a level that the attainment and satisfaction of other basic needs are not threatened or compromised ...

(d) Habitability. Adequate housing must be habitable, in terms of providing the inhabitants with adequate space and protecting them from cold, damp, heat, rain, wind or other threats to health, structural hazards, and disease vectors. The physical safety of occupants must be guaranteed as well.

(e) Accessibility. ... such disadvantaged groups as the elderly, children, the physically disabled, the terminally ill, HIV-positive individuals, persons with persistent medical problems, the mentally ill, victims of natural disasters, people living in disaster-prone areas and other groups should be ensured some degree of priority consideration in the housing sphere.

(f) Location. Adequate housing must be in a location which allows access to employment options, health-care services, schools, child-care centres and other social facilities. This is true both in large cities and in rural areas where the temporal and financial costs of getting to and from the place of work can place excessive demands upon the budgets of poor households. Similarly, housing should not be built on polluted sites nor in immediate proximity to pollution sources that threaten the right to health of the inhabitants.

(g) Cultural adequacy. The way housing is constructed, the building materials used and the supporting policies must appropriately enable the expression of cultural identity and diversity of housing.[39]

---

37 See South African cases on the right to housing discussed below in Chapter 4.5.1.

38 CESCR, *General Comment 4: The Right to Adequate Housing (art 11(1))*, UN ESCOR, 6th sess, UN Doc E/1992/23 (13 December 1991).

39 Ibid para 8.

SNAPSHOT: USA AND THE RIGHT TO ADEQUATE HOUSING

It seems clear that no state party is free of significant problems of one kind or another in relation to the right to housing. In 2009 the UN Special Rapporteur on adequate housing, Raquel Rolnik, conducted a fact-finding mission to the US to examine housing conditions, particularly in light of the continuing global financial crisis, and warned that, '[m]illions of people in the US are spending high percentages of their income to make their monthly rent and mortgage payment, face foreclosure or eviction, and live in overcrowded and substandard conditions'. The Special Rapporteur's report particularly noted the need to focus on eliminating discrimination when assessing eligibility for subsidised housing, the need for greater accountability, transparency and participation in planning decisions, increased public responsibility to provide for the needs of the most vulnerable and improvements required to provide adequate housing for the Native American population.

REPORT OF THE SPECIAL RAPPORTEUR ON ADEQUATE HOUSING, MISSION TO THE UNITED STATES OF AMERICA[40]

79. The Special Rapporteur acknowledges the high quality of the majority of housing in the United States, as well as the availability and quality of utilities and services. However, she expresses her deep concern about the millions of people living in the United States today who face serious challenges in accessing affordable and adequate housing, issues long faced by the poorest people and today affecting a greater proportion of society. A new face of homelessness is appearing, with increasing numbers of working families and individuals finding themselves on the streets, or living in shelters or in transitional housing arrangements with friends and family. Federal funding for low-income housing has been cut over the past decades, leading to a reduced stock and quality of subsidized housing. In addition, several cities have experienced a real estate boom which has led to increased housing prices. The subprime mortgage crisis has increased an already large gap between the supply and demand of affordable housing, and the economic crisis which followed has led to increased unemployment and an even greater need for affordable housing.

79. The Special Rapporteur noted throughout the visit that there is a longstanding commitment to provide adequate housing within their means for all Americans and an acknowledgement that the history of housing policy in the United States has been problematic. ... in many cases, neighbourhoods of concentrated poverty were the result of government policy.

80. Housing is not simply about bricks and mortar, nor is it simply a financial asset. Housing includes a sense of community, trust and bonds built between neighbours over time; the schools which educate the children; and the businesses which support the local economy and provide needed goods and services. Government policy has sometimes resulted in tearing apart this important sense of community, removing a source of stability for subsidized housing residents, and engendering a sense of mistrust of Government.

40 Report of the Special Rapporteur on adequate housing as a component of the right to an adequate standard of living, and on the right to non-discrimination in this context, Raquel Rolnik—Addendum—Mission to the United States of America, A/HRC/13/20/Add.4 (12 February 2010), available at <http://daccess-dds-ny.un.org/doc/UNDOC/GEN/G10/107/39/PDF/G1010739.pdf?OpenElement>.

4.2.7 The Right to Health: Article 12

Article 12(1) provides that state parties 'recognize the right of everyone to the enjoyment of the highest attainable standard of physical and mental health'. Since the adoption of the ICESCR in 1966 global health issues have changed significantly, and while article 12(2) notes the issues (among others) of maternal and reproductive health and environmental and industrial hygiene as issues of significance, other major determinants of health that may also now be taken into account in interpreting article 12 include formerly unknown threats to health such as HIV/AIDS and other threats that have become more pervasive, such as cancer.

Like many other economic, social and cultural rights, the right to health is interrelated with and dependent upon the realisation of a number of other human rights, including the rights to an adequate standard of living, work, education, life, privacy, non-discrimination and equality, and freedoms of information and movement and the prohibition against torture.

The right of everyone to the enjoyment of the highest attainable standard of physical and mental health is not to be confused with a right to be healthy. The CESCR's General Comment 14 notes that the definition in article 12(1) 'takes into account both the individual's biological and socio-economic preconditions and a state's available resources ... good health cannot be ensured by a state, nor can states provide protection against every possible cause of human ill health. Thus, genetic factors, individual susceptibility to ill health and the adoption of unhealthy or risky lifestyles may play an important role with respect to an individual's health. Consequently, the right to health must be understood as a right to the enjoyment of a variety of facilities, goods, services and conditions necessary for the realisation of the highest attainable standard of health.'[41]

Similar to its discussion in General Comment 4 on the content of the right to housing, the CESCR[42] has indicated in General Comment 14 that states parties must take into account a number of factors in realising this particular right, such as: availability, having regard to, for example, the state party's developmental level; accessibility, having regard to non-discrimination, physical and economic accessibility, and availability of information; acceptability, having regard to ethical and cultural considerations; and quality, having regard to scientific and medical considerations.

SNAPSHOT: A REPORT CARD ON AUSTRALIA AND ITS REALISATION OF THE RIGHT TO HEALTH

In 2009 the United Nations Special Rapporteur on the right of everyone to the enjoyment of the highest attainable standard of physical and mental health conducted a mission to Australia, primarily to investigate indigenous health and access to healthcare for those held in detention, including asylum seekers, refugees and prisoners. One of the many issues raised by the Special Rapporteur was the absence of a

41 CESCR, *General Comment No 14: The Right to the Highest Attainable Standard of Health (article 12 of the International Covenant on Economic, Social and Cultural Rights)*, UN ESCOR, 22nd sess, Agenda Item 3, UN Doc E/C/.12/2000/4 (11 August 2000) para 9.

42 Ibid para 12.

legal right to health in Australia.[43] Recent reviews of Australia by UN treaty bodies, including reports from the CESCR[44] and the Human Rights Committee[45] in 2009, raised a number of negative issues with respect to the realisation of the right to health in Australia. Responsibility for health care in Australia is split between Commonwealth and State governments and critics argue that the 'provision of public health care ... is suffering from chronic under funding, a decaying public health system, rising medical costs, inadequate coverage and inaccessibility ...'[46]

UN SPECIAL RAPPORTEUR'S 2009 PRELIMINARY REPORT ON AUSTRALIA[47]

... The focus of this mission was on two main issues—indigenous health and access to healthcare in detention establishments, including those for asylum-seekers, refugees and prisoners. I looked at these issues through the prism of the right to health. But that was one of my major challenges as there is no legal right to health in Australia. In addition, Australia is apparently the only developed liberal democracy that does not provide constitutional guarantee for human rights. Nevertheless, Australia's obligations to respect and protect human rights derives from its adherence to the core human rights treaties such as the International Covenant on Civil and Political Rights, the International Covenant on Economic, Social and Cultural Rights, the Convention against torture or the Convention on the Rights of the Child ...

The health of Australia's refugee and asylum seeker population in detention has been a significant concern for many years ... I would like to emphasize my overriding concerns regarding the situation of persons in detention centres: the fact that detention remains mandatory, with no maximum limits on duration of stay, and that there are no binding legal standards that must be met in providing services. These factors impact negatively on the status of health of persons in detention ...

Knowing Australia to be a developed, prosperous country, I was moved by the stories told to me by indigenous communities, the living conditions I saw, and the extent of preventable disease and health-related disability I witnessed among those of Aboriginal and Torres Strait Islander descent. The right of a significant proportion of Australia's indigenous populations to the highest attainable standard of physical and mental health is being violated. Basic needs, such as adequate housing, safe drinking water and sanitation and access to education are not being met. Unresolved issues

43 However, within Australia, both the Australian Capital Territory (ACT) and Victoria have enacted human rights legislation. While both the *Charter of Human Rights and Responsibilities Act 2006* (Vic) and the *Human Rights Act 2004* (ACT) only expressly protect civil and political rights, the recent case *Kracke v Mental Health Review Board* [2009] VCAT 646 (23 April 2009) demonstrates the interdependence of the right to health with other human rights. This case concerned the compulsory medical treatment of Mr Kracke without his consent and without his treatment having been reviewed by the Mental Health Review Board as required by the *Mental Health Act 1986* (Vic). While Mr Kracke's right to health was not able to be considered, the circumstances of his treatment and health care were able to be considered in the context of his right to a fair hearing. Also see H Charlesworth et al, *Australian Capital Territory Economic, Social and Cultural Rights Research Project Report* (21 September 2010) <http://acthra.anu.edu.au/PESCR/Final%20report/Final%20Report%20of%20the%20ACT%20ESCR%20Research%20Project_9%20December%202010.pdf>. See Chapter 10.3.4.

44 CESCR, *Concluding Observations of the Committee on Economic, Social and Cultural Rights: Australia*, UN ESCOR, 42nd sess, UN Doc E/C.12/AUS/CO/4 (22 May 2009).

45 Human Rights Committee, *Concluding Observations of the Human Rights Committee: Australia*, 95th sess, UN Doc CCPR/C/AUS/CO/5 (7 May 2009).

46 Human Rights Law Resource Centre, *Briefing Paper on Key Issues on the Right to Health in Australia* (September 2009) <http://www.hrlrc.org.au/files/Briefing-Paper-Health-in-Austalia-September-2009.pdf>.

47 Anand Grover, *United Nations Special Rapporteur On The Right Of Everyone To The Enjoyment Of The Highest Attainable Standard Of Physical And Mental Health, Preliminary observations and recommendations*, Canberra, 4 December 2009, <http://www2.ohchr.org/english/issues/health/right/docs/PressStatementAustralia041209.doc>.

> surrounding native titles and land rights continue to have a detrimental impact. Communities are not benefitting from the equal access to primary healthcare facilities which are at times inaccessible or inappropriate. This is sometimes due to lack of transportation and communication infrastructure, but more often due to direct discrimination and culturally inappropriate services being provided. Institutions and processes, particularly those linked to tertiary care, and staff are not adequately supported to address the specific needs and vulnerabilities of the indigenous communities they serve. Such inequities are incompatible with basic principles of the right to health including equality and non-discrimination ...

4.2.8 The Right to Education: Articles 13 and 14

The realisation of the right to education is crucial for the exercise of all other human rights. Katarina Tomasevski, former United Nations Special Rapporteur on the right to education, argues that

> [t]here is a large number of human rights problems which cannot be solved unless the right to education is addressed as the key to unlock other human rights. Education operates as multiplier, enhancing the enjoyment of all individual rights and freedoms where the right to education is effectively guaranteed, while depriving people of the enjoyment of many rights and freedoms where the right to education is denied or violated.[48]

The more limited a person's education, the less likely it is that he or she will fully participate in and realise other human rights. The CESCR's General Comment 13 emphasises this 'multiplier' effect by affirming the vital role education has 'in empowering women, safeguarding children from exploitative and hazardous labour and sexual exploitation, promoting human rights and democracy, protecting the environment, and controlling population growth'.[49]

Articles 13 and 14 of the ICESCR delineate the states parties' requirements with respect to the right to education that encompass the full levels of education from primary education (which should be compulsory and freely available) to secondary and tertiary study, which should be equally accessible to all.

The relevant criteria most commonly used in determining the scope of the right are those set out by the CESCR in its General Comment 13 (paragraph 6). The criteria are expressed as availability (encompassing aspects of availability in terms of both programs and the physical infrastructure required); accessibility (incorporating non-discriminatory access to education), acceptability (relating to form and substance of education) and adaptability (incorporating cultural concerns). Chapter 3 illustrates the interaction between the right to freely express one's religious beliefs and a woman's right to education.

---

48 K Tomasevski, *Removing Obstacles in the Way of the Right to Education (Right to Education Primer No 1, 2001)* <www.right-to-education.org/sites/r2e.gn.apc.org/files/B6e%20Primer.pdf>.

49 CESCR, *General Comment No 13: The Right to Education (Art. 13)*, UN ESCOR, 21st sess, UN Doc E/C.12/1999/10 (8 December1999) para 1.

SNAPSHOT: EDUCATING CHILDREN WITH DISABILITIES

The right to education is guaranteed in the *European Social Charter* in similar terms to the ICESCR.[50] In *International Association Autism Europe v France*,[51] the NGO Autism Europe alleged that France had failed to provide adequate access to education to adults and children with autism. The Committee ruled that the Government's overall lack of progress in this area constituted a violation of the *European Social Charter*, namely the right of persons with disabilities to education, the right of children and young persons to education, and the right of all persons to non-discrimination. The Committee acknowledged that the realisation of a Charter right may be complex and expensive, but said that realisation of social rights must occur within a reasonable time, with measurable progress and to an extent consistent with the maximum available resources.

4.2.9 The Right to Take Part in Cultural Life: Article 15

There has been less focus on realising the so-called 'cultural' rights of the ICESCR rights, such as those contained in article 15(1), which recognise the right of everyone:

(a) to take part in cultural life;
(b) to enjoy the benefits of scientific progress and its applications;
(c) to benefit from the protection of the moral and material interests resulting from any scientific, literary or artistic production of which he is the author.

Part of the reluctance in addressing cultural rights may be the potentially all-encompassing and, some may argue, overly broad notion of culture. Vagueness around the meaning of culture, what it does and does not incorporate, and how it forms part of a human right were all discussed at CESCR's Day of General Discussion on the 'right to take part in cultural life' held in May 2008.[52] In November 2009, the CESCR released General Comment 21,[53] noting that 'cultural rights are an integral part of human rights'[54] and that 'the right to take part in cultural life can be characterized as a freedom'.[55] The CESCR's view still tends to encompass a broad view of culture, defining it as including:

> ways of life, language, oral and written literature, music and song, non-verbal communication, religion or belief systems, rites and ceremonies, sport and games, methods of production or technology, natural and man-made environment, food, clothing and shelter, the arts, customs and traditions, through which individuals,

50 *European Social Charter (revised)*, opened for signature 3 May 1996, (entered into force 1 July 1999) CETS No 163; art 17.

51 European Committee of Social Rights, *International Association Autism Europe v France*, Complaint No 13/2002, Decision on the Merits (4 November 2003).

52 CESCR, *Day of General Discussion on the Right to Take Part in Cultural Life* (9 May 2008) <http://www2.ohchr.org/english/bodies/cescr/discussion090508.htm>.

53 CESCR, *General Comment No 21: Right of Everyone to Take Part in Cultural Life (art 15, para 1(a) of the International Covenant on Economic, Social and Cultural Rights)*, UN ESCOR, 43rd sess, UN Doc E/C.12/GC/21 (12 June 2009).

54 Ibid para 1.

55 Ibid para 6.

groups of individuals and communities express their humanity and the meaning they give to their existence, and build their world view representing their encounter with the external forces affecting their lives. Culture shapes and mirrors the values of well-being, as well as the economic, social and political life of individuals, groups of individuals and communities.[56]

4.3 NATURE OF OBLIGATIONS

4.3.1 Tripartite Typology of Obligations

Economic, social and cultural rights impose three different obligations on states: the obligations to respect, protect and fulfil. This tripartite typology of obligations has been incorporated by the CESCR in its General Comments and is now broadly accepted.[57] The obligation to respect requires states to refrain from interfering directly or indirectly with the enjoyment of economic, social and cultural rights. For example, the right to health may be violated if the state takes action to limit or deny access to health care services. The obligation to protect requires states to prevent violations of such rights by third parties. Thus, the failure to ensure that private employers comply with basic labour standards may amount to a violation of the right to work or the right to just and favourable conditions of work. The obligation to fulfil requires states to take appropriate legislative, administrative, budgetary, judicial and other measures to ensure the enjoyment by all of economic, social and cultural rights in practice.

The obligation to fulfil may be further divided into the obligations to facilitate, promote and provide.[58] The obligation to facilitate requires states to undertake positive measures and enabling strategies, for example by ensuring that education in schools is of good quality and culturally appropriate for minorities. The obligation to promote requires states to create and maintain the realisation of a right. For example, in General Comment 16, the CESCR urges states to promote the equal rights of men and women by conducting human rights education and training for judges and public officials and to conduct

56 Ibid para 13.

57 This development of this typology has generally been attributed to the UN Special Rapporteur on the Right to Food, see A Eide, *The Right to Adequate Food as a Human Right*, UN Doc E/CN.4/Sub.2/1987/23 (7 July 1987) para 66. See also: CESCR, see above, n 22, paras 43–51; CESCR, *General Comment No 18: The Right to Work (Article 16 of the International Covenant on Economic, Social and Cultural Rights)*, UN ESCOR, 35th sess, Provisional Agenda Item 3, UN Doc E/C.12/GC/18 (6 February 2006) para 22; CESCR, *General Comment No 17: The Right of Everyone to Benefit from the Protection of the Moral and Material Interests Resulting from Any Scientific, Literary or Artistic Production of which He or She is the Author*, UN ESCOR, 35th sess, UN Doc E/C.12/GC/17 (12 January 2006) para 28; CESCR, *General Comment No 16*, see above, n 29, paras 18–21; CESCR, *General Comment No 15: The Right to Water (arts 11 and 12 of the International Covenant on Economic, Social and Cultural Rights)*, UN ESCOR, 29th sess, Agenda Item 3, UN Doc E/C.12/2002/11 (20 January 2003) paras 20–29; CESCR, see above, n 41, para 33; CESCR, see above, n 49, para 46.

58 CESCR, see above, n 31, para 37.

awareness-raising programs on equality for workers at a grass roots level.[59] The obligation to provide obliges states to provide for rights directly when an individual or a group are unable, for reasons beyond their control, to enjoy a right by the means at their disposal.[60] This may be particularly relevant to groups that are more likely to suffer disproportionate harm, such as lower-income groups, women, indigenous and tribal peoples, occupied populations, asylum seekers, refugees and internally displaced persons, minorities, the elderly, children, landless peasants, persons with disabilities and the homeless.[61]

This tripartite typology of obligations was also adopted by the African Commission on Human and Peoples' Rights in its landmark decision in *The Social and Economic Rights Action Centre (SERAC) and the Centre for Economic and Social Rights v Nigeria*.[62]

4.3.2 Obligation 'to Take Steps ... by All Appropriate Means'

The words of article 2(1) of the ICESCR have been, and still are, the source of extensive debate over the exact nature and scope of states' obligations under the Covenant.[63]

ARTICLE 2(1) ICESCR

Each State Party to the present Covenant undertakes to take steps, individually and through international assistance and co-operation, especially economic and technical, to the maximum of its available resources, with a view to achieving progressively the full realization of the rights recognized in the present Covenant by all appropriate means, including particularly the adoption of legislative measures.

As noted by Alston and Quinn, the *travaux préparatoires*[64] reveal a sharp division between states regarding the phraseology of article 2(1).[65] The article has been closely examined by groups of experts who adopted the Limburg Principles on the Implementation of the International Covenant on Economic, Social and Cultural Rights and the Maastricht Guidelines on Violations of Economic, Social and Cultural

59 CESCR, see above, n 29.

60 United Nations Economic and Social Council, *Report of the Office of the High Commissioner for Human Rights, Substantive Session of 2007*, Provisional Agenda Item 14(g), UN Doc E/2007/82 (25 June 2007) paras 10–13.

61 'Maastricht Guidelines on Violations of Economic, Social and Cultural Rights, Maastricht, 22–6 January 1997' (1998) 20 *Human Rights Quarterly*, 691, [20].

62 CESCR, see above, n 39. See discussion at Chapter 4.2.6.

63 M Ssenyonjo, *Economic, Social and Cultural Rights in International Law*, Hart Publishing, Oxford, 2009, 51.

64 The *travaux préparatoires* are the official record of a negotiation. They are often useful in clarifying the intentions of a treaty or other instrument. This is reflected in article 32 of the Vienna *Convention on the Law of Treaties*.

65 P Alston & G Quinn, 'The Nature and Scope of States Parties' Obligations under the International Covenant on Economic, Social and Cultural Rights' (1987) 9 *Human Rights Quarterly*, 156, 165–80.

Rights,[66] and also by the CESCR in General Comment 3. While each of the phrases in article 2(1) tends to be analysed separately, they are all inextricably linked.

In General Comment 3, the CESCR clarified the nature of states' obligations:

> 1 Article 2 is of particular importance to a full understanding of the Covenant and must be seen as having a dynamic relationship with all of the other provisions of the Covenant. It describes the nature of the general legal obligations undertaken by States parties to the Covenant. Those obligations include both what may be termed (following the work of the International Law Commission) obligations of conduct and obligations of result. While great emphasis has sometimes been placed on the difference between the formulations used in this provision and that contained in the equivalent article 2 of the International Covenant on Civil and Political Rights, it is not always recognized that there are also significant similarities. In particular, while the Covenant provides for progressive realization and acknowledges the constraints due to the limits of available resources, it also imposes various obligations which are of immediate effect. Of these, two are of particular importance in understanding the precise nature of States parties obligations. One of these, which is dealt with in a separate general comment, and which is to be considered by the Committee at its sixth session, is the 'undertaking to guarantee' that relevant rights 'will be exercised without discrimination …'
>
> 2 The other is the undertaking in article 2(1) 'to take steps', which in itself, is not qualified or limited by other considerations. The full meaning of the phrase can also be gauged by noting some of the different language versions. In English the undertaking is 'to take steps', in French it is 'to act' ('s'engage à agir') and in Spanish it is 'to adopt measures' ('a adoptar medidas'). Thus while the full realization of the relevant rights may be achieved progressively, steps towards that goal must be taken within a reasonably short time after the Covenant's entry into force for the States concerned. Such steps should be deliberate, concrete and targeted as clearly as possible towards meeting the obligations recognized in the Covenant.

In this General Comment, the Committee confirms that the requirement 'to take steps' is an immediate obligation. Although the phrase is qualified by the concepts of 'progressive realisation' and the 'availability of resources', this does not alter the immediacy of the obligation, nor can resource constraints alone justify inaction. A 2007 statement by the CESCR noted that even where the available resources are inadequate, the obligation remains for a state party to ensure the widest possible enjoyment of economic, social and cultural rights under the prevailing circumstances.[67] The CESCR argues that even under conditions where there are very limited resources, states parties must protect the most disadvantaged and marginalised members or groups of society by adopting relatively low-cost targeted programs.[68] The following are factors that the CESCR considers relevant in determining if the actions taken by the State are adequate or reasonable.

---

66 Commission on Human Rights, *The Limburg Principles on the Implementation of the International Covenant on Economic, Social and Cultural Rights*, 43rd sess, Provisional Agenda Items 8 and 18, UN Doc E/CN.4/1987/17 (8 January 1987) Annex. A group of 29 distinguished experts in international law, convened by the International Commission of Jurists, the Faculty of Law of the University of Limburg (Maastricht, the Netherlands) and the Urban Morgan Institute for Human Rights, University of Cincinnati (Ohio, United States of America), met in Maastricht on 2–6 June 1986 to consider the nature and scope of the obligations of states parties to the ICESCR. Like the Maastrict Guidelines, the Limburg Principles are not legally binding but as 'teachings of the most highly qualified publicists', are influential in interpreting the Covenant.

67 CESCR, *An Evaluation of the Obligation to Take Steps to the 'Maximum of Available Resources' under an Optional Protocol to the Covenant*, UN ESCOR, 38th sess, UN Doc E/C.12/2007/1 (10 May 2007) para 3.

68 Ibid para 4.

CESCR: *AN EVALUATION OF THE OBLIGATION TO TAKE STEPS TO THE 'MAXIMUM OF AVAILABLE RESOURCES' UNDER AN OPTIONAL PROTOCOL TO THE COVENANT*[69]

[8] In considering a communication concerning an alleged failure of a State party to take steps to the maximum of available resources, the Committee will examine the measures that the State party has effectively taken, legislative or otherwise. In assessing whether they are 'adequate' or 'reasonable', the Committee may take into account, inter alia, the following considerations:

(a) the extent to which the measures taken were deliberate, concrete and targeted towards the fulfilment of economic, social and cultural rights;
(b) whether the State party exercised its discretion in a non-discriminatory and non arbitrary manner;
(c) whether the State party's decision (not) to allocate available resources is in accordance with international human rights standards;
(d) where several policy options are available, whether the State party adopts the option that least restricts Covenant rights;
(e) the time frame in which the steps were taken;
(f) whether the steps had taken into account the precarious situation of disadvantaged and marginalized individuals or groups and, whether they were non-discriminatory, and whether they prioritized grave situations or situations of risk.

Article 2(1) of ICESCR goes on to state that in meeting the requirement 'to take steps' states must do so 'by all appropriate means, including particularly the adoption of legislative measures.' While the adoption of legislation is considered 'highly desirable and in some cases indispensable,'[70] its adoption will not automatically exhaust the obligations of states under the Covenant. States are granted a 'margin of discretion'[71] in determining the most appropriate means of implementing their obligations under the ICESCR. Other measures that might be appropriate include the provision of judicial remedies, and administrative, financial, educational or social measures. This view was reinforced by the Constitutional Court of South Africa in *Grootboom*, where the Court stressed that in so far as socio-economic rights are concerned:

69 (2007) UN Doc E.C.12/2007/.

70 CESCR, *General Comment 3: The Nature of States Parties Obligations (art 2, para 1 of the Covenant)*, UN ESCOR, 5th sess, UN Doc E/1991/23 (14 December 1990) para 3:
The Committee recognizes that in many instances legislation is highly desirable and in some cases may even be indispensable. For example, it may be difficult to combat discrimination effectively in the absence of a sound legislative foundation for the necessary measures. In fields such as health, the protection of children and mothers, and education, legislation may also be an indispensable element for many purposes.

71 CESCR, see above, n 41, para 53; CESCR, see above, n 57, para 45; CESCR, *General Comment 16: The Equal Right of Men and Women to the Enjoyment of All Economic, Social and Cultural Rights (art 3 of the International Covenant on Economic, Social and Cultural Rights)*, UN ESCOR, 34th sess, Agenda Item 5, UN Doc E/C.12/2005/4 (11 August 2005) para 32.

> The State is required to take reasonable legislative and other measures. Legislative measures by themselves are not likely to constitute constitutional compliance. Mere legislation is not enough. The State is obliged to act to achieve the intended result, and the legislative measures will invariably have to be supported by appropriate, well-directed policies and programmes implemented by the Executive. These policies and programmes must be reasonable both in their conception and their implementation. The formulation of a programme is only the first stage in meeting the State's obligations. The programme must also be reasonably implemented. An otherwise reasonable programme that is not implemented reasonably will not constitute compliance with the State's obligations.[72]

4.3.3 Progressive Realisation

Not all of the obligations regarding economic, social and cultural rights are qualified by the notion of progressive realisation. Some obligations, such as the obligation to take steps towards realisation, the prohibition of discrimination and the satisfaction of minimum core obligations, are of immediate effect.

For those rights that are subject to 'progressive realisation', there are very different interpretations of what might be entailed in the obligation of states 'to achieve progressively the full realization of the rights' in article 2(1). On the one hand it could be said that the notion of progressive achievement seriously hampers implementation of the Covenant and provides states with a flexible 'loophole' they can use to deprive the ICESCR of any meaningful obligation. On the other hand, progressive achievement can be viewed not as a limitation but a pragmatic recognition, or necessary accommodation, of the differing levels of social and economic development of states parties, and gives states a margin of discretion to realise economic, social and cultural rights over time.[73] The CESCR has adopted the latter view and notes in General Comment 3 that:

> The concept of progressive realization constitutes a recognition of the fact that full realization of all economic, social and cultural rights will generally not be able to be achieved in a short period of time. In this sense the obligation differs significantly from that contained in article 2 of the International Covenant on Civil and Political Rights which embodies an immediate obligation to respect and ensure all of the relevant rights. Nevertheless, the fact that realization over time, or in other words progressively, is foreseen under the Covenant should not be misinterpreted as depriving the obligation of all meaningful content. It is on the one hand a necessary flexibility device, reflecting the realities of the real world and the difficulties involved for any country in ensuring full realization of economic, social and cultural rights. On the other hand, the phrase must be read in the light of the overall objective, indeed the *raison d'être*, of the Covenant which is to establish clear obligations for States parties in respect of the full realization of the rights in question. It thus imposes an obligation to move as expeditiously

72 *Government of the Republic of South Africa and Others v Grootboom* [2001] 1 SA 46, [42] (Constitutional Court) ('Grootboom').

73 See for example the comments, cited in of the Lebanese representative during the preparatory phase of drafting Article 2(1) that 'the deletion of "progressively" was desirable as that expression added nothing and might be intrepreted as discouraging immediate implementation' versus the comments of the Guatemalan representative who argued that 'the word "progressively" was not really dangerous. "It should enable certain States to ratify the Covenant, even if they were quite unable to implement its provisions forthwith. It did not in any way mean that states whose social development was adequate would not be bound by the obligations laid on them in the Covenant. It was all a matter of good faith"' quoted in Philip Alston and Gerard Quinn, see above, n 65, 175–6.

and effectively as possible towards that goal. Moreover, any deliberately retrogressive measures in that regard would require the most careful consideration and would need to be fully justified by reference to the totality of the rights provided for in the Covenant and in the context of the full use of the maximum available resources.[74]

'Progressive realisation' is an inexact term that can render economic, social and cultural rights difficult to monitor.[75] In a world of increasing needs but limited resources, states have a margin within which they may determine the use of their resources, prioritise some demands over others, and use a wide range of possible measures to progressively realise economic, social and cultural rights. As noted by the Constitutional Court of South Africa in *Minister of Health v Treatment Action Campaign*, 'It is impossible to give everyone access even to a "core" service immediately. All that is possible, and all that can be expected of the State, is that it act reasonably to provide access to ... socio-economic rights ... on a progressive basis ... The State is obliged to take reasonable measures progressively to eliminate or reduce the large areas of severe deprivation that afflict our society.'[76]

In sum, the notion of progressive realisation requires progress, that is, improvement over time that is evidenced by deliberate, concrete and targeted measures adopted by the state making efficient use of available resources. Put simply, as stated by the UN Special Rapporteur on the right to health in 2006, progressive realisation means that 'states are expected to do better [towards realising the rights] next year than they are doing today.'[77]

4.3.4 Maximum of Available Resources

Realisation of economic, social and cultural rights hangs on the question of resources. Article 2(1) obliges each State party to take the necessary steps 'to the maximum of its available resources'. In order for a state party to be able to attribute its failure to meet at least its minimum core obligations to a lack of available resources, it must be able to demonstrate that every effort has been made to use all resources that are at its disposition.[78] But while this phrase establishes the tangible response states must make to the challenge of realising economic, social and cultural rights, it is imprecise. As noted by Robertson, '[I]t is a difficult phrase—two warring adjectives describing an undefined noun. "Maximum" stands for idealism; "available" stands for reality. "Maximum" is the sword of human rights rhetoric; "available" is the wiggle room for the State.'[79]

---

74 CESCR, see above, n 70.

75 A R Chapman, 'A "Violations Approach" for Monitoring the International Covenant on Economic, Social and Cultural Rights' (1996) 18 *Human Rights Quarterly* 23, 23.

76 *Minister of Health v Treatment Action Campaign (No 2)* [2002] 5 SA 721 (Constitutional Court) ('Treatment Action Campaign'), and see discussion at Chapter 4.3.5 and 4.5.1.

77 Human Rights Council, *Report of the Special Rapporteur on the Right of Everyone to the Enjoyment of the Highest Attainable Standard of Physical and Mental Health, Paul Hunt*, 7th sess, Agenda Item 3, UN Doc A/HRC/7/11 (31 January 2008) para 126; Human Rights Council, *Implementation of General Assembly Resolution 60/251 of 15 March 2006 entitled "Human Rights Council": Opinions Adopted by the Working Group on Arbitrary Detention*, 4th sess, Provisional Agenda Item 2, UN Doc A/HRC/4/40/Add.1 (2 February 2007).

78 CESCR, see above, n 70, para 10.

79 R E Robertson, 'Measuring State Compliance with the Obligation to Devote the "Maximum Available Resources" to Realizing Economic, Social and Cultural Rights' (1994) 16 *Human Rights Quarterly* 693, 694.

It is clear that the undertaking by a state party to use 'the maximum' of its available resources includes access to resources from the international community. In this regard, the CESCR notes that the phrase 'to the maximum of its available resources' refers to the resources within a state as well as those available from the international community through international cooperation and assistance.[80] The CESCR has commented that:

> should a state party use 'resource constraints' as an explanation for any retrogressive steps, it would consider such information on a 'country-by-country basis in the light of objective criteria such as:
>
> (a) the country's level of development;
> (b) the severity of the alleged breach, in particular whether the situation concerned the enjoyment of the minimum core content of the Covenant;
> (c) the country's current economic situation, in particular whether the country was undergoing a period of economic recession;
> (d) the existence of other serious claims on the State party's limited resources; for example, resulting from a recent natural disaster or from recent internal or international armed conflict;
> (e) whether the state party had sought to identify low-cost options; and
> (f) whether the state party had sought cooperation and assistance or rejected offers of resources from the international community for the purposes of implementing the provisions of the Covenant without sufficient reason.[81]

While the term is inexact and does provide states with a significant margin of discretion in allocating resources, a number of decisions in a variety of jurisdictions have started to give the phrase more precision. The cases noted below discuss the concept with respect to the right to health, and gradually, on a case-by-case basis, clarify the scope of a state's obligations in realising this right. Although these cases are from developing countries, balancing the realisation of the right to health with available resources is faced by most economies around the world.

In *Soobramoney v Minister of Health*[82] the Constitutional Court of South Africa acknowledged that the obligations imposed on the state regarding access to health care depend on the resources available. Because of limited resources, the hospital in question had adopted a policy of admitting for renal treatment only those patients who could be cured within a short period and those with chronic renal failure who were eligible for a kidney transplant. The Court declared that it could not interfere with decisions taken in good faith by political organs and medical authorities as to how to allocate budgets and decide on priorities. In his judgment, Madala J noted that the concepts of 'available resources' and 'progressive realisation' are recognition of the fact that no government can 'solve all of our society's woes overnight, but must go on trying to resolve these problems'.[83] In the principal judgment, Chaskalson P commented that:

80 CESCR, see above, n 70, para 13.

81 CESCR, *An Evaluation of the Obligation to Take Steps to the "Maximum of Available Resources" under an Optional Protocol to the Covenant*, UN ESCOR, 38th sess, UN Doc E/C.12/2007/1 (10 May 2007) para 10.

82 *Soobramoney v Minister of Health (KwaZulu-Natal)* [1998] 1 SA 765 (Constitutional Court).

83 Ibid [43] (Constitutional Court).

> [24] There are many more patients suffering from chronic renal failure than there are dialysis machines to treat such patients. This is a nation-wide problem and resources are stretched in all renal clinics throughout the land. Guidelines have therefore been established to assist the persons working in these clinics to make the agonising choices which have to be made in deciding who should receive treatment, and who not. These guidelines were applied in the present case.
>
> [25] By using the available dialysis machines in accordance with the guidelines more patients are benefited than would be the case if they were used to keep alive persons with chronic renal failure, and the outcome of the treatment is also likely to be more beneficial because it is directed to curing patients, and not simply to maintaining them in a chronically ill condition. It has not been suggested that these guidelines are unreasonable or that they were not applied fairly and rationally when the decision was taken by the Addington Hospital that the appellant did not qualify for dialysis.
>
> [31] The state has to manage its limited resources in order to address all these claims. There will be times when this requires it to adopt a holistic approach to the larger needs of society rather than to focus on the specific needs of particular individuals within society.

In *Purohit and Moore v Gambia*[84] (a case concerning the right to health in article 16 of the *African Charter on Human and Peoples' Rights*), the African Commission on Human and Peoples' Rights recognised that poverty is a serious limitation on states seeking to provide all the necessary amenities, infrastructure and resources to facilitate enjoyment of the right to health. However, the Commission did not allow a general lack of resources as an excuse not to realise a specific duty. For example, in the course of analysing the adequacy of mental health care in Gambia, the government disclosed that it actually had enough medicines for mental health patients, but that they had not been distributed. Consequently the Commission could justifiably order that the state provide these medicines to those who needed them, even though it noted the state's severe resource constraints. Similarly, in *Paschim Banga Khet Mazdoor Samity v State of West Bengal*[85] the Supreme Court of India held that the Government was under an obligation to provide emergency health treatment despite being limited by financial constraints.

4.3.5 Minimum Core Obligations

States parties to the ICESCR are under an immediate obligation to satisfy, as a matter of priority, 'minimum essential levels of each of the rights' recognised in the Covenant, also referred to as 'minimum core obligations'. Failure by a state party to fulfil such minimum essential levels of rights constitutes a prima facie violation of the Covenant. In General Comment 3, the CESCR stated that it is of the view that:

> a minimum core obligation to ensure the satisfaction of, at the very least, minimum essential levels of each of the rights is incumbent upon every State party. Thus, for example, a State party in which any significant number of individuals is deprived of essential foodstuffs, of essential primary health care, of basic shelter and housing, or of the most basic forms of education is, *prima facie*, failing to discharge its obligations

84 *Purohit and Moore v Gambia*, Communication 241/2001 (2003) AHRLR 96 (ACHPR 2003).

85 *Paschim Banga Khet Mazdoor Samity v State of West Bengal* (1996) 4 SCC 37 and see discussion at Chapter 4.5.2.

> under the Covenant. If the Covenant were to be read in such a way as not to establish such a minimum core obligation, it would be largely deprived of its *raison d'être*. By the same token, it must be noted that any assessment as to whether a State has discharged its minimum core obligation must also take account of resource constraints applying within the country concerned.[86]

The minimum core obligations apply at all times to developing and developed states, and are considered a baseline that states should reach and rise above. The obligation to realise the minimum core obligations is immediate and non-derogable and persists in times of conflict, emergency and natural disaster. After a state has met its minimum core obligations, it is obliged to progressively realise the remainder of a right. The CESCR emphasised in General Comment 3 that 'even where the available resources are demonstrably inadequate, the obligation remains for a state party to strive to ensure the widest possible enjoyment of the relevant rights under the prevailing circumstances'.[87]

What constitutes the definitive content of the core of the rights to food, health, housing and education is debatable. The Covenant provides limited guidance, apart from broad statements such as 'the right of everyone to be free from hunger' (article 11) and the provision that 'primary education shall be compulsory and available free to all' (article 13). Since 2000 the CESCR has in its General Comments sought to provide guidance on what it would consider minimum essential levels of fulfilment for a number of rights. They include, for example in relation to the right to health, the obligations:

- to ensure the right of access to health facilities, goods and services on a non-discriminatory basis, especially for vulnerable and marginalised groups;
- to ensure access to the minimum essential food that is nutritionally adequate and safe, to ensure freedom from hunger to everyone;
- to ensure access to basic shelter, housing and sanitation, and an adequate supply of safe and potable water;
- to provide essential drugs, as from time to time defined under the WHO Action Program on Essential Drugs.[88]

---

86 CESCR, *General Comment No 3: The Nature of States Parties Obligations*, UN ESCOR, 5th sess, UN Doc E/1991/23 (14 December 1990) para 10. See also UN Commission on Human Rights, *The Right of Everyone to the Enjoyment of the Highest Attainable Standard of Physical and Mental Health: Report of the Special Rapporteur, Paul Hunt, Submitted in Accordance with Commission Resolution 2002/31*, UN ESCOR, 59th sess, Provisional Agenda Item 10, UN Doc E/CN.4/2003/58 (13 February 2003) para 53; UN Commission on Human Rights, *Report of the Special Rapporteur on the Right to Food, Mr. Jean Ziegler, Submitted in Accordance with Commission on Human Rights Resolution 2001/25*, UN ESCOR, 58th sess, Provisional Agenda Item 10, UN Doc E/CN.4/2002/58 (10 January 2002) para 39. The notion of minimum core obligations is also reflected in the UN Commission on Human Rights, see above, n 66, as an obligation towards ensuring 'respect for minimum subsistence rights'. See CESCR, *The Right of Everyone to Benefit from the Protection of the Moral and Material Interests Resulting from Any Scientific, Literary or Artistic Production of which He or She is the Author (Art 15.1(c) of the Covenant)*, UN ESCOR, 24th sess, Provisional Agenda Item 3, UN Doc E/C.12/2000/13 (2 October 2000) para 25.

87 CESCR, *General Comment No 3*, ibid para 11.

88 CESCR, see above, n 41, para 43.

Disagreement about the scope of core entitlements also raises questions about the concept of establishing minimum core obligations themselves.[89] In the context of a discussion on the decision of the Constitutional Court of South Africa in *Minister of Health v Treatment Action Campaign* (the '*TAC*' case),[90] Dixon argues, for example, that there are likely to be divergent notions of what constitutes the core right of access to health care services. This case centred on a claim that the failure by the state to provide access, outside of certain designated test sites, to an antiretroviral medication (nevirapine), which had been shown to substantially decrease the risk of mother-to-child transmission of HIV, was a breach of the right to access health care services protected under the South African Constitution. The Court had to consider the scope of the state's obligations regarding the core elements of the right to health, and Dixon argues:

> How that core is defined will depend on whether South Africans give priority to the right to life (that is, the need to respond to urgent and concrete threats to life); to urgent demands for palliative care and treatment for debilitating and painful disease (dignity as a baseline); to demands that count as inherently reasonable from a cost-benefit point of view, thus entailing the refusal of that which might tend to demean citizens' sense of self-worth (dignity in the Kantian sense); or to the need to respond to claims made on behalf of the poorest and most neglected South Africans from a health care point of view (equality). In a case such as *TAC*, for example, a focus on dignity in the Kantian sense might well favor treating access to nevirapine as within the minimum core right of access to health care services, whereas focusing on dignity as a baseline would reject giving priority to such access, at least over and above access to life-improving antiretrovirals for those already suffering from full-blown AIDS. Conversely, in the context of the current debates in South Africa about broader access to antiretrovirals, a focus on dignity in the baseline sense, or on rights to life and equality, might favor treating such access as within the scope of the State's minimum core obligations, whereas a focus on dignity in the Kantian sense would imply that such a right of general access was far more contingent, varying according to the costs to the State associated with the treatment's provision.
>
> It is quite possible, as an abstract theoretical matter, that there are answers to these questions that are both morally and constitutionally 'right'. However, as free and equal citizens, with extremely different life experiences and perspectives, it is also both likely and reasonable that South Africans should reach a variety of different answers to these questions.[91]

In *Mazibuko v City of Johannesburg*,[92] one of the more recent cases in South Africa's economic and social rights jurisprudence, the Constitutional Court of South Africa debated the scope and content of the right to water. In doing so, it considered the difficulties of practically applying the CESCR's concept of a definitive 'minimum core' and emphasised that the content of a particular right will vary according to circumstance and context.

89 For an overview of some of the arguments against the minimum core obligations, see A Chapman and S Russell, 'Introduction' in A Chapman and S Russell (eds), *Core Obligations: Building a Framework for Economic, Social and Cultural Rights*, Intersentia, Antwerp, 2002, 1, 8–19. Chapman and Russell, however, support the minimum core obligations approach. Also see generally: K G Young, 'The Minimum Core of Economic and Social Rights: A Concept in Search of Content' (2008) 33 *Yale Journal of International Law*, 113; A Muller, 'Limitations to and Derogations from Economic, Social and Cultural Rights' [2009] *Human Rights Law Review*, 557.

90 See above, n 76. Also see discussion in Chapter 4.5.1.

91 R Dixon, 'Creating Dialogue About Socioeconomic Rights: Strong-Form Versus Weak-Form Judicial Review Revisited' [2007] *International Journal of Constitutional Law* 391, 400.

92 *Mazibuko v City of Johannesburg* [2010] 4 SA 1 (Constitutional Court) and see Chapter 4.6.2.

The Constitutional Court of South Africa has generally rejected the concept of a 'minimum core' and has instead developed a model of 'reasonableness review' for evaluating positive socio-economic claims. As noted by Liebenberg, '[i]n reviewing the positive duties imposed by social rights provisions on the state, the central question that the Court asks is whether the means chosen are reasonably capable of facilitating the realisation of the rights in question.'[93] In *Mazibuko*, O'Regan J first summarised the earlier positions of the Constitutional Court with respect to determining a minimum core (in relation to the right to housing (*Grootboom*) and the right to health (*TAC*)) and then discussed the 'minimum core' in the context of what constitutes a sufficient supply of water to satisfy an individual's right to water.

> [53] In *Grootboom*, this Court rejected the argument that the social and economic rights in our Constitution contain a minimum core which the state is obliged to furnish, the content of which should be determined by the courts. The Court reasoned as follows:
>
> It is not possible to determine the minimum threshold for the progressive realisation of the right of access to adequate housing without first identifying the needs and opportunities for the enjoyment of such a right. These will vary according to factors such as income, unemployment, availability of land and poverty. The differences between city and rural communities will also determine the needs and opportunities for the enjoyment of this right. Variations ultimately depend on the economic and social history and circumstances of a country. All this illustrates the complexity of the task of determining a minimum core obligation for the progressive realisation of the right of access to adequate housing without having the requisite information on the needs and the opportunities for the enjoyment of this right. [para. 32]
>
> [54] In *Treatment Action Campaign No 2*, as well, this Court refused to accept that section 27 of the Constitution had a minimum core content. It reasoned:
>
> Although Yacoob J indicated that evidence in a particular case may show that there is a minimum core of a particular service that should be taken into account in determining whether measures adopted by the State are reasonable, the socioeconomic rights of the Constitution should not be construed as entitling everyone to demand that the minimum core be provided to them. *Minimum core was thus treated as possibly being relevant to reasonableness under section 26(2), and not as a self standing right conferred on everyone under section 26(1).* (My [O'Regan J] emphasis) [para 34]
>
> [56] The applicants' argument that this Court should determine a quantity of water which would constitute the content of the section 27(1)(b) right is, in effect, an argument similar to a minimum core argument though it is more extensive because it goes beyond the minimum. The applicants' argument is that the proposed amount (50 litres per person per day) is what is necessary for dignified human life; they expressly reject the notion that it is the minimum core protection required by the right. Their argument is thus that the Court should adopt a quantified standard determining the content of the right not merely its minimum content. The argument must fail for the same reasons that the minimum core argument failed in *Grootboom* and *Treatment Action Campaign No 2*.
>
> [57] Those reasons are essentially twofold. The first reason arises from the text of the Constitution and the second from an understanding of the proper role of courts in our constitutional

93 S Liebenberg, 'Needs, Rights and Transformation: Adjudicating Social Rights' (2006) 17 *Stellenbosch Law Review* 5, 22.

> democracy. As appears from the reasoning in both *Grootboom* and *Treatment Action Campaign No 2*, section 27(1) and (2) of the Constitution must be read together to delineate the scope of the positive obligation to provide access to sufficient water imposed upon the State. That obligation requires the State to take reasonable legislative and other measures progressively to achieve the right of access to sufficient water within available resources. It does not confer a right to claim "sufficient water" from the State immediately. ...
>
> [59] At the time the Constitution was adopted, millions of South Africans did not have access to the basic necessities of life, including water. The purpose of the constitutional entrenchment of social and economic rights was thus to ensure that the state continue to take reasonable legislative and other measures progressively to achieve the realisation of the rights to the basic necessities of life. It was not expected, nor could it have been, that the State would be able to furnish citizens immediately with all the basic necessities of life. Social and economic rights empower citizens to demand of the State that it acts reasonably and progressively to ensure that all enjoy the basic necessities of life. In so doing, the social and economic rights enable citizens to hold government to account for the manner in which it seeks to pursue the achievement of social and economic rights.
>
> [60] Moreover, what the right requires will vary over time and context. Fixing a quantified content might, in a rigid and counter-productive manner, prevent an analysis of context. The concept of reasonableness places context at the centre of the enquiry and permits an assessment of context to determine whether a government programme is indeed reasonable.
>
> [61] Secondly, ordinarily it is institutionally inappropriate for a court to determine precisely what the achievement of any particular social and economic right entails and what steps government should take to ensure the progressive realisation of the right. This is a matter, in the first place, for the legislature and executive, the institutions of government best placed to investigate social conditions in the light of available budgets and to determine what targets are achievable in relation to social and economic rights. Indeed, it is desirable as a matter of democratic accountability that they should do so for it is their programmes and promises that are subjected to democratic popular choice.
>
> [62] Just as *Grootboom* illustrated that what would be required of the State to achieve the right of access to adequate housing varies depending on context, this case illustrates that the obligation in relation to the right of access to sufficient water will vary depending upon circumstance ... what constitutes sufficient water depends on the manner in which water is supplied and the purposes for which it is used.

The Constitutional Court of South Africa, via cases such as *Grootboom, TAC* and now *Mazibuko*, has repeatedly expressed concerns with the concept of minimum core obligations. Liebenberg suggests that the Court has recognised three principal issues with the concept of the minimum core.[94] First, as noted in *Grootboom*, the Court has argued that it is difficult to categorically define a minimum core of any right because of the varying social needs of different groups in society. Second, as demonstrated by the *TAC* case, it is 'impossible to give everyone access to even a "core" service immediately',[95] and as such the concept of a state providing even minimum core obligations in respect of specific rights is unrealistic. Finally, as argued in *Mazibuko*, 'it is institutionally inappropriate for a court to determine

94 Ibid 22.

95 See above, n 76.

precisely what the achievement of any particular social and economic right entails'[96] and as such, the determination of the concept of a 'minimum core was incompatible with the institutional competencies and roles of the courts.'[97]

In these cases, where the Constitutional Court of South Africa was considering the state's constitutional obligations to provide access to housing, healthcare and water, it is important to note that the South African Constitution includes a 'reasonableness' qualifier. For example, section 26(1) (dealing with the right to have access to adequate housing) and section 27(1) (dealing with the right to have access to healthcare, food, water and social security) are accompanied by subsections 26(2) and 27(2) respectively, which state that '[T]he State must take reasonable legislative and other measures, within its available resources, to achieve the progressive realisation of this right.' This qualifier raises questions such as whether the immediacy of the obligation in ICESCR to 'take reasonable legislative and other measures' to achieve the 'progressive realisation' of these rights is altered, or should be. Another question the qualifier raises is whether the path taken by the Constitutional Court of South Africa, which aims to contextually (and perhaps over-pragmatically) consider the availability of resources, is a more 'reasonable' (and effective) approach to enforcing economic, social and cultural rights than the more rigid but arguably idealistic approach of the CESCR.

Opinions vary widely on the 'minimum core' versus 'reasonableness review' approach. Some argue that the minimum core approach should be adopted in part because it protects basic rights and ensures individuals 'are not exposed to the general conditions that threaten their survival',[98] while others argue that the minimum core represents an 'intrusive rule-based approach' that will lead to a lack of collaboration between government, the executive and the courts.[99] Some, such as Liebenberg, have taken a more nuanced approach and argue in favour of 'reconceiving' rather than abandoning the reasonableness review to ensure a more substantive engagement with the scope, content and underlying values of socio-economic rights: 'such an approach should aim at preserving the openness and sensitivity to context of reasonableness review ...'.[100]

---

96 See above, n 92, [61] (Constitutional Court). Refer to discussion below of Mazibuko.

97 S Liebenberg, see above, n 94.

98 David Blichitz, *Poverty and Fundamental Rights: The Justification and Enforcement of Socio-Economic Rights*, Oxford University Press, Oxford, 2007) 187. Also see the International Commission of Jurists, *Courts and the Legal Enforcement of Economic, Social and Cultural Rights* (2008) 23–5, which discusses examples of some jurisdictions that have embraced the approach of the CESCR. Also see Alicia Ely Yamin and Oscar Parra-Vera, 'How Do Courts Set Health Policy? The Case of the Colombian Constitutional Court' (2009) 6(2) *PLoS Medicine* <http://www.plosmedicine.org/article/info%3Adoi%2F10.1371%2Fjournal.pmed.1000032#pmed-1000032-b001>, which discusses the 2008 decision by the Constitutional Court of Colombia that ordered a restructuring of the Colombian health system, and reaffirmed its jurisprudence on the establishment of an essential minimum core of the right to health and state obligations in respect of that right. See Judgement T-760/2008 (Second Review Chamber of the Colombian Constitutional Court, 31 July 2008).

99 C Steinberg, 'Can Reasonableness Protect the Poor? A Review of South Africa's Socio-Economic Rights Jurisprudence' (2006) 123 *South African Law Journal*, 264, 274.

100 S Liebenberg, *Socio Economic Rights: Adjudication under a Transformative Constitution*, Juta, Claremont, 2010, 173–86.

4.3.6 Limitations to and Derogations from the ICESCR

As discussed in Chapter 3.3, there are a number of ways in which human rights can be limited, and in relation to economic, social and cultural rights in particular, there are a number of factors such as armed conflicts and natural disasters, as well as economic difficulties, that can affect a state's ability to comply with its obligations under the ICESCR. In such circumstances, the question is whether and to what extent state parties have the ability under the ICESCR to limit or derogate rights.

Limitations

The nature of economic, social and cultural rights means that limitations that might be relevant to civil and political rights (such as restricting rights for reasons of public order or public morals) are not applicable to economic, social and cultural rights.[101] The ICESCR contains a general limitations clause in article 4. By way of contrast, the ICCPR, does not contain a general limitation but attaches specific limitations to particular articles.[102] Article 4 of the ICESCR provides that:

> The States Parties to the present Covenant recognize that, in the enjoyment of those rights provided by the State in conformity with the present Covenant, the State may subject such rights only to such limitations as are determined by law only in so far as this may be compatible with the nature of these rights and solely for the purpose of promoting the general welfare in a democratic society.

As Muller notes, the broad rationale for permitting limitations of human rights is to reinforce the notion that human rights are not absolute or unconditional, and that there is a need to balance the enjoyment of rights by the individual with the legitimate interests of the community.[103] The flexibility provided to states via this general limitations clause is restricted in that there is only one legitimate purpose for which limitations may be imposed, that is, for the purpose of promoting general welfare in a democratic society.

While the CESCR has not commented directly on the meaning of 'general welfare', Alston and Quinn argue that it should be interpreted restrictively, with the burden of proof resting on the state; they suggest that broad concepts such as 'national security' or 'economic development' are unlikely to be sufficient to justify limitations.[104] Similarly, without a definition in the Covenant there are multiple interpretations of the meaning of a 'democratic society', although, a reasonable approach might be to look for evidence of a transparent and participative decision-making process involved

101 See generally A Muller, above, n 89.

102 *International Covenant on Civil and Political Rights* (ICCPR), opened for signature 12 December 1966, 999 UNTS 171 (entered into force 23 March 1976) art 5; see Chapter 3.3.3.

103 A Muller, see above, n 89, 559.

104 P Alston & G Quinn, see above, n 65, 202.

in the decision to limit rights.[105] Limitations under article 4 must also be 'determined by law'; this is generally interpreted as requiring a definition of such limitations through a form of national law (including common law, statutes and delegated legislation) and that such restrictions must be accessible and foreseeable.

While there may appear to be some inevitable practical overlap between article 4 and article 2(1) (the notion of progressive realisation to the maximum of available resources), based on the *travaux préparatoires*, article 4 should not apply to restrictions a state may impose for reasons of lack of resources. Alston and Quinn refer to this distinction as being between 'formal limitations on rights on the one hand and the "general level of attainment" of those rights on the other', saying that a 'resource-motivated reduction in the level of enjoyment/attainment of a particular right would not constitute a limitation under Article 4'.[106]

Article 8, which deals with trade union rights, is the only substantive provision in the ICESCR, which contains a specific detailed limitations clause.[107] Article 8(1)(a) provides that with respect to the formation of and participating in trade unions, 'No restrictions may be placed on the exercise of this right other than those prescribed by law and which are necessary in a democratic society in the interests of national security or public order or for the protection of the rights and freedoms of others'. Similarly, article 8(1)(c) stipulates the 'right of trade unions to function freely subject to no limitations other than those prescribed by law and which are necessary in a democratic society in the interests of national security or public order or for the protection of the rights and freedoms of others'.

Derogations

Unlike the ICCPR,[108] the ICESCR does not contain a clause allowing or prohibiting derogations in a state of emergency.[109] There is debate over what to make of this omission.

In General Comment 3, the CESCR confirmed that states parties have a core obligation to ensure the satisfaction of minimum essential levels of each of the rights set out in the Covenant, including at least the provision of essential foodstuffs, of essential primary health care, of basic shelter and

105 A Muller, see above, n 89.

106 P Alston & G Quinn, see above, n 65, 205.

107 Article 13(4) dealing with the right to education contains a minor limitation, provides that:

> No part of this article shall be construed so as to interfere with the liberty of individuals and bodies to establish and direct educational institutions, subject always to the observance of the principles set forth in paragraph I of this article and to the requirement that the education given in such institutions shall conform to such minimum standards as may be laid down by the State.

108 ICCPR, see above, n 102, art 4. See Chapter 3.3.3.

109 *European Social Charter (revised)*, opened for signature 3 May 1996, (entered into force 1 July 1999) CETS No: 163; which deals with rights comparable to the ICESCR does contain a derogation clause (Part V, art F) however the *African [Banjul] Charter on Human and Peoples' Rights*, opened for signature 27 June 1981, 1520 UNTS 217 (entered into force 21 October 1986) does not. The *Additional Protocol to the American Convention on Human Rights in the Area of Economic, Social and Cultural Rights*, 'Protocol of San Salvador,' OAS Treaty Series No 69 (1988), entered into force November 16, 1999 does not specifically refer to derogations but allows for restrictions and limitations on rights.

housing and of the most basic forms of education.[110] In subsequent general comments and statements, the CESCR has affirmed that these core obligations arising under the Covenant are non-derogable.

> General Comment 14 (right to health): It should be stressed, however, that a State party cannot, under any circumstances, whatsoever, justify its non-compliance with the core obligations set out...which are non-derogable. (para 47)
>
> General Comment 15 (right to water): A State party cannot justify its non-compliance with the core obligations set out ... which are non-derogable. (para 40)
>
> Statement adopted by CESCR on poverty: First, because core obligations are non-derogable, they continue to exist in situations of conflict, emergency and natural disaster. (para 18)[111]

The absence of a specific derogation clause from a treaty is not itself determinative of whether derogations are permitted or prohibited,[112] and the absence of a specific derogations clause may mean either that derogations are not permitted at all, or that they are permissible only for non-core obligations (since they are not explicitly prohibited). State and international bodies have taken different views on whether the absence of a derogations clause from a treaty thus prohibits the derogation of rights. The ILO has acknowledged that the absence of a specific derogations provision from a convention is not determinative of whether derogation is justifiable and permitted,[113] while more recently the African Commission on Human and Peoples' Rights has held that the absence of a derogation clause from the *African Charter on Human and Peoples' Rights* means that derogations are not permitted.[114]

The *travaux préparatoires* do not reveal any specific discussion on the omission of a derogations clause, and Alston and Quinn speculate that its absence may be due to a number of factors, including:

> (1) the nature of the rights contained in the Covenant and the fact that the case for derogation in times of emergency from, for example, the rights to food or to health care would seem inherently less compelling than the case for derogation from the right of peaceful assembly or the right to vote; (2) the existence of a general limitations clause in the Covenant unlike the approach adopted in the Covenant on Civil and Political Rights; and (3) the more flexible and accommodating nature of the basic obligation contained in Article 2(1) of the Covenant.[115]

In the context of the non-core obligations in the ICESCR, it is arguable that the absence of a specific derogation clause does not rule out the possibility of derogation, but the nature of the rights and the flexibility and broadness of the limitations clause in article 4 means that any such derogation is

---

110 CESCR, *General Comment No 3*, see above, n 86, para 10.

111 CESCR, *Substantive Issues Arising in the Implementation of the International Covenant on Economic, Social and Cultural Rights: Poverty and the International Covenant on Economic, Social and Cultural Rights*, UN ESCOR, 25th sess, Agenda Item 5, UN Doc E/C.12/2001/10 (10 May 2001).

112 M Ssenyonjo, see above, n 63, 40.

113 ILO Explanatory Note, 'The International Labour Code 1951', Geneva, 1952, xcvi–xcvii.

114 See A Muller, above, n 89, 596 n 182 citing *Commission Nationale des Droits de l'Homme et des Libertes v Chad*, Communication 74/92 (2000) AHRLR 66 (ACHPR 1995).

115 P Alston & G Quinn, see above, n 65, 217.

unlikely and, if sought, should be justified according to similar criteria to that set out in article 4 of the ICCPR.

SNAPSHOT: SLOVENIA

Muller notes that 'many states seem to assume the derogability of the right to strike or other rights related to labour issues set out in articles 6, 7 and 8 of the ICESCR. The state report from Slovenia, for example, explains a procedure under Slovenian law by which workers may be required to perform compulsory labour during emergencies when this is necessary to deal with the consequences of a severe natural or other disaster, or to guarantee the effective defence of the country when it faces a direct military threat.[116]

CESCR, *INITIAL REPORT, SLOVENIA*,[117]

100 The *Employment Act* (Ur I RS, 42/2002) provides that employers must provide for employees the work on which the two sides have agreed in an employment contract. In the event of a natural or other disaster, or where such disaster is imminent, workers are bound to perform work beyond the full or agreed part-time hours at their place of work, or other work in connection with the elimination or prevention of the consequences of a disaster. Such work may only last for as long as it is essential to save human life, protect people's health or prevent material damage.

100 The [Slovenian] Constitution provides that human rights and fundamental freedoms may be temporarily suspended or restricted in a state of war or emergency (art 16) ...

104 ... In the chapter on the duties and rights of citizens in the defence of the country, the [Slovenian Defence] Act lays down the working duties that citizens have to fulfil by performing work essential for the supply of the Slovene armed forces and population, the functioning of State bodies, local self-government bodies and other defence needs ...

4.4 *OPTIONAL PROTOCOL*

The *Optional Protocol* to ICESCR[118] allows for an individual to lodge communications with the CESCR, complaining of a state's violation of the ICESCR. It was unanimously adopted by the UN General Assembly in December 2008.[119] The terms of the *Optional Protocol* require 10 ratifications or accessions before it comes into force.[120] As at the time of writing only three states (Ecuador, Mongolia and Spain) had ratified it.

116 A Muller, see above, n 89, 568.

117 26 May 2006, E/1990/5/ADD.62 at [100–4].

118 See *Report of the Human Rights Council: Report of the Third Committee*, UN GAOR, 63rd sess, Agenda Item 53, UN Doc A/63/435 (28 November 2008), 3, where the Committee recommended to the General Assembly adoption of the *Optional Protocol to the International Covenant on Economic, Social and Cultural Rights*.

119 *Optional Protocol to the International Covenant on Economic, Social and Cultural Rights*, GA Res 63/117, UN GAOR, 63rd sess, Agenda Item 58, UN Doc A/RES/63/117 (5 March 2009).

120 Ibid art 18(1).

The development of an *Optional Protocol* to the ICESCR has been a slow process.[121] The ICCPR has been coupled with an *Optional Protocol* that allows such communications since 1966, and other significant human rights treaties such as the *Convention against Torture and Other Cruel, Inhuman or Degrading Treatment or Punishment*, the *International Convention on the Elimination of All Forms of Racial Discrimination* and the *Convention on the Elimination of All Forms of Discrimination against Women* each allow, in different ways, the aiming of individual communications.[122] Formal discussions focused on the creation of an *Optional Protocol* to the ICESCR were initiated in 1990 by the CESCR.[123] Draft text was eventually forwarded to the UN Human Rights Council for consideration in April 2008, and was approved by the Council in June of the same year.[124] The UN General Assembly adopted the text on 10 December 2008, the 60th Anniversary of the Universal Declaration of Human Rights.

There have been several reasons for the initial (and continuing) state reluctance to pursue the drafting and ratification of the *Optional Protocol*. The two most frequent arguments are that economic, social and cultural rights are not justiciable and that they are not susceptible to individual case-based complaints because they are too vague. These issues are discussed in Chapter 1.4.3. Ultimately, as Simmons notes, the *Optional Protocol* is 'a way to help interpret the law through the lives and experiences of living individuals'.[125]

4.4.1 Jurisdictional Limits Imposed on Complainants

Article 2 of the *Optional Protocol* limits its scope to the jurisdictional reach of the state party. While the ICCPR (in article 2(1)) states the scope of that treaty is limited to the territory and jurisdiction of the state party, the ICESCR does not contain any such express limitations. It is interesting then to note that article 2 of the *Optional Protocol* states that '[c]ommunications may be submitted by or on behalf of individuals or groups of individuals, under the jurisdiction of a State Party, claiming to be victims of a violation of any of the economic, social and cultural rights set forth in the Covenant by that State Party.' As noted by Courtis and Sepúlveda:

> With respect to ICESCR obligations, the argument that a State party has jurisdiction beyond its territory has been implicitly developed in the jurisprudence of the CESCR. The Committee has consistently maintained that jurisdiction includes any territory over which a State party has geographical, functional or personal jurisdiction, including dependent territories and territories where a State has de facto control. Moreover, the Committee has

121 M Langford & B Thiele, 'Introduction: The Road to a Remedy' in J Squires, M Langford & B Thiee (eds), *The Road to a Remedy: Current Issues in the Litigation of Economic, Social and Cultural Rights*, UNSW Press, Sydney, 2005, 1.

122 See the further discussion in Chapter 7.3.

123 A Vandenbogaerde & W Vandenhole, 'The Optional Protocol to the International Covenant on Economic, Social and Cultural Rights: An Ex Ante Assessment of its Effectiveness in Light of the Drafting Process' (2010) 10(2) *Human Rights Law Review*, 207, 208.

124 *Optional Protocol to the International Covenant on Economic, Social and Cultural Rights*, Human Rights Council Res 8/2, UN GAOR, 8th sess, Agenda Item 3, UN Doc A/HRC/8/L.2/Rev.1(12 June 2008).

125 B A Simmons, 'Should States Ratify?—Process and Consequences of the *Optional Protocol to the ICESCR*' [2009] *Nordic Journal of Human Rights* 64, 69.

suggested that a State party may have jurisdiction over nationals of a State party residing in another territory when the negative fulfilment of a Convention obligation results in violations with the State party's territory.

However, the extent of the extra-territorial jurisdiction of States regarding ESC rights is far from having a solid grounding under international law. In the absence of a specific act by a State to recognise jurisdiction on subjects operating or deeds occurring beyond its borders—when for example, a statute allows its courts to consider cases for violations committed outside its territory—there is no generally accepted presumption in favour of State jurisdiction beyond its own territory. Consequently, under the Optional Protocol petitioners will bear the burden of proof in establishing a violation occurring outside a State's territory occurs *de jure* within the State's jurisdiction.[126]

4.5 TRANSFORMING RIGHTS INTO REALITY: DOMESTIC ADJUDICATION OF ECONOMIC, SOCIAL AND CULTURAL RIGHTS

As discussed in Chapter 1.4.3, a consistent observation made of economic, social and cultural rights is that they are not (easily) justiciable. The following overview of South African and Indian jurisprudence shows that courts can effectively and responsibly assess and give effect to such rights. The recognition and enforcement of economic, social and cultural rights remains more difficult in countries where, unlike South Africa, the rights are not enshrined in their constitution or laws or where international law is not automatically incorporated in the domestic law. In India for example, a different approach has been adopted and civil and political rights have been shown to possess socio-economic dimensions, thus extending the 'traditional' rights into the socio-economic arena. But there are many countries, such as Australia, where economic, social and cultural rights are still regarded differently from civil and political rights: if not inferior to them then, at least, not justiciable in the same way.[127]

4.5.1 South Africa

The *Constitution of the Republic of South Africa* was adopted in 1996 and since that time much attention has been paid to the emerging jurisprudence dealing with socio-economic rights and the tension that has 'arisen between its transformative vision and the macroeconomic policies adopted by the South African government'.[128] Liebenberg acknowledges the transformative nature of the Constitution and notes that its primary concern is 'not to restrain State power, but to facilitate a fundamental change in unjust political, economic and social relations in South Africa'.[129] In the Constitutional Court decision of *S v Makwanyane* (1995)[130] Chaskalson P noted that:

126 C Courtis & M Sepulveda, 'Are Extra-Territorial Oblgiations Reviewable under the Optional Protocol to the ICESCR?' [2009] *Nordic Journal of Human Rights* 54, 58.

127 See discussion at Chapter 10.3.3.

128 D M Davis, 'Socioeconomic Rights: Do They Deliver the Goods?' [2008] *International Journal of Constitutional Law* 687, 697.

129 S Liebenberg, see above, n 93, 6, and above, n 100, 44–51.

130 *The State v T Makwanyane and M Mchunu* [1995] 3 SA 391, [7] (Constitutional Court).

> [7] The Constitution
> ... provides a historic bridge between the past of a deeply divided society characterised by strife, conflict, untold suffering and injustice, and a future founded on the recognition of human rights, democracy and peaceful co-existence and development opportunities for all South Africans, irrespective of colour, race, class, belief or sex.

The Constitution contains a bill of rights which includes a number of economic, social and cultural rights such as: the right to fair labour practices; right to an environment that is not harmful to health or well-being; right to property; right of access to adequate housing; right of access to health care, food, water and social security; children's rights to basic nutrition, shelter, basic health care services and social services; right to education; right to take part in cultural life; and rights of prisoners to adequate accommodation, nutrition, reading material and medical treatment.

The inclusion of economic, social and cultural rights in the Constitution was a matter of intense debate during the drafting period. Advocates for the inclusion of economic, social and cultural rights, such as Albie Sachs, argued that the Constitution should provide the means of ensuring substantive equality for all South Africans and as such should establish 'a minimum floor of rights to a series of carefully defined social and economic goods'.[131] As succinctly stated by Nelson Mandela:

> a simple vote, without food, shelter and health care is to use first generation rights as a smokescreen to obscure the deep underlying forces which dehumanise people. It is to create an appearance of equality and justice, while by implication socio-economic inequality is entrenched. We do not want freedom without bread, nor do we want bread without freedom. We must provide for all the fundamental rights and freedoms associated with a democratic society.[132]

Liebenberg aptly summarises various aspects of this debate in the following extract.

S LIEBENBERG 'NEEDS, RIGHTS AND TRANSFORMATION: ADJUDICATING SOCIAL RIGHTS'[133]

> The inclusion of a range of socio-economic rights as justiciable rights in the 1996 Constitution can be seen as a successful struggle by various political actors and civil society organisations to establish the meeting of these needs as objects of constitutionally mandated State responsibility. By placing a constitutional obligation on the State to ensure that everyone has 'access to' a variety of socio-economic rights, the meeting of the needs in question are clearly recognised as a public matter, and not simply to be relegated to the 'private' domestic or market sphere.
>
> The very distinction between 'justiciable' civil and political rights versus non-justiciable socio-economic rights is in itself deeply political. It privileges negative liberty and the existing economic *status quo*, and obscures the costs and policy dimensions of civil and political rights. In constitutional democracies where adjudication is an important component of a country's fundamental governance structures, the exclusion

131 D M Davis, see above, n 128, 688.

132 N Mandela, 'Address: On the Occasion of the ANC's Bill of Rights Conference' in *A Bill of Rights for a Democratic South Africa: Papers and Report of a Conference Convened by the ANC's Constitutional Committee*, May 1991 (Centre for Development Studies, UWC, 1991) 9, 12.

133 (2006) 17 *Stellenbosch Review* 5 at 16–17.

or weak enforcement of socio-economic rights can have the effect of marginalising the interests of the poor and masking the socio-economic barriers to more egalitarian social relations. By contrast, the inclusion of social rights transforms the issue of unmet needs into a question of entitlement.

The constitutional status of these rights clearly does not avoid ongoing contestation and the emergence of 'reprivatization' discourses aimed at re-establishing the needs in question as matters for the family or the market to deal with. In the current era of neo-liberalism, social assistance and social insurance programmes in many countries are being privatised or cut back. This presents a new set of challenges for asserting the State's role in the public provision of social benefits to mitigate current inequalities in resources. The constitutional recognition of justiciable social rights provides oppositional social movements with a potentially powerful tool to assert the State responsibility for meeting basic needs.

In the years since the adoption of the Constitution, the Constitutional Court has delivered a number of landmark judgements dealing with economic, social and cultural rights but particularly relating to the rights to housing, health care and water and the interplay of these with children's rights.[134]

In a number of landmark judgments delivered since 2000, the Constitutional Court of South Africa has tussled with the obligations set out in the Constitution regarding the enjoyment of economic, social and cultural rights and the reality of the limited resources available to ensure such rights.

As noted above to illustrate the idea of core minimum standards, in *Soobramoney v Minister of Health*[135] and *Minister of Health v Treatment Action Campaign* ('TAC')[136] the Constitutional Court grappled with the question (among others) of whether there was an unrestricted right to minimum core medical services. In *Soobramoney* the Court accepted that rationing of resources is integral to health service delivery in the public sector, even if this might support ongoing disparities between the private and public sector. However, given the 'reasonableness' requirement (in s 27(2) of the Constitution)[137] the Court implied that there could be room to contest executive policies if such policies were unreasonable or if they were not applied fairly and reasonably, and it was this latter point that came to the forefront in the subsequent case of TAC.

In TAC, with South Africa in the midst of an HIV/AIDS epidemic, the Treatment Action Campaign (TAC) and a number of other NGOs initiated a constitutional challenge to restrictions on the provision of anti-retroviral drugs to HIV-positive pregnant women. The South African government, as part of its response to the pandemic, devised a program to deal with mother-to-child transmission of HIV at

134 For the judgments of the Constitutional Court: <http://www.constitutionalcourt.org.za/site/thecourt/history.htm#cases>.

135 See above, n 82.

136 See above, n 76.

137 *Constitution of the Republic of South Africa*, 1996 (No. 108 of 1996). Section 27 (Health care, food, water and social security):
1 Everyone has the right to have access to: a health care services, including reproductive health care; b sufficient food and water; and c social security, including, if they are unable to support themselves and their dependants, appropriate social assistance.
2 The state must take reasonable legislative and other measures, within its available resources, to achieve the progressive realisation of each of these rights.
3 No one may be refused emergency medical treatment.

birth via the limited provision of Nevirapine. The drug was offered to the government for free for five years, but the government announced it would introduce the mother-to-child-transmission program only in certain pilot sites and would delay setting these up for a year, thereby denying most mothers access to treatment. The Constitutional Court held that the restriction of Nevirapine to pilot sites excluded those who could reasonably be included in the program. The Court ordered the Government to extend availability of Nevirapine to hospitals and clinics, to provide counsellors and to take reasonable measures to extend the testing and counselling facilities throughout the public health sector.[138]

Similarly, in decisions dealing with the right to have access to housing, the Court has assessed the right by asking whether the means chosen by the state are reasonably capable of facilitating the realisation of the rights in question. The first major case before the Court dealing with the right to have access to adequate housing was *Government of the Republic of South Africa and Others v Grootboom and Others ('Grootboom')*.[139] *Grootboom* was only the second social rights case the Court dealt with (following *Soobramoney*). In *Grootboom*, the Court laid the foundation for the justiciability of the obligation to progressively realise economic, social and cultural rights, and set out the basis of the 'reasonableness' test. The ruling modified the approach adopted in the earlier *Soobramoney* case, and *Grootboom* is now probably one of the most cited economic, social and cultural rights cases.

Grootboom raised the issue of the state's obligations under s 26[140] and s 28(1)(c)[141] of the *South African Constitution*, to provide housing generally and for children in particular. Mrs Grootboom was one of a group of 390 adults and 510 children living in an informal settlement in Wallacedene. When evicted from this settlement, the group then illegally occupied nearby land earmarked for low-cost housing but were forcibly evicted and in the process their shacks and possessions were destroyed. Faced with few options, they then set up camp on a sports field and adjacent community hall that lacked basic sanitation or electricity. The Constitutional Court found no violation by the state of s 28 but did find a violation of the right to adequate housing in s 26. In a unanimous decision, written by Justice Yacoob, it was noted that 'this case shows the desperation of hundreds of thousands of people living in deplorable conditions throughout the country. The Constitution obliges the state to act positively to ameliorate these conditions. The obligation is to provide access to housing, health-care, sufficient food and water, and social security to those unable to support themselves and their dependants.'[142]

138 See generally L Forman, 'Ensuring Reasonable Health: Health Rights, the Judiciary and South African HIV/AIDS Policy' [2005] *Journal of Law, Medicine and Ethics*, 711.

139 *Government of the Republic of South Africa v Grootboom* [2001] 1 SA 46 (Constitutional Court).

140 *Constitution of the Republic of South Africa*, 1996 (No. 108 of 1996). Section 26 (Housing):
1 Everyone has the right to have access to adequate housing.
2 The state must take reasonable legislative and other measures, within its available resources, to achieve the progressive realisation of this right.
3 No one may be evicted from their home, or have their home demolished, without an order of court made after considering all the relevant circumstances. No legislation may permit arbitrary evictions...

141 Ibid Section 28. Children.—(1) Every child has the right—(c) to basic nutrition, shelter, basic health care services and social services ...

142 See above, n 139, [93] (Constitutional Court).

While acknowledging that neither s 26 nor s 28(1)(c) provides anyone with a right to claim shelter immediately, the Court held that the state must give effect to these rights and, in appropriate circumstances, the courts can and must enforce these obligations.[143] The question is always whether the measures taken by the state to realise the rights afforded by s 26 are reasonable. In determining whether a set of measures or a program is reasonable, the Court noted the following:

> [43] ... A programme that excludes a significant segment of society cannot be said to be reasonable. Conditions do not remain static and therefore the programme will require continuous review.
>
> [44] Reasonableness must also be understood in the context of the Bill of Rights as a whole. The right of access to adequate housing is entrenched because we value human beings and want to ensure that they are afforded their basic human needs. A society must seek to ensure that the basic necessities of life are provided to all if it is to be a society based on human dignity, freedom and equality. To be reasonable, measures cannot leave out of account the degree and extent of the denial of the right they endeavour to realise. Those whose needs are the most urgent and whose ability to enjoy all rights therefore is most in peril, must not be ignored by the measures aimed at achieving realisation of the right. It may not be sufficient to meet the test of reasonableness to show that the measures are capable of achieving a statistical advance in the realisation of the right. Furthermore, the Constitution requires that everyone must be treated with care and concern. If the measures, though statistically successful, fail to respond to the needs of those most desperate, they may not pass the test.

The Constitutional Court issued a declaratory order that required the state to devise and implement a program that included measures to provide relief for those people who had not been catered for in the state, but declined to play any role in supervising or overseeing the implementation of the order. As a result, while the decision of the Constitutional Court in *Grootboom* has been hailed as a great victory for the homeless and landless people of South Africa, the actual impact of the judgment on the housing situation of the litigants—and others who find themselves in a similar situation—has been less significant.[144] The decision though did have an immediate impact on housing policy in South Africa, as many municipalities put in place a 'Grootboom allocation' in their budgets to address those in desperate need.

In a subsequent case dealing with housing rights and forced evictions,[145] the Constitutional Court clarified the obligations of the state when dealing with evictions, holding that before the government evicts residents from their homes, it has the duty to engage meaningfully with them about possible steps that can be taken to alleviate their homelessness. That is, meaningful participation, or engagement, with rights holders is constitutionally required.

The economic, social and cultural rights cases brought in South Africa since the adoption of the Constitution in 1996 have been ground breaking and not without controversy. With justiciability for economic, social and cultural rights built into the Constitution, the emphasis shifted from whether such rights can be enforced to how enforcement is best achieved, and the role of the courts

143 See above, n 139, [94]–[95] (Constitutional Court).

144 See K Pillay, 'Implementing Grootboom' (2002) 3(1) *ESR Review: Economic and Social Rights in South Africa*, 13.

145 *Occupiers of 51 Olivia Road, Berea Township and 197 Main Street, Johannesburg v City of Johannesburg* [2008] 3 SA 208 (Constitutional Court).

in achieving it. The 2009 decision of the Constitutional Court in *Mazibuko v City of Johannesburg ('Mazibuko')*[146] (discussed in detail in Chapter 4.6), in which the Court dismissed the challenge to the sufficiency of free water provided by the city, arguably marks a continuing retreat from the earlier 'transformative' approach of the Court to enforcing socio-economic rights taken in *Grootboom*. *Mazibuko*, and indeed many of the other South African landmark judgments on socio-economic rights, highlight the advantages and disadvantages of relying on public-interest litigation to advance these rights. In criticising the decision in *Mazibuko* and highlighting some of the challenges that lie ahead for South Africa, Liebenberg notes that:

> litigation is an expensive, time consuming and draining process...The resources and energy that are expended on litigation can frequently produce more sustainable benefits when invested in building strong community organisations and development projects ...
>
> The deferential and normatively thin concept of reasonableness review applied in the *Mazibuko* case weakens the capacity of socio-economic rights jurisprudence to contribute meaningfully to transformative social change ...
>
> The Court's early jurisprudence on socio-economic rights has the potential to evolve into a rich, substantive set of normative criteria for guiding fundamental social and economic reforms in South Africa ...
>
> Revisiting and developing the early potential of the Court's approach to socio-economic rights is a major challenge for the constitutional adjudication of claims to decent social and economic services and benefits over the next decade.[147]

4.5.2 India

The acceptance of the justiciability of economic, social and cultural rights in India is due in large part to the pioneering efforts of the Supreme Court of India and the corresponding rise of public-interest litigation. Without the broad and explicit constitutional guarantees of economic, social and cultural rights like those established in South Africa's Constitution, the Supreme Court of India has adopted an innovative approach to read socio-economic dimensions into civil and political rights (in particular, the right to life, which is guaranteed under article 21 of the Constitution of India). In 2000, the Committee on the Convention on the Elimination of All Forms of Racial Discrimination acknowledged the role played by the Court when it stated:

> The Committee appreciates the contribution made by the Supreme Court of India in developing the concept of social action litigation and a jurisprudence integrating the Convention into domestic law by interpreting Constitutional provisions on gender equality and non-discrimination.[148]

146 See above, n 92.

147 S Liebenberg, see above, n 100, 479–80. While recognising the prominent role the Constitutional Court of South Africa has played in progressing ESCR, there is reason to be critical of the relief granted in the Constitutional Court's socio-economic jurisprudence where litigants in cases such as *Grootboom* and the *Treatment Action Campaign* case have not received the shelter or drugs awarded in the judgments. See M Swart, 'Left Out in the Cold? Crafting Constitutional Remedies for the Poorest of the Poor' (2005) 21(2) *South African Journal on Human Rights*, 215.

148 CERD, *Concluding Observations of the Committee on the Elimination of Discrimination Against Women: India*, 22nd sess, UN Doc A/55/38 (4 February 2000), para 46.

The *Constitution of India*[149] guarantees the judicial enforcement (by way of application to the High Court and the Supreme Court) of a category of rights referred to as 'fundamental rights'. These rights (contained in Part III of the *Constitution*, articles 14–35) include classic civil and political rights such, as the right to equality, the prohibition against discrimination, the right to life, protections against trafficking and forced labour, freedom of speech and religion, and the protection of minorities. In 2002 Article 21A was added to provide the right to free education for children aged 6–14 years.[150]

Part IV of the *Constitution* sets out the 'Directive Principles of State Policy' (articles 36–51) and contains mainly economic, social and cultural rights such as the right to work, education, health and the environment. Article 37 notes that Directive Principles 'shall not be enforceable by any court, but the principles therein laid down are nevertheless fundamental in the governance of the country and it shall be the duty of the State to apply these principles in making laws'.

DIRECTIVE PRINCIPLES OF STATE POLICY, *CONSTITUTION OF INDIA* (PART IV)

39 The State shall, in particular, direct its policy towards securing—

(*d*) that there is equal pay for equal work for both men and women;

(*e*) that the health and strength of workers, men and women, and the tender age of children are not abused and that citizens are not forced by economic necessity to enter avocations unsuited to their age or strength; not denied to any citizen by reason of economic or other disabilities.

41 The State shall, within the limits of its economic capacity and development, make effective provision for securing the right to work, to education and to public assistance in cases of unemployment, old age, sickness and disablement, and in other cases of undeserved want.

42 The State shall make provision for securing just and humane conditions of work and for maternity relief.

43 The State shall endeavour to secure, by suitable legislation or economic organisation or in any other way, to all workers, agricultural, industrial or otherwise, work, a living wage …

47 The State shall regard the raising of the level of nutrition and the standard of living of its people and the improvement of public health as among its primary duties and, in particular, the State shall endeavour to bring about prohibition of the consumption except for medicinal purposes of intoxicating drinks and of drugs which are injurious to health.

48A The State shall endeavour to protect and improve the environment and to safeguard the forests and wild life of the country.

The movement to allow greater enforceability of economic, social and cultural rights, and the role played by the Supreme Court of India, are well summarised in a 2005 report of the International Council on Human Rights Policy.[151]

149 *Constitution of India* (adopted by the Constituent Assembly 26 November 1949, entered into force 26 January 1950).

150 *Eighty-Sixth Amendment Act*, 2002 (India).

151 S Verma, 'Justiciability of Economic, Social and Cultural Rights: Relevant Case Law' (The International Council on Human Rights Policy, Review Meeting, Rights and Responsibilities of Human Rights Organisations, Geneva, 15 March 2005).

[68] In its early judgements [[*State of Madras v Champakam Dorairajan*, AIR 1951 SC 525, *In re Keral Education Bill* AIR 1958 SC 956, *Deep Chand v State of Uttar Pradesh*, AIR 1959 SC 648, *UPSE Board v Hari*, AIR 1979 SC 65] the Supreme Court held that where there is a conflict between Fundamental Rights and Directive Principles of State Policy (DPSP), fundamental rights stand supreme and that the directive principles are not enforceable in the court of law and hence their alleged breaches does not invalidate any law. The Court also held that such breaches do not entitle a citizen to complain of violation of DPSPs by the State so as to seek relief against the State. However in a series of later judgements [*State of Kerala v NM Thomas*, AIR 1976 SC 496, *Manchegowda v State of Karnataka* AIR 1984 SC 1151, *Lingappa v State of Maharshtra* AIR 1985 SC 389, *Laxmi Kant v Union of India*, AIR 1987 SC 232 the Supreme Court (SC) held that the Directive Principles supplement Fundamental Rights in achieving a Welfare State and that parliament could amend Fundamental Rights for implementing the Directives as long as the amendment does not touch the basic feature of the Constitution. The SC also held that legislations enacted to implement the DPSPs should be upheld as far as possible. It was also said that 'in building up a just social order it is sometimes imperative that the fundamental rights should be subordinated to the directive principles' [*State of Kerala v N.M. Thomas* (1976) 2SCC 310 at 367]. Implicit here is the pioneering role played by the SC in recognising the justiciability of ESCRs at par with civil and political rights.

[69] The SC has invoked Article 21 (the right to life) with reference to ESC Rights. The expanded notion of the right to life enabled the courts, in its PIL jurisdiction, to overcome objections on grounds of justiciability to its adjudicating the enforceability of ESCRs. In reading several of the related rights of dignity, living conditions, health into the ambit of the right to life, the court has overcome the difficulty of the justiciability of these as economic and social rights, which in their manifestation as DPSP, considered non enforceable.

Article 21 of the *Constitution of India*, 1950 provides that, 'No person shall be deprived of his life or personal liberty except according to procedure established by law.' The Supreme Court of India has in more recent decades adopted a liberal interpretation of article 21 to cement the notion that the right to life must be read in conjunction with a right to live with human dignity and free from exploitation; the article was applied broadly to allow the enforceability of traditional economic, social and cultural rights such as the right to housing, education and health, among others. This attitude was evident in *Francis Coralie Mullin v Administrator*[152] where Justice Bhagwati (delivering the judgment of the Supreme Court), in considering the ambit and scope of article 21, commented:

> that a Constitutional provision must be construed, not in a narrow and constricted sense but in a wide and liberal manner so as to anticipate and take account of changing conditions and purposes so that the Constitutional provision does not get atrophied or fossilized but remains flexible enough to meet the newly emerging problems and challenges, applies with greater force in relation to a fundamental right enacted by the Constitution. The fundamental right to life which is the most precious human right and which forms the arc of all other rights must therefore be interpreted in a broad and expansive spirit so as to invest it with significance and vitality which may endure for years to come and enhance the dignity of the individual and the worth of the human person.
>
> We think that the right to life includes the right to live with human dignity and all that goes along with it, namely, the bare necessaries of life such as adequate nutrition, clothing and shelter and facilities for

152 *Francis Coralie Mullin v Administrator, Union Territory of Delhi* (1981) 2 SCR 516.

> reading, writing and expressing one-self in diverse forms, freely moving about and mixing and commingling with fellow human beings. Of course, the magnitude and content of the components of this right would depend upon the extent of the economic development of the country, but it must, in any view of the matter, include the right to the basic necessities of life and also the right to carry on such functions and activities as constitute the bare minimum expression of the human-self. Every act which offends against or impairs human dignity would constitute deprivation protanto of this right to live and it would have to be in accordance with reasonable, fair and just procedure established by law which stands the test of other fundamental rights.[153]

For the Supreme Court, '(the) right to life guaranteed in any civilised society implies the right to food, water, decent environment, education, medical care and shelter',[154] and the right to life protected by article 21 also includes the right to water.[155]

This broad interpretation of article 21 was put to the test in a landmark judgment of the Supreme Court dealing with the right to housing. In *Olga Tellis v Bombay Municipal Corporation*[156] (*'Olga Tellis'*) the Supreme Court heard arguments that the eviction of pavement dwellers by the State of Maharashta and the Bombay Municipal Council would violate the pavement dwellers' right to life under the *Constitution* by depriving them of their livelihood, since a home in the city allowed them to attain a livelihood. The case was brought by 11 residents, the Peoples Union for Civil Liberties, the Committee for the Protection of Democratic Rights and two journalists, one of whom was Olga Tellis. The Supreme Court held that the right to life, in article 21 of the *Constitution*, encompassed means of livelihood since:

> 21 The sweep of the right to life conferred by Article 21 is wide and far reaching. It does not mean merely that life cannot be extinguished or taken away as, for example, by the imposition and execution of the death sentence, except according to procedure established by law. That is but one aspect of the right to life. An equally important facet of that right is the right to livelihood because, no person can live without the means of living, that is, the means of livelihood. If the right to livelihood is not treated as a part of the constitutional right to life, the easiest way of depriving a person of his right to life would be to deprive him of his means of livelihood to the point of abrogation. Such deprivation would not only denude the life of its effective content and meaningfulness but it would make life impossible to live.

However, the Supreme Court held that the right to a livelihood was not absolute, and deprivation of the right to livelihood could occur if there was a just and fair procedure undertaken according to law: the government's action must be reasonable and any person affected must be afforded an opportunity of being heard as to why that action should not be taken. The Supreme Court found that the residents had been given the opportunity to be heard by virtue of the proceedings, and found it was reasonable for the government to evict those living on public pavements, footpaths and public roads. Conditions were attached to the evictions that required them to be delayed until one month after the monsoon season.

153 Ibid 527, 529.

154 *Chameli Singh v State of Uttar Pradesh* (1996) 2 SCC 549, [8].

155 *Narmada Bachao Andolan v Union of India* (2000) 10 SCC 664.

156 *Olga Tellis v Bombay Municipal Corporation* (1985) 3 SCC 545.

Although the Court declined to hold that evicted dwellers had a right to an alternative site, it made orders that: (i) sites should be provided to residents presented with census cards in 1976; (ii) slums in existence for 20 years or more were not to be removed unless land was required for public purposes and, in that case, alternative sites must be provided; and (iii) high priority should be given to resettlement.

While *Olga Tellis* is often cited as a classic illustration of the social activism of the Indian Supreme Court in supporting the more vulnerable members of the Indian population, ironically it can also be seen as supporting the right of property holders to evict. The caveat is that such evictions cannot take place summarily.

The significant role played by the Supreme Court in blurring the often fine line between Fundamental Rights and the *Constitution*'s Directive Principles is also illustrated by a case dealing with the right to education: *Unni Krishnan, JP v State of Andhra Pradesh*.[157] The Supreme Court was asked to determine whether the 'right to life' in article 21 of the *Constitution of India* guarantees a fundamental right to education to citizens of India. In declaring that the right to education is implicit in and flows from the right to life, the Supreme Court held that the state is under a constitutional mandate to provide education, but that it is not an absolute right and must be read in conjunction with the financial constraints of a state, as stated in article 41. The Supreme Court held:

> The right to education further means that a citizen has the right to call upon the State to provide educational facilities to him within the limits of its economic capacity and development. By saying so we are not transferring Article 41 from Part IV to Part III—we are merely relying upon Article 41 to illustrate the content of the right to education flowing from Article 21.[158]

The Supreme Court employed ICESCR language for progressive realisation of the right to higher education while declaring the fundamental right to free primary education. Nine years after this decision, the government responded by inserting article 21A into the *Constitution*, providing for the fundamental right to education for children between the ages of six and fourteen.

The right to health (and a healthy environment) is protected as a Directive Principle in the *Constitution* (articles 47 and 48) but has also been read into article 21 as concomitant with the right to life. In *Consumer Education and Research Centre v Union of India*[159] the Supreme Court explicitly held that '[t]he right to health … is an integral fact of [a] meaningful right to life'. In this case, the Supreme Court held that the right to health and medical care is a fundamental right. Addressing the occupational health hazards faced by workers in the asbestos industry, the Supreme Court read article 21 in conjunction with the relevant Directive Principles to guarantee the right to health as a fundamental right.

In *Paschim Banga Khet Mazdoor Samity v State of West Bengal*[160] (*'Paschim Banga'*) the Supreme Court confirmed that article 21 imposes an obligation on the state to safeguard the right to life of every person, irrespective of constraints in financial resources. This case involved an agricultural

157 *Unni Krishnan, JP v State of Andhra Pradesh* (1993) 1 SCC 645.

158 Ibid 735.

159 *Consumer Education and Research Centre v Union of India* (1995) 3 SCC 42.

160 See above, n 85.

labourer who had sustained serious injuries after falling off a train and was refused treatment at seven successive state hospitals because the hospitals either had inadequate medical facilities or did not have a vacant bed. With regard to the constitutional obligations of the state with respect to the right to health, the Supreme Court held:

> 9 The Constitution envisages the establishment of a welfare State at the federal level as well as at the State level. In a welfare State the primary duty of the Government is to secure the welfare of the people. Providing adequate medical facilities of the people is an essential part of the obligations undertaken by the Government in a welfare State. The Government discharges this obligation by running hospitals and health centres which provide medical care to the person seeking to avail those facilities. Article 21 imposes an obligation on the State to safeguard the right to life of every person. Preservation of human life is thus of paramount importance. The Government hospitals run by the State and the Medical Officers employed therein are duty bound to extend medical assistance for preserving human life. Failure on the part of a Government hospital to provide timely medical treatment to a person in need of such treatment results in violation of his right to life guaranteed under Article 21. In the present case there was breach of the said right of Hakim Seikh guaranteed under Article 21 when he was denied treatment at the various Government hospitals which were approached even though his condition was very serious at that time and he was in need of immediate medical attention.

With regard to the tension between fulfilling the right to life and the financial constraints of the state, the Court stated:

> 16 It is no doubt true that financial resources are needed for providing these facilities. But at the same time it cannot be ignored that it is the constitutional obligation of the State to provide adequate medical services to the people. Whatever is necessary for this purpose has to be done. In the context of the constitutional obligation to provide free legal aid to a poor accused this Court has held that the State cannot avoid its constitutional obligation in that regard on account of financial constraints. (See *Khatri (II) v. State of Bihar*, (1981) 1 SCC 627 at p 631: (AIR 1981 SC 928 at p 931)). The said observations would apply with equal, if not greater, force in the matter of discharge of constitutional obligation of the State to provide medical aid to preserve human life.

In the later decision of the Constitutional Court of South Africa in *Soobramoney v Minister of Health, Paschim Banga* was distinguished both on its facts and because in the South African Constitution the right to medical treatment does not have to be inferred from the nature of the state established by the Constitution or from the right to life that it guarantees.[161] In *Paschim Banga*, the Supreme Court of India placed extensive positive obligations on the state to improve emergency health care infrastructure and services, while in *Soobramoney*, the Constitutional Court of South Africa adopted a more restrictive approach in interpreting the state's duties with respect to sudden medical emergencies.[162]

In light of these decisions from the Supreme Court of India, it appears that perhaps every social or economic right that significantly contributes to an adequate life is capable of being interpreted as contingent on the right to life. The question remains, however, whether a clear line can be drawn to

---

161 See above, n 82.

162 See the discussion comparing *Soobramoney v Minister of Health (KwaZulu-Natal)* [1998] 1 SA 765 (Constitutional Court) and *Paschim Banga* (1996) 4 SCC 37 in S Liebenberg, see above, n 100, 134–9.

now distinguish economic, social and cultural rights (cast as Directive Principles in the Constitution of India) from 'fundamental rights'? Despite the best intentions and deliberate judicial activism of the Supreme Court in ensuring the justiciability of economic, social and cultural rights, there are, as in South Africa, still problems with their enforcement, including high costs, lack of implementation, delays in court proceedings and the lack of full independence of the judiciary at the local level limiting access to the judicial system.[163]

4.6 CASE STUDY: THE RIGHT TO WATER

As noted earlier, human rights and their ensuing obligations are more complex than a simple reading of the text of the treaty provision implies. In interpreting a human right, difficult questions arise as to the specific content of the right, the obligations attached to the right and the limitations to the right, all of which may vary from one right to another. While a brief summary of the substantive economic, social and cultural rights is provided above, this case study examines the right to water stemming from article 11 of the ICESCR.

4.6.1 Is There a Human Right to Water?

Discussions about the right to water often begin with statistics. More than 1 billion people are denied the right to clean water and 2.6 billion people (or 42 per cent of the world's population) lack access to adequate sanitation.[164] The World Health Organisation estimates that every year some 1.8 million children die as a result of diarrhoea and other diseases related to unsafe water.[165] Beyond these immediate effects that the limited availability of water or access to unsafe water have on health, are the flow-on effects on other human rights: '[E]very day millions of women and young girls collect water for their families—a ritual that reinforces gender inequalities in employment and education. Meanwhile, the ill health associated with deficits in water and sanitation undermines productivity and economic growth, reinforcing the deep inequalities that characterize current patterns of globalization and trapping vulnerable households in cycles of poverty.'[166] Despite these alarming statistics, the academic debate continues as to whether an explicit right to water exists.

The UN human rights system now has a separate mechanism exclusively dedicated to issues related to the right to water and sanitation. In March 2008, the Human Rights Council adopted

163 CESCR, *Concluding Observations of the Committee on Economic, Social and Cultural Rights: India*, UN ESCOR, 40th sess, UN Doc E/C.12/IND/Co/5 (May 2008) paras 9–11. Also see, *Report of the Special Rapporteur on the Right to Food, Jean Ziegler, Addendum: Mission to India*, 20 August to 2 September 2005, UN ESCOR, 62nd sess, Provisional Agenda Item 10, UN Doc E/CN.4/2006/44/Add.2 (20 March 2006).

164 Centre on Housing Rights and Evictions, American Association for the Advancement of Science, Swiss Agency for Development and Cooperation, & United Nations Human Settlements Programme (UN-HABITAT), *Manual on the Right to Water and Sanitation*, 2007 xix.

165 United Nations Development Programme, *Human Development Report 2006, Beyond Scarcity: Power, Poverty and the Global Water Crisis*, Macmillan, New York, 2006, v ('Foreword').

166 Ibid v ('Foreword').

a resolution[167] establishing an Independent Expert on human rights obligations related to access to safe drinking water and sanitation, which affirms the human rights obligations that are attached to this right. In September 2010 the Human Rights Council also adopted, without a vote, a resolution on 'Human Rights and access to safe drinking water and sanitation' presented by Spain and Germany with more than 50 co-sponsors. Importantly, the resolution recalled UN General Assembly *Resolution 64/292* of 28 July 2010, which recognised the right to safe and clean drinking water and sanitation 'as a human right that is essential for the full enjoyment of life and all human rights'. Interestingly the US, which had abstained from the UN General Assembly resolution on the grounds that existing international law does not recognise 'a right to water and sanitation', joined the consensus on the later resolution. The United Kingdom did not join the consensus and reiterated its view that the right to water is only an element of an adequate standard of living and that there is no international recognition of a right to sanitation.

The national legislation of several countries has explicitly recognised a right to water and/or the obligation of the state to provide everyone with access to clean water. In South Africa, section 27(1)(b) of the Constitution provides that everyone has the right to have access to sufficient food and water. Other African countries too have enshrined the right to water in their constitutions.[168] The Belgian Constitution protects economic, social and cultural rights that have been interpreted by the Constitutional Court as including the right to water. In 2006, Bolivia appointed its first Minister for Water. While a right to water is not explicitly protected in the *Constitution of India* (1950), the Kerala High Court recognised the right of people to clean water as a right to life.[169] Some regions have also recognised the right to water.[170]

The international community has increasingly accepted that water is a basic need, and that inadequate management of water resources has drastic consequences for states, communities, individuals and the environment. Particularly since the 1970s, there has been a marked evolution of political commitments concerning water, starting with the UN Conference on Human Environment (Stockholm 1972), and the Water Conference in Mar del Plata (1977), through to the Millennium Development Goals adopted in 2000,[171] and the findings of the 2006 UN Human Development Report,[172]

167 *Human Rights and Access to Safe Drinking Water and Sanitation*, Human Rights Council Res 7/22, UN GAOR, 7th sess, Agenda Item 3, UN Doc A/HRC/7/L.16 (20 March 2008).

168 *Constitution of the Second Republic of the Gambia*, 1997 (Gambia) art 216(4); *Constitution of Zambia Act, 1996* (Zambia) art 112; *Constitution of the Republic of Uganda, 1995* (Uganda) art 14; *Constitution of Ethiopia, 1998* (Ethiopia) art 90(1).

169 *Attakoya Thangal v Union of India* (1990) 1 KLT 580.

170 *African [Banjul] Charter on Human and Peoples' Rights*, opened for signature 27 June 1981, 1520 UNTS 217 (entered into force 21 October 1986) art 24; European Council of Environmental Law (ECEL), 'Resolution on the Right to Water, adopted 28 April 2000' (2000) 30(5) *Environmental Policy and Law*, 265; *African Charter on the Rights and Welfare of the Child*, opened for signaure 11 July 1990, OAU Doc CAB/LEG/24.9/49 (entered into force 29 November 1999) art 14.

171 Included in the MDG targets was MDG Goal 7, which sets out a goal to halve the number of people globally without sufficient access to safe drinking water by 2015 but generally the MDGs continue to characterise the issue of water and accessibility as it has traditionally been seen—that is, as an issue of sustainable development—rather than one that relates to the fulfilment of a basic human right; on the Millennium Development Goals, see Chapter 20.2.2.

172 UN Development Programme, *Beyond Scarcity: Power, Poverty and the Global Water Crisis (Human Development Report*, 2006).

which focused on water. However, none has given rise to an instrument that sets out an express human right to water applicable to all men, women and children.[173] Instead, a right to water has been set out in a limited form by three of the core international human rights instruments: the *Convention on the Rights of the Child* (CROC), the *Convention on the Elimination of All Forms of Discrimination Against Women* (CEDAW) and the *Convention on the Rights of Persons with Disabilities* (CRPD).

While one might attempt to rely on these instruments to point to a more general right to water, this is arguably misleading. For example, article 24(2) of the CROC requires states to combat disease and malnutrition 'through the provision of ... clean drinking-water', but it applies only to children and does not extend to the provision of, for example, water required for sanitation or other domestic uses (for example, the production of household food). In contrast, article 14(2) of the CEDAW requires states to ensure rural women the right to 'enjoy adequate living conditions, particularly in relation to ... water supply'. This would appear to guarantee a right to water for all domestic and personal uses, yet applies to only rural women. Similarly, article 28(2) of the CRPD, which places an obligation on states to take measures to ensure equal access by persons with disabilities to clean water services applies only in relation to people with disabilities.

General Comment 15 on the right to water, adopted by the CESCR in 2002,[174] provides guidelines for states parties on the interpretation of the right to water under two articles of the ICESCR: article 11 (the right to an adequate standard of living) and article 12 (the right to health). The CESCR affirmed that the right to water is an implicit component of these two rights and hence gives rise to a human right to water.[175]

> 3 Article 11, paragraph 1, of the Covenant specifies a number of rights emanating from, and indispensable for, the realization of the right to an adequate standard of living 'including adequate food, clothing and housing'. The use of the word 'including; indicates that this catalogue of rights was not intended to be exhaustive. The right to water clearly falls within the category of guarantees essential for securing an adequate standard of living, particularly since it is one of the most fundamental conditions for survival. Moreover, the Committee has previously recognized that water is a human right contained in article 11, paragraph 1, (see General Comment No. 6 (1995)). The right to water is also inextricably related to the right to the highest attainable standard of health (art 12, para 1) and the rights to adequate housing and adequate food (art 11, para 1). The right should also be seen in conjunction with other rights enshrined in the International Bill of Human Rights, foremost amongst them the right to life and human dignity.

173 See generally D Shelton 'Human Rights and the Environment: What Specific Environmental Rights Have Been Recognised?' (2007) 35 *Denver Journal of International Law and Policy*, 129; J Gupta & L Ahmed 'The Human Right to Water: Moving Towards Consensus in a Fragmented World' (2010) 19(3) *Review of European Community and International Environmental Law*, [294–305].

174 CESCR, *General Comment No 15*, see above, n 57.

175 On the value of this General Comment in establishing a human right to water, see: S Tully, 'A Human Right to Access Water? A Critique of General Comment No. 15' (2005) 23(1) *Netherlands Quarterly of Human Rights*, 35; M Langford, 'Ambition that Overlaps Itself? A Response to Stephen Tully's Critique of the General Comment on the Right to Water' (2006) 24(3) *Netherlands Quarterly of Human Rights*, 433.

4.6.2 Determining the Scope and Content of the Right to Water

In General Comment 15, the CESCR sought to define the normative content of the right to water. It stated that 'the elements of the right to water must be *adequate* for human dignity, life and health [and]…. [t]he adequacy of water should not be interpreted narrowly, by mere reference to volumetric quantities and technologies. Water should be treated as a social and cultural good, and not primarily as an economic good.'[176] It went on to state that the adequacy of water required for the right to water may vary but should be assessed on the basis of availability (sufficiency of water supply for individuals); quality (which may differ between domestic and commercial usage); accessibility (available on a non-discriminatory basis to all and includes both physical and economic aspects of accessibility).[177]

Determining 'sufficiency': *Mazibuko v City of Johannesburg*

The right to water, as defined by CESCR in its 2002 General Comment 15, entitles every person, on a non-discriminatory basis, to water that is sufficient, safe, acceptable, physically accessible and affordable. In *Mazibuko v City of Johannesburg*[178] the Constitutional Court of South Africa considered for the first time the obligations imposed by the right to access sufficient water as set out in Section 27(1)(b) of the *South African Constitution*. The applicants were five residents of Phiri, Soweto, a poor urban area of Johannesburg that had developed as a black township during the period of apartheid. In May 2003, Johannesburg Water, a company wholly owned by the city, initiated 'Operation Gcin'amanzi' ('to save water') to revamp Soweto's distribution of water services. The company aimed to reduce water losses and demand, rehabilitate the water network, and improve the rate of payment. Phiri was selected in February 2004 as the first area for implementation of the project. Central to the City's plan was the abandonment of the flat rate policy of deemed consumption charges, and the installation of pre-paid meters that would provide each household with 6 kilolitres of free water per month (or 25 litres per person per day) with the requirement that any more than that be paid in advance ('the free basic water policy'). The case was brought against the City of Johannesburg, Johannesburg Water, and the national Minister for Water Affairs and Forestry. Two of the key issues argued by the applicants were whether the City's policy of supplying 6 kilolitres of water free to every household in the City was in compliance with section 27 of the *Constitution*, and whether the installation of pre-paid meters was lawful.

The Constitutional Court found that the City's Free Basic Water policy fell within the bounds of reasonableness and was therefore not in conflict with section 27 of the *Constitution*, and that the installation of pre-paid meters in Phiri was lawful. The Court held that the right of access to sufficient water does not require the state to provide upon demand every person with sufficient water. Rather it requires the state to take reasonable legislative and other measures progressively to realise the achievement of the right of access to sufficient water, within available resources. The Court described a basic water supply as the prescribed minimum amount of water necessary for the supply of a sufficient

176 CESCR, *General Comment No 15*, see above, n 57, [11].

177 CESCR, *General Comment No 15*, see above, n 57, [12].

178 See above, n 92.

quality of water to support life and personal hygiene.[179] The applicants argued that the City's policy was unreasonable because the amount of 6 kilolitres a month was insufficient for large households, and was inflexible by allocating 6 kilolitres to rich and poor households alike and allocating water per household rather than per person. The Court expressly rejected these arguments. Speaking for the majority, O'Regan J stated:

> [62] ... this case illustrates that the obligation in relation to the right of access to sufficient water will vary depending upon circumstance ... what constitutes sufficient water depends on the manner in which water is supplied and the purposes for which it is used. Water can be supplied in a variety of ways, including through reservoirs, boreholes, water trucks, neighbourhood taps and by piping it into houses. Even where the manner in which and the purpose for which it is supplied are clear—as in this case where we know that in Phiri piped water is generally provided to brick houses with water-borne sanitation—the expert evidence on the record provides numerous different answers to the question of what constitutes 'sufficient water'. Courts are ill-placed to make these assessments for both institutional and democratic reasons.

Justice O'Regan also contended that a water service is merely suspended rather than disconnected by the operation of the meters, and that consumers are not denied basic water services because their free water allocation will still be available the following month. The majority's view that there is a tangible difference between the disconnection and the suspension of water services appears to disregard the impact of the ongoing water deprivations experienced by poor households in Phiri. Such a characterisation stands in contrast to a decision in the United Kingdom in 1998,[180] where Justice Harrison found that pre-paid meters disconnected or otherwise cut off the supply of water to the premises. It is ironic that the opposite conclusion could be reached ten years later in South Africa—a country that is widely viewed as a leader in social rights jurisprudence.

Mazibuko, along with South Africa's other recent economic and social rights jurisprudence, is likely to be vigorously critiqued. One interpretation is that the Court is easing away from its 'transformative' role,[181] and in *Mazibuko* is adopting a more conservative and deferential approach to enforcing socio-economic rights rather than giving any substantive consideration of the content and scope of the right itself. Alternatively it could be argued that *Mazibuko* should be read simply in light of its own facts and not as a harbinger for the demise of economic, social and cultural rights jurisprudence in South Africa.

179 See above, n 92, [22] (Constitutional Court).

180 *R v Director General of Water Services* (1998) (Queen's Bench Division, Crown Office List).

181 For example see former CJ Arthur Chaskalson in *Soobramoney v Minister of Health* (KwaZulu-Natal) [1998] 1 SA 765, [8] (Constitutional Court):

> We live in a society in which there are great disparities in wealth. Millions of people are living in deplorable conditions and great poverty. There is a high level of unemployment, inadequate social security, and many do not have access to clean water or to adequate health services. These conditions already existed when the Constitution was adopted and a commitment to address them, and to transform our society into one in which there will be human dignity, freedom and equality, lies at the heart of our new constitutional order. For as long as these conditions continue to exist that aspiration will have a hollow ring.

See more generally above, n 93.

4.6.3 Privatising Water Services

States are not the only actors that can endanger or restrict the right to water. Pollution from factories or over-use of local water supplies can damage or restrict the quality and quantity of water used for drinking. A private individual can deny access to a river needed for washing, or a corporation may increase prices for water services to unaffordable levels.[182] International law establishes that states have a duty to protect against non-state human rights abuses within their jurisdiction,[183] and the obligation to protect requires that governments ensure that third parties, including corporations, individuals and groups under their jurisdiction do not interfere with a person's or community's water supply. Privatisation of water services is often a controversial issue, and while in some countries private sector involvement may initially have been limited to simply selling water from trucks or the supply of infrastructure, it has now extended to the full operation and management of water delivery systems. While the World Health Organization (WHO) has challenged water commoditisation from a health perspective,[184] and some might agree that privatisation is more likely to result in poor service and significant price increases without resolving the lack of access, the converse argument is that private companies might simply be better suited than states to provide water and sanitation services, particularly in developing nations.

While governments may, under international human rights law, permit private sector involvement, their responsibilities remain the same. States are obliged to ensure that water services are delivered in an equitable and non-discriminatory manner, prioritising the most vulnerable groups. When privatising water services, states are encouraged to establish a clear and efficient regulatory framework that can maintain sustainable access to safe, sufficient, physically accessible and affordable water and sanitation.[185] In 2007 the United Nations Global Compact[186] launched the CEO Water Mandate, a public-private initiative designed to help companies in the development, implementation and disclosure of water sustainability policies and practices. The CEO Water Mandate covers six areas: direct operations, supply chain and watershed management, collective action, public policy, community engagement, and transparency.

---

182 Office of the High Commissioner for Human Rights, 'Briefing Note on the Right to Water' (March 2008) United Nations Global Compact <http://www.unglobalcompact.org/docs/issues_doc/Environment/ceo_water_mandate/Right_to_Water_Briefing_Note.pdf >.

183 J Ruggie, *Report of the Special Representative of the Secretary-General on the Issue of Human Rights and Transnational Corporations and other Business Enterprises*, 'Business and Human Rights: Mapping International Standards of Responsibility and Accountability for Corporate Acts', UN Doc A/HRC/4/35 (19 February 2007).

184 See Ranier Fehr et al, 'Towards Health Impact Assessment of Drinking-Water Privatization—The Example of Waterborne Carcinogens in North Rhone-Westphalia (Germany)' (2003) 81(6) *Bulletin of the World Health Organization*, 408.

185 *Annual Report of the United Nations High Commissioner for Human Rights and Reports of the Office of the United Nations High Commissioner for Human Rights and the Secretary General: Report of the United Nations High Commissioner for Human Rights on the Scope and Content of the Relevant Human Rights Obligations Related to Equitable Access to Safe Drinking Water and Sanitation under International Human Rights Instruments*, 6th sess, Provisional Agenda Item 2, UN Doc A/HRC/6/3 (16 August 2007).

186 The United Nations Global Compact defines itself as 'a strategic policy initiative for businesses that are committed to aligning their operations and strategies with ten universally accepted principles in the areas of human rights, labour, environment and anti-corruption' see <www.unglobalcompact.org>.

The extract below dealing with the privatisation of water supplies in Bolivia illustrates the tensions that can arise when private companies take on essential public service functions and operate in a manner that prizes water as a commodity rather than a basic need.

SNAPSHOT: BOLIVIA'S WATER PRIVATISATION[187]

In 1999, the city of Cochabamba, Bolivia, awarded a newly privatised water service concession to Aguas del Tunari (a consortium of International Water, Abengoa and five Bolivian firms). The consortium faced allegations that it limited the local community's access to water through overpricing.

Bechtel Enterprises (which had a 27.5% stake in Aguas del Tunari) notes that the consortium began operating the city's water and wastewater system in 1999, taking over from the municipal water company SEMAPA, under which 'low-volume, poorer users paid more per unit than high volume, wealthier users'. According to Bechtel, the consortium succeeded in improving quality and increasing the availability of water by 30%, while instituting a new rate structure by which most price increases would fall to larger, wealthier users. To secure the concession, Aguas del Tunari agreed to repay SEMAPA's accumulated debts and finance maintenance and expansion of the water system in exchange for income generated from government approved tariffs.

Bechtel holds that much of the perceived increases in costs to end users were the result of poorly managed consumption—residents unaccustomed to ready access to water were ill prepared for the consequences of over-consumption. Bechtel notes that the municipality failed properly to communicate the cost implications of increased water consumption that often accompany improvements to the availability of water.

The Democracy Center, an NGO, has a different version of events in Cochabamba. It alleges that within weeks of taking control of the city's water system, Aguas del Tunari raised water rates by an average of over 50%. The NGO claims that by February 2000 the price of water had increased so significantly that many poorer families were priced out of the market and that this sparked civil unrest. Bechtel points out that rates were soon rolled back to pre-concession levels and argues that the civil unrest was not caused exclusively by the effects of the price increases, but was precipitated by multiple factors, 'including unrelated national groundwater legislation'.

The Democracy Center has disputed Bechtel's statements. In particular it has placed electronic copies of customers' water bills and SEMAPA computer records on its website, records which it claims demonstrate that the price increases were far higher and more damaging than was claimed by Bechtel.

In April 2001, the violence in Cochabamba and other parts of the country escalated, which led to the government dispatching the military and culminated in several deaths. Amidst the deteriorating security situation Aguas del Tunari personnel vacated their office and the government cancelled the water contract.

In November 2001, Aguas del Tunari filed a request for arbitration with the International Centre for Settlement of Investment Disputes (ICSID) (under the terms of a Netherlands–Bolivia bilateral investment treaty) for the recovery of lost assets, investments and future profits. In 2002, an

187 Extract from *Human Rights Translated: A Business Reference Guide,* Monash University Castan Centre for Human Rights Law, International Business Leaders Forum, Office of the United Nations High Commissioner for Human Rights and United Nations Global Compact Office, 2008, 120.

international petition was filed by activists with the World Bank demanding that the ICSID case be open to public scrutiny and participation.

In 2006 the ICSID case was settled. A statement from Bechtel read:

'The Government of Bolivia and the international shareholders of Aguas del Tunari declare that the concession was terminated only because of the civil unrest and the state of emergency and not because of any act done or not done by the international shareholders of Aguas del Tunari (Bechtel, Befesa, Abengoa and Edison)' and that there would be *'no compensation paid by the Government of Bolivia or Aguas del Tunari for the termination of the concession and the withdrawal of the claim [before the ICSID].'* Jim Schultz, director of the Democracy Center, conversely described the settlement as 'a huge victory for activists worldwide'.

In 2006, the Movement for Socialism (*Movimiento al Socialismo*) won the Bolivian national elections and established the country's first Water Minister, emphasising that water is a resource and a public good and not to be treated as merchandise. The issues raised in the snapshot from Bolivia resonate in other jurisdictions, and the application and scope of human rights obligations of states pursuing the privatisation of water services in relation to access to safe drinking water and sanitation are still evolving. For the first time, in a case involving water privatisation in Argentina, the International Centre for the Settlement of Investment Disputes agreed to receive amicus curiae briefs from civil society organisations, noting that the circumstances of the case raised issues of public interest as 'those systems provide basic public services to millions of people and as a result may give rise to a variety of complex public and international law questions, including human rights considerations'.[188]

4.7 CONCLUSION AND ISSUES

While economic, social and cultural rights have long been considered the poor cousin of civil and political rights, this traditional understanding of the nature of economic, social and cultural rights is being 'fundamentally challenged as a result of academic and judicial developments over the last three decades'.[189] The adoption of the *Optional Protocol* to the ICESCR is a significant step in confirming the justiciability of these rights.

Despite these advances, a number of interesting issues raised in this chapter indicate the progress on accepting economic, social and cultural rights as 'real' human rights is not universal. For example, it is apparent that not all states are ready to embrace the notion that '[a]ll human rights are universal, indivisible and interdependent and interrelated [and that] [t]he international community must treat

188 See above, n 185, para 63. And see ICSID cases No ARB/03/19 and ARB/03/17.

189 A Byrnes, 'Second-Class Rights Yet Again? Economic, Social and Cultural Rights in the Report of the National Human Rights Consultation Committee' (2010) 33 *UNSWLJ*, 193, 196.

human rights globally in a fair and equal manner, on the same footing, and with the same emphasis'[190]. The approach of the United States to economic, social and cultural rights stands in contrast to the judicial developments in South Africa and India. Other questions raised relate to the content of what might constitute the minimum core obligations of states in relation to economic, social and cultural rights, the discretion available to states in interpreting such obligations, and the content of the rights themselves, including the status of the right to water.

190 See above, n 5.

PART THREE

THE INTERNATIONAL HUMAN RIGHTS FRAMEWORK

5
THE FRAMEWORK OF THE UNITED NATIONS SYSTEM

CONTENTS

5.1 INTRODUCTION

This part focuses on UN bodies with human rights functions that are established under the *UN Charter*. A number of UN bodies with human rights functions are established not under the Charter, but under the UN human rights treaties; those are discussed detail in Chapter 7.

The *UN Charter*—the history of which is discussed in Chapter 1—establishes in article 1 that one of the four purposes of the organisation is to promote and encourage 'respect for human rights and for fundamental freedoms for all without distinction as to race, sex, language, or religion'. While references to human rights are scattered throughout the *UN Charter*,[1] the importance attached to securing human rights has long been viewed as secondary to the primary purpose of the UN, that of maintaining international peace and security. Over time, however, the protection of human rights has come to be recognised as a core function of the organisation and its responsibility for human rights is now focused in a few key bodies.

Article 7 of the *UN Charter* establishes the six principal organs of the UN: a General Assembly, a Security Council, an Economic and Social Council, a Trusteeship Council (now obsolete with the transition to independence of the non-self-governing territories), an International Court of Justice, and a Secretariat, known as 'Charter Bodies'. Not all of the Charter bodies are significantly involved in human rights issues,

1 See Chapter 1.2.2.

and in some cases primary responsibility for rights has been taken over by a range of ancillary bodies. This section focuses on the role played by the UN Security Council, the UN General Assembly, the Office of the High Commissioner for Human Rights and the International Court of Justice in promoting and encouraging respect for human rights. The central role of the UN General Assembly's Human Rights Council, and of the 'treaty bodies' which extist under the human rights treaties, in establishing and realising rights is discussed in Chapters 6 and 7 respectively.

5.1.1 UN Structure

Although the *UN Charter* establishes the six principal organs of the organisation, it does not establish a hierarchy among them nor regulate how they should relate to each other. In practice, the difference between the UN General Assembly's merely 'making recommendations', and the UN Security Council's more authoritatively 'making decisions' that can bind all States, establishes its own de facto system of hierarchy. The following chart[2] sets out the UN institutions most involved with human rights issues, which we discuss in this chapter.

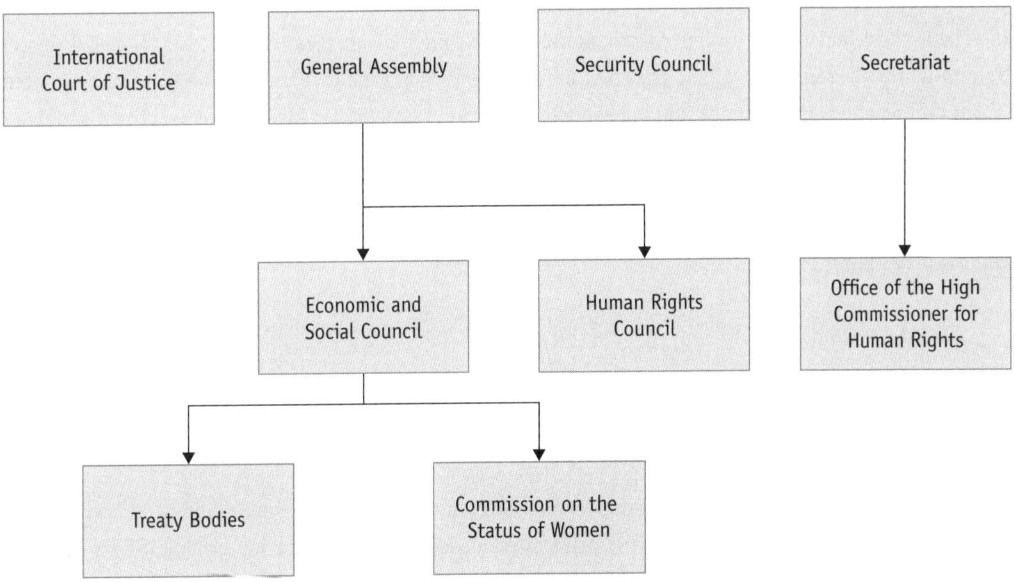

5.1.2 UN Membership

The UN was formed in 1945 with 51 founding member states.[3] By 2011, membership had grown to 193 states,[4] with an attendant rise in the complexity of achieving consensus. Membership of the organisation

2 For an organisational chart of the entire UN system see: <http://www.un.org/aboutun/chart_en.pdf>.

3 See the discussion in Chapter 1.2.2.

4 United Nations, 'UN At A Glance' (2010) United Nations Website <http://www.un.org/en/aboutun/index.shtml>.

'is open to all peace-loving states that accept the obligations contained in the *United Nations Charter* and, in the judgment of the Organization, are able to carry out these obligations'.[5] States are admitted to the UN by decision of the General Assembly on the recommendation of the Security Council. The *UN Charter* also provides that the UN Security Council can recommend that the UN General Assembly suspend the rights and privileges of membership of any member against which the UN Security Council has taken preventative or enforcement action. Only the UN Security Council, not the UN General Assembly, has the power to restore these rights (article 5). Any member that 'has persistently violated the Principles' of the *UN Charter* may be expelled from the UN by the same procedure. As at July 2011 no cases of suspension of rights or expulsion had been recommended by the UN Security Council.

Controversy did arise over the status of South Africa during its apartheid era. Many states called for its expulsion, but no formal proposal to this effect was made. In 1974, the UN General Assembly called on the UN Security Council to review the relationship between the UN and South Africa in light of the constant violations by South Africa of the principles of the *UN Charter* and the *Universal Declaration of Human Rights* (UDHR).

The challenge to South Africa's status within the UN came about because of the rejection of its credentials of its delegation, the acceptance of which is normally a straightforward procedural matter. In effect, the rejection of the South African delegation's credentials meant that for as long as it denied its non-white citizens most of the rights of participation in governance under its regime of apartheid, it was denied the right to speak and vote in the UN General Assembly.[6] Although it remained a member of the UN, South Africa was not represented at subsequent sessions of the UN General Assembly due to the rejection of its delegates' credentials. Following South Africa's successful democratic elections in May 1994, the UN General Assembly unanimously welcomed South Africa back to full participation in the UN on 23 June 1994.

5.2 UN GENERAL ASSEMBLY

5.2.1 Overview

The UN General Assembly is the deliberative and policy-making organ of the UN and is comprised of all 193 members, each having one vote. It is primarily an assembly, not an action group, and its principal responsibilities are to discuss, debate and make recommendations on a range of subjects concerning international peace and security, including human rights and international law. It elects the non-permanent members of the UN Security Council and other bodies such as the Human Rights Council. It also appoints the UN Secretary-General based on the recommendation of the UN Security Council. Decisions on such issues as international peace and security, admitting new members, and the UN budget are decided by a two-thirds majority. Other matters are decided by a simple majority.

5 *Charter of the United Nations* (UN Charter), June 26, 1945, entered into force Oct. 24, 1945, art 4.

6 S Chesterman, T M Franck & D M Malone, *Law and Practice of the United Nations*, Oxford University Press, Oxford, 2008, 191–6.

While the Assembly is empowered to make only non-binding recommendations to states on international issues, its decisions can be persuasive as indicative of global opinion (particularly those adopted unanimously or without a dissenting vote) and may lead to the development of 'hard' law in the form of a treaty.[7]

In addition to the plenary work of the UN General Assembly discussed below, the committee system of the UN General Assembly also plays a significant role on human rights issues. The UN General Assembly has six standing committees, commonly referred to by number, and it is the Third Committee, responsible for social, humanitarian and cultural issues, which is most directly concerned with human rights. At the Third Committee's annual session, it considers the reports made under each of the Special Procedures, described in chapter 6.1.3. and state representatives can ask questions of the various Special Rapporteurs. The Third Committee is also the forum where many of the resolutions and debates of the UN General Assembly on human rights issues originate. All member states are entitled to be represented and to participate in the UN General Assembly standing committees, because they are committees of the whole and so are broader forums than bodies with elected membership, such as the Human Rights Council. However, there is certainly some duplication in the functions of the Third Committee and the Human Rights Council (and the UN Commission on Human Rights before it).

5.2.2 Human Rights

Under article 13 of the *UN Charter*, the UN General Assembly may 'initiate studies and make recommendations for the purpose of: ... promoting international co-operation in the economic, social, cultural, educational, and health fields, and assisting in the realization of human rights and fundamental freedoms for all without distinction as to race, sex, language, or religion.' As discussed in detail in Chapter 1.3 in 1948, two years after the UN General Assembly convened its inaugural session, it promulgated the UDHR,[8] which contained thirty articles stating the UN's view on human rights. As well, it established the UN Commission on Human Rights, since replaced by the Human Rights Council, which is discussed below in Chapter 6.2.

The debates of the UN General Assembly can play a vital role in promoting human rights awareness. The advantage of holding such discussions in the UN General Assembly is its universal membership.

7 A distinction is sometimes made in international law between 'soft law' (ie declarations, guidelines) and 'hard law' (ie treaties, domestic legislation). Soft law is generally considered to be non-binding, and the use of soft law is attractive because it sometimes contains inspirational goals and aspirations that aim for the best possible scenario. Soft law can serve as a testing ground for the development of new mechanisms of accountability; it also functions as a useful and necessary tool for the development of ensuing hard law that legally binds parties to their commitments. For example see the *Declaration on the Rights of the Child*, GA Res 1386 (XIV), 14 UN GAOR Supp (No 16) at 19, UN Doc. A/4354 (1959) and the *Declaration on the Elimination of All Forms of Racial Discrimination*, GA Res 1904, UNGAOR, 18th sess, Agenda Item 43, UN Doc A/Res/18/1904 (1963), which were subsequently followed by treaties on these topics. For a discussion on how soft law can influence the development of international standards see: J Nolan & L Taylor 'Corporate Responsibility for Economic, Social and Cultural Rights: Rights in Search of a Remedy?' (2009) 87 *Journal of Business Ethics* 433 at 437.

8 *Universal Declaration of Human Rights* (UDHR), GA Res. 217A (III), UN Doc A/810 at 71 (1948).

The UN General Assembly's resolutions, although not binding, can still provoke intense and heated debate. For example, in 2007 the UN General Assembly passed a resolution[9] calling for a moratorium on the death penalty by a vote of 104 in favour to 54 against, with 29 abstentions, calling on all States that still allowed capital punishment to 'progressively restrict the use of the death penalty and reduce the number of offences for which it may be imposed'. In December 2008, the UN General Assembly adopted (106 to 46 with 34 abstentions) another resolution calling for a global moratorium on capital punishment. The following extract from the UN media release reveals the intensity of the debate. Although the resolution is non-binding, the debate that led up to its adoption provided a useful forum for pressing states on human rights reforms.

GENERAL ASSEMBLY ADOPTS LANDMARK TEXT CALLING FOR MORATORIUM ON DEATH PENALTY[10]

'Echoes of the intense two-day debate that preceded approval … of the resolution on a moratorium on executions reverberated in the Assembly hall, with a number of delegations arguing that the death penalty was not illegal under international human rights legislation and that it was the sovereign right of each and every State to determine its own judicial system. Two similar proposals had reached the Assembly in 1994 and 1999; in the first case, it was defeated by eight votes, while in the second, it was withdrawn at the last minute.

Among those delegations opposing the resolution, the representative of Barbados said the European Union and other main sponsors were trying to impose their will on other countries. 'Capital punishment remains legal under international law and Barbados wishes to exercise its sovereign right to use it as deterrent to the most serious crimes,' he said just ahead of the vote.

Singapore's representative said it was unfortunate that the resolution's co-sponsors had handled the issue not as a debate, but as a lecture. There had never been any attempt to reach consensus. They had ignored the diversity of States and their judicial systems. In addition, they had resorted to pressure tactics and demarches. While the co-sponsors would celebrate their victory, it had come at the expense of acrimony in the Third Committee. Each State had a sovereign right to choose its own political, criminal and judicial systems, he said, stressing that Singapore would continue to follow its own course in the matter.

The UN General Assembly proclaimed that its fifty-fifth session in 2000 would be designated the Millennium Assembly. At a summit that year, the UN Secretary-General at the time, Mr Kofi Annan, unveiled the UN's Millennium Declaration.[11] It set forth what are known as the Millennium Development Goals (MDGs), a collection of eight 'time-bound and measurable' set targets for everything from combating poverty and HIV/AIDS to improving universal education, gender equality, child and maternal health, ensuring environmental sustainability and developing a global partnership for development, all by the

9 *Resolution 62/149—Moratorium on the Use of the Death Penalty*, UNGAOR, 66nd sess, Agenda Item 70(b), UN Doc A/Res/62/149 (2008).

10 UN Department of Public Information, 'General Assembly adopts landmark text calling for moratorium on death penalty', 18 December 2007 <http://www.un.org/News/Press/docs/2007/ga10678.doc.htm>.

11 *Resolution 55/2—United Nations Millennium Declaration*, GA Res 55/2, UNGAOR, 55th sess, 8th plenary mtg, UN Doc A/Res/55/2 (2000), available online at <http://www.un.org/millennium/declaration/ares552e.pdf>.

target date of 2015. The development goals are often invoked by governments, NGOs and other groups in an effort to secure more aid and assistance for the developing world. In its *Millennium Development Goals Report* for 2010, the UN noted that although progress towards meeting the goals had been made, it was uneven, and 'without a major push forward, many of the MDG targets are likely to be missed'.[12]

The Millennium Declaration set up an important framework for accountability for ensuring all peoples the basic right to live with dignity, and is a useful tool for measuring the commitment of all states towards meeting this goal. The MDGs appear unlikely to be met by their target date of 2015 and pressure from many sources, including the UN General Assembly, may be useful in encouraging states to maintain their commitment to meeting their targets.

5.3 UN SECURITY COUNCIL

5.3.1 Overview

The UN Security Council is widely seen as the most influential part of the UN system and assumes primary responsibility under the Charter for the maintenance of international peace and security. One of the questions constantly posed about the UN Security Council, 65 years or so after it was created, concerns its legitimacy: 'Can the victors of the Second World War legitimately continue to be the privileged guardians of international peace and security well into the 21st century?'[13] The UN Security Council has fifteen members, but the ten rotating members are overshadowed by its five permanent members (China, France, Russia, the United Kingdom and the United States) and their so-called veto power.

While it is clear that the non-observance of human rights may constitute a threat to international peace and security, the UN Security Council has long pursued a non-intervention policy with regards to the internal affairs of states. It thus accepts the principle that a sovereign state is empowered in international law to exercise exclusive and total jurisdiction within its territorial borders. The norm of non-intervention is enshrined in article 2(7) of the Charter and is somewhat at odds with article 1(3), which commits the UN to 'promoting and encouraging respect for human rights and for fundamental freedoms'.[14]

In the early decades of the UN, Security Council practices were largely dominated by a strict adherence to the non-intervention principle. However, since the 1990s, the Council's deliberations suggest a gradual shift from policies dominated by a culture of sovereign impunity to those characterised by national and international accountability, with an increasing awareness of and stridency regarding the protection of human rights.

In 1950 the UN General Assembly adopted Resolution 377(V), known as the 'Uniting for Peace Resolution'.[15] It states that if the UN Security Council (because of a lack of unanimity of its permanent

12 United Nations, *The Millenium Development Goals Report 2010*, United Nations, New York, 2010, 4; on the Millennium Development Goals, see Chapter 20.2.2.

13 D Hovell, 'International law and the United Nations: a new era of engagement?' in R Niblett (ed), *America and a Changed World: A Question of Leadership*, Wiley-Blackwell, London, 2010, 216.

14 See Chapter 1.2.2.

15 *Uniting for Peace Resolution*, GA Res 377 (V), UNGAOR, 5th sess, 302nd plenary mtg, UN Doc A/Res/377(V), available online at <http://www.undemocracy.com/A-RES-377(V).pdf>.

members) fails to exercise its primary responsibility of maintaining international peace and security, the UN General Assembly can and should take up the matter itself and urge member states to consider collective action. The assembly has enacted this resolution in a handful of instances, including in relation to the Suez crisis of 1956, and the conflict between India and Pakistan in 1971, and in respect of Afghanistan in 1980. The language of the resolution clearly dictates that the UN General Assembly can never be a full substitute for the UN Security Council: only recommendations are mentioned so its pronouncements are devoid of any binding legal force.

UN Security Council deliberations and resolutions can be divided into four defined periods: the dormant period (1945–1989), the awakening period (1989–1995), the active period (1995–1998) and the assertive period (1998–present).[16] In her study of UN Security Council resolutions, Mansson concludes that the general absence of explicit human rights provisions was a main feature of UN Security Council resolutions passed during the Cold War (the dormant period) and that it was not until the 1990s that the Council formally recognised the link between human rights and peace. During this awakening period, Mansson argues that the UN Security Council was overtly conscious of human rights, but as a passive observer. The adoption of resolutions establishing the International Criminal Tribunal for the former Yugoslavia (1993) and the International Criminal Tribunal for Rwanda (1994) indicate the ascendancy of an accountability culture within the UN Security Council that values rights (at least in circumstances linked to gross violations of human rights) over sovereign impunity. Unfortunately, in both cases this action was predominantly reactive rather than proactive.

The appointment of Annan to the role of UN Secretary-General on 1 January 1997 coincided with the adoption by the UN Security Council of a more active human rights agenda. 'From 1995 onwards, the UN Security Council itself proactively condemned and deplored violations of human rights, calling upon and demanding that parties to conflicts respect human rights.'[17] The appointment of Mary Robinson as the United Nations High Commissioner for Human Rights in September 1997 led to greater interaction and communication between the UN Security Council and the Office of the High Commissioner, such as the establishment of regular monthly human rights briefings for the incoming UN Security Council President.

Annan underlined the relevance of the integration of human rights into all UN activities in his 2005 report, *In Larger Freedom: Towards Development, Security and Human Rights for All* when he stated: 'we will not enjoy development without security, we will not enjoy security without development, and we will not enjoy either without respect for human rights'.[18] In September 2005, when the UN General Assembly embraced the 'responsibility to protect' doctrine at the World Summit,[19] it (like the UN Security Council) was signalling a shift from acknowledging sovereignty as control to accepting sovereignty as responsibility for the protection of human rights.

16 K Mansson, 'UN Peace Operations and Security Council Resolutions: A Tool for Measuring the Status of International Human Rights Law?' (2008) 26(1) *Netherlands Quarterly of Human Rights*, 79, 83.

17 See UN Doc. S/RES/1019, 9 November 1995 and UN Doc. S/RES/1034, 21 December 1995 on Bosnia as discussed in K Mansson, ibid 92.

18 K Annan, *In Larger Freedom: Towards Development, Security and Human Rights for All*, UN Doc.A/59/2005 (2005), <http://www.un.org/largerfreedom/chap5.htm>, [17].

19 GA Res 60/1, UN Doc A/RES/60.1 [138–139] 24 October 2005.

In 2006 the UN Security Council unanimously adopted Resolution 1674[20] on the Protection of Civilians in Armed Conflict, which contains the historic first official UN Security Council reference to the responsibility to protect individuals from mass atrocity crimes.[21] The responsibility to protect is a doctrine that is arguably still in search of greater definition, but for a body such as the UN Security Council, the emphasis may lie first in preventing mass atrocities and includes the responsibility to warn, to generate effective prevention strategies and, when necessary, to mobilise effective reaction. If prevention fails, the responsibility to protect requires whatever measures are necessary—economic, political, diplomatic, legal, security-based or, in the last resort, military—to stop mass atrocities from occurring. However, history suggests that despite the greater theoretical clarity around the institutional responsibility for preventing massive human rights violations, the inherently political nature of the UN Security Council often means that inaction trumps action.

5.3.2 Action v Inaction: The Perennial Dilemma

The UN Security Council will often condemn violations of human rights, though action may be less forthcoming. Since the formation of the UN there have been numerous opportunities where it might have intervened to prevent and/or redress violations of peace and security. Some notable examples include the intervention in Korea in 1950 and more recent actions (or inactions) in Kosovo, East Timor and Iraq.

In March 1999 the North Atlantic Treaty Organisation (NATO) began airstrikes in the territory of the former Yugoslavia without prior UN Security Council permission, sparking an intense debate among international lawyers about the legality and legitimacy of the military intervention. A report by the Independent Commission on Kosovo in 2000[22] concluded that

> the NATO military intervention was illegal but legitimate. It was illegal because it did not receive prior approval from the United Nations Security Council. However, the Commission considers that the intervention was justified because all diplomatic avenues had been exhausted and because the intervention had the effect of liberating the majority population of Kosovo from a long period of oppression under Serbian rule.

The Commission then went on to say that:

> the NATO war was neither a success nor a failure; it was in fact both. It forced the Serbian government to withdraw its army and police from Kosovo and to sign an agreement closely modelled on the aborted Rambouillet accord. It stopped the systematic oppression of the Kosovar Albanians. However, the intervention failed to achieve its avowed aim of preventing massive ethnic cleansing. Milosevic remained in power. The Serbian people were the main losers. Kosovo was lost. Many Serbs fled or were expelled from the province. Serbia suffered considerable economic losses and destruction of civilian infrastructure. Independent media and NGOs were suppressed and the overall level of repression in Serbia increased.

20 SC Res 1674, UN SCOR, 5430th mtg (2006), UN Doc S/RES/1674.

21 See Chapter 20.3.

22 Independent International Commission on Kosovo, *The Kosovo Report: Conflict, International Response, Lessons Learned*, Oxford University Press, Oxford, 2000, 4.

The rift that emerged in the UN Security Council over the action/inaction in Kosovo was mild compared to the schism that preceded and followed the US-led invasion of Iraq in 2003. The invasion split the UN Security Council, divided NATO and the European Union, and prompted the creation of a high-level panel to rethink the very basis of collective security, including reassessing the role of the UN and the UN Security Council in maintaining peace and security and thus protecting human rights.[23]

More recently still, an NGO, the International Service for Human Rights, characterised the year 2009 as 'yet another tragedy of inaction when it came to UN Security Council responsiveness to three major crises at the end of 2008 and the beginning of 2009'.[24] This extract from the International Service's 2009 annual report reveals the frustration sometimes felt about the UN Security Council's apparent lack of action to protect human rights:

INTERNATIONAL SERVICE FOR HUMAN RIGHTS *ANNUAL HUMAN RIGHTS MONITOR* (2009)[25]

The developments in the Democratic Republic of the Congo (DRC), Gaza, and Sri Lanka all tested the body's political will to translate its work on protecting civilians in armed conflict into practice. However, in all three cases, the Security Council did not act in a timely and decisive manner, and the inadequate response in the face of killings of at least 6,000 civilians at the hands of national authorities and the rebel force in Sri Lanka was a failure of historic proportions. In the DRC, the Security Council met with silence the news that its peacekeeping mission—the UN Organisation Mission in the Democratic Republic of the Congo (MONUC)—was providing support to Congolese military operations commandeered by known war criminals in the national army's offensive against a rebel group in Eastern DRC. Only in December, through its annual resolution renewing the mission's mandate, did the Security Council finally decide to call on MONUC to immediately withdraw support from those army units that were not in strict compliance with international humanitarian, human rights, and refugee law, and to request that the Secretary-General establish a mechanism to assess the implementation of MONUC policy governing support to the DRC army. Such belated action was little recompense for the civilian victims who were killed or raped. The Security Council also did not play a satisfactory part in breaking the cycle of impunity in the Middle East conflict, with the majority of members deciding to reject taking up substantively the recommendations addressed to it in the UN Fact finding Mission to Gaza, led by Justice Richard Goldstone. The recommendations of the so-called 'Goldstone Report' included important proposals on how the Security Council could help ensure accountability and justice in both sides of the conflict.

The perennial dilemma faced not only by the UN Security Council, but by the UN as a whole, about when and how to intervene in situations to prevent or redress human rights violations, is well summed up in this extract from the UN Secretary-General's address to the UN General Assembly in September 1999.

23 Report of the Secretary General's High-level Panel on Threats, Challenges and Change, 'A more secure world: Our shared responsibility', UN, 2004 available at <http://www.un.org/secureworld/report2.pdf>.

24 International Service for Human Rights, *Annual Human Rights Monitor* (2009) No 67/2009, 115. <http://www.ishr.ch/component/search/?searchword=human+rights+monitor&ordering=&searchphrase=all>.

25 Ibid.

KOFI ANNAN, *ADDRESS TO THE GENERAL ASSEMBLY*, SEPTEMBER 1999[26]

While the genocide in Rwanda will define for our generation the consequences of inaction in the face of mass murder, the more recent conflict in Kosovo has prompted important questions about the consequences of action in the absence of complete unity on the part of the international community.

It has cast in stark relief the dilemma of what has been called humanitarian intervention: on one side, the question of the legitimacy of an action taken by a regional organization without a United Nations mandate; on the other, the universally recognized imperative of effectively halting gross and systematic violations of human rights with grave humanitarian consequences.

The inability of the international community in the case of Kosovo to reconcile these two equally compelling interests—universal legitimacy and effectiveness in defence of human rights—can only be viewed as a tragedy.

It has revealed the core challenge to the Security Council and to the United Nations as a whole in the next century: to forge unity behind the principle that massive and systematic violations of human rights—wherever they may take place—should not be allowed to stand.

The Kosovo conflict and its outcome have prompted a wide debate of profound importance to the resolution of conflicts from the Balkans to Central Africa to East Asia. And to each side in this critical debate, difficult questions can be posed.

To those for whom the greatest threat to the future of international order is the use of force in the absence of a Security Council mandate, one might ask—not in the context of Kosovo—but in the context of Rwanda: If, in those dark days and hours leading up to the genocide, a coalition of States had been prepared to act in defence of the Tutsi population, but did not receive prompt Council authorization, should such a coalition have stood aside and allowed the horror to unfold?

To those for whom the Kosovo action heralded a new era when States and groups of States can take military action outside the established mechanisms for enforcing international law, one might ask: Is there not a danger of such interventions undermining the imperfect, yet resilient, security system created after the Second World War, and of setting dangerous precedents for future interventions without a clear criterion to decide who might invoke these precedents, and in what circumstances? …

In response to this turbulent era of crises and interventions, there are those who have suggested that the Charter itself—with its roots in the aftermath of global inter-State war—is ill-suited to guide us in a world of ethnic wars and intra-State violence. I believe they are wrong.

The Charter is a living document, whose high principles still define the aspirations of peoples everywhere for lives of peace, dignity and development. Nothing in the Charter precludes a recognition that there are rights beyond borders.

Indeed, its very letter and spirit are the affirmation of those fundamental human rights. In short, it is not the deficiencies of the Charter which have brought us to this juncture, but our difficulties in applying its principles to a new era; an era when strictly traditional notions of sovereignty can no longer do justice to the aspirations of peoples everywhere to attain their fundamental freedoms.

The sovereign States who drafted the Charter over half a century ago were dedicated to peace, but experienced in war.

26 K Annan, *Address to the General Assembly*, United Nations Press Release, SG/SM/7136, 20 September 1999, available at <http://www.un.org/news/Press/docs/1999/19990920.sgsm7136.html>.

They knew the terror of conflict, but knew equally that there are times when the use of force may be legitimate in the pursuit of peace. That is why the Charter's own words declare that 'armed force shall not be used, save in the common interest'. But what is that common interest? Who shall define it? Who will defend it? Under whose authority? And with what means of intervention? These are the monumental questions facing us as we enter the new century ...

Ultimately, the UN Security Council is a political body with limited accountability and transparency surrounding its decisions about whether to intervene to protect rights. The power wielded by its permanent five members, including their discretionary use of the veto power, largely determines whether action is taken in any particular situation. Despite ongoing discussions, reform of the UN Security Council still appears to be a somewhat distant prospect.[27]

SNAPSHOT: THE UN SECURITY COUNCIL'S 1267 SANCTIONS REGIME AND HUMAN RIGHTS

In 1999 the UN Security Council, acting under Chapter VII of the UN Charter, adopted Resolution 1267, which required all states to impose aviation and financial sanctions and an arms embargo against the Taliban. Under the resolution a Sanctions Committee was established and states were specifically directed to freeze the assets of, prevent the entry into or transit through their territories by, and prevent the direct or indirect supply, sale and transfer of arms and military equipment to, any individual or entity associated with al Qaeda, Osama bin Laden and/or the Taliban as designated by the Al-Qaida and Taliban Sanctions Committee.[28] The aim of the sanctions was to limit travel and immobilise the assets of suspected terrorists, and the Sanctions Committee has broad powers to list and delist the individuals and entities subjected to sanctions.

The sanctions regime established under Resolution 1267 contains minimal provision for due process rights. Targeted individuals are not informed before their listing, and even after an individual or entity is listed, states do not have an obligation to provide any detailed information to that person or entity about the reasons for their inclusion. Decisions to list or delist are made (primarily) by Sanctions Committee consensus and listees are not represented before the Committee. Michaelsen argues that '[i]n spite of the improvements made to the listing and delisting mechanism over the years, the procedure continues to raise serious concerns in relation to fundamental human rights. These include in particular the right to judicial review, the right to procedural fairness, the right to be heard and the right to judicial remedy.[29] These rights form the very basis of due process of law and are guaranteed ... by the leading international human

27 See above, n 23, and K Annan, see above, n 18.

28 SC Res 1267, UN SCOR, 54th Sess, 4051st mtg, UN Doc S/RES/1267 (1999).

29 For an in-depth legal analysis of these rights as they are engaged by the 1267 Listing and De-Listing Procedure, see especially L van den Herik & N Schrijver, 'Human Rights Concerns in Current Targeted Sanctions Regimes from the Perspective of International and European Law' in T J Biersteker & S E Eckert *Strengthening Targeted Sanctions through Fair and Clear Procedures* (Watson Institute for International Studies, Brown University White Paper, 30 March 2006) 9.

rights instruments such as the *Universal Declaration on Human Rights*, the *ICCPR*, the *ECHR*, the *American Convention on Human Rights* and the *African Charter*.'[30]

In 2008 a decision of the European Court of Justice (ECJ), *Kadi & Al Barakaat International Foundation v Council of the European Union & Commission of the European Communities*,[31] challenged the framework of the sanctions regime and confirmed that the process violates fundamental human rights as set out in European Community law.[32] An individual (Yassin Abdullah Kadi, a Saudi national) and an entity (Al Barakaat International Foundation, registered in Sweden) challenged their listing. The court held that although efforts had been made to improve the listing system procedures, fundamental rights were still inadequately protected. Individuals and other entities should have an opportunity to be heard, and the court commented that in this case, 'the right to be heard, and the right to effective judicial review of those rights, were patently not respected'.[33] The *Kadi* decision challenges the compatibility of targeted sanctions with human rights and, in this case, found that the means employed by the Security Council's Sanctions Committee did not justify the end sought. As noted by Michaelsen, 'the decision is remarkable in that it is the first time that a court has (indirectly) found that UN Security Council resolutions on counter-terrorism violate fundamental rights'.[34]

5.4 SECRETARIAT

The Secretariat, housing the UN Secretary-General and his staff, has an *ad hoc* rather than day-to-day involvement with human rights, although it provides essential administrative support to the Office of High Commissioner for Human Rights.

The Secretariat carries out the day-to-day work of the organisation, including servicing the other principal organs, administering peacekeeping operations, surveying economic and social trends and preparing studies on human rights. The Secretariat thus plays a dual and potentially conflicting role in the organisation; providing service support to the principal organs including the UN Security Council and the General Assembly to ensure the effective functioning of the UN, but also acting independently as its own principal organ to lead and administer the organisation.

30 C Michaelsen, '*Kadi & Al Barakaat v Council of the European Union & Commission of the European Communities*: The Incompatiblity of the United Nations Security Council's 1267 Sanctions Regime with European Due Process Guarantees' (2009) 10 *Melbourne Journal of International Law*, 329, 334.

31 Judgment of the ECJ in Joined Cases C-402/05 P and C-415/05 P, *Yassin Abdullah Kadi and Al Barakaat International Foundation v Council of the EU and Commission of the EC* (ECJ Judgment), 3 September 2008, available at <http://curia.europa.eu/en/content/juris/index.htm> ('*Kadi*').

32 For a discussion of the specifics of the laws violated see above, n 30.

33 See above, n 31.

34 See above, n 30. Also see J Weiler 'Editorial, Kadi—Europe's Medellin?' (2008) 19 *European Journal of International Law* 895.

The UN Secretary-General is appointed by the UN General Assembly on the recommendation of the UN Security Council (article 97). Article 99 of the *UN Charter* recognises the potentially broad authority of the UN Secretary-General to 'bring to the attention of the UN Security Council any matter that in his opinion may threaten the maintenance of peace and security', which, of course, may encompass human rights issues. Such powers go beyond the characterisation of the UN Secretary-General as a mere chief administrative officer for the organisation. Chesterman, Franck and Malone query whether the UN Secretary-General can be both a 'secretary' and a 'general':

> The Secretary-General of the United Nations is a unique figure in world politics. At once the world's senior diplomat, servant of the UN Security Council (and member states more generally), and commander-in-chief of up to a hundred thousand peacekeepers, he or she depends on states for both the legitimacy and resources that enable the United Nations to function. The tension between these roles—of being secretary or general—has challenged every incumbent. The first, the Norwegian Trygve Lie (1946–1952), memorably welcomed his successor to New York's Idlewild Airport with the words: 'You are about to enter the most impossible job on this earth.'[35]

5.5 THE INTERNATIONAL COURT OF JUSTICE

The International Court of Justice (ICJ) is the principal judicial organ of the United Nations. It was established in June 1945 by article 92 of the *UN Charter* and began operations in April 1946. The Court is located in The Hague (Netherlands) and is composed of 15 judges, who are elected for terms of office of nine years by a majority of both the UN General Assembly and the UN Security Council.

The ICJ's role is to settle, in accordance with international law, legal disputes submitted to it by states and to give advisory opinions on legal questions referred to it by authorised UN organs and specialised agencies. States members of the United Nations, and other states that have become parties to the Statute of the Court[36] or that have accepted its jurisdiction under certain conditions, may be parties to what is referred to as 'contentious cases'. The ICJ is competent to entertain a dispute only if the states concerned have accepted its jurisdiction but any state can recognise the competence of the Court to deal with any case.

The ICJ does not deal with disputes raised by individuals. This is an important difference between the ICJ and other human rights institutions that allow some type of direct access. The limitation reflects the state-centric view of international law prevailing when the statute of the ICJ's predecessor, the Permanent Court of International Justice (PCIJ), was drawn up after the First World War.

While there have been a few ICJ (and PCIJ) decisions significantly contributing to human rights law, historically they have constituted only a small part of the Court's docket. Human rights issues have been an intermittent rather than routine part of the Court's work. In recent years there have been

35 S Chesterman, see above, n 6, 133. See also, T M Franck 'The Secretary-General's Role in Conflict Resolution: Past, Present and Future' (1995) 6 *European Journal of International Law* 360.

36 The *Statute of the International Court of Justice* is annexed to the *UN Charter* and deals primarily with the composition and functioning of the Court.

a few more such cases, and any contemporary discussion of the ICJ and human rights invariably makes mention of three: *Legal Consequences of the Construction of a Wall in the Occupied Palestinian Territory*;[37] *Armed Activities on the Territory of the Congo (Democratic Republic of the Congo v Uganda)*;[38] and *Application of the Convention on the Prevention and Punishment of the Crime of Genocide (Bosnia and Herzegovina v Serbia and Montenegro)*.[39] In *Application of the International Convention on the Elimination of All Forms of Racial Discrimination (Georgia v Russian Federation)*, Georgia attempted to enforce treaty obligations (under the *Convention for the Elimination of All Forms of Racial Discrimination* [CERD]) between the two parties. Georgia alleged that Russia violated its treaty obligations during its interventions in South Ossetia, Abkhazia and adjacent areas in Georgia from 1990 to 2008. This was the first time the Court has been called on to exercise its jurisdiction in respect of a core human rights treaty. In April 2011, the majority of the Court held that it had no jurisdiction to consider the case, because the parties had failed to negotiate or make use of the CERD procedures before Georgia took its case to the ICJ, which the majority considered a precondition to the consideration of the matter before the ICJ.[40]

The following extract from Rosalyn Higgins, President of the ICJ, 2006–2009, demonstrates how (depending on the particular issue at stake) human rights can be a central feature of the Court's deliberations and less of a mere aberration:

ROSALYN HIGGINS, 'HUMAN RIGHTS IN THE INTERNATIONAL COURT OF JUSTICE'[41]

Until comparatively recently the Court was a 'Court of sovereign States'. But, as it is above all a court of international law, it has in recent years become also a court concerned with human rights, as human rights law has finally found its proper place within international law. Advisory Opinions, and interstate cases which claim human rights treaty violations *inter se*, have provided the vehicle for this development within the Court.

Over the past twelve years, we have seen the arrival at the Court of judges with strong backgrounds in human rights. I came to the Court in 1995, after serving ten years on the UN Human Rights Committee. Then came Judge Kooijmans, who sat at the Court until 2006, and had been president of the UN Commission on Human Rights and a very important rapporteur on torture. Judge Buergenthal came to us in 2000. He was the former President of the Inter-American Court on Human Rights and later a member of the UN Human Rights Committee. Judge Simma came to the Court in the same year, with a background as a prominent member of the Committee under the Covenant on Economic, Social and Cultural Rights of the UN. The presence of these judges on the bench, providing a 'critical mass' of persons particularly versed in human rights law, has contributed, I believe, to human rights being viewed as in the centre of what the Court does, not at the margin. The passage of time, and the change of judicial culture more generally, have played their role, too. Human rights are now routinely addressed in judgments of the Court ...

37 Advisory Opinion of 9 July 2004, [2004] ICJ Rep 136.

38 Judgment, [2005] ICJ Rep 168.

39 Judgment, 26 February 2007. The application of the Genocide Convention is still being considered in *Croatia v Serbia and Montenegro*, an application filed in July 1999.

40 Judgment of 1 April 2011 on preliminary objections at 115–84. The procedural precondition referred to was contained in art 22 of the ICERD.

41 (2007) 20 *Leiden Journal of International Law* 745–51.

One cannot discuss the ICJ and human rights without mentioning three recent cases: the Advisory Opinion on the *Palestine Wall*, *Congo v Uganda*, and *Bosnia and Herzegovina v Serbia and Montenegro*. Human rights and humanitarian law were at the centre of each of these cases. The first addressed an element of the immensely complex Israel–Palestine dispute. The second concerned allegations of massive human rights violations set against the backdrop of the history of violence in the Great Lakes Region. And the third concerned what is widely regarded as the most serious violation of human rights—the commission of genocide.

The Court's Advisory Opinion on the *Palestine Wall* delivered in 2004 found that the 'wall' or 'security barrier' built by Israel violated various international obligations, that the wall must be dismantled immediately, and that Israel must make reparation for any damage caused to Palestinian property. The Court examined the relationship between international humanitarian law and international human rights law, and found that both branches of international law would have to be taken into consideration. It further held that international human rights instruments are applicable 'in respect of acts done by a State in the exercise of its jurisdiction outside its own territory', particularly in occupied territories (this reasoning was later applied in the *Congo v Uganda* Judgment) ... an Advisory Opinion is *not* without legal effect. The *Palestine Wall* Opinion was an authoritative statement of the applicable law, and contributes to the framework for peace in the Middle East.

In 2005 the Court delivered its Judgment in the *Congo v Uganda* case. The [Democratic Republic of the Congo] claimed that Uganda, during its military intervention in Congolese territory, was responsible *inter alia* for large-scale massacres of civilians, acts of torture and other forms of inhuman treatment, unlawful seizure of civilian property, and the abduction and forcible conscription of children. The Court closely examined the extensive evidence submitted by both parties and concluded that atrocities had been committed by Ugandan troops. There was the interesting and difficult legal question of the legal definition of belligerent occupation, which had an impact on the extent of Uganda's responsibility for human rights violations. The Court found that Uganda established and exercised authority in one province, Ituri, as an occupying power. As a result, the Court had to deal with two separate areas to which different legal regimes applied. In Ituri, Article 43 of the 1907 *Hague Regulations* imposed on Uganda a duty to restore and ensure public order and safety while respecting the laws of the Congo. Uganda could therefore be held responsible not only for its own acts and omissions in that region, but also for any lack of vigilance in preventing violations of human rights and humanitarian law by other actors in that territory, including rebel groups. On the rest of the Congolese territory invaded by Uganda, not qualified as occupied, that specific duty of vigilance did not apply and Uganda could only be held responsible for the acts and omissions of its own forces.

The *Bosnia and Herzegovina v Serbia and Montenegro* Judgment ... was the first legal case in which allegations of genocide had been made by one state against another. The International Court was acutely sensitive to its responsibilities. The Court—as it always does—meticulously applied the law to each and every one of the issues before it. The concept of genocide has caught the public and political imagination. While this is a positive development, great care has to be taken, by commentators and governments alike, not to assume that all massive violations of human rights constitute genocide. The Convention requirement of special intent—intent to destroy, in whole or in part, the group as such—remains the essence of genocide, and what distinguishes it from crimes against humanity. Further, the concentration on 'genocide' should not lead down a path whereby crimes against humanity, or a finding of a violation of the *Genocide Convention* by failure to prevent genocide, come to be perceived as somehow 'insignificant'. The Court's judgment in the *Bosnia* case seeks not only to answer the claims before it, but also systematically to elaborate and explain each and every element in the Convention, believing this latter task is also a necessary contribution to clarity and understanding.

5.6 ECONOMIC AND SOCIAL COUNCIL

Under the *UN Charter,* responsibility for human rights largely falls within the duties of the Economic and Social Council (ECOSOC). Article 62 of the *UN Charter* states:

> The Economic and Social Council may make or initiate studies and reports with respect to international economic, social, cultural, educational, health, and related matters and may make recommendations with respect to any such matters to the General Assembly to the Members of the United Nations, and to the specialized agencies concerned.
> It may make recommendations for the purpose of promoting respect for, and observance of, human rights and fundamental freedoms for all.
> It may prepare draft conventions for submission to the General Assembly, with respect to matters falling within its competence.
> It may call, in accordance with the rules prescribed by the United Nations, international conferences on matters falling within its competence.

The UN Commission on Human Rights, established under the auspices of ECOSOC, assumed the primary responsibility for developing international human rights standards: see Chapter 6.1. The Commission was a subsidiary body of ECOSOC, and it was an ECOSOC resolution that established the first complaint procedure for dealing with human rights violations.[42]

ECOSOC's importance for human rights has been waning, particularly since the establishment in 2006 of the Human Rights Council, a body that reports directly to the UN General Assembly rather than to ECOSOC. Nevertheless, the role played by ECOSOC in coordinating the activities of the specialised agencies of the UN and in consulting with non-governmental organisations (NGOs)[43] is still relevant, not only to the protection of human rights but also increasingly in achieving the UN's many development goals.

The former UN Secretary-General Kofi Annan, in his policy document advocating reform of the UN, had the following to say about ECOSOC in 2005:

KOFI ANNAN, *IN LARGER FREEDOM: TOWARDS DEVELOPMENT, SECURITY AND HUMAN RIGHTS FOR ALL*[44]

171 The Charter of the United Nations gives the Economic and Social Council a range of important functions that involve coordination, policy review and policy dialogue. Most of these seem more critical than ever in this age of globalization, in which a comprehensive United Nations development agenda has emerged from the summits and conferences of the 1990s. More than ever, the United Nations needs to be able to develop and implement policies in this area in a coherent manner. The functions of the Council are generally thought to be uniquely relevant to these challenges, but it has not as yet done justice to them.

42 See Chapter 6.1.1.

43 See Chapter 9.3.2.

44 K Annan, see above, n 18.

172 In 1945, the framers of the Charter did not give the Economic and Social Council enforcement powers. Having agreed at Bretton Woods in the previous year to create powerful international financial institutions and expecting that those would be complemented by a world trade organization in addition to the various specialized agencies, they clearly intended that international economic decision-making would be decentralized. But this only makes the Council's potential role as coordinator, convener, forum for policy dialogue and forger of consensus the more important. It is the only organ of the United Nations explicitly mandated by the Charter to coordinate the activities of the specialized agencies and to consult with non-governmental organizations. And it has a network of functional and regional commissions operating under its aegis which are increasingly focused on the implementation of development goals.

5.7 HUMAN RIGHTS COUNCIL

From its establishment in 1946 as a subsidiary body of ECOSOC, until it was abolished in 2006, the UN Commission on Human Rights led the UN's standard-setting activity for human rights, and was the principal forum for international human rights debate. In 2006 it was replaced by the Human Rights Council, a subsidiary body of the UN General Assembly. We discuss the role and activity of the Commission and the Council in detail in Chapter 6.

5.8 OFFICE OF THE HIGH COMMISSIONER FOR HUMAN RIGHTS

The High Commissioner for Human Rights is the official 'with principal responsibility for United Nations human rights activities' and has a mandate 'to coordinate the human rights promotion and protection activities throughout the United Nations system'.[45] Although the post was not created until 1993, discussions about the need for such a position began at the time of the UN's formation. Concerns about the breadth and impact of the proposed office, Cold War tensions, and the general difficulty in gathering consensus among the ever expanding UN membership all contributed to the delay in establishing the post. The office was formally created by a UN General Assembly resolution on 20 December 1993.[46]

The High Commissioner is appointed by the UN Secretary-General, approved by the UN General Assembly with due regard for geographical rotation, and serves for a term of four years (with the possibility of one renewal). The High Commissioner serves as an Under-Secretary-General and has primary responsibility for United Nations human rights activities under the direction and authority of the UN Secretary-General.[47]

It might be said that the mandate of the High Commissioner gives the office holder a broad array of tasks, as set out in the following extract, and limited resources with which to achieve them.

45 *High Commissioner for the Promotion and Protection of All Human Rights*, GA Res 48/141, GAOR, 48th sess, 85th plenary mtg, UN Doc A/Res/48/141 (1993), available online at <http://www.un.org/documents/ga/res/48/a48r141.htm>.

46 Ibid.

47 Ibid.

GENERAL ASSEMBLY RESOLUTION 48/141(1993)[48]

[4] The High Commissioner's responsibilities shall be:

(a) To promote and protect the effective enjoyment by all of all civil, cultural, economic, political and social rights;

(b) To carry out the tasks assigned to him/her...with a view to improving the promotion and protection of all human rights;

(c) To promote and protect the realization of the right to development ...;

(d) To provide....advisory services and technical and financial assistance, at the request of the State concerned and, where appropriate, the regional human rights organizations ...;

(e) To coordinate relevant United Nations education and public information programmes in the field of human rights;

(f) To play an active role in removing the current obstacles and in meeting the challenges to the full realization of all human rights and in preventing the continuation of human rights violations throughout the world, as reflected in the *Vienna Declaration and Programme of Action;*

(g) To engage in a dialogue with all Governments in the implementation of his/her mandate with a view to securing respect for all human rights;

(h) To enhance international cooperation for the promotion and protection of all human rights;

(i) To coordinate the human rights promotion and protection activities throughout the United Nations system;

(j) To rationalize, adapt, strengthen and streamline the United Nations machinery in the field of human rights with a view to improving its efficiency and effectiveness; ...

So far six people have filled this position, often with quite different approaches to their role: Jose Ayala-Lasso (Ecuador) 1994–1997; Mary Robinson (Ireland) 1997–2002; Sergio Vieira de Mello (Brazil) 2002–2003 (killed in the bombing of the UN's Baghdad office); B G Ramcharan, acting High Commissioner (Guyana) 2003–2004; Louise Arbour (Canada) 2004–2008; and Navanethem Pillay (South Africa) from 2008.

Much of the effectiveness of the role depends on the particular office-holder and his/her relationship with states and the UN Secretary-General. The conservative approach of the first High Commissioner can be contrasted with that of his successor, Robinson, who was an outspoken advocate for human rights and who did not flinch from holding states publicly accountable for human rights abuses.

The role is a difficult one to fill. The following extract about the expectations surrounding the appointment of the first High Commissioner highlights the almost impossible breadth of experience and talent that is expected of the office-holder.

48 Ibid para 4.

FELICE GAER, 'BOOK REVIEW OF *THE UNITED NATIONS HIGH COMMISSIONER FOR HUMAN RIGHTS: THE CHALLENGES OF INTERNATIONAL PROTECTION*'[49]

Human rights advocates wanted a high commissioner who would focus on human rights violations and develop strategies for immediate and effective responses. The officeholder had to live up to the post's title: many NGOs argued that a high commissioner should be high level, independent and able not only to heighten attention to human rights in the United Nations and throughout the world, but to galvanize concern, act rapidly in emerging crises, and produce actions and results that would help individual victims...Many spoke of the high commissioner as a 'champion' of human rights for all, and as a 'conscience' or moral voice able to speak out honestly when political forces kept others silent or fearful. For these purposes, the high commissioner would have to be a critic, a communicator and a colleague and confidant of human rights defenders the world over. The high commissioner was thus expected to enhance the global visibility of human rights, to integrate human rights concerns throughout the UN system, to develop new strategies for action and effectiveness, and at the same time, to be a manager and coordinator of the UN human rights programs, rationalizing and streamlining them...

What individual could meet all the expectations? And did the individual matter more than the bureaucratic section established and its particular mandate within the UN system?

The work of the Office of the High Commissioner for Human Rights (OHCHR) focuses on three areas: human rights standard setting, monitoring, and implementation on the ground. This includes supporting (both substantively and administratively) the Human Rights Council, treaty monitoring bodies and the work of the special procedures. Its field offices also play an essential role in monitoring and developing responses to human rights challenges in collaboration with governments, the UN system and civil society.

The OHCHR's Research and Right to Development Branch promotes and protects the right to development. The UN General Assembly resolution establishing the OHCHR explicitly includes the mandate 'to promote and protect the realization of the right to development and to enhance support from relevant bodies of the UN system for this purpose' (US $109 million in 2010).[50]

The OHCHR is funded from the UN's regular budget, which provides about a third of its resources (funding for 2010–2011 was US$142.7 million), and from voluntary contributions from member states, intergovernmental organisations, foundations and individuals.[51] Its headquarters are in Geneva, and it also has a presence in New York and a network of regional and country offices spread over five continents. By way of overview, in 2010, the OHCHR employed close to 1000 staff, of which about 48 per cent were based in the field, 50 per cent in Geneva and 2 per cent in New York.[52]

49 (2004) 98 *American Journal of International Law*, 391.

50 GA Res 48/141, see above, n 48, para 4(c).

51 United Nations Office of the High Commissioner for Human Rights, 'About OHCHR Funding', <http://www.ohchr.org/EN/AboutUs/Pages/FundingBudget.aspx>.

52 *United Nation Office of the High Commissioner for Human Rights, High Commissioner's Strategic Management Plan 2010–2011 (2009)* available online at <http://www.ohchr.org/Document/press SMP2010–2011>.

5.9 COMMISSION ON THE STATUS OF WOMEN

The Commission on the Status of Women (CSW) was established in 1946 as a subcommittee of the UN Commission on Human Rights, but in the same year it was given the status of a full commission of ECOSOC. It focuses on preparing recommendations and reports to ECOSOC on promoting women's rights in political, economic, civil, social and educational fields. The role and activities of the CSW are discussed in detail in Chapter 13.3.1.

In 2010, Iran secured a seat on the 45-member commission.[53] Iran is a state that has not yet ratified the *Convention on the Elimination of All Forms of Discrimination Against Women* [CEDAW]), and one might argue that as such, it does not merit membership of a body dedicated to advancing the status of women. Iran's ascension to membership of the CSW highlights the shortcomings associated with the *fait accompli* approach of the regional bloc voting mechanisms associated with most UN bodies, and is indicative of the UN's strategy of adopting a broad, 'inside the tent' membership base rather than focusing on improvement via exclusion.

5.10 TREATY BODIES

This part has focused on UN bodies with human rights functions that are established under the *UN Charter*. A number of UN bodies with human rights functions are established not under the Charter, but under the UN human rights treaties; those are discussed in detail in Chapter 7.4.

5.11 CONCLUSION AND ISSUES

The UN has a complex framework for the promotion and protection of human rights. Beginning with the institutions established in the *UN Charter*, to more recent developments such as the establishment of the Office of the High Commissioner for Human Rights, the promotion and protection of human rights, while an integral part of the UN, is not without its challenges. With a membership of 193 states, a plenary body such as the UN General Assembly is often more likely to be the site of vigorous debate and disagreement around human rights than a vision of consensus. The UN Security Council, often considered the powerhouse of the UN, can be equally prone to bickering. For many years it has prized inaction over action with respect to human rights but has also, in more recent decades, placed human rights firmly on its agenda. The involvement of the Secretariat and the Office of the High Commissioner for Human Rights in an active mandate to protect human rights has been dependent to a certain extent on the personality of the principal office holder, but these offices have also proved to be invaluable defenders of rights. The UN framework for promoting and protecting human rights draws on an effervescent mix of social, political and legal factors which, whether viewed singly or in combination, allow for vigorous debate, disagreement and, occasionally, consensus on human rights issues, and are reflective of the vitality and dynamism of the field more generally.

53 See the press release for the Economic and Social Council ECOSOC/6419 28 April 2010, available online at: <http://www.un.org/News/Press/docs/2010/ecosoc6419.doc.htm>.

6
THE HUMAN RIGHTS COUNCIL

CONTENTS

6.1 THE UN COMMISSION ON HUMAN RIGHTS

The UN Commission on Human Rights was established in 1946, in one of the first acts of the newly formed United Nations. The intention behind the establishment of the Commission, under the auspices of the Economic and Social Council (ECOSOC), was to create a body that was smaller than the full membership of the United Nations to oversee the promotion and realisation of human rights, which formed one of the pillars of the new international legal order under the UN Charter.[1] The mandate of the Commission covered the human rights situation in all UN member states, drawing authority

1 See the discussion in Chapter 1.2.2, concerning the position of human rights under *UN Charter*.

from the commitments to human rights contained in the *UN Charter*.[2] The Commission was therefore considered a 'Charter body', as opposed to the 'treaty bodies', which oversee the implementation of specific human rights treaties and therefore have a mandate over only those states that are parties to the relevant treaty.

For the first 20 years of its life, the Commission concentrated on the development of international human rights standards. Its first task was to draft the *Universal Declaration of Human Rights* (UDHR).[3] The Commission was the principal forum for the discussion and debate of various human rights standards and for drafting new normative instruments, many of which went on to become UN General Assembly declarations or international treaties. The *International Covenant on Civil and Political Rights* (ICCPR), *International Covenant on Economic, Social and Cultural Rights* (ICESOC), *Convention on the Elimination of All Forms of Racial Discrimination* (CERD), *Convention Against Torture* (CAT), and *Convention on the Rights of the Child* (CROC), among others, all began as draft texts in the Commission.[4]

6.1.1 Inquiries into Gross and Systematic Human Rights Abuses

Until 1967, the Commission perceived this standard-setting and debate function to be its proper role and did not see a role for itself in investigating human rights violations or hearing complaints from victims.

ECOSOC resolution 1235 of 1967 introduced the first complaint procedure for gross and systematic human rights abuses in a particular country, which became known as the 1235 procedure. Resolution 1235 was prompted by a need to respond to the systematic racial discrimination occurring in South Africa and the territories then known as South West Africa and Southern Rhodesia. Its legacy, however, was not confined to that issue. The resolution authorised the Commission in appropriate cases 'to make a thorough study of situations which reveal a consistent pattern of violations of human rights, ... and report, with recommendations thereon, to the Economic and Social Council.'[5]

Despite the apparently soft language, the ability to conduct a 'thorough study' and make 'recommendations' was a marked departure from the realm of abstract standards, launching a new era of state-specific criticism for human rights abuses. Notably, however, the 1235 procedure was expressly for consistent patterns of abuse, rather than for allegations of human rights violations in a specific instance against a specific victim, such as might be considered by a treaty-monitoring committee.

Another procedure for the investigation of alleged systematic human rights abuses was introduced in 1970 through ECOSOC resolution 1503. That resolution allowed the Commission to consider complaints relating to 'situations which appear to reveal a consistent pattern of gross and reliably attested violations of human rights', and the procedure for the consideration of such complaints became known as the '1503 procedure'.

The 1503 procedure formalised a complaints mechanism, establishing a working group to receive complaints from any purported victim or any person with knowledge of gross and systematic human

2 *Charter of the United Nations (UN Charter)* June 26 1945, entered into force October 24 1945, arts 1(3), 55 and 56.

3 *Universal Declaration of Human Rights* (UDHR), GA Res. 217A (III). See also Chapter 1.3.

4 For a discussion of these treaties see Chapter 7.3.

5 *Economic and Social Council Resolution 1235* (XLII), UN doc E/4393 (1967), para 3.

rights abuses by any state. If the working group, drawn from the Subcommission (see below), considered that the complaint disclosed 'a consistent pattern of gross and reliably attested violations of human rights and fundamental freedoms'[6] and met the other criteria for admissibility, the Commission would engage confidentially with the relevant government to attempt to resolve the situation. The insistence on confidentiality was an attempt to use diplomatic pressure rather than naming and shaming or quasi-judicial mechanisms for declaring a violation of human rights. As a result, the 1503 procedure had its share of detractors as well as supporters.

As well as confidentiality, a key feature of the 1503 procedure was that it related to systemic human rights abuses, as opposed to a single, specific allegation of a human rights violation (which are the subject of individual communications procedures before the various treaty monitoring committees discussed in Chapter 7.4.7).

The rationale for confidentiality was to facilitate genuine, constructive engagement between the government, the purported victims, and the representatives of the Commission, which might not be possible if the government was forced to defend its position publicly. Confidentiality, however, also had its share of critics:

> Based on the premise that confidentiality would induce governments to cooperate with the United Nations, the 1503 procedure was a comfortable hiding place for governments, which relied on the argument that a discussion or investigation of a particular human rights situation under the 1503 procedure would pre-empt a public discussion or even the establishment of a country-specific procedure of the same situation.[7]

The complaints procedures pioneered by the 1235 and 1503 procedures in the Commission no longer operate, but have been adapted by the Human Rights Council as 'special procedures', discussed below.

6.1.2 Subcommission on the Promotion and Protection of Human Rights

At the first session of the UN Commission on Human Rights in 1947, a Subcommission then known as the Subcommission on the Prevention of Discrimination and Protection of Minorities was created under the authority of ECOSOC to assist the Commission in its work. While the Commission was an inherently political body comprised of member states, the Subcommission comprised a number of independent experts serving in their personal capacities, not as representatives of their governments.[8] In 1999 the name of the Subcommission was changed to the Subcommission on the Promotion and Protection of Human Rights.

The intention behind the Subcommission was to create a repository of independent, expert advice and a capacity to investigate human rights issues. A 2005 brochure produced by the Office of the High Commissioner for Human Rights described the Subcommission's role in the following terms:

---

6 *Economic and Social Council Resolution 1503* (XLVIII), (1970), UN Doc E/4832/ Add. 1, para 1.

7 J Gutter, 'Special Procedures and the Human Rights Council: Achievements and Challenges Ahead' (2007) 7 *Human Rights Law Review* 93, 98.

8 The original Subcommission had 12 members. By the time it was abolished in 2006, the Subcommission comprised 26 independent experts.

> The Subcommission is often described as a 'think tank' for the UN Commission on Human Rights as its central task is to assist the Commission in its work in specific areas relating to the prevention of discrimination of any kind in the exercise of human rights and fundamental freedoms and the protection of racial, national, religious and linguistic minorities. The Subcommission provides substantive input to the Commission's work by undertaking studies on human rights issues, making recommendations to the Commission and carrying out any other tasks that may be entrusted to it by the [Economic and Social] Council or the Commission.[9]

That official description of the Subcommission as a servant of the Commission belied the sometimes antagonistic relationship between the independent experts on the Subcommission and the diplomatic Commission to which they reported. Particularly in the last 15 years of its existence, the Subcommission took the initiative to pass its own resolutions, initiate its own studies on subjects that its members considered pertinent, and in some cases began drafting documents with a view to developing new legal instruments. Such initiatives were sometimes politically sensitive and were not always welcomed by the Commission. For example, between 1998 and 2003, the Subcommission drafted Norms of Responsibilities of Corporations with regard to Human Rights,[10] purporting to set out human rights standards applicable to corporations. The Commission's gruff response to the final version of the draft Norms was to '[a]ffirm that [it] has not been requested by the Commission and, as a draft proposal, has no legal standing, and that the Subcommission should not perform any monitoring function in this regard.'[11]

The bulk of the Subcommission's work was carried out by individual members nominated as Special Rapporteurs on a particular issue, or by Working Groups of several members, reporting back to the Subcommission as a whole for discussion and debate before the various reports were adopted and referred to the Commission for consideration.

In 2006 the Commission was replaced by the Human Rights Council, discussed below at Chapter 6.2. As part of the Human Rights Council's institution-building resolution of June 2007,[12] the Subcommission was abolished and replaced with an Advisory Committee, which is similarly composed of independent experts but lacks the Subcommission's ability to initiate its own studies, to draft standards or to pass resolutions. The Advisory Committee is discussed below at Chapter 6.4. Writing in January 2007, when the abolition of the Subcommission had not yet happened but was widely expected, Steiner, Alston and Goodman made the following comment on the work of the Subcommission:

> For many years it stood out because of its relative independence, its flexible agenda and working methods, its preparedness to act as a pressure group vis-à-vis its parent body (the Commission), and its ambiguous and often antagonistic relationship with that parent. It came under increasing attack in the 1990s and

9 Office of the High Commissioner for Human Rights, *The Subcommission on the Promotion and Protection of Human Rights*, 2005, <http://www2.ohchr.org/english/bodies/subcom/docs/leaflet2005-En.pdf>.

10 United Nations Subcommission on the Promotion and Protection of Human Rights, *Norms on the Responsibilities of Transnational Corporations and Other Business Enterprises with Regard to Human Rights*, UN Doc E/CN.4/Sub.2/2003/12/Rev.2 (26 August 2003); see Chapter 19.

11 UN Commission on Human Rights, Res 2004/116, para (c).

12 Human Rights Council, *Institution-Building of the United Nations Human Rights Council*, Res 5/1, 18 June 2007.

since 1999 has been instructed not to adopt resolutions on country situations under consideration by the Commission. It previously played an important role by adopting resolutions which put pressure on the Commission to act in relation to specific situations.[13]

6.1.3 Special Procedures

The capacity of the Commission to engage with human rights in the field, as distinct from the debates and standard-setting activities carried out in Geneva, was largely met through the so-called 'special procedures'. Special procedures was the collective name given to the various country-specific and thematic mandates of individual experts and expert working groups appointed by the Commission to investigate and report back. (A list of current thematic mandates appears below at Chapter 6.5.) The mandates created by the Subcommission, as well as the working group responsible for communications under the 1503 complaint procedure, also fell under the umbrella of special procedures. The tasks entrusted to the various special procedure mandate holders varied considerably from one mandate to another.

When the Human Rights Council was established, the question of whether to continue some or all (or none) of the special procedures attracted significant debate. The interim solution was for the Council to assume the mandates of the Commission and to undertake a review of all those mandates within the Council's first year.[14] Many of the special procedures in the Commission continue under the Human Rights Council, and are discussed further below.

6.1.4 Inaction in the Face of Atrocities

A frequently cited criticism of the Commission was its failure to act, or the watered down nature of its actions when it finally did act, in the face of atrocities demanding urgent action. The case that perhaps best encapsulates this criticism is that of the ongoing genocide in Rwanda in 1994.

The United Nations, through its field commander, was aware of the trouble brewing several months before the genocide started. The special session of the UN Commission on Human Rights convened in late May 1994, at the height of the Rwandan genocide, is with hindsight often cited as a classic example of weak action in the face of dire and urgent need, caused by political paralysis.[15]

However, as far as practical measures to stem the violence is concerned, particularly relating to the use of force, it should be noted that the UN Security Council rather than the UN Commission on Human Rights was the body with the relevant authority. The rhetoric of the Commission at that session, and of course the UN Security Council and other bodies meeting contemporaneously, was not accompanied by sufficient concrete action to stop the genocide.

13 H Steiner, P Alston & R Goodman, *International Human Rights in Context: Law, Politics, Morals*, 3rd edn, Oxford University Press, Oxford, 2008, 740.

14 GA Res 60/251 (15 March 2006), para 6.

15 UN Commission on Human Rights, *Report of the Third Special Session*, 24–25 May 1994, UN Document E/CN.4/S-3/4. The focus of much of the retrospective criticism on the Commission on this issue is on the wording of the fifth paragraph of the preamble of the Commission's resolution S-3/1 (25 May 1994) at a time when the estimated number killed already exceeded 500,000: 'Believing that genocidal events may have occurred in Rwanda'. The Rwandan genocide is discussed further in Chapter 11.4.2.

This example and others like it were raised frequently when the architecture of the new Human Rights Council was being debated, in the hope that such inaction would not be repeated in the future.

6.1.5 Politicisation of the Commission and Calls for Reform

Although criticism of the Commission persisted throughout its existence, as it does for any significant international institution, a sustained wave of criticism emerged from the Western states, especially the United States, from the beginning of the twenty-first century.[16] The principal assertion was that the Commission was tainted by political bias. It was alleged that states sought membership of the Commission not to advance the realisation of human rights, but to protect themselves and their allies from being targeted by the Commission. Critics argued that the Commission was selective in the states it singled out for criticism, focusing disproportionately on Israel, while ignoring the grave human rights abuses occurring in states such as Sudan, Iran, Zimbabwe and Cuba. The United States Department of State for example, noted in relation to UN Commission on Human Rights activity in 2005:[17]

> Despite the fact that the Secretary General and member states decried the UNCHR's declining credibility, the U.S. Government achieved virtually all of its priority objectives at the 2005 session of UN Commission on Human Rights. Together with its allies the United States defeated efforts to pass no-action motions and adopted resolutions on freedom of association, democracy, and the human rights situations in Cuba, Belarus, North Korea, and Burma. The U.S. and its allies secured passage of resolutions that supported human rights technical assistance but also condemned the human rights situations in Sudan and Nepal. International condemnation of anti-Semitism was referenced in a resolution on religious intolerance, and the CHR also defeated a resolution introduced by Cuba on detainees at Guantanamo.

The Commission, according to its critics, had turned into an institution that did not focus on the most serious and grave human rights atrocities in the world, but used human rights rhetoric as an instrument for advancing the political agenda of whichever group of states had the numbers on the Commission, at the expense of their ideological opponents. Balakrishnan Rajagopal has pointed out that in its early years, the Commission displayed political bias in favour of the West, failing to examine human rights abuses occurring in the course of colonial rule and systematic racial discrimination in the United States.[18] With the change in numbers as a result of the newly independent states joining the UN following decolonisation in the 1960s and 70s, the focus of political selectivity also shifted. In the last 15 years of its operation, the Commission therefore had a strong focus on issues of concern to the developing states that comprised its majority, such as the right to development, while the identity of states subjected to frequent criticism also changed to reflect the interests of the majority

16 See for example the letter from US Ambassador to the United Nations, John Bolton, to all UN member states dated 30 August 2005, stating, inter alia, 'States have sought membership of the Commission not to strengthen human rights, but to protect themselves against criticism or to criticize others. As a result, a credibility deficit has developed, which casts a shadow on the reputation of the United Nations system as a whole.'

17 United States Department of State, *FY 2005 Performance and Accountability Report*, 'November 2005, Strategic Goal 7: Democracy and Human Rights—Performance Results for Performance Goal 2', <http://www.state.gov/s/d/rm/rls/perfrpt/2005/html/56359.htm>.

18 B Rajagopal, 'Lipstick on a Caterpillar? Assessing the New Human Rights Council through Historical Reflection' (2007) 13 *Buffalo Human Rights Law Review*, 7, 8–9.

bloc. South Africa was therefore a primary target of Commission resolutions during the apartheid era, while Israel was criticised in more resolutions than any other state during the Commission's life, and increasingly so from the 1990s to 2005.

> The focus on South Africa and Israel came out of the simple fact that the Commission - along with the ECOSOC and the General Assembly—was one of the arenas where the Third World could bring in issues of racial discrimination and self-determination, as the most powerful U.N. organ, the Security Council, was unavailable due to the veto powers of the U.S. and other allies of Israel and South Africa.[19]

It should be remembered that the UN Commission on Human Rights was a political institution, in that it was composed of representatives of those UN member states elected to the Commission. This is a stark contrast to the treaty monitoring bodies examined in Chapter 4, which are composed of independent experts who do not represent their home states. Accordingly, it should hardly be surprising that the work of an inherently political body was politicised. The same is certainly true of all other UN bodies whose work is conducted by diplomats representing their respective governments, including the UN Security Council and the UN General Assembly.

Whatever the merits of the 'politicisation' argument, including the premise that the politicisation of the Commission was both new and unintended,[20] it became the basis of calls for reform of the Commission. The most prominent example of such a call is the document entitled *In Larger Freedom*, issued by the then UN Secretary-General, Kofi Annan, in March 2005, extracted below. *In Larger Freedom* set out a blueprint for UN reform, aimed at better achieving security and human rights in a world that had changed significantly since the UN was founded in 1945.

IN LARGER FREEDOM: TOWARDS DEVELOPMENT, SECURITY AND HUMAN RIGHTS FOR ALL:[21]

PROPOSED HUMAN RIGHTS COUNCIL

181 The Commission on Human Rights has given the international community a universal human rights framework, comprising the Universal Declaration on Human Rights, the two International Covenants and other core human rights treaties. During its annual session, the Commission draws public attention to human rights issues and debates, provides a forum for the development of United Nations human rights policy and establishes a unique system of independent and expert special procedures to observe and analyse human rights compliance by theme and by country. The Commission's close engagement with hundreds of civil society organizations provides an opportunity for working with civil society that does not exist elsewhere.

182 Yet the Commission's capacity to perform its tasks has been increasingly undermined by its declining credibility and professionalism. In particular, States have sought membership of the Commission not to strengthen human rights but to protect themselves against criticism or to criticize others. As a result,

19 Ibid 13.

20 See F Hampson, 'An Overview of the Reform of the UN Human Rights Machinery' (2007) 7 *Human Rights Law Review* 7, 8, arguing that politicisation was not only present from the outset of the Commission, but that it was an intended and necessary element of such a body.

21 Report of the Secretary-General, 21 March 2005, UN Doc A/59/2005.

a credibility deficit has developed, which casts a shadow on the reputation of the United Nations system as a whole.

183 If the United Nations is to meet the expectations of men and women everywhere—and indeed, if the Organization is to take the cause of human rights as seriously as those of security and development—then Member States should agree to replace the Commission on Human Rights with a smaller standing Human Rights Council. Member States would need to decide if they want the Human Rights Council to be a principal organ of the United Nations or a subsidiary body of the General Assembly, but in either case its members would be elected directly by the General Assembly by a two-thirds majority of members present and voting. The creation of the Council would accord human rights a more authoritative position, corresponding to the primacy of human rights in the *Charter of the United Nations*. Member States should determine the composition of the Council and the term of office of its members. Those elected to the Council should undertake to abide by the highest human rights standards.

6.2 THE HUMAN RIGHTS COUNCIL

The UN General Assembly voted on 15 March 2006[22] to create a Human Rights Council to replace the UN Commission on Human Rights, which would be abolished after its final session in March 2006. The vote was 170 states in favour, four states opposed (the United States, Israel, the Marshall Islands and Palau) and three states abstaining (Belarus, Iran and Venezuela).

GENERAL ASSEMBLY RESOLUTION 60/251[23]

[Preamble]

...

Recognizing the work undertaken by the Commission on Human Rights and the need to preserve and build on its achievements and to redress its shortcomings,

Recognizing also the importance of ensuring universality, objectivity and non-selectivity in the consideration of human rights issues, and the elimination of double standards and politicization,

Recognizing further that the promotion and protection of human rights should be based on the principles of cooperation and genuine dialogue and aimed at strengthening the capacity of Member States to comply with their human rights obligations for the benefit of all human beings

[Operative paragraphs]

8. Decides that the membership in the Council shall be open to all States Members of the United Nations; when electing members of the Council, Member States shall take into account the contribution of candidates to the promotion and protection of human rights and their voluntary pledges and commitments made thereto; the General Assembly, by a two-thirds majority of the members present and voting, may suspend the rights of membership in the Council of a member of the Council that commits gross and systematic violations of human rights;

22 GA Res 60/251 (15 March 2006).

23 Ibid.

9 *Decides also* that members elected to the Council shall uphold the highest standards in the promotion and protection of human rights, shall fully cooperate with the Council and be reviewed under the universal periodic review mechanism during their term of membership;

6.2.1 Structure of the Human Rights Council: Depoliticisation?

The Council was established as a subsidiary body of the UN General Assembly, rather than of ECOSOC, giving it a higher status than the Commission, but a lesser status than the option canvassed by the UN Secretary-General of making the Council a principal organ of the United Nations, on a par (at least in hierarchical terms) with the UN Security Council and ECOSOC.

In response to the criticisms that gave rise to the replacement of the Commission with a new Human Rights Council, some of the key objectives in designing the structure of the Council were to make it smaller, to make it less politically motivated and less selective in its focus, and to prevent habitual human rights abusers from being elected to the Council.

The size of the Council was set at 47 states, only marginally reduced from the 53 on the Commission at the time of its demise. The opportunity was also taken to reallocate regional representation on the Council to reflect proportions of world population and number of UN member states more accurately, resulting in an increase in the proportion of seats allocated to developing regions compared with the former Commission. The regional representation on the Human Rights Council is 13 seats for the Asian Group (1 more than on the Commission), 13 for the African Group (2 fewer), 6 for the Eastern European Group (1 more), 8 for the Latin American and Caribbean Group (3 fewer) and 7 for the Western European and Others Group, which includes Australia, Canada and the USA (3 fewer).

In the Commission, as in most UN bodies, the practice had been for regional groupings to decide among themselves which states would occupy the seats allocated to that region for a given year. ECOSOC would then be presented with a group of candidate states matching the number of vacancies for the particular region, making their election a *fait accompli*. In effect, election to the Commission (and many other UN bodies) was therefore determined by lobbying within regional blocs. In attempting to depoliticise the Council and to make a state's human rights record a relevant factor in determining whether or not it could be elected to the Council, a different election system was established.

Provision was made for the suspension of members that have committed 'gross and systematic violations of human rights.'[24] Such suspension is effected by a vote of two-thirds of the members of the UN General Assembly. At the time of writing, the suspension mechanism had yet to be used.

6.2.2 Election to the Human Rights Council

Members of the Human Rights Council are elected by a secret ballot in the UN General Assembly. In exercising that vote, member states are directed to 'take into account the contribution of candidates to the promotion and protection of human rights and their voluntary pledges and commitments made

24 Ibid para 8.

thereto',[25] although the weight given to such considerations as opposed to political considerations is obviously impossible to verify. In practice, there is nothing to prevent regional blocs agreeing among themselves to have the same number of states nominate as there are vacancies.

In the first four years of elections to the Human Rights Council, nominations matched vacancies for a given region approximately half of the time. The African Group received the same number of nominations as vacancies on 3 out of 4 occasions; Asia 2 out of 4; Latin America and Caribbean 3 out of 4; Western European and Others 1 out 4; Eastern Europe received more nominations than vacancies on all 4 occasions.

In the 2007 election, non-governmental organisations (NGOs) and other states prevailed on Bosnia and Herzegovina to stand for election to the Council at the last minute, along with Slovenia and Belarus, to ensure that the two vacancies for the Eastern European Group would be contested, thereby presenting a challenge to Belarus, which had a particularly poor human rights record—a strategy that ultimately succeeded when Bosnia and Herzegovina defeated Belarus in the second round of balloting for the final vacancy. In the 2009 election, on the other hand, the number of nominations in the Western European and Others Group matched the number of vacancies for the first time. This was also the first time that the United States was a candidate.

As part of the plan to have more human rights 'leaders' on the Council, states are encouraged to make voluntary pledges when standing for election, pledging action in relation to the implementation of human rights at the national level, as well as cooperation with and participation in international mechanisms.[26] In the 2009 election, 16 of the 20 states competing for vacancies on the Council submitted voluntary pledges.[27] Although such pledges are not legally binding in the manner of treaty commitments, they do come within the ambit of the Universal Periodic Review, described below, when the pledging state is reviewed.

HUMAN RIGHTS COMMITMENTS AND PLEDGES OF THE UNITED STATES OF AMERICA, 22 APRIL 2009[28]

The deep commitment of the United States to championing the human rights enshrined in the Universal Declaration of Human Rights is driven by the founding values of our nation and the conviction that international peace, security and prosperity are strengthened when human rights and fundamental freedoms are respected and protected. As the United States seeks to advance human rights and fundamental freedoms around the world, we do so cognizant of our own commitment to live up to our ideals at home and to meet our international human rights obligations. We therefore make the following pledges:

25 Ibid para 8.

26 The Office of the High Commissioner for Human Rights issued 'suggested elements for voluntary pledges and commitments by candidates for election to the Human Rights Council', available at <http://www2.ohchr.org/english/bodies/hrcouncil/docs/pledges.pdf>.

27 Such pledges become official General Assembly documents and are made publicly available. The 2009 pledges can be viewed at <http://www.un.org/ga/63/elections/hrc_elections.shtml>. The four candidate states not submitting voluntary pledges in 2009 were Saudi Arabia, Kyrgyzstan, Nigeria and Bangladesh, all of which were subsequently elected. The 2010 election results can be viewed at <http://www.un.org/en/ga/64/elections/hrc/index.shtml>.

28 UN Doc A/63/831.

COMMITMENT TO ADVANCING HUMAN RIGHTS IN THE UNITED NATIONS SYSTEM

1 The United States commits to continuing its efforts in the United Nations system to be a strong advocate for all people around the world who suffer from abuse and oppression, and to be a stalwart defender of courageous individuals across the globe who work, often at great personal risk, on behalf of the rights of others.

2 The United States commits to working with principled determination for a balanced, credible and effective United Nations Human Rights Council to advance the purpose of the Universal Declaration of Human Rights. To that same end, in partnership with the international community, we fully intend to promote universality, transparency and objectivity in all of the Council's endeavours. The United States commits to participating fully in the universal periodic review process and looks forward to the review in 2010 of its own record in promoting and protecting human rights and fundamental freedoms in the United States.

3 The United States is committed to advancing the promotion and protection of human rights and fundamental freedoms in the General Assembly and the Third Committee, and in this vein intends to actively participate in the 2011 review by the General Assembly of the work of the Human Rights Council.

4 The United States is also committed to the promotion and protection of human rights through regional organizations. Through our membership in the Organization for Security and Cooperation in Europe and the Organization of American States, the United States commits to continuing efforts to uphold human rights and fundamental freedoms, and to strengthening and developing institutions and mechanisms for their protection. In particular recognition of its human rights commitments within the inter-American system, the United States strongly supports the work of the Inter-American Commission on Human Rights.

5 The United States recognizes and upholds the vital role of civil society and human rights defenders in the promotion and protection of human rights and commits to promoting the effective involvement of non-governmental organizations in the work of the United Nations, including the Human Rights Council, and other international organizations.

6 As part of our commitment to the principle of universality of human rights, the United States commits to working with our international partners in the spirit of openness, consultation and respect and reaffirms that expressions of concern about the human rights situation in any country, our own included, are appropriate matters for international discussion.

COMMITMENT TO ADVANCING HUMAN RIGHTS AND FUNDAMENTAL FREEDOMS IN THE UNITED STATES

1 The United States executive branch is committed to working with its legislative branch to consider the possible ratification of human rights treaties, including but not limited to the Convention on the Elimination of All Forms of Discrimination against Women and ILO Convention No. 111 concerning Discrimination in Respect of Employment and Occupation.

2 The United States is committed to meeting its United Nations treaty obligations and participating in a meaningful dialogue with treaty body members.

3 The United States is committed to cooperating with the human rights mechanisms of the United Nations, as well as the Inter-American Commission on Human Rights and other regional human rights bodies, by responding to inquiries, engaging in dialogues and hosting visits.

4 The United States is also strongly committed to fighting racism and discrimination, and acts of violence committed because of racial or ethnic hatred. Despite the achievements of the civil rights movement and many years of striving to achieve equal rights for all, racism still exists in our country and we continue to fight it.

5 The United States is committed to continuing to promote human prosperity and human rights and fundamental freedoms of all persons within the United States, including through enforcement of the Americans with Disabilities Act and its amendments, engaging religious and community leaders in upholding religious freedom and pluralism, and encouraging the members of the private sector to serve as good corporate citizens both in the United States and overseas.

6.2.3 Universality and non-selectivity

The other key elements of the Council that were supposed to distinguish it from the Commission were the principles of universality and non-selectivity. These apply to the categorisation of human rights issues, such that civil, political, economic, social and cultural rights are to be treated as indivisible and equally important.[29] The right to development, which has been as issue of great importance to developing countries, is also singled out for special attention by the Human Rights Council.[30]

Universality and non-selectivity are also supposed to apply to the Council's treatment of human rights implementation and reports of and responses to violations. In other words, the Council's mandate expressly directs it not to engage in the politically motivated targeting of certain states for human rights violations that was considered to have plagued the Commission.

6.3 SESSIONS OF THE HUMAN RIGHTS COUNCIL

The Council is mandated by the UN General Assembly resolution that established it to sit for at least three sessions per year, for a total of at least ten weeks,[31] compared to the single six-week session previously held by the Commission. The Council is also able to hold special sessions whenever needed, with the support of one third of its membership.[32] That provision is supposed to enable the Council to respond quickly to emergency situations, while the low threshold for calling a special session should prevent political stonewalling, although states' behaviour once the session is underway is another matter.

6.3.1 The First Session: June 2006

The first session of the Council was held from 19 to 30 June 2006. As a temporary measure, most of the functions of the former Commission, including the special procedures, most of the ongoing

29 Ibid preambular paras 3 and 12, paras 2 and 4.

30 Ibid preambular 12, para 4.

31 Ibid para 10.

32 Ibid para 10. The Commission was also empowered to convene special sessions from 1990 pursuant to ECOSOC Resolution 1990/48 (25 May 1990), although those special sessions required support from a majority of the Commission's members.

thematic and country mandates, and the 1503 complaint procedure, were rolled over and continued operation under the Council while the Council decided how it would conduct itself.[33] That question of the operational mechanisms of the new Council occupied much of the time in the ordinary sessions during the Council's first year, culminating in the 'institution-building' resolution passed at the fifth session in June 2007, which addressed the procedural workings of the Council.

Despite the primary focus on mechanics in the early sessions, a number of substantive issues were debated, and the role of the Council in setting human rights standards, which it inherited from the Commission, was taken up immediately. The *International Covenant for the Protection of All Persons from Enforced Disappearance* was adopted, paving the way for a new human rights treaty.[34] The *Declaration on the Rights of Indigenous Peoples* was also adopted,[35] while progress was made on standard setting in other areas.

The first session of the Human Rights Council was watched closely by supporters and opponents alike. While there were considerable successes in establishing the institutional mechanisms and in certain areas of standard setting, the Council's first session also attracted considerable criticism, primarily related to the campaign by the Organisation of the Islamic Conference to target the issue of human rights in Israel and the Occupied Palestinian Territories, not least because the manner in which those efforts were conducted was the very reason cited by many for the loss of credibility of the former Commission. The following extract by observers Chris Sidoti and Nicholas Calacouras of the International Service for Human Rights provides an account of the proceedings of the first session.

THE HUMAN RIGHTS COUNCIL: WHERE ARE WE NOW? CHRIS SIDOTI AND NICHOLAS CALACOURAS, INTERNATIONAL SERVICE FOR HUMAN RIGHTS[36]

The new Human Rights Council (the Council) held its first session from 19 to 30 June 2006, amid hope and scepticism. The session failed to live up to the rhetoric of a 'new start' and a 'new commitment' to human rights but it was certainly far better than many had feared. The pity was that the many accomplishments and good spirit of most of the two-week session were dissipated by the highly politicised, selective actions initiated by the member States of the Organisation of the Islamic Conference (OIC) during the last hours of the session.

The former Commission on Human Rights (the Commission) had been abolished and replaced by the Human Rights Council precisely because of its perceived politicisation and selectivity. General Assembly *Resolution 60/251* proclaimed a new working methodology of collaboration, objectivity, and even-handedness. The debates of the Council in the plenary generally reflected this. There was less heat, less provocation and less confrontation than in

33 See above, n 14, para 6; Commission on Human Rights, *Procedural Resolution on the Closure of the Work of the Commission*, UN Document E/CN.4/2006/L.2 (24 March 2006); Human Rights Council, *Extension by the Human Rights Council of All Mandates, Mechanisms, Functions and Responsibilities of the Commission on Human Rights*, UN Document A/HRC/1/L.6 (29 June 2006).

34 *International Covenant for the Protection of All Persons from Enforced Disappearance*, opened for signature 20 December 2006 (entered into force 23 December 2010).

35 GA Res 61/295 (2 October 2007), adopted by the Human Rights Council on 29 June 2006, see Chapter 13.2.2.

36 <www.ishr.ch>.

recent years. The informal consultations on draft resolutions running parallel to the plenary were different. There, the discussions sounded more like the rejected past than a new hopeful future.

Whether the new Council will be different from the old Commission remains an open question. Fortunately, however, its first session produced some very good results.

STANDARD-SETTING

While important institution-building work had to be done, the Council's first session was also marked by the adoption of two important new human rights instruments, after years of negotiations. First, the Council adopted by consensus the *International Convention for the Protection of All Persons from Enforced Disappearance* 6. Then it finalised 21 years of work, first through the Subcommission and then through a Commission working group by adopting the *Declaration on the Rights of Indigenous Peoples*. Regrettably this was not so consensual, with Council members Canada and Russia, supported by non-members Australia, New Zealand, and the United States, fighting adoption to the end and forcing a vote. The end vote was 30 in favour, two against with 12 abstentions …

The Council also made progress on a possible new instrument, an *Optional Protocol* to the *International Covenant on Economic, Social and Cultural Rights* to permit individual complaints under the Covenant. It extended the open-ended intergovernmental Working Group for two years with a specific mandate to prepare a draft *Optional Protocol*. The Working Group will meet for ten working days per year and will report back to the Council.

The Council took two other decisions by consensus in relation to human rights standards. The Working Group on the Effective Implementation of the Durban Declaration and Programme of Action was also extended for a further three years. A report is to be presented to this Working Group at its next session, prepared by five experts appointed by the High Commissioner, on the 'content and scope of the substantive gaps in the existing international instruments to combat racism, racial discrimination, xenophobia and related intolerance'. The Committee on the Elimination of Racial Discrimination has also been requested to make recommendations to strengthen the implementation of the *Convention on the Elimination of Racial Discrimination*. The Council also renewed the mandate of the Working Group on the Right to Development for one year.

SUBSTANTIVE ISSUES

Many feared that the Council was at risk of addressing only procedural matters during its first session, ignoring pressing or substantive human rights issues. In response to this, the Council dedicated a part of the work program to the discussion of five substantive issues: the situation of human rights in Palestine and other Occupied Arab Territories; the *Abuja Peace Agreements* in the Sudan; the human rights of migrants; the role of human rights defenders; and avoiding incitement to religious or racial hatred and violence through the promotion of tolerance and dialogue.

These discussions were intended to result in a Presidential Statement, reflecting a consensus on the issues. Instead the Council adopted resolutions on incitement to religious hatred and the human rights situation in Palestine and other Occupied Arab Territories. These resolutions dealt with very serious human rights issues. They could and should have been developed as consensus resolutions. But the sponsors, predominantly member States of the organisation of the Islamic Conference, rejected the opportunity to have good, strong resolutions passed by consensus. As a result, unbalanced, deficient resolutions were passed on a vote of Council member States, with significant numbers voting against them.

Positively, the resolutions represent important endorsements of the system and functions of the special procedures, both thematic and country-specific mandates, and the concept of the new Council as a standing or permanent body that becomes seized of a matter and receives regular reports in relation to it. These are important precedents for the future.

The Council also adopted statements on hostage-taking and on the entry into force of the *Optional Protocol* to the *Convention against Torture*, both declaratory statements with little follow-up envisaged.

A LAST WORD

The first session of the new Human Rights Council was better than expected, though certainly not all that we could have hoped for. Much of its success is due to the astute management of the process by the President, Ambassador de Alba. The Council is fortunate to have him as its leader during this formative first year. Building this institution will be a long and complex task and its success is not assured. The work has only just begun.

6.3.2 Conduct of a Council Session

The standing agenda for the regular sessions of the Human Rights Council comprises the following ten items:[37]

1 Organizational and procedural matters
2 Annual report of the United Nations High Commissioner for Human Rights and reports of the Office of the High Commissioner and the Secretary-General
3 Promotion and protection of all human rights, civil, political, economic, social and cultural rights, including the right to development
4 Human rights situations that require the Council's attention
5 Human rights bodies and mechanisms
6 Universal Periodic Review
7 Human rights situation in Palestine and other occupied Arab territories
8 Follow-up and implementation of the *Vienna Declaration and Programme of Action*[38]
9 Racism, racial discrimination, xenophobia and related forms of intolerance, follow-up and implementation of the Durban Declaration and Programme of Action
10 Technical assistance and capacity-building

Several of the agenda items are built around receiving and discussing the reports of mandate holders under the Special Procedures, which are discussed below. The complaint procedure, addressed under agenda item 5, and the Universal Periodic Review are also discussed below.

Agenda items 3 and 4 are sufficiently broad to accommodate specific issues that states wish to discuss. Agenda item 3, dealing with human rights broadly, is used for initiatives in standard setting. States can propose issues for the consideration of the Council, leading to debate and in some cases to a resolution of the Council. 'Human rights situations that require the Council's attention' in agenda

37 Human Rights Council, see above, n 12, part V.

38 See also chapter 1.5.2.

item 4 is used for discussion of state-specific human rights situations, generally involving allegations of serious human rights abuses.

States that are present as observers, as well as member states of the council, are allowed to participate in debate, as are accredited NGOs.[39]

6.3.3 Special Sessions

The capacity of the Human Rights Council to call a special session with the support of one-third of Council members was utilised immediately, and the first special session was convened on 5 July 2006, the week after the first ordinary session concluded. The first special session was requested by Tunisia on behalf of the Group of Arab States 'to consider the latest escalation of the situation in the Palestinian and other occupied Arab territories'.[40] The request was supported by 21 members of the Council,[41] thus meeting the threshold for a special session.

The first special session passed a single resolution that expressed concern at the violations of the human rights of the Palestinian people caused by the Israeli occupation of the Occupied Palestinian Territories, demanded an end to the occupation, called for compliance with international law by 'all concerned parties' (after a more one-sided draft was amended during the session) and decided to 'dispatch an urgent fact-finding mission' headed by the Special Rapporteur on the human rights situation in the Palestinian Territories.[42] The resolution was adopted by a vote of 29 to 11, with five abstentions. The vote followed geographical groupings, with Western and Eastern European states mostly voting against the resolution, while Asian, African and Latin American states either supported it or abstained.[43]

The second special session, held in August 2006, focused on the conflict at the time between Israel and Lebanon. The session was again requested by Tunisia on behalf of the Group of Arab States, this time 'to consider and take action on the gross human rights violations, by Israel in Lebanon, including the Qana massacre, the countrywide targeting of innocent civilians and the destruction of vital civilian infrastructure'.[44] Once again, the resolution condemning actions by the Israeli military was adopted by a vote essentially along geographical lines, this time 27 votes to 11, with eight abstentions.

When the third special session in November 2006 followed the same pattern, once again focusing on the human rights situation in the Occupied Palestinian Territories, critics of the Council had plenty of ammunition in support of their claims that the Human Rights Council was dysfunctional and a forum for political game-playing, rather than a body genuinely attempting to address the most pressing human

39 See Chapter 6.8 and Chapter 9.

40 Letter dated 30 June 2006 from the Permanent Representative of Tunisia to the President of the Human Rights Council, UN Document A/HRC/S-1/1 (4 July 2006).

41 The request was supported by Algeria; Azerbaijan; Bahrain; Bangladesh; Brazil; China; Cuba; Gabon; India; Indonesia; Jordan; Malaysia; Mali; Morocco; Pakistan; Russian Federation; Saudi Arabia; Senegal; South Africa; Sri Lanka; and Tunisia.

42 Human Rights Council Res S-1/Res.1 (6 July 2006).

43 The exceptions were Russia (Eastern European group), which supported the Resolution; Japan (Asian group), which opposed it; and Switzerland (Western European and Others group), which abstained.

44 Letter dated 7 August 2006 from the Permanent Representative of Tunisia to the President of the Human Rights Council, UN Document A/HRC/S-2/1 (9 August 2006).

rights issues of the day. While the human rights problems in the Middle East are indeed profound—and were particularly pressing in mid-2006 given the hostilities between Israel and Lebanon—it is difficult to justify all of the Human Rights Council's first three special sessions being spent on that region, to the exclusion of egregious human rights violations occurring elsewhere. If nothing else, for a fledgling institution looking for the support of the international community that had abandoned its predecessor, the early fixation on Israel in special sessions was probably unwise in pragmatic terms.

Perhaps recognising this problem, the special sessions of the Human Rights Council that took place after the Council's first six months, initiated by Western states but with support across all regions, focused on some of the other protracted human rights problems around the world. The fourth special session was requested by a broad group of states[45] and focused on Darfur, which had been the scene of long-running internal conflict frequently described as genocide. The decision of the Council to dispatch a High-Level Mission to monitor the human rights situation in Darfur was adopted by the Human Rights Council by consensus.[46] The consensual nature of the Darfur special session, both in the manner of calling it and in the way it was conducted, including the ability to adopt the text of a decision without calling for a vote, stands in stark contrast to the predictable political divides of the three special sessions that preceded it.

The pattern of focusing on pressing human rights problems in special sessions continued after the Darfur session. The fifth special session, in October 2007, focused on human rights in Myanmar, triggered by a violent crackdown on political protests the previous month. Subsequent special sessions focused on the world food crisis (seventh special session, May 2008), the human rights impact of the global financial crisis (tenth special session, February 2009), post-disaster recovery in Haiti (thirteenth special session, January 2010) and the situations in the Congo (eighth special session, November-December 2008), Sri Lanka (tenth special session, May 2009) the Cote d'Ivoire (fourteenth special session, December 2010), Libya (fifteenth special session February 2011) and Syria (sixteenth special session, April 2011).

The topic of Israel and the Palestinian Territories has featured in recent special sessions, prompted by Israeli military incursions into Gaza in January 2008. However, a total of three special sessions in four years since the end of 2006 is not the smoking gun of the Council's disproportionality and selectivity that critics pointed to in the first 6 months. After a rocky start, it seems that the ability to convene a special session quickly, with broad but not necessarily majority support, has been used capably by the Human Rights Council to deal with pressing human rights issues as they arise. The effectiveness of the Council's response to those issues once a special session has been convened is another matter, turning as it does on the availability of tools to the Human Rights Council and the prevalence of political will.

---

45 Letter dated 30 November 2006 from the Permanent Representative of Finland to the President of the Human Rights Council, UN Document A/HRC/S-4/1 (4 December 2006). 35 states drawn from all regional groups signed the formal request from Finland for a special session.

46 Human Rights Council, *Situation of Human Rights in Darfur*, Decision S-4/101 (13 December 2006).

6.4 ADVISORY COMMITTEE

It was noted above that the Subcommission on the Promotion and Protection of Human Rights—the body comprising independent experts reporting to the former UN Commission on Human Rights—was abolished in 2007 and replaced with an Advisory Committee. While the independence and the quality of the work produced by the Subcommission was highly valued by at least some states and a large number of NGOs, many states had long been uneasy about the Subcommission's penchant for undertaking work on its own initiative, leaving the Commission (and later the Council) to respond to sensitive or unpalatable issues that had not been filtered through diplomatic channels. When the Human Rights Council was created in 2006 to replace the Commission, the Subcommission was initially left standing; however, it met its demise in 2007 in the Institution-Building Resolution, in which the Subcommission was replaced by the Advisory Committee.

The formal description of the Advisory Committee's role in the instrument by which it was established is as follows:[47]

> 65 The Human Rights Council Advisory Committee, composed of 18 experts serving in their personal capacity, will function as a think-tank for the Council and work at its direction.
>
> 75 The function of the Advisory Committee is to provide expertise to the Council in the manner and form requested by the Council, focusing mainly on studies and research-based advice. Further, such expertise shall be rendered only upon the latter's request, in compliance with its resolutions and under its guidance.
>
> 76 The Advisory Committee should be implementation-oriented and the scope of its advice should be limited to thematic issues pertaining to the mandate of the Council; namely promotion and protection of all human rights.
>
> 77 The Advisory Committee shall not adopt resolutions or decisions. The Advisory Committee may propose within the scope of the work set out by the Council, for the latter's consideration and approval, suggestions for further enhancing its procedural efficiency, as well as further research proposals within the scope of the work set out by the Council.

It is apparent from that description that much of the Advisory Committee's role is defined in terms of what it must not do: namely, render unsolicited advice, exceed the scope of its instructions or adopt resolutions or decisions—all of which brought its predecessor, the Subcommission, into regular conflict with its parent body.

The intention behind the Advisory Committee is to retain the capacity for independent study of issues, engagement, field work, drafting and standard-setting that the Subcommission had provided, while neutering the body's potential as a gadfly to states on the Council. Since the Advisory Committee held its first session in August 2008, that 'think-tank' work has indeed continued, including the important role of overseeing the complaint procedure and coordinating much of the work of the Special Procedures, both of which are discussed below.

47 Human Rights Council, see above, n 12, paras 65 and 75–7.

6.5 SPECIAL PROCEDURES

The capacity of the Human Rights Council to investigate human rights issues and engage with people on the ground in relation to a particular human rights situation is delivered through the mechanisms known as Special Procedures. The Special Procedures are a series of mandates for independent experts or groups of experts to investigate either a specific human rights issue worldwide (known as a thematic mandate) or the human rights situation in a specific country (known as a country mandate). The mandate holders are given various titles, such as Independent Expert, Special Rapporteur or Special Representative of the UN Secretary-General, although the title has no substantial bearing on the powers, status or procedures employed under a particular mandate. Some mandates are allotted to a Working Group rather than an individual.

The terms of every mandate are different, being the result of a unique political negotiation when that particular mandate was established. Conducting studies of a human rights situation, often including country visits and receiving complaints of human rights violations, is a core part of the task of most Special Procedures. But the issues chosen for investigation by the creation of a special procedure mandate have always been the subject of controversy, particularly from the perspective of a country being investigated or from its allies. For that reason, some rapporteurs received greater cooperation than others, and some mandates were considered to be more productive than others in terms of achieving positive human rights outcomes.

The degree of cooperation that mandate holders have received over the years from the governments of countries they wished to visit—for instance to survey the human rights situation in a particular region, inspect a particular institution or interview affected individuals—has, not surprisingly, varied greatly. As the Special Procedures do not come with coercive powers, mandate holders can only enter a country, or a region or a facility within a country, with the consent and cooperation of the relevant government. When such cooperation has not been forthcoming, the effectiveness of the relevant mandate has often been compromised. This has been one of the key criticisms of the existence of country mandates, given that a state singled out for scrutiny and criticism by a mandate is unlikely to be kindly disposed towards the mandate holder, thereby limiting the effectiveness of the procedure. For this reason, among others, there has been a sustained shift away from country mandates in favour of thematic mandates in recent years, decreasing from a high of 26 country mandates in 1998 to just eight by the time of the Council's institution-building resolution in 2007.[48]

Some of the Special Procedures are important for the role they play in facilitating communication between governments in the countries they visit, communities and NGOs whom they interview and consult with, and the international community represented by the Human Rights Council and the UN General Assembly, to whom the mandate holders report. Others play a significant role in standard setting, with their normative studies and recommendations leading to resolutions and draft texts before the Council, ultimately influencing the development of international law.

48 J Gutter, see above, n 7, 104; Human Rights Council, See above, n 12, Appendix I.

Following the review of the Special Procedures mandates during the first year of the Human Rights Council, a total of 38 mandates were renewed—30 thematic mandates and eight country mandates.

LIST OF SPECIAL PROCEDURES MANDATES HUMAN RIGHTS COUNCIL INSTITUTION BUILDING RESOLUTION[49]

RENEWED MANDATES UNTIL THEY COULD BE CONSIDERED BY THE HUMAN RIGHTS COUNCIL ACCORDING TO ITS ANNUAL PROGRAMME OF WORK

Independent expert appointed by the Secretary-General on the situation of human rights in Haiti

Independent expert appointed by the Secretary-General on the situation of human rights in Somalia

Independent expert on the situation of human rights in Burundi

Independent expert on technical cooperation and advisory services in Liberia

Independent expert on the situation of human rights in the Democratic Republic of the Congo

Independent expert on human rights and international solidarity

Independent expert on minority issues

Independent expert on the effects of economic reform policies and foreign debt on the full enjoyment of all human rights, particularly economic, social and cultural rights

Independent expert on the question of human rights and extreme poverty

Special Rapporteur on the situation of human rights in the Sudan

Special Rapporteur on the situation of human rights in Myanmar

Special Rapporteur on the situation of human rights in the Democratic People's Republic of Korea

Special Rapporteur on the situation of human rights in the Palestinian territories occupied since 1967 (The duration of this mandate has been established until the end of the occupation.)

Special Rapporteur on adequate housing as a component of the right to an adequate standard of living

Special Rapporteur on contemporary forms of racism, racial discrimination, xenophobia and related intolerance

Special Rapporteur on extrajudicial, summary or arbitrary executions

Special Rapporteur on freedom of religion or belief

Special Rapporteur on the adverse effects of the illicit movement and dumping of toxic and dangerous products and wastes on the enjoyment of human rights

Special Rapporteur on the human rights aspects of the victims of trafficking in persons, especially women and children

Special Rapporteur on the human rights of migrants

Special Rapporteur on the independence of judges and lawyers

Special Rapporteur on the promotion and protection of human rights and fundamental freedoms while countering terrorism

Special Rapporteur on the promotion and protection of the right to freedom of opinion and expression

Special Rapporteur on the right of everyone to the enjoyment of the highest attainable standard of physical and mental health

Special Rapporteur on the right to education

Special Rapporteur on the right to food

49 HRC RES 5/1, see above, n 12, appendix I.

Special Rapporteur on the sale of children, child prostitution and child pornography
Special Rapporteur on the situation of human rights and fundamental freedoms of indigenous people
Special Rapporteur on torture and other cruel, inhuman or degrading treatment or punishment
Special Rapporteur on violence against women, its causes and consequences
Special Representative of the Secretary-General on the issue of human rights and transnational corporations and other business enterprises
Special Representative of the Secretary-General for human rights in Cambodia
Special Representative of the Secretary-General on the situation of human rights defenders
Representative of the Secretary-General on human rights of internally displaced persons
Working Group of Experts on People of African Descent
Working Group on Arbitrary Detention
Working Group on Enforced or Involuntary Disappearances
Working Group on the question of the use of mercenaries as a means of violating human rights and impeding the exercise of the right of peoples to self-determination

6.6 COMPLAINT PROCEDURE

The former Commission first entertained complaints of specific violations of human rights from 1970 under the auspices of ECOSOC resolution 1503.[50] As part of the Institution-Building Resolution, a new complaint procedure for the Council based on the old 1503 procedure was introduced in 2007.

Like the earlier 1503 procedure, the Council's complaint procedure is not a mechanism for victims to complain of a single incident that violates their human rights, but is aimed at repeated breaches by a state in similar cases, and is limited to gross breaches. The complaint procedure enables any person or group that was a victim of the alleged violations, as well as any person with direct and reliable knowledge of the violations or an NGO acting in good faith, to make a communication to the Council, alleging 'a consistent pattern of gross and reliably attested violations of human rights'.[51]

Domestic remedies must be exhausted before the complaint will be admissible,[52] and it must not be a matter that is already being dealt with under some other human rights mechanism in the UN or regional system.[53]

Once received, the complaint is considered by a working group of the Council's Advisory Committee, called the Working Group on Communications. The Working Group then weeds out any inadmissible or manifestly unfounded complaints and refers the prima facie complaints to another working group of the Advisory Committee, called the Working Group on Situations. The Working Group on Situations investigates the complaint and engages confidentially with the relevant government, seeking a response to the substantive allegations. It then compiles a report for the Council with conclusions as to the

50 Economic and Social Council, *Resolution 1503* (XLVIII), 27 May 1970.

51 Human Rights Council, see above, n 12, para 87(d) and (f).

52 Human Rights Council, see above, n 12, para 87(g).

53 Human Rights Council, see above, n 12, para 87(f).

substantive allegations and recommending what action the Council should take, which normally takes the form of a draft resolution for the consideration of the Council.

Up until the point of transmission of the Working Group's report to the Human Rights Council, the entire process has to be conducted confidentially. In the normal course of events, consideration of the report and subsequent action of the Council will also be conducted confidentially, although the Council is empowered to decide otherwise on a case-by-case basis, for instance in a case where the state concerned has been consistently uncooperative.[54]

While the Council's complaints procedure, like the earlier 1503 procedure it is modelled on, is criticised for being too lenient,[55] particularly because of the confidential manner in which it is conducted, it does have some advantages that make it complementary to other mechanisms in the UN human rights system. Remembering that the complaint procedure is intended for systemic and ongoing human rights abuse rather than individual breaches, the ability to engage with the state concerned through a more diplomatic process can yield better results than a more adversarial process of public accusation. At the very least, it is useful to have that tool at the disposal of the international community for situations where naming and shaming has proved ineffective. Perhaps the biggest advantage of this complaint procedure, though, is that it can be used against any state, regardless of whether it has ratified a particular treaty. It could therefore be useful for states that have not agreed to the individual complaints mechanisms under the various treaties discussed in Chapter 7.4.

6.7 UNIVERSAL PERIODIC REVIEW

The most significant addition to the mandate of the Human Rights Council compared to that of the Commission, and the principal tool given to the Human Rights Council to give effect to the principles of universality and non-selectivity, is the Universal Periodic Review (UPR).

The UPR was an integral part of the proposal for replacing the Commission with the Council, as it was intended to address the perceived problems of selectivity and political bias discussed above. Instead of certain 'usual suspect' states being singled out for condemnation year after year, while other states relied on alliances to deflect criticism, every state would take its turn being scrutinised by the broader international community. This reasoning is evident in the language used by the UN General Assembly in establishing the Human Rights Council, in which it directed that the Council shall:

> Undertake a universal periodic review, based on objective and reliable information, of the fulfilment by each State of its human rights obligations and commitments in a manner which ensures universality of coverage and equal treatment with respect to all States; the review shall be a cooperative mechanism, based on an interactive dialogue, with the full involvement of the country concerned and with consideration given to its capacity-building needs.[56]

54 Human Rights Council, see above, n 12, para 104.

55 See for example International Service for Human Rights, *A New Chapter for Human Rights*, 2006, Geneva, 66.

56 See above, n 14, para 5(e).

The idea behind the UPR is that every state should be subjected to a review of its human rights record on a rotating basis, to demonstrate that no state is above the scrutiny of its peers. The reporting mechanism of the UPR is based on the principle of peer review, in that it is conducted by other states. It is therefore not a substitute for state reports under specific treaties conducted by the respective treaty bodies, described in Chapter 7.4, even though there may well be some overlap in the content discussed in both forums. As a regular, rotating review of state performance, the UPR is also not a substitute for responses to gross human rights abuses as they arise, or monitoring of ongoing situations of concern. The ability of the Council to respond to a situation by passing resolutions and to monitor situations through the Special Procedures is therefore preserved in addition to the UPR, as is the specific complaints procedure.

While the UPR might prove successful in reducing the selectivity that was characteristic of the former Commission, it will nevertheless retain at least some degree of politicisation, as the Council is itself a political body. On the other hand, it is conceivable that states might be more amenable to the diplomatic approach of peer review than the approach adopted by the treaty-monitoring committees, which could be seen as judgmental or adversarial.

6.7.1 Basis of the UPR

In the UPR, states are judged on their performance in relation to all of their human rights obligations. These include the explicit treaty obligations that each state has undertaken in ratifying certain human rights treaties, and the human rights obligations that all UN member states have pursuant to the *UN Charter* and the UDHR.[57] This broad scope means that even if a state had not ratified a single human rights treaty (although there is no UN member state that has not), the human rights obligations that are inherent in membership of the UN and that derive from the *UN Charter*, the UDHR and customary international law are still expected to be realised, and such a state would still be held to account by its peers through the UPR process. This is consistent with the philosophy of universality and non-selectivity that underpins the UPR, as distinct from the opt-in nature of reporting to the respective treaty-monitoring committees.

In addition to legal obligations derived from treaties, the *UN Charter* and the UDHR, the UPR may review voluntary commitments that states may make as part of the process of seeking election to the Human Rights Council.[58]

6.7.2 UPR Process

The reviews are conducted in three two-week sessions per year, with 16 states reviewed each session, meaning that 48 states are reviewed every year. At that rate, the entire UN membership is able to be reviewed every four years. As a gesture of commitment to the UPR, to the Human Rights Council and to human rights in general, incumbent members of the Council were among the first group of states

57 Human Rights Council, see above, n 12, para 1.

58 Human Rights Council, see above, n 12, para 1(d).

to be reviewed. The first round of the UPR took place in April 2008, with Bahrain becoming the first state to be reviewed.

The essence of the UPR is the dialogue that takes place between the state under review and its peers. The review is technically conducted by the UPR Working Group of the Human Rights Council, although all 47 member states of the Council currently comprise that Working Group. States that are not members of the Council are also allowed to participate in the discussion and may ask questions of the state under review, and make comments and recommendations. Three hours are set aside for the interactive dialogue for each state. A randomly assigned group of three states (known as the 'troika') facilitates the review and prepares the report.

Because the UPR is intended to be a peer review process NGOs are not permitted to participate in the review itself. However, their submissions through the OHCHR effectively form a 'shadow report' for the state under review, and that report is commonly the trigger for questions put by other states during the dialogue. NGOs are therefore able to have a very significant influence without participating in the actual UPR discussion. Furthermore, when the outcome of a given UPR is discussed in a regular plenary session of the Human Rights Council before being formally adopted, NGOs are permitted to make statements.[59]

The review of each state is based on three documents: those conducting the review are armed with reports on a state's performance produced by the state itself, by UN expert bodies, and by civil society, hopefully providing a solid and reasonably balanced platform for the discussions.

The first document is prepared by the state concerned, up to a maximum of 20 pages. This report is effectively the state's self-evaluation of its human rights progress and performance. The second document, produced by the Office of the High Commissioner for Human Rights (OHCHR), compiles detailed information on the international human rights obligations undertaken by the state under review and all of the material pertaining to that state emanating from UN treaty bodies, including individual communications and state reports, and the special procedures of the Council and the former Commission and other UN human rights bodies. The OHCHR report therefore aims to provide a comprehensive reference point for all of the human rights-related activity in the somewhat fragmented UN system pertaining to that state. It is intended to be a neutral, factual document rather than one containing analysis or opinion.

The third document in the UPR process is also produced by the OHCHR. It is a summary of 'credible and reliable information provided by other relevant stakeholders',[60] primarily NGOs and national human rights institutions. Again, the OHCHR is supposed to compile the information rather than engage in any judgment or analysis. To the extent that stakeholder information contains allegations of human rights abuses by a particular state, the OHCHR simply passes on those allegations for the purpose of the UPR without commenting on their veracity or merit.

Extracts from the stakeholder summary for the 2011 review of Australia are set out below by way of example.

59 See the discussion of NGOs in Chapter 9.

60 Human Rights Council, see above, n 12, para 15(c).

OHCHR SUMMARY OF STAKEHOLDERS' SUBMISSIONS TO UPR—AUSTRALIA[61]

I BACKGROUND AND FRAMEWORK

A SCOPE OF INTERNATIONAL OBLIGATIONS

1 The Australian Human Rights Commission (AHRC) recommended that the Government ratify OP-ICESCR; expedite ratification of OP-CAT and the establishment of a National Preventive Mechanism for places of detention; and consider ratifying ILO Convention No 169 and the ICRMW. Joint Submission 1 (JS1) added that CED should be ratified.

2 JS3 recommended that Australia withdraw its reservations to article 4(a) of the ICERD, articles 10(2), 10(3), and 20 of the ICCPR, article 37(c) of the CRC. JS1 recommended that Australia withdraw its interpretive declaration in relation to articles 12 and 18 of CRPD.

B CONSTITUTIONAL AND LEGISLATIVE FRAMEWORK

3 JS1 noted that despite being a party to seven of the core human rights treaties, Australia had not incorporated these treaties into domestic law and had failed to adopt a comprehensive legal framework for the protection of human rights. Amnesty International (AI) noted that the *Australian Constitution* and common law provided limited human rights protection. JS1 further stated that many individuals were unable to access effective remedies. It recommended that Australia should fully incorporate international human rights obligations into domestic law (with the aim of eventual Constitutional entrenchment) by introducing a comprehensive, judicially enforceable federal *Human Rights Act*.

4 JS1 noted that further to the appointment in 2008, by the Federal Government, of an independent Committee to conduct a National Human Rights Consultation and in response to the Committee's report, the Federal Government announced a 'Human Rights Framework' which did not include a federal *Human Rights Act*—the Committee's key recommendation. Among the initiatives included in the Framework was the development of a comprehensive *Equality Act*.

5 AHRC noted that the absence of an entrenched guarantee of equality/nondiscrimination in the *Constitution* was of particular concern due to current laws that discriminated against Indigenous peoples on the basis of race. AHRC further noted that while there were federal, state and territory anti-discrimination laws, there were inconsistencies between them and their coverage varied and was not comprehensive. There was no other comprehensive human rights protection legislation and access to remedies for human rights breaches was accordingly limited. JS1 recommended that Australia should enact comprehensive legislation that addressed all prohibited grounds of discrimination, promoted substantive equality, and provided effective remedies against systemic and intersectional discrimination.

6 AI noted that the *Constitution* still contained a provision which contemplated the disqualification by States within Australia of 'all persons of any race' from voting in a federal election. Section 51(xxvi) of the Constitution also enabled discrimination on the basis of race, granting the Australian Commonwealth the power to make special laws for people of any race, which, according to AI, had facilitated the suspension of the *Racial Discrimination Act* in 2007 in relation to the Northern Territory Emergency Response (NTER) legislation which had introduced measures such as income quarantining and acquisition of Indigenous land.

61 A/HRC/WG.6/10/Aus/3, 3 November 2010.

7 JS1 noted that there was a lack of integration of children's rights in Australian law and recommended the enactment of stronger legislative protections for groups such as disabled children.

8 JS1 recommended amending anti-discrimination laws to include 'homelessness' or 'social status' as prohibited attributes. AHRC recommended that sexuality be included as a ground of discrimination federally; that sex or gender diversity be included as grounds of discrimination in federal laws; and that the Sex Files report be implemented.

9 JS4 recommended that Australia develop a legislative framework by 2012 to ensure the mitigation of the effects of the emission of greenhouse gases from Australian sources, with a view to protecting fundamental rights of the citizens of countries affected by human induced climate change.

10 According to JS1, some Australian companies, particularly mining companies, had a severe impact on human rights in many parts of the world. Australian Corporate Accountability Network's (ACAN), while commending the Australian Government for introducing the Division 268 offences into the *Criminal Code*, and applying them to Australian corporate conduct overseas, strongly urged the Australian Government to remove s.268.121 (1) from the *Criminal Code Act 1995* (Cth) indicating that this action would rightfully remove undue political interference from future decisions of the Federal Public Prosecutor to pursue criminal charges of grave human rights abuses committed by Australian companies overseas.

II PROMOTION AND PROTECTION OF HUMAN RIGHTS ON THE GROUND

A COOPERATION WITH HUMAN RIGHTS MECHANISMS

16 While welcoming the issuance of a standing invitation by Australia to the Special Procedures, JS1 recommended that Australia should extend the mandate of the proposed Joint Parliamentary Committee on Human Rights to include the consideration, follow up and oversight of implementation of recommendations and views of UN human rights mechanisms

B IMPLEMENTATION OF INTERNATIONAL HUMAN RIGHTS OBLIGATIONS

1 Equality and non-discrimination

11 Human rights and counter-terrorism

66 AHRC noted that the Government had introduced more than 50 new counterterrorism laws since 2001, often without adequate consideration of their potential impact on human rights. JS1 stated that the impact of these laws had been felt disproportionately by the Muslim, Kurdish, Tamil and Somali communities in Australia. AHRC further noted that those laws had enabled: detention without charge for 12 days; secret searching of homes and planting of surveillance devices, restricting movement through control orders issued by courts; and special powers of detention for the Australian Security Intelligence Organisation. AHRC recommended that all counter-terrorism laws be rigorously monitored and amended to ensure they complied with Australia's human rights obligations. [Other human rights issues were addressed under the headings: Right to life, liberty and security of the person; Administration of justice and the rule of law; Right to privacy, marriage and family life; Freedom of religion or belief, expression, association and peaceful assembly and right to participate in public and political life; Right to work and to just and favourable conditions of work; Right to social security and to an adequate standard of living; Right to education and to participate in the cultural life of the community; Minorities and indigenous peoples; and Migrants, refugees and asylum-seekers.]

III ACHIEVEMENTS, BEST PRACTICES, CHALLENGES AND CONSTRAINTS

67 ACSJC applauded the Government for its introduction of Crimes Legislation that extend [sic] the prohibition of the death penalty to Australian states and territories in accordance with the ICCPR-OP 2.

68 AHRC commended the development of a National Disability Strategy.

69 AHRC stated that Australia had strong traditions of liberal democracy, an independent judiciary and a robust media and that its largely harmonious and prosperous society can mask weaknesses and gaps in the protection of human rights that are compounded by the federated system of Government.

IV KEY NATIONAL PRIORITIES, INITIATIVES AND COMMITMENTS

70 AHRC noted that the Government released the Australian Human Rights Framework in 2010. The Framework commits to human rights education for the community and public sector; developing a National Action Plan on Human Rights; establishing a federal parliamentary scrutiny committee on human rights; requiring that all new federal legislation be accompanied by a statement of compatibility with Australia's human rights obligations; and developing a consolidated federal anti-discrimination law. AHRC stated that these measures will contribute to improved protection of human rights in Australia and address some, but not all, of the weaknesses in Australia's human rights protection system.

71 AHRC noted the Government's commitment to develop a National Plan to reduce violence against women and children.

6.7.3 Outcomes of the UPR

After the dialogue between the UPR Working Group and representatives of the state, a summary of the review is prepared by the OHCHR in consultation with the state under review, under the supervision of the troika. The outcome report contains a summary of the questions posed and comments made by other states during the review, as well as recommendations proposed by other states. The report then gives the response of the state under review to each point—for instance, accepting a recommendation, 'not supporting' a recommendation, pledging to consider a particular course of action, or making some other voluntary commitment.

The following extract from the outcome report of the 2009 review of China is provided by way of example.

UNIVERSAL PERIODIC REVIEW
REPORT OF THE WORKING GROUP ON THE UNIVERSAL PERIODIC REVIEW
CHINA[62]

B INTERACTIVE DIALOGUE AND RESPONSES BY THE STATE UNDER REVIEW

26 During the interactive dialogue, statements were made by 60 delegations. Fifty-five delegations were not able to make their statements. A large number of delegations congratulated China for its informative and

62 A/HRC/11/25, 3 March 2009.

comprehensive national report and its open presentation. Numerous delegations welcomed China's commitment to the UPR process and its constructive and cooperative participation. Statements were made welcoming the broad-based consultation with stakeholders in the preparation of the national report.

27 Australia welcomed the considerable improvements made by China over the past 30 years, but expressed concern that Chinese officials continue to repress religious activities considered to be outside the State-controlled religious system. Noting grave concerns about reports of harassment, arbitrary arrest, punishment and detention of religious and ethnic minorities, including Tibetans, it recommended that China: (a) strengthen the protection of ethnic minorities' religious, civil, socio-economic and political rights. While encouraged by positive developments in the handling of death-penalty cases, it remained concerned about the reportedly high number of executions and lack of transparency in such cases and recommended that China; (b) abolish the death penalty and, as interim steps, reduce the number of crimes for which the death penalty can be imposed and publish figures on executions. Welcoming the softening of media regulations for foreign journalists and encouraging China to ensure restrictions are not imposed on journalists' access to the Tibetan Autonomous Region and to rural areas, it recommended (c) that the new regulations be extended to Chinese journalists. Australia further recommended that China (d) respond positively to outstanding visit requests by special procedures and issue a standing invitation; (e) ratify the International Covenant on Civil and Political Rights (ICCPR)as quickly as possible and with minimal reservations; (f) establish a national human rights institution, in accordance with the Paris Principles; and (g) investigate reports of harassment and detention of human rights defenders, including alleged mistreatment while in police custody, with a view to ending impunity.

28 Canada welcomed the measures taken to reduce immediate death sentences, reserving them for 'exceptionally grave' crimes and reinstating Supreme People's Court authority to review death sentences. Canada expressed deep concern about reports of arbitrary detention of ethnic minorities members, including Tibetans, Uighurs and Mongols as well as religious believers, including Falun Gong practitioners, without information about their charges, their location and wellbeing. Canada recommended that China: (a) accelerate legislative and judicial reforms, particularly on death penalty and administrative detention, to be in compliance with the ICCPR; (b) reduce the number of crimes carrying the death penalty and (c) regularly publish detailed statistics on death penalty use; (d) abolish all forms of administrative detention, including 'Re-Education Through Labour'; (e) eliminate abuse of psychiatric committal; (f) provide those held on State-security charges with all fundamental legal safeguards, including access to counsel, public trial and sentencing, and eligibility for sentence reduction and parole; (g) take immediate measures to implement the recommendations of November 2008 of the Committee against Torture, particularly on the inadmissibility in court of statements made under torture and the non-refoulement of refugees from the Democratic People's Republic of Korea; and (h) respond positively to outstanding requests made by several United Nations Special Procedures, including the Special Rapporteur on freedom of religion or belief, to visit China, and (i) facilitate an early visit by the High Commissioner for Human Rights.

29 Singapore noted China's priority on realizing the people's right to development has brought about since 1978 rapid growth averaging 9.8 per cent per annum. It noted that this result could not have been possible without the empowerment of women. It welcomed the elaboration of a National Human Rights Action Plan for 2009–2010 that seeks to balance urban and rural development and to accelerate social development, with an emphasis on people's welfare and on promoting social equity and justice. Singapore recommended that China

finalize and publish the national human rights action plan for 2009–2010 at an early date and then swiftly implement it. It commended China for its efforts at strengthening its human rights legislation. It noted that over the past three decades the National People's Congress and its Standing Committee have enacted some 250 laws relating to human rights protection, with the Constitution as its core. Singapore appreciated China's active role in supporting the work of the United Nations in the area of human rights, including hosting in Beijing the 4th World Conference on Women in 1995.

30 The Netherlands noted the Chinese position on the protection of ethnic minority rights, and looked forward to further explanations on the death penalty and on UNHCR's role with regard to refugees from the Democratic People's Republic of Korea. It welcomed progress made in human rights. It recommended that China: (a) continue to advance the rule of law and to deepen the reform of the judicial system; (b) ratify the ICCPR as soon as possible and bring its legislation into line with its provisions; and (c) extend a standing invitation to all United Nations special rapporteurs. It said it looked forward to the publication of the Human Rights Action Plan 2009–2010.

[A further 83 paragraphs summarising the interactive dialogue are contained in the outcome report.]

II CONCLUSIONS AND/OR RECOMMENDATIONS

114 The recommendations formulated during the interactive dialogue have been examined by China and the recommendations listed below enjoy the support of China:

1 Create conditions for an early ratification of the International Covenant on Civil and Political Rights (ICCPR) (Sweden); In accordance with its imperatives dictated by its national realities, to proceed to legislative, judicial and administrative reform as well as create conditions permitting the ratification, as soon as possible, of the ICCPR (Algeria); Analyse the possibility of ratifying/consider ratifying/ratify ICCPR (Argentina, Brazil, Austria);

2 Continue its efforts: for the promotion of human rights (Oman); in legal and judicial reforms, economic development and other areas towards promoting a harmonious society, democracy, the rule of law and human rights (Viet Nam);

3 Continue enhancing the quality of life of its people through the enjoyment of economic, social and cultural rights and pursuant to international standards (Nicaragua).

4 Continue its national efforts for the promotion and protection of human rights, including in the area of strengthening its national human rights architecture (Egypt);

...

13 Attach more importance to the protection of rights of the child through national plans for economic and social development (Qatar);

14 Continue the efforts aimed at further enhancing the status of women and gradually do away with some traditional concepts in the rural areas that are likely to entrench practices that may still hamper progress in gender equality (Mozambique);

15 Continue efforts in supporting persons with disabilities and ensuring their contribution in social life, as effective partners (Yemen).

16 Adopt further measures to ensure universal access to health and education and other welfare for rural communities, minority regions, disadvantaged families and the internal migrant population (New Zealand);

17 Adopt special measures in the context of the international financial crisis in order to guarantee job opportunities in rural areas (Morocco);

18 Continue its endeavour to build a sound social security system and supporting services commensurate with national conditions, as well as its level of social and economic development (Philippines);

19 Strengthen its efforts in poverty alleviation in order to continue reducing the number of persons living in poverty (Bhutan); Continue its poverty reduction programmes (Zimbabwe).

20 Intensify its efforts to eradicate poverty, to improve its health infrastructure, including access to health services especially for vulnerable groups like women, children, the elderly, the disabled and ethnic minorities, and in fostering civil society participation (South Africa);

...

25 Continue to explore methods of development and implementation of human rights in harmony with its characteristics, its realities and the needs of Chinese society (Algeria);

26 Continue to invest financial and material resources, in conditions of the financial crisis, with the view to support the economic and social development in the country as a whole and the Tibet Autonomous Region in particular (Russian Federation);

27 Bridge the gap in economic and social development between rural and urban areas and among regions (Bhutan);

28 Share best practices with other developing countries on poverty reduction programmes and strategies, especially in rural areas (Philippines); Share with the international community its experience in promoting the right to development and poverty reduction (Viet Nam); Share its experiences and best practices in the field of reduction of poverty and improvement of standards of living with other developing countries (Malaysia);

29 Continue its policies in the field of international cooperation in order to assist the efforts made by other countries to fulfil the right to development (Angola);

30 In the light of its national realities, continue to implement the policy of strictly controlling and applying the death penalty (Egypt);

31 Actively and prudently push forward reform of re-education through labour according to its national realities, so that everything goes according to its system (Sudan);

...

33 Continue to support and encourage the further development of China's media use of English and other foreign languages to help the outside world better understand China, including the objective coverage of China, a country too often deliberately and grossly misunderstood by some international media (Zimbabwe);

...

36 While guaranteeing this freedom of speech, strengthen Internet governance to make sure the contents that incite war, racial hatred or defamation of religions are prohibited, and pornographic websites that are harmful to children and minors are banned or restricted (Islamic Republic of Iran);

37 Continue its efforts to further ensure ethnic minorities the full range of human rights including cultural rights (Japan);

38 Make more widely available to the world its experience in combining a strong state with ethnic regional autonomy (Sri Lanka);

...

115 The following recommendations are noted and China indicated that they are pertaining to measures already being implemented or which had already been implemented:

1 Guarantee that all detainees, regardless of their crimes, are held in facilities with decent standard and treatment (Germany);

2 Develop and adopt a comprehensive policy to combat child labour (Finland);

3 Strengthen the protection of ethnic minorities' religious, civil, socio-economic and political rights (Australia); In accordance with the Constitution, allow ethnic minorities to fully exercise their human rights, to preserve their cultural identity and to ensure their participation in decision-making; (and address these issues in the National Plan of Action) (Austria).

116 The following recommendations will be examined by China which will provide responses in due time. The responses of China to these recommendations will be included in the outcome report adopted by the Human Rights Council at its eleventh session:

1 Inscribe a legal definition of discrimination in its national law (Portugal)/Evaluate the possibility of establishing a legal description of discrimination taking into account international legal standards in this area (Argentina);

2 Reduce the number of crimes carrying the death penalty (Australia, Canada);

3 Adopt specific legislation on domestic violence (Brazil);

4 Follow-up on this UPR (Austria).

117 The recommendations noted in the report in paragraphs 27(b),(c),(d),(e),(f), (g), 28 (a), (c), (d), (e), (f), (g), (h), 30(b),(c), 31, 38, 42, 43(a),(b),(e),(f),(g),(h) 56, 79(a), (c), 81(b), 82, 83(a),(c),(d),(e), (g), 84(a), 85(b),86(b),(e), 92(b),(c),(d),(e),(f),(g), (h), 95(b), (c), (d), 96, 97 did not enjoy the support of China.

[Paragraphs 27–30, referred to in paragraph 117, are extracted above.]

The outcome report is then listed as an agenda item for discussion in a plenary session of the Human Rights Council. States and NGOs are permitted to comment on the report, including expressing views about the responses of the state contained in the outcome report. The report is then adopted by the Council.

The recommendations in the UPR outcome report, whether or not they were accepted by the state being reviewed, are quite different in nature to the views of treaty-monitoring committees discussed in Chapter 7.4, which are designed to remedy specific violations of the human rights of a particular individual. The recommendations emanating from the UPR tend to be more programmatic and couched in more diplomatic language. On their own, the UPR recommendations do not have any binding legal effect. They may well provide a good indication of state practice on specific issues, particularly after a substantial body of practice has built up over a number of years, thereby contributing to the formation of customary international law. However any effect on state practice is quite indirect.

Although the outcomes of the UPR are not enforceable as such, they are still potentially meaningful in a number of ways. First, states are forced to address uncomfortable human rights questions and explain themselves before the international community. Secondly, peer pressure is applied for constant improvement of states' human rights performance, for instance by ratifying new treaties, engaging with special procedures, reforming problematic domestic institutions and reporting back on a national plan of action. Finally, an opportunity for follow-up is provided by the periodic nature of the process: four years after being reviewed and making undertakings to the Council in the outcome report, a state will once again be up for review. While the second round of the UPR has not yet started at the time of writing, it is likely that states and stakeholders will focus on successes and failures in implementing the first round of recommendations, which will in turn feed into the dialogue in the second round.

The UPR does not have sanctions available to deal with an uncooperative state that is not concerned about the public airing and debate of its human rights practices. The following extract from the International Service for Human Rights, an NGO that observes and reports on the UPR process, relaying the response of North Korea to the outcome report on its 2010 review, demonstrates the difficulty of applying a collegiate system to a state that refuses to engage.

THE DEMOCRATIC PEOPLE'S REPUBLIC OF KOREA ACCEPTS NONE OF UPR'S 167 RECOMMENDATIONS [63]
INTERNATIONAL SERVICE FOR HUMAN RIGHTS

The adoption by the Human Rights Council of the report of the universal periodic review of the Democratic Peoples' Republic of Korea (DPRK) took place on 18 March 2010. The DPRK had rejected 50 recommendations at the initial UPR Working Group phase, and failed to submit in writing its position on 117 pending recommendations prior to the Human Rights Council adoption. Likewise, in his presentation to the Council, the Ambassador of the DPRK stressed his State's willingness to cooperate, having already 'given answers and explanations in good faith to questions' during the UPR, but he then proceeded to ignore all outstanding recommendations. The Ambassador stated in vague terms that efforts were underway to improve economic and social rights, as well as women's and children's rights, and that there is no discrimination in the DPRK. It claimed that 50 recommendations had been rejected as they were 'in full conflict with the DPRK's principled stand against politicisation of human rights'. He made no reference to other specific recommendations.

The interventions of States were clearly divided among those who interpreted the DPRK's participation as a sufficient sign of cooperation (Algeria, Cuba, Sudan, Pakistan, Venezuela, Qatar, Saudi Arabia, Sri Lanka), and those who were clearly unhappy with the State's lack of clarity in relation to all pending recommendations (Japan, Republic of Korea, United States, France). Human Rights Watch was most condemnatory of the DPRK's behaviour, stating that it neither cooperated with nor understood the UPR process, that it claimed to have held national consultations with civil society but that in reality suppression is so severe that civil society does not exist in the country, and that they had purposefully ignored important recommendations related to labour camps, arbitrary detention, collective punishment, and restrictions on religious practices.

France asserted that the Ambassador needed to answer the question of which recommendations had been accepted, or they would interpret the DPRK's actions as non-cooperation with the Council. In his closing comments the Ambassador of the DPRK claimed that he simply 'took note' of such recommendations. On moving to the adoption of the report, Norway intervened to support France's assertion that the DPRK's position was unclear, and therefore requested a two minute suspension to clarify the matter. Cuba, on the other hand, expressed that

63 International Service for Human Rights, 22 March 2010, available at <http://www.ishr.ch/council-news/725-the-peoples-democratic-republic-of-korea-accepts-none-of-uprs-167-recommendations?utm_source=ISHR+Publications+and+News&utm_campaign=fd423365e7-COUNCIL_RSS_EMAIL_CAMPAIGN&utm_medium=email>.

the DPRK's noting of recommendations was in accordance with the UPR and their right as a sovereign State. Upon resuming, the Ambassador of the DPRK simply reiterated that he took note of the outstanding recommendations. This prompted France to state that it understood this to mean that the DPRK had not accepted any of the UPR's 167 recommendations. The DPRK did not respond and the report was adopted.

6.7.4 Value of the UPR

In summary, the UPR is not an enforcement mechanism in the sense of obtaining redress for a specific human rights grievance; that is the role of the treaty bodies' complaints procedures discussed at Chapter 7.4. The UPR is also not particularly suitable for independent, authoritative judgments on violations of human rights, given its governmental composition. As such, one should be very cautious about suggesting that other mechanisms are rendered redundant by the UPR.

However, the UPR has great potential value as a forum for airing human rights concerns. The universal, periodic nature of the system also has something to offer the broader international human rights system. Whereas the pre-2006 human rights system was facing a crisis of confidence due to a perception of selectivity and political polarisation (regardless of the merits of that perception), the advent of a flagship process to which all states are subjected in equal measure has the potential to defuse those criticisms and reinstate confidence in the rest of the human rights system.

If it is embraced conscientiously by states (a proposition that is greeted with varying levels of scepticism), the UPR also offers a forum for collegiality among states in developing a truly universal understanding of human rights and their corresponding obligations. Even in the absence of such a utopian accord, the UPR process should reveal something about where the areas of consensus lie and where genuine normative disputes persist in contemporary international human rights law. Therefore, in addition to the obvious practical value of the UPR, in that it applies pressure on states to commit to specific improvements in the human rights situations in their jurisdiction, there is also a potential normative value for the development and the identification of international human rights law.

6.8 NGO PARTICIPATION

Non-government organisations are not members of the Human Rights Council, and therefore cannot vote, cannot directly propose resolutions or amendments and cannot participate directly in the peer review mechanism of the Universal Periodic Review. However, their important role in protecting of human rights and highlighting human rights violations is widely recognised. NGOs are therefore given a great deal of leeway in participating in the work of the Council and have a significant impact on the issues that are debated and the direction of that debate.

An NGO that has been accredited with consultative status[64] is permitted to make oral statements on the substantive agenda items within the Council in much the same way as observer states (that is, states that have not been elected to the Council). Their presence at Council sessions also presents opportunities for lobbying state representatives, potentially giving rise to significant impact beyond what is visible from the sessions themselves. As was noted above, NGOs also have an opportunity to

64 See Chapter 9.3.2.

make submissions on a state's human rights record via the Office of the High Commissioner as part of the documentation for the UPR, helping to determine the direction that the review takes.

The role of NGOs in international human rights law more broadly is discussed separately in Chapter 9.

6.9 CONCLUSION AND ISSUES

The creation of the Human Rights Council in 2006 followed years of criticism of the UN human rights system, particularly the UN Commission on Human Rights. The reforms did not go as far as some had hoped: the status of the Council, subordinate to the UN General Assembly, does not match that of the UN Security Council, and it is still a very large (and some would say therefore unwieldy) body. While efforts were made in the design of the Council to prevent or discourage states with long-standing poor human rights records from being elected to the Council, it is unclear whether that is working. After the first few years, many states have reverted to their old ways of back-room deals in regional groups to determine which states are elected to the Council, rather than multiple candidates facing the full UN General Assembly for election as intended, purportedly to be judged on human rights criteria, although practice in that regard has fluctuated from year to year in the first years of the Council. The selectiveness of issues focused on by the Council also arguably remains a problem.

At the core of many of these criticisms, though, is that the Human Rights Council, like its predecessor Commission and most other UN bodies, is an inherently political body. As long as states come to the Council with their own interests and agendas, politicisation of the Council's agenda and some degree of selectivity is inevitable. It remains a debatable question whether states have shown more restraint and a more universal approach to human rights issues in the first few years of the Council than they did before the Council's creation.

Probably the most significant development under the Human Rights Council has been the creation of the Universal Periodic Review. The fact that it is universal—that is, not selective as to which states it targets, but focusing on every state—and periodic—that is, each state taking its turn in a rotation—makes the UPR a potentially potent antidote to accusations of selectivity. The peer-focused nature of the UPR, in that states interrogate one another on their human rights record rather than having independent experts conduct the review as occurs under the Special Procedures, further neutralises any claims of bias that 'targeted' states often level at Special Rapporteurs. The success of the UPR depends on the extent to which states are prepared to examine their own human rights records and those of other countries frankly and conscientiously, rather than viewing the exercise as an opportunity to shield allies and take potshots at political opponents. The extent to which states act on recommendations from the UPR will also be a key test of its success. The second and subsequent rounds of the UPR will be more revealing of those outcomes than the first round.

7 THE HUMAN RIGHTS TREATY SYSTEM

CONTENTS

7.1 INTRODUCTION

International human rights treaties make extensive demands of states in the organisation of their domestic affairs, and in their conduct towards individuals. Those demands are never actually enforceable in a system of international law that is founded on national sovereignty. Nevertheless, an extensive system of monitoring and reporting on treaty compliance provides states with some incentive to comply with their obligations.

After describing treaty practice generally, this chapter gives an account of the structure and operation of the human rights treaty system: the treaties, the treaty bodies as well as the ILO, and the treaty bodies' interactions with states and individuals. It concludes with a discussion of the continuing efforts to achieve higher levels of compliance from states, and respect for the system, generally, through attempts to reform the slow and cumbersome treaty system processes.

7.2 INTERNATIONAL TREATY PRACTICE

Chapter 1.3 describes how the first task of the predecessor to the current Human Rights Council, the UN Commission on Human Rights, was to oversee the drafting of the *Universal Declaration of Human Rights* (UDHR), which sets out the human right standards that UN members states aspire to. The UDHR is a 'declaration' of the UN, adopted by the UN General Assembly on a vote of its members.

7.2.1 Declarations

A unilateral declaration by the UN General Assembly does not create binding obligations on UN member states. But it has been said of the UDHR that even though, as a declaration voted in the UN General Assembly, it lacks the formal authority of a treaty that binds its parties, '[n]evertheless, it remains in some sense the constitution of the entire movement, as well as the single most cited human rights instrument'.[1] Indeed, there is an argument that the UDHR has attained a different status under international law.[2]

Brownlie points out that although the UDHR 'is not a legally binding instrument *as such*',[3] it has what he calls 'considerable indirect legal effect'[4] because it is 'an authoritative guide, produced by the [UN] General Assembly, to the interpretation of the provisions in the Charter'.[5] Others go further and argue for more than indirect effect, saying that the UDHR creates binding obligations on member states of the UN because the states have expressly accepted the obligations set out in it.[6] There is as well a view that the UDHR is binding on nation states because it has become a part of international customary law,[7] and Brownlie regrets the tendency of '[t]he literature of human rights ... to neglect the role, or potential role, of customary law'.[8]

Subsequent UN documents have developed more detailed accounts of the human rights standards set out in the UDHR; for example, the guarantee in article 5 of the UDHR that 'no-one shall be subjected to torture or to cruel, inhuman or degrading treatment or punishment' was later set out in greater detail in the *Convention against Torture and Other Cruel, Inhuman or Degrading Treatment or Punishment* (CAT), discussed below. Whatever the 'bindingness' of the UDHR, there is no doubt that the subsequent human rights documents are binding on states that choose to be a party to them. These subsequent documents are not declarations: they are 'treaties'.

7.2.2 Covenants, Conventions and 'Treaties'

The principal statement in international law on treaties is the *Vienna Convention on the Law of Treaties*,[9] which 'purports to constitute a comprehensive set of principles and rules governing all the most significant aspects of the law of treaties'.[10]

---

1 H J Steiner, P Alston & R Goodman, *International Human Rights in Context: Law, Politics, Morals*, 3rd edn, Oxford University Press, Oxford, 2008, 136.

2 See the discussion of the UDHR's legal status in Chapter 1.3.2.

3 I Brownlie (ed), *Basic Documents in International Law*, 6th edn, Oxford University Press, Oxford, 2008, 192 (emphasis in original).

4 Ibid 192.

5 I Brownlie, *Principles of Public International Law*, 7th edn, Oxford University Press, Oxford, 2008, 559.

6 See, eg, P Sieghart, *The International Law of Human Rights*, Clarendon Press, Oxford, 1983, 53–5; T Zuijdwijk, *Petitioning the United Nations*, Gower Publishing Company, Aldershot, 1982, 100–5; but to the contrary, see: V Pechota, 'The Development of the Covenant on Civil and Political Rights' in L Henkin (ed), *The International Bill of Rights: The Covenant on Civil and Political Rights*, Columbia University Press, New York, 1981, 32–71, 37.

7 See, eg, L Sohn, 'The New International Law: Protection of the Rights of Individuals Rather Than States' (1982) 32(1) *American University Law Review* 1, 16; 'Montreal Statement of the Assembly for Human Rights' (1968) reprinted in (1968) 9(1) *Journal of the International Commission of Jurists* 94.

8 See above, n 5, 563; see the discussion in Chapter 1.3.2.

9 *Vienna Convention on the Law of Treaties* (*Vienna Convention*), opened for signature 23 May 1969, 1155 UNTS 331, art 2(1)(a) (entered into force 27 January 1980).

10 I M Sinclair, *The Vienna Convention on the Law of Treaties*, Manchester University Press, Manchester, 1984, 5.

For purposes of international law, the Vienna Convention defines a treaty as 'an international agreement concluded between States in written form and governed by international law, whether embodied in a single instrument or in two or more related instruments, and whatever its particular designation'.[11] By defining a document as a treaty 'whatever its particular designation', the definition can encompass written agreements between states that are designated, for example, 'treaty, convention, protocol, covenant, charter, statute, act, declaration, concordat, exchange of notes, agreed minute, memorandum of agreement, *modus vivendi* or any other appellation'.[12] A human rights treaty is usually called a 'covenant' or a 'convention', and an ancillary treaty is usually called a 'protocol'; for ease of reference they can all be referred to by the generic term 'treaty'.

A treaty between two states is a 'bilateral' treaty, and one between three or more states is a 'multilateral' treaty, creating binding obligations on states in international law. Human rights treaties (eg, covenants, conventions and protocols) are multilateral treaties. When a human rights treaty has been adopted by the UN General Assembly, or by a special meeting for the purpose (such as the Rome Conference, which adopted the treaty—in that case called a 'statute'—to establish the International Criminal Court), it is then 'open for signature' by states.

Signature does not bind a state to ratify or comply with a treaty; it is a state's indication that it intends to become a party to the treaty and will not in the meantime act inconsistently with it. A state is bound to give effect to a treaty only when it becomes a party to it through ratification or accession and when the treaty itself has entered into force.

A treaty is not in force simply because it has been adopted by the UN General Assembly, or even after it has been signed by states: the terms of a treaty set out the minimum number of ratifications or accessions that are required before the treaty enters into force. For example, as we discuss in more detail below, the *International Covenant on Economic, Social and Cultural Rights* (ICESCR) did not enter into force, with the required ratification or accession by 35 states, until 10 years after it was adopted by the UN General Assembly.

7.2.3 Ratification, Accession, Acceptance and Succession

If a state decides it is ready to be bound by a treaty it has signed, it will *ratify* that treaty; if a state decides it is ready to be bound by a treaty it has not signed, it will *accede* to that treaty. In some states (such as Australia) a treaty is ratified or acceded to by a formal domestic act by the head of state; in Australia this is an executive act by the Governor-General on the advice of the federal government. In states where an act by the head of state is not required, the obligations of a treaty are taken on by *acceptance*.[13] When a new state succeeds a former state—Slovakia and the Czech Republic succeeded

11 *Vienna Convention*, see above, n 9.

12 International Law Commission, *Provisional Draft of the Vienna Convention*, quoted in I Brownlie, see above, n 5, 608.

13 *Vienna Convention*, see above, n 9, art 14(2).

the former Czechoslovakia, for example—then the new state is bound by the treaty obligations of the former state by way of *succession* to the treaty.

7.2.4 Reservations, Declarations and Understandings

Each of ratification, accession, acceptance and succession has the same effect in international law: the state consents to be bound by the treaty,[14] but only to the extent it has not entered a *reservation*.[15]

A reservation to a treaty is a 'unilateral statement, however phrased or named, made by a State, when signing, ratifying, accepting, approving or acceding to a treaty, whereby it purports to exclude or to modify the legal effect of certain provisions of the treaty in their application to that State'.[16] A state may, on ratification or accession, enter a reservation as long as the terms of the treaty do not prohibit reservations and the reservation does not effectively negate the state's obligations under the treaty.[17]

In treaties outside the human rights field, the consequence of a reservation is to modify the relevant obligation as between the state entering the reservation and all other states, on a reciprocal basis. For example, a treaty between three states may grant state tariff-free access to each other's markets for agricultural goods. If one of the three states entered a reservation to exclude bananas from the operation of the treaty, the other two states would also be relieved of the obligation to accord tariff-free access to bananas from that state, but would continue to accord tariff-free access to each other's banana exports.

Reservations to human rights treaties create technical difficulties that do not arise for treaties on other topics, because the intended beneficiaries of obligations in human rights treaties are the people in each state, rather than the other states parties to the treaty. It is therefore more problematic to allow states to enter reservations to a human rights treaty, which allows states to modify the extent of their obligations, than it would be for an ordinary treaty that has been entered into between states on a reciprocal basis. Thus, if state A was to enter a reservation to a human rights treaty saying 'state A reserves the right to torture', it would not make sense to relieve all other states of their obligations regarding freedom from torture in relation to state A.

Nevertheless, states do enter reservations to human rights treaties. In some cases, these are along operational lines, for example, that measures will be taken to the extent that they do not conflict with the state's constitution, or that a given right will be realised through administrative measures rather than new legislation. Many of those are therefore more accurately described as declarations or understandings, discussed in this part, below. Other reservations specifically exclude or severely

14 *Vienna Convention*, see above, n 9, art 2(1)(b).

15 On treaty-making, see generally, Senate Legal and Constitutional Affairs Committee, Parliament of Australia, *Trick or Treaty? Commonwealth Power to Make and Implement Treaties* (1995); P Reuter, *Introduction to The Law of Treaties*, Kegan Paul International, London, 1995.

16 *Vienna Convention*, see above, n 9, art 2(4)(1).

17 *Vienna Convention*, see above, n 9; UN Human Rights Committee, *General Comment 24: Issues Relating to Reservations Made Upon Ratification or Accession to the Covenant or the Optional Protocols Thereto, or in Relation to Declarations Under Article 41 of the Covenant*, 52nd sess, para 6, UN doc CCPR/C/21/Rev.1/Add.6 (1994).

modify the operation of a particular right, such as the examples in Chapter 3.2.3, of reservations that states have entered to the *International Covenant on Civil and Political Rights* (ICCPR).

In 1994 the UN Human Rights Committee, which monitors the ICCPR, issued General Comment 24, described by Charlesworth as 'a fascinating and bold statement'.[18] The Committee published its Comment to provide guidance on the making of reservations under the ICCPR, prompted to do so by the fact that '[a]s of 1 November 1994, 46 of the 127 States Parties to the ICCPR had, between them, entered 150 reservations of varying significance to their acceptance of obligations of the Covenant'.[19] Although expressed in relation to the ICCPR it is a useful comment on reservations to human right treaties generally.

HUMAN RIGHTS COMMITTEE: *GENERAL COMMENT 24: ISSUES RELATING TO RESERVATIONS MADE UPON RATIFICATION OR ACCESSION TO THE COVENANT OR THE OPTIONAL PROTOCOLS THERETO, OR IN RELATION TO DECLARATIONS UNDER ARTICLE 41 OF THE COVENANT*[20]

8 Reservations that offend peremptory norms would not be compatible with the object and purpose of the Covenant. Although treaties that are mere exchanges of obligations between States allow them to reserve *inter se* application of rules of general international law, it is otherwise in human rights treaties, which are for the benefit of persons within their jurisdiction. Accordingly, provisions in the Covenant that represent customary international law (and *a fortiori* when they have the character of peremptory norms) may not be the subject of reservations ...

9 Applying more generally the object and purpose test to the Covenant, the Committee notes that, for example, reservation to article 1 denying peoples the right to determine their own political status and to pursue their economic, social and cultural development, would be incompatible with the object and purpose of the Covenant. Equally, a reservation to the obligation to respect and ensure the rights, and to do so on a non-discriminatory basis (article 2 (1)) would not be acceptable. Nor may a State reserve an entitlement not to take the necessary steps at the domestic level to give effect to the rights of the Covenant (article 2 (2)).

...

12 The intention of the Covenant is that the rights contained therein should be ensured to all those under a State party's jurisdiction. To this end certain attendant requirements are likely to be necessary. Domestic laws may need to be altered properly to reflect the requirements of the Covenant; and mechanisms at the domestic level will be needed to allow the Covenant rights to be enforceable at the local level. Reservations often reveal a tendency of States not to want to change a particular law. And sometimes that tendency is elevated to a general policy. Of particular concern are widely formulated reservations which essentially render ineffective all Covenant rights which would require any change in national law to ensure compliance with Covenant obligations. No real international rights or obligations have thus been accepted. And when there is an absence of provisions

18 H Charlesworth, 'The UN Treaty-Based Human Rights System: An Overview', in S Pritchard (ed), *Indigenous Peoples, the United Nations and Human Rights*, Zed Books/Federation Press, Sydney, 1998, 66–73, 72.

19 UN Human Rights Committee, see above, n 17.

20 See above, n 17.

to ensure that Covenant rights may be sued on in domestic courts, and, further, a failure to allow individual complaints to be brought to the Committee under the first *Optional Protocol*, all the essential elements of the Covenant guarantees have been removed.

...

17 ... [human rights] treaties, and the Covenant specifically, are not a web of inter-State exchanges of mutual obligations. They concern the endowment of individuals with rights. The principle of inter-State reciprocity has no place, save perhaps in the limited context of reservations to declarations on the Committee's competence under article 41.

18 ... Because of the special character of a human rights treaty, the compatibility of a reservation with the object and purpose of the Covenant must be established objectively, by reference to legal principles, and the Committee is particularly well placed to perform this task. The normal consequence of an unacceptable reservation is not that the Covenant will not be in effect at all for a reserving party. Rather, such a reservation will generally be severable, in the sense that the Covenant will be operative for the reserving party without benefit of the reservation.

19 Reservations must be specific and transparent, so that the Committee, those under the jurisdiction of the reserving State and other States parties may be clear as to what obligations of human rights compliance have or have not been undertaken. Reservations may thus not be general, but must refer to a particular provision of the Covenant and indicate in precise terms its scope in relation thereto ...

Reservations that effectively negate the treaty obligations, contrary to article 19(c) of the *Vienna Convention*, are, for example, those in relation to the *Convention on the Elimination of All Forms of Discrimination Against Women* (CEDAW), which say that effect will be given to the 'non-discrimination' requirement only to the extent that it is consistent with religious law, Islamic law and other laws'.[21] When a state's reservation appears to be inconsistent with the state's treaty obligations, another state can *object* to the reservation,[22] although there is some controversy in international law as to the position that General Comment 24 takes on how the question of inconsistency is to be determined.[23]

Differently from a reservation, a *declaration* does not affect a state's obligations under a treaty it has ratified, but merely 'give[s] notice of a State's interpretation of the Covenant ... [with] no legal effect in international law'.[24] To similar effect, states also record an *understanding*, which operates as a type of declaration. Neither a declaration nor an understanding is a procedure recognised in the *Vienna Convention*.

Australia has entered reservations and made declarations for a number of human rights treaties, described in Chapter 10.2.3.

21 See the discussion of such reservations in Chapter 16.5.3.

22 *Vienna Convention*, see above, n 9, art 2; UN Human Rights Committee, see above, n 17.

23 See the discussion in S Joseph, J Schultz & M Castan, *The International Covenant on Civil and Political Rights: Cases, Materials and Commentary*, 2nd edn, Oxford University Press, Oxford, 2004, para 25.37.

24 Ibid para 25.08.

7.2.5 Denunciation and Derogation

Denunciation of a treaty is the withdrawal by a ratifying state from that treaty, denouncing its ratification. The Vienna Convention recognises the right of a state to denounce a treaty only when the treaty's terms allow for it;[25] although some treaties specifically allow for denunciation, the *International Covenant on Civil and Political Rights* (ICCPR) does not. When North Korea purported to withdraw from the ICCPR, the United Nations Human Rights Committee expressed the view that denunciation of the ICCPR cannot cause the rights to not be available to people within the state.[26]

A state has the right to limit the effect of its human rights treaty obligations during times of emergency; to do so is to *derogate* from the treaty obligations. The ICCPR, for example, allows derogation '[i]n time of public emergency which threatens the life of the nation and the existence of which is officially proclaimed', but specifies rights that cannot be derogated[27] without thereby indicating a hierarchy of importance of rights.[28] We discuss derogation in time of public emergency in more detail in relation to human rights and terrorism in Chapter 18.

In 2001 the UN Human Rights Committee issued General Comment 29 (extracted in Chapter 3.3.3), to make clear that '[m]easures derogating from the provisions of the Covenant must be of an exceptional and temporary nature'.[29] A more detailed discussion of derogations under the ICCPR is in Chapter 3.3.3, and under the ICESCR in Chapter 4.3.6.

7.2.6 State Obligations to Give Effect to a Human Rights Treaty

When states ratify international human rights treaties they take on an obligation to give effect to them, by way of legislative measures and without discrimination.[30] The ICCPR specifically requires the state to 'respect and to ensure to all individuals' the rights in the Covenant, and to provide effective remedies for violations of those rights. Less emphatically, the ICESCR requires states only to 'take steps with a view to achieving progressively' the rights in the Covenant.[31]

25 *Vienna Convention*, see above, n 9, art 56.

26 See above, n 23, para 25.38.

27 *International Covenant on Civil and Political Rights* (ICCPR), opened for signature 16 December 1966, 999 UNTS 171 (entered into force 23 March 1976), art 4.

28 See above, n 17, para 10, UN Doc CCPR/C/21/Rev.1/Add.6 (1994).

29 UN Human Rights Committee, *General Comment 29: States of Emergency (Article 4)*, art 2, UN Doc CCPR/C/21/Rev.1/Add.11 (2001). Also see discussion at Chapter 3.3.3 regarding the Siracusa Principles.

30 *Vienna Convention*, see above, n 9, art 26; see, eg *International Covenant on Economic, Social and Cultural Rights* (ICESCR), opened for signature 16 December 1966, 999 UNTS 3, arts 2 & 3 (entered into force 3 January 1976); see above, n 27, arts 2 & 3.

31 See the discussion at Chapter 4.3.

The following General Comment from the CESCR Committee observes how state parties might best understand their international human rights obligations:[32]

COMMITTEE ON ECONOMIC, SOCIAL AND CULTURAL RIGHTS: *GENERAL COMMENT NO 9: THE DOMESTIC APPLICATION OF THE COVENANT*

A THE DUTY TO GIVE EFFECT TO THE COVENANT IN THE DOMESTIC LEGAL ORDER

1 ... The central obligation in relation to the Covenant is for States parties to give effect to the rights recognized therein. By requiring Governments to do so 'by all appropriate means', the Covenant adopts a broad and flexible approach which enables the particularities of the legal and administrative systems of each State, as well as other relevant considerations, to be taken into account.

2 But this flexibility coexists with the obligation upon each State party to use all the means at its disposal to give effect to the rights recognized in the Covenant ... the Covenant norms must be recognized in appropriate ways within the domestic legal order, appropriate means of redress, or remedies, must be available to any aggrieved individual or group, and appropriate means of ensuring governmental accountability must be put in place.

3 States should modify the domestic legal order as necessary in order to give effect to their treaty obligations. [A] State party seeking to justify its failure to provide any domestic legal remedies for violations of economic, social and cultural rights would need to show either that such remedies are not 'appropriate means' within the terms of article 2, paragraph 1, of the International Covenant on Economic, Social and Cultural Rights or that, in view of the other means used, they are unnecessary. It will be difficult to show this and the Committee considers that, in many cases, the other means used could be rendered ineffective if they are not reinforced or complemented by judicial remedies.

B THE STATUS OF THE COVENANT IN THE DOMESTIC LEGAL ORDER

4 In general, legally binding international human rights standards should operate directly and immediately within the domestic legal system of each State party, thereby enabling individuals to seek enforcement of their rights before national courts and tribunals. The rule requiring the exhaustion of domestic remedies reinforces the primacy of national remedies in this respect. The existence and further development of international procedures for the pursuit of individual claims is important, but such procedures are ultimately only supplementary to effective national remedies.

5 The Covenant does not stipulate the specific means by which it is to be implemented in the national legal order. And there is no provision obligating its comprehensive incorporation or requiring it to be accorded any specific type of status in national law ...

6 An analysis of State practice with respect to the Covenant shows that States have used a variety of approaches. Some States have failed to do anything specific at all. Of those that have taken measures, some States have

32 UN Committee on Economic, Social and Cultural Rights, CESCR *General Comment No 9: The Domestic Application of the Covenant*, 19th sess, UN Doc E/C.12/1998/24 (1998).

transformed the Covenant into domestic law by supplementing or amending existing legislation, without invoking the specific terms of the Covenant. Others have adopted or incorporated it into domestic law, so that its terms are retained intact and given formal validity in the national legal order. This has often been done by means of constitutional provisions according priority to the provisions of international human rights treaties over any inconsistent domestic laws …

7 But whatever the preferred methodology, several principles follow from the duty to give effect to the Covenant and must therefore be respected. First, the means of implementation chosen must be adequate to ensure fulfilment of the obligations under the Covenant. The need to ensure justiciability … is relevant when determining the best way to give domestic legal effect to the Covenant rights. Second, account should be taken of the means which have proved to be most effective in the country concerned in ensuring the protection of other human rights …

8 Third, while the Covenant does not formally oblige States to incorporate its provisions in domestic law, such an approach is desirable. Direct incorporation avoids problems that might arise in the translation of treaty obligations into national law, and provides a basis for the direct invocation of the Covenant rights by individuals in national courts …

7.2.7 Giving Effect to a Treaty in a Dualist System

For any state there exists, at the same time, international law and domestic (or municipal) law. From time to time a question will arise: which has precedence? The answer depends on which of two views is preferred: a 'dualist' view or a 'monist' view:

> Dualist doctrine points to the difference of international law and municipal law, consisting primarily of the fact that the two systems regulate different subject-matter. International law is a law between sovereign states: municipal law applies within a state and regulates the relations of its citizens with each other and the executive. On this view neither legal order has the power to create or alter the rules of the other.
>
> … monism [is] an assertion of the supremacy of international law even within the municipal sphere … International law is seen as the best available moderator of human affairs, and also as a logical condition of the *legal* existence of states and therefore of the municipal systems of law …[33]

Countries with an English common law heritage are typically 'dualist', which means treaty obligations are not part of the domestic law unless they are enacted into domestic law: 'the stipulations of a treaty duly ratified do not … by virtue of the treaty alone, have the force of law'.[34] When and how international law becomes part of domestic law is a matter for the domestic constitutional arrangements.

Countries with a continental European legal heritage are likely to be 'monist' in their approach to international law. This means treaty obligations should automatically form part of the domestic law. States that are ostensibly monist have been inconsistent in the way their constitutions have

33 I Brownlie, see above, n 5, 32.

34 *Attorney-General (Canada) v Attorney-General (Ontario)* [1937] AC 326, 34. For Australia see *Brown v Lizars* (1905) 2 CLR 837, 851 (Griffith CJ); *Dietrich v The Queen* [1992] HCA 57; 177 CLR 292, 304 (Mason CJ and McHugh J), 359–60 (Toohey J); *Minister for Immigration and Ethnic Affairs v Teoh* [1995] HCA 20; 183 CLR 273, 297 (Mason CJ and Deane J).

expressed the monist intention and in the extent to which the courts have recognised it. Instead of relying on a monist assumption for the incorporation of human rights treaty obligations into domestic law, it is preferable to ask—for each state and each treaty to which the state is a party—whether the circumstances of the state's entering the treaty, and the domestic circumstances of the state, indicate that the treaty is self-executing or if it requires domestic implementation.

7.3 THE 'CORE' HUMAN RIGHTS TREATIES

Under the UDHR the UN has developed what the Office of the United Nations High Commissioner for Human Rights (OHCHR) calls the 'nine core international human rights treaties'[35] and the UN Secretary-General calls the 'main international human rights conventions'.[36] The treaties that were developed and are, if in force, monitored within the human rights processes of the UN are, in chronological order of their having been adopted by the UN General Assembly:[37]

International Convention on the Elimination of All Forms of Racial Discrimination (ICERD), 1965
International Covenant on Civil and Political Rights (ICCPR), 1966
International Covenant on Economic, Social and Cultural Rights (ICESCR), 1966
Convention on the Elimination of All Forms of Discrimination against Women (CEDAW), 1979
Convention Against Torture and Other Cruel, Inhuman or Degrading Treatment or Punishment (CAT), 1984
Convention on the Rights of the Child (CROC), 1989
International Convention on the Protection of the Rights of All Migrant Workers and Members of Their Families (ICRMW), 1990
International Convention for the Protection of All Persons from Enforced Disappearance (ICPED), 2006
International Convention on the Rights of Persons with Disabilities (CRPD), 2006.

7.3.1 Optional Protocols

Many of these treaties are supplemented by 'optional protocols', effectively supplementary treaties that address specific issues arising under the principal treaty:

(First) Optional Protocol to the International Covenant on Civil and Political Rights (to establish a complaint mechanism for individuals) (ICCPR-OP1), 1966
Second Optional Protocol to the International Covenant on Civil and Political Rights (to achieve abolition of the death penalty) (ICCPR-OP2), 1989

35 *International Law*, UN Office of the United Nations High Commissioner for Human Rights, <www2.ohchr.org/english/law/index.htm>.

36 UN Secretary-General, *Compilation of Guidelines on the Form and Content of Reports to be submitted by States Parties to the International Human Rights Treaties*, Appendix 2, HRI/GEN/2/Rev.6, 3 June 2009.

37 For abbreviations from the Office of the United Nations High Commissioner for Human Rights see, *International Law*, Office of the United Nations High Commissioner for Human Rights, <www2.ohchr.org/english/law/index.htm>.

Optional Protocol of the Covenant on Economic, Social and Cultural Rights (to establish a complaint mechanism for individuals and groups) (ICESCR-OP), not yet in force

Optional Protocol to the Convention on the Elimination of All Forms of Discrimination against Women (to establish a complaint mechanism for individuals) (OP-CEDAW), 1999

Optional Protocol to the Convention on the Rights of the Child on the involvement of children in armed conflict (OP-CRC-AC), 2000

Optional Protocol to the Convention on the Rights of the Child on the sale of children, child prostitution and child pornography (OP-CRC-SC), 2000

Optional Protocol to the Convention against Torture and Other Cruel, Inhuman or Degrading Treatment or Punishment (to establish a Subcommittee on Prevention of Torture and Other Cruel, Inhuman or Degrading Treatment, to conduct regular inspections of places of detention) (OP-CAT), 2002

Optional Protocol to the Convention on the Rights of Persons with Disabilities (to establish a complaint mechanism for individuals and groups) (OP-CRPD), 2006.

7.3.2 States Parties to the Core Human Rights Treaties[38]

A majority of the core human rights treaties have been ratified, acceded to or succeeded to by a majority of states:

Treaty	No of States parties[39]
ICERD	174
ICESCR	160
ICESCR-OP	3 of 160
ICCPR	167
ICCPR-OP1	114 of 167
ICCPR-OP2	73 of 167
CEDAW	186
CEDAW OP	102 of 186
CAT	147
CAT-OP	57 of 147
CROC	193[40]
CROC-OPAC	141[41] of 193
CROC-OPSC	143[42] of 193
ICRMW	44

38 As at 31 July 2011. Table adapted from Office of the United Nations High Commissioner for Human Rights, *Report on the Working Methods of the Human Rights Treaty Bodies Relating to the State Party Reporting Process*, Table 2, UN Doc HRI/ICM/2010/2 (2010), with additional information from the United Nations Treaty Collection <http://treaties.un.org>.

39 There are 193 UN member states.

40 Three non-UN member states are party to CROC: Cook Islands, the Holy See and Niue.

41 The USA has ratified the CROC-OPAC even though it is only a signatory to the CROC: see CROC-OPAC art 9(1).

42 The USA has ratified the CROC-OPSC even though it is only a signatory to the CROC: see CROC-OPSC art 13(2).

Treaty	No of States parties[39]
CRPD	100
CRPD-OP	61 of 100
ICPED	26

7.3.3 Overlap Among Treaties

As the UN Secretary-General acknowledges,[43] there are 'other United Nations human rights and related conventions', such as the genocide,[44] slavery[45] and refugee conventions,[46] and the many conventions of the International Labor Organisation (ILO) relating to rights at work. These treaties were developed and are monitored outside the human rights processes of the UN. Provisions in these other human rights treaties, particularly the ILO conventions, overlap with the core human rights treaties. They overlap too with regional human rights treaties, most significantly the *European Convention on Human Rights*.[47] Overlap among the treaties risks 'forum shopping',[48] where individuals select a treaty that offers the best prospect of success (no bad thing perhaps) and, more significantly, results in overlap in state reporting requirements,[49] leading to the calls for reform discussed below, and to diverging views on the nature of the same human rights standards stated in different instruments.[50]

In 1989 the Secretary-General prepared a report[51] that met a request by the Committee on Economic, Social and Cultural Rights, endorsed by the Economic and Social Council, to show clearly 'the extent and nature of any overlapping of issues dealt with in the [at the time, six] principal human rights treaties, with a view to reducing, as appropriate, duplication in the different supervisory bodies of issues raised with respect to any given State party'.[52] The Canadian Government has published the following 'Table

43 UN Secretary-General, see above, n 36.

44 *Convention on the Prevention and Punishment of the Crime of Genocide*, opened for signature 9 December 1948, 78 UNTS 277 (entered into force 12 January 1951).

45 *Slavery Convention*, signed at Geneva on 25 September 1926 and amended by the Protocol, opened for signature 7 December 1953, 212 UNTS 17 (entered into force 7 July 1955).

46 *Convention Relating to the Status of Refugees*, opened for signature 28 July 1951, 189 UNTS 137, art 1A(2) (entered into force 22 April 1954); *Protocol Relating to the Status of Refugees*, opened for signature 31 January 1967, art 1(2) (entered into force 4 October 1967).

47 See eg the discussion of the overlap between the ICCPR and the European Convention in L R Helfer, 'Forum Shopping for Human Rights' (1999–2000) 148(2) *University of Pennsylvania Law Review* 285, 301–2.

48 L R Helfer, ibid.

49 See generally A Bayefsky, *The UN Human Rights Treaty System: Universality at the Crossroads*, Kluwer Law International, The Hague, 2001, <http://www.bayefsky.com/report/finalreport.pdf>; R L Johnstone 'Cynical Savings or Reasonable Reform—Reflections on a Single Unified UN Human Rights Treaty Body' (2007) 7 *Human Rights Law Review* 173, 181–2; for a critique of efforts to avoid overlap, see M O'Flaherty and C O'Brien, 'Reform of UN Human Rights Treaty Monitoring Bodies: A Critique of the Concept Paper on the High Commissioner's Proposal for a Unified Standing Treaty Body' 7 *Human Rights Law Review* 141.

50 See eg M K Addo, 'Practice of United Nations Human Rights Treaty Bodies in the Reconciliation of Cultural Diversity with Universal Respect for Human Rights' (2010) 32(3) *Human Rights Quarterly* 601.

51 E/C.12/1989/3. See also P Alston, 'Comparative Analysis of the International Covenants on Human Rights and International Labour Conventions and Recommendations' (1969) 52 (2) *ILO Official Bulletin*, 215.

52 Economic and Social Council Resolution 1988/4, 24 May 1988.

of Concordances',[53] which assesses overlap among UN treaties at that time (ie, not including the ICMRW, CRPD and ICPED), by reference to themes used in the Secretary-General's 1989 report:

[Themes]	CERD	CCPR	ESCR	CEDAW	CAT	CROC
Self-determination	–	Art 1	Art 1	–	–	–
Limits on Rights	–	Art 4, Art 5	Art 4, Art 5	–	Art 2	Art 4
Equality	Art 2, Art 3	Art 2, Art 3, Art 26	Art 2, Art 3	Art 2, Art 3, Art 15	–	Art 2
Implementation prevention	Art 7	–	–	Art 5	Art 10, Art 11	Art 11, Art 19
Implementation legislation	Art 2, Art 5	Art 2	Art 2	Art 3	Art 2	Art 3, Art 4
Implementation legal sanctions	Art 4	–	–	Art 3	Arts 2–9	–
Effective remedy	Art 6	Art 2	–	–	–	–
Procedural guarantees	Art 5a	Arts 14–16	–	Art 15	Arts 12–15	Art 12, Art 25
Right to life	–	Arts 6–8	–	Art 6	Art 1, Art 16	Art 6, Art 33
Liberty, security	Art 5b	Arts 9–11	–	–	–	Arts 11, 19, 33–38, 40
Freedom of movement	Art 5d and 5f	Art 12, Art 13	–	Art 15	Art 3	Art 10
Privacy, religion, conscience	Art 5d	Art 17, Art 18	–	–	–	Art 14
Opinion, expression	Art 5d	Art 19, Art 20	–	–	–	Art 12, Art 13
Assembly, association	Art 4, Art 5d	Art 21, Art 22	–	–	–	Art 15
Marriage, family	Art 5d	Art 23, Art 24	Art 10	Art 4, Art 12, Art 16	–	Arts 5, 9, 10, 16, 20, 21, 22
Nationality	Art 5d	Art 24	–	Art 9	–	Art 7, Art 8
Political rights	Art 5c	Art 25	–	Art 7, Art 9	–	–
Property	Art 5d	–	–	Art 8, Art 13, Art 15	–	–
Vulnerable groups	Art 1	Art 27	Art 2	Art 4, Art 14	–	Arts 17d, 23, 30
Work	Art 5e	–	Art 6, Art 7	Art 11	–	Art 32
Trade unions	Art 5e	Art 22	Art 8	–	–	–
Social security	Art 5e	–	Art 9	Art 11	–	Arts 18, 20, 26
Food and shelter	Art 5e	–	Art 11	–	–	Art 27
Health	–	Art 6	Art 12	Art 12	–	Arts 17, 19, 24, 31, 39
Education, culture	Art 5e	–	Art 13, Art 14, Art 15	Art 10, Art 13	–	Arts 17, 20, 28, 29, 31

53 Concordances (2009) Canadian Heritage <www.pch.gc.ca/pgm/pdp-hrp/docs/corcond-eng.cfm>.

7.3.4 International Bill of Rights

The ICESCR and the ICCPR detail the rights in the UDHR. The three documents constitute the International Bill of Rights,[54] described as 'the currently definitive international statement of the scope of human rights', and 'the central legal statement for the world of the content of human rights'.[55] The history of the development of the International Bill of Rights is described in Chapter 1. The nature of and protection for the civil and political rights that are protected by the ICCPR are described in detail in Chapter 3. The nature of the economic, social and cultural rights that are protected by the ICESCR, and of the protection that is offered, are described in detail in Chapter 4.

7.3.5 ICESCR: Economic, Social and Cultural Rights

The ICESCR required ratification or accession by 35 states before it entered into force,[56] and did not enter into force until 3 January 1976, nine years after it opened for signature. As at 31 July 2011, 160 states were a party to ICESCR. The ICESCR entered into force for Australia on 10 March 1976, without any reservations or declarations; Australia's implementation of its ICESCR obligations is discussed in Chapter 10.3.3.

In the ICESCR, article 2 summarises the obligations on states to give effect to the treaty. The UN Economic Social and Cultural Rights Council (ECOSOC) has published General Comment 3 on the nature of these obligations and is discussed in detail in Chapter 4.3.2.[57]

Optional Protocol to ICESCR

The *Optional Protocol* to the ICESCR[58] was adopted by the UN Human Rights Council in 2008,[59] and was recommended to the UN General Assembly, which adopted it later the same year.[60] The terms of the ICESCR-OP require 10 ratifications of accessions before it comes into force.[61] Within days of its being

54 See, eg, *UN High Commissioner for Human Rights Fact Sheet No 2 (Rev)* at <www.ohchr.org/Documents/Publications/FactSheet2Rev.1en.pdf>; Philip Alston includes in the International Bill of Rights the First Optional Protocol to the ICCPR, which allows individuals to communicate alleged violations to the Human Rights Committee, see P Alston 'Making and Breaking Human Rights: The UN's Specialised Agencies and Implementation of the International Covenant on Economic Social and Cultural Rights' (*Human Rights and Development Working Paper No 1, Anti-Slavery Society, 1979*) n 1.

55 P Bailey, *The Human Rights Enterprise: In Australia and Internationally*, LexisNexis, Chatswood, 2009, 9–10.

56 ICESCR, see above, n 30, art 27(1).

57 Committee on Economic, Social and Cultural Rights, *General Comment No 3: The Nature of States Parties Obligations* (art 2, par.1), 5th sess, UN Doc E/1991/23(1990).

58 *Optional Protocol to the International Covenant on Economic, Social and Cultural Rights* (ICESCR-OP), opened for signature 24 September 2009 (not yet in force); <www2.ohchr.org/english/law/docs/A.RES.63.117_en.pdf>.

59 UN Human Rights Council, *Optional Protocol to the International Covenant on Economic, Social and Cultural Rights*, HRC Res 8/2, 8th sess, UN Doc A/HRC/RES/8/2 (2008).

60 ICESCR-OP, see above, n 58, GA Res 63/117, UN GA, 63rd sess, UN Doc A/63/435 (2008).

61 Ibid art 18(1).

open for signature, thirty states signed the *Optional Protocol*.[62] As at 31 July 2011, 36 states had signed it, but only three (Ecuador, Mongolia and Spain) had ratified it. Australia has not signed it, but said in January 2011, responding to the recommendations of the Universal Period Review, that it will be considering its position.[63] The history and scope of the ICESCR-OP is discussed in more detail in Chapter 4.4.

7.3.6 ICCPR: Civil and Political Rights

As with the ICESCR, the ICCPR[64] was adopted by the General Assembly and opened for signature in 1966.[65] It required 35 ratifications or accessions before it came into force,[66] except for article 41 establishing the Human Rights Committee, which required 10 states parties to the ICCPR to make the necessary declaration. The ICCPR came into force (but for article 41) on 23 March 1976, more than nine years after being opened for signature, and a few months after the ICESCR came into force. As at 31 May 2011, 167 states were party to the ICCPR. The ICCPR entered into force for Australia on 13 November 1980, subject to a number of reservations and declarations; Australia's implementation of its ICCPR obligations is discussed in Chapter 10.3.3.

In the ICCPR, article 2 summarises the obligations on states to give effect to the treaty; the Human Rights Committee has published General Comment 31 on the nature of the article 2 obligations,[67] discussed in more detail in Chapter 3.2.1.

First Optional Protocol to the ICCPR

The ICCPR-OP1[68] gives people the right to communicate with the UN Human Rights Committee (HRC), alleging that the state has violated their rights guaranteed under the ICCPR. The right can be exercised only after the person has exhausted their remedies under the domestic law of the state.[69] A communication is effectively a complaint that the state has breached the ICCPR by violating a person's

62 Argentina, Armenia, Azerbaijan, Belgium, Chile, Congo, Ecuador, El Salvador, Finland, Gabon, Ghana, Guatemala, Guinea-Bissau, Italy, Luxembourg, Madagascar, Mali, Montenegro, the Netherlands, Paraguay, Portugal, Senegal, Slovakia, Slovenia, Solomon Islands, Spain, Timor-Leste, Togo, Ukraine, Uruguay.

63 P Woolcott, *Response of Australia to Recommendations of the United Nations Human Rights Council*, 31 January 2011, <http://www.geneva.mission.gov.au/gene/Statement159.html>.

64 ICCPR, see above, n 27.

65 ICCPR, see above, n 27.

66 ICCPR, see above, n 27, art 49.

67 UN Human Rights Committee, *General Comment 31: Nature of the General Legal Obligation Imposed on States Parties to the Covenant*, 80th sess, UN Doc CCPR/C/21/Rev.1/Add.13 (2004).

68 *First Optional Protocol to the International Covenant on Civil and Political Rights* (ICCPR-OP1), opened for signature 16 December 1966, 999 UNTS 171 (entered into force 23 March 1976).

69 ICCPR, see above, n 27, art 41(1)(c).

enjoyment of one of the rights set out in the ICCPR. The HRC investigates these communications and publishes 'views' on them, discussed below.

The *Optional Protocol* required 10 ratifications[70] and came into force at the same time as the ICCPR, on 23 March 1976. The Human Rights Committee has observed that '[a]lthough the *Optional Protocol* is organically related to the Covenant, it is not automatically in force for all States parties to the Covenant. Article 8 of the *Optional Protocol* provides that States parties to the Covenant may become parties to the *Optional Protocol* only by a separate expression of consent to be bound'.[71]

As at 31 May 2011, 114 states had ratified or acceded to the ICCPR-OP1. Australia has ratified the Protocol, and it came into force for Australia on 25 December 1991. Communications made against Australia are discussed in Chapter 10.5.4.

Second Optional Protocol to the ICCPR

The ICCPR-OP2[72] imposes an obligation on a ratifying state not to execute anyone within its jurisdiction, and allows the HRC to receive communications from individuals alleging violations of this obligation.[73] The Protocol was adopted by the UN General Assembly in 1989.[74] It required 10 ratifications, and came into force on 11 July 1991. As at 31 May 2011, 73 states had become parties to the *Second Optional Protocol*. Australia has ratified the ICCPR-OP2, and it came into force for Australia on 11 July 1991. The death penalty is not currently provided for in any Australian jurisdiction and no execution has been carried out in Australia since 1967.[75]

7.3.7 ICERD: Racial Discrimination

The *International Convention on the Elimination of All Forms of Racial Discrimination* (ICERD)[76] was the first human rights treaty (preceding both the ICESCR and the ICCPR), and the first to address the rights of a specifically identified group; others that followed address the rights of women, children, people with disabilities, migrant workers and enforced disappearances. ICERD does not define 'race', grouping the term with other like terms: article 1 refers to 'race, colour, descent, or national or ethnic origin'.

70 ICCPR-OP, see above, n 68, art 9.

71 UN Human Rights Committee, *General Comment 33 The Obligations of States Parties under the Optional Protocol to the International Covenant on Civil and Political Rights*, UN Doc CCPR/C/GC/33 (2008).

72 *Second Optional Protocol to the International Covenant on Civil and Political Rights, Aiming at the Abolition of the Death Penalty* (ICCPR-OP2), opened for signature 15 December 1989, 1642 UNTS 414 (entered into force 11 July 1991); <www2.ohchr.org/english/law/ccpr-death.htm>.

73 Ibid art 5.

74 *Elaboration of a Second Optional Protocol to the International Covenant on Civil and Political Rights, Aiming at the Abolition of the Death Penalty*, GA Res 44/128, UN GA, 44th sess, 82nd plen mtg, 206, UN Doc A/RES/44/128 (1989).

75 The last person executed in Australia was Ronald Ryan on 3 February 1967 in Melbourne, Victoria.

76 *International Convention on the Elimination on All Forms of Racial Discrimination* (ICERD), opened for signature 21 December 1965, 660 UNTS 195 (entered into force 4 January 1969); <www2.ohchr.org/english/law/cerd.htm>.

As the first such treaty, ICERD offered a template for subsequent human rights treaties. Most significantly, it pioneered a committee system for monitoring states' compliance with treaty obligations and for receiving communications from individuals about states' violations of treaty obligations. While the ICCPR was subsequently drafted to include the same approach of establishing a committee to monitor compliance and receive communications, the ICESCR was not: 'fears were expressed that such a body might encroach upon the work of ECOSOC and the functions of the specialised United Nations agencies'.[77]

ICERD was adopted by the UN General Assembly and opened for signature in 1965.[78] Requiring 27 ratifications or accessions,[79] it came into force on 4 January 1969. As at 31 May 2011, 174 states were party to ICERD. Australia ratified the treaty in 1975 and it came into force for Australia in the same year; Australia's implementation of its ICERD obligations is discussed in Chapter 10.3.3.

ICERD is different from subsequent human rights treaties (other than CAT) in that the capacity of its monitoring committee to receive communications from individuals about a state's violation of the treaty is in the terms of the treaty itself, and not in a separate protocol. However, the ICERD Committee has that capacity in relation to a state party only if, separately from ratifying ICERD, the state party specifically declares that it recognises the Committee's competence for that purpose.[80] Australia did not make that declaration until 1993.

Article 8 of ICERD established the ICERD Committee. In its Part II of General Recommendation 32, extracted and discussed in Chapter 13.2.3, the Committee has commented on the nature of the essential non-discrimination provisions of the treaty.

7.3.8 CEDAW: Discrimination Against Women

The Convention on the Elimination of All Forms of Discrimination Against Women (CEDAW)[81] was adopted by the UN General Assembly in December 1979. It was opened for signature on 1 March 1980 and, having obtained the required 20 ratifications or accessions,[82] came into force on 3 September 1981.

As at 31 May 2011, 186 countries had ratified or acceded to CEDAW. Australia ratified CEDAW in 1983, and it came into force for Australia in the same year; discuss Australia's implementation of its CEDAW obligations is discussed in Chapter 10.3.3.

77 A Devereaux, *Australia and the Birth of the International Bill of Rights 1946–1966*, Federation Press, Annandale, 2005, 178.

78 *International Convention on the Elimination of All Forms of Racial Discrimination* (ICERD), GA Res 2106 (XX), UN GA, 20th sess, 1046th plen mtg, UN Doc A/RES/20/2106 (1965).

79 ICERD, see above, n 76, art 19(1).

80 ICERD, see above, n 76, art 14(1).

81 *Convention on the Elimination of All Forms of Discrimination Against Women* (CEDAW), opened for signature 1 March 1980, 1249 UNTS 13 (entered into force 3 September 1981); <www2.ohchr.org/english/law/cedaw.htm>.

82 Ibid art 27(1).

Although CEDAW is second only to the *Convention on the Rights of the Child* in the number of state parties, it has the highest number of reservations. Most of the reservations relate to articles 2 and 16, which 'delineate the spirit and essence of effective implementation of women's rights'.[83] Article 2 is the essential provision of CEDAW, stating that, 'State parties condemn discrimination against women in all its forms, [and] agree to pursue by all appropriate means and without delay a policy of eliminating discrimination against women …' To lodge a reservation against this article is incompatible with accepting the object and purpose of the treaty. Similarly incompatible is a reservation in relation to article 16, which requires states to 'take all appropriate measures to eliminate discrimination against women in all matters relating to marriage and family relations …'[84]

Optional Protocol to CEDAW

The CEDAW Committee drafted an *Optional Protocol*[85] procedure for individual communications ('CEDAW-OP'), which was adopted by the UN General assembly in 1999.[86]

CEDAW-OP required 10 ratifications[87] and came into force on 22 December 2000. As at 31 May 2011, 100 states had become parties to the CEDAW *Optional Protocol*. Australia acceded to CEDAW-OP only in December 2008, after having previously explicitly declined to do so, discussed further in Chapter 10.5.5.

7.3.9 CAT: Protection Against Torture

The *Convention Against Torture and Other Cruel, Inhuman or Degrading Treatment or Punishment* (CAT)[88] was adopted by the UN General Assembly in December 1984.[89] It required 20 ratifications or accessions to come into force,[90] and did so on 26 June 1987. As at 31 May 2011, 147 states had ratified or acceded to CAT. Australia ratified CAT and it came into force for Australia on 7 September 1989; Australia's implementation of its CAT obligations is discussed in Chapter 10.3.3.

---

83 F Acar, 'The Convention on the Elimination of All Forms of Discrimination Against Women', in R K Smith & C van den Anker (eds), *The Essentials of Human Rights*, Hodder Arnold, London, 2005, 58–61.

84 See the Snapshot of reservations to CEDAW in Chapter 13.5.3.

85 *Optional Protocol to the Convention on the Elimination of All Forms of Discrimination Against Women* (OP-CEDAW or CEDAW-OP), opened for signature 10 December 1999, 2131 UNTS 83 (entered into force 22 December 2000).

86 Ibid GA Res 54/4, UN GA, 54th sess, UN Doc A/RES/54/4 (1999).

87 See above, n 85, art 16(1) (entered into force 22 December 2000).

88 *Convention Against Torture and Other Cruel, Inhuman or Degrading Treatment or Punishment* (CAT), opened for signature 4 February 1985, 1465 UNTS 85 (entered into force 26 January 1987); <www2.ohchr.org/english/law/cat.htm>.

89 CAT, see above, n 88, GA Res 39/462, UN GA, 39th sess, UN Doc A/RES/39/46.

90 CAT, see above, n 88, art 27(1) (entered into force 26 January 1987).

The CAT Committee has published its General Comment 2 on the nature of state obligations under Art 2 of CAT:[91]

2 Article 2, paragraph 1 obliges each State party to take actions that will reinforce the prohibition against torture through legislative, administrative, judicial, or other actions that must, in the end, be effective in preventing it …

3 The obligation to prevent torture in Article 2 is wide-ranging. The obligations to prevent torture and other cruel, inhuman or degrading treatment or punishment (hereinafter 'ill-treatment') under Article 16, paragraph 1, are indivisible, interdependent and interrelated … Experience demonstrates that the conditions that give rise to ill-treatment frequently facilitate torture and therefore the measures required to prevent torture must be applied to prevent ill-treatment …

4 States parties are obligated to eliminate any legal or other obstacles that impede the eradication of torture and ill-treatment; and to take positive effective measures to ensure that such conduct and any recurrences thereof are effectively prevented …

5 Article 2, paragraph 2, provides that the prohibition against torture is absolute and nonderogable. It emphasizes that *no exceptional circumstances whatsoever* may be invoked by a State Party to justify acts of torture in any territory under its jurisdiction …

…

8 States parties must make the offence of torture punishable as an offence under its criminal law, in accordance, at a minimum, with the elements of torture as defined in Article 1 of the Convention, and the requirements of Article 4.

…

15 The Convention imposes obligations on States parties and not on individuals. States bear international responsibility for the acts and omissions of their officials and others, including agents, private contractors, and others acting in official capacity or acting on behalf of the State, in conjunction with the State, under its direction or control, or otherwise under colour of law …

16 Article 2, paragraph 1, requires that each State party shall take effective measures to prevent acts of torture not only in its sovereign territory but also 'in any territory under its jurisdiction.' …

17 The Committee observes that States parties are obligated to adopt effective measures to prevent public authorities and other persons acting in an official capacity from directly committing, instigating, inciting, encouraging, acquiescing in or otherwise participating or being complicit in acts of torture as defined in the Convention …

…

20 The principle of non-discrimination is a basic and general principle in the protection of human rights and fundamental to the interpretation and application of the Convention. Nondiscrimination is included within the definition of torture itself in Article 1, paragraph 1, of the Convention, which explicitly prohibits specified acts when carried out for '*any reason based on discrimination of any kind* …' The Committee emphasizes that the discriminatory use of mental or physical violence or abuse is an important factor in determining whether an act constitutes torture.

21 The protection of certain minority or marginalized individuals or populations especially at risk of torture is a part of the obligation to prevent torture or ill-treatment …

91 UN Committee against Torture, *General Comment No 2: Implementation of Article 2 by States Parties*, UN Doc CAT/C/GC/2 (2008).

CAT Monitoring

CAT, like CERD but differently from other human rights treaties, establishes in the terms of the treaty itself, and not in a separate protocol, the capacity of its monitoring committee ('treaty body') to receive communications from individuals about a state's violation of the treaty. The operation of treaty bodies is discussed below.

CAT required five states parties to make a declaration under articles 21 and 22 before those provisions would come into effect. Those declarations were made among the initial ratifications of CAT, so came into force with the whole of the treaty. Australia did not make the declarations under articles 21 and 22 until 1993.

Optional Protocol to CAT

On 18 December 2002 the UN General Assembly adopted the *Optional Protocol* to CAT ('CAT-OP').[92] In adopting the *Optional Protocol* the UN General Assembly was acting on a recommendation from ECOSOC that had been opposed only by Australia, China, Cuba, Egypt, Japan, Libya, Nigeria and Sudan.

The CAT-OP needed 20 ratifications or accessions to come into force.[93] It was opened for signature on 4 February 2003, and entered into force on 22 June 2006. As at 31 May 2011, 57 states had ratified the *Optional Protocol*. Under a different government from that which opposed the CAT-OP at the UN General Assembly, Australia signed it on 19 May 2009. In January 2011, responding to the recommendations of the Universal Period Review, Australia said that it is committed to ratifying it as a matter of priority, but as at 20 July 2011 had not ratified it.[94]

Subcommittee on Prevention of Torture

The CAT-OP establishes the UN Subcommittee on Prevention of Torture and other Cruel, Inhuman or Degrading Treatment or Punishment (SPT). The *Optional Protocol* requires state parties to establish national preventive mechanisms that will monitor the treatment of people in detention and make recommendations to government authorities to strengthen protection against torture. It also requires state parties to permit regular visits by independent international and national bodies to places of detention to prevent torture and other cruel, inhuman or degrading treatment or punishment.

In its *Third Annual Report*,[95] the SPT discussed its mandate:

---

92 *Optional Protocol to the Convention Against Torture and Other Cruel, Inhuman or Degrading Treatment or Punishment*, GA Res 57/199, UN GAOR, 57th sess, UN Doc A/RES/57/199 (2003).

93 *Optional Protocol to the Convention Against Torture and Other Cruel, Inhuman or Degrading Treatment or Punishment*, opened for signature 4 February 1985, 2375 UNTS 237, art 28(1) (entered into force 22 June 2006).

94 P Woolcott, see above, n 63.

95 UN Subcommittee on Prevention of Torture and Other Cruel, Inhuman or Degrading Treatment or Punishment, *Third Annual Report, Committee Against Torture*, 44th sess, UN Doc CAT/C/44/2 (2010) (headings and citations ommitted).

THE SPT MANDATE

Article 11 [of CAT-OP] … establishes that the Subcommittee shall:

(a) Visit places where persons are or may be deprived of liberty and make recommendations to the States parties on the protection of persons deprived of their liberty from torture and other cruel, inhuman or degrading treatment or punishment;

(b) In regard to national preventive mechanisms:

(i) Advise and assist States parties, when necessary, in their establishment;

(ii) Maintain direct contact with national preventive mechanisms and offer them training and technical assistance; advise and assist national preventive mechanisms in evaluating the needs and necessary means to improve safeguards against ill-treatment; and make necessary recommendations and observations to States parties with a view to strengthening the capacity and mandate of national preventive mechanisms;

(c) Cooperate with relevant United Nations bodies as well as with international, regional and national bodies, in the prevention of ill-treatment.

…

13 … Each State party is obliged to allow visits by the Subcommittee to any places under its jurisdiction and control where persons are or may be deprived of their liberty, either by virtue of an order given by a public authority or at its instigation or with its consent or acquiescence.

14 States parties further undertake to grant the Subcommittee unrestricted access to all information concerning persons deprived of their liberty and to all information referring to the treatment of those persons, as well as their conditions of detention. They are also obliged to grant the Subcommittee private interviews with persons deprived of liberty without witnesses. The Subcommittee is free to choose the places it wishes to visit and the persons it wishes to interview …

…

16 The process of prevention of torture and other cruel, inhuman or degrading treatment or punishment ranges from the analysis of international instruments on protection to the examination of the material conditions of detention, taking in along the way public policy, budgets, regulations, written guidelines and theoretical concepts explaining the acts and omissions that impede the application of universal standards to local conditions.…

18 … there is always a need for States to be vigilant in order to guard against the risk of it occurring and to put in place and maintain effective and comprehensive safeguards to protect persons deprived of their liberty. It is the role of preventive mechanisms to ensure that such safeguards are actually in place and operating effectively and to make recommendations to improve the system of safeguards …

7.3.10 CROC: Children's Rights

The UN General Assembly adopted the *Convention on the Rights of the Child* (CROC) in 1989,[96] and on being ratified by 20 states[97] it entered into force on 2 September 1990. As at 31 May 2011, 193 states

96 *Convention on the Rights of the Child* (CROC), GA Res 44/25, UN GA, 44th sess, 61st plen mtg, UN Doc A/RES/44/25 (1989).

97 *Convention on the Rights of the Child* (CROC), opened for signature 20 November 1989, 1577 UNTS 3, art 49(1) (entered into force 2 September 1990).

had ratified or acceded to the CROC, more than for any of the other human rights treaties.[98] The CROC entered into force for Australia on 16 January 1991; Australia's implementation of its CROC obligations is discussed in Chapter 10.5.

The Committee on the Rights of the Child has published its General Comment 5 on 'General measures of implementation for the *Convention on the Rights of the Child*'.[99] The Committee addressed in particular article 4 of the CROC, which requires state parties to 'undertake all appropriate legislative, administrative, and other measures for the implementation of the rights recognized in the present Convention'. The operation of the CROC is discussed in detail in Chapter 12.

Optional Protocols to the CROC

Two Optional Protocols under the CROC have been adopted. The first, CROC-OPSC, prohibits the sale of children, child prostitution and child pornography.[100] After adoption by the UN General Assembly in 2000,[101] it came into force on 18 January 2002 on being ratified by the required number of 10 states.[102] As at 31 May 2011, 142 states had become party to it; Australia ratified CROC-OPSC on 8 January 2007.

The second *Optional Protocol*,[103] CROC-OPAC, obliges states to take all possible measures to ensure that people under 18 do not take part in armed conflict. After adoption by the UN General Assembly in 2000,[104] it came into force on 12 February 2002 on being ratified by the required number of 10 states.[105] As at 31 May 2011, 139 states had become party to it; Australia ratified CROC-OPAC on 26 September 2006. The human rights of children are discussed in detail in Chapter 17.

7.3.11 ICRMW: Rights of Migrant Workers

The *Convention on the Protection of the Rights of All Migrant Workers and Members of Their Families* (ICRMW)[106] was adopted by the UN General Assembly in 1990,[107] and entered into force on 1 July 2003

98 See above, n 38.

99 UN Committee on the Rights of the Child, *General Comment No 5: General Measures of Implementation for the Convention on the Rights of the Child (Articles 4, 42 and 44(6))*, 34th sess, UN Doc CRC/GC/2003/5 (2003).

100 *Optional Protocols to the Convention on the Rights of the Child on the Involvement of Children in Armed Conflict and on the Sale of Children, Child Prostitution and Child Pornography* (OP-CRC-AC or CROC-OPAC and OP-CRC-SC or CROC-OPSC), GA Res 54/263, UN GA, 54th sess, UN Doc A/RES/54/263 (2000).

101 Ibid.

102 *Optional Protocol to the Convention on the Rights of the Child on the Sale of Children, Child Prostitution and Child Pornography* (OP-CRC-SC or CROC-OPSC), opened for signature 25 May 2000, 2171 UNTS 227, art 14(1) (entered into force 18 January 2002).

103 *Optional Protocol to the Convention on the Rights of the Child on the Involvement of Children in Armed Conflict* (OP-CRC-AC or CROC-OPAC), opened for signature 25 May 2000, 2173 UNTS 222, art 10(1) (entered into force 12 February 2002).

104 Ibid.

105 Ibid.

106 *International Convention on the Protection of the Rights of All Migrant Workers and Members of Their Families* (ICRMW), opened for signature 18 December 1990, 2220 UNTS 3 (entered into force 1 July 2003).

107 *International Convention on the Protection of the Rights of All Migrant Workers and Members of Their Families* (ICRMW), GA Res 45/158, UN GA, 45th sess, 69th plen mtg, UN Doc A/RES/45/158 (1990).

on having been ratified by the required number of 20 states.[108] Its aim is to prevent the exploitation of migrant workers through trafficking and illegal recruitment, and irregular or undocumented employment situations.

The ICRMW took 13 years to achieve the necessary number of ratifications, and many of the countries ratifying are those whose citizens make up a large part of the 150 million migrants working in a country other than their own. As at 31 May 2011, 44 states were party to the treaty. Australia is not yet a party, and its view of the Convention is discussed in Chapter 10.2.2.

7.3.12 CRPD: Rights of People with Disabilities

The purpose of the *Convention on the Rights of Persons with Disabilities* (CRPD)[109] is to 'promote, protect and ensure the full and equal enjoyment of all human rights and fundamental freedoms by all persons with disabilities, and to promote respect for their inherent dignity'.[110] The term 'persons with disabilities' is defined to include people who have 'long-term physical, mental, intellectual or sensory impairments which in interaction with various barriers may hinder their full and effective participation in society on an equal basis with others'.[111]

The CRPD was adopted by the UN General Assembly,[112] and entered into force on 3 May 2008 on having been ratified by the required number of 20 states.[113] As at 31 May 2011, 100 states were party to the treaty. Australia ratified on 17 July 2008. The human rights of people with disabilities are discussed in detail in Chapter 14.

Optional Protocol to the CRPD

The *Optional Protocol* to the CRPD[114] ('CRPD-OP') empowers the Committee on the Rights of Persons with Disabilities to 'receive and consider communications from or on behalf of individuals or groups of individuals subject to its jurisdiction who claim to be victims of a violation by that State Party of the provisions of the Convention'.[115]

The UN General Assembly adopted the CRPD-OP on 18 December 2002. It was opened for signature on 30 March 2007, and entered into force on 3 May 2008 having achieved the required 10 ratifications

108 ICRMW, see above, n 106, art 87(1).

109 *Convention on the Rights of Persons with Disabilities* (CRPD), opened for signature 30 March 2007, 189 UNTS 137 (entered into force 3 May 2008).

110 Ibid.

111 Ibid.

112 CRPD, see above, n 109, GA Res 61/106, UN GA, 61st sess, UN Doc A/RES/61/106 (2006).

113 CRPD, see above, n 109, art 45(1).

114 *Optional Protocol to the Convention on the Rights of Persons with Disabilities* (OP-CRPD), opened for signature 30 March 2007 (entered into force 3 May 2008).

115 Ibid art 1.

or accessions.[116] As at 31 May 2011, 61 states had ratified the *Optional Protocol*. Australia acceded to the *Optional Protocol* on 21 August 2009.

7.3.13 ICPED: Protection from Enforced Disappearance

The *International Convention for the Protection of All Persons from Enforced Disappearance* (ICPED)[117] was adopted by the UN General Assembly on 20 December 2006.[118] It required ratification by 20 states to enter into force,[119] and came into force on 23 December 2010.[120] As at 31 May 2011, 26 states were party to the treaty. Australia has not signed the ICPED, but said in January 2011, responding to the recommendations of the Universal Period Review, that it will be considering its position.[121]

7.4 THE TREATY BODIES

Except for ICESCR, each of the core human rights treaties establishes a committee[122] that has, in general terms, the obligation to oversee states' effective implementation of the treaty. The terms of ICESCR do not establish a committee, and refer only to ECOSOC.[123] In 1976 ECOSOC resolved to establish a committee similar to that already operating at the time in relation to ICERD and ICCPR.[124]

116 Ibid art 13(1).

117 *International Convention for the Protection of All Persons from Enforced Disappearance* (ICPED), opened for signature 6 February 2007 (entered into force 23 December 2010); <www2.ohchr.org/english/law/disappearance-convention.htm>.

118 *International Convention for the Protection of All Persons from Enforced Disappearance* (ICPED), GA Res 61/177, UN OGA, 61st sess, UN Doc A/RES/61/177 (2007).

119 See above, n 117, art 39.

120 For a discussion the terms of the ICPED see K Anderson, 'How Effective is the International Convention for the Protection of all Persons from Enforced Disappearance Likely to be in Holding Individuals Criminally Responsible for Acts of Enforced Disappearance?' (2006) 7(2) *Melbourne Journal of International Law*, 245.

121 P Woolcott, see above, n 63.

122 ICERD, see above, n 76, art 8(1); ICCPR, see above, n 27, art 28(2); CEDAW, see above, n 81, art 17(1); CAT, see above, n 88, art 17(1); CROC, see above, n 97, art 43(1); ICRMW, see above, n 106, art 72; ICPED, see above, n 117, art 26; CRPD, see above, n 109, art 34.

123 ICESCR, see above, n 30, art 16.

124 Resolution 1988 (LX) (1976), E/C.12/1989/4.

The committees are commonly known as 'treaty bodies', or 'treaty monitoring bodies' and, except for the committee established by the ICCPR, they are named in terms that are the same as or similar to the name of their enabling treaty:

Treaty	Treaty body
ICERD	Committee for the Elimination of Racial Discrimination (CERD)
ICCPR	Human Rights Committee (HRC)
ICESCR	Committee on Economic Social and Cultural Rights (CESCR)
CEDAW	Committee for the Elimination of Discrimination Against Women (CEDAW)
CAT	Committee Against Torture (CAT)
CROC	Committee on the Rights of the Child (CRC)
ICRMW	Committee on Migrant Workers (CMW)
ICPED	Committee on Enforced Disappearances (CED)[125]
CRPD	Committee on the Rights of Persons with Disabilities (CRPD)

It is apparent from the discussion below concerning treaty body reform that there has been little planning in the creation of the treaty bodies. Establishing a treaty body is simply a standard part of designing a treaty's enforcement mechanisms. The sensitivities of international diplomacy, especially on questions of human rights, have meant that there has been very little development or innovation in the design of human rights mechanisms; if consensus has been achieved on a particular approach, it is far easier to replicate that approach than to revisit it. As a result, subsequent treaties have substantially followed the templates established by CERD and ICCPR.

7.4.1 Treaty Bodies' Purpose

The treaty body system was born of compromise. Early proposals for implementing the human rights treaties focused on a right to petition the UN for human rights violations, although any form of implementation that would encroach on national sovereignty was strongly resisted by many states parties.[126] The Human Rights Committee, established under the ICCPR following the ICERD model, was an acceptable approach only because it was established with the limited monitoring power of receiving states parties' reports, and with 'no power of investigation, no capacity for independent monitoring, no judicial authority, no ability to impose even symbolic penalties, no resources for research to verify state reporting, and no authority to compel states to submit reports ...'[127]

125 Independently of CED, a Working Group of the Human Rights Council has a mandate to 'assist the relatives of disappeared persons to ascertain the fate and whereabouts of their disappeared family members'. See Working Group on Enforced or Involuntary Disappearances, <http://www2.ohchr.org/english/issues/disappear/index.htm>.

126 See generally, R Normand & S Zaidi, *Human Rights at the UN*, Indiana University Press, Bloomington, 2008, 235–8.

127 Ibid 240.

The eight existing treaty bodies are constituted similarly to each other,[128] as the ICPED Committee will be if and when it is established. A principal treaty body function is to review states parties' progress in implementing the treaty: each committee is to receive, consider and comment on reports that states parties make on measures they have taken to implement the treaty.[129] This activity is commonly referred to as 'monitoring'. Two other principal functions for most committees are to receive, consider and comment on 'communications' (complaints) made by individuals against states parties, and made by one state party against another, both discussed below. As well as these three principal functions, most committees are required to report on their own activities to the states parties and to the General Assembly of the United Nations.

Only ICPED makes specific provision for evaluation of its committee's performance, requiring states parties to 'evaluate the functioning of the Committee' after not more than six years and to decide 'whether it is appropriate to transfer to another body—without excluding any possibility—the monitoring of this Convention'.[130]

A group of human rights experts ('the Nottingham group') called for clarity about the ultimate goals of treaty bodies,[131] reflecting the extent to which the treaty bodies' activities have—despite their limited formal powers and very limited resources—developed beyond mere monitoring of states parties implementation. The activities have extended to articulating interpretations of the treaties, developing human rights jurisprudence, providing a forum for individual petitions, establishing expectations for states parties' performance and promoting treaty compliance.

---

128 ICERD, see above, n 76, art 8(1); ICCPR, see above, n 27, art 28(2); CEDAW, see above, n 81, art 17(1); CAT, see above, n 88, art 17(1); CROC, see above, n 97, art 43(1); ICRMW, see above, n 106, art 72 (entered into force 1 July 2003); ICPED, see above, n 117, art 26; CRPD, see above, n 109, art 34.

129 ICERD, see above, n 76, art 9(1); ICCPR, see above, n 27, art 40(1); CEDAW, see above, n 81, art 18; CAT, see above, n 88, art 19 (entered into force 26 January 1987); CROC, see above, n 97, art 44; ICRMW, see above, n 106, arts 73 & 74; ICPED, see above, n 117, art 29; CRPD, see above, n 109, arts 35 & 36.

130 ICPED, see above, n 117, art 27.

131 *Expert Workshop on Reform of United Nations Human Rights Treaty Monitoring Bodies*, University of Nottingham Human Rights Law Centre, 11–12 February 2006, 3.1.

7.4.2 Membership

Except for CESCR, whose members are elected by ECOSOC, treaty body members are elected by states parties to the relevant treaty, from nominations made by states parties. Members are elected for four-year terms, with half the committee members being up for election every two years. Members can serve unlimited terms, assuming they are re-nominated by a state party, except in the CRPD, which limits members to being re-elected only once.[132] There is provision in every treaty that committee members serve in their personal capacity,[133] meaning that they are not agents of, or subject to direction by, the state party that nominated them.[134]

All the human rights treaties have very broad eligibility requirements for members. The criteria for membership are a matter for discussion in relation to treaty body reform generally, discussed below. The treaties require members to be either of high moral standing[135] or high moral character,[136] and all but ICERD require competence in human rights or the field covered by the treaty.[137] ICERD, ICRMW and

132 CRPD, see above, n 109, arts 34(7).

133 ICERD, see above, n 76, art 8(1); ICCPR, see above, n 27, art 28(3); CEDAW, see above, n 81, art 17(1); CAT, see above, n 88, art 17(1); CROC, see above, n 97, art 43(2); ICRMW, see above, n 106, art 72(2)(b); ICPED, see above, n 117, art 26(1); CRPD, see above, n 109, art 34 (3).

134 K J Partsch, 'The Committee on the Elimination of Racial Discrimination' in P Alston, *The United Nations and Human Rights: A Critical Appraisal*, Clarendon Press, 1992, 341–68, 341–2, 366–7; R Jacobson, 'The Committee on the Elimination of Discrimination Against Women' in P Alston, *The United Nations and Human Rights: A Critical Appraisal*, Clarendon Press, 1992, 444–72, 450.

135 ICERD, see above, n 76, art 8(1); CEDAW, see above, n 81, art 17(1); CAT, see above, n 88, art 17(1); CROC, see above, n 97, art 43(2); ICRMW, see above, n 106, art 72(1)(b); ICPED, see above, n 117, art 26(1); CRPD, see above, n 109, art 34 (3).

136 ICCPR, see above, n 27, art 28(2).

137 ICCPR, see above, n 27, art 28(2); CEDAW, see above, n 81, art 17(1); CROC, see above, n 97, art 43(2); ICRMW, see above, n 106, art 72(1)(b).

ICPED require impartiality, and ICRMW and ICPED require independence.[138] The ICCPR requires that an elected member declare 'in open committee that he (sic) will perform his functions impartially and conscientiously'.[139] Only ICCPR, CAT and ICPED require that consideration be given to the usefulness of a member's having legal experience.[140] The most recent treaty, ICRPD, stipulates (article 34(3)) that 'when nominating their candidates, States Parties are invited to give due consideration to the provision set out in article 4(3)', which requires state parties to 'closely consult with and actively involve persons with disabilities, including children with disabilities, through their representative organizations'.

All the treaties except ICCPR call the treaty body members 'experts'.[141] Hilary Charlesworth has referred to members as 'so-called independent experts', and has said that '[s]ometimes it is questionable whether in the end you get people of the highest calibre, as there is a fair amount of politicking in ensuring that particular candidates are elected'.[142] Although she has questioned the expertise of some treaty body members, Charlesworth has said that 'the Australian Government ... has chosen people of enormous calibre'.[143] Australian appointees to the treaty bodies have been Professor Philip Alston, foundation director of the Centre for International and Public Law at the Australian National University, who was Chair of CESCR from 1991 to 1998; the Hon Elizabeth Evatt AC, founding Chief Justice of the Family Court of Australia and former President of the Australian Law Reform Commission, who was a member of the CEDAW from 1984 to 1992 and its chair from 1989 to 1990, and a member of the HRC from 1992 to 2000, its Rapporteur from 1997 to 1998, and its Vice-Chairperson from 1999 to 2000; Professor Ivan Shearer AM, formerly Challis Professor of International Law at the University of Sydney, who was

138 ICERD, see above, n 76, art 8(1); ICRMW, see above, n 106, art 72(1)(b); ICPED, see above, n 117, art 26(1).

139 ICCPR, see above, n 27, art 38.

140 ICCPR, see above, n 27, art 28(2); CAT, see above, n 88, art 17(1); ICPED, see above, n 117, art 26(1).

141 ICERD, see above, n 76, art 8(1); CEDAW, see above, n 81, art 17(1); CAT, see above, n 88, art 17(1); CROC, see above, n 97, art 43(2); ICRMW, see above, n 106, art 72(1)(b); ICPED, see above, n 117, art 26(1); CRPD, see above, n 109, art 34(3).

142 H Charlesworth, see above, n 18, 67; see also, S Joseph, J Schultz & M Castan, see above, n 23, para 1.34.

143 H Charlesworth, see above, n 18, 67.

a member of the HRC from 2000 to 2008; and Professor Ron McCallum AO, formerly Dean of Law at the University of Sydney, who was elected as a member of the UN Committee on the Rights of Persons with Disabilities in 2008 and its chair in 2010.

The treaties attempt to ensure diversity in treaty body membership, but only by requiring that some factors be considered in the process of electing members. Members are elected by secret ballot, so even if these considerations weighed on the mind of a state party when casting its vote, the result of an election cannot be managed to ensure diverse representation on the treaty body. Only an open selection process, if not for treaty body members then for nominees for election, could ensure the type of diversity anticipated by the treaties.

Most treaties require that in the election of members to a committee, consideration be given to equitable geographical distribution.[144] The criterion of 'geographic balance' is different from those of legal system and civilisation discussed below; it is a simple exercise in formal equality, ensuring an even spread of representation according to region without addressing assumptions that are made about a state's values and perspectives when identifying its geographic locus (eg north = developed, south = developing). ICPED requires geographical equity among members,[145] and ICRMW requires equitable geographical distribution according to both states of origin (where migrant workers come from) and states of employment (where migrant workers are employed).[146] For a period a Western representative bias could be detected in membership of the HRC, '[t]he geographic balance [having been] thrown into some disarray by the effective disappearance of the Eastern bloc as a separate political force in 1989'.[147]

Only the two most recent treaties, ICPED and CRPD, require that consideration be given to 'balanced gender representation'.[148] CEDAW membership is always predominantly female, while the other committees rarely if ever reach 50 percent female membership. Apart from CEDAW, only CRC has significant female membership. Only seven of the 24 nominees for election to the first CRPD in 2008 were women, five of whom were elected to a committee of 12; when membership expanded to 18 the number of women rose to eight, or 44 percent.

Particular to the circumstances addressed by the treaty, CRPD requires that consideration be given to 'participation of experts with disabilities'.[149] ICERD, ICCPR, CEDAW and CRPD require that

144 ICERD, see above, n 76, art 8(1); ICCPR, see above, n 27, art 28(3); CEDAW, see above, n 81, art 17(1); CAT, see above, n 88, art 17(1); CROC, see above, n 97, art 43(2); CRPD, see above, n 109, art 34(3).

145 ICPED, see above, n 117, art 26(1).

146 ICRMW, see above, n 106, art 72(2)(a).

147 See above, n 23, para 1.21.

148 ICPED, see above, n 117, art 26(1); CRPD, see above, n 109, art 34(3).

149 CRPD, see above, n 109, art 34(3).

consideration be given to 'the representation of the different forms of civilization as well as of the principal legal systems',[150] while CROC and ICRMW refer only to representation of the principal legal systems.[151]

The requirement for diversity is a vague requirement that seems to be an earnest but clumsy attempt to capture the universality of human rights in a committee made up of representatives of sovereign states. It invites, for example, apprehension that 'the body telling [a state party] what it must do to comply with the treaty will include those who not only do not share, but who absolutely oppose, the cultural and political principles underlying [that state party's] form of government'.[152]

7.4.3 Procedures

Each treaty provides that its committee 'shall establish ['adopt'[153]] its own rules of procedure'.[154] CAT and ICCPR define a quorum[155] and require that decisions be by majority vote.[156] Each committee has promulgated their own rules of procedure (eg the rules of the HRC[157]), but the various rules are generally similar.[158] Variations and inconsistencies in committee procedures have, however, led to calls for reform, discussed below.

150 ICERD, see above, n 76, art 8(1); ICCPR, see above, n 27, art 28(3); CEDAW, see above, n 81, art 17(1).

151 CROC, see above, n 97, art 43(2); ICRMW, see above, n 106, art 72(2)(b).

152 T L Jipping & W Wright, *CEDAW Treaty Would Undermine American Sovereignty*, The Federalist Society for Law and Public Policy Studies, Washington DC, 2002.

153 ICRMW, see above, n 106, art 75(1); CEDAW, see above, n 81, art 19(1); ICERD, see above, n 76, art 10(1).

154 ICPED, see above, n 117, art 26(6); CROC, see above, n 97, art 43(8); CRPD, see above, n 109, art 34(1); CEDAW, see above, n 81, art 19(1).

155 The quorum is six for CAT, and 12 for the HRC. See above, n 88, art 18(2); see above, n 27, art 39(2)(a) (entered into force 23 March 1976).

156 CAT, see above, n 88, art 18(2); ICCPR, see above, n 27, art 39(2)(b).

157 UN Human Rights Committee, *Rules of Procedure of the Human Rights Committee*, UN Doc CCPR/C/3/Rev.9 (2011).

158 *Human Rights Treaty Bodies—Individual Communications: 23 FAQ about Treaty Body Complaints Procedures*, UN Office of the High Commissioner for Human Rights <http://www2.ohchr.org/english/bodies/petitions/individual.htm>.

7.4.4 State Reports

A function common to all the treaty bodies is to receive and study periodic reports by states parties on measures they have taken to give effect to the rights recognised in the relevant treaty, and on progress made in the enjoyment of those rights.[159] This practice—of sovereign states submitting reports on their domestic performance against international standards—was described as 'revolutionary' and 'nearly inconceivable' as recently as the mid-twentieth century.[160]

States parties are required to report at intervals of two to five years, specified by each committee. The CAT Committee allows for urgent and confidential state reports when it is alerted to the systemic practice of torture.[161] Expressed differently in each treaty, each of the treaty bodies has power to ask for additional reports from state parties as they think fit, out of step with the regular reporting cycle. Conscious of the burden of submitting reports under the various treaties, harmonised guidelines for preparing reports under the human rights treaties have been compiled into a common 'core' UN document,[162] although separate reports still have to be made to each treaty body.

The state reports have been criticised as often being superficial,[163] characterised by incomplete coverage, and by abstraction and formality that stress formal constitutional provisions rather than a realistic description of practices.[164] Charlesworth has suggested abandoning the process altogether.[165]

Reporting by Federal States

A difficult issue in the negotiation of the human rights treaties was the extent to which the treaties could impose obligations on federal states such as Australia, Canada and the USA. Australia was vocal in pushing for a 'federal clause' that would limit the obligation on federal states to account for the conduct of their constituent provinces, saying that to extend the treaty obligations to federated provinces 'would be a breach of the whole spirit of federation'.[166] It was anomalous that federal states

159 ICCPR, see above, n 27, art 40(4); ICERD, see above, n 76, art 9; CEDAW, see above, n 81, art 18.

160 H Steiner, P Alston & R Goodman, see above, n 1, 850.

161 CAT, see above, n 88, art 20.

162 UN Secretary-General, see above, n 36.

163 H Steiner, P Alston & R Goodman, see above, n 1, 919.

164 See above, n 1, 850.

165 H Charlesworth, see above, n 18, 72.

166 Mr Moodie (Australia) addressing the UN General Assembly, 134, UN Doc A/C.5/SR.292 (1950), quoted in R Normand & S Zaidi, see above, n 126, 226.

had not made the same argument in relation to their other, non-human-rights treaty obligations, and after a lengthy debate over some years the proposal was dropped.[167]

The effect of international human rights treaties extends 'to all parts of federal States without limitations or exceptions'.[168] The intention behind such a provision is that Australia, for example, is accountable for implementation of the treaties, and for violations of them, in areas of activity that are constitutionally the concern of the states and territories rather than of the federal government. Australia has in fact attempted to avoid accountability for state and territory action or inaction by declarations it has made on ratification; this is discussed in Chapter 10.2.3.

Overlap in Reporting

States resent having to make multiple reports, many of which overlap in areas covered.[169] The treaty bodies do not—and perhaps could not—fully coordinate their respective reporting timetables, so that a state that is party to a number of treaties may indeed have more than one treaty body report in a year. Parker has analysed the figures, and the results suggest that the problem is not as extensive as might be thought: in 2007, 90 states parties were scheduled to appear before a treaty body to address a report they had lodged, of which 26 (29 percent) were scheduled to appear twice in the year and seven (8 percent) three times.[170]

Certainly the likelihood of a state facing multiple appearances in a year will increase as more states ratify more human rights treaties, and will increase again if state parties make any effort to catch up on late reports. The burden of multiple reports and consequent appearances before the treaty bodies has been addressed through harmonisation of the reports and the creation of a common core form of reporting,[171] but not yet through a single report, discussed below.

States' Delay in Reporting

Most state parties have been consistently late with their reports; in 2006 some of the states were overdue with their reports under the ICCPR by more than 15 years; 20 states had not even submitted an initial report more than five years after ratification.[172] A report by the OHCHR in March 2006 illustrated

167 See generally, R Normand & S Zaidi, ibid 224–30.

168 ICCPR, see above, n 27, art 50; ICESCR, see above, n 30, art 28; *Vienna Convention*, see above, n 9, art 2.

169 See E Tistounet, 'The Problem of Overlapping Among Different Treaty Bodies' in P Alston & J Crawford (eds), *The Future of UN Human Rights Treaty Monitoring*, Cambridge University Press, Cambridge, 2000, 383–401.

170 P Parker, *The State of the UN Human Rights Treaty Body System 2007: An NGO Perspective*, Minnesota Advocates for Human Rights, Minneapolis, 2007, 5.

171 UN Secretary-General, see above, n 36.

172 H Steiner, P Alston & R Goodman, see above, n 1, 854.

the significant extent of the states parties' failure to report, and showed that CEDAW and CROC have attracted the highest level of reporting compliance.[173]

Not only are delays in submitting reports chronic; the quality of the reports that are submitted is often poor: '[t]he national reporting mechanisms ... frequently receive reports that are inaccurate, incomplete, late, or not submitted at all'.[174] Parker suggests that the problem of states parties' delayed reports is not getting any worse.[175] Analysing the overdue reports, she takes into account the increasing number of new ratifications over the same period and concludes that the number of overdue reports has increased only in proportion to the increase in the numbers of ratifying countries and the consequent reporting obligations in the system.

Treaty Bodies' Backlog

It may be that the delay in states' submission of reports is only as bad now as it has been for some time, but even so, the treaty bodies are falling behind in reviewing those reports. The treaty bodies' backlog in considering reports perhaps takes some pressure off the recalcitrant states to comply with their reporting schedule, but does not explain or excuse states' failure to submit even an initial report under a treaty.

Bayefsky, a consistent but constructive critic of the UN treaty body system,[176] produced extensive statistical analyses of the treaty bodies' operations, represented in graphical form and current to 2000.[177] There have been no developments since then that would alter the upward climb of the charts, which suggests that the treaty bodies are falling further and further behind in dealing with reports. If the thousand or more overdue state reports were to arrive in a hurry the treaty bodies' work would come to a standstill. Although Parker has shown that the rate of delayed states parties' reports is constant, the treaty bodies are not dealing with states parties' reports as quickly as they are being filed, so the 'steady' rate of states parties' delay results in an increased rate of the treaty bodies' backlog.

Treaty Bodies' Hearings

Treaty bodies supplement the state reports with a discussion in a public meeting with state representatives, when treaty body members raise issues for clarification.

173 UN Office of High Commissioner for Human Rights, *Concept Paper on the High Commissioner's Proposal for Unified Standing Treaty Body*, HRI/MC/2006/2 (2006), Annex 1.

174 J Mertus, *The United Nations and Human Rights: A Guide for a New Era*, Routledge, London, 2005, 80.

175 P Parker, see above, n 170, 4.

176 A Bayefsky, 'Report on the human rights treaties: Facing the implementation crisis. First Report of the Committee on International Human Rights Law and Practice', *Report of the Sixty-Seventh Conference of the International Law Association*, International Law Association, London, 336–57; A Bayefsky, 'The UN and the International Protection of Human Rights', in B Galligan & C Sampford (eds), *Rethinking Human Rights*, Federation Press, Sydney, 1997, 74–85; A Bayefsky, see above, n 49.

177 A Bayefsky, see above, n 49, 193–562.

Bayefsky has observed that meetings of the treaty bodies 'in general are often poorly attended, particularly by national non-governmental organisations (NGOs) and national and international media'.[178] Alston, a consistently staunch defender of the UN treaty body system, responds by questioning the relevance of merely counting the number of attendees at treaty body meetings and the number of news media reports of treaty body proceedings. He points out that NGOs do in fact participate in treaty body proceedings, to an extent that threatens to overwhelm the treaty bodies.[179]

Based on her extensive experience in the HRC and the CEDAW Committee, Evatt has given an outline of the questions addressed by the committees: Do the domestic laws comply with the treaty? Are domestic remedies available for violation of treaty rights? Is the treaty known to all relevant government officials? and Is there actual enjoyment of the treaty rights by people in the state?[180] Alston has described relatively informal processes for deliberating on state reports in the CESCR and the CROC Committee, with an openness to dialogue, inquiry and NGO involvement.[181]

Bayefsky criticises the treaty bodies for failing to press for answers to questions that they have put to states parties and failing to provide an accessible record of the proceedings in which states parties' reports are considered.[182] Alston on the other hand sees the dialogue as a continuing process where a committee's adverse comment on a state party's failure to answer a question may lead state party to 'after reflection respond in ways that it refused to do earlier'. He protests that '[t]he process can be frustrating, and takes time. But it is a process, and its strengths need to be appreciated as well as its weaknesses'. [183]

Fact Finding by Treaty Bodies

The treaty bodies are substantially dependent on the material provided in the reports. They do not have access to reliable independent information and do not have the resources to undertake their own research. As a result, the treaty bodies are dependent on the self-serving documentation provided by the states parties, the knowledge of committee members and their willingness to use it, and information sought from or volunteered by other UN agencies and NGOs such as the International Commission of Jurists and Amnesty International.

---

178 A Bayefsky, 'Introduction', in A Bayefsky (ed), *The UN Human Rights Treaty System in the 21st Century*, Kluwer Law International, The Hague, 2000, xvii–xx, xviii.

179 P Alston, 'Beyond "Them" and "Us": Putting Treaty Body Reform into Perspective' in P Alston & J Crawford (eds), *The Future of UN Human Rights Treaty Monitoring*, Cambridge University Press, Cambridge, 2000, 501–25, 505–9.

180 E Evatt, 'Periodic Reporting: The International Covenant on Civil and Political Rights and the Convention on the Elimination of All Forms of Discrimination against Women' in S Pritchard (ed), *Indigenous Peoples, the United Nations and Human Rights*, Zed Books/Federation Press, Sydney, 1998, 135–49, 138.

181 P Alston, 'Periodic Reporting: The International Covenant on Economic, Social and Cultural Rights and the Convention on the Rights of the Child' in S Pritchard (ed), *Indigenous Peoples, the United Nations and Human Rights*, Zed Books/Federation Press, Sydney, 1998, 130–4, 133–4.

182 A Bayefsky, see above, n 178, xvii–xx, xix.

183 P Alston, see above, n 179, 501–25, 512.

The treaty bodies rely significantly on material provided to them by NGOs as a counter to state party reports that are 'less than candid'.[184] These alternative, or 'shadow' reports are 'often invaluable in providing information' on the underlying conditions causing human rights issues, and 'frequently provide useful information and data on state failures to protect and promote' human rights. As a result, 'when Committees receive evidence from NGOs that contradicts claims in governmental reports, it allows the Committee to question state credibility and compliance'.[185]

Although recognising the usefulness of NGOs' shadow reports,[186] Bayefsky considers that treaty bodies are overly reliant on them, and should engage in their own fact finding.[187] Alston argues that the treaty bodies, vastly underfunded to do their work, could not hope also to conduct credible fact-finding missions, and that such an active role for the treaty bodies would be fundamentally at odds with the terms on which states parties agreed to enter the treaties.[188]

Concluding Comments and Observations

The most sensitive part of the state reporting process is the production by a committee, by consensus, of Concluding Comments, or Concluding Observations, in which the treaty bodies, in diplomatic language, applaud the state for progress made and express concern in relation to matters that have arisen or steps that still need to be taken.

The Nottingham workshop of human rights experts identified the insufficiently detailed nature of concluding observations as a failing of the treaty body system,[189] and that the treaty bodies consistently fail to challenge or follow up on state reports. Although hampered by limited resources, the treaty bodies could themselves address the question of follow-up more actively. They have no process for following up their observations, or for requiring states to respond to recommendations and to report on measures taken to address matters that have been observed on adversely.

SNAPSHOT: AUSTRALIA

In its Concluding Observations on Australia in 2009, the CESCR highlighted positive and negative aspects of the country's adherence to its treaty obligations under ICESCR. For example, it commended Australia on the parliamentary apology issued in February 2008 to the indigenous peoples who were victims of the

184 A Bayefsky, see above, n 178, xvii–xx, xviii.

185 I Merali, 'Advancing Women's Reproductive and Sexual Health Rights: Using the International Human Rights System' (2000) 10(5) *Development in Practice*, 609, 619.

186 A Bayefsky, see above, n 49, 48.

187 A Bayefsky, see above, n 178.

188 P Alston, see above, n 179, 501–25, 510–12.

189 See above, n 131, 3, 2.2.

'Stolen Generation' policies, and noted 'with satisfaction that the State party has repealed legal provisions which discriminated against same-sex couples in relation to financial and work related benefits'. At the same time, it highlighted areas where Australia might improve:[190]

10 While welcoming the National Human Rights Consultation regarding the legal recognition and protection of human rights which is currently being carried out in the State party, the Committee regrets that the terms of reference for the National Human Rights Consultation do not specifically call for the consideration of economic, social and cultural rights.

The Committee affirms the principle of interdependency and indivisibility of human rights and calls on the State party to include economic, social and cultural rights when considering the submissions received.

11 The Committee regrets that the Covenant has not yet been incorporated into domestic law by the State party, despite the Committee's recommendations adopted in 2000 (E/C.12/1/Add.50). It notes with concern the lack of a legal framework for the protection of economic, social and cultural rights at the Federal level, as well as of an effective mechanism to ensure coherence and compliance of all jurisdictions in the Federation with the State party's obligations under the Covenant.

Bearing in mind the provisions of Article 28 of the Covenant, the Committee reiterates that the principal responsibility for its implementation lies with the State party's Federal government and recommends that it: (a) enact comprehensive legislation giving effect to all economic, social and cultural rights uniformly across all jurisdictions in the Federation; (b) consider the introduction of a Federal charter of rights that includes recognition and protection of economic, social and cultural rights, as recommended by the Australian Human Rights Commission; (c) establish an effective mechanism to ensure the compatibility of domestic law with the Covenant and to guarantee effective judicial remedies for the protection of economic, social and cultural rights.

...

26 The Committee notes with concern that the incidence of homelessness has increased in the State party over the last decade, mainly affecting indigenous peoples, in spite of the measures undertaken by the State party to address homelessness in Australia, including its National Housing Strategy, as well as its commitment to halve homelessness by 2020 and to improve housing affordability for vulnerable individuals (art 11 [of the Covenant]).

The Committee recommends that the State party take effective measures, in line with the Committee's general comment No 4 (1991) on the right to adequate housing (art 11, para 1, of the Covenant), to address homelessness in its territory. The State party should implement the recommendations of the Special Rapporteur on the Right to Adequate Housing contained in the report of his mission to Australia (A/HRC/4/18/Add.2). The Committee requests the State party to provide, in its next periodic report, disaggregated data and information which will allow the Committee to assess the progress made by the State party in improving the housing situation in its territory, in particular with respect to indigenous peoples.

190 UN Committee on Economic, Social and Cultural Rights, *Concluding Observations of the Committee on Economic, Social and Cultural Rights: Australia*, 42nd sess, UN Doc E/C.12/AUS/CO/4 (2009).

7.4.5 General Comments and Recommendations

Under a generous interpretation of the state reporting requirements in the treaties, the treaty bodies issue General Comments (General Recommendations in CEDAW, ICERD and ICESCR), which are views and recommendations on how provisions of the particular treaty should be interpreted and given effect to by states.[191] These General Comments, along with the views that some treaty bodies can take on individual communications, discussed below, are widely accepted as authoritative statements on interpretation of the terms of the particular treaty.

The General Comments have been described as 'a distinct judicial instrument, enabling the [Human Rights] Committee to announce its interpretations of different provisions of the Covenant in a form that bears some resemblance to the advisory opinion practice of international tribunals'.[192] The availability of the General Comments on the internet has greatly increased their relevance to a general understanding of the meaning and effect of the human rights treaties.[193]

7.4.6 State-to-State Communications

The HRC and the CERD and CAT Committees have a power they are yet to use, to deal with a state party communication that alleges that another state party is not fulfilling its obligations under the relevant treaty.[194] But only state parties that have declared that they recognise this jurisdiction of the particular committee can be party to this procedure. Australia is one such state party.

No ratifying state has yet invoked the procedure, '[p]resumably … because of the diplomatic and political implications of such an action; States fear retaliatory attacks on their own human rights records'.[195] In the face of this argument, however, the equivalent provision in the *European Convention for the Protection of Human Rights and Fundamental Freedoms*[196] has been used a number of times,[197]

191 See generally P Alston, 'The Historical Origins of the Concepts of "General Comments" in Human Rights Law' in L Boisson de Chazournes & V Gowland Debbas (eds), *The International Legal System in Quest of Equity and Universality, Liber Amicorum Georges Abi-Saab*, Kluwer Law International, The Hague, 2001, 763, extracted in H J Steiner, P Alston & R Goodman, see above, n 1, 873.

192 T Buergenthal, 'The Human Rights Committee', in H J Steiner & P Alston, *International Human Rights in Context: Law, Politics, Morals*, 2nd edn, Oxford University Press, Oxford, 2000, 732.

193 *Documents by Treaty*, UN Office of the High Commissioner for Human Rights <www.unhchr.ch/tbs/doc.nsf/>.

194 ICCPR, see above, n 27, art 41 (entered into force 23 March 1976); see above, n 76, art 11 and art 21 (entered into force 4 January 1969).

195 S Joseph, J Schultz & M Castan, see above, n 24, para 1.43.

196 *European Convention for the Protection of Human Rights and Fundamental Freedoms*, art 33 (entered into force 3 September 1950).

197 H Steiner, P Alston & R Goodman, see above, n 1, 946–8; see Chapter 8.2.3.

indicating perhaps a different ethos existing among the smaller collection of European states than exists in the global community.

7.4.7 Individual Communications

Under the terms of the relevant treaty or its Optional Protocol, some of the treaty bodies are able to receive and consider complaints ('communications') from individuals that a state party has violated their rights as set out in the relevant treaty.[198] A communication can be made only against a state party that has explicitly recognised the jurisdiction of the CAT and CERD, or has ratified the *Optional Protocol* to the ICCPR or the *Optional Protocols* to CEDAW and CRPD. The communications procedure under the ICCPR is used much more frequently than the procedures under other treaties: there is considerable overlap between the CCPR on the one hand and CAT and CERD on the other, and the communication process under the ICCPR-OP1 is, quite simply, a better-known process.[199]

Communication Procedures

Before considering the merits of a communication, a treaty body will decide the communication's 'admissibility' against a range of criteria. The communication must be in writing, must not be anonymous, must be about a right recognised in the treaty, must relate to the conduct of a state party to the treaty, must relate to a violation that occurred or continued after the date the treaty came into effect for the relevant state, must be by a victim or their authorised representative, must not be an abuse of the right to make a complaint (eg a complaint already rejected), and cannot relate to a matter already being considered by another committee.[200] An essential admissibility requirement is that the 'author' of the communication must have exhausted all domestic remedies, that is, they must have sought redress, unsuccessfully, in their own domestic system and taken the matter as far as they reasonably can in that system.

---

198 ICCPR-OP1, see above, n 68; CEDAW-OP, see above, n 85; ICERD, see above, n 76, art 14; CAT, see above, n 88, art 22; CRPD, see above, n 109; ICRMW, see above, n 106, art 76.

199 The HRC procedures have been described and commented on extensively, eg S Joseph, J Schultz & M Castan, see above, n 24, paras 1.31—1.55; H J Steiner, P Alston & R Goodman, see above, n 1, Ch 10; E Evatt, 'Reflecting on the Role of International Communications in Implementing Human Rights' (1995) 5(2) *Australian Journal of Human Rights*, 20; S Pritchard & N Sharp, *Communicating with the Human Rights Committee: A Guide to the Optional Protocol to the International Covenant on Civil and Political Rights* (Human Rights Booklet No 1), Australian Human Rights Information Centre, <www.austlii.edu.au/au/other/ahric/booklet/index.htm>.

200 For communications to treaty bodies, see above, n 158.

A treaty body's consideration of a communication's admissibility and merit is done 'in committee', that is, privately. The communication is conveyed to the relevant state party for submissions, and the state party's reply is provided to the author of the communication for comment. The treaty body then adopts its views, both on admissibility and on the merits, by consensus; on occasion the dissenting opinions of individual members of the committee are added as an appendix.

A treaty body's views are not and cannot be binding on the state; they are recommendatory. It has been said of the HRC that it is 'the pre-eminent interpreter of the ICCPR which is itself legally binding. The HRC's decisions are therefore strong indicators of legal obligations, so rejection of those decisions is good evidence of a State's bad faith attitude towards its ICCPR obligations'.[201] The same could be said for each of the treaty bodies and their treaties. There is, however, 'an unsatisfactory rate of non-compliance with *Optional Protocol* decisions'.[202]

Reflecting on the efficacy of individual communications to the HRC, Evatt paints what she calls a 'rather gloomy picture' but sees positive aspects.[203] She concludes that the communications procedures have real potential to oblige a state to act and to cause wrongs done to individuals to be redressed. In the following Snapshot, the recent history of communications to the HRC against Australia challenges Evatt's optimism that states feel under pressure to redress human rights violations.

SNAPSHOT: AUSTRALIAN COMMUNICATIONS TO THE HUMAN RIGHTS COMMITTEE[204]

In over 40 communications against Australia under the ICCPR, the HRC has found a number to be substantiated.[205] Australia's violations of human rights have included:

- Mistreatment of children: In *Bakhtiyari v Australia*[206] the detention of two children in immigration detention for two years and eight months violated their right to protection as minors.
- Inhumane treatment of prisoners: In *Cabal and Bertran v Australia*,[207] the detention of two prisoners in a triangular cage the size of a telephone booth was inhumane, and in *Brough v Australia*,[208] holding a disabled young Aboriginal man in solitary confinement in an adults' prison without clothing and blankets was inhumane.
- Denial of the right to family life: In *Winata v Australia*, deportation of the parents of a 13-year-old child who was born in and had grown up in Australia constituted an interference with the right to family life.
- Undue trial delay: In *Rogerson v Australia*,[209] a two-year delay by the Northern Territory Court of Appeals to deliver its decision on a criminal contempt charge constituted undue delay.

201 S Joseph, J Schultz & M Castan, see above, n 24, para 1.51.

202 S Joseph, J Schultz & M Castan, see above, n 24, para 1.51.

203 E Evatt, see above, n 199, 32.

204 Based on H Charlesworth, 'Human Rights: Australia Versus the UN', Discussion Paper 22/06, RegNet, Australian National University, 2006, 2–3, <www.democraticaudit.anu.edu.au>.

205 See Chapter 10.5.4.

206 CCPR/C/79/D/1069/2002 (2003).

207 CCPR/C/78/D/1020/2001 (2003).

208 CCPR/C/86/D/1184/2003 (2006).

209 CCPR/C/74/D/802/1998 (2002).

- Discrimination: In *Young v Australia*,[210] refusal to pay a pension to a war veteran's same-sex dependent was a breach of the right to non-discrimination.
- Arbitrary detention: In *D & E v Australia*,[211] the 'immigration detention' of an Iranian woman, together with her husband and two young children, for over three years was arbitrary.

Australia's response to these findings is consistently to state that the Human Rights Committee is not a court and its views are not binding, and to take no action to remedy or compensate for the violations.

Communications Under ECOSOC

Under a series of ECOSOC Resolutions the previous UN Commission on Human Rights, and its Sub-commission on the Promotion and Protection of Human Rights, dealt with the communications that the UN received regarding human rights violations. In 2006 the functions and responsibilities of the UN Commission on Human Rights were assumed by the newly-established Human Rights Council, which has adapted the procedures under ECOSOC Resolutions into the Council's own communication procedures, discussed in detail in Chapter 6.6.

7.4.8 Treaty Body Reform

Treaty body reform is a constant item on the UN's agenda,[212] and on the agenda of many of the state parties. The need for reform has been identified and discussed since at least 1984, when the chairpersons of the treaty bodies had their first of what are now annual meetings. The UN Secretariat noted that '[t]he treaty body system has developed *ad hoc* and it does not function as an integrated and indivisible framework for human rights protection'.[213]

In 1994 Bayefsky published a strong critique of the treaty bodies.[214] The then Secretary to the CERD, Michael O'Flaherty, found Bayefsky's criticisms 'rather unfair and damaging', saying that they threatened to undermine faith in the treaty bodies and failed to acknowledge recent improvements.[215] In 2000 Bayefsky again set out her list of the treaty body system's 'shortfalls',[216] and Alston responded saying that it 'does not provide an accurate or balanced picture ... based on a

210 CCPR/C/78/D/941/2000 (2003).

211 CCPR/C/87/D/1050/2002 (2006).

212 See the reports collected at *Reform of the UN Human Rights Treaty System: Reports* <http://www.bayefsky.com/tree.php/id/48610753>.

213 UN Secretariat, *Concept Paper on the High Commissioner's Proposal for a Unified Standing Treaty Body*, para 23, UN Doc HRI/MC/2006/2 (2006).

214 A Bayefsky, 'Making the Human Rights Treaties Work', in L Henkin & J L Hargrave (eds), *Human Rights: An Agenda for the Next Century*, American Society of International Law, Washington DC, 1994, 229–97.

215 M O'Flaherty, in S Pritchard (ed), *Indigenous Peoples, the United Nations and Human Rights*, Sydney, Zed Books and the Federation Press, 1998, 73.

216 See above, n 131, pp xvii–xx, pp xviii–xix. See also A Bayefsky, 'Panel Discussion Remarks, the UN Human Rights Regime: Is it Effective' (1997) 91 *Proceedings of the Annual Meeting of the American Society of International Law 1997*, 466–72; see above, n 214, 246–9.

fundamental misunderstanding of the nature and objectives of the system'.[217] Bayefsky is far from alone in these complaints, however. The Nottingham workshop of human rights experts identified as weaknesses the treaty bodies' varied procedural requirements, and their deficiencies in capacity (backlogs) and in compliance (non-reporting, late reporting).[218] Both Charlesworth[219] and Crawford have identified the problem of the backlog of states' reports, Crawford pointing out what he calls its 'corrosive effects'.[220]

The treaty bodies have contributed to perceptions of their poor performance through the variable quality of their work and the cumbersome nature of their procedures. Their inadequate performance is related to the poor support they receive from the states parties, but it is impossible to ignore the problem of grossly inadequate resources that are available to enable them to carry out their functions.

States parties undermine the effectiveness of the treaty bodies through non-reporting and late reporting, and through their unwillingness to subject themselves wholly to the terms of the treaties and to comply wholly with the intended design of the treaty bodies. For example, reservations to a treaty compromise the authority of the treaty and its treaty body, as do the states parties' disregard of the criteria for nominating independent experts as members of the committees, and their practice of nominating government officials to carry out the role of independent expert. Many states parties have accepted the invitation, implicit in the non-binding nature of the treaty bodies' powers, to ignore the treaty bodies' views, comments and requests, and to persist in the practices that have been criticised.

Formal Steps Towards Reform

In response to the widely-appreciated need for reform, there have been many proposals and reports, and substantial agreement on what needs to be done. The Nottingham meeting of human rights experts noted, however, that in 2006 '[e]ven small, apparently routine improvements ... have remained unimplemented, notwithstanding repeated recommendations over many years'.[221] In 2009 the Dublin Statement reported that subsequent reform efforts 'have been confined to the greater harmonisation of working methods', and noted that the innovation of the common core document for state reports is a limited advance in a reform process which 'proceeds inevitably at a slow pace'.[222]

217 P Alston, see above, n 188, 503.

218 See above, n 131, 3.

219 H Charlesworth, see above, n 18, 71.

220 J Crawford, 'The Human Rights Treaty System: A System in Crisis?' in P Alston & J Crawford (eds), see above, n 179, 1–13, 4–7.

221 See above, n 131, 4–5.

222 *The Dublin Statement on the Process of Strengthening of the United Nations Human Rights Treaty Body System*, University of Nottingham Human Rights Law Centre, 19 November 2009, para 4, <http://www.nottingham.ac.uk/hrlc/documents/specialevents/dublinstatement.pdf>; reprinted in 2010 *Netherlands Human Rights Quarterly*, 116.

In 1988 the UN General Assembly initiated a review of the system for monitoring the human rights treaties.[223] The then UN Commission on Human Rights requested the UN Secretary-General to appoint an expert,[224] and Philip Alston was appointed in 1989 to report on 'possible long-term approaches to enhancing the effective operation of existing resources, and prospective bodies established under the United Nations human rights instruments'. After an initial report[225] and a further interim report,[226] Alston reported to the UN Commission on Human Rights in 1997,[227] recommending the allocation of additional resources and significant reforms to committee procedures, state reporting requirements and committee relations with intergovernmental agencies and NGOs.

Proposed structural reforms to the Office of the High Commissioner for Human Rights (OHCHR) were endorsed by the UN General Assembly in 2003,[228] which at the same time requested a 'review of the human rights special procedures in order to rationalize their work and enhance their effectiveness, consistent with their mandates'.[229] The OHCHR organised a meeting of experts (the treaty bodies, states, UN organisations and NGOs) to discuss treaty reform, and the meeting reported to the UN General Assembly in 2003.[230] The meeting agreed on a range of procedural reforms for the treaty bodies, noted a number of matters that could be considered further, and rejected some proposed reforms.

In 2006 the OHCHR documented 'challenges' facing the treaty system:[231] increased and underfunded treaty monitoring responsibilities with associated increases in workload, poor support from states parties with an associated inadequacy in and backlog of reports, overlap and duplication in treaty body mandates, ignorance of the system outside a small circle of governments and specialist academics and NGOs, uneven expertise and independence among committee members, *ad hoc* development of the system with associated lack of coherence, coordination and efficiency, and conflicting jurisprudence from the various treaty bodies. Those concerns were reiterated in 2009 by the High Commissioner for Human Rights.[232]

---

223 *Reporting Obligations of States Parties to International Instruments on Human Rights and Effective Functioning of Bodies Established Pursuant to such Instruments*, GA Res 43/115, UN GA, 43rd sess, 75th plen mtg, para 15(a), UN Doc A/RES/43/115 (1988).

224 UN Commission on Human Rights, Res 1989/47, para 5, UN Doc E/CN.4/RES/1989/47.

225 P Alston, *Initial Report on Enhancing the Long-Term Effectiveness of the United Nations Human Rights Treaty System*, UN GA, 44th sess, UN Doc A/44/668 (1989).

226 P Alston, *Interim Report for Enhancing the Long-Term Effectiveness of the United Nations Human Rights Treaty Regime, World Conference on Human Rights*, UN Doc A/CONF.157/PC/62/Add.1I/Rev.1 (1993).

227 P Alston, *Final Report on Enhancing the Long-Term Effectiveness of the United Nations Human Rights Treaty System: Effective Functioning of Bodies Established Pursuant to United Nations Human Rights Instruments*, UN Commission on Human Rights, 53rd sess, UN Doc E/CN.4/1997/74 (1996).

228 *Strengthening the United Nations: An Agenda for Future Change*, GA Res 57/300, UN GA, 57th sess, 79th plen mtg, para 10, UN Doc A/RES/57/300 (2003).

229 Ibid.

230 *Report of a Brainstorming Meeting on Reform of the Human Rights Treaty Body System*, Malbun, Liechenstein, UN GA, 58th sess, UN Doc A/58/123 (2003).

231 See above, n 213.

232 N Pillay, United Nations High Commissioner for Human Rights, *Dublin Statement on the Process of Strengthening the United Nations Human Rights Treaty Body System*, Dublin, 19 November 2009, <http://www.ohchr.org/en/NewsEvents/Pages/DisplayNews.aspx?NewsID=9642&LangID=E>.

The one significant procedural reform has been the consolidation of guidelines for preparing state reports under the human rights treaties into a single 'core' UN document.[233]

The Need for Resources

It is impossible to avoid the pervasive problem that underlies the many failings of the treaty system outlined above: the unplanned and under-resourced increase in the number of treaty bodies. In 1995 Australia's then Minister for Foreign Affairs, Senator Gareth Evans, said that '[w]hat is needed is not so much the further proliferation of treaty bodies, thematic and country rapporteurs, experts and working groups, but giving those that now exist the capacity to do their jobs really effectively'.[234] Eight treaties and related protocols have been adopted since Charlesworth suggested in 1998 that the treaty system was in 'crisis [as] a result of the tendency in the UN system to respond to a problem by drafting a new treaty without considering how it will impact on the system, as a whole'.[235]

In 2002 the UN Secretary-General presented a report to the UN General Assembly, titled *Strengthening of the United Nations: An Agenda for Further Change*, that called for coordination and standardisation across the committees and set in train a review by the treaty bodies of their processes.[236] In 2006 the Secretariat identified the proliferation of treaties and treaty bodies as one of a number of 'challenges' facing the system.[237]

The single step that would make the greatest difference to the effectiveness of the treaty bodies would be more funds, to employ additional staff, improve technical resources and increase the number and length of meetings. The Nottingham meeting of human rights experts identified the problems: '[t]he part-time, unremunerated nature of service' on the treaty bodies, and generally '[c]hronic resource shortfalls', saying that '[t]he OHCHR Secretariat budget falls far below those of other treaty systems, such as the Council of Europe'.[238] The same call was made by a similar meeting of experts in Dublin in 2010, recommending that the OHCHR enhance and further consolidate the secretariat support provided to the treaty bodies ... [and] enhance mainstreamed attention to the treaty body activities across all the Office's work areas'. The call was made not only of the OHCHR but also of 'UN member States as a

233 UN Secretary-General, see above, n 36.

234 G Evans, 'Reform of the United Nations: Where to Next?' (Address delivered at the Royal Institute of International Affairs, Chatham House, London, 19 December 1995). See also Joint Standing Committee on Foreign Affairs and Trade, Parliament of Australia, *A Review of Australia's Efforts to Promote and Protect Human Rights* (1994) recommendation 2 and accompanying text.

235 H Charlesworth, see above, n 18, 70.

236 UN Secretary-General, *Strengthening of the United Nations: An Agenda for Future Change*, UN GA, 57th sess, UN Doc A/57/387-Corr 1 (2002).

237 See above, n 213, para 15, UN Doc HRI/MC/2006/2 (2006).

238 See above, n 131, 5.

matter of high priority [to] provide necessary resources to adequately service the functioning of the treaty body system'.[239] In 2010 the chairperson of the treaty bodies, at their annual inter-committee meeting, 'agreed that there was an urgent need for additional resources to be allocated to the Human Rights Treaties Branch of OHCHR for the support of the follow-up mechanisms of respective treaty bodies'.[240]

Quite simply, there is not enough money available to treaty bodies to enable them to do their work at even the most basic level, which would be to read and comment constructively on the state reports. Unless the treaty bodies are funded to carry out their essential tasks, calls for reform will continue in the same vein. It is quite possible that the treaty body system itself will fail, overwhelmed by work and under-regarded by states parties, before adequate funds are made available. In the meantime, the feat of '[m]aintaining the supervisory procedures of the human rights treaty bodies [calls for] a certain sleight of hand—to turn less into more'.[241]

Despite the promotion of efficiency through the promulgation of a 'core' reporting document, the effectiveness of the treaty bodies continues to be compromised by prohibitive costs and political realities: 'treaty bodies will have to live with the *status quo* in terms of services available in the foreseeable future'.[242]

Procedural Reforms

As a means of improving efficiency, a consolidated treaty body is not a new idea. Alston had proposed consideration of the 'most radical option' of consolidating the various treaty bodies into a 'super-committee' in 1989,[243] and again in 1993,[244] saying that '[s]uch a consolidation could be limited in scope so that two or three committees would replace six ... or it could be comprehensive so that [only] a single committee would be required'. In 1997 Alston recommended 'the convening

239 See above, n 216, paras 22, 23, <http://www.nottingham.ac.uk/hrlc/documents/specialevents/dublinstatement.pdf>; reprinted in 2010 *Netherlands Human Rights Quarterly*, 116; see also M O'Flaherty, 'Reform of the UN Human Rights Treaty Body System: Locating the Dublin Statement' (2010) 10(2) *Human Rights Law Review* 319.

240 *Promotion and Protection of Human Rights: Implementation of Human Rights Instruments: Effective Implementation of International Instruments on Human Rights, Including Reporting Obligations under International Instruments on Human Rights; Report of the Chairs of the Human Rights Treaty Bodies on their 22nd Meeting*, UN GA 65th sess, para 22, A/65/190 (2010).

241 E Evatt, 'Ensuring Effective Supervisory Procedures: The Need for Resources' in P Alston & J Crawford (eds), above, n 179, 461–79, 463; see above, n 220.

242 M Schmidt, 'Servicing and Financing Human Rights Supervisory Bodies' in P Alston & J Crawford (eds), above, n 179, 481–99, 484.

243 P Alston, see above, n 225, paras 179–83, UN Doc A/44/668 (1989).

244 P Alston, see above, n 226.

of a small expert group ... to prepare a report on the modalities that might be considered' for consolidation.[245]

In its 2005 Plan of Action the OHCHR undertook to convene an intergovernmental meeting to consider options for a unified standing treaty body. The OHCHR Secretariat's 'concept paper' set out arguments for a unified standing treaty body,[246] revisiting (without acknowledgement) many of the arguments Alston had made 17 years earlier, and noting the many issues that would have to be addressed in achieving a unified body: loss of identity for specified groups, compatibility of diverse procedures, membership, and technical issues of jurisdiction and constitution.

There are, however, reservations and concerns about moving to a single treaty body, such as overlooking specific needs of certain groups for targeted protection and reporting, the risk of having to re-negotiate the treaties themselves, and the suggestion that consolidation could be a move towards a 'world court'. Attention has shifted to formulating harmonised reporting guidelines.[247]

Efforts directed to finding agreed common approaches across the committees have been made principally through the inter-committee meetings of the chairpersons of the treaty bodies.[248] A repeated proposal that state reports to the various committees be merged into a single report[249] has so far not eventuated, in part for fear that 'certain groups of rights-holders, such as children and women, would be rendered invisible in a single homogenised report'.[250]

Australia's Role in Treaty Body Reform

In August 2000 the Australian government announced 'strong measures to improve the effectiveness of the United Nations human rights treaty bodies'.[251] Its view was that the committees should 'accord

245 P Alston, see above, n 227.

246 UN Secretariat, see above, n 213, see M O'Flaherty and C O'Brien, above, n 49.

247 M O'Flaherty, see above, n 239, 325; see also R L Johnstone, 'Cynical Savings or Reasonable Reform? Reflections on a Single Unified UN Human Rights Treaty Body' (2007) 7(1) *Human Rights Law Review* 17; A Hudson, 'Dangerous Potential: Streamlining the United Nations Human Rights Committees' (2002) 8(2) *Australian Journal of Human Rights* 55.

248 See above, n 240.

249 See, eg, P Alston, above, n 226; A Bayefsky, see above, n 49, 17–18; UN Secretary-General, K Annan, *Strengthening the United Nations: An Agenda for Further Change*, 9 September 2002, A/57/387 at para 54.

250 M O'Flaherty, see above, n 239, 323.

251 A Downer, D Williams & P Ruddock, 'Improving the Effectiveness of United Nations Committees' (Joint Media Release, 29 August 2000).

due weight and respect to submissions from democratically elected governments which, such as Australia, have excellent human rights records'.[252]

In its media release the government announced that, in light of its review of its interaction with the UN treaty committee system, 'Australia's strategic engagement with the treaty committee system should be dependent on the extent to which effective reform occurs'. Measures designed to 'improve' Australia's interactions with the UN human rights treaty system include taking a more economical and selective approach to treaty reporting, agreeing to UN human rights visits only when there is a compelling reason to do so and not signing the CEDAW *Optional Protocol*. These measures, and Australia's approach generally to the UN human rights treaty system, have been the subject of much comment.[253]

Australia took a role in discussions, at the UN and among other states, that were intended to improve the efficiency of the treaty system.[254] To this end Australia convened workshops in Geneva that 'involve[d] discussions by middle-ranking diplomatic representatives' and the 'contribution of [which was] likely to be modest at best'.[255] Australia's initiatives produced no apparent results, the momentum for treaty body reform belonging to the much larger and more effective UN processes discussed above. Australia has since been more modest in the campaign for reform of the treaty bodies, although its temporary retreat from the treaty body system continues to suggest an anxiety in Australia about the international order,[256] discussed further in Chapter 10.5.5.

7.5 CONCLUSION AND ISSUES

In describing the complex network of international treaties and protocols, this chapter suggests that aspirational treaties alone are not enough to secure human rights; a credible monitoring and reporting system is essential if the international human rights regime is to be effective in securing states' respect for and compliance with the treaties.

Even the most willing of states are deterred by the slow processes of an under-resourced system, but more than resources are required to ensure the integrity of the system: the account in this chapter raises a number of issues for consideration: whether national and international politics necessarily compromise appointments to and the processes of the treaty bodies; whether the treaty bodies can rely on states to reporting an accurate or sufficient account of their human rights records; and what powers and capacity the treaty bodies need to sufficiently investigate and monitor states' conduct.

252 Australia, *Hansard*, Senate, 31 August 2000, p 17121 (qs 1928, 1929, 1930).

253 See, eg, S Zifcak, *Mr Ruddock Goes to Geneva*, UNSW Press, Sydney, 2003; D Kinley & P Martin, 'International Human Rights Law at Home: Addressing the Politics of Denial' (2002) 26(2) *Melbourne University Law Review*, 466; A Kent, *Australia's International Human Rights Policies* (2003) <http://isaa.org.au/wp-content/uploads/2007/04/kent.pdf>.

254 A Downer, D Williams & P Ruddock, 'Australian Initiative to Improve the Effectiveness of the UN Treaty Committees' (Joint Media Release, 5 April 2001); D Williams, 'Reforming Human Rights Treaty Bodies' (1999) 5(2) *Australian Journal of Human Rights* 158.

255 S Zifcak, see above, n 253, 35.

256 H Charlesworth, M Chiam, D Hovell & G Williams, 'Deep Anxieties: Australia and the International Legal Order' (2003) 25(4) *Sydney Law Review* 423.

8
REGIONAL MECHANISMS

CONTENTS

8.1 OVERVIEW OF REGIONAL SYSTEMS

There are three main regional systems focused on promoting and protecting human rights: the Council of Europe, the Organisation of American States, and the African Union. Other regional groupings of states have chosen to either adopt instruments that demonstrate their professed respect for human rights (such as the Arab Charter) or are in a more embryonic state of developing regional human rights mechanisms (Asia and the Pacific).

Regional systems have a number of advantages over a system purporting to cover the entire globe, all essentially emanating from the greater ease of obtaining political consensus across a smaller regional grouping. Negotiating any international treaty, including human rights treaties, can be a long, drawn-out process full of political compromises. A smaller group will normally reach consensus more easily than a larger one. When a group of states has a perceived common culture or history, such as the values presumed to underpin the Western European states that founded the Council of Europe, agreement on what constitutes the essence of human dignity, and therefore the rights and obligations that stem from dignity, should be comparatively easy. If human rights instruments are viewed as a response, at least in part, to historical events, a shared historical experience should be a further reason for states within a region to reach agreement on the rights they wish to protect and the obligations they wish to impose. The shared experience of Western Europe in the Second World War in the lead-up to the 1950 European Convention, and the experience of Africa in emerging from colonialism prior to the 1981 African Charter, are notable examples.

The same benefits of size and a perceived common heritage also make workable enforcement mechanisms more achievable for regional groups than they are at the global level. It may be considered less of an infringement on sovereignty for a state to subject itself to the judgment of a court or commission comprised of its neighbouring states, as opposed to being subject to the judgment of those from states perceived to have significantly different cultures, values or priorities. Perhaps for this reason, the most onerous transnational human rights enforcement mechanisms in terms of the sanctions available to require state compliance are those at the regional level, especially the oldest regional system in Europe.

Regional systems, however, cannot replace national human rights mechanisms for the implementation of human rights and adjudication of breaches. All regional enforcement mechanisms face severe strain from their caseloads, remembering that their relatively small resources, compared to most domestic courts, must deal with people from an entire region. Furthermore, regional systems rely on cooperation from their member states to be successful. If the member states of a regional system do not respect and implement the rulings of that system, the system will be an empty shell, as regional bodies typically have no mechanisms of their own to enforce decisions.

Current international human rights law therefore recognises an important role for regional systems, while at the same time emphasising the importance of a global system to maintain universality of human rights and national systems to maximise implementation. The World Conference on Human Rights in 1993 made the following observation about the place of regional systems in the broader human rights architecture:

> Regional arrangements play a fundamental role in promoting and protecting human rights. They should reinforce universal human rights standards, as contained in international human rights instruments, and

their protection. The World Conference on Human Rights endorses efforts under way to strengthen these arrangements and to increase their effectiveness, while at the same time stressing the importance of cooperation with the United Nations human rights activities.

The World Conference on Human Rights reiterates the need to consider the possibility of establishing regional and subregional arrangements for the promotion and protection of human rights where they do not already exist.[1]

8.2 EUROPE

8.2.1 The Council of Europe

The Council of Europe was founded in 1949 with ten member states, all from Western Europe: Belgium, Denmark, France, Ireland, Italy, Luxembourg, the Netherlands, Norway, Sweden and the United Kingdom. The organisation was intended to promote unity between European states, based on their common ideals and principles,[2] clearly driven by a desire to avoid the fragmentation and clashes between European powers that had led to the Second World War, as well as articulating a set of values to define Western Europe in contrast to the communism of the east as the Cold War ramped up.

Today, membership of the Council of Europe extends to 47 states covering all of Europe, including Turkey, Russia, many of the former Soviet republics and the states comprising the former Yugoslavia; at the time of writing the only state physically located in Europe not a member of the Council of Europe is Belarus. Membership is thus significantly larger than that of the European Union and extends across much broader historical, social, cultural and religious heritage than the relatively homogenous ten founding members.

Chief among the ideals and principles to be promoted by the Council of Europe were human rights, democracy and the rule of law. It is a precondition for membership of the Council of Europe that states 'must accept the principles of the rule of law and of the enjoyment by all persons within its jurisdiction of human rights and fundamental freedoms.'[3] In providing more detailed content to that broadly stated obligation, the *Convention for the Protection of Human Rights and Fundamental Freedoms* was adopted in 1950.

8.2.2 The *Convention for the Protection of Human Rights and Fundamental Freedoms*

While the development of a binding treaty at the international level following the adoption of the UDHR was bogged down in political debate, the states of Europe were able to conclude a binding regional treaty by the end of 1950—the *Convention for the Protection of Human Rights and Fundamental Freedoms* (commonly referred to as the European Convention on Human Rights or ECHR).

1 *Vienna Declaration and Programme of Action*, adopted by the World Conference on Human Rights, 25 June 1993, para 37.

2 *Statute of the Council of Europe*, art 1(a).

3 Ibid art 3.

Drafting the ECHR was the first substantive task undertaken by the newly formed Council of Europe and was concluded very quickly. In contrast to the drawn-out negotiation period in drafting the *International Covenant on Civil and Political Rights* (ICCPR), and the *International Covenant on Economic Social and Cultural Rights* (ICESCR), the ECHR was concluded and opened for signature within 18 months of the commencement of the Council of Europe. Ratification of the ECHR is a condition of membership of the Council of Europe.

The ECHR focuses strongly on civil and political rights as opposed to economic, social and cultural rights. The content of the rights and the expression of states' obligations to secure those rights closely resemble those in the ICCPR. Although the ECHR predated the ICCPR by 16 years, the initial draft of the ICCPR had been completed by the UN Commission on Human Rights in June 1949 and it was utilised by the drafters of the ECHR.[4]

The content of the ECHR is able to be amended by protocols, which are optional for states when they address substantive rights, but compulsory when they address procedural issues such as the workings of the Court. To date, five protocols have amended the content of the substantive rights.[5]

Like the ICCPR, the original ECHR omitted the right to property, which is included in the UDHR, and did not include any economic, social and cultural rights. An additional protocol was adopted in 1952 adding the rights to property, education and free elections to the coverage of the ECHR, which has now been ratified by all but two member states.[6] A further protocol was adopted in 1963 to include a handful of rights that were omitted in the ECHR but were set to be included in the almost-finished ICCPR.[7] Otherwise the most substantial difference between the content of the ICCPR and the ECHR is the omission from the ECHR of the right to self-determination.

8.2.3 The European Court of Human Rights

The most remarkable innovation of the ECHR was the creation of an international judicial body, the European Court of Human Rights, which could hear complaints from individuals against their own states for violation of the rights in the ECHR. When the ECHR first came into force, individuals were required to submit their complaints to the European Commission on Human Rights, which in turn could refer the matter to the Court for adjudication if it was deemed admissible.

The competence of the Commission to receive individual petitions, and therefore the competence of the Court to accept a referral from the Commission, was originally dependent on the state concerned

4 C Tomuschat, *Human Rights: Between Idealism and Realism*, 2nd edn, Oxford University Press, Oxford, 2008, 31.

5 First Protocol (1952); Protocol No 4 (1963); Protocol No 6 (1983); Protocol No 7 (1984); and Protocol No 12 (2000).

6 *Protocol to the Convention for the Protection of Human Rights and Fundamental Freedoms* (opened for signature 20 March 1952) [First Protocol]. Monaco and Switzerland have both signed but not ratified the First Protocol.

7 Protocol No 4 to the *Convention for the Protection of Human Rights and Fundamental Freedoms Securing Certain Rights and Freedoms Other than Those Already Included in the Convention and in the First Protocol Thereto* (opened for signature 16 September 1963). All but four member states (Greece, Switzerland, Turkey and the United Kingdom) have ratified Protocol No 4.

having declared that it had accepted the competence of the Commission.[8] Despite the optional nature of the Court's jurisdiction and the requirement to direct petitions via the Commission, the creation of an international judicial system that recognised the standing of individuals to allege violations of their human rights pursuant to an international treaty, and was able to adjudicate on those allegations, was a watershed development in international human rights law.

From November 1998, the jurisdiction of the European Court of Human Rights became compulsory for all member states and the requirement for individual complaints to be submitted via the European Commission was removed, creating a direct right of individuals to petition the European Court.[9]

The ECHR also created a right for states parties to bring complaints against one another for violation of human rights obligations under the Convention; such a right exists under some of the international human rights treaties but has never been used (see Chapter 7.4.6). As at January 2011, only 15 applications have been brought under the ECHR state complaints procedure, concerning only eight distinct cases,[10] out of a total of approximately 400,000 ECHR applications. The only inter-state complaints made in the last decade were brought by Georgia against Russia in 2007 and 2008 and are still pending at the time of writing.[11]

Compliance

The ECHR provides that parties agree to abide by the Court's decisions, and that judgments of the court are to be transmitted to the Committee of Ministers, which supervises their execution.[12] The judgments typically award 'just satisfaction' when a breach is found, which normally constitutes financial compensation.[13] The Court may also find that a state has a duty to take specific measures to remedy the breach.

Once a judgment has been given, the responsibility for its implementation shifts from the Court to a political body of the Council of Europe known as the Committee of Ministers. While there is no capacity to impose sanctions on non-complying states, the existence of a political body mandated to follow up the implementation of judgments and apply political pressure in the process probably contributes to the relatively high compliance rate in the European system.[14]

8 *Convention for the Protection of Human Rights and Fundamental Freedoms* (ECHR), opened for signature 4 November 1950 (entered into force 1953), art 25.

9 Protocol No 11 to the *Convention for the Protection of Human Rights and Fundamental Freedoms,* opened for signature 11 May 1994 (entered into force 1 November 1998).

10 Several of the inter-state cases involve the same parties and allege violations arising out of the same long-running disputes, such as those between Ireland and the UK in 1970 and 1971 and between Cyprus and Turkey in 1974, 1975 and 1977.

11 *Georgia v Russia*, European Court of Human Rights, application no 13255/07, held admissible on 30 June 2009; application no 38263/08, ruling on admissibility still pending.

12 ECHR, see above, n 8, art 46.

13 ECHR, see above, n 8, art 41 provides for the award of just satisfaction where the law of the relevant state would allow the victim to recover only partial reparation.

14 V Mantouvalou & P Voyatzis, 'The Council of Europe and the Protection of Human Rights: A System in Need of Reform' in S Joseph and A McBeth (eds), *Research Handbook on International Human Rights Law*, Edward Elgar, Cheltenham (UK), 2010, 330–1.

Caseload Reform

A growing concern with the European Court, particularly since the expansion of the Council of Europe (and therefore of the coverage of the ECHR) after the Cold War, has been the Court's staggering and exponentially growing caseload. In 2009, there were more than 57 000 applications to the Court, compared to a total of 45 000 for the 40 years 1958–98.[15] As part of the solution to that problem, Protocol 14 to the ECHR came into force in June 2010, designed to streamline the process and filter out unmeritorious cases.

One of the key provisions of Protocol 14 requires the Court to dismiss as inadmissible any application in which 'the applicant has not suffered a significant disadvantage, unless respect for human rights as defined in the Convention and the Protocols thereto requires an examination of the application on the merits and provided that no case may be rejected on this ground which has not been duly considered by a domestic tribunal.'[16] Other provisions provided for admissibility hearings before single judges and determinations of the merits by panels of three judges in cases where the violation appears to be clear (for example, if the Court has already found a breach against the relevant state in a previous case on similar facts).[17] These changes free up Court resources previously occupied by large panels of judges (between three and 17, depending on the stage of proceedings) for preliminary procedures or uncontroversial cases. However, the rapid growth of the Court's caseload remains a daunting problem that shows no signs of changing in the near future.

The Margin of Appreciation: A European Contribution to International Human Rights Jurisprudence

It is well-accepted in international human rights law that while human rights standards are universal, states have some degree of discretion in the most appropriate way to implement those standards within their own societies. The jurisprudence of the European Court has formalised that principle of discretion through a doctrine known as the 'margin of appreciation'.

The doctrine has been invoked most commonly when the rights of different people potentially conflict, deferring to the national authorities to decide how to resolve such a clash.[18] However, it must be applied consistently with the rights and limitations set out in the ECHR and so is not an infinite discretion. For some time, other international human rights jurisdictions did not formally adopt the margin of appreciation, although in practice they accorded a similar type of discretion to

---

15 European Court of Human Rights, *50 Years of Activity: The European Court of Human Rights—Some Facts and Figures*, April 2010, 4, available at <http://www.echr.coe.int/NR/rdonlyres/ACD46A0F-615A-48B9-89D6-8480AFCC29FD/0/FactsAndFiguresENAvril2010.pdf>.

16 *Protocol No 14 to the Convention for the Protection of Human Rights and Fundamental Freedoms, Amending the Control System of the Convention* (opened for signature 13 May 2004, entered into force 1 June 2010), article 12, amending article 35(3) ECHR.

17 Ibid articles 6–8, amending articles 26–8 ECHR.

18 O De Schutter, *International Human Rights Law*, Cambridge University Press, Cambridge, 2010, 447.

the implementation of human rights at the local level and the resolution of conflicting rights. In recent years, however, the margin of appreciation has become an accepted part of international human rights jurisprudence,[19] albeit not developed to the extent it has been in the European system.

SNAPSHOT: *HANDYSIDE V UNITED KINGDOM*[20]

Mr Handyside was the English publisher of a Danish publication called *The Little Red Schoolbook*, intended for school children aged 12 and over, published in the UK in 1971. Editions of the book had been published in 14 other European countries and several non-European countries.[21] Mr Handyside was convicted of possessing obscene books for publication. He alleged that this conviction violated his freedom of expression under article 10 of the ECHR.

The offending passages cited in the English criminal trial concerned the use of marijuana, pornography and sexual activity between minors, which were said to be likely to deprave or corrupt and to encourage the commission of criminal offences, having regard to the intended young audience.

Freedom of expression under article 10 is qualified to allow restrictions for considerations that are 'necessary in a democratic society' such as national security, public safety, and the protection of health or morals.[22] The Court had to decide whether it was open to the UK authorities to prevent the publication of the book on grounds 'necessary in a democratic society', notwithstanding that its publication was permitted in most other European states. The court held as follows:[23]

> 48 ... Article 10 para. 2 leaves to the Contracting States a margin of appreciation. This margin is given both to the domestic legislator ('prescribed by law') and to the bodies, judicial amongst others, that are called upon to interpret and apply the laws in force.
>
> 49 Nevertheless, Article 10 para. 2 does not give the Contracting States an unlimited power of appreciation. The Court ... is empowered to give the final ruling on whether a 'restriction' or 'penalty' is reconcilable with freedom of expression as protected by Article 10. The domestic margin of appreciation thus goes hand in hand with a European supervision ...
>
> The Court's supervisory functions oblige it to pay the utmost attention to the principles characterising a 'democratic society'. Freedom of expression constitutes one of the essential foundations of such a society, one of the basic conditions for its progress and for the development of every man. Subject to paragraph 2 of Article 10, it is applicable not only to 'information' or 'ideas' that

19 See for example the speech of the High Commissioner for Human Rights, 16 July 2008, regarding the optional protocol to the ICESCR, available at <http://www.ohchr.org/EN/NewsEvents/Pages/DisplayNews.aspx?NewsID=6155&LangID=E> in which the High Commissioner said: 'each State would enjoy a broad "margin of appreciation" in determining the policies which it considers most suitable in its specific circumstances. The Committee thus clarifies that, in assessing communications under an optional protocol, it would adhere to the "margin of appreciation" doctrine—also reflected in the jurisprudence of regional human rights courts and the Human Rights Committee'.

20 *Handyside v United Kingdom*, judgment of the European Court of Human Rights, 7 December 1976, application no 5493/72.

21 After the *Handyside* case, the book was banned in France and Italy, but published in Australia and elsewhere.

22 ECHR art 10(2).

23 See above, n 20, paragraphs 48–52 (internal references omitted).

are favourably received or regarded as inoffensive or as a matter of indifference, but also to those that offend, shock or disturb the State or any sector of the population. Such are the demands of that pluralism, tolerance and broadmindedness without which there is no 'democratic society'. This means, amongst other things, that every 'formality', 'condition', 'restriction' or 'penalty' imposed in this sphere must be proportionate to the legitimate aim pursued.

...

52 ... Basically the book contained purely factual information that was generally correct and often useful ... However, it also included ... sentences or paragraphs that young people at a critical stage of their development could have interpreted as an encouragement to indulge in precocious activities harmful for them or even to commit certain criminal offences. In these circumstances, despite the variety and the constant evolution in the United Kingdom of views on ethics and education, the competent English judges were entitled, in the exercise of their discretion, to think at the relevant time that the Schoolbook would have pernicious effects on the morals of many of the children and adolescents who would read it.

Accordingly, the decision of the English courts was held to be within the UK's margin of appreciation, and Mr Handyside's freedom of expression was held not to have been breached.

8.2.4 The *European Social Charter*

The *European Social Charter* was adopted by the Council of Europe in 1961. A revised Social Charter was adopted in 1996. Unlike the ECHR, ratification of the Social Charter is not a condition for membership of the Council of Europe, with the result that not all Council of Europe members are parties. The Social Charter as amended contains economic, social and cultural rights similar to, but somewhat more extensive than, those contained in the ICESCR, but with a very different approach to the nature of the obligations.

In part I, states 'accept as the aim of their policy, to be pursued by all appropriate means both national and international in character, the attainment of conditions' in which a list of 31 rights may be effectively realised.[24] From that broad, general obligation, part II of the Social Charter adopts an *a-la-carte* approach. Each of the 31 articles is broken down into a series of undertakings by which the state pledges to realise the relevant right. However, states are permitted to select the specific articles or paragraphs in part II to which they wish to be bound, with a minimum threshold specified.[25] In that way, the specificity of the undertakings goes some way to allaying the criticisms often made of human rights law that the treaty provisions are too vague to be meaningful. At the same time, the ability of states to be selective in those undertakings potentially undermines claims to the universality of the content of human rights.

Unlike the ECHR, the Social Charter does not give rise to a petition to the European Court and contains no individual complaints mechanism of its own. Instead, there is an optional system allowing for collective complaints to a committee of experts, the European Committee of Social Rights, which has

24 *European Social Charter* (revised), (opened for signature 3 May 1996, entered into force 1 July 1999), part I.

25 Ibid part III, article A(1).

the power to prepare a report for the Committee of Ministers.[26] As at January 2011, 14 of the 47 Council of Europe member states have accepted the complaints jurisdiction of the European Committee of Social Rights, with only Finland having taken the additional step of recognising the right of national NGOs to lodge a complaint against it. International NGOs recognised by the Council of Europe are permitted to lodge collective complaints as of right. Between the commencement of the Committee's operations in 1998 and July 2011, it had received 72 complaints, 46 of which had been held to be admissible and proceeded to a decision on the merits.[27]

8.3 THE AMERICAS

8.3.1 The Organization of American States

The Organization of American States (OAS) was established at the Bogotá Inter-American Conference in 1948, effectively replacing a series of successive intergovernmental organisations in the Americas dating back to 1890. Like the United Nations and the Council of Europe, the OAS was largely the result of a desire to secure regional peace and security in the aftermath of the Second World War. Its professed goal is 'to achieve an order of peace and justice, to promote their solidarity, to strengthen their collaboration, and to defend their sovereignty, their territorial integrity, and their independence.'[28] Among the eight declared essential purposes of the OAS are the promotion and consolidation of representative democracy, the promotion of economic, social and cultural development and the eradication of extreme poverty.[29] The OAS has expanded from 21 founding member states to cover all 35 states of the Americas.

8.3.2 The American Declaration of the Rights and Duties of Man

At the Bogotá Inter-American Conference in 1948, the *American Declaration of the Rights and Duties of Man* was adopted, predating the UDHR by six months. Like the UDHR, the American Declaration was originally not in a legally binding form, but like the UDHR, more recent state practice has treated the American Declaration as legally binding for members of the OAS, as have the Inter-American Court of Human Rights and the Inter-American Commission of Human Rights.[30]

26 *Additional Protocol to the European Social Charter Providing for a System of Collective Complaints* (opened for signature 9 November 1995) [applicable to the original 1961 Social Charter]; see above, n 24, part IV, article D.

27 Council of Europe, List of Complaints and State of Procedure. <http://www.coe.int/t/dghl/monitoring/socialcharter/complaints/complaints_en.asp>

28 *OAS Charter*, art 1.

29 Ibid art 2.

30 J Pasqualucci, 'The Americas', in D Moeckli, S Shah & S Sivakumaran (eds), *International Human Rights Law*, Oxford, Oxford University Press, Oxford, 2010, 435.

The rights contained in the American Declaration are broadly equivalent to those contained in the UDHR, covering civil and political as well as economic, social and cultural rights. However, as the title of the instrument indicates, equal emphasis is given to personal duties as to rights, contrasting with the UDHR. After enumerating 27 rights, with an additional article declaring the scope of those rights, chapter two of the American Declaration sets out ten duties. These cover duties to one's family and fellow individuals, as well as duties to the state (such as the duty to pay taxes[31]), civic duties (such as the duty to vote and the duty to render national service[32]) and duties to better oneself (such as the duty 'to acquire at least an elementary education'[33]).

8.3.3 The American Convention on Human Rights

The *American Convention on Human Rights* was opened for signature in 1969. Like the ECHR, the American Convention focuses primarily on civil and political rights. The drafters drew on the text of the American Declaration of the Rights of Man, the ECHR and the ICCPR.[34]

For the most part, the content of the rights in the American Convention reflects the ICCPR, discussed in Chapter 3. The main differences are the inclusion of the right to property,[35] omitted from the ICCPR although found in the UDHR, and the addition of a single article incorporating economic, social and cultural rights. Article 26 of the Convention commits states parties to adopt measures for the progressive realisation of 'the rights implicit in the economic, social, educational, scientific, and cultural standards set forth in the Charter ...' . The American Convention further contains a specific provision on personal responsibilities. Article 32 provides:

> Every person has responsibilities to his family, his community, and mankind.
> The rights of each person are limited by the rights of others, by the security of all, and by the just demands of the general welfare, in a democratic society.

There is also a subtle but potentially significant difference in the expression of the right to life. Article 4 of the American Convention guarantees the right to life 'from the moment of conception.'[36] That explicit definition puts the American Convention at odds with the approach taken to the right to life and the question of abortion in other human rights jurisdictions,[37] no doubt influenced by the influence of Catholicism in a majority of OAS member states.

Not all OAS member states are parties to the Convention. The United States and Canada are notable non-parties, while Trinidad and Tobago renounced its ratification in 1998.[38] Twenty-four of the 35 OAS

31 *American Declaration of the Rights and Duties of Man,* art XXXVI.

32 Ibid arts XXXII and XXXIV, respectively.

33 Ibid art XXXI.

34 D Shelton, 'The Jurisprudence of the Inter-American Court of Human Rights' (1994) 10 *American University Journal of International Law and Policy* 333, 334.

35 *American Convention on Human Rights* (ACHR), art 21.

36 Ibid art 4(1).

37 See the 'right to life' case study in Chapter 3.5.

38 Trinidad and Tobago's renunciation related to its use of the death penalty, which did not comply with conditions set down in the American Convention.

member states are parties to the Convention. For OAS member states that are not parties to the Convention, the Charter of the OAS[39] and the American Declaration are the only sources of regional human rights obligations, although these do not come with their own enforcement mechanisms.

There have been two protocols to the American Convention, supplementing its content for those states choosing to ratify them. The first is the *Additional Protocol to the American Convention on Human Rights in the Area of Economic, Social and Cultural Rights*, more commonly known as the *Protocol of San Salvador*. Following the model of the *European Social Charter* supplementing the ECHR, the *Protocol of San Salvador* was opened for signature in 1988 and came into effect in 1999. A second protocol (the *Protocol to the American Convention on Human Rights*) aimed at the abolition of the death penalty was opened for signature in 1990 and comes into effect for each state at the time of ratifying it.

8.3.4 The Inter-American Commission of Human Rights

The Inter-American Commission on Human Rights was established in 1959, before there was a regional human rights treaty to monitor. Its original role, to 'promote the observance and defense of human rights and serve as an organ of consultation for the Organization in this field',[40] was effectively one of study and investigation with a view to furthering human rights, rather than specifically a complaints mechanism. However, the Commission almost immediately received many complaints of human rights abuses and requests for investigation, resulting in its evolution into ade facto complaints mechanism.

The Commission had no power to deal with complaints beyond investigation, but it was able to use its investigatory power to make a report finding that human rights violations had occurred and recommending appropriate action. Among the human rights monitoring powers of the Inter-American Commission are the capacity to conduct on-site visits and appoint Special Rapporteurs, much like the equivalent powers of the UN Human Rights Council and its predecessor the Commission on Human Rights, discussed above in Chapter 6.2.

After the American Convention came into effect, and following various amendments to the role of the Commission over the years, the Commission now has a formal role in considering individual complaints. Complaints may be received from individuals, from a group of individuals or from an NGO legally recognised by one or more OAS member states.[41] That complaints system applies differently for different OAS member states, depending on whether they have ratified the Convention. The Commission has authority under the OAS Charter to oversee the obligations of all OAS member states, whether or not they have ratified the American Convention. The Commission is therefore able to investigate alleged violations of human rights obligations arising from the OAS Charter or the American Declaration.

For states that have ratified the American Convention, the Commission can also receive complaints alleging violations of the obligations in the Convention. If the Commission finds that the complaint

39 *Charter of the Organization of American States* (1948), art 3(1) recognises that all human beings have fundamental rights as one of the principles of the OAS, but like the *UN Charter*, does not elaborate on those rights.

40 *OAS Charter*, art 112.

41 ACHR, see above, n 35, art 44.

is admissible and has been unable to facilitate 'friendly settlement', the Commission may forward the case to the Inter-American Court of Human Rights if the state has accepted the contentious jurisdiction of the Court.

8.3.5 The Inter-American Court of Human Rights

An additional layer of human rights supervision was introduced to the Inter-American system in the form of the Inter-American Court of Human Rights when the American Convention on Human Rights came into force. The Inter-American Court became the second regional judicial body with human rights jurisdiction after the European Court of Human Rights. The Court has both an advisory jurisdiction, enabling it to give advisory opinions on human rights matters, and a contentious jurisdiction, allowing it to hear complaints of human rights violations from individuals or between states. However, as in the European system, the inter-state complaint system is extremely rarely used.[42]

As the Court was created by the American Convention, only parties to the American Convention that have made a declaration accepting the contentious jurisdiction of the Court are subject to that jurisdiction. In June 2011, 21 of the 24 states parties to the American Convention had accepted the Court's contentious jurisdiction. OAS member states that are not parties to the American Convention will not be bound by the Court's contentious jurisdiction. However, all OAS member states, as well as certain OAS organs, are permitted to request an advisory opinion from the Court.

Individuals cannot file a petition directly with the Inter-American Court. For individuals whose state has accepted the Court's jurisdiction, an application must first be filed with the Commission, and the Commission will determine admissibility, seek friendly settlement, and if a prima facie breach is found, make recommendations as to how the state can comply with its human rights obligations. If such recommendations are not complied with, the Commission will typically refer the case to the Court.

As in the European system, the caseload in the Inter-American complaints system is becoming crippling. It was reported in 2008 that the average time for processing a complaint from the time of submission to the Commission to the time or referral to the Court was over eight years,[43] with an average of an additional 19 months until the Court's judgment is handed down,[44] leaving victims waiting approximately 10 years from the time of suffering the violation to the time of the judgment, even if the complaint was filed almost immediately.

42 According to D Rodríguez-Pinzón and C Martin, 'The Inter-American Human Rights System: Selected Examples of its Supervisory Work' in S Joseph & A McBeth (eds), see above, n 14, 367, only one inter-state complaint has ever been filed with the Commission, by Nicaragua against Costa Rica in 2006, and that case was declared inadmissible for failure to exhaust domestic remedies, thus never making it to the Court.

43 J Pasqualucci, see above, n 30, 438.

44 J Pasqualucci, see above, n 30, 444.

8.3.6 The Legacy of Military Dictatorships

The history of human rights abuses by military dictatorships in many Latin American states during the 1970s and 1980s provided the backdrop for the early jurisprudence of the Inter-American Court, which began operation in 1979, as well as much of the work of the Inter-American Commission during that period.[45] The role of the Commission, which was able to investigate complaints from states that had not ratified the Convention or acceded to the jurisdiction of the Court, was particularly valuable in examining the phenomenon of 'forced disappearances,' extrajudicial killings and other atrocities committed by military regimes. That legacy remains influential in the inter-American system today, with its organs prepared to take stronger stands in favour of democracy and against coups-d'état than is typical in international organisations.

8.4 AFRICA

Africa has the most recently developed regional human rights system. The continent has a long history of oppression and human rights violations and a nascent system for holding violators accountable for human rights abuses. Heyns and Killander provide a succinct summary of the situation.

> While there is an increasing recognition of human rights in Africa in the strong sense of the word, the continent is still facing a myriad of challenges to the realization of the human rights of its people. This is despite widespread formal commitment to human rights across the continent in the form of bills of rights, establishment of national human rights institutions, declarations by intergovernmental organizations, and the establishment of a regional human rights system.
>
> Human rights violations in Africa, as elsewhere, take many forms. State repression was the hallmark of colonial rule in many parts of Africa. After independence, opposition politicians, journalists, and human rights defenders continue to be persecuted in many countries on the continent. However, human rights violations are not limited to the state. Many human rights violations, which in particular affect women and children, take place in private. These violations may take the form of domestic violence or be a result of harmful traditional practices such as female genital mutilation ... Armed conflicts which may or may not involve the state also give rise to serious human rights violations ...
>
> Poverty and human rights violations go hand in hand in Africa, as is the case in other parts of the world ... Most African countries have not made significant progress towards achievement of the Millennium Development Goals (MDGs) and the realization of other socio-economic rights. While improvement in governance offers the best chance for realization of socio-economic rights in Africa, a more equitable globalization process would also be beneficial.[46]

45 D Shelton, see above, n 34, 337 notes that in the first 15 years of the Court's operation, all of the contentious cases concerned 'disappearances or arbitrary killings of individuals or groups, linked to government actions in Argentina, Colombia, Honduras, Nicaragua, Peru, Suriname, and Venezuela. Some of the events in question took place during periods of military control and remained unresolved after the restoration of democratic governments.'

46 C Heyns & M Killander, 'Africa' in D Moeckli, S Shah & S Sivakumaran (eds), *International Human Rights Law*, Oxford University Press, Oxford, 2010, 478, 479; on the Millennium Development Goals, see Chapter 20.2.2.

This section focuses on the African mechanisms established for protecting human rights, but the UN has also had a presence in Africa, principally via the work of its treaty bodies and special procedures. The International Criminal Court and the International Criminal Tribunal for Rwanda are also playing a significant role in Africa in addressing human rights atrocities.[47]

8.4.1 The African Union

The Organisation of African Unity (OAU) was established 1963 by 32 African countries as the official regional body of African states with a principal focus on decolonisation. The OAU's Charter made only sparse references to human rights and in 2001 the OAU was replaced by the African Union (AU), which comprises 53 states parties; Morocco is not a member.

The AU Charter[48] did not make admission contingent on fulfilling any human rights standards, so all members of the OAU became members of the AU without any examination of their human rights practices. However, compared to the OAU's Charter, the AU's Charter has a number of explicit human rights references and includes in its objectives, in article 3(e) and (h), to encourage international cooperation, taking due account of the *Charter of the United Nations* and the *Universal Declaration of Human Rights*; and to promote and protect human and peoples' rights in accordance with the *African Charter on Human and Peoples' Rights*, and other relevant human rights instruments. While these are phrased as objectives rather than requirements, theoretically at least non-compliance with these human rights goals could lead to sanctions. Article 23 of the *AU Charter* provides that 'any Member State that fails to comply with the decisions and policies of the Union may be subjected to ... sanctions'.

8.4.2 *The African Charter on Human and Peoples' Rights*

In 1981 the OAU Assembly adopted the *African Charter on Human and Peoples' Rights* (ACHPR) and it entered into force on 21 October 1986. The ACHPR has been ratified by all 53 members of the African Union.[49]

The ACHPR can be distinguished from the regional human rights conventions of Europe and the Americas because of its incorporation of socio-economic rights and civil and political rights in a manner that emphasises their indivisibility, interdependence and interrelatedness.[50] The Preamble to the ACHPR states that 'civil and political rights cannot be disassociated from economic, social and cultural rights in their conception as well as universality and that the satisfaction of economic, social and cultural rights is a guarantee for the enjoyment of civil and political rights'.

---

47 See Chapter 11.4.2.

48 *Constitutive Act of the African Union*, opened for signature 11 July 2000, 2158 UNTS 3 (entered into force 26 May 2001).

49 For a discussion on the background to the *African Charter* see R M D'Sa, 'The African Charter on Human and Peoples' Rights: Problems and Prospects for Regional Action' (1981) 10 *Australian Year book of International Law* 101, 103.

50 See generally D Mzikenge Chirwa, 'African Regional Human Rights System: The Promise of Recent Jurisprudence on Social Rights' in M Langford (ed), *Social Rights Jurisprudence: Emerging Trends in International and Comparative Law*, Cambridge University Press, New York, 2008, 323.

The ACHPR also emphasises the right to development as particularly relevant to Africa. While much is made of the inclusion of socio-economic rights alongside civil and political rights in the *African Charter*, it should be noted that only a modest number of the former are explicitly included in the Charter. Articles 15, 16 and 17 explicitly recognise the right to work, health and education respectively, but the African Commission has implicitly recognised some other socio-economic rights in its decisions.

In 2001 the African Commission handed down its landmark decision in *SERAC v Nigeria*,[51] which concerned the actions of the military government in Nigeria in facilitating and failing to protect the Ogoni communities against the environmental pollution of their lands and destruction of their food sources by the Shell Petroleum Development Corporation in a consortium with the state oil company, the Nigerian National Petroleum Company. While the African Commission found violations of the right to health, the right to freely dispose of the communities' wealth, and resources and environment rights, it also deduced an implicit right to housing or shelter in the ACHPR from the provisions on health, property and family life, and implied a right to food (which was read into the right to dignity).

A significant source of future guidance on the interpretation of the economic, social and cultural rights set out in the ACHPR is likely to be the *Draft Principles and Guidelines on the Economic, Social and Cultural Rights in the African Charter*, which by early 2011 has been circulated for comment but not yet adopted by the African Commission.[52]

The ACHPR is also unique in a regional treaty in recognising not only individual rights but also peoples' rights. Articles 19–24 recognise rights—such as the right to be equal; to existence; to freely dispose of wealth and natural resources; to economic, social and cultural development; to national and international peace and security; and to a satisfactory environment—that are possessed not only by individuals but by 'peoples' in their collectivity.

8.4.3 The *Children's Charter* and the *Women's Protocol*

The OAU has also adopted two other significant human rights instruments that address the rights of women and children. The *African Charter on the Rights and Welfare of the Child* (*Children's Charter*) was adopted in 1990 and entered into force in 1999. As of July 2011 it had 45 ratifications. The *Children's Charter*, as compared to the UN *Convention on the Rights of the Child*, provides for some increased protections relating to child soldiers, child marriages and internally displaced children.[53]

The *Protocol to the African Charter on Human and Peoples' Rights on the Rights of Women in Africa* (*Women's Protocol*) was adopted in 2003 and entered into force in 2005. As of April 2011 it had 28 ratifications. The *Women's Protocol* includes comprehensive provisions on domestic violence, trafficking, elimination of harmful practices, reproductive rights and HIV/AIDS.[54]

51 *Social and Economic Rights Action Center and the Center for Economic and Social Rights v Nigeria*, Communication 155/96 (2001) AHRLR 60 (ACHPR 2001); see the Snapshot in Chapter 4.2.6.

52 See <http://www.achpr.org/english/other/Draft_guideline_ESCR/Draft_Pcpl%20&%20Guidelines.pdf>.

53 See the special issue of the *International Journal of Children's Rights*, volume 10(2) of 2002, which focuses on children's rights in Africa, and generally Chapter 12 below.

54 For further discussion see: C Ocran, 'The Protocol to the African Charter on Human and Peoples' Rights on the Rights of Women in Africa' (2007) 15 *African Journal of International and Comparative Law* 147; K Davis, 'The Emperor is Still Naked: Why the Protocol on the Rights of Women in Africa Leaves Women Exposed to More Discrimination' (2009) 42 *Vanderbilt Journal of Transnational Law* 949.

8.4.4 The African Commission on Human and Peoples' Rights

The African Commission on Human and Peoples' Rights (African Commission), established in 1987 under article 30 of the ACHPR, is the principal human rights body in Africa, although it has been chronically underfunded,[55] and under-regarded by the AU.[56] The Commission was established to promote the *African Charter* and to manage the business arising under it; the arrangement mirrors the familiar UN mechanisms for promoting human rights.[57] It is tasked with promoting human and peoples' rights and ensuring their protection in Africa. It is composed of eleven members, serving in their personal and independent capacity and not as representatives of their countries.

The Commission meets twice a year in regular sessions for a period of up to two weeks, alternating its meetings between its headquarters in Banjul, capital of the Gambia, and other capitals. In addition to the two principal mechanisms outlined below, the African Commission has appointed a number of 'special mechanisms' that may include the appointment of Special Rapporteurs and Working Groups to deal with thematic human rights issues.[58]

8.4.5 The African Commission Complaints Procedures

States and individuals may bring complaints to the African Commission for violations of the provisions of the ACHPR. Articles 47–54 deal with complaints by a state or states alleging violation of the Charter provisions by another state or states. Only one such case has been decided so far by the Commission.[59]

Articles 55–8 set out the conditions under which 'other communications' may be considered by the African Commission. The ACHPR does not explicitly state who may make these communications, but in practice it has been established that communications can be received from individuals, non-governmental organisations (NGOs) or groups of individuals (none of which need be the victim of the violation). If the communication meets the admissibility criteria set out in article 56 it will be formally accepted for consideration. The state is then informed of the communication and invited to respond, following which the complainant is also given an opportunity to respond to the state's comments. The complainant and the respondent are both invited to make presentations at the hearing, which is not public.

The admissibility and procedures for dealing with these 'other communications' are set out under in the *AU Charter*, and in the *African Commission Rules of Procedure* (Rules 102–20). Article 56 of the

55 Rachel Murray, *Human Rights in Africa: From the OAU to the African Union*, Cambridge University Press, Cambridge, 2004, 55–7.

56 Ibid 69–71; H Steiner, P Alston & R Goodman, *International Human Rights in Context: Law, Politics, Morals*, 3rd edn, Oxford University Press, Oxford, 2007, 1063–72; Frans Viljoen, *International Human Rights Law in Africa*, Oxford University Press, Oxford, 2007, 416–17.

57 See above, n 55, Ch 2.

58 See the website of the African Commission <http://www.achpr.org/>, which lists a number of 'special mechanisms' on topics including prisons, women, freedom of expression, human rights defenders, refugees, extrajudicial executions, indigenous populations, economic, social and cultural rights and the death penalty.

59 *Democratic Republic of the Congo v Burundi, Rwanda and Uganda, Communication No 227/99* (2004) AHRLR 19 (ACHPR 2003) detailing the violations of the three respondent states of individual and peoples' rights during the presence of their armed forces in the DRC.

Charter requires that for a complaint to be admissible, a complainant must exhaust local remedies. Articles 56–7 require state parties who receive a complaint to respond within 6 months. Once a communication is held to be admissible the Commission may then make recommendations on how a state party should respond. Recommendations may include, for example, an order requesting the cessation of the violation, or that laws be amended or repealed or compensation be paid. States are obliged to respond to these recommendations arising as a consequence of article 45 of the *AU Charter*, which obliges the state party to protect human rights of everyone in their territory.[60]

Individuals and NGOs based in or outside Africa are entitled to submit complaints to the African Commission and, over the years, many have done so. Complaints tend to increase against a state party depending on the political situation in the country. For example, during the era of military rule in Nigeria, it monopolised the communication procedure; more recently it was Zimbabwe that took the lead.

One reason for the use of this procedure is that 'the Charter is one of the most comprehensive instruments as far as catering for all categories of human and collective rights is concerned'.[61] Despite its widespread utility, the procedure does have some limitations. For instance, state parties often claim they have not received information about a complaint being lodged against them.[62] However the final decisions of the Commission are (mostly) available online, and a brief survey of the decisions indicates the breadth of issues submitted.[63]

A landmark decision of the African Commission on Human and Peoples' Rights in 2001[64] held that the destruction of crops by government and non-state actors violated the Nigerian government's duties with respect to the right to food (a right the Commission implied from the *African Charter*). The Commission also found violations of the more obtuse right to a satisfactory environment under the *Charter*. The decision was significant for the broad requirements it imposed on African governments to respect economic, social and cultural rights including monitoring the activities of multinational corporations to prevent such violations.[65]

Since its establishment in 1987, the African Commission has considered more than 370 communications.[66] Some critics of the communications procedure have argued that the process is

60 A Bösl & J Diescho, *Human Rights in Africa: Legal Perspectives on Their Protection and Promotion*, Macmillan Education, Namibia, 2009, 259.

61 Ibid.

62 Ibid 261.

63 <http://www.achpr.org/english/_info/List_Decision_Communications.html>.

64 *Social and Economic Rights Action Center and the Center for Economic and Social Rights*, see above, n 51.

65 For further discussion see D Shelton, 'Decision Regarding Communication 155/96 (*Social and Economic Rights Action Center/Center for Economic and Social Rights v Nigeria*)' (2002) 96 *American Journal of International Law*, 937, and see the Snapshot in Chapter 4.2.6.

66 By comparison, the United Nations Human Rights Committee has dealt with 1960 communications since the first Optional Protocol entered into force (1976) until 2010. This averages to approximately 57 complaints considered per year versus 16 considered per year by the African Commission. These figures are averages and not exact figures for each year in this period. See: *Report of the Human Rights Committee* (Volume I) 97th session (12–30 October 2009); 98th session (8–26 March 2010); 99th session (12–30 July 2010); *General Assembly Official Records* 56th session Supplement No 40 (A/65/40) at iii.

underused (indicating a lack of awareness of the system) and that the recommendations of the Commission are often vague and lacking in any significant follow-up mechanisms.[67]

8.4.6 Periodic State Reporting to the African Commission

As part of its protective mandate, the African Commission also receives and considers periodic reports submitted by state parties in conformity with article 62 of the *Charter*. State parties are required to submit reports every two years on their efforts to comply with the ACHPR. Several states—Botswana, Comoros, Cote D'Ivoire, Djibouti, Equatorial Guinea, Eritrea, Gabon, Guinea-Bissau, Liberia, Malawi, Sao Tome and Principe, Sierra Leone and Somalia[68]—have never submitted a report, and many are late or overdue. Since 2001 the African Commission has adopted concluding observations after considering the reports, and more recently has started to publish the observations on its website. The Commission's review of states' periodic reports 'has not actually been a great success to date, essentially because the states parties have seldom demonstrated the requisite diligence and rigour.'[69] The reports that have been submitted share the same characteristics as all states reports (not only those from Africa) in the UN system: they are 'far too descriptive and do not devote enough space to the concrete steps taken to give effect to [human rights] ... most of the reports are essentially a reproduction *in extensor* of the rights guaranteed by constitutions of the states concerned'.[70]

8.4.7 The African Court on Human and Peoples' Rights

The *Protocol to the African Charter on Human and Peoples' Rights on the Establishment of an African Court on Human and Peoples Rights'* (1998) (*African Protocol*) was signed in 1998, but came into force only in January 2005 when it was ratified by 15 members states of the AU. By July 2011, 25 of the 53 African states had ratified the *African Protocol*: Algeria, Burkina Faso, Burundi, Comoros, Côte d'Ivoire, Gabon, Gambia, Ghana, Kenya, Lesotho, Libyan Arab Jamahiriya, Malawi, Mali, Mauritania, Mauritius, Mozambique, The Niger, Nigeria, Rwanda, Senegal, South Africa, Tunisia, The United Republic of Tanzania, Togo, and Uganda.

The African Court on Human and Peoples' Rights (African Court) commenced operation only in January 2006, when the first 11 judges of the Court were appointed by the AU Assembly. The Court is able 'to give legally binding judgements coupled with appropriate remedies as well as advisory opinions, and has the potential to provide substantial impetus to the developing body of jurisprudence' on the rights set out in the ACHPR.[71] However, this potential is limited by the fact that individuals and NGOs can take cases directly to the court only in respect of those states that have made an additional

67 C Heyns & M Killander, see above, n 46, 488.

68 As at May 2010, <http://www.achpr.org/english/_info/statereport_considered_en.html>.

69 F Ouguergouz, *The African Charter on Human and Peoples' Rights: A Comprehensive Agenda for Human Dignity and Sustainable Democracy in Africa*, Martinus Nijhoff Publishers, The Hague, 2003, 530.

70 Ibid see the discussion of the inadequacy of states' reports generally in Chapter 7.4.4.

71 S Liebenberg, *Socio-Economic Rights: Adjudication under a Transformative Constitution*, Juta, Claremont, 2010, 110.

declaration specifically authorising them to do so. To date, only Burkina Faso and Mali have made such a declaration. The likely procedure otherwise is that cases will be taken to the court by the African Commission if it has found a violation and established that the state has not yet complied with its recommendations.

It has been observed that '[a]side from the appointment of judges, very few activities have taken place at the Court. It only adopted its *Interim Rules of Procedure* in June 2008 and handed down its first judgment in December 2009'.[72] In *Michelot Yogogombaye v The Republic of Senegal*[73] the applicant was a Chadian National who wanted to prevent the Government of Senegal from conducting the trial against the former Chadian head of state, Hissene Habre. The Court decided it lacked jurisdiction, because Senegal had not made the declaration under article 34.6 of the Protocol giving an individual standing to claim in the Court.[74]

In July 2004 the AU decided that the African Court should merge with the African Court of Justice, which is provided for in the Constitutive Act of the AU but has not yet been established. The new court would be the African Court of Justice and Human Rights. The Protocol on the Statute of the African Court of Justice and Human Rights was opened for signature and ratification on 1 July 2008 but has not yet entered into force. Once it has received the requisite 15 ratifications it will replace the African Protocol and a new, merged court will be established.

8.5 THE ARAB REGION

8.5.1 The *Arab Charter on Human Rights*

The League of Arab States (also known as the Arab League) was established in March 1945 to develop closer relations and collaboration between its (now) 22 member states and to generally supervise the affairs and interests of Arab countries.[75] The Arab League 'did not show any interest in human rights until 1968 [when it established the Permanent Arab Human Rights Commission (Resolution 2443 of 3 September 1968)] and it took another twenty-five years to adopt the Arab Charter on Human Rights' in 1994.[76] This Charter was widely criticised for falling short of international standards, including the lack of provision of any human rights enforcement mechanism.[77] The 1994 version did not receive any ratifications and thus never entered into force.

In 2002 the Council of the League of Arab States adopted resolutions encouraging the 'modernisation' of the Charter in an attempt to bring its provisions into closer compliance with international human

72 J Ddamulira Mujuzi, '*Michelot Yogogombaye v The Republic of Senegal*: The African Court's First Decision' (2010) 10 *Human Rights Law Review* 372, 372.

73 African Court on Human and People's Rights, Application No 001/2008, Judgment, (15 December 2009).

74 See above, n 72.

75 League of Arab States <http://www.arableagueonline.org/las/index_en.jsp> (Arabic only).

76 A Ahmed An-Na'im, 'Human Rights in the Arab World: A Regional Perspective' (2001) 23 *Human Rights Quarterly* 701, 712.

77 'Arab Charter on Human Rights' (trans M Amin Al-Midani & M Cabanettes, revised by S M Akram) (2006) 24 *Boston University International Law Journal* 147, 147–8.

rights standards.[78] A revised text of the *Arab Charter on Human Rights* was adopted by the League of Arab States in 2004 and entered into force in March 2008.[79] At the time of writing it had received 10 (of potentially 22) ratifications from: Algeria, Bahrain, Jordan, Libya, Palestine, Qatar, Saudi Arabia, Syria, the United Arab Emirates and Yemen.

Article 1 of the revised Charter notes that its provisions 'seek to place human rights at the centre of key national concerns of Arab States, making them lofty and fundamental ideals that shape the will of the individual in Arab States and enable him to improve his life in accordance with noble values'. While the 2004 version is a step forward from the original, it still contains provisions that fall short of international human rights standards. In the extract below, Rishmawi highlights some of the more problematic provisions in the Charter.[80]

M RISHMAWI, 'THE ARAB CHARTER ON HUMAN RIGHTS AND THE LEAGUE OF ARAB STATES: AN UPDATE'

There is a reference [in the Preamble] to Zionism as 'an impediment to human dignity and a major barrier to the exercise of the fundamental rights of all peoples'. This has been criticised by a number of human rights non-governmental organisations (NGOs) which have called for reference to be made to universal values rather than focussing on particular ideologies. Article 8 prohibits torture or cruel, degrading, humiliating or inhuman treatment, but not punishment. Some economic and social rights, such as the right to work (Article 34), the right to free basic health care (Article 39(1)), and the right to free education at the primary and basic levels (Article 41(2)) are only granted to citizens, and not to all persons under the jurisdiction of the State. Furthermore, some of the rights contained in the Charter are contingent upon interpretation of Islamic Shari'a. For example, Article 3(3) provides that '[m]en and women are equal in respect of human dignity, rights and obligations within the framework of the positive discrimination established in favour of women by the Islamic Shari'a, other divine laws and by applicable laws and legal instruments'. Article 7 permits the imposition of the death penalty against children aged below 18 years if national law so provides. This is in clear violation of Articles 37(a) of the Convention on the Rights of the Child 1989 and Article 6(5) of the International Covenant on Civil and Political Rights 1966. Article 30 of the Charter also allows for the imposition of limitations on freedom of thought, conscience and religion, if these are 'provided for by law', and does not limit the possibility of limitation to the manifestation aspect of such freedoms. In contrast, Article 18 of the ICCPR distinguishes between the right to freedom of thought, conscience and religion, and the manifestation of one's religion or beliefs. Only this second may be subject 'to such limitations as are prescribed by law and are necessary to protect public safety, order, health, or morals or the fundamental rights and freedoms of others'.

The 2004 Charter attempts to address the historical and ongoing issue of the compatibility of Islamic principles with the universality of international human rights standards, but it is questionable how successfully this has been done.

78 M Rishmawi, 'The Revised Arab Charter on Human Rights: A Step Forward?' (2005) 5 *Human Rights Law Review*, 361, 362. Rishmawi notes the Council of Ministers of the Arab League's Resolutions 6184 of March 2002 and 6243 of September 2002 (only available in Arabic).

79 For an English version of the Arab Charter prepared by the OHCHR see: 'The Arab Charter on Human Rights, May 2004' (2005) 12 *International Human Rights Reports* 893.

80 (2010) 10 *Human Rights Law Review* 169, 171–2.

While overall the provisions of the 2004 Charter demonstrate that there is a degree of willingness to incorporate and reflect international human rights principles among the laws of Arab states, there is still a strong element of conservatism in the practical integration and enforcement of human rights at the local level. In 2009, for example, the Arab League rejected the arrest warrant for Sudanese President Omar al-Bashir issued by the International Criminal Court and reaffirmed this position in 2010.[81] It is clear, as Rishmawi notes, that the 2004 Charter reflects the extent to which certain Arab states accept international human rights law and standards, as shown by their reservations to UN human rights treaties.[82]

8.5.2 The Arab Human Rights Committee

The Arab Charter establishes an Arab Human Rights Committee (article 45(1)) with its principal focus being to review states' periodic reports. It does not include any mechanism to consider individual or state-based complaints. It held its first session in April 2009[83] and has adopted procedural standards for its operation but has not yet held any substantive reviews.

8.6 THE ASIA-PACIFIC REGION

The Asia-Pacific region, as defined by the United Nations, encompasses a broad geographical expanse with borders that extend from the Mediterranean Sea to the eastern edge of the Pacific Ocean.[84] It includes 52 member states and contains half of the world's population. The level of national human rights protection mechanisms varies widely between countries: ranging from those of Australia and New Zealand for example, to Myanmar (Burma), a country noted more for its human rights violations than protections.

Given the vastness and diversity of the area, one of the recurrent challenges has been to develop a regional framework for the promotion and protection of human rights. It has long been described as the only UN-designated region that had no specific human rights treaty or a regional mechanism to protect rights.

The establishment of the Association of South-East Asian Nations (ASEAN) Intergovernmental Commission on Human Rights (AICHR) in October 2009 was a step forward for the promotion and protection of human rights in the region. Other inter-governmental networks in the region that have at times focused on human rights issues include the South Asian Association on Regional Cooperation

81 The initial warrant issued by the ICC accuses Bashir of war crimes and crimes against humanity relating to the Darfur conflict in Western Sudan. The second warrant issued in 2010 includes genocide.

82 M Rishmawi, 'The Arab Charter on Human Rights and the League of Arab States: An Update' (2010) 10 *Human Rights Law Review* 169, 171.

83 Ibid 172.

84 *Summary of Recommendations Made and Progress Achieved under the Framework on Regional Cooperation for the Promotion and Protection of Human Rights in the Asia-Pacfic Region* (Office of the High Commissioner for Human Rights, 2010) <http://bangkok.ohchr.org/news/events/asia-pacific-regional-framework-workshop-2010/files/summary_recommendations_progress.pdf>.

(SAARC) and the Pacific Islands Forum (PIF).[85] Despite the establishment of the AICHR, there are a number of significant challenges that lie ahead in developing a comprehensive regional plan for the promotion and protection of human rights in the Asia-Pacific region. It remains an open question as to whether 'this herald[s] a new era of steady progress towards the realisation of human rights in Southeast Asia, or are these developments little more than a legitimacy-seeking, "window-dressing" exercise, not to be followed by any concrete implementation?'[86]

8.6.1 The Asian Reluctance About Rights?

For many years, the United Nations and many NGOs have emphasised the need for a human rights mechanism in Asia, and particularly in South-East Asia,[87] and from the 1980s the UN has continuously called on states in Asia to consider establishing a regional human rights mechanism.[88]

In 1998, the Asian Human Rights Commission, a Hong Kong-based NGO, drafted an Asian Human Rights Charter with the involvement of hundreds of individuals and regional NGOs, but there are many NGO efforts that predate this effort. Despite this, progress has been sporadic and non-institutionalised. Various explanations are offered for the slow pace of development towards a regional framework, some categorising it as an Asian reluctance about rights. Some commentators argue that some of the common theories about why the Asia-Pacific has appeared resistant to embracing a human rights regional protective framework 'typically include [1] that the region is too diverse to subscribe to uniform standards; contrarily that [2] "Asian values" differ from western "international human rights standards"; that [3] principles of sovereignty and non-intervention preclude external scrutiny; and that [4] Asians have a cultural preference for conciliation over adjudication, ruling out quasi-judicial methods for protecting human rights'.[89]

The assertion that the Asia-Pacific region is too diverse to share common standards could arguably also apply to Africa and to a lesser extent Europe and the Americas, and some commentators argue that '[i]t is difficult to accept that Asia is objectively more diverse than all of the other regions

---

85 SAARC has developed its own instruments: *SAARC Convention on Preventing and Combating Trafficking in Women and Children for Prostitution* (5 January 2002); *SAARC Convention on Regional Arrangements for the Promotion of Child Welfare in South Asia* (5 January 2002). PIF has consistently called for the establishment of national human right institutions and has developed its own action plan to address human rights issues common to member states.

86 Y Ginbar 'Human Rights in ASEAN—Setting Sail or Treading Water?' *Human Rights Law Review* 10 (2010) 504–18, 505.

87 See generally J Tang, 'Towards an Alternative Approach to International Human Rights Protection in the Asia-Pacific' in J Tang (ed), *Human Rights and International Relations in the Asia-Pacific*, Pinter, London, 1995, 185 and A Durbach, C Renshaw & A Byrnes, 'A Tongue but No Teeth?: The Emergence of a Regional Human Rights Mechansim in the Asia Pacific Region' (2009) 31 *Sydney Law Review* 211–38, 222–5.

88 See, eg, GA Res 41/153, UN GAOR, 41st sess, 97th plen mtg, UN Doc A/RES/41/153 (4 December 1986); GA Res 45/168, UN GAOR, 45th sess, 69th plen mtg, UN Doc A/RES/45/168 (18 December 1990).

89 B Saul, J Mowbray & I Baghoomians, 'Resistance to Regional Human Rights Cooperation in the Asia-Pacific: Demythologising Regional Exceptionalism by Learning from the Americas, Europe and Asia' (Legal Studies Research Paper No 10/107, University of Sydney Law School, October 2010) 2. Also see A H Y Chen, 'Conclusion: Comparative Reflections on Human Rights in Asia' in R Peerenboom, C J Petersen & A H Y Chen (eds), *Human Rights in Asia*, Routledge, Abingdon, 2006, 487.

in the world.'[90] The argument that 'Asian values' are incompatible with 'Western international standards' is reflected in the Bangkok Declaration of 1993[91] and the Terms of Reference of the AICHR[92] discussed below. Such an argument assumes there is a common Asian identity that spans the vast geographical, political and legal region that makes up the Asia-Pacific and stands in direct contrast to the arguments noted above about Asia's diversity. It is arguable however that there are some commonalities reflected in an 'Asian approach' to human rights (applicable to a subset of countries in the Asia-Pacific) that might set it apart from other regions. Such commonalities are reflected in the initial reservations of ASEAN states to the proposal to establish an ASEAN human rights body: their concerns were centred largely around the requirement for 'the universal application of international human rights norms, the over-emphasis on civil and political rights "at the expense of the right to development" and the right to individual freedom operating as a restriction on the right to govern and protect national security'.[93] Concerns about interference in the domestic affairs of neighbouring states alleged to have violated human rights are also relevant.' Finally, the suggestion of a cultural preference for informal dispute settlement over adjudication is best responded to by noting that 'binding settlement is hardly foreign to Asia, its values or traditional practices and that indeed it has been warmly embraced where natural resources or economic transactions are involved'.[94]

Some may argue that 'claims about the uniqueness of the Asian experience are often exaggerated or inaccurate [and] ... Asian exceptionalism on human rights questions is often more fruitfully explained as an expression of strategic policy choices by Asian governments to avoid strengthening human rights protections, rather than by any inherent truths about the unsuitability of rights and institutions to Asian traditions, values, diversity or cultural preferences'.[95] But there is no doubt that the 52 countries that comprise the Asia-Pacific region include vastly different political systems and cultures and that establishing a regional mechanism that will satisfy all is a challenging task.

---

90 B Saul, J Mowbray & I Baghoomians, ibid 6.

91 The *Bangkok Declaration on Human Rights* declared that while human rights were 'universal in nature', rights should be considered 'in the context of a dynamic and evolving process of international norm-setting, bearing in mind the significance of national and regional peculiarities and various historical, cultural and religious backgrounds'. See *Final Declaration of the Regional Meeting for Asia of the World Conference on Human Rights*, UN GAOR, UN Doc A/CONF.157/ASRM/8 (7 April 1993) para 8.

92 *Terms of Reference of ASEAN Intergovernmental Commission on Human Rights* (2009) art 1.4 <http://www.aseansec.org/DOC-TOR-AHRB.pdf>.

93 A Durbach, C Renshaw & A Byrnes, see above, n 87, at 224 quoting M Mohamad, 'Towards a Human Rights Regime in Southeast Asia: Charting the Course of State Commitment' (2002) 24 *Contemporary Southeast Asia* 230 at 233.

94 B Saul, J Mowbrary & I Baghoomians, see above, n 89, 16.

95 B Saul, J Mowbrary & I Baghoomians, see above, n 89, 2. Also see the discussion in Chapter 2.4.2.

8.6.2 ASEAN Intergovernmental Commission on Human Rights (AICHR)

In November 2007, after 15 years of deliberations, leaders of the ten ASEAN member states[96] signed the *Charter of the Association of Southeast Asian Nations*[97] (*ASEAN Charter*), which entered into force in December 2008. The *ASEAN Charter* includes references to the promotion and protection of human rights in the preamble, purposes and principles. It committed ASEAN members to the establishment of a human rights body (article 14), the structure and functions of which were to be determined later. Following the endorsement by ASEAN's Foreign Ministers of the Terms of Reference for the ASEAN Intergovernmental Commission on Human Rights (AICHR),[98] the organisation was launched on 23 October 2009 during the fifteenth ASEAN Summit in Thailand with a mandate to promote and protect the human rights of the people of ASEAN countries.

The AICHR is far less robust than the other three regional mechanisms and is limited by its narrow mandate. While one of its purposes is 'to promote and protect human rights and fundamental freedoms of the people of ASEAN' (Terms of Reference article 1.1), it is a consultative body with no mandate to review individual complaints or publicly criticise state practices.[99] The Terms of Reference do not stipulate that its members must be independent and its focus is on developing a 'constructive and non-confrontational approach' (Terms of Reference article 2.4) that emphasises cooperation over criticism and echoes the consensual decision-making process that ASEAN is well known for. The Terms of Reference reiterate the principles of state independence and sovereignty and non-interference and respect for different cultures that feature in article 2 of the *ASEAN Charter*. Article 1.4 of the Terms of Reference reflects the cultural relativist theory evident in the 1993 Bangkok Declaration, noting that it is the responsibility of AICHR 'to promote human rights within the regional context, bearing in mind national and regional particularities and mutual respect for different historical, cultural and religious backgrounds'.

While the establishment of the AICHR is a positive step for the region, there remain significant issues to be addressed if it is to develop into an effective regional mechanism for addressing human rights issues. For example, its mandate could be explicitly expanded to incorporate the receipt of state and individual complaints, the independence of its members could be guaranteed, greater transparency could be incorporated in its future decision-making processes and consultations with civil society might be institutionalised. If ASEAN member states can take steps towards these goals, there would be real cause for optimism about the development of a regional Asian human rights mechanism.

96 The ten members of ASEAN are Brunei, Cambodia, Indonesia, Laos, Malaysia, Myanmar, Philippines, Singapore, Thailand and Vietnam.

97 *Charter of the Association of Southeast Asian Nations*, opened for signature 20 November 2007 (entered into force 15 December 2008) <http://www.aseansec.org/21069.pdf>.

98 See above, n 92.

99 However there is also nothing in the AICHR's Terms of Reference to prevent it from investigating complaints of human rights violations, see above, n 86, 517.

8.7 CONCLUSION AND ISSUES

Regional human rights systems, particularly the longer-established systems in Europe and the Americas, have proven that a more concentrated system of human rights monitoring and accountability can have advantages over the global system. That is particularly true in terms of enforcement, where governments have shown much greater political will to comply with rulings of regional courts, especially the European Court of Human Rights, than is typically accorded to the views of the UN treaty monitoring committees. Standard-setting has also proven more efficient at the regional level than at the global level, partly because of the smaller number of states that need to agree, but purportedly also because of the greater degree of shared history and similar values between states in the same region.

The suggestion that shared regional values are relevant to the interpretation of human rights, however, also gives rise to the biggest philosophical question mark over regionalism. If human rights really are universal, rather than relative to a particular culture or region, how can it make any difference whether or not there is a shared historical or cultural understanding between member states of a given organisation? A further potential threat to universalism posed by regional human rights systems is the potential for divergent jurisprudence to emerge between different regional systems, or between a region and a global body such as a UN treaty monitoring committee. If these different human rights jurisdictions reach different interpretations of a given right in similar conditions, how are they to be reconciled (if indeed they need to be reconciled)? And what does such a divergence say about the idea that human rights are inherent in all human beings everywhere in the world and not relative?

The emphasis on regional human rights systems seems to be increasing, with a newly energised African Court and a sustained push for regional systems in Asia and the Pacific. These movements are likely to improve the enforcement of human rights, and in turn a culture of human rights in those regions, but at the same time, will increase the pressure on the modern consensus position that human rights are universal.

9 THE ROLE OF NON-GOVERNMENT ORGANISATIONS (NGOS)

CONTENTS

9.1 INTRODUCTION

States are the principal 'established legal persons' in international law.[1] But accountability mechanisms in international law are limited, and on the issue of human rights compliance the United Nations machinery relies principally on self-reporting by states (see Chapter 7.4). UN oversight is necessarily undertaken in a diplomatic environment, characterised by respectful requests and expressions of regret. At the same time, states' self-reporting is almost invariably non-existent, delayed, incomplete or self-serving.

Increasingly, states' performance under international human rights standards is being scrutinised by *non*-governmental organisations (NGOs), and states are held accountable by these organisations in UN forums, and in the news media and public debate. As a result, NGOs have assumed a significant role in the international human rights regime. In turn, this exposes NGOs to scrutiny and criticism.

This chapter discusses the origins and types of NGOs, and describes the nature of their involvement in the UN machinery. After illustrating aspects of NGOs' work the tensions of NGOs-state relations is reviewed, along with some of the criticism directed towards NGOs and their activity.

1 I Brownlie, *Principles of Public International Law*, 7th edn, Oxford University Press, Oxford, 2008, Ch 3.

9.2 THE IDEA OF AN NGO

The term 'non-governmental organisation' is of relatively recent origin, coming into wide use only since the Second World War.[2] Before then, terms such as 'international associations', 'private international organizations', and 'voluntary agencies' were used,[3] and at the 1945 San Francisco Conference on the *UN Charter*, the terms 'pressure groups', 'private organizations' and 'unofficial organizations' were still in use.[4]

9.2.1 Defining an NGO

The label 'NGO' is applied to a wide variety of organisations, and is not a very descriptive term; it simply defines an entity in the negative, as an organisation that is not a 'governmental' organisation. There is no generally accepted definition of an NGO, and its meaning 'tends to vary according to who is using the term and in what context'.[5] It seems that 'experts and the public at large constantly use the term, confident that others know what they are talking about'.[6]

NGOs have limited recognition under international law; in fact, 'legal scholars have not reached consensus on the question of whether NGOs ... enjoy (some components of) international legal personality'.[7] The question is often approached as one of 'legal status' rather than 'legal personality', even though legal status 'may vary according to the circumstances and needs to be specified for each particular entity'.[8] Categorising NGOs in international law is a fairly theoretical exercise, with few practical implications. It seems to matter to theorists, who need to find a legitimate place for NGOs in the pattern of international law and institutions.[9] Dupuy suggests, however, that whatever their

2 N Götz, 'Reframing NGOs: The Identity of an International Relations Non-Starter' (2008) 14(2) *European Journal of International Relations* 231, 237.

3 Ibid 237 citing P Chiang, *Non-Governmental Organizations at the United Nations: Identity, Role, and Function*, Praeger, New York, 1981, 33, L C White, *International Non-Governmental Organizations: Their Purposes, Methods, and Accomplishments*, Rutgers University Press, New Brunswick, 1951, 3, and B Seary, 'The Early History: From the Congress of Vienna to the San Francisco Conference' in P Willetts (ed), *The Conscience of the World: The Influence of Non-Governmental Organisatons in the UN System*, Hurst, London, 1996 15–30.

4 See above, n 2, 238, citing UNCIO (1945–1955) *Documents of the United Nations Conference on International Organization, San Francisco*, 1945, London: United Nations Information Organization, Vol V, 153–4.

5 S Calnan, *The Effectiveness of Domestic Human Rights NGOs: A Comparative Study*, Martinus Nijhoff, Leiden, 2008, 5, citing M A Ölz, 'Non-Governmental Organisations in Regional Human Rights Systems' (1997) 28(2) *Columbia Human Rights Law Review* 307, 313. See also A Lindblom, *Non-Governmental Organisations in International Law*, Cambridge University Press, Cambridge, 2005, 36; F D Gaer 'Reality Check: Human Rights Non-Governmental Organisations Confront Governments at the United Nations' (1995) 16(3) *Third World Quarterly* 389, 395.

6 C Bakker & L Vierucci, 'Introduction: A Normative or Programmatic Definition of NGOs?' in P Dupuy & L Vierucci (eds), NGOs in *International Law: Efficiency in Flexibility?*, Edward Elgar Publishing, Cheltenham, 2008, 1–17, 12.

7 Ibid 1.

8 Ibid 1.

9 See the approaches surveryed in Z Pearson, 'Book Review: Anna-Karin Lindblom, *Non-Governmental Organizations in International Law*; S Ripinsky & P Van den Bossche, *NGO Involvement in International Organizations*; A Vedder (ed), *NGO Involvement in International Governance and Policy: Sources of Legitimacy*; and P Dupuy & L Vierucci (eds), *NGOs in International Law: Efficiency in Flexibility?*, Edward Elgar Publishing, Cheltenham, 2008, 317.

technical status, all that NGOs really want is to be recognised as 'worthy interlocutors' and 'useful and legitimate partners'.[10]

Taken literally, the idea of a non-governmental organisation can include 'profit-seeking entities ... multinational enterprises, international public corporations, cartels, criminal alliances ... religions, charities, foundations, research organisations (that is, universities, institutes and laboratories), and groups seeking formal power, such as political parties or liberation movements'.[11] NGOs can be classified according to a range of attributes, such as 'function, size, resource base, geographical spread, membership, area of interest, degree of institutionalization, and philosophical orientation ... [but] these typologies are, at best, partial'.[12]

In 2010 the UN Department of Public Information (UNDPI) described an NGO as a 'not-for-profit, voluntary citizens' group, which is organized on a local, national or international level to address issues in support of the public good'.[13] In similar terms, the World Association of Non-Governmental Organisations (WANGO) defines an NGO as a 'not-for-profit organization that is not established by a governmental entity or intergovernmental agreement and which is organized on a local, national, sub-regional, regional, or international level';[14] numerous authors have explored similar definitions in some detail.[15]

Distinguishing between NGOs that operate internationally (INGOs) and those that operate only within a state is common, most importantly for purposes of accreditation by the UN Economic and Social Council (ECOSOC), discussed below. As well, the 1986 *European Convention on the Recognition of the Legal Personality of International Non-Governmental Organisations*[16] defines NGOs as non-profit-making 'associations, foundations and other private institutions' that 'carry on their activities with effect *in at least two States*'.[17] There is not, however, always a 'a clear cut distinction' between domestic and international

10 P Dupuy, 'Conclusion: Return on the Legal Status of NGOs and on the Methodological Problems which Arise for Legal Scholarship', in P Dupuy & L Vierucci (ed), *NGOs in International Law: Efficiency in Flexibility?* Edward Elgar Publishing, Cheltenham, 2008, 204–15, 213.

11 S Charnovitz, 'Two Centuries of Participation: NGOs and International Governance' (1997) 18(2) *Michigan Journal of International Law* 183, 187.

12 D Otto, 'Nongovernmental Organisations in the United Nations System: The Emerging Role of International Civil Society' (1996) 18 (1) *Human Rights Quarterly*, 107, 111–12. See also Calnan's 'taxonomy' of human rights NGOs in S Calnan, *The Effectiveness of Domestic Human Rights NGOs: A Comparative Study*, Martinus Nijhoff, Leiden, 2008.

13 <http://www.un.org/wcm/content/site/dpingorelations/criteria>.

14 *Connecting & Serving NGOs Beyond Borders*, World Association of Non-Governmental Organizations, <www.wango.org/download/pdf/WANGO_Brochure_v2.pdf>.

15 See, eg, A Lindblom, above, n 5; S Calnan, above, n 5; see above, n 6; 1–17; see above, n 2; E Rebasti, 'Beyond Consultative Status: Which Legal Framework for Enhanced Interaction Between NGOs and Interntional Organisations?' in P Dupuy & L Vierucci (eds), *NGOs in International Law: Efficiency in Flexibility?* Edward Elgar Publishing, Cheltenham, 2008, 21–70.

16 *European Convention on the Recognition of the Legal Personality of International Non-Governmental Organisations*, opened for signature 24 April 1986, ETS 124 (entered into force 1 January 1991).

17 Ibid art 1 (emphasis added).

NGOs,[18] and there is an inevitable degree of overlap between them;[19] domestic NGOs, for example, turn to international NGOs 'when they are frustrated in being able to achieve accountability for human rights violations through domestic means of redress'.[20]

In Australia, the Institute of Public Affairs (IPA) has defined NGOs very broadly, as 'non-profit groups that combine resource mobilisation, information provision and activism to advocate for changes in certain areas'.[21] The IPA included as NGOs 'business, industry, and professional associations, trade unions, "think-tanks" as well as citizen and community organisations [but not] [a]academic and research organisations ... because their primary purposes are not those of "resource mobilization, information provision, and activism"'.[22]

In its 2005 National Human Rights Action Plan, the Australian Government described NGOs that are active in the field of human rights by reference, in part, to their relationship with government:[23]

> Some [non-government organisations (NGOs)] focus exclusively on specific human rights issues, whereas others have broader interests which inevitably encompass human rights. Other NGOs focus on discrete areas such as the rights of women, children or Indigenous peoples.
>
> There are many NGOs in Australia that work cooperatively with the Government in enhancing human rights by providing a range of support services, such as: food and shelter for the homeless; support for people with disabilities; refuges for women who are victims of domestic violence; AIDS support services; community legal centres; and community health care.
>
> Other private bodies assume an advocacy role in the protection and promotion of human rights, seeking to effect change through lobbying Governments on human rights issues. As their names imply, NGOs are independent of governments and therefore do not always share the same views as national governments or international bodies such as the UN.
>
> Consistently with this diversity, Australian human rights NGOs operate at all levels in society and across all sectors, engaging in advocacy, education and training, and research. Some are concerned with a special interest, perhaps only of the moment, while others address systemic issues and may have been doing so for decades.

Human Rights NGOs

A wide range of organisations could be described in some sense as 'human rights NGOs', and it is as difficult to define precisely a human rights NGO as it is to define an NGO generally. There is, for example,

18 H J Steiner, *Diverse Partners: Non-Governmental Organizations in the Human Rights Movement: The Report of a Retreat of Human Rights Activists*, Harvard Law School Human Rights Program, Cambridge, 1991, 5.

19 S Calnan, above, n 5, 8.

20 M H Posner & C Whittone, 'The Status of Human Rights NGOs' (1994) 25(2) *Columbia Human Rights Law Review* 269, 269–74.

21 G Johns & J Roskam, *Report to the Prime Minister's Community Business Partnership: The Protocol: Managing Relations with NGOs*, The Institute of Public Affairs, Melbourne, 2004, 5, quoting D L Spar & L T La Mure, 'The Power of Activism: Assessing the Impact of NGOs on Global Business' (2003) 45(3) *California Management Review* 78, at 79.

22 G Johns & J Roskam, ibid.

23 *Australia's National Framework for Human Rights: National Action Plan*, Commonwealth Attorney-General's Department, Canberra, 2005, 7; see Chapter 10.4.1 for discussion of Australia's next proposed National Action Plan.

debate whether the work of a human rights NGO necessarily relies on the formal sources of international human rights law;[24] research in Australia found that 'NGOs choose between using the language of human rights and the language of social justice according to the circumstances'.[25]

Despite the difficulties of definition, Bell and Keenan describe different essential types of human rights NGOs:[26]

> ... there are human rights groups whose core mandate is the promotion and protection of human rights, as defined internationally. They clearly self-identify as human rights groups first and foremost. These groups tend to be internationally networked, to have consultative status at the United Nations, or to be affiliated with a group with such status ...
>
> Beyond this 'classic' form, there are a range of other groups with varied connections to human rights. In a second category are 'equality' NGOs, whose work is focused around the equality claims of a specific marginalized community, where the community is defined around an aspect of identity, such as gender, sexuality, ethnicity, disability, or age ...
>
> In a third category are groups whose core mandate is something other than 'human rights,' but where the group sees human rights as either a sub-issue within their broader mandate, or a way of characterizing their work. This covers a broad range of very different groups, from those dealing with issues such as democracy or development, to single issue groups, such as campaigns against land mines or plastic bullets, or for adequate housing. Groups dealing with the needs of victims, or ex-prisoners, or refugees, can be included in this category.

Human rights NGOs, such as Amnesty International and Human Rights Watch for example, operate politically and diplomatically to draw attention to human rights abuses, and through collaboration and criticism bring pressure to bear on governments.[27]

Humanitarian NGOs

The term 'humanitarian' NGO encompasses NGOs that, according to their particular focus, can be referred to as well as 'aid', 'relief', or 'development' NGOs. Many NGOs are active 'in the field', engaging in direct provision of services as well advocacy for human rights; humanitarian NGOs such as Médecins Sans Frontières and Oxfam, for example, 'provide immediate care to the world's worst-off people'.[28]

The humanitarian NGOs fill a 'vacuum left by nation-states in international relief and development work by both corporations and nation-states',[29] and their growth has been a phenomenon since the

---

24 See, eg, S Calnan, above, n 5, 6; see above, n 18.

25 S Rice & S Calnan, *Sustainable Advocacy: Capabilities and Attitudes of Australian Human Rights NGOs*, Australian Lawyers for Human Rights and Australian Human Rights Centre, Sydney, 2007, para 4.3.2.

26 C Bell & J Keenan, 'Human Rights Nongovernmental Organisations and the Problems of Transition' (2004) 26(2) *Human Rights Quarterly* 33, 336–7.

27 D A Bell & J H Carens, 'The Ethical Dilemmas of International Human Rights and Humanitarian NGOs: Reflections on a Dialogue Between Practitioners and Theorists' (2004) 26(2) *Human Rights Quarterly*, 300, 320–4.

28 Ibid 317. See also M Lindenberg & C Bryant, *Going Global: Transforming Relief and Development NGOs*, Kumarian Press, Bloomfield, 2001.

29 M Lindenberg & C Bryant, ibid 1.

1970s; the Organisation for Economic Cooperation and Development estimated that 'the number of Northern NGOs with international programs grew from 1600 in 1980 to more than 2500 in 1990'.[30]

Within this broad category of humanitarian NGOs, 'relief' NGOs 'frequently specialise in one or more of the five activities that are commonly understood to compose the relief discipline: food distribution, shelter, water, sanitation and medical care. To this may be added the rehabilitation efforts to bring a society traumatised by a complex emergency to minimum self-sufficiency: animal husbandry, agriculture and primary health care'.[31]

A 'new humanitarian discourse' has seen a shift in relief work to a more explicit commitment to 'development', where effort has been directed not only to meeting human needs but also to securing human rights.[32] Reflecting this broader agenda, development NGOs 'are focused on long-term economic and social development of developing countries, and want to attack the root problems of poverty rather than treat its symptoms'.[33]

SNAPSHOT: OXFAM AND THE SOLOMON ISLANDS[34]

As a humanitarian NGO, Oxfam's response to the 2007 tsunami in the Solomon Islands was to provide emergency shelter, water and sanitation. Similarly, when a tsunami and landslides destroyed homes and left people homeless in 2010, Oxfam supplied tarpaulins and rope for shelter.

Beyond humanitarian assistance, however, Oxfam has been enhancing the community's own capacity to deal with natural disasters. The flooding from tsunamis puts communities at risk of contracting diseases from dirty water, so Oxfam has provided health lessons to promote practices that guard against disease, such as washing hands, covering food, boiling water before drinking, and healthy toilet habits. And to protect the social and economic rights of people displaced by the tsunami Oxfam ran a program (funded by the Australian Government aid agency AusAid) to increase rights awareness, and to increase women's participation in decision-making on land rights issues.

Oxfam's work transitions from humanitarian to developmental when it runs leadership training for young people, provides domestic violence counselling and legal assistance for women, programs that challenge a culture of gender-based violence, and lobbies for legislative and policy responses to the risk of increasing HIV and AIDS infection rates among women and young people.

30 M Lindenberg, 'Declining State Capacity, Voluntarism, and the Globalization of the Not-for-Profit Sector', (1999) 28 (suppl 1) *Nonprofit and Voluntary Sector Quarterly*, 147, 148.

31 A Natsos, 'NGOs and the UN System in Complex Humanitarian Emergencies: Conflict or Cooperation?' (1995) 16(3) *Third World Quarterly* 405, 407.

32 D Chandler, 'The Road to Military Humanitarianism: How the Human Rights NGOs Shaped a New Humanitarian Agenda' (2001) 23(3) *Human Rights Quarterly* 678, 694. See also D A Bell & J H Carens, above, n 27, 317, n 42.

33 K Kennedy & D Dornan, 'An Overview: Tourism, Non-Governmental Organizations and Poverty Reduction in Developing Countries' (2009) 14(2) *Asia Pacific Journal of Tourism Research* 183, 185.

34 <http://www.oxfam.org.au/about-us/countries-where-we-work/solomon-islands>.

9.2.2 IGOs, NHRIs and CSOs

Intergovernmental organisations (IGOs) are not NGOs. Rather, they are organisations that comprise representatives of nation states, are active in establishing international law, policy and practice, and so are usually the focus of NGOs' activities.[35] The largest IGO is the United Nations. Many IGOs are within the UN system, such as the United Nations Educational, Scientific and Cultural Organization (UNESCO) and the United Nations Children's Fund (UNICEF), and many more are external to it, ranging from the Asia-Pacific Economic Cooperation Council (APEC) to the World Trade Organisation (WTO),[36] and many have a standing invitation to participate as observers in the sessions and the work of the UN General Assembly.[37]

Nor are National Human Rights Institutions (NHRIs) NGOs. NHRIs are expected to comply with the UN-promulgated 'Paris Principles',[38] a 1991 resolution of the UN Commission on Human Rights, which was then adopted by the UN General Assembly. The Principles require a state to ensure that its NHRI (such as the Australian Human Rights Commission) is autonomous, has its independence guaranteed by statute, has a broad mandate based on human rights standards, and has adequate powers and sufficient resources. There is no similar prescription for NGOs that, differently from NHRIs, operate independently of the state. Nevertheless, the activities of NGOs and NHRIs can be similar: 'both organizations conduct human rights education activities, public awareness campaigns, and oversee government performance in relation to human rights'.[39]

It is becoming increasingly hard to distinguish between the terms NGO and a more recent term, 'civil society organization', or 'CSO'. The term CSO has been described as 'somewhat unimaginative and verbose',[40] but also as a 'more inclusive' and 'broader notion' than NGO, extending to include 'local authorities, business companies and private organisations performing public functions'.[41] Despite increasing use of the term 'civil society organisation' the term 'NGO' is used widely and loosely; the UN consistently refers to NGOs in the context of 'civil society'.

---

35 For an extensive discussion of IGO/NGO relations, see A Lindblom, above, n 5, 366–486 & 487–509.

36 See R V Williams, *The Information Systems of International Inter-Governmental Organizations: A Reference Guide*, Ablex Publishing, Stamford, 1998.

37 *Intergovernmental Organizations having Received a Standing Invitation to Participate as Observers in the Sessions and the Work of the General Assembly and Maintaining Permanent Offices at Headquarters*, United Nations <http://www.un.org/en/members/intergovorg.shtml>.

38 *Principles Relating to the Status and Functioning of National Institutions for Protection and Promotion of Human Rights*, GA Res 48/134, UN GA, 48th sess, 85th plen mtg, UN Doc A/RES/48/134 (1993).

39 M Qafisheh, *Defining the Role of National Human Rights Institutions with Regard to the United Nations* (2004) Graduate Institute of International Studies, Legal Report Series (36) <http://www.miftah.org//Doc/Reports/2004/nhr35.pdf>.

40 See above, n 2, 251, citing J Habermas, *Between Facts and Norms: Contributions to a Discourse Theory of Law and Democracy*, Polity Press, Cambridge, 1996, 366–7 and M Nefin, 'Neither Prince nor Merchant: Citizen—An Introduction to the Third System' (1987) 1 *Development Dialogue*, 170, 173.

41 E Rebasti, see above, n 15, 21–70, 21, n 1.

9.2.3 A Brief History of NGOs

The contemporary idea of an NGO emerged during the nineteenth century. Such organisations were active internationally on issues such as slavery, peace, labour and oppressed minorities, and by the time of the League of Nations in 1919, they were firmly established as important participants in international affairs.[42] International NGOs, which engage with a number of states or with the international community of states, were formally recognised in 1923 when the they were defined in a draft treaty, the *Convention Relative à la Condition Juridique des Association Internationales* [Convention on the Legal Status of International Associations].[43]

Between 1945 and 1949, NGOs formalised their role, beginning with their participation in the San Francisco Conference and culminating in their formal though limited recognition in article 71 of the *UN Charter* discussed at Chapter 9.3.1 below. From 1950–1971, NGOs' effectiveness in the UN system was 'limited by Cold War politics and the institutional weakness of ECOSOC';[44] in Otto's view, 'Communist and Third World states adopted a general policy of opposition to NGOs, for different reasons, and the attitude of Western states was often characterized by prevarication and opportunism'.[45] The effects of Cold War politics 'devastated ECOSOC [and] the UN-NGO relationship deteriorated further'.[46]

From 1972 NGOs 'grew in number, size and diversity ... increas[ing] their impact, especially on the environment and human rights'.[47] Reimann offers a 'top-down' analysis of the growth in NGO numbers, saying that 'it is impossible to understand the explosive growth of NGOs in the past several decades without taking into account the ways in which states, international organizations, and other structures have actively stimulated and promoted NGOs from above ... grants and subsidies from the state, foundations, and other elite institutions have played an essential and critical role in the development of the non-profit and voluntary sector'.[48]

42 S Charnovitz, see above, n 11, 216–46.

43 S Charnovitz, see above, n 11, 188, citing J B Scott, 'The Institute of International Law' (1923) 17 *American Journal of International Law* 751, 753–6.

44 S Charnovitz, see above, n 11, 258.

45 D Otto, see above, n 12, 113 (citations omitted).

46 Ibid 113.

47 S Charnovitz, see above, n 11, 261.

48 K D Reimann, ' A View from the Top: International Politics, Norms and the Worldwide Growth of NGOs' (2006) 50(1) *International Studies Quarterly* 45, 55, citing J L Walker, *Mobilizing Interest Groups in America: Patrons, Professions, and Social Movements*, University of Michigan Press, Ann Arbor, 1991, T Skocpol, 'Advocates Without Members: The Recent Transformation of American Civic Life' in T Skocpol &M Fiorina (eds), *Civic Engagement in American Democracy*, Brookings Institution Press and Russell Sage Foundation, Washington, 1999, 461–505, N Berkovitch 'The Emergence and Transformation of the International Women's Movement' in J Boli & G Thomas (eds), *Constructing World Culture, International Nongovernmental Organizations since 1875*, Stanford University Press, Stanford, 1999, 100–26, and J W Meyer et al, 'The Structuring of a World Environmental Regime, 1870–1990' (1997) 51(4) *International Organization* 623.

9.2.1 NGOs' Functions and Activities

NGOs are now a legitimate and necessary part of international relations, and of the allocation, distribution and control of power in the world.[49] Former UN Secretary-General Boutros Boutros-Ghali took this view further, saying that the participation of NGOs 'is, in a way, a guarantee of the political legitimacy of those international organisations'.[50] This acknowledges the indirect effect of NGOs' activity and expertise as 'providing legitimacy for international civil servants and intergovernmental organisations ... [and] strategic value for [the] accrediting institutions'.[51]

Participants in international relations, such as NGOs, have particular activities and functions: *intelligence*—obtaining, processing and disseminating information; *promotion*—advocating policy; *prescription*—crystallising community expectations in policy; *invocation*—proposing the application of policy to specific circumstances; *application*—applying policy to specific circumstances; *termination*—ending a policy and managing the expectations created by it; and *appraisal*—evaluating policy.[52] These functions have been used as 'a useful framework' for 'understanding of what NGOs do'.[53]

Human rights NGOs in particular 'commonly identify their primary goals as monitoring and reporting of government behaviour on human rights, particularly violations, building pressure and creating international machinery to end the violations and to hold governments accountable ...'[54] The activities of monitoring, investigating and reporting on states, lobbying government and IGOs, mobilising interest groups, educating the public and representing clients, are 'characteristic' of human rights NGOs.[55] The mission of Amnesty International, for example, is 'to conduct research and generate action to prevent and end grave abuses of human rights and to demand justice for those whose rights have been violated',[56] and Human Rights Watch 'is dedicated to protecting the human rights of people

49 M S McDougal, H D Lasswell & W M Reisman, 'The World Constitutive Process of Authoritative Decision', (1967) 19(3) *Journal of Legal Education* 253 (Pt 1) and (1967) 19(4) *Journal of Legal Education* 403 (Pt 2). See also the discussion in S Charnovitz, 'Two Centuries of Participation: NGOs and International Governance' (1997) 18(2) *Michigan Journal of International Law* 183, 271–4 referring to the same article published in M S McDougal & W M Reisman (eds), *International Law Essays: A Supplement to International Law in Contemporary Practice*, The Foundation Press Inc, Mineola, 1981; B Cronin, 'The Two Faces of the United Nations: The Tension between Intergovernmentalism and Transnationalism' (2002) 8(1) *Global Governance* 53, 62.

50 N Götz, see above, n 2, 244, citing B Boutros-Ghali, 'Keynote Address to the 47th DPI/NGO Conference' (1995) 47(6) *Transnational Associations* 345, 345–9.

51 N Götz, see above, n 2, 244.

52 M S McDougal, H D Lasswell & W M Reisman, see above, n 49, 261 & 417–37.

53 S Charnovitz, see above, n 11, 271. See also C Lung-Chu, *An Introduction to Contemporary International Law*, Yale University Press, New Haven, 1989, 69–73.

54 F D Gaer, see above, n 5, 394–5.

55 H Steiner, see above, n 18, 1.

56 <www.amnesty.org/en/who-we-are/about-amnesty-international>.

around the world ... stand[ing] with victims and activists to prevent discrimination, to uphold political freedom, to protect people from inhumane conduct in wartime, and to bring offenders to justice ... investigat[ing] and expose human rights violations and hold abusers accountable ... challeng[ing] governments and those who hold power to end abusive practices and respect international human rights law'.[57] In Australia, the aims of the Human Rights Council of Australia include 'to promote a better understanding and the implementation of human rights' and 'to monitor and make public the performance of governments'.[58]

SNAPSHOT: AMNESTY INTERNATIONAL

CAMPAIGNING AGAINST THE DEATH PENALTY[59]

Amnesty International (AI) has been campaigning against the death penalty since 1977. Its members engage in demonstrations, vigils, and direct lobbying to governments and authorities about the cases of people facing execution. As well, AI collects data and publishes annual figures on the use of the death penalty, both to as a resource and to draw attention to the continuing practice of executions.

In 1977 only 16 countries had abolished the death penalty in law or in practice; in 2001 the number was 108 and in 2010 it was 139. Few of the 58 countries that retained the death penalty in 2010 actually use it.

Amnesty's grass-roots campaign complements the operation of the *Second Optional Protocol* to the *International Covenant on Civil and Political Rights* (ICCPR), and the view of the UN Human Rights Committee that the death penalty can violate article 6(1) of the ICCPR.

MONITORING STATES' CONDUCT

In 2000 AI published a report on Saudi Arabia that examined what it said was 'systematic violation of human rights that occurs in Saudi Arabia on a daily basis'.[60] Based on interviews of victims, the violations were said to include arbitrary arrest and detention, persecution of political opponents and religious minorities, torture and the death penalty. In light of this report, AI called on the UN Commission on Human Rights to adopt a resolution 'condemning gross and systematic human rights violations in Saudi Arabia' and to request Saudi Arabia to issue an invitation to the Special Rapporteur on the independence of judges and lawyers.

In response, The Gulf Cooperation Council Ministers issued a statement saying that 'Amnesty International has recently launched an unjustified campaign on Saudi Arabia, lacking in objectivity and neutrality, for its implementation of the just Islamic Sharia law'. The Ministers asked AI and other organisations 'to be more accurate and objective and to respect the beliefs and cultures of other nations'.[61]

Although the Commission did not condemn human rights violations in Saudi Arabia, it did renew the mandate of the Special Rapporteur on the independence of judges and lawyers. Saudi Arabia invited the

57 <www.hrw.org/en/about>.

58 <www.hrca.org.au>.

59 Amnesty International Ltd, London, *Death Sentences and Executions 2010*, March 2011.

60 Amnesty International, *Saudi Arabia: A Secret State of Suffering*, London, 2000.

61 'Gulf Ministers condemn Amnesty report on Saudi Arabian abuses', *The Birmingham Post*, 10 Apr 10, 2000, at <www.thefreelibrary.com>.

Special Rapporteur to visit, which he did in 2002, reporting that steps could be taken to improve judicial independence, prosecutors' impartiality, the legal profession's diversity, and the human rights compliance of the criminal justice system.[62]

A measure of the diversity of NGOs' activities is the many acronyms that are built on the three-letter base 'NGO' (eg BONGO, QUANGO, GRINGO etc[63]) that provide 'a good impression of conflict and demarcation within the sphere of NGOs [and] of different paradoxes and types of non-governmental organizations'.[64]

NGOs often distinguish their work along the lines of 'civil and political rights' on the one hand and 'economic, social and cultural rights' on the other. Western or 'First World' NGOs have usually concentrated more on 'civil and political rights, a commitment to fair (due) process, an individualistic rather than group or community orientation in rights advocacy, and a belief in a pluralist society functioning within a framework of rules impartially applied to protect individuals against state interference'.[65] By way of contrast, Third World NGOs[66] commonly stress 'the importance of economic-social rights [and] ... transformative goals for society'.[67] They are likely to see human rights issues from a perspective that is different from that of First World NGOs, identifying, for example, 'the underlying human rights problem [in the Third World] as one of North-South economic relations'.[68]

In their work in the front line of human need and human rights violations, NGOs' physical proximity to conflicts and disasters expose them to political engagement: '[t]he relationship between NGOs, those they are supposed to be helping, and other actors can be very complicated and morally

62 Special Rapporteur on the Independence of Judges and Lawyers, *Report on the Mission to the Kingdom of Saudi Arabia*, E/CN.4/2003/65/Add.3, 14 January 2003.

63 BONGO = business-organised NGO; QUANGO = quasi-NGO; GRINGO = government operated NGO: see above, n 2, 231–2 citing variously, C F Alger, 'Strengthening Relations between NGOs and the UN System: Toward a Research Agenda' (1999) 13(4) *Global Society* 393, M B Ginsburg, 'NGOs: What's in an Acronym?' (1998/99) 1(1) *Current Issues in Comparative Education* 29, O D Ikeorha, *NGOs in the Twenty-First Century*, Network Publishers, Kaduna, 2005, J Keane, *Global Civil Society?*, Cambridge University Press, Cambridge, 2003 and D Otto, see above, n 12.

64 N Götz, see above, n 2, 233.

65 H Steiner, see above, n 18, 19. On 'First World NGOs' and advocacy for economic social and cultural rights, see K Roth, 'Defending Economic Social and Cultural Rights: Practical Issues Faced by an International Human Rights Organisation' (2004) 26(1) *Human Rights Quarterly* 63.

66 Third World NGOs typically operate within their Third World countries of formation because few INGOs originate outside the First World: see above, n 18, 28–9.

67 H Steiner, see above, n 18, 29.

68 H Steiner, see above, n 18, 29.

ambiguous,'[69] challenging their claims to being impartial and neutral.[70] NGOs' determined effort to preserve neutrality can mean 'tolerating, or refraining from criticising, evil actions',[71] or even making things worse,[72] leading to the question: 'why not drop the aspiration of political neutrality and devote one's efforts entirely to addressing the political and economic causes of poverty and suffering?'[73]

SNAPSHOT: THE INTERNATIONAL COMMITTEE OF THE RED CROSS

The experience of the International Committee of the Red Cross (ICRC) illustrates the tension between maintaining neutrality and exposing human rights violations.

The ICRC is very protective of its neutrality, and was embarrassed by the leaking in 2009 of a 2007 ICRC report on the torture of detainees in Guantanamo Bay. The report documented specific instances of torture, and the participation—passive and active—of health personnel in that conduct.

The ICRC had decided to not reveal what it knew, saying 'it is important for us to be able to discuss matters confidentially with governments, which gives us the credibility to influence them'.[74]

Five years before, it was reported that a similar leak had provoked 'a stormy debate' within the Red Cross, with some officials arguing that it should publish its concerns; one official said 'It's a daily dilemma for us to put in the balance the positive effects our visits have for detainees against the confidentiality'.[75]

9.3 NGOS AT THE UN

9.3.1 Article 71 of the *UN Charter*

As participants in the San Francisco Conference,[76] NGOs were instrumental in the drafting of article 71 of the *UN Charter*, which reads:

> The [UN] Economic and Social Council [ECOSOC] may make suitable arrangements for consultation with non-governmental organisations which are concerned with matters within its competence. Such arrangements may be made with international organisations and, where appropriate, with national organisations after consultation with the Member of the United Nations concerned.

69 K Mills, 'Neo-Humanitarianism: The Role of International Humanitarian Norms and Organisation in Contemporary Conflict' (2005) 11 *Global Governance* 161, 174.

70 See K Anderson, 'Humanitarian Inviolability in Crisis: The Meaning of Impartiality and Neutrality for UN and NGO Agencies Following the 2003–2004 Afghanistan and Iran Conflicts' (2004) 17 *Harvard Human Rights Journal* 41.

71 D A Bell & J H Carens, see above, n 27, 317.

72 D A Bell & J H Carens, see above, n 27, 318.

73 D A Bell & J H Carens, see above, n 27, 319.

74 M Tran, 'Leaked ICRC Report Claims Medical Staff Monitored Terror Suspects During Waterboarding', *The Guardian*, 7 April 2009, <www.guardian.co.uk>.

75 N Lewis, 'Red Cross Finds Detainee Abuse in Guantánamo', *New York Times*, 30 November, 2004, <www.nytimes.com>.

76 See Chapter 1.2.2.

Article 71 was a significant development in NGO-state relations, and in the international standing and involvement of NGOs. Prior to this, NGOs' established role as important—and often leading—participants in international affairs had had little formal recognition; the Covenant of the League of Nations in 1919, for example, did not recognise the role of NGOs in international relations even though they worked closely and cooperatively with the League and member states and on their own account.[77] A significant exception was and remains the recognition of NGOs in the 1919 constitution of the International Labour Organisation, under which employer and worker delegates are chosen by governments through agreement with industrial organisations.[78]

Article 71 gives recognition to NGOs in the UN Charter, but '[n]ot everyone viewed Article 71 as a step forward for NGOs', principally because the recognition is limited to ECOSOC matters, and does not extend to the wide range of issues addressed by NGOs.[79] Article 71 'codif[ied] the custom of NGO participation', affording opportunities that were 'no better than those afforded to NGOS in the early years of the League [of Nations]'.[80]

To give effect to article 71, ECOSOC defined an NGO as 'any international organisation which is not established by intergovernmental agreement',[81] a definition that excluded national NGOs. A national NGO could do not be given consultative status without the approval of their government,[82] a limitation that was set aside in 1996 when sub-regional, regional, national and international NGOs were allowed to apply for ECOSOC consultative status. Differently from the practice under the League of Nations, ECOSOC excludes NGOs from its subsidiary commissions, limiting membership to state representatives, a 'guarded state-centric' approach that 'reflects a continuing and pervasive tension in UN arrangements for cooperation between states and NGOs'.[83]

9.3.2 NGO Consultative Status Under ECOSOC

NGOs had been granted consultative status by the Economic and Social Council (ECOSOC) as early as in 1948, and the first set of rules on this relationship was adopted in 1950.[84] The adverse effect of Cold War politics on the UN-NGO relationship precipitated an ECOSOC review of NGO consultative arrangements,

77 S Charnovitz, see above, n 11, 220–46.

78 International Labour Organisation Constitution, art 3.5, discussed in S Charnovitz, see above, n 11, 216.

79 S Charnovitz, see above, n 11, 250.

80 S Charnovitz, see above, n 11, 258.

81 S Charnovitz, see above, n 11, 252, citing ESC Res. 1/4, Feb 16, 1946 [8].

82 S Charnovitz, see above, n 11, 253 citing *Commentary on Article 71 of the Charter of the United Nations*, Union of International Associations, Brussels, 1956, 11.

83 D Otto, See above, n 12, 110 citing D O'Donovan, 'The Economic and Social Council' in P Alston (ed), *The United Nations and Human Rights: A Critical Appraisal*, Clarendon Press, Oxford, 1992, 107–25, 110.

84 ECOSOC Resolution 288 B(X), 27 February 1950.

resulting in Resolution 1296.[85] After a further review by an ECOSOC Working Group, arrangements were updated by ECOSOC Resolution 1996/31,[86] which is the current basis for partnership between NGOs and the United Nations, although the UN Secretary-General has since elaborated on arrangements and practices for NGOs.[87] Resolution 1996/31 aspires to the 'just, balanced, effective and genuine involvement of non-governmental organisations from all regions and areas of the world'.[88] But it was arrived at only after the usual diplomatic negotiations, meaning that its final form is a compromise: its 'ambiguous language ... reflects the disagreement among UN member states on how wide the door shall stand open for non-state actors. The political compromise ... after several years of debate merely postponed further controversy ...'[89]

The ECOSOC Committee on Non-Governmental Organisations ('NGO Committee') is 'responsible for monitoring the relationship between NGOs and the UN'.[90] Its 19 elected members have equitable geographical representation: five members from African states; four members from Asian states; two members from Eastern European states; four members from Latin American and Caribbean states, and four members from Western European and other states.

The NGO Committee considers and recommends NGOs' applications for consultative status under article 71, considers quadrennial reports submitted by NGOs, implements the provisions of Council resolution 1996/31, and monitors the consultative relationship.[91] For purposes of considering applications for consultative status, Resolution 1996/31 does not define an NGO, but sets out eligibility criteria:

> The aims of the organisation must be concerned with matters falling within the competence of ECOSOC and its subsidiary bodies and must be able to demonstrate that its programme of work is of direct relevance to

85 ECOSOC Resolution 1296, 44th sess, UN Document E/4548, 23 May 1968. See also D Otto, above, n 12, 110–11.

86 *Consultative Relationship Between the United Nations and Non-Governmental Organizations*, UN ESCOR, 51st sess, 49th plen mtg, ESC Res 1996/31, pt II, UN Doc E/1996/L.25 (1996).

87 See *Report of the Secretary-General, Arrangements and Practices for the Interaction of Non-Governmental Organizations in All Activities of the United Nations System*, UN GA, 53rd sess, UN Doc A/53/170 (1998); *Report of the Secretary-General: Views of Member States, Members of the Specialized Agencies, Observers, Intergovernmental and Non-Governmental Organizations from all Regions on the Report of the Secretary-General on Arrangements and Practices for the Interaction of Non-Governmental Organizations in all Activities of the United Nations System*, UN Doc A/54/329 (1999); Office of the President of the Millennium Assembly—55th session of the UN General Assembly, *Reference Document on the Participation of Civil Society in United Nations Conferences and Special Sessions of the General Assembly during the 1990s* (Version 1, August 2001) <http://www.un.org/ga/president/55/speech/civilsociety1.htm>.

88 See above, n 86.

89 J D Aston, 'The United Nations Committee on Non-Governmental Organisations: Guarding the Entrance to a Politically Divided House' (2001) 12(5) *European Journal of International Law* 943, 946.

90 Office of the President of the Millenium Assembly, see above, n 87.

91 Committee on Non-Governmental Organisations <www.un.org/esa/coordination/ngo/committee.htm>.

> and can contribute to the aims and purposes of the UN. The aims and purposes of the organisation must be in conformity with the spirit, purposes and principles of the [UN] Charter. The organisation must be of recognised standing within its field of competence and must have an established headquarters, with an executive officer. Furthermore the organisation must have a democratically adopted constitution, a representative and accountable inner structure and the authority to speak for its members. As regards the funding of the organisation, the basic resources must be derived from either national affiliates or other components or from individual members. Lastly, the organisation must attest that it has been in existence for at least two years at the date of receipt of its application.[92]

Resolution 1996/31 identifies 'three different types of consultative status [for NGOs], depending on the level of participation. 'General Status' accords 'rights and privileges [which] are the most far-reaching of the three categories.'[93] It applies to large international NGOs whose interests cover most of ECOSOC's agenda, requiring them to provide a quadrennial report and allowing them to speak before delegates, circulate statements up to 2000 words long, and place items on the agenda. 'Special Status' concerns NGOs with 'special competence in some fields of activity of the Council'; they must provide a quadrennial report, and may make written statements of up to 500 words but cannot place items on the agenda. 'Roster NGOs' are those addressing one or more specific issues; they may 'attend meetings, but cannot speak or circulate statements'.[94] The category of Roster NGOs is a loose one, because '[m]any NGOs are on the Roster not because they have fulfilled ECOSOC requirements, but by virtue of their status with specialised agencies and other UN bodies ... the criteria for establishing consultative relationships vary considerably with respect to the different UN bodies'.[95]

These three levels of participation have been in place, under different names, since the ECOSOC first established procedures under article 71. The levels are problematic: the criteria for categorisation are vague, the significance of the categorisations is debatable, the categories discriminate between 'haves' and 'have nots', and seeking categorisation has a potentially pacifying and acquiescing effect on NGOs.[96] At the same time, 'NGOs gain prestige in politics and before the larger public by being able to cite a consultative relationship with the United Nations [and] in this capacity they wield a certain potential to influence multilateral processes'.[97]

---

92 J D Aston, 'The United Nations Committee on Non-Governmental Organisations: Guarding the Entrance to a Politically Divided House' (2001) 12(5) *European Journal of International Law* 943, 947, citing various paragraphs of the 1996/31.

93 Ibid.

94 Economic and Social Council (ECOSOC), UN Non-Government Liaison Service <http://www.un-ngls.org/spip.php?page=article_s&id_article=799>.

95 See above, n 92, 48.

96 N Götz, see above, n 2, 243, citing B Dunér, 'The Fight for Greater NGO Participation in the UN (1997) 28(3) *Security Dialogue* 301, 310, P Willetts, 'Consultative Status for NGOs at the United Nations' in P Willetts (ed), *'The Conscience of the World': The Influence of Non-Governmental Organisations in the UN System*, Hurst, London, 1996, 31–62 and P Ghils, 'International Civil Society: International Non-Governmental Organizations in the International System' (1992) 44 *International Social Science Journal* 417.

97 N Götz, see above, n 2, 243, citing J J Shestack, 'Sisyphus Endures: The International Human Rights NGO' (1978) 24(1) *New York Law School Law Review*, 89, 99 & 116–17 and J Boli & G M Thomas 'INGOs and the Organization of World Culture, in J Boli & G M Thomas (eds), *Constructing World Culture: International Nongovernmental Organizations Since 1875*, Stanford University Press, Stanford, 1999, 13–29, 30.

As of 1 September 2010 there were 139 NGOs in general consultative status, 2218 in special consultative status and 1025 on the Roster.[98] That is a significant number of organisations making their way around the UN corridors in Geneva and New York; the absence of a definition of an NGO, combined with 'a dramatic increase in the number of applications', may have led the NGO Committee to grant consultative status to 'too many organisations'.[99] It is not only the number of accredited NGOs that is cause for concern, but also the bias in the type of organisations that are accredited. Under Resolution 1996/31, sub-regional, regional, national and international NGOs can apply for ECOSOC consultative status only with the support of their state, which means that at least some states grant access only to what de Frouville calls 'servile' NGOs,[100] a problem compounded by 'the inability of the NGO Committee to make objective decisions and its tendency instead to 'be hostage of its members own interests'.[101] Alston points out a further consideration that affects the range of NGOs that achieve consultative status: 'those states that are frequently targeted by human rights NGOs are by the same token those states that decide on what NGO shall be granted consultative status'.[102]

Many of the 'rights' granted by ECOSOC consultative status 'are, in practice, less useful than they might at first appear. The right to make oral statements at the [then] United Nations Commission on Human Rights, for example, is often rendered virtually useless because of the fact that the debate is so crowded, with so many governments and NGOs wanting to speak, that NGOs are frequently allotted the least popular time, late at night, when there are few government delegates to hear or respond to them'.[103] In fact NGOs 'do not need consultative status to participate in many ... human rights activities of the United Nations. They may, for example, submit information to various thematic rapporteurs and treaty monitoring bodies, have been able to participate, to some extent, in major events such as the Vienna Conference on Human Rights and the Rio Conference on the Environment and Development',[104] and can be accredited with the UN Department of Public Information under accreditation criteria that are less restrictive than those for ECOSOC.[105]

98 UN Economic and Social Council, *List of Non-Governmental Organizations in Consultative Status with the Economic and Social Council as of 1 September 2010*, UN Doc E/2010/INF/4 (2010); as at 31 July 2011 DESA reported that it supported '13,400 non-govermental organizations' in consultative status with ECOSOC'; see Chapter 9.3.4 below.

99 See above, n 92, 951 (citations omitted).

100 O de Frouville, 'Domesticating Civil Society at the United Nations' in P Dupuy & L Vierucci (eds), see above, n 9, 71–115. See also K Martens, 'Examining the (Non-)Status of NGOs in International Law' (2003) 10(2) *Indiana Global Legal Studies Journal* 1, 8.

101 O de Frouville, ibid.

102 See above, n 92, 949–50.

103 M H Posner & C Whittone, see above, n 20, 286.

104 M H Posner & C Whittone, see above, n 20, 287.

105 <http://www.un.org/wcm/content/site/dpingorelations/criteria>.

9.3.3 UN Observer Status

Apart from the usual three levels of NGO participation, six organisations have been granted, outside the ECOSOC procedures, 'Observer status' for the sessions and the work of the UN General Assembly: the International Committee of the Red Cross,[106] the International Federation of Red Cross and Red Crescent Societies (IFRC),[107] the Inter-Parliamentary Union,[108] the International Criminal Court,[109] the International Olympic Committee,[110] and the Sovereign Military Hospitaller Order of St John of Jerusalem of Rhodes and of Malta (the Sovereign Order of Malta).[111] These organisations are a mix of NGOs and IGOs, although they see their Observer status as distinguishing them from NGOs that have the usual levels of ECOSOC consultative status.[112]

9.3.4 NGO Relations with the UN

A number of UN-related agencies support NGO/UN relations: the UN-sponsored NGO Informal Regional Network (UN-NGO-IRENE),[113] the integrated Civil Society Organizations (iCSO) System,[114] which facilitates interactions between NGOs the UN Department of Economic and Social Affairs (DESA); DESA's web portal Civil Society Network (CSO Net);[115] the semi-autonomous United Nations Non-Governmental Liaison Service (UN-NGLS);[116] and the UNDPI website, which is operated by NGOs associated with the United Nations' Department of Public Information.

Independently of the UN, CoNGO—the Conference of NGOs in Consultative Relationship with the United Nations[117]—describes itself as 'an independent, international, non-profit membership association

106 *Observer Status for the International Committee of the Red Cross, in Consideration of the Special Role and Mandates Conferred Upon It by the Geneva Conventions of 12 August 1949*, GA Res 45/6, UN GA, 45th sess, 31st plen mtg, UN Doc A/RES/45/6 (1990).

107 *Observer Status for the International Federation of Red Cross and Red Crescent Societies in the General Assembly*, GA Res 49/2, UN GA, 49th sess, 38th plen mtg, UN Doc A/RES/49/2 (1994).

108 *Observer Status for the Inter-Parliamentary Union in the General Assembly*, GA Res 57/32, UN GA 57th sess, 52nd plen mtg, UN Doc A/RES/57/32 (2002).

109 *Cooperation Between the United Nations and the International Criminal Court*, GA Res 58/318, UN GA, 58th sess, 95th plen mtg, UN Doc A/RES/58/318 (2004).

110 *Observer Status for the International Olympic Committeee in the General Assembly*, GA Res 64/5, UN GA, 64th sess, 21st plen mtg, UN Doc A/RES/64/3 (2009).

111 *Observer Status for the Sovereign Military Order on Malta in the General Assembly*, GA Res 48/265, UN GA, 60th sess, 103rd plen mtg, UN Doc A/Res/48/265 (1994).

112 See C Lamb, 'Observers at the United Nations General Assembly—IFRC Experience' (speech delivered at UN-IOC Forum on Sport for Development, Lausanne, 20 May 2010).

113 UN Public Administration Programme, Division for Public Administration and Development Management, UN Department of Economic and Social Affairs <http://www.unpan.org/NGO.asp>.

114 Integrated Civil Society Organizations System, NGO Branch, UN Department of Economics and Social Affairs <http://esango.un.org/civilsociety/>.

115 NGO Branch, UN Department of Economics and Social Affairs <http://esango.un.org/>.

116 UN Non-Government Liason Service <http://www.un-ngls.org>.

117 The Conference of Non-Governmental Organizations in Consultative Relationship with the United Nations <http://www.ngocongo.org/index.php?what=about>.

of non-governmental organizations [which] facilitates the participation of NGOs in United Nations debates and decision-making',[118] although Franda describes it as an effort by NGOs 'to bolster their privileges and influence'.[119] The World Association of Non-Governmental Organizations (WANGO)[120] is an international organisation that supports NGO members 'to advance peace and global well being', and has affiliates such as governmental and intergovernmental bodies, business, and universities.[121]

In 2004 a 'panel of eminent persons', whose task was to 'review the relationship between the United Nations and civil society'[122] reported to the UN Secretary-General. The Secretary-General was complimentary in his formal response to what became known as the Cardoso Report,[123] although the report has been strongly criticised,[124] and parts of it were queried or rejected, such as the proposal to establish a single system of NGO accreditation for all UN intergovernmental bodies.[125]

9.4 NGOS AND NATION STATES

As 'non'-governmental organisations, NGOs have a different perspective, or advocate a different approach, from that of the state: 'governments and NGOs have different but complementary roles. The special capacity for witnessing and advocacy which rests with NGOs cannot easily be replicated by government'.[126]

---

118 About CoNGO, the Conference of Non-Governmental Organizations in Consultative Relationship with the United Nations <http://www.ngocongo.org/index.php?what=about>.

119 M F Franda, *The United Nations in the Twenty-First Century: Management and Reform Processes in a Troubled Organization*, Rowman & Littlefield, Lanham, 2006, 10.

120 World Association of Non-Governmental Organisations <www.wango.org/about.aspx>.

121 Ibid.

122 Panel of Eminent Persons on United Nations—Civil Society Relations, Transmittal Letter Dated 7 June 2004 from the Chair of the Panel of Eminent Persons on United Nations–Civil Society Relations Addressed to the Secretary-General ('the Cardoso Report'), UN GA, 58th sess, UN Doc A/58/817 (2004). See also *Report of the Secretary General: Arrangements and Practices for the Interaction of Non-Governmental Organizations in All Activities of the United Nations System*, UN GA, 53rd sess, UN Doc A/53/170 (1998); *Report of the Secretary-General: Views of Member States, Members of the Specialized Agencies, Observers, Intergovernmental and Non-Governmental Organizations from All Regions on the Report of the Secretary-General on Arrangements and Practices for the Interaction of Non-Governmental Organizations in All Activities of the United Nations System*, UN Doc A/54/329 (1999); B Sadoun 'UN Conferences on the Spot—Voices from Civil Society: Whispering, Talking and Shouting Out' in V Katrandjiev (ed), *Multistakeholder Diplomacy: Challenges and Opportunities*, Diplo Foundation, Geneva, 2006, 69–83.

123 *Report of the Secretary-General in Response to the Report of the Panel of Eminent Persons on United Nations–Civil Society Relations*, UN GA, 59th sess, UN Doc A/59/354 (2004).

124 See P Willetts, 'The Cardoso Report on the UN and Civil Society: Functionalism, Global Corporatism, or Global Democracy?' (2006) 12(3) *Global Governance: A Review of Multilateralism and International Organizations* 305.

125 See above, n 123, para B27, UN Doc A/59/354 (2004); for a strong critique of the Cardoso Report, see ibid.

126 A Downer, 'Strengthening Australia's Human Rights Credentials' (speech delieved to a Forum on Australia's Human Rights Obligations for Human Rights Day, Canberra, 10 December 1996).

The respective roles can be seen as complementary, although there is a tension that can be seen as part of a debate about the scope and adequacy of democracy, both within a state and internationally: '[m]any politicians resent an alternative voice from their country, challenging their policies in diplomatic forums', even though '[i]n a democratic world, intergovernmental organisations have to be transparent and open to public debate, articulated by NGOs'.[127] In 2004 the International Council on Human Rights Policy (ICHRP) reported that 'human rights NGOs have begun to reposition themselves in relation to the state ... various forms of co-operation have emerged between civil society and government in recent years, particularly in countries where governments have formally integrated human rights principles into their domestic law, and their domestic and international policies'.[128]

The idea of NGO-state cooperation is different from the activities of a 'servile' NGO (or 'GONGO'—government-organised NGO), which 'systematically adopts a laudatory view of its own government, or which never criticises it'.[129] But even genuinely independent NGOs risk losing their non-governmental perspective when cooperating with government, having to 'remain vigilant and identify violations by official institutions even while co-operating with them to improve their capacity'.[130]

9.4.1 Criticisms

The increasingly large and influential presence of NGOs in the UN has raised important issues of identity and accountability[131] that, although arising in that context, are indicative of issues that NGOs are facing around the world.

There has been a longstanding resentment by governments concerning the role of NGOs in the UN,[132] a 'feeling that NGOs are getting away with too much, making too much of a splash, causing too much heartache', and 'have grown far too big for their Doc Martens'.[133] It is possible to suggest a 'strong ideological undercurrent'[134] to these attacks when it is remembered that 'the really serious problems of organisational accountability exist elsewhere, in business and government ... corporations, government and intergovernmental bodies are much more powerful than NGOs, and affect many more people'.[135]

The type of 'accountability' NGOs are said to lack is the type of accountability that elected representatives have to a constituency, but to expect this of NGOs arguably misunderstands—perhaps

127 P Willetts, 'Civil Society Networks in Global Governance: Remedying the World Trade Organisation's Deviance from Global Norms', in P Griffith & J Thurston (eds), *Free and Fair: Making the Progressive Case for Removing Trade Barriers*, The Foreign Policy Centre, London, 2004, 131–40, 132–3.

128 *Enhancing Access to Human Rights*, International Council on Human Rights Policy, Versoix, 2004, 44.

129 O de Frouville, 'Domesticating Civil Society at the United Nations', in P Dupuy & L Vierucci (ed), *NGOs in International Law: Efficiency in Flexibility?*, Edward Elgar Publishing, Cheltenham, 2008, 71–115, 73–81.

130 See above, n 128, 45.

131 J Bendell, *Debating NGO Accountability*, UN Non-Governmental Liaison Service (UN-NGLS), Geneva, 2006, 48.

132 F D Gaer, see above, n 5, 402–3.

133 M Mowbray, 'War on Non-Profits: NGOs: What Do We Do About Them?' (2003) 30 *Just Policy* 3, 3.

134 J Butcher, *Government, the Third Sector and the Rise of Social Capital*, Centre for Research in Public Sector Management, Canberra, 2005, 10.

135 See above, n 131, 75.

wilfully—the role that NGOs play in democracy,[136] where they are a voice in public policy debate, perhaps representing ideas and values rather than identifiable 'constituencies'. Nevertheless, human rights NGOs do run the risk of losing touch—or of being seen to have lost touch—with the experiences of those whose rights they advocate;[137] a degree of openness about their processes can help alleviate these apprehensions, or perhaps usefully illustrate there is some truth to them.

NGOs are commonly criticised for lacking transparency in their operations and, most particularly, their funding. To the extent that NGOs do claim to represent a constituency of interests—such as the poor, the homeless, workers, women, etc—a measure of the legitimacy of that claim is the extent to which they succeed in raising funds for that purpose.[138] While this type of disclosure may allay concerns about the 'real' purpose of NGOs' activity, there is a principled argument for it: it is the same type of conduct that NGOs commonly demand from government, public officials, and corporations,[139] and reforms in structure and governance may be necessary to harmonise 'praxis and culture'.[140]

NGOs make the point that they do not operate out of self-interest or for profit, and represent ideals of human rights and social justice that are marginalised by states[141] and that want for sustained advocacy.[142] Even so, it is hard for them to wield the influence they do without at the same time being at least as open about their operations as other private entities have to be. There is a risk that restructuring and internal governance reforms of NGOs could undermine their 'useful and largely accepted role in holding business and government accountable for their actions,'[143] but that risk seems to be a reason for NGOs to be careful in how they go about ensuring their accountability,[144] not a reason to not volunteer some acceptable degree of openness.

136 J Staples, 'NGOs Out in the Cold: The Howard Government Policy Towards NGOs', Discussion Paper 19/06, Democratic Audit, 2006, 6–7; see above, n 131, p 40, citing M Edwards. 'NGO Legitimacy—Voice or Vote', BOND, February 2003, 1.

137 See above, n 128, 45. See also G Johns & J Roskam, above, n 21.

138 *Investing in Ourselves: Giving and Fund Raising in the Philippines*, Venture for Fund Raising Foundation, Pasig City, 2001, 2.

139 Ibid 2.

140 C Frangonikolopoulos, 'Non-Governmental Organisations and Humanitarian Action: The Need for a Viable Change of Praxis and Ethos', (2005) 19(1) *Global Society* 49.

141 See R Archer, *Deserving Trust: Issues of Accountability for Human Rights NGOs: Draft Report for Consultation*, International Council on Human Rights Policy, Versoix, 2003.

142 See generally H Steiner & P Alston, *International Human Rights in Context: Law, Politics, Morals*, 2nd edn, Oxford University Press, 2000, Ch 11; H Steiner, P Alston & R Goodman, *International Human Rights in Context: Law, Politics, Morals*, 3rd edn, Oxford University Press, 2008, 1420–32; R Archer, ibid.

143 Tony Hill, 'Preface' in J Bendall, *Debating NGO Accountability*, UN Non-Governmental Liaison Service Development Dossier, New York and Geneva, 2006, vii–viii.

144 See eg 'International Guidance Standard on Social Responsibility, ISO 26000', <www.iso.org/iso/iso_catalogue/management_and_leadership_standards/social_responsibility/sr_iso26000_overview.htm>.

9.4.2 Silencing NGOs

Despite the possibility of genuine cooperation, '[s]ome governments ... perceive 'non-governmental' organisations to be 'anti-government' organisations that are a threat to security and stability'. This inevitably puts NGOs who engage in advocacy in conflict with states, and the response of states may be to classify NGOs as service providers, and so more readily accuse them of exceeding their mandate, or to characterise them as effectively a political opposition.[145]

While conflict with NGOs may be a reason for a state to establish servile GONGOs, it may also lead to a state's taking active measures to constrain NGOs: 'NGOs routinely face government-created obstacles to their efforts to operate freely, including restrictions on their rights to raise funds from abroad, on their ability to disseminate materials freely and on their ability to gain permission to operate as a legal entity'.[146]

As Posner and Whittone point out, '[e]ven a government that is publicly committed to allowing NGOs to operate freely may react with hostility when national NGOs draw attention to their abuses of human rights.'[147]

SNAPSHOT: SILENCING NGO DISSENT IN AUSTRALIA[148]

A survey of non-governmental advocacy in Australia, between 1996 and 2004 under the then conservative federal government in Australia, concluded that the government and like-minded commentators had deliberately targeted the non-government sector to silence its dissent.

In 2004 the Australia Institute conducted a survey of Australian NGOs that include some advocacy in their role, asking for their perceptions of Government attitudes to debate, and whether they believed that dissenting views were welcomed or discouraged. The respondents reported a perception that governments subdue their often-critical voices through bullying, harassment, intimidation, public denigration and the threatened withdrawal of funding.

They reported on what they felt was implicit pressure to censor themselves, saying that '[w]hile not openly stated, it has been unequivocally conveyed [by government] that 'we do not fund organisations to criticise us'. The perception is that you toe the line or you risk getting defunded'. Most NGOs believed that they were being pressured to conform with Government policy, by public criticism, ministerial interference, excessive auditing, and threats of defunding.

In 2003 the federal Government commissioned the Institute of Public Affairs (IPA) to audit how NGOs relate to government departments. The IPA recommended limiting the 'privileged' access and funding that

145 P van Tuijl, 'NGOs and Human Rights: Sources of Justice and Democracry' (1999) 52(2) *Journal of International Affairs* 493.

146 M H Posner & C Whittone, see above, n 20, 273–4.

147 M H Posner & C Whittone, see above, n 20, 273–4.

148 C Hamilton & S Maddison 'Non-Government Organisations' in C Hamilton & S Maddison (eds), *Silencing Dissent: How the Australian Government is Controlling Public Opinion and Stifling Debate*, Allen & Unwin, Crows Nest, 2007, Ch 5.

NGOs have, and that there be a protocol for increasing scrutiny of the relationships between NGOs and government. No such proposal were made in relation to, for example, for-profit organisations and their dealings with government.

It is both understandable that the government would want to ensure public accountability for NGO activity, and concerning that the government would take that opportunity to constrain their ability to engage in public debate.

SNAPSHOT: MANAGING NGOS IN CAMBODIA[149]

Since 2008 the Cambodian Government has proposed what has since been called a 'Law on Non-Government Organizations' which will require the country's more than 3000 associations and NGOs to complete a complex registration process and submit to stringent financial reporting requirements. The law is said by the Government to prevent extremist activity and to ensure transparency. Although it applies to all NGOs, it is aimed principally at international NGOs, which Hun Sen said 'are out of control … they insult the government just to ensure their financial survival'.

The government of Hun Sen has had a difficult relationship with international NGOs, upset by accusations from the INGO Global Witness of government links to illegal logging, and by criticism from Amnesty International of state-sponsored forced evictions. Many fear the discretionary powers that the 'Law on Organizations' will give the government monitoring and sanctioning NGOs.

Local Cambodian NGOs are concerned the law could be used to restrict freedom of speech, assembly and association, and will make it difficult to organise small community groups into associations. Similarly, international NGOs are concerned that the law will hinder their work and limit progress to an open society. A senior US human rights official has visited Cambodia to make representations opposing the law.

But there are in fact problems with international NGOs in Cambodia. Their workers have a poor image, partly because of their comparatively high salaries and lifestyles, and some are accused of impeding the development of a self-sustaining private sector, mainly through the alleged abuse of their not-for-profit status to pursue business opportunities. The World Bank has said that international aid is often poorly managed, with the problem of 'fragmented' assistance especially acute in health and education. In the health sector in 2008, for example, 22 donors were working with over 100 NGOs to deliver $110 million a year in aid per through 109 projects, but use of the national health system remained at under 18 percent.

The Cambodian Government intends to pass the draft Law on Non-Government Organizations into law in 2011, but faces strong pressure from the US and NGOs to reduce the proposed level of regulation.

The Cambodian experience illustrates a further criticism of international NGOs that are funded and headquartered in the West. They are often criticised for imposing their own interests in local environments,

149 C Guthrie, 'The end of an NGO era in Cambodia', *Asia Times Online*, 14 November 2008, <www.atimes.com>; <www.sithi.org>; <www.ccc-cambodia.org>; <www.voanews.com>.

and for influencing local culture, economics and politics.[150] The perception is not helped by the fact that Western NGOs rarely include representatives of developing countries in their management, and fail to value local experience, local perspectives and differences in history.[151]

9.4.3 NGO–State Relations in Australia

NGOs have a long and valued history in Australia, as providers of social and humanitarian services, and as advocates for constituencies and values. The standing that NGOs have in Australia, and the extent to which they are supported and even relied on by government, even when they criticise and campaign against government policy, reflects very favourably on the strength of Australian democracy.[152] When, for example, Australia reported to the United Nations in 2010 under the Universal Period Review,[153] it made a virtue of its having 'engaged extensively with civil society to prepare Australia's National Report', citing its reliance on an NGO workshop and government-hosted NGO forums on human rights.[154] Australia's report recognised that 'NGOs ... play important roles in promoting and protecting human rights in Australia'.[155]

There has, however, been a shift in NGO–state relations in Australia since the relationship has become more commonly a funded contractual one, in Australia as much as elsewhere. As a result of this new relationship, the state has been able to impose conditions on NGOs' activities; conditions imposed on the Australian Government's funding contract with the Australian Council of Social Service (ACOSS), for example, included ACOSS's having to give 24 hours' notice of any media release and two weeks' notice of submissions, and having to accept a government veto over material containing departmental facts and figures.[156]

As well as imposing limiting conditions on NGOs' activity, the Australian Government has opposed the use of public funds to support a dissenting voice, for example declining to fund the national conference of community legal centres because it was 'inappropriate for Australian Government funds to be directed to the support of campaigns against legislation enacted by the Parliament of Australia'.[157] Hamilton and Maddison offer examples of what they identify as a 'strategy of divide and rule' in which organisations that have been critical of government 'have been frozen out of debates and positions of

150 J Bendell, see above, n 131, 11.

151 C Frangonikolopoulos, see above, n 140, 62.

152 C Hamilton & S Maddison, see above, n 148, 78–81.

153 UN Human Rights Council, *National Report Submitted in Accordance with Paragraph 15 (a) of the Annex to Human Rights Council Resolution 5/1: Australia*, 10th sess, Working Group on the Universal Periodic Review, UN Doc A/HRC/WG.6/10/AUS/1 (2010).

154 Ibid pt 1, paras 3–5.

155 Ibid pt 2D, para 35.

156 E Sidoti, 'Australian Democracy: Challenging the Rise of Contemporary Authoritarianism', *Catholics in Coalition for Justice and Peace*, Sydney, 2003, 17.

157 D Marr, 'Ruddock snubs legal centres', *Sydney Morning Herald*, Sydney, 2 August 2006.

influence. Others that have been friendly to the Government have been favoured with funding, contracts and appointments of senior staff to various boards and inquiries'.[158]

The limitations on NGO activity imposed by charity and tax law has been a significant constraint on NGO activity in Australia. The scope of 'charitable' purpose was, however, recently broadened considerably by the High Court in *Aid/Watch Incorporated v Commissioner of Taxation*,[159] where the Court decided that what might have been seen as activity to influence government was in fact activity that generated public debate about the relief of poverty, thereby contributing to the public welfare and being of a charitable purpose.

9.5 CONCLUSION AND ISSUES

Human rights NGOs clearly have an important role to play in the monitoring and enforcement of states' compliance with international human rights standards, both internationally through the UN and in international relations, and nationally through domestic politics and public debate. Humanitarian NGOs are perhaps now an indispensible part of global responses to natural and man-made disasters, and play an important role in promoting and supporting development.

It is not surprising therefore, particularly as they grow in number and influence, that NGOs are increasingly coming under scrutiny. Governments, inter-governmental agencies, corporations, funding bodies, commentators and NGOs themselves are asking questions raised in this chapter, such as whether there is a need to define 'NGO' more precisely and prescriptively in international forums; the type and degree of accountability and transparency that should be expected of NGOs; the legitimacy of state controls over NGO activity; the sensitivity of ostensibly 'Western' NGOs to local customs and needs in developing countries; and the wisdom of relying on ostensibly private NGOs to deliver UN and state-sanctioned aid and development programs.

158 C Hamilton & S Maddison (eds), *Silencing Dissent: How the Australian Government is Controlling Public Opinion and Stifling Debate*, Allen & Unwin, Crows Nest, 2007, 88. See also J Staples, 'NGOs Out in the Cold: The Howard Government Policy Towards NGOs', Discussion Paper 19/06, Democratic Audit, 2006, 4–5; J Butcher, *Government, the Third Sector and the Rise of Social Capital*, Centre for Research in Public Sector Management, Canberra, 2005.

159 *Aid/Watch Incorporated v Commissioner of Taxation* [2010] HCA 42.

PART FOUR

AUSTRALIA

10 IMPLEMENTATION OF INTERNATIONAL HUMAN RIGHTS LAW IN AUSTRALIA

CONTENTS

10.1 INTRODUCTION

Australia has been described as having a 'patchwork quilt' approach to the protection of human rights.[1] It is pieced together from an unplanned and uncoordinated collection of constitutional provisions, common law, legislation, policies and procedures, and institutions, across state territory and national jurisdictions, with the notable absence of a national human rights law. This chapter describes the patchwork, and assesses its adequacy as a means of protecting human rights in Australia. It is arguable that Australia's approach is emerging as a model of sorts, where adequate human rights protection can be achieved without relying on a national human rights law or extensive domestic implementation of international human rights treaty obligations.

Australia's long history of supporting the international human rights regime dates from its involvement in the drafting and adoption of the *Universal Declaration of Human Rights* (UDHR). Since the mid-1990s, however, Australia's support has been qualified, and it has been quick to assert its sovereignty as a basis for resisting some of the demands made of it by international human rights standards. The nature and extent of Australia's challenge to international human rights is discussed towards the end of the chapter, which finishes by noting Australia's clear but slow return to willing participating in the United Nations human rights system.

10.2 TREATY RATIFICATION IN AUSTRALIA

Under international law, treaties impose obligations on a state in relation to other states, but not necessarily in relation to its own citizens. If a state is 'dualist' (discussed in Chapter 7.2.7), treaties impose no direct obligations on it in relation to its own citizens unless the state implements the treaty obligations in domestic legislation. As Australia is a dualist state, 'statements of international law [are not] automatically rendered part of Australian domestic law'.[2] This is so 'even where the ratification has received Parliamentary approval'.[3]

1 *National Human Rights Consultation Report*, Commonwealth of Australia, 2009, 349.

2 *Wurridjal v Commonwealth* [2009] HCA 2, (2009) 237 CLR 309, 412 (Kirby J).

3 *Nulyarimma & Others v Thompson & Others* [1999] FCA 1192; (1999) 96 FCR 153, 162 (Wilcox J).

In *Nulyarimma v Thompson*, indigenous people—members of the stolen generations who were taken from their families to be assimilated into white society—filed an action in the Federal Court to prosecute members of the Australian Parliament for the crime of genocide because of their involvement in amendments to native title legislation.[4] Their case failed because there was no Australian law implementing the 1948 UN Convention on the Prevention and Punishment of the Crime of Genocide, and '[i]f genocide is to be regarded as punishable in Australia ... it must be shown that Australian law permits that result'.[5]

10.2.1 Constitutional Power

The Australian federal government has executive prerogative power to ratify international treaties.[6] Once a treaty has been ratified, parliament can then legislate to give domestic effect to the treaty obligations, under the 'external affairs' power in section 51(xxix) of the *Constitution*. The extent of the external affairs power was originally unclear,[7] but was confirmed first in *Koowarta v Bjelke-Petersen*[8] and then in *Commonwealth v Tasmania* (the '*Tasmanian Dam Case*').[9]

In *Koowarta*, Ministers of the Queensland Government 'alleged that the [*Racial Discrimination Act*] is not a law of the kind mentioned in s 51(xxvi) of the Constitution and is outside the legislative power of the Commonwealth and invalid'.[10] In a 4:3 decision the High Court disagreed, and upheld the constitutional validity of the RDA as an enactment of Australia's obligations under ICERD, which it had ratified. The minority view was that although Australia can enact domestic laws to give effect to a treaty obligation, it can do so only when the subject matter of the treaty is an area for which the Commonwealth otherwise has power to legislate.

In the *Tasmanian Dam* case a majority of the High Court confirmed that the external affairs power means Australia can enact domestic laws to give effect to a treaty obligation, even if the subject matter of the treaty is not otherwise an area for which the Commonwealth has power to legislate. This time the minority view was that if the legislation were to be valid, the treaty it gives effect to must address a 'matter of international concern' and not something that is principally a domestic issue. In *Richardson v Forestry Commission*,[11] the High Court endorsed the majority view in the *Tasmanian Dam Case*, confirming that the federal parliament has the power to legislate to give effect to a treaty obligation regardless of its subject matter.

4 [1999] FCA 1192; see also *Buzzacott v Hill* [1999] FCA 639, a concurrent claim that other members of the Australian Parliament had committed genocide in failing to protect traditional lands of the Arabunna People.

5 [1999] FCA 1192 [22]; see the discussion of *Nulyarimma*, and of the incorporation of international law into domestic law, in H Charlesworth, M Chiam, D Hovell & G Williams, 'Deep Anxieties: Australia and the International Legal Order' (2003) 25(4) *Sydney Law Review* 423, 455–6.

6 S Joseph & M Castan, *Federal Constitutional Law: A Contemporary View*, 3rd edn, Thompson Reuters, Sydney, 2010, paras 4.25 & 5.45.

7 See, eg, *R v Burgess; Ex parte Henry* [1936] HCA 52; 55 CLR 608.

8 [1982] HCA 27; (1982) 153 CLR 168.

9 [1983] HCA 21; (1983) 158 CLR 1.

10 [1982] HCA 27; (1982) 153 CLR 168, 177.

11 [1988] HCA 10; (1988) 164 CLR 261.

There are, however, conditions attached to the exercise of this power.[12] The treaty must be reasonably specific about the steps necessary to implement the obligations it creates, and the law must be similarly specific in the regime it establishes to give effect to the treaty.[13] As well, a domestic law is valid only to the extent that it gives effect to the treaty; it 'must be reasonably capable of being considered appropriate and adapted to implementing the treaty'.[14]

10.2.2 Parliamentary Process

When the Australian government signs a treaty, thereby indicating its intention to ratify, or proposes to take some other action in relation to a treaty such as withdrawing a reservation, the treaty or notice of the proposed action is tabled in the Federal Parliament for different periods depending on the type of treaty. Human rights treaties are in Category 1,[15] and are tabled with a National Interest Analysis (NIA), prepared by the Department of Foreign Affairs and Trade.[16] The NIA addresses considerations in Australia's becoming a party to the treaty or taking the proposed action,[17] and reflects to an extent the deliberations of the Commonwealth-State-Territory Standing Committee on Treaties, which is briefed quarterly on international treaties that are currently under negotiation or review.

Parliament can refer the proposed treaty action to its Joint Standing Committee on Treaties (JSCOT) to conduct an inquiry and report within the tabling period.[18] On 4 June 2008, for example, JSCOT reported on its Inquiry into the United Nations *Convention on the Rights of Persons with Disabilities*, saying, 'The Treaties Committee supports [the Convention] and recommends that binding treaty action be taken'.[19] The Australia Government ratified the Convention on 17 July 2008 and it entered into force for Australia on 20 September 2009.

12 See above, n 6, paras 4.40–4.60.

13 *Victoria v Commonwealth* [1996] HCA 56; 187 CLR 416, 486 (Brennan CJ, Toohey, Gaudron, McHugh and Gummow JJ) (*'Industrial Relations Case'*).

14 *Victoria v Commonwealth* [1996] HCA 56; 187 CLR 416 (*'Industrial Relations Case'*); *Commonwealth v Tasmania* [1983] HCA 21; 158 CLR 1, 258–9 (Deane J) (*'Tasmania Dam Case'*).

15 For a discussion and evaluation of Australia's procedures for considering adoption of treaties, see above, n 5, 438–44.

16 NIAs are available at Australian Treaty National Interest Analyses, <http://www.austlii.edu.au/au/other/dfat/nia/>.

17 See generally, Department of Foreign Affairs and Trade, *Australia and International Treaty Making Information Kit* <www.austlii.edu.au/au/other/dfat/reports/infokit.html> at 31 March 2011; A Twomey, *Federal Parliament's Changing Role in Treaty Making and External Affairs*, Research Paper 15, Parliamentary Library, Canberra, 2000; G Cranwell, 'The Treaty Making Process in Australia—A Report Card on Recent Reforms' (2001) *Australian International Law Journal* 177; H Charlesworth et al (eds), *The Fluid State: International Law and National Legal Systems*, Federation Press, Annandale, 2005; H Charlesworth et al, see above, n 5, 439–40.

18 Joint Standing Committee on Treaties, Parliament of Australia <www.aph.gov.au/house/committee/jsct/index.htm>.

19 Joint Standing Committee on Treaties, Parliament of Australia, *Report 92: United Nations Convention on the Rights of Persons with Disabilities* (New York, 13 December 2006) (2008), 2, recommendation 1.

10.2.3 Human Right Treaties Binding on Australia

Australia has ratified or acceded to most of the 'core' human right treaties and related protocols.[20] Of the core treaties, it has not yet signed the *International Convention on the Protection of the Rights of All Migrant Workers and Members of Their Families* (ICRMW) or the *International Convention for the Protection of All Persons from Enforced Disappearance* (ICPED). In its response to recommendations arising from the 2011 Universal Periodic Review,[21] Australia said that it 'will consider becoming party to the [ICPED], but views existing protections in place for migrant workers as adequate and does not intend to become a party to the ICRMW'.[22]

Australia's failure to ratify the *Optional Protocol of the Covenant on Economic, Social and Cultural Rights* was not addressed in the 2011 Universal Periodic Review. However, its failure to ratify the *Optional Protocol to the Convention Against Torture and Other Cruel, Inhuman or Degrading Treatment or Punishment* was the subject of comment, and Australia responded by saying that it 'is working with States and Territories to take the necessary steps towards ratifying [it]'.[23]

Treaty	Ratified/Acceded (Signed) by Australia
ICERD	30 September 1975 (ratified)
ICESCR	10 December 1975 (ratified)
ICESCR-OP	n/a
ICCPR	13 August 1980 (ratified)
ICCPR-OP1	25 September 1991 (acceded)
ICCPR-OP2	2 October 1990 (acceded)
CEDAW	28 July 1983 (ratified)
CEDAW-OP	4 December 2008 (acceded)
CAT	8 Aug 1989 (ratified)
CAT-OP	(signed 19 May 2009)
CROC	17 December 1990 (ratified)
CROC-OPAC	26 September 2006 (ratified)
CROC-OPSC	8 January 2007 (ratified)
ICRMW	n/a
CRPD	17 July 2008 (ratified)
CRPD-OP	21 August 2009 (acceded)
ICPED	n/a

20 See Chapter 7.3.

21 See Chapter 10.5.1.

22 Human Rights Council, Seventeenth session, Geneva, 30 May—17 June 2011, *Report of the Working Group on the Universal Periodic Review: Australia, Addendum: Views on conclusions and/or recommendations, voluntary commitments and replies presented by the State under review*, A/HRC/17/10/Add.1, 31 May 2011.

23 Ibid.

10.2.4 Australia's Declarations and Reservations[24]

A Federated State

When Australia ratified the *International Covenant on Civil and Political Rights* (ICCPR) it declared that, as Australia is a 'federal constitutional system in which legislative, executive and judicial powers are shared or distributed between the Commonwealth and the constituent States', implementation of the treaty obligations is the responsibility of all the federated jurisdictions—the Commonwealth, the States and the Territories—having regard to their constitutional powers.

Australia repeats this qualification to its treaty obligations in its periodic reports to the treaty-monitoring bodies. Consistently with its reservation, the federal government has frequently declined to intervene when a State or Territory law has operated in violation of Australia's human rights obligations (for example, mandatory sentencing laws in Western Australia[25] and the Northern Territory[26]). An exception was the Australian Government's 1994 legislation to override a Tasmanian law that criminalised consensual homosexual sex.[27] Australia's claimed 'federation' qualification to treaty compliance is not recognised under the international law of treaties[28] and is inconsistent with the jurisprudence on the 'external affairs' power in the *Australian Constitution*, which makes it clear that the federal government can, in order to give effect to international treaties, legislate to override State or Territory legislation that is inconsistent with Australia's treaty obligations.[29]

In its Concluding Observations on Australia's combined sixth and seventh reports under the *Convention on the Elimination of All Forms of Discrimination Against Women* (CEDAW), the CEDAW Committee said it

> remains concerned about the lack of harmonization or consistency in the way that the Convention is incorporated and implemented across the country, particularly when the primary competence to address a particular issue lies with the individual states and territories ... The Committee reiterates its previous recommendation that the State party promote and guarantee the implementation of the Convention throughout the country, including through its power to legislate for the implementation of treaty obligations in all states and territories.[30]

Various Treaties

As is outlined below, Australia has entered a number of reservations to the human rights treaties it has ratified. In January 2011, responding to the recommendations of the Universal Period Review that

24 Treaty reservations and declarations are discussed in Chapter 7.2.4.

25 *Criminal Code Amendment Act (No 2) 1996* (WA), which inserted new ss 400 and 401 into the *Criminal Code*.

26 *Sentencing Amendment Act 1996* (NT) which inserted new ss 78A, 78B and Schedule 1 into the *Sentencing Act 1995* (NT). Mandatory sentencing of juveniles and adult property offenders has since been repealed: *Sentencing Amendment Act (No 3) 2001* (NT); see generally G Zdenkowski, 'Mandatory Imprisonment of Property Offenders in the Northern Territory' (1999) 22(1) *University of New South Wales Law Journal* 302.

27 Discussed in Chapter 10.5.4 below.

28 *Vienna Convention on the Law of Treaties* art 27.

29 See discussion above on *Koowarta* and *Tasmanian Dam Case* at Chapter 10.2.1.

30 UN Committee on the Elimination of Discrimination Against Women, *Concluding Observations of the Committee on the Elimination of Discrimination Against Women: Australia*, 46th sess, paras 16 & 17, UN Doc CEDAW/C/AUS/CO/7 (2010).

it withdraw its reservations, Australia said only that it will 'systematically review its reservations to human rights treaties, having regard to whether reservations remain necessary'.[31]

When it ratified the ICCPR, Australia entered a number of reservations. Although it has since withdrawn some, it maintains reservations to article 10(2)(a) (segregating convicted from unconvicted detainees), the second sentence of article 10(2)(b) (segregating juvenile from adult offenders), article 14(6) (compensating convicted people who have been pardoned), and article 20 (criminalising racial hatred).[32]

Australia's ratification of the *Convention on the Rights of the Child* (CROC) is subject to a reservation to article 37(c), (segregating detained children separately from adults); the Committee on the Rights of the Child (CROC) has said it sees this reservation as 'unnecessary'.[33] On ratifying the *International Convention on the Elimination of All Forms of Racial Discrimination* (ICERD), Australia entered a reservation to article 4(a), (declaring racial hatred an offence).[34] The Racial Hatred Bill 1994 (Cth) at one stage made provision for criminalising racial hatred, but those provisions were dropped from the final Bill, which made racial hatred a matter for complaint and inquiry and not prosecution.

When it ratified CEDAW, Australia entered a reservation to article 11(2)(b), (maternity leave).[35] It made but later withdrew a reservation relating to women in combat. When it ratified the *Convention on the Rights of Persons with Disabilities* (CRPD), Australia made declarations about its interpretation of a number of articles, relating to substituted decision-making arrangements, compulsory treatment, and immigration health tests.[36]

10.3 AUSTRALIA'S HUMAN RIGHTS LAWS

10.3.1 Constitutional 'Rights'

Unlike the constitutions of any Western state, Australia's *Constitution* has no entrenched guarantees of rights that are recognised internationally as human rights. A 2003 a review of countries that do not have constitutionally entrenched rights reported:[37]

31 Human Rights Council, see above, n 22.

32 See *International Covenant on Civil and Political Rights* (ICCPR) United Nations Treaty Series, vol 999, 171 <http://treaties.un.org/pages/ViewDetails.aspx?src=UNTSONLINE&tabid=1&mtdsg_no=IV-4&chapter=4&lang=en#Participants> at 31 March 2011.

33 UN Committee on the Rights of the Child, *Concluding Observations: Australia*, 40th sess, para 7, UN Doc CRC/C/15/Add.268 (2005).

34 See *International Convention on the Elimination of All Forms of Racial Discrimination*, (ICERD) opened for signature 21 December 1965, 660 UNTS 195 (entered into force 4 January 1969).

35 See *International Convention on Elimination of All Forms of Discrimination against Women*, (CEDAW) opened for signature 1 March 1980, 1249 UNTS 13 (entered into force 3 September 1981).

36 See *Convention on the Rights of People with Disabilities*, (CRPD) opened for signature 30 March 2007, 993 UNTS 3 (entered into force 3 May 2008).

37 Gareth Griffith, *The Protection of Human Rights: A Review of Selected Jurisdictions*, NSW Parliamentary Library Research Service, Briefing Paper No 3/2000, 3.

It seems that Afghanistan, where there is no valid constitution and which is ruled by Islamic law, also belongs to that category; as does Burma (Myanmar) where the constitution is suspended. From a survey of their constitutions, Bhutan and Brunei may also belong to the 'no' list; and perhaps Libya should be added to it on the ground that the rights articulated in its constitution are primarily social and economic in nature. Moreover, the position in some countries is hard to determine, including those in a state of constitutional flux at present, as in the cases of Pakistan and Indonesia. The general point to make is that the 'no' list is as short as the 'yes' list is long.

The *Australian Constitution* is essentially a description of the mechanism for national government of federated states. It is a functional, not an aspirational, document, although some of its provisions provide for qualified 'rights' of a specific kind:[38]

- a right to be compensated on just terms for acquisition of property for Commonwealth purposes[39]
- a right to trial by jury for a Commonwealth offence charged under indictment[40]
- a right to free movement of people and free trade between states[41]
- rights in relation to religion,[42] which limit the Commonwealth from establishing a State religion or State church,[43] imposing any religious observance, limiting the free exercise of religion subject to 'restrictions ... essential to the preservation of the community',[44] and requiring no religious test for appointment to Commonwealth office
- a right to not be discriminated against on basis of state residence,[45] and
- a right to vote in Commonwealth elections subject to restrictions on that right imposed by Commonwealth law.[46]

As well as these explicit rights, the High Court has identified a right to free political communication that is implicit in the representative parliamentary democracy established by the *Constitution.*[47] Unsurprisingly, considering they were drawn up before 1901, the rights found in the Constitution are not the rights enunciated in later human rights treaties. The most that can be said is that some of them bear some similarity to international human rights.

38 For an historical account of these rights, see N O'Neill, S Rice & R Douglas, *Retreat from Injustice: Human Rights in Australia*, 2nd edn, Federation Press, Annandale, 2004, Ch 3.

39 *Australian Constitution* s 51(xxxi).

40 Ibid s 80; *R v Archdall & Roskruge* [1928] HCA 18; 41 CLR 128.

41 *Australian Constitution* s 92.

42 *Australian Constitution* s 116.

43 *Attorney-General (Vic); Ex rel Black v Commonwealth* [1981] HCA 2; 146 CLR 559 ('DOGS Case').

44 *Adelaide Company of Jehovah's Witnesses Incorporated v Commonwealth* [1943] HCA 12; 67 CLR 116, 149–50 (Rich J) (*'Jehovah's Witnesses Case'*).

45 *Australian Constitution* s 117; *Street v Queensland Bar Association* [1989] HCA 53; 168 CLR 461.

46 *Australian Constitution* ss 24 & 41; *R v Pearson; Ex parte Sipka* [1983] HCA 6; 152 CLR 254; *Attorney-General (Cth); Ex rel McKinlay v Commonwealth* [1975] HCA 53; 135 CLR 1.

47 *Australian Capital Television Pty Ltd v Commonwealth* (1992) 177 CLR 106; *Lange v Australian Broadcasting Corporation* (1997) 189 CLR 520.

Although there is in article 17 of the *Universal Declaration of Human Rights* a right to own property and not to be arbitrarily deprived of it, the right in the *Australian Constitution* to be compensated on just terms for the state's taking of property is referable to a long-standing common law principle, traceable to Chapters 28–31 of *Magna Carta* and found in numerous constitutions of the British Commonwealth.[48] There is no human right to trial by jury, although there is a less specific right in article 14(1) of the ICCPR to a 'fair and public hearing by a competent, independent and impartial tribunal'.

The Constitutional right to free movement between states was a political and commercial imperative to establish a single national entity composed of different provincial powers, and has no connection with the right to freedom of movement in article 12(1) of the ICCPR. The Constitutional right not to be discriminated against on the basis of state residence is also pragmatic, not connected with the human right of non-discrimination, in the same way that the qualified right to vote is not connected with article 25 of the ICCPR. The human right to religion in article 18 of the ICCPR is not limited in the same way as the rights are under section 117 of the *Constitution*.

10.3.2 A 'Legitimate Expectation' of Human Rights Conformity

In the High Court decision of *Minister for Immigration and Ethnic Affairs v Teoh*, Mason CJ and Deane J said that Australia's ratification of a convention 'is an adequate foundation for a legitimate expectation ... that administrative decision-makers will act in conformity with the Convention'.[49] It could be argued that this principle is not limited to administrative decision-making but extends to judicial decision making.[50]

The High Court's decision in *Re Minister for Immigration and Multicultural Affairs; Ex parte Lam*[51] reinforced the view that the principle in *Teoh* is 'only an entitlement to procedural fairness and cannot generate a right to any particular substantive outcome',[52] and in *Re East; Ex parte Nguyen* the High Court referred to *Teoh* as authority for the proposition that ratification of a treaty creates no enforceable rights in Australian law.[53] The *Teoh* decision itself was clear that no new and enforceable rule of law was being created, and treaties were not being elevated to the status of law in Australia.[54]

Despite this, in periodic reports to UN committees the Commonwealth Government protested that *Teoh* gives treaties 'an effect in Australian law which they did not previously have and that the development

48 See generally T Allen, *The Right to Property in Commonwealth Constitutions*, Cambridge University Press, Cambridge, 2000.

49 [1995] HCA 20; 183 CLR 273, 291.

50 *Wickham v Canberra District Rugby League Football Club Limited* [1998] ACTSC 95 [68]; *R v Haughbro* [1997] ACTSC 112. Contra, *R v Smith* [1998] SASC 6649; *R v Togias* [2001] NSWCCA 522 [33].

51 *Re Minister for Immigration and Multicultural Affairs; Ex parte Lam* [2003] HCA 6; 214 CLR 1. On the implications of Lam, see H Burmester, 'Teoh Revisited after Lam' (2004) 40 AIAL Forum 33.

52 J Ford 'Review of R Creyke & P Keyzer (eds), 'The Brennan Legacy: Blowing the Winds of Legal Orthodoxy' (2003) 25(3) *Sydney Law Review* 413.

53 [1998] HCA 73; 196 CLR 354, 362 (Gleeson CJ, Gaudron, McHugh, Gummow, Hayne & Callinan JJ).

54 [1995] HCA 20; 183 CLR 273, 291 (Mason CJ and Deane J). See also A Mason, 'Judicial Review: The Contribution of Sir Gerard Brennan', in R Creyke & P Keyzer (eds), *The Brennan Legacy: Blowing The Winds of Legal Orthodoxy*, Federation Press, Sydney, 2002.

was not consistent with the proper role of Parliament in implementing treaties in Australian law'.[55] Commonwealth Government Bills designed to negate any legitimate expectations arising from Australia's ratification of human rights treaties were repeatedly introduced, and repeatedly lapsed.[56] It appears that, consistently with the reassurance in the decision itself that no new rule was being created, '[c]ourts and tribunals have continued to apply the [*Teoh*] legitimate expectation test without apparent difficulty'.[57]

10.3.3 Federal Legislation

After the decisiveness of the *Racial Discrimination Act 1975* (Cth), which implemented Australia's obligations under ICERD, Australia has taken faltering, sporadic and inconsistent steps to implement its international human rights obligations.[58] Australia has no national law that proclaims and protects human rights, and has not legislated to implement either the ICCPR or ICESCR.

National Consultation and Framework

On 10 December 2008, the Australian Commonwealth Attorney-General announced a National Human Rights Consultation, to report on three questions: 'which human rights (including corresponding responsibilities) should be protected and promoted?'; 'are these human rights currently sufficiently protected and promoted?'; and 'how could Australia better protect and promote human rights?'.[59]

In its report the Consultation Committee made 31 recommendations. Under the heading 'Creating a human rights culture', recommendation 1 was that 'education be the highest priority for improving and promoting human rights in Australia'. In relation to 'policy and legislation' the committee recommended that the government should 'compile a definitive list of Australia's international human rights obligations' and that it conduct an 'audit of all federal legislation, policies and practices to determine their compliance with Australia's international human rights obligations'. It also said a 'statement of compatibility' should be required for Bills and legislative instruments and that a Joint Committee on Human Rights should be established, in both cases to assess the law's compatibility with Australia's human rights obligations.

In relation to government decision making, the committee recommended that the government should develop 'a whole-of-government framework for ensuring that human rights ... are better integrated into public sector policy and legislative development, decision making, service delivery, and practice more generally', and in particular that 'in the absence of a federal Human Rights Act, the *Acts Interpretation Act 1901* (Cth) be amended to require that, as far as it is possible to do so

55 Australia's *Combined Second and Third Reports Under the Convention on the Rights of the Child*, Attorney-General's Department, 2003, para 38.

56 Administrative Decisions (Effect of International Instruments) Bill 1995 (Cth); Administrative Decisions (Effect of International Instruments) Bill 1997 (Cth); Administrative Decisions (Effect of International Instruments) Bill 1999 (Cth). See also W Lacey, 'In the Wake of *Teoh*: Finding an Appropriate Government Response' (2001) 29(2) *Federal Law Review* 219.

57 H Charlesworth, M Chiam, D Hovell & G Williams, see above, n 5, 438.

58 See M Kirby, 'Domestic Implementation of International Human Rights Norms' (1999) 5(2) *Australian Journal of Human Rights* 109; P Bailey, 'Implementing Human Rights—The Way Forward' (1999) 5(2) *Australian Journal of Human Rights* 167; M Kirby, 'The Australian Use of International Human Rights Norms: From Bangalore to Balliol—A View from the Antipodes' (1993) 16(2) *New South Wales Law Journal* 363.

59 See above, n 1, 3.

consistently with the legislation's purpose, all federal legislation is to be interpreted consistently with ... Australia's human rights obligations'. As is discussed in more detail below, the committee also recommended a national Human Rights Act.

The government's response to the consultation committee's report, in April 2010, was to announce an Australian Human Rights Framework,[60] which was said to be based on 'five key principles':

- reaffirming a commitment to our human rights obligations
- the importance of human rights education;
- enhancing our domestic and international engagement on human rights issues
- improving human rights protections, including greater parliamentary scrutiny, and
- achieving greater respect for human rights principles within the community.

The government has said it will review the framework in 2014.

The tangible results of the framework have been increased funding for human rights education (consistently with the priority this received from the consultation committee) and the introduction into Parliament of bills to enable the scrutiny of proposed legislation for human rights compliance,[61] discussed further below. Reporting to the UN, the government identified the 'measures to make information about human rights more readily available across the Australian community' as the 'centrepiece of the framework'.[62]

A Federal Human Rights Act (not)

Australia does not have a national human rights statute and, as was discussed above, the *Australian Constitution* does not contain provisions in the nature of a bill of rights. The National Human Rights Consultation Committee Report referred to Australia's 'patchwork quilt' approach to the protection of human rights[63] and Charlesworth has described Australia's 'reluctance about rights'.[64] There have been many proposals for a national human rights statute,[65] and arguments for and against one;[66] the National Human Rights Consultation was seen as another occasion to consider such legislation.

The Consultation Committee's report recommended a legislative bill of rights, similar to the 'dialogue model' of the United Kingdom's *Human Rights Act*.[67] However, the Committee anticipated the possibility that the Government would not implement this recommendation, and that is what

60 *Australia's Human Rights Framework*, Australian Government Attorney-General's Department <www.ag.gov.au/humanrightsframework>.

61 Human Rights (Parliamentary Scrutiny) Bill 2010; Human Rights (Parliamentary Scrutiny) (Consequential Provisions) Bill 2010.

62 *Universal Periodic Review National Report—Australia*, 2010, para 43, A/HRC/WG.6/10/AUS/1

63 See above, n 1, 349.

64 H Charlesworth, 'The Australian Reluctance about Rights' (1993) 31(1) *Osgoode Hall Law Journal* 195.

65 N O'Neill, S Rice & R Douglas, see above, n 38, 90–2.

66 See, eg, M Wilcox, *An Australian Charter of Rights?*, Law Book Company, Sydney, 1993; F Brennan, *Legislating Liberty A Bill of Rights for Australia*, University of Queensland Press, Brisbane, 1998; 'Special Edition: A Bill of Rights for Australia' (2003) 9(1) *Australian Journal of Human Rights*; J Leeser & R Haddrick (eds), *Dont Leave Us with the Bill: The Case Against an Australian Bill of Rights*, Menzies Research Centre, Barton, 2009; James Allan, 'A Defence of the Status Quo', in T Campbell, J Goldsworthy & A Stone (eds), *Protecting Human Rights*, Oxford University Press, Oxford, 175–94.

67 *Human Rights Act 1998* (UK); for criticism of the accuracy of the term 'dialogue model' see *Momcilovic v R* [2011] HCA 34.

happened. In its response to the report the Government rejected enacting a federal Human Rights Act, saying only that 'a legislative charter of rights is not included in the framework as the Government believes that the enhancement of human rights should be done in a way that, as far as possible, unites rather than divides our community'.[68]

Domestic Laws Giving Effect to Human Rights Treaties

Australia has a very uneven record in legislating to give domestic effect to its international human rights treaty obligations, as the account which follows illustrates. In January 2011, Australia was questioned by delegates to the Universal Periodic Review as to whether it gives proper legal effect to its treaty obligations in its domestic law. Australia's response was that it 'incorporates international obligations into domestic law to the extent considered necessary, noting that some obligations are reflected in policy',[69] and that human rights are appropriately protected in Australian domestic law and policy through a combination of parliamentary scrutiny of new legislation for human rights compatibility, federal protection against discrimination, human rights education, and a proposed National Human Rights Action Plan.[70] These various human rights mechanisms are discussed in the remainder of this section, and in Chapter 10.4. Australia's failure to give full domestic effect to its treaty obligations has been the subject of repeated comment by a range of treaty bodies when observing on Australia's state reports.[71]

ICESCR

Unlike the ICCPR, discussed below, the *International Covenant on Economic, Social and Cultural Rights* (ICESCR) is not a schedule to the AHRC Act, and so people in Australia do not have access to the AHRC complaint or inquiry processes to raise alleged violations of economic, social or cultural rights, even on the limited basis that is available for the ICCPR. Neither the ACT nor Victorian human rights statutes makes explicit provision for the rights set out in the ICESCR, although there is some coverage due to the overlap between ICESCR and some of the ICCPR rights, which are provided for—and some ICESCR rights.

68 R McClelland, 'Launch of Australia's Human Rights Framework' (speech delivered at the National Press Club of Australia, Canberra, 21 April 2010); for an assessment of the prospects of a national human rights law in Australia after its rejection in 2010, see D Erdos, 'The Rudd Government's Rejection of an Australian Bill of Rights: A Stunted Case of Aversive Constitutionalism?' *Oxford Legal Studies Research Paper No 17/2011*, <http://ssrn.com/abstract=1766566>.

69 Human Rights Council, see above, n 22.

70 P Woolcott, *Response of Australia to Recommendations of the United Nations Human Rights Council*, 31 January 2011 <http://www.geneva.mission.gov.au/gene/Statement159.html>.

71 UN Human Rights Committee, *Concluding Observations of the Human Rights Committee: Australia*, 69th sess, paras 498–528, UN Doc A/55/40 (2000); UN Committee on the Rights of the Child, *Concluding Observations: Australia*, 40th sess, UN Doc CRC/C/15/Add.268 (2005); UN Committee on the Elimination of Discrimination Against Women, *Concluding Comments of the Committee on the Elimination of Discrimination against Women: Australia*, 34th sess, paras 10 & 11, CEDAW/C/AUL/CO/5 (2006); UN Human Rights Committee, *Concluding Observations of the Human Rights Committee: Australia*, 95th sess, para 8, UN Doc CCPR/C/AUS/CO/5 (2009); UN Committee on Economic, Social and Cultural Rights, *Concluding Observations of the Committee on Economic, Social and Cultural Rights: Australia*, 42nd sess, UN Doc E/C.12/AUS/CO/4 (2009); see above, n 30.

Many of the economic, social and cultural rights in the ICESCR are reflected in the provision of, for example, health and education services in Australia. But such services are not made available as a right, and at any time the service can be withdrawn. In the absence of the guarantees in the ICESCR—such as might be found in a human rights statute—there is no enforceable claim to the service as a human right.[72]

ICESCR has been the constitutional basis for some Australian legislation: in part for the *Disability Discrimination Act 1992* (Cth) (DDA) and *Age Discrimination Act 2004* (Cth) (ADA),[73] and for the since-repealed 'right to strike' measures in the *Industrial Relations Act 1988* (Cth).[74] The *Fair Work Act 2009* (Cth) enables employees covered by that Act to take industrial action when negotiating a collective agreement;[75] the ILO standards on freedom of association set out the minimum requirements for a right to strike under Article 8 of ICESCR,[76] but the *Fair Work Act 2009* (Cth) falls well short of those standards.[77]

In 1993 the federal government introduced provisions entitled 'Equal remuneration for work of equal value' into the *Industrial Relations Act*,[78] 'to give effect, or further effect, to [articles 3 and 7 of ICESCR]'.[79] Those provisions are still in place in Part 2-7 of the *Fair Work Act 2009* (Cth), though they have been little used.[80]

That is the extent of explicit legislative effect being given to ICESCR in Australia. ICESCR is referred to as a standard for the purposes of indigenous social justice monitoring[81] and is mentioned in the preamble or long title to some laws with a rights focus.[82] Despite persuasive international experience,[83] Australia has been reluctant to recognise the justiciability of economic, social and cultural rights. Their exclusion from the scope of the Australian Capital Territory and Victorian human rights statutes, discussed below, is an example.[84]

72 See P Bailey 'The Right to an Adequate Standard of Living: New Issues for Australian Law' (1997) 4(1) *Australian Journal of Human Rights* 25.

73 *Disability Discrimination Act 1992* (Cth) s 12 (8)(c); *Age Discrimination Act 2004* (Cth) s 10(7)(c).

74 In 1993 the federal government introduced Pt VIB Div 4 into what was then the *Industrial Relations Act 1988* (Cth) 'to give effect, in particular situations, to Australia's international obligation to provide for a right to strike' (the obligation arises under International Labour Organisation (ILO) conventions, international customary law and ICESCR, art 8). Part VIB Div 4 was upheld in *Victoria v MacBean* (1996) 68 IR 442, 448–53, and *Victoria v Commonwealth* [1996] HCA 56; 187 CLR 416 (*'Industrial Relations Case'*) as a valid law giving effect to Australia's international obligations under ICESCR. However, the law was repealed in 1996 by the *Workplace Relations and Other Legislation Amendment Act 1996* (Cth).

75 *Fair Work Act 2009* (Cth) pt 3–3.

76 C Fenwick, 'Minimum Obligations with Respect to Article 8 of the International Covenant on Economic, Social and Cultural Rights', in A Chapman & S Russell (eds), *Core Obligations: Building a Framework for Economic, Social and Cultural Rights*, Intersentia, Antwerp, 2002, 53–85, 61, cited in S McCrystal '*The Fair Work Act 2009* (Cth) and the Right to Strike' (Legal Studies Research Paper No 10/18, Sydney Law School, 2010) 3.

77 See generally S McCrystal 'The Fair Work Act 2009 (Cth) and the Right to Strike', (2009-2010) 23(1) *Australian Journal of Labour Law* 3.

78 *Industrial Relations Act 1988* (Cth) pt VIA, div 2.

79 See the definition of 'anti-discrimination conventions', *Industrial Relations Act 1988* (Cth) s 4.

80 See T McDermott, 'Labour Law and Human Rights' in D Kinley (ed), *Human Rights in Australian Law*, Federation Press, Sydney, 1998, 195 & 203–5.

81 *Australian Human Rights and Equal Opportunity Commission Act 1986* (Cth) s 46C (4)(a).

82 For example, *Aboriginal and Torres Strait Islander Commission Act 1989* (Cth); *Native Title Act 1993* (Cth); *Supported Accommodation Assistance Act 1994* (Cth); *Housing Assistance Act 1996* (Cth).

83 See the discussion in Chapter 1.4.3.

84 For previous consideration of protection for economic, social and cultural rights in Australia, see Queensland Electoral and Administrative Review Commission, *Report on Review of the Preservation and Enhancement of Individuals' Rights*

SNAPSHOT: AUSTRALIA AND ICESCR

The Committee on Economic, Social and Cultural Rights has consistently urged Australia to incorporate ICESCR into domestic law. In 2009, in response to Australia's Fourth Report under ICESCR, the Committee said it 'regrets that the Covenant has not yet been incorporated into domestic law ... [and] notes with concern the lack of a legal framework for the protection of economic, social and cultural rights at the Federal level, as well as of an effective mechanism to ensure coherence and compliance of all jurisdictions in the Federation with the state party's obligations under the Covenant.'[85]

The Australian Human Rights Commission, discussed below, has wide-ranging responsibilities in relation to promoting awareness of, and a respect for, human rights in the community, but its mandate does not include the rights contained in the ICESCR.

The 2009 *National Human Rights Consultation Report* found that 'protection and promotion of economic, social and cultural rights is important to the community, and the way they are protected and promoted has a major impact on the lives of many Australians'.[86] But on advice from the Commonwealth Solicitor-General, the *National Human Rights Consultation Report* expressed '[c]oncerns about the justiciability of economic, social and cultural rights',[87] and recommended instead monitoring such rights were monitored 'through administrative complaints mechanisms'.

The Consultation Committee's apprehensions about economic, social and cultural rights contrast starkly with the views of the United Kingdom Parliament's Joint Committee on Human Rights in 2008, which was also assessing the possible inclusion of economic, social and cultural rights in their domestic human rights legislation.[88]

The 2010 *National Human Rights Framework*, discussed above, outlines measures to strengthen domestic protection and promotion of human rights. It reaffirms a commitment to 'promoting human rights awareness' in the community and to respecting the seven core instruments to which Australia is party, including ICESCR and CEDAW.[89] The parliamentary scrutiny legislation under which all legislative instruments will be assed for compatibility with Australia's human rights obligations, the Human Rights (Parliamentary Scrutiny) Bill 2010 is not limited to a narrow list of 'core' human rights but refers to the full list of obligations under the seven instruments, giving equal weight to civil and political rights and economic, social and cultural rights.

and Freedoms (1993); Legal, Constitutional and Administrative Review Committee, Parliament of Queensland, *The Preservation and Enhancement of Individuals' Rights and Freedoms in Queensland: Should Queensland Adopt a Bill of Rights* (1998); Standing Committee on Law and Justice, NSW Parliament, *A NSW Bill of Rights* (2001).

85 UN Committee on Economic, Social and Cultural Rights, *Concluding Observations of the Committee on Economic, Social and Cultural Rights: Australia*, 42nd sess, UN Doc E/C.12/AUS/CO/4 (2009), para 11.

86 See above, n 1, 96.

87 Ibid 317. See also A Byrnes, 'Second-Class Rights Yet Again? Economic, Social and Cultural Rights in the Report of the National Human Rights Consultation Committee' (2010) 33(1) *University of New South Wales Law Journal* 193.

88 Joint Committee on Human Rights, Parliament of the UK, *A Bill of Rights for the UK? Twenty-Ninth Report of the Session 2007–08* (2008), Ch 5, particularly paras 147, 155 & 191. See also ACT Human Rights Act Research Project ANU, *The Human Rights Act 2004 (ACT): The First Five Years of Operation: A 'Report to the ACT Department of Justice and Community* (2009).

89 Australian Government Attorney-General's Department, *Australia's Human Rights Framework (2010)*, 3.

ICCPR

The rights guaranteed by the ICCPR have a small and almost random presence in Australian law. Their most significant presence is in the *Human Rights Act 2004* (ACT) and the *Charter of Rights and Responsibilities 2006* (Vic), discussed below.

Australia has not enacted the ICCPR into federal law, but has scheduled it to the *Australian Human Rights Commission Act* 1986 (Cth) (AHRC Act). This gives the Australian Human Rights Commission (AHRC) the power to conduct an inquiry into an alleged breach, but not to offer any enforceable remedy. The fact that the ICCPR is a schedule to the AHRC Act does not mean it has been enacted into domestic law.[90] A suggestion that a treaty's being a schedule to the AHRC 'may give it a special significance in Australian law' has been raised but not resolved.[91]

Because of Australia's ratification of the *First Optional Protocol* to the ICCPR, Australians have access to the international complaints process that gives them another unenforceable remedy, discussed below.

Some provisions in the ICCPR have been given effect in Australian laws: in the ACT and Victorian human rights statutes, and the *Disability Discrimination Act* (DDA) and *Age Discrimination Act* (ADA). In addition, the ICCPR was the constitutional basis for the *Human Rights (Sexual Conduct) Act 1994* (Cth), which was introduced to override sections of the *Tasmanian Criminal Code* that violated the right to privacy,[92] and the *Privacy Act 1988* (Cth) operates in relation to organisations other than a government authority to the extent that it gives effect to the ICCPR.[93] In Federal, State and Territory laws, the ICCPR has been relied on as a standard for, variously, the purposes of improperly obtained evidence,[94] the issue of a passport,[95] law reform proposals,[96] indigenous social justice monitoring,[97] permissible limits of what might otherwise be torture[98] and conduct that can be prosecuted as a crime against humanity,[99] and is mentioned in the preamble or long title to various laws with a rights focus.[100]

CEDAW

The *Convention on the Elimination of all Forms of Discrimination Against Women* (CEDAW) is the constitutional basis in part for the *Sex Discrimination Act 1984*(Cth)[101] and for the *Equal Opportunity for*

90 *Minogue v Williams* [2000] FCA 125; 60 ALD 366, [23]–[25].

91 *B & B v Minister for Immigration & Multicultural & Indigenous Affairs* [2003] FamCA 451; 30 Fam LR 181, 224 (Nicholson CJ and O'Ryan J).

92 After the UN Human Rights Commission's decision in *Toonen*, discussed in Chapter 10.5.4 below.

93 *Privacy Act 1988* (Cth) s 12B.

94 *Evidence Act 1995* (Cth) s 138(3)(f); *Evidence Act 1995* (NSW) s 138(3)(f); *Evidence Act 2001* (Tas) s 138(3)(f).

95 Section 14(1)(a)(iii) *Australian Passport Act 2005* (Cth).

96 Section 24(1)(b) *Australian Law Reform Commission Act 1996* (Cth).

97 See above, n 81.

98 Section 274.2(4) *Criminal Code Act 1995* (Cth).

99 Section 268 *Criminal Code Act 1995* (Cth).

100 See, eg, *Privacy Act 1988* (Cth); *Aboriginal and Torres Strait Islander Commission Act 1989* (Cth); *Native Title Act 1993* (Cth); *Supported Accommodation Assistance Act 1994* (Cth); *Housing Assistance Act 1996* (Cth); *Anti-Discrimination Act 1991* (Qld).

101 *Sex Discrimination Act 1984* (Cth) ss 3, 9 & 11.

women in the Workplace Act 1999 (Cth).[102] It has not been given legislative effect in other Acts and is not scheduled to the AHRC Act. Australians therefore have no access to the AHRC complaints process for breaches of CEDAW, but because of Australia's ratification of the CEDAW *Optional Protocol* they do have access to an international complaints process: see the discussion of individual communications below.

CROC

Although it is the most ratified of the international human rights treaties,[103] only a few of the rights set out in the *Convention on the Rights of the Child* (CROC) are reflected in Australian legislation, and the treaty itself has not been specifically implemented.

The CROC provides part of the constitutional basis for the *Age Discrimination Act 2004*,[104] but there is no other significant reference to the convention in Australian legislation. None of the extensive State and Territory legislation establishing mechanisms to promote and protect children's welfare is based on the human rights standards of the CROC.[105] It is referred to as a standard for the purposes of indigenous social justice monitoring,[106] and is mentioned in the preamble or long title to a few laws with a rights focus.[107] It has been declared as a relevant human rights instrument under the AHRC Act and so, as is the case with the ICCPR, Australians have access to a complaints process through the AHRC that gives them an unenforceable remedy, discussed below.

There is a suggestion that the declaration of the CROC under the AHRC Act gives it some significance in Australian law. In stating the objects and principles of the Part VII of the *Family Law Act 1975* (Cth), and in introducing the 'best interests of the child' test, amending legislation reflected the wording of the CROC.[108] In *B and B v Minister for Immigration & Multicultural & Indigenous Affairs*[109] the government had argued that Part VII did not actually implement CROC[110] and the trial judge had agreed, relying on *B and B; Family Law Reform Act 1995*[111] to say that '[t]he Reform Act may have been influenced by some of the sentiments in the Convention but this is far from indicating that the *Family*

102 *Equal Opportunity for Women in the Workplace Act 1999* (Cth) s 5, originally the *Affirmative Action (Equal Employment Opportunity For Women) Act 1986* (Cth).

103 See the overview in J Behrens & P Tahmindjis, 'Family Law and Human Rights', in D Kinley, *Human Rights in Australian Law*, Federation Press, Sydney, 1998, 169–93, 175–80; M Jones, 'The Myths and Facts Concerning the Convention on the Rights of the Child in Australia' (1999) 5(2) *Australian Journal of Human Rights* 126; Joint Standing Committee on Foreign Affairs and Trade, Parliament of Australia, *A Review of Australia's Efforts to Promote and Protect Human Rights* (1994), recommendation 40 and accompanying text.

104 *Age Discrimination Act 2004* (Cth) s 10(7)(d).

105 See, eg, *Children and Young People Act 2008* (ACT); *Commission for Children and Young People Act 1998* (NSW); *Commission for Children and Young People Act 2000* (Qld); s 78 *Children, Young Persons and Their Families Act 1997* (Tas).

106 See above, n 81.

107 See, eg, *Supported Accommodation Assistance Act 1994* (Cth); *Housing Assistance Act 1996* (Cth); *Anti-Discrimination Act 1991* (Qld). See also H Blagg & M Wilkie, 'Young People and Policing in Australia: The Relevance of the UN Convention on the Rights of the Child' (1997) 3(2) *Australian Journal of Human Rights* 134.

108 *Family Law Reform Act 1995* (Cth).

109 *B & B v Minister for Immigration & Multicultural & Indigenous Affairs* [2003] FamCA 451; 30 Fam LR 181.

110 Ibid [2003] FamCA 451; 30 Fam LR 181, 225 (Nicholson CJ and O'Ryan J).

111 [1997] FamCA 451; 21 Fam LR 676.

Law Act implements the Convention'.[112] A Full Court of the Family Court rejected the trial judge's interpretation of *B and B* and favoured a view that 'the 1995 amendments to Part VII did intentionally incorporate certain articles of [the CROC] into municipal law'.[113] Addressing this issue on appeal, the majority in the High Court said only that 'there may be [such] a question' and that 'it is unnecessary ... to embark upon consideration of those various matters'.[114]

In its most recent comment on legislative implementation of CROC in Australia, the Committee on the Rights of the Child expressed concern that the treaty 'cannot be used by the judiciary to override inconsistent provisions of domestic law'.

CAT

The *Convention Against Torture and Other Cruel, Inhuman or Degrading Treatment or Punishment* (CAT) has been legislated into Australian domestic law to an extent. Previously, the *Crimes (Torture) Act 1988* (Cth) made an act of torture a crime, but in very limited circumstances and there were no prosecutions under the Act. That Act was repealed in 2010 when Australia, on signing the *United Nations Optional Protocol to the Convention Against Torture*, passed the *Crimes Legislation Amendment (Torture Prohibition and Death Penalty Abolition) Act 2010* (Cth). That Act more fully implements CAT by adding the crime of torture to the Commonwealth *Criminal Code ('the Code')*.

The effect of section 274.2 of the *Code* is to impose 'absolute liability [on] persons who commit torture when acting in the capacity of a public official; acting in an official capacity; or acting at the instigation, or with the consent or acquiescence, of a public official or other person acting in an official capacity'.[115] Consistently with the absolute prohibition on torture in CAT, it is not a defence that the torture was done because of war or public emergency, or under orders.

SNAPSHOT: TORTURE OF AUSTRALIANS[116]

Australian citizens Mamdouh Habib and David Hicks were transferred to US custody following their apprehension in Pakistan in October 2001 and in Afghanistan in December 2001, respectively. It was not until 10 June 2004 that Mr Hicks was charged with conspiracy to commit war crimes, attempted murder and aiding the enemy. Mr Habib was released on 28 January 2005 on the basis that there was insufficient evidence to lay charges against him.

112 *B & B v Minister for Immigration & Multicultural & Indigenous Affairs* [2003] FamCA 451; 30 Fam LR 181, 195 (Nicholson CJ and O'Ryan J).

113 Ibid [2003] FamCA 451; 30 Fam LR 181, 227 (Nicholson CJ and O'Ryan J).

114 *Minister for Immigration and Multicultural and Indigenous Affairs v B & Another* [2004] HCA 20; 219 CLR 365, 406–407 (Gummow, Hayne and Heydon JJ). See also L Ruddle & S Nicholes, 'B & B and Minister for Immigration and Multicultural and Indigenous Affairs: Can International Treaties Release Children from Immigration Detention Centres? (2004) 5(1) *Melbourne Journal of International Law* 256.

115 Senate Standing Committee for the Scrutiny of Bills, Parliament of Australia, *Alert Digest No 15 of 2009* (2009) 17.

116 Based on Parliamentary Library, Commonwealth of Australia, *Bills Digest No 91 2009–10*, Crimes Legislation Amendment (Torture Prohibition and Death Penalty Abolition) Bill 2009 (2010) (citations omitted).

In February 2006, a report by the UN Commission on Human Rights stated that in April 2003, the United States Secretary of Defense authorised:

- removal of incentives, that is, comfort items
- exposure to extreme temperatures and deprivation of light and auditory stimuli
- altering the environment to create moderate discomfort by, for example, adjusting temperature or introducing an unpleasant smell
- adjusting the sleeping times of the detainee by reversing sleep cycles from night to day, and
- isolating the detainee from other detainees while still complying with basic standards of treatment.

Separately, the Parliamentary Assembly of the Council of Europe concluded that many detainees in Guantánamo Bay had been subjected to torture, which occurred systematically and with the knowledge and complicity of the United States Government. Lord Hope of Craighead, of the United Kingdom's House of Lords, stated that 'some of [the practices authorized for use in Guantánamo Bay by the United States authorities] would shock the conscience if they were ever to be authorized for use in our own country'.

Both Mr Hicks and Mr Habib alleged they were tortured during their detention, although the United States Government denied the allegations. The specific allegations remain undetermined, but the findings of the United States District Court for the District of Columbia in *Fouad Mahmoud al Rabiah v United States*[117] would seem to put beyond doubt that conduct amounting to torture was practised at Guantánamo Bay.

Mr Hicks and Mr Habib had no remedy under Australia law at the time. If the same conduct were to occur again, under the Code an arrest warrant could be issued and executed in relation to an official said to have engaged in or permitted the conduct. The Attorney-General's consent is necessary before any proceedings commence.

There is coverage of torture in State and Territory legislation. In Queensland the *Criminal Code* makes torture, defined consistently with the CAT definition, an offence.[118] Other State and Territory legislation referring to torture is in relation to, say, censorship restrictions or cruelty to animals, where the term 'torture' is not defined.

CAT is not scheduled or declared under the AHRC Act, so Australians have no access to the AHRC complaints process. Australians have access to an international complaints process under article 22 of CAT: see the discussion of individual communications in Chapter 7.4.7.

There is a prohibition in article 3 of CAT against *refoulement*—a state's sending a person to another state—if on being *refouled* the person is likely to be tortured. This prohibition is reflected to a limited extent in the *Extradition Act 1988* (Cth), under which the Attorney-General must be satisfied that a person will not be subjected to torture before allowing the person to be extradited.[119] Extradition is

117 *Fouad Mahmoud Al Rabiah, et al v United States et al, United States District Court for the District of Columbia, Civil Action No 02-828* (2009) <http://www.pillsburylaw.com/siteFiles/News/1259B22146574C540A8871C2C3131CA2.pdf>.

118 *Criminal Code 1899* (Qld) s 320A.

119 *Extradition Act 1988* (Cth) s 22(3).

not, however, the only way people are *refouled*: deportation and an administrative order for removal are other methods. Australian law is therefore not as broad in its protection as article 3 of CAT requires, and a person in Australia whose deportation or removal exposes them to the risk of torture can only make a communication to the CAT Committee.[120] In its observations on Australia's third periodic report under CAT,[121] the CAT Committee repeated concerns it had expressed previously[122] about the absence of a review mechanism for the Attorney-General's discretion in relation to *refoulement*, and called on Australia to 'explicitly incorporate [*non-refoulement*] into domestic legislation ... and implement it in practice'.[123] *Refoulement* is discussed in more detail in Chapter 15.4.4.

ILO

Australia has ratified seven of the eight ILO 'fundamental conventions'[124]—it has not ratified Convention 138 *Minimum Age Convention*, 1973—and the ILO convention rights are protected in a wide range of state and federal statutes. Australia's ratification of ILO 111, for example, underpins the *Disability Discrimination Act 1992* (Cth), the *Age Discrimination Act 2004* (Cth), parts of the *Australian Human Rights Commission Act 1986* (Cth) and affirmative action programs. Its ratification of *ILO 156 Workers with Family Responsibilities (1980)* is reflected in sections 4A and 7A of the *Sex Discrimination Act* and Part 6-4 of the *Fair Work Act*, and *ILO 158 Termination of Employment at the Initiative of the Employer* is also reflected in Part 6-4 of the *Fair Work Act*.

Perhaps it is Australia's long history of awareness and protection of the rights of workers—having been a founding member of the International Labour Organisation ('ILO') in 1919—that has led to its very high rate of implementing ILO conventions. Certainly the rate is in striking contrast with Australia's very poor implementation of its obligations under the major human rights treaties.

As is discussed in more detail below, Australia reports regularly to the ILO, and from time to time finds itself a party to complaints made by industrial organisations about labour law, policy and practices.

120 See UN Committee against Torture, *Elmi, Communication No 120/1998: Australia*, 22nd sess, UN Doc CAT/C/22/D/120/1998 (1999); J Kinslor, *Non-refoulement* and Torture: The Adequacy of Australia's Laws and Practices in Safeguarding Asylum-Seekers from Torture' (2000) 6(2) *Australian Journal of Human Rights* 161.

121 UN Committee against Torture, *Concluding Observations of the Committee Against Torture: Australia* 40th sess, Doc CAT/C/AUS/CO/3 (2008).

122 UN Committee against Torture, *Concluding Observations of the Committee Against Torture: Australia*, 25th sess, paras 47–53, UN Doc A/56/44 (2000).

123 See above, n 121, para 15, UN Doc CAT/C/AUS/CO/3 (2008).

124 See Chapter 17.2.3. The eight fundamental conventions of the ILO are: the Freedom of Association and Protection of the Right to Organise Convention 1948 (No 87); the Right to Organise and Collective Bargaining Convention 1949 (No 98); the Forced Labour Convention 1930 (No 29); the Abolition of Forced Labour Convention 1957 (No 105); the Equal Remuneration Convention 1951 (No 100); the Discrimination (Employment and Occupation) Convention 1958 (No 111); the Minimum Age Convention 1973 (No 138); and the Worst Forms of Child Labour Convention 1999 (No 182).

10.3.4 State and Territory Human Rights Laws

In the absence of a national human rights law for Australia, some of the States and Territories are taking matters into their own hands, although human rights legislation was rejected by inquiries in Victoria in 1987,[125] in Queensland in 1993[126] and 1998,[127] and in New South Wales in 2001.[128]

The Australian Capital Territory has enacted the *Human Rights Act 2004* (ACT) and Victoria has enacted the *Charter of Human Rights and Responsibilities Act 2006* (Vic). In 2007 inquiries in Tasmania[129] and Western Australia[130] recommended a human rights statute. The Western Australia recommendations have not been acted on, while in Tasmania the Government responded to the report of the Tasmania Law Reform Institute by announcing in June 2010 a project to examine a model for a Human Rights Charter for Tasmania; the project was continuing during 2011.[131]

The 'Dialogue' Model

The approach to human rights legislation in the ACT and Victoria is called the 'dialogue model', based on the approach taken in the UK under its *Human Rights Act*. The National Human Rights Consultation report explained the dialogue model:

NATIONAL HUMAN RIGHTS CONSULTATION REPORT[132]

What is common to the human rights Acts adopted in New Zealand, the United Kingdom, Victoria and the ACT is that they aim to facilitate a 'dialogue' between the three arms of government—the executive, the parliament and the judiciary. The Acts set out a range of rights to be protected and then give distinct roles to each arm of government in relation to those rights:

The executive (the government and its agencies) is required to act in a manner consistent with human rights in its decision making and can face court action if it fails to do so. When introducing new legislation into parliament, the government is (or members of parliament are) generally required to include a statement about whether the legislation is 'human rights compliant'. When a court makes a declaration that specific legislation is inconsistent with human rights, some models require the government to report to parliament on the inconsistency.

125 Legal and Constitutional Committee, Parliament of Victoria, *Report on the Desirability or Otherwise of Legislation Defining and Protecting Human Rights* (1987).

126 Queensland Electoral and Administrative Review Commission, see above, n 84.

127 Legal, Constitutional and Administrative Review Committee, Parliament of Queensland, *The Preservation and Enhancement of Individuals' Rights and Freedoms in Queensland: Should Queensland Adopt a Bill of Rights* (1998).

128 Standing Committee on Law and Justice, NSW Parliament, *A NSW Bill of Rights* (2001).

129 Tasmania Law Reform Institute, *A Charter of Rights for Tasmania, Report No 10* (2007).

130 Consultation Committee for a Proposed WA Human Rights Act, *A WA Human Rights Act* (2007).

131 <http://www.justice.tas.gov.au/corporateinfo/projects/human_rights_charter>.

132 Commonwealth of Australia, 2009, Ch 11 ; for criticism of the accuracy of the term 'dialogue model' see *Momcilovic v R* [2011] HCA 34.

The parliament is given the final say on laws. It can decide to pass legislation that overrides human rights. If a court makes a declaration that specific legislation is inconsistent with human rights, parliament can choose whether to amend the legislation. Parliamentary committees are involved in scrutinising Bills for human rights compliance before they are passed.

The judiciary is required to interpret legislation in a manner consistent with human rights. It may be empowered to provide remedies if the executive breaches human rights and to make declarations of incompatibility if legislation is found to be inconsistent with human rights. Importantly, such a declaration does not affect the operation or validity of the legislation: it is merely a signal to the government that it should consider amending the legislation.

In this way the three arms of government prompt responses from each other when a proposed law or policy is inconsistent with human rights.

[The National Human Rights Consultation report also noted arguments for and against the dialogue model:]

The dialogue model has been the subject of much debate. Supporters say it strikes a suitable balance between the judicial protection of human rights and parliamentary sovereignty because parliament retains the power to amend the Human Rights Act, to pass laws that are inconsistent with it, and to respond in any way it considers appropriate to a court's finding of inconsistency. The model has already been tested in several jurisdictions, and any federal model could draw on the lessons learnt from that experience. The Human Rights Law Resource Centre suggested that the dialogue model has been proven to create 'important systemic and cultural change within governments towards the protection and promotion of human rights'.

On the other hand, the dialogue model has been criticised on several grounds. The facts that parliament can amend the Human Rights Act at any time and that any legislative response to a court's finding of inconsistency depends on political will are regarded as weaknesses in the model. Some commentators have also suggested that some technical aspects of the model might encounter practical or constitutional difficulties. Others—including the Commonwealth Solicitor-General—are more confident that a carefully drafted Human Rights Act could avoid some of these problems.[133]

The ACT *Human Rights Act*

The *Human Rights Act 2004* (ACT) (HRA) gives explicit but limited effect to human rights in the ICCPR. Although the ACT Bill of Rights Consultative Committee recommended that the HRA protect economic, social and cultural rights,[134] the HRA in its final form does not do so, setting out only civil and political rights.

The HRA requires all public authorities to act consistently with the human rights protected under the Act, and to give proper consideration to relevant human rights in making decisions.[135] Although

133 See above, n 1, Chs 11 & 14 (citations omitted).

134 ACT Bill of Rights Consultative Committee, *Towards an ACT Human Rights Act* (2003), paras 2.97–2.108, 527, recommendation 1, cl 4 & the schedule to the draft Human Rights Bill at appendix 4. See also J Debeljak, 'Rights Protection without Judicial Supremacy: A Review of the Canadian and British Models of Bills of Rights' (2002) 26(2) *Melbourne University Law Review* 285, and *Australian Capital Territory Economic, Social And Cultural Rights Research Project, Report*, September 2010, at <http://acthra.anu.edu.au>.

135 *Human Rights Act 2004* (ACT) s 40B.

the HRA does not permit individuals to sue for damages for a breach of human rights, it does permit alleged victims to claim that a public authority has failed to act consistently with their human rights, and to seek an appropriate remedy other than damages.[136] Administrative law remedies, such as setting aside a decision or ordering that a decision be remade, are most likely to be useful in this context.

The HRA further enables the ACT Supreme Court to make a declaration of incompatibility in relation to an ACT law, without actually invalidating the law.[137] As well,[138] the HRA requires: ACT laws to be interpreted in a way compatible with human rights '[s]o far as it is possible to do so consistently with its purpose';[139] notice to be given to the government and the ACT Human Rights Commission when a question involving the application of the HRA arises in the Supreme Court;[140] and the ACT government to table a 'compatibility statement' with any new legislation.[141]

The ACT Supreme Court has made only one declaration of incompatibility,[142] and the HRA has had little influence on court decisions.[143] The Act is said, however, to have led to laws that are more respectful of human rights.[144]

SNAPSHOT: ACT *HUMAN RIGHTS ACT* DECLARATION OF INCOMPATIBILITY

Mr Islam was charged with a range of offences including attempted murder, and was refused bail.[145] The refusal was based on the operation of s9C of the *Bail Act 1992* (ACT), which requires a person charged with a serious offence to show 'exceptional circumstances' to be eligible for bail.

The Court considered the operation of section 9C in light of section 30 of the *Human Rights Act 2004* (ACT), which requires an ACT law to be 'interpreted in a way that is compatible with human rights', so far as it is possible to do so consistently with the legislation's purpose. The Court decided that the purpose of

136 Ibid 40C.

137 Ibid s 32.

138 See generally G McKinnon, 'Comment: Strengthening Human Rights: Amendments to the *Human Rights Act 2004* (ACT)' (2008) 19 *Public Law Review* 186; H Charlesworth & R Thilagaratnam, 'Human Rights Protection in Australia: The ACT *Human Rights Act*' (paper presented at the Protecting Human Rights Conference, Gilbert + Tobin Centre of Public Law, Sydney, 2 October 2009; ACT Human Rights Act Research Project ANU, *The Human Rights Act 2004 (ACT): The First Five Years of Operation: A Report to the Act Department of Justice and Community* (2009).

139 See above, n 135, s 30. See *R v Fearsside* [2009] ACTCA 3.

140 See above, n 135, s 34.

141 See above, n 135, s 37.

142 *In the Matter of an Application for Bail by Isa Islam* [2010] ACTSC 147.

143 See cases reported at <http://acthra.anu.edu.au/>.

144 H Charlesworth & G McKinnon, 'Australia's First Bill of Rights: The Australian Capital Territory's *Human Rights Act*' (Law and Policy Paper No 28, Centre for International and Public Law, ANU, 2006) 10, cited by G McKinnon, 'Strengthening Human Rights: Amendments to the *Human Rights Act 2004* (ACT)' (2008) 19 *Public Law Review* 186, 186. See also ACT *Human Rights Act* Research Project ANU, *Creating a Human Rights Culture Within the ACT Government—Report on Interview Research Assessing the Impact of the Human Rights Act 2004 on the ACT Public Service*, 2008.

145 See above, n 142, (19 November 2010); based on a summary of *R v Islam* by Sean Costello at <www.hrlrc.org.au>.

section 9C was to set 'exceptional circumstances' as a threshold barrier for bail. The Court decided it was not possible to interpret section 9C in a way that is compatible with the requirement in section 18(5) of the *Human Rights Act* that no one be detained in custody as a general rule.

Because s 9C could be not be interpreted consistently with the *Human Rights Act*, the Court issued a declaration of incompatibility under section 32 of that Act. The ACT Attorney-General tabled the declaration to the Legislative Assembly within six sitting days as required[146] and tabled a written response within a further six months, in June 2011, as required advising that no action would be taken until the result was known of the High Court appeal in Momcilovic (see snapshot below). There is no requirement for the Legislative Assembly to amend the law, and it can remain in its original form.

Despite the declaration, section 9C continues to operate. The Court went on to give effect to it and decided that there were no exceptional circumstances that entitled Mr Islam to make a bail application. His application for bail was refused.[147]

The Victorian *Charter of Rights and Responsibilities*

Like the HRA, the *Charter of Human Rights and Responsibilities Act 2006* (Vic) (the *Charter*) gives explicit effect to civil and political rights but does not extend to cover economic, social and cultural rights. Unlike the report leading to human rights legislation in the ACT, the Victorian report recommended against legislating for economic, social and cultural rights, although it recommended that a subsequent review revisit the issue.[148]

The *Charter* operates similarly to the HRA. It does not permit individuals to sue for damages, but it permits individuals to challenge the actions of public authorities for failure to comply with their obligation to act compatibly with human rights or give proper consideration to a relevant right,[149] provided that the individual would otherwise have standing to challenge the public authority (for example under administrative law).[150]

As in the ACT, the *Charter* enables the Victorian Supreme Court, without actually invalidating a law, to make declarations of inconsistent interpretation when a law cannot be interpreted and applied consistently with human rights.[151] It requires the Scrutiny of Acts and Regulations Committee[152] to report on the human rights compatibility of all new legislation;[153] and requires courts and tribunals to

146 Legislative Assembly for the ACT, *2011 Week 1 Hansard (15 February)*, 70–1.

147 In late 2010 the ACT Government lodged an appeal against the declaration of incompatability: ibid.

148 *Rights, Responsibilities and Respect: The Report of the Human Rights Consultation Committee, State of Victoria*, 2005, 29. See J Tobin 'Economic, Social and Cultural Rights and the Victorian *Charter of Human Rights and Responsibilities*—A Framework for Discussion' (Occasional Paper, Victorian Equal Opportunity and Human Rights Commission, 2010).

149 The obligations of public authorities are contained in *Charter of Human Rights and Responsibilities Act 2006* (Vic) s 38.

150 *Charter of Human Rights and Responsibilities Act 2006* (Vic) s 39.

151 Ibid s 36; see Snapshot below; note that three of seven judges in *Momcilovic v R* [2011] HCA 34 found s36 to be invalid.

152 Ibid s 30.

153 Ibid s 28.

interpret and apply laws consistently with human rights 'so far as it is possible to do so consistently with their purpose'.[154]

The *Charter* rights are, however, subject 'to such reasonable limits as can be demonstrably justified in a free and democratic society'[155] and may be overridden by legislation that is specifically declared to have that effect.[156] But 'the general limitation power is broader than the equivalent limitation powers under international human rights law [and] the inclusion of an override power is [both] unnecessary [and its] application ... to all rights is too broad. Further, the safeguards included to regulate the use of the override fall far short of those contained in international, regional and comparable domestic human rights instruments'.[157]

Debeljak points out that the general limitations provision in the *Charter* operates much more broadly than international law, which does not allow limits (as the *Charter* does) on absolute rights such as the prohibitions against torture, slavery, arbitrary detention, racial discrimination and retrospective laws, and the right to be treated equally before the law.[158] She also points out that the conditions under which the *Charter's* override provision operates are much less restrictive than in international law, which requires a 'public emergency which threatens the life of a nation'.[159] The situation under the *Charter* can be compared to the *HRA*, which 'does not contain an additional override/derogation provision [and] implicitly recognises that the retention of parliamentary sovereignty is achieved by limiting the powers of the judiciary to interpretation and declaration alone'.[160]

The Victorian Human Rights and Equal Opportunity Commission reported favourably on parliamentary performance under the *Charter* in 2009,[161] saying that 'members have generally tabled well-drafted statements of compatibility, some containing a robust analysis of human rights issues ... Parliamentary debates have made increasing references to the Charter, sometimes articulating complex and considered comment in relation to human rights issues'. In April 2011, the newly elected Liberal–National government in Victoria asked the parliamentary Scrutiny of Acts and Regulations Committee to report by the end of the year on the first four years of operation of the *Charter*, including the effects of the *Charter Act* on the development, drafting and parliamentary consideration of statutory provisions; the provision of services and performance of functions by public authorities, litigation and the conduct of courts and tribunals; the availability of accessible, just and timely remedies for infringements of rights; the overall benefits and costs of the *Charter*; and options for reform or improvement.[162]

154 Ibid s 32.

155 Ibid s 7(2); the interaction of ss 7(2) and 32 was examined in *Momcilovic v R* [2011] HCA 34.

156 Ibid s 31.

157 J Debeljak, 'Balancing Rights in a Democracy: The Problems with Limitations and Overrides of Rights under the Victorian *Charter of Human Rights and Responsibilities Act 2006*' (2008) 32(2) *Melbourne University Law Review* 422, 432.

158 Ibid 434.

159 Ibid 441.

160 Ibid 422, n 150.

161 Victorian Equal Opportunity & Human Rights Commission, *The 2009 Report on the Operation of the Charter of Human Rights and Responsibilities: Making Progress*, 2010.

162 *Victoria Government Gazette*, No. S 128, Tuesday 19 April 2011.

SNAPSHOT: VICTORIAN CHARTER DECLARATION OF INCOMPATIBILITY

Drugs were found in Ms Momcilovic's apartment.[163] The *Drugs, Poisons and Controlled Substances Act 1981* (Vic) (DPCS Act) deems a person to be in possession of drugs that are found unless they 'satisf[y] the court to the contrary'. Ms Momcilovic was so deemed, and she was convicted of one count of drug trafficking.

Section 32 of the *Charter of Rights and Responsibilities 2006* (Vic) requires all statutory provisions to be interpreted in a way that is compatible with human rights, 'so far as it is possible to do so consistently with their purpose'. Ms Momcilovic appealed on the ground, among others, that by imposing a legal burden to show that she was not in possession of a drug, the DPCS Act is inconsistent with the presumption of innocence in s25(1) of the *Charter*.

The Court said that the relevant provision of the DPCS Act was 'not so much an infringement of the presumption of innocence as a wholesale subversion of it', contrary to section 25 of the *Charter*. Accordingly, the Court notified the Attorney-General of its intention to issue a 'Declaration of Inconsistent Interpretation' under section 36(2) of the *Charter*. The Attorney-General must table the Declaration, and a written response, in Parliament within six months.

Despite the declaration, the deeming provision of the DPCS Act continues to operate. The Court was obliged to give effect to it, and upheld Ms Momcilovic's conviction.[164]

10.3.5 Anti-Discrimination Laws

Federal, State and Territory anti-discrimination and affirmative action laws implement many, but not all, of Australia's obligations under ICERD, CEDAW and CRPD, and some aspects of ICCPR, CROC and ILO Conventions.

Commonwealth Anti-Discrimination Laws

The Commonwealth has no explicit constitutional power to legislate against discrimination generally, although it could pass laws in respect of discrimination against specific groups of people for whom it has power to legislate, such as migrants or married people,[165] and can rely on a range of constitutional powers to legislate more generally.[166]

The *Racial Discrimination Act 1975* (RDA) was the first anti-discrimination law enacted by the Commonwealth, giving almost literal effect to ICERD. The constitutional validity of the RDA was confirmed in 1982 in *Koowarta v Bjelke-Petersen*.[167] As with the RDA, the constitutional validity of the *Sex*

163 *R v Momcilovic* [2010] VSCA 50 (17 March 2010); based on a summary of *R v Momcilovic* by Phil Lynch at <www.hrlrc.org.au>.

164 The High Court quashed the conviction, but by a 4-3 majority upheld the validity of the Victorian Supreme Court's power to make a declaration of inconsistency: *Momcilovic v R* [2011] HCA 34; on the Victorian decision, see Julie Debeljak, 'Who is sovereign now? The Momcilovic Court hands back power over human rights that Parliament intended it to have' (2011) 22 *Public Law Review* 15.

165 *Australian Constitution* ss 51(xxi) and 51(xxvii).

166 See Chapter 10.3.3.

167 [1982] HCA 27; 153 CLR 168; see Chapter 10.2.1.

Discrimination Act 1984 (SDA) is supported by various heads of Commonwealth power in s 51 of the *Constitution*, and by Australia's ratification of CEDAW.

The *Disability Discrimination Act 1992* (DDA) relies on heads of power in s 51 of the *Constitution*, and implements various provisions of the ICCPR, ICESCR, ILO Discrimination (Employment and Occupation) Convention 1958 (ILO convention 111) and CROC. The DDA was enacted some years before the UN's development and adoption of the CRPD. Similarly to the DDA, the *Age Discrimination Act 2004* (ADA) relies for its validity on the extent to which it gives effect to various provisions of the ICCPR, ICESCR, ILO convention 111 and CROC.[168] The objects of the ADA reflect 'the international commitment to eliminate age discrimination reflected in the Political Declaration adopted in Madrid, Spain on 12 April 2002 by the Second World Assembly on Ageing'.[169]

In 2010 the Commonwealth Government said it would consolidate the four specific discrimination Acts into a single omnibus statute,[170] a possibility that had been raised in a 2008 Senate Committee report on the effectiveness of the SDA.[171] The consultation process towards the proposed consolidation was continuing during 2011.

The mechanism for obtaining a remedy for a breach of federal anti-discrimination legislation is in the *Australian Human Rights Act 1986* (AHRC Act),[172] which establishes the Australian Human Rights Commission (AHRC). The AHRC inquires into and attempts to conciliate complaints of unlawful discrimination made under federal anti-discrimination legislation,[173] and inquires into and attempts to conciliate more general 'human rights complaints'[174] and complaints about conduct that nullifies or impairs the right to equality in employment.[175]

State and Territory Anti-Discrimination Laws

The States and Territories have been enacting and amending anti-discrimination legislation since the South Australian *Prohibition of Discrimination Act* in 1966. Tasmania was the last jurisdiction to enact a comprehensive anti-discrimination law, in 1998.[176] Victoria has most recently overhauled its legislation, in 2010.[177]

168 *Age Discrimination Act 2004* (Cth) s 10(7).

169 Ibid s 3(e).

170 R McClelland & L Tanner, 'Reform of Anti-Discrimination Legislation' (Media Release, 21 April 2010); see above, n 89, 9.

171 Senate Standing Committee on Legal and Constitutional Affairs, Parliament of Australia, *Effectiveness of the Sex Discrimination Act 1984 in Eliminating Discrimination and Promoting Gender Equality*, (2008), recommendation 111.

172 Previously the *Human Rights and Equal Opportunity Commission Act 1986* (Cth).

173 *Australian Human Rights Commission Act 1986* (Cth) ss 11(1)(a) & 11(1)(aa) see the description of the AHRC's process at Chapter 10.4.2 below.

174 Ibid s 11(1)(f).

175 Ibid s 31(b).

176 For a history of the development of anti-discrimination laws in Tasmania, see G Bernardi, 'From Conflict to Convergence: The Evolution of Tasmanian Anti-Discrimination Law' (2001) 7(1) *Australian Journal of Human Rights* 134.

177 The substance of the *Equal Opportunity Act 2010* (Vic) will commence during 2011.

The federal anti-discrimination laws apply in all States and Territories, and operate concurrently with State and Territory laws to the extent that there is no inconsistency.[178] The coverage of the State and Territory laws is wider than that of the four federal laws, protecting against discrimination in many areas of public activity on the basis of a wide range of additional personal attributes, such as carer's responsibility, sexuality, gender status, criminal or medical record, industrial activity, sexual activity, relationship status, parental status, physical features and religious or political belief.[179]

The proposed consolidation of the four federal discrimination statutes into a single statute may or may not be a step towards harmonising, if not consolidating, all anti-discrimination laws in Australia. In 2004 the Productivity Commission concluded that 'the problems of trying to negotiate a uniform national framework and the disruption that this effort would cause suggest that the best course of action is for both levels of government to continue to legislate in this area'.[180]

10.4 AUSTRALIAN HUMAN RIGHTS MECHANISMS

10.4.1 National Action Plan

The Office of the United Nations High Commissioner for Human Rights (OHCHR) has recommended a 'best practice' process for developing a national action plan (NAP) in its *Handbook on National Human Rights Plans of Action*.[181] Australia's first NAP in 1994, and its updates in 1995 and 1996, were pioneering documents, setting a benchmark for the plans that followed from other countries. After a brief preamble and overview they ran through a series of issues, identifying in each case current policy, challenges ahead and proposed national action. They gave a clear account of how and when steps would be taken to address human rights issues in Australia and were well regarded in the account given in the OHCHR handbook.[182]

Australia's most recent NAP, *Australia's National Framework for Human Rights—National Action Plan*, was published in December 2004. After a wholly inadequate preparation, that NAP failed to describe the (then) present situation drawing on a baseline study, failed to set out proposed action within short, medium and long timeframes, failed to set out institutional responsibility for proposed action, failed to identify resources and failed to describe monitoring and evaluation processes. In its 2010 report to the United Nations Universal Periodic Review, the Australian Government committed to 'develop a new National Action Plan on Human Rights, working with States and Territories to outline

178 *Racial Discrimination Act 1975* (Cth) s 6A; *Sex Discrimination Act 1984* (Cth) ss 10(3), 10(4) & 10(5); *Disability Discrimination Act 1992* (Cth) s 13; *Viskauskas v Niland* [1983] HCA 15; 153 CLR 280; *University of Wollongong v Mohamed Naguib Fawzi Ahmed Metwally & Others* [1984] HCA 74; 158 CLR 447. See also *Attorney-General (NT) v Hand, Minister for Aboriginal Affairs & Others* (1989) 25 FCR 345.

179 See generally N Rees, K Lindsay & S Rice, *Australian Anti-Discrimination Law*, Federation Press, Sydney, 2008.

180 Australian Government Productivity Commission, *Review of the Disability Discrimination Act 1992*, Report No 30 (2004) 177.

181 UN Office of the High Commissioner for Human Rights, New York, 2002.

182 *Handbook on National Human Rights Plans of Action*, UN Office of the High Commissioner for Human Rights, New York, 2002, pt 4.1.

future action for the promotion and protection of human rights'.[183] After consultation on a background paper,[184] a baseline study and a draft plan, a new NAP will be released in late 2011 or early 2012.[185]

10.4.2 Australian Human Rights Commission

The Australian Human Rights Commission (AHRC)—previously the Human Rights and Equal Opportunity Commission (HREOC)—is Australia's national human rights institution (NHRI). International standards for the structure and operation of NHRIs are known as the Paris Principles[186] under a 1991 resolution of the United Nations Commission on Human Rights adopted by the UN General Assembly. The Paris Principles require a state to ensure that its NHRI is autonomous, that its independence is guaranteed by statute and that it has a broad mandate based on universal human rights standards with adequate powers and sufficient resources.

The AHRC has been given an 'A' status as an NHRI by the International Coordinating Committee of National Human Rights Institutions. Its status was last reviewed in 2006 and its application to for re-accreditation will be in late 2011.[187]

Australia is one of the few states to operate an NHRI that has powers of monitoring, policy development, education and complaint handling. Most other institutions, with a notable exception in Canada, have a more narrow range of functions such as consultation and advice, reviewing maladministration in the role of an ombudsman, or conducting education programs.

An independent report on NHRIs in 2000 queried whether the AHRC at the time met a key criterion in the Paris Principles for independence: sufficiency and security of funding.[188] The financial security of the AHRC has only become more uncertain since, and there is still some doubt as to whether it meets the international standards for an effective NHRI. Despite having reduced funding to its own NHRI and trying to limit its autonomy (discussed below), in 2004 then the federal government reaffirmed the important and constructive role played by NHRIs, and encouraged other states to strengthen existing institutions and to consider providing their NHRIs with more autonomy and independence.[189]

Structure

The AHRC is established under the AHRC Act and administers its own Act, the four discrimination Acts and parts of the *Native Title Act 1993* and the *Fair Work Act 2008*. The AHRC has a President,

---

183 See above, n 62, para 47.

184 Attorney-General's Department, *A new National Human Rights Action Plan for Australia: Background Paper*, Commonwealth of Australia, 2010.

185 Ibid 6; for news and developments on the NAP see <www.humanrightsactionplan.org.au>.

186 *Institutions for the Promotion and Protection of Human Rights*, GA Res 48/134, UN GA, 48th sess, 85th plen mtg, UN Doc A/RES/48/134 (1993). These principles were also endorsed by the UN Commission on Human Rights in resolution 1992/54, entitled 'Principles Relating to the Status and Functioning of National Institutions for Protection and Promotion of Human Rights'.

187 National Human Rights Institutions Forum <www.nhri.net/>.

188 *Performance and Legitimacy: National Human Rights Institutions*, International Council on Human Rights Policy, Versoix, 2000, 108.

189 *National Institutions for the Promotion and Protection of Human Rights*, CHR Res 2004/75, UN Commission on Human Rights, 60th sess, 58th plen mtg, UN Doc E/CN.4/2004/L.11/Add.7 (2004).

and six 'portfolio' Commissioner positions responsible for human rights, Aboriginal and Torres Strait Islander social justice, racial discrimination, sex discrimination, disability discrimination and age discrimination respectively. The position of Aboriginal and Torres Strait Islander Social Justice Commissioner was established in 1992 in response to recommendations from the Royal Commission into Aboriginal Deaths in Custody.[190]

The AHRC is established as a body corporate, but there are aspects of its structure and operation that compromise its independence. AHRC has no entitlement to operational funds from the government, and depends from year to year on the parliament, advised by the executive, making funds available. In the 2000–01 year the government's appropriation to the AHRC was reduced by more than 26 per cent, from $14.4m to $10.6m. The cut in funding has not been restored; in 2011–12 the government appropriation to the AHRC was $16.5m,[191] still lower in real terms than it was in 1999–2000.[192]

The AHRC has reported that '[as] a small agency, [it] does not compete on an equal footing with large agencies for additional funding from government ... because its project proposals are required to be fully offset within the portfolio'. Government funding, it said, does not keep up with 'the demand-driven growth in services provided by AHRC and the increases in its operating expenses'.[193]

Functions

The AHRC's principal functions are set out in section 11 of the AHRC Act, and include inquiring into and attempting to conciliate complaints of unlawful discrimination; examining enactments for their consistency with human rights; conducting inquiries into contemporary human rights issues; promoting understanding, acceptance and public discussion of human rights in Australia; preparing guidelines for good human rights practice; and intervening in court proceedings that involve human rights issues.

Complaints of Unlawful Discrimination

The AHRC is the body to which complaints are made by people who claim they have been unlawfully discriminated against under the four federal anti-discrimination statutes.

The commission's predecessor body, HREOC, used to investigate complaints, attempt to resolve them and hold public hearings about unresolved complaints. It would make findings of fact and law, and a complainant who was successful would register the favourable findings in the Federal Court and enforce them. In *Brandy v HREOC*,[194] the High Court decided that HREOC did not have the constitutional power to make legally binding decisions because it is not established as a court under Chapter III of the

190 Royal Commission into Aboriginal Deaths in Custody, Commonwealth of Australia, 1991, <www.austlii.edu.au/au/other/IndigLRes/rciadic/>.

191 Appropriation Bill (No 1) 2011–2012 (Cth).

192 Australian Bureau of Statistics, *6401.0—Consumer Price Index, Australia, March 2011*, Table 13, Data sheet 6, column AD.

193 Human Rights and Equal Opportunity Commission, *Submission to the Joint Committee of Public Accounts and Audit Inquiry on the Effects of the ongoing Efficiency Dividend on Smaller Public Sector Agencies*, Parliament of Australia, 2008.

194 [1995] HCA 10; 183 CLR 245.

Australian Constitution. Amending legislation gave power to the Federal Court and the Federal Magistrates Court to hear complaints that cannot be resolved by investigation and conciliation at the AHRC.[195]

Complaints of Human Rights Violations

As well as dealing with complaints under the federal anti-discrimination laws, the AHRC can inquire into 'any act or practice that may be inconsistent with or contrary to any human right'[196] if it is an act or practice of the Commonwealth or its agencies.[197] For this purpose, human rights are those recognised in the ICCPR, *the Declarations of the Rights of the Child, on the Rights of Mentally Retarded Persons, and on the Rights of Disabled Persons*,[198] and 'any relevant international instrument' declared by the Attorney-General 'to be an international instrument relating to human rights and freedoms for the purposes of [AHRC Act]';[199] instruments that have been declared for this purpose are CROC, the CRPD, *and the Declaration on the Elimination of all Forms of Intolerance and of Discrimination Based on Religion of Belief*. The ICESCR has not been declared, which means that the AHRC has no power to inquire into a breach of it.

The AHRC can also 'inquire into any act or practice, including any systemic practice, that may constitute discrimination [in employment]'. Discrimination for this purpose is defined by the AHRC Act in the same terms as in ILO Convention No 111[200] and does not apply to conduct that is the subject of the four federal discrimination statutes. ILO Convention No 111 proscribes conduct based on specified grounds (race, sex, religion etc) and on 'any other distinction, exclusion or preference' that nullifies or impairs equality of opportunity in employment. For purposes of the AHRC's power to inquire, that has been defined to include an extensive list of personal attributes: age, medical record, criminal record, marital status, disability, nationality, sexual preference and trade union activity, whether past, current or imputed.[201]

For human rights violations and ILO employment complaints, the AHRC has the power to investigate the complaint and attempt to resolve it through conciliation.[202] If a complaint cannot be conciliated, the President will either decline it or make a finding that it constitutes a breach and report to the federal Attorney-General, who will table the report in the Federal Parliament.[203] The report will recommend what the respondent to the complaint—the breaching party—should do to remedy the breach and avoid it in future. A finding that conduct constitutes a breach is a reviewable decision under the *Administrative Decisions (Judicial Review) Act 1977* (Cth).[204]

195 *Human Rights Legislation Amendment Act (No 1) 1999* (Cth).

196 *Australian Human Rights Commission Act 1986* (Cth) s 11(1)(f).

197 Ibid s 3(1) (definitions of 'act' and 'practice').

198 Ibid s 3(1).

199 Ibid s 47.

200 Ibid s 3(1).

201 *Australian Human Rights Commission Regulations 1989* (Cth) reg 4(a).

202 See above, n 196 ss 11(1)(f) & 31(b).

203 Ibid s 46.

204 *Commonwealth v Human Rights & Equal Opportunity Commission & Others* [1999] FCA 1524 ; (1999) 167 ALR 268.

Of the 220 human rights and discrimination in employment complaints that the AHRC received in 2009–10, most were made under the ICCPR (35.5 per cent) and ILO 111 (57 per cent).[205] In the same year AHRC resolved 194 such complaints, of which 49 per cent were declined or closed (too old, not a breach, trivial, withdrawn etc). Of the remainder, 46 per cent were resolved through conciliation and 5 per cent could not be resolved and will become the subject of report to the Attorney-General.[206]

SNAPSHOT: DISCRIMINATION IN EMPLOYMENT ON THE GROUND OF A CRIMINAL RECORD—*KL V STATE OF NEW SOUTH WALES (DEPARTMENT OF EDUCATION)*

A significant number of the complaints made under ILO Convention No 111 are for discrimination on the ground of criminal record (for example, 30.5% in 2009–10[207]). In 2010 the AHRC reported to the Attorney-General on its investigation of a complaint by Mr 'KL' against the NSW Department of Education.[208]

Between the ages of 21 and 30 Mr KL was convicted of a number of offences including drug use and possession, stealing and dishonesty. He was sentenced to terms of imprisonment for many of those offences. More than 10 years after the last offence, he completed a Bachelor of Music Education and a Graduate Diploma in Education. The NSW Department of Education refused him a position as a teacher because of his record of convictions.

The Department and the AHRC agreed that it is an inherent requirement of the job of a teacher that a person espouses the highest standards of conduct and integrity, demonstrates a commitment to upholding the standards expected by the community of teachers in NSW public schools and enhances and protects the reputation of the Department of Education as an employer and of public education. They disagreed on whether that is now the case for Mr KL: the AHRC said that 'a person with Mr KL's criminal record is [not] necessarily rendered incapable forever of fulfilling the inherent requirements of the job of a teacher'.

The AHRC decided that the Department's decision was a breach of the prohibition against discrimination in employment as defined in the AHRC Act and recommended payment of financial compensation. The Department said it would not follow the recommendations, but that it would give casual approval to Mr KL to teach in NSW Government Schools for an initial period of 12 months.

The AHRC's ability to inquire into and report on human rights violations is the only national mechanism in Australia for assessing conduct against the human rights standards of the ICCPR, CROC and CRPD. But as is apparent from Mr KL's experience, the exercise gives no enforceable remedy to a victim of a breach, and respondents to a tabled report rarely comply with the AHRC's recommendations. The process is therefore an inadequate implementation of Australia's obligations, as UN Committees have observed.

205 Australian Human Rights Commission, *Annual Report 2009–2010*, 2010, 33 (table 33).

206 Ibid 89 (table 36).

207 Ibid 33 (table 33).

208 *Mr KL v State of NSW (Department of Education)* [2010] AusHRC 42.

Court Intervention and Amicus Curiae

The AHRC occasionally acts in an *amicus curiae* ('friend of the court') role in the Federal Court or Federal Magistrates Court under the federal anti-discrimination statutes, if the case may significantly affect the human rights of people who are not parties to it or if it has significant implications for the administration of one of the discrimination Acts.[209] The AHRC can also intervene as a party in proceedings, although its criteria for intervening are strict.[210]

Significant interventions by the AHRC (and its predecessor HREOC)[211] include the matters of *Re McBain; Ex parte Australian Catholic Bishops Conference* (the IVF Case),[212] in which AHRC addressed the construction to be given to provisions of the SDA; *Members of the Yorta Yorta Aboriginal Community v Victoria*,[213] in which AHRC addressed the application of international human rights principles to the construction to be given to the *Native Title Act 1993* (Cth); and the *Family Provisions Case—PR082005*,[214] in which the AHRC invoked Australia's international obligations in support of award provisions that would assist working parents and carers to balance their paid work with their family and caring responsibilities, and reported on the 'right to request' model in the UK.

Reporting on Indigenous Issues

The Aboriginal and Torres Strait Islander Social Justice Commissioner reports to Federal Parliament each year on human rights issues for Australia's indigenous peoples.[215] Under the *Native Title Act 1993*,[216] the Commissioner reports to the responsible Minister on the operation of the legislation and its impact on the human rights of the Aboriginal and Torres Strait Islander peoples.

Public Education, Reports and Inquiries

One of the AHRC's functions is 'to undertake ... educational programs ... for the purpose of promoting human rights',[217] and it does so extensively.[218] It makes submissions to parliamentary committees on proposed human rights legislation and amendments, and monitors the implementation of human rights legislation. It is able to report on laws that should be made, or action that should be taken by

209 See above, n 201, s 46PV.

210 *Intervention in Court Proceedings: The Australian Human Rights Commission Guidelines*, Australian Human Rights Commission <http://www.humanrights.gov.au/legal/submissions_court/intervention/interventions_in_court_proc.htm>.

211 See a list at *Information about the Intervention Role*, Australian Human Rights Commission <http://www.humanrights.gov.au/legal/submissions_court/intervention/intervention_info.html>.

212 [2002] HCA 16; 209 CLR 372.

213 [2002] HCA 58; 214 CLR 422.

214 [2005] AIRC 692.

215 *Social Justice Reports*, Australian Human Rights Commission <http://www.hreoc.gov.au/social_justice/sj_report/index.html>.

216 *Native Title Act 1993* (Cth) s 209.

217 See above, n 196.

218 See Australian Human Rights Commission <www.humanrights.gov.au>.

Australia, on matters relating to human rights and can report on action that needs to be taken by Australia to comply with international instruments scheduled to or declared under the AHRC Act. Recent reports address human rights issues facing African Australians,[219] age discrimination issues for mature-age workers[220] and offshore detention of asylum seekers.[221]

10.4.3 Other Federal Human Rights Agencies

The Office of the Australian Information Commissioner (which incorporates the previous Office of the Privacy Commissioner) oversees information policy, privacy protection and freedom of information.[222] Its privacy functions give effect to Australia's obligations regarding the right to privacy under article 17 of the ICCPR,[223] and its role in overseeing the right of access to information under the *Freedom of Information Act 1982*, although not expressed in the Act in human rights terms, is an aspect of the human right to freedom of expression in article 19 of ICCPR.

The Equal Opportunity for Women in the Workplace Agency (EOWA) (formerly the Affirmative Action Agency) works to achieve equal opportunity for women through education and assistance to organisations. EOWA's role is intended to give effect to certain of Australia's obligations under CEDAW.[224]

The Commonwealth Ombudsman's office receives and investigates complaints by people about the conduct of the executive branch of government.[225] Speaking in 2009, the then Commonwealth Ombudsman, John McMillan, said that '[i]n broad terms, Ombudsman offices are especially interested in safeguarding *administrative law rights*. This includes the right to complain about the actions of a government agency without reprisal, the right to natural justice (a fair hearing, and an unbiased decision) before adverse action is taken by a government agency, and the right to equal and non-discriminatory treatment by government'.[226] The Ombudsman does not, however, offer an enforceable remedy for a breach of 'administrative law rights'. On concluding an investigation into a complaint, and finding that there was maladministration by the government agency, the Ombudsman will report to the agency recommending that they take remedial action.[227]

219 Australian Human Rights Commission, *In Our Own Words: African Australians—A Review of Human Rights and Social Inclusion Issues*, 2010.

220 Australian Human Rights Commission, *Age Discrimination—Exposing the Hidden Barrier for Mature Age Workers*, 2010.

221 Australian Human Rights Commission, *Immigration Detention and Offshore Processing on Christmas Island*, 2009.

222 *Australian Information Commissioner Act 2010* (Cth) s 4. Cf *Freedom of Information Act 1982* (Cth); *Privacy Act 1988* (Cth).

223 *Privacy Act 1988* (Cth), long title.

224 *Equal Opportunity for Women in the Workplace Act 1999* (Cth) s 5(9). For a recent review of EOWA, see Office for Women, Department of Families, Housing, Community Services and Indigenous Affairs, *Review of the Equal Opportunity for Women in the Workplace Act 1999—KPMG Consultation Report*, 2009; for the government's response to the review, and proposed renaming of EOWA to the Workplace Gender Equality Agency, see Department of Families, Housing, Community Services and Indigenous Affairs, Fact Sheet: Retaining and Improving the 'Equal Opportunity for Women in the Workplace Act 1999', March 2011, <http://www.fahcsia.gov.au/sa/women/progserv/economic/Documents/EOWA_fact_sheet.pdf>.

225 Commonwealth Ombudsman <www.ombudsman.gov.au/>.

226 J McMillan, 'The Ombudsman's Role in Human Rights Protection: An Australian Perspective' (paper presented at the 11th Asian Ombudsman Association Conference, Bangkok, November 2009, 2 (emphasis in original).

227 *Ombudsman Act 1976* (Cth) s 15.

10.4.4 State and Territory Human Rights Agencies

A wide range of Commonwealth, State and Territory agencies have functions under legislation to engage in conduct (eg elections and policing) and to provide services (eg education, social security and public housing) that protect and promote human rights. These agencies are not established explicitly to give effect to an obligation arising under an international human rights treaty, but exist and operate because Australia is a liberal democracy and, to a significant degree, a welfare state.

In each State and Territory a statutory agency receives and investigates complaints of discrimination under local legislation. The effect of human rights legislation in the ACT and Victoria has been to highlight a human rights perspective on the provision of public services, but such services exist at the discretion of the government, rather than guaranteed by legal recognition of a human right.

10.4.5 Legislation Scrutiny Committees

In 1981 the Australian Senate established the Senate Standing Committee for the Scrutiny of Bills[228] to consider whether, among other things, Bills 'trespass unduly on personal rights and liberties; or make rights, liberties or obligations unduly dependent upon insufficiently defined administrative powers ... [or] non-reviewable decisions'.[229] The Committee issues an alert on new Bills and receives a comment from the responsible Minister before publishing a report on its concerns about the Bills. The report is not binding and makes no recommendations, but it puts on the record any concerns and implicitly invites the Minister to address them.

Responding to a recommendation of the National Human Rights Consultation,[230] the federal government introduced legislation[231] to establish a new Joint Parliamentary Committee on Human Rights, which will examine and report to Parliament on the compatibility of legislation and legislative instruments with Australia's international human rights obligations. The legislation was referred to a Senate Committee, which by majority supported it, with some proposed amendments.[232] The minority view supported establishing a new Joint Parliamentary Committee on Human Rights, but rejected both defining human rights by reference to international human rights treaties, and making provision for Statements of Compatibility.[233] The Bills were pending in the Australian Senate in mid-2011.[234]

Victoria's Scrutiny of Acts and Regulations Committee has criteria for review and processes very similar to those of the existing Senate Standing Committee for the Scrutiny of Bills, with specific

228 Senate Standing Committee for Scrutiny of Bills, Parliament of Australia <www.aph.gov.au/senate/committee/scrutiny> at 2 April 2011. See also D Kinley, 'Comments: Human Rights Scrutiny in Parliament: Westminster Set to Leap Ahead' (1999) 10 *Public Law Review* 252.

229 Senate Standing Order 24, s 1(a).

230 See above, n 1, recommendation 6, xxxi.

231 Human Rights (Parliamentary Scrutiny) Bill 2010. See also Human Rights (Parliamentary Scrutiny) (Consequential Provisions) Bill 2010.

232 Senate Legal and Constitutional Affairs Legislation Committee, Parliament of Australia, Human Rights (Parliamentary Scrutiny) Bill 2010 [Provisions] and Human Rights (Parliamentary Scrutiny) (Consequential Provisions) Bill 2010 [Provisions] (2011).

233 Ibid paras 1.10 & 1.23.

234 See <http://parlinfo.aph.gov.au> and search 'Human Rights (Parliamentary Scrutiny) Bill'.

duties under the *Charter of Human Rights and Responsibilities Act 2006*.[235] In New South Wales, the Legislation Review Committee, which was established as a result of the Bill of Rights Inquiry report in 2001, reports on possible encroachments on individual liberties.[236]

A Scrutiny of Legislation Committee in Queensland under the *Parliamentary Committees Act 1995* monitored Bills for concerns about civil and political freedoms.[237] The same committee now operates under the *Parliament of Queensland Act 2001*,[238] monitoring compliance with the requirement under the *Legislative Standards Act 1992* for legislation to have 'sufficient regard to rights and liberties of individuals'.[239]

The Australian Capital Territory parliament has a Standing Committee on Justice and Community Safety, which scrutinises bills and subordinate legislation for matters related to, among many other things, 'community and individual rights, consumer rights ... civil liberties and human rights'.[240] The Northern Territory parliament's Legal and Constitutional Affairs Committee has a mandate limited to 'legal or constitutional issues, including law reform, parliamentary reform, administrative law, legislative review and inter-governmental relations'.[241] The Subordinate Legislation and Publications Committee has a duty to consider whether a legislative or administrative instrument 'trespasses unduly on personal rights or liberties [or] unduly makes rights and liberties of citizens dependent upon administrative and not upon judicial decisions'.[242]

Legislation review committees in South Australia, Tasmania and Western Australia do not have scrutiny functions that refer specifically to human rights issues.

10.4.6 Statutory Interpretation by the Courts

The reluctance of Australian courts to refer to international law is well documented.[243] In its Concluding Observations on Australia's fifth report under ICCPR in May 2009, the UN Human Rights Committee said that it 'regrets that judicial decisions [in Australia] make little reference to international human

235 *Parliamentary Committees Act 2003* (Vic) s 17; *Charter of Human Rights and Responsibilities Act 2006* (Vic) s 30; *Scrutiny of Acts and Regulation*, Parliament of Victoria <www.parliament.vic.gov.au/sarc/>.

236 Standing Committee on Law and Justice, Parliament of New South Wales, *A New South Wales Bill of Rights* (2001) 132, recommendation 1; *Legislation Review Act 1987* (NSW) s 8a; Committees, Parliament of New South Wales <www.parliament.nsw.gov.au/committees>.

237 *Parliamentary Committees Act 1995* (Qld) s 4; Scrutiny of Legislation Committee, Queensland Parliament <http://www.parliament.qld.gov.au/view/committees/SLC.asp>.

238 *Parliament of Queensland Act 2001*(Qld) s 103(2)(a).

239 *Legislative Standards Act 1992* (Qld) s 4(3).

240 *Resolution of Appointment*, Standing Committee on Justice and Community Safety, Legislative Assembly for the ACT, <http://www.parliament.act.gov.au/downloads/resolution-of-appointment/ROAjustice07.pdf>.

241 Legal and Constitutional Affairs Committee, Legislative Assembly of the Northern Territory, 1(a) <www.nt.gov.au/lant/parliament/committees/lca/lca.shtml>.

242 *Subordinate Legislation and Publications, Terms of Reference*, s 20 Standing Orders, 2(a) & 2(b), Legislative Assembly of the Northern Territory, <http://www.nt.gov.au/lant/parliament/committees/slp/slp.shtml>.

243 See, eg, H Charlesworth et al, above, n 5; K Eastman & C Ronalds, 'Using Human Rights Laws in Litigation: The Practitioners Perspective' in D Kinley (ed), *Human Rights in Australian Law*, Federation Press, Sydney, 1998, 319–41, 321–7.

rights law'[244] and recommended that Australia 'organise training programmes for the Judiciary on the [ICCPR] and the jurisprudence of the Committee'.

In *Polites v Commonwealth*,[245] Dixon J said, 'It is a rule of construction that, unless a contrary intention appears, general words occurring in a statute are to be read subject to the established rules of international law.' But courts in Australia are still uncertain about how far to go in having regard to international law when interpreting statutes.

When legislation actually incorporates the terms of an international treaty in the form of 'transposed text', the court will ensure that the legislation is given effect in accordance with the treaty obligations.[246] Short of transposing the text of a treaty, a statute may be enacted 'pursuant to, or in contemplation of, the assumption of international obligations under a treaty',[247] in which case it is clear that a court, when resolving an ambiguity, 'should favour a construction which accords with Australia's [treaty] obligations'.[248] That is because 'Parliament, prima facie, intends to give effect to Australia's obligations under international law'.[249]

When legislation does not incorporate the terms of a treaty, it is not clear that international law will have a bearing on any necessary interpretation exercise. An established limitation on interpretation is that:

> courts do not impute to the legislature an intention to abrogate or curtail fundamental rights or freedoms unless such an intention is clearly manifested by unmistakable and unambiguous language. General words will rarely be sufficient for that purpose. What courts will look for is a clear indication that the legislature has directed its attention to the rights or freedoms in question, and has consciously decided upon abrogation or curtailment.[250]

Although the reference to fundamental rights or freedoms has been to such rights in common law,[251] 'a number of recent cases have extended the presumption to the protection of fundamental human rights, and it is likely that courts will have regard to international human rights norms when applying this presumption in future'.[252] Nevertheless, this merely limits interpretation so as not to curtail rights; it is not a rule that enables interpretation so as to promote rights.

244 UN Human Rights Committee, *Concluding Observations of the Human Rights Committee: Australia*, 95th sess, para 8, UN Doc CCPR/C/AUS/CO/5 (2009).

245 [1945] HCA 3; (1945) 70 CLR 60, 77.

246 *A v Minister for Immigration and Ethnic Affairs* [1997] HCA 4; (1997) 190 CLR 225, 230–1 (Brennan CJ). See also *Acts Interpretation Act 1901* (Cth) s 15AB(2)(d).

247 *Plaintiff S157/2002 v Commonwealth* [2003] HCA 2; 211 CLR 476, 492 (Gleeson CJ).

248 Ibid 492 (Gleeson CJ).

249 *Minister of State for Immigration & Ethnic Affairs v Ah Hin Teoh* ('*Teoh's Case*') [1995] HCA 20; (1995) 183 CLR 273, 287 (Mason CJ and Deane J). For an application of this approach see, eg, *Aurukun Shire Council & Anor v CEO Office of Liquor Gaming and Racing in the Department of Treasury* [2010] QCA 37, *Cheedy on behalf of the Yindjibarndi People v State of Western Australia* [2010] FCA 690.

250 See above, n 247.

251 See generally, N O'Neill, S Rice & R Douglas, above, n 38, Ch 5.

252 H Charlesworth et al, see above, n5, 461, referring to *Minister for Foreign Affairs and Trade v Magno* [1992] FCA 566; 37 FCR 298, *Kruger v Commonwealth* [1997] HCA 27; 190 CLR 1, *Kartinyeri v Commonwealth* [1998] HCA 22; 195 CLR 337, *Plaintiff S157/2002 v Commonwealth* [2003] HCA 2; 211 CLR 476, *Minister for Immigration and Multicultural and Indigenous Affairs v Al Masri* [2003] FCAFC 70; 126 FCR 54.

The position on relying on international law as an interpretive guide to the *Constitution* is in a state of flux. Kirby J has been the only High Court judge to be prepared to do so.[253] In *Kateb Al-Kateb v Godwin*,[254] a strongly worded exchange between McHugh and Kirby JJ illustrates the differing views. McHugh J said that '[t]he claim that the Constitution should be read consistently with the rules of international law ... must be regarded as heretical'. He distinguished the rule of construction in *Polites*, saying that it 'had some validity when the rules of international law were few and well-known. Under modern conditions, however, this rule of construction is based on a fiction. Gone are the days when the rules of international law were to be found in the writings of a few well-known jurists'.[255] He rejected 'amending the Constitution under the guise of interpretation'.[256]

Kirby J responded, denying that his approach was 'a judicial attempt to amend the Constitution under the guise of interpretation'.[257] He said, pointedly, that 'with every respect to those of a contrary view, opinions that seek to cut off contemporary Australian law (including constitutional law) from the persuasive force of international law are doomed to fail', and that 'it is often helpful for national judges to check their own constitutional thinking against principles expressing the rules of a "wider civilization" '.[258]

10.4.7 Common Law Development by the Courts

Australian courts are as uncertain about referring to international law when they deal with common law as they are when they deal with statutes. Again, the authorities in Australia go back some time, to at least 1948, when Dixon J recognised that 'international law is not a part, but is one of the sources, of English law'.[259] More recently, in 1992 in *Mabo (No 2)*, Brennan J made the same point but specifically in relation to human rights: 'international law is a legitimate and important influence on the development of the common law, especially when international law declares the existence of universal human rights', short of 'fractur[ing] the skeleton of principle which gives the body of our law its shape and internal consistency'.[260]

In *Dietrich v the Queen*, Brennan J referred specifically to the ICCPR as 'a legitimate influence on the development of the common law',[261] a view echoed by Kirby J who said that '[i]nternational law is a

253 See J Curtin, '"Never Say Never": *Al-Kateb v Godwin*' (2005) 27(2) *Sydney Law Review* 355; H Charlesworth et al, see above, n 5, 461–3.

254 [2004] HCA 37; 219 CLR 562.

255 *Al-Kateb v Godwin* [2004] HCA 37; 219 CLR 562, 590.

256 Ibid 595.

257 Ibid 629.

258 Ibid 629.

259 *Chow Hung Ching v The King* [1948] HCA 37; 77 CLR 449, 477.

260 *Mabo v Queensland (No 2)* (*'Mabo Case'*) [1992] HCA 23; (1992) 175 CLR 1, 42–3 (Brennan J). See also *Minister of State for Immigration & Ethnic Affairs v Ah Hin Teoh* (*'Teoh's Case'*) [1995] HCA 20; (1995) 183 CLR 273, 287 (Mason CJ & Deane J); *Kartinyeri v Commonwealth* [1998] HCA 22; 195 CLR 337, 383 (Gummow & Hayne JJ). For similar international practice see, eg, *Baker v Canada (Minister of Citizenship and Immigration)* [1999] 2 SCR 817 [69]–[71], referring to *Tavita v Minister of Immigration* [1994] 2 NZLR 257 (CA) and *Vishaka v Rajasthan* [1997] 3 LRC 361 (SC India).

261 *Dietrich v The Queen* [1992] HCA 57; 177 CLR 292, 321; see also 360 (Toohey J).

legitimate and important influence on the development of the common law ... especially when international law declares the existence of universal and fundamental rights.'[262] Soon afterwards, Mason CJ and Deane J set out a cautious prescription for the use of international law in developing the common law:

> Apart from influencing the construction of a statute or subordinate legislation, an international convention may play a part in the development by the courts of the common law. The provisions of an international convention to which Australia is a party, especially one which declares universal fundamental rights, may be used by the courts as a legitimate guide in developing the common law. But the courts should act in this fashion with due circumspection when the Parliament itself has not seen fit to incorporate the provisions of a convention into our domestic law. Judicial development of the common law must not be seen as a backdoor means of importing an unincorporated convention into Australian law. A cautious approach to the development of the common law by reference to international conventions would be consistent with the approach which the courts have hitherto adopted to the development of the common law by reference to statutory policy and statutory materials. Much will depend upon the nature of the relevant provision, the extent to which it has been accepted by the international community, the purpose which it is intended to serve and its relationship to the existing principles of our domestic law.[263]

Mason CJ and Deane J refer to the part international law 'may' play in developing the common law. Callinan J has since, in *Western Australia v Ward*, rejected the *necessity* for the common law to develop in accordance with international law, saying that international law is 'often vague and conflicting' and that is it 'unacceptable' for it to 'mould' the common law 'apparently without regard for precedent, the conditions in this country, or the fact that governments and individuals may have reasonably relied on the law as it stands'.[264] This apprehension has the ring of Australian 'anxiety about the international order'[265] that was prevalent in Australia federal politics at the time and is discussed further below in Chapter 10.5.5.

10.5 AUSTRALIA'S PERFORMANCE UNDER ITS HUMAN RIGHTS TREATY OBLIGATIONS

The following account sets out the various ways in which Australia engages with the UN human rights monitoring system, principally by reporting and responding to individual complaints. The overall effectiveness of the UN's monitoring of a state's human rights is debatable, and is discussed in Chapter 7.4.8. For Australia, there is no real measure of the extent to which UN monitoring is effective in increasing human rights compliance by, or even awareness among, governments and individuals. As is discussed below, the Australian government has been through a period of challenging, quite aggressively, the legitimacy of the UN's monitoring of human rights.

---

262 *Newcrest Mining (WA) Ltd v Commonwealth* [1997] HCA 38; 190 CLR 513, 657.

263 *Teoh's Case,* see above, n 260, 288 (citations omitted).

264 [2002] HCA 28; 213 CLR 1, 389.

265 H Charlesworth et al, see above, n 5, 424.

10.5.1 Universal Periodic Review

The Universal Periodic Review (UPR) examines the human rights records of all UN Member States every four years. The system was created by the UN General Assembly in March 2006 when it established the Human Rights Council.[266] The UPR is described by the UN as 'a State-driven process ... which provides the opportunity for each State to declare what actions they have taken to improve the human rights situations in their countries and to fulfil their human rights obligations. [It] is designed to ensure equal treatment for every country when their human rights situations are assessed.'[267] It is discussed in detail in Chapter 6.7.

Australia submitted its first report to the UPR in October 2010.[268] Much like its state reports, discussed below, Australia's UPR report was all good news, not reflecting on or analysing at all the country's compliance with human rights. Only in the last of 151 paragraphs did it note briefly 'challenges and constraints', but then simply by saying that it 'recognises the challenges of implementing human rights in a meaningful way across all sections of Australian society'.[269]

SNAPSHOT: AUSTRALIA'S UPR REPORT

In its 2010 report to the UN Human Rights Council, Australia described in positive terms its human rights-related activity across Australia society. Under the heading 'Challenges and constraints' it stated only:

> Australia recognises the challenge of implementing human rights in a meaningful way across all sections of Australian society. This Report identifies practical human rights challenges, together with laws, policies and programs Australia has put in place to address these challenges. Australia's commitment to achieving full respect for human rights is reflected in the list of priorities set out in the following section.[270]

Australia listed as its priorities only the same activities it had reported on, such as human rights education and parliamentary statements of human rights compatibility. In short, Australia did not identify any areas in which it was concerned that people do not enjoy respect for and enjoyment of their human rights.

A coalition of Australian NGOs collaborated to submit a 'shadow' report to the UN Human Rights Council. By way of contrast with Australia's official report, the NGOs' report drew attention to a wide range of 'challenges' to which priority could be given, including Australia's decision to not enact a national human rights law; its failure to ratify number of international human rights and ILO treaties; its failure to give full effect to the *Convention on the Rights of Persons with Disabilities* and the *Convention on the Rights of the Child*; its failure to fully implement the National Plan to reduce Violence Against Women; the continuing

266 *Human Rights Council*, GA Res 60/251, UN GA, 60th sess, 72nd plen mtg, UN Doc A/Res/60/251 (2006).

267 *Universal Periodic Review*, UN Office of the High Commissioner for Human Rights <www.ohchr.org/en/hrbodies/upr> at 2 April 2011. See generally Basic Facts About the UPR, UN Office of the High Commissioner for Human Rights <www.ohchr.org/en/hrbodies/upr/Pages/BasicFacts.aspx>.

268 Documents relating to the UPR process are at <www.ohchr.org/EN/HRBodies/UPR/Pages/UPRMain.aspx>.

269 See above, n 62, para 151, A/HRC/WG.6/10/AUS/1.

270 See above, n 62.

discriminatory operation of the Northern Territory Intervention; the persistent social-economic, criminal justice and land title disadvantages suffered by indigenous peoples; the prison-like detention of asylum seekers; the situation of homeless people and people needing mental health care; the constraints on human rights imposed by anti-terrorism legislation; human rights accountability of corporations operating off-shore; and the need for a human rights-based approach to foreign aid.

The UN Human Rights Council examined Australia's record in January 2011. It subsequently issued a draft report,[271] which records statements made by delegations from 53 states. In stark contrast to the steps that Australia volunteered it could take, the report makes 145 recommendations for action by Australia to better implement human rights protection in Australia. In its preliminary response at the time,[272] Australia said that it acknowledged the concerns raised and would carefully analyse the recommendations.

Australia formally responded in June 2011, and 'accepted in full or in part more than 90 per cent of the recommendations made to it'.[273] In its response,[274] Australia said, for example, that it will consider ratifying the *Convention for the Protection of All Persons from Enforced Disappearance* but that it will not ratify the *Convention on the Protection of the Rights of All Migrant Workers and Members of Their Families* because it regards 'existing protections in place for migrant workers as adequate'. It rejected recommendations to introduce a Human Rights Act and to amend the *Marriage Act* to allow same-sex partners to marry, and said that it is 'currently exploring a possible role for a national children's commissioner'.

10.5.2 Human Rights Treaty Reporting

Australia has reported to the treaty bodies under all the human rights treaties to which it is a party. Charlesworth has said of Australia's reports that they are 'much more honest than the norm', although 'they tend to provide very positive spins on particular fact situations'.[275] In this, Australia's approach is no different from that of other states, discussed in detail in Chapter 7.4.4.

The real importance in human rights treaty reporting is not in a state's report, which, even if 'more honest than the norm', is largely self-serving, but in the published response (called 'concluding observations') by the treaty body. It is there that the treaty body—informed by its questioning of the state and by non-state perspectives proposed by NGOs and UN Special Rapporteurs—outlines what it sees as both praiseworthy and concerning about a state's performance. A further important measure of a state's attitude to human rights compliance is whether and how it responds to a treaty body's observations, although there is no formal measure of this apart from the state's own reporting on the next occasion.

271 Human Rights Council Working Group on the Universal Periodic Review, 10th sess, Geneva, 24 January–4 February 2011, *Report of the Working Group on the Universal Periodic Review: Australia*, A/HRC/17/10.

272 P Woolcott, see above, n 70.

273 R McClelland & K Rudd MP, 'Australia's Response to its Universal Periodic Review at the UN', (Joint Media Release, 6 June 2011).

274 See above, n 22.

275 H Charlesworth, 'The UN Treaty-Based Human Rights System: An Overview' in S Pritchard (ed), *Indigenous Peoples, the United Nations and Human Rights*, Zed Books/Federation Press, Sydney, 1998, 66–73, 70.

The Australian government's aggressive challenges to the legitimacy of the UN's human rights monitoring system, discussed below at Chapter 10.5.5, is some indication of its responsive to the treaty bodies' observations.

A recurring theme in the treaty bodies observations on Australia's reports is that, despite a wide range of impressive measures to promote and protect human rights, Australia continues not to give legislative effect to its fundamental human rights treaty obligations. Time and again the treaty bodies observe with concern that the ICCPR and ICESCR have not been incorporated into domestic law, a situation that seems unlikely to change for some time in light of the federal government's response in 2010 to the *National Human Rights Consultation Committee Report* discussed above at Chapter 10.3.3.

ICESCR

In May 2009 the Committee on Economic, Social and Cultural Rights considered Australia's fourth report under the ICESCR, the format of which 'did not provide the Committee with a substantive report on the measures adopted by the State party to give effect to the Covenant rights and on the progress made in achieving the observance of those rights'.[276] The Committee noted that Australia has repealed laws that discriminated against same-sex couples in relation to financial and work-related benefits, and that the *Fair Work Act 2009* improves the protection of the right to work.[277] However, among a number of concerns[278] it noted Australia's failure to incorporate the treaty into domestic law,[279] the limited coverage of federal anti-discrimination law,[280] aspects of the Northern Territory intervention inconsistent with the treaty, poor living standards of people with disabilities,[281] and the continuing gap between men and women for work of equal value.[282] The Committee invited Australia to next report by June 2014.

ICCPR

According to the Human Rights Committee (HRC), Australia's fifth report under the ICCPR, made in July 2007, did 'not meet the requirements of article 40 of the Covenant regarding the provision of sufficient and adequate information on the measures adopted to give effect to the Covenant rights, as well as on the progress made in the enjoyment of those rights'.[283] Commenting on the report in May 2009, the HRC

276 See above, n 85, para 2, UN Doc E/C.12/AUS/CO/4 (2009). For comment on Australia's earlier report, and Australia's compliance generally with the requirements of ICESCR, see D Otto & D Wiseman, 'In Search of 'Effective Remedies': Applying the International Covenant on Economic, Social and Cultural Rights to Australia' (2001) 7(1) *Australian Journal of Human Rights* 5.

277 See above, n 85, paras 5 & 6, UN Doc E/C.12/AUS/CO/4 (2009).

278 Ibid paras 10–33, UN Doc E/C.12/AUS/CO/4 (2009).

279 Ibid para 11.

280 Ibid para 14.

281 Ibid para 16.

282 Ibid para 17.

283 See above, n 244, para 2, UN Doc CCPR/C/AUS/CO/5 (2009).

had only three positive things to mention: the (then) current National Human Rights Consultation; the parliamentary apology to indigenous peoples' victims of the Stolen Generations policies; and the establishment of the National Council to Reduce Violence against Women and their Children.[284] Among the many concerns were Australia's continuing reservations to ICCPR, the terms of Australia's anti-terrorism legislation, the inconsistency of aspects the Northern Territory intervention with ICCPR, the situation of homeless people, the trafficking of women, and continuing mandatory detention of asylum seekers.[285] The Committee invited Australia to submit its next ICCPR report by April 2013 and recommended that it involve civil society and NGOs in the reporting process.

CERD

Australia made its fifteenth, sixteenth and seventeenth reports, the last of which had been due in October 2008, to the Committee on the Elimination of All Forms of Racial Discrimination as a single combined report in 2009 although not, the Committee noted, in complete conformity with the reporting guidelines.[286] The Committee welcomed Australia's support for the UN *Declaration on the Rights of Indigenous Peoples* and the government's commitment to address indigenous disadvantage through the six 'Closing the Gap' targets.[287] But it was concerned by a number of matters, including 'the absence of any entrenched protection against racial discrimination in the federal Constitution', noting that in the *Constitution*, sections 25 (disqualification from voting by reference to race) and 51(xxvi) (making laws for people according to race) raise issues of racial discrimination.[288] Other matters of concern included the risk of racial profiling through biometric data collection,[289] the discrimination experienced by people of African, Asian, Middle Eastern and Muslim background,[290] the Northern Territory intervention, and racially motivated violence.[291] The Committee also noted Australia's continuing reservation to article 4(a).[292] The Committee called on Australia to ratify the *International Convention on the Protection of the Rights of All Migrant Workers and Members of Their Families* and invited Australia to next report by October 2012, reporting in particular on the Committee's recommendations regarding Australia's indigenous peoples.

284 See above, n 244, paras 5–7.

285 See above, n 244, paras 8–27.

286 UN Committee on the Elimination of Racial Discrimination, *Concluding Observations of the Committee on the Elimination of Racial Discrimination*, 77th sess, para 2, UN Doc CERD/C/AUS/CO/15-17 (2010).

287 Ibid paras 3 & 6.

288 Ibid para 10; in 2011 the Australian Government convened a Panel on Constitutional Recognition of Indigenous Australians to consult the Australian community and advise the government on possible options for change that can be put to a referendum for constitutional amendment: see <http://youmeunity.org.au>.

289 Ibid para 12.

290 Ibid para 14.

291 Ibid para 23.

292 Ibid para 17.

CAT

Australia provided its third report under the CAT, due in 2004, in April 2005.[293] In its Concluding Observations published in May 2008, the CAT Committee noted favourably changes regarding children in immigration detention; the closure of the offshore migration processing centres, and the end of the 'Pacific Solution'; the Government's apology to the Aboriginal and Torres Strait Islander peoples for past policies and laws that resulted in the removal of children; the commitment to become a party to the *Optional Protocol* to the Convention; and ratification of the *Rome Statute of the International Criminal Court*.[294] Among the many issues of concern to the Committee were conditions in which people are detained under anti-terrorism laws and immigration detention policy; the AHRC's lack of power to investigate complaints under the treaty; the possibility that a person could be extradited despite being at risk of torture; and overcrowding and absence of mental health care in prisons.[295] The Committee invited Australia to report again under CAT by 30 June 2012.

CEDAW

Australia's sixth and seventh reports under CEDAW, due in 2004 and 2008 respectively, were submitted as a combined report in March 2009. Commenting on the report in 2010,[296] the CEDAW Committee welcomed Australia's ratification of the CEDAW *Optional Protocol* and 'laws enacted since the last report to advance the status of women and combat discrimination, such as the *Fair Work Act 2009* and the *Paid Parental Leave Act 2010*'. Among a number of areas of concern,[297] the Committee noted the continuing reservations to CEDAW, and reiterated an earlier recommendation[298] that Australia consider the adoption of temporary special measures[299] 'to increase further the number of women in political and public life and to ensure that the representation of women in political and public bodies reflect the full diversity of the population, including indigenous women and women from ethnic minorities'. Inviting Australia to submit its next report under CEDAW by July 2014, the Committee asked Australia to consult widely when preparing it.

293 See above, n 121.

294 Ibid paras 4–7.

295 Ibid paras 8–35.

296 See above, n 30.

297 Ibid para 14–49.

298 UN Committee on the Elimination of Discrimination Against Women, *Concluding Observations of the Committee on the Elimination of Discrimination against Women: Australia*, 34th sess, para 17, CEDAW/C/AUL/CO/5 (2006).

299 *Convention on the Elimination of All Forms of Discrimination Against Women*, opened for signature 1 March 1980, 1249 UNTS 13, arts 2 & 3 (entered into force 3 September 1981) art 4(1); UN Committee on the Elimination of Discrimination Against Women, *Concluding Observations of the Committee on the Elimination of Discrimination against Women: Australia*, 46th sess, para 27, UN Doc CEDAW/C/AUS/CO/7 (2010).

CROC

Australia's fourth report under the *Convention on the Rights of the Child* was made in late 2009 and is yet to be considered by the Committee on the Rights of the Child. Australia's last report was a combined second and third report, submitted in March 2003. Responding to that report in 2005,[300] the Committee commented favourably on national initiatives relating to families and children, and on national action plans against people trafficking and the exploitation of children.[301] The Committee reiterated its view that Australia had no reason to maintain its reservations to the treaty, and expressed concern about a wide range of matters, including the absence of a national children's commissioner, the continuing availability of corporal punishment, the immigration detention of children, homelessness, substance abuse and the health and education of indigenous children.[302]

ILO Convention Reporting

The ILO monitors compliance with its conventions through the Committee of Experts on the Application of Conventions and Recommendations (CEACR). CEACR reported to the 100th session of the International Labour Conference in 2010[303] on Australia's compliance with some of the ILO Conventions.[304] For example, in relation to the *Equal Remuneration Convention*, CEACR asked the Australian Government to provide information on the implementation of the *Fair Work Act* 'in practice with respect to applying the principle of the Convention, in particular through awards, enterprise agreements, low-paid authorizations, minimum wages and equal remuneration orders'.[305] In relation to the *Discrimination (Employment and Occupation)* Convention, CEACR noted 'with interest' the Government's support for the United Nations *Declaration on the Rights of Indigenous Peoples*, and the national apology to indigenous peoples, and further noted 'the wide range of initiatives at the federal and state levels that have been undertaken to address inequality and discrimination that have been experienced by indigenous peoples'.[306]

In its report to the ninety-ninth session of the International Labour Conference in 2010,[307] CEACR invited the Australian Government to respond to concerns of the Australian Council of Trade Unions that 'excessively long working hours are causing numerous problems for workers',[308] and sought more information about the activities of the then newly established Fair Work Ombudsman, and about

300 UN Committee of the Rights of the Child, *Concluding Observations: Australia*, 40th sess, UN Doc CRC/C/15/Add.268 (2005).

301 Ibid para 3.

302 Ibid paras 5–77.

303 *International Labour Conference: ILC Sessions*, International Labour Organisation, <www.ilo.org/ilc/ILCSessions>; the Conventions are reported on by states under a rotating roster over intervals of three years.

304 *Report of the Committee of Experts on the Application of Conventions and Recommendations, Report III (Part 1A): General Report and Observations Concerning Particular Countries, International Labour Conference*, 100th sess (2010).

305 Ibid 412.

306 Ibid 413.

307 See above, n 303.

308 *Report of the Committee of Experts on the Application of Conventions and Recommendations, Report III (Part 1A): General Report and Observations Concerning Particular Countries, International Labour Conference*, 99th sess (2010) 627.

the conduct of the Australian Building and Construction Commission, which, established in 2005 in response to the Cole Royal Commission into the Building and Construction Industry,[309] has the power to compel a person to provide information, produce documents and answer questions in a closed investigation, backed up by sanctions of imprisonment for non-compliance, arguably violating rights to privacy and to a fair trial.[310]

10.5.3 Visits under Thematic Mandates

Australia extended a standing invitation to all thematic special procedures in August 2008, meaning that Australia has announced that it will always accept requests to visit from the thematic mandate holders.[311] Seventy-two other states have extended standing invitations. In recent years four thematic mandate holders have made official visits to Australia: Mr Miloon Kothari, Special Rapporteur on Adequate Housing, in 2006; Mr James Anaya, Special Rapporteur on Indigenous Human Rights, in August 2009; Mr Anand Grover, Special Rapporteur on the Right to Health, in December 2009; and Dr Cephas Lumina, Independent Expert on the Effects of Foreign Debt on Human Rights, in February 2011.

Mr Anaya visited to examine the human rights situation of indigenous peoples in Australia. He commended the Australian government on its various programs to address the social and economic disadvantages faced by its indigenous peoples, but was concerned about the lack of integration of the programs, the failure to promote self-determination and indigenous involvement in design and delivery of programs, the lack of indigenous security over land, and the threats to culture to indigenous peoples living in remote areas.[312]

The visit by Mr Grover was to understand how Australia 'endeavours to implement the right to health, the measures taken for its successful realization and the obstacles encountered both at the national and international level', with particular regard to 'the impact of poverty and discrimination, including inequalities, on the enjoyment of the right to health, and in particular in the context of indigenous health, and health care in detention establishments, including those for asylum-seekers, refugees and prisoners'.[313] His visit and report in is discussed in more detail in Chapter 4.2.7.

Dr Lumina assessed the impact of Australian development aid on the realisation of human rights and the Millennium Development Goals in the recipient countries in the Pacific, as well as the human rights impact of Australia's trade negotiations with Pacific countries. He criticised the emphasis on the 'national interest' in Australia's aid program, as distinct from a human rights-based approach to development. He also recommended that Australia legislate to prevent private commercial creditors,

309 <www.royalcombci.gov.au>.

310 See above, n 308, 487–90. The Australian Building and Construction Commission was.

311 For an explanation of the role of thematic mandates in the UN human rights system, see Chapter 6.5.

312 J Anaya, *Report of the Special Rapporteur on the Situation of Human Rights and Fundamental Freedoms of Indigenous People; Addendum: The Situation of Indigenous Peoples in Australia*, UN Human Rights Council, 15th sess, Summary, UN Doc A/HRC/15 (2010).

313 A Grover, *Report of the Special Rapporteur on the Rights of Everyone to the Enjoyment of the Highest Attainable Standard of Physical and Mental Health: Mission to Australia*, UN Human Rights Council, 14th sess, paras 1 & 2, UN Doc A/HRC/14/20/Add.4 (2010).

known as 'vulture funds', from buying up the defaulted debt of poor countries and seeking to recover the full debt with interest through litigation, which curtails the resources available for the realisation of human rights in those heavily indebted poor countries.[314]

SNAPSHOT: SPECIAL RAPPORTEUR ON ADEQUATE HOUSING

The purpose of Mr Kothari's mission to Australia was 'to examine the status of realization of adequate housing',[315] with particular attention to housing for indigenous peoples, women, children and youth, people with disabilities and health problems including mental health, refugees and asylum seekers, prisoners and persons released from detention. He also looked into the housing needs of the elderly, persons with complex needs (such as HIV/AIDS, sexual minorities), single parents, migrants and people with low incomes.[316]

In his report to the Human Rights Council, Mr Kothari noted 'a serious national housing crisis in Australia [which] affects many sections of the population ... especially low-income households and, increasingly, middle-income households'.[317] He noted that:

> Australia lacks a clear consistent, long-term and holistic housing strategy. There is no national legislative and policy framework against which the outcomes of government programs and strategies can be evaluated to assess to what extent Governments are progressively realizing the human right to adequate housing for all. Current indicators from diverse sources show regressive results: reductions in public housing stock, soaring private rental rates, an acknowledged housing affordability crisis and no real reduction in the number of homeless.[318]

He concluded that 'Australia has failed to implement the human right to adequate housing'. He recommended the establishment of a federal Ministry with a portfolio solely devoted to housing, a national body that truly represents the voices of indigenous people and a rigorous attempt to tackle problems of housing affordability and housing and land speculation.[319]

10.5.4 Treaty Body Communications

When domestic remedies have been exhausted or are not available, people in Australia have access, in some circumstances, to the international complaint mechanisms available for the violation of rights in ICCPR, CAT, ICERD, CEDAW and CRPD, discussed in detail in Chapter 7.4.7. A complaint

314 *Independent Expert on the Effects of Foreign Debt and Other Related International Financial Obligations of States on the Full Enjoyment of All Human Rights, Particularly Economic, Social and Cultural Rights: Mission to Australia*, 7–11 February 2011, UN Office of the High Commissioner for Human Rights, <http://www.ohchr.org/EN/NewsEvents/Pages/DisplayNews.aspx?NewsID=10720&LangID=E>.

315 M Kothari, *Report of the Special Rapporteur on Adequate Housing as a Component of the Right to an Adequate Standard of Living: Mission to Australia*, UN Human Rights Council, 4th sess, 2, UN Doc A/HRC/4/18/Add.2 (2007).

316 Ibid 31.

317 Ibid 2.

318 Ibid 2.

319 Ibid 2.

(called a 'communication') is made to the relevant treaty committee, which will consider it and express an opinion (called a 'view'). The committees' views are not binding on a state, so that if a state rejects it—as has usually been the case for Australia—there is no tangible result for the person who complained.

Most communications against Australia have been made under the ICCPR, and a few have been made under CAT and ICERD. Australia became a party to the communication mechanisms for CEDAW and CRPD only in 2008 and 2009 respectively. Of the communications made, most have been found by the relevant treaty body to be inadmissible or without merit.

ICCPR

The first communication against Australia was *Toonen.*[320] It was lodged in 1992 and decided in 1994, when the HRC published its view that section 123 of the *Criminal Code* (Tas), which criminalised homosexual acts between males, violated ICCPR article 17 (the right to privacy) and ICCPR article 26 (the right to non-discrimination).[321] The Australian Government responded by introducing legislation that would override the offending Tasmanian provisions,[322] but the Tasmanian Government itself repealed the provision.

Three years later the HRC considered the communication of *A*, an asylum seeker who was held in immigration detention. The HRC said that *A*'s communication had merit,[323] because detention without court review, beyond the period necessary to assess refugee status, is arbitrary detention in violation of the ICCPR. As it has done consistently since then, the Australian Government rejected the HRC's view. The matter of *A* was the first of many successful communications relating to the fact and conditions of immigration detention in Australia—*C,*[324] *Baban,*[325] *Bakhtiyari,*[326] *D, E and Children,*[327] *Shafiq,*[328] and *Shams and Others*[329]—where the Human Rights Committee considered, consistently from 1997 until 2007, that Australia's immigration detention regime is in violation of, variously, articles 7, 9(1) and (4), 17 and 24 of the ICCPR.

320 *UN Human Rights Committee, Toonen, Communication No 488/1992: Australia,* 50th sess, UN Doc CCPR/C/50/D/488/1992 (1994).

321 See H Charlesworth, 'First Australian Case under the Optional Protocol' (1992) 3 *Public Law Review* 278.

322 *Human Rights (Sexual Conduct) Act 1994* (Cth).

323 UN Human Rights Committee, *A (name deleted), Communication No 560/1993: Australia,* 59th sess, UN Doc CCPR/C/59/D/560/1993 (1997). See also N Poynder, '*A (name deleted) v Australia*: A Milestone for Asylum Seekers' (1997) 4(1) *Australian Journal of Human Rights* 155.

324 UN Human Rights Committee, *C (name withheld), Communication No 900/1999: Australia,* 76th sess, UN Doc CCPR/C/76/D/900/1999 (2002).

325 *UN Human Rights Committee, Baban, Communication No 1014/2001: Australia,* 78th sess, UN Doc CCPR/C/78/D/1014/2001 (2003).

326 *UN Human Rights Committee, Ali Aqsar Bakhtiyari and Roqaiha Bakhtiyari, Communication No 1069/2002: Australia,* 79th sess, UN Doc CCPR/C/79/D/1069/2002 (2003).

327 *UN Human Rights Committee, D and E, and Their Two Children, Communication 1050/2002: Australia,* 87th sess, UN Doc CCPR/C/87/D/1050/2002 (2006).

328 UN Human Rights Committee, *Danyal Shafiq, Communication No 1324/2002: Australia,* 88th sess, UN Doc CCPR/C/88/D/1324/2004 (2006).

329 *UN Human Rights Committee, Shams and Others, Communication Nos 1255, 1256, 1259, 1260, 1266, 1268, 1270, 1288/2004: Australia,* 90th sess, UN Doc CCPR/C/90/D/1255, 1256, 1259, 1260, 1266, 1268, 1270 & 1288/2004 (2007).

In a case involving immigration detention pending deportation, the HRC considered that Ms Fong had been detained contrary to article 9(1) when she was refused permission to remain in Australia, and that her proposed return to China, which would put her at risk of the death penalty, was a potential violation of articles 6 and 7.[330] By way of contrast, the Committee did not see that violations to rights under article 7 of the ICCPR were a foreseeable and necessary consequence of deportation in the matters of *TT*[331] and *ARJ*.[332]

In another deportation case, *Winata*,[333] the HRC found Australia was in violation of articles 17, 23 and 24 when it decided to deport Indonesian nationals who had been living in Australia without lawful immigration status. Their 10-year-old son was an Australian citizen, so they would have to leave him behind or take him to Indonesia, where he had never been. The Committee's decision was subject to an unusually strong dissent from four of its members.

A wide range of other circumstances have been held to be violations by Australia of its obligations under ICCPR, for example: Queensland legislation, under which a protester was convicted for speaking in public without a permit, violated the right to free speech in article 19(2);[334] limited entitlements of same-sex partners under the *Veterans' Entitlements Act 1986* (Cth) breached the guarantee of non-discrimination under article 26;[335] and incarcerating prisoners in a cell so small that they had to stand and sit in turn violated article 10(1).[336] Another violation of article 10, along with article 24, related to the conditions of incarceration of a juvenile indigenous offender with an intellectual disability.[337]

In *Dudko*,[338] the conduct of a hearing by the High Court (in circumstances where the prosecutor appeared and was heard but the applicant was absent in custody) was a violation of the guarantee in article 14(1) of equality before the courts. One of the three judges in the High Court hearing, Kirby J, had in fact asked why arrangements had not been made to have the applicant present or represented, and said he was 'troubled by the inequality'.[339]

330 UN Human Rights Committee, *Kwok Yin Fong, Communication No 1442/2005: Australia*, 97th sess, UN Doc CCPR/C/97/D/1442/2005 (2009).

331 *UN Human Rights Committee, G T, Communication No 706/1996: Australia*, 61st sess, UN Doc CCPR/C/61/D/706/1996 (1997).

332 UN Human Rights Committee, *A R J, Communication No 692/1996: Australia*, 60th sess, UN Doc CCPR/C/60/D/692/1996 (1997).

333 UN Human Rights Committee, *Hendrick Winata and So Lan Li, Communication No 930/2000: Australia*, 72nd sess, UN Doc CCPR/C/72/D/930/2000 (2001).

334 UN Human Rights Committee, *Patrick Coleman, Communication No 1157/20003: Australia*, 87th sess, UN Doc CCPR/C/87/D/1157/2003 (2005).

335 UN Human Rights Committee, *Young, Communication No 941/2000: Australia*, 78th sess, UN Doc CCPR/C/78/D/941/2000 (2003).

336 UN Human Rights Committee, *Carlos Cabal and Marco Pasini Bertran, Communication 1020/2011: Australia*, 78th sess, UN Doc CCPR/C/78/D/1020/2001 (2003).

337 UN Human Rights Committee, *Corey Brough, Communication No 1184/2003: Australia*, 86th sess, UN Doc CCPR/C/86/D/1184/2003 (2006).

338 UN Human Rights Committee, *Lucy Dudko, Communication No 1347/2005: Australia*, 90th sess, UN Doc CCPR/C/90/D/1347/2005 (2007).

339 Transcript of Proceedings, *Dudko v The Queen* (High Court of Australia, Kirby J, 16 March 2004).

In other criminal matters, a delay of almost two years in the delivery of a decision by the Northern Territory Court of Appeal on a contempt of court charge was a violation of the article 14(3)(c) right to a trial without undue delay,[340] and detaining prisoners beyond the term of their sentence under special legislation,[341] although constitutionally permissible in Australia,[342] was found to be in violation of article 9.[343]

CAT

Of 11 communications against Australia under CAT to mid-2011, only the first, *Elmi*,[344] was successful. Mr Elmi was a Somali national whose application for refugee status had been rejected. He faced deportation to Somalia, and the CAT Committee was of the view that Australia would be in breach of CAT if it were to send him back to Somalia as he faced a real risk of torture there. The response of the Australian government was to keep Mr Elmi in immigration detention while a solution was found. Mr Elmi, who had been in detention for two years, opted to leave Australia voluntarily and seek refugee status elsewhere.

In similar communications since, the CAT Committee has not been satisfied that the person faced 'a foreseeable, real and personal risk of being tortured': *NP*[345] and *MPS*[346] (removal to Sri Lanka); MS (removal to Algeria);[347] *HMHI*[348] and *YHA*[349] (removal to Somalia); *AK* (removal to Sudan);[350] *LJR* (removal to the United States);[351] and *X* (removal to Lebanon).[352]

340 UN Human Rights Committee, *Andrew Rogerson, Communication No 802/1998: Australia*, 74th sess, UN Doc CCPR/C/74/D/802/1998 (2002).

341 *Crimes (Serious Sex Offenders) Act 2006* (NSW); *Dangerous Prisoners (Sexual Offenders) Act 2003* (Qld).

342 *Fardon v Attorney-General (Qld)* [2004] HCA 46; 223 CLR 575.

343 UN Human Rights Committee, *Robert John Fardon, Communication No 1629/2007: Australia*, 98th sess, UN Doc CCPR/C/98/D/1629/2007 (2010); UN Human Rights Committee, *Kenneth Davidson Tillman, Communication No 1635/2007: Australia*, 98th sess, UN Doc CCPR/C/98/D/1635/2007 (2010).

344 UN Committee Against Torture, *Sadiq Shek Elmi, Communication No 120/1998: Australia*, 22nd sess, UN Doc CAT/C/22/D/120/1998 (1999).

345 UN Committee Against Torture, *NP (name withheld), Communication No 106/1998: Australia*, 22nd sess, UN Doc CAT/C/22/D/106/1998 (1999).

346 UN Committee Against Torture, *MPS, Communication No 138/1999: Australia*, 28th sess, UN Doc CAT/C/28/D/138/1999 (2002).

347 UN Committee Against Torture, *MS (name withheld), Communication No 154/2000: Australia*, 27th sess, UN Doc CAT/C/27/D/154/2000 (2001).

348 UN Committee Against Torture, *HMHII (name withheld), Communication No 177/2001: Australia*, 28th sess, UN Doc CAT/C/28/D/177/2001 (2002).

349 UN Committee Against Torture, *YHA (name withheld), Communication No 162/2000: Australia*, 27th sess, UN Doc CAT/C/27/D/162/2000 (2002).

350 UN Committee Against Torture, *AK, Communication No 148/1999: Australia*, 32nd sess, UN Doc CAT/C/32/148/1999 (2004).

351 UN Committee Against Torture, *LJR, Communication N 316/2007: Australia*, 41st sess, UN Doc CAT/C/41/D/316/2007 (2008).

352 UN Committee Against Torture, *X, Communication No 324/2007: Australia*, 42nd sess, UN Doc CAT/C/42/D/324/2007 (2009).

ICERD

There have been only six communications against Australia under ICERD to mid-2011, all but one of which have been inadmissible or unsubstantiated. Mr Hagan, an Indigenous Australian, successfully complained to the CERD Committee about the refusal of trustees of a sports ground to remove the word 'nigger' from the ES 'Nigger' Brown Stand at the ground. The stand's name recorded ES Brown's nickname from the 1950s and 1960s, but the CERD Committee decided 'that use and maintenance of the offending term can at the present time be considered offensive and insulting, even if for an extended period it may not have necessarily been so regarded'.[353] In a decision described as 'curiously ambiguous', [354] the CERD Committee did not actually say that there was a breach of articles 2 and 5.

ILO Complaints

Articles 24 and 26 of the ILO Constitution provide a mechanism for workers' organisations and, less frequently, employer organisations to complain to the ILO Committee on Freedom of Association (CFA) about a state's failure to observe an ILO Convention. The CFA comprises an independent chair and three representatives of each of governments, employers and workers. If it finds that a state has violated freedom of association standards, it issues a report with recommendations to the state.[355]

Complaints have been made by unions representing workers in a wide range of service and manufacturing industries. Complaints to the CFA about Australia have twice been made by employer groups: once by the Confederation of Australian Industry and the International Organisation of Employers,[356] and once by the Australian Chamber of Commerce and Industry.[357] In the former, the complaint was that amendments to the *Industrial Relations Act 1988* (Cth) unreasonably restricted the registration of new employee organisations by requiring minimum membership of 10 000 except in special circumstances. The Committee agreed that the 10 000 threshold could 'influence unduly the workers' free choice of union to which they wish to belong' in breach of articles 2 and 3 of ILO 87 *Freedom of Association and Protection of the Right to Organise Convention*.

In its 2009 complaint,[358] the Communications, Electrical, Electronic, Energy, Information, Postal, Plumbing and Allied Services Union alleged that the Fair Work Bill 2008[359] contravened freedom of association principles, replicating provisions in the repealed *Workplace Relations Act 1996* that did not

353 UN Committee on the Elimination of Racial Discrimination, *Stephen Hagan, Communication 26/2002: Australia*, 62nd sess, UN Doc CERD/C/62/D/26/2002 (2003).

354 S Joseph, 'UN Human Rights Treaty Bodies: Recent Decisions' (2003) 3(2) *Human Rights Law Review* 291, 299.

355 See, 'Special Procedures for the Examination in the International Labour Organization of Complaints Alleging Violations of Freedom of Association', ILOLEX Document No 2320062001, *CFA Digest of Decisions* (2006).

356 'The Confederation of Australian Industry (CAI) and the International Organisation of Employers (IOE), Case No 1559', *Committee on Freedom of Association Report No 284*, Vol LXXV, 1992, Series B, No 3, paras 200–63.

357 'The Australian Chamber of Commerce and Industry, Case No 1774', *Committee on Freedom of Association Report No 302*, Vol LXXIX, 1996, Series B, No 1, para 11.

358 'Communications, Electrical, Electronic, Energy, Information, Postal, Plumbing and Allied Services Union of Australia (CEPU), Case number 2698', *Committee on Freedom of Association Report No 357*, Vol XCIII, 2010, Series B, No 2, paras 165–229.

359 Now the *Fair Work Act 2009* (Cth).

conform with ILO 87 *Freedom of Association and Protection of the Right to Organise Convention* and ILO 98 *Right to Organise and Collective Bargaining Convention*. The CFA decided that the impact of the new laws depended to an extent on their application by Fair Work Australia and should be kept under review. The Committee was concerned about provisions restricting the right to strike, and asked the Australian Government to consult on and review the provisions. Australia reported back to the Committee.[360] The Committee will not consider that response until at least its 361st meeting in November 2011.[361]

10.5.5 Australia's Challenge to the International Human Rights System

Before 1996 there would have been little to criticise about Australia's relationship with the international human rights system; Australia had taken a leading role in establishing that system, as was discussed in Chapter 1.2.2, and has been a committed supporter and participant. From 1996 to 2007 the conservative federal government took 'a combative approach' to the international human rights system,[362] questioning its integrity and rejecting the validity of its oversight of Australia's performance against human rights standards.

Australia's attitude during this period has been described as 'politics of denial ... evident in ... decidedly petulant and self-righteous statements of the ... government regarding the actions and activities of the various human rights organs of the UN that dare to question Australia's compliance with its international human rights obligations'.[363] Australia's maintaining a system of immigration detention for indefinite periods, and without access to periodic court review, despite the repeatedly expressed views of the Human Rights Committee that the practice violated ICCPR, indicates the disregard the government had for the Committee's authority as a supervisory body for treaty compliance.[364]

There are numerous examples of Australia challenging the legitimacy of the views of the UN treaty bodies.[365] Australia's rejection of the views of the Human Rights Committee in *A*, that Australia's

---

360 *Committee on Freedom of Association Report No 359*, Vol. XCIV, 2011, Series B, No. 1.

361 See 'Reports of the supervisory bodies' at <http://www.ilo.org/global/standards>.

362 H Charlesworth, 'Human Rights: Australia Versus the UN', Discussion Paper 22/06 (August 2006) RegNet, Australian National University Discussion Paper, 2006, 3 <www.democraticaudit.anu.edu.au>.

363 D Kinley, 'Human Rights Fundamentalisms' (2007) 29(4) *Sydney Law Review* 545, 570.

364 See D Hovell, 'The Sovereignty Stratagem: Australia's Response to UN Human Rights Treaty Bodies' (2003) 28(6) *Alternative Law Journal* 297. See also H Charlesworth, 'Human Rights: Australia versus the UN' (Discussion Paper No 22/06, RegNet, Australian National University, 2006) 7; S Zifcak, 'The New Anti-Internationalism: Australia and the United Nations Human Rights Treaty System' (Discussion Paper No 54, The Australia Institute, 2003).

365 On Australia's relationship with the Human Rights Committee generally, see J Kinslor, '"Killing Off" International Human Rights Law: An Exploration of the Australian Government's Relationship with United Nations Human Rights Committees' (2002) 8(2) *Australian Journal of Human Rights* 79. On Australia's response to the Human Rights Committee's view on the communication of *A*, see N Poynder, '*A (name deleted) v Australia*: A Milestone for Asylum Seekers' (1997) 4(1) *Australian Journal of Human Rights* 155; W Morgan, 'Passive/Aggressive: The Australian Government's Responses to Optional Protocol Communications' (1999) 5(2) *Australian Journal of Human Rights* 5. On Australia's response to the CERD Committee's noting Australia's failure to apologise to the Stolen Generations see H Charlesworth, 'Human Rights: Australia versus the UN' (Discussion Paper No 22/06, RegNet, Australian National University, 2006). On Australia's response to the Human Rights Committee's view on the communication of *Young*, see Comments of the Attorney-General, Australia, *Hansard*, House of Representatives, 3 November 2003, 21832 (q 2383). On Australia's response to the CERD Committee's view on the communication of *Hagan* (discussed above in relation to ICERD in Chapter 10.5.4), see UN Committee of the Elimination of Racial

immigration detention regime is in breach of ICCPR,[366] elicited a sharp comment from the Committee in its Concluding Observations to Australia's next periodic report, when it said that 'Rejecting the Committee's interpretation of the Covenant when it does not correspond with the interpretation presented by the State party in its submissions to the Committee undermines the State party's recognition of the Committee's competence under the *Optional Protocol* to consider communications'.[367]

The 'high-water mark in Australian unease about accepting international obligations'[368] came in 2002, when Australia voted in the UN against the adoption of an *Optional Protocol* to the Torture Convention. Inaccurately stating the effect of the Protocol, Alexander Downer, Minister for Foreign Affairs, said that 'UN officials should seek the agreement of the federal, [and] ... the state governments, to have access to our prisons, not just get off the plane ... and walk into the prison'.[369]

Australia engaged in a 'steady withdrawal from the [UN human rights] system', announcing that, among other things, it would 'only agree to visits by human rights treaty committees and the provision of information where there is a compelling reason to do so. Australia would reject "unwarranted" requests from treaty committees to delay removal of unsuccessful asylum-seekers from Australia [and] Australia would not sign or ratify the *Optional Protocol* to CEDAW, which establishes an individual complaints procedure'.[370]

The election of a new federal government in 2007 signalled a more cooperative attitude to the UN and its human rights mechanisms. In its first term, from 2007–2010, the government ratified or acceded to the *Convention for the Rights for Persons with Disabilities* and its *Optional Protocol*, and to the *CEDAW Optional Protocol*, and signed the *CAT Optional Protocol*. It changed Australia's previous position and formally advised the UN of its support for the UN *Declaration on the Rights of Indigenous Peoples*, issued a standing invitation to the Special Rapporteurs and other Special Procedures of the UN Human Rights Council to visit Australia, and hosted visits from the UN Special Rapporteur on Indigenous Human Rights and the UN Special Rapporteur on the Right to Health. Nevertheless, Australia continues to dispute the views of the treaty monitoring bodies,[371] and there continues to be a view in national

Discrimination, *Report of the Committee on the Elimination of Racial Discrimination*, 65th sess, para 461, UN Doc A/59/18 (2004).

366 UN Human Rights Committee, above, n 323, discussed above in relation to the ICCPR in Chapter 10.5.4.

367 See above, n 244, paras 498–528, UN Doc A/55/40 (2000).

368 H Charlesworth et al, see above, n 5, 434.

369 See above, n 5, 434, citing *Australia Defends Torture Vote*, CNN.com (26 July 2002).

370 H Charlesworth, 'Human Rights: Australia Versus the UN' (Discussion Paper No 22/06, RegNet, Australian National University, 2006) 5 (citations omitted), citing A Downer, D Williams & P Ruddock, 'Improving the Effectiveness of United Nations Committees' (Joint Media Release, 29 August 2000).

371 See, eg, *Response of the Australian Government to the Views of the Committee in Communications Numbers 1255/2004, 1256/2004, 1259/2004, 1260/2004, 1266/2004, 1268/2004, 1270/2004, 1288/2004; Shams, Atvan, Shahrooei, Saadat, Ramezani, Boostani, Behrooz, Sefed v Australia; Response of the Australian Government to the Views of the Committee in Communication No 1324/2004 Shafiq v Australia; Response of the Australian Government to the Views of the Committee in Communication No 1184/2003 Brough v Australia; Response of the Australian Government to the Views of the Committee in Communication No 1157/2003 Coleman v Australia; Response of the Australian Government to the Views of the Committee in Communication No 1050/2002 D & E v Australia*, available at Human Rights Communications, Australian Government, Attorney-General's Department <http://www.ag.gov.au/www/agd/agd.nsf/Page/Human_rights_and_anti-discriminationCommunications>.

politics that is 'very sceptical of the wholesale invocation of the international jurisdiction surrounding [the human rights treaties]', preferring 'the accumulation of rights through both the common law and statutory protection going back literally centuries'. [372]

10.6 CONCLUSION AND ISSUES

This chapter traces Australia's human rights activity from its ratification of international treaties, through its human rights laws and mechanisms, to its international reporting. The overall picture bears out the 'patchwork quilt' metaphor used by the National Human Rights Consultation Committee; human rights protection in Australia is pieced together from domestic laws, common law and judicial practice, oversight by a number of institutions, and accountability under international treaty obligations.

Alone among industrialised nations Australia has no legislative guarantee of human rights protection. Australia's national human rights institution has no powers of regulation and enforcement, judges debate the relevance of international human rights to statutory interpretation and the development of the common law, and Australia repeatedly rejects the views of UN human rights monitoring bodies. At the same there is no doubt that most Australians, most of the time, enjoy the rights and freedoms described in the international human rights treaties, and that a significant majority of laws, policies and practices in Australia are compliant with human rights standards.

In light of the comfortable, rights-compliant state of most of Australian society, the question arises whether the Australia government was in fact right in fearing that passing a national human rights law would be 'divisive' in the community. On the other hand, the premise of that question can lead to a debate about just how much, and for whom in the community, Australia is rights-compliant, and what efforts should be made to ensure that there is human rights protection for all.

The formal steps that the Australian government proposes taking under the National Framework are, essentially, education for the community and legislative scrutiny for the Parliament. This raises the questions of how effective human rights education is in promoting human rights awareness and understanding, and of what can and will be done to ensure that the full extent of government activity, beyond the making of legislation, will be human rights compliant. This leads in turn to the issues covered at the end of the chapter, including examining the effectiveness of Australia's reporting to the UN as a means of ensuring human rights compliance in Australia.

372 Senator the Hon George Brandis SC, *Hansard*, Senate Legal and Constitutional Affairs Legislation Committee, Reference: Human Rights (Parliamentary Scrutiny (Consequential Provisions) Bill 2010; Human rights ((Parliamentary Scrutiny) Bill 20101, Thursday 4 November 2010, 14–15.

PART FIVE

HUMAN RIGHTS ABUSES

11 ACCOUNTABILITY FOR GROSS HUMAN RIGHTS ABUSES

CONTENTS

11.1 INTERNATIONAL HUMANITARIAN LAW

11.1.1 Development of International Humanitarian Law

International humanitarian law is the law of armed conflict. Despite the different historical origins of international humanitarian law and international human rights law, their aims frequently coincide. The primary concern of international humanitarian law is to minimise human suffering during armed conflict. Its rules therefore prohibit the targeting of civilians and the killing or mistreatment of prisoners of war or combatants who have surrendered, require that sick and wounded combatants be allowed to be treated and medical facilities not be attacked, prohibit torture and certain particularly cruel weapons, and impose a wide range of other requirements on the parties to a conflict.

The foundation of modern international humanitarian law is the four Geneva Conventions.[1] The first Geneva Convention was adopted in 1864. Like many major developments in international law, including

1 *Convention for the Amelioration of the Condition of the Wounded and Sick in Armed Forces in the Field*, opened for signature 12 August 1949, 75 UNTS 31 (entered into force 21 October 1950); *Convention for the Amelioration of the Condition of Wounded, Sick and Shipwrecked Members of Armed Forces at Sea*, opened for signature 12 August 1949, 75 UNTS 85 (entered into force 21 October 1950); *Convention Relative to the Treatment of Prisoners of War*, opened for signature 12 August 1949, 75 UNTS 135 (entered into force 21 October 1950); *Convention Relative to the Protection of Civilian Persons in Time of War*, opened for signature 12 August 1949, 75 UNTS 287 (entered into force 21 October 1950).

international human rights law, the first Geneva Convention was a response to the horror felt by observers of a particular atrocity. In 1859 Henry Dunant, a Geneva businessman, went to Northern Italy to seek an audience regarding business matters with Napoleon III, who was at the time commanding French troops against the Austrians at the Battle of Solferino. Dunant witnessed the battle and was horrified at the lack of assistance to wounded and dying soldiers, who were left to die and were trampled underfoot as the battle raged on. Assisted by local women, Dunant organised improvised care for the many wounded of both sides who had been abandoned on the battlefield after the battle ended.

HENRY DUNANT, *A MEMORY OF SOLFERINO* (1862)[2]

[3] Here is a hand-to-hand struggle in all its horror and frightfulness; Austrians and Allies trampling each other under foot, killing one another on piles of bleeding corpses, felling their enemies with their rifle butts, crushing skulls, ripping bellies open with sabre and bayonet. No quarter is given; it is a sheer butchery; a struggle between savage beasts, maddened with blood and fury. Even the wounded fight to the last gasp. When they have no weapon left, they seize their enemies by the throat and tear them with their teeth.

A little further on, it is the same picture, only made the more ghastly by the approach of a squadron of cavalry, which gallops by, crushing dead and dying beneath its horses' hoofs. One poor wounded man has his jaw carried away; another his head shattered; a third, who could have been saved, has his chest beaten in. Oaths and shrieks of rage, groans of anguish and despair, mingle with the whinnying of horses.

Here come the artillery, following the cavalry, and going at full gallop. The guns crash over the dead and wounded, strewn pell-mell on the ground. Brains spurt under the wheels, limbs are broken and torn, bodies mutilated past recognition—the soil is literally puddled with blood, and the plain littered with human remains.

...

[11] When the sun came up on the twenty-fifth, it disclosed the most dreadful sights imaginable. Bodies of men and horses covered the battlefield; corpses were strewn over roads, ditches, ravines, thickets and fields; the approaches of Solferino were literally thick with dead. ...

The poor wounded men that were being picked up all day long were ghastly pale and exhausted. Some, who had been the most badly hurt, had a stupefied look as though they could not grasp what was said to them; they stared at one out of haggard eyes, but their apparent prostration did not prevent them from feeling their pain. Others were anxious and excited by nervous strain and shaken by spasmodic trembling. Some, who had gaping wounds already beginning to show infection, were almost crazed with suffering. They begged to be put out of their misery, and writhed with faces distorted in the grip of the death-struggle.

There were poor fellows who had not only been hit by bullets or knocked down by shell splinters, but whose arms and legs had been broken by artillery wheels passing over them. The impact of a cylindrical bullet shatters bones into a thousand pieces, and wounds of this kind are always very serious. Shell-splinters and conical bullets also cause agonizingly painful fractures, and often frightful internal injuries. All kinds of splinters, pieces of bone, scraps of clothing, equipment or footgear, dirt or pieces of lead, often aggravate the severity of a wound and double the suffering that must be borne.

2 H Dunant, *A Memory of Solferino* (1862), republished by the International Committee of the Red Cross, Geneva, 1986. Extracts from 3, 11, 27 and 29.

...

[27] Would it not be possible, in time of peace and quiet, to form relief societies for the purpose of having care given to the wounded in wartime by zealous, devoted and thoroughly qualified volunteers? ...

Societies of this kind, once formed and their permanent existence assured, would naturally remain inactive in peacetime. But they would be always organized and ready for the possibility of war. They would have not only to secure the goodwill of the authorities of the countries in which they had been formed, but also, in case of war, to solicit from the rulers of the belligerent states authorization and facilities enabling them to do effective work. The societies, therefore, should include, in each country, as members of their governing board, men enjoying the most honourable reputation and the highest esteem. The committees would appeal to everybody who, for sincerely philanthropic motives, would undertake to devote himself for the time to this charitable work. The work itself would consist in bringing aid and relief (in agreement with the military commissaries, ie, when necessary with their support and under their instructions) onto the battlefield whenever battle was joined, and subsequently to continue to care for the wounded in the hospitals until their convalescence was complete.

...

[29] On certain special occasions, as, for example, when princes of the military art belonging to different nationalities meet at Cologne or Châlons, would it not be desirable that they should take advantage of this sort of congress to formulate some international principle, sanctioned by a Convention inviolate in character, which, once agreed upon and ratified, might constitute the basis for societies for the relief of the wounded in the different European countries? It is the more important to reach an agreement and concert measures in advance, because when hostilities once begin, the belligerents are already ill-disposed to each other, and thenceforth regard all questions from the one limited standpoint of their own subjects.

The *Convention for the Amelioration of the Condition of Wounded Armies in the Field* (1864—the first Geneva Convention) provided for the protection of hospitals, ambulances, medical personnel and local people providing assistance to the sick and wounded in time of war.[3] It also provided for safe evacuation of sick and wounded soldiers from the battlefield and created the symbol of the red cross as a symbol to guarantee neutrality for medical operations,[4] addressing the main concerns raised by Dunant following the battle of Solferino. The major powers of Europe had thereby agreed to constrain their wartime activities in deference to humanitarian concern for the soldiers on all sides of a conflict.

In the years between the first Geneva Convention and the Second World War, additional treaties were concluded to regulate the conduct of war, particularly to protect those who were no longer actively involved in hostilities, because they had been wounded or taken prisoner of war.[5] However, those treaties did not adequately provide for the protection of civilians during armed conflict. After the experience of the Second World War, revision of international humanitarian law became a priority of the international community, resulting in the four Geneva Conventions of 1949. The four Geneva

3 *Convention for the Amelioration of the Condition of Wounded Armies in the Field*, opened for signature 22 August 1864 (entered into force 22 June 1865), arts 1–5.

4 Ibid arts 6–7.

5 For example: Hague Convention of 1899; *Hague Convention for the Adaptation to Maritime Warfare of the Principles of the Geneva Convention*, 18 October 1907; *Convention on the Treatment of Prisoners of War*, 27 July 1929, 47 Stat. 2021.

Conventions included expanded conventions dealing with wounded and sick in the field and at sea, and the treatment of prisoners of war, replacing the earlier Geneva and Hague Conventions on those subjects, as well as a new convention on the protection of civilians, and extended the limited protection previously recognised in customary international law.

A particularly significant development of the 1949 Geneva Conventions was the inclusion of identical text in article 3 of each of the four conventions, known as 'common article 3'. The breakthrough of common article 3 was its application to non-international armed conflicts—that is, conflicts occurring entirely within a state's borders or between a state and a non-state group. At the same time that states were conceding that human rights abuses within their own borders were a legitimate concern of the international community and international law by adopting the UDHR in the UN General Assembly, states made a similar concession of sovereignty regarding the treatment of protected persons in times of armed conflict.

COMMON ARTICLE 3 TO THE GENEVA CONVENTIONS 1949

In the case of armed conflict not of an international character occurring in the territory of one of the High Contracting Parties, each Party to the conflict shall be bound to apply, as a minimum, the following provisions:

(1) Persons taking no active part in the hostilities, including members of armed forces who have laid down their arms and those placed 'hors de combat' by sickness, wounds, detention, or any other cause, shall in all circumstances be treated humanely, without any adverse distinction founded on race, colour, religion or faith, sex, birth or wealth, or any other similar criteria.

To this end, the following acts are and shall remain prohibited at any time and in any place whatsoever with respect to the above-mentioned persons:

(a) violence to life and person, in particular murder of all kinds, mutilation, cruel treatment and torture;

(b) taking of hostages;

(c) outrages upon personal dignity, in particular humiliating and degrading treatment;

(d) the passing of sentences and the carrying out of executions without previous judgment pronounced by a regularly constituted court, affording all the judicial guarantees which are recognized as indispensable by civilized peoples.

(2) The wounded and sick shall be collected and cared for.

An impartial humanitarian body, such as the International Committee of the Red Cross, may offer its services to the Parties to the conflict.

The Parties to the conflict should further endeavour to bring into force, by means of special agreements, all or part of the other provisions of the present Convention.

The application of the preceding provisions shall not affect the legal status of the Parties to the conflict.

The 1949 Geneva Conventions were supplemented by two additional protocols adopted in 1977. The first of these[6] elaborated on the rules for the protection of civilians and other protected persons in international

6 *Protocol Additional to the Geneva Conventions of 12 August 1949, and Relating to the Protection of Victims of International Armed Conflicts*, 8 June 1977 ('Additional Protocol I').

armed conflicts, while the second[7] elaborated on the rules applicable in non-international armed conflicts, considerably expanding the rules contained in common article 3 of the Geneva Conventions.

The common theme in international humanitarian law is that human suffering and harm to civilian life should be no greater than is necessary to achieve military objectives. In achieving that end, a distinction is drawn between those individuals, buildings, vehicles and facilities that are involved in the conflict and those that are not. Included in the latter protected group are soldiers who are no longer taking part in hostilities, because they have surrendered, been wounded or been taken prisoner. Hence there is a general presumption that non-combatants and civilian property will be protected, which can only be rebutted if those people or objects become a legitimate military target—for example if civilians take up arms and join the battle, or if a school is used as a de facto military base—or if the harm to those people or objects was a necessary and proportionate consequence of pursuing a legitimate military objective.

This theme of minimising suffering is manifested in rules prohibiting acts that cause harm to protected persons, such as murder, torture, hostage-taking and denial of a fair trial, among others,[8] and there are clear parallels between such prohibitions and international human rights standards such as those in the *International Covenant on Civil and Political Rights*. It is also manifested in rules regarding the manner in which a military attack is carried out. Particularly cruel weapons, such as hollow bullets, poisonous gas and other chemical weapons, have long been expressly prohibited[9] and their use is recognised as a war crime.[10] Those categories reflect the experience of unnecessary suffering from conflicts preceding the 1949 Geneva Conventions, including the Battle of Solferino and the First World War, but they are silent on some of the most catastrophic weapons in use today, such as nuclear weapons, cluster bombs and land mines. Additional treaties have been developed to regulate the use of some such weapons, although ratification is not universal and some of the most significant deployers of those weapons are not parties to those treaties.[11] In addition to the weapons that are specifically banned, it is prohibited to use weapons that will cause indiscriminate damage or unnecessary suffering.[12]

LEGALITY OF THE THREAT OR USE OF NUCLEAR WEAPONS, ADVISORY OPINION OF THE INTERNATIONAL COURT OF JUSTICE[13]

78 The cardinal principles contained in the texts constituting the fabric of humanitarian law are the following. The first is aimed at the protection of the civilian population and civilian objects and establishes the distinction

7 Ibid ('Additional Protocol II').

8 See for example common article 3 of the Geneva Conventions, extracted above.

9 Hague Declaration (1899); Hague Regulations (1907); Geneva Protocol (1925).

10 *Rome Statute of the International Criminal Court*, (*Rome Statute*) 2187 UNTS 90 (entered into force July 1 2002), art 8(2)(b)(xvii)–(xix), drawing on earlier prohibitions in the Hague rules and customary international law.

11 *The Convention on the Prohibition of the Use, Production and Transfer of Anti-Personnel Mines and on their Destruction* opened for signature 18 September 1997 2056 UNTS 211, (entered into force 1 March 1999) has 156 states parties as at July 2011, but the United States, China, India, Pakistan, Sri Lanka, Israel, Iran, Lebanon, North Korea and South Korea are among the non-parties. The Convention on Cluster Munitions 2008 has only 59 states parties as at July 2011, mainly because it is so new, but none of the states listed above are parties except Lebanon; see <www.clusterconvention.org>.

12 International Committee of the Red Cross, Customary IHL database, <www.icrc.org/customary-ihl> (1996), rules 70 and 71.

13 [1996] ICJ Rep 22s

between combatants and non-combatants; States must never make civilians the object of attack and must consequently never use weapons that are incapable of distinguishing between civilian and military targets. According to the second principle, it is prohibited to cause unnecessary suffering to combatants: it is accordingly prohibited to use weapons causing them such harm or uselessly aggravating their suffering.

In application of that second principle, States do not have unlimited freedom of choice of means in the weapons they use.

...

humanitarian law, at a very early stage, prohibited certain types of weapons either because of their indiscriminate effect on combatants and civilians or because of the unnecessary suffering caused to combatants, that is to say, a harm greater than that unavoidable to achieve legitimate military objectives. If an envisaged use of weapons would not meet the requirements of humanitarian law, a threat to engage in such use would also be contrary to that law.

79 It is undoubtedly because a great many rules of humanitarian law applicable in armed conflict are so fundamental to the respect of the human person and 'elementary considerations of humanity' as the Court put it in its Judgment of 9 April 1949 in the Corfu Channel case, that the Hague and Geneva Conventions have enjoyed a broad accession. Further these fundamental rules are to be observed by all States whether or not they have ratified the conventions that contain them, because they constitute intransgressible principles of international customary law.

...

92 Another view holds that recourse to nuclear weapons could never be compatible with the principles and rules of humanitarian law and is therefore prohibited. In the event of their use, nuclear weapons would in all circumstances be unable to draw any distinction between the civilian population and combatants, or between civilian objects and military objectives, and their effects, largely uncontrollable, could not be restricted, either in time or in space, to lawful military targets. ...That view lay at the basis of the assertions by certain States before the Court that nuclear weapons are by their nature illegal under customary international law, by virtue of the fundamental principle of humanity.

...

94 The Court would observe that none of the States advocating the legality of the use of nuclear weapons under certain circumstances, including the 'clean' use of smaller, low yield, tactical nuclear weapons, has indicated what, supposing such limited use were feasible, would be the precise circumstances justifying such use; nor whether such limited use would not tend to escalate into the all-out use of high yield nuclear weapons. This being so, the Court does not consider that it has a sufficient basis for a determination on the validity of this view.

95 Nor can the Court make a determination on the validity of the view that the recourse to nuclear weapons would be illegal in any circumstance owing to their inherent and total incompatibility with the law applicable in armed conflict. Certainly, as the Court has already indicated, the principles and rules of law applicable in armed conflict—at the heart of which is the overriding consideration of humanity—make the conduct of armed hostilities subject to a number of strict requirements. Thus, methods and means of warfare, which would preclude any distinction between civilian and military targets, or which would result in unnecessary suffering to combatants, are prohibited. In view of the unique characteristics of nuclear weapons, to which the Court has referred above, the use of such weapons in fact seems scarcely reconcilable with respect for such requirements. Nevertheless, the Court considers that it does not have sufficient elements to enable it to

conclude with certainty that the use of nuclear weapons would necessarily be at variance with the principles and rules of law applicable in armed conflict in any circumstance.

...

105 For these reasons, THE COURT, ...

(2) Replies in the following manner to the question put by the General Assembly :

...

D Unanimously,

A threat or use of nuclear weapons should also be compatible with the requirements of the international law applicable in armed conflict, particularly those of the principles and rules of international humanitarian law, as well as with specific obligations under treaties and other undertakings which expressly deal with nuclear weapons ;

E By seven votes to seven, by the President's casting vote,

It follows from the above-mentioned requirements that the threat or use of nuclear weapons would generally be contrary to the rules of international law applicable in armed conflict, and in particular the principles and rules of humanitarian law;

However, in view of the current state of international law, and of the elements of fact at its disposal, the Court cannot conclude definitively whether the threat or use of nuclear weapons would be lawful or unlawful in an extreme circumstance of self-defence, in which the very survival of a State would be at stake.

The theme of minimising suffering is also applied in the selection of targets for military attacks: civilians and protected civilian objects cannot themselves be the target of an attack. However, if civilians are killed in the process of conducting an attack on a legitimate military target, the civilian casualties will not be unlawful if they were incidental to the military attack (ie 'collateral damage' rather than the direct target) and if the casualties were not 'excessive in relation to the concrete and direct military advantage anticipated.'[14]

11.1.2 Application of International Human Rights Law in Times of Armed Conflict

The International Court of Justice has affirmed on numerous occasions that international human rights law continues to apply in times of armed conflict.[15] Furthermore, international humanitarian law, as the law governing the conduct of armed conflicts, does not displace international human rights law; rather it modifies the application of human rights law.

---

14 See above, n 6, article 51(5)(b).

15 *Legal Consequences of the Construction of a Wall in the Occupied Palestinian Territory* (Advisory Opinion), (2004) ICJ, para 106; *Legality of the Threat or Use of Nuclear Weapons* (Advisory Opinion), (1996) ICJ, para 25; *Armed Activities on the Territory of the Congo (Democratic Republic of the Congo v Uganda),* (1999) ICJ, para 216.

At first glance, it might appear that international human rights law and international humanitarian law are irreconcilable. For instance, international humanitarian law presumes that it is lawful for combatants to kill one another in armed conflict, while international human rights law guarantees the right to life. However, international human rights law only prohibits the arbitrary deprivation of life, not killing per se.[16] While in the normal course of events, extrajudicial killing, absent any urgent necessity such as self-defence, will be an arbitrary deprivation of life, the definition of what is 'arbitrary' necessarily shifts in times of armed conflict. In its advisory opinion on the *Legality of the Threat or Use of Nuclear Weapons*, the ICJ held:

> the protection of the International Covenant of [sic] Civil and Political Rights does not cease in times of war ... In principle, the right not arbitrarily to be deprived of one's life applies also in hostilities. The test of what is an arbitrary deprivation of life, however, then falls to be determined by the applicable *lex specialis*, namely, the law applicable in armed conflict which is designed to regulate the conduct of hostilities.[17]

The principle *'lex specialis derogare lege generali'* (specific law derogates from general laws) operates in international law to ensure that a specific rule will prevail over a generally applicable rule. Sometimes that principle operates so that the specific rule simply clarifies how the general rule operates in a particular context, while in rare cases, the specific rule contradicts and acts as an exception to the general rule.[18] In the example of the right to life, the general rule prohibiting arbitrary deprivation of life is clarified in the context of armed conflict by the context-specific rules of international humanitarian law. Accordingly, when read together, international humanitarian law and international human rights law will render the deliberate targeting of civilians, or engaging in an attack that is indiscriminate or results in a disproportionate number of casualties, arbitrary deprivation of life in the context of armed conflict.

In the same way, the international human rights standards continue to apply in situations of armed conflict, with their parameters determined by the principles of international humanitarian law. Some human rights standards will be altered by the understanding of the types of conduct that are permissible in armed conflict, and others will remain unaltered when international humanitarian law has no specific rule to apply to that situation.

One further note regarding the relationship between international human rights law and the law of armed conflict is that states are permitted to derogate from certain human rights norms in times of 'public emergency that threatens the life of the nation'. This process of derogation, which is discussed in detail in Chapter 3.3.3, will most often arise in a situation of armed conflict. However, derogation is not automatic; positive acts are required of the state to opt out of its human rights obligations, and the measures taken must be necessary to address the emergency and of a temporary nature.[19] Furthermore, there are some human rights norms that are non-derogable.[20] Therefore, in the absence of a positive act of derogation, when permitted, international human rights law will continue to apply in times of armed

16 See Chapter 3.2.2 and 3.5.

17 *Legality of the Threat or Use of Nuclear Weapons*, (1996) ICJ, Advisory Opinion, para 25.

18 International Law Commission, *Fragmentation of International Law: Difficulties Arising from the Diversification and Expansion of International Law*, 13 April 2006, UN document no A/CN.4/L.682, paras 56–67.

19 Human Rights Committee: *General Comment No 29: States of Emergency*, 31 August 2001, UN document no CCPR/C/21/Rev.1/Add.11, para 2.

20 ICCPR, article 4(2).

conflict alongside international humanitarian law. It is not permissible to derogate from obligations of international humanitarian law, since their only application is in times of armed conflict; if such norms could be derogated from in times of national emergency, they would never apply.

11.2 CRIMINAL LAW AS A HUMAN RIGHTS ENFORCEMENT TOOL

11.2.1 The Nature of International Criminal Law

International criminal law overlaps substantially with international human rights law, in that those heinous acts that amount to international crimes—war crimes, crimes against humanity and genocide—also constitute grave violations of human rights. International criminal law is therefore one mechanism for accountability for a particular subset of gross human rights abuses.

International human rights law guarantees certain entitlements to all human beings and focuses primarily on states as the holders of the corresponding obligation. Accordingly, when an individual alleges a violation, the usual response of international human rights law is to look to the state to determine whether the state had some part in the wrongful act or whether it failed to put in place measures to prevent it or to investigate and punish it after the event. International criminal law, on the other hand, holds accountable individual perpetrators rather than states. For a gross human rights abuse that falls within the jurisdiction of international criminal law, two separate fields of international law are engaged: international criminal law to hold the individual perpetrator accountable; and international human rights law to hold accountable the state or states that failed to respect and protect the human rights of the victims in that case.

At the time of the trial of the accused Nazi war criminals at Nuremberg, the resort to individual liability for breaches of international law was somewhat novel, as international law was essentially seen as applying to states. In the course of its judgment the International Military Tribunal famously observed: 'crimes against international law are committed by men, not by abstract entities, and only by punishing individuals who commit such crimes can the provisions of international law be enforced.'[21]

As well as an overlap with international human rights law, international criminal law overlaps with international humanitarian law, as sufficiently grave conduct amounting to international crimes in the currently recognised categories typically occurs during or in the lead-up to armed conflict. Thus, for example, the prohibitions in the Geneva Conventions are directly relevant in defining war crimes for the purpose of international criminal liability. Cassese explains how rules drawn from international humanitarian law were drawn into the realm of individual criminal responsibility with the following example:

> [P]reviously the indiscriminate bombing of civilians was only considered a wrongful act attributable to the relevant belligerent state and entailed the international responsibility of that state vis-à-vis the enemy belligerent. Gradually the same act also came to be regarded as a war crime for which those ordering and executing the indiscriminate attack had to bear individual criminal responsibility.[22]

---

21 International Military Tribunal at Nuremberg, *Trial of Major War Criminals before the International Military Tribunal*, Nuremberg, 1947, 223.

22 A Cassese, *International Criminal Law*, 2nd edn, Oxford University Press, Oxford, 2008, 149 (regarding torture) and 166 (regarding terrorism).

In order for conduct to attract international criminal liability, it must be criminalised either in a treaty or in customary international law. To prosecute individuals for conduct that was not criminalised under international law at the time it was committed would be to invoke retrospective criminality, which is contrary to international human rights law.[23] Having identified an international crime, it is then necessary for a relevant court or tribunal to have jurisdiction to try the case. The International Criminal Court (ICC) has jurisdiction over certain categories of crime—genocide, crimes against humanity, war crimes and aggression—committed after July 2002; that is, the ICC has only prospective jurisdiction, from the date it was established.

International law also permits trials before courts or tribunals that were established after the commission of the relevant crime: such a trial does not violate the rule against retrospectivity, as the conduct itself was criminal at the relevant time; it is only the machinery for the trial of the alleged crime that has been established after the fact. In that way, ad hoc courts and tribunals established to try crimes committed in conflicts in the former Yugoslavia, Rwanda, Cambodia, Sierra Leone and Kosovo are able to exercise jurisdiction over crimes that were committed before the courts or tribunals themselves came into existence. The key to the legality of such trials is the ability to locate a source of international law criminalising the relevant act that was in force at the time the act was committed.

SNAPSHOT: ESTABLISHING 'CRIMES AGAINST HUMANITY' AT NUREMBERG

The London Charter of the International Military Tribunal (concluded by the four major allies—the United Kingdom, United States, France and the USSR) established a tribunal for the trial of 'major war criminals of the European Axis countries' for crimes under international law committed in the course of the war. In order not to be retrospective, the London Charter had to rely on legal principles that were already established, and not create new principles of law. It therefore needed to rely on legal principles that were already reflected in treaties ratified by the relevant states or in customary international law. A charge of 'crimes against peace', which concerned the actions taken in conducting a war of aggression, and of 'war crimes', which concerned the mistreatment of enemy civilians or enemy prisoners, the destruction of property and related crimes, could rely on existing treaty law relating to the legality of war (*jus ad bellum*) and the conduct of war (*jus in bello*). But those crimes could not deal with the crimes of the holocaust in which some of the most egregious conduct was committed by the Nazis against their own people, rather than against the soldiers or inhabitants of enemy or even neutral countries. For that reason, the charge of 'crimes against humanity' was included, defined in the following terms:

> Crimes Against Humanity: namely, murder, extermination, enslavement, deportation, and other inhumane acts committed against any civilian population, before or during the war, or persecutions on political, racial or religious grounds in execution of or connection with any crime within the jurisdiction of the Tribunal, whether or not in violation of the domestic law of the country where perpetrated.[24]

The Tribunal interpreted its jurisdiction in relation to crimes against humanity narrowly, holding that only crimes that occurred after the outbreak of war in 1939 were properly within its jurisdiction.

23 ICCPR article 15.

24 *Agreement for the prosecution and punishment of the major war criminals of the European Axis* (1945) (the 'London Agreement'), Annex, art 6(c).

JUDGMENT OF THE INTERNATIONAL MILITARY TRIBUNAL AT NUREMBERG, 1946[25]

With regard to Crimes against Humanity, there is no doubt whatever that political opponents were murdered in Germany before the war, and that many of them were kept in concentration camps in circumstances of great horror and cruelty. The policy of terror was certainly carried out on a vast scale, and in many cases was organised and systematic. The policy of persecution, repression and murder of civilians in Germany before the war of 1939, who were likely to be hostile to the Government, was most ruthlessly carried out. The persecution of Jews during the same period is established beyond all doubt. To constitute Crimes against Humanity, the acts relied on before the outbreak of war must have been in execution of, or in connection with, any crime within the jurisdiction of the Tribunal. The Tribunal is of the opinion that revolting and horrible as many of these crimes were, it has not been satisfactorily proved that they were done in execution of, or in connection with, any such crime. The Tribunal therefore cannot make a general declaration that the acts before 1939 were Crimes against humanity within the meaning of the Charter, but from the beginning of the war in 1939 War Crimes were committed on a vast scale, which were also crimes against humanity; and insofar as the inhumane acts charged in the Indictment, and committed after the beginning of the war, did not constitute War Crimes, they were all committed in execution of, or in connection with, the aggressive war, and therefore constituted Crimes against Humanity.

11.2.2 The Main Categories of International Crimes

The main categories of crimes considered by the modern international criminal courts and tribunals, as prescribed in the governing statute of the relevant tribunal, are genocide, crimes against humanity and war crimes. However, it would be lawful for other categories of crimes to be tried in future tribunals, as long as the crime in question was clearly prohibited under treaty or customary international law at the time it was committed. There is some disagreement as to the categories of crimes that might meet that threshold: the most commonly suggested include torture, terrorism offences and drug trafficking.[26]

Genocide

Genocide refers to crimes committed with the intention of destroying an entire group because of its members' inherent characteristics, such as race, ethnicity or religion. The particularly egregious nature of genocide and the emotive response it generates in the international community has in fact been the driving force for many of the major breakthroughs in modern international criminal law. The genocide against Jews that characterised the Holocaust was a very significant factor in the decision of the Allies to establish the International Military Tribunal at Nuremberg, although genocide was not prosecuted

25 (1947) 41 *American Journal of International Law* 172, 249.

26 A Cassese, see above, n 22; P Robinson, 'The Missing Crimes', in A Cassese et al (eds), *The Rome Statute of the International Criminal Court: A Commentary*, Oxford University Press, Oxford, 2002, 497–525.

as a separate crime at Nuremberg.27 Likewise, the 'ethnic cleansing' that was pervasive in the Balkans conflict and the slaughter of Tutsis in Rwanda were the clear motivating factors for the UN Security Council's action in establishing the International Criminal Tribunals for the Former Yugoslavia and Rwanda.

The definition of genocide under the Genocide Convention, which is replicated in modern international criminal courts and tribunals, provides that

> genocide means any of the following acts committed with intent to destroy, in whole or in part, a national, ethnical, racial or religious group, as such:
>
> (a) Killing members of the group;
>
> (b) Causing serious bodily or mental harm to members of the group;
>
> (c) Deliberately inflicting on the group conditions of life calculated to bring about its physical destruction in whole or in part;
>
> (d) Imposing measures intended to prevent births within the group;
>
> (e) Forcibly transferring children of the group to another group.[28]

As this definition illustrates, measures short of direct physical violence can constitute genocide if accompanied by the intention to destroy the group. The essence of genocide is therefore not the individual acts of violence themselves, but the context in which they occur, namely a campaign to eradicate a particular racial, ethnic or religious group.

Crimes Against Humanity

As it is in defining genocide, context is important in the definition of crimes against humanity. To qualify as crimes against humanity, the *Rome Statute of the International Criminal Court* requires the proscribed acts to be 'committed as part of a widespread or systematic attack directed against any civilian population, with knowledge of the attack.'[29] In that context, 'attack' does not necessarily mean a military attack occurring during an armed conflict. Rather, it means a 'course of conduct involving the multiple commission' of the acts that are proscribed as crimes against humanity, in connection with the policy of a state or other organisation to commit such acts against civilians.[30] Thus a systematic campaign of violence or persecution against a civilian population, even if not amounting to an armed conflict, can give rise to crimes against humanity.

---

27 W Schabas, *Convention on the Prevention and Punishment of the Crime of Genocide* (2008) United Nations Audiovisual Library of International Law, <http://untreaty.un.org/cod/avl/pdf/ha/cppcg/cppcg_e.pdf> has explained: 'The term "genocide" was first used by Raphael Lemkin in his book *Axis Rule in Occupied Europe*, published in late 1944. Although the word appears in the drafting history of the *Charter of the International Military Tribunal*, the final text of that instrument uses the cognate term "crimes against humanity" to deal with the persecution and physical extermination of national, ethnic, racial and religious minorities. Prosecutors also used the term occasionally in their submissions to the Nuremberg Tribunal, but "genocide" does not appear in the final judgment, issued on 30 September – 1 October 1946.'

28 *Genocide Convention*, art II; *Rome Statute*, art 6; *ICTY Statute*, art 4; *ICTR Statute*, art 2.

29 *Rome Statute*, art 7.

30 *Elements of Crimes, Annex to Rome Statute of the International Criminal Court*, art 7, introduction, para 3.

Unlike genocide, there is no requirement in the *Rome Statute* or the *Statute of the International Criminal Tribunal for the Former Yugoslavia* (ICTY Statute) for the attack on the civilian population to be motivated by the nationality, race, ethnicity or religion of the targeted group. The *Statute of the International Criminal Tribunal for Rwanda* (ICTR Statute), however, does require the attack to be 'on national, political, racial or ethnical grounds.'[31] That has not proven a significant obstacle in the ICTR, however, since the Hutu–Tutsi conflict in which the atrocities took place has been recognised as ethnically based.[32]

The acts enumerated in the *Rome Statute* as crimes against humanity, if the requisite context is satisfied, are:

(a) murder
(b) extermination
(c) enslavement
(d) deportation or forcible transfer of population
(e) imprisonment or other severe deprivation of liberty in violation of fundamental rules of international law
(f) torture
(g) rape, sexual slavery, enforced prostitution, forced pregnancy, enforced sterilisation, or any other form of sexual violence of comparable gravity
(h) persecution against any identifiable group or collectivity on political, racial, national, ethnic, cultural, religious, gender, or other grounds that are universally recognised as impermissible under international law, in connection with any act referred to in this paragraph or any crime within the jurisdiction of the court
(i) enforced disappearance of persons
(j) the crime of apartheid
(k) other inhumane acts of a similar character intentionally causing great suffering, or serious injury to body or to mental or physical health.[33]

The connection of these enumerated crimes against humanity to human rights standards is quite apparent; each of them involves the mistreatment of individuals in a manner that defies the inherent dignity of the human person. Each crime is clearly referable to one or more of the civil and political rights set out in the ICCPR. In the case of the crime against humanity of persecution, international human rights law is specifically invoked: the reference to 'international law' in the *Rome Statute* text primarily relates to international human rights law, and specifically to the right of non-discrimination.[34]

---

31 *ICTR Statute*, art 3.

32 *Prosecutor v Akayesu*, ICTR, Judgment of the Trial Chamber, 2 September 1998, Case no ICTR-96-4-T.

33 *Rome Statute*, art 7(1). The ICTY Statute (art 5) and ICTR Statute (art 3) contain similar lists but are less specific, particularly regarding sexual offences, which are described simply as 'rape'; it has been left to the case law of the tribunals to define rape broadly. The ICTY and ICTR Statutes also contain a catch-all provision of 'other inhumane acts' as a crime against humanity if committed in the requisite context.

34 Elements of Crimes, see above, n 30, article 7(1)(h), element 1.

When the category of crimes against humanity was originally developed in the *Charter of the International Military Tribunal at Nuremberg*, there was a requirement that the crimes be committed 'in execution of or connexion with' war crimes or 'crimes against peace'.[35] The main reason for that was the sensitivity to the accusations of retrospectivity, discussed further below at Chapter 11.3.1 in connection with Nuremberg. While the prohibition of war crimes under customary international law was well accepted at the time of the Second World War, crimes committed against civilians—particularly a state's own civilians—not as part of a war were more controversial. The ICTY Statute retained the requirement for a connection to armed conflict,[36] which was not problematic given the clear context of armed conflict in which the Balkans crimes were committed. In Rwanda, however, the mob violence character of many of the atrocities made the connection to armed conflict somewhat uncertain. The ICTR Statute therefore omitted the requirement for crimes against humanity to be committed in a context of armed conflict.[37] It is now clear that international law treats crimes against humanity as quite separate from crimes in armed conflict, although the two will often overlap.

War Crimes

International humanitarian law forms the basis for war crimes. War crimes include the grave breaches of the Geneva Conventions, which focus mainly on the mistreatment of protected persons, as well as serious breaches of customary international law. The *Rome Statute* divides the enumerated war crimes into those applicable to international armed conflicts, totalling 34 separate crimes,[38] and those applicable to non-international armed conflicts, totalling 16 separate crimes.[39] The division is due to the more detailed historic laws and prohibitions in international armed conflict compared to those in internal conflicts.

The Charters of the Nuremberg and Tokyo tribunals, which predated the 1949 revisions of the Geneva Conventions, relied on the prohibitions contained in the Hague Conventions and the 1929 Geneva Conventions, but were instrumental in confirming that those prohibitions could give rise to individual liability.[40]

11.2.3 International Criminal Law as Catharsis

International criminal trials taking place in post-conflict scenarios are not solely about the question of guilt or innocence of the accused for the crimes charged. The trials also serve important historical and social purposes. Putting on trial those responsible for mass atrocities, and potentially convicting them, also serves the purpose of publicly condemning the acts, as well as putting the details on the public record for posterity, so that future generations will not doubt the extent of the harm inflicted.

35 *Charter of the International Military Tribunal* (1945), art 6(c); see Chapter 11.3.1 below.

36 *ICTY Statute*, art 3.

37 Ibid art 5.

38 *Rome Statute*, art 8(2)(a) and (b).

39 Ibid art 8(2)(c) and (e).

40 S Ratner & J Abrams, *Accountability for Human Rights Atrocities in International Law: Beyond the Nuremberg Legacy*, 2nd edn, Oxford University Press, Oxford, 2001, 81.

It has been noted that such trials

> present moments of transformative opportunity in the lives of individuals and societies, a potential not lost upon the litigants themselves. Prosecutors and judges in these cases thus rightly aim to shape collective memory of horrible events in ways that can be both successful as public spectacle and consistent with liberal legality.[41]

In that way, the theme of 'never again', which is so prevalent in shaping the development of international law, permeates international criminal law.

> Many have thought, in particular, that the best way to prevent recurrence of genocide, and other forms of state-sponsored mass brutality, is to cultivate a shared and enduring memory of its horrors—and to employ the law self-consciously to that end.[42]

In modern courts and tribunals, recognition of the importance of victims being allowed to tell their story, both in service of history and also for the cathartic effect on the victims themselves, has given rise to a much stronger emphasis on the involvement of victims than is common in most domestic criminal proceedings. In the ICC, the interests of victims are one of the principal considerations for the court in decisions about the conduct of the case, including admissibility and the type of evidence that is heard.[43] Victims can also apply to participate in the proceedings, including making opening and closing statements and cross-examining witnesses through a legal representative.[44] The ability to question one's tormentor in a safe, public environment can be a powerful experience for a victim of gross human rights abuses.

Post-conflict trials are also promoted as a means of closure or moving on, for both individual victims and the society as a whole. The need for closure has been proffered as a major reason for the establishment of the Extraordinary Chambers in the Courts of Cambodia (ECCC) in 2006, almost 30 years since the crimes it is tasked with trying, which occurred during the Khmer Rouge regime of 1975–80.[45]

Criminal trials are not the only method for achieving closure of that sort, however. An alternative approach is to pursue non-punitive investigatory commissions or 'truth and reconciliation' commissions. Those commissions are designed to pursue truth, story-telling, compilation of a historical record, catharsis for victims and an opportunity to confront one's tormentors, but without a criminal trial for the accused. In fact, those accused of committing atrocities are commonly offered amnesty for their conduct in return for their testimony, on the theory that truth and acknowledgement are more important than punishment and vengeance. Investigatory commissions have been used following the removal of abusive regimes in Argentina, Chile, El Salvador, South Africa and Timor Leste, among others.[46]

41 M Osiel, 'In Defense of Liberal Show Trials—Nuremberg and Beyond', reprinted in G Mettraux (ed), *Perspectives on the Nuremberg Trial*, Oxford University Press, Oxford, 2008, 704.

42 Ibid 705.

43 *Rome Statute*, see above, n 10, arts 53–4.

44 ICC, *Rules of Procedure and Evidence*, document no ICC-ASP/1/3, rules 89–91.

45 Open Society Justice Initiative, *Justice Initiatives*, Spring 2006, available at <www.justiceinitiative.org>. See further L Banner, 'What Kind of Justice Long After Genocide?' (2009) 76(1) *Criminal Justice Matters* 4.

46 See further R Goldstone, 'Advancing the Cause of Human Rights: The Need for Justice and Accountability' in S Power & G Allison (eds), *Realizing Human Rights*, St Martin's Press, New York, 2000, 195–224.

TRUTH AND RECONCILIATION COMMISSION OF SOUTH AFRICA, *REPORT*[47]

65 In evaluating the role played by those who were involved in the conflicts of the past, the Commission was guided, in particular, by section 4 of its enabling Act, the relevant portions of which read as follows:

The functions of the Commission shall be to achieve its objectives, and to that end it shall –

(a) facilitate and where necessary initiate or co-ordinate, inquiries into …

(iii) the identity of all persons, authorities, institutions and organisations involved in [gross violations of human rights]

(iv) the question whether such violations were the result of deliberate planning on the part of the State or a former state or any of their organs, or of any political organisation, liberation movement or other group or individual; and

(v) accountability, political or otherwise, for any such violations.

66 In the light of the above and of the evidence received, the Commission is of the view that gross violations of human rights were perpetrated or facilitated by all the major role-players in the conflicts of the mandate era. These include:

(a) The state and its security, intelligence and law-enforcement agencies, the [South African Police], the [South African Defence Force], and the [National Intelligence Service].

(b) Groups and institutions which, to a greater or lesser extent, were affiliated or allied to the state in an official capacity. These include homeland governments and their security forces as well as groups and institutions informally allied to the state or receiving financial or logistic assistance from the state in order to oppose and/or withstand the liberation movements and their internal allies. Groups falling into this category include the [Inkatha Freedom Party] and conservative surrogate organisations and groupings like the witdoeke, AmaAfrika and the Eagles.

(c) White right-wing organisations which, while actively opposing the state, actively and violently took action to preserve the status quo in the 1990s. These include the Afrikaner Weerstandsbeweging (AWB), the Afrikaner Volksfront and the Boere Bevrydingsbeweging.

(d) Liberation movements and organisations which sought to bring about change through armed struggle and which operated outside South Africa and by covert and underground means inside the country.

(e) Organisations which sought to bring about change by non-violent means prior to and post-1990, including the United Democratic Front; and

(f) Non-state paramilitary formations such as the ANC's self-defence units and the IFP's self-protection units (SPUs).

67 Evidence before the Commission indicates that all of the above were responsible for gross violations of human rights—including killing, attempted killing, torture and severe ill treatment—at different stages during the mandate period and that, to varying degrees, such violations entailed deliberate planning on the part of the organisations and institutions concerned, or were of such a nature that the organisations are accountable for them.

68 At the same time, the Commission is not of the view that all such parties can be held to be equally culpable for violations committed in the mandate period. Indeed, the evidence accumulated by the Commission and documented in this report shows that this was not the case. The preponderance of responsibility rests with the state and its allies.

…

47 Vol 5, Ch 6.

74 It would, however, be misleading and wrong to assign blame for the gross violation of human rights only to those who confronted each other on the political and military battlefields, engaged in acts of commission. Others, like the church or faith groups, the media, the legal profession, the judiciary, the magistracy, the medical/health, educational and business sectors, are found by the Commission to have been guilty of acts of omission in that they failed to adhere or live up to the ethics of their profession and to accepted codes of conduct.

75 It is also the view of the Commission that these sectors failed not so much out of fear of the powers and wrath of the state—although those were not insignificant factors—but primarily because they were the beneficiaries of the state system. They prospered from it by staying silent. By doing nothing or not enough, they contributed to the emergence of a culture of impunity within which the gross violations of human rights documented in this report could and did occur.

11.3 NUREMBERG AND TOKYO TRIBUNALS

11.3.1 Nuremberg

In the closing stages of the Second World War, the victorious Allies met to discuss the fate of the main Nazi leaders. The British Prime Minister Winston Churchill reportedly favoured summary execution, but the preference of the Americans and Soviets to hold a public trial ultimately prevailed.[48] The International Military Tribunal (IMT, commonly called the Nuremberg Tribunal) was thus a creation of the four major Allies—the United Kingdom, the United States, France and the Soviet Union—who sat in judgment over their vanquished enemies. The accusation of 'victor's justice' was therefore inevitable and has persisted at some level ever since.[49]

The Nuremberg Tribunal was the first international criminal tribunal seeking to hold individuals, rather than states, directly responsible for serious violations of the laws of war and fundamental human rights. It was therefore a paradigm-setting development, changing the approach to international law as a system that held individuals accountable as well as states, and a system that did not consider state sovereignty an absolute shield in circumstances of human rights atrocities. Given the novelty of the Nuremberg trials, the identification of applicable law was both crucial and difficult. The laws of war, having been well established at the time of the outbreak of the Second World War, were clearly binding on the states involved in the conflict as customary international law. The assertion of jurisdiction to hold individuals criminally liable for such breaches was controversial, but the rules themselves were not. 'Crimes against peace', which today would be referred to as the crime of aggression, was more controversial, as the prohibition on the use of aggressive force enshrined in 1945 in the *UN Charter* was somewhat more equivocal at the outbreak of the war.

48 See for example J Crossland, 'Churchill: Execute Hitler Without Trial', *The Sunday Times*, London, 1 January 2006, reporting on the release of Churchill's 1942 cabinet documents.

49 See for example M Cherif Bassiouni, *Introduction to International Criminal Law*, Transnational Publishers, New York, 2003, 406–12, particularly in relation to Soviet efforts to frame the tribunal's jurisdiction to focus on German aggression to the exclusion of Soviet actions in parts of Poland and Finland during the war.

'Crimes against humanity' were included as a third category in the IMT Charter in order to cover the Nazi atrocities that were committed against their own people in their own territory, as opposed to the soldiers and civilians of enemy countries, which would have been covered as war crimes. This category, covering 'murder, extermination, enslavement, deportation, and other inhumane acts committed against any civilian population, before or during the war, or persecutions on political, racial or religious grounds',[50] is the category most directly connected to human rights norms. However, the status of crimes against humanity as stand-alone crimes in international law during the period of Nazi ascendancy, 1933–45, was highly controversial, given the supremacy of sovereignty in international relations at that time. As a result, the IMT Charter required the crimes against humanity to be connected to war crimes or crimes against peace for the tribunal to have jurisdiction. Furthermore, the prosecutors chose not to prosecute crimes committed by the Nazis before the outbreak of war, between 1933 and 1939, thus minimising the basis for accusations of retrospectivity.

The Nuremberg Tribunal tried 22 defendants in its main proceeding in 1945–46, known as the 'Trial of the Major War Criminals', 19 of whom were convicted. Twelve were sentenced to death, including one (Martin Bormann) in absentia, and the remaining seven to prison sentences ranging from 10 years to life.

ROBERT H JACKSON (JUSTICE OF THE US SUPREME COURT AND AMERICAN CHIEF PROSECUTOR AT THE NUREMBERG TRIBUNAL), 'NUREMBERG IN RETROSPECT: LEGAL ANSWER TO INTERNATIONAL LAWLESSNESS'[51]

We must not forget that we did not invoke the outlawry of war as a sword to punish acts that were otherwise innocent and harmless. On the contrary, it was the accused who had to establish the lawfulness of their belligerency to excuse a course of murders, enslavements, arsons and violence which, except in war, is criminal by every civilized concept. They were like pirates or buccaneers who are punishable wherever, whenever and by whomever caught unless they can show that their acts fall within the protection the law always has afforded those who commit acts of violence in prosecuting war. The very least legal consequences that follow outlawing wars of aggression is to withdraw from one knowingly and voluntarily causing or promoting such aggression the defense of lawful warfare. Thus if the treaties outlawing this war did not expressly create a new crime, they took away the immunity of war makers from prosecution for old crimes.

...

Thus 'the old order changeth, yielding place to the new.' Like much legal work ours at Nuremberg has far-reaching implications rarely apparent to laymen and often missed by lawyers. Its value to the world will depend less on how faithfully it interpreted the past than on how accurately it forecasts the future.

Following the Trial of the Major War Criminals at Nuremberg, Control Council Law No 10 enacted by the Allied powers in December 1945 authorised each of the four Allied powers to try further accused war criminals within their own zones of occupation in Germany. Each of the Allies conducted numerous trials under that law.

50 See above, n 35, article 6(c).

51 R H Jackson, 'Nuremberg in Retrospect: Legal Answer to International Lawlessness', reprinted in G Mettraux (ed), *Perspectives on the Nuremberg Trial*, Oxford University Press, Oxford, 2008, 370–1.

11.3.2 Tokyo

The International Military of the Far East (the Tokyo Tribunal) commenced trials at Yokohama, Japan, in April 1946, after the major trial at Nuremberg had concluded. The Tokyo Tribunal comprised 11 judges, all drawn from Allied countries and appointed by the Supreme Commander of the Allied Powers, General MacArthur of the United States, whose considerable influence over the tribunal led to criticism of the tribunal as merely an instrument of US foreign policy in post-war Japan.[52] The Tokyo Tribunal tried the same three categories of offences as the Nuremberg Tribunal: war crimes, crimes against peace and crimes against humanity.

Criticism of the Tokyo Tribunal for meting out victor's justice has been widespread;[53] indeed some such criticism came from the bench of the tribunal itself. Professor Röling, the Dutch judge, issued a dissenting judgment criticising the structure of the tribunal, particularly the fact that it was comprised exclusively of judges from Allied countries, and concluded that several of the accused convicted by the majority should have been acquitted. The Indian judge, Radhabinod Pal, issued a scathing dissent, concluding that the tribunal on which he served was an illegitimate exercise in victor's justice, that it was retrospective, particularly in relation to the assertion that waging aggressive war was a crime under international law before the Second World War, and that all of the accused should therefore be acquitted.[54]

The legacy of the Nuremberg and Tokyo tribunals is therefore mixed. While the legality and legitimacy of the trials remain contested, given the state of international law at the time the alleged crimes were committed, leading to criticisms of retrospectivity and selectivity, the post-war trials had an enormous prospective impact. From that moment on, it was clear that international law could impose obligations upon individuals as well as states, and that gross violations of human rights could be prosecuted as international crimes.

11.4 AD HOC CRIMINAL TRIBUNALS

It had been a goal of the international community for many years to establish a permanent international criminal court, before one was finally established in 2002, discussed below. Indeed, the language of much of the Nuremberg judgment seemed to presume that such a court was inevitable and imminent, as did the *Genocide Convention* that followed shortly after.[55] As it happened, consensus to establish a permanent international criminal court was not forthcoming for another half century. In particular, the mutual suspicion between the two main blocs during the Cold War, which characterised so much of

52 See for example T Maga, *Judgment at Tokyo: The Japanese War Crimes Trials*, University of Kentucky Press, Lexington, 2001, 64.

53 M Bassiouni, see above, n 49, 414–20.

54 E Kopelman, 'Ideology and International Law: The Dissent of the Indian Justice at the Tokyo War Crimes Trial' (1991) 23 *New York University Journal of International Law and Politics* 373.

55 For example, the *Genocide Convention* (1948), art VI, provides trial for the crime of genocide in 'such international penal tribunal as may have jurisdiction'.

international relations during that period, prevented the emergence of such a court. As the Cold War came to a close, new momentum for international criminal law emerged due to the improved political possibilities.

11.4.1 The Former Yugoslavia

The horrific ethnic cleansing and related crimes committed in the course of the conflict as the former Yugoslavia broke up from 1991 provided the impetus for the international community to act. In May 1993, the UN Security Council exercised its powers under Chapter VII of the *UN Charter* to create the *International Criminal Tribunal for the Former Yugoslavia* (ICTY).[56] The tribunal, with its seat in The Hague, has an independent prosecutor and judges. Judges preside over pre-trial motions in the pre-trial chamber, hear the trial in the trial chamber, and provision is made for appeals to a differently comprised Appeals Chamber, avoiding some of the criticisms about the unfairness of the process of the Nuremberg and Tokyo Tribunals to defendants.

Unlike the Nuremberg and Tokyo tribunals that went before it and the International Criminal Court that came after it, the ICTY was not a creature of international treaty, but a creation of the UN Security Council. Its Statute was annexed to the UN Security Council resolution creating the tribunal. The ICTY Statute asserts jurisdiction over war crimes from two legal sources, namely 'grave breaches of the Geneva Conventions'[57] and 'violations of the laws or customs of war'.[58] It also asserts jurisdiction over genocide[59] and crimes against humanity.[60]

SNAPSHOT: *PROSECUTOR v KRSITĆ*—SREBRENICA MASSACRE

During the Yugoslavian conflict, an enclave around the town of Srebrenica in Bosnia was declared to be a UN safe area, immune from the fighting and under the protection of Dutch peacekeepers. In March 1995, Serb forces cut off food and water supplies, aid and communications from the enclave. Then in July 1995, the Bosnian Serb army moved to take over the enclave, committing mass rapes and other atrocities in the process. Bosnian Muslim men were separated from women and children and executed en masse. One of the Bosnian Serb commanders, General Radovan Krsitć, was prosecuted for his responsibility for the atrocities.

The following is an extract from the judgment of the ICTY Trial Chamber.[61]

66 The Bosnian Muslim men who had been separated from the women, children and elderly in Potočari (numbering approximately 1000) were transported to Bratunac and subsequently joined by Bosnian Muslim men captured from the column. No discernible effort was made to keep the prisoners from

56 Security Council resolution 827 (25 May 1993). The resolution was unanimously supported by UN Security Council members.

57 *ICTY Statute*, art 2.

58 Ibid art 3.

59 Ibid art 4.

60 Ibid art 5.

61 *Prosecutor v Krsitć*, ICTY Trial Chamber, judgment of 2 August 2001, Case no IT-98-33-T.

Potočari and the men captured from the column in woods separate. These men were held in various locations, such as an abandoned warehouse, an old school and even in the buses and trucks that had brought them there. During the nights, individual prisoners in Bratunac were called out, and cries of pain and gunfire could be heard. After being detained in Bratunac for between one and three days, the prisoners were transported elsewhere, as the buses used to evacuate the women, children and elderly from Potočari became available.

67 Almost to a man, the thousands of Bosnian Muslim prisoners captured, following the takeover of Srebrenica, were executed. Some were killed individually or in small groups by the soldiers who captured them and some were killed in the places where they were temporarily detained. Most, however, were slaughtered in carefully orchestrated mass executions, commencing on 13 July 1995, in the region just north of Srebrenica. Prisoners not killed on 13 July 1995 were subsequently bussed to execution sites further north of Bratunac, within the zone of responsibility of the Zvornik Brigade. The large-scale executions in the north took place between 14 and 17 July 1995.

68 Most of the mass executions followed a well-established pattern. The men were first taken to empty schools or warehouses. After being detained there for some hours, they were loaded onto buses or trucks and taken to another site for execution. Usually, the execution fields were in isolated locations. The prisoners were unarmed and, in many cases, steps had been taken to minimise resistance, such as blindfolding them, binding their wrists behind their backs with ligatures or removing their shoes. Once at the killing fields, the men were taken off the trucks in small groups, lined up and shot. Those who survived the initial round of gunfire were individually shot with an extra round, though sometimes only after they had been left to suffer for a time. Immediately afterwards, and sometimes even during the executions, earth moving equipment arrived and the bodies were buried, either in the spot where they were killed or in another nearby location.

69 At several of the sites, a few wounded people survived by pretending to be dead and then crawled away. The Trial Chamber heard from some of these survivors about their ordeals. It also heard from a member of the [Bosnian Serb Army] who participated in one of the largest executions, which took place on 16 July 1995.

70 In addition to being an unspeakable human evil, the decision to execute these Bosnian Muslim men is unfathomable in military terms. As Mr Richard Butler ..., the Prosecution's military expert, pointed out:

> it is hard to envision a better bargaining chip in dealing with the political authorities of certainly the BiH government and of the International Community than having 10 000 to 15 000 Muslim men in the middle of Potočari in a legitimate prisoner of war facility under the control or under the supervision of certainly the UN troops that were there and the ICRC at a point in time. That is the ultimate bargaining chip, to be able to get significant political leverage from people, one would think, and this chip was thrown away for another reason.

...

95 Almost without exception, the witnesses who appeared before the Trial Chamber did not seriously contest that, following the take-over of Srebrenica, the mass killings described above actually occurred outside of combat activities and on the basis of orders given by high level Bosnian Serb officers or officials. ... 201 Nonetheless, in the words of Nuremberg Prosecutor Telford Taylor, it is 'important that these incredible events be established by clear and public proof, so that no one can ever doubt that they were fact and not fable ...'. It is therefore imperative to document these 'incredible events' in detail.

...

648 First, General Krsitć exercised effective control over Drina Corps troops involved in the killings. Second, in terms of *mens rea*, not only was General Krsitć fully aware of the ongoing killing campaign and of its impact on the survival of the Bosnian Muslim group at Srebrenica, as well as the fact that it was related to a widespread or systematic attack against Srebrenica's Bosnian Muslim civilian population, but the Drina Corps (and Main Staff) officers and troops involved in conducting the executions had to have been aware of the genocidal objectives. Third, General Krsitc´ failed to prevent his Drina Corps subordinates from participating in the crimes or to punish them thereafter.

[General Krsitc´ was found guilty of genocide, various crimes against humanity and the war crime of murder. He was sentenced to 46 years in prison.]

The *ICTY Statute* gives the tribunal jurisdiction over specified crimes committed in the former Yugoslavia from 1 January 1991,[62] giving it jurisdiction over events taking place before the tribunal itself was established. Accusations of retrospectivity (*'nullem crimen sine lege'*) were inevitably made by defendants and their supporters, but given the precedents of Nuremberg and Tokyo and the much greater consensus regarding the individual criminal responsibility for crimes under international law by 1991, these arguments were significantly less potent than their Second World War counterparts.

As it was created as an ad hoc tribunal rather than a permanent court, the ICTY was always intended to wind up after completing its work. In 2003, ten years after it began, the UN Security Council set out a 'completion strategy' for the ICTY. All investigations were completed in 2004, but the 2008 deadline for completion of all trials was not met, and at the time of writing, trials in current cases are expected to run until at least late 2013, with appeals continuing until 2015.[63]

11.4.2 Rwanda

The genocide in Rwanda in 1994, in which 800,000 people were killed in just 100 days, led to significant criticism of the United Nations for its failure to act to prevent the slaughter despite warnings and to stop it once it began. It remains a talismanic significance for criticism of UN ineptitude to this day.

SNAPSHOT: *BYSTANDERS TO GENOCIDE*— THE STORY OF US AND UN INACTION IN RWANDA[64]

In response to the initial killings by the Hutu government, Tutsi rebels of the Rwandan Patriotic Front—stationed in Kigali under the terms of the Arusha Accords—surged out of their barracks and resumed their civil war against the Hutu regime. But under the cover of that war were early and strong indications that systematic genocide was taking place. From April 7 onward the Hutu-controlled army, the gendarmerie, and the militias worked together to wipe out Rwanda's Tutsi. Many of the early Tutsi victims found themselves specifically, not spontaneously, pursued: lists of targets had been prepared in advance, and Radio Mille

62 ICTY Statute, art 1.

63 ICTY website, 'Completion Strategy', <http://www.icty.org/sid/10016>.

64 S Power, 'Bystanders to Genocide', *The Atlantic*, September 2001, available at <http://www.theatlantic.com/magazine/archive/2001/09/bystanders-to-genocide/4571/1/>.

> Collines broadcast names, addresses, and even license-plate numbers. Killers often carried a machete in one hand and a transistor radio in the other. Tens of thousands of Tutsi fled their homes in panic and were snared and butchered at checkpoints. Little care was given to their disposal. Some were shoveled into landfills. Human flesh rotted in the sunshine. In churches bodies mingled with scattered hosts. If the killers had taken the time to tend to sanitation, it would have slowed their 'sanitization' campaign.
>
> ...
>
> Even after the reality of genocide in Rwanda had become irrefutable, when bodies were shown choking the Kagera River on the nightly news, the brute fact of the slaughter failed to influence US policy except in a negative way. American officials, for a variety of reasons, shunned the use of what became known as 'the g-word.' They felt that using it would have obliged the United States to act, under the terms of the 1948 *Genocide Convention*. They also believed, understandably, that it would harm US credibility to name the crime and then do nothing to stop it.
>
> ...
>
> When the killing began, Romeo Dallaire [the Canadian commander of the UN peacekeeping force in Rwanda] expected and appealed for reinforcements. Within hours of the plane crash he had cabled UN headquarters in New York: 'Give me the means and I can do more.' He was sending peacekeepers on rescue missions around the city, and he felt it was essential to increase the size and improve the quality of the UN's presence. But the United States opposed the idea of sending reinforcements, no matter where they were from. The fear, articulated mainly at the Pentagon but felt throughout the bureaucracy, was that what would start as a small engagement by foreign troops would end as a large and costly one by Americans. This was the lesson of Somalia, where US troops had gotten into trouble in an effort to bail out the beleaguered Pakistanis. The logical outgrowth of this fear was an effort to steer clear of Rwanda entirely and be sure others did the same. Only by yanking Dallaire's entire peacekeeping force could the United States protect itself from involvement down the road.

Having failed to intervene during the genocide itself, the UN Security Council voted in November 1994 to establish the International Criminal Tribunal for Rwanda (ICTR).[65]

The ICTR essentially mirrored the ICTY, which had been established the year before. Like the ICTY, the ICTR has jurisdiction over genocide and crimes against humanity, expressed in virtually identical terms in both the ICTY and ICTR statutes.[66] The ICTR also has jurisdiction over war crimes, although the statute limits that jurisdiction to 'violations of article 3 common to the Geneva Conventions and of Additional Protocol II',[67] in recognition of the non-international nature of the conflict in Rwanda.

With its seat in Arusha, Tanzania, the ICTR is also in the midst of its completion strategy at the time of writing. A recent projection by the tribunal would see it completing all trials and appeals by the end of 2013.[68]

65 Security Council resolution 955 (8 November 1994). China abstained from the vote and Rwanda voted against. All other Security Council members voted for the resolution.

66 ICTR Statute, arts 2 and 3.

67 Ibid art 4.

68 *Report on the Completion Strategy of the International Criminal Tribunal for Rwanda*, 1 November 2010, UN document no S/2010/574, para 72.

11.4.3 Hybrid Courts and Tribunals

Following the renewed momentum for international criminal law after the establishment of the tribunals for Yugoslavia and Rwanda, a new model of tribunal emerged which sought to combine the best elements of an international tribunal with elements of a domestic system. In some cases, the institution is essentially part of the domestic legal system, but employs a mix of international and domestic judges and prosecutors and a mix of international and domestic criminal law, as in the Extraordinary Chambers of the Courts of Cambodia. In other cases, the institution is effectively international in nature and separate from the domestic judiciary, but still applying the mixture of international and domestic judges, prosecutors and law, as in the Special Court for Sierra Leone.[69]

The international system lends a degree of credibility to the institution in countries not known for an impartial legal system, as well as providing assistance in institution-building by having international professionals working side by side with their domestic counterparts. At the same time, the domestic element may promote a greater degree of engagement, as the institution will not be seen as having been imposed from outside, as well as utilising the local knowledge and skills of professionals in the country.

While the idea behind hybrid tribunals is for them to be the best of both systems, they risk creating new problems if the international and domestic components clash or do not cooperate. Anecdotal evidence from the early trials of the Cambodian tribunal, for example, suggests that the very different approaches of co-prosecutors from Cambodia and their international counterparts, and to a lesser extent those of the judges, are creating difficulties for the smooth conduct of trials.[70]

11.5 INTERNATIONAL CRIMINAL COURT

In 1998, in the wake of the establishment of the two ad hoc tribunals for the former Yugoslavia and Rwanda, the United Nations Conference of Plenipotentiaries on the Establishment of an International Criminal Court (known as the Rome Conference) adopted the *Rome Statute of the International Criminal Court*. The ICC became a reality in July 2002 when the *Rome Statute* came into force and it commenced operation in 2003. The ICC has jurisdiction over four categories of crime: genocide, crimes against humanity, war crimes and aggression.

The ICC is intended as a court of last resort. The primary responsibility for the trial of individuals accused of the heinous crimes within the ICC's jurisdiction lies with domestic courts. However, in situations of genocide and other widespread atrocities, domestic authorities are sometimes unable—due to societal breakdown—or unwilling—due to state authorities' own involvement in the

69 The Special Court for Sierra Leone, a hybrid criminal tribunal, was established to try persons accused of serious crimes during the conflict in Sierra Leone. One of the interesting preliminary issues concerned the validity of the amnesty granted to combatants by the Lome Peace Agreement. For a discussion of the amnesty and the state of amnesties more generally in international law, see: S Williams, 'Amnesties in International Law: The Experience of the Special Court for Sierra Leone', (2005) 5(2) *Human Rights Law Review* 271–309.

70 A Cassese foresaw these difficulties before the ECCC began operation: A Cassese, *International Criminal Law*, Oxford University Press, Oxford, 2003, 345. Also see generally S Williams, *Hybrid and Internationalised Criminal Courts and Tribunals*, Hart Publishing, Oxford, forthcoming, 2012.

crimes—to prosecute and try such cases. Consistently with a 'last resort' purpose, the ICC operates under a jurisdictional principle known as 'complementarity', in the sense that the ICC's jurisdiction is complementary to that of domestic courts.[71] Under complementarity, a case will not be admissible if it is being prosecuted or investigated by a state with jurisdiction over it, or if the case has already been tried by a domestic court, or if a domestic investigation concluded that prosecution was not warranted, unless the investigation or prosecution was not genuine.[72]

There are three ways a case can be commenced in the ICC. The first is where a situation involving one or more crimes within the jurisdiction of the court is referred to the Prosecutor by a state party to the *Rome Statute*.[73] The second is where the Prosecutor decides to investigate a situation on his own motion.[74] Because of that possibility, the Prosecutor regularly receives many requests from individuals and NGOs to investigate various situations, often accompanied by dossiers detailing alleged crimes. The third method is where the UN Security Council refers a situation to the Prosecutor in exercising its powers under chapter VII of the *UN Charter*.[75] The UN Security Council has the unique power to refer situations involving states that are not parties to the *Rome Statute*, over which the ICC would otherwise lack jurisdiction.

As at June 2011, investigations have been commenced in relation to six situations, all of them in Africa. Situations in Uganda, the Democratic Republic of the Congo and the Central African Republic were all referred to the Prosecutor by those states. An investigation into the situation in Kenya was commenced on the Prosecutor's own motion. The UN Security Council referred situations in Darfur (Sudan) and Libya to the Prosecutor, despite the fact that neither of those states is a party to the *Rome Statute*.[76]

SNAPSHOT: OVERVIEW OF EARLY CASES IN THE ICC

PROSECUTOR v THOMAS DYILO, SITUATION IN THE DEMOCRATIC REPUBLIC OF THE CONGO[77]

Lubanga was the first accused to be arrested and transferred to the ICC in March 2006. He was charged with war crimes arising from the conflict in the Congo in 2002–03 relating to the recruitment and conscription of children under 15 into the armed group known as the *Forces patriotiques pour la libération du Congo* (FPLC). Lubanga was alleged to be a leader of the FPLC and to have forcibly recruited children from towns captured by the FPLC during the conflict, with those children subsequently being forced to fight on the front lines for the FPLC.

Lubanga's trial commenced in January 2009. The trial chamber stayed the proceeding in 2008 because important potentially exculpatory evidence had not been disclosed to the defence by the prosecutor, on the grounds that the informants had insisted on confidentiality. The trial chamber therefore found that a fair trial

71 *Rome Statute*, see above, n 10, art 1.

72 *Rome Statute*, see above, n 10, art 17.

73 *Rome Statute*, see above, n 10, arts 13(a) and 14.

74 *Rome Statute*, see above, n 10, arts 13(c) and 15.

75 *Rome Statute*, see above, n 10, art 13(b).

76 Information regarding the situations referred to the ICC can be found on the ICC website at <http://www2.icc-cpi.int/Menus/ICC/Situations+and+Cases/>.

77 Case no ICC-01/04-01/06.

would be impossible and stayed the first ever trial in the ICC. The emphasis on procedural fairness, at the cost of proceeding with a closely watched trial, was a marked contrast with the Nuremberg and Tokyo Tribunals, perhaps self-consciously so. However, the stay was lifted in late 2008, allowing the trial to proceed. The proceeding was stayed again in July 2010 because the prosecutor had failed to comply with the court's order to disclose information about confidential informants to the defence. That stay was reversed by the appeals chamber in October 2010 and the trial resumed. The trial remains in progress at the time of writing.

[*PROSECUTOR v JOSEPH KONY, VINCENT OTTI, OKOT ODHIAMBO AND DOMINIC ONGWEN*, SITUATION IN UGANDA[78]]

The co-accused, Kony, Otti, Odhiambo and Ongwen, were alleged commanders of the Lord's Resistance Army (LRA), a rebel group fighting an insurgency in Uganda from 2002. A fifth alleged commander, Raska Lukwiya, was also the subject of an arrest warrant, but the case against him was dropped following confirmation of his death. Rumours of the death of the other co-accused circulate periodically but have never been confirmed. None of the co-accused has been arrested at the time of writing.

Kony, the alleged commander-in-chief of the LRA, and his alleged lieutenants have been charged with a long list of crimes against humanity and war crimes for attacks allegedly carried out on civilians. The charges include murder, enslavement, sexual enslavement, rape, intentionally directing attacks against civilian populations, pillaging and forced enlistment of children.

Efforts to conclude a peace agreement between the Ugandan government and the LRA between 2007 and 2009 raised significant issues for the proceeding against the LRA commanders. The government proposed to establish a special division of the Ugandan High Court for trying offenders during the conflict after a final peace agreement was concluded. That raised questions regarding the admissibility of the case against Kony and his co-accused, given the principle of complementarity of the ICC. The government confirmed in 2008 that a comprehensive peace agreement had not been signed and that it remained committed to the execution of the ICC warrants, however there have been unconfirmed reports that the Ugandan authorities believe that arrest of the LRA leaders would compromise peace efforts and have therefore not sought out the accused particularly diligently.

[*PROSECUTOR v OMAR HASSAN AHMAD AL BASHIR*, SITUATION IN DARFUR, SUDAN[79]]

The UN Security Council referred the situation in Darfur to the prosecutor in 2005, despite the fact that Sudan is not a party to the *Rome Statute*. The referral focused on the armed conflict in the Darfur region between the Sudanese government and a range of armed groups. A feature of the conflict was the particularly violent attacks on civilians in Darfur, as well as alleged acts of genocide against the Fur, Masalit and Zaghawa ethnic groups in the region.

The prosecutor applied for an arrest warrant against Omar Al-Bashir, the incumbent president of Sudan, in July 2008 and a warrant was issued by the pre-trial chamber in July 2009. He is charged with crimes against humanity, war crimes and genocide.

78 Case No ICC-02/04-01/05.

79 Case No ICC-02/05-01/09. Also see: S Williams and L Sherif, 'The Arrest Warrant for President al-Bashir: Immunities of Incumbent Heads of State and the International Criminal Court' (2009) 14 *Journal of Conflict and Security Law* 71.

The issue of an arrest warrant against an incumbent head of state was a significant symbolic development for the ICC. It signalled that sovereign immunity, which was a feature of customary international law but expressly abrogated in the *Rome Statute*, would not protect individuals accused of international crimes. However, the nature of an international court without its own police force poses practical difficulties highlighted by the Al-Bashir case. As long as he remains in Sudan, he is unlikely to be arrested.

11.6 CONCLUSION AND ISSUES

International humanitarian law and international criminal law are parallel fields of international law to international human rights law, but share similar objectives. All three aim to minimise human suffering within their respective spheres of operation. In armed conflict, international humanitarian law places a particular emphasis on protection of the vulnerable—civilians, prisoners of war and wounded combatants. International criminal law provides one mechanism for holding individual perpetrators accountable. The three fields will often overlap, as all international crimes will be gross violations of human rights, and many of them occur in the course of armed conflict, making them also breaches of international humanitarian law.

International criminal law also advances human rights law by imposing individuals directly accountable for violations, compared with the traditional focus of international human rights law on the responsibility of states.

While international criminal law has developed rapidly since the 1994 ad hoc tribunals for Rwanda and the former Yugoslavia, especially with the commencement of the permanent International Criminal Court, there remain significant questions surrounding its direction. The theme of victor's justice that has persisted since Nuremberg is still with us, having developed into a theme of selectivity. The International Criminal Court currently has 114 states parties, but three of the five permanent members of the UN Security Council—the United States, Russia and China—are not parties. Therefore, whenever the UN Security Council refers a situation to the ICC, as it has in relation to Darfur and Libya, those countries are subjecting other countries to jurisdiction that they have not accepted for themselves.

Furthermore, all six of the ICC's current situations under investigation are in Africa. This pattern is fuelling a view that international criminal justice operates on a double standard. Opponents have labelled the ICC 'Europe's Court for Africa', and several African states have threatened to withdraw from the *Rome Statute* after criticising Prosecutor Luis Moreno Ocampo as 'prejudiced against Africa'.[80]

Other potential developments facing international criminal law include an expansion of its scope. New crimes could be added to the jurisdiction of the ICC or other international tribunals in the future,

80 'Dim Prospects', *The Economist*, 17 February 2011, available at <http://www.economist.com/node/18176088>.

such as torture and trafficking in drugs, weapons and people.[81] The expansion of the Court's jurisdiction to cover legal persons, such as corporations, as well as natural persons has also been proposed.[82]

Finally, the influence that international criminal law and domestic law have on one another is an issue to watch. The complementarity of ICC jurisdiction is designed to ensure that national courts are the first option for pursuit of accountability for gross human rights abuses, while the existence of the ICC as a last resort is intended to act as a disincentive for laxity in investigation and prosecution, or holding show trials or disingenuously dismissing an investigation.[83] At the same time, hybrid tribunals are operating in several countries with a view to building the infrastructure and culture of justice systems in those countries in the long terms. The degree to which international criminal law succeeds in transforming domestic justice will ultimately be a measure of its success at least as much as the outcome of trials in The Hague, and probably more so.

81 States parties to the *Rome Statute* are able to propose amendments for consideration by the Assembly of States Parties to the ICC: *Rome Statute*, article 121.

82 J Kyriakakis, Corporate Criminal Liability and the ICC Statute: The Comparative Law Challenge' (2009) 56(3) *Netherlands International Law Review* 333–66.

83 *Rome Statute*, see above, n 10, art 17.

PART SIX

VULNERABLE PEOPLE

12 CHILDREN

CONTENTS

12.1 INTRODUCTION

The *Convention on the Rights of the Child* (CROC)[1] is the most widely and rapidly ratified human rights treaty in history, yet many children around the world are routinely denied their human rights. Almost half of the 34 million people around the world that are of concern to the United Nations High Commissioner for Refugees are children.[2] Thousands of children have been affected by armed conflict. Children are trafficked as sex slaves and work long hours in harsh and inhumane conditions. They are subjected to the death penalty and other forms of violence. Children are denied their rights to food, water, health and education. Despite the widespread ratification of the convention and its two accompanying optional protocols, these abuses continue. The path to the adoption of the Convention was slow, but the basic principle that children are entitled to special care and assistance has long been accepted. The evolution of the principle that children as human beings possess their own particular

1 *Convention on the Rights of the Child* (CROC), opened for signature 20 November 1989, 1577 UNTS 3 (entered into force 2 September 1990).

2 UN Refugee Agency, *Children* (2011) <http://www.unhcr.org/pages/49c3646c1e8.html>.

rights has been more recent. However, the gap between the acceptance of children's rights and the reality of their enforcement remains broad.

This chapter begins with an overview of the legal framework for protecting children's rights, focusing primarily on the CROC and noting its two accompanying optional protocols and other international and regional agreements in place to protect children. It then discusses the mandate of the Committee on the Rights of the Child and its reporting procedures for checking state compliance with their treaty obligations. The recent initiative to draft a third optional protocol to allow the Committee to receive individual communications regarding violations of the CROC and its two existing optional protocols is ongoing. Finally, the chapter concludes with a case study highlighting the impact of armed conflict on children.

12.2 INTERNATIONAL LEGAL FRAMEWORK: FROM THE DECLARATION TO THE CONVENTION

12.2.1 *Declaration of Geneva*

In 1924 the League of Nations endorsed the *Declaration of the Rights of the Child*, commonly referred to as the *'Declaration of Geneva'*, which noted that 'mankind owes to the Child the best that it has to give'.[3] The Declaration, although imprecise and drafted as a set of duties (rather than rights) and directed to 'men and women of all nations' rather than states, was the first significant step taken towards developing international norms for the protection of children.

DECLARATION OF THE RIGHTS OF THE CHILD[4]

By the present Declaration of the Rights of the Child, commonly known as '*Declaration of Geneva*', men and women of all nations, recognizing that mankind owes to the Child the best that it has to give, declare and accept it as their duty that, beyond and above all considerations of race, nationality or creed:

1 The child must be given the means requisite for its normal development, both materially and spiritually;
2 The child that is hungry must be fed; the child that is sick must be nursed; the child that is backward must be helped; the delinquent child must be reclaimed; and the orphan and the waif must be sheltered and succored;
3 The child must be the first to receive relief in times of distress;
4 The child must be put in a position to earn a livelihood, and must be protected against every form of exploitation;
5 The child must be brought up in the consciousness that its talents must be devoted to the service of fellow men.

12.2.2 *Declaration of the Rights of the Child*

The efforts to develop more concrete and binding standards continued beyond the adoption of the *Declaration of Geneva*. In 1959 the UN General Assembly adopted the *Declaration of the Rights of the*

3 *Declaration of the Rights of the Child* (1959) GA Res 1386 (XIV), final preambular paragraph.

4 Adopted 26 September 1924, League of Nations.

Child, in which it noted in its Preamble that 'the child, by reason of his physical and mental immaturity, needs special safeguards and care, including appropriate legal protection, before as well as after birth.' The notion that children are entitled to special care and assistance because of their vulnerability to exploitation and abuse had also been recognised in the earlier 1948 *Universal Declaration of Human Rights* (UDHR).[5]

The 1959 Declaration sets out 10 principles that 'parents ... men and women as individuals ... voluntary organizations, local authorities and national Governments' should recognise. As a Declaration it is non-binding, but the fact that it was adopted unanimously by the UN General Assembly was indicative of the continuing push to recognise the special vulnerability of children as a group worthy of protection. The evolving rights-focused agenda of children's advocates within and outside the United Nations is evident in a comparison of the text of the Geneva Declaration with that of the 1959 Declaration. The 1959 document focuses not so much on the duties a child is owed but on the rights he or she inherently possess. These rights encompass civil and political issues and economic, social and cultural matters of relevance to the child and their family.

DECLARATION OF THE RIGHTS OF THE CHILD (1959)[6]

Principle 1 The child shall enjoy all the rights set forth in this Declaration. Every child, without any exception whatsoever, shall be entitled to these rights, without distinction or discrimination on account of race, colour, sex, language, religion, political or other opinion, national or social origin, property, birth or other status, whether of himself or of his family.

Principle 2 The child shall enjoy special protection, and shall be given opportunities and facilities, by law and by other means, to enable him to develop physically, mentally, morally, spiritually and socially in a healthy and normal manner and in conditions of freedom and dignity. In the enactment of laws for this purpose, the best interests of the child shall be the paramount consideration.

Principle 3 The child shall be entitled from his birth to a name and a nationality.

Principle 4 The child shall enjoy the benefits of social security. He shall be entitled to grow and develop in health; to this end, special care and protection shall be provided both to him and to his mother, including adequate pre-natal and post-natal care. The child shall have the right to adequate nutrition, housing, recreation and medical services.

Principle 5 The child who is physically, mentally or socially handicapped shall be given the special treatment, education and care required by his particular condition.

Principle 6 The child, for the full and harmonious development of his personality, needs love and understanding. He shall, wherever possible, grow up in the care and under the responsibility of his parents, and, in any case, in an atmosphere of affection and of moral and material security; a child of tender years shall not, save in exceptional circumstances, be separated from his mother. Society and the public authorities shall have the duty to extend particular care to children without a family and to those without adequate means of support. Payment of State and other assistance towards the maintenance of children of large families is desirable.

5 Art 25(2).

6 GA Res 1386 (XIV), UN GAOR, 14th sess, 841st plen mtg, Supp No 16, UN Doc A/4354 (20 November 1959).

Principle 7 The child is entitled to receive education, which shall be free and compulsory, at least in the elementary stages. ... The best interests of the child shall be the guiding principle of those responsible for his education and guidance; that responsibility lies in the first place with his parents.

Principle 8 The child shall in all circumstances be among the first to receive protection and relief.

Principle 9 The child shall be protected against all forms of neglect, cruelty and exploitation. He shall not be the subject of traffic, in any form. The child shall not be admitted to employment before an appropriate minimum age; he shall in no case be caused or permitted to engage in any occupation or employment which would prejudice his health or education, or interfere with his physical, mental or moral development.

Principle 10 The child shall be protected from practices which may foster racial, religious and any other form of discrimination. He shall be brought up in a spirit of understanding, tolerance, friendship among peoples, peace and universal brotherhood, and in full consciousness that his energy and talents should be devoted to the service of his fellow men.

12.2.3 *Convention on the Rights of the Child*

The CROC was adopted by the UN General Assembly on 20 November 1989 and entered into force an unusually short time later, on 2 September 1990.[7] Over 10 years earlier, in 1978, Poland had submitted draft text to the United Nations Commission on Human Rights to be used as the starting point for developing a binding treaty on children's rights, and in 1979 (the International Year of the Child) work began in earnest on drafting the Convention. An open-ended Working Group was established that, unusually for the United Nations at the time, worked closely with an ad hoc group of non-governmental organisations (NGOs) in the drafting process.

The CROC is a broad document (much expanded from the original draft text, which had been based primarily on the 1959 Declaration); it incorporates the spectrum of human rights—civil, political, economic, social and cultural—and sets out the specific ways these rights should be ensured for children and young people. The CROC recognises that the degree to which children can exercise these rights independently is influenced by their evolving maturity. It also emphasises the rights and responsibilities of parents, where applicable.

Definition of a Child

The 1924 and 1959 Declarations did not directly address the question of when childhood begins and ends. No mention was made of this issue in the *Declaration of Geneva* and it is only in the Preamble of the *Declaration of the Rights of Child* that it is noted that a child is worthy of special protection 'before as well as after birth'. Article 1 of the CROC states that 'a child means every human being below the age of eighteen years unless under the law applicable to the child, majority is attained earlier'.

One of the divisive issues that arose during the drafting of the CROC is the question of whether childhood should be recognised as commencing at the moment of conception or at the time of birth. While, as a drafting compromise, the preamble to the CROC repeats the statement in the 1959

---

7 CROC, see above, n 1.

Declaration that a child deserves protection before and after birth, the substantive articles in the text of the CROC do not explicitly reiterate this view. Although article 1 states that 'a child means every human being', it is generally accepted that the CROC 'does not restrict a state's discretion to provide under its domestic law the point in time when childhood begins'.[8] A number of states have made explicit reservations to article 1 to clarify when childhood begins. Argentina[9] and Guatemala,[10] for example, note that the state should protect human life from the time of its conception, and Ecuador[11] declared that the need to protect the unborn child should be borne in mind in interpreting all the articles of the Convention.

Likewise, the question of when childhood ends may also differ among nation states. Cuba, for example, notes in its declaration to the CROC that majority is not attained at 18 years of age for purposes of the full exercise of civic rights.[12] On the issue of age limits regarding the recruitment of child soldiers (article 38), the CROC is particularly weak. The convention sets the age limit for recruitment to combat service as low as 15, and indirectly legitimises the use of 15- and 16-year-olds as combat soldiers. The *Optional Protocol to the Convention on the Rights of the Child on the Involvement of Children in Armed Conflict*[13] sets 18 as the age limit for compulsory recruitment into the armed forces (see Chapter 12.4.2).

General Principles

The substantive articles of the CROC cover all human rights without any of the divisions between economic, social and cultural rights and civil and political rights that have long plagued discussions on

8 G Van Bueren, *The International Law on the Rights of the Child*, Martinus Nijhoff, The Hague, 1998, 34.

9 CROC, see above, n 1; *Argentina Declaration*: 'Concerning article 1 of the Convention, the Argentine Republic declares that the article must be interpreted to the effect that a child means every human being from the moment of conception up to the age of eighteen' <http://treaties.un.org/Pages/ViewDetails.aspx?src=TREATY&mtdsg_no=IV-11&chapter=4&lang=en>.

10 CROC, see above, n 1; *Guatemala Declaration*: 'With reference to article 1 of the Convention, and with the aim of giving legal definition to its signing of the Convention, the Government of Guatemala declares that article 3 of its Political Constitution establishes that: "The State guarantees and protects human life from the time of its conception, as well as the integrity and security of the individual"' <http://treaties.un.org/Pages/ViewDetails.aspx?src=TREATY&mtdsg_no=IV-11&chapter=4&lang=en>.

11 CROC, see above, n 1; *Ecuador Declaration:* 'In signing the Convention on the Rights of the Child, Ecuador reaffirms ... [that it is] especially pleased with the ninth preambular paragraph of the draft Convention, which pointed to the need to protect the unborn child, and believed that that paragraph should be borne in mind in interpreting all the articles of the Convention, particularly article 24 ...' <http://treaties.un.org/Pages/ViewDetails.aspx?src=TREATY&mtdsg_no=IV-11&chapter=4&lang=en>.

12 CROC, see above, n 1; *Cuba Declaration*: 'With reference to article 1 of the Convention, the Government of the Republic of Cuba declares that in Cuba, under the domestic legislation in force, majority is not attained at 18 years of age for purposes of the full exercise of civic rights' <http://treaties.un.org/Pages/ViewDetails.aspx?src=TREATY&mtdsg_no=IV-11&chapter=4&lang=en>.

13 *Optional Protocol to the Convention on the Rights of the Child on the Involvement of Children in Armed Conflict*, GA Res 54/263, UN GAOR, 54th sess, 97th plen mtg, Agenda Item 116a, Supp No 49, UN Doc A/54/49 (25 May 2000) art 1.

international human rights. Some of the rights recognised in the CROC are similar to those contained in other human rights treaties but are often adapted to the particular needs of the child. The prohibition against discrimination, for example, is a fundamental human right recognised in all major human rights instruments, but article 2 notes that the child should be protected against discrimination based on the status of the child or the parent/guardian. Articles 7 and 8 ensure that the child has a right to an identity and articles 9 and 10 the right to a family life. The child's right to health (article 24), an adequate standard of living (article 27) and education (article 28) are similar to those contained in the ICESCR, but article 27 highlights, for example, the responsibility of a parent or guardian to secure living conditions necessary for the child's development.

The Committee on the Rights of the Child (CRC) in *General Comment No 5* (2003)[14] has recognised four general or guiding principles of the Convention. These are: non-discrimination (article 2); adherence to the best interests of the child (article 3); the right to life, survival and development (article 6); and the right to participate (article 12). They represent the underlying requirements for any and all rights to be realised. In *General Comment No 5* at paragraph 12 the CRC explained the obligations these four principles place on states.

COMMITTEE ON THE RIGHTS OF THE CHILD, *GENERAL COMMENT NO 5: GENERAL MEASURES OF IMPLEMENTATION FOR THE CONVENTION ON THE RIGHTS OF THE CHILD*

12 The development of a children's rights perspective ... is required for effective implementation of the whole Convention and, in particular, in the light of the following articles in the Convention identified by the Committee as general principles:

- **Article 2:** the obligation of States to respect and ensure the rights set forth in the Convention to each child within their jurisdiction without discrimination of any kind. This non-discrimination obligation requires States actively to identify individual children and groups of children the recognition and realization of whose rights may demand special ... It should be emphasized that the application of the non-discrimination principle of equal access to rights does not mean identical treatment. A general comment by the Human Rights Committee has underlined the importance of taking special measures in order to diminish or eliminate conditions that cause discrimination.
- **Article 3 (1):** the best interests of the child as a primary consideration in all actions concerning children. ... Every legislative, administrative and judicial body or institution is required to apply the best interests principle by systematically considering how children's rights and interests are or will be affected by their decisions and actions—by, for example, a proposed or existing law or policy or administrative action or court decision, including those which are not directly concerned with children, but indirectly affect children.
- **Article 6:** the child's inherent right to life and States parties' obligation to ensure to the maximum extent possible the survival and development of the child. The Committee expects States to interpret "development" in its broadest sense as a holistic concept, embracing the child's physical, mental, spiritual, moral, psychological and social development. Implementation measures should be aimed at achieving the optimal development for all children.

14 (arts 4, 42 and 44(6)), 34th sess, UN Doc CRC/GC/2003/5 (3 October 2003).

- **Article 12:** the child's right to express his or her views freely in 'all matters affecting the child', those views being given due weight. This principle, which highlights the role of the child as an active participant in the promotion, protection and monitoring of his or her rights, applies equally to all measures adopted by States to implement the Convention.

... Listening to children should not be seen as an end in itself, but rather as a means by which States make their interactions with children and their actions on behalf of children ever more sensitive to the implementation of children's rights.

... The emphasis on 'matters that affect them' in article 12 (1) implies the ascertainment of the views of particular groups of children on particular issues—for example children who have experience of the juvenile justice system on proposals for law reform in that area, or adopted children and children in adoptive families on adoption law and policy. It is important that Governments develop a direct relationship with children, not simply one mediated through non-governmental organizations (NGOs) or human rights institutions ...

Best Interests of the Child

Of particular interest are the principles relating to the best interests of the child and to participation rights, as they are peculiar to the drafting of the CROC.

Article 3(1) states that 'in all actions concerning children, whether undertaken by public or private social welfare institutions, courts of law, administrative authorities or legislative bodies, the best interests of the child shall be a primary consideration'. Simply put, all adults, particularly law makers and policy bodies, should do what is best for children; but it is apparent that there is a lack of agreement, internationally and nationally, about what constitutes children's interests, let alone their 'best' interests. While the CROC is clear in recognising children as human beings in possession of their own rights, it also accepts that inevitably adults will be making decisions on a child's behalf. The 'best interests' principle 'provides decision and policy makers with the authority to substitute their own decisions for either the child's or the parents', providing it is based on considerations of the best interest of the child'.[15]

Article 3(1) provides for a child's interests to be among the first considerations rather than requiring them to be the first considered or favoured. There are circumstances in which the community or other parties might have equal or even superior interests so that a child's interests may not prevail. By providing that the best interests of the child are 'a primary consideration' rather than *the* primary or the *paramount* consideration, article 3.1 allows decision-makers to balance the best interests of the child against 'equally weighty' primary considerations of their own choosing, such as religious or economic considerations.[16] Van Bueren comments that

it has to be accepted that the world lacks and always will lack an accurate scientific measure or philosopher's stone which can be utilised to determine what is truly in the child's best interests. Perhaps

15 G Van Bueren, see above, n 8, 46.

16 In Australia an example of a decision taken out of parents' hands altogether is whether to have a child with a disability sterilised. In *Marion's Case* the High Court stipulated that sterilisation is a 'step of last resort': *Secretary, Department of Health and Community Services v JWB* (1992) 175 CLR 218 (*'Marion's Case'*).

we ought to be honest and realise that although the best interests is the desired standard, in reality we are applying what we perceive as the better interests of the child or at least the less harmful.[17]

Right to Participate

Throughout the CROC there is apparent an underlying tension between balancing the rights of the child to participate in the decision-making process with the responsibilities of the adult who will often have the ultimate legal authority for making particular decisions. In *General Comment No 12* (2009) the CRC notes that 'Article 12 of the *Convention on the Rights of the Child* … is a unique provision in a human rights treaty; it addresses the legal and social status of children, who, on the one hand lack the full autonomy of adults but, on the other, are subjects of rights.'[18]

CONVENTION ON THE RIGHTS OF THE CHILD

ARTICLE 12

1 States Parties shall assure to the child who is capable of forming his or her own views the right to express those views freely in all matters affecting the child, the views of the child being given due weight in accordance with the age and maturity of the child.

2 For this purpose, the child shall in particular be provided the opportunity to be heard in any judicial and administrative proceedings affecting the child, either directly, or through a representative or an appropriate body, in a manner consistent with the procedural rules of national law.

ARTICLE 13

1 The child shall have the right to freedom of expression; this right shall include freedom to seek, receive and impart information and ideas of all kinds, regardless of frontiers, either orally, in writing or in print, in the form of art, or through any other media of the child's choice.

2 The exercise of this right may be subject to certain restrictions, but these shall only be such as are provided by law and are necessary:

(a) For respect of the rights or reputations of others; or

(b) For the protection of national security or of public order (*ordre public*), or of public health or morals.

Children are entitled to the freedom to express opinions and to have a say in matters affecting their social, economic, religious, cultural and political life. Participation rights include the right to express opinions and be heard, the right to information and freedom of association. A child also has the right not to exercise this right: expressing views is a choice for the child, not an obligation. As children mature, engaging these rights helps them to bring about the realisation of all their rights and

17 G Van Bueren, see above, n 8, 49.

18 Committee on the Rights of the Child, *General Comment No 12: The Right of the Child to be Heard*, 51st sess, UN Doc CRC/C/GC/12 (20 July 2009) para 1. Also see more generally N Thomas, 'Towards a Theory of Children's Participation' (2007) 15 *International Journal of Children's Rights* 199.

prepares them for an active role in society. Article 12 stipulates that the right to be heard is owed to every child 'capable of forming his or her own views'. The CRC emphasises that

> this phrase should not be seen as a limitation, but rather as an obligation for States parties to assess the capacity of the child to form an autonomous opinion to the greatest extent possible. This means that States parties cannot begin with the assumption that a child is incapable of expressing her or his own views. On the contrary, States parties should presume that a child has the capacity to form her or his own views and recognize that she or he has the right to express them; it is not up to the child to first prove her or his capacity.[19]

Articles 12 and 13 (along with article 14, freedom of thought, conscience and religion; article 15, freedom of association; article 16, privacy; and article 17, access to the media) emphasise the participation rights of children. Underpinning these articles and several others in the Convention is the need to balance such participation rights with appropriate direction and guidance from parents and others. The difficulty arises when trying to determine whose opinions and rights should take precedence.

In analysing the impact of the CROC, Van Bueren notes that

> it accomplishes five goals. It creates new rights under international law for children where no such rights existed ... Secondly, the Convention on the Rights of the Child enshrines rights in a global treaty which had until the Convention's adoption only been acknowledged or refined in case law under regional human rights treaties ... Thirdly, the Convention also creates binding standards in areas, which, until the Convention's entry into force, were only non-binding recommendations ... The Convention also imposes new obligations in relation to the provision and protection of children ... Finally, the Convention adds an additional express ground by which states parties are under duty not to discriminate against children in their enjoyment of the Convention's rights.[20]

12.2.4 Optional Protocols

In 2000, the UN General Assembly adopted two Optional Protocols to the CROC, one on the *Involvement of Children in Armed Conflict*,[21] and another on the *Sale of Children, Child Prostitution and Child Pornography*.[22] Both Optional Protocols provide stronger protection for children on these particular issues than that previously agreed to by states when drafting the CROC.

For example, the *Optional Protocol on the Involvement of Children in Armed Conflict* (see section 12.4.2, below) requires governments to ensure that while their armed forces can accept volunteers below the age of 18, they cannot be conscripted and that 'States Parties shall take all feasible measures to ensure that members of their armed forces who have not attained the age of 18 years do not take a

---

19 Committee on the Rights of the Child, ibid para 20.

20 See above, n 8, 16.

21 *Optional Protocol on the Involvement of Children in Armed Conflict*, GA Res 54/263, UN GAOR, 54th sess, 97th plen mtg, Agenda Item 116a, Supp No 49, UN Doc A/54/49 (25 May 2000).

22 *Optional Protocol to the Convention on the Rights of the Child on the Sale of Children, Child Prostitution and Child Pornography*, GA Res 54/263, UN GAOR, 54th sess, 97th plen mtg, Agenda Item 116a, Supp No 49, UN Doc A/54/49 (25 May 2000).

direct part in hostilities'.[23] Non-state actors and guerrilla forces are forbidden from recruiting anyone under the age of 18 for any purpose.[24]

The *Optional Protocol on the Sale of Children, Child Prostitution and Child Pornography* recognises the right of the child to be protected from economic exploitation and focuses in particular on prohibiting trafficking in children, child prostitution and child pornography, and specifically highlights how the practices of sex tourism contribute to these offences. The *Optional Protocol* recommends the criminalisation of trafficking, child prostitution and child pornography, requires states to establish procedures for the extradition of those guilty of such offences, calls for international cooperation in tracking and prosecuting offenders, recommends mechanisms for protecting and assisting child victims and calls for the promotion of greater public awareness on these issues.

A peculiarity of the Optional Protocols is that they contain a provision that allows them to be ratified by the United States and Somalia, as the only two states yet to ratify the CROC. The US has ratified both Optional Protocols and Somalia has signed but not ratified the *Optional Protocol on the Involvement of Children in Armed Conflict.*

12.2.5 State Responses to the CROC: Focus on the United States

The CROC has been ratified by 193 states and is widely lauded for its near universal acceptance.[25] Only Somalia and the United States (US) have not ratified the convention. Somalia signed the treaty in 2002 but is unable to ratify as it has no recognised government. The US, by signing the Convention in 1995, has signalled its intention to ratify—but has yet to do so. Why, and what is the significance of the US's non-ratification of the treaty?

Although the US has ratified both of the Optional Protocols attached to the CROC, and the ILO *Convention No 182* dealing with the worst forms of child labour, its non-ratification of the CROC is significant. The US is one of the most powerful actors in world affairs, and its lack of acceptance of the convention can impact the validity of the principles set out in the treaty. As noted by Alston and Tobin, 'the US is not a country which can be ignored and its opposition to the [CROC] will, over time, manifest itself in a more damaging and destructive way vis-à-vis the overall enterprise of promoting children's rights in general and the Convention in particular'.[26]

23 See above, n 21, art 1.

24 See above, n 21, art 4.

25 What is sometimes overlooked is the significant number of declarations and reservations that have been made to the CROC; on reservations generally see Chapter 7.2.4. Some reservations, such as Iran's, are so broad as to make the ratification of the CROC nearly meaningless: *Convention on the Rights of the Child,* opened for signature 20 November 1989, 1577 UNTS 3 (entered into force 2 September 1990) *Iran Reservation:* 'The Government of the Islamic Republic of Iran reserves the right not to apply any provisions or articles of the Convention that are incompatible with Islamic Laws and the international legislation in effect.' <http://treaties.un.org/Pages/ViewDetails.aspx?src=TREATY&mtdsg_no=IV-11&chapter=4&lang=en>. See also William A Schabas, 'Reservations to the Convention on the Rights of the Child' (1996) 18 *Human Rights Quarterly* 472.

26 P Alston & J Tobin, *Laying the Foundations for Children's Rights: An Independent Study of Some Key Legal and Institutional Aspects of the Impact of the Convention on the Rights of the Child,* UNICEF, 2005, 11.

However, the lack of ratification of the treaty by the US should also be seen as part of its general reluctance to ratify international human rights treaties.[27] In the context of the CROC, a number of conservative religious groups in the US continue to raise objections to formal acceptance of the treaty. Some of the objections relate broadly to the tension between balancing children's rights and parental rights and the acceptance (or not) of public intrusion into the private domain.

Kilbourne summarises some of the objections in the US to articles 14 (freedom of thought, conscience and religion) and 15 (freedom of association and freedom of peaceful assembly) as being based on the theory that the CROC prevents parents from supervising or guiding their children in a manner appropriate to their culture and upbringing.

SUSAN KILBOURNE, 'THE WAYWARD AMERICANS—WHY THE USA HAS NOT RATIFIED THE UN CONVENTION ON THE RIGHTS OF THE CHILD'[28]

Article 14 appears to be one of the most objectionable Articles. American critics almost uniformly interpret this Article as giving children 'a legal right to object to all religious training. Alternatively, children may assert their right against parental objection to participate in occult, Muslim or Buddhist worship services'. Opponents worry that '[p]arents would not be able to require their child to learn about the Bible or attend church if the child did not want to do so' ...

American opponents interpret Article 15 as preventing parents from restricting their children's freedom of association, even 'from forbidding their child to associate with people deemed to be objectionable companions'. According to one author, '[t]his implies parents would not be allowed to restrict a child's choice of friends. If your 14-year-old daughter wants to date an 18-year-old dropout with a police record, who are you to say she can't?'

Specific opposition to article 37 of the CROC relating to the prohibition on capital punishment of persons for offences committed before the age of 18 have been rendered redundant by the 2005 US Supreme Court decision of *Roper v Simmons*.[29] In this case the Supreme Court held that it is unconstitutional to impose capital punishment for crimes committed while under the age of 18. The 5:4 decision overruled the Court's prior ruling in *Stanford v Kentucky*,[30] which held that that the execution of 16- and 17-year-old offenders was not constitutionally barred. The Court concluded that since *Stanford*, a national consensus had formed against the execution of juvenile offenders, and the practice violates society's 'evolving standards of decency'. In addition to considering evidence of a national consensus as expressed by legislative enactments and jury practices, the majority noted that the execution of juvenile offenders violated

27 For example, the US signed *Convention on the Elimination of All Forms of Discrimination Against Women* in 1980 but is still yet to ratify it; see the discussion and references at Chapter 16.5. Of the nine major human rights treaties, the US has ratified three: *International Convention on the Elimination of All Forms of Racial Discrimination, International Covenant on Civil and Political Rights* and the *Convention Against Torture and Other Cruel, Inhuman or Degrading Treatment or Punishment*.

28 S Kilbourne, 'The Wayward Americans—Why the USA Has Not Ratified the UN *Convention on the Rights of the Child*' (1998) 10(3) *Child and Family Law Quarterly* 243.

29 543 US 551 (2005).

30 492 US 361 (1989) ('*Stanford*').

several international treaties, including the CROC and the ICCPR, and stated that the overwhelming weight of international opinion against the juvenile death penalty provides confirmation for the Court's own conclusion that the death penalty is disproportional punishment for offenders under 18.

12.2.6 Other Instruments and Developments

International

Pre-dating the CROC, the rights of the child are recognised to a limited extent in the International Bill of Rights. Article 25 of the UDHR echoes the sentiments of the *Declaration of Geneva* by declaring that children are entitled to special care and assistance. Article 23 of the ICCPR recognises that the family unit is worthy of special protection, and article 24 stipulates that every child must be treated in a non-discriminatory manner, that they should be registered immediately after birth, and shall have a name and have the right to acquire a nationality. Article 10 of the ICESCR reiterates the special protection due to children, particularly in relation to economic and social exploitation. These rights are also reflected and expanded upon in the CROC.

One of the primary aims in establishing the International Labour Organisation in 1919 was the abolition of child labour, but it took until 1973 for the first major convention that targeted this issue to be adopted. The two principal ILO conventions dealing with child labour are the *Minimum Age Convention* (No 138)[31] and the *Worst Forms of Child Labour Convention* (No 182).[32] Taken together, these provide a framework for determining what work is acceptable for children under the age of 18 years.

The United Nations Children's Fund (UNICEF) was established in 1946 by the United Nations to provide food, shelter and health care for the millions of children affected by war. It is now the lead United Nations agency responsible for the global monitoring of the child-related Millennium Development Goals (MDGs).[33] It is mandated by the UN General Assembly to advocate for the protection of children's rights and its work is guided by the CROC and the decisions and recommendations emanating from the CRC.

In 1990 the UN hosted a World Summit for Children, which included heads of state and government, and set 10-year goals for children's health, nutrition and education. In 2002 a landmark Special Session of the UN General Assembly was convened to review progress since the World Summit and re-energise global commitment to children's rights. It was the first such session devoted exclusively to children and the first to include them as official delegates permitted to address the UN General Assembly directly. At this session, where world leaders committed themselves to a compact on child rights: 'A World Fit for Children'.[34] In 2007, the five-year follow-up to the Special Session ended with a declaration on children

31 *Convention Concerning Minimum Age for Admission to Employment* (*Minimum Age Convention*, 1973) (No 138), opened for signature 26 June 1973, 1015 UNTS 297 (entered into force 19 June 1976).

32 *Convention Concerning the Prohibition and Immediate Action for the Elimination of the Worst Forms of Child Labour* (*Worst Forms of Child Labour Convention*, 1999) (No 182), opened for signature 17 June 1999, 2133 UNTS 161 (entered into force 19 November 2000). The ILO Conventions, including the two child labour conventions, are discussed in detail in Chapter 17.2.3.

33 See UN, *We Can End Poverty 2015: Millennium Development Goals* (2010) <http://www.un.org/millenniumgoals/>; on the Millennium Development Goals, see Chapter 20.2.2.

34 *A World Fit For Children*, GA Res S-27/2, UN GAOR, 27th special sess, Agenda Items 8 and 9, UN Doc A/RES/S-27/2 (11 October 2002).

adopted by more than 140 governments, identifying the many gains that had been realised in the five years since the first Special Session but noting that much needed to be done to build upon them.[35] The declaration identified eradicating poverty as the greatest global challenge facing children and families. It was only the second time in UN history that children had directly addressed the UN General Assembly.[36]

Regional

Africa

The *African Charter on the Rights and Welfare of the Child*[37] ('African Children's Charter') was the first regional treaty on the human rights of the child and was adopted by the Organization of African Unity in 1990. It entered into force in 1999 after receiving the requisite 15 ratifications and to date has been ratified by 45 of the 53 African countries. All of the African countries (except Somalia) have ratified the CROC.

The *African Children's Charter* codifies the responsibilities of the state, community and individual in the protection of the civil and political and economic, social and cultural rights of the child, and although it was completed after the adoption of the CROC, the fact that it was based on an earlier draft version of that convention means there are some differences between the two treaties. The *African Children's Charter* categorises all persons under 18 as children (article 2); notes that the best interests of the child are 'the' rather than 'a' primary consideration (article 4); prohibits marriage below the age of 18 and calls for harmful social and cultural practices (not identified) to be eliminated (article 21); and prohibits the recruitment and participation of children in armed conflict (article 22).

Chapter two of the *African Children's Charter* provides for the creation of the African Committee of Experts on the Rights and Welfare of the Child, which is tasked with (among other duties) examining state reports on their compliance with the Charter. The Committee, which was formally established in 2001, is also empowered to consider complaints 'from any person, group or nongovernmental organization recognized by the Organization of African Unity, by a Member State, or the United Nations relating to any matter covered by this Charter' (article 44).

The Americas

The region of the Americas does not have a specialist charter or convention dealing with children's rights. The 1968 *American Convention on Human Rights*[38] and the 1988 *Additional Protocol to the American Convention on Human Rights in the Area of Economic, Social, and Cultural Rights*[39] (more commonly known

35 *Declaration of the Commemorative High-Level Plenary Meeting Devoted to the Follow-Up to the Outcome of the Special Session on Children*, GA Res 62/88, UN GAOR, 62nd sess, 73rd plen mtg, Agenda Item 66(b), UN Doc A/RES/62/88 (25 January 2008).

36 UNICEF, 'UN General Assembly Plenary Closes with Renewed Commitment to Children' (Media Release, 13 December 2007) <http://www.unicef.org/worldfitforchildren/index_42198.html>.

37 *African Charter on the Rights and Welfare of the Child*, opened for signature 11 July 1990, OAU Doc CAB/LEG/24.9/49 (entered into force 29 November 1999).

38 *American Convention on Human Rights*, opened for signature 22 November 1968, 1144 UNTS 123 (entered into force 18 July 1978) ('*American Convention*').

39 *Additional Protocol to the American Convention on Human Rights in the Area of Economic, Social and Cultural Rights*, opened for signature 17 November 1988, 28 ILM 156 (entered into force 16 November 1999).

as the 'Protocol of San Salvador') contain several broad provisions that relate to children. For example, article 19 of the American Convention stresses that children have the right to special protection from the state but does not stipulate which rights children are entitled to or how these should be upheld. The provisions in both instruments that relate to children are drafted in a pre-CROC style that focuses more on the welfare of the child than on the rights they possess. However, as noted by Alston and Tobin, there is an anomaly between the limited and dated rights set out in the instruments of the Organisation of American States and the more expansive and contemporary protection provided by institutions of the inter-American system such as the Inter-American Commission on Human Rights and the Inter-American Court on Human Rights.[40]

Unlike the CROC, the American Convention includes provisions for reporting individual cases in which children's rights have been breached. Such cases have helped to establish precedents for protecting children's rights in many countries in the region and states have been ordered to pay compensation to the victims and to make changes to their legislation.[41] In August 2002, the Inter-American Court produced an Advisory Opinion (in response to a request from the Inter-American Commission), entitled 'Legal Status and Human Rights of the Child',[42] which noted the 'conceptual evolution' of children's rights and said that children should be dealt with in approaches that reflect the modernity of the principles reflected in the CROC that emphasise respect for individual rights.

Europe

The *European Convention on Human Rights*[43] makes no specific mention of children's rights. However, the rights in the convention apply to children, and complaints have been brought to the European Court of Human Rights alleging breaches of these rights in the case of children.[44] The other major treaty adopted by the Council of Europe is the *European Social Charter*, which contains limited references to children's rights that largely reflect the outdated welfare/protectionist mode of drafting rather than the contemporary child rights agenda as reflected in the CROC.[45] In addition, the Council of Europe has

40 P Alston & J Tobin, see above, n 26, 14.

41 See for example, *Villagrán Morales v Guatemala* (Inter-American Court of Human Rights, 19 November 1999) on extra-judicial executions of street children in Guatemala; *Instituto de Reeducación del Menor v Paraguay* (Inter-American Court of Human Rights, Series C No 112, 2 September 2004) on the conditions of detention facilities for children in Paraguay; *The Yean and Bosico Girls v Dominican Republic* (Inter-American Court of Human Rights, 8 September 2005) concerning discrimination on the basis of nationality in the Dominican Republic.

42 Inter-American Court of Human Rights, *Advisory Opinion on the Juridical Condition and Human Rights of the Child* (Advisory Opinion Oc-17/2002 requested by the Inter-American Commission on Human Rights, 28 August 2002) [36], [137] <http://www.crin.org/docs/advisory-opinion17.pdf>.

43 *Convention for the Protection of Human Rights and Fundamental Freedoms (European Convention on Human Rights)*, opened for signature 4 November 1950, 213 UNTS 221 (entered into force 3 September 1953).

44 See for example, *Tyrer v UK* (1978) 26 Eur Court HR (ser A) relating to corporal punishment of a 15-year-old at his school; *Okkali v Turkey* (European Court of Human Rights, Application No 52067/99, 17 October 2006) where the complaint related to the treatment of a 12-year-old boy in police custody; *Mubilanzila Mayeka and Kaniki Mitunga v Belgium* (European Court of Human Rights, Application No 13178/03, 12 October 2006) relating to the detention and deporation of children seeking asylum. For a summary of case law see: Child Rights Information Network, *European Court of Human Rights* <http://www.crin.org/resources/infoDetail.asp?ID=18061&flag=report>.

45 *European Social Charter*, opened for signature 18 October 1961, 529 UNTS 89 (entered into force 2 February 1965) pt 1 paras 7, 17; see Chapter 8.2.4.

adopted a number of treaties specifically to protect children's rights and which may be invoked at the European Court of Human Rights to challenge breaches of these rights, one of the most recent being the *Convention on the Protection of Children against Sexual Exploitation and Sexual Abuse*.[46]

In 2000 the European Union adopted the *Charter of Fundamental Rights of the European Union*[47] (a non-binding statement of rights), which contains several provisions relating to children. The range of rights represented is selective and restrictive, but the recognition of the need to include separate rights for children is at least a limited step forward from their previous exclusion from the European Convention.

12.3 COMMITTEE ON THE RIGHTS OF THE CHILD

12.3.1 Mandate and Reporting Procedures

The CROC is monitored through a system of reporting by states parties to the Committee on the Rights of the Child (CRC).[48] The CRC is composed of 18 independent experts who are elected in their personal capacity to four-year terms by states parties. An equitable geographical distribution and representation of the principal legal systems is taken into consideration in their selection. Like the other treaty bodies attached to each of the main human rights conventions, the CRC is primarily responsible for examining the achievements of states parties in relation to the CROC and assisting and advising states in overcoming any limitations in implementing the CROC. Each state party is required to submit an initial report two years after ratification of the convention, followed by five yearly progress reports. The CRC has encouraged NGOs to submit alternative reports or other supplementary information to provide it with a complete picture of how the Convention is being implemented in a particular country.

In its annual report to the General Assembly the CRC sets out its conclusions from examining each state's periodic report and generally covers positive as well as negative developments, ranging from the general to the specific. The extract below, from the Committee's 2010 annual report,[49] sets out a selection of the concluding observations adopted by the CRC in response to the third and fourth periodic reports of the United Kingdom.

COMMITTEE ON THE RIGHTS OF THE CHILD, *REPORT ON THE FORTY-NINTH SESSION (2010)*

[28] The Committee, while welcoming the introduction of statutory child death reviews in England and Wales, is very concerned that six more children have died in custody since the last examination, as well as at the high prevalence of self-injurious behaviour among children in custody.

46 *Council of Europe Convention on the Protection of Children Against Sexual Exploitation and Sexual Abuse*, opened for signature 25 October 2007, CETS No 201 (entered into force 1 July 2010).

47 *Charter of Fundamental Rights of the European Union* [2000] OJ C 364/01.

48 See the discussion of treaty bodies generally in Chapter 7.4.

49 UN Doc CRC/C/49/3 (25 February 2010).

(29) The Committee recommends that the State party use all available resources to protect children's rights to life, including by reviewing the effectiveness of preventive measures. The State party should also introduce automatic, independent and public reviews of any unexpected death or serious injury involving children—whether in care or in custody …

(36) The Committee is concerned that:

(a) DNA data regarding children is kept in the National DNA Database irrespective of whether the child is ultimately charged or found guilty;

(b) The State party has not taken sufficient measures to protect children, notably those subject to ASBOs, from negative media representation and public 'naming and shaming';

(c) Children's appearances on television reality shows may constitute an unlawful interference with their privacy.

(37) The Committee recommends that the State party:

(a) Ensure, both in legislation and in practice, that children are protected against unlawful or arbitrary interference with their privacy, including by introducing stronger regulations for data protection;

(b) Intensify its efforts, in cooperation with the media, to respect the privacy of children in the media, especially by avoiding messages publicly exposing them to shame, which is against the against the best interests of the child;

(c) Regulate children's participation in television programmes, notably reality shows, as to ensure that they do not violate their rights.

12.3.2 New Draft Communications Procedure

The CROC does not have a communications (that is, complaints) procedure attached to the treaty.[50] However, the Human Rights Council decided in 2009 to establish an open-ended working group to explore the possibility of setting up a communications procedure that would complement the convention's states reporting procedure.[51] Although children and their representatives can use the mechanisms provided by other international instruments to pursue many of their rights, those instruments do not cover, separately or together, the full range and detail of rights in the CROC. At the time of writing, a draft optional protocol had been circulated by the working group for comment.[52]

Most of the provisions in the draft are standard, in that they already exist in similar instruments establishing communications procedures under other human rights treaties. But some are specific

50 See the discussion of communications to the treaty bodies generally in Chapter 7.4.7.

51 *Open-Ended Working Group on an Optional Protocol to the Convention on the Rights of the Child to Provide a Communications Procedure*, Human Rights Council Res 11/1, 11th sess, 27th mtg, UN Doc A/HRC/RES/11/1 (17 June 2009).

52 Human Rights Council, *Proposal for a Draft Optional Protocol Prepared by the Chairperson-Rapporteur of the Open-Ended Working Group on an Optional Protocol to the Convention on the Rights of the Child to Provide a Communications Procedure*, UN Doc A/HRC/WG.7/2/2 (1 September 2010) (CROC Draft Optional Protocal); Human Rights Council, *Comments by the Committee on the Rights of the Child on the Proposal for a Draft Optional Protocol Prepared by the Chairperson-Rapporteur of the Open-Ended Working Group on an Optional Protocol to the Convention on the Rights of the Child to Provide a Communications Procedure*, UN Doc A/HRC/WG.7/2/3 (13 October 2010).

to children and do not exist in other international instruments. For example, it is proposed that although communications may claim a violation of any of the rights guaranteed in the CROC and/or its two associated optional protocols, states can declare that they do not recognise the CRC's competence to examine communications claiming a violation of any of the rights guaranteed in the CROC or its optional protocols.[53] The CRC's commentary on the draft optional protocol states that it is 'essential that no right protected under these three instruments be excluded from the ambit of the communication procedure [as] [t]hese rights are interrelated, interdependent and indivisible; to exclude any right would risk creating a hierarchical relationship among them.'[54] For that reason, the CRC recommends deleting the opt-out clause from the draft text.

The draft text also suggests that national human rights institutions, ombudsman institutions and NGOs should be able to submit collective communications alleging grave or systematic violations of any of the rights set out in the CROC and its two optional protocols.[55] However, the capacity of NGOs to submit collective communications is currently limited to those that have consultative status with the UN's Economic and Social Council[56] and any collective communication is limited to grave or systematic violations of the Convention. The CRC argues that both limitations are too restrictive and that the 'specificity of the collective communication procedure should not be based on the nature of the alleged violation, but mainly on the fact that it concerns a group of alleged victims who cannot be all identified by name'.[57]

The move to develop a communications procedure for the CROC and its two optional protocols is a welcome step towards recognising that the rights of children are equivalent to those of all other individuals.

12.4 CASE STUDY: CHILDREN AND ARMED CONFLICT

12.4.1 Overview

International law generally prohibits the participation in armed conflict of children aged under 18 years. However, although there are no exact figures, it is estimated that hundreds of thousands of

53 Human Rights Council, CROC Draft Optional Protocol, UN Doc A/HRC/WG.7/2/2, art 2.

54 Human Rights Council, see sbove, n 52, UN Doc A/HRC/WG.7/2/3 para 10.

55 Human Rights Council, UN Doc A/HRC/WG.7/2/3, see above, n 52.

56 See Chapter 9.3.2.

57 Human Rights Council, see sbove, n 52, UN Doc A/HRC/WG.7/2/3 para 15.

children under that age are still serving in government forces or armed rebel groups. UNICEF states on its website that 'an estimated 300 000 child soldiers—boys and girls under the age of 18—are involved in more than 30 conflicts worldwide'. UNICEF also states that 'an estimated 20 million children have been forced to flee their homes because of conflict and human rights violations and are living as refugees in neighbouring countries or are internally displaced within their own national borders. More than 2 million children have died as a direct result of armed conflict over the last decade. More than three times that number, at least 6 million children, have been permanently disabled or seriously injured. More than 1 million have been orphaned or separated from their families. Between 8000 and 10 000 children are killed or maimed by landmines every year.'[58]

In her 1996 seminal report[59] on the 'Impact of Armed Conflict on Children', Machel[60] noted that while children participate in armed conflict as soldiers, they may also 'serve armies in supporting roles, as cooks, porters, messengers and spies.'[61] Child soldiers may be recruited in many different ways into government armed forces, paramilitaries, civil militia and a variety of other armed groups. 'While some children are recruited forcibly, others are driven into armed forces by poverty, alienation and discrimination. Many children join armed groups after having experienced or witnessed abuse at the hands of state authorities'.[62] Machel noted that 'one of the most basic reasons that children join armed groups is economic. Hunger and poverty may drive parents to offer their children for service', and in some cases their wages are paid directly to the family.[63]

Although the involvement of children in armed conflict has received widespread attention, the 2010 report of the UN Secretary-General to the UN General Assembly on 'Children and Armed Conflict' highlighted the grave and systematic violations that beset children in many parts of the world.[64]

58 See UNICEF, *Child Protection from Violence, Exploitation and Abuse: Children in Conflict and Emergencies* (2011) <http://www.crin.org/resources/infoDetail.asp?ID=18061&flag=report>.

59 *Impact of Armed Conflict on Children: Report of the Expert of the Secretary-General, Ms Graça Machel, Submitted Pursuant to the General Assembly Resolution 48/157*, UN GAOR, 51st sess, Provisional Agenda Item 108, UN Doc A/51/306 (26 August 1996).

60 In 1993, following a recommendation by the Committee on the Rights of the Child, the General Assembly adopted a resolution recommending that the Secretary-General appoint an independent expert to study the impact of armed conflict on children. Following the release of Graça Machel's report in 1996, the Assembly recommended that the Secretary-General appoint a Special Representative for Children and Armed Conflict.

61 See above, n 59, para 34.

62 *Coalition to Stop the Use of Child Soldiers: Global Report on Child Soldiers*, April 2001, 10.

63 See above, n 59, para 39. Also see Committee on the Rights of the Child, *Report on the Forty-Eighth Session*, UN Doc CRC/C/48/3 (16 November 2009) regarding CRC's response to the US's obligations under the Optional Protocol on the Involvement of Children in Armed Conflict, GA Res 54/263, UN GAOR, 54th sess, 97th plen mtg, Agenda Item 116a, Supp No 49, UN Doc A/54/49 (25 May 2000). The CRC Report deals with issues such as voluntary recruitment under the age of 18; methods of recruitment that target children from minorities, under-privileged backgrounds and the need to update national criminal legislation to include crimes covered in the Protocol: at para 25 ('United States of America: Optional Protocol on the Involvement of Children in Armed Conflict').

64 *Report of the Secretary General: Children and Armed Conflict*, UN GAOR, 64th sess, Agenda Item 65(a), UN Doc A/64/742 (13 April 2010).

CHILDREN AND ARMED CONFLICT[65]

DEVELOPMENTS IN AFGHANISTAN

47 While detailed documentation is still difficult to obtain, available information indicates that a number of children were recruited or used by armed opposition groups throughout the country, including the Taliban, the Haqqani network, Hezb-i-Islami, the Tora Bora Front and Jamat Sunat al-Dawa Salafia. Cases were documented of children as young as 13 and 14 years of age who carried out suicide attacks or were used to plant explosives.

DEVELOPMENTS IN THE CENTRAL AFRICAN REPUBLIC

57 Child recruitment continues to be a serious concern in 2009, with active mobilization of a large number of children into the ranks of self-defence militias throughout the country ...

DEVELOPMENTS IN THE DEMOCRATIC REPUBLIC OF THE CONGO

69 In 2009 the United Nations Organization Mission in the Democratic Republic of Congo (MONUC) documented 848 newly recruited children (including 52 girls) ...

73 Sexual violence against children continued to be a widespread phenomenon ...

DEVELOPMENTS IN IRAQ

81 Police and military sources, community members, the media and United Nations partners have reported the continuing recruitment of children by armed groups for acts of terror, including as suicide bombers. The children were reported to have been tricked, coerced or enticed with financial incentives. Some of the children used as suicide bombers were girls.

DEVELOPMENTS IN MYANMAR

88 The United Nations country task force on monitoring and reporting continues to face challenges related to access to Government armed forces (Tatmadaw Kyi) recruitment units, schools and camps in order to carry out its monitoring and verification exercises. The task force also had extremely limited access to non-State armed groups during the reporting period and was unable to establish contact with many of those groups owing to Government restrictions ...

90 ILO has verified a report that an under-age boy who was recruited into the Tatmadaw Kyi and had taken a direct part in hostilities, had been convicted of murdering a colleague and sentenced to death.

The map[66] below highlights the principal areas where the UN currently estimates children are most at risk from armed conflict.

65 Ibid.

66 UN, *Grave Violations Against Children in Armed Conflict* (2010) <http://www.un.org/children/conflict/_media/maps/CAACWorldMap2010_english.pdf>.

12.4.2 Legal Framework

At the time of drafting the CROC, the question of the minimum age for recruitment into armed forces and participation in conflict provoked considerable controversy. The standards in article 38 are weak, and in some cases lower than those already established under international humanitarian law.[67] Hammarberg argues that pressure from the US delegation during the drafting of article 38 resulted in the formulation that only those aged under fifteen be protected against service in armed forces, even though more and more delegations were coming to support NGOs' arguments that the maximum age for recruitment should be raised.[68]

CROC, ARTICLE 38

1 States Parties undertake to respect and to ensure respect for rules of international humanitarian law applicable to them in armed conflicts which are relevant to the child.

2 States Parties shall take all feasible measures to ensure that persons who have not attained the age of fifteen years do not take a direct part in hostilities.

67 Article 4(3)(c) of *Protocol Additional to the Geneva Convention of 12 August 1949, and Relating to the Protection of Victims of Non-International Armed Conflicts (Protocol II)* 8 June 1997, opened for signature 8 June 1977, 1125 UNTS 609 (entered into force 7 December 1978) notes that 'children who have not attained the age of 15 years shall neither be recruited in the armed forces or groups nor allowed to take part in hostilities'. This provides a total ban on recruitment and does not limit the governmental obligation to 'feasible measures' to prevent their direct involvement in hostilities.

68 Thomas Hammarberg, 'The UN Convention on the Rights of the Child—And How to Make it Work' (1990) 12 *Human Rights Quarterly* 97, 101.

3 States Parties shall refrain from recruiting any person who has not attained the age of fifteen years into their armed forces. In recruiting among those persons who have attained the age of fifteen years but who have not attained the age of eighteen years, States Parties shall endeavour to give priority to those who are oldest.

4 In accordance with their obligations under international humanitarian law to protect the civilian population in armed conflicts, States Parties shall take all feasible measures to ensure protection and care of children who are affected by an armed conflict.

In 1990, just one year after the adoption of the CROC, the *African Charter on the Rights and Welfare of the Child* established that 'States Parties to the present Charter shall take all necessary measures to ensure that no child shall take a direct part in hostilities and refrain in particular from recruiting any child'.[69] A child is defined as being less than 18 years. The ILO *Convention on the Worst Forms of Child Labour*, adopted in 1999, prohibits the forced or compulsory recruitment of children under the age of 18 for use in armed conflict. It has been ratified by 173 countries.

In 2000, in response to pressure from within and outside the United Nations, the *Optional Protocol to the Convention on the Rights of the Child on the involvement of children in armed conflict* was adopted. The protocol prohibits the forced recruitment of children under the age of 18 or their use in hostilities. To date, it has been ratified by 141 countries.[70]

OPTIONAL PROTOCOL TO THE CONVENTION ON THE RIGHTS OF THE CHILD ON THE INVOLVEMENT OF CHILDREN IN ARMED CONFLICT

ARTICLE 1

States Parties shall take all feasible measures to ensure that members of their armed forces who have not attained the age of 18 years do not take a direct part in hostilities.

ARTICLE 2

States Parties shall ensure that persons who have not attained the age of 18 years are not compulsorily recruited into their armed forces.

ARTICLE 3

1 States Parties shall raise the minimum age for the voluntary recruitment of persons into their national armed forces from that set out in article 38, paragraph 3, of the Convention on the Rights of the Child, taking account of the principles contained in that article and recognizing that under the Convention persons under 18 are entitled to special protection.

...

69 See above, n 37, art 22(2).

70 In 2010 the Office of the Special Representative for Children and Armed Conflict in cooperation with the Special Representative on Violence against Children, UNICEF, the Office of the High Commissioner for Human Rights and the Committee on the Rights of the Child launched a campaign to achieve universal ratification of the *Optional Protocol 'Zero under 18'*. See Coomaraswamy, 'The *Optional Protocol to the Convention on the Rights of the Child on the Involvement of Children in Armed Conflict*—Towards Universal Ratification' (2010) 18 *International Journal of Children's Rights* 535.

2 States Parties that permit voluntary recruitment into their national armed forces under the age of 18 shall maintain safeguards to ensure, as a minimum, that:

(a) Such recruitment is genuinely voluntary;

(b) Such recruitment is done with the informed consent of the person's parents or legal guardians;

(c) Such persons are fully informed of the duties involved in such military service;

(d) Such persons provide reliable proof of age prior to acceptance into national military service.

ARTICLE 4

1 Armed groups that are distinct from the armed forces of a State should not, under any circumstances, recruit or use in hostilities persons under the age of 18 years.

2 States Parties shall take all feasible measures to prevent such recruitment and use, including the adoption of legal measures necessary to prohibit and criminalize such practices ...

The *Rome Statute of the International Criminal Court* establishes that war crimes include 'conscripting or enlisting children under the age of fifteen years into [the national] armed forces or using them to participate actively in hostilities'.[71]

In 2007 a major project to gather and compile experiences from the demobilisation, disarmament and reintegration of child soldiers around the world culminated in *The Paris Principles: The Principles and Guidelines on Children Associated with Armed Forces or Armed Groups (February 2007).*[72] Endorsed by 66 governments, the Paris Principles offer guidance on protecting children from recruitment and providing them with assistance during or after their involvement with armed groups. The principles stress that '[t]he unlawful recruitment or use of children is a violation of their rights: therefore preventive activities must be carried out continuously. The release, protection and reintegration of children unlawfully recruited or used must be sought at all times, without condition and must not be dependent on any parallel release or demobilisation process for adults'.[73]

12.4.3 Accountability

Two high-profile cases involving the conscription of children into armed conflict have featured recently in the International Criminal Court (ICC) and the Special Court for Sierra Leone. Both trials are powerful symbols in the continuing struggle to end impunity for those involved in recruiting and using children in armed conflict.

In the case before the ICC—*The Prosecutor v Thomas Lubanga Dyilo*[74]—Lubanga is charged with the war crime of conscripting and enlisting children under the age of fifteen years and using them to participate actively in hostilities. Lubanga is a former rebel leader from the Democratic Republic of

71 *Rome Statute of the International Criminal Court*, art 8(2)(b)(xxvi) for international armed conflicts; art 8(2)(e)(vii) for non-international armed conflicts. The *Rome Statute* and its crimes are discussed in more detail in Chapter 11.5 and 12.4.3.

72 Available online at <http://www.un.org/children/conflict/_documents/parisprinciples/ParisPrinciples_EN.pdf>.

73 UNICEF, *The Paris Principles: The Principles and Guidelines on Children Associated with Armed Forces or Armed Groups* (2007) [3.6].

74 *Prosecutor v Thomas Lubanga Dyilo* (International Criminal Court) Case No ICC-01/04-01/06. See Chapter 11.5.

the Congo (DRC) who is alleged to have founded and led the Union of Congolese Patriots (UPC) and to have been the Commander-in-Chief of its military wing, the *Forces Patriotiques pour la Libération du Congo* (FPLC). The current case against Lubanga comes as a result of an investigation by the Prosecutor of the ICC into the situation in the DRC. On 17 March 2006, Lubanga became the first person ever arrested under a warrant issued by the ICC. His trial began on 26 January 2009 and at the time of writing continues. The Prosecution alleges that Lubanga actively recruited children under the age of fifteen years, subjected them to military training and subsequently used them to participate actively in hostilities, including as bodyguards for military officers.

In the Special Court for Sierra Leone the case against Charles Taylor, the former President of Liberia is continuing.[75] Charles Taylor, the former President of Liberia, was indicted on 7 March 2003 by the Special Court on a number of charges, including conscripting or enlisting children under the age of 15 years into armed forces or groups, or using them to participate actively in hostilities. The case commenced on 4 June 2007 and, because Taylor initially boycotted the proceedings and dismissed his legal team, proceedings were elongated and finally concluded on 12 November 2010. At the time of writing the judges were continuing their deliberations.

SNAPSHOT: OMAR KHADR[76]

Omar Khadr faced charges before a US Military Commission relating to his conduct as a child soldier in Afghanistan. The trial attracted criticism from NGOs such as Human Rights Watch and Amnesty International and the Special Representative of the Secretary-General for Children and Armed conflict for failing to apply age-appropriate treatment to Khadr.[77]

Omar Khadr is a Canadian citizen who was detained by US forces in Afghanistan in July 2002 and transferred to the Guantánamo Naval Base in October 2002 at the age of 15 years. He was accused of killing a US soldier by throwing a hand grenade during combat with US forces, planting mines to target US convoys and gathering surveillance at an airport in Afghanistan. Khadr alleged he was subjected to torture and cruel treatment during multiple interrogation sessions in US military custody at Bagram Air Field in Afghanistan and at Guantánamo Bay. Human Rights Watch notes that 'both US and international law allow for detention of juveniles only as a last resort, require juveniles to be provided educational opportunities and housed separately from adults, and mandate a prompt determination of all cases involving children. Yet Khadr has been incarcerated with adults, reportedly subjected to abusive interrogations, and not provided with any educational opportunities (unlike other children at Guantanamo). In addition, he was detained for more than two years

75 *Prosecutor v Charles Ghankay Taylor* (Special Court for Sierra Leone, Trial Chamber II, Case No SCSL-03-01-T, 27 February 2009).

76 See US Department of Defense, Omar Ahmed Khadr (2010) <http://www.defense.gov/news/commissionsKhadr.html>. For a detailed account of the background to Omar Khadr's case, see Human Rights First, 'The Case of Omar Ahmed Khadr, Canada' available at: <http://www.humanrightsfirst.org/us_law/detainees/cases/khadr.aspx>.

77 Letter from American Civil Liberties Union, Human Rights Watch and the Juvenile Law Center to Attorney General Eric Holder and Secretary of Defense Robert Gates, 12 March 2010 <http://www.hrw.org/node/89081>; Amnesty International, *Omar Khadr Military Trial Condemned* (12 August 2010) <http://www.amnesty.org/en/news-and-updates/omar-khadr-guant%C3%A1namo-military-trial-condemned-2010-08-12>; Office of the Special Representative of the Secretary-General for Children and Armed conflict (Press Release, 5 May 2010) <http://www.un.org/children/conflict/english/pr/2010-05-05236.html>.

before he was provided with access to an attorney, and for more than three years before he was charged.'[78] On 25 October 2010 Khadr accepted a plea deal and pleaded guilty to murder, conspiracy and spying. Under the deal, he will serve eight years in custody, one in Guantanamo and the rest in Canada.

At the start of Khadr's trial the Special Representative of the UN Secretary-General for Children and Armed conflict argued that the trial of a juvenile before the US Military Commission was an anomaly. She noted that

> [t]he statute of the International Criminal Court (ICC) makes it clear that no one under 18 will be tried for war crimes, and prosecutors in other international tribunals have used their discretion not to prosecute children. Since World War II, no child has been prosecuted for a war crime. Child soldiers must be treated primarily as victims and alternative procedures should be in place aimed at rehabilitation or restorative justice.[79]

It is arguable that the US failed throughout Khadr's detention to afford him the protections given to children under international law. Under the *Optional Protocol to the Convention on the Rights of the Child on the Involvement of Children in Armed Conflict*, which the US ratified in 2002, the US is obliged to recognise the special situation of children who have been recruited or used in armed conflict.[80] The Optional Protocol requires former child soldiers to be rehabilitated within a state party's jurisdiction, stipulating that states provide 'all appropriate assistance for their physical and psychological recovery and their social reintegration.'

Under the CROC, to which the US is a signatory (but not a party), governments should ensure that the imprisonment of a child offender 'shall be used only as a measure of last resort and for the shortest appropriate period of time'.[81] Likewise Canada's role in Khadr's confinement might also be highlighted. In 2010, the Supreme Court of Canada held that the Canadian Government, by interrogating Khadr while he was being improperly treated by US officials, had breached its human rights obligations and Khadr's rights under the Canadian *Charter of Rights and Freedoms*.[82]

The 2009 *Report of the Special Representative of the Secretary-General for Children and Armed Conflict* reiterates the view that

> children should be considered primarily as victims, and decisions to prosecute a child or not must be guided by the principle of their best interests, bearing in mind the child's emotional, mental and intellectual maturity, the extent of their moral culpability and the possibility of alternative accountability and reconciliation mechanisms focusing on their rehabilitation. If a child is to be tried in any jurisdiction

---

78 Human Rights Watch, *Omar Ahmed Khadr—Canadian* (2 November 2010) <http://www.hrw.org/en/news/2008/12/04/omar-ahmed-khadr>.

79 Office of the Special Representative of the Secretary-General for Children and Armed Conflict, *Statement of SRSG Ms Radhika Coomaraswamy on the Occasion of the Trial of Omar Khadr before the Guantanamo Military Commission* (10 August 2010) <http://www.un.org/children/conflict/english/09-august-2010-trial-of-omar-khadr.html>.

80 See above, n 13, art 7.

81 CROC, see above, n 1, art 37(b).

82 *Canada (Prime Minister) v Khadr* [2010] 1 SCR 44. See also McGregor, 'Are Declaratory Orders Appropriate for Continuing Human Rights Violations? The Case of *Khadr v Canada*' *Human Rights Law Review* (2010) 10(3): 487–503.

for crimes, their treatment should adhere to international human rights standards specific to the rights of the child, in particular with regard to the age of criminal responsibility, fair trials, sentencing and detention. Similarly, national courts trying children for international crimes must also uphold their rights in accordance with international standards for juvenile justice.[83]

12.5 CONCLUSION AND ISSUES

Children's rights are simply the human rights of children. Children have long been recognised as a group worthy of special protection and assistance and the near universal ratification of the CROC signals a widespread international consensus for ensuring the rights of children are protected. The ongoing drafting of a third optional protocol to allow the CRC to receive communications regarding violations of the CROC and its two existing optional protocols is an encouraging initiative to strengthen the enforcement of children's rights. Despite these advances in promulgating the legal rights of children there remain a number of issues of concern.

As noted at the outset, children around the world continue to be routinely denied their human rights. Amnesty International estimates that between 1990 and 2010, 84 individuals who were children at the time they committed their crimes were executed in clear contravention of international law.[84] While this number is small compared to the overall number of executions, 'their significance goes beyond their number and calls into question the commitment of the executing states to respect international law'.[85]

Despite the adoption of the CROC's two Optional Protocols aimed at reducing the number of children involved in trafficking and armed conflict, UNICEF acknowledges that 'trafficking in children is a global problem affecting large numbers of children [and] some estimates have as many as 1.2 million children being trafficked every year'.[86] As discussed in the case study above, UNICEF also estimates that there are as many 300 000 child soldiers involved in various armed conflicts around the world. Alongside these gross violations of children's rights is the struggle of children in many parts of the world to receive an education, to benefit from the equal treatment of boys and girls, to be ensured access to adequate health care and to have an avenue for their voices and opinions to be heard.

Much progress has been made in the field of children's rights and much remains to be done to ensure the rights and safeguards set out in the CROC, its Optional Protocols and the various international, regional and national agreements, are implemented to the fullest possible level.

---

83 *Report of the Special Representative of the Secretary-General for Children and Armed Conflict*, UN GAOR, 64th sess, Provisional Agenda Item 67(a), UN Doc A/64/254 (6 August 2009) para 15.

84 Amnesty International, *Executions of Juveniles Since 1990* <http://www.amnesty.org/en/death-penalty/executions-of-child-offenders-since-1990>.

85 Ibid.

86 UNICEF, *Child Protection from Violence, Exploitation and Abuse: Child Trafficking* (2010) <http://www.unicef.org/protection/index_exploitation.html>.

13 INDIGENOUS PEOPLES

CONTENTS

13.1 INTRODUCTION

A notable feature of the international human rights regime is the emerging recognition of indigenous peoples as special subjects of concern,[1] and this brief chapter can only touch on the breadth and complexity of human rights law as it relates to indigenous peoples. After an outline of the formal international instruments and institutions that are dedicated or relevant to the human rights of indigenous peoples, the chapter gives an overview of some the current and emerging human rights issues that are of particular importance to indigenous peoples.

13.1.1 The Place of Indigenous Peoples

The human rights of indigenous peoples are, of course, the same as the human rights of all peoples. But, as with any particular group of people, attention is paid to certain rights that are of greater relevance to their history and circumstances.

1 J Anaya & R A Williams, 'The Protection of Indigenous Peoples' Rights over Lands and Natural Resources under the Inter-American Human Rights System' (2001) (14) *Harvard Journal of Human Rights* 33, 33.

The history of indigenous peoples from the seventeenth to the twentieth centuries is principally one of colonisation, subjugation, assimilation and genocide. It is a history of widespread and deliberate denial and violation of what we now recognise as human rights. Indigenous peoples have been the victims of more powerful peoples who have entered and taken over their land, most commonly European invaders of land in Africa, the Americas and Australasia, although the subjugation and displacement of indigenous peoples has been a world-wide phenomenon.

Indigenous peoples are not defined by reference to a closed set of criteria, but by reference to distinguishing social and cultural features. In international law, a person's identity as a member of a particular racial or ethnic group or groups is based on 'self-identification'.[2] Close to 400 million indigenous people in about 90 countries 'retain social, cultural, economic and political characteristics that are distinct from those of the dominant societies in which they live'. They are descended from the people who were in a geographical region when new arrivals 'became dominant through conquest, occupation, settlement or other means'.[3]

In the course of a significant report on indigenous peoples, the then Special Rapporteur of the (Commission for Human Rights') Sub-Commission on Prevention of Discrimination and Protection of Minorities, Jose R Martinez Cobo, described indigenous peoples in this way:[4]

> Indigenous communities, peoples and nations are those which, having a historical continuity with pre-invasion and pre-colonial societies that developed on their territories, consider themselves distinct from other sectors of the societies now prevailing on those territories, or parts of them. They form at present non-dominant sectors of society and are determined to preserve, develop and transmit to future generations their ancestral territories, and their ethnic identity, as the basis of their continued existence as peoples, in accordance with their own cultural patterns, social institutions and legal system.

It is, however, arguable that the emphasis on prior inhabitation is 'a description ... valid for North and South America, and in some areas of the Pacific', while elsewhere 'there is very little distinction between the time at which tribal and other traditional peoples arrived in the region and the time at which other populations arrived'.[5]

Although there is very significant diversity of history, language, culture and traditions among the world's indigenous peoples, they share the common feature of having been oppressed by a more powerful social grouping. This has subjected them to discrimination, denied them political representation and participation, denied them access to social and economic benefits, denied them the opportunity to

---

2 Committee on the Elimination of Racial Discrimination, *General Recommendation No 08: Identification with a Particular Racial or Ethnic Group*, 22 August 1990, contained in document A/45/18.

3 UN Permanent Forum on Indigenous Issues, *Factsheet: Who Are Indigenous Peoples?* 2006, <http://www.un.org/esa/socdev/unpfii/documents/5session_factsheet1.pdf>.

4 Special Rapporteur of the Subcommission on Prevention of Discrimination and Protection of Minorities, *Study on the Problem of Discrimination against Indigenous Populations*, UN Doc. E/CN.4/Sub.2/1986/7 and Add 1–4, para 379.

5 P Thornberry, *Indigenous Peoples and Human Rights*, Manchester University Press, Manchester, 2002, 45, citing M Tomei and L Swepston, *Indigenous and Tribal Peoples: A Guide to ILO Convention No 169*, Geneva, 1996, 5.; see also A Barnard, 'Kalahari revisionism, Vienna and the "indigenous peoples" debate' (2006) 14(1) *Social Anthropology* 1.

maintain their identity through their language, culture and traditions, and denied them the use of their traditional lands, territories and natural resources.[6]

13.1.2 Race Theory

Indigenous peoples identify according to their 'race', as that term is broadly understood for purposes of, for example, the *Convention for the Elimination of All Forms of Racial Discrimination*. That is, they identify according to a commonly held 'colour, descent, or national or ethnic origin'.[7] It is immediately apparent that this level of particularising identity poses a challenge to the universalism of human rights, although as has been said of the diversity of women's experiences, while there may be no 'monolithic' single point of view, there are commonalties across cultures.[8]

Building on the same anti-essentialist, post-modern perspectives that have informed critiques of universalism in human rights generally,[9] and women's human rights in particular,[10] a theoretical school of critical race theory has developed.[11] It is impossible to capture the 'sprawling literature'[12] of critical race theory here but, in short, the theory identifies the inadequacy of attempts to achieve formal equality by negating the existence and relevance of a person's race, and it looks at underlying social structures of power and material interests that maintain racial inequality. A critical race perspective can, for example, lead to an intellectual attack on racism said to be implicit in the 'grand narrative' of human rights and the international human rights system, saying that it assumes the superior state of whiteness as a standard that indigenous peoples should be helped to achieve.[13]

Some approaches to critical race theory question the categorisation of 'race' as a real identifier, suggesting that ideas of race are themselves constructed from a range of other personal identifiers, and others propose that ideas of race shift within cultures from time to time according to a range of other factors. A positive critical perspective on race is that in a post-colonial world, non-white people have fundamentally different perspectives that cannot be known by a white majority and that can make unique contributions to an understanding of the world.[14]

---

6 See above, n 3.

7 *International Convention for the Elimination of All Forms of Racial Discrimination*, (ICERD) opened for signature 21 December 1965, 660 UNTS 195 (entered into force 4 January 1969) art 1.

8 H Charlesworth, 'What Are Women's International Human Rights?' in R Cook (ed), *Women's Rights in International Law*, University of Pennsylvania Press, Philadelphia, 1994 58–84, 63.

9 See Chapter 2.4.2.

10 See Chapter 16.2.

11 See generally R Delgado and J Stefancic, *Critical Race Theory: An Introduction*, NYU Press, 2001; P E Andrews, 'Globalization, Human Rights and Critical Race Feminism: Voices from the Margins Journal of Gender, Race and Justice' (1999–2000) *Journal of Gender Race and Justice* 373, 374–7.

12 A Harris, 'Foreword' in R Delgado and J Stefancic, ibid xvii–xxi, xx.

13 See eg M Mutua, 'Savages, Victims, and Saviors: The Metaphor of Human Rights' (200) 41 *Harvard International Law Journal*, 201.

14 On the transformative potential of indigenous peoples' narratives, see R A Williams, 'Encounters on the Frontiers of International Human Rights Law: Redefining the Terms of Indigenous Peoples' Survival in the World' [1990] *Duke Law Journal* 660.

13.2 THE INTERNATIONAL FRAMEWORK

13.2.1 Recent History

The following chronology describes the rapidly growing international importance of the rights of indigenous peoples:[15]

J ANAYA & R A WILLIAMS, 'THE PROTECTION OF INDIGENOUS PEOPLES' RIGHTS OVER LANDS AND NATURAL RESOURCES UNDER THE INTER-AMERICAN HUMAN RIGHTS SYSTEM'[16]

In 1948, the Organization of American States General Assembly took initial steps toward recognition of indigenous peoples as special subjects of international concern in article 39 of the *Inter-American Charter of Social Guarantees* ... This regional recognition was followed by the adoption of the first multilateral treaty devoted specifically to recognizing and protecting indigenous peoples' human rights, *International Labour Organization Convention No 107 of 1957*.[17]

The modern indigenous rights movement gained momentum in the 1960s and 1970s, when indigenous peoples in the Americas, Australia, New Zealand, and other parts of the world began to draw increased attention to their demands for continued survival as distinct communities with historically based cultures, political institutions, and entitlements to land. These efforts led to a number of important international conferences and heightened attention from scholars and international nongovernmental organizations.

By the late 1970s, indigenous peoples' representatives began appearing before United Nations and other human rights bodies in increasing numbers and with increasing frequency, grounding their concerns on generally applicable human rights principles. Since that time, a steady stream of important developments and responses to the concerns of indigenous peoples has issued from the international human rights system. Indigenous peoples prompted the International Labour Organization (ILO) to discard *Convention No 107*'s assimilationist bias [and adopt] *ILO Convention No 169 of 1989*[18] ... The establishment of the United Nations Working Group on Indigenous Populations in 1982 and the ... United Nations Declaration on the Rights of Indigenous Peoples ... have focused even greater international attention on the protection of indigenous peoples' rights.

New international standards concerning the rights of indigenous peoples have significantly influenced the work of several international human rights bodies and other international institutions. The UN Human Rights Committee and the UN Committee on the Elimination of Racial Discrimination now regularly apply the prevailing understandings of indigenous peoples' rights reflected in the newly articulated standards. They draw heavily on these understandings when they monitor human rights situations involving indigenous groups. Even beyond the formal human rights process, the discourse of indigenous human rights now affects the lending processes of the

15 See also R Morgan, 'Advancing Indigenous Rights at the United Nations: Strategic Framing and its Impact on the Normative Development of International Law' (2004) 13 *Social and Legal Studies* 481; R Morgan, 'On Political Institutions and Social Movement Dynamics: The Case of the United Nations and the Global Indigenous Movement' (2007) 28 *International Politcial Science Review* 273, 276–8.

16 (2001) (14) *The Harvard Journal of Human Rights* 33, 33–5.

17 *Convention Concerning the Protection and Integration of Indigenous Populations and Other Tribal and Semi-Tribal Populations in the Independent Countries*, 1957 (No 107), General Conference of the International Labour Organization, 40th sess, C107 (adopted 26 June 1957, entered into force 2 June 1959).

18 *Convention Concerning Indigenous and Tribal Peoples in Independent Countries*, 1991, 169 *ILO* 1989 5 September.

World Bank, the Inter-American Development Bank, the European Union, and the domestic legislation and policies and judge-made law of states.

13.2.2 Declaration on the Rights of Indigenous Peoples

In 1982 the UN Subcommission on the Prevention of Discrimination and Protection of Minorities established a Working Group on Indigenous Populations (WGIP), comprising indigenous peoples and states' representatives, to develop a 'Draft Declaration on the Rights of Indigenous Peoples'.[19] In 1994, in time for the first International Decade of the World's Indigenous Peoples, the WGIP produced a draft, which remained under consideration by an inter-sessional Working Group of the Commission on Human Rights for a number of years.[20]

The delay is unsurprising when account is taken of what was at stake: 'The issues of indigenous peoples strike at the very core of the Westphalian state system and state sovereignty. Indigenous rights pertaining to consultation and participation, and more substantive rights relating to land, territories and resources are inextricably linked with dispossession and the exclusion of indigenous peoples from the institutions of the colonising state'.[21] As a result, agreement on the draft stalled on issues such as the respective roles in the drafting of states and representatives of indigenous peoples,[22] and the scope of the term 'indigenous peoples'.[23]

The most significant obstacle was recognition of the right to self-determination; a number of states, including Australia,[24] opposed recognition of that right, despite its being recognised as the right of 'all peoples' in article 1(1) of the ICCPR. Australia compounded the delay by proposing, in 2003, a substantial redrafting of the articles relating to land rights and resource development based primarily on a rejection of the principle of self-determination. Although supported by the 'CANZUS Group' (Canada, Australia, New Zealand and the United States), Australia's proposal did not have the support of the majority of states, and arose after 21 years of deliberation and nine years after the text was first proposed.[25]

19 See generally S Pritchard, 'The United Nations and the Making of a Declaration on Indigenous Rights' (1997) 3(89) *Aboriginal Law Bulletin* 4; the WGIP has been succeeded by the Expert Mechanism on the Rights of Indigenous Peoples: see Chapter 13.2.5 below.

20 For an account of the 'the long journey toward the Declaration undertaken by the international indigenous peoples movement' see M Davis, 'Indigenous Struggles in Standard-Setting: The United Nations Declaration on the Rights of Indigenous Peoples' (2008) 9(2) *Melbourne Journal of International Law* 439; see also R L Barsh, 'Indigenous Peoples and the UN Commission on Human Rights: A Case of the Immovable Object and the Irresistible Force' (1996) 18(4) *Human Rights Quarterly* 782; C Charters, 'The Road to the Adoption of the Declaration on the Rights of Indigenous Peoples' (2007) 4 *New Zealand Yearbook of International Law* 121.

21 M Davis, ibid 454.

22 Ibid 447.

23 Ibid 443.

24 See M Dodson & S Pritchard, 'Recent Developments in Indigenous Policy: The Abandonment of Self-Determination' (1998) 4(15) *Indigenous Law Bulletin* 4.

25 See the *Report of the WGIP to the 60th Session of the Commission on Human Rights*, E/CN.4/2004/81, [119]–[122]; see also *Technical Workshop on the Draft Declaration on the Rights of Indigenous Peoples, Workshop Report and Recommendations*, Human Rights and Equal Opportunity Commission, March 2004, Sydney, at <www.hreoc.gov.au/social_justice/technical/workshop.html>.

Australia, the US and New Zealand issued a notorious joint statement to explain their position on self-determination, saying that 'No government can accept the notion of creating different classes of citizens'.[26] No other state believed that that notion was a part of the draft declaration. Rather, the draft declaration recognised that 'different classes were created from the very beginning, as indigenous people were cleared off their lands and either treated as second class citizens, or, not even considered to be citizens in the first place'.[27]

In June 2006 the Human Rights Council resolved to adopt the draft Declaration;[28] of the CANZUS Group only Canada was a member of the Human Rights Council at the time, and it opposed the resolution. But the draft Declaration had to make its way through the United Nations General Assembly, and the Third Committee,[29] where it was unexpectedly opposed by a number of African states. They too were concerned about the provisions for self-determination, in terms very similar to those of the CANZUS Group.[30] The African concerns resulted in an amendment to the Preamble of the draft Declaration, which recognised that 'the situation of indigenous peoples varies from region to region and from country to country'.

When the *Declaration on the Rights of Indigenous Peoples* was adopted by the UN General Assembly on 13 September 2007,[31] the only votes against it were from the four members of the CANZUS Group.[32] Australia has since changed its position (after a change of government) and has formally advised the UN of its support for the Declaration.[33]

Having achieved a declaration, the next step might be to draft a treaty that would impose binding obligations on states, a pattern that was followed in relation to, for example, the rights of women and of people with disabilities. There are concerns, however, that by going down that path indigenous peoples would be setting themselves up to fail—there is a risk that a treaty on the rights of indigenous peoples would not attract enough ratifications to come into effect.[34] It may be, however, that state practice and conformity of domestic laws will demonstrate the necessary widespread acceptance of core principles to establish the Declaration as customary international law.[35]

---

26 H Rizvi, 'US, Australia, New Zealand Reject Indigenous Declaration' *InterPress Service Newsagency*, 24 May 2006, <http://ipsnews.net/news.asp?idnews=3335>.

27 A Shah, *Rights of Indigenous People*, Global Issues, 2010, <http://www.globalissues.org/article/693/rights-of-indigenous-people>.

28 A/HRC/1/L.3.

29 See Chapter 5.2.1.

30 M Davis, see above, n 20, 456–8.

31 *United Nations Declaration on the Rights of Indigenous Peoples*, GA Res 61/295, UN GAOR, 61st sess, 107th plen mtg, UN Doc A/RES/61/295 (13 September 2007).

32 K Wessendorf (ed), *The Indigenous World 2009*, International Working Group For Indigenous Affairs, Copenhagen, 584.

33 The Hon J Macklin MP, *Statement on the United Nations Declaration on the Rights of Indigenous Peoples*, 3 April 2009; Jenny Macklin, 'Federal Government Formally Endorses the Declaration on the Rights of Indigenous Peoples' (2009) 7(11) *Indigenous Law Bulletin* 6.

34 M Davis, see above, n 20, 467.

35 J Anaya & R A Williams, see above, n 1, 54–5; A Xanthaki, 'Indigenous Rights in International Law over the Last 10 Years and Future Developments Feature: Reflections on a Decade of International Law' (2009) 10 *Melbourne Journal of International Law* 27, 35–7.

13.2.3 Convention on the Elimination of All Forms of Racial Discrimination

The *Declaration on the Rights of Indigenous Peoples* is a non-binding, aspirational statement. The *International Convention on the Elimination of All Forms of Racial Discrimination* (ICERD), on the other hand, is a multilateral treaty that binds states to comply with its obligations.[36] Although not specifically concerned with the rights of indigenous peoples, the terms of ICERD encompass them.

Indigenous peoples are identified as such by reference to peoples living in the same state who are *not* indigenous—indigenous peoples are the people who were present when newly arrived people became dominant, and who retain social, cultural, economic and political characteristics that are distinct from the newer arrivals. Indigenous peoples are, therefore, of a different 'race' from that of the newer arrivals, within the broad idea of 'race, colour, descent, or national or ethnic origin' in the ICERD, remembering that a person's racial identity is based on 'self-identification'.[37]

It is therefore particularly appropriate to look to ICERD for provisions that protect the human rights of indigenous peoples, and the Committee on the Elimination of Racial Discrimination (ICERD Committee), which monitors states' compliance with the treaty,[38] has confirmed that discrimination against indigenous peoples falls under the scope of ICERD, and has called on states to include in their periodic reports full information on the situation of indigenous peoples.[39]

The terms of ICERD protect indigenous peoples from discrimination (article 2); racial segregation (article 3); and being the subject of incitement to racial hatred (article 4). ICERD guarantees indigenous peoples the rights to equality before the law (article 5(a)); physical security (article 5(b)); public participation (article 5(c)); and a host of civil, political, economic, social and cultural rights (articles 5(d) and (e)). The IERD Committee has commented on the treaty's fundamental non-discrimination provisions:[40]

> 6 … The principle of equality underpinned by the Convention combines formal equality before the law with equal protection of the law, with substantive or *de facto* equality in the enjoyment and exercise of human rights as the aim to be achieved by the faithful implementation of its principles.
>
> 7 The principle of enjoyment of human rights on an equal footing is integral to the Convention's prohibition of discrimination on grounds of race, colour, descent, and national or ethnic origin … Discrimination under the Convention includes purposive or intentional discrimination and discrimination in effect. Discrimination is constituted not simply by an unjustifiable 'distinction, exclusion or restriction' but also by an unjustifiable 'preference' …

36 See Chapter 7.37.

37 Committee for the Elimination of Racial Discrimination, *General Recommendation No 8: Identification with a Particular Racial or Ethnic Group*, 22 August 1990.

38 See Chapter 7.4.4.

39 Committee for the Elimination of Racial Discrimination, *General Recommendation No 23: Indigenous Peoples*, 51st sess, 18 August 1997.

40 Committee for the Elimination of Racial Discrimination, *General Recommendation No 32: The meaning and scope of special measures in the International Convention on the Elimination of Racial Discrimination*, 2–3.

8 ... The term 'non-discrimination' does not signify the necessity of uniform treatment when there are significant differences in situation between one person or group and another, or, in other words, if there is an objective and reasonable justification for differential treatment. To treat in an equal manner persons or groups whose situations are objectively different will constitute discrimination in effect, as will the unequal treatment of persons whose situations are objectively the same ...

9 The principle of non-discrimination ... protects the enjoyment on an equal footing of human rights and fundamental freedoms 'in the political, economic, social, cultural or any other field of public life.' The list of human rights to which the principle applies under the Convention is not closed and extends to any field of human rights regulated by the public authorities in the State party. The reference to public life does not limit the scope of the non-discrimination principle to acts of the public administration but should be read in light of provisions in the Convention mandating measures by States parties to address racial discrimination 'by any persons, group or organization' ...

As well as receiving communications from aggrieved individuals,[41] the CERD committee monitors the human rights of indigenous peoples by scrutinising state reports made under the treaty. States rarely volunteer the existence of human rights violations in their own country, and the Committee depends on information provided by NGOs, and its own questioning of the state representatives, to get a reasonable idea of the situation. The following Snapshot illustrates the interest that the CERD Committee can take in the situation of indigenous peoples, as well as the complacent attitude a state can adopt and the importance of an NGO's information.

SNAPSHOT: CERD OBSERVATIONS ON INDIGENOUS PEOPLES IN THE PHILIPPINES

In 2009 the CERD Committee considered the fifteenth to twentieth periodic reports of the Philippines.[42]

The Committee's report was informed by a 'shadow' report from a coalition of NGOs representing over 40 indigenous communities in the Philippines, people who 'are historically distinct from the majority of Filipinos in their success in resisting the Spanish colonial administration of the Philippines [and] maintained their indigenous belief systems, worldviews and ways of life while the Filipino majority was assimilated into the socio-cultural, economic and political system brought about by the Spanish conquistadores'.

The shadow report methodically addressed the state report and drew attention to the extensive discrimination, direct and indirect suffered by indigenous peoples.

In its observations on the Philippines' report the Committee was 'concerned' by the Philippines' denial that there is or ever has been racial discrimination in the country.

A significant number of the Committee's observations related to the Philippines' indigenous peoples: human rights violations against indigenous peoples innocently in armed conflict zones, internal displacement

41 See Chapter 7.4.7.

42 Committee on the Elimination of Racial Discrimination, *Concluding Observations: Philippines*, 23 September 2009, CERD/C/PHL/CO/20.

of indigenous peoples, threats to indigenous lands and resources by economic activity such as mining and failure to fully consult, the burdensome process for claiming land title, and the failure to ratify *ILO Convention No 169 concerning Indigenous and Tribal Peoples in Independent Countries*. The Committee drew particular attention to its recommendations concerning indigenous peoples and asked the Philippines for a detailed report on those issues in its next report.

13.2.4 Special Rapporteur

Operating under a mandate from the Human Rights Council, the Special Rapporteur on the Situation of Human Rights and Fundamental Freedoms of Indigenous People examines ways of overcoming obstacles to the full and effective protection of the rights of indigenous peoples, gathers information on alleged violations of the rights of indigenous peoples, and makes recommendations on appropriate measures such violations.[43] At the request of the Special Rapporteur, states issue an invitation for what is, effectively, a compliance inspection on the human rights situation of indigenous peoples, which is subsequently reported to the Human Rights Council.

Since 2002 the Special Rapporteur has visited and published country reports on Australia, Bolivia, Botswana, Brazil, Canada, Chile, Colombia, Ecuador, Ecuador, Guatemala, Guatemala, Kenya, Mexico, Nepal, New Zealand, Nordic countries' Saami People, Philippines, Russian Federation, and South Africa.[44]

SNAPSHOT: SPECIAL RAPPORTEUR VISIT TO NEW ZEALAND

The Special Rapporteur visited New Zealand in July 2010. During his visit, the Special Rapporteur heard complaints about the inherent lack of bargaining power on the part of Maori in the treaty settlement process, and in particular the recent refusal of the Government to allow for the possibility of the return of lands within the Urewera National Park to the Tuhoe iwi.

In a 'preliminary note' in advance of his full report,[45] the Special Rapporteur respectfully urged the New Zealand Government to reconsider its regarding the Tuhoe claim.

The Special Rapporteur recorded his agreement that the principles enshrined in the Treaty of Waitangi must be provided with constitutional security, noting that they appear to be in their perpetual insecurity and instability and vulnerable to political discretion.

43 On Special Rapporteurs generally, see Chapter 6.5; on the role and activity of the Special Rapporteur on the Situation of Human Rights and Fundamental Freedoms of Indigenous People, see J Preston, D Vinding, L Garcia-Alix, *The UN Special Rapporteur: Indigenous Peoples' Rights: Experiences and Challenges*, International Work Group for Indigenous Affairs, 2007; see above, n 32, 603.

44 See <http://www2.ohchr.org/english/issues/indigenous/rapporteur/countryreports.htm> at 12 April 2011; for the Special Rapporteur's first report to the General Assembly, see R Stavenhagen, 'Report of the Special Rapporteur on the Situation of Human Rights and Fundamental Freedoms of Indigenous People' (2005) 9(1) *Australian Indigenous Law Reporter* 102.

45 Special Rapporteur on the Situation of Human Rights and Fundamental Freedoms of Indigenous People, *Preliminary Note on the Mission to New Zealand*, Human Rights Council, 15th sess, A/HRC/15/37/Add 9.

Finally, the Special Rapporteur 'could not help but note' the extreme disadvantage in the social and economic conditions of Maori people, which are dramatically manifested in the continued and persistent high levels of incarceration of Maori individuals. In his view this undoubtedly resulted from the historical and ongoing denial of the human rights of Maori, which have to be addressed as a matter of upmost priority.

13.2.5 Expert Mechanism on the Rights of Indigenous Peoples

The Expert Mechanism on the Rights of Indigenous Peoples, a successor body to the previous Working Group on Indigenous Populations, is a subsidiary body of Human Rights Council.[46] It comprises five independent experts, and holds annual sessions with representatives from states, indigenous peoples, NGOs inter-governmental organisations and academics.

While the Special Rapporteur investigates and reports on violations and the situations in states, the Expert Mechanism provides the Council, on request, with studies and research on the rights of indigenous peoples, according to particular themes. In 2009 the Expert Mechanism made recommendations on how an indigenous peoples' right to education might be realised,[47] and it will report in 2011 on indigenous peoples' right to participate in decision making. These recommendations are directed to states to assist them in complying with and reporting under their treaty obligations.

13.2.6 United Nations Permanent Forum on Indigenous Issues

The UN Permanent Forum on Indigenous Issues (UNPFII) advises the Economic and Social Council on indigenous issues related to economic and social development, culture, the environment, education, health and human rights,[48] and so has a broader mandate than the activities of the Special Rapporteur and the Expert Mechanism associated with the Human Rights Council. It is comprised of sixteen independent experts, eight of whom are nominated by states and eight by indigenous organisations from prescribed regions: Africa; Asia; Central and South America and the Caribbean; the Arctic; Central and Eastern Europe, Russian Federation, Central Asia and Transcaucasia; North America; and the Pacific. Australia successfully nominated Professor Mick Dodson as an expert member of UPPFII for 2005–2010, and Associate Professor Megan Davis for the period 2011–2013.

From time to time the UNPFII has appointed its members as Special Rapporteurs, to report on specific themes. At the Sixth Session, Special Rapporteurs' reports were submitted on the impact of commercial tree plantations on indigenous peoples,[49] and on indigenous traditional knowledge.[50]

46 K Wessendorf, see above, n 32, 603.

47 The *Expert Mechanism Advice No 1 (2009) on the Right of Indigenous Peoples to Education* is annexed to the *Study on Lessons Learned and Challenges to Achieve the Implementation of the Right of Indigenous Peoples to Education* (A/HRC/12/33).

48 K Wessendorf, see above, n 32, 592.

49 V Tauli-Corpuz & P Tamang, *Oil Palm and Other Commercial Tree Plantations, Monocropping: Impacts on Indigenous Peoples' Land Tenure and Resource Management Systems and Livelihoods*, Permanent Forum on Indigenous Issues, 6th sess, 14–25 May 2007, UN Doc E/C 19/2007/CRP 6.

50 M Dodson, *Report of the Secretariat on Indigenous Traditional Knowledge*, Permanent Forum on Indigenous Issues, 6th sess, 14–25 May 2007, UN Doc E/C 19/2007/10 (2007).

UNPFII meets annually for 10 day sessions, and since 2007 has alternated biennially with an agenda of policy discussion and review. The implementation sessions do not have a theme. After its first session in 2002 the UNPFII has addressed the following issues, with 2009 and 2011 being review years:

Second Session 2003: Indigenous Children and Youth
Third Session 2004: Indigenous Women
Fourth Session 2005: Millennium Development Goals and Indigenous Peoples with a focus on Goal 1 to Eradicate Poverty and Extreme Hunger, and Goal 2 to achieve universal primary education
Fifth Session 2006: The Millennium Development Goals and indigenous peoples: Re-defining the Millennium Development Goals
Sixth Session 2007: Territories, Lands and Natural Resources
Seventh Session 2008: Climate change, bio-cultural diversity and livelihoods: the stewardship role of indigenous peoples and new challenges
Ninth Session 2010: Indigenous peoples: development with culture and identity; articles 3 and 32 of the United Nations Declaration on the Rights of Indigenous Peoples.

13.2.7 United Nations Voluntary Fund for Indigenous Populations

The Fund for Indigenous Populations is funded by voluntary contributions from Governments, non-governmental organisations and other private or public entities. It was established by the UN General Assembly in 1985 to assist representatives of indigenous communities and organisations to participate in the deliberations of relevant UN human rights bodies. The Fund is administered by the UN Secretary-General through the OHCHR, assisted by a Board of Trustees: five people with relevant experience on indigenous issues. The UN Secretary-General reports every two years to the UN General Assembly on the activities of the Fund.[51]

The Fund has allocated more than 1100 grants[52] to representatives of indigenous communities and organisations to participate in the deliberations of the Working Group on Indigenous Populations, to observe sessions of the Permanent Forum on Indigenous Issues, and to participate in the Expert Mechanism on the Rights of Indigenous Peoples. In 2010, with the support of the OHCHR, the Fund was extended to facilitate the participation of representatives of indigenous peoples' organisations in sessions of the Human Rights Council and of human rights treaty bodies.

13.2.8 International Decades of the World's Indigenous People

The UN General Assembly declared the period 1995–2004 the International Decade of the World's Indigenous People,[53] to strengthen international efforts to address issues of human rights, the environment, development, education and health for indigenous peoples. In a 2004 report on the Decade,[54] the UN Secretary-General summarised activities undertaken by the OHCHR, UN bodies, states

51 See eg *Status of the United Nations Voluntary Fund for Indigenous Populations—Report of the United Nations High Commissioner for Human Rights*, 65th sess, UNGA, 23 July 2010, A/65/163.

52 Office of the High Commissioner on Human Rights, *Practical Implications of a Change in the Mandate the Voluntary Fund for Indigenous Populations*, 15th sess, Human Rights Council, A/HRC/15/38.

53 GA Res 52/108, A/RES/52/108, 18 February 1998.

54 *Report of the Secretary-General on the Preliminary Review by the Coordinator of the International Decade of the World's Indigenous People on the Activities of the United Nations system in Relation to the Decade*, UN Doc E/2004/82; see also R Dunbar, 'The First Decade of Indigenous Peoples at the United Nations' (2006) 31(1) *Peace & Change* 58.

and NGOs. He reported that despite 'important institutional developments', indigenous peoples in many countries continue to be among the poorest and most marginalised. At that stage the *Declaration on the Rights of Indigenous Peoples*, one of the main objectives of the Decade, had yet not been achieved.

In 2004 the UN General Assembly resolved[55] that a second International Decade of the World's Indigenous People would commence on 1 January 2005,[56] with five main objectives: non-discrimination and inclusion of indigenous peoples in international, regional and national processes; full and effective participation of indigenous peoples, with free, prior and informed consent, in decisions that directly or indirectly affect them; ensuring development policies that are equitable and are culturally appropriate; setting 'concrete benchmarks' for the development of indigenous peoples, particularly women, children and youth; and strong monitoring and accountability mechanisms for international, regional and national legal, policy and operational frameworks.

Half way through the Second Decade, in 2010, the UN Secretary-General reported on information received from states, UN agencies and intergovernmental organisations, and NGOs.[57] He analysed progress made towards the objectives of the Decade, and concluded that while 'substantive advances' were made, there was a substantial gap between policy intentions and actual implementation of the specific objectives.

The Voluntary Fund for the Decade of Indigenous Peoples has supported NGO activities in both decades; those that were funded in 2011 are some indication of the work that is being done to advance the situation of indigenous peoples worldwide:[58] a Pacific regional committee for promotion and coordination of the Second Decade of the World's Indigenous Peoples; indigenous youth-led development in Cambodia; and an arts and cultural aboriginal youth leadership project in Saskatchewan. Other NGO projects were funded in Indonesia, Paraguay, Russia, Zimbabwe and Sierra Leone.

13.2.9 Regional Mechanisms

Outside the UN institutions and mechanisms, indigenous issues are dealt with extensively in individual states. There are as well some regional forums where policy and programs are designed and promoted, although not in Asia, where there is resistance to the idea of there being 'indigenous peoples',[59] or in the Pacific.

Africa

The African Commission on Human and Peoples' Rights, for example, has given a mandate to its Working Group on Indigenous Populations/Communities in Africa to promote and protect the rights of

55 A/RES/59/174.

56 Res 59/174; Programme of Action was adopted by GA Res 60/142 and is contained in document A/60/270, sect II.

57 *Report of the Secretary-General: Midterm Assessment of the Progress made in the Achievement of the Goal and Objectives of the Second International Decade of the World's Indigenous People*, 23 July 2010, UN Doc A/65/166.

58 Trust Fund on Indigenous Issues relating to the Second International Decade of the World's Indigenous People: see <http://www.un.org/esa/socdev/unpfii/en/second_trustfund.html>.

59 P Thornberry, see above, n 5, 38.

indigenous populations/communities. The Working Group conducts country visits on which it reports to the African Commission, engages in and publishes research, runs seminars and produces guidelines, and collaborates with international bodies such as the ILO and the Expert Mechanism on the Rights of Indigenous Peoples.[60]

SNAPSHOT: ACKNOWLEDGING INDIGENOUS PEOPLES IN RWANDA[61]

The issue of indigenous peoples' rights is not well known in Africa, and the Working Group has had an important role in sensitising many African states to it.

In Rwanda, for example, the term 'indigenous' is not encouraged and the Constitution refers to one national language, one culture, and a long common history. The term 'indigenous' has a negative connotation because it is understood to refer to one group in particular, the Batwa, and to emphasise their specific culture and issues they face, differently from the dominant groups, Hutus and Tutsis. It is feared that a discussion about 'indigenous peoples' will bring back ethnic tensions in Rwanda.

In 2008, the Working Group undertook a country visit to Rwanda. The mission met with the relevant stakeholders and visited indigenous communities outside Kigali. One of the Working Group members is himself from a Batwa community in Rwanda.

The Working Group's visit was crucial in discussing indigenous peoples in a way that would clarify the concept and consequently minimise apprehension towards indigenous peoples' rights.

Rwanda was called on to recognise its indigenous peoples in the *Declaration Of Indigenous Peoples* at The Second International Forum Of Indigenous Peoples Of Central Africa,[62] comprising indigenous peoples of Burundi, Cameroon, Gabon, Equatorial Guinea, the Central African Republic, Congo, Rwanda, Sao Tome and Principe and Chad.

The Americas

Neither the Organisation of American States (OAS) nor the Inter-American Commission has any particular mandate to monitor protect or promote the human rights of the region's indigenous peoples, although indigenous peoples have access to the Inter-American Commission's complaints process.[63]

60 See, eg, *46th Intersession Activity Report of the Chairperson of the Working Group on Indigenous Populations/ Communities in Africa*, November 2009, <http://www.achpr.org/english/_info/wgip_intersess.htm>.

61 Based on K Wessendorf (ed), see above, n 32, 639.

62 *Second International Forum of Indigenous Peoples of Central Africa* (FIPAC 2), para 1(d), Impfondo, 15 to 18 March 2011, <www.indigenouspeoplesissues.com> at 12 April 2011.

63 See the cases discussed in P Thornberry, see above, n 5, 274–9; and see Chapter 8.3.4 above.

The OAS has, however, been working for some years towards an *American Declaration on the Rights of Indigenous Peoples.*

A draft declaration was approved by the Inter-American Commission on Human Rights in 1997,[64] but progress, though continuing, is slow. The OAS appointed a Working Group of OAS member states in 1999, and for some years it deliberated privately, with no formal indigenous consultation or representation. It was not until 2003 that indigenous peoples from 25 states were included in the Working Group. A new draft ('the New Basic text') was agreed on in 2008, and negotiations are continuing over the final wording.[65] At the thirteenth meeting of the Working Group in January 2011, agreement was reached on three articles in the draft.

The Arctic

The Arctic Council is an intergovernmental forum made up of six international organisations representing Arctic indigenous peoples, and the states of Canada, Denmark (including Greenland and the Faeroe Islands), Finland, Iceland, Norway, the Russian Federation, Sweden and the United States of America. The Council deliberates and reports on issues such as sustainable development and environmental protection, maintenance of Arctic indigenous languages, and responding to climate change.[66]

Independently of the Arctic Council, the governments of Finland, Sweden and Norway have long been in negotiation with the Saami people over a proposed Nordic Saami Convention.[67] A draft convention, to 'allow the Saami people to safeguard and develop their language, culture, livelihoods and way of life with the least possible interference by national borders',[68] was proposed by a working party of experts in 2005, but negotiations have stalled on internal political considerations in Finland.[69] A convention will have to be adopted by the three national parliaments and the three Saami parliaments.

Europe

Although there is no specific provision in Europe for the human rights of indigenous peoples, indigenous groups have access to the individual rights mechanisms of the European Court of Human Rights.[70] But

64 *Proposed American Declaration on the Rights of Indigenous Peoples*, 26 February, 1997, 1333rd sess, 95th Regular Session OEA/Ser/L/V/.II.95 Doc.6 (1997).

65 Indian Law Resource Centre, *Current Situation of the Draft Declaration*, <http://ilrc.xinsys.net/projects/ihr/oas/draft> at 12 April 2011.

66 K Wessendorf, see above, n 32, 642–5.

67 See generally M Åhrén, M Scheinin & J B Henriksen, 'The Nordic Saami Convention: International Human Rights, Self-Determination and Other Central Provision' (2007) 3 *Gáldu čála—Journal of Indigenous Peoples Rights;* T Koivurova, 'The Draft Nordic Saami Convention: Nations Working Together' (2008) 10(3) *International Community Law Review*, 279.

68 Article 1, draft Nordic Saami Convention.

69 K Wessendorf, see above, n 32, 38–40.

70 P Thornberry, see above, n 5, 290, and see the cases discussed at 290–306.

there is increasing recognition of indigenous peoples in Europe, not only the Saami people of the Arctic but also the Roma.[71]

13.3 CURRENT ISSUES

A large number of very difficult human rights issues confront the world's indigenous peoples; self-determination, cultural practices and customary law are three such areas, discussed briefly below. Those areas are themselves very broad; they overlap significantly, and they encompass other important areas that are not discussed, such as land ownership,[72] environmental integrity,[73] ownership and exploitation of cultural knowledge,[74] the right to health,[75] and a right to development.[76]

In the area of intellectual property, the UN *Convention on Biological Diversity*[77] is particularly important: article 8(j) of the Convention affirms indigenous peoples' rights over their 'knowledge, innovations and practices', and their right to be involved, and share the benefits from, their application. In the area of development, the UN Development Group (UNDG) has produced *Guidelines on Indigenous Peoples' Issues* to states to assist in integrating indigenous peoples' issues into their policies and programs.[78]

71 P Thornberry, see above, n 5, 291.

72 See eg J Gilbert, *Indigenous Peoples' Land Rights under International Law: From Victims to Actors*, Brill, 2006; A Xanthaki, *Indigenous Rights and United Nations Standards: Self-Determination, Culture and Land*, Cambridge University Press, Cambridge, 2007, Ch 6, 237–78.

73 L Westra, *Environmental Justice and the Rights of Indigenous Peoples: International and Domestic Legal Perspectives*, Earthscan, London, 2008; D Schlosberg, *Defining Environmental Justice: Theories, Movements, and Nature*, Oxford University Press, USA, 2007, 79–99; G Di Chiro, 'Indigenous Peoples and Biocolonialism: Defining the "Science of Environmental Justice" in the Century of the Gene' in R Sandler and P C Pezzullo (eds), *Environmental Justice and Environmentalism: The Social Justice Challenge to the Environmental Movement*, MIT Press, 2007, 251–83; and see the discussion of socio-economic and environmental issues and the right to life for indigenous peoples in Chapter 3.5.6 above.

74 See, eg, P-T Stoll and A von Hahn, 'Indigenous Peoples, Indigenous Knowledge and Indigenous Resources in International Law' in S von Lewinski, *Indigenous Heritage and Intellectual Property: Genetic Resources, Traditional Knowledge, and Folklore*, Kluwer Law International, Netherlands, 2008, 8–57; M A Bengwayan, *Intellectual and Cultural Property Rights of Indigenous and Tribal Peoples in Asia*, Minority Rights Group International, London, 2003, <www.unhcr.org/refworld/pdfid/469cbf970.pdf> at 12 April 2011; L R Helfer, G W Austin, *Human Rights and Intellectual Property: Mapping the Global Interface*, Cambridge University Press, Cambridge, 2011, Ch 7, 432–502; I Mgbeoji, *Global Biopiracy: Patents, Plants and Indigenous Knowledge*, UBC Press, Vancouver, 2006; A Gupta, *Human Rights of Indigenous Peoples*, Vol 1, Gyan Publishing, New Delhi, 2005, 120–68.

75 See, eg, J Taylor, 'Indigenous Peoples and Indicators of Well-Being: Australian Perspectives on United Nations Global Frameworks' (2008) 87 *Social Indicators Research* 111; M Cooke, F Mitrou, D Lawrence, E Guimond & D Beavon, 'Indigenous Well-Being in Four Countries: An Application of the UNDP's Human Development Index to Indigenous Peoples in Australia, Canada, New Zealand and the United States' (2007) 7 *BMC International Health and Human Rights* 9.

76 D Aguirre, *The Human Right to Development in a Globalized World*, Ashgate, Aldershot, England ; Burlington, VT, 2008; M E Salomon and A Sengupta, *The Right to Development: Obligations of States and the Rights of Minorities and Indigenous Peoples*, Minority Rights Group International, 2003; A Gupta, *Human Rights of Indigenous Peoples*, Vol 1, Gyan Publishing, New Delhi, 2005, 169–220.

77 *United Nations Convention on Biological Diversity*, 5 June 1992 (entered into force 29 December 1993), 1760 UNTS 79.

78 United Nations Development Group, *Guidelines on Indigenous Peoples' Issues*, February 2008, <http://www 2.ohchr.org/english/issues/indigenous/docs/guidelines.pdf>.

13.3.1 Self-Determination

For indigenous peoples, the right to self-determination is the cornerstone of the *Declaration on the Rights of Indigenous Peoples*. Article 3 of the Declaration is in the same terms as article 1 of both the ICESCR and the ICCPR—but with specific reference to 'indigenous' peoples—stating their right to self-determination, and that it carries with it the right to 'freely determine their political status and freely pursue their economic, social and cultural development'.[79]

The reference to self-determination in the covenants was from a time when the drafters were looking ahead to post-colonial times, and were anticipating new states exercising their own democratic autonomy. The idea of 'self-determination' took on different implications when it arose in the context of indigenous peoples within established states.[80] States' opposition to the Declaration's reference to self-determination, described in Chapter 13.2.2 above, was based principally on these issues of state sovereignty and territorial integrity, and as well on the possible financial implications of compensation.

There are complex and unresolved issues concerning the right to self-determination in international law, most fundamentally between the a group's right of self-determination and a state's of sovereignty and security. As well, there are differences between definitions of self-determination in international law and in a broader political and advocacy context. But arguments for indigenous peoples' self-determination were sufficiently persuasive to see the right enshrined in the Declaration; those arguments included the emerging idea of a 'right of democratic governance' in international law, and the right to political participation recognised in the *UN Charter*, the UDHR and the ICCPR.[81] As a result, far from supporting secessionist movements, the Declaration assists states to implement the indigenous right to self-determination 'within a democratic system without disrupting public institutions or the rule of law'.[82] That means, for example, not necessarily self-government, but representative government, which is the 'clearest requirement'[83] for self-determination.

13.3.2 Right to Culture

The right to culture is particularly important to indigenous peoples: their enjoyment of their culture is commonly overwhelmed, and often actively suppressed or limited, by the dominant groups in society. The right to culture is protected under a number of the human rights treaties, in slightly different terms in keeping with the particular focus of the treaty, but the source of the various guarantees is

79 See Chapters 1.5.1 and 3.2.1.

80 See generally Elena Cirkovic, 'Self-Determination and Indigenous Peoples in International law' (2006–2007) 31 *American Indian Law Review* 375.

81 M Davis, see above, n 20, 459; R Morgan, see above, n 15, 485–92.

82 M Davis, see above, n 20, 459–60; C E Foster, 'Articulating Self-Determination in the Draft Declaration on the Rights of Indigenous Peoples' (2001) 12(1) *European Journal of International Law* 141, 148.

83 C E Foster, ibid 157.

article 27(1) of the *Universal Declaration of Human Rights*: 'everyone has the right freely to participate in the cultural life of the community'.

The United Nations Educational, Scientific and Cultural Organization (UNESCO) 2005 *Convention on the Protection and Promotion of the Diversity of Cultural Expressions* addresses the nature of culture/s:[84]

> 41 Cultures have no fixed borders. The phenomena of migration, integration, assimilation and globalization have brought cultures, groups and individuals into closer contact than ever before, at a time when each of them is striving to keep their own identity.
>
> 42 ... Far from having produced a single world culture, globalization has demonstrated that the concept of culture implies the coexistence of different cultures.
>
> 43 ... cultural activities, goods and services have economic and cultural dimensions, conveying identity, values and meanings. They must not be treated as having solely a commercial value.

In its *General Comment No 21*[85] the Committee on Economic Social and Cultural Rights (the CESCR Committee) considered the idea of culture, saying that

> 11 ... culture is a broad, inclusive concept encompassing all manifestations of human existence. The expression 'cultural life' is an explicit reference to culture as a living process, historical, dynamic and evolving, with a past, a present and a future.
>
> 13 ... culture, for the purpose of implementing article 15 (1) (a), encompasses, inter alia, ways of life, language, oral and written literature, music and song, non-verbal communication, religion or belief systems, rites and ceremonies, sport and games, methods of production or technology, natural and man-made environments, food, clothing and shelter and the arts, customs and traditions through which individuals, groups of individuals and communities express their humanity and the meaning they give to their existence, and build their world view representing their encounter with the external forces affecting their lives. Culture shapes and mirrors the values of well-being and the economic, social and political life of individuals, groups of individuals and communities.

Article 15(1)(a) of the ICESCR 'recognise[s] the right of everyone to take part in cultural life'. In *General Comment No 21* the CESCR Committee identifies 'persons and communities requiring special protection':[86] women, children, older persons, persons with disabilities, minorities, migrants, indigenous peoples, and persons living in poverty. In relation to indigenous peoples, the Committee says:[87]

> 36 ... The strong communal dimension of indigenous peoples' cultural life is indispensable to their existence, well-being and full development, and includes the right to the lands, territories and resources which they have traditionally owned, occupied or otherwise used or acquired. Indigenous peoples' cultural values and rights associated with their ancestral lands and their relationship with nature should be regarded with respect and protected, in order to prevent the

84 *UNESCO Convention on the Protection and Promotion of the Diversity of Cultural Expressions*, para 18, adopted at the General Conference of the United Nations Educational, Scientific and Cultural Organization, 33rd sess, Paris, 20 October 2005; also the *Universal Declaration on Cultural Diversity*, art 8.

85 Committee on Economic, Social and Cultural Rights, *General Comment No 21: Right of Everyone to Take Part in Cultural Life*, E/C.12/GC/21, 21 December 2009.

86 E1-8.

87 See above, n 85, footnotes omitted.

> degradation of their particular way of life, including their means of subsistence, the loss of their natural resources and, ultimately, their cultural identity ...
>
> 37 Indigenous peoples have the right to act collectively to ensure respect for their right to maintain, control, protect and develop their cultural heritage, traditional knowledge and traditional cultural expressions, as well as the manifestations of their sciences, technologies and cultures, including human and genetic resources, seeds, medicines, knowledge of the properties of fauna and flora, oral traditions, literature, designs, sports and traditional games, and visual and performing arts. States parties should respect the principle of free, prior and informed consent of indigenous peoples in all matters covered by their specific rights.

Article 27 of the ICCPR guarantees a person the right to 'enjoy their culture, to profess and practice their own religion, [and] to use his or her own language' in community with the other members of their group. As well, the ICCPR guarantees other rights that support a person's right to enjoy their own culture: the right to privacy (article 17); the right to freedom of thought, conscience and religion (article 18); right to hold opinions without interference (article 19); right not to be the subject of incitement to national, racial or religious hatred (article 20); the right of peaceful assembly (article 21); and the right to freedom of association (article 22).

Article 5(e)(iv) of the *International Convention on the Elimination of All Forms of Racial Discrimination* (ICERD) guarantees equality, without distinction as to race, in the enjoyment of economic social and cultural rights, in particular the right to 'equal participation in cultural activities'. The CERD Committee, in its *General Recommendation 23 on Indigenous Peoples*,[88] affirmed that the provisions of ICERD apply to indigenous peoples. It called on states to '[r]ecognize and respect indigenous distinct culture, history, language and way of life as an enrichment of the State's cultural identity and to promote its preservation', and to '[e]nsure that indigenous communities can exercise their rights to practise and revitalize their cultural traditions and customs and to preserve and to practise their languages'.[89]

Other treaties that recognise the right to culture are the *Convention on the Elimination of All Forms of Discrimination against Women* ('the right to participate in ... all aspects of cultural life': article 13(c)), the *Convention on the Rights of the Child* (the right 'to participate freely in cultural life and the arts': article 31(2), and in article 30 a right in the same terms as ICCPR article 27)), the *International Convention on the Protection of the Rights of All Migrant Workers and Members of Their Families* (equality in 'access to and participation in cultural life': article 43(1)(g)), and the *Convention on the Rights of Persons with Disabilities* (the right 'to take part on an equal basis with others in cultural life': article 30(1)).

SNAPSHOT: CHILDREN'S CONNECTION WITH THEIR INDIGENOUS CULTURE

In 1996 the UN Human Rights Committee in Geneva published its view[90] in relation to a communication it had received from X, an indigenous Australian man who was initiated as a member of the Arrente people. He was involved in court proceedings with his former wife, a non-indigenous woman, concerning the division of

88 Fifty-first sess, 1997 UN Doc.A/52/18, annex V.

89 Ibid para 4(a) and (e).

90 *X v Australia, Communication No 557/1993*, UN Doc CCPR/C/57/D/557/1993; 1 August 1996.

marital property and the custody of children. The court, concerned to protect the 'best interests' of the children, refused to allow evidence to be given in count of the children's Aboriginality, of the effect on indigenous peoples of their having been raised as 'whites' under Australia's assimilation policy, and of the way in which Australian Aboriginal children are raised and cared for in an extended family.

X complained to the Human Rights Committee that the refusal to allow this evidence denied him the right to a fair hearing before a court, which is guaranteed by ICCPR article 14(1).

Further, the court refused to allow evidence of X's concerns to ensure that his children be educated in Aboriginal religious and moral customs. X complained that this denied him the right to adopt and manifest his beliefs guaranteed by ICCPR art 18(1). And X complained that the judge had insisted on a full explanation of his initiation ceremony, making public sacred knowledge of the Arrente people and so denying him the right to enjoy his culture and practise his religion, guaranteed by ICCPR article 27.

Although the Human Rights Committee ruled the communication inadmissible because X had not exhausted all domestic remedies, the issues raised by X resulted in amendments to the Australian *Family Law Act 1975* (Cth), so that ss 61F and 68CC(3)(h) now require the court, when deciding the best interests of a child, to consider the child's need to maintain a connection with Aboriginal lifestyle, culture and traditions. Subsequent Family Court cases have been decided very differently from the way X complained that the court approached his matter.[91]

Limits on the Right to Culture

A limitation on the right in article 27 of the ICCPR to enjoy culture is that it cannot be exercised inconsistently with other human rights.[92] These include, relevantly for some indigenous cultural practices, equality of rights between men and women,[93] and the right not to be subjected to torture.

Both article 7 of the ICCPR and the *Convention Against Torture and Other Cruel, Inhuman or Degrading Treatment or Punishment* (CAT)[94] set bounds on the legitimacy of some cultural practices. CAT prohibits torture and cruel, inhuman or degrading treatment, as it will be arguable in some circumstances that customary practices, such as the infliction of physical punishment, female genital mutilation[95] and culturally sanctioned domestic violence, amount to the infliction of torture. Whether it is in fact torture is 'context-specific', depending on the particular circumstances, as the Australian Aboriginal and Torres Strait Islander Social Justice Commissioner has argued.[96] Nevertheless, human rights standards do set outer boundaries for indigenous customary practices.

91 See, for example, *Davis & Spring* [2007] FamCA 1149.

92 See the discussion in *General Comment No 23: The Rights of Minorities* (art 27), Human Right Committee, Geneva, 1994, CCPR/C/21/Rev 1/Add.5

93 Article 3.

94 Articles 1 and 16.

95 See, for example, *Fact Sheet 23: Harmful Traditional Practices Affecting the Health of Women and Children*, Office of the High Commissioner for Human Rights, Geneva, at <http://www.ohchr.org/Documents/Publications/FactSheet23en.pdf>, where the practice is identified as a breach as well of art 24 of the *Convention on the Rights of the Child*.

96 *Submission to the Northern Territory Law Reform Committee Inquiry into Aboriginal Customary Law in the Northern Territory*, Aboriginal and Torres Strait Islander Social Justice Commissioner of the Human Rights and Equal Opportunity Commission, Sydney, 2003, 29.

13.3.3 Customary Law

Article 12 of the *Declaration on the Rights of Indigenous Peoples* recognises indigenous peoples'

> right to manifest, practise, develop and teach their spiritual and religious traditions, customs and ceremonies; the right to maintain, protect, and have access in privacy to their religious and cultural sites; the right to the use and control of their ceremonial objects; and the right to the repatriation of their human remains.

These rights are not, however, merely declared aspirations. As a matter of customary international law, 'each culture has a dignity and a value which must be respected and preserved; every people has the right and the duty to develop its culture; [and] … all cultures form part of the common heritage belonging to all mankind'.[97] Further, article 27 of the ICCPR obliges states to respect minorities' right to 'enjoy their culture, to profess and practise their own religion'. There is, therefore, clear support in international law for the relevance of tradition and custom to matters that are decided in domestic legal system, such as custody of children or the imposition of punishment for a crime.

As a general proposition, there is a fundamental difference between the usual approaches of customary law and the law of developed states to dealing with crime:[98]

> … indigenous law consists of a series of unwritten oral principles that are abided by and socially accepted by a specific community. Although these norms may vary from one community to another, they are all based on the idea of recommending appropriate behaviour rather than on prohibition.
>
> … customary indigenous law aims to restore the harmony and balance in a community; it is essentially collective in nature, whereas the Western judicial system is based on individualism. Customary law is based on the principle that the wrongdoer must compensate his or her victim for the harm that has been done so that he or she can be reinserted into the community, whereas the Western system seeks punishment.

Customary law does, however, have its punitive dimensions, and when customary punishment inflicts physical harm it is likely to violate international human rights standards. The issue of reconciling competing rights is a challenging one, not only in Australia but throughout the world. It inevitably invites debate about the 'relativity' of rights, but can be understood as a debate concerning the implementation of measures in a particular place, and how best in the circumstances to reconcile universal and fundamental human rights with local custom.

This is the approach recommended by the Australian Law Reform Commission (ALRC) in its very substantial report on Aboriginal customary laws. The ALRC's report considered the application of criminal law to indigenous defendants, including whether a new defence should be recognised based on customary laws and whether customary laws should themselves be imported into the general legal system in some way. On reconciling customary law and human rights standards, the ALRC proposed that 'each case must be considered in its own context and in relation to the most precise or "directly

97 *Declaration of the Principles of International Cultural Co-operation*, UNESCO, 1966, art 1.

98 A Shah, 'Rights of Indigenous People' *Global Issues* 2010, <http://www.globalissues.org/article/693/rights-of-indigenous-people>, quoting Guisela Mayén, quoted by L Reynolds in 'Mayan Law Still Lacks Official Recognition' *Latin America Press*, October 6, 2006.

applicable" [ICCPR] provision. Whether the [ICCPR] has been violated depends not merely on the terms of the local law but on the method and circumstances in which it has been applied'.[99]

One of the more difficult issues that arises in relation to customary law is when its practice is inconsistent with human rights standards. In some parts of Australia, courts are well practised in the pragmatic exercise of resolving indigenous customary practices and Australian law. Nevertheless, there are times when the issues are confronting and difficult, as the following snapshot illustrates.

SNAPSHOT: CUSTOMARY LAW AND CRIMINAL SENTENCING

In the Australian Northern Territory (NT), an Aboriginal man was sentenced to 13 months' imprisonment for sexual relations with a minor, a 15-year-old girl. The defendant did not rely on his compliance with customary law as a defence, but as a factor in mitigation in sentencing. An appeal court reduced the sentence to imprisonment for a day, in response to the defendant's claim that the sexual relations were 'culturally appropriate' as the girl had been promised to him as his wife.

A further appeal court reviewed the evidence of indigenous people and anthropologists regarding the relevant customs, and considered the Australian Law Reform Commission's report *The Recognition of Aboriginal Customary Laws*.[100] Imposing a 12-month sentence, the Chief Justice said that: 'notwithstanding the cultural circumstances surrounding this particular event, the protection given by the law to girls under the age of 16 from sexual intercourse is a value of the wider community, which prevails over that of this section of the Aboriginal community'.[101]

When debating a proposed amendment to the NT *Sentencing Act* that would remove customary law as a relevant factor in sentencing for sexual assault of a minor, the NT parliament referred to article 23(2) of the ICCPR, which guarantees a right to enter marriage only with free and full consent, and article 24 of the CROC, which guarantees freedom from sexual exploitation and abuse.

The amendment was not made, but the Australian Parliament subsequently legislated to prohibit, only in the NT, any account being taken of customary law as an exculpatory or aggravating factor in sentencing.[102] Judicial interpretation has determined, however, that the provision does 'not remove all consideration of customary law and cultural practice from the sentencing process'.[103]

13.4 CONCLUSION AND ISSUES

Recognising the human rights of indigenous peoples is a very challenging task for states. The difficulty stems from the fact that an assertion by indigenous peoples of their human rights is fundamentally at odds with their having lived, for at least decades and sometimes centuries, as part of a different

99 *The Recognition of Aboriginal Customary Laws*, Australian Law Reform Commission, Report No 31, Canberra, AGPS, 1986, Summary [192].

100 Ibid.

101 *Jamilmira v Hales* [2003] NTCA 9 [26].

102 Section 91 *Northern Territory National Emergency Act 2007* (Cth).

103 *R v Wunungmurra* [2009] NTSC 24.

dominant socio-political system. Many of the human rights that are especially important to indigenous peoples are in the areas of life that have been the subject of norms and rules imposed by the later dominant society, ranging from organisation of family to use of land, from criminal justice to religious worship.

The human right of self-determination is in many ways emblematic of the challenge that indigenous peoples' human rights pose: it demands that difference be recognised, valued and respected, not only on an individual basis, and not only in some area of life, but fundamentally in the structure and governance of states. Within the right to self-determination issues arise that bring in an additional, and in some ways even more difficult, consideration: the right of indigenous peoples to use, exploit and profit from land and knowledge that was theirs until it was lost to the later dominant society. Claims to such a right challenge not only the state, but extensive and powerful private profit-making interests, locally and internationally.

14 PEOPLE WITH DISABILITIES

CONTENTS

14.1 INTRODUCTION

People with disabilities have only recently come from the wings into the centre stage of international human rights. This chapter first notes the history of people with disabilities as people who were locked away, out-of-sight-out-of-mind, oppressed by a medical model that focused only on impairment, and took no account of social barriers, the most pervasive of which was—and still is—attitude and perception.

When the medical model of disability gave way to a social model, people with disabilities could claim their entitlement to enjoy universal human rights, an entitlement that was recognised very quickly through the adoption of the *Convention on the Rights of Persons with Disabilities*.

There are difficulties with terminology when discussing people with disabilities, and those difficulties were a matter of some debate in the drafting of the Convention. The difficulty turns on the difference between a person's having a disability and their having an impairment. An impairment is a medical status, while a disability is a social phenomenon. A person with an impairment may not, in particular circumstances, or often, or at all, be disabled. A person who is disabled has an impairment that proves to be a barrier to, for example, their social participation or access. In discussion of law and policy there will be times when what is being dealt with is the fact that a person has an impairment, and times when what is being dealt with is the fact that a person with an impairment has a disability. It was just such a distinction that caused confusion in debates at the drafting of the Convention. For the sake of consistency this chapter refers throughout to people with disabilities.

14.1.1 The Idea of Disability

There is extensive continuing debate about how 'disability' can and should be understood. The debate is important to the human rights of people with disabilities, because deciding what human rights are of particular importance to people with disabilities, and how they are best realised, will turn on how the idea of being disabled is understood:

> How societies divide 'normal' and 'abnormal' bodies is central to ... what it means to be human in society. It defines access to nations and communities. It determines choice and participation in civic life. It determines what constitutes 'rational' men and women and who should have the right to be part of society and who should not.[1]

Medical and Social Disability Models

The traditional approach to disability[2] has been to see it as a personal impairment, as

> a health and welfare issue, to be addressed through care provided to persons with disabilities in the form of charitable handouts and similar measures. Persons with disabilities have been viewed as abnormal, deserving of pity and care, and not as individuals who are entitled to enjoy the same opportunities to live a full and satisfying life as other members of society. As a consequence, persons with disabilities have been marginalized and excluded both from the mainstream of society, and have been denied, or significantly limited in the enjoyment of, their fundamental human rights and freedoms.[3]

This is what has come to be called the 'medical model', which 'identif[ies] people with disabilities as ill, different from their non-disabled peers, and in need of care [with] a corresponding neglect of their wider social needs'.[4] It is supported by underlying assumptions of: 'otherness'—that people with disabilities are inferior; of 'spread'—that a person disabled in one way is disabled in others; and of

1 H Meekosha & R Shuttleworth, 'What's So "Critical" about Critical Disability Studies?' (2009) 15(1) *Australian Journal of Human Rights* 47, 65.

2 For an overview of approaches to disability in the nineteenth and twentieth centuries, see D Pfeiffer, 'Overview of the Disability Movement: History, Legislative Record, and Political Implications' (1993) 21(4) *Policy Studies Journal* 724.

3 *Report of the United Nations Consultative Expert Group Meeting on International Norms and Standards Relating to Disability* 8–12 December 1998 <http://www.un.org/esa/socdev/enable/disberk0.htm>.

4 Ibid.

'devaluation'—that a person who is flawed is without value and, at an extreme, has a life not worth living.[5] As the United Nations Consultative Expert Group describes:[6]

> [i]n recent years ... this approach has been superseded by a broader understanding of disability, sometimes referred to as the 'social model'. This analysis recognises that the circumstances of people with disabilities and the discrimination they face are socially created phenomena and have little to do with the impairments of people with disabilities.
>
> This is a critical reorientation of perspective, which has important implications for the way in which law and policy in relation to disability are developed, as well as for its substantive content. It focuses on the many ways in which the existing social environment places barriers in the way of persons with disabilities who seek to carry out the usual activities of everyday life and to participate in the full range of activities in society. Thus, this model sees the problem not as residing in the person with a disability, but as resulting from the structures, practices and attitudes that prevent the individual from exercising his or her capabilities: the cure to the problem of disability lies in restructuring society.

The social model of disability recognises that

> many impairments are not misfortunes foisted on individuals by the hand of fate, but are bound up in the way societies are structured, that is, in the way entitlements are determined and resources are distributed. They are bound up with technologies used in everyday life and with the way individuals interact with one another. Their social construction is accordingly revealed in the extent to which they are patterned in accord with gender, class, age, race and religion in any given society and, on a global scale, in accord with levels of resources and access to potentially mediating technologies.[7]

Disability is recognised, therefore, 'not so much an inherent quality of individuals [but] as a consequence, on the one hand, of societal failure to accommodate the needs created by impairment and, on the other, of the creation of obstructions (lack of opportunity, lack of access, lack of respect and assurance of dignity)'.[8]

The social model of disability has been described as an 'emancipatory force in the lives of many disabled people', enabling people with disabilities to see that the discrimination and social exclusion they face is not 'their own fault', and placing responsibility for that discrimination and exclusion 'at the door of a normalising society that has rigidly developed and maintained structures designed to create a docile workforce', and that has 'reward[ed] those who most closely conform to socially prescribed ideal models of appearance and behaviour'.[9]

---

5 H G Gallagher, '"Slapping Up Spastics": The Persistence of Social Attitudes toward People with Disabilities' (1994–1995) 10 *Issues of Law and Medicine* 401, 411.

6 See above, n 3, quoting *South African Integrated National Disability Strategy*, White Paper Office of the Deputy President of South Africa, 1997.

7 C Baylies, 'Disability and the Notion of Human Development: Questions of Rights and Capabilities' (2002) 17(7) *Disability & Society* 725, 726; and see R Kayess & P French, 'Out of Darkness into Light? Introducing the Convention on the Rights of Persons with Disabilities' (2008) 8(1) *Human Rights Law Review* 1, 5–12.

8 C Baylies, ibid 728.

9 C Tregaskis, 'Social Model Theory: The Story So Far ...' (2002) 17(4) *Disability & Society* 457, 457; and see T Burchardt, 'Capabilities and Disability: The Capabilities Framework and the Social Model of Disability' (2004) 19(7) *Disability & Society* 735, 735–7.

Further Thinking

Understandings of disability continue to develop, and the social model has been subject to intellectual analysis—not rejection so much as refinement.[10] A complementary way of seeing disability within a 'capabilities' framework was developed by economists and political philosophers[11] in reaction to the utilitarian basis of modern welfare economics and liberal political thought.[12] The capability framework is a political policy theory that expects the state to take steps to ensure that everyone is able to enjoy their full capabilities. It is not exclusively concerned with disability, as a range of other factors (eg poverty) may limit persons' being able to achieve their capabilities. But it has implications for conceptualising disability, and for how the state sets priorities for addressing barriers faced by people with disabilities,[13] and can be seen as a theoretical approach that encompasses the pragmatic dimensions of social model of disability.[14]

Critical disability studies are further development of the social model, 'incorporating a more complex conceptual understanding of disability oppression [in a way] that nevertheless still employs key ideas about disability that saw the light of day with the ascendance of the social model'.[15] A critical approach to disability looks beyond recognising social, economic and political barriers, and is open to psychological, cultural and psychoanalytic analyses.[16] It aims to 'bring some of the challenges faced by disabled people to the forefront of public discourse', representing 'the latest marginalised group with a political agenda to connect with critical social theory in its present form'.[17]

Another intellectual development is the proposition that there are elements of resistance theory in the social model, grounded as it is in addressing oppressive social processes.[18] And beyond the

10 But see T Shakespeare & N Watson, 'The Social Model of Disability: An Outdated Ideology?' in S N B & B M Altman (ed), *Exploring Theories and Expanding Methodologies: Where We Are and Where We Need to Go, Research in Social Science and Disability*, Vol 2, Emerald Group Publishing Limited, Bingley, UK, 9–28.

11 eg M Nussbaum & A Sen, (eds), *The Quality of Life*, Oxford University Press, 1993; M Nussbaum, 'Human Capabilities, Female Human Beings' in M Nussbaum and J Glover (eds), *Women, Culture and Development: A Study of Human Capabilities*, Clarendon Press, Oxford 61–104.

12 T Burchardt, see above, n 9, 735; and see C Baylies, above, n 7; M Stein & P Stein, 'Beyond Disability Civil Rights' (2006–2007) 58 *Hastings Law Journal* 1203, 1216–21.

13 See D Wasserman, 'Disability, Capability and Thresholds for Distributive Justice' in A Kaufman, (ed) *Capabilities Equality: Basic Issues and Problems*, Routledge, 2006, 214–34; M S Stein, *Distributive Justice & Disability: Utilitarianism Against Egalitarianism*, Yale University Press, New Haven, 2006, 187–9.

14 T Burchardt, see above, n 9, 736.

15 H Meekosha & R Shuttleworth, see above, n 1, 50; see generally R F Devlin and D Pothier, *Critical Disability Theory: Essays in Philosophy, Politics, Policy and Law*, UBC Press, 2006; M Corker and T Shakespeare, *Disability/Postmodernity: Embodying Disability Theory*, Continuum International Publishing, London, 2002.

16 H Meekosha & R Shuttleworth, see above, n 1, 57.

17 H Meekosha & R Shuttleworth, see above, n 1, 65.

18 S Gabel & S Peters 'Presage of a Paradigm Shift? Beyond the Social Model of Disability Toward Resistance Theories of Disability' (2004) 19(6) *Disability & Society* 585, 592.

social model is an approach that promotes 'disability culture', a 'non-tragic' view of disability that 'encompasses positive social identities, both individual and collective, for disabled people grounded in the benefits of life style and life experience of being impaired and disabled'.[19]

It seems that theorists and people with disabilities are using 'eclectic theories ... while they are identifying their work as within the social model', a process that, '[r]ather than weakening the social model ... actually strengthens it'.[20] The importance of the social model is that, developed from the 'struggle of disabled people for the realisation of their civil rights',[21] it informed the design of the UN *Convention on the Rights of Persons with Disabilities*.

14.2 THE INTERNATIONAL FRAMEWORK

14.2.1 Towards a Treaty

The new thinking about disability described above influenced the UN, causing it to reflect on the ideas of disability that had informed earlier international instruments.[22] The UN saw, for example, that instruments such as the 1971 *Declaration on the Rights of Mentally Retarded Persons*, and the 1975 *Declaration on the Rights of Disabled Persons*, were 'based on assumptions and analyses ... which persons with disabilities would today consider inappropriate or offensive.'[23] Both were heavily qualified by their medical/welfare approach, and tended to be paternalistic, legitimising segregation through specialised services and institutions.[24]

Impetus towards an international convention began with the UN International Year of Disabled Persons in 1981,[25] an event that raised disability as a human rights issue in the global public discourse.[26] It led to adoption by the UN of a World Programme of Action Concerning Disabled Persons (WPA),[27] which had as a goal the equalisation of opportunities for people with disabilities,[28] and placed priority

19 J Swain & S French, 'Towards an Affirmation Model of Disability' (2000) 15(4) *Disability & Society* 569, 569.

20 See above, n 18, 597.

21 C Baylies, see above, n 7, 725.

22 For an overview of the building momentum towards the *Convention on the Rights of Persons with Disabilities*, see A Lawson, 'The United Nations and the Convention on the Rights of Persons with Disabilities: New Era or False Dawn?' (2006–2007) 34 *Syracuse Journal of International Law and Commerce* 563.

23 See above, n 3.

24 R Kayess & P French, see above, n 7, 14.

25 UNGA Res 31/123 of 16 December 1976.

26 H Meekosha & R Shuttleworth, see above, n 1, 47.

27 *World Program of Action Concerning Disabled Persons*, UNGA Res. 37/52, 3 December 1982, A/RES/37/52, 37th Sess Supp No 51.

28 Ibid para 12.

on the use of UN instruments and international organisations.[29] The emphasis in the WPA on achieving accessibility in 'the physical and cultural environment, housing and transportation, social and health services, educational and work opportunities, cultural and social life, including sports and recreational facilities' was the start of the move in international law and practice towards recognising and acting on a social model of disability,[30] and set a direction for the UN International Decade of Disabled Persons 1983–1992.

The social model of disability was given further impetus as a basis for international action when, at the request of the UN Economic and Social Council, the UN Sub-Commission on Prevention of Discrimination and Protection of Minorities appointed a Special Rapporteur 'to conduct a comprehensive study on the relationship between human rights and disability'. In the resulting report, *Human Rights and Disabled Persons*, the Special Rapporteur 'warned' the international community that 'to deal correctly with this topic it is essential to rid ourselves of any feelings of pity or commiseration'. He continued:[31]

> 5 ... We are not dealing with a strictly humanitarian problem, still less with a situation requiring our charity. Far from that, the treatment given to disabled persons defines the innermost characteristics of a society and highlights the cultural values that sustain it.
>
> 6 It might appear elementary to point out that persons with disabilities are human beings - as human as, and usually even more human than, the rest. The daily effort to overcome impediments and the discriminatory treatment they regularly receive usually provides them with special personality features, the most obvious and common of which are integrity, perseverance, and a deep spirit of comprehension and patience in the face of a lack of understanding and intolerance. However, this last feature should not lead us to overlook the fact that as subjects of law they enjoy all the legal attributes inherent in human beings and hold specific rights in addition.

One result of the Decade of Disabled Persons 1983–1992 was promulgation of the *Standard Rules on the Equalization of Opportunities for Persons with Disabilities*,[32] which operated as a precursor to a formal convention, and in 1991 the United Nations adopted the *Principles for the Protection of Persons with Mental Illness and the Improvement of Mental Health Care*.[33] Although they were concerned to protect people with mental illness against human rights abuses, the Principles were

29 See above, n 27, paras 163–66.

30 R Kayess & P French, see above, n 7, 15; and see G Quinn & T Degener 'The Application of Moral Authority: The Shift to the Human Rights Perspective on Disability through United Nations "Soft Law"' in G Quinn & T Degener (eds), *Human Rights and Disability: The Current Use and Future Potential of United Nations Human Rights Instruments in the Context of Disability*, Office of the High Commissioner for Human Rights, United Nations, 2002, 19–36; note also a version online at <http://unipd-centrodirittiumani.it/public/docs/HRDisabilityen.pdf>.

31 L Despouy, Special Rapporteur of the UN Subcommission on Prevention of Discrimination and Protection of Minorities, *Human Rights and Disabled Persons*, Human Rights Studies Series, Number 6, Centre for Human Rights, Geneva 1993, E/CN.4/Sub.2/1991/31, paras 5 and 6; New York: Bantam Books, 1988; <http://www.un.org/esa/socdev/enable/dispaperdes0.htm>.

32 UN GA Res 48/96 of 20 December 1993.

33 GA Res 46/119, 17 December 1991.

controversial for their perpetuation of the medical model of disability through their focus on treatment and protection.[34]

In 1994 the UN Committee on Economic, Social and Cultural Rights, responsible for monitoring the implementation of the *International Covenant on Economic, Social and Cultural Rights* (ICESCR), issued *General Comment 5*,[35] described as 'a milestone in the process of developing disability as a human rights issue':[36]

> The [ICESCR] does not refer explicitly to persons with disabilities. Nevertheless, the *Universal Declaration of Human Rights* recognizes that all human beings are born free and equal in dignity and rights and, since the Covenant's provisions apply fully to all members of society, persons with disabilities are clearly entitled to the full range of rights recognized in the Covenant. In addition, insofar as special treatment is necessary, States parties are required to take appropriate measures, to the maximum extent of their available resources, to enable such persons to seek to overcome any disadvantages, in terms of the enjoyment of the rights specified in the Covenant, flowing from their disability. Moreover, the requirement contained in article 2 (2) of the Covenant that the rights 'enunciated … will be exercised without discrimination of any kind' based on certain specified grounds 'or other status' clearly applies to discrimination on the grounds of disability.

The UN Consultative Expert Group Meeting on International Norms and Standards Relating to Disability proposed a new international instrument on the human rights of people with disabilities in 1998, but were not able to get it onto the agenda of the UN General Assembly.[37] Momentum was building however. The UN Commissioner of Human Rights commissioned research and a report into the effectiveness of UN human rights instruments in responding to and addressing disability, which was published in 2002.[38]

Perhaps the tipping point came when the UN's Millennium Development Goals failed to identify people with disabilities as a specific target group for action 'even though this group is significantly over-represented among the world's so-called "poorest of the poor"'.[39] This omission led to a campaign

34 R Kayess & P French, see above, n 7, 15.

35 *Official Records of the Economic and Social Council*, 1995, Supp No 3 (E/1995/22), annex IV.

36 *Report of the Special Rapporteur of the Commission for Social Development on Monitoring the Implementation of the Standard Rules on the Equalization of Opportunities for Persons with Disabilities on His Third Mandate*, 2000–2002, E/CN.5/2002/4 at [62].

37 G Quinn & T Degener, see above, n 30, 21; note also a version online at <http://unipd-centrodirittiumani.it/public/docs/HRDisabilityen.pdf>.

38 G Quinn & T Degener (eds), *Human Rights and Disability: The Current Use and Future Potential of United Nations Human Rights Instruments in the Context of Disability*, Office of the High Commissioner for Human Rights, United Nations, 2002; note also a version online at <http://unipd-centrodirittiumani.it/public/docs/HRDisabilityen.pdf>.

39 R Kayess & P French, see above, n 7, 17, citing World Health Organisation (WHO) estimates that, of the 650 million people with disabilities in the world, 80 percent live in the developing world.

for a specific human rights instrument, to ensure that people with disabilities were not left behind in global development efforts.[40]

Why a 'Special' Treaty?

The omission from the Millennium Development Goals of mention of people with disabilities only continued the pattern of omissions that had been seen in previous human rights instruments.[41] But it might be asked why, if human rights are universal, there is a need for specific consideration of the human rights of a particular group. The same question has been asked in relation to women (Chapter 16.5.4), indigenous peoples (Chapter 13.1) and children (Chapter 12.2.2).

The need is not to create new or special human rights, but to give visibility to groups in society who, because of their marginalised and dis-empowered social and political status, do not enjoy the benefits of their human rights.[42] Critical perspectives on disability, noted above, show the limits inherent in the liberal assumption that 'all' people have real access to 'universal' rights. The medical model of disability effectively disentitled people with disabilities from being included among all people for purposes of access to human rights. The limited access that people with disabilities have had to existing human rights mechanisms is illustrated by the strikingly small number of individual complaints of human rights violations made by people with disabilities under the ICCPR: just eight of the 244 communications that had been by 2002.[43]

As there is a feminist debate about the relative merits of mainstreaming and separatism,[44] so there is among disability advocates. The debate took place as steps were being taken towards the very mainstream approach of a new international human rights treaty, and those who would maintain a specialised single-issue campaign were pitted against those who would emphasise the legitimacy of their claims in the broader human rights movement.[45] Ultimately, however, in large part because of the inclusive drafting process for the treaty described in the next section, bringing disability advocacy into the mainstream of human rights advocacy appears to have been an empowering experience for people with disabilities.[46]

40 R Kayess & P French, see above, n 7, 17.

41 R Kayess & P French, see above, n 7, 12.

42 See A Lawson, above, n 22, 583–5.

43 A Lawson, see above, n 22, 578, citing T Degener 'Disability and Freedom: The International Covenant on Civil and Political Rights' in G Quinn & T Degener (eds), *Human Rights and Disability: The Current Use and Future Potential of United Nations Human Rights Instruments in the Context of Disability*, Office of the High Commissioner for Human Rights, United Nations, 2002, 48.

44 See Chapter 16.1.

45 J Mertus, 'Politics' in D Moeckli, S Shah & S Sivakumaran, *International Human Rights Law*, Oxford University Press, Oxford, 2010, 87–100, 95–6.

46 Ibid 96.

The Drafting Process

In 2001 the UN General Assembly established the Ad Hoc Committee on a Comprehensive and Integral International Convention on the Protection and Promotion of the Rights and Dignity of Persons with Disabilities, which in turn established a Working Group of 27 governmental and 12 NGO representatives to prepare a draft text of a treaty. The draft was developed in regular meetings until 2006, when a final draft was referred to the UN General Assembly.

It was a distinctive aspect of the drafting process, unprecedented in the normal course of UN treaty development,[47] that NGOs representing people with disabilities had a formal and significant role. Their inclusion was a sign of the philosophy of inclusiveness that underpins the treaty and it was decisive in the terms of the treaty.[48]

SNAPSHOT: PARTICIPATION OF PEOPLE WITH DISABILITIES IN THE DRAFTING PROCESS

Victor Pineda was not allowed to go to school in his native Venezuela because of his weak muscles. He was diagnosed with muscular dystrophy when he was seven years old and subsequently moved to the United States with his family where new doors opened for him. Twenty years later, Victor, an economist, human rights expert and film director, participated as the youngest delegate to the Ad Hoc Committee to draft the new disability treaty.[49]

Rosemary Kayess is an Australian lawyer and lecturer with a disability, who has had extensive involvement in disability issues. She has been the Chairperson of the New South Wales Disability Discrimination Legal Centre and a lecturer in law and social sciences and policy at the University of New South Wales in Sydney. As a delegate to the Ad Hoc Committee, Rosemary facilitated discussion at the sixth session in 2005, on what became article 24 of the new treaty, relating to education.[50]

Adoption of a Convention and an Optional Protocol

On 13 December 2006 the UN General Assembly adopted *the Convention on the Rights of Persons with Disabilities* (CRPD),[51] which opened for signature on 30 March 2007.[52]

47 M A Stein & J Lord, 'Jacobus Tenbroek, Participatory Justice, and the *UN Convention on the Rights of Persons with Disabilities*' (2008) 13 *Texas Journal on Civil Liberties and Civil Rights* 167, 177.

48 For a description of the Ad Hoc Committee's process, see R Kayess & P French, above, n 7; A S Kanter, 'The Promise and Challenge of the United Nations Convention on the Rights of Persons with Disabilities', (2006–2007) 34 *Syracuse Journal of International Law and Commerce* 287, 297–306.

49 Based on 'A New Legal Tool to Protect Persons with Disabilities' at <http://www.ohchr.org/EN/NewsEvents/Pages/DisabilitiesLegalTool.aspx> at 12 April 2011, and on material at <www.pinedafoundation.org>.

50 And see 'On the Couch with Rosemary Kayess' UNSW TV, 2009 at <http://www.youtube.com/watch?v=RMYu-tJKErs>.

51 The *Convention on the Rights of Persons with Disabilities* has been nicknamed in Australia the 'DisCo': <http://www.hreoc.gov.au/disability_rights/convention.htm>.

52 *Convention on the Rights of People with Disabilities* (CRPD), opened for signature 30 March 2007, 189 UNTS 137 (entered into force 3 May 2008).

An *Optional Protocol* to the Convention[53] enables individual complaints to be made against a state about alleged violations of the Convention, a process described in detail in Chapter 7.4.6. The *Optional Protocol* does not limit the rights in relation to which violation can be complained of. This means that all of the broad range of rights stated in the CRPD are justiciable, a significant development in light of the disputed justiciability of economic, social and cultural rights.[54]

Reservations

A number of states have entered reservations or, more commonly, made declarations of interpretation, in relation to the CRPD.[55]

It is Australia and Canada's position, for example, that while they recognise that people with disabilities enjoy legal capacity on an equal basis with others in all aspects of life (article 12), the CRPD allows for fully supported or substituted decision-making arrangements, when necessary and appropriate and subject to safeguards. Australia also declares that even though people with disabilities have the rights to liberty of movement, freedom to choose their residence, and a nationality, on an equal basis with others (article 18) it understands that the Convention does not create a right for a person to enter or remain in a country of which he or she is not a national, and does not affect Australia's legitimate, objective and reasonable health requirements for non-nationals seeking to enter or remain in Australia.

Remarkably, Malaysia ratified the CRPD subject to the reservation that 'it does not consider itself bound by articles 15 and 18'. Article 15 prohibits torture and being subjected without consent to medical or scientific experimentation, and article 18 recognises right to freedom of movement and to a nationality. More remarkably, no state has yet objected to this reservation.

14.2.2 The *Convention on the Rights of Persons with Disabilities*

The CRPD has been described as a 'startling instrument'[56] containing 'extraordinary innovations and applications of civil and political rights to persons with disabilities'.[57] In its form, it was 'modelled consciously after recent United Nations human rights treaties, most particularly the *Convention on the Rights of the Child*'. Following the CROC model, the CRPD' sets forth a full set of human rights obligations and applies them to the specific circumstances of a targeted group, in this case persons with disabilities ... [setting] forth articles that are introductory, of universal application, spell out substantive rights, and establish implementation and monitoring plans'.[58]

---

53 *Optional Protocol to the Convention on the Rights of Persons with Disabilities* (OP-CRPD), opened for signature 30 March 2007, art 1 (entered into force 3 May 2008).

54 See the discussion in Chapter 1.4.3.

55 See *Status of Treaties*, Chapter 4, at <http://treaties.un.org>, and the discussion of reservations and declarations in Chapter 7.2.4.

56 A Lawson, see above, n 22, 619.

57 R Kayess & P French, see above, n 7, 29.

58 M A Stein & J Lord, see above, n 47, 174, references omitted.

The social model of disability is apparent throughout the CRPD with its focus on removing barriers to participation and inclusion,[59] and explicitly in paragraph (e) of the Preamble, which recognises that 'disability results from the interaction between persons with impairments and attitudinal and environmental barriers that hinders their full and effective participation in society on an equal basis with others'.

No Definition of Disability

The CRPD does not define 'disability' or 'persons with disabilities'. The absence of a definition is the result of an impasse in the drafting negotiations.

Arguments against a definition were that, practically, a definition risked inadvertently excluding some people; politically, a definition risked the impression that a different human rights regime was being created for a distinct group;[60] in principle, a definition would have to be based on the externally imposed and disempowering medical model; and conceptually, the idea of disability as a social category is evolving over time and varies between societies.[61] Arguments in favour of a definition disability were advocates' concern that, without one, states could so narrow the coverage of a treaty as to make it meaningless,[62] and states' concern that, without one, they would have to recognise impairment groups they have not previously understood to be people with disabilities, such as those with psycho-social disability or blood borne organisms causing disease, like HIV/AIDS.[63]

The result of this debate is an inclusive definition:

> **Article 1:** Persons with disabilities include those who have long-term physical, mental, intellectual or sensory impairments which in interaction with various barriers may hinder their full and effective participation in society on an equal basis with others.

The reference to 'long-term' is 'regrettable'[64] and, if applied strictly, 'would certainly exclude those persons with short-term impairments arising from traumatic injuries and disease, and it may also exclude persons with episodic conditions (for example, mood disorders, asthma)'.[65] It is, however, part of an open, inclusive definition, and attention will be on the treaty monitoring committee, the CRPD Committee, to ensure that states are encouraged to take a broad approach to it.

59 R Kayess & P French, see above, n 7; but see 23–4 for a discussion of possible confusion if the intention of the drafters was in fact to refer to impairment.

60 A Lawson, see above, n 22, 593.

61 R Kayess & P French, see above, n 7, 23.

62 A Lawson, see above, n 22, 93.

63 R Kayess & P French, see above, n 7, 23.

64 A Lawson, see above, n 22, 595.

65 R Kayess & P French, see above, n 7, 23.

The social model of disability draws attention to barriers in society that prevent or limit people's full participation. It is therefore fundamental to the CRPD that it requires states to 'take all appropriate steps to ensure that reasonable accommodation is provided' (article 5(3)). But the definition of 'reasonable accommodation' in article 2 as steps that do not impose 'a disproportionate or undue burden' has been criticised, as a 'two element test that may allow the obligation to be evaded at the lower of either threshold', and as insufficient to 'penetrate to the core of exclusionary practices affecting persons requiring significant structural adjustments ... more likely to produce results for persons who require relatively marginal changes to the prevailing social environment'.[66]

The idea of reasonable accommodation, or 'reasonable adjustment', is central to the social model of disability, because it explores the extent to which barriers to access and participation can be set aside. In Australia, the *Disability Discrimination Act 1992* (Cth) requires reasonable adjustment to be made in, for example, the provision of education services according to standards that have been established.[67]

SNAPSHOT: *WALKER v STATE OF VICTORIA*[68]

The Disability Standards under the *Disability Discrimination Act 1992* (Cth) require that schools must take reasonable steps to ensure that a student with a disability is able to participate in the courses offered by the school. The school must determine whether any adjustment is necessary in order to ensure that the student is able, in a meaningful way, to participate in the programs offered by the school.

Alex Walker suffers from a number of disabilities including learning disabilities, dyslexia, attention deficit hyperactivity disorder and Asperger's syndrome. Through his parents, he complained about many things that were done and not done by schools he had attended, which were said to have involved discrimination against Alex because of his disabilities. His claim was considered by the Federal Court of Australia.

The Court looked at the requirement on the schools to make reasonable adjustments, and said that there will be cases where an adjustment is necessary, but that in the circumstances of the case no *reasonable* adjustment could ensure that the Disability Standards will be achieved.

The Court considered evidence of the adjustments that were made by the schools to enable Alex's participation in the educational and other programs, and was satisfied that all reasonable adjustments had been made to assist him. As a result, the Court decided that the schools had not breached the Disability Standards.

New Rights?

Despite having a drafting mandate that precluded the creation of 'new' human rights,[69] the CPRD 'subtly reformulates and extends existing human rights to take into account the specific rights experience of people with disabilities [and arguably] comes close to creating new rights, or at least

66 R Kayess & P French, see above, n 7, 27.

67 *Disability Standards for Education 2005* (Cth), August 2005; see E Dickson, 'Disability Standards for Education and the Obligation of Reasonable Adjustment' (2006) 11(2) *Australia & New Zealand Journal of Law & Education* 23.

68 [2011] FCA 258.

69 R Kayess & P French, see above, n 7, 20.

very new ways of seeing common rights'.[70] The CPRD incorporates rights that, although arguably an extension of the conventional categories of 'civil and political' rights and 'economic, social and cultural rights', go beyond them, into a recognised 'third-generation' of collective rights—such as rights to research and development (articles 4(10(f) and (g)), awareness raising (article 8), social protection and poverty reduction (article 28(2)(b), and international cooperation (article 32)—and, perhaps further than third-generation rights, to the right to an accessible environment (articles 3 and 9), and rights to leisure, tourism and recreation (article 30).[71]

A particularly controversial provision in the drafting process was article 17, which reads simply: 'Every person with disabilities has a right to respect for his or her physical and mental integrity on an equal basis with others'. An earlier draft of the provision included an attempt to regulate states' involuntary treatment of people with disabilities. In doing so, however, the provision implicitly authorised such treatment, thereby accepting a lower standard of human rights protection for people with disabilities. States, on the other hand, were reluctant to renounce their right to intervene in circumstances where a person refusing medical treatment poses a risk to themselves or others.[72]

The resulting simple terms of article 17—credited to 'very vigorous advocacy against compulsory treatment' by advocates for people with psycho-social impairments[73]—avoid addressing the issue. This leaves decisions in relation to 'the use of coercive State power for the purpose of "treatment"' [74]—a critical area of potential human rights violations—to the discretion of states and the views expressed by the CRPD Committee.[75] In the larger context of the CRPD, however, the omission of a specific reference to involuntary treatment should not mean that differential treatment for people with disabilities is permissible.[76]

Monitoring Committee

The CRPD establishes a treaty body, the Committee on the Rights of Persons with Disabilities (CRPD Committee),[77] body of independent experts that monitors implementation of the Convention by the states parties. When nominating members to the CRPD Committee, states are expected to consult with

70 F Mégret, 'The Disabilities Convention: Human Rights of Persons with Disabilities or Disability Rights?' *Human Rights Quarterly* 30 (2008) 494, 494.

71 R Kayess & P French, see above, n 7, 32.

72 A Lawson, see above, n 22, 609.

73 R Kayess & P French, see above, n 7, 29.

74 R Kayess & P French, see above, n 7, 30.

75 See generally T Minkowitz, 'The United Nations Convention on the Rights of Persons with Disabilities and the Right to Be Free from Nonconsensual Psychiatric Interventions' (2006–2007) 34 *Syracuse Journal of International Law and Commerce* 405.

76 See A Kämpf, 'The Disabilities Convention and its Consequences for Mental Health Laws in Australia' in B McSherry (ed), 26(2) (2008) *Law in Context Special Issue: International Trends in Mental Health Laws* 10, 32.

77 Art 34(1).

people with disabilities to consider ensuring balanced gender representation and to nominate experts with disabilities.[78] In 2008 Australia successfully nominated Professor Ron McCallum AO, formerly Dean of Law at the University of Sydney, to membership of the inaugural committee, and he was elected its chair in 2010.

States submit regular reports to the Committee, a process for all treaty bodies described in detail in Chapter 7.4.4. The Committee is also empowered to receive and consider individual complaints made under the *Optional Protocol* to the Convention. A Secretariat for CRPD and its *Optional Protocol* is operated jointly by the Division for Social Policy and Development in the UN Department of Economic and Social Affairs, and the Office of the High Commissioner for Human Rights.[79]

The Committee meets twice yearly, and had its first meeting in February 2009. After a period of establishing it procedures and guidelines, the Committee received at its April 2011 meeting its first state reports for future consideration, from Argentina, Australia, Austria, Azerbaijan, China El Salvador, Hungary, Paraguay, Peru, Spain, Sweden and Tunisia. The Committee issued questions to Tunisia and Spain arising from their reports and, as the brief extract below illustrates, Tunisia responded to those questions.

SNAPSHOT: REPLIES OF TUNISIA TO THE LIST OF ISSUES TO BE TAKEN UP DURING CONSIDERATION BY THE COMMITTEE ON THE RIGHTS OF PERSONS WITH DISABILITIES OF THE INITIAL REPORT OF TUNISIA[80]

5. *Please explain how equality and freedom from all forms of discrimination in all areas of life is guaranteed to persons with disabilities.*

   Persons with disabilities enjoy the same constitutional right to equality and protection from all forms of discrimination in all areas of life as any Tunisian citizen; article 6 of the Constitution provides that 'all citizens have equal rights and duties and are equal before the law'. Their equality is reflected in numerous areas, including:

[EDUCATION]

Under article 1 of *General Principles Act No 80 of 2002* on education and teaching, which provides that 'education shall be compulsory from the age of 6 to 18 years and is a fundamental right guaranteed to all Tunisians without discrimination', all 6-year-olds may enrol in primary school, including those with disabilities.

Should a child's file contain information that would indicate that his disability could have an impact on his school career, he is directed to the Regional Committee for Persons with Disabilities [which] considers and decides on the cases of children with disabilities who are candidates for inclusion in regular schools and directs them to the appropriate educational, vocational and training institutions.

78 Art 34(3).

79 See <http://www.un.org/disabilities> at 12 April 2011.

80 *Replies Submitted by the Government of Tunisia to the List of Issues (CRPD/C/TUN/Q/1) to be Taken Up During the Consideration of the Initial Report of Tunisia (CRPD/C/TUN/1)*, Committee on the Rights of Persons with Disabilities, 5th sess, Geneva, 11–15 April 2011, CRPD/C/TUN/Q/1/Add.1.

WORK

Under Tunisian law, persons with disabilities are guaranteed the right to work like other individuals … 'no citizen who is suitably qualified may be denied employment in the public or private sector on the basis of disability'. In cases where that principle is breached, individuals may resort to the courts …

HEALTH

Persons with disabilities benefit from health insurance cover and treatment free of charge in Tunisia as a matter of principle, whether they and their beneficiaries are covered by social security or not. Persons denied this right can exercise their right to free treatment and medication through recourse to the provincial and central public health authorities. In addition, they may apply to the Administrative Tribunal in order to benefit from this right.

CULTURE AND SPORTS

Pursuant to the agreement concluded between the Ministry of Social Affairs and the Ministry of Culture and Heritage Preservation, cultural spaces and centres have been opened for cultural activities to the beneficiaries of associations working in the field of disability. Furthermore, persons with disabilities benefit from a range of incentives and facilities, including free entry to museums and archaeological sites, playgrounds and leisure areas, and are allocated spaces at sports facilities.

In its subsequent views on Tunisia's state report, the Committee, informed by NGO reports,[81] recorded a number of areas of concern, suggestions and recommendations.[82] In relation to the matters reported by Tunisia in the Snapshot above, for example, the Committee 'note[d] with deep concern that, in practice, the inclusion strategy is not equally implemented in schools', and was 'concerned at the low level of [employment] of persons with disabilities in the private sector'.[83]

14.3 THE UNITED NATIONS AND DISABILITY

Established UN human rights procedures that are likely to be concerned with people with disabilities include the treaty bodies' work under human rights treaties such as the ICCPR, ICESCR, CEDAW and the CROC,[84] and the Human Rights Council's Special Rapporteurs on the Right to Education, and on the Right of Everyone to the Enjoyment of the Highest Attainable Standard of Physical and Mental Health.[85]

81 Committee on the Rights of Persons with Disabilities, 5th session (11–15 April 2011), <http://www.ohchr.org/EN/HRBodies/CRPD/Pages/Session5.aspx>.

82 *Concluding Observations of the Committee on the Rights of Persons with Disabilities: Tunisia*, Committee on the Rights of Persons with Disabilities, 5th sess, Geneva, 11–15 April 2011, CRPD/C/TUN/CO/1, 29 April 2011.

83 Ibid [30], [33].

84 See Chapter 7.4.

85 See Chapter 6.5.

Beyond the dedicated human rights bodies of the UN, most of what the UN does has some bearing on the interests of people with disabilities, particularly in economic, social and cultural rights such as health, work and education. In the area of health, for example, the Preamble of the Constitution of the World Health Organisation (WHO) recognises the 'enjoyment of the highest attainable standard of health as a fundamental human right', and WHO maintains a significant focus on meeting the health needs of people with disabilities within a human rights framework.[86]

In the area of sustainable development, the UN Food and Agricultural Organisation (FAO) researches and runs programs that address social and economic human rights issues for rural disabled people, for example to prevent disability though use of agro-chemicals, to reduce accidents from agricultural tools and implements, to promote nutritional adequacy, to reduce water-borne disease, and to prevent agro- and forestry industry accidents.[87] In education the United Nations Educational, Scientific and Cultural Organisation (UNESCO) has a focus on accessible education of children with disabilities,[88] and in relation to work, the International Labour Organisation (ILO) promotes labour standards, advocacy, and knowledge-building for the training and employment of people with disabilities.[89]

The UN Programme on Youth has a special focus on Youth and Disability,[90] although the 'World Programme of Action for Youth to the Year 2000 and Beyond', which was adopted by the UN in 1995 made only incidental reference to youth with disabilities in its 10 priorities.[91] The Global Initiative for Inclusive Information and Communication Technologies, known as 'G3ict', is an initiative of UN-GAID, the United Nations Global Alliance for ICT and Development,[92] and promotes disability accessibility standards and practices in information and communication technologies.

14.3.1 Regional Activity

The UN Economic Commission of Africa (ECA) was established by the Economic and Social Council to promote the economic and social development in Africa. In 2008, jointly with British charity Leonard Cheshire Disability, ECA convened a conference which discussed implementation of the CRPD in Africa. Five hundred participants from 58 countries issued a 'call to action on poverty, discrimination and lack of access'.[93]

---

86 <http://www.who.int/topics/human_rights/en/> at 12 April 2011.

87 'Empowering The Rural Disabled in Asia and the Pacific' <http://www.fao.org/sd/PPdirect/PPre0035.htm>; and see 'Database on the Rural Disabled', <http://www.fao.org/sd/PPdirect/rurald/>.

88 <http://www.unesco.org/new/en/education/themes/strengthening-education-systems/inclusive-education/children-with-disabilities/> and <http://www.unesco.org/education/efa/know_sharing/flagship_initiatives/depliant_flagship.pdf>.

89 <http://www.ilo.org/skills/areas/lang--en/WCMS_DOC_SKL_ARE_DBL_EN/index.htm>.

90 See <http://www.un.org/esa/socdev/unyin/disability.htm>.

91 See <http://www.un.org/events/youth98/backinfo/ywpa2000.htm>.

92 <http://g3ict.com>.

93 <http://www.lcint.org/?lid=5152>; and see 'Selected Papers from UN Convention on the Rights of Persons with Disabilities: A Call for Action' (2009) *Disability Studies Quarterly*.

Although the European Union has an extensive human rights regime,[94] with general prohibitions against discrimination on attributes such as disability, there is very little that is tailored specifically to the circumstances of people with disabilities. People with disabilities can and do of course use the usual human rights mechanisms. There has been little progress towards implementing, on a regional basis, a 2000 European Commission Communication *Towards a Barrier Free Europe for People With Disabilities*, which was intended to remove environmental, technical and legal barriers to the effective participation of people with disabilities.[95]

The United Nations Economic and Social Commission for Asia and the Pacific (ESCAP) estimates that of the 650 million people living with a disability in the world, 400 million live in Asia and the Pacific. ESCAP promotes policy options and networks, and provides data and information to promote human rights for people with disabilities.[96]

In the concluding year of the Decade of Disabled Persons, ESCAP declared the period 1993 to 2002 as the Asian and Pacific Decade of Disabled Persons.[97] ESCAP adopted a *Proclamation on the Full Participation and Equality of People with disabilities in the Asian and Pacific Region*, and an associated Agenda for Action.[98] Projects to implement the Agenda for Action and a trust fund for the decade were funded by donor states NGOs, supporting training, research, community development programs, expert consultancies and support networks.

At the conclusion of the Asian and Pacific Decade of Disabled Persons, ESCAP convened a High-level Intergovernmental Meeting in 2002, which adopted the *Biwako Millennium Framework for Action Towards an Inclusive, Barrier-Free and Rights-Based Society for Persons with Disabilities in Asia and the Pacific*. The *Biwako Framework* provides recommendations for action by states and concerned stakeholders 'to achieve an inclusive, barrier-free and rights-based society for persons with disabilities in the new decade, 2003–2012'. It identifies seven priority areas, with targets and required action: self-help organisations; women with disabilities; early detection, early intervention and education; training and employment; access to built environments and public transport; access to information and communications; and poverty alleviation.[99]

In 2007 ESCAP conducted a midpoint review of the Asian and Pacific Decade of Disabled Persons ('Biwako Plus Five') where it documented further efforts to be made to achieve the *Biwako Framework* goals,[100] guided by the CRPD.

94 See Chapter 8.2.

95 F Brennan, 'Disability and Human Rights Law' in R Smith and C van den Anker, *The Essentials of Human Rights*, Hodder Arnold, London, 2005, 93–97, 96.

96 <http://www.unescap.org/esid/psis/disability/>.

97 Commission Res 48/3, 48th session, April 1992.

98 49th sess, April 1993.

99 <http://www.unescap.org/esid/psis/disability/bmf/bmf.html>.

100 E/ESCAP/APDDP(2)/2*, Bangkok, 13 November 2007.

14.4 DOMESTIC LAWS

As noted above, in 1993 the UN promulgated *Standard Rules on the Equalization of Opportunities for Persons with Disabilities*.[101] Standard Rule 15, 'Legislation', required states to legislate for 'full participation and equality for persons with disabilities'. As a result of this unprecedented international attention on people with disabilities, the 1990s saw a remarkable number of states enact laws prohibiting disability discrimination.[102]

Important legislative steps were also taken to ensure the full participation of people with disabilities. There is now, for example, constitutional recognition of the right to equality of people with disabilities in article 3(3) of the *German Basic Law* (*Grundgesetz*), section 13(g) of the *Constitution of Malawi* where it is a 'Fundamental Principle of National Policy', section 9 of the Bill of Rights in the *South African Constitution*, and section 21 (2) of the *Ugandan Constitution*. The *Ugandan Constitution* goes further, and reserves five seats in Parliament for people with disabilities, and legislation requires the inclusion of at least one representative who is disabled at all levels of government, resulting in the late 1990s in the election of 'thousands of local representatives who are disabled'.[103]

It is of course one thing to enact a law, and another altogether to give effect to it; the real question to be asked is not about legislative action, but actual implementation.[104] Implementation of CRPD at a national level is supported by resources such as handbooks[105] and guidelines,[106] and by monitoring,[107] which is reported to the CRPD Committee through the process of states' reports.

101 UN GA Res 48/96 (20 December 1993).

102 For example, the *Disability Discrimination Act 1992* in Australia; the *Law of the Peoples' Republic of China on the Protection of Disabled Persons* (1990); the *Law on Equal Opportunities for Persons with Disabilities* (1996) in Costa Rica; the *Disability Discrimination Ordinance* (1995) in Hong Kong; the *Act on Provisions of the Rights of Persons Living with Disability and their Equality of Opportunity* (1998) in Hungary; the *Persons with Disabilities (Equal Opportunities, Protection of Rights and Full Participation) Act* in India; the *Employment Equality Act of 1998* and Equal Status Bill of 1999 in Ireland; the *Equal Rights for People with Disabilities Law* (1998) in Israel; the *Act Relating to Employment Promotion etc. of the Handicapped* (1990) in South Korea; the *Magna Carta for Disabled Persons* (1991) in the Philippines; the *Protection of the Rights of Persons with Disabilities Act* (1996) in Sri Lanka; the *Law on the Prohibition of Discrimination Against Persons with Disabilities in Employment* (1999) in Sweden, the *Disability Discrimination Act* (1995) in the United Kingdom; the *Americans with Disabilities Act* (1999) in the United States, and the *Disabled Persons Act* (1992) in Zimbabwe: *International Norms and Standards Relating to Disability*, United Nations, 2003, p 12, <www.wwda.org.au/internorms1.doc>.

103 C Baylies, see above, n 7, 730–1.

104 See, eg, the review of states' implemetation in A S Kanter, 'The Promise and Challenge of the United Nations Convention on the Rights of Persons with Disabilities' (2006–2007) 34 *Syracuse Journal of International Law and Commerce* 287, 309–14.

105 See UN Department of Economic and Social Affairs, Office of the United Nations High Commissioner for Human Rights, and Inter-Parliamentary Union, *From Exclusion to Equality: Realizing The Rights of Persons with Disabilities; Handbook for Parliamentarians on the Convention on the Rights of Persons with Disabilities and Its Optional Protocol*, United Nations, Geneva, 2007, HR/PUB/07/6, at <http://www.un.org/disabilities/default.asp?id=212>.

106 See R Rieser, *Implementing Inclusive Education: A Commonwealth Guide to Implementing Article 24 of the UN Convention on the Rights of People with Disabilities*, Commonwealth Secretariat, 2008, available online at <http://www.worldofinclusion.com/res/internat/Commonwealth_Guide.doc>.

107 See eg Office of the High Commissioner of Human Rights, *Monitoring the Convention on the Rights of Persons with Disabilities: Guidance for Human Rights Monitors*, United Nations, NY and Geneva, 2010, HR/P/PT/17, at <http://www.ohchr.org/Documents/Publications/Disabilities_training_17EN.pdf>.

14.5 CASE STUDY: THE RIGHT TO LIFE

Article 10 of the CRPD restates the provision in article 6(1) of the ICCPR that 'every human being has the inherent right to life',[108] but adds significantly to it:

> **Article 10:** States Parties reaffirm that every human being has the inherent right to life and shall take all necessary measures to ensure its effective enjoyment by persons with disabilities on an equal basis with others.

After reaffirming the right to life, article 10 then 'transforms the right into a positive State obligation to secure the conditions under which people with disabilities may effectively realise their rights to life and survival'.[109] Kayess and French suggest that 'this formulation to the right to life clearly adverts to action in the economic, social and cultural spheres ... the CRPD therefore has much greater potential to penetrate to social, economic and culturally based threats to the lives of people with disabilities'.[110]

During the drafting process there was 'considerable agitation' by some NGOs seeking explicit recognition of issues that are concerning to people with disabilities, such as 'genetic science aimed at the elimination of impairment-related human diversity, and ... pre-birth negative selection of foeti with identified or imputed impairment'.[111] The failure of the CRPD to 'engage with these, and other, contemporary eugenic threats' to the lives of people with disabilities may be 'its greatest failing',[112] and certainly leaves states—led perhaps by the views of the CRPD Committee—to address them.

But as well as these complex emerging issues, there are simple life and death challenges in the daily lives of people with disabilities:

> Evidence suggest that the lives of [people with disabilities] are often not protected or valued to the same degree as those of non-disabled people. There are indications that, in some countries, 90% of disabled people die before they reach the age of 20. This is partly due to factors such as neglect and inadequate medical care. However, deliberate practices (often unofficial), which have the effect of bringing the lives of disabled people to an end, appear to operate in many countries all over the world. These include withholding care for food from a newly born child or an adult unable to communicate and withholding life-saving treatment.[113]

108 See the discussion of this provision in Chapter 3.2.2.

109 P French & R Kayess, 'Deadly Currents Beneath Calm Waters: People with Disabilities and the Right to Life in Australia' in L Clements and J Read (eds), *Disabled People and the Right to Life: The Protection and Violation of Disabled People's Most Basic Human Rights*, Routledge 2008, 57–84, 59; a longer version of this article is available at <http://www.austlii.edu.au/au/journals/UNSWLRS/2008/34.html>.

110 Ibid.

111 R Kayess & P French, see above, n 7, 29.

112 P French & R Kayess, 'Deadly Currents Beneath Calm Waters: People with Disabilities and the Right to Life in Australia' [2008] UNSWLRS 34, [2.2]; this article is a longer version of P French & R Kayess, see above, n 109.

113 A Lawson, see above, n 22, 570–1, references omitted.

A recurring debate in relation to people with disabilities concerns 'end-of-life' decisions—active euthanasia—where the taking of life is not the informed and voluntary decision of a person with a disability, but one imposed on a person and characterised, for example, as 'an act of mercy'.[114]

14.5.1 The Case of Jason Dawes[115]

In a complex and tragic case, Daniela Dawes suffocated her 10-year-old autistic son, Jason, by holding her hand over his nose and mouth until he died. This was not merely a case of a mother killing her severely disabled son, but of a mother suffering from major depression occasioned not only by the need to care for her son and the devotion she gave to that task, but overwhelmed by a number of other stressors.

Kayess and French argue that, when sentencing Ms Dawes for manslaughter, Jason was portrayed as a principal cause of Ms Dawes' depression, and of other stressors to which she was subject. Before the sentencing court and on appeal, Jason's characteristics were treated as mitigating, rather than aggravating, the seriousness of the offence: the courts effectively constructed Jason as a demonic 'other,' by implication offering a degree of excuse for his killing.

In sentencing Ms Dawes to a five-year bond to be of good behaviour,[116] the court said that '[i]n all the circumstances of this case, [her] moral culpability was very low. Accordingly, the need to denounce her conduct and make her accountable for her actions does not have the significance it might otherwise have had'.[117] The appeal court, however, criticised the sentencing court for not taking seriously enough the courts' 'responsibility to uphold the sanctity of human life,' to 'denounc[e] the conduct of the offender, mak[e] the offender accountable for her actions and ensur[e] adequate punishment for the offence'.[118] Although the appeal court considered the sentence to be 'manifestly inadequate', by the time the appeal was heard Ms Dawes's circumstances were such that a gaol sentence was not imposed.

---

114 See, eg, L J Clements and J Read (eds), *Disabled People and the Right to Life: The Protection and Violation of Disabled People's Most Basic Human Rights*, Routledge, London, 2008.

115 P French & R Kayess, see above, n 109, 63–66.

116 *R v Daniella Dawes* (unreported), District Court of New South Wales, Criminal Jurisdiction, Judge Ellis, Parramatta, Wednesday, 2 June 2004; and see 'When love is not enough' *Sydney Morning Herald*, 1 June 2004 <http://www.smh.com.au/articles/2004/05/31/1085855494917.html> and L Lemont, 'Dawes "has suffered too much to go to jail"' *Sydney Morning Herald*, 3 June 2004, <http://www.smh.com.au/articles/2004/06/02/1086058923624.html>.

117 P French & R Kayess, see above, n 109, 64, quoting from *R v Daniella Dawes* (unreported), District Court of New South Wales, Criminal Jurisdiction, Parramatta, Wednesday, 2 June 2004 (Ellis J).

118 *R v Daniella Dawes* [2004] NSWCCA 363, [4] (Dundord J, Hoeben J concurring); and see L Lemont, 'jail mother, prosecutor urges' *Sydney Morning Herald*, 30 September 2004 <http://www.smh.com.au/articles/2004/09/29/1096401654311.html>.

14.5.2 The Case of Matthew Sutton[119]

The parents of Matthew Sutton, a 28-year-old man with severe multiple impairments, pleaded guilty to his manslaughter and were sentenced to a good behaviour bond for a period of five years.[120] Matthew's parents told the court that Matthew had needed surgery to correct chronic ear pain and prevent meningitis, resulting in total hearing loss for a period of at least three months and a significant risk of permanent hearing loss. They decided that he would not have had 'quality of life', and that he should be spared further 'suffering' by euthanasia.

In Kayess and French's view, the court focused on the perceived impact on his parents of Matthew's impairment and disability, and on the abuse and neglect Matthew experienced in supported accommodation. Matthew is constructed as a suffering, living tragedy—as other than human—and as a source of profound grief, shame and burden to his parents. The court approved of the opinion of a psychiatrist,

> that Matthew's mother 'suffered the terrible and indescribable horror of having a son who had the most serious deprivation of senses imaginable and then having the remaining senses having to be removed'. In the psychiatrist's opinion, Matthew's mother did not think they were acting to kill their son, but primarily to stop his suffering.

As was the case for Jason Dawes, Matthew was portrayed as the cause of his parents' depressive illnesses, stress disorders, thoughts of suicide, relationship difficulties and social withdrawal, and his father's alcoholism. And as was the case for Jason Dawes, Matthew's characteristics, and the position of trust and authority occupied by his parents, are dealt with not as aggravating the offence, but as factors that mitigated, and even excused it.

The court said that there is no deterrent in imposing a sentence in such cases, as nobody in the parents' situation in future is likely to give consideration to sentences imposed on others and thereby be deterred.[121] The parents' killing of Matthew was characterised by the court as an act of love, to protect him 'from a future life without sensation'.[122]

Kayess and French argue that the sentences imposed by the courts in these cases:[123]

> are not reflective of the inherent dignity and value of Jason and Matthew's lives, or of their equality with others'. The courts in both cases are obviously deeply repelled by Jason and Matthew's impairment and disability, acquiesce or collude in their construction as other than human, and appear to strongly identify

119 P French & R Kayess, see above, n 109, 65–66.

120 *R v Raymond Douglas Sutton; R v Margaret E Sutton* [2007] NSWSC 295; and see G Jacobsen, 'Parents "released" son' *Sydney Morning Herald*, 17 March 2007, <http://www.smh.com.au/news/national/parents-released-son/2007/03/16/1173722744991.html>.

121 *R v Raymond Douglas Sutton*, *ibid* [33].

122 *R v Raymond Douglas Sutton*, *ibid* [36].

123 P French & R Kayess, see above, n 109, 66.

with those responsible for depriving them of life. Implicitly, the courts appear to consider Jason and Matthew's impairment and disability a powerful excuse, if not complete justification, for their homicide.

Perhaps the question to be asked in terms of article 10 of the CRPD is whether, during Jason and Matthew's lives, the state took 'all necessary measures to ensure' that they effectively enjoyed the right to life on an equal basis with others.

14.6 CONCLUSION AND ISSUES

The law of human rights for people with disabilities is now focused on the CRPD. The Convention's ambitious and perhaps novel standards for state behaviour may be difficult for states to implement. The CRPD Committee has a significant role in monitoring states' performance, and in providing guidance on the meaning to be given to the expression of rights in the CRPD. Among the challenges for the CRPD Committee are, on the one hand, the justiciability of some of the rights in the treaty and, on the other, the apparently limited coverage and prescription of some others.

Realising the human rights of people with disabilities will, however, require much more than the operation of a treaty. The social model of disability reveals how attitudes and perceptions lead to exclusion and discrimination, but at the same time it exposes the great difficulty of actually changing those attitudes and perceptions. What real barriers to realising their human rights do people with disabilities face on a day-to-day basis, and how far can an initiative such as the CRPD go in overcoming them, even if it were to be enacted into national law?

15
REFUGEES

CONTENTS

15.1 INTRODUCTION

People fleeing persecution are vulnerable to human rights violations wherever they turn. Although refugees have the same 'universal' human rights as all people have, they are in fear of persecution by the very state against which they would claim such rights. They are not protected by their home state, and can only hope that the state they escape to will offer to grant them asylum; in the interim they are completely without protection. Refugees in their millions fill refugee camps around the world, and international law strains to provide a solution, to where they can live, and to how they are treated.

Promotion and protection of human rights occurs largely within a state's borders, the novelty of which is that a state's domestic conduct is under international scrutiny. The special challenge posed by refugees is that they cross borders, and so make themselves a domestic issue for a state that finds that it is an involuntary host to foreign nationals. Few states willingly take responsibility for refugees, and there are severe limits to the capacity of international law to compel and control states' conduct towards them.

This chapter describes the international arrangements for refugees, and identifies the occasions when refugee law and practice are complemented by international human rights law, principally to ensure minimum standards of treatment at least until a refugee is granted asylum, and has a state to call home.

15.2 THE IDEA OF A 'REFUGEE'

In international law, a 'refugee' is defined by the 1951 *Convention Relating to the Status of Refugees*[1] (the *Refugee Convention*); it is essential to the conception of a 'refugee' under the *Refugee Convention* that a person fears persecution, and is without protection from the cause of that fear, either because their country of nationality will not protect them, or because they have no nationality. This is narrower than the usual meaning of a refugee as person who is 'in flight, who seeks to escape conditions or personal circumstances found to be intolerable ... to freedom, to safety'.[2]

A person is a refugee because of their circumstances—a person does not apply to be a refugee, they apply for recognition of their existing status as a refugee. The UNHCR has observed that a determination of a person's refugee status is only a formal declaration of a state of affairs: '[t]he absence of formal recognition as a refugee does not preclude that the person concerned possesses refugee status'.[3]

While a determination of refugee status is an assessment of a person's current fear of persecution, in many cases that same fear will have been well founded for some time previously: 'A person is a

1 *Convention Relating to the Status of Refugees* (*Refugee Convention*), opened for signature 28 July 1951, 189 UNTS 137, art 1 (entered into force 22 April 1954).

2 G S Goodwin-Gill & J McAdam, *The Refugee in International Law*, 3rd edn, Oxford University Press, Oxford, 2007, 15.

3 UN High Commissioner for Refugees, *UNHCR Note on the Principle of Non-Refoulement*, (1997) <http://www.unhcr.org/refworld/docid/438c6d972.html>.

refugee ... as soon as he fulfils the criteria contained in the definition ... Recognition of his refugee status does not therefore make him a refugee but declares him to be one'.[4] It follows from this that people claiming refugee status in good faith[5] should be accorded the rights of refugees until and unless they are found *not* to be refugees.

People seeking recognition of their status as refugees are seeking 'asylum', and are referred to as asylum-seekers; the terms 'refugee' and 'asylum-seeker' are used interchangeably, although the latter carries with it the mistaken suggestion that the person is 'merely' claiming refugee status and is not yet a refugee; as noted above, they may well be a refugee, and the question is whether and when that status will be recognised.

15.2.1 Refugees are not 'Illegal'

Refugees are doing what is anticipated by the *Refugee Convention*: seeking protection because they fear persecution in their own country. They have not acted illegally.[6] They have broken no law and are not subject to any criminal charge. There is no concept in international law of an 'illegal' person,[7] and it is well established in common law that a person is not an outlaw only because they are in a country unlawfully.[8]

In Australia and elsewhere, misleading and prejudicial language has been used to describe refugees, commonly those who arrive in a state without a visa such as, for example, those who enter Australian waters by boats without permission.[9] Terms used in Australia newspapers to describe refugees include 'queue jumpers, illegal immigrants, people smugglers, boat people, jumbo people, jet loads of illegals, illegal foreigners, bogus, and phoney applicants'.[10] This position has been clouded in Australia by language in the *Migration Act*, which 'divide[s] non-citizens into two categories: one described as 'lawful non-citizens' and the other described as 'unlawful non-citizens'.[11]

4 UN High Commissioner for Refugees, *Handbook on Procedures and Criteria for Determining Refugee Status Under the 1951 Convention and the 1967 Protocol Relating to the Status of Refugees*, UN Doc HCR/IP/4/Eng/REV.1 (1979), reedited Geneva, 1992.

5 See above, n 2, 265, citing *R v Uxbridge Magistrates Court; Ex parte Adimi* [2001] QB 667.

6 See *Al-Kateb v Godwin* [2004] HCA 37; (2004) 219 CLR 562, 633 (Hayne J).

7 Although the Department of Immigration uses the terms consistently in its Fact Sheets, for example, Department of Immigration and Multicultural and Indigenous Affairs, *Fact Sheet 74: Unauthorised Arrivals by Air and Sea* (2002).

8 See *Potter v Minahan* [1908] HCA 63; (1908) 7 CLR 277, 289–290 (Griffith CJ); *Kioa v West* [1985] HCA 81; (1985) 159 CLR 550, 631 (Deane J); *Chu Kheng Lim v Minister for Immigration Local Government & Ethnic Affairs* [1992] HCA 64; (1992) 176 CLR 1, 19 (Brennan, Deane and Dawson JJ).

9 See, eg, S Pickering, 'Common Sense and Original Deviancy: News Discourses and Asylum Seekers in Australia' (2001) 14(2) *Journal of Refugee Studies* 169; M Leach, 'Disturbing Practices: Dehumanizing Asylum Seekers in the Refugee "Crisis" in Australia, 2001–2002' (2003) 21(3) *Refuge: Canada's Periodical on Refugees* 25; M Clyne, 'The Use of Exclusionary Language to Manipulate Opinion: John Howard, Asylum Seekers and the Reemergence of Political Incorrectness in Australia' (2005) 4(2) *Journal of Language and Politics* 73; P Mares, 'Reporting Australia's Asylum Seeker "Crisis"' (2002) 29(2) *Media Asia* 71; C Dauvergne, 'Making People Illegal', in P Fitzpatrick & P Tuitt, *Critical Beings: Law, Nation, and the Global Subject*, Ashgate, Burlington, 2004, 83–99.

10 S Pickering, 'The Hard Press of Asylum' (2000) 8 *Forced Migration Review*, 32, 32.

11 See above, n 6.

Nor are refugees fairly described as 'queue jumpers'. There is no 'queue': refugees are escaping persecution, and they rarely have the opportunity to find and apply to a nearby embassy or consular official and wait for a decision.[12]

15.3 INTERNATIONAL ARRANGEMENTS FOR REFUGEES

15.3.1 The *Refugee Convention* and Protocol

The *Refugee Convention* was a direct response to the refugee crisis in Europe during and after World War Two (1939–45). It originally applied only to those who became refugees as a result of events occurring in Europe before 1 January 1951, but the 1967 *Protocol Relating to the Status of Refugees*[13] (the Protocol) extended the reach of the *Refugee Convention* to apply to people who became, and will become, refugees as a result of events occurring after 1 January 1951, without any geographic limitation.

The *Refugee Convention* has been ratified by 144 states and the Protocol by 146.[14] Australia ratified the *Refugee Convention* on 22 January 1954, and the Protocol on 13 December 1973.

Under the *Refugee Convention*,[15] a refugee is:

> any person who ... owing to well-founded fear of being persecuted for reasons of race, religion, nationality, membership of a particular social group or political opinion, is outside the country of his nationality and is unable or, owing to such fear, is unwilling to avail himself of the protection of that country; or who, not having a nationality and being outside the country of his former habitual residence, is unable or, owing to such fear, is unwilling to return to it.[16]

The *Refugee Convention* as a Human Rights Treaty

Refugee law and practice have not yet converged with human rights law and practice.[17] The United Nations High Commission for Refugees (UNHCR) itself observed that '[e]xtreme caution traditionally marked UNHCR's approach to any suggestion that it should cooperate and collaborate with established mechanisms for the promotion and protection of general human rights principles'. This caution was

12 See Edmund Rice Centre, 'Debunking the Myths about Asylum Seekers' (2001) 4(3) *Just Comment*, <www.erc.org.au/just_comments/1029891642.shtml>.

13 *Protocol Relating to the Status of Refugees*, opened for signature 31 January 1967 (entered into force 4 October 1967).

14 <http://treaties.un.org>.

15 From this point on, reference to the *Refugee Convention* is a reference to the *Refugee Convention* and the Protocol.

16 *Refugee Convention*, see above, n 1, art 1A(2) (entered into force 22 April 1954) as amended by the *Protocol Relating to the Status of Refugees*, opened for signature 31 January 1967, art 1(2) (entered into force 4 October 1967).

17 J McAdam, 'The Refugee Convention as a Rights Blueprint for Persons in Need of International Protection' *New Issues in Refugee Research*, Working Paper No 125, UNHCR, 2006, 7–8.

due to a fear that doing so would politicise UNHCR activities and 'compromise [its] to work with ... government counterparts'.[18]

The *Refugee Convention* has always stood apart from the 'human rights' treaties and, in spite of the human rights origins and principles of the *Refugee Convention*,[19] there has been a general reluctance by states, academics and institutions to view human rights law, refugee law and humanitarian law as branches of an interconnected, holistic regime.[20] Nevertheless, the regimes overlap and complement each other, not only in practical terms relating to *non-refoulement* and complementary protection (both discussed below), but also historically and in the underlying commitment to universal standards and the treatment of people with dignity.

McAdam argues strongly for 'fundamental conceptual connections between international refugee law and human rights law', saying that there are 'clear policy reasons why this should be the case [and] also cogent legal arguments that support the extension of Convention status to extra-Convention refugees. These are based on a conceptualization of international law as a body of interrelated norms that must be interpreted in relation to, and be informed by, each other'.[21] As a matter of principle, therefore, McAdam would characterise the *Refugee Convention* as 'a specialist human rights treaty that reflects the tenets of the UDHR, ICCPR and ICESCR [and] reinforces States' protection of refugees as an international legal duty'.[22]

It is the last point, however, which suggests an essential difference between the *Refugee Convention* and the human rights treaties. The 'international legal duty' that states have under the *Refugee Convention* is not accompanied by a concomitant right on the part of those to whom the duty is owed. The human rights treaties' obligations are enforceable but those of the *Refugee Convention* are not, and the *Refugee Convention* does not offer a rights-based solution to people in need of state protection. Differently from the human rights treaties and the ILO Conventions (discussed in Chapter 7.4 and Chapter 16.2.4 respectively), the *Refugee Convention* has no mechanism for oversight of states, for states' reports, or for communication about violations of rights: states parties can ignore their obligations under the *Refugee Convention* with impunity.

Although the *Refugee Convention* is not a human rights treaty,

> [h]uman rights doctrine has frequently been resorted to in order to fill in the "grey areas" of refugee protection, in particular, in giving fuller meaning to the terms "persecution" and "social group" within the refugee definition, in determining appropriate asylum procedures, and in ensuring protection to

18 *UNHCR and Human Rights: A Policy Paper Resulting from Deliberations in the Policy Committee on the Basis of a Paper Prepared by the Division of International Protection*, (1997) UNHCR, AHC/97/325 <http://www.unhcr.org/refworld/docid/3ae6b332c.html>.

19 See above, n 17, 6–8; A Edwards, 'Human Rights, Refugees, and the Right "to Enjoy" Asylum' (2005) 17(2) *International Journal of Refugee Law* 293, 297–9.

20 See above, n 17, 1, references omitted.

21 See above, n 17, 3.

22 See above, n 17, 7–8. See also the reconception of refugee law as human rights protection in J C Hathaway, 'Reconceiving Refugee Law as Human Rights Protection' (1991) 4(2) *Journal of Refugee Studies* 113, 120–7.

> those who fail the narrow definition of a "refugee" in the 1951 Convention and/or 1967 Protocol but who nonetheless need protection ...[23]

Chapter 15.7 below discusses the human rights protections that are available to refugees from the human rights treaties.

15.3.2 The United Nations High Commission for Refugees

The UNHCR has the 'function of providing international protection ... to refugees ... and of seeking permanent solutions for the problem of refugees ...'[24] This function is commonly referred to as the UNHCR's 'mandate'. For purposes of that mandate, the definition of a refugee[25] is the same as that in the *Refugee Convention* except that the *Refugee Convention* adds, as a reason for persecution, 'membership of a particular social group'. There is, however, 'little practical difference'[26] in the scope of protection offered by the UNHCR mandate and the *Refugee Convention*, although having its own mandate enables the UNHCR to work with people who are not covered by the terms of the *Refugee Convention* but are nevertheless in need of protection, discussed below.

A related organisation is United Nations Relief and Works Agency for Palestine Refugees in the Near East (UNRWA), which provides 'relief, human development and protection services to Palestine refugees and persons displaced by the 1967 hostilities in its fields of operation: Jordan, Lebanon, the Syrian Arab Republic, West Bank and the Gaza Strip'.[27]

15.3.3 Arrangements for Refugees in Regional Instruments

The African Union's *Convention on Refugee Problems in Africa*[28] is similar to the *Refugee Convention* in its conception of a refugee, 'although it has there been realistically extended to cover those compelled to leave their country of origin on account of external aggression, occupation, foreign domination, or events seriously disturbing public order'.[29] A non-binding declaration in Central America, the 1984 *Cartagena Declaration*[30], takes a broader approach to the idea of being a refugee, extending the Refugee

---

23 A Edwards, see above, n 19, 295 (citations omitted).

24 *Statute of the Office of the United Nations High Commissioner for Refugees*, GA Res 428(V), UN GAOR, 5th sess, art 1, UN Doc A/1775 (1950).

25 Ibid art 6B, UN Doc A/1775 (1950).

26 G S Goodwin-Gill & J McAdam, see above, n 2, 36.

27 *Frequently Asked Questions: History and Establishment of UNRWA, UN Relief and Works Agency for Palestine Refugees in the North East* <www.unrwa.org> at 14 March 2011.

28 Organisation of African Unity, *Convention on Specific Aspects of Refugee Problems in Africa*, 10 September 1969, 1001 UNTS 60 (No. 14691), entered into force 20.6.74.

29 G S Goodwin-Gill & J McAdam, see above, n 2, 37.

30 *Cartagena Declaration on Refugees*, Nov. 22, 1984, Annual Report of the Inter-American Commission on Human Rights, OAS Doc. OEA/Ser.L/V/II.66/doc.10, rev. 1

Convention grounds to include threats to 'lives, safety or freedom ... by generalised violence, foreign aggression, internal conflicts, massive violation of human rights, other circumstances seriously disturbing public order'.[31] Similarly, the *Bangkok Principles*[32] are non-binding on Asian countries, but include the broad approach of the African Convention.[33]

In Europe, the European Union has established minimum standards for identifying people in need of protection through its 1999 *Refugee Qualification Directive* ('RQD').[34] The RQD is 'the first supranational instrument binding on [European Union] Member States to cover those in need of international protection but who fall outside the provisions of the 1951 *Refugee Convention* and its 1967 Protocol ... [and] that deals with refugee protection and subsidiary protection under one umbrella'.[35] It is 'unquestionably the most important instrument in the new legal order in European asylum because it goes to the heart of the [*Refugee Convention*]';[36] it does not, however, replace the operation of the *Refugee Convention*, to which members states of the EU remain party: '[n]ot only is the *Refugee Convention* part of the European legal order; it is also superior to [European] Community law'.[37]

The RQD is narrower in its scope than the *Refugee Convention*, applying only to 'third country nationals or stateless persons' and not to nationals of EU members states.[38] At the same time, however, the RQD broadens the scope of the *Refugee Convention* by providing detail and 'interpretive guidance'[39] to the meaning to be given to the idea of a 'refugee' under the *Refugee Convention*, and by entrenching an obligation to protect people who, although falling outside the scope of the *Refugee Convention*, are nevertheless in need of protection ('subsidiary protection').[40]

31 G S Goodwin-Gill & J McAdam, see above, n 2, 38.

32 Asian-African Legal Consultative Committee (AALCO), *Bangkok Principles on Status and Treatment of Refugees*, 1966, revised and adopted at the AALCO's 40th session, New Delhi, 24 June 2001.

33 G S Goodwin-Gill & J McAdam, see above, n 2, 39.

34 *Directive of the European Council of 29 April 2004 on the Minimum Standards for the Qualification and Status of Third Country Nationals or Stateless Persons as Refugees or as Persons who Otherwise Need International Protection and the Content of the Protection Granted* [2004] OJ L 304/12.

35 H Storey, 'EU Refugee Qualification Directive: A Brave New World?' (2008) 20(1) *International Journal of Refugee Law* 1, 5.

36 H Lambert, 'The EU Asylum Qualification Directive, its Impact on the Jurisprudence of the United Kingdom and International Law' (2006) 55(1) *International and Comparative Law Quarterly* 161, 161.

37 Ibid 176 & 189.

38 Ibid 178.

39 See above, n 35.

40 For criticism of the limited scope of this subsidiary protection, see J McAdam, *Complementary Protection in International Refugee Law*, Oxford University Press, Oxford, 2007, Introduction; see above, n 36, 176.

15.4 THE IDEA OF 'ASYLUM'

There is a gap between a state's recognising a person's status as a refugee, and a state's offering to give the refugee permanent protection, ie, asylum. There is no 'right' to asylum,[41] only a right to *seek* asylum,[42] and the distinction between the two is a fine but important one.

States' reluctance to be obliged to grant asylum was apparent from the earliest steps towards international cooperation on the issue of refugees. The draft text of the *Universal Declaration of Human Rights* (UDHR) gave people 'the right to seek and to be granted ... asylum from persecution', but in the final text of article 14(1) the 'right *to be granted* asylum' was replaced by the 'right *to enjoy* asylum', a change supported by '[a] number of States ... on the ground that it imposed no legal obligation on them actually to grant asylum'.[43] This decision was the beginning of a decades-long debate about asylum as a human right.

In drafting the *Refugee Convention*,[44] refugees' need for asylum was trumped by state sovereignty: 'the plight of displaced or "needy" people was subordinated to the needs and wants of the state parties who drafted the Convention, and ... refugees were defined by reference to the interests of nation states pre-occupied with Cold War politics'.[45]

Of the many debates, resolutions and declarations on asylum as a human right, the 1967 *Declaration on Territorial Asylum*[46] was to have been a precursor to a binding treaty on the right to asylum, but momentum was lost after the 'abject failure' of the 1997 UN Conference on Territorial Asylum.[47] Asylum continues to be something that refugees have a right 'to seek and enjoy',[48] but not a right to be granted.

The effect of granting asylum is to grant a right of entry to the state, and 'states have consistently guarded their "sovereign prerogative" to decide whether to admit a person to its territory'.[49] The position was stated simply—and tellingly, as it was in the context of an election campaign—by a

41 See generally A Edwards, above, n 19.

42 S Da Lomba, *The Right to Seek Refugee Status in the European Union*, Intersentia New York, 2004, 8.

43 G S Goodwin-Gill & J McAdam, see above, n 2, 359, citing records of debates of the United Nations.

44 For a history of the Refugee Convention see R Germov & F Motta, *Refugee Law in Australia*, Oxford University Press, South Melbourne, 2003, 12–23.

45 J Vrachnas et al, *Migration and Refugee Law: Principles and Practice in Australia*, 2nd edn, Cambridge University Press, Cambridge, 2008, 173.

46 *Declaration on Territorial Asylum*, GA Res 2312 (XXII), UN GAOR, 22nd sess, UN Doc A/Res/3314 (1967).

47 G S Goodwin-Gill & J McAdam, see above, n 2, 363–4.

48 See, eg, World Conference on Human Rights, *Vienna Declaration and Programme of Action*, para 23, UN Doc A/CONF.157/23 (1993); UN Subcommission on the Promotion and Protection of Human Rights, *International Protection for Refugees and Displaced Persons*, Res 2001/16, UN Doc E/CN.4.Sub.2/2001/L.11 (2001); UN Subcommission on the Promotion and Protection of Human Rights, *International Protection for Refugees*, Res 2002/23, UN Doc E/CN.4/Sub.2/RES/2002/23 (2002).

49 See above, n 44, 24.

former Australian Prime Minister: 'We will decide who comes to this country and the circumstances in which they come'.[50]

So, while being granted asylum is conditional on being recognised as a refugee, being recognised as a refugee is no guarantee of being granted asylum. The position was outlined by Gummow J in the Australian High Court decision *Applicant A and Another v Minister for Immigration & Ethnic Affairs and Another*.[51] Pointing out that 'the term "asylum" does not appear in the text of the [Refugee] Convention or the Protocol. Rather, as the title of the Convention suggests, it is concerned with the status and civil rights to be afforded to refugees within member states', Gummow J confirms that 'decisions to admit persons as refugees to the territory of member states are left to those states', and cites Lord Mustill,[52] who said that '[n]either under international nor ... municipal law does a fugitive have any direct right to insist on being received by a country of refuge'.

15.4.1 The Reluctance of States

International recognition of refugees, and arrangements for their protection, are humanitarian measures; the mechanism under the *Refugee Convention* can be seen as a surrogate for the state, 'attempting to make good the deficiency of national protection'[53] by obliging another state to step in and offer 'substitute protection'[54] because the person's own state will not. States have, however, consistently 'insisted on fairly restrictive criteria for identifying those who benefit from refugee status and asylum or local protection'.[55] Indeed, developing states have taken the lead from the industrialised world in 'mobilising popular support by promoting nationalistic and xenophobic sentiments, and by blaming their country's ills on the presence of refugees, asylum seekers, and illegal immigrants'.[56]

In responding to 'mass population movements of the type witnessed in the Balkans and the Great Lakes region of Africa', for example, 'UNHCR has encountered a serious problem: a declining willingness on the part of states to admit and accommodate large numbers of refugees'.[57] There is a history of 'political and economic trends' that have led to '[t]he declining commitment to asylum among the world's developing countries';[58] one of which was the example set by 'the industrialised countries attempting to keep asylum seekers and refugees away from their territory', despite their being better placed 'to assume responsibility of large numbers of refugees'.[59]

50 J Howard, Liberal Party election launch 28 October 2001, quoted in J Vrachnas et al, *Migration and Refugee Law: Principles and Practice in Australia*, 2nd edn, Cambridge University Press, Cambridge, 2008, 1.

51 [1997] HCA 4; (1997) 190 CLR 225, 273–4 (citations omitted).

52 *T v Home Secretary* [1996] UKHL 8; [1996] AC 742 at 754.

53 G S Goodwin-Gill & J McAdam, see above, n 2, 23.

54 J C Hathaway, *The Law of Refugee Status*, Butterworths, Toronto, 1991, 124, citing J Patrnogic, 'Refugees—a Continuing Challenge' (1982) *Annuaire de droit internationale médical* 73, 75.

55 G S Goodwin-Gill & J McAdam, see above, n 2, 15.

56 J Crisp, 'Refugees and the Global Politics of Asylum' (2003) 74 (Issue Supplement s1) *Political Quarterly* 75, 78.

57 Ibid 76.

58 Ibid 77.

59 Ibid 77–8.

15.4.2 'Safe Third Country'

Australia has developed the idea of a 'safe third country': the *Migration Act 1958* (Cth) provides that Australia does not have protection obligations to a claimant for refugee status 'who has not taken all possible steps to avail himself or herself of a right to enter and reside in, whether temporarily or permanently ... any country apart from Australia, including countries of which the [claimant for refugee status] is a national'.[60] A person is prevented from applying for recognition of their refugee status in Australia if they have been in a prescribed 'safe third country' for at least seven days and have a right of re-entry to that country.[61] Arrangements to similar effect exist in the United States of America and Canada, where they survived a constitutional challenge.[62]

Kirby J of the Australian High Court has criticised such provisions, saying that they lead to the 'absurd result' that 'the generosity of other States' refugee laws [relieve a state] of international obligations that it voluntarily accepted with other nations'.[63]

15.4.3 No 'Right of Entry'

Article 31(1) of the *Refugee Convention* protects a refugee from being penalised, and from being detained arbitrarily, if they enter a state without permission. This protection is necessary if the *Refugee Convention* is to work: 'it would make a nonsense of the [Refugee] Convention if [entry] was not intended, at least for the purposes of refugee status determination, especially where an individual has reached a country's territory, such as its territorial seas or a waiting zone in an international airport'.[64] To obtain the protection the refugee must 'present themselves without delay to the authorities'.

The meaning of 'without delay' can be defined by a state; in Australia, for example, refugees who arrive in Australia without a visa must make their claim for asylum within 45 days to avoid the penalty of being denied permission to work and being excluded from public health benefits.[65]

15.4.4 *Non-Refoulement*

With some exceptions,[66] a refugee can be expelled from a state as long as there has been both due process and a reasonable period within which to seek admission to another country.[67] But under the

60 *Migration Act 1958* (Cth) s 36 (3). See *NAGV and NAGW of 2002 v Minister for Immigration and Multicultural and Indigenous Affairs* [2005] HCA 6; 222 CLR 161.

61 *Migration Act 1958* (Cth) ss 91A–G.

62 *Canadian Council for Refugees v Canada*, 2008 FCA 229, [2009] 3 FCR 136.

63 *NAGV and NAGW of 2002 v Minister for Immigration and Multicultural and Indigenous Affairs* [2005] HCA 6; 222 CLR 161, 190 (Kirby J).

64 A Edwards, see above, n 19, 302.

65 *Migration Regulations 1994* (Cth) reg 2.20.

66 For example, if a person is a danger to the security or community of the returning state, *Convention Relating to the Status of Refugees*, opened for signature 28 July 1951, 189 UNTS 137, art 33(2) (entered into force 22 April 1954). For an analysis of this exception to the right of *non-refoulement*, see S Taylor, 'Exclusion from Protection of Persons of "Bad Character": Is Australia Fulfilling its Treaty-Based Obligations?' (2002) 8(1) *Australian Journal of Human Rights* 83.

67 *Refugee Convention*, see above, n 1, art 32 (entered into force 22 April 1954).

principle of *'non-refoulement'*, a state may not return a refugee to the country they fled from if to do so would threaten their life or freedom.[68]

The principle of *non-refoulement* is '[t]he most essential component of refugee status and of asylum';[69] in UNHCR's view, it has become a norm of customary international law.[70] A 2001 declaration by parties to the *Refugee Convention* confirmed the 'core ... principle of *non-refoulement*, whose applicability is embedded in customary international law'.[71]

The UNHCR's 'Note on the Principle of *Non-refoulement*' gives an extensive and authoritative account of the history and meaning of the principle:

> ... respect for the principle of *non-refoulement* requires that asylum applicants be protected against return to a place where their life or freedom might be threatened until it has been reliably ascertained that such threats would not exist and that, therefore, they are not refugees ... Without such a rule, the principle of *non-refoulement* would not provide effective protection for refugees, because applicants might be rejected at the frontier or otherwise returned to persecution on the grounds that their claim had not been established ...
>
> The need to provide international protection to persons fleeing armed conflict and civil strife, whether or not they come within the terms of the [Refugee] Convention definition, is generally accepted in practice by States as a humanitarian responsibility. The protection accorded in these countries to persons who are not deemed to be refugees under the [Refugee] Convention is normally granted as a humanitarian act, or as a duty under national law (including constitutional provisions) ...
>
> Measures of *refoulement* are various and include expulsion/deportation orders against refugees, return of refugees to countries of origin or unsafe third countries, electrified fences to prevent entry, non-admission of stowaway asylum-seekers and push-offs of boat arrivals or interdictions on the high seas.
>
> Whenever refugees—or asylum-seekers who may be refugees—are subjected, either directly or indirectly, to such measures of return, be it in the form of rejection, expulsion or otherwise, to territories where their life or freedom are threatened, the principle of *non-refoulement* has been violated.
>
> Furthermore, having regard to the nature and purpose of the principle, it also applies to extradition. Indeed, the protection of a refugee cannot be regarded as complete unless he or she is also protected against extradition to a country where he or she has reason to fear persecution ...
>
> Since the purpose of the principle of *non-refoulement* is to ensure that refugees are protected against forcible return to situations of danger it applies both within a State's territory and to rejection at its borders. It also applies outside the territory of States. In essence, it is applicable wherever States act.

The principle of *non-refoulement* suggests that there is a 'de facto duty to admit the refugee',[72] at least where there is a real risk that to refuse entry will expose the person to persecution.[73] But 'the duty of *non-refoulement* imposed on States ... must not be confused with asylum. Whereas the

68 *Refugee Convention*, see above, n 1, art 33 (entered into force 22 April 1954). On the principle of *non-refoulement* see generally E Lauterpacht & D Bethlehem, 'The Scope and Content of the Principle of *Non-Refoulement*: Opinion', in E Feller, V Türk & F Nicholson (eds), *Refugee Protection in International Law: UNHCR's Global Consultations on International Protection*, Cambridge University Press, Cambridge, 2003, 78–177, 87.

69 UN High Commissioner for Refugees, see above, n 3.

70 UN High Commissioner for Refugees, see above, n 3.

71 UN High Commissioner for Refugees, *Declaration of States Parties to the 1951 Convention and/or its 1967 Protocol Relating to the Status of Refugees*, para 4, UN Doc HCR/MMSP/2001/09 (2002).

72 J C Hathaway, *The Rights of Refugees under International Law*, Cambridge University Press, Cambridge, 2005, 301.

73 G S Goodwin-Gill & J McAdam, see above, n 2, 215.

former prevents a state from removing a person to a situation of danger, the latter describes the act of a state protecting a person by granting her/him refuge on its territory'.[74]

There are exceptions to the principle of *non-refoulement*: it is not available to a refugee who is reasonably regarded as a danger to national security or to the community,[75] although the exception 'should be applied with the greatest caution'.[76]

Non-Refoulement under Human Rights Treaties

It is in relation to *non-refoulement* that the human rights treaties have the most to offer the refugee process.[77] Article 3 of the *Convention Against Torture* (CAT) explicitly prohibits *refoulement*, and the same principle of *non-refoulement* has been developed by the UN Human Rights Committee in its jurisprudence on the prohibition against torture in article 7 of the ICCPR,[78] and by the Committee on the Rights of the Child in its jurisprudence on articles 6, 37 and 38 of the *Convention on the Rights of the Child*.[79] The reasoning of the Human Rights Committee makes clear that, differently from the *Refugee Convention*, the guarantee of *non-refoulement* in the ICCPR is 'not subject to any exception whatsoever'.[80]

15.5 Applying for asylum

15.5.1 Proving a Claim

An applicant for refugee status must establish their claim,[81] and there is extensive debate about the standard of proof that is expected in what is 'an essay in hypothesis ... an attempt to prophesy what

74 S Persaud, 'Protecting Refugees and Asylum Seekers under the International Covenant on Civil and Political Rights' (*New Issues in Refugee Research*, Working Paper No 132, UNHCR, 2006) 14 (citations omitted).

75 *Refugee Convention*, see above, n 1, art 33(2) (entered into force 22 April 1954).

76 UN High Commissioner for Refugees, see above, n 3.

77 See generally J Hearn & K Eastman, 'Human Rights Issues for Australia at the United Nations—Australia's *Non-Refoulement* Obligations under the Torture Convention and the ICCPR' (2000) 6(1) *Australian Journal of Human Rights* 216.

78 UN Human Rights Committee, *General Comment No 31: Nature of the General Legal Obligation Imposed on States Parties to the Covenant*, para 12, UN Doc CCPR/C/21/Rev.1/Add.13 (2004); see the discussion generally in S Persaud, above, n 74, 8.

79 Committee on the Rights of the Child, *General Comment No 6: Treatment of Unaccompanied and Separated Children Outside Their Country of Origin*, paras 27–8, UN Doc CRC/GC/2005/6 (2005).

80 See above, n 74, 6–12.

81 UN High Commissioner for Refugees, see above, n 4, para 196.

might happen to the applicant in the future, if returned to his or her country of origin'.[82] The nature of the exercise 'call[s] for account to be taken of consequences, and of degrees of likelihood far short of any balance of probability'.[83]

The standard of proof required of an applicant for refugee status is to a large extent in the terms of the *Refugee Convention*: the applicant must show that their fear is 'well-founded'. It is up to the state to which the application has been made to decide if the applicant's fear is well-founded, so it is the states' domestic courts that have developed standards for what will persuade them of this.

15.5.2 A 'Well-Founded Fear'

The courts of the UK, the USA, Canada and Australia have arrived at broadly similar standards for being satisfied of the existence of a well-founded fear. In *Chan Yee Kim v Minister for Immigration and Ethnic Affairs*,[84] Mason CJ of the Australian High Court surveyed these approaches, and said that 'a fear of persecution is "well-founded" if there is a real chance that the refugee will be persecuted if he returns to his country of nationality'.[85] The Court agreed that the term 'well-founded fear of persecution' contains both subjective and objective elements: not only the existence of a real fear by the applicant, but also objective circumstances that indicate a 'real chance' that the applicant would be persecuted, thereby confirming the applicant's subjective fear as 'well-founded'.

Despite this judicial exploration of the meaning of the *Refugee Convention's* terms, Australia has legislated to set its own standard for what constitutes a 'well-founded' fear. The *Migration Act 1958* (Cth) prescribes a fear as 'well-founded' only if persecution is 'the essential or significant reason' for the fear.[86]

Proving 'Identity'

Proving identity is integral to a refugee's proving the validity of their fear. To prove identity, the Australian *Migration Act 1958* sets a higher threshold than the *Refugee Convention*, by allowing adverse inferences to be drawn from the fact that a refugee has no documentary evidence of their identity, nationality or citizenship, without a reasonable explanation.[87] The written request a refugee receives for the documentary evidence is in terms that are 'often regarded as threatening',[88] and

82 G S Goodwin-Gill & J McAdam, see above, n 2, 54–60.

83 G S Goodwin-Gill & J McAdam, see above, n 2, 58–59 (citations omitted).

84 (1989) 169 CLR 379. See also *S395 v Minister for Immigration and Multicultural Affairs* [2003] HCA 71; 216 CLR 473, 486 (McHugh and Kirby JJ).

85 *Chan Yee Kim v Minister for Immigration and Ethnic Affairs* (1989) 169 CLR 379, 389; citing *R v Home Secretary; Ex parte Sivakumaran* [1987] UKHL 1; (1988) AC 958; *Immigration and Naturalization Service v Cardoza-Fonseca* [1987] USSC 32; (1987) 94 L Ed 2d 434.

86 *Migration Act 1958* (Cth) s 91R(1).

87 Ibid s 91w.

88 Department of Immigration and Citizenship, *Review of Personal Identifier Provisions Introduced in 2004 to Migration Act 1958: Final Report* (2009), para 6.1.12.

drawing an adverse inference from the absence of documents is at odds with the procedure, and the underpinning rationale, set out in the UNHCR *Handbook on Procedures and Criteria for Determining Refugee Status*.[89]

The Australian government allows the adverse inference to be drawn because of a concern that 'some applicants are engaging in sophisticated identity, nationality and claims fraud in order to bolster their chances of gaining protection in Australia'.[90] However, McKay points out that it is 'well nigh impossible for refugees to travel to countries of refuge without false documents', and that women in particular 'may never have had possession of their travel documentation, let alone played any role in their acquisition or loss'.[91]

15.5.3 A Fear of 'Persecution'

A person's well-founded fear is of 'persecution', a term that is not defined in the *Refugee Convention*. It is up to states to interpret 'this fundamental term, and the jurisprudence, not surprisingly, is inconsistent'.[92] Persecution can range from 'the threat of deprivation of life or physical freedom ... [to] restrictions on freedoms traditionally guaranteed in a democratic society', but '[w]hether such restrictions amount to persecution ... will ... turn on an assessment of a complex of factors, including (1) the nature of the freedom threatened, (2) the nature and severity of the restriction, and (3) the likelihood of the restriction eventuating in the individual case'.[93]

Clearly it would be persecution to engage in or threaten conduct that is prohibited by CAT,[94] although states are free to set their own standards for what they will accept as 'persecution'. Australia, for example, defines conduct as persecution only if it is systematic and discriminatory conduct that involves serious harm to the person.[95]

15.5.4 The Grounds of Persecution

Having been formulated in the 1950s in response to the Second World War, the *Refugee Convention* is limited in the number and type of grounds that are recognised as a basis for persecution. There are

89 UN High Commissioner for Refugees, see above, n 4.

90 Explanatory Memorandum, Migration Legislation Amendment Bill [No 6] 2001 (Cth) para 44 quoted in L McKay, 'Women Asylum Seekers in Australia: Discrimination and the *Migration Legislation Amendment Act [No 6] 2001* (Cth)' (2003) 4(2) *Melbourne Journal of International Law* 439, 448.

91 L McKay, ibid 449–50.

92 G S Goodwin-Gill & J McAdam, see above, n 2, 91.

93 G S Goodwin-Gill & J McAdam, see above, n 2, 92. See also *Chan Yee Kim v Minister for Immigration and Ethnic Affairs* (1989) 169 CLR 379, 429–431. (McHugh J).

94 See above, n 34, art 9.

95 *Migration Act 1958* (Cth) s 91R(1); see also the discussion in C Hunter, 'Khawar and Migration Legislation Amendment Bill (No 6): Why Narrowing the Definition of a Refugee Discriminates Against Gender-Related Claims' (2002) 8(1) *Australian Journal of Human Rights* 107.

'Convention grounds': race, religion, nationality, membership of a particular social group, or political opinion.[96] Dawson J of the Australian High Court observed that: 'No matter how devastating may be epidemic, natural disaster or famine, a person fleeing them is not a refugee within the terms of the Convention. And by incorporating the five Convention reasons the Convention plainly contemplates that there will even be persons fearing persecution who will not be able to gain asylum as refugees.'[97]

Large numbers of people now fear—and are subject to—persecution for reasons other than the five Convention grounds. The situation of people who are outside the scope of the *Refugee Convention* is discussed below.

Race

In this context, race 'has to be understood in its widest sense to include all kinds of ethnic groups that are referred to as "races" in common usage.'[98] Although a person's 'race' is usually verifiable as a fact, Goodwin-Gill and McAdam note as well a 'shift towards the greater use of "subjective criteria", including self-perception and the perception of others'.[99]

Religion

As is the case with race, 'religion' is understood broadly for purposes of the *Refugee Convention*, and the UNHCR takes its guidance from the way 'religion' is described in various human rights treaties.[100] The UNHCR's view[101] is that claims based on religion involve one or more of: religion as belief (including non-belief), religion as identity, and religion as a way of life.

Persecution on the basis of religion 'may assume various forms, eg prohibition of membership of a religious community, of worship in private or in public, of religious instruction, or serious measures of discrimination imposed on persons because they practise their religion or belong to a particular religious community'.[102]

96 *Refugee Convention*, see above, n 1, art 1A(2) (entered into force 22 April 1954).

97 *Applicant A and Another v Minister for Immigration and Ethnic Affairs and Another* [1997] HCA 4; 190 CLR 225, 248.

98 UN High Commissioner for Refugees, see above, n 4, para 68. See also *International Convention on the Elimination of All Forms of Racial Discrimination* (ICERD), opened for signature 21 December 1965, 660 UNTS 195, art 1(1) (entered into force 4 January 1969).

99 G S Goodwin-Gill & J McAdam, see above, n 2, 70, quoting G Verdirame, 'The Genocide Definition in the Jurisprudence of the Ad Hoc Tribunals' (2000) 49(3) *International & Comparative Law Quarterly* 578, 592–4.

100 UN High Commissioner for Refugees, *Guidelines on International Protection No 6: Religion-Based Refugee Claims Under Article 1A(2) of the 1951 Convention and/or the 1967 Protocol Relating to the Status of Refugees*, para 4, UN Doc HCR/GIP/04/06 (2004).

101 Ibid paras 5–8, UN Doc HCR/GIP/04/06 (2004).

102 UN High Commissioner for Refugees, see above, n 4, para 72.

Nationality

Nationality as a reason for persecution may seem 'somewhat odd, given the absurdity of a State persecuting its own nationals on account of their membership of the body politic'.[103] But the UNHCR takes a broad approach,[104] seeing 'nationality' as referring not only to 'citizenship' but also 'to membership of an ethnic or linguistic group and may occasionally overlap with the term "race"'.

Membership of Particular Social Group

In its Guidelines on International Protection, the UNHCR has commented on two approaches to identifying 'membership of a particular social group' in '[j]udicial decisions, regulations, policies, and practices in common law jurisdictions'.[105] One is the 'protected characteristics' or 'immutability' approach, which 'examines whether a group is united by an immutable characteristic or by a characteristic that is so fundamental to human dignity that a person should not be compelled to forsake it'. The other is the 'social perception' approach, which 'examines whether or not a group shares a common characteristic which makes them a cognizable group or sets them apart from society at large'.

The UNHCR points out that the two approaches may frequently converge, each resulting in, say women, families and homosexual people being recognised as particular social groups, 'depending on the circumstances of the society in which they exist'. The UNHCR proposes a single approach:[106]

> a particular social group is a group of persons who share a common characteristic other than their risk of being persecuted, or who are perceived as a group by society. The characteristic will often be one which is innate, unchangeable, or which is otherwise fundamental to identity, conscience or the exercise of one's human rights.

The approach to defining a social group that matters, however, is the one taken by the domestic courts: '[t]he jurisprudence of recent years shows courts and tribunals in different jurisdictions wrestling with the concept of particular social group, and a coherent, general approach is beginning to emerge'.[107] There is 'probably no single coherent definition, but rather a set of variables, a "range of permissible descriptors" [which] include, for example, (1) the fact of voluntary association ... (2) involuntary linkages, such as family, shared past experience, or innate, unalterable characteristics;

103 UN High Commissioner for Refugees, see above, n 2, 72.

104 UN High Commissioner for Refugees, see above, n 4, paras 74–6.

105 UN High Commissioner for Refugees, *Guidelines on International Protection No 2: 'Membership of a Particular Social Group' Within the Context of Article 1A(2) of the 1951 Convention and/or its 1967 Protocol Relating to the Status of Refugees*, UN Doc HCR/GIP/02/02 (2002).

106 Ibid para 11, UN Doc HCR/GIP/02/02 (2002); see above, n 34, art 10(1)(d).

107 G S Goodwin-Gill & J McAdam, see above, n 2, 84–5.

and (3) the perception of others'.[108] In the view of Gleeson CJ of the Australian High Court, 'It is power, not number, that creates the conditions in which persecution may occur'.[109]

SNAPSHOT: PARTICULAR SOCIAL GROUP

In *S395 v Minister for Immigration and Multicultural Affairs* it was not contested that homosexual men in Bangladesh are a 'particular social group' within the meaning of the *Refugee Convention*.[110]

In *Applicant A*, the Australian Refugee Review Tribunal decided that a married couple from China were refugees because they were members of a group of people 'who, having only one child, do not accept the limitations placed on them [by China's 'one-child' policy] or who are coerced or forced into being sterilised'.[111] The High Court overturned this decision, saying 'numerous individuals with similar characteristics or aspirations ... do not comprise a particular social group of which they are members'.[112]

But there was a different result in *Chen Shi Hai*, when the refugee claimant was the second child of Chinese parents. The High Court decided unanimously that a three-year-old Chinese national, born in an Australian immigration detention centre, was a member of a particular social group—so-called 'black children' born in breach of China's 'one child' policy—and that he would face persecution in China.[113] The fears of the child's parents on his behalf was sufficient to found his claim for refugee status.

Political Opinion

A 'typical political refugee' is a person who is 'pursued by the government of a State or other entity on account of his or her opinions, which are an actual or perceived threat to that government or its institutions, or to the political agenda and aspirations of the entity in question'.[114]

The UNHCR points out that this 'presupposes that the applicant holds opinions not tolerated by the authorities, which are critical of their policies or methods ... [and] that such opinions have come to the notice of the authorities or are attributed by them to the applicant ...'[115] In fact, persecution more frequently 'take[s] the form of sanctions for alleged criminal acts against the ruling power.

108 G S Goodwin-Gill & J McAdam, see above, n 2, 85.

109 *Minister for Immigration and Multicultural Affairs v Khawar and Others* [2002] HCA 14; 210 CLR 1, 13 (Gleeson CJ). See also *Shah and Islam* [1999] 2 AC 629.

110 *S395/2002 v Minister for Immigration and Multicultural Affairs* [2003] HCA 71; 216 CLR 474. In *Minister for Immigration and Citizenship v SZMDS* [2010] HCA 16; 240 CLR 611, a Pakistani man who engaged in homosexual relationships while working abroad was not successful in seeking asylum because there was not a 'real chance' that he would face persecution in Pakistan.

111 *Applicant A v Minister for Immigration & Ethnic Affairs* [1997] HCA 4; 190 CLR 225, 239 (Dawson J).

112 Ibid 285 (Gummow J).

113 *Chen Shi Hai v Minister for Immigration and Multicultural Affairs* [2000] HCA 19; 201 CLR 293; 170 ALR 553; 74 ALJR 775.

114 G S Goodwin-Gill & J McAdam, see above, n 2, 87.

115 UN High Commissioner for Refugees, see above, n 4, para 80.

It will, therefore, be necessary to establish the applicant's political opinion, which is at the root of his behaviour, and the fact that it has led or may lead to the persecution that he claims to fear'.[116]

15.5.5 Grounds Arising After Fleeing—a Refugee *'Sur Place'*

It can happen that because of a change in circumstances, a person 'may not have been a refugee on leaving his or her country, however, he or she may be a refugee at the time of determination [of their application for refugee status]'.[117]

A person is then a 'refugee *sur place*', because of 'a change in the conditions of that country after their departure from it ... [or] as a consequence of their own activities after their departure because those activities may come to the attention of the authorities in that country'.[118] Such activities may be, for example, 'associating with refugees already recognized, or expressing ... political views'.[119] People in this situation may be '[d]iplomats and other officials serving abroad, prisoners of war, students [and] migrant workers'.[120]

There is of course a risk that a person in a country of residence has not acted in good faith, and 'has engaged in activities ... with a view to building a refugee case'.[121] Whether this is so is usually assessed with the person's application, but in Australia there is a presumption that a person has acted in *bad* faith, and an assessment of their application will 'disregard any conduct engaged in by the person in Australia unless ... the person satisfies the Minister that the person engaged in the conduct otherwise than for the purpose of strengthening the person's claim to be a refugee'.[122]

15.5.6 'Extra territorial Processing'

Ostensibly to deter asylum seekers from sailing to Australia from Asia, Australia engages in 'extra-territorial processing' of 'boat arrivals' who claim refugee status. Extra territorial processing has been proposed in the United Kingdom and debated widely in Europe, and 'a number of States have developed pilot schemes, such as Italy's removal of asylum seekers ... to transit centres in Libya'.[123]

116 UN High Commissioner for Refugees, see above, n 4, para 81.

117 J Vrachnas, see above, n 45, 257.

118 *Minister for Immigration and Citizenship v SZJGV; Minister for Immigration and Citizenship v SZJXO* [2009] HCA 40; 238 CLR 642, 661 (Crennan and Kiefel JJ).

119 UN High Commissioner for Refugees, see above, n 4, para 96.

120 UN High Commissioner for Refugees, see above, n 4, para 95.

121 G S Goodwin-Gill & J McAdam, see above, n 2, 65.

122 *Migration Act 1958* (Cth) s 91R(3). For the history and reasoning behind this approach, see above, n 118.

123 G S Goodwin-Gill & J McAdam, see above, n 2, 411.

An Australian scheme, known colloquially as 'the Pacific Solution', was established in 2001. Australia's migration zone—within which the *Migration Act* operates—is defined as all Australian territory to the low water mark.[124] Amendments to the *Migration Act*[125] removed the external territories of Ashmore, Cartier, Christmas and Cocos (Keeling) Islands, and over 3000 islands—including the Coral Sea Islands Territory and all islands north of Queensland, the Northern Territory and Western Australia—from the migration zone and classified them as 'excised offshore places', removing them from the scope of the *Migration Act*.

People travelling to Australia by boat are intercepted before they reach the migration zone. Until early 2008 the people who were intercepted in this way were relocated to 'offshore processing centres' in the sovereign states of Nauru and Papua New Guinea, where their applications for refugee status were considered under the UNHCR mandate (discussed below).[126] A newly elected federal government in Australia discontinued the practice of extra territorial processing in February 2008, but did not repeal the enabling legislation.[127] Facing an election in 2010 the same government proposed—unsuccessfully—the establishment of a 'regional processing centre' in South-East Asia, similar to proposal that the United Kingdom had made to (and which was rejected by) the European Union in 2003.[128]

People who are intercepted before they reach the migration zone are now taken to Christmas Island, which is an excised place. As a technical matter, their application for refugee status is then processed outside the migration zone, even if they are moved into detention on the Australian mainland. An asylum seeker in this situation cannot apply for a visa unless the Minister considers that it is in the public interest to allow them to do so.[129] In practice the Minister allows them to apply only if, in an administrative process guided by administrative 'manuals',[130] they are assessed as likely to be a refugee.[131] The administrative assessment is, however, bound by the *Migration Act* and is subject to the requirements of procedural fairness.[132] This process has been commented on adversely by the CAT Committee.[133]

---

124 *Migration Act 1958* (Cth) s 5.

125 *Migration Amendment (Excision from Migration Zone) Act 2001* (Cth) sch 2; *Migration Amendment Regulations 2003 (No 8) 2003* (Cth).

126 On the Pacific Solution see generally D Marr and M Wilkinson, *Dark Victory*, Allen & Unwin, Crows Nest, 2003; S Metcalf, *The Pacific Solution*, Australian Scholarly Publishing, North Melbourne, 2010.

127 On the cost and closure of the offshore processing centres see: The Hon Chris Evans, Minister for Immigration and Citizenship, *Last Refugees Leave Nauru*, Media Release, 8 February 2008, cited in E Karlsen, *Background Note: Developments in Australian Refugee Law and Policy 2007–10, Labor's First Term in Office*, Law and Bills Digest Section, Parliamentary Library, Parliament of Australia, 2010.

128 Communication from the Commission to the Council and the European Parliament: *Towards More Accessible, Equitable and Managed Asylum Systems*, /*COM/2003/0315 final*/ (2003).

129 *Migration Act 1958* (Cth) s 46A.

130 The 'RSA Manual' and the 'IMR Manual'.

131 Officers of the Australian Immigration Department carry out a 'Refugee Status Assessment' ('RSA'), which is subject to an externally contracted 'Independent Merits Review' ('IMR').

132 *Plaintiff M61 and Plaintiff M69 v Commonwealth* [2010] HCA 41.

133 UN Committee Against Torture, *Concluding Observations of the Committee Against Torture: Australia*, UN Doc CAT/C/AUS/CO/3 (2008).

In 2011, the Australian federal government arranged to send asylum seekers from Australia to Malaysia for their refugee claims to be assessed by the UNHCR. In return, Malaysia will send to Australia recognised refugees who are already in camps in Malaysia awaiting re-settlement. The intention behind this extra territorial processing plan is to 'help put people smugglers out of business and prevent asylum seekers making the dangerous journey to Australia by boat'.[134] But the High Court declared that the arrangement was invalid, and ordered that no asylum seeker could be removed from Australia under the arrangement.[135]

15.5.7 Losing Refugee Status

A refugee can lose the protection of the *Refugee Convention* only in limited circumstances, through, for example, the exception to the *non-refoulement* protection noted above, or because they committed either a 'crime against peace, a war crime, or a crime against humanity', a 'serious non-political crime' in another country before becoming a refugee, or 'an act contrary to the purposes and principles of the United Nations'.[136]

These reasons for losing refugee status can be related to concerns about terrorism and national security, and they readily conflate with the instinctive concerns over sovereignty that are raised by the phenomenon of unauthorised arrivals of asylum seekers. Mr Faisal almost lost his refugee status; he ultimately retained it, but will never know why it was in doubt.

SNAPSHOT: NATIONAL SECURITY CONCERNS

Mr Faisal was an Iraqi who was persecuted there for his political opinions. He travelled to Indonesia where he paid a people smuggler to take him by boat to Australia. The boat was intercepted by the Royal Australian Navy and Mr Faisal was taken to Nauru (under Australia's 'Pacific Solution'—Chapter 15.5.6) where he made application for asylum in 2001. His application was refused and he was told that more information was required.

Mr Faisal remained in detention in Nauru. In 2003 his application for asylum was accepted, subject to his being assessed for national security risk. He was interviewed by the Australian Security Intelligence Organisation (ASIO) for eight hours, answering questions about his personal history. He was later told that the delay in transferring him to Australia was because he had not co-operated with ASIO. In 2004 ASIO again interviewed him, for about six and a half hours, and was again told that he was failing to co-operate. Mr Faisal refused to participate in any further interviews.

Sometime in 2005 or 2006 Mr Faisal was taken to Australia, where he was admitted to hospital for six months. He agreed to a further ASIO interview, which lasted six hours, and was asked the same questions

134 The Prime Minister, the Minister for Immigration, 'The Regional Cooperation Framework' *Media Release*, 7 May 2011.

135 *Plaintiff M70/2011 v Minister for Immigration and Citizenship*; [2011] HCA 32; the Court held that asylum seekers can be removed from Australia only to a country that is bound by international law or its own law to provide: effective refugee determination procedures, protection pending determination, protection for people determined to be refugees, and certain human rights standards.

136 *Refugee Convention*, see above, n 1, art 1F (entered into force 22 April 1954).

that he had been asked on the previous occasions. He was then advised by ASIO that he had been accepted in Australia as a refugee.

Mr Faisal subsequently tried to get access to the ASIO security assessment, but was unsuccessful; the Court agreed that the assessment could be kept from him in the interests of national security.[137]

15.6 THE LAWFULNESS OF DETENTION

The issue of isolated and lengthy detention of refugees is a worldwide one, from Nordic countries[138] to Australia.[139] The *Refugee Convention* recognises a state's limited right to detain refugees and asylum seekers: only 'in time of war or other grave and exceptional circumstances [as] is necessary … in the interests of national security',[140] and otherwise only when 'necessary and … only … until their status in the country is regularized or they obtain admission into another country'.[141]

The UNHCR is clear in stating that: '[i]n view of the hardship which it involves, detention should usually be avoided … detention measures should be subject to judicial or administrative review [and] … conditions of detention of refugees and asylum seekers must be humane'.[142] Despite this, '[t]he increasing use of detention as a restriction on the freedom of movement of asylum seekers on the grounds of their illegal entry is a matter of major concern to UNHCR, NGOs, other agencies as well as Governments'.[143] Recognising that some asylum seekers and refugees will be detained, the UNHCR has set out the proper limits on their detention, saying that '[d]etention that is automatic and prolonged and/or which takes place in conditions which are inadequate … is not in line with international

137 *Mohammed Yussef Sagar and Muhammad Faisal v Paul O'Sullivan sued in his capacity as Director-General of Security* [2011] FCA 182.

138 See eg R Lööf and B Gorlick, 'Implementing International Human Rights Law on behalf of Asylum Seekers and Refugees: The Record of the Nordic Countries', in J Grimheden & R Ring (eds), *Human Rights Law: From Dissemination to Application: Essays in Honour of Göran Melander*, Martinus Nijhoff Publishers, Leiden, 2006, 251–88, 262.

139 See eg M Crock, B Saul and A Dastyari, *Future Seekers II: Refugees and Irregular Migration in Australia*, The Federation Press, 2006.

140 *Refugee Convention*, see above, n 1, art 9 (entered into force 22 April 1954).

141 *Refugee Convention*, see above, n 1, art 31(2) (entered into force 22 April 1954).

142 UN High Commissioner for Refugees: *Detention of Refugees and Asylum Seekers*, Executive Committee Conclusion no 44 (XXXVII), UN Doc 12A (A/41/12/Add.1) (1986).

143 UN High Commissioner for Refugees, *UNHCR's Revised Guidelines on Applicable Criteria and Standards Relating to the Detention of Asylum Seekers*, Conclusion (1999) <www.unhcr.org.au/pdfs/detentionguidelines.pdf> at 14 March 2011. On the lawfulness of detention, see generally G S Goodwin-Gill & J McAdam, *The Refugee in International Law*, 3rd edn, Oxford University Press, Oxford, 2007, 462–71; UN High Commissioner for Refugees, *Global Consultations on International Protection/Third Track: Reception of Asylum-Seekers, Including Standards of Treatment, in the Context of Individual Asylum Systems*, para 7, UN Doc EC/GC/01/17 (2001); UN High Commissioner for Refugees, ibid.

standards'. Australia has taken a 'distinctive' approach[144] to detaining refugees and asylum seekers when compared with approaches in other western industrial countries.[145] Australia's detention centre regime was created because 'the Parliament considers that it is in the national interest that each non-citizen who is a designated person should be kept in custody until he or she (a) leaves Australia; or (b) is given an entry permit'.[146] Putting to one side the issue of whether detention of unauthorised arrivals is in the public interest,[147] this view fails to respond to the UNHCR's requirement that detention be for maximum period set by law and not of an unlimited or excessive length.

The UN Human Rights Committee (HRC) has consistently found Australia's lengthy detention of asylum seekers to be 'arbitrary', in violation of the ICCPR, and the conditions of detention to be in violation of Australia's human rights treaty obligations—discussed further below.

15.7 THE HUMAN RIGHTS OF REFUGEES

The *Refugee Convention* recognises 'rights' of refugees—in articles 4 (freedom to exercise religion), 14 (artistic rights), 16 (access to courts and legal advice), 22 (education), 24 (employment conditions and social security), 26 (freedom of movement), 27 (travel documents), 29 (equality in taxation), 30 (transfer of assets) and 34 (naturalisation). But, as noted above, none of these guarantees is enforceable; they operate more as a statement of expectations of states' conduct than as a statement of states' obligations.

Nevertheless, if refugees and asylum seekers are in a state that has ratified human rights treaties then, as the UNHCR points out,[148] they have the protection of those treaties. Each of the ICCPR, ICESCR, CAT, CEDAW and CRC establish standards relevant to the situation of refugees, and violation of those treaties can be the subject of complaint to the relevant treaty body, discussed in Chapter 7.4.7.

The human rights of asylum-seekers may also be protected by regional human rights instruments, such as the *Refugee Qualification Directive* in Europe, the *African Charter on Human and Peoples' Rights*,

144 F Brennan, *Tampering with Asylum*, University of Queensland Press, Brisbane, 2003, 6.

145 See, eg, A Nicholas, 'Protecting Refugees: Alternatives to a Policy of Mandatory Detention' (2002) 8 (1) *Australian Journal of Human Rights* 69; F Brennan, ibid Ch 5.

146 Previously *Migration Act 1958* (Cth) s 54J, since renumbered as s 176 by *Migration Legislation Amendment Act 1994* (Cth). See also *Al-Kateb v Godwin* [2004] HCA 37; 219 CLR 562 in which the High Court decided that the *Australian Constitution* does not limit the Parliament's power to legislate for the indefinite detention of asylum seekers.

147 See J Bailey, 'Australia and Asylum Seekers: Is a Policy of Protection in the "National Interest"' (2002) 8(1) *Australian Journal of Human Rights* 57.

148 UN High Commissioner for Refugees, *Global Consultations on International Protection/Third Track: Reception of Asylum-Seekers, Including Standards of Treatment, in the Context of Individual Asylum Systems*, paras 5–6, UN Doc EC/GC/01/17 (2001); UN High Commissioner for Refugees, *UNHCR's Revised Guidelines on Applicable Criteria and Standards Relating to the Detention of Asylum Seekers*, Conclusion (1999) <www.unhcr.org.au/pdfs/detentionguidelines.pdf>, which 'address exclusively the detention of asylum seekers'. See generally, A Edwards, above, n 19, 304–7; see above, n 72, 119–23, 439–912.

the *African Charter on the Rights and Welfare of the Child*, the *American Convention on Human Rights* ('Pact of San Jose'), and the *Latin American Conventions on Territorial Asylum and on Diplomatic Asylum*.[149]

15.7.1 Arbitrary Detention and Torture

The most directly relevant human rights treaty provisions to the practice of detention are article 9(1) of the ICCPR and article 37(b) of the CROC, both of which prohibit 'arbitrary' detention.[150] As described below, the situation in Australia illustrates that there is real debate over what constitutes 'arbitrary' detention.

The UN Commission of Human Rights' Working Group on Arbitrary Detention has set out 'criteria for determining whether or not the deprivation of liberty of asylum seekers and immigrants may be arbitrary',[151] saying that an asylum-seeker must, among other things 'have the possibility, while in custody, of communicating with the outside world ... be brought promptly before a judicial or other authority, and [be detained for] a maximum period ... set by law'.

For some refugees, the very fact of detention—arbitrary or not—could constitute torture; for many, the conditions of detention can amount to torture. Torture and cruel, inhuman or degrading treatment or punishment is prohibited by the CAT and by article 7 of the ICCPR and article 37(a) of the CRC.

SNAPSHOT: ARBITRARY DETENTION IN AUSTRALIA

UN human rights bodies have consistently expressed the view that the nature and conditions of detention violate Australia's international human rights treaty obligations, and Australia has as consistently rejected that view.[152]

As early as 1998 the Australian Human Rights Commission inquired into the detention of refugees and asylum seekers in Australia.[153] The report gave a detailed account of the conditions in each centre, and found that Australia's immigration detention regime 'would be considered arbitrary and unreasonable under the provisions of international law, including ICCPR article 9.1 and CRoC article 37(b)'.[154]

149 *Global Consultations on International Protection/Third Track*, ibid paras 5–6.

150 See also UN Human Rights Committee, *General Comment No 8: Right to Liberty and Security of Persons*, 60th sess, UN Doc HRI/GEN/1/Rev.6 at 130 (1982).

151 UN Commission on Human Rights Working Group on Arbitrary Detention, *Body of Principles for the Protection of All Persons under Any Form of Detention or Imprisonment Regarding the Situation of Immigrants and Asylum Seekers*, UN Doc E/CN.4/2000/4/Annex 2 (1999).

152 Australia is not alone in rejecting such views: Belarus, Canada, the Netherlands and the Philippines have all done so: S Persaud, see above, n 74, n 27.

153 Australian Human Rights Commission, *Those Who've Come Across the Seas: Detention of Unauthorised Arrivals*, Commonwealth of Australia, 1998.

154 Ibid 53.

The AHRC has tabled in the Commonwealth Parliament[155] a number of reports of complaints under the ICCPR where it has found a violation of ICCPR article 10 in the failure to provide adequate medical services to persons in migration detention,[156] and violations of ICCPR articles 9(1) and 10(1) arising from the solitary confinement of refugees and asylum seekers.

In 2003 the UN Working Group on Arbitrary Detention reported to the UN Commission of Human Rights that in Australia:[157]

> the conditions of detention are in many ways similar to prison conditions: detention centres are surrounded by impenetrable and closely guarded razor wire; detainees are under permanent supervision; if escorted outside the centre they are, as a rule, handcuffed; escape from a centre constitutes a criminal offence under the law and the escapee is prosecuted. In certain respects, their regime is less favourable (indeterminate detention; exclusion from legal aid; lack of judicial control of detention; etc). Several detainees who had been in both situations told the delegation that their time in prison had been less stressful than the time spent in the centres.

Observing on Australia's third and fourth reports under the ICCPR, the HRC said that it 'considers that the mandatory detention under the *Migration Act* of ... asylum-seekers raises questions of compliance with article 9, paragraph 1, of the Covenant' and it 'urged Australia to reconsider mandatory detention and instituting alternative means of maintaining an orderly immigration process'.[158] On numerous occasions since, the UN Human Rights Committee has said, in response to communications made to it by refugees and asylum seekers in detention, that their detention is arbitrary.

Australia has responded to the Committee's views on these communications by repeatedly defending its immigration detention regime.[159] Regarding the communication of *A*, the Australian Government said it is 'firmly of the view that immigration detention is justified for compelling reasons of domestic policy', and that it considers ... that the Australian system for assessing the claims of applicants for refugee status is fair and thorough and involves responsible management of individual cases. Regarding the communication of *Baban*, the Australian Government said it 'considers its system of immigration detention [a] reasonable legislative judgement' to control entry into Australia. And regarding the communication of *Bakhtiyari*, the Australian Government 'reiterate[d] its view that immigration detention is not arbitrary'.

Observing on Australia's report, the Committee said it remained concerned, and it called on Australia 'to enact in legislation a comprehensive immigration framework in compliance with the [ICCPR]'.[160] Similarly the

155 The Australian Human Rights Commission has the power to receive and report on complaints of violations of the ICCPR and CROC (see Chapter 10.4.2).

156 Australian Human Rights Commission, *Report of an Inquiry into a Complaint by Mr Hassan Ghomwari Concerning his Immigration Detention and the Adequacy of the Medical Treatment He Received While Detained*, Report No 23 (2002).

157 UN Commission of Human Rights, *Civil and Political Rights, Including the Question of Torture and Detention: Report of the Working Group on Arbitrary Detention, Visit to Australia*, 18, UN Doc E/CN.4/2003/8/Add.2 (2002). See also N Poynder, 'The Incommunicado Detention of Boat People' (1997) 3(2) *Australian Journal of Human Rights* 53.

158 UN Commission of Human Rights, *Concluding Observations of the Human Rights Committee: Australia*, paras 498–528, UN Doc A/55/4024 (2000).

159 Australia's Fifth Periodic Report under the *International Covenant on Civil and Political Rights*, UN Doc CCPR/C/AUS/5 (2008).

160 See above, n 158.

CAT Committee, observing on Australia's third report under CAT,[161] called on Australia to '[c]onsider abolishing its policy of mandatory immigration detention for those entering irregularly the State party's territory'.[162]

15.7.2 Conditions of Detention

As Persaud points out, '[i]n order to best respond to the asylum-seekers' claims and their possible plight, the conditions of detention are of utmost importance. Being under distress and in a situation of uncertainty, asylum seekers are at risk to develop traumas or mental illnesses in detention'.[163]

Article 10 of the ICCPR requires that people in detention 'be treated with humanity and with respect for the inherent dignity of the human person',[164] and the prohibition against torture and cruel, inhuman or degrading treatment or punishment in CAT, article 7 of the ICCPR, and article 37(a) of the CROC. Other considerations are the right to have, maintain and re-establish family derived from articles 17 and 23,[165] the right to non-discrimination derived from articles 2 and 26,[166] and minority groups' right, in article 27, to enjoy their culture, profess their religion and use their language.[167]

Article 22(1) of the CROC makes specific provision for 'a child who is seeking refugee status or who is considered a refugee', to guarantee that they 'receive appropriate protection and humanitarian assistance in the enjoyment of applicable rights set forth in the present Convention and in other international human rights or humanitarian instruments'. Also relevant to detention of children, article 9(1) of the CROC requires that 'a child shall not be separated from his or her parents against their will [unless] necessary for the best interests of the child', and article 24(1) requires a state to 'strive to ensure that no child is deprived of his or her right of access to ... health care services'.

Under article 12 of the International Covenant on Economic, Social and Cultural Rights (ICESCR), states are obliged to 'recognise the right of everyone to the enjoyment of the highest attainable standard of physical and mental health'.

161 Australia's Fourth Report under the *Convention Against Torture and Other Cruel, Inhuman or Degrading Treatment or Punishment*, UN Doc CAT/C/67/Add.7 (2005).

162 UN Committee Against Torture, see above, n 133, para 11.

163 S Persaud, see above, n 74, 19.

164 UN Human Rights Committee, *General Comment No 21: Replaces General Comment 9 Concerning Humane Treatment of Persons Deprived of Liberty (Art 10)*, 44th sess, UN Doc HRI/GEN/1/Rev.6 at 153 (1992).

165 See UN Human Rights Committee, *General Comment No 19: Protection of the Family, the Right to Marriage and Equality of the Spouses*, 39th sess, UN Doc HRI/GEN/1/Rev.6 at 149 (1990); S Persaud, see above, n 74, 21; A Edwards, see above, n 19, 309–19.

166 See UN Human Rights Committee, *General Comment No 18: Non-Discrimination*, 37th sess, UN Doc HRI/GEN/1/Rev.6 at 149 (1989); S Persaud, see above, n 74, 22–3.

167 See also UN Human Rights Committee, *General Comment No 23: The Rights of Minorities*, 50th sess, UN Doc CCPR/21/Rev.1/Add.5 (1994); S Persaud, see above, n 74, 23–4.

In 2002 Australia's detention centres were visited by both an ECOSOC Working Group on Arbitrary Detention, and Justice PN Bhagwati on behalf of the UN High Commissioner for Human Rights. Among many concerns the Working Group identified 'the psychological impact of detention on asylum-seekers, who suffer "collective depression syndrome"; the denial of family unity in several cases; [and] children in detention'.[168] Justice Bhagwati's 'general impression' was that 'the human rights situation of persons in immigration detention in Australia is a matter of serious concern', and specifically that the conditions of detention were inhuman and degrading, in light of ICCPR article 7 and the provisions of CAT.[169]

In *Behrooz v Secretary, Department of Immigration and Multicultural and Indigenous Affairs*,[170] an asylum seeker failed in arguing before the Australian High Court that the harshness of the conditions of detention rendered the detention unlawful because they exceed any conditions that could be necessary to carry out the requirements of the *Migration Act 1958* (Cth).

15.8 PROTECTING PEOPLE WHO ARE NOT 'REFUGEES'

People flee their state of nationality and seek protection elsewhere for many reasons other than the five 'Convention grounds'.

15.8.1 'Economic' Refugees

The strict categorisation of refugees in the *Refugee Convention* is increasingly being challenged by modern complexity. It is quite simply no longer the case, if it ever was, that there is a single simple reason for a person's fleeing persecution. People's fear is based on factors other than—or intertwined with—their race, religion, nationality, social group or political opinion.

Because of the status accorded people who fit the limited categories of the *Refugee Convention*, identifying people as 'refugees' for another reason is often a pejorative: the term 'economic refugee' disdainfully refers to someone seen to be looking for a better economic environment in which to live. If a person's persecution is kept in mind as the fundamental criterion for refugee status, then there are people who do fall into a category of 'economic refugee'. They face economic persecution because of their race, religion, nationality, political opinion or membership of a particular social group, and so could meet the definition under the *Refugee Convention*.[171]

---

168 UN Commission of Human Rights, see above, n 157, 2.

169 Justice P N Bhagwati, Regional Advisor for Asia and the Pacific of the United Nations High Commissioner for Human Rights, *Human Rights and Immigration Detention in Australia: Mission to Australia 24 May to 2 June 2002*, para 20. The report was rejected by the Australian government as 'fundamentally flawed', Joint Media Release of Ministers Downer, Ruddock and Williams, 31 July 2002.

170 [2004] HCA 36; 219 CLR 486.

171 See J McAdam, 'From Economic Refugees to Climate Refugees? Review of International Refugee Law and Socio-Economic Rights: Refuge from Deprivation by Michelle Foster' (2009) 10(2) *Melbourne Journal of International Law* 579, 580.

This is, however, a narrow way of thinking about an economic refugee, necessarily wedded to the categories of the *Refugee Convention*. It may well be that poverty and socio-economic deprivation itself is the root cause of a person's fear of persecution—effectively a class-based persecution—but unless the person can invoke the limited categories of the *Refugee Convention* they will not be recognised as a 'genuine' refugee.

Whether a person who seeks refuge from economic persecution is labelled an 'economic refugee' or 'economic migrant', the label challenges their having any status under the *Refugee Convention*, and discounts their fear of persecution. There is a widely accepted and dichotomy between so-called economic migrants/refugees and 'genuine' refugees; despite having its own mandate that enables it to act outside the *Refugee Convention*, '[e]ven the UNHCR tends to accept the dichotomy'.[172] The result is that the claims of people who are truly economic refugees, fleeing economic persecution because of a Convention ground, are easily dismissed by states, and by commentators within states, who seek ways to minimise their obligations to people fleeing other regimes.

15.8.2 'Environmental' or 'Climate' Refugees

Although environmental phenomena cause people to migrate involuntarily, 'several researchers have rejected the very concept of environmental refugees'.[173] Objections to the concept are that it is hard to identify an 'environmental' factor as the principal cause of involuntary migration, and it 'conflates the idea of disaster victim and refugee'.[174] Nevertheless, it is undoubtedly the case that environmental phenomena such as hurricanes, torrential rains, floods, drought, desertification and rising sea levels can cause migration.[175]

There is often a political dimension to 'climate-induced displacement', where '[p]olitical instability, military conflict, ecological stress and socio-economic change' combine with 'increasing vulnerability to poverty and social deprivation [and] weak state institutions that are inadequate in managing competition over diminishing resources'.[176] Despite the visible environmental reason for a person's leaving their home, there are often political and social circumstances that force some to flee while others are able to stay. It may be that the climatic circumstances force a person to flee only because the state does not assist, or actively discriminates against a person. It is this complexity of factors that

172 M Foster, *International Refugee Law and Socio-Economic Rights: Refuge from Deprivation*, Cambridge University Press, Cambridge, 2007, 4.

173 E Piguet, 'Climate Change and Forced Migration', *New Issues in Refugee Research*, Working Paper No 153, UNHCR, 2008, 3 (citations omitted).

174 Ibid.

175 Ibid 8; and see J McAdam (ed) *Climate Change and Displacement: Multidisciplinary Perspectives*, Hart Publishing, Oxford, 2010; J McAdam, *Climate Change, Forced Migration, and International Law*, Oxford University Press, Oxford, 2012. (forthcoming 2012).

176 Human Rights and Equal Opportunity Commission, *Background Paper: Human Rights and Climate Change* (2008) 8. See also the example of the 'complex dynamics of conflict, disasters and human mobility' in Somalia, in V Kolmannskog, 'Climate Change, Disaster, Displacement and Migration: Initial Evidence from Africa', (*New Issues in Refugee Research*, Working Paper No 180, UNHCR, 2009).

highlight the narrow and rigid nature of the five grounds for persecution recognised by the *Refugee Convention*.[177]

People's movement away from adverse environmental events are readily characterised as migration: the term 'environmental' or 'climate' refugee has the same pejorative tone—and is put to the same dismissive use—as the term economic refugee.

15.8.3 Internally Displaced Persons

People who fear persecution but remain within the country of their nationality do not have access to the *Refugee Convention*, and '[n]either the UNHCR nor any other UN agency has any legal authority to "protect" persons within their own country'.[178] People in this situation are commonly referred to as 'internally displaced persons' (IDPs), perhaps the largest group of vulnerable people in the world.[179]

IDPs can be separated into different groups requiring different humanitarian responses: 'IDPs in rural camps [and] urban IDPs ... not formally separated from the local community or housed in easily recognizable regions'. For urban IDPs, it is 'often difficult to analytically distinguish ... the forced internally displaced from regular rural-to-urban migrants'.[180]

The *UN Guiding Principles on Internal Displacement*[181] are intended to guide states in discharging their responsibilities to IDPs. Of course many states do not recognise or discharge those responsibilities, and the response to IDPs is shared among a range of UN agencies, including the UNHCR, the World Health Organisation (WHO), the UN Development Programme (UNDP) and the United Nations Children's Fund (UNICEF).

15.8.4 The UNHCR Mandate

The UNHCR has been authorised by the UN to use its 'good offices' to assist people whose situation is not within the *Refugee Convention* but is nevertheless 'such as to be of concern to the international community'.[182] The need often arises as a result of mass exodus from conflict, such as the flight from Cambodia, Laos and Vietnam in and after 1975,[183] and more recently from Burma and Afghanistan.

177 See eg J McAdam and B Saul, 'Displacement with Dignity: Climate Change, Migration and Security in Bangladesh' (2010) 53 *German Yearbook of International Law* 1.

178 G S Goodwin-Gill & J McAdam, see above, n 2, 34.

179 A Fielden, 'Ignored Displaced Persons: The Plight of IDPs in Urban Areas', *New Issues in Refugee Research*, Working Paper No 161, UNHCR, 2008, 1, quoting UN High Commissioner for Refugees, *Internally Displaced Persons: Questions and Answers*, Geneva, 2007, 1.

180 Ibid.

181 *Guiding Principles on Internal Displacement*, UN Doc E/CN.4/1998/53/Add.2 (1998).

182 G S Goodwin-Gill & J McAdam, see above, n 2, 24 quoting *Chinese Refugees in Hong Kong*, GA Res 1167(XII), UM GAOR, 12th sess, 727th plen mtg, UN Doc A/Res/1167(XII) (1957).

183 G S Goodwin-Gill & J McAdam, see above, n 2, 27–8.

The scale of the humanitarian need is enormous: more than 26 million people—10.4 million refugees and 15.6 million IDPs—were receiving protection or assistance from UNHCR at the end of 2009.[184]

The increasing extent to which the UNHCR exercises its mandate is controversial. Humanitarian issues within a country of origin and in areas of armed conflict 'was largely the preserve of the International Committee of the Red Cross'[185] but the UNHCR is now increasingly involved. Its involvement is due to a range of factors including that 'many refugee-hosting countries [in western Africa, for example] are themselves in the throes of armed conflict and violence ... refugees have left their own country only to find that their country of asylum is equally dangerous'.[186]

There seems to be little argument that the UNHCR's priority 'must surely be to save lives',[187] but the effectiveness of its work, and the considerations that inform it, such as international law, inter-national relations and human rights principles, are the subject of debate.[188]

15.8.5 Complementary Protection

As well as their *Refugee Convention* obligations, 'States have always recognised, to varying degrees, the protection needs of people falling outside the "refugee" definition of article 1A(2) of the Convention'.[189] This is recognition of an obligation of complementary protection, which 'may be based on a human rights treaty or on more general humanitarian principles, such as providing assistance to persons fleeing from generalized violence ... simply operat[ing] as a form of human rights or humanitarian protection triggered by States' expanded *non-refoulement* obligations'.[190]

States therefore offer complementary protection in an indirect way because of their obligations under human rights treaties such as the ICCPR and the CAT, discussed below. As well, some states volunteer to take on complementary protection in specific provisions. Complementary protection does not, therefore, 'mandate a lesser duration or quality of status but simply assesses international protection needs on a wider basis than the 1951 Convention'.[191]

184 UN High Commissioner for Refugees, *2009 Global Trends: Refugees, Asylum Seekers, Returnees, Internally Displaced and Stateless Persons* (2010).

185 J Crisp, see above, n 56, 79.

186 J Crisp, see above, n 56, 80.

187 M Barutciski, 'A Critical View on UNHCR's Mandate Dilemmas' (2002) 14(2 & 3) *International Journal of Refugee Law* 365, 365–6.

188 Ibid; M Barutciski, 'The Reinforcement of Non-Admission Polices and the Subversion of UNHCR: Displacement and Internal Assistance in Bosnia-Herzegovina (1992–1994)' (1996) 8 (1–2) *International Journal of Refugee Law* 49; N Morris, 'Protection Dilemmas and UNHCR's Response: A Personal View From Within UNHCR' (1997) 9(3) *International Journal of Refugee Law* 492; M Weiner, 'The Clash of Norms: Dilemmas in Refugee Policies' (1998) 11(4) *Journal of Refugee Studies* 443.

189 G S Goodwin-Gill & J McAdam, see above, n 2, 285.

190 J McAdam, 'Complementary Protection and Beyond: How States Deal with Human Rights Protection, *New Issues in Refugee Research*, Working Paper No 118, UNHCR, 2005, 1.

191 Ibid 2.

SNAPSHOT: AUSTRALIA AND COMPLEMENTARY PROTECTION

Australia does not offer complementary protection. Protection of that sort is a discretionary matter for the Minister for Immigration;[192] the Minister under the new federal government in early 2008 expressed reservations about the high level of discretion he enjoyed, saying that he had 'too much power'.[193] In 2009 the Migration Amendment (Complementary Protection) Bill (Cth) was introduced into the Australian Parliament, to amend the *Migration Act 1958* (Cth) by extending Australia's protection obligations beyond the *Refugee Convention* to people who, if they were removed from Australia, face a real risk of irreparable harm. A Senate committee inquiry recommended, by majority, that the Bill be passed with only minor amendments.[194] The Bill was not passed before the election in late 2010, and was reintroduced as the Migration Amendment (Complementary Protection) Bill (Cth) 2011.

Other states and regions have responded in different ways. The EU *Refugee Qualification Directive* offers only 'subsidiary' protection to a person in need of protection who is not a refugee,[195] and 'has failed to implement a common status for all beneficiaries of international protection'.[196] Canada, on the other hand, 'has a single determination procedure for [Refugee] Convention refugees and other persons in need of protection, together called 'protected persons'.[197]

15.8.6 *Non-Refoulement*

People who are not covered by the *Refugee Convention* are nevertheless protected against *refoulement* by the equivalent—and at times stronger—human rights treaty guarantees, discussed above in Chapter 15.4.4. But protection from *refoulement* does not necessarily lead to a long-term solution to the situation of a person who is not recognised as a refugee.

SNAPSHOT: AUSTRALIA AND *NON-REFOULEMENT*

Mr Elmi, a Somali national, sought asylum in Australia and was kept in immigration detention. His claim was rejected, and he exhausted his appeal rights, all the way to being refused leave to appeal to the High Court.

Mr Elmi complained to the CAT Committee that Australia would be in breach of article 3 of CAT if it were to send him back to Somalia, as he faced a real risk of torture there. The Committee agreed, saying that

192 *Migration Act 1958* (Cth) s 417.

193 Evidence to Senate Standing Committee on Legal and Constitutional Affairs Estimates (Additional Budget Estimates), Parliament of Australia, Canberra, 19 February 2008, *Committee Hansard*, 19 L & CA 22 (Senator Chris Evans). For criticisms of the discretion by the UN Committee Against Torture see above, n 133.

194 Senate Standing Committee on Legal and Constitutional Affairs Legislation Committee, Migration Amendment (Complementary Protection) Bill 2009 [Provisions], Commonwealth of Australia, October 2009.

195 See Chapter 15.3.3 above.

196 J McAdam, see above, n 190, 5.

197 Ibid 11. See also *Immigration and Refugee Protection Act 2001* (Canada).

substantial grounds existed for believing that Mr Elmi would be in danger of being subjected to torture if forcibly returned to Somalia.[198]

The response of the Australian government was to keep Mr Elmi in immigration detention while a solution was found; Mr Elmi decided to leave Australia voluntarily and seek refugee status elsewhere.[199] Mr Elmi left Australia but did not arrive at his destination; he seems to have avoided the risk he faced of returning to Somalia, and his whereabouts are unknown.

Since *Elmi*, similar communications against Australia have been made to the CAT Committee by asylum seekers who say that they face torture in their country of origin, but in none of them has the CAT Committee been satisfied that the person faced 'a foreseeable, real and personal risk of being tortured'.[200]

15.9 CONCLUSION AND ISSUES

The *Refugee Convention* is not a human rights treaty. This is not because it is not among the UN's international human rights treaties; the same is true of the conventions of the International Labour Organisation, but they are regarded as human rights treaties, because they confer rights on individuals and corresponding obligations on states. The *Refugee Convention* sets up a regime for recognising a person as refugee, but does not give a refugee a right to asylum. The international politics of the time, and the pervasive influence of state sovereignty, mean that the *Refugee Convention* leaves states to decide for themselves what their response will be, if any, to a person's being in need of asylum.

Nor do the processes of the *Refugee Convention* equate to those of the human rights treaties: it has no mechanism for monitoring states' conduct and compliance, and states can ignore their obligations under the *Refugee Convention* with impunity.

There are, however, significant human rights dimensions to the situation of refugees. Refugees have the rights and freedoms declared by the UDHR, but they cannot enjoy and be protected by those rights when they are being persecuted by their own state and have no right of asylum from another. This is the great hiatus in the operation of the *Refugee Convention*, where it fails to ensure protection for people who are, by definition, extremely vulnerable. A resulting issue is whether the refugee regime could operate otherwise—what would be the implications of grating a right to asylum, and how likely is it that states would agree to accept that refugees have such a right?

For the millions of refugees who are caught in the limbo of seeking asylum but having no right to it, human rights issue arise daily. They are detained arbitrarily, and/or in conditions that threaten their physical and mental health. They have little or no access to work, education and public services. The challenge posed by those who are fleeing persecution is how to ensure that their human rights are protected. Who will take that responsibility, and at whose cost?

---

198 UN Committee Against Torture, *Communication No 120/1998: Australia* 22nd sess, UN Doc CAT/C/22/D/120/1998 (1999).

199 An unresolved question later arose as to Mr Elmi's bona fides in his claim of persecution, see F Brennan, above, n 144, 186.

200 See Chapter 10.5.4.

As the discussion in this chapter illustrates, an increasing challenge facing the global community is the needs of people who fall outside the narrow categories of persecution in the *Refugee Convention*. People do not fell only if they know they will meet the *Refugee Convention* definition of refugee; they flee because they fear persecution. People who flee 'internally', or leave a state for reasons that are not obviously covered by the *Refugee Convention*, are no less in need of protection, and impose no less of a demand on states. But how likely is it that states would agree to extend the coverage of the *Refugee Convention*, or would agree to another international treaty to ensure protection from those who are outside its strict scope?

Complementary protection measures are one response to the needs of people who are not refugees strictly speaking, but those measures seem to be limited by states' reluctance to take on too great a responsibility. Even if complementary protection measures are taken, how likely are they to extend to meet the emerging needs of people fleeing persecution in adverse economic and climatic conditions?

16 WOMEN

CONTENTS

16.1 INTRODUCTION

Claims for special recognition of the rights of women have a long history, stemming principally from men's domination of women in almost all areas of life. In 1791 Olympe de Gouge published *The Declaration of the Rights of Woman*, declaring that woman is 'born free and lives equal to man in her rights',[1] and Mary Wollstonecraft wrote in 1792 that 'If the abstract rights of man will bear discussion and explanation, those of woman, by a parity of reasoning, will not shrink from the same test'.[2] These, with John Stuart Mill's *The Subjection of Women*, are examples of early liberal feminist theory, the starting point of which 'is the understanding that women are in fact the same as men, and therefore equal to men'.[3]

This chapter begins with a brief overview of the feminist theories that have contributed to an increasingly sophisticated understanding of women's place/s in the world, and then gives an account

1 M Ishay, *The History of Human Rights: From Ancient Times to the Globalization Era*, 2nd edn, University of California Press, Berkeley, 2008, 112.

2 K Minogue, 'The History of the Idea of Human Rights' in W Laqueur & B Rubin (eds), *The Human Rights Reader*, Temple University Press, Philadelphia, 1979, 3–16, 15.

3 K Mahoney, 'Theoretical Perspectives on Women's Human Rights and Strategies for the Implementation' 21 (1995–1996) *Brooklyn Journal of International Law* 799, 802.

of the international law and institutions that are designed to address oppression and exploitation and/or discrimination against, women.

In a chapter such as this, there is scope for debate about differences in emphasis and implications among various similar terms, such as 'women's rights', 'human rights of women', and 'women's human rights'. The debate turns on a sensitivity to the relationship between the established language and regimes for international human rights, and the situation(s) of women: whether that relationship is, for example, inclusionary, dependent, adversarial and so on. Acknowledging this debate, and its important political implications, this chapter follows Engle's lead in generally using the term 'women's human rights',[4] out of convenience and to conflate the terms 'women's rights' and 'human rights of women'.[5]

There is a pervasive ambiguity in relationship between international human rights and the goal of achieving equality for women. On the one hand there is enthusiasm and support for the posited rights in international instruments, and for the related institutions. On the other hand there are both theoretical and pragmatic reservations about attaching hopes for women's freedom and full expression of identity to systems of law and practice that are part of the system that has denied those hopes: to 'law-making institutions of the international legal order [which] have always been, and continue to be, dominated by men'.[6]

One way of seeing the dilemma—'the paradox of feminism'[7]—is whether to pursue women's equality through working in the mainstream of human rights, or through a separate and specialised set of institutions and procedures:

> In many ways, the creation of a specialised 'women's' branch of human rights law, of which the Women's Convention is the flagship, has allowed its marginalisation. 'Mainstream' human rights institutions have tended to ignore the application of human rights norms to women. The UN's separation of 'general' and 'women's' matters seems to have disadvantaged women. There is a strategic dilemma with respect to international legal structures and women. On the one hand, the attempt to improve the position of women through more generally applicable measures has allowed women's concerns to be submerged by what are regarded as more 'global' issues. On the other hand, the price of the creation of separate institutional mechanisms and special measures dealing with women within the UN system has typically been the creation of a 'women's ghetto', given less power, fewer resources and a lower priority than 'mainstream' human rights bodies.[8]

4 See H Charlesworth, 'What Are Women's International Human Rights?' in R Cook (ed), *Women's Rights in International Law*, University of Pennsylvania Press, Philadelphia, 1994, 58–84.

5 K Engle, 'International Human Rights and Feminism: When Discourse Meet' (1991–1992) 13 *Michigan Journal of International Law* 517, 517 n 2.

6 H Charlesworth, 'Human Rights as Men's Rights' in J Peters and A Wolper (eds), *Women's Rights, Human Rights: International Feminist Perspectives*, Routledge, 1995, 103–13, 103.

7 H Charlesworth, 'Not Waving but Drowning: Gender Mainstreaming and Human Rights' (2005) *18 Harvard Human Rights Journal* 1, 1, <http://www.law.harvard.edu/students/orgs/hrj/iss18/charlesworth.shtml>.

8 H Charlesworth, 'Women's Rights' [2001] *Human Rights Law Resources* 9, <http://portsea.austlii.edu.au/au/other/HRLRes/2001/9/>; and see F Gaer, 'Women, International Law and International Institutions: The Case of the United Nations' (2009) 32 *Women's Studies International Forum* 60, 61.

To the extent that there has been an effort to 'mainstream' women's issues in the UN human rights system, Charlesworth has questioned the 'rather bland, bureaucratic acceptance of the method of gender mainstreaming [which] has deployed the idea of gender in a very limited way and has allowed the mainstream to tame and deradicalise claims to equality'. In her view, gender mainstreaming 'has made issues of inequality between women and men harder to identify and to deal with [and] has effectively drowned out the project of equality between women and men'.[9]

16.2 A FEMINIST FRAMEWORK

It remains debatable how far mainstream international human rights law procedures can and do advance women's human rights, but it is clear that feminist perspectives have contributed significantly to the development of the idea of human rights. Even if feminist analyses suggest that women's human rights could be better pursued outside mainstream human rights instruments and institutions, those same analyses bring new light to bear on the mainstream:

> In looking at the human rights framework from women's perspectives, women have shown how current human rights definitions and practices fail to account for the ways in which already recognized human rights abuses often affect women differently because of their gender. This approach acknowledges the importance of the existing concepts and activities, but also points out that there are dimensions within these received definitions that are gender-specific and that need to be addressed if the mechanisms, programs, and the human rights framework itself are to include and reflect the experiences of the female half of the world's population.[10]

There are many 'feminisms', from Marxist to existentialist.[11] Each is a 'mode of analysis' rather than a single school of thought (although there are competing views of this, and European feminists take quite different theoretical approaches[12]). Four related approaches have, however, had the closest and most consistent influence on the development of international law relating to women: liberal cultural, radical and post-modern feminism. The international instruments, institutions and procedures for the law of woman's human rights have been consistently analysed through these approaches to feminist thought.

9 See above, n 7.

10 C Bunch & S Frost, 'Women's Human Rights: An Introduction' in *Routledge International Encyclopaedia of Women: Global Women's Issues and Knowledge*, Routledge, New York and London, 2000, 1078–1083, 1079–1080.

11 K Mahoney, see above, n 3, 801 n 8.

12 On the many feminisms, see H Charlesworth, C Chinkin & S Wright, 'Feminist Approaches to International Law' (1991) 85 *American Journal of International Law* 613, 613–14 citing Hartsock, 'Feminist Theory and the Development of Revolutionary Strategy' in Z R Eisenstein (ed), *Capitalist Patriarchy and the Case for Socialist Feminism*, Monthly Review Press, New York, 1979, 56, 58; on competing views on the 'unity' of feminist perspectives, and on European theoretical approaches, see Charlesworth, Chinkin & Wright, this note above, at 613, n 6.

16.2.1 Four Stages of Feminism

Liberal feminists seek to achieve formal equality of treatment between men and women through gender-neutral rules, focusing on achieving opportunities that are equal to men's, under laws and in the legal system. But the formal equality of liberal feminism assumes that women's equal access to the basic institutions of society will result in their achieving equal status, and does not take into account actual differences between the situations of men and women: the fact that, for example, 'a right to hold and use property is irrelevant if women have no economic opportunities to acquire it in the first place'.[13]

Cultural feminism is a response to the limited recognition that liberal feminism gives to the social and political situation of women. Rather than claim equality as if a woman is 'the same as' a man, cultural feminism emphasises the positive aspects of stereotypical female characteristics, affirming '[p]assivity, motion, and connectedness ... as being as important and valuable as aggression, abstractedness and individuality'.[14] This approach, however, has been criticised for actually affirming male dominance by identifying woman's characteristics in terms that 'accept a male vision of womanhood which has been foisted upon women', and are 'qualities and characteristics of powerlessness'.[15]

Radical feminism focuses not on difference but on power, seeing women's oppression as caused by social and cultural arrangements that require women to submit to men. The radicalism of this feminism lies in its proposal to achieve equality not through reforming legal and political social structures, but through challenging the '[g]endered power, dominance, hierarchy, and competition imbued in social and cultural systems especially the family, the church, and the academy'.[16]

Post-modern feminism is a variant of radical feminism that rejects any universal feminist definitions. Claiming that it is typically male thinking to seek 'one true, feminist story of reality', a post-modern view values diversity and the individuality of a particular situation, believing that 'the more feminist thoughts we have, the better because women are not all the same'.[17] The post-modern anti-essentialist view is one that challenges the universalism that is at heart of

13 K Mahoney, see above, n 3, 804, reference omitted.

14 K Mahoney, see above, n 3, 799, 809, referring to L Bender, 'From Gender Difference to Feminist Solidarity: Using Carol Gilligan and an Ethic of Care in Law' (1990) 15 *Vermont Law Review* 1, 36; see above, n 4, 65–6.

15 K Mahoney, see above, n 3, 812–13, citing Catharine MacKinnon, *Feminism Unmodified: Discourses on Life and Law* (1987), 39.

16 K Mahoney, see above, n 3, p 814–15; see above, n 4, 66–7.

17 K Mahoney, see above, n 3, 827, citing S Harding, *The Science Question in Feminism* (1986), 28

the contemporary idea of human rights, discussed in Chapter 2.[18] Charlesworth points out that even though there may be no 'monolithic women's point of view', there are commonalties across cultures.[19]

Each of these stages of feminism have contributed to the development of women's human rights. The formal equality of liberal feminism has led to most states giving legal recognition to the equality of women in public life, for example, 'the right to vote, to hold public office, to participate in the professions, to hold, use and enjoy property on the same basis as men during and outside of marriage, and to have equal custody and guardianship of children'.[20] This idea of legally recognised equality is the aspect of women's rights that is given the greatest attention in the *Convention for the Elimination of All Forms of Discrimination Against Women* (CEDAW).[21]

The cultural critique of liberal feminism relied on women's lived experience to highlight the divide between public and private life that characterises conventional (male) conceptions of the legitimate scope of human rights, and exposed the private worlds in which women are contained, repressed and exploited.[22] Feminists' identification of the public/private divide has revolutionised understanding of the operation of international law, demanding recognition of women's rights for women in the full extent of their lives, and not merely the public life that has been the focus of civil and political rights.

Pursuing the private side of women's life, radical feminism has exposed and condemned violence against women, pornography, prostitution, sexual harassment, rape, practices such as *sutee*,[23] and *purdah*,[24] genital mutilation and sexual abuse of children: by promoting the differences in the lived experiences of women, post-modern feminism has helped to identify 'the relationship between gender and race, class, ethnicity, religion and other situated experiences'.[25]

These feminist perspectives enrich an understanding of women's lives, and of the human rights issues that actually women face. The following account shows, however, that the formal mechanisms of human rights law continue to be substantially premised on a liberal idea of achieving formal equality for women within established systems.

18 See eg K Nash, 2002. 'Human Rights for Women: An Argument for "Deconstructive Equality"' (2002) 31(4) *Economy and Society* 414.

19 H Charlesworth, see above, n 4, 63.

20 K Mahoney, see above, n 3, 803.

21 H Charlesworth, see above, n 4, 63–65.

22 H Charlesworth, see above, n 4, 58–84, 68–76.

23 A rarely practised Hindi custom, when a woman immolates herself after the death of her husband.

24 A Hindi and Islamic custom in which clothing and enclosures seclude women from public view.

25 K Mahoney, see above, n 3, 829.

16.3 UN BODIES

16.3.1 Commission on the Status of Women (CSW)

The Commission on the Status of Women (CSW) is a commission of the UN's Economic and Social Council (ECOSOC), and operates independently of other agencies of the UN dedicated to women's issues that have been brought together under the name 'UN Women', discussed below. Differently from the UN agencies, which are part of the UN bureaucracy, the CSW is an inter-governmental body made up of states' representatives.

Elizabeth Evatt gives credit for the establishment of the CSW to the female delegates involved in the founding of the United Nations.[26] It was established in 1946 by ECOSOC as a subcommittee of the then UN Commission on Human Rights but quickly and successfully lobbied for the status of a full commission.[27]

The CSW consists of 45 members elected by the ECOSOC for a period of four years. Members are nominated by their respective national governments and are elected on the basis of representation from different regions. One of the original 15 members of the CSW was an Australian, Jessie Street.

It was said of the CSW in its early days that '[t]here was no more independent body in the UN',[28] and the CSW is credited for having been the champion of women's human rights in the UN.[29] Its mandate was, however, limited to preparing recommendations and reports to ECOSOC on promoting women's rights. It worked slowly, with limited resources,[30] to pursue this limited mandate. Although ostensibly of equal status with the UN Commission on Human Rights, it has operated under very different conditions. Every aspect of the CSW's operations compares unfavourably to the UN Commission on Human Rights and its successor body, the Human Rights Council: its funding, its staffing, the frequency of meetings, its powers to initiate action and conduct investigations, even its security of existence.[31] The CSW's marginal status perhaps reflects an apprehension in its formative years that it 'might empower women in unexpected ways, and perhaps even challenge the mainstream approach to violations of human rights'.[32]

---

26 E Evatt, 'Finding a Voice for Women's Rights: The Early Days of CEDAW' 34 (2002–2003) *George Washington International Law Review* 515, 515.

27 R S Mama, 'Women and Children Next: The Significance of US Ratification of the Convention on the Elimination of All Forms of Discrimination Against Women and the Convention on the Rights of the Child' (2009) 2(2) *Journal of Global Social Work Practice*, <http://www.globalsocialwork.org/vol2no2.html>.

28 F Gaer, 'Women, International Law and International Institutions: The Case of the United Nations' (2009) 32 *Women's Studies International Forum* 60, 61, quoting J Humphrey, 'Memoirs of John P Humphrey, the First Director of the United Nations Division of Human Rights' (1983) 5 *Human Rights Quarterly* 387.

29 Ibid quoting Margaret Galey, 'International Enforcement of Women's Rights' (1984) 4 *Human Rights Quarterly* 463.

30 L Reanda, 'Human Rights and Women's Rights: The United Nations Approach' (1981) 3 *Human Rights Quarterly* 11, 24.

31 Ibid; H Charlesworth, C Chinkin & S Wright, see above, n 12, 24; A Byrnes and J Connors, 'Enforcing the Human Rights of Women: A Complaints Procedure for the Women's Convention?' (1995–1996) 21 *Brooklyn Journal of International Law* 679, 684–8; K Engle, 'International Human Rights and Feminism: When Discourses Meet' (1991–1992) 13 *Michigan Journal of International Law* 517, 565–70.

32 See above, n 28.

An illustration of the type of work the CSW did for many years was the nomination in 1968 of a Special Rapporteur for the Status of Women and Family Planning Project, and the numerous studies on the subject that resulted. But the CSW's principal focus was on achieving formal statements—in ECOSOC resolutions and international instruments—in support of women's rights. To this end it drafted many of the women's human rights instruments listed below.

In the 1970s the CSW followed the UN's direction and shifted its focus to issues of economic and social development. It may be that this new direction contributed to the marginalisation of women's human rights issues in the UN, leaving the human rights field to the UN Commission on Human Rights under little pressure to take account of the special situation and needs of women.[33] As a result of the focus on development, the CSW seems to have lost a degree of rights awareness in women's issues:

> [i]nstead of recognizing that women's informed participation in development projects would be enhanced by pressing governments to meet their obligation to provide women their equality rights, the development approach emphasized needs resulting from women's participation in society, sometimes implying that help offered to advance women was not a right but a privilege, maybe even a political prize won by those who made the best case for financial and political support.[34]

The CSW became quite marginal to activities designed to promote women's human rights. Although it proposed the first International Women's Conference, discussed below, it had no role in preparing for it. In 1980 there was a proposal to abolish the CSW and transfer its functions to ECOSOC.[35] In 1980 the second women's conference recommended that the CSW be strengthened,[36] and by the early 1990s the CSW had re-established its role in relation to women's human rights: it took a leading role in the fourth conference in 1995 in Beijing and its subsequent reviews, and in drafting the individual complaints mechanism under CEDAW.

16.3.2 'UN Women'

In 2010, under its reform agenda, the UN created a single agency, the United Nations Entity for Gender Equality and the Empowerment of Women, known as 'UN Women'.[37] UN Women merges into one entity what were previously the Division for the Advancement of Women (DAW), the International Research and Training Institute for the Advancement of Women (INSTRAW), the Office of the Special Adviser on Gender Issues and Advancement of Women (OSAGI), and the United Nations Development Fund for Women (UNIFEM).

33 See above, n 30, 28.

34 See above, n 28, 63.

35 *Short History of the Commission on the Status of Women*, UN Division for the Advancement of Women, 2006, <www.un.org/womenwatch/daw/CSW60YRS/CSWbriefhistory.pdf>, citing *The United Nations and the Advancement of Women, 1945–1996*, United Nations Blue Book Series, 52.

36 *Short History of the Commission on the Status of Women*, based on the and the United Nations CD-ROM *Women Go Global*, UN Division for the Advancement of Women, 2006, <www.un.org/womenwatch/daw/CSW60YRS/CSWbriefhistory.pdf>, citing J Devaki, *Women, Development and the UN: A Sixty-Year Quest for Equality and Justice*, Bloomington, Indiana Press University, 2005, 132.

37 <www.unwomen.org/>.

UN Women now has responsibility for all UN action to promote equality for women, led by Under-Secretary-General Michelle Bachelet, a former President of Chile. UN Women liaises across the UN system to promote gender equality, as DAW did, chairing the UN Inter-Agency Network on Women and Gender Equality. As well, it provides training, technical expertise and financial support to states and NGOs to implement gender equality standards, as UNIFEM. It maintains data, provides information to the UN General Assembly, and promotes gender equality at intergovernmental negotiations.

The essential difference between UN Women and the CSW is that the former is a part of the UN bureaucracy while the latter is an inter-governmental body. UN Women engages daily in liaison, training, grant-making and advising. CSW meets annually to make policy for adoption by ECOSOC and to propose standards and goals for global action to achieve gender equality.

16.4 WOMEN'S RIGHTS UNDER HUMAN RIGHTS TREATIES

There are more than twenty international treaties that are intended to address and improve the treatment of women, many of which were drafted by the CSW:[38] the 1952 *Convention on the Political Rights of Women*, the 1957 *Convention on the Nationality of Married Women*,[39] the 1962 *Convention on Consent to Marriage, Minimum Age for Marriage, and Registration of Marriages*,[40] the 1965 *Recommendation on Consent to Marriage, Minimum Age for Marriage, and Registration of Marriages*,[41] and the 1967 *Declaration on the Elimination of Discrimination Against Women*.[42] Two other instruments of relevance to women developed outside CSW were the 1950 *Convention for the Suppression of Traffic in Persons and the Exploitation of the Prostitution of Others*,[43] and the 1956 *Supplementary Convention on the Abolition of Slavery, the Slave Trade and Institutions and Practices Similar to Slavery*.[44]

Even though the list of human rights instruments is long, they have been criticised for their restricted scope and the lack of provision for international review, being limited in their ability to improve recognition of women's human rights and representing 'little more than a statement of good intentions on the part of states parties and of the international community'.[45] The instrument that departed from this mould is CEDAW,[46] discussed in detail below.

An approach to analysing the many treaties relating to women is to categorise them according to whether their dominant goal is protective (an exclusionary approach that treats women as a group in

38 L Reanda, see above, n 30, 21.

39 Opened for signature 29 January 1957, (entered into force 11 August 1958) UNTS, vol 309, p. 65.

40 Opened for signature 7 November 1962, (entered into force 9 December 1964) UNTS, vol 521, p. 231.

41 UN General Assembly resolution 2018 (XX), 1 November 1965.

42 UN General Assembly, 7 November 1967, A/RES/2263.

43 Opened for signature 2 December 1949, (entered into force 25 July 1951) UNTS, vol 96, p 271.

44 Adopted on 7 September 1956; entered into force on 30 April 1957.

45 Ibid 11, 19–21.

46 United Nations, Treaty Series, vol 1249, 13; <www2.ohchr.org/english/law/cedaw.htm>.

society unable to engage in certain activities), corrective (an inclusionary approach that treats women as a group in society needing help to overcome oppressive or restrictive conduct), or non-discriminatory (a gender-neutral approach that treats women as deserving of equal status with men).[47]

An example of a protective treaty is one that prevents women from working at night,[48] or underground,[49] for their own protection. An example of a corrective treaty is one that bans exploitation of and violence towards women.[50] The *UN Charter*, the International Bill of Rights, and CEDAW are all examples of non-discriminatory treaties that are focused on abolishing sex-based discrimination. Charlesworth breaks down the non-discriminatory treaties into two groups, general instruments (the *UN Charter* and the International Bill of Rights), and women-specific instruments such as those drafted by the CSW noted above, and of course CEDAW.[51] The terms of CEDAW encompass the three categories of protective, corrective and non-discriminatory, and effectively eliminate reliance on archaic protective treaties. Some corrective treaties remain relevant in specific areas, particularly in relation to work.[52]

16.4.1 Economic, Social and Cultural Rights

Among the principal human rights treaties, the subject matter of the *International Covenant on Economic, Social and Cultural Rights* (ICESCR) is significant for women because, out of the public eye and without ready access to a public voice, women are particularly vulnerable to violations of such rights. In its *General Comment No 16*, the UN Committee on Economic, Social and Cultural Rights, has commented on an obligation on states to ensure that women have equal access to the guarantees under the ICESCR:[53]

COMMITTEE ON ECONOMIC, SOCIAL AND CULTURAL RIGHTS *GENERAL COMMENT NO 16: THE EQUAL RIGHT OF MEN AND WOMEN TO THE ENJOYMENT OF ALL ECONOMIC, SOCIAL AND CULTURAL RIGHTS*

1 The equal right of men and women to the enjoyment of all human rights is one of the fundamental principles recognized under international law and enshrined in the main international human rights instruments …

…

4 The Committee … has taken particular note of factors negatively affecting the equal right of men and women to the enjoyment of economic, social and cultural rights in many of its general comments, including those on the

47 N Kaufman Hevener, 'An Analysis of Gender Based Treaty Law: Contemporary Developments in Historical Perspective' 8(1) (1986) *Human Rights Quarterly* 70, 71–2.

48 ILO *Convention Concerning Night Work of Women Employed in Industry*, 1919, modified 1935 and 1948, 40 UNTS 63.

49 ILO *Convention Concerning the Employment of Women on Underground Work in Mines of All Kinds*, 1946, 81 UNTS 147.

50 UN *Convention for the Suppression of Traffic in Persons and of the Exploitation of the Prostitution of Others*, entered into force 29 July 1951, 96 UNTS 271.

51 H Charlesworth, see above, n 8.

52 See above, n 47, 83–4.

53 Committee on Economic, Social and Cultural Rights, *Substantive Issues Arising in the Implementation of the International Covenant on Economic, Social and Cultural Rights: General Comment No 16, The Equal Right of Men and Women to the Enjoyment of All Economic, Social and Cultural Rights* (art 3 of the International Covenant on Economic, Social and Cultural Rights), 34th sess, Geneva, 25 April – 13 May 2005, E/C.12/2005/4; headings and footnotes omitted.

right to adequate housing, the right to adequate food, the right to education, the right to the highest attainable standard of health, and the right to water …

5 Women are often denied equal enjoyment of their human rights, in particular by virtue of the lesser status ascribed to them by tradition and custom, or as a result of overt or covert discrimination. Many women experience distinct forms of discrimination due to the intersection of sex with such factors as race, colour, language, religion, political and other opinion, national or social origin, property, birth, or other status, such as age, ethnicity, disability, marital, refugee or migrant status, resulting in compounded disadvantage.

…

8 Substantive equality for men and women will not be achieved simply through the enactment of laws or the adoption of policies that are, prima facie, gender-neutral. In implementing article 3, States parties should take into account that such laws, policies and practice can fail to address or even perpetuate inequality between men and women because they do not take account of existing economic, social and cultural inequalities, particularly those experienced by women.

…

14 Gender affects the equal right of men and women to the enjoyment of their rights. Gender refers to cultural expectations and assumptions about the behaviour, attitudes, personality traits, and physical and intellectual capacities of men and women, based solely on their identity as men or women. Gender-based assumptions and expectations generally place women at a disadvantage with respect to substantive enjoyment of rights, such as freedom to act and to be recognized as autonomous, fully capable adults, to participate fully in economic, social and political development, and to make decisions concerning their circumstances and conditions. Gender-based assumptions about economic, social and cultural roles preclude the sharing of responsibility between men and women in all spheres that is necessary to equality.

16.5 CEDAW

Consistently with the discussion in Chapter 1 of the history and origin of contemporary human rights, the formal contemporary statement of the human rights of women is in the International Bill of Rights—the UDHR, ICCPR and ICESCR—and the subsequent *Convention for the Elimination of All Forms of Discrimination Against Women*. CEDAW was adopted by the UN General Assembly in December 1979 and came into force on 3 September 1981. Its ratification, and reservations to it, are discussed in Chapter 7.3.8.

The only industrialised democracy not to have ratified CEDAW is the United States, despite President Carter's having signed it in 1979. The US Senate Foreign Relations Committee recommended its ratification in 1994 and again in 2002, but the issue has not yet been voted on by the US Senate.[54] Although Iran is among the few that have not ratified CEDAW,[55] in 2010 it secured a seat on the

54 For a discussion of the USA's reluctance to ratify CEDAW see eg, H Hongju Koh, 'Why America Should Ratify the Women's Rights Treaty (CEDAW)' (2002) 34 *Case Western Reserve Journal of International Law* 263; M Cohn, 'Resisting Equality: Why the US Refuses to Ratify the Women's Convention' (2004–2005) 27 *Thomas Jefferson Law Review* 15; L Blanchfield, 'The UN Convention on the Elimination of All Forms of Discrimination Against Women (CEDAW): Issues in the US Ratification Debate' Report for Congress R40750, *Congressional Report Service*, 7 August 2009; see above, n 27.

55 See the table at Chapter 7.3.2.

45-member UN Commission on the Status of Women.[56] There was an immediate outcry from human rights organisations and women's rights advocates inside and outside Iran about the incongruity of a country that consistently fails to uphold women's rights becoming a member of the UN body that is charged with advancing women's rights and empowerment.[57]

16.5.1 The CEDAW Committee

States' compliance with CEDAW is monitored by the CEDAW Committee, established under article 17. Although there is no relevant requirement, CEDAW Committee membership is always predominantly female.

States are scheduled to report regularly to the CEDAW Committee, and with CROC, CEDAW has attracted the highest level of reporting compliance.[58] As well as publishing views on state's reports,[59] the Committee issues 'General Recommendations' on how CEDAW should be interpreted and given effect to by states.[60]

The CEDAW Committee's first General Recommendation, in 1986, was two lines of text on the frequency of reporting. None of the first 18 General Recommendations issued by the Committee runs for more than a page, and many run for no more than two or three paragraphs, some on the machinery of reporting and some on issues such as violence, disability, AIDS and 'female circumcision'. General Recommendation 19 in 1992 broke the mould and elaborated at length on gender-based violence as a form of discrimination. This trend continued: General Recommendation 26 in 2008, for example, is a substantial comment on women migrant workers,[61] and General Recommendation 28 in 2010 addresses the Core Obligations of States Parties under article 2 of the Convention.[62]

16.5.2 The Provisions of CEDAW

In article 2, CEDAW obliges states to treat women equally, to prohibit discrimination against women, and to ensure that they receive equal legal status.

56 See the press release for the Economic and Social Council ECOSOC/6419 28 April 2010 available online at: <http://www.un.org/News/Press/docs/2010/ecosoc6419.doc.htm>.

57 See for example some news reports: A Applebaum, 'Another Human Rights Irony at the UN' *The Washington Post*, May 4 2010 available online at <http://www.washingtonpost.com/wp-dyn/content/article/2010/05/03/AR2010050303950.html>; J Abrams 'UN Elects Iran to Commission on Women's Rights' 29 April 2010 available online at <http://www.foxnews.com/world/2010/04/29/elects-iran-commission-womens-rights/#>, and S B Anderlini, H Ghaemi, D Fassihian 'Iran, Gender Discrimination, and the UN's Women's Commission' April 27, 2010 available online at <http://mideast.foreignpolicy.com/posts/2010/04/27/iran_gender_discrimination_and_the_uns_womens_commission>.

58 OHCHR, *Concept Paper on the High Commissioner's Proposal for Unified Standing Treaty Body*, HRI/MC/2006/2, 22 March 2006, Annex 1.

59 <http://www2.ohchr.org/english/bodies/cedaw/followup.htm>.

60 See the discussion in Chapter 7.4.5.

61 CEDAW/C/2009/WP.1/R, 5 December 2008.

62 CEDAW/C/2010/47, 19 October 2010.

ARTICLE 2 OF CEDAW

States Parties condemn discrimination against women in all its forms, agree to pursue by all appropriate means and without delay a policy of eliminating discrimination against women and, to this end, undertake:

(a) To embody the principle of the equality of men and women in their national constitutions or other appropriate legislation ...

(b) To adopt appropriate legislative and other measures, including sanctions where appropriate, prohibiting all discrimination against women;

(c) To establish legal protection of the rights of women on an equal basis with men and to ensure through competent national tribunals and other public institutions the effective protection of women against any act of discrimination;

(d) To refrain from engaging in any act or practice of discrimination against women and to ensure that public authorities and institutions shall act in conformity with this obligation;

(e) To take all appropriate measures to eliminate discrimination against women by any person, organization or enterprise;

(f) To take all appropriate measures, including legislation, to modify or abolish existing laws, regulations, customs and practices which constitute discrimination against women;

(g) To repeal all national penal provisions which constitute discrimination against women.

The CEDAW Committee has explained the meanings to be given to 'discrimination':[63]

> ... Direct discrimination against women constitutes different treatment explicitly based on grounds of sex and gender differences. Indirect discrimination against women occurs when a law, policy, programme or practice appears to be neutral as it relates to men and women, but has a discriminatory effect in practice on women, because pre-existing inequalities are not addressed by the apparently neutral measure. Moreover, indirect discrimination can exacerbate existing inequalities owing to a failure to recognize structural and historical patterns of discrimination and unequal power relationships between women and men.

However, addressing discrimination against women is often not as straightforward as simply looking at treatment of or effect on women. The concept of 'intersectionality' responds to the fact that the universal category of 'woman' precludes the 'raced, sexualised, able-bodied and aged identity of the female subject'.[64] As the Committee points out:[65]

63 Committee on the Elimination of Discrimination Against Women, *General Recommendation No 28 on the Core Obligations of States Parties under Article 2 of the Convention on the Elimination of All Forms of Discrimination Against Women*, para 16, 47th sess, 4–22 October 2010, CEDAW/C/2010/47/GC.2.

64 M Thornton, 'Can We Feminise Human Rights?' in M Thornton (ed), *Sex Discrimination in Uncertain Times*, ANU ePress, Canberra, 2010, 319, 324.

65 See above, n 63, paras 18; and see above, n 53.

The discrimination of women based on sex and gender is inextricably linked with other factors that affect women, such as race, ethnicity, religion or belief , health, status, age, class, caste, and sexual orientation and gender identity. Discrimination on the basis of sex or gender may affect women belonging to such groups to a different degree or in different ways than men. States parties must legally recognize and prohibit such intersecting forms of discrimination and their compounded negative impact on the women concerned ...

The focus in article 2 on formal equality, reflecting the early, liberal stage of feminist theory discussed above, is picked up in article 7, which requires states to ensure women's public participation 'on equal terms with men', and in articles 8, 9 and 15, which concern representation, nationality and legal capacity. In some of these provisions the desire for formal equality can be traced back to the earlier treaties relating to women noted above.[66]

Articles 3, 4 and 5 reflect the later cultural critique of liberal feminism, and require states to recognise and address social and cultural barriers to women's achieving equality. Article 6 addresses specific instances of men's social domination of women: trafficking, exploitation and prostitution. Socio-economic issues of particular concern to women are addressed in articles 10, 11, 12 and 13: education, employment, health, and participation in financial and cultural activities. Article 14 addresses these same concerns but with particular reference to the needs of women in rural areas.[67]

It is principally in article 16 that CEDAW reaches into private areas of life and recognises rights that women have in marriage and family, leading to the many reservations that states have made, discussed below.

ARTICLE 16 OF CEDAW

States Parties shall take all appropriate measures to eliminate discrimination against women in all matters relating to marriage and family relations and in particular shall ensure, on a basis of equality of men and women:

(a) The same right to enter into marriage;

(b) The same right freely to choose a spouse and to enter into marriage only with their free and full consent;

(c) The same rights and responsibilities during marriage and at its dissolution;

(d) The same rights and responsibilities as parents, irrespective of their marital status, in matters relating to their children; in all cases the interests of the children shall be paramount;

(e) The same rights to decide freely and responsibly on the number and spacing of their children and to have access to the information, education and means to enable them to exercise these rights;

(f) The same rights and responsibilities with regard to guardianship, wardship, trusteeship and adoption of children, or similar institutions where these concepts exist in national legislation; in all cases the interests of the children shall be paramount;

(g) The same personal rights as husband and wife, including the right to choose a family name, a profession and an occupation;

66 See the analysis in N Kaufman Hevener, above, n 47.

67 Lisa Pruitt, 'Deconstructing CEDAW's Article 14: Naming and Explaining Rural Difference' (2011) 17 *William & Mary Journal of Women and the Law* 347.

(h) The same rights for both spouses in respect of the ownership, acquisition, management, administration, enjoyment and disposition of property, whether free of charge or for a valuable consideration.

16.5.3 Reservations to CEDAW

CEDAW has been ratified by almost all states, but it is also the human rights treaty that has the highest number of reservations. Most of the reservations relate to article 2 and article 16. The CEDAW Committee has expressed strong views on the appropriateness of the reservations made by states to CEDAW:[68]

> 41 The Committee considers article 2 to be the very essence of the obligations of States parties under the Convention. The Committee therefore considers reservations to article 2 or to subparagraphs of article 2 to be, in principle, incompatible with the object and purpose of the Convention and thus impermissible in accordance with article 28, paragraph 2. States parties that have entered reservations to article 2 or to subparagraphs of article 2 should explain the practical effect of those reservations on the implementation of the Convention and should indicate the steps taken to keep the reservations under review, with the goal of withdrawing them as soon as possible.
>
> 42 The fact that a State party has entered a reservation to article 2 or to subparagraphs of article 2 does not remove the need for that State party to comply with its other obligations under international law, including its obligations under other human rights treaties that the State party has ratified or acceded to and under customary international human rights law relating to the elimination of discrimination against women. Where there is a discrepancy between reservations to provisions of the Convention and similar obligations under other international human rights treaties ratified or acceded to by a State party, it should review its reservations to the Convention with a view to withdrawing them.

The CEDAW Committee was moved to make this statement by the many and diverse reservations that have been made, as the following snapshot illustrates.

SNAPSHOT: RESERVATIONS TO CEDAW

Articles 2 and 16 of CEDAW states the most fundamental of obligations: to not discriminate generally, and specifically in marriage and family life. The following are just some of the reservations and declarations that have been made to these essential terms:[69]

India, with regard to article 16 (2) ... declares that though in principle it fully supports the principle of compulsory registration of marriages, it is not practical in a vast country like India with its variety of customs, religions and level of literacy.

Ireland is of the view that the attainment in Ireland of the objectives of the Convention does not necessitate [under article 16(1) (d) and (f)] the extension to men of rights identical to those accorded by law to women in respect of the guardianship, adoption and custody of children born out of wedlock.

68 See above, n 63, paras 41, 42.

69 <http://www.un.org/womenwatch/daw/cedaw/reservations-country.htm#N16>.

Israel hereby expresses its reservation with regard to article 16 of the Convention, to the extent that the laws on personal status which are binding on the various religious communities in Israel do not conform with the provisions of that article.

Lesotho declares that it does not consider itself bound by article 2 to the extent that it conflicts with Lesotho's constitutional stipulations relative to succession to the throne of the Kingdom of Lesotho and law relating to succession to chieftainship.

Micronesia ... reserves the right not to apply the provisions of Articles 2(f), 5, and 16 to the succession of certain well-established traditional titles, and to marital customs that divide tasks or decision-making in purely voluntary or consensual private conduct ...

Monaco does not consider itself bound by Article 16, paragraph 1(e), to the extent that the latter can be interpreted as forcing the legalisation of abortion or sterilization.

Morocco makes a reservation with regard to the provisions of [article 16], particularly those relating to the equality of men and women, in respect of rights and responsibilities on entry into and at dissolution of marriage. Equality of this kind is considered incompatible with the Islamic Shariah, which guarantees to each of the spouses rights and responsibilities within a framework of equilibrium and complementary in order to preserve the sacred bond of matrimony.

The Cook Islands reserves the right not to apply article 2 ... to the extent that the customs governing the inheritance of certain Cook Islands chief titles may be inconsistent with those provisions.

Niger expresses reservations concerning ... article 16, particularly those concerning the same rights and responsibilities during marriage and at its dissolution, the same rights to decide freely and responsibly on the number and spacing of their children, and the right to choose a family name.

Singapore reserves the right not to apply the provisions of articles 2 and 16 where compliance with these provisions would be contrary to the religious or personal laws of a multi-racial and multi-religious society.

Switzerland: article 16, paragraph 1 (g) shall be applied subject to the regulations on family name ...

The United Kingdom declares [re article 16(1)(f)] that the legislation of the United Kingdom regulating adoption, while giving a principal position to the promotion of the children's welfare, does not give to the child's interests the same paramount place as in issues concerning custody over children.

16.5.4 Women's Human Rights?

In its General Recommendation No 28 the CEDAW Committee states clearly the coverage of the treaty:[70]

> ... the Convention covers gender-based discrimination against women. The term sex refers to biological differences between men and women. The term gender refers to socially constructed identities, attributes and roles for women and men and society's social and cultural meaning for these biological differences resulting in hierarchical relationships between women and men and in the distribution of power and rights favouring men and disadvantaging women. This social positioning of women and men is affected by political, economic, cultural, social, religious, ideological and environmental factors and can likewise be changed by culture, society and community ...

70 See above, n 63, para 5.

Although CEDAW is concerned with discrimination against women, the rights it sets out are not particular to women. Rather, consistently with the liberal feminism of its time, its purpose is to ensure that human rights are enjoyed equally by women and men. The text of CEDAW is pervaded by the phrases 'equal rights with men', 'on equal terms with men', and 'the same right [as men]': every 'right' is a right to equality with men in an area of life. This 'andocentric' approach[71]—taking the position of men as a benchmark—was exactly the target of cultural and radical feminist critiques. It risks making women's rights dependent on a measure of men's rights, rather than on a true universality of human rights. A different critique is that the binary categories of man/woman limit the effectiveness of CEDAW as an instrument for equality, and that an inclusive term such as 'gender' should have been used.[72]

If women are as entitled as anyone to the universal human rights set out in the International Bill of Rights, it can be asked whether a specially focused treaty for women is necessary.[73] Feminist theory points out, however, that the social and cultural experiences of women put many human rights out of their reach; special attention has to be given to women if they are to actually enjoy universally proclaimed human rights. For as long as human rights are stated in universal terms they will be seen, exercised and enforced by men more than by women, simply because of the more powerful positions men hold.

The Preamble to CEDAW acknowledges that its impetus comes in part from the failure of the International Bill of Rights to meet the needs of women, expressing concern 'that despite these various instruments extensive discrimination against women continues to exist'.[74] Women are effectively marginalised in or absent from the language and practice of human rights, in areas ranging from the male/neutral terms of the UDHR, ICCPR and ICESCR to the subject matter of states' reports under the treaties and the male-dominated membership of the treaty bodies.[75] The discriminatory operation of human rights instruments themselves is reason enough for a treaty that is dedicated to promoting the rights of women. As well, a separate treaty draws attention to issues of distinct concern to women, such as trafficking in women and prostitution, and to the fact that not all women have the same problems, such as the situation of rural women.[76]

This is an argument for a specially focused treaty for women's human rights, but the question is then whether merely the content, or also the approach, should be special to women. To a significant extent the approach of CEDAW is a conventional liberal approach that mirrors previous human rights

71 K Mahoney, see above, n 3, 838; see above, n 30, 12; H Charlesworth, C Chinkin & S Wright, see above, n 12, 631–2.

72 D Rosenblum, 'Unsex CEDAW, or What's Wrong with Women's Rights', (2011) *Columbia Journal of Gender and Law* (forthcoming); see <http://ssrn.com/abstract=1545302>.

73 See the account of T Meron's critique in K Engle, see above, n 31, 524–431.

74 Preamble, CEDAW.

75 L Reanda, see above, n 30, 15–16.

76 H Charlesworth, C Chinkin & S Wright, see above, n 12, 632.

treaties and promotes recognition of formal equality between men and women. There are, however, differences in approach that give CEDAW a distinctive feminist dimension.

16.5.5 Into the Private Sphere

Each of the ICCPR, the ICESCR, and the *International Convention for the Elimination of All Forms of Racial Discrimination* were in force before the adoption of CEDAW. The development of CEDAW was to an extent a response to the perception that those instruments had failed to deal effectively with women's rights,[77] most significantly because they were 'directed mainly at actions by public agencies, whereas discrimination against women occurs in the private as well as the public arena'.[78]

In this sense CEDAW was an initiative that went beyond the formal equality pursued by earlier instruments, and recognised the cultural context of women's lives by extending its effect into the private sphere. It reflects the unfolding feminist critiques of the times, being a document of traditional liberalism,[79] seeking formal equality for women with 'benchmark' men, while also adopting a cultural awareness of the place of women in society and the need to address their particular circumstances.

The incursion of CEDAW into private life is illustrated by article 16, which requires states to 'take all appropriate measures to eliminate discrimination against women in all matters relating to marriage and family relations'. This was controversial during the drafting stage of CEDAW[80] and has been the subject of numerous reservations by states ratifying the treaty, discussed above.

The usual object of a treaty's obligations is states. The feminist insight into the private nature of much of a woman's life leads to an awareness that human rights protection similarly needs to extend to into the private sphere. In its General Recommendation No 28 the CEDAW Committee states clearly that the scope of the treaty extends to requiring states to regulate the conduct of private actors:[81]

> 10 States parties have an obligation not to cause discrimination against women through acts or omissions; they are further obliged to react actively against discrimination against women, regardless of whether such acts or omissions are perpetrated by the State …
>
> 13 … States parties are … obliged to ensure that private actors do not engage in discrimination against women, as defined in the Convention. The appropriate measures States parties are obliged to take include the regulation of the activities of private actors in regard to education, employment and health policies and practices, working conditions and work standards, and other areas where private actors provide services or facilities, such as banking and housing.

77 E Evatt, see above, n 26, 516.

78 E Evatt, see above, n 26, 517.

79 See, eg, L Merola, 'Liberalism and Feminism: Theoretical Conflicts within CEDAW' paper to the Annual Conference of the International Studies Association, Montreal, Quebec, March 17–21, 2004.

80 E Evatt, see above, n 26, 518, citing Japanese Association of International Women's Rights (ed), *Convention on the Elimination of Discrimination Against Women: A Commentary*, 1995.

81 See above, n 63, paras 10, 13.

The landmark communication of Ms A T against Hungary, described in the Snapshot below in Chapter 16.5.7, illustrates how a state will be held accountable for its failure to act to prevent conduct that harms women.

16.5.6 CEDAW's Effect on States' Behaviour

Research and reports shows that in states where CEDAW has been ratified women have benefited:[82]

> Some parts of [CEDAW] have been used to form policies or have been written into national law in a number of countries. For example, in Turkey, CEDAW was used to rescind a government policy that forced female students to undergo virginity exams. In Colombia, the courts have cited CEDAW in court rulings to provide legal recourse to domestic violence victims.
>
> Advocates have used the treaty to urge their governments to take actions such as investing in education for girls or passing laws to curb trafficking of women. Further, some countries have incorporated provisions of the treaty directly into their national law, and courts have cited CEDAW in decisions ranging from requiring protection from domestic violence to enabling women to inherit property.
>
> Amnesty International cites a number of countries that have used CEDAW to improve the lives of women, including the development of citizenship rights in Botswana and Japan; inheritance rights in Tanzania; property rights and political participation in Costa Rica; development of domestic violence laws in Turkey, Nepal, South Africa, and the Republic of Korea; and anti-trafficking laws in Ukraine and Moldova.

Against these reports of CEDAW's beneficial impact, Rosenblum questions its efficacy, and details its limitations, conceding only that CEDAW has been internalised within national legal systems to an extent.[83] This is faint praise, consistent with a view that 'inequality is too embedded to be removed by a mere comprehensive catalogue of women's rights that has very weak, if not non-existent, enforcement capabilities'.[84] This is, effectively, a criticism of reliance on the positivism of an instrument of international law as a means of changing states' behaviour.

A common response to the limitations of positivist doctrine is for advocates to turn to 'strategic positivism', where they rely on non-institutional strategies, rather than the terms of the instrument itself, a liberal feminist approach, which aims to 'assimilate women's rights to the dominant human rights structures'.[85] CEDAW remains 'a resource for activists' who invoke it to exploit the legitimacy of

---

82 R S Mama, see above, n 27, citing N O'Connell and R Sharma, 'Treaty for the Rights of Women Deserves full US support'. (2003) 10(2) *Human Rights Brief*, 22–25, Amnesty International, *A Fact Sheet on CEDAW: Treaty for the Rights of Women*, 2005, <http://www.amnestyusa.org/sites/default/files/pdfs/cedaw_fact_sheet.pdf>, at <http://www.globalsocialwork.org/vol2no2.html>.

83 D Rosenblum, 'Unsex CEDAW, or What's Wrong with Women's Rights', (2011) *Columbia Journal of Gender and Law* (forthcoming; <http://ssrn.com/abstract=1545302>), citing D Rosenblum, 'Internalising Gender: Why International Law Theory Should Adopt Comparative Methods' (2007) 45 *Columbia Journal of Transnational Law*, 759.

84 K Mahoney, see above, n 3, 842.

85 K Engle, see above, n 5, 533–534.

the international process of consensus building and related social movements to define social justice for women.[86]

This means that '[t]he power of the CEDAW Convention as an instrument for promoting women's human rights lies in the hands of those who use it',[87] and can influence state conduct.

SNAPSHOT: JAPAN'S EQUAL EMPLOYMENT OPPORTUNITY LAW[88]

In 1987 Japan adopted a new *Equal Employment Opportunity Law*, purportedly in an effort to meet its CEDAW obligations. The law merely 'encouraged' employers to not discriminate against women in hiring and promotion. The only remedy it offered was a mediation process by a local government agency; the employer could refuse to participate, and the agency could refuse to perform the mediation if it determined that no violation of the law had occurred.

In its 1994 review of Japan, the CEDAW Committee noted that the *Equal Employment Opportunity Law* did not address 'discrimination in effect' (indirect discrimination), and said that it was discriminatory in recognising 'equal' treatment of women simply if they are employed in equal numbers with men, even though women could be assigned to a career track with little or no opportunity for advancement, regardless of their qualifications and performance.

Japan responded to the CEDAW Committee's report by amending the *Equal Employment Opportunity Law* to 'require' rather than merely encourage non-discriminatory treatment in recruiting and promotion, and to remove an employer's privilege to refuse mediation.

Inspired by the CEDAW Committee's report, several Japanese women sued their employer, the Sumitomo conglomerate, claiming that the Sumitomo companies' policy of assigning men and women to separate employment tracks discriminated against women. In 2000 the court issued an opinion that compared the women's labour status to that of blue-collar men in the company and denied their wage disparity claim. While acknowledging that the two-track system was discriminatory, the court stated, 'in the light of the social conditions [between] 1965 [and] 1975, when the plaintiffs were hired ... it cannot be said that the defendant company was in violation of public order and good morals ...' The plaintiffs appealed.

Japan was reviewed by the CEDAW Committee again in 2003. Approximately 70 NGO representatives from Japan attended to observe the session, a record in CEDAW history. An NGO, Working Women's International Network, submitted a shadow report and spoke directly with the Committee members about the case. In its Concluding Observations, the Committee noted that despite the amendment of the Equal Employment Opportunity Law, the two-track employment system remained as a source of discrimination and wage gap.

86 See S Engle Merry, 'Constructing a Global Law-Violence against Women and the Human Rights System' (2003) 28(4) *Law & Social Inquiry* 941.

87 M A Freeman, 'The Committee on the Elimination of Discrimination Against Women and the Role of Civil Society in Implementing International Women's Human Rights Norms' 16 (2010) *New Eng J Int'l & Comp L* 25, 43; and see Engle's discussion of examples of 'strategic positivism' in K Engle, 'International Human Rights and Feminism: When Discourse Meet' (1991–1992) 13 *Michigan Journal of International Law* 517, 533–55.

88 Adapted from M A Freeman, ibid 43–8; see also <http://wwn-net.org/english/>.

In 2003, as the plaintiffs' appeal was pending, the judge recommended a settlement, referring to the 2003 recommendations of the CEDAW Committee. In 2006 a settlement resulted in the plaintiffs being paid compensation and guaranteed future fair treatment.

After lobbying by Working Women's International Network, the government amended the Equal Employment Opportunity Law in 2007 to prohibit indirect discrimination, to a limited extent. In its 2009 review of Japan, the CEDAW Committee again noted the two-track employment system and recommended in some detail actions the government must take to eliminate employment discrimination.

16.5.7 Individual Communications Under CEDAW

The procedure for individual communications under CEDAW did not come into effect until almost 20 years after the treaty itself. The terms of the treaty were controversial and challenging enough; it may have been a step too far at the time to include a mechanism for individual complaint, despite support for the idea from some states at the time.[89] There were as well concerns about the justiciability of the types of matters addressed by CEDAW,[90] in much the same way that similar concerns have held back the development of an individual complaints mechanism for ICESCR, discussed in Chapter 4.4. It seems that the CSW itself was not wholly committed to an individual complaints mechanism, because of its preference for a broader systemic approach to addressing women's inequality, and because continuing power struggles within the organisation to keep it weak with respect to the UN Commission on Human Rights.[91]

In theoretical terms, an individual complaints mechanism 'is largely founded upon liberal notions of rights protection as individual, injury-based causes of action ... [which] may aid in the ability of specific individuals or groups to effectively assert claims to CEDAW, [but] will do little to directly advance the immediate, substantive societal transformation sought by feminism'.[92] In a similarly critical vein, it is also possible to see the desire to give CEDAW the same enforcement capability as other treaties as itself a liberal desire for formal institutional equality between men and women,[93] although there is a greater complexity than mere formality in using institutions that are both mainstream in their structure and operation, and specialist in their focus and activity.

89 See A Byrnes and J Connors, above, n 31, 684–8.

90 Ibid 734–737.

91 See above, n 28, 64.

92 See above, n 5, 557; and see Engle's discussion of examples of the use of human rights institutions to promote women's rights, in K Engle, 'International Human Rights and Feminism: When Discourse Meet' (1991–1992) 13 *Michigan Journal of International Law* 517, 555–75. In promoting a communications mechanism under CEDAW Byrnes and Connors made no conscious allusion to an uncritical liberal bias in their aspirations: A Byrnes & J Connors, see above, n 31.

93 See above, n 5, 557; and see Engle's discussion of examples of the use of human rights institutions to promote women's rights, in K Engle, 'International Human Rights and Feminism: When Discourse Meet' (1991–1992) 13 *Michigan Journal of International Law* 517, 555–75. In promoting a communications mechanism under CEDAW Byrnes and Connors made no conscious allusion to an uncritical liberal bias in their aspirations: A Byrnes & J Connors, see above, n 31.

The *CEDAW Optional Protocol*[94] was adopted by the UN General Assembly in 1999 and came into force on 22 December 2000.[95] The *Optional Protocol* sets out a procedure for individuals to communicate with the CEDAW Committee, complaining of a state's breach of the treaty. The CEDAW Committee has published views in only a handful of matters.[96] It has usually found that the communication was inadmissible,[97] although dissenting views from individual members are common. The following snapshot is an example of one of the few matters found by the Committee to be admissible and to have merit.

SNAPSHOT COMMUNICATION NO: 2/2003, *MS A T v HUNGARY*[98]

Ms A T was subjected to regular severe domestic violence and serious threats by her husband, the father of her two children, one of whom is disabled. Ms A T was unable to leave home because no shelter in Hungary was equipped to take in a family with a disabled child. There were no protection orders or restraining orders available under Hungarian law. Ms A T requested assistance from local child protection authorities, but the authorities allegedly felt unable to help.

Ms A T's husband left the family home, taking most of the furniture and household items with him. He did not pay child support for three years, and continued to attack and threaten her. A court ordered that the husband be allowed back into the family home, citing lack of substantiation of the claim of domestic assaults, and the husband's right to the property.

Criminal proceedings against the husband had been continuing for three years without resolution, during which time no action was taken to keep the husband away from Ms A T.

Ms A T alleged to the CEDAW Committee that Hungary had violated her rights under CEDAW. She claimed that for four years Hungary failed in its duty to provide her with effective protection from the serious risk to her physical integrity, her physical and mental health, and her life, posed by her husband. Hungary did not contest the admissibility of the communication or the facts alleged by Ms A T, and admitted that the remedies that Ms A T had pursued in Hungary were not capable of providing her with immediate protection. More generally, Hungary agreed that its legal and institutional arrangements did not ensure the internationally expected, coordinated, comprehensive and effective protection and support for the victims of domestic violence.

The Committee noted Hungary's concession that domestic violence is not given high priority in court

94 United Nations, Treaty Series, vol 2131, 83; <www2.ohchr.org/english/law/cedaw-one.htm>.

95 Resolution A/RES/54/4 of 6 October 1999 at the 54th sess of the General Assembly of the United Nations; see Chapter 7.3.8.

96 *Optional Protocol to the Convention on the Elimination of Discrimination Against Women—Jurisprudence*, <http://www2.ohchr.org/english/law/jurisprudence.htm>.

97 On admissibility of communications generally, see Chapter 7.4.7.

98 CEDAW/C/32/D/2/2003 (2005). Discussed in B Rudolf & A Eriksson, 'Women's Rights under International Human Rights Treaties: Issues of Rape, Domestic Slavery, Abortion, and Domestic Violence' (2007) 5 *International Journal of Constitutional Law* 507, 519–22.

proceedings, and said that '[w]omen's human rights to life and to physical and mental integrity cannot be superseded by other rights, including the right to property and the right to privacy'. The Committee said that Ms A T's rights under articles 5 (a) and 16 of CEDAW had been violated. It recommended that Hungary take immediate and effective measures to guarantee the physical and mental integrity of Ms A T and her family, and ensure that she is given a safe home in which to live with her children, receiving child support, legal assistance and reparation.

More generally, the Committee recommended that Hungary take a number of steps that would respect, protect, promote and fulfil women's human rights.

16.6 THE INTERNATIONAL WOMEN'S CONFERENCES

Outside the formal and cumbersome processes of CEDAW, women's human rights have been the subject of a parallel program of global activities that has been sustained from one international women's conference to the next.

The UN had declared 1975 International Women's Year, and agreed to the CSW's request for an international conference. The conference in Mexico City[99] produced the *Declaration on the Equality of Women and their Contribution to Development and Peace*, stating women's (formal) equality in their right to work, and their right to economic activity. The *United Nations Decade for Women: Equality, Development and Peace* followed, in the period 1976–1985,[100] for which the conference produced a World Plan of Action. The Mexico Conference and the Women's Decade gave impetus to the drafting of the CEDAW.

In 1980 in Copenhagen,[101] the World Conference on Women discussed the subject of violence against women, not from a rights perspective but in a health and the social context.[102] Marking the mid-point of the Women's Decade, the Copenhagen conference produced a Program of Action for the five years to the end of the decade, focusing on employment, health and education as areas that underpinned the broad goals of equality, development and peace from the first World Conference.

At the 1985 Nairobi Conference[103] issues of violence against women were addressed in a human rights context, but did not go as far as to suggest that states themselves bear responsibility for failing

99 *Report of the World Conference of the International Women's Year*, Mexico City, 19 June – 2 July 1975, E/CONF.66/34, <http://www.un.org/womenwatch/daw/beijing/mexico.html>.

100 A/RES/3520, 15 December 1975.

101 *Report of the World Conference of the United Nations Decade for Women: Equality, Development and Peace*, Copenhagen, 14–19 July 1980, A/CONF.94/35, <http://www.un.org/womenwatch/daw/beijing/copenhagen.html>.

102 F Gaer, see above, n 28, 63.

103 *Report of the World Conference to Review and Appraise the Achievements of the United Nations Decade for Women: Equality, Development and Peace*, Nairobi, 15–26 July 1988, A/CONF.116/28/Rev.1, <http://www.un.org/womenwatch/daw/beijing/nairobi.html>.

to take measures to stop the violence.[104] The conference produced *Forward-Looking Strategies for the Advancement of Women to the Year 2000*, which was reviewed by the CSW in 1990.

In the period after the Nairobi Conference, the importance of women's human rights was endorsed by the 1993 *Vienna Declaration and Programme of Action* adopted by the World Conference on Human Rights.[105] In terms that invite a relativist debate[106] about the place of women in the international system of human rights, paragraph 18 of the Vienna Declaration recognised that 'the human rights of women and of the girl child are an inalienable, integral and indivisible part of universal human rights'.[107]

The year after the Vienna Declaration the UN General Assembly adopted the *Declaration on the Elimination of Violence against Women*.[108] In the same year delegates to the International Conference of Parliamentarians on Population and Development in Cairo adopted the *Cairo Declaration on World Population*.[109] Informed by the growing rights-consciousness of women's advocates, the Vienna Declaration and the Nairobi *Forward-Looking Strategies*, the *Cairo Declaration* stated that women's equality is necessary for human development, and redefined population policy, 'giving prominence to reproductive health and the empowerment of women while downplaying the demographic rationale'.[110]

After its review of the Nairobi *Forward-Looking Strategies* in 1990, the CSW commenced planning for 'one of [its] greatest achievements',[111] the Fourth UN Conference on Women's Human Rights, which was held in Beijing in 1995.[112] The Beijing Conference continues to be the largest, most comprehensive and far-sighted exercise in using international cooperation to realise women's human rights, notable for the extensive presence and involvement of NGOs. The Conference adopted the Beijing Platform for Action[113] (BPFA) as a blueprint for action by the UN, states, the private sector and NGOs, and has become the plan against which progress has been measured since.

104 F Gaer, see above, n 28, 63.

105 See generally K Boyle, 'Stock-Taking on Human Rights: The World Conference on Human Rights, Vienna 1993' (1995) 43 (suppl) *Political Studies* 79.

106 See Chapter 2.4.2 for an explanation of relativism and universality.

107 *Report of the World Conference on Human Rights*, Vienna, 14–25 June 1993, A/CONF.157/24.

108 *Declaration on the Elimination of Violence Against Women*, UNGA 85th plenary meeting, A/RES/48/104 (1993).

109 *Cairo Declaration on World Population*, Cairo, 3–4 September 1994, A/CONF/171/13, <www.un.org/popin/icpd/conference/bkg/egypt.html>.

110 C A McIntosh & J L Finkle, 'The Cairo Conference on Population and Development: A New Paradigm?' (1995) 21(1) *Population and Development Review* 223, 223.

111 *Short History of the Commission on the Status of Women*, based on the United Nations CD-ROM *Women Go Global*, UN Division for the Advancement of Women, 2006, <www.un.org/womenwatch/daw/CSW60YRS/CSWbriefhistory.pdf>.

112 *Report of the Fourth World Conference on Women*, Beijing, 4–15 September 1995, A/CONF.177/20/Rev.1, <http://www.un.org/womenwatch/daw/beijing/fwcwn.html>.

113 Ibid.

SNAPSHOT: BEIJING PLAN OF ACTION

The Australian Human Rights Commission views the BPFA as 'one of the most influential, international policy documents regarding women's human rights'.[114] It was adopted unanimously by the 189 countries present at the conference, and was seen as consolidating the momentum built up from the preceding conferences and their plans of action. Its strategy was to secure a commitment from participating states to develop local implementation strategies. States subsequently reported on action they had taken under the BFPA's 11 areas of concern for women.[115]

In preparation for Beijing +5, Australia, for example, reported against the BFPA's areas of concern as follows:[116]

1 *Poverty:* focus on social security, superannuation schemes, achieve equitable distribution of food within households, reform industrial relations; provide parenting allowance, legal services, access to credit and savings.
2 *Education and Training:* promote gender-sensitive education, flexible school schedules, target disadvantaged, introduce migrant English programmes, vocational/continuing training.
3 *Health:* focus on reproductive health, cervical and breast cancer, preventive health initiatives, disabled women.
4 *Violence:* assist victims of violence, provide culturally sensitive community education on female genital mutilation, introduce gun control, provide training for judicial, legal, medical and other personnel.
5 *Armed Conflict:* enforce international measures, national legislation, reduce military expenditures.
6 *Economy:* institute Workplace Relations Act 1996, safety net measures, independent advisory mechanism, Working Women's Centres for assisting in the labour market, high quality child care.
7 *Power and decision-making:* pilot programme for boosting number of women in public sector, build alliances with private sector, small business owners.
8 *Institutional mechanisms:* publish women's budget statement.
9 *Human Rights:* modify reservations to CEDAW.
10 *Media:* combat stereotyping, increase women's participation in the media.
11 *Environment*: participation in management and safeguarding the environment.
12 *Girl Child:* [prohibit] female genital mutilation, prostitution, legislation, child sexual abuse.

After the Beijing Conference the CSW received a UN General Assembly mandate to follow up and regularly review the BPFA. In 2000 the twenty-third special session of the General Assembly was nick

114 <http://www.hreoc.gov.au/sex_discrimination/publication/archive/cedaw/what_about_beijing.html>.

115 For a discussion of the BPFA's areas of concern for women, see M Platiner, 'Status of Women under International Human Rights Law and the 1995 UN World Conference on Women, Beijing, China' (1995–1996) 84 *Kentucky Law Journal* 1249.

116 Division for the Advancement of Women (Informal paper for the 42nd session of the Commission on the Status of Women, March 1998) <http://www.un.org/womenwatch/confer/beijing/national/westsum.htm>; see also Commission on the Status of Women, *Follow-up to the Fourth World Conference on Women: Implementation of Strategic Objectives and Action in the Critical Areas of Concern; Synthesized Report on National Action Plans and Strategies for Implementation of the Beijing Platform for Action,* Economic and Social Council, 42nd session, 2–13 March 1998, E/CN.6/1999/2/Add.1.

named 'Beijing +5'.[117] Based on preparatory sessions, research and reports from states, the session reviewed progress on the BPFA, and the UN General Assembly reaffirmed its commitment to the BPFA.[118] In 2005 at its forty-ninth session, the CSW conducted its own 'Ten-year Review and Appraisal of the Implementation of the Beijing Declaration and Platform for Action' (Beijing +10). Further research and reports were considered, and the CSW reported on measures taken and progress achieved.[119] CSW repeated the exercise in 2010 (Beijing +15), welcoming progress made towards achieving gender equality and women's empowerment, but stressing that obstacles remain in the implementation of the BPFA.[120]

Whether there will be a Beijing +20 in 2015, and what form it will take, is a matter for the CSW to decide. There is, however, a call by NGOs for a 'Fifth World Conference on Women and Girls' instead of a further review of the BPFA. Their argument is that there is a new generation of women who were not old enough to attend Beijing, and that the internet and globalisation now present an opportunity to network a new generation of women leaders.[121]

16.7 CONCLUSION AND ISSUES

The dilemma for advocates of women's human rights—whether to seek recognition of their human rights from within or apart from a male-designed and dominated system—is perennial. States' reservations to CEDAW's fundamental claim for non-discrimination raise real questions about women's reliance on the instruments and institutions of international law. Broader initiatives such as the International Women's Conferences and the Beijing Plan of Action show more promise, engaging a coalition of states, NGOs, and international bodies to take local action.

But women's disadvantage is deeply entrenched, in social systems, cultural practices, and economic structures. For many women in western developed societies, the idea that a woman's world—and the conditions under which she lives—is largely private is less relevant now than it was only thirty years ago, as they now have, at least, formal equality and access to equal opportunity. But there remain many women in those societies, and many more in developing countries, without the support of the state to emerge from the oppression of economic dependence and social subservience. More than reliance on CEDAW is needed to overcome barriers to achieving women's human rights such as suburban and rural poverty.

---

117 *Women 2000: Gender Equality, Development and Peace for the Twenty-First Century*, UNGA New York, 5–9 June 2000, A/55/341; see <www.un.org/womenwatch/daw/followup/beijing+5.htm>.

118 *Political Declaration*, UNGA 23rd sess, 16 November 2000, A/RES/S-23/2, and see *Follow-Up to the Fourth World Conference on Women and Full Implementation of the Beijing Declaration and Platform for Action and the Outcome of the Twenty-Third Special Session of the General* Assembly, UNGA 55th sess, A/Res/55/71.

119 *Measures Taken and Progress Achieved in the Follow-Up to and Implementation of the Fourth World Conference on Women and to the Twenty-Third Special Session of the General Assembly, with an Assessment of Progress Made on Mainstreaming a Gender Perspective within the United Nations System*, UN Doc. E/CN.6/2005/3, December 10, 2004; see <www.un.org/womenwatch/daw/Review/english/49sess.htm>.

120 *Declaration on the Occasion of the Fifteenth Anniversary of the Fourth World Conference on Women*, Commission on the Status of Women, 54th sess, 1–12 March 2010, E/CN.6/2010/L.1; see <www.un.org/womenwatch/daw/beijing15/index.html>.

121 See <http://5wcw.org/>.

17 WORKERS

CONTENTS

17.1 INTRODUCTION

Core labour standards are a subset of fundamental human rights, some of which are expressly recognised in the International Bill of Rights. However, it is a 'regrettable paradox that the human rights movement and the labour movement run on tracks that are sometimes parallel and rarely meet' despite the substantial overlap between the two.1 In her essay on the paradox of workers' rights as human rights, Virginia Leary comments on the relationship between human and labour rights by noting that:

> The status of workers' rights in a country is a bellwether for the status of human rights in general. The first sign of a deteriorating situation is often the violation of freedom of association, the most fundamental of workers' rights. Repressive regimes inevitably attempt to suppress or control trade unions ... Although South Africa maintained its membership in the United Nations during the period of apartheid, it withdrew from the International Labour Organization in 1966 following persistent criticism of its treatment of union and labour leaders.[2]

The establishment of the International Labour Organisation (ILO) pre-dates the creation of the United Nations (UN) by 27 years and took an active role early on in standard setting, but the late 1940s and 1950s were a particularly intense period of activity for both organisations. During this

1 V A Leary, 'The Paradox of Workers' Rights as Human Rights' in L A Compa & S F Diamond (eds), *Human Rights, Labor Rights and International Trade*, University of Pennsylvania Press, Philadelphia, 1996, 22, 22.

2 Ibid 22–3.

time a number of significant human rights and ILO treaties were drafted that provide protection for a similar array of rights. The *Universal Declaration of Human Rights* (UDHR), adopted in 1948, includes in it protections against discrimination and slavery and provides for the rights to freedom of association and to form and join trade unions, the right to work, to free choice of employment, to just and favourable conditions of work, to protection against unemployment and the right to equal pay for equal work. The UDHR also provides that everyone has the right to rest and leisure, including reasonable limitation of working hours and periodic holidays with pay. The many intersections between the UDHR and the standards set by the ILO arise partly from the fact that the UDHR took account of what the ILO had already done, and partly because the ILO subsequently incorporated aspects of the UDHR in drafting later treaties and recommendations.

The *International Covenant on Civil and Political Rights* (ICCPR) and the *International Covenant on Economic, Social and Cultural Rights* (ICESCR) were drafted to transform the rights incorporated in the UDHR into binding law and both incorporate some labour rights. The ICCPR prohibits discrimination, slavery and forced labour and protects the right to freedom of association and the right to form and join trade unions. The ICESCR also prohibits discrimination and protects the right of freedom of association and the right of everyone to form and join the trade union of their choice. The ICESCR is more expansive on workers' rights than the ICCPR; it proclaims the right to work more generally in its article 6, while article 7 recognises the right of everyone to the enjoyment of just and favourable conditions of work.[3]

INTERNATIONAL COVENANT ON ECONOMIC, SOCIAL AND CULTURAL RIGHTS (ARTS 6–8)

ARTICLE 6

1 The States Parties to the present Covenant recognize the right to work, which includes the right of everyone to the opportunity to gain his living by work which he freely chooses or accepts, and will take appropriate steps to safeguard this right …

ARTICLE 7

The States Parties to the present Covenant recognize the right of everyone to the enjoyment of just and favourable conditions of work which ensure, in particular:

(a) Remuneration which provides all workers, as a minimum, with:

(i) Fair wages and equal remuneration for work of equal value without distinction of any kind, in particular women being guaranteed conditions of work not inferior to those enjoyed by men, with equal pay for equal work;

(ii) A decent living for themselves and their families in accordance with the provisions of the present Covenant;

3 Also see *Universal Declaration on Human Rights* (UDHR), GA Res 217A (III), UN GAOR, 3rd sess, 183rd plen mtg, UN Doc A/810 (10 December 1948) art 23; *American Convention on Human Rights* (ACHR), 1144 UNTS 123 (entered into force 18 July 1978) arts 6, 7; *African Charter on Human and Peoples' Rights* (ACHPR), 21 ILM 58 (adopted 27 June 1981, entered into force 21 October 1986) art 15; *International Covenant on Economic, Social and Cultural Rights* (ICESCR), opened for signature 16 December 1966, 993 UNTS 3 (entered into force 3 January 1976) arts 1–6.

(b) Safe and healthy working conditions;

(c) Equal opportunity for everyone to be promoted in his employment to an appropriate higher level, subject to no considerations other than those of seniority and competence;

(d) Rest, leisure and reasonable limitation of working hours and periodic holidays with pay, as well as remuneration for public holidays.

ARTICLE 8

1 The States Parties to the present Covenant undertake to ensure:

(a) The right of everyone to form trade unions and join the trade union of his choice, subject only to the rules of the organization concerned, for the promotion and protection of his economic and social interests. No restrictions may be placed on the exercise of this right other than those prescribed by law and which are necessary in a democratic society in the interests of national security or public order or for the protection of the rights and freedoms of others;

...

(c) The right of trade unions to function freely subject to no limitations other than those prescribed by law and which are necessary in a democratic society in the interests of national security or public order or for the protection of the rights and freedoms of others;

(d) The right to strike, provided that it is exercised in conformity with the laws of the particular country ...

The right to work has direct intersections with civil and political rights, such as the right to life and freedom of expression, and with economic, social and cultural rights such as the rights to health and an adequate standard of living. The Committee on Economic, Social and Cultural Rights (CESCR) (the Committee tasked with interpreting and assessing the implementation of ICESCR by states parties) has emphasised the importance of the right to work and its direct interplay with other human rights:

> The right to work is essential for realizing other human rights and forms an inseparable and inherent part of human dignity. Every individual has the right to be able to work, allowing him/her to live in dignity. The right to work contributes at the same time to the survival of the individual and to that of his/her family, and since work is freely chosen or accepted, to his/her development and recognition within the community.[4]

In *General Comment No 18*, the CESCR goes on to note that the right to work is both an individual right and a collective right and that it should not be understood as an absolute and unconditional right to obtain employment.[5] While states are ultimately accountable for respecting, protecting and fulfilling the right to work, the CESCR has emphasised that non states parties such as individuals,

---

4 CESCR, *General Comment No 18: The Right to Work*, 35th sess, Provisional Agenda Item 3, UN Doc E/C.12/GC/18 (6 February 2006, adopted 24 November 2005) para 1.

5 Ibid para 6.

local communities, trade unions, civil society and private sector organisations also have particular responsibilities regarding the realisation of this right.[6]

Beyond the rights established in the UDHR and the ICCPR and the ICESCR, there are a number of other human rights treaties that also overlap with ILO standards. The *Convention on the Elimination of All Forms of Discrimination against Women* (CEDAW) requires states to abolish employment discrimination against women and provide safe and healthy working conditions and maternity leave with pay.[7] The *Convention on the Rights of All Migrant Workers and Members of Their Families* protects more generally the rights of migrant workers and their families and in particular gives migrants and their families the right to join unions and to seek their aid and assistance without any restrictions and prohibits slavery, servitude and forced or compulsory labour.[8] The *Convention on the Rights of Persons with Disabilities* (CRPD) obliges states to protect the right to work of persons with disabilities, prohibit discrimination and ensure reasonable accommodation of persons with disabilities in the workplace.[9] There are also regional human rights treaties that incorporate reference to labour rights[10] and the decision by the European Committee on Social Rights in *International Commission of Jurists v Portugal*[11] that Portugal had violated its obligations under article 7(1) of the *European Social Charter* relating to the minimum age of employment for children emphasised the interconnection between labour rights and human rights.

The ILO liaises closely with *UN Charter*-based and treaty based bodies,[12] reporting on issues such as child labour, discrimination, forced labour, migrant workers and freedom of association. Although the essence of both the UN and ILO monitoring systems is based on dialogue and persuasion, some commentators argue that states are subject to more effective monitoring through the supervisory systems of the ILO than via the UN.[13] While various UN committees and bodies deal with a wide variety of labour issues, the ILO is the main international institution given the responsibility for enforcing labour rights, so this chapter principally focuses on the activities of the ILO in promoting and protecting labour rights.

6 Ibid para 52.

7 *Convention on the Elimination of All Forms of Discrimination Against Women*, opened for signature 1 March 1980, 1249 UNTS 13 (entered into force 3 September 1981) art 11 (CEDAW). See Chapter 16 for a more thorough discussion of CEDAW.

8 *International Convention on the Protection of the Rights of All Migrant Workers and Members of their Families*, opened for signature 18 December 1990, 2220 UNTS 3 (entered into force 1 July 2003) arts 11, 26.

9 *Convention on the Rights of Persons with Disabilities*, opened for signature 30 March 2007, 993 UNTS 3 (entered into force 3 May 2008) art 27.

10 *European Social Charter*, opened for signature 3 May 1996 (entered into force 1 July 1999) CETS No 163; the *African [Banjul] Charter on Human and Peoples' Rights*, opened for signature 27 June 1981, 1520 UNTS 217 (entered into force 21 October 1986) and the *Additional Protocol to the American Convention on Human Rights in the Area of Economic, Social and Cultural Rights*, 'Protocol of San Salvador,' OAS Treaty Series No 69 (1988, entered into force November 16, 1999).

11 *International Commission of Jurists v Portugal*, No 1/1998 (European Committee on Social Rights).

12 See Chapter 7.4.

13 See for example: A Kent, *China, the United Nations, and Human Rights: The Limits of Compliance*, University of Pennsylvania Press, Philadelphia,1999; V A Leary, 'Learning from the Experience of the ILO' in P Alston (ed), *The United Nations and Human Rights: A Critical Appraisal*, Clarendon Press, Oxford, 1992.

17.2 THE INTERNATIONAL LABOUR ORGANISATION

17.2.1 Formation and goals

The ILO was created in 1919 by the Paris Peace Conference under the *Treaty of Versailles*. The preamble to the *ILO Constitution* gives an insight into the reasoning behind the establishment of the organisation: that economic progress must be accompanied by social justice. The preamble states that 'conditions of labour exist involving such injustice, hardship and privation to large numbers of people as to produce unrest so great that the peace and harmony of the world are imperilled' and the contracting parties acknowledge that in signing the treaty they are 'moved by sentiments of justice and humanity as well as by the desire to secure the permanent peace of the world'.

Australia was a founding member of the ILO and a party to that treaty, but the United States (US) was not. The US joined the ILO in 1934 in the era of President Roosevelt's New Deal and its emphasis on social policy.

In 1944 the ILO adopted the *Declaration of Philadelphia*,[14] which refined the aims and purposes of the organisation. The Declaration states that:

ILO *DECLARATION OF PHILADELPHIA* 1944

(a) Labour is not a commodity.

(b) Freedom of expression and of association are essential to sustained progress.

(c) Poverty anywhere constitutes a danger to prosperity everywhere.

(d) The war against want requires to be carried on with unrelenting vigour within each nation, and by continuous and concerted international effort in which the representatives of workers and employers, enjoying equal status with those of governments, join with them in free discussion and democratic decision with a view to the promotion of the common welfare.

In 1946 the ILO became a specialised agency of the newly formed UN and in the last 90 or so years it has produced 188 conventions and 199 recommendations that provide states with a comprehensive framework for ensuring respect for labour standards. In 1998 the ILO adopted the *Declaration on Fundamental Principles and Rights at Work*[15] and in 2008 the *Declaration on Social Justice for a Fair Globalization*. As the Director General of the ILO notes in the introduction to the 2008 Declaration, it 'is the third major statement of principles and policies adopted by the International Labour Conference since the ILO's Constitution of 1919. It builds on the *Philadelphia Declaration* of 1944 and the *Declaration on Fundamental Principles and Rights at Work* of 1998. The 2008 *Declaration* expresses the contemporary vision of the ILO's mandate in the era of globalization'.[16] The 2008 *Declaration* takes account of the conundrum faced by the ILO in reconciling globalisation and decent working

14 Available at <http://www.ilocarib.org.tt/projects/cariblex/conventions_23.shtml>.

15 Adopted by the International Labour Conference at its Eighty-sixth Session, Geneva, 18 June 1998 (Annex revised 15 June 2010).

16 ILO, *ILO Declaration on Social Justice for a Fair Globalization* (International Labour Conference, 97th sess, 10 June 2008) preface.

conditions, which although separated by almost 90 years, are not unlike the initial challenges it faced in 1919 in reconciling economic progress with social justice and decent working conditions. The 2008 Declaration notes:

ILO'S *DECLARATION ON SOCIAL JUSTICE FOR A FAIR GLOBALIZATION*, 2008[17]

Considering that the present context of globalization, characterized by the diffusion of new technologies, the flow of ideas, the exchange of goods and services, the increase in capital and financial flows, the internationalization of business and business processes and dialogue as well as the movement of persons, especially working women and men, is reshaping the world of work in profound ways:

- on the one hand, the process of economic cooperation and integration has helped a number of countries to benefit from high rates of economic growth and employment creation, to absorb many of the rural poor into the modern urban economy, to advance their developmental goals, and to foster innovation in product development and the circulation of ideas;
- on the other hand, global economic integration has caused many countries and sectors to face major challenges of income inequality, continuing high levels of unemployment and poverty, vulnerability of economies to external shocks, and the growth of both unprotected work and the informal economy, which impact on the employment relationship and the protections it can offer ...

17.2.2 ILO's Structure

The principal organs of the ILO are the International Labour Conference (ILC), the Governing Body, and the International Labour Office (the permanent secretariat of the ILO headed by the Director General).

The ILC is the organisation's policy-making and legislative body, in which every member state is represented. It holds one session a year at ILO headquarters in Geneva. The ILC considers and adopts conventions, recommendations and resolutions and debates general topics of interest. Each member state is represented at the ILC by two government delegates, one workers' delegate and one employers' delegate. Each delegate has one independent vote.

The Governing Body of the ILO (which acts as the secretariat's executive and establishes the agenda of the ILC) is composed of 28 government members, 14 worker members and 14 employer members.

The organisation's unique tripartite structure aims to ensure the full participation of not only governments but also employer and employee representatives in the drafting and implementation of labour standards. Tripartism is synonymous with the ILO, and is confirmed in a number of its international instruments.[18] The principle was reaffirmed in 2002 when the ILC adopted a resolution confirming the importance of social dialogue in drafting and promulgating labour standards: the 'Resolution concerning tripartism and social dialogue' restates the preeminent position of tripartite negotiations in the ILO:

17 Adopted by the International Labour Conference at its Ninety-seventh Session, Geneva, 10 June 2008, p5. Available at <http://www.ilo.org/wcmsp5/groups/public/@dgreports/@cabinet/documents/publication/wcms_099766.pdf>.

18 For example, *Tripartite Consultation (International Labour Standards) Convention* (No 144 of 1976), General Conference of the International Labour Organization, 61st sess, C144 (adopted 21 June 1976, entered into force 16 May 1978).

> Aware that social dialogue and tripartism have proved to be valuable and democratic means to address social concerns, build consensus, help elaborate international labour standards and examine a wide range of labour issues on which the social partners play a direct, legitimate and irreplaceable role ...[19]

Tripartism is not a panacea and its effectiveness relies on the ability of each of the parties to negotiate as independent entities. In some regions of the world, 'industrial relations law and practice are closely bound up with industrialisation and development strategies that are generally accompanied by state control over labour unions in order to maintain the stability that national governments may feel is needed for rapid economic development'.[20] In such situations where the independence of the three parties to labour negotiations is blurred, tripartism may be compromised.

17.2.3 ILO Standards

International labour standards take the form of conventions (legally binding treaties that may be ratified by member states and to which member states are then monitored for compliance) or recommendations (non-binding guidelines) that may supplement a particular convention or provide more general guidance on labour standards and their implementation. In either case, the process of developing the standards is initiated by the Governing Body, which first must decide to put an issue on the agenda of a future ILC.[21] The International Labour Office then takes the lead in preparing a series of reports for circulation to the ILC initially providing background for discussion and ultimately (if the decision is made to proceed) developing a draft international standard for consideration by the ILC. A two-thirds majority of votes is required for a standard to be adopted and the convention is then open for ratification by member states. Ratifying states may not enter reservations to ILO conventions but may make declarations.

'Core' Conventions

In the more than 90 years since its creation, the ILO has drafted numerous conventions and recommendations covering a diverse range of topics. In 1998 the ILO attempted to refine the focus of its labour standards to denote those that should be considered fundamental to the organisation and 'adopted, and gave particular emphasis to, a different form of instrument that is neither a treaty nor a recommendation: a *Declaration on Fundamental Principles and Rights at Work* (the Declaration). The Declaration enunciated for the first time within the ILO the concept of 'core labour standards'—freedom of association, elimination of discrimination in employment, elimination of forced labour,

---

19 'Resolution Concerning Tripartism and Social Dialogue' General Conference of the International Labour Organization, 90th sess, Provisional Record 21 (15 June 2002), 24 <http://www.ilo.org/public/english/standards/relm/ilc/ilc90/pdf/pr-21res.pdf>.

20 WR Simpson, 'The ILO and Tripartism: Some Reflections' (1994) 117(9) *Monthly Labor Review* 40.

21 For the process of how ILO standards are created see the ILO website 'How ILO Standards Are Created' <http://www.ilo.org/global/standards/introduction-to-international-labour-standards/international-labour-standards-creation/lang--en/index.htm>.

and elimination of child labour—as obligations of membership in the organisation, whether or not member states have ratified the relevant ILO conventions.'[22]

ILO DECLARATION ON FUNDAMENTAL PRINCIPLES AND RIGHTS AT WORK 1998

... all Members, even if they have not ratified the Conventions in question, have an obligation arising from the very fact of membership in the Organization to respect, to promote and to realize, in good faith and in accordance with the Constitution, the principles concerning the fundamental rights which are the subject of those Conventions, namely:

(a) freedom of association and the effective recognition of the right to collective bargaining;
(b) the elimination of all forms of forced or compulsory labour;
(c) the effective abolition of child labour; and
(d) the elimination of discrimination in respect of employment and occupation.

These four fundamental issues are linked to the following eight conventions, commonly referred to as the ILO's fundamental or core conventions:

C87 *Freedom of Association and Protection of the Right to Organise Convention*, 1948
C98 *Right to Organise and Collective Bargaining Convention*, 1949
C29 *Forced Labour Convention*, 1930
C105 *Abolition of Forced Labour Convention*, 1957
C138 *Minimum Age Convention*, 1973
C182 *Worst Forms of Child Labour Convention*, 1999
C100 *Equal Remuneration Convention*, 1951
C111 *Discrimination (Employment and Occupation) Convention*, 1958

As at July 2011, of the ILO's 183 member States, 135 have ratified the eight fundamental ILO Conventions and 18, including Australia, have ratified seven. By comparison, 14 member states have ratified four or fewer fundamental Conventions including three countries that joined the ILO only recently and have not yet ratified any of the fundamental Conventions.[23]

The impetus for the 1998 Declaration arose from a sustained period of debate, increasing in volume in the early 1990s, around the possibility of linking labour standards with trade commitments (often called the 'social clause debate'). In 1995, delegates at the United Nations World Summit on Social Development in Copenhagen reaffirmed the relevance of the ILO in dealing with labour issues and agreed on a set of commitments to safeguard the basic rights of workers. Further impetus was given to reviving the relevance of the ILO by the refusal of member states at the first Ministerial Conference of the newly established World Trade Organization (WTO) in 1996 in Singapore, to consider international

22 V A Leary, 'Form Follows Function: Formulations of International Labor Standards—Treaties, Codes, Soft Law and Trade Agreements' in R J Flanagan & W B Gould (eds), *International Labor Standards*, Stanford University Press, Stanford, 2003, 179, 179.

23 For the most up to date information, please see: International Labour Organization, *Ratifications of the ILO Fundamental Conventions* (25 July 2011) <http://webfusion.ilo.org/public/db/standards/normes/appl/appl-ratif8conv.cfm?lang=EN>.

labour standards as part of their domain. The Singapore Ministerial Declaration[24] (adopted on 13 December 1996) by the WTO noted that:

> We renew our commitment to the observance of internationally recognized core labour standards. The International Labour Organization (ILO) is the competent body to set and deal with these standards, and we affirm our support for its work in promoting them. We believe that economic growth and development fostered by increased trade and further trade liberalization contribute to the promotion of these standards. We reject the use of labour standards for protectionist purposes, and agree that the comparative advantage of countries, particularly low-wage developing countries, must in no way be put into question. In this regard, we note that the WTO and ILO Secretariats will continue their existing collaboration.

These developments opened the door for the ILO's adoption of the Declaration in 1998 and its acknowledgment that certain 'core' standards required commitment from member states regardless of the status of ratifications of the eight fundamental conventions. The Declaration has an uncertain legal status (as it is not a treaty, yet 'requires' commitment from all member States). But the emphasis by the ILO on the four core issues, and the follow-up procedures provided for in the Declaration, which provide for annual reports on the implementation of the core labour standards by all member states (whether or not they have ratified the relevant conventions), leaves no doubt as to the ILO's commitment to improving adherence to these core labour standards.

The ILO's declaration of these standards as the baseline of acceptable working conditions has attracted some criticism for what it left out as much as for what is included. In declaring the four issues as fundamental labour rights, the ILO may have diminished the relevance of the many other ILO conventions or its focused approach may be a useful means of refining the ILO's core mission to provide decent working condition around the globe. Lance Compa argues that a 'core' or 'extended core' of labour standard should also prioritise wages, benefits, health and safety rights, social insurance and other economic and social rights.

LANCE COMPA, 'CORE LABOUR RIGHTS: PROMISE AND PERIL'[25]

Workers' rights advocates are converging on the International Labour Organization's 1998 declaration of 'core' labour standards as an authoritative statement of workers' rights in the global economy. The ILO set out four core rights: to organise and bargain collectively, and to be free of forced labour, child labour, and discrimination.

The promise of a labour rights core lies in its universality. Contending trade union, business, government and civil society forces engaged in the debate over trade and labour standards need a common goal for workers' rights to become part of the global economic agenda.

Here is where peril arises. The rush to core labour standards invites the logical response that other workers' concerns, most involving economic and social rights, are not worthy of equal standing and advocacy. Instead, these standards can vary based on economic circumstances and development strategies.

24 *Singapore Ministerial Declaration* WTO Doc WT/MIN(96)/DEC (18 December 1996, adopted 13 December 1996) (Ministerial Declaration) para 4.

25 (2002) International Union Rights 9(3) 20–1.

Labour rights advocates should not shrink the terrain for action by focusing only on the ILO's declaration of core standards. Advocates should expand the grounds for advocacy by insisting on a 'core-plus' or 'expanded core' covering a greater range of workers' vital interests, embracing economic and social rights...

Supporters of a narrow 'core' approach to workers' rights emphasise that these are not economic and social rights that depend on a country's level of development and ability to pay. Even the poorest countries should be able to afford the core rights, the argument goes, so charges of protectionism—that labour standards' links to trade and investment are being imposed by developed countries to block imports from developing countries—are misplaced.

But the supposed bright line between no-cost, basic human rights standards for workers and cost-filled economic and social rights and benefits begins to blur up close. Freedom of association and the right to organise and bargain collectively are surely fundamental rights that must be protected in the international trading system, but they are not divorced from economic benefits. Higher wages are a primary goal of workers and their trade union negotiators ...

Core labour rights have cost dimensions. So be it; workers' rights advocates should not shrink from demanding that payment be made for social justice. At the same time, rights and protections seen as outside the 'core' because they carry economic costs have strong human rights dimensions. For example, why isn't workplace health and safety counted among core labour norms?

Similarly, disabled workers should have a fundamental right to social insurance providing compensation for workplace injuries, illnesses and deaths. The same logic applies to unemployment insurance or severance pay for workers who are displaced by the 'creative destruction' of global trade and investment, and pensions for workers who reach old age.

Freedom of Association and the Effective Recognition of the Right to Collective Bargaining

The principle of freedom of association—the right of workers to form and join trade unions for the protection of their interests—is a fundamental labour right and lies at the core of the ILO's values. The recognition of freedom of association and the associated right to collective bargaining—which aims to ensure that employers and workers have an equal voice in negotiations—provides a platform for establishing just and equitable working conditions. The rights are protected not only by two of the ILO's fundamental conventions (C87 *Freedom of Association and Protection of the Right to Organise Convention*, 1948 and C98 *Right to Organise and Collective Bargaining Convention*, 1949) but also by a number of other ILO treaties and recommendations and are enshrined in the ILO Constitution, the Declaration of Philadelphia and the *Declaration on Fundamental Principles and Rights at Work*. Interestingly, Convention No 87 remains the least ratified of the eight fundamental conventions. If all nations ratified and enforced Convention No 87, the flow-on effects from a freely organised workplace might reduce their enforcement workload with respect to the remaining core labour standards.

Freedom of association is a fundamental right also recognised in the principal international and regional human rights instruments.[26] In September 2010, the Human Rights Council adopted a

26 UDHR, UN Doc A/810, arts 20, 23; *International Covenant on Civil and Political Rights*, opened for signature 16 December 1966, 999 UNTS 171 (entered into force 23 March 1976) arts 21, 22 (ICCPR); ICESCR art 8; ACHR arts 15, 16; ACHPR arts 10, 1; ESC arts 5, 6.

resolution[27] by consensus establishing for the first time a Special Rapporteur on the rights to freedom of peaceful assembly and of association. The new Special Rapporteur's role is to report on violations of these rights and on threats, harassment and reprisals against those exercising their right to freedom of peaceful assembly. The mandate was established at the initiative of a cross-regional group of states including the United States, the Czech Republic, the Maldives, Nigeria, Lithuania, Mexico, Indonesia and Latvia. However, China, Pakistan, Cuba and Libya disassociated themselves from the consensus.

The ILO's 2008 Global Report on Freedom of Association provides a global overview of the realisation of the rights of freedom of association and collective bargaining and notes that although recognition of the importance of these rights is growing, there are still serious issues regarding its implementation.

'FREEDOM OF ASSOCIATION IN PRACTICE: LESSONS LEARNED'[28]

… serious and major cases involving large-scale dismissals, harassment, imprisonment and violence, including killings of trade unionists. Trade unions and employers' organizations continue to experience obstacles in their day-to-day activities. Problems arise with: restrictions on the establishment of organizations or the right to join them; interference by governments and other parties in the functioning of employers' and workers' organizations; restrictions on collective bargaining; discrimination against union members; and undue restrictions on the right to strike.

In recent years the ILO supervisory bodies have recorded an increase in the number of complaints concerning acts of anti-union discrimination and interference. These allegations concern prejudicial acts (including dismissals, demotions, transfers and refusals to hire) against trade union officers and members.

Government intervention in trade union activities is a recurrent problem. Less visible but equally pernicious restrictions of freedom of association exist where this right is denied or discouraged in practice as a result of pressure and interference in the activities of trade unions. Registration systems still allow the authorities to exercise undue discretion. Restrictions frequently take the form of excessively high membership requirements or requirements for previous authorization. Many countries have in fact abandoned legislation or practice which guarantees the dominant or monopoly position of one union, although significant exceptions still remain.

SNAPSHOT: CHINA

The ILO's 2008 global report on freedom of association refers to exceptions to the move away from guaranteeing the dominant or monopoly position of a single union. One of these exceptions is China.

In practice, Chinese workers are not free to organise or join trade unions of their choosing. Workers cannot choose an independent union to represent them, as independent unions are illegal. The All China Federation of Trade Unions (ACFTU), controlled by the Chinese Communist Party and chaired by a member of the Politburo, is the sole legal workers' organisation.

27 Human Rights Council, *Oral Revisions for Distribution in the Room*, UN GAOR, 15th sess, Agenda Item 3, UN Doc A/HRC/15/L.23 (27 September 2010).

28 ILO, *Freedom of Association in Practice: Lessons Learned* (International Labour Conference, 97th session 2008, Report I (B), 2008) <http://www.ilo.org/wcmsp5/groups/public/---dgreports/---dcomm/documents/publication/wcms_096122.pdf>.

China has not ratified ILO Conventions No 87 or No 98, but in 2001 it did ratify ICESCR, which guarantees in article 8: 'the right of everyone to form trade unions and join the trade union of his choice'. However, when the Chinese government ratified the ICESCR it made a statement that the application of article 8(1)(a) 'shall be consistent with the relevant provisions of the *Constitution of the People's Republic of China, Trade Union Law of the People's Republic of China* and *Labor Law of the People's Republic of China*.'[29]

Forced Labour

The right to work assumes that everyone has the opportunity to gain his or her living by work that he or she 'freely chooses or accepts'.[30] The ILO's first treaty on forced labour, Convention No 29 of 1930, clearly defines the term of forced labour as 'all work or service which is exacted from any person under the menace of any penalty and for which the said person has not offered himself voluntarily'.[31] Convention No 29 is the most widely ratified of all the ILO Conventions, having almost universal acceptance.

International and regional human rights treaties also provide protection from slavery or servitude or forced or compulsory labour.[32] For example, article 8 of the ICCPR (which is non-derogable) provides:

1. No one shall be held in slavery; slavery and the slave-trade in all their forms shall be prohibited
2. No shall be held in servitude
3. No one shall be required to perform forced or compulsory labour …

Additionally, forced or compulsory labour is considered as one of the worst forms of child labour in the *Worst Forms of Child Labour Convention*, 1999 (No 182).

Convention No 105 of 1957, the *Abolition of Forced Labour Convention*, prohibits forced or compulsory labour as a means of political coercion or education or as a punishment for holding or expressing political views or views ideologically that are opposed to the established political, social or economic system. It also prohibits forced or compulsory labour as a method of mobilising and using labour for purposes of economic development; as a means of labour discipline; as a punishment for having participated in strikes; and as a means of racial, social, national or religious discrimination.

A particular focus of the ILO in recent years has been on the forced labour that results from trafficking in persons. The ILO's 2009 Global Report noted significant growth in trafficking for labour or sexual exploitation and the particular impact of trafficking on migrant workers. The Reports notes:

> The size of this migrant labour force has grown in recent years, increasingly involving young women for domestic service and other activities. They can be charged excessively high recruitment fees, be deceived about the conditions of employment, and face restrictions to move freely or change jobs in the destination country. There can also be collusion between recruiters in sending countries and employers in destination

29 <http://treaties.un.org/Pages/ViewDetails.aspx?src=TREATY&mtdsg_no=IV-3&chapter=4&lang=en#8>.

30 ICESCR art 6(1).

31 *Forced Labour Convention, 1930 (No 29)*, General Conference of the International Labour Organization, 14th sess (adopted 28 June 1930, entered into force 1 May 1932) art 2.

32 UDHR art 4; ICCPR art 8; ACHR art 6; ACHPR art 5; ECHR art 4.

countries to trick these vulnerable migrants out of fair wages and employment conditions. This is widely seen as a modern form of debt bondage.[33]

SNAPSHOT: BURMA (MYANMAR)

The ILO and Myanmar (formerly Burma) have been at odds for decades over the issue of forced labour. Forced labour is widely acknowledged as being employed in Myanmar, primarily in development projects, agricultural enterprises and the military. In its 1998 report[34] of a Commission of Inquiry appointed to examine forced labour in Myanmar, the ILO found that:

528 There is abundant evidence before the Commission showing the pervasive use of forced labour imposed on the civilian population throughout Myanmar by the authorities and the military for portering, the construction, maintenance and servicing of military camps, other work in support of the military, work on agriculture, logging and other production projects undertaken by the authorities or the military, sometimes for the profit of private individuals, the construction and maintenance of roads, railways and bridges, other infrastructure work ...

530 Failure to comply with a call-up for labour is punishable under the *Village Act* with a fine or imprisonment for a term not exceeding one month, or both, and under the *Towns Act*, with a fine. In actual practice, the manifold exactions of forced labour often give rise to the extortion of money in exchange for a temporary alleviation of the burden, but also to threats to the life and security and extrajudicial punishment of those unwilling, slow or unable to comply with a demand for forced labour; such punishment or reprisals range from money demands to physical abuse, beatings, torture, rape and murder.

531 Forced labour in Myanmar is widely performed by women, children and elderly persons as well as persons otherwise unfit for work ...

533 Forced labour is a heavy burden on the general population in Myanmar, preventing farmers from tending to the needs of their holdings and children from attending school; it falls most heavily on landless labourers and the poorer sections of the population, which depend on hiring out their labour for subsistence and generally have no means to comply with various money demands made by the authorities *in lieu* of, or over and above, the exaction of forced labour. The impossibility of making a living because of the amount of forced labour exacted is a frequent reason for fleeing the country.

534 The burden of forced labour also appears to be particularly great for non-Burman ethnic groups, especially in areas where there is a strong military presence, and for the Muslim minority, including the Rohingyas.

Article 33 of the ILO Constitution provides that '[i]n the event of any Member failing to carry out within the time specified the recommendations, if any, contained in the report of the Commission of

33 ILO, 'The Cost of Coercion: Executive Summary of 2009 Global Report on Forced Labour' 2 <http://www.ilo.org/wcmsp5/groups/public/---ed_norm/---declaration/documents/publication/wcms_106387.pdf>.

34 ILO, *Forced Labour in Myanmar (Burma): Report of the Commission of Inquiry Appointed under Article 26 of the Constitution of the International Labour Organization to Examine the Observance by Myanmar of the Forced Labour Convention*, 1930 (No 29) (Report, ILO, 2 July 1998).

Inquiry, or in the decision of the International Court of Justice, as the case may be, the Governing Body may recommend to the Conference such action as it may deem wise and expedient to secure compliance therewith'. Before 2000 this power had never been invoked. In 2000, the ILC—by a vote of 257 in favour, 41 against, and 31 abstentions—acted under article 33 and called on Myanmar to 'take concrete action' to implement the recommendations of the 1998 Commission of Inquiry, which found that the use of forced labour in the country was 'widespread and systematic'.[35]

The wording of the Myanmar Resolution in 2000 deliberately left member states with a wide discretion as to how they might respond. Member states were asked to 'review' their relations with Myanmar and to take 'appropriate measures'. This raised the issue of what 'measures' might be taken by member states and, if in the form of trade sanctions, whether they would be compatible with the member's obligations under international law, particularly membership of the WTO.[36] For example, in 2003, the US passed the *Burmese Freedom and Democracy Act*,[37] which imposes sanctions against Burma (Myanmar) but authorises the US President to waive those sanctions in certain circumstances. This response was partially in response to the ILO resolution but also related to the latest incarceration of Burmese opposition leader Aung San Suu Kyi. In its 2009 *Global Report on Forced Labour: 'The Cost of Coercion'*,[38] the ILO notes that:

> Under an accord between the ILO and the government of Myanmar in 2007, the ILO's Liaison Officer has been able to receive, examine and assess complaints of forced labour. The officer's findings are then relayed to the government for investigation as well as to the ILO Governing Body, which also is kept informed about the outcome of the complaint. The agreement is part of the ILO's longstanding drive against the use of forced labour by the authorities in Myanmar. As of November 2008, 120 complaints had been received, 70 of which were assessed as falling under the definition of forced labour. Of these, 21 were cases of forced labour under the orders of civil authorities, 10 involved forced labour under the military authorities and 39 involved recruitment of minors into the military.

Child Labour

Child labour is evident across a diverse range of sectors; some of the more prominent include agriculture, domestic labour, mining, armed conflict (child soldiers) and the commercial sexual exploitation of children. While estimating that there are approximately 218 million child labourers worldwide, 126

35 ILO News (ILO/00/27) 'International Labour Conference adopts Resolution targeting forced labour in Myanmar (Burma)' June 14, 2000 <http://www.ilo.org/global/about-the-ilo/press-and-media-centre/press-releases/WCMS_007899/lang--en/index.htm>. Also see: ILO Governing Body, *Effect Given by the Government of Myanmar to the Recommendations of the Commission of Inquiry established to examine the observance of the Forced Labour Convention, 1930 (No 29), Follow-Up to the Resolution Adopted by the International Labour Conference at its 88th Session (May–June 2000)* GB.279/6/2 279th Session Geneva, November 2000 <http://www.ilo.org/public/english/standards/relm/gb/docs/gb279/pdf/gb-6-2.pdf>.

36 For a discussion of the labour/trade linkage associated with the Myanmar Resolution, see F Maupin, 'Is the ILO Effective in Upholding Workers' Rights?: Reflections on the Myanmar Experience' in P Alston (ed), *Labour Rights as Human Rights*, Oxford University Press, New York 2005, 85.

37 *Burmese Freedom and Democracy Act of 2003*, HR 2330, 108th Congress (2003); *Burmese Freedom and Democracy Act of 2003*, 50 USC § 1701 (Supp 2003).

38 <http://www.ilo.org/wcmsp5/groups/public/---dgreports/---dcomm/documents/publication/ wcms_106243.pdf>.

million of whom are engaged in hazardous work, the ILO, in its 2006 *Global Report on Child Labor*, claims child labour is declining globally.[39]

The UN's predecessor, the League of Nations, adopted the *Geneva Declaration of the Rights of the Child* in 1924, which stated that children must be protected against exploitation.[40] The ICCPR and the ICESCR also protect children against exploitation, and the ICESCR reflects the requirements of numerous ILO conventions that set a minimum age for the paid employment of children. The *Convention on the Rights of the Child* (CROC) provides broad coverage with respect to protecting children from harm.[41]

One of the primary aims in establishing the ILO in 1919 was the abolition of child labour but it took until 1973 for the first major convention to be adopted that targeted this issue. However, in the time since the adoption of this convention, child labour has become a major global issue and is one where the traditional divide between the work of human rights and labour rights activists is less marked.

The two principal ILO conventions dealing with child labour are the *Minimum Age Convention* (No 138) and the *Worst Forms of Child Labour Convention* (No 182). Taken together, these provide a framework for determining what acceptable work is for children under the age of 18 years. *Convention No 138* provides generally that the minimum age for employment shall not be less than the age of completion of compulsory schooling and in any case shall not be less than 15 years (article 2). However, the Convention does build in some flexibility and provides that children aged 13–15 years may be permitted to undertake light work as long as it is not likely to be harmful to their health or development and will not prejudice their attendance at school or participation in vocational or training programs (article 7).

Convention No 182 adopted in 1999 requires ratifying states to eliminate the worst forms of child labour, including all forms of slavery or practices similar to slavery, such as the sale and trafficking of children, debt bondage and serfdom and forced or compulsory labour, including forced or compulsory recruitment of children for use in armed conflict; child prostitution and pornography; using children for illicit activities, in particular for the production and trafficking of drugs; and work that is likely to harm the health, safety or morals of children.

Approximately 87 per cent of member states have ratified the *Convention No 138*, compared to 95 per cent of member states that have ratified *Convention No 182* targeting the worst forms of child labour. India, which has the biggest child population in the world, has not yet ratified either of these ILO conventions but did accede to the CROC in 1992.

The ILO's focus on eliminating child labour has not been limited to the ratification of its fundamental conventions but has also emphasised the provision of technical assistance to member states to test various approaches to reduce child labour. Following the adoption by the UN General Assembly in 1989 of the CROC, the *International Programme on the Elimination of Child Labour* (IPEC) was launched by the ILO in 1992 and developed specific initiatives working with governments, employers, workers and non-governmental organisations (NGOs) to reduce child labour.

39 Report of the Director General, *The End of Child Labour: Within Reach. Global Report under the Follow-Up to the ILO Declaration on Fundamental Principles and Rights at Work*, International Labour Conference 95th Session 2006 Report I (B) xi.

40 Adopted 26 September 1924, League of Nations OJ Spec Supp 21, 43 (1924). See also the *Declaration of the Rights of the Child*, GA Res 1386 (XIV), UN GAOR, 14th sess, Supp No 16, UN Doc A/4354 (20 November 1959) principle 2.

41 ICCPR art 24(1); ICESCR art 10(3); CROC art 32.

SNAPSHOT: CHILD LABOUR IN COCOA PRODUCTION

Of the 218 million child labourers estimated by the ILO, about 70 per cent are working in agriculture. The problems related to agricultural child labour are particularly acute in sub-Saharan Africa, where nearly 30 per cent of all children under the age of 15 are thought to be working. From 2002 to 2006, the ILO-IPEC technical assistance program focused on reducing child labour in West African cocoa production and worked across its tripartite structure to achieve this. The impetus for the ILO project flowed from strong calls from the NGO sector to address this issue and mobilised governments, international organisations, business and civil society to work together.

In 2001, in an attempt to avoid government regulation and intense media scrutiny, major cocoa companies made a voluntary commitment (the Cocoa Industry Protocol) to certify their cocoa 'child labour-free' by July 2005, but that deadline passed with little fanfare. The deadline was then extended to certify 50% of farms 'child-labour free' by July 2008. The cocoa companies have initiated a few pilot programs but NGOs argue that they continue to purchase and reap profits from child labour cocoa.

The International Labor Rights Fund (ILRF) is a US-based NGO active in the area of labour standards compliance in global supply chains. It has played a prominent role in working against child labour in efforts such as the Rugmark program and the Sialkot soccer ball initiative in the mid-1990s.[42] In 2001, when the Cocoa Industry Protocol was first announced, ILRF was a critical voice, pointing out that this particular initiative did not conform with best practice approaches to labour rights compliance in global commodity chains. In 2008 the ILRF published its recommendations to the principal stakeholders involved.

INTERNATIONAL LABOR RIGHTS FUND: 'THE COCOA PROTOCOL: SUCCESS OR FAILURE?' (JUNE 30, 2008)[43]

VII. Lessons Learned and Recommendations

... with seven years of analysis and observations behind us, what have we learned?

Recommendations

To companies:

- Take the Hippocratic Oath: First, do no harm. Ensure that your own supply chains provide fair and sustainable incomes for farmers and sustainable wages for workers.
- Focus on integrity of your own supply chains and engage programs that will monitor labor standards to the farm or cooperative level.
- Openly support multilateral initiatives to hold non-state actors accountable, and ensure your own operations and supply chains comply fully with existing guidelines such as ILO Tripartite Declaration of Principles Regarding Multinational Enterprises and also the OECD Guidelines for Multinational Enterprises.

42 Rugmark is a network of non-profit organizations dedicated to ending illegal child labour in the rug making industry. It provides a certification program that allows companies that pass inspection to attach a logo certifying that their product is made without child labour. Rugmark International re-branded the certification program and introduced the GoodWeave label in 2009, see: <www.rugmark.org>. In 1996 a number of NGOs called attention to violations of child labour occurring in the soccer ball industry in Sialkot, Pakistan; see below at 17.3.

43 <http://www.laborrights.org/sites/default/files/publications-and-resources/Cocoa%20Protocol%20Success%20or%20Failure%20June%202008.pdf>.

To West African governments:

- Work with and support ILO-IPEC programs to eliminate child labor.
- Work with and support the International Migration Organization (IOM) on strategies to combat trafficking regionally.
- Work toward reinstatement of supply management mechanisms in the cocoa sector to protect farmers from price fluctuations and support revenue transparency.

To the US government and EU governments:

- Invest in funding the ILO-IPEC program and do not divert funding for child labor to public-private partnerships.
- Reengage in commodity agreements and publicly support the efforts of UNCTAD to promote development through farmer-sensitive commodity policies.
- Support and fund the Education for All initiative.
- Support revenue transparency for all commodity production worldwide, and hold US multinational corporations accountable to providing such transparency of payments.

To multilateral agencies:

- The ILO should continue to work with the governments of Cote d'Ivoire and Ghana to ensure full implementation of the ILO conventions.
- The World Bank and other international financial institutions should reverse policy and publicly support the efforts of developing country governments to regulate commodity prices, and should support and fund government efforts to implement the Education for All initiative. The World Bank should also offer its public support to national and international efforts to increase revenue transparency in all commodity sectors.

To consumers:

- Reward companies with ethical integrity in supply chains—companies that can tell you how the farmers and workers that produced your chocolate were treated.
- Continue to demand that world's largest chocolate manufacturers answer to the question as to how you can be assured no exploited or trafficked child labour was used in the making of their products.

Equality and the Elimination of Discrimination

Freedom from discrimination is a fundamental human right and is enshrined in the UN's international and regional human rights treaties as well as the labour rights conventions of the ILO.[44] Two of the ILO's core conventions are the *Equal Remuneration Convention*, 1951 (No 100) and the *Discrimination (Employment and Occupation) Convention*, 1958 (No 111).

The focus of the *Equal Remuneration Convention* (No 100) is on parity between male and female work and it requires ratifying states to 'ensure the application to all workers of the principle of equal remuneration for men and women workers for work of equal value'.[45] In its 2007 *Global Report on Equality* the ILO noted that 'equal pay for work of equal value' is one of the least understood concepts in the

44 ICCPR art 2; ICESCR arts 2, 3 and 6; CEDAW art 11 and the CRPD generally requires states to prohibit discrimination against persons with disabilities. Also, CESCR, see above, n 4 para 12(b)(i).

45 *Equal Remuneration Convention, 1951* (No 100), General Conference of the International Labour Organization, 34th sess, C100 (adopted 29 June 1951, entered into force 23 May 1953) art 2 (ILO Convention No 100).

field of action against discrimination: it is often given a narrow interpretation in laws and regulations, and the lack of reliable sex-disaggregated data on wages makes it difficult to monitor trends'.[46] The report also comments that 'despite advances in women's educational achievements, their earnings are still on average less than men's. It is also difficult for women to reconcile family duties with paid work without affecting their chances of promotion or skill enhancement. However, even where they manage to overcome these obstacles, they earn less than men'.[47]

Although the *Equal Remuneration Convention* (No 100) has one of the highest rates of ratification of the international labour standards and the principle of equal remuneration for work of equal value is widely incorporated into national legislation, gender disparity still exists globally; in a number of developed countries women workers earn up to 25 percent less than male colleagues performing equal work.[48] The *Discrimination (Employment and Occupation) Convention*, 1958 (No 111) defines discrimination as 'any distinction, exclusion or preference made on the basis of race, colour, sex, religion, political opinion, national extraction or social origin, which has the effect of nullifying or impairing equality of opportunity or treatment in employment or occupation'.[49] The ILO in its second global report on equality and discrimination, notes that discrimination in the workplace continues to evolve and

> while long-recognized patterns of discrimination based on sex, race and religion persist, often acquiring new expressions, newer forms are emerging such as discrimination on account of actual or perceived HIV/AIDS status or against workers at both ends of the age spectrum. At the same time, other practices, such as those that penalize individuals with habits regarded as unhealthy, have begun to surface in several countries.[50]

17.2.4 Monitoring Compliance with ILO Standards

The principal mechanism for ensuring compliance with ILO standards is the system of state reporting. Committee bodies established in the ILO operate in a similar manner to the human rights treaty bodies,[51] with the regular supervisory system focused on receiving and examining state reports, and the special procedures mechanism established to deal with complaints, representations and a special procedure regarding freedom of association.

46 ILO, 'Equality at Work: Tackling the Challenges'. *Global Report under the Follow-Up to the ILO Declaration on Fundamental Principles and Rights at Work* (International Labour Conference, 96th sess, 2007) xiv.

47 Ibid xii.

48 L Wirth, *Breaking Through the Glass Ceiling: Women in Management* (ILO Publications, 2001) <http://www.ilo.org/public/libdoc/ilo/2001/101B09_102_engl.pdf>.

49 *Discrimination (Employment and Occupation) Convention*, 1958 (No 111), General Conference of the International Labour Organization, 42nd sess, C111 (adopted 25 June 1958, entered into force 15 June 1960) art 1 (ILO Convention No 111).

50 See above, n 46, 15. For a discussion on the application of ILO discrimination laws to Australia see: Simon Rice & Cameron Roles, '"It's a Discrimination Law, Julia, But Not As We Know It": Part 3-1 of the Fair Work Act' (2010) 21(1) *Economic and Labour Relations Review*, 13.

51 See Chapter 7.4.

Regular System of Supervision: State Reports

Article 22 of the ILO Constitution provides:

> Each of the Members agrees to make an annual report to the International Labour Office on the measures which it has taken to give effect to the provisions of Conventions to which it is a party. These reports shall be made in such form and shall contain such particulars as the Governing Body may request.

The Committee of Experts on the Application of Conventions and Recommendations (CEACR) is the body primarily responsible for monitoring a state's performance under the ILO treaties.[52] Established in 1926, the CEACR comprises 20 members who are appointed by the Governing Body for three year terms. States are required to submit reports every two years on their compliance with the 'fundamental conventions' they have ratified, and every five years for other treaties. The CEACR reviews the state reports and any supplementary information supplied by employer or worker organisations and the Committee may then make 'direct requests' to states for more information, perhaps pointing to a particular problem in complying with a standard and giving the state time to respond. These direct requests are not published. The CEACR does publish 'observations' on the application of a particular convention by a state in the Committee's annual report. The annual report is submitted to the ILC's Conference Committee on the Application of Standards.

Special Procedures: Representation and Complaint Procedures

The complaint mechanisms of the ILO provide generally for three types of complaint procedures: representations by employer or worker organisations about state compliance with a ratified treaty under article 24; complaints made by a state against other states under article 26; and complaints dealing specifically with freedom of association issues.[53]

Article 24 of the ILO Constitution allows for an industrial association of employers or workers to present the ILO Governing Body a 'representation' against any member state that in its view has failed to comply with its obligations under a convention the state has ratified. The admissibility criteria for a representation are similar to that used by the human rights treaty bodies.[54] If the representation is admissible, it is referred to a three-member tripartite committee of the Governing Body for examination. Individuals cannot make representations under article 24 but can pass on complaints to employer or worker organisations for referral.

Article 26 of the ILO Constitution provides that 'any of the Members shall have the right to file a complaint with the International Labour Office if it is not satisfied that any other Member is securing the effective observance of any Convention that both have ratified in accordance with the foregoing

---

52 See ILO website 'Committee of Experts on the Application of Conventions and Recommendations': <http://www.ilo.org/global/standards/applying-and-promoting-international-labour-standards/committee-of-experts-on-the-application-of-conventions-and-recommendations/lang--en/index.htm>.

53 For some examples of complaints made by Australian bodies under articles 24 and 26 of the ILO Constitution see Chapter 10.5.4.

54 See Chapter 7.4.

articles.' After receiving a complaint the ILC or the Governing Body may initiate a Commission of Inquiry, which investigates the complaint and recommends any further action. The Commission of Inquiry is the ILO's premier investigative mechanism and is used to investigate the actions of states that persistently violate ILO standards. If a state refuses to follow the recommendations of a Commission of Inquiry, action may be taken under article 33 of the Constitution, which the Governing Body 'may deem wise and expedient to secure compliance.' Article 33 was invoked for the first time in 2000 in response to Myanmar's refusal to comply with ILO recommendations.[55]

Representations on freedom of association issues are generally sent to the Committee on Freedom of Association (CFA), which has become the principal ILO complaints body. The CFA is also a tripartite body with three members from each of the government, employer and worker sectors. Complaints may be brought against a state by employer or worker organisations. The CFA can receive complaints about violations of freedom of association whether or not the state has ratified the relevant conventions.

SNAPSHOT: FREEDOM OF ASSOCIATION IN PRACTICE—ZIMBABWE

In a Shadow Report to the African Commission on Human and Peoples' Rights in 2007,[56] Amnesty International argued that the government of Zimbabwe had long been targeting trade unions in continued attempts to restrict the right to freedom of association in that country. The government believed that labour activists from the Zimbabwe Congress of Trade Unions (ZCTU) and other unions were working with the political opposition to mobilise votes against the government. The report cites several examples where ZCTU officials were subject to arbitrary arrest, torture and excessive use of force by the police.

> For example, on 13 September 2006, 15 members of the ZCTU ... were arrested in Harare after attempting to engage in a peaceful demonstration. They were severely assaulted during arrest. They were detained at Matapi police station and tortured. Doctors confirmed that the ZCTU activists were beaten on the soles of the feet—a torture method called 'falanga', which leaves many victims with life-long problems with walking.
>
> On the same day, 13 September 2006, in the farming town of Chegutu, 11 members of a ZCTU affiliate union, the General Agricultural and Plantations Workers' Union (GAPWUZ), were arrested after handing over a petition at a government office. They were taken to Chegutu Police Station and reportedly tortured while in police custody over a three-day period. They were made to lie on the stomach and were beaten on the soles of the feet while held in leg irons and handcuffs. The 11 trade unionists were later charged under the *Public Order and Security Act* (POSA) and granted bail.
>
> The previous day, 12 September 2006, police had arrested ZCTU leaders across the country in an apparent pre-emptive action to forestall the ZCTU protest.
>
> On 8 November 2005 more than 100 people were arrested in Harare when the ZCTU tried to hold a peaceful demonstration protesting against the grave economic situation in Zimbabwe. Lawyers

55 See discussion above at 17.2.3.

56 Amnesty International, *Zimbabwe: Human Rights in Crisis. Shadow Report to the African Commission on Human and Peoples' Rights* (Report No AFR 46/016/2007, 22 May 2007) 35–41 <http://www.amnesty.org/en/library/asset/AFR46/016/2007/en/6f1c11c5-d38e-11dd-a329-2f46302a8cc6/afr460162007en.pdf>. For an overview of the African system, see Chapter 8.4.

> were initially denied access to the detainees, who were moved by police from one police station to another in an apparent attempt to prevent contact with lawyers. …
>
> At least 100 trade union and human rights activists were arrested throughout the country on 18 November 2003 in order to prevent them from staging a peaceful demonstration against the economic crisis and human rights abuses in Zimbabwe.
>
> In Harare approximately 50 activists were arrested including ZCTU President Lovemore Matombo and Secretary General Wellington Chibebe …
>
> On 8 October 2003 at least 200 trade union activists were arrested in various parts of Zimbabwe ahead of planned demonstrations against high taxes and inflation …[57]

In November 2008 a Commission of Inquiry was established by the ILO's Governing Body in accordance with article 26 (para 4) of the ILO Constitution following the filing of complaints by 13 Workers' and 13 Employers' delegates to the ninety-seventh session (June 2008) of the International Labour Conference. The Commission of Inquiry (comprising three eminent individuals) conducted two missions to Zimbabwe in May and August 2009, and in its report filed with the ILO Governing Body in March 2010 found that there had been systematic, and even systemic, violations of ILO Conventions No 87 and 98.[58] The report confirmed calculated attempts on the part of the government to intimidate and threaten trade union members including the use of violence and unjustified detentions. The Zimbabwe government, in its prompt reply of 20 April 2010, accepted the recommendations made by the Commission of Inquiry 'in the spirit of engagement among the people of Zimbabwe.' It indicated that the commission's recommendations would be implemented as part of its current legislative and institutional reform program.[59]

Given the substantive nature of the Commission's recommendations, including the need for legislative reform; the cessation of anti-union arrests, detentions, violence, torture, intimidation and harassment, interference and discrimination; strengthening of national institutions and social dialogue; training on freedom of association and collective bargaining, civil liberties and human rights; and the reinforcement of the rule of law and the role of the Courts, the onus remains with Zimbabwe to now deliver these reforms in accordance with its 2010 response.

17.3 EFFECTIVENESS OF THE ILO

As with the UN human rights system, the efficacy of the ILO relies primarily on a 'voluntary approach' that depends on the consent of states. Consistently with the procedures established in international

57 Ibid 37–8.

58 ILO, *Truth, Reconciliation and Justice in Zimbabwe: Report of the Commission of Inquiry Appointed under Article 26 of the Constitution of the International Labour Organization to Examine the Observance by the Government of Zimbabwe of the Freedom of Association and Protection of the Right to Organise Convention, 1948 (No 87), and the Right to Organise and Collective Bargaining Convention, 1949 (No 98)* (ILO, December 2009) <http://www.ilo.org/wcmsp5/groups/public/---ed_norm/---relconf/documents/meetingdocument/wcms_123293.pdf>.

59 ILO, 'Zimbabwe Government Accepts ILO Commission of Inquiry's Recommendations' (Press Release, ILO/10/18, 27 April 2010) <http://www.ilo.org/global/About_the_ILO/ Media_and_public_information/Press_releases/lang--en/WCMS_126394/index.htm>.

law, states that have voluntarily ratified a convention accept its obligations as binding and should then incorporate the standards into national legislation.[60] The challenge for the ILO, and likewise the UN, lies in ensuring this voluntary acceptance of state obligations becomes a reality. A system of standards involves not only establishing the standards, but monitoring compliance, assisting with technical aspects of compliance and enforcing the standards.

There are generally polarised sets of opinions regarding the efficacy of the ILO.[61] On one side, one might characterise the ILO as having no 'teeth' and argue that it operates as little more than a debating society with no meaningful remedies or sanctions at hand. Others argue that the ILO not only has 'teeth' but 'also a tongue; and [that] a good tongue lashing, based on evaluations that are credible, impartial and unbiased, can push a country into better policies through shame, guilt and the activities of NGOs that act on such findings'.[62]

In evaluating the effectiveness of the ILO it is important to consider how its operations have changed and expanded in recent decades partly due to continuing pressures on labour standards wrought by globalisation since the 1990s. In the last 20 years there has been an increasing involvement of the private sector in upholding international labour standards.[63] Voluntary codes of conduct—which may not only establish standards but also set up a monitoring and review mechanism—are now routinely employed by many companies as a way of improving workplace standards. Is it is illegitimate for private companies to be conducting labour inspections? Should resources instead be devoted to strengthening public labour administration systems reaffirming the responsibility of the state to protect rights? Unfortunately, years of ILO technical assistance to countries around the world have not been able to stem the decline of labour inspection, and the global labour market has quite simply overwhelmed most national systems of labour market regulation.[64] Even developed market economies have trouble maintaining adequate levels of inspection.[65] So the need for private actors to take responsibility for labour inspection remains and will probably grow. No socially responsible company would want child labour or forced labour or toxic conditions of work involved in the production of their goods, so it is still necessary to perform due diligence to ensure that labour standards are respected, even in jurisdictions where labour inspectors are active.[66]

---

60 A refinement on this is that for monist states the treaty obligations will have domestic effect without the need for legislation: see the discussion in Chapter 7.2.7.

61 See above n 1, 22–47 at 41.

62 J Bhagwati, *Free Trade Today*, Princeton University Press, Princeton, 2002, 79. Also, V A Leary 'The Paradox of Workers' Rights as Human Rights' in L A Compa & S F Diamond (eds), *Human Rights, Labor Rights and International Trade*, University of Pennsylvania Press, Philadelphia, 1996, 22–47 at 41.

63 See Chapter 19.4.3.

64 J Nolan & A van Heerden 'Engaging Business in the Business of Human Righs' in D Kinley & M Pedersen (eds), *Principled Engagement*, United Nations University Press, [forthcoming 2012].

65 See: L Compa, *Unfair Advantage: Workers Freedom of Association in the United States under International Human Rights Standards*, Cornell University Press, New York, 2004); Human Rights Watch, *Blood, Sweat, and Fear: Workers' Rights in US Meat and Poultry Plants* (2005).

66 See also the emphasis placed on due diligence to mitigate risk by the UN Special Representative, Professor Ruggie. *Report of the Special Representative of the Secretary-General on the Issue of Human Rights and Transnational Corporations and other Business Enterprises, John Ruggie 'Business and Human Rights: Further Steps toward the Operationalization of the "Protect, Respect and Remedy" Framework'* 9 April 2010, A/HRC/14/27, paras 7–86.

Perhaps the ideal situation would be one in which private actors complemented the work of public agencies by mobilising resources to protect social, labour and environmental rights. If the private and public actors cooperated and coordinated it may be possible to weave social safety nets in countries that have never had them before. That synergy has been hard to capture, however, and most public agencies are either in denial or in bad faith about the lamentable state of labour law enforcement in their jurisdictions.[67] This has certainly stymied ILO action on the topic, since no member state wants to admit in public that its labour laws are not being enforced and that it requires assistance from international organisations or private corporations.

The two snapshots below illustrate the willingness of the ILO (in particular and defined sectors) to move beyond standard setting to active involvement in the implementation of labour standards, and the need to seek out and work with other partners in order to achieve more sustained and sustainable compliance with such standards.

SNAPSHOT: LINKING LABOUR WITH TRADE AND THE EFFECTIVENESS OF THE ILO'S TECHNICAL ASSISTANCE IN CAMBODIA'S TEXTILE INDUSTRY

A constant criticism of the ILO since its inception has been its limited ability to enforce compliance with its standards and its reluctance to tackle hands-on monitoring at the level of individual factories or corporations. In Cambodia in the late 1990s, a confluence of forces involving the ILO, the US and Cambodian governments, trade unions, business, NGOs and workers came together to demonstrate how compliance with labour standards can be improved based on 'carrots, not sticks'.

In January 1999 the US and Cambodia signed the US–Cambodia Bilateral Textile Agreement (initially for a three-year period and extended until 2004).[68] Under this agreement, the US promised Cambodia better access to US markets in exchange for improved working conditions in Cambodia's garment sector. The value of textile and apparel imports increased by almost 200 percent in the first two years of the agreement and the labour incentives clause in the agreement has in part caused the growth in US purchasing from Cambodia to be accompanied by improvements in working conditions. The improvement in working conditions has been in a large part due to the establishment in 2001, by the ILO, of the 'Better Factories Cambodia' program, which aimed to help the garment sector make and maintain the required improvements.

Linking labour standards with trade has long been a controversial issue. Opinions differ on free trade versus fair trade and on whether such linkages are merely a facade for implementing the protectionist policies of developed countries. So why was this agreement successful? In part, because of the stake each of the parties had in ensuring the agreement was successful and the very active role assumed by the ILO via its Better Factories program. The US President, Bill Clinton, was heavily reliant on maintaining the backing of organised labour, and was thus committed to using Cambodia as a test case to show that improving

67 J Nolan & A van Heerden, see above, n 64.

68 *Principled Engagement*, United Nations University Press, *US–Cambodia Bilateral Textile Agreement* (20 January 1999). For more information see: <http://cambodia.usembassy.gov/uploads/images/M9rzdrzMKGi6AjfOSIuJRA/uskh_texttile.pdf>.

working conditions did not come at the price of economic development. For years, Cambodia's garment industry had been plagued by corruption, violence, strikes and allegations of human rights violations including sexual harassment and targeted attacks against union representatives. If these problems were not solved, business, government and labour in Cambodia all stood to lose.

The credibility of the US–Cambodia pact hinged on third party monitoring of labour conditions, and accordingly the ILO runs a series of unannounced factory visits to check on working conditions. The standards monitored are based on Cambodia labour law and the ILO's standards and specific feedback is provided to factories for improvements. International buyers have made sourcing decisions based on the factory's participation in the program. The Cambodian Ministry of Commerce requires factories to register with the program in order to export. The ILO publishes semi-annual public reports tracking improvement in working conditions.[69]

While the US–Cambodia example demonstrates how the ILO's technical assistance can be a valuable tool in enforcing labour standards, the snapshot below dealing with child labour in Pakistan, emphasises the ongoing need for the ILO to work with other partners, including corporations, to reduce labour rights violations.

SNAPSHOT: PUBLIC/PRIVATE ENFORCEMENT OF LABOUR RIGHTS AN EFFECTIVE MEANS OF REDUCING CHILD LABOUR IN PAKISTAN'S FOOTBALL PRODUCTION

In 1977 the ILO established its *Tripartite Declaration of Principles Concerning Multinational Enterprises and Social Policy*[70] (ILO MNE Declaration). The ILO MNE Declaration was adopted in response to the growing role and influence of corporations in the 1960s and 1970s. The Declaration is aimed at encouraging member states to support the contributions of multinational enterprises to economic and social progress and to minimise and resolve the difficulties that their operations may give rise to. Although voluntary, the ILO MNE Declaration offers a set of core principles and guidelines for corporations in the areas of employment, training, working conditions and industrial relations. While the Declaration provides a useful framework for good practice, there is no evidence that it has had any considerable effect in influencing the behaviour of corporations. The 1977 Declaration was timid and it took more time and media attention to focus the ILO on the more substantial and direct role it might play in influencing corporate behaviour.

In 1997 the ILO, UNICEF and Pakistan's Sialkot Chamber of Commerce and Industry signed a Partners' Agreement on a joint project to improve working conditions and, in particular, prevent and eliminate child labour in the football manufacturing industry in Sialkot, Pakistan. At that time, Sialkot was the centre of

69 For an update on the program see: *Better Factories Cambodia* <http://www.betterfactories.org>.

70 Adopted by the Governing Body of the International Labour Office at its 204th session (November 1977) as amended at its 279th (November 2000) and 295th session (March 2006).

Pakistan's football producing industry, producing nearly 75 percent of the world's hand-stitched footballs and the ILO estimated that as many as 7000 children were working in the industry around this time.[71] The Sialkot Partners' Agreement followed a media campaign by the International Confederation of Free Trade Unions and a number of NGOs (the 'foul ball campaign') to highlight the use of child labour in this production process. Following negative media attention, the World Federation of Sporting Goods Industry and the Soccer Industry Council of America, which represented more than 50 sporting goods brands, was launched to eliminate child labour from the production of soccer balls in Pakistan. The Partners' Agreement evolved via this process.

The Agreement required football manufacturers to establish a comprehensive internal monitoring system, including training programs, to agree to independent monitors to verify compliance and to work closely with the ILO and other organisations in a Social Protection Program to provide children with educational and other opportunities. The Social Protection Program also provided support services to children and their families, including non-formal education, vocational training and microcredit facilities.

While the Sialkot experiment has been generally successful in improving working conditions in that region[72] and established a successful framework for tackling child labour in other regions and industries, violations in the soccer ball manufacturing industry continue. A 2010 report[73] by the International Labor Rights Fund detailed the reality of the poor working conditions faced by soccer ball stitchers in Pakistan, India, China and Thailand, including the use of temporary labour (which means the workers lack access to healthcare or social security), excessive working hours, underpayment of wages, discrimination and isolated examples of child labour.

17.4 CONCLUSION AND ISSUES

As is discussed above, the interdependence of the right to work with other human rights is apparent from the terms of both the ICCPR and the ICESCR: the rights to life, health and education are some of the more obvious rights affected by deleterious working conditions. Labour rights are well defined in international and regional human rights treaties and more specifically in the conventions and recommendations of the ILO. However, while the delineation of labour rights is well advanced, the enforcement of these rights remains challenging.

The ILO's distinctive tripartite approach raises the question of whether it is a more effective mechanism for drafting and enforcing labour rights than the current mechanisms in the UN for enforcement of human rights more generally. On the one hand the formal involvement of the three primary stakeholders in both drafting and enforcing labour standards is an advantage; on the other

71 ILO/IPEC 'From Stitching to School: Combating Child Labor in the Soccer Ball Industry in Pakistan' 8.

72 However, a 2008 report by an NGO argues that the contractors who make soccer balls have simply moved their operations from Sialkot to northern India but conditions have not improved. The report details abuses such as child labour and debt bondage are still continuing in this industry. See B Bachao Andolan, *Child Labor in Football Stitching Activity in India* (2008) at <http://www.laborrights.org/sites/default/files/publications-and-resources/FOOTBALLREPORT2008.pdf>.

73 ILRF, *Missed the Goal for Workers: The Reality of Soccer Ball Stitchers in Pakistan, India, China and Thailand* (7 June 2010) <http://www.laborrights.org/stop-child-forced-labor/foulball-campaign/resources/12331>.

it may lead to compromises in drafting that lower the basic standards for compliance. Over the years, it appears that the tripartite system of governance has generally been a positive rather than negative contribution to the evolution of international labour rights.

Looking ahead to future issues, it is apparent that the private sector is potentially crucial in enforcing labour standards, raising the question of whether soft law mechanisms—such as codes of conduct—that may or may not have been developed and enforced in collaboration with the ILO, are useful tools in protecting labour rights? Such soft law might be seen as a substitute for, rather than a supplement to, international labour standards but it is arguable that an advantage is that such standards might at least be a stepping stone along the road of compliance with international labour standards.

The right to work forms an essential part of human rights law and greater respect and protection for labour rights is a key component in ensuring all individuals can live and work with dignity.

PART SEVEN

CONTEMPORARY ISSUES IN INTERNATIONAL HUMAN RIGHTS LAW

18 TERRORISM, COUNTER-TERRORISM AND THE IMPACT ON HUMAN RIGHTS

CONTENTS

18.1 INTRODUCTION

It is self-evident that 'terrorism' affects the enjoyment of fundamental human rights, but whether certain counter-terrorism measures also violate human rights is a question being asked with new vigour since the 11 September 2001 attacks in the United States. Terrorism is not new, nor is its impact on human rights, but the 2001 attacks and the subsequent pronouncements and reactions of individual states, non-state actors and international organisations have thrust the issues of terrorism and counter-terrorism to the fore.

'Since 11 September 2001 many people have come to believe, if they did not already, that terrorism is one of the most serious threats we face in the world today. Others have come to believe that counter-terrorism—the "war on terror"—is one of the most serious threats we face in the world today'.[1] Former UN Secretary General Kofi Annan stated in 2003 that 'our responses to terrorism as well as our efforts to thwart it and prevent it, should uphold the human rights that terrorists aim to destroy. Respect for

1 S Marks & A Clapham, *International Human Rights Lexicon*, Oxford University Press, Oxford, 2005, 345.

human rights, fundamental freedoms and the rule of law are essential tools in the effort to combat terrorism—not privileges to be sacrificed at the time of tension.'[2] However, as some of the counter-terrorism measures adopted before and after 2001 show, such respect for human rights is not always obvious.

This chapter focuses largely on the impact counter-terrorism mechanisms have on human rights and the role international human rights law could or should play in the development and implementation of counter-terrorism measures. It begins by examining the struggle to define the concept of terrorism and how the failure to develop an international comprehensive convention on terrorism affects rights. Human rights and the defence of those rights is used by protagonists and reactionaries alike as their raison d'être. Depending on which side of the fence one sits, both states and non-state actors have been cast as terrorists. The old adage that 'one man's terrorist is another man's freedom fighter' is perhaps over-used but, given the lack of clarity around the concept, is still relevant. Indeed, it shows that 'terrorism' is an inherently political rather than legal term. While there is no inherent contradiction in protecting people's rights and ensuring public safety, some of the responses to terrorism studied in this chapter reveal a lack of respect for the human rights they seek to protect.

18.2 DEFINING TERRORISM

Terrorism is not a new phenomenon but its legal definition (at least internationally) still lacks consistency and clarity. Numerous attempts have been made to define the concept, ranging from the precise to the general and from the international to the local, but no legal terminology is universally agreed upon.[3] Disagreement is largely political rather than legal. Over time various activities have been labelled as 'terrorism', including hostage taking and hijacking, attacks on civilian aircraft, bombing of embassies and civilians, attacks by non-state actors in peacetime, abduction of UN personnel and assassination of political leaders.

Terrorism is a powerful concept and a term that is 'ideologically and politically loaded; pejorative; implies moral, social and value judgment; and is slippery and much abused'.[4] In some respects, terrorism has become a term of convenience, used by governments (and others) at will to describe conduct, whether by states or individuals, that is disapproved of, perceived of as unlawful and worthy of retribution. Disagreement about defining terrorism runs deep and while some may be satisfied with the 'we-know-it-when-we-see-it'[5] definitional approach, for others, the search for an adequate definition remains a priority.

2 See K Annan, speech delivered at the Special Meeting of the UN Security Council's Counter-Terrorism Committee with International Regional and Sub-Regional Organisations, New York, 6 March 2003 <http://www.un.org/apps/sg/sgstats.asp?nid=275>.

3 For a contrary view see R Young, 'Defining Terrorism: The Evolution of Terrorism as a Legal Concept' (2006) 29 *Boston College International and Comparative Law Review* 23.

4 B Saul, *Defining Terrorism in International Law*, Oxford University Press, Oxford, 2006, 3.

5 A P Schmid & A J Jongman, *Political Terrorism: A New Guide to Actors, Authors, Concepts, Data Bases, Theories and Literature*, 2nd edn, Transaction Publishers, New Brunswick, 2005, 1.

18.2.1 Drafting an International Law Definition

International attempts to define terrorism have been drawn-out and inconclusive but there is no shortage of treaties or UN General Assembly or Security Council resolutions that delineate certain aspects or elements of terrorism, even if they do not always label it as terrorism.[6] In 2004 the UN Secretary General's High Level Panel on Threats, Challenges and Change commented that the '[l]ack of agreement on a clear and well-known definition undermines the normative and moral stance against terrorism and has stained the United Nations' image. Achieving a comprehensive convention on terrorism, including a clear definition, is a political imperative'.[7] But it is a political imperative that remains unrealised.

One of the earliest significant steps taken to define terrorism was the drafting exercise undertaken by the League of Nations between 1934 and 1937 to develop a convention for the prevention and punishment of terrorism.[8] The Convention was adopted in 1937, but never came into force as it did not receive the requisite number of ratifications.[9] Like many terrorism treaties that followed it, the impetus for drafting the League of Nations' Convention was a specific event—in this case, the assassination of King Alexander I of Yugoslavia in October 1934. Following the assassination, the League Council lamented that 'the rules of international law concerning the repression of terrorist activity are not at present sufficiently precise to guarantee efficiently international cooperation'[10] and thus sought to develop a comprehensive convention on terrorism. Article 1(2) of the League's Convention defines terrorism as '[A]ll criminal acts directed against a State and intended or calculated to create a state of terror in the minds of particular persons or a group of persons or the general public', and the influence of this general description is evident in later international attempts to define the concept.

In 1996 the UN General Assembly established an Ad Hoc Committee[11] with a mandate to draft a comprehensive international convention on terrorism. In the years before and since there have been other attempts to define and prohibit specific types of 'terrorist-like' conduct, but a single comprehensive convention is still out of reach. Between 1963 and 2005, 13 international legal thematic instruments were created to deal with terrorism, several in response to specific terrorist attacks. Cumulatively, these documents have identified a number of acts commonly considered as terrorist acts, even if they are not specifically referred to as such in the conventions and protocols.

---

6 For an overview of the international legal framework to combat terrorism, see, eg, S Scott, A Billingsley & C Michaelsen, Ch 8 in *International Law and the Use of Force: A Documentary and Reference Guide*, Praeger Security International, Santa Barbara, 2010, 215–54.

7 The Secretary General, *A More Secure World: Our Shared Responsibility—Report of the Secretary General's High-Level Panel on Threats, Challenges and Change*, UN GAOR, 59th sess, Agenda Item 55, UN Doc A/59/565 (2 December 2004) [159] <http://www.un.org/secureworld/>.

8 B Saul, see above, n 4, 171.

9 *League of Nations Convention for the Prevention and Punishment of Terrorism*, opened for signature 16 November 1937, LoN Doc C546(I) M 383(I) 1937 V (did not enter into force).

10 League of Nations Committee for the International Repression of Terrorism, LoN Doc CRT 1 (10 April 1935) quoted in B Saul, 'The Legal Response of the League of Nations to Terrorism' (2006) 4 *Journal of International Criminal Justice* 78, 80.

11 Ad Hoc Committee established by Measures to Eliminate International Terrorism, GA Res 51/210, 51st sess, 88th plen mtg, UN Doc A/RES/51/210 (17 December 1996).

18.2.2 International Conventions and Protocols on Terrorism

The following documents were developed under the auspices of the United Nations and its specialised agencies and are open to participation by all Member States. The UN Action to Counter Terrorism provides the following summary of these major conventions.[12]

MAJOR INTERNATIONAL TERRORISM CONVENTIONS

1963 Convention on Offences and Certain Other Acts Committed on Board Aircraft (applies to acts affecting in-flight safety)

1970 Convention for the Suppression of Unlawful Seizure of Aircraft creates an offence for any person on board an aircraft in flight to 'unlawfully, by force or threat thereof, or any other form of intimidation, [to] seize or exercise control of that aircraft' or to attempt to do so.

1971 Convention for the Suppression of Unlawful Acts against the Safety of Civil Aviation creates an offence for any person to unlawfully and intentionally perform an act of violence against a person on board an aircraft in flight, if that act is likely to endanger the safety of the aircraft; to place an explosive device on an aircraft; to attempt such acts; or to be an accomplice of a person who performs or attempts to perform such acts.

1973 Convention on the Prevention and Punishment of Crimes Against Internationally Protected Persons defines an 'internationally protected person' as a Head of State, Minister for Foreign Affairs, representative or official of a State or international organization who is entitled to special protection in a foreign State, and his/her family; and requires parties to criminalise and make punishable the intentional murder, kidnapping or other attack upon the person or liberty of an internationally protected person, a violent attack upon the official premises, the private accommodations, or the means of transport of such person; a threat or attempt to commit such an attack; and an act 'constituting participation as an accomplice'.

1979 International Convention against the Taking of Hostages states that 'any person who seizes or detains and threatens to kill, to injure, or to continue to detain another person in order to compel a third party, namely, a State, an international intergovernmental organization, a natural or juridical person, or a group of persons, to do or abstain from doing any act as an explicit or implicit condition for the release of the hostage commits the offence of taking of hostage within the meaning of this Convention'.

1980 Convention on the Physical Protection of Nuclear Material and amendments of 2005 criminalises the unlawful possession, use, transfer or theft of nuclear material and threats to use nuclear material to cause death, serious injury or substantial property damage.

1988 Protocol for the Suppression of Unlawful Acts of Violence at Airports Serving International Civil Aviation, supplementary to the Convention for the Suppression of Unlawful Acts against the Safety of Civil Aviation extends and supplements the provisions of the *Montreal Convention* (see No 3 above) to encompass terrorist acts at airports serving international civil aviation.

1988 Convention for the Suppression of Unlawful Acts against the Safety of Maritime Navigation **and 2005** ***Protocol to the Convention for the Suppression of Unlawful Acts against the Safety of Maritime Navigation*** establish a legal

12 *UN Action to Counter Terrorism* <http://www.un.org/terrorism/index.shtml>.

regime applicable to acts against international maritime navigation that is similar to the regimes established for international aviation.

1988 Protocol for the Suppression of Unlawful Acts Against the Safety of Fixed Platforms Located on the Continental Shelf and **2005** ***Protocol to the Protocol for the Suppression of Unlawful Acts against the Safety of Fixed Platforms Located on the Continental Shelf*** establish a legal regime applicable to acts against fixed platforms on the continental shelf that is similar to the regimes established against international aviation.

1991 Convention on the Marking of Plastic Explosives for the Purpose of Detection designed to control and limit the use of unmarked and undetectable plastic explosives (negotiated in the aftermath of the 1988 Pan Am flight 103 bombing).

1997 International Convention for the Suppression of Terrorist Bombings creates a regime of universal jurisdiction over the unlawful and intentional use of explosives and other lethal devices in, into, or against various defined public places with intent to kill or cause serious bodily injury, or with intent to cause extensive destruction of the public place.

1999 International Convention for the Suppression of the Financing of Terrorism requires parties to take steps to prevent and counteract the financing of terrorists, whether direct or indirect, through groups claiming to have charitable, social or cultural goals or which also engage in illicit activities such as drug trafficking or gun running; and provides for the identification, freezing and seizure of funds allocated for terrorist activities, as well as for the sharing of the forfeited funds with other States on a case-by-case basis. Bank secrecy is no longer adequate justification for refusing to cooperate.

2005 International Convention for the Suppression of Acts of Nuclear Terrorism covers a broad range of acts and possible targets, including nuclear power plants and nuclear reactors and threats and attempts to commit such crimes or to participate in them, as an accomplice.

18.2.3 Draft Comprehensive Convention on International Terrorism

The events of 11 September 2001 brought terrorism to the fore in the UN Security Council. On 12 September 2001 in UN Security Council Resolution 1368, the Council condemned 'in the strongest terms the horrifying terrorist attacks' and regarded 'such acts, like any act of international terrorism, as a threat to international peace and security'.[13] The Council called on all states 'to bring to justice the perpetrators, organizers and sponsors' and 'to prevent and suppress terrorist acts'.[14]

The events of 11 September spurred on the drafting process within the Ad Hoc Committee to develop a comprehensive terrorism convention, and by 2002 agreement was reached on most of the articles, but universal consensus was lacking. Drafting continues, as do the disagreements, particularly on articles dealing with the scope of the application of the draft comprehensive convention in relation to liberation movements and the activities of state military forces. In a 2009 report from the Ad Hoc Committee, it is clear that these concerns are still a substantial roadblock to negotiation. The report

13 *Threats to International Peace and Security Caused by Terrorist Acts*, UN SCOR, SC Res 1368, 4370th mtg, UN Doc S/RES/1368 (12 September 2001) para 1.

14 Ibid paras 3–4.

emphasises the need to develop a comprehensive convention to include a legal definition of terrorism but also recognises objections from some delegations about 'the necessity to distinguish between acts of terrorism and the legitimate struggle of people in the exercise of their right to self-determination by people under foreign occupation and colonial or alien domination'. Some other delegations stressed that no cause can justify terrorism, and it was also stated that the comprehensive convention should not exclude criminal acts on the basis of self-determination.[15]

The *Draft Comprehensive Convention on International Terrorism*[16] proposes a broad definition of terrorism that has been criticised for its lack of precision, particularly in relation to the minimal threshold of requiring only 'serious damage' and 'any damage' to property that results in major economic loss.

ARTICLE 2(1) *DRAFT COMPREHENSIVE CONVENTION ON INTERNATIONAL TERRORISM*

Any person commits an offence within the meaning of this Convention if that person, by any means, unlawfully and intentionally, causes:

(a) Death or serious bodily injury to any person; or

(b) Serious damage to public or private property, including a place of public use, a State or government facility, a public transportation system, an infrastructure facility or the environment; or

(c) Damage to property, places, facilities, or systems referred to in paragraph 1 (b) of this article, resulting or likely to result in major economic loss, when the purpose of the conduct, by its nature or context, is to intimidate a population, or to compel a Government or an international organization to do or abstain from doing any act.

18.2.4 UN Security Council Resolution 1373

The problems created by the lack of universal agreement on an international legal definition of terrorism are now acute following the adoption (under chapter VII of the *UN Charter*) of UN Security Council Resolution 1373 in 2001. Resolution 1373 requires states to prevent, suppress, freeze and criminalise terrorist financing and refrain from supporting terrorists, prevent terrorist acts, deny safe haven to those who finance, plan, support or commit terrorist acts and prevent the use of their territory to plan, facilitate or commit such acts.[17]

15 *Report of the Ad Hoc Committee established by General Assembly resolution 51/210 of 17 December 1996 Thirteenth Session (29 June to 2 July 2009)*, UN GAOR, 64th sess, Supp No 37, UN Doc A/64/37 (2009) para 6. Also see S P Subedi, 'The UN Response to International Terrorism in the Aftermath of the Terrorist Attacks in America and the Problem of the Definition of Terrorism in International Law' (2002) 4 *International Law Forum* 159.

16 For the 2002 draft see: *Report of the Ad Hoc Committee established by General Assembly resolution 51/210 of 17 December 1996, Sixth Session (28 January–1 February 2002)*, UN GAOR, 57th sess, Supp No 37 (11 February 2002) Annexes I–VI. For subsequent negotiations on the drafting of the *Draft Comprehensive Convention on International Terrorism by the Ad Hoc Committee established by General Assembly Resolution 51/210 of 17 December 1996*, see: <http://www.un.org/terrorism/index.shtml>. See also, James Martin Centre for Nonproliferation Studies, *Draft Comprehensive Convention on International Terrorism: Overview* (Inventory of International Nonproliferation Organizations and Regimes, 05 October 2010) <http://www.nti.org/e_research/official_docs/inventory/pdfs/intlterr.pdf>.

17 SC Res 1373, UN SCOR, 4385th mtg, UN Doc S/RES/1373 (28 September 2001) paras 1–2.

Despite extensive references to terrorism, Resolution 1373 does not itself define terrorism. The problem is, as noted by one commentator, that before 11 September 2001 the 'lack of definition was inconsequential' but since then 'the Security Council has *required* States to implement measures against *terrorist acts* and *terrorists* according those terms operative legal significance without defining them'.[18]

The lack of definition or common understanding of whom or what states should be fighting can result in broad counter-terrorism legislation being used to mask human rights abuses. The International Commission of Jurists has commented: '[F]or some States that routinely abused human rights in the past, counter-terrorism is simply the newest excuse behind which to hide; for other states, counter-terrorism is claimed to be the justification for departing from long-cherished norms'.[19]

The reaction of some member states after 11 September 2001 was to introduce new or special domestic legislation, often with great speed and minimal legislative scrutiny or debate that set out their own particular definitions of terrorism and the offences that accompanied it without any standard objective reference. The flurry of new laws has sometimes produced expansive definitions and 'a wide range of new ancillary or inchoate terrorist offences, often accompanied by special rules for investigation and/or trials of such offences'.[20]

18.2.5 UN Security Council Resolution 1566

What is perhaps the closest to an existing international working definition of terrorism is provided via UN Security Council Resolution 1566:[21]

UN SECURITY COUNCIL RESOLUTION 1566 (2004) PARA 3

The Security Council ... acting under Chapter VII ... [r]ecalls that criminal acts, including against civilians, committed with the intent to cause death or serious bodily injury, or taking of hostages, with the purpose to provoke a state of terror in the general public or in a group of persons or particular persons, intimidate a population or compel a government or an international organization to do or to abstain from doing any act, which constitute offences within the scope of and as defined in the international conventions and protocols relating to terrorism, are under no circumstances justifiable by considerations of a political, philosophical, ideological, racial, ethnic, religious or other similar nature, and *calls upon* all States to prevent such acts and, if not prevented, to ensure that such acts are punished by penalties consistent with their grave nature.

18 B Saul, see above, n 4, 5.

19 *Assessing Damage Urging Action: Report of the Eminent Jurists Panel on Terrorism, Counter-Terrorism and Human Rights*, International Commission of Jurists, 2009, 17.

20 Ibid 124–36. See also: K Roach, 'The World Wide Expansion of Anti-Terrorism Laws After 11 September 2001' (2004) 3 *Studi Senesi* 487. For a criticism of Australia's laws see:
P Emerton, 'Australian Terrorism Offences—A Case Against' in A Lynch, E Macdonald and G Williams, *Law and Liberty in the War on Terror*, Federation Press, Sydney, 2007, 75.

21 SC Res 1566, UN SCOR, 5053rd mtg, UN doc S/RES/1566 (8 October 2004).

The impetus for this resolution (introduced by Russia) was the 'school hostage crisis' in September 2004 when a Chechnyan armed group took control of a Russian school in Beslan and in which more than 300 people, mostly children, were killed. Although Resolution 1566 did not resolve the debate regarding the legitimacy (or illegitimacy) of self determination struggles, it partly fills the void left by the lack of conceptual clarity in Resolution 1373. Even if not recognised formally as such, this definition is likely to be, in the short-term, a de facto if not de jure UN definition of terrorism.[22]

Other commentators, such as Cassese, argue that although treaty laws have failed to establish a comprehensive definition of terrorism, there is a 'widespread consensus on a generally acceptable definition of terrorism'[23] that has emerged via reference to customary international law. Cassese maintains that international terrorism is a customary crime with distinct elements, the requisite practice resulting from 'the converging adoption of national laws, the handing down of judgements by national courts, the passing of UN General Assembly resolutions, as well as the ratification of international conventions by a great number of states'.[24] He recognises that there is still disagreement about whether the actions of 'freedom fighters'[25] are an exception to the definition of terrorism but argues that there is general international agreement on the definition of terrorism. According to Cassese:

> International law defines and regulates international terrorism. International terrorism as a discrete international crime perpetrated *in time of peace* exhibits the following requisites: (i) it is an action normally criminalized in national legal systems; (ii) it is transnational in character ...; (iii) it is carried out for the purpose of coercing a state or an international organization to do or refrain from doing something; (iv) it uses for this purpose two possible modalities: either spreading terror among civilians or attacking public or eminent private institutions or their representatives; (v) it is not motivated by personal gain but by ideological or political aspirations.[26]

In contrast, Saul argues that there is no distinct international crime or unified legal concept of terrorism that has developed through customary law:

> A number of conflicting definitions of terrorism have emerged in the practice of the UN General Assembly and the Security Council, and in national case law and legislation. While there is a definite movement toward generic definition over time, the divergent approaches to definition, and persistent disagreement over the scope of exceptions, have inhibited the emergence of a customary crime. At best, there is international

22 R Young, 'Definining Terrorism: The Evolution of Terrorism as a Legal Concept in International Law and its Influence on Defnitions in Domestic Legislation' (2006) 29 *Boston College International and Comparative Law Review* 23, 45.

23 A Cassese, *International Criminal Law*, 2nd edn, Oxford University Press, Oxford, 2008, 163.

24 Ibid.

25 See G Robertson's discussion of freedom fighters in *Crimes Against Humanity: The Struggle for Global Justice*, 2nd edn, Penguin Books, London, 2002, where he argues that looking to targets helps overcome the difficulty in distinguishing between a terrorist (targeting for example civilians in shopping centres or commuter transport) versus a freedom fighter (targeting military installations) at 514–16.

26 See above, n 23, 177. Also see the 2011 decision of the Appeals Chamber of the UN Special Tribunal for Lebanon where it identifies an existing customary international crime of terrorism: UN Special Tribunal for Lebanon (Appeals Chamber), *Interlocutory Decision on the Applicable Law: Terrorism, Conspiracy, Homicide, Perpetration, Cumulative Charging*, STL-11-01/I, 16 February 2011 and for the contra argument, see: B Saul 'Legislating from a Radical Hague: The UN Special Tribunal for Lebanon Invents an International Crime of Transnational Terrorism' Vol 24 Issue 3 (2011) *Leiden Journal of International Law*, 677.

> consensus on condemning terrorism, or support for a *prohibition* on terrorism, but which is insufficiently precise to support individual criminal liability.[27]

While universal consensus on an international definition of terrorism is lacking, many states now have an operative definition of terrorism in place under which people are being prosecuted. One of the dangers of the international community failing to provide guidance on a comprehensive and clear definition of terrorism is that states have few specific and objective criteria on which to base domestic legislation. The resulting domestic legislation may sometimes produce overly broad counter-terrorism measures that discriminate against particular sections of the community or individuals.

18.3 CASE STUDY: DRAFTING A DEFINITION OF TERRORISM IN AUSTRALIAN LAW

In the wake of the 11 September attacks, the Australian government introduced an expansive range of new counter-terrorism laws. Between 2002 and 2010 Australia enacted 44 counter-terrorism laws, some passing through Parliament in debates that lasted for only a few hours.[28] Before 2001, Australia did not have any specific counter-terrorism laws at the national level and terrorism was not an offence under Australia's *Criminal Code Act 1995* (Cth). The threat of terrorism was virtually unknown in Australia,[29] unlike the United Kingdom, for example, which had lived with, and legislated for, the threat of the Irish Republican Army for several decades. Many of Australia's new counter-terrorism laws are unprecedented in Australia's legal history and were passed with the assumption that the terrorist threat was exceptional and that the general criminal law provisions already in place were insufficient to prevent terrorist attacks.

Since 2002, Australian laws have: established a definition of a 'terrorist act'; introduced a range of offences that criminalise acts involving the planning, preparation and commission of a terrorist act and criminalise a person's involvement or association with a terrorist organisation; enabled the proscription of a terrorist organisation; enabled the detention or placement of restrictions (such as

---

27 B Saul, see above, n 4, 191. See also R E Schreiber, 'Ascertaining *Opinio Juris* of States Concerning Norms Involving the Prevention of International Terrorism: A Focus on UN Process' (1998) 16 *Boston University International Law Journal* 309.

28 G Carne, 'Hasten Slowly: Urgency, Discretion and Review—A Counter-Terrorism Legislatve Agenda and Legacy' (2008) 13(2) *Deakin Law Review* 49. For an analysis of the compatibility of some of the early Australian anti-terrorism laws with international human rights obligations see, eg, S Joseph, 'Australian Counter-Terrorism Legislation and the International Human Rights Framework' (2004) 27 *University of New South Wales Law Journal* 428.

29 In *Counter-Terrorism White Paper: Securing Australia—Protecting Our Community* (Commonwealth of Australia, Department of the Prime Minister and Cabinet, 2010) 7 <http://www.dpmc.gov.au/publications/counter_terrorism/docs/counter-terrorism_white_paper.pdf>, the Australian government notes several terrorist attacks that occurred in Australia prior to 2001 including the 1978 bombing of the Sydney Hilton hotel during a Commonwealth Heads of Government meeting. Since 2001, more than 100 Australians have been killed in terrorist attacks overseas, noting in particular the Bali bombings of 2002 in which 88 Australians were killed.

control orders) on suspects and non-suspects; and introduced special powers for intelligence agencies to question individuals.[30]

18.3.1 A 'Terrorist Act'

The *Security Legislation Amendment (Terrorism) Act 2002* (Cth) inserted new provisions into the *Criminal Code* and a 'terrorist act' is defined in section 100.1(1) of the *Criminal Code* as an action or threat of action if:

> (b) the action is done or the threat is made with the intention of advancing a political, religious or ideological cause; and
>
> (c) the action is done or the threat is made with the intention of:
>
> > (i) coercing, or influencing by intimidation, the government of the Commonwealth or a State, Territory or foreign country, or of part of a State, Territory or foreign country; or
> >
> > (ii) intimidating the public or a section of the public.

Under section 100.1(2) of the *Criminal Code*, an action will only be defined as a terrorist act if it:

> (a) causes serious harm that is physical harm to a person; or
>
> (b) causes serious damage to property; or
>
> (c) causes a person's death; or
>
> (d) endangers a person's life, other than the life of the person taking the action; or
>
> (e) creates a serious risk to the health or safety of the public or a section of the public; or
>
> (f) seriously interferes with, seriously disrupts, or destroys, an electronic system ...

An action will not be a terrorist act if it is an act of advocacy, protest or dissent or if it is an industrial action, and is not intended to cause serious physical harm or death, endanger the lives of others or create a serious risk to public health or safety.

This definition of terrorism is broad and potentially criminalises actions that fall far short of the catastrophic attacks that motivated the initial legislative changes. McGarrity notes:[31]

> The unwieldy drafting and indeterminate scope of Australia's counter-terrorism laws have been the focus of much criticism (albeit largely in the abstract). The first layer of complexity in Australia's terrorism laws arises from the definition of a 'terrorist act' ... Although no individual has been prosecuted, or even charged, in Australia for the 'simple' offence of engaging in a terrorist act under s 101.1 of the *Criminal Code*, the complexities of the definition of a 'terrorist act' have nonetheless plagued *every* terrorist prosecution. This is because the preparatory offences in Div 101 and the terrorist organisation offences in Div 102 both hinge upon the definition of a 'terrorist act'. A significant area of debate in relation to the definition of a 'terrorist act' has been the inclusion of the requirement that the act be done or threatened with the

30 The principal Australian federal terrorism legislation made after 11 September 2001 is contained in the *Criminal Code Act 1995* (Cth) sch 1 pt 5.3 divs 100–3. Incitement to criminal acts (including incitement to terrorism) is contained in Part 2.4 of the Criminal Code. The *Australian Security Intelligence Organisation Act 1979* (Cth) pt III div 3 deals with ASIO's special powers relating to terrorism offences.

31 N McGarrity, 'Testing Our Counter-Terrorism Laws: The Prosecution of Individuals for Terrorism Offences in Australia' (2010) 34 *Criminal Law Journal* 92, 113–14.

intention of advancing a political, religious or ideological cause. This requirement has been criticised, to some extent, by both prosecutors and defence lawyers.

Further difficulties, and layers of complexity, are created by the particular offences with which individuals have been charged in Australia. First, the preparatory offences in Div 101 of the *Criminal Code* are problematic because they go significantly further than the inchoate offences of 'attempt', 'incitement' and 'conspiracy' by eliminating the requirement that the prosecution prove the defendant planned to commit a specific terrorist act. The indeterminacy of these offences becomes even more apparent when the preparatory offences are combined with one of the inchoate offences, for example, the charges of conspiring to do an act in preparation for a terrorist act or attempting to incite another to engage in a terrorist act.

Australia's counter-terrorism laws have—consistently with the recent international trend to define terrorism generically rather than thematically in response to a specific event—adopted a broad definition of a terrorist act. The United Nations High Commissioner for Human Rights has warned that '[D]efining crimes with insufficient precision can also lead to an inappropriate broadening of the proscribed conduct by means of judicial interpretation'[32] and that this opens the way to limit or violate human rights. As noted by Golder and Williams, while a more general definition of terrorism may be preferred by government because it offers more flexibility to respond to current and future threats,[33] the danger is that generality can result in indeterminate meaning. The work of clarifying the specifics is likely to be done in the courts as they apply the definition to individual cases. In his country report on Australia, the UN Special Rapporteur on the Protection and Promotion of Human Rights and Fundamental Freedoms while Countering Terrorism ('Special Rapporteur on Terrorism') has noted the obligation on the Australian Government, when introducing new laws aimed at countering terrorism, to assess whether proposed measures are necessary and proportionate to the threat it seeks to counter.[34]

18.3.2 Case Law in Australia

Since 2002, more than 30 individuals have been prosecuted (but only a few actually convicted) in Australia in relation to terrorism offences.[35] The first terrorism case pursued in Australia since the adoption of the new laws in Div 101 of the Criminal Code was against Zeky Mallah and involved a discussion of the intentional elements of the terrorism definition. The inclusion of political, religious or ideological motive, alongside an intention to coerce or influence by intimidation a government or the public, is a key part of the Australian definition of a terrorist act and is one that has provoked debate

32 United Nations High Commissioner for Human Rights, *Report of the United Nations High Commissioner for Human Rights on the Protection of Human Rights and Fundamental Freedoms while Countering Terrorism*, 8th sess, Agenda Item 2, UN Doc A/HRC/8/13 (2 June 2008) para 23.

33 B Golder & G Williams, 'What is "Terrorism"? Problems of Legal Definition' (2004) 27(2) *University of New South Wales Law Journal* 270, 292.

34 M Scheinin, *Report of the Special Rapporteur on the Promotion and Protection of Human Rights and Fundamental Freedoms while Countering Terrorism—Australia: Study on Human Rights Compliance while Countering Terrorism*, 4th sess, Provisional Agenda Item 2, UN Doc A/HRC/4/26/Add.3 (14 December 2006). For example, the Special Rapporteur urges vigilance in ensuring control orders are necessary and proportionate and that preventative detention orders are sought in a manner that guarantees the right to a fair trial: at para 71.

35 For an overview of Australian terrorism cases see N McGarrity, above, n 31.

from a human rights perspective. Some argue that including an intent requirement allows the law to more accurately target the wrongful act as one specifically focused on terrorism. But the inclusion of motive may also invite racial, religious and political profiling that can lead to an infringement of human rights such as non-discrimination and freedom of expression, association and religion.[36]

SNAPSHOT: *R v MALLAH*[37]

In this case the defendant was charged with two counts of doing an act in preparation for a terrorist offence under section 101.6(1) of the *Criminal Code Act 1995* (Cth). Part of the allegations against Mallah related to a video message that he had recorded recounting his plan to enter particular government offices and kill staff. Assuming that Mallah did have a genuine plan to kill government officers, the intentional elements of the Australian definition of a 'terrorist act' would then require the prosecution to establish that Mallah also intended: to advance a political, religious or ideological cause; and, to coerce, or influence by intimidation the government.

The prosecution sought to prove such an intention by reference to Mallah's possession of items that it argued supported Mallah's 'jihad-like-intentions'. The defendant was found in possession of, among other things, a rifle, ammunition and several documents including a handwritten will, a printed document 'How can I prepare myself for jihad?' and a typed manifesto setting out his grievances with ASIO.[38] Ultimately Mallah was acquitted as it was not accepted that his plan to kill was genuine and thus the intentional elements of the offence were not required to be established, but the case is evidence of how subjective and difficult it can be to establish the requisite intent and how it might easily be misused to put religion on trial. The case is also illustrative of the gap that can exist between 'extremist views' and the carrying out of violent action.

18.4 HUMAN RIGHTS AND (COUNTER) TERRORISM

18.4.1 Setting the Context: Rights and Security

Terrorist violence aims to destroy fundamental aspects of human rights. It has a direct impact on the enjoyment of a number of human rights, as do some counter-terrorism measures employed to prevent and respond to acts of terrorism. In 2004 the UN Security Council adopted resolutions reminding states that they must ensure that any measures taken to combat terrorism comply with all their obligations under international law, in particular international human rights, refugee, and humanitarian law.[39] The reminders

36 For arguments in favour of including motive in a terrorism definition see B Saul, 'The Curious Element of Motive in Definitions of Terrorism: Essential Ingredient or Criminalising Thought' (at 28–8), and for arguments against, see K Roach, 'The Case for Defining Terrorism With Restrain and Without Reference to Political or Religious Motive' (at 39–48), both in A Lynch, E Macdonald & G Williams (eds), *Law and Liberty in the War on Terror*, Federation Press, Sydney, 2007.

37 *R v Mallah* [2005] NSWSC 317 (21 April 2005).

38 See M Gani, 'How Does it End? Reflections on Completed Prosecutions under Australia's Anti-Terrorism Legislation' in M Gani & P Mathew (eds), *Fresh Perspectives on the 'War on Terror'*, ANU E-Press, Canberra, 2008, 269, 285.

39 SC Res 1535, UN SCOR, 4936th mtg, UN Doc S/RES/1535 (26 March 2004) Preamble para 4; SC Res 1566, UN SCOR, 5053rd mtg, UN doc S/RES/1566 (8 October 2004) Preamble para 6.

were deemed necessary as a result of some of the legal and policy changes in many countries, especially since 11 September 2001. Some anti-terrorism laws and practices have targeted specific groups such as political activists, refugees and religious minorities. The presumption of innocence, the right to privacy, the right to a fair trial (or indeed any trial at all), the right to be free from torture, the right to liberty and the freedoms of expression, association and religion have all been breached in the name of counter-terrorism. A number of economic, social and cultural rights, including the right to work, the right to an adequate standard of living, the right to health and the right to education, have also been put at risk by particular counter-terrorism measures. Chapter 18.4 details some of these impacts.

The 'war on terror' paradigm, invoked principally by the United States from 2001, effectively sidelined human rights principles as inflexible, esoteric and unsuitable for countering the immediate threat terrorism posed. The war paradigm radically altered a 'previously shared international consensus on the legal framework underlying both human rights and humanitarian law ... [m]oreover the use of the war paradigm has given a spurious justification to a range of serious human rights and humanitarian law violations ...'[40] and raised the question of whether human rights are an optional extra in the 'war on terror'.[41]

PAUL HOFFMAN, 'HUMAN RIGHTS AND TERRORISM'[42]

Can we afford universal human rights norms in a time of perpetual crisis and exceptional danger? Will there be a 'war on terrorism' exception to the international human rights framework?

These questions will define the landscape of human rights practices for a long time. Terrorist threats have existed throughout modern history, and the importance of deterring and preventing terrorist acts is of central importance. The impulse to abandon human rights norms in times of fear and crisis is short-sighted and self-defeating. As the revelations of shocking abuses at Abu Ghraib prison have demonstrated, the world will not easily accept inhumane treatment in any context, and such treatment will tarnish and undermine even legitimate security operations. ...

The United States-led 'war on terrorism' is premised on the notion that the events of September 11 should be seen as a wake-up call that the world has changed ...

The way this 'war' is being waged is itself a threat to human security. By challenging the framework of international human rights and humanitarian law, so painstakingly developed over the last several decades, the 'war on terrorism' undermines our security more than any terrorist bombing. The horror of the September 11 attacks understandably overshadows the human rights consequences of the 'war on terrorism' in the public's consciousness. It is time to restore the balance between liberty and security provided by existing international human rights and humanitarian standards.

40 See above, n 19.

41 H Charlesworth, 'Is the War on Terror Compatible with Human Rights?: An International Law Perspective' (paper presented at the Castan Centre for Human Rights Law Conference 'Human Rights 2003: The Year in Review', Melbourne, 4 December 2003).

42 P Hoffman, 'Human Rights and Terrorism' (2004) 26 *Human Rights Quarterly* 932, 933–4.

The human rights vision of the Universal Declaration of Human Rights, and the body of human rights norms it spawned, is even more relevant and important today than it was on 10 September 2001. The fulfilment of universal human rights is essential to building a world in which terrorism will not undermine our freedom and security. The human rights framework does not inhibit legitimate and effective efforts to respond to terrorist attacks. The limits that international human rights law places on certain forms of executive power (eg, the prohibition against torture) embody profound agreements about the values the international community in all of its diversity accepts as fundamental.

History shows that when societies trade human rights for security, most often they get neither.

As this extract shows, the use of 'war rhetoric' has led to debates about the need to 'balance' human rights and the threat to public safety, with the balance often tipping in favour of security. Several commentators have argued that the 'balance' metaphor is misleading and counterproductive to an understanding of how human rights law works to protect individual and public safety.[43] International human rights law was developed in the aftermath of horrific global conflict, and built into the law are mechanisms ensuring the preservation of fundamental rights and security interests.

18.4.2 The Flexibility of International Human Rights Law

In exceptional circumstances, it may be possible to derogate from certain obligations under international human rights standards. Article 4 of the ICCPR allows states to go beyond simply limiting rights (where it is lawful to do so) to derogating from them or suspending them in times of emergency that threaten the life of the nation.[44] Before a state can seek to apply article 4, two fundamental conditions must be met: the situation must amount to a public emergency that threatens the life of the nation, and the state party must have officially proclaimed a state of emergency.

Article 4(1) of the ICCPR states:

> In time of public emergency which threatens the life of the nation and the existence of which is officially proclaimed, the States Parties to the present Covenant may take measures derogating from their obligations under the present Covenant to the extent strictly required by the exigencies of the situation, provided that such measures are not inconsistent with their other obligations under international law and do not involve discrimination solely on the ground of race, colour, sex, language, religion or social origin.

The United Nations Human Rights Committee, in *General Comment No 29* on article 4 of the ICCPR, observed that '[m]easures derogating from the provisions of the Covenant must be of an exceptional and temporary nature'.[45]

43 J Waldron, 'Security and Liberty: The Image of Balance' (2003) 11 *Journal of Political Philosophy* 191; L Zedner, 'Securing Liberty in the Face of Terror: Reflections from Criminal Justice' (2005) 32 *Journal of Law and Society* 507, 510–11; C Michaelsen, 'Reforming Australia's National Security Legislation: The Case for a Proportionality-Based Approach' (2010) 29(1) *University of Tasmania Law Review* 32.

44 See Chapter 7.2.5 for further discussion of derogation from ICCPR obligations.

45 Human Rights Committee, *General Comment No 29: States of Emergency (article 4)*, 72nd sess, 1950th mtg, UN Doc CCPR/C/21/Rev.1/Add.11 (31 August 2001) para 2. An extract of *General Comment 29* appears in Chapter 3.3.3.

SNAPSHOT: WHAT CONSTITUTES A PUBLIC EMERGENCY?

In *A v The United Kingdom*[46] the European Court of Human Rights discussed what amounts to a public emergency in light of the ongoing terrorist threat both globally and particularly as it related to the United Kingdom. The applicants argued that there had been no public emergency threatening the life of the British nation, for three main reasons: first, the emergency was neither actual nor imminent; second, it was not of a temporary nature; and, third, the practice of other states, none of which had derogated from the ICCPR, together with the informed views of other national and international bodies, suggested that the existence of a public emergency had not been established. The Court first canvassed other cases that had examined this issue in the context of article 15 of the European Convention of Human Rights and then went onto conclude that there was a legitimate public emergency threatening the life of the nation.

A v THE UNITED KINGDOM

176 The Court recalls that in *Lawless*,[47] it held that in the context of article 15 the natural and customary meaning of the words 'other public emergency threatening the life of the nation' was sufficiently clear and that they referred to 'an exceptional situation of crisis or emergency which affects the whole population and constitutes a threat to the organised life of the community of which the State is composed'. In the *Greek Case*,[48] the Commission held that, in order to justify a derogation, the emergency should be actual or imminent; that it should affect the whole nation to the extent that the continuance of the organised life of the community was threatened; and that the crisis or danger should be exceptional, in that the normal measures or restrictions, permitted by the Convention for the maintenance of public safety, health and order, were plainly inadequate. In *Ireland v United Kingdom*,[49] the parties agreed, as did the Commission and the Court, that the Article 15 test was satisfied since terrorism had for a number of years represented 'a particularly far-reaching and acute danger for the territorial integrity of the United Kingdom, the institutions of the six counties and the lives of the province's inhabitants'. ...

177 Before the domestic courts, the Secretary of State adduced evidence to show the existence of a threat of serious terrorist attacks planned against the United Kingdom. ... Although when the derogation was made no al'Qaeda attack had taken place within the territory of the United Kingdom, the Court does not consider that the national authorities can be criticised, in the light of the evidence available to them at the time, for fearing that such an attack was 'imminent', in that an atrocity might be committed without warning at any time. The requirement of imminence cannot be interpreted so narrowly as to require a State to wait for disaster to strike before taking measures to deal with it. Moreover, the danger of a terrorist attack was, tragically, shown by the bombings and attempted bombings in London in July 2005 to have been very real. Since the purpose of Article 15 is to permit States to take derogating measures to protect their populations from future risks, the existence of the threat to the life of the nation must be assessed primarily with reference to those facts which were known at the time of the derogation. The Court is not precluded, however, from having regard to information which comes to light subsequently ...

46 (European Court of Human Rights, Grand Chamber, Application 3455/05, 19 February 2009).

47 *Lawless v Ireland (No 3)* (1961) 3 Eur Court HR (ser A).

48 (1969) 12 YB 1, § 153.

49 (1978) 25 Eur Court HR (ser A) § 191.

178 While the United Nations Human Rights Committee has observed that measures derogating from the provisions of the ICCPR must be of 'an exceptional and temporary nature' ... the Court's case-law has never, to date, explicitly incorporated the requirement that the emergency be temporary, although the question of the proportionality of the response may be linked to the duration of the emergency. Indeed, the cases cited above, relating to the security situation in Northern Ireland, demonstrate that it is possible for a 'public emergency' within the meaning of Article 15 to continue for many years. The Court does not consider that derogating measures put in place in the immediate aftermath of the al'Qaeda attacks in the United States of America, and reviewed on an annual basis by Parliament, can be said to be invalid on the ground that they were not 'temporary'.

...

180 As previously stated, the national authorities enjoy a wide margin of appreciation under Article 15 in assessing whether the life of their nation is threatened by a public emergency. While it is striking that the United Kingdom was the only Convention State to have lodged a derogation in response to the danger from al'Qaeda, although other States were also the subject of threats, the Court accepts that it was for each Government, as the guardian of their own people's safety, to make their own assessment on the basis of the facts known to them. Weight must, therefore, attach to the judgment of the United Kingdom's executive and Parliament on this question. In addition, significant weight must be accorded to the views of the national courts, who were better placed to assess the evidence relating to the existence of an emergency.

181 On this first question, the Court accordingly shares the view of the majority of the House of Lords that there was a public emergency threatening the life of the nation.

Article 4 of the ICCPR and equivalent provisions in other international human rights treaties acknowledge that certain rights are non-derogable but states are able to derogate from other rights.[50] While courts may be willing to grant states leniency in determining the existence of a public emergency, measures derogating from the provisions of international human rights law must be of an exceptional and temporary nature to ensure that the system of protection for human rights is safeguarded.[51] One question is whether some states have exploited this flexibility so that security not only trumps, but occasionally obliterates, certain rights.

18.4.3 Impact on Rights

Terrorism and counter-terrorism both affect the enjoyment of rights.[52] Under international law, states have the right and the duty to protect the security of all persons within their jurisdiction, which

50 See the discussion of derogation of rights in Chapter 3.3.3.

51 *A v The United Kingdom* (European Court of Human Rights, Grand Chamber, Application 3455/05, 19 February 2009) [173]–[184]. However, note the House of Lords discussion above regarding the notion that such measures need not necessarily be temporary.

52 For a discussion on the distinction between terrorism as destruction of human rights and counter-terrorism measures taken by states as violating human rights, see M Scheinin, 'Terrorism' in D Moeckli et al (eds) *International Human Rights Law*, Oxford University Press, Oxford, (2010) 583, 584–6.

includes any territory under their occupation or control. States are obliged to protect such persons from acts of terrorism. However, counter-terrorism measures must always take strict regard of the principles of legality, necessity, proportionality and non-discrimination in accordance with international human rights standards. Dworkin, commenting in 2003 on the impact on rights of some of the counter-terrorism measures introduced by US President George W Bush, argued for a proportionate response from government to perceived threats. Dworkin noted that:

> every government has a special responsibility to look after its own citizens' safety and a nation may, when necessary, use violence in self-defense. But the harm it deliberately inflicts on others must be comparable to the harm it thereby prevents to its own people, and when our [the US] government shows itself ready to impose grave harm on foreigners or on suspected Americans for only speculative, marginal, or remote benefits to the rest of us, its action presupposes that their lives count for nothing compared to ours.[53]

In its Berlin Declaration of 2004, the International Commission of Jurists argued that, '[t]he odious nature of terrorist acts cannot serve as a basis or pretext for States to disregard their international obligations, in particular in the protection of fundamental human rights.'[54] Efforts to combat terrorism can affect a broad spectrum of rights, if not all rights, to a greater or lesser extent. The erosion of rights is always critical, but particularly because 'what is once lost can be much harder to regain'.[55]

Freedom from Torture and Cruel, Inhuman or Degrading Treatment[56]

The prohibition on torture is one of the most challenged (and challenging) aspects of human rights since the 'war on terror' was proclaimed. The *Convention Against Torture*[57] and article 7 of the ICCPR provide the main framework in international human rights law prohibiting torture. The right to freedom from torture and cruel, inhuman or degrading treatment or punishment is considered absolute and non-derogable. The prohibition against torture is treated as a customary norm of international law:

---

53 R Dworkin, 'Terror and the Attack on Civil Liberties', *New York Review of Books* (online), 6 November 2003 <http://www.nybooks.com/articles/archives/2003/nov/06/terror-the-attack-on-civil-liberties/>.

54 International Commission of Jurists, *The Berlin Declaration: The ICJ Declaration on Upholding Human Rights and the Rule of Law in Combating Terrorism* (adopted 28 August 2004) <http://www.justice.org.uk/images/pdfs/icjberlin.pdf>.

55 See above, n 53.

56 See further Chapter 7.3.9. See also: *European Convention for the Protection of Human Rights and Fundamental Freedoms*, opened for signature 4 November 1950, 213 UNTS 222 (entered into force 3 September 1953) art 3; IACHR art 5; *Geneva Conventions* Common art 3. Special additional protection is also found in other treaties including: *Convention on the Elimination of All Forms of Discrimination against Women*, opened for signature 1 March 1980, 1249 UNTS 13 (entered into force 3 September 1981); *International Convention on the Elimination of All Forms of Racial Discrimination*, opened for signature 21 December 1965, 660 UNTS 195 (entered into force 4 January 1969); *Convention on the Rights of the Child*, opened for signature 20 November 1989, 1577 UNTS 3 (entered into force 2 September 1990).

57 *Convention Against Torture and Other Cruel, Inhuman or Degrading Treatment or Punishment*, opened for signature 4 February 1984, 1465 UNTS 85 (entered into force 26 June 1987).

it applies universally and allows for no exceptions, even in times of emergency.[58] Despite this, torture is still widespread.[59] In a 2010 report, the Special Rapporteur on torture and other cruel, inhuman or degrading treatment or punishment ('Special Rapporteur on Torture') noted:

> Despite the fact that torture constitutes one of the most brutal attacks on human dignity and one of the most serious human rights crimes, and notwithstanding the absolute prohibition of torture and ill-treatment even in the most exceptional circumstances, such as war, internal disturbances and terrorism, *torture and ill treatment are widespread practices in the majority of the countries on our planet*. Almost no society is immune against torture, but in many societies torture is practiced systematically, both in fighting ordinary crime and in combating terrorism ...[60]

The absolute prohibition on torture has been under intense pressure in the context of the fight against terrorism. Efforts by states to redefine the physical limits of torture, the use of secret places of detention and 'extraordinary renditions', the acceptance of diplomatic assurances to circumvent the principle of *non-refoulement* and the use of evidence extracted by torture have compromised the absolute ban on torture.[61] The changing attitude, particularly of the US government before and after the attacks of September 2001, has been a decisive factor in pushing the now seemingly porous boundaries of torture.[62] The approach of the United States to this issue in its notorious 'torture memos' is explored in a snapshot in Chapter 3.2.3.

The Special Rapporteur on Torture commented in 2010 that '[h]istory, including the recent context of the global "war on terror" shows that putting the absolute prohibition of torture in question means opening Pandora's Box'. While other UN reports have been extremely critical of US practices in the last decade, the Special Rapporteur on Torture noted recently that the 'present [Obama] Administration of the United States

58 One of the most commonly cited authorities for stating that the prohibition against torture has evolved into a preemptory norm of international law or *jus cogens* is the decision of the International Criminal Tribunal for the former Yugoslavia (ICTY) in *Prosecutor v Anto Furundzija* Case No IT-95-17/1-T10, Trial Chamber, Judgement [153–154]. A preemptory norm of international law is defined in article 53 of the *Vienna Convention on the Law of* Treaties as 'a norm accepted and recognized by the international community of States as a whole as a norm from which no derogation is permitted and which can be modified only by a subsequent norm of general international law having the same character'.

59 On this point, Steiner, Alston & Goodman note that 'whether the prohibition of torture by states could be viewed as part of customary international law (indeed, of *jus cogens*) [is questioned by some commentators] because, despite the consistent *opinio juris* about its illegality, so much state practice remained to the contrary'. H J Steiner, P Alston & R Goodman, *International Human Rights in Context: Law, Politics, Morals* 3rd edn, Oxford University Press, Oxford, 2008, 225.

60 M Nowak, *Report of the Special Rapporteur on Torture and Other Cruel, Inhuman or Degrading Treatment or Punishment: Study on the Phenomena of Torture, Cruel, Inhuman or Degrading Treatment or Punishment in the World, Including an Assessment of Conditions of Detention*, 13th sess, Agenda Item 3, UN Doc A/HRC/13/39/Add.5 (5 February 2010) para 9 (emphasis as per original).

61 Ibid paras 240–5.

62 The US, while the focus of this discussion, was only one of many states to push the boundaries of the prohibition against torture in the name of countering terrorism. See for example, Michael S, '"Torture" Victims Say They Will Not Have Their "Silence Bought" by Cameron', *Mail Online*, 8 July 2010 <http://www.dailymail.co.uk/news/article-1292832/Guantanamo-Bay-torture-victims-say-silence-bought-Cameron.html>, whereby the UK Prime Minister David Cameron ordered an investigation into torture allegations made by 12 men held in foreign prisons in response to the so called 'War on Terror'. The catch, however, is that the men will have to drop all court proceedings that claim the UK government, MI5 and MI6 were complicit in their torture.

of America has taken decisive steps to reverse this policy', but it will take many years until the global damage that was inflicted on the prohibition of torture as a rule of *jus cogens* is repaired.[63]

Right to Life

Article 6(1) ICCPR provides: 'Every human being has the inherent right to life. This right shall be protected by law. No one shall be arbitrarily deprived of his life.' Not every action that results in death will be arbitrary, and therefore not every death will be a violation of the right to life.[64] The right to life is non-derogable under all circumstances, including states of emergency. However, when a state's population is threatened by violence, the state has the right and obligation to protect the population against those threats.[65] Two areas where the right to life has been particularly affected by terrorism and counter-terrorism measures are: the use of lethal force by State agents; and extra-judicial executions or, more specifically, targeted killings of terrorist suspects.

The Inter-American Commission on Human Rights has noted that the use of lethal force by law enforcement officials may be lawful

> where strictly unavoidable to protect themselves or other persons from imminent threat of death or serious injury, or to otherwise maintain law and order where strictly necessary and proportionate ... Unless such exigencies exist, however, the use of lethal force may constitute an arbitrary deprivation of life or a summary execution; that is to say, the use of lethal force must be necessary as having been justified by a state's right to protect the security of all.
>
> The justification for the use of lethal force may be for reasons such as self defence or neutralising a conflict but must be necessary and proportionate.[66]

A targeted killing is not a term defined under international law but is understood as encompassing the 'intentional, premeditated and deliberate use of lethal force, by States or their agents acting under colour of law, or by an organized armed group in armed conflict, against a specific individual who is not in the physical custody of the perpetrator'.[67] Targeted killings of known or suspected terrorists undermine the right to life, because their extrajudicial nature renders them 'arbitrary' within the meaning of article 6 of the ICCPR. In a 2010 report on targeted killings, the UN Special Rapporteur on extrajudicial, summary or arbitrary executions noted:

63 M Nowak, see above, n 60, para 45. For a critical examination of US practices in countering terrorism, see M Scheinin, *Report of the Special Rapporteur on the Promotion and Protection of Human Rights and Fundamental Freedoms while Countering Terrorism: Addendum—Mission to the United States of America*, 6th sess, Agenda Item 3, UN Doc A/HRC/6/17/Add.3 (22 November 2007).

64 See the detailed case study of the right to life in Chapter 3.5.

65 See the discussion of derogation from the ICCPR in Chapter 3.3.3.

66 The Inter-American Commission on Human Rights, *Report on Terrorism and Human Rights*, OEA/Ser.L/V/II.116 Doc 5 rev 1 corr (22 October 2002) [87]–[88]. Also see Human Rights Committee, *Views: Communication No 45/1979*, 15th sess, UN Doc CCPR/C/15/D/45/1979 (31 March 1982) (*'Guerrero v Colombia'*).

67 P Alston, *Report of the Special Rapporteur on Extrajudicial, Summary or Arbitrary Executions: Addendum—Study on Targeted Killings*, 14th sess, Agenda Item 3, UN Doc A/HRC/14/24/Add.6 (28 May 2010) para 1.

> [1] ... In recent years, a few States have adopted policies, either openly or implicitly, of using targeted killings, including in the territories of other States.
>
> [2] Such policies have been justified both as a legitimate response to 'terrorist' threats and as a necessary response to the challenges of 'asymmetric warfare.' In the legitimate struggle against terrorism, too many criminal acts have been re-characterized so as to justify addressing them within the framework of the law of armed conflict. New technologies, and especially unarmed combat aerial vehicles or 'drones', have been added into this mix, by making it easier to kill targets, with fewer risks to the targeting State.[68]

The report goes on to note some recent examples of state-sponsored targeted killings, ostensibly in the name of countering terrorism. These include: the November 2002 killing of alleged al Qaeda leader Ali Qaed Senyan al-Harithi and five other men in Yemen, reportedly by a CIA-operated Predator drone using a Hellfire missile; and the January 2010 killing of Mahmoud al-Mahbouh, a Hamas leader, at a Dubai hotel in an operation allegedly carried out by 18 Israeli Mossad intelligence agents. According to the Special Rapporteur, 'a targeted killing in the sense of an intentional, premeditated and deliberate killing by law enforcement officials cannot be legal because, unlike in armed conflict, it is never permissible for killing to be the *sole objective* of an operation'.[69]

Freedom from Arbitrary Detention and the Right to a Fair Trial

Freedom from arbitrary detention and the right to a fair trial are guaranteed by articles 9 and 14 of the ICCPR respectively. Emergency powers used by states to combat terrorism have particularly challenged both of these rights. The instinctive reaction of states to quickly detain those who might be suspected of terrorism may at times violate the procedural guarantees set out in ICCPR. Article 9 provides that no person should be detained except in accordance with the law and the arresting authority must notify the person being arrested of the reasons for the arrest, to inform the person promptly of any charges against him or her, and to bring the person promptly before a court or otherwise release him or her. The detention must not be arbitrary. The fair trial guarantees of article 14 include ensuring access to a lawyer, access to court review and the ability to challenge decisions, information about the charges and the right to be tried without undue delay. All of these rights have been put under pressure by states' counter-terrorism efforts.

Although neither of these rights is classified as non-derogable by article 4 of the ICCPR, the Human Rights Committee has said that in its view, the right of people in detention to be treated humanely is non-derogable and that certain aspects of article 14 on due-process rights are obligatory for states, even in times of emergency.[70] In the landmark case of *A v Secretary of State for the Home Department*,[71] discussed above at 18.4.2 in relation to the existence of a 'public emergency', the House of Lords

---

68 Ibid.

69 Ibid para 33.

70 Human Rights Committee, *General Comment No 29: States of Emergency (article 4)*, 1950th mtg, UN Doc CCPR/C/21/Rev.1/Add.11 (31 August 2001); Human Rights Committee, General Comment No 32 (Article 14: Right to Equality before Courts and Tribunals and to a Fair Trial), 90th sess, UN Doc CCPR/C/GC/32 (20 August 2007).

71 *A v Secretary of State for the Home Department* [2004] UKHL 56 (16 December 2004). This case is often referred to as the '*Belmarsh detainees*' case.

discussed restrictions on liberty relating to the indefinite detention of a number of foreign nationals on the grounds that the UK Secretary of State had a reasonable suspicion that they were international terrorists. The judgment is extremely supportive of the right to liberty. Lord Nicholls starts his judgment: 'Indefinite imprisonment without charge or trial is anathema in any country that observes the rule of law. It deprives the detained person of the protection a criminal trial is intended to afford. Wholly exceptional circumstances must exist before this extreme step can be justified.'[72] He continues:

> the human right in question, the right to individual liberty, is one of the most fundamental of human rights. Indefinite detention without trial wholly negates that right for an indefinite period. With one exception all the individuals currently detained have been imprisoned now for three years and there is no prospect of imminent release. It is true that those detained may at any time walk away from their place of detention if they leave this country. Their prison, it is said, has only three walls. But this freedom is more theoretical than real. This is demonstrated by the continuing presence in Belmarsh of most of those detained. They prefer to stay in prison rather than face the prospect of ill treatment in any country willing to admit them.[73]

SNAPSHOT: AUSTRALIA: THE USE OF CONTROL ORDERS TO COUNTER TERRORISM

Control orders are extraordinary powers that displace the principle that the deprivation of liberty should only occur as a result of a criminal conviction. Control orders became part of Australia's Commonwealth *Criminal Code Act 1995* (Cth) by inserting the new Division 104 in 2005. Under this legislation, the Australian Federal Police (AFP), with the Attorney-General's consent, may ask a court to issue a control order to allow obligations, prohibitions and restrictions to be imposed on someone to protect the public from a terrorist act.[74] The issuing court must be satisfied on the balance of probabilities that the control order would substantially assist in preventing a terrorist attack, or that the person has provided training to, or received training from, a listed terrorist organisation. In addition, the court must be satisfied that each of the obligations, prohibitions or restrictions to be imposed by the control order is reasonably necessary and reasonably appropriate to protect the public from a terrorist act.[75] The obligations imposed by a control order can vary and include prohibiting or restricting a person visiting specified places, communicating or associating with particular individuals, wearing a tracking device, using or accessing certain forms of communication (such as the internet or a mobile phone) and requiring the person to remain at specified premises for certain times each day.[76]

72 Ibid [74].

73 Ibid [81].

74 A Lynch, '*Thomas v Mowbray*: Australia's 'War on Terror' Reaches the High Court' (2008) 32 *Melbourne University Law Review* 1182, 1183–6.

75 *Criminal Code Act 1995* (Cth) sch 1 ('Criminal Code') s 104.4(1)(c), (d). Interim control orders are issued ex parte (the person against whom the control order is sought is not present in the court). If the Australian Federal Police want to confirm the control order, they must then go back to court to seek a confirmed order. The person who is the subject of the control order is given 48 hours notice of the confirmation hearing however the information provided to them regarding the necessity of the control order may be restricted so as not to prejudice national security or jeopardise police operations.

76 *Criminal Code* s 104.5(3).

Two control orders have been issued in Australia to date, against Jack Thomas[77] in August 2006 following the quashing of his conviction on the provision of support to a terrorist organisation, and against David Hicks in December 2007 following his release from Yatala Prison. The interim control order issued against Jack Thomas required him, among other things, to keep a curfew at his home address between midnight and 5am each day, restricted the use of telephone and internet services to those pre-approved by the police, required him to report to the police three times a week and prohibited him from communicating with a member of a terrorist organisation or any one of the 50 specified people, including Osama Bin Laden.

Australia has relied heavily on the laws of other jurisdictions (particularly the UK) in constructing its national security law framework, and although there are significant differences between control orders in the UK and Australia there are also obvious similarities.[78] Of particular significance is that unlike the UK, Australia lacks a national Human Rights Act, so Australians have fewer objective grounds on which to challenge control orders that restrict their human rights.

The right to a fair trial has also been tested in some jurisdictions by counter-terrorism legislation. The US detention facility at Guantánamo Bay, Cuba, has become a notorious symbol of the long term and indefinite detention of terrorist suspects without trial.[79] The establishment and use of military commissions by the US to try Guantánamo detainees has also been extensively criticised as violating article 14 of the ICCPR.[80] The independence and impartiality of judges has been questioned, not only in deciding which cases to try but also in their ability to intervene in the conduct of trials. The use and availability of evidence, including the withholding of certain evidence due to its classified status, is also of concern. The ability of US military commissions to impose the death penalty despite not guaranteeing the fair trial procedures of article 14 means that any conviction resulting in the imposition of the death penalty may also be in violation of article 6 of the ICCPR.

77 See *Thomas v Mowbray* (2007) 233 CLR 307.

78 See generally: A Lynch, 'Control Orders in Australia: A Further Case Study in the Migration of British Counter-Terrorism Law' (2008) 8(2) *Oxford University Commonwealth Law Journal* 159; B Jaggers, 'Anti-Terrorism Control Orders in Australia and the United Kingdom' (Parliamentary Library, Research Paper No 28, 2007–8) <http://www.aph.gov.au/library/pubs/rp/2007-08/08rp28.htm>.

79 There are numerous references on this topic, see for example: Lord Steyn, 'Guantánamo Bay: The Legal Black Hole' (2004) 53 *International and Comparative Law Quarterly* 1; Inter-American Commission on Human Rights, 'Pertinent Parts of July 23, 2002 Reiteration of Precautionary Measures Regarding Detainees in Guantánamo Bay, Cuba' (2006) 45 ILM 667; Human Rights Watch, *Fighting Terrorism Fairly and Effectively: Recommendations for President-Elect Barack Obama* (2010).

80 M Scheinin, see above, n 63, paras 19–32. Also see *Boumediene v Bush*, 549 US 1328 (2007) in which parts of the military commission framework were criticised by the US Supreme Court and where the majority held that Guantánamo Bay detainees have habeas corpus rights.

SNAPSHOT: AUSTRALIA AND THE USE OF MILITARY COMMISSION TRIALS TO COUNTER TERRORISM

An Australian national, David Hicks, was detained at Guantánamo Bay for more than five years without trial, which violated the guarantees of article 14 and 9 ICCPR. Hicks was captured among Taliban forces in Afghanistan in 2001. In January 2002 he was transported to Guantánamo Bay where he was detained without charge as an 'unlawful combatant'. In June 2004 he was charged with conspiracy to commit war crimes, attempted murder and aiding the enemy. In June 2006 in *Hamdan v Rumsfield*[81] the Supreme Court found the original form of military commissions set up by the US to try terrorist suspects such as David Hicks to be illegal, and subsequently Congress authorised a modified form of these commissions. In 2007 Hicks was charged for a second time under the *Military Commissions Act 2006* (US), this time with providing material support for terrorism and associating and training with a terrorist organisation. Hicks pleaded guilty to association and training with a terrorist organisation and was sentenced to seven years imprisonment, all but nine months of which was suspended in accordance with the plea bargain agreement.

A 2007 report by the Law Council of Australia was highly critical of the 'trial' of Hicks: '[t]he "*trial*" of David Hicks, which took place in March 2007, was a charade. A pre-trial agreement had been signed and the balance of the legal proceedings was entirely surplus to requirements, although designed to lay a veneer of due process over a political and pragmatic bargain. The veneer cracked immediately'.[82]

Right to Non-Discrimination

All human rights treaties include a non-discrimination clause, and the right to equality and protection from discrimination should be part of any counter-terrorism policy, because discriminatory counter-terrorism measures are particularly likely to adversely affect the freedoms of association, expression, religion and movement. Several UN human rights mechanisms, including the Human Rights Committee and the Committee on the Elimination of Racial Discrimination, have warned that counter-terrorism measures must not infringe on the prohibition of discrimination on grounds of race, colour, sex, religion, political opinion or national origin.[83] The increasing use of racial profiling (the inclusion of race, ethnicity, nationality or religion in the profile of an individual considered likely to commit a crime) by police and state security forces has been highlighted as of concern by the Special Rapporteur on the

81 548 US 557 (2006).

82 L Lasry, '*David Hicks v the United States*: Summary of the Report of the Independent Observer for the Law Council of Australia' (Law Council of Australia, 24 July 2007) 5.

83 See, eg, *Concluding Observations of the Committee on the Elimination of Racial Discrimination: Denmark*, 60th sess, 1522nd mtg, UN Doc CERD/C/60/CO/5 (21 May 2002); *Concluding observations of the Committee on the Elimination of Racial Discrimination: Republic of Moldova*, 60th sess, 1517th mtg, UN Doc CERD/C/60/CO/9 (21 May 2002). See also D Dieène, *Report by Mr Doudou Dieène, Special Rapporteur on Contemporary Forms of Racism, Racial Discrimination, Xenophobia and Related Intolerance, Submitted Pursuant to Commission on Human Rights Resolution 2002/9*, UN ESCOR, 59th sess, Provisional Agenda Item 6, UN Doc E/CN.4/2003/23 (3 January 2003) para 2, which called attention to the 'grave situation of Muslims and Arabs in non-Muslim countries, which is a direct, proven and recognized consequence of the events of 11 September'.

promotion and protection of human rights and fundamental freedoms while countering terrorism. The two examples below from Germany and the UK illustrate the use of profiling by state agencies.

SNAPSHOT: RACIAL PROFILING

REPORT OF THE SPECIAL RAPPORTEUR ON THE PROMOTION AND PROTECTION OF HUMAN RIGHTS AND FUNDAMENTAL FREEDOMS WHILE COUNTERING TERRORISM[84]

35 The Special Rapporteur notes that terrorist profiles have been employed, for example, in the context of data-mining initiatives, i.e. searches of personal data sets according to presumed characteristics of suspects. An illustrative case is the so-called *Rasterfahndung* programme, initiated by the German authorities in the wake of 11 September 2001 to identify terrorist 'sleepers'. The German police forces collected personal records of several million persons from public and private databases.[85] The criteria for the search included: being male; age 18–40; current or former student; Muslim denomination; link through birth or nationality to one of several specified countries with a predominantly Muslim population. Approximately 32 000 persons were identified as potential terrorist sleepers and more closely examined. In *none* of these cases did the *Rasterfahndung* lead to the bringing of criminal charges for terrorism-related offences.

....

37 In some cases, police forces have relied on profiles based on a person's ethnic and/or religious appearance when conducting stops, document checks or searches for counter-terrorism purposes. In the United Kingdom of Great Britain and Northern Ireland, government officials have openly acknowledged that law-enforcement efforts in the counter-terrorism context focus on particular ethnic or religious groups. Accordingly, stops and searches under section 44 of the *Terrorism Act 2000*, which authorizes the police in designated areas to stop and search people without having to show reasonable suspicion, have affected ethnic minorities. Between 2001–2002 and 2002–2003, for example, the number of persons of Asian ethnicity subjected to section 44 searches rose by 302 per cent as compared to a rise of 118 per cent for white people. By 2003–2004, Asian people were about 3.6 times more likely and black people about 4.3 times more likely, to be stopped and searched under counter-terrorism legislation than white people. Similarly, police forces in the Russian Federation have subjected ethnic minorities to stops and document checks, which are often carried out in response to terrorist threats. A study of police practices on the Moscow metro system in 2005 found that persons of non-Slavic appearance were, on average, 21.8 times more likely to be stopped than Slavs.

Economic, Social and Cultural Rights

Discussion of the impact of counter-terrorism measures on human rights tends to focus primarily on civil and political rights, but economic, social and cultural rights are equally susceptible. A number of economic, social and cultural rights enshrined in the ICESCR have been put at risk by

84 M Scheinin, *Report of the Special Rapporteur on the Promotion and Protection of Human Rights and Fundamental Freedoms while Countering Terrorism*, 4th sess, Provisional Agenda Item 2, UN Doc A/HRC/4/26 (29 January 2007).

85 See the decision of the Bundesverfassungsgericht (German Constitutional Court), 1 BvR 518/02, 4 April 2006.

counter-terrorism measures, namely the right to work (articles 6 and 7); protection and assistance accorded to the family and to children and young persons (article 10); the right to an adequate standard of living, including adequate food and housing (article 11); the right to health (article 12); and the right to education (articles 13 and 14).[86]

SNAPSHOT: CONSTRUCTION BY ISRAEL OF THE 'WALL'

A 2007 report of the Special Rapporteur on Terrorism examined the effect of the construction of a wall, described by Israel as a counter-terrorism measure, along and partly inside the Occupied Palestinian Territory, on the economic, social and cultural rights of Palestinians.[87] In its advisory opinion of July 2004, the International Court of Justice concluded that Israel was in breach of its obligations under the *ICESCR* due to the construction of the wall.[88] The Court identified a number of economic, social and cultural rights affected by the construction of the wall, namely: the right to work; protection and assistance accorded to the family and to children and young persons; the right to an adequate standard of living; the right to health; and the right to education.[89]

Some of the effects detailed in the Special Rapporteur's report show how extraordinary measures taken by a state in the name of security can drastically affect the everyday lives of those in the vicinity. In this example, the security barrier resulted in a system of road closures and permit requirements regulating the movement of people from one area to another. These restrictions on movement affected the ability of the Palestinian people to gain access to education, health services (including emergency medical treatment), other social services and places of employment. Reports from the Special Rapporteur and other UN mechanisms note that 'delays at checkpoints have complicated childbirth for Palestinian women ... [resulting] in the delivery of children at checkpoints and unattended roadside births, putting at risk the health of both child and mother, and leading to numerous miscarriages and the death of at least five mothers'.[90]

86 M Scheinin, *Report of the Special Rapporteur on the Promotion and Protection of Human Rights and Fundamental Freedoms while Countering Terrorism*, 6th sess, Agenda Item 3, UN Doc A/HRC/6/17 (21 November 2007). See the discussion of these rights more generally in Chapter 4.

87 M Scheinin, *Report of the Special Rapporteur on the Promotion and Protection of Human Rights and Fundamental Freedoms while Countering Terrorism: Addendum—Mission to Israel, Including Visit to Occupied Palestinian Territory*, 6th sess, Agenda Item 3, UN Doc A/HCR/6/17/Add.4 (16 November 2007).

88 *Legal Consequences of the Construction of a Wall in the Occupied Palestinian Territories (Advisory Opinion)* [2004] ICJ Rep 136, [116].

89 Ibid [112], [130], [134].

90 See above, n 86, para 38. Also see H Aswad, 'Checkpoints Compound the Risks of Childbirth for Palestinian Women' (15 May 2007) United Nations Population Fund <http://www.unfpa.org/public/site/global/News/pid/310>; *Report of the Secretary-General on the Situation of and Assistance to Palestinian Women*, UN ESCOR, 46th sess, Provisional Agenda Item 3(a), UN Doc E/CN.6/2002/3 (4 January 2002) paras 18–20.

18.5 CONCLUSION AND ISSUES

Particularly since the attacks of 11 September 2001, the issues of terrorism, counter-terrorism measures and the impact of both on human rights have been at the forefront of international and many national agendas. Terrorism, however legally defined, is a phenomenon that adversely impacts on many human rights. As noted at the beginning of this chapter, while 'respect for human rights, fundamental freedoms and the rule of law are essential tools in the effort to combat terrorism',[91] too often human rights have come to be regarded as an optional extra in the 'war on terror'.

One of the many issues arising in this area is whether there will ever be sufficient legal and political consensus to formally define terrorism within the UN. Perhaps it is no longer necessary and the informal definition arising out of UN Security Council Resolution 1566 is sufficient. However, arrival at and agreement on a formal legal definition of terrorism by the UN would at the very least, be symbolic of the international community consensus of a way forward.

The continued negative impact of many domestic counter-terrorism measures on human rights remains significant. The undue and disproportionate restrictions placed on many rights limits their full enjoyment and can lead to a diminished understanding of what such rights entail. The erosion of rights is always critical, but particularly because 'what is once lost can be much harder to regain'.[92] The acceptance in countries such as Australia that expansive questioning and detention powers are necessary in order to combat terrorism, raises the question of whether existing criminal laws in such jurisdictions would have sufficed. Is there any danger in 'temporary' measures become permanent features of law and practice?

Terrorism is not new, nor is the desire of states and the UN to combat it; however, the protection of human rights should remain synonymous with efforts to counter terrorism. 'History shows that when societies trade human rights for security, most often they get neither'.[93]

91 See K Annan, *Speech delivered at the Special Meeting of the Security Council's Counter Terrorism Committee with International Regional and Sub-Regional Organisations*, New York, 6 March 2003 <http://www.un.org/apps/sg/sgstats.asp?nid=275>.

92 R Dworkin, see above, n 53.

93 P Hoffman, see above, n 42, 934.

19 TRANSNATIONAL CORPORATIONS AND HUMAN RIGHTS

CONTENTS

19.1 INTRODUCTION

Traditional considerations of human rights take place in the context of a state-based system of global governance; however, the rise of the 'global' corporation (more commonly referred to as the transnational corporation ('TNC'))[1] as a powerful non-state actor in recent decades has seen increased interest in understanding the emerging relationship between human rights and corporations. There are

1 While 'transnational corporation' is variously defined, this chapter adopts the definition proposed in Sub commission on the Promotion and Protection of Human Rights, *Norms on the Responsibilities of Transnational Corporations and Other Business Enterprises with Regard to Human Rights*, UN ESCOR, 55th sess, 22nd mtg, Agenda Item 4, UN Doc E/CN.4/Sub.2/2003/12/Rev.2 (26 August 2003, adopted 3 August 2003) ('Norms'), which refers to 'an economic entity operating in more than one country or cluster of economic entities operating in two or more countries—whatever their legal form, whether in their home country or country of activity, and whether taken individually or collectively': para 20.

now '80 000 transnational enterprises, 10 times as many subsidiaries and countless millions of national firms'[2] that span the globe. In addition, there are an even larger number of businesses operating in the informal sector in developing countries.[3] With significant economic power at their disposal, TNCs are able to do great harm as well as good for human rights at the global and domestic levels.[4] It is for this reason that some sectors of the international community have increasingly called for corporations to be held responsible for the human rights consequences of their actions.

PETER MUCHLINSKI 'HUMAN RIGHTS AND MULTINATIONALS: IS THERE A PROBLEM?'[5]

In recent years there has been an upsurge of concern over human rights and multinational enterprises (MNEs). A number of significant cases have been documented of apparent collusion between MNEs and host governments in major violations of human rights. These have been brought to public attention in the media through the actions of concerned individuals and groups, most notably by non-governmental organizations (NGOs) concerned with human rights. Among the most publicized cases have been the operations of Shell in Ogoniland, BP in Columbia and Unocal in Burma (Myanamar), the last of these having led to landmark litigation in the United States. Thus, *prima facie*, there is a problem: multinationals can take part in alleged violations of human rights. Such allegations are not really new: concerns about the complicity of corporate and/or commercial actors in human rights violations can be traced back through the era of apartheid in southern Africa, to the use of slave labour by the Nazis in the Second World War, which has itself generated recent legal action, to the exploitation of workers on colonial plantations and to the movement for the abolition of slavery in the eighteenth century. What is new is the context in which these more recent cases are being discussed. The traditional notion that only states and state agents can be held accountable for violations of human rights is being challenged as the economic and social power of MNEs appears to rise in the wake of the increasing integration of the global economy that they have helped bring about.

19.2 THE ROLE OF CORPORATIONS IN SOCIETY

While corporations play a fundamental role in domestic and international economies their impact on human rights is equally significant.

> Through commercial activity driven by corporations, jobs and wages are made available, goods and services are provided and taxes are paid, allowing governments to provide more goods and services. Directly or indirectly, a vast array of human rights may be supported, such as the rights to work, welfare, food and

2 J Ruggie, *Report of the Special Representative of the Secretary-General on the Issue of Human Rights and Transnational Corporations and other Business Enterprises, 'Guiding Principles for the Implementation of the United Nations "Protect, Respect and Remedy" Framework'* A/HRC/17/31 (21 March 2011) [15], <http://www.business-humanrights.org/media/documents/ruggie/ruggie-guiding-principles-21-mar-2011.pdf>.

3 J Ruggie, *Report of the Special Representative of the Secretary-General on the Issue of Human Rights and Transnational Corporations and Other Business Enterprises, 'Business and Human Rights: Mapping International Standards of Responsibility and Accountability for Corporate Acts'*, UN Doc A/HRC/4/035 (9 February 2007) [64].

4 J Nolan & D Kinley, 'Trading and Aiding Human Rights: Corporations in the Global Economy' [2007] *Nordic Journal of Human Rights* 353, 358.

5 (2001) 77 *International Affairs* 31, 31.

> shelter, health and education, and the freedoms of speech, association and movement. In short, not only do corporations help to provide many of the things that make human life more tolerable, enjoyable and fulfilling; the work and wages that corporate enterprise brings to all communities are key elements in the establishment and maintenance of individual human dignity to which end human rights strive to meet.[6]

However, the influence of corporations on human rights is not entirely benign. Corporations (local and transnational) are also abusers of human rights. Violations of labour rights are not uncommon; nor are claims of environmental degradation and discrimination to name a few. These violations might be caused by the corporations themselves or the governments they work alongside as partners, joint venturers or in some other legal relationship.

As the role and influence of corporations have increased, so too has confusion about their obligations (if any) to respect and protect human rights. They are not a government, and although a corporation is ultimately beholden to its shareholders, its role in contemporary society—and its social licence to operate—depends on its ability to meet the expectations of an increasingly wide range of stakeholders including consumers, customers, business partners and the community in which it operates. What role is expected of corporations?

SNAPSHOT: APPAREL COMPANIES IN HONDURAS

In July 2009, four apparel companies (NIKE Inc,, The adidas Group, Gap Inc and Knights Apparel), all of which had business interests in Honduras, sent a letter to the US Secretary of State, Hillary Clinton, urging support for the restoration of democracy in Honduras. On 28 June 2009, soldiers of the Honduran military had ousted President Zelaya and forced him into exile. Some viewed the events as a constitutional crisis, while others perceived them as a military *coup d'état*. The removal of President Zelaya was criticised by the United Nations, the Organization of American States ('OAS'), the United States and the European Union. The following letter from these companies illustrates the proactive approach taken in this instance to protect human rights (and stability) in a country in which the companies have business interests.

> July 27, 2009
> The Honorable Hillary R Clinton
> The Secretary of State
> 2201 C St NSW
> Washington, DC 20520
> Dear Secretary Clinton
> As companies that have products made in Honduras, we are deeply concerned about recent events in that country. We understand that serious disagreements exist between the elected President, Congress and the Supreme Court, but these should be resolved through peaceful, democratic dialogue, rather than through military action.
>
> While we do not and will not support or endorse the position of any party in this internal dispute, we feel it is necessary in this case to join with the President of the United States, the governments of countries throughout the Americas, the Organization of American States, the UN General Assembly and the European Union in calling for the restoration of democracy in Honduras.

6 Ibid 358.

We are also very concerned about the continuation of violence if this dispute is not resolved immediately, and with restrictions on civil liberties under the July 1 Emergency Decree. We urge for an immediate resolution to the crisis and that civil liberties, including freedom of the press, freedom of speech, freedom of movement, freedom of assembly, and freedom of association be fully respected.

We welcome the participation of the contending parties in mediation talks and are hopeful they will achieve a prompt and just solution to all issues in dispute.

Sincerely,

NIKE, Inc, The adidas Group, Gap Inc, Knights Apparel[7]

19.3 CONTEMPORARY DEVELOPMENTS: APPOINTMENT OF THE UN SPECIAL REPRESENTATIVE FOR BUSINESS AND HUMAN RIGHTS

In 2004, the UN Commission on Human Rights asked the Office of the High Commissioner on Human Rights to compile a report on the potential human rights responsibilities of TNCs. Following up on this report, in April 2005 the UN Commission on Human Rights called on the UN Secretary-General to appoint a Special Representative on the issue of human rights and transnational corporations and other business enterprises to investigate the legal responsibilities of businesses for social and environmental issues.

The resolution[8] provided the Special Representative with a mandate to:

(i) clarify the standards of corporate responsibility;
(ii) elaborate on the role of States in regulating business;
(iii) define concepts such as 'complicity' and 'spheres of influence';
(iv) develop ways to assess the impact of business activities on human rights; and
(v) compile a compendium of best practices.

On 28 July 2005 the UN Secretary-General appointed Professor John Ruggie of the Kennedy School of Government at Harvard University as Special Representative. Consulting widely and extensively, Professor Ruggie has published an annual report each year since 2006. The 2008 report of the Special Representative presented a conceptual and policy framework 'to anchor the business and human rights debate and to help guide all relevant actors'.[9] His 2009 report aims to provide an operational guide to achieving this. The framework comprises three core principles: the state's duty to protect against

7 Letter from Nike Inc, the Adidas Group, Gap Inc, and Knights Apparel Inc to the Honorable Hillary R Clinton, 27 July 2009 <http://www.nikebiz.com/responsibility/2009SecretaryClintonHondurasLetter.html>.

8 UN Commission on Human Rights, *Human Rights Resolution 2005/69: Human Rights and Transnational Corporations and Other Business Enterprises*, UN ESCOR, 61st sess, 59th mtg, UN Doc E/CN.4/RES/2005/69 (20 April 2005).

9 J Ruggie, *Report of the Special Representative of the Secretary-General on the Issue of Human Rights and Transnational Corporations and Other Business Enterprises, 'Protect, Respect and Remedy: A Framework for Business and Human Rights'*, UN Doc A/HRC/8/5 (7 April 2008).

human rights abuses by third parties, including business; the corporate responsibility to respect human rights; and the need for more effective access to remedies, often referred to as the 'protect, respect, remedy' framework.

JOHN RUGGIE, *REPORT OF THE SPECIAL REPRESENTATIVE OF THE SECRETARY-GENERAL ON THE ISSUE OF HUMAN RIGHTS AND TRANSNATIONAL CORPORATIONS AND OTHER BUSINESS ENTERPRISES, 'PROTECT, RESPECT AND REMEDY: A FRAMEWORK FOR BUSINESS AND HUMAN RIGHTS'*[10]

3 The root cause of the business and human rights predicament today lies in the governance gaps created by globalization—between the scope and impact of economic forces and actors, and the capacity of societies to manage their adverse consequences. These governance gaps provide the permissive environment for wrongful acts by companies of all kinds without adequate sanctioning or reparation. How to narrow and ultimately bridge the gaps in relation to human rights is our fundamental challenge.

...

5 The business and human rights debate currently lacks an authoritative focal point. Claims and counter-claims proliferate, initiatives abound, and yet no effort reaches significant scale. Amid this confusing mix, laggards—States as well as companies—continue to fly below the radar.

6 Some stakeholders believe that the solution lies in a limited list of human rights for which companies would have responsibility, while extending to companies, where they have influence, essentially the same range of responsibilities as States. For reasons this report spells out, the Special Representative has not adopted this formula. Briefly, business can affect virtually all internationally recognized rights. Therefore, any limited list will almost certainly miss one or more rights that may turn out to be significant in a particular instance, thereby providing misleading guidance...

7 There is no single silver bullet solution to the institutional misalignments in the business and human rights domain. Instead, all social actors—States, businesses, and civil society—must learn to do many things differently...

8 Every stakeholder group, despite their other differences, has expressed the urgent need for a common conceptual and policy framework, a foundation on which thinking and action can build ...

9 The framework rests on differentiated but complementary responsibilities. It comprises three core principles: the State duty to protect against human rights abuses by third parties, including business; the corporate responsibility to respect human rights; and the need for more effective access to remedies. Each principle is an essential component of the framework: the State duty to protect because it lies at the very core of the international human rights regime; the corporate responsibility to respect because it is the basic expectation society has of business; and access to remedy, because even the most concerted efforts cannot prevent all abuse, while access to judicial redress is often problematic, and non-judicial means are limited in number, scope and effectiveness. The three principles form a complementary whole in that each supports the others in achieving sustainable progress ...

10 UN Doc A/HRC/8/5 (7 April 2008).

In 2010 with his mandate drawing to a close the Special Representative released a set of draft 'Guiding Principles' for the implementation of his three-pronged 'protect, respect and remedy' framework. The Guiding Principles (submitted to the Human Rights Council in 2011)[11] were both applauded and criticised by various sectors of the community often with quite strident but divergent views. The submission from the United States Chamber of Commerce, for example, welcomed the Guiding Principles as potentially an 'important tool to guide business and governments in their activities worldwide'[12] but expressed concerns over any attempts to over regulate the role of business in terms of respecting human rights. The Chamber of Commerce argues that '[w]e do not support a premise that business will not respect human rights without a comprehensive regulatory scheme to force them to do so'.[13] A joint submission from a number of NGOs including Amnesty International, Human Rights Watch and the International Commission of Jurists argued on the other hand that the Guiding Principles are in part vague, lacking in robust guidance for the protection of human rights and 'risk undermining efforts to strengthen corporate responsibility and accountability for human rights'.[14] In June 2011, the UN Human Rights Council unanimously endorsed the Guiding Principles and announced the formation of a working group and an annual meeting of business, government, and civil society representatives focused on disseminating and discussing those principles. While there remains opposing views among stakeholders on what kind of legal framework might be necessary to ensure that business complies with international human rights obligations or indeed if any legal framework is needed to achieve this end, the endorsement of the Guiding Principles is a significant step in establishing a framework against which business behaviour will be assessed.

19.4 SOURCES OF CORPORATE RESPONSIBILITIES AND STANDARDS FOR HUMAN RIGHTS

In most jurisdictions there is a substantial body of domestic legislation that regulates (or could regulate) corporate activities that affect human rights. These laws are typically concerned with areas such as anti-discrimination, health and safety at work, environmental protection and labour rights, and are not usually described as 'human rights' laws. However, except in certain circumstances, these domestic human rights laws are designed to operate intra-territorially (that is, within state borders) rather than extra-territorially. 'At the international level the corporate form is barely recognised,

11 J Ruggie, see above, n 2.

12 Letter from the Chamber of Commerce of the United States of America to Professor J Ruggie, 31 January 2011, 2 <http://www.business-humanrights.org/media/documents/ruggie/us-chamber-of-commerce-re-guiding-principles-31-jan-2011.pdf>.

13 Ibid.

14 Amnesty International, CIDSE, ESCR-Net, Human Rights Watch, International Commission of Jurists, International Federation for Human Rights (FIDH), and Rights and Accountability in Development (RAID), *Joint Civil Society Statement on the Draft Guiding Principles on Business and Human Rights* (14 January 2011), 1, <http://www.fidh.org/IMG/pdf/Joint_CSO_Statement_on_GPs.pdf>.

still less directly bound, in respect of human rights …'[15] Nevertheless, and partly in response to this governance gap, other mechanisms, such as soft law standards,[16] have evolved in an attempt to clarify the role corporations can play in respecting human rights.

19.4.1 *Universal Declaration of Human Rights* and Corporations

It has been argued that there is a basis under international law for extending international legal obligations to corporations in relation to human rights. The *Universal Declaration of Human Rights* ('UDHR') sets out a list of 30 substantive human rights,[17] which it promulgates as

> a common standard of achievement for all peoples and all nations, to the end that every individual and every organ of society, keeping this Declaration constantly in mind, shall strive by teaching and education to promote respect for these rights and freedoms and by progressive measures, national and international, to secure their universal and effective recognition and observance.[18]

The UDHR is expressed entirely in terms of entitlements for individuals and peoples, rather than in terms of obligations for states or any other entities. As we discuss in more detail in Chapter 1, the UDHR, as a declaration of the UN General Assembly, does not in and of itself create legal obligations. Nevertheless, the UDHR is frequently cited as the source of human rights obligations that a given entity is being urged to follow.[19]

The view has been expressed that '[e]very individual includes juridical persons. Every individual and every organ of society excludes no one, no company, no market, and no cyberspace. The Universal Declaration applies to them all.'[20] Other arguments attempting to extend the moral, if not legal, authority of the UDHR rely on article 29, which acknowledges that '[e]veryone has [non-specific] duties to the community', and article 30, which prohibits 'any state, group or person' from engaging in any activity or performing any act aimed at the destruction of any of the rights and freedoms in the UDHR. Ultimately, it is difficult to avoid the conclusion that the provisions in the UDHR express no more than a desire that business might strive to promote respect for human rights, rather than imposing any binding legal obligation directly on business entities.

19.4.2 Human Rights Treaties and Corporations

The development of human rights treaties since 1945 has focused almost exclusively on the primary responsibility of states to protect human rights while remaining at least partially blind to the opportunity to speak more directly to powerful non-state actors such as corporations. International law establishes that states have a duty to protect against non-state human rights abuses in their

---

15 J Nolan & D Kinley, see above, n 4, 359.

16 See the discussion below in Chapter 19.4.3, on soft law.

17 See the discussion of the UDHR in Chapter 1.3.

18 *Universal Declaration of Human Rights*, GA Res 217 A (III), UN GOAR, 3rd sess, 183rd plen mtg, UN Doc A/Res/217A (10 December 1948) Preamble final paragraph.

19 See the discussion on the status of UDHR in Chapter 1.3.

20 L Henkin, 'The Universal Declaration at 50 and the Challenge of Global Markets' (1999) 25 *Brook Journal of International Law* 17.

jurisdiction, and that this duty extends to protection against abuses by business entities. The duty to protect exists under the core United Nations human rights treaties as elaborated by the treaty bodies and is generally agreed to exist under customary international law. The United Nations Human Rights Committee, in its *General Comment No 31* commenting on a state's legal obligation to protect civil and political rights, affirmed that the obligation 'will only be fully discharged if individuals are protected by the state, not just against violations of Covenant rights by its agents, but also against acts committed by private persons or entities'.[21] So to fulfil the duty to protect, states must regulate and adjudicate the acts of business enterprises.

International human rights treaties do not themselves create direct obligations for corporations. However, more recent treaties, and occasionally now treaty bodies, have begun to refer more directly to the role of states in specifically guarding against human rights abuses by corporations. For example, the *Convention on the Rights of Persons with Disabilities* states clearly that states parties have an obligation 'to take all appropriate measures to eliminate discrimination on the basis of disability by any person, organization or private enterprise'.[22]

Jurisdictional Dilemma

One crucially unresolved legal issue is whether a state's general obligation under international human rights law to protect against corporate-related human rights abuses extends beyond its jurisdiction (that is, extra-territorially or internationally).

Professor Ruggie's 2007 report suggests that international human rights law is ambiguous in this regard. The report notes that human rights treaties neither require states to exercise extra-territorial jurisdiction over corporate human rights abuses nor prohibit them from doing so.[23] That is, a state may choose to require corporations (domiciled in their jurisdiction) to abide by certain standards regardless of the country in which they are operating. For example, the anti-bribery provisions of the United States' (US) *Foreign Corrupt Practices Act of 1977*[24] make it unlawful for a US national, and certain foreign issuers of securities, to make a payment to a foreign official for the purpose of obtaining or retaining business for or with, or directing business to, any person whether such action occurs within or outside of the US. However, the basis for exercising such jurisdiction over human rights standards generally and the particular subject matter that might justify such action are still matters for debate. Any suggestion of holding home states responsible under international human rights law for the extra-territorial actions of non-state actors is regarded by some as 'a radical step which would probably necessitate relevant treaty amendments, or the adoption of appropriate optional protocols'.[25]

21 Human Rights Committee, *General Comment No 31: Nature of the General Legal Obligation on States Parties to the Covenant*, 80th sess, UN Doc CCPR/C/21/Rev.1/Add.13 (26 May 2004), [8].

22 *Convention on the Rights of Persons with Disabilities*, opened for signature 30 March 2007, 993 UNTS 3 (entered into force 3 May 2008) art 4 para 1(e).

23 J Ruggie, see above, n 3 [15], <http://www.business-humanrights.org/Documents/SRSG-report-Human-Rights-Council-19-Feb-2007.pdf>.

24 *Foreign Corrupt Practices Act of 1977*, 15 USC §§ 78dd-1.

25 S Joseph, 'An Overview of the Human Rights Accountability of Multinational Enterprises' in M Kamminga & S Zia-Zarifi (eds), *Liability of Multinational Corporations Under International Law*, Kluwer Law International, The Hague, 2000, 75, 85.

19.4.3 The Development of Soft Law

Since the 1970s there have been a variety of attempts to 'regulate' the impact of business on human rights—whether at the international, national or company level including industry-specific guidelines, declarations or codes of conduct, as well as the threat of lawsuits or public reporting requirements, to name just a few. Since the 1990s, the development and reliance on 'soft law' instruments, such as codes of conduct that guide corporate behaviour but do not necessarily legally bind corporations, has increased. Codes are widely used in supply chain management as a way to achieve corporate compliance with human rights standards. All codes, to varying extents, rely on corporate engagement, but the credibility and the potential longevity of the code depend on how business engages with other stakeholders in the development and enforcement of such codes.

Three different modes of such guidelines have developed in parallel, each envisaging a quite different role for how companies might engage in human rights. At the international level, examples include the United Nations Global Compact, the OECD Guidelines on Multinational Enterprises and the United Nations' Draft Norms on the Responsibilities of Transnational Corporations and Other Business Enterprises with Regard to Human Rights.[26] At the other end of the scale, a growing number of corporations now have their own voluntary codes that may have been primarily developed in-house with or without involvement from external stakeholders such as NGOs, trade unions, consumers or workers.

In between are the thematic or sector-specific codes that have been developed particularly in industries that have poor social or environmental track records, such as the extractive industries and the clothing, footwear and toy industries.[27] These codes, which are increasingly likely to originate from a multi-stakeholder forum, are seen as a way of tailoring the codes beyond what is possible in the one-size-fits-all approach of initiatives such as the Global Compact, while endeavouring to achieve a degree of consensus, consistency and credibility that is often lacking in single-enterprise corporate-driven codes. The multi-stakeholder basis for developing such codes (for example, which stakeholders were involved) and the monitoring and reporting and public verification systems attached to these codes, are two crucial indicators of their long term sustainability and effectiveness. Examples of some of the more prominent codes and guidelines are discussed below.[28]

---

26 Subcommission on the Promotion and Protection of Human Rights, see above, n 1.

27 See for example the Cambodian and Pakistani Snapshots in Chapter 17.3.

28 There is substantial literature available discussing the values and intricacies of codes of conduct, see for example: S P Sethi, *Globalization and Self-Regulation: The Crucial Role that Corporate Codes of Conduct Play in Global Business* (Palgrave Macmillan, 2011); T Sagafi-nejad & J H Dunning, *The UN and Transnational Corporations: From Code of Conduct to Global* Compact, Indiana University Press, Bloomington, 2008; D Lepziger, *The Corporate Responsibility Code Book*, Greenleaf Publishing, Sheffield, 2003); J Blendell, *Barricades and Boardrooms: A Contemporary History of the Corporate Accountability Movement* (Paper No 13, United Nations Research Institute for Social Development, 2004) 21 <http://www.unrisd.org/unrisd/website/document.nsf/0/504AF359BB33967FC1256EA9003CE20A?OpenDocument>.

The Draft UN Code of Conduct on Transnational Corporations[29]

In 1973 the UN Economic and Social Council gave a 'Group of Eminent Persons' the task of advising on matters related to TNCs and their impact on development. In 1974 the UN established the Centre on Transnational Corporations, which by 1977 was coordinating the negotiation of the Draft Code of Conduct on Transnational Corporations ('Draft Code'). Negotiations lingered until the early 1990s but no final agreement was concluded.[30] The Draft Code was never officially adopted and its legal nature was never established. There were proponents of a universally applicable, legally binding code on one side and a voluntary code on the other. If binding, it would have served as a convention with national and international mechanisms for implementation. If voluntary, it would have merely served as a set of broad guidelines to be observed by participating parties.

The *Organisation for Economic Cooperation and Development Guidelines for Multinational Enterprises* ('OECD Guidelines')

The OECD Guidelines describe themselves as 'recommendations addressed by governments to multinational enterprises'.[31] The Guidelines cover a wide range of issues, including labour and environmental standards, human rights, corruption, consumer protection, technology transfer, competition and taxation. They require multinational enterprises generally to '[r]espect the human rights of those affected by their activities consistent with the host government's international obligations and commitments'.[32]

The OECD Guidelines are voluntary in their application and do not require companies to 'sign on' like the Global Compact. Instead, multinational enterprises are invited to adopt the guidelines in their management systems and incorporate the principles into their operations. The Guidelines form part of the *Declaration on International Investment and Multinational Enterprises*. The Declaration on International Investment is a political commitment, adopted by the governments of OECD member countries in 1976, with the objective of facilitating direct investment among OECD members.

The OECD Guidelines were revised in 2000 (and updated again in 2011).[33] In 2000 a new complaint procedure was introduced that allows NGOs and others to submit complaints concerning alleged breaches

29 United Nations Centre on Transnational Corporations, *The United Nations Code of Conduct on Transnational Corporations*, Graham & Trotman, London, 1988.

30 See *Code of Conduct on Transnational Corporations*, GA Res x, UN GAOR, 45th sess, 71st plen mtg, UN Doc A/RES/45/186 (21 December 1990), <http://www.un.org/documents/ga/res/45/a45r186.htm>.

31 OECD Guidelines, para 1. For a critical discussion of the OECD Guidelines see: OECD Watch, *Assessing the Contribution of the OECD Guidelines for Multinational Enterprises to Responsible Business Conduct* (June 2010) <http://oecdwatch.org/publications-en/Publication_3550/at_download/fullfile>. And for a discussion of the application of the Guidelines to a particular company, see A McBeth, 'Crushed by an Anvil: A Case Study on Responsibility for Human Rights in the Extractive Sector,' (2008) 11 *Yale Human Rights and Development Law Journal* 127.

32 Organisation for Economic Co-operation and Development (OECD), *OECD Guidelines for Multinational Enterprises*, 2nd edn, 2000, Part II, para 2.

33 Organisation for Economic Co-Operation and Development (OECD), *OECD Guidelines for Multinational Enterprises, Recommendations for Responsible Business Conduct in a Global Context 2011*; available at <http://www.oecd.org/dataoecd/43/29/48004323.pdf>

of the OECD Guidelines to a government's National Contact Point ('NCP'). Before the revision in 2000, only trade unions could submit complaints.[34] If the NCP believes a complaint warrants investigation, it will examine the matter and attempt to broker a resolution between the relevant parties in accordance with the guidelines. If resolution is not possible, the matter can be referred to the OECD Investment Committee to issue a 'clarification' of the application of the guidelines in the situation in question. Clarifications are publicly available but generally will not name the enterprise involved and are therefore more conciliatory and advisory than punitive.

While the dispute resolution process at the NCP level might involve a recommendation that some measure of restitution or remedial action be taken, any such recommendation will not be binding. Since the 2000 version of the OECD Guidelines was adopted, over 200 specific instance complaints had been raised with the various NCPs, many of which concerned violations of labour rights. Of these, 160 were accepted for consideration and 138 were concluded or closed by the relevant NCPs.[35]

The 2011 update enhanced the scope of the Guidelines, by introducing a specific chapter on human rights, and requiring adhering governments to strengthen the NCP mechanism for complaints-handling and investigation, by making human and financial resources available to their NCPs to enable them to effectively fulfil their responsibilities. A general policy of the OECD Guidelines is that enterprises should respect the internationally recognised human rights of those affected by their activities. The new Chapter IV aligns the Guidelines with the UN Special Representative's 'protect, respect and remedy' framework.

OECD GUIDELINES FOR MULTINATIONAL ENTERPRISES: IV HUMAN RIGHTS

States have the duty to protect human rights. Enterprises should, within the framework of internationally recognised human rights, the international human rights obligations of the countries in which they operate as well as relevant domestic laws and regulations:

1 Respect human rights, which means they should avoid infringing on the human rights of others and should address adverse human rights impacts with which they are involved.
2 Within the context of their own activities, avoid causing or contributing to adverse human rights impacts and address such impacts when they occur.
3 Seek ways to prevent or mitigate adverse human rights impacts that are directly linked to their business operations, products or services by a business relationship, even if they do not contribute to those impacts.
4 Have a policy commitment to respect human rights.
5 Carry out human rights due diligence as appropriate to their size, the nature and context of operations and the severity of the risks of adverse human rights impacts.
6 Provide for or co-operate through legitimate processes in the remediation of adverse human rights impacts where they identify that they have caused or contributed to these impacts.

34 See two examples of British cases in L Catá Backer, '*Rights and Accountability in Development v DAS Air* and *Global Witness v Afrimex*: Small Steps towards an Autonomous Transnational Legal System for the Regulation of Multinational Corporations' [2009] *Melbourne Journal of International Law* 13.

35 Organisation for Economic Co-operation and Development, *Report of the Chair of the 2010 meeting of National Contact Points*, 4 <http://www.oecd.org/dataoecd/15/23/46385752.pdf>.

The OECD Guidelines have been criticised, particularly by NGOs, as being toothless, partly because of the design of the implementation system and also because of the way they have been applied by the various NCPs.[36] NGOs argue that if sanctions for violations will not be imposed, there should at least be a 'name and shame' option. Yet despite their shortcomings, the guidelines are noteworthy for being a set of standards applied by industrialised home countries to the operations of their corporations at home and abroad. The availability of a dispute resolution mechanism at an international level for those aggrieved by violations of human rights standards by corporate entities is also significant.

The extract below summarises the allegations that arose against Global Solutions Limited over the management of immigration detention centres in Australia. The Australian NCP negotiated a mediated outcome whereby the company agreed that international human rights law should provide the framework for its operations and agreed to change its internal monitoring processes, including allowing for external scrutiny and to engage human rights experts to train its staff.

STATEMENT BY THE AUSTRALIAN NATIONAL CONTACT POINT 'GSL AUSTRALIA SPECIFIC INSTANCE'[37]

INTRODUCTION

1 In June 2005, the Australian National Contact Point (ANCP) for the *OECD Guidelines for Multinational Enterprises* ('the Guidelines') received a submission from several Australian and overseas non-government organisations ('the complainants') alleging that a UK-controlled multinational, Global Solutions Limited, in providing immigration detention services to the Australian Government through its Australian incorporated wholly-owned subsidiary GSL (Australia) Pty Ltd ('GSL Australia'), had breached the Human Rights and Consumer Interests provisions of the Guidelines.

2 The submission alleged that GSL Australia:

- in detaining children was complicit in violations of the 1989 *Convention on the Rights of the Child* particularly where there is no legal limit on the length of the detention;
- was acquiescing in the mandatory detention of asylum seekers and was therefore complicit in subjecting detainees to a regime of indefinite and arbitrary detention in contravention of Article 9 of the 1996 *International Covenant on Civil and Political Rights* and Article 9 of the 1948 *Universal Declaration of Human Rights*. Furthermore, this regime is allegedly punitive in nature and is thus in contravention of Article 31 of the 1951 *Convention Relating to the Status of Refugees*;
- did not adequately respect the human rights of those detained in its operation of Australian immigration detention facilities; and

36 J Oldenziel, J Wilde-Ramsing & P Feeney, *Assessing the Contribution of the OECD Guidelines for Multinational Enterprises to Responsible Business Conduct*, OECD Watch, June 2010, 29–53, <http://oecdwatch.org/publications-en/Publication_3550/at_download/fullfile>; C Freeman, *A Guide to the Guidelines* (Friends of the Earth, undated) <http://raid-uk.org/docs/Guidelines/Guide_to_Guidelines.pdf>.

37 G Antioch, *Statement by the Australian National Contact Point 'GSL Australia Specific Instance'*, Australian National Contact Point, 6 April 2006 <http://www.ausncp.gov.au/content/reports_newsletters/downloads/reports/GSL_Statement.pdf>.

- was misstating its operations in a way that was 'deceptive, misleading, fraudulent, or unfair' by claiming to be 'committed to promoting best practice in human rights in its policies, procedures and practices' ...

OUTCOMES OF THE SPECIFIC INSTANCE

9 The mediation session was conducted in a spirit that promoted the wellbeing of the detainee population whose care is currently entrusted to GSL Australia. A significant outcome was the value both parties gained in engaging openly on the human rights aspects of GSL Australia's operations. The discussion was frank and robust and enabled consideration of potential solutions.

10 GSL Australia committed to upholding the human rights of those in its care. GSL Australia's Managing Director, Mr Olszak, summed up the company's position by pledging to always consider the question of 'Is it right?' within the framework of human rights and embedding this approach within the company's policy and procedures, including training of its officers.

United Nations Global Compact

In 2000, the UN established the Global Compact, with then UN Secretary-General Kofi Annan calling on world business leaders to voluntarily 'embrace and enact', in their individual corporate practices, a set of 10 principles relating to human rights, labour rights, the protection of the environment and corruption. The Compact is an attempt to produce a broad but brief, universally applicable code of conduct for all corporations operating in all industries in all countries. The initiative includes more than 8000 participants, with more than 5300 businesses in 130 countries around the world.

The Global Compact is a voluntary initiative that invites corporations to sign on to participate. By participating, corporations agree to incorporate the principles into their day-to-day operations and report publicly on their implementation of the principles in annual reports or some equivalent means.

GLOBAL COMPACT, 2000[38]

The Global Compact asks companies to embrace, support and enact, within their sphere of influence, a set of core values in the areas of human rights, labour standards, the environment, and anti-corruption:

HUMAN RIGHTS

Principle 1: Businesses should support and respect the protection of internationally proclaimed human rights; and

Principle 2: make sure that they are not complicit in human rights abuses.

38 Extracted from the UN Global Compact website: <http://www.unglobalcompact.org/AboutTheGC/TheTenPrinciples/index.html>.

LABOUR STANDARDS

Principle 3: Businesses should uphold the freedom of association and the effective recognition of the right to collective bargaining;

Principle 4: the elimination of all forms of forced and compulsory labour;

Principle 5: the effective abolition of child labour; and

Principle 6: the elimination of discrimination in respect of employment and occupation.

ENVIRONMENT

Principle 7: Businesses should support a precautionary approach to environmental challenges;

Principle 8: undertake initiatives to promote greater environmental responsibility; and

Principle 9: encourage the development and diffusion of environmentally friendly technologies.

ANTI-CORRUPTION

Principle 10: Businesses should work against corruption in all its forms, including extortion and bribery.

The Compact did not initially include a mechanism for dispute settlement and there were no consequences for non-compliance. As a result, the Compact was criticised by some as being ineffective, toothless or 'blue-wash', allowing companies to benefit from their association with a UN program without making any meaningful changes to their operations.[39] Partly in response to such criticisms, 'integrity measures' were introduced in 2005. In addition to the public reporting requirement, the integrity measures created a complaints process for 'credible complaints of egregious and systematic abuse of the [Global Compact's] overall aims and principles'.[40]

The focus of the complaints system is on engagement with the company and working with it to achieve change. The strongest remedy available under the complaints process is designation as an 'inactive' participant—the same sanction applied to companies that fail to comply with the public reporting requirements. The Global Compact emphasises a non-confrontational approach to engaging corporations in human rights issues. While other stakeholders, such as civil society, are involved in the process, the mode of engagement is largely that of one conglomerate (business) with another (the UN).

39 S Deva, 'Global Compact's Integrity Measures: Signs of Progress, but Still Long Way to Go' in C Gregoratti & B Slob (eds), *The UN Global Compact: Alternative Voices*, Pluto Press, London, 2011; J Nolan, 'The United Nations' Global Compact: Hindering or Helping the Protection of Human Rights?' [2005] *University of Queensland Law Journal* 445. Also see the more recent report from the United Nations Joint Inspection Unit (P L Fell & M M Zahran), *United Nations Corporate Partnership: The Role and Functioning of the Global Compact* Geneva 2010 (JIU/REP/2010/9).

40 The Global Compact, *The Global Compact's Next Phase* (6 September 2005) 2, <http://www.unglobalcompact.org/docs/about_the_gc/gc_gov_framew.pdf>.

The United Nations Norms on the Responsibilities of Transnational Corporations and Other Business Enterprises with Regard to Human Rights

In 1998 the UN Subcommission on the Promotion and Protection of Human Rights[41] 'established, for a three year period, a sessional working group of the Subcommission, composed of five of its members, to examine the working methods and activities of transnational corporations' to 'draft Norms … on the responsibilities of transnational corporations and other business enterprises with regard to human rights'.[42]

In August 2003, the UN Subcommission unanimously adopted a comprehensive set of international norms specifically applying to TNCs and other businesses (thus applying to any business entity regardless of its international or domestic nature). The Norms[43] state that they are based not only on international instruments, non-binding declarations and guidelines adopted by multilateral organisations, but also on industry initiatives, framework agreements between corporations and workers' organisations, corporate codes of conduct and NGO and union guidelines.

NORMS ON THE RESPONSIBILITIES OF TRANSNATIONAL CORPORATIONS AND OTHER BUSINESS ENTERPRISES WITH REGARD TO HUMAN RIGHTS

A GENERAL OBLIGATIONS

1 States have the primary responsibility to promote, secure the fulfilment of, respect, ensure respect of and protect human rights recognized in international as well as national law, including ensuring that transnational corporations and other business enterprises respect human rights. Within their respective spheres of activity and influence, transnational corporations and other business enterprises have the obligation to promote, secure the fulfilment of, respect, ensure respect of and protect human rights recognized in international as well as national law, including the rights and interests of indigenous peoples and other vulnerable groups.

B RIGHT TO EQUAL OPPORTUNITY AND NON-DISCRIMINATORY TREATMENT

2 Transnational corporations and other business enterprises shall ensure equality of opportunity and treatment …

C RIGHT TO SECURITY OF PERSONS

3 Transnational corporations and other business enterprises shall not engage in nor benefit from war crimes, crimes against humanity, genocide, torture, forced disappearance, forced or compulsory labour, hostage-taking, extrajudicial, summary or arbitrary executions …

---

41 See the discussion of the Subcommission in Chapter 6.1.2.

42 Subcommission on the Prevention of Discrimination and Protection of Minorities, *The Relationship Between the Enjoyment of Economic, Social and Cultural Rights and the Right to Development, and the Working Methods and Activities of Transnational Corporations*, UN ESCOR, 50th sess, 26th mtg, UN Doc E/CN.4/Sub.2/Res/1998/8 (20 August 1998) [4].

43 Subcommission on the Promotion and Protection of Human Rights, see above, n 1.

D RIGHTS OF WORKERS

5 Transnational corporations and other business enterprises shall not use forced or compulsory labour ...

6 Transnational corporations and other business enterprises shall respect the rights of children to be protected from economic exploitation ...

7 Transnational corporations and other business enterprises shall provide a safe and healthy working environment

8 Transnational corporations and other business enterprises shall provide workers with remuneration that ensures an adequate standard of living for them and their families. Such remuneration shall take due account of their needs for adequate living conditions with a view towards progressive improvement.

9 Transnational corporations and other business enterprises shall ensure freedom of association and effective recognition of the right to collective bargaining ...

E RESPECT FOR NATIONAL SOVEREIGNTY AND HUMAN RIGHTS ...

12 Transnational corporations and other business enterprises shall respect economic, social and cultural rights as well as civil and political rights and contribute to their realization, in particular the rights to development, adequate food and drinking water, the highest attainable standard of physical and mental health, adequate housing, privacy, education, freedom of thought, conscience, and religion and freedom of opinion and expression, and shall refrain from actions which obstruct or impede the realization of those rights.

F OBLIGATIONS WITH REGARD TO CONSUMER PROTECTION ...

G OBLIGATIONS WITH REGARD TO ENVIRONMENTAL PROTECTION ...

H GENERAL PROVISIONS OF IMPLEMENTATION ...

I DEFINITIONS

20 The term 'transnational corporation' refers to an economic entity operating in more than one country or a cluster of economic entities operating in two or more countries—whatever their legal form, whether in their home country or country of activity, and whether taken individually or collectively ...

The introduction of the Norms signalled a renewal of interest (by a select body within the UN) in addressing human rights violations by corporate abuses. However, the Norms also provoked intense debate among stakeholders including concern from some business representatives about their content and potential application.[44] The International Chamber of Commerce and the International Organization

44 D Kinley, J Nolan & N Zerial, '"The Norms are Dead! Long Live the Norms!" The Politics Behind the UN Human Rights Norms for Corporations' in D McBarnet, A Voiculescu & T Campbell (eds), *The New Corporate Accountability; Corporate Social Responsibility and the Law*, Cambridge University Press, Cambridge, 2007; L C Backer, 'Multinational Corporations, Transnational Law: The United Nations' Norms on the Responsibilities of Transnational Corporations as a Harbinger of Corporate Social Responsibility in International Law' (2006) 37 *Columbia Human Rights Law Review* 287.

of Employers, for example, criticised the Norms as an inappropriate effort to privatise vague human rights standards in a manner that would invite highly subjective, politicised claims.[45]

The Norms and the accompanying interpretative Commentary have no formal legal status and are, in their current form, unlikely to be developed any further. In 2005 the UN Commission on Human Rights took note of the 'code', but in its recommendations to the ECOSOC affirmed that the code had not been requested by the Commission and, as a draft proposal, had no legal standing.[46] The UN High Commissioner on Human Rights has also expressed the view that the Norms have no legal standing.[47] The UN Secretary-General's Special Representative on the issue of human rights and business has been patently critical of some aspects of the Norms, viewing the initiative as 'engulfed by its own doctrinal excesses' and creating 'confusion and doubt' through 'exaggerated legal claims and conceptual ambiguities'. Indeed, he has concluded that the Norms should be abandoned rather than pursued.[48]

Multi-Stakeholder Codes of Conduct

The UN Special Representative on business and human rights has repeatedly stated that there is no 'silver bullet' that will provide a systemic solution to reducing the incidence of business-related human rights abuses.[49] For much of the past few decades a plethora of tactics have been used to regulate or at least reduce the negative impact that business can have on human rights, with varying levels of success.

In 1977, for example, Reverend Sullivan developed the Sullivan Principles,[50] a code of conduct encompassing human rights and equal opportunity standards for companies operating in South Africa. The Sullivan Principles, which were aimed at ending discrimination against blacks in the workplace, were one of the earlier high-profile corporate responsibility initiatives.

The 1990s saw an explosion in the development of codes of conduct. While initially many were company-specific and often developed in-house without input from civil society, the more recent trend is toward the development of 'multi-stakeholder' codes. Who or what constitutes a stakeholder may be broadly defined to encompass individuals or groups whose interests are or will be substantially affected by the activities of the company or who simply have an interest in promoting greater

---

45 International Organisation of Employers and International Chamber of Commerce, *Joint Views of the IOE and ICC on the Draft Norms on the Responsibilities of Transnational Corporations and Other Business Enterprises with Regard to Human Rights* (2003) <http://www.unhchr.ch/Huridocda/Huridoca.nsf/0/918bbd410b5a8d2cc1256d78002a535a?Opendocument>

46 See the discussion on the Subcommission on the Promotion and Protection of Human Rights in Chapter 6.1.2.

47 Sub commission on the Promotion and Protection of Human Rights, *Report of the United Nations High Commissioner on Human Rights on the Responsibilities of Transnational Corporations and Related Business Enterprises with Regard to Human Rights*, UN ESCOR, 61st sess, 59th mtg, Item 16 of the Provisional Agenda, UN Doc E/CN.4/2005/91 (15 February 2005).

48 J Ruggie, *Interim Report of the Secretary-General's Special Representative on the Issue of Human Rights and Transnational Corporations and Other Business Enterprises*, UN Doc E/CN.4/2006/97 (22 February 2006) [57]–[59].

49 J Ruggie, see above, n 3 [88].

50 L H Sullivan Foundation, *The Global Sullivan Principles of Social Responsibility* <http://www.thesullivanfoundation.org/about/global_sullivan_principles>.

respect for human rights. Multi-stakeholder codes might have input from consumer groups, customers, governments, neighbouring communities, indigenous peoples and communities, NGOs, trade unions, trade associations and others.

Programs such as the Fair Labor Association's Workplace Code of Conduct, Social Accountability 8000, the Ethical Trading Initiative, the Global Reporting Initiative, Accountability 1000, the Voluntary Principles on Security and Human Rights, and the Business Principles for Countering Bribery are just a few of the codes that have been established in an attempt to develop consensus on code standards, guidelines and monitoring mechanisms relevant to particular companies and industries.[51] All are largely focused on TNCs that are responsible, either directly or via their supply chain, for the protection and promotion of human rights. These codes provide a useful guide to the developing consensus on the human rights issues most relevant to business; their guidance, though, is necessarily limited by the self-selecting nature of the standards.

Specific issues may have been addressed in a code as a direct result of public criticism of a company's practices. However, given the 'copycat' nature of code development, the inclusion of an issue in one company's code of conduct may be enough to warrant inclusion (barring absolute irrelevance) in another code.

While the proliferation of codes of conduct—whether company-specific or as part of a multi-stakeholder initiative—in the last two decades has meant that hundreds of companies have now publicly committed to upholding basic human rights. The challenge is to ensure the standards espoused in codes or guidelines adopted by business are consistent, comprehensive and, most importantly, implemented.

FAIR LABOR ASSOCIATION (FLA) *WORKPLACE CODE OF CONDUCT*[52]

The FLA developed its *Workplace Code of Conduct* based on International Labour Organization (ILO) standards. The Code, presented below, delineates the specific code elements that FLA-affiliated companies are required to enforce in factories that supply their products. The FLA Code is supplemented by FLA Compliance Benchmarks, which identify specific benchmarks for each code element.

FORCED LABOR

There shall not be any use of forced labor, whether in the form of prison labor, indentured labor, bonded labor or otherwise.

CHILD LABOR

No person shall be employed at an age younger than 15 (or 14 where the law of the country of manufacture allows) or younger than the age for completing compulsory education in the country of manufacture where such age is higher than 15.

51 For a wealth of information on all aspects of corporate interaction on human rights issues see the website of the Business and Human Rights Resource Centre, an independent not-for-profit organisation: <www.business-humanrights.org/>.

52 Fair Labor Association, *Workplace Code of Conduct* (2008) <http://www.fairlabor.org/about_us_code_conduct_e1.html>.

HARASSMENT OR ABUSE

Every employee shall be treated with respect and dignity. No employee shall be subject to any physical, sexual, psychological or verbal harassment or abuse.

NONDISCRIMINATION

No person shall be subject to any discrimination in employment, including hiring, salary, benefits, advancement, discipline, termination or retirement, on the basis of gender, race, religion, age, disability, sexual orientation, nationality, political opinion, or social or ethnic origin.

HEALTH AND SAFETY

Employers shall provide a safe and healthy working environment to prevent accidents and injury to health arising out of, linked with, or occurring in the course of work or as a result of the operation of employer facilities.

FREEDOM OF ASSOCIATION AND COLLECTIVE BARGAINING

Employers shall recognize and respect the right of employees to freedom of association and collective bargaining.

WAGES AND BENEFITS

Employers recognize that wages are essential to meeting employees' basic needs. Employers shall pay employees, as a floor, at least the minimum wage required by local law or the prevailing industry wage, whichever is higher, and shall provide legally mandated benefits.

HOURS OF WORK

Except in extraordinary business circumstances, employees shall (i) not be required to work more than the lesser of (a) 48 hours per week and 12 hours overtime or (b) the limits on regular and overtime hours allowed by the law of the country of manufacture or, where the laws of such country do not limit the hours of work, the regular work week in such country plus 12 hours overtime and (ii) be entitled to at least one day off in every seven day period.

OVERTIME COMPENSATION

In addition to their compensation for regular hours of work, employees shall be compensated for overtime hours at such premium rate as is legally required in the country of manufacture or, in those countries where such laws do not exist, at a rate at least equal to their regular hourly compensation rate.

Legal Effect of Codes

Codes of conduct are generally regarded as part of the 'soft law' paradigm for protecting human rights. Nevertheless, arguments are emerging that question whether their generally 'normative' effect may transform into a legal effect. For example, the standards set out in a particular code may be incorporated into an employment, supplier or agency contract. The standards may also be given legal effect if adopted by a regulatory agency as a mandatory disclosure requirement for corporate public reporting.[53]

In the case of *Kasky v Nike*,[54] an action was brought against Nike in California under consumer protection legislation, whereby Nike was accused of misleading and deceptive practices in denying human rights abuses within its supply chains.[55]

> At issue in [this case] were communications Nike made to customers, newspaper editors, college presidents and athletic directors, and others responding to allegations that Nike had engaged in, or was complicit in, the mistreatment of foreign workers. Respondent Marc Kasky contended that Nike's communications contained significant misstatements of fact and thus were actionable under California's unfair competition and false advertising laws.[56]

While the case focused primarily on the question of whether Nike's statements constituted commercial speech rather than on the human rights standards promulgated under Nike's code of conduct, the case highlights the dangerous position in which a corporation can find itself if it signs up to a code or makes sweeping statements about its labour standards or other human rights practices and those commitments do not match reality. Ultimately the case was settled and while the terms of settlement were undisclosed, there was an acknowledgement that Nike had paid US$1.5 million, not to Mr Kasky but to the Fair Labor Association, an NGO that monitors labour conditions.[57]

19.5 HUMAN RIGHTS ENFORCEMENT THROUGH LITIGATION IN TORT

Violations of human rights standards that have been incorporated into a state's domestic law, whether in criminal law, labour law, tort law or company law, will of course expose the violator to the enforcement process and sanctions prescribed by that law.[58] International law, to the extent that it is considered (perhaps indirectly) to impose human rights obligations on corporations, does not have any such enforcement mechanisms that can be imposed directly on corporations. In the absence of such specific measures, a sense of creativity has been employed to the application of domestic tort law in particular to address human rights violations. 'Human rights standards and liability in domestric tort share a common purpose: to protect people from harm by deterring others from certain conduct'[59] and

53 For example, the Johannesburg Securities Exchange adopted a 'Code of Corporate Practices and Conduct' that requires all publicly listed companies to disclose non-financial information in accordance with the Global Reporting Initiative.

54 539 US 654 (2003).

55 R K L Collins & D M Rover, 'Landmark Free-Speech Case That Wasn't: The *Nike v Kasky* Story' (2004) 54 *Case Western Reserve Law Review* 965; T Spencer, 'Talking about Social Responsibility: Liability for Misleading and Deceptive Statements in Corporate Codes of Conduct' [2003] *Monash University Law Review* 297.

56 D C Vladeck, 'Lessons from a Story Untold: *Nike v Kasky* Reconsidered' (2004) 54 *Case Western Reserve Law Review* 1049, 1049–50.

57 See the FLA code above at Chapter 19.4.3.

58 S Joseph, *Corporations and Transnational Human Rights Litigation*, Hart Publishing, Oxford, 2004, 8–16.

59 S McMurray & S Rice, 'Lifting the Veil: Human Rights Violations and Tort Law in Australia' (2005) 70 *Precedent* 27.

the overlap between human rights violations and tortuous liability is currently a matter of debate in cases brought under the *Alien Torts Claims Act of 1789* ('ATCA').[60] The fact that the ATCA draws directly on international legal norms differentiates it from other avenues of domestic law, such as negligence principles, which can also be used when appropriate to hold corporations liable for conduct that violates human rights.

19.5.1 The US approach: The *Alien Tort Claims Act*

The US *Alien Tort Claims Act of 1789* ('ATCA') provides the link between international obligations and domestic enforcement by characterising a 'violation of the law of nations' as a tort under United States federal law. The ATCA allows a plaintiff who is not resident in the United States to sue a defendant over whom a US court has personal jurisdiction for a violation of the 'law of nations', even if the event in question had no connection to United States territory.

The application of the ATCA to international human rights standards was first upheld in the 1980 case of *Filartiga v Peña-Irala*,[61] in which a Paraguayan police official was successfully sued for the torture and murder of the plaintiffs' relative.

The question of whether human rights violations constitute a violation of the law of nations was revisited by the United States Supreme Court in the 2004 case of *Sosa v Alvarez Machain*,[62] concerning an action for damages against perpetrators of a cross-border kidnapping. The Court left open the question of whether an action can be brought under the ATCA for violations of clear norms of customary international law or violations of provisions of self-executing treaties to which the United States is a party. While that window clearly includes a number of human rights norms (such as the prohibitions against torture, genocide or slavery), it was held in *Sosa* not to extend to arbitrary arrest or detention in violation of the UDHR and the ICCPR.

Implications for Corporations

A number of United States cases have proceeded on the assumption that corporations can be liable under the ATCA for breaches of international customary law. Significant cases include *Doe v Unocal*, *The Presbyterian Church of Sudan v Talisman Energy* and *Wiwa v Royal Dutch Petroleum*.[63] In respect of corporate defendants, plaintiffs have to a large extent relied on principles of aiding and abetting, or complicity, in state violations of human rights.

In September 2010, the assumption of corporate liability under the ATCA was directly addressed by the Second Circuit Court of Appeals decision in *Kiobel v Royal Dutch Petroleum*.[64] The plaintiffs alleged

60 28 USC § 1350.

61 *Filartiga v Peña-Irala*, 630 F 2d 876 (2nd Cir, 1980).

62 *Sosa v Alvarez Machain*, 542 US 692 (2004)

63 *Doe I v Unocal Corp*, 963 F Supp 880 (CD Cal, 1997), denying the defendants' motion to dismiss the complaint; *Presbyterian Church of Sudan v Talisman Energy*, 582 F 3d 244, 261 n 12 (2nd Cir, 2009); *Wiwa v Royal Dutch Petroleum*, 226 F 3d 88 (2nd Cir, 2000). See further S Joseph, above, n 58.

64 *Kiobel v Royal Dutch Petroleum Co*, 621 F 3d 111 (2nd Cir, 2010).

that the defendants were complicit in human rights breaches by the Nigerian government in the Ogoni region including procuring the Nigerian military to suppress the local human rights and environmental activists and providing support to the Nigerian military such as transport, food and compensation. The majority (2:1) held that because corporations are not liable under the customary international law of human rights, they cannot be subject of liability under the ATCA. The majority recognised that although states are the primary subjects of international law, in a limited number of circumstances individuals can be held liable for certain crimes, such as crimes against humanity, war crimes and torture. However, the liability of individuals related to actual persons, not 'juridical' persons such as corporations.

The minority opinion delivered by Circuit Judge Leval was critical of this reasoning. He stated:

> The majority opinion deals a substantial blow to international law and its undertaking to protect fundamental human rights. According to the rule my colleagues have created, one who earns profits by commercial exploitation of abuse of fundamental human rights can successfully shield those profits from victims' claims for compensation simply by taking the precaution of conducting the heinous operation in the corporate form.[65]

The dissent of Judge Leval is reflected in two more recent decisions, one in the Seventh Circuit[66] and the other in the DC Circuit.[67] These opinions support corporate liability under ATCA and as a number of cases currently before other United States circuits are based on the assumption that corporations may be liable either directly or indirectly under the ATCA, it is likely that this issue will not be completely settled until addressed by the United States Supreme Court. No case brought against a corporation under the ATCA for violation of human rights has yet resulted in a merits decision in favour of the plaintiff. Nevertheless, the potential for a corporation to be considered capable of violating the law of nations and thus liable under the ATCA has led to considerable emphasis on this piece of legislation in the literature on corporate responsibility for human rights violations.[68]

---

65 Ibid 51. On 4 February 2011, the United States Court of Appeals for the Second Circuit denied *en banc* reconsideration of September 2010 ruling in *Kiobel v Royal Dutch Petroleum Co*, 621 F 3d 111 (2nd Cir, 2010), letting the earlier decision of a three-judge panel of that court barring corporate liability under the ATCA stand. The vote of the full 10-judge panel of the Second Circuit was split 5–5, thus leaving intact the original ruling from September. The initial panel voted separately not to rehear the case: *Kiobel v Royal Dutch Petroleum Co*, No 06-4800-cv, 06-4876-cv, 2011 US App LEXIS 2200 (2nd Cir Feb 4, 2011). The decision confirms that plaintiffs are unable to seek redress directly against corporations under the ATCA, at least in the Second Circuit. In June 2011 the plaintiffs in Kiobel filed a petition for certiorari with the US Supreme Court (http://harvardhumanrights.files.wordpress.com/2011/06/kiobel-petition-for-writ-final-6-6-2011.pdf) and in July 2011, a group of international human rights organisations filed an amicus brief in the US Supreme Court in which they urge the Court to review the Second Circuit Court of Appeal findings in Kiobel. See <http://www.ccrjustice.org/files/FINAL%20Kiobel%20Amicus.pdf>.

66 See Judge Posner in *Flomo v Firestone Natural Rubber Co* LLC, No 10-3675 (7th Cir, July 11, 2011).

67 See Judge Rogers in *Doe v Exxon*, (No 09-7125 (DC Cir, July 8, 2011) <http://www.cadc.uscourts.gov/internet/opinions.nsf/567B411C56CD7A6F852578C700513FC8/$file/09-7125-1317431.pdf>.

68 A small sample of some of the more recent literature includes: J G Ku 'The Curious Case of Corporate Liability Under the Alien Tort Statute: A Flawed System of Judicial Lawmaking' (2011) 51(2) *Virginia Journal of International Law* 353; D Wallach, 'The Alien Tort Statute and the Limits of Individual Accountability in International Law (2010) 46(1) *Stanford Journal of International Law* 121; P Hoffman & A Quarry, 'The Alien Tort Statute: An Introduction for Civil Rights Lawyers' (2009) 2 *Los Angeles Public Interest Law Journal* 129; B Athreya & J Su, 'The Perils and Promise of the Alien Tort Statute in Practice: A Comment on "The Alien Tort Statute: An Introduction for Civil Rights Lawyers" by Paul Hoffman & Adrienne Quarry' (2009) 2 *Los Angeles Public Interest Law Journal* 203.

SNAPSHOT: UNOCAL IN BURMA (MYANMAR)

In the case of *Doe v Unocal*,[69] a civil claim was brought by a group of Myanmar (Burmese) villagers under the ATCA alleging abuses on the part of a multinational oil consortium led by US-based Unocal and its security forces (provided by the Myanmar military). The allegations focused on the conduct of the security forces and alleged behaviour resulting in forced labour on the construction of the pipeline and on roads servicing the area, the murder, rape and torture of villagers who refused to work or tried to escape, and the execution of those who grew too weak to work. Unocal was not alleged to have committed these abuses directly; the physical contact with the victims came only from the military personnel engaged to provide security for the pipeline.

The court agreed that the evidence could support a finding that Unocal knew that forced labour was being used and that the enterprise benefited from it, and that it knew or should have known that its conduct would assist or encourage the military to subject the plaintiffs to forced labour. Similar conclusions were reached for the allegations of murder and rape. As a result, the court held that a reasonable person could conclude, on the evidence before the court, that Unocal had aided and abetted the abuses allegedly committed by the Myanmar military. In doing so, the court applied the standard of aiding and abetting from international criminal law, drawing largely from the jurisprudence of the International Criminal Tribunal for the Former Yugoslavia. Following the decision of the Court of Appeals described here, the *Doe v Unocal* decision was settled in April 2005, before the merits of the case were argued.

In *Presbyterian Church of Sudan v Talisman Energy*,[70] the US Court of Appeals for the Second Circuit affirmed the lower court's dismissal of the plaintiffs' claim under the ATCA, and found that to establish liability under the ATCA the plaintiffs must show that the defendant 'purposefully' aided and abetted a violation of international law.[71] The Presbyterian Church of Sudan (along with a number of Sudanese individuals) had alleged Talisman was complicit in the Sudanese government's human rights violations against the non-Muslim Sudanese living in the area of Talisman's oil concession in southern Sudan and that these abuses amounted to genocide. In April 2010 the plaintiffs filed a petition for *certiorari* with the Supreme Court asking the Court to hear an appeal of the lower court's dismissal of the case, but in October 2010 the Supreme Court announced that it would not hear the appeal. However, in DC Circuit decision of *Doe v Exxon*, on the question of aiding and abetting, Judge Rogers diverged from *Talisman* reasoning and argued that it is enough that a corporation abets a wrongful act knowingly—and not purposefully.[72]

The issue of corporate complicity has been recognised as crucial in defining precisely when a corporation should be held legally responsible for violations of international human rights standards. The question remains unresolved for the time being.

---

69 *Doe I v Unocal Corp*, 963 F Supp 880 (CD Cal, 1997).

70 *Presbyterian Church of Sudan v Talisman Energy*, 582 F 3d 244 (2nd Cir, 2009).

71 Ibid.

72 See above, n 67.

19.5.2 Other Tort-Based Approaches For Enforcing Human Rights

Litigation Conducted in 'Host' States[73]

Corporations are obliged to comply with laws enacted by host states that give effect to obligations those states have assumed under international law. Litigation in the host state, where the damage is generally suffered, is therefore the obvious first port of call for a victim seeking redress, even though power differentials and the difficulty of enforcing domestic laws against corporations may make it hard for enforcing those standards against corporations. However, host state litigation has tended to be overlooked in discussions about the enforcement of international human rights standards against multinational enterprises because it is often assumed that the victim of a human rights violation will only seek to invoke international law or the domestic law of a foreign jurisdiction if the opportunity for redress in a local forum is inadequate.[74]

There are a number of examples of civil litigation under domestic law in the host country against an entity of a multinational enterprise, illustrated by the following snapshots.

SNAPSHOT: INDONESIA

Sulawesi residents brought a case against Newport Minahasa Raya, a local subsidiary of US-based multinational enterprise Newport Mining; the case was brought by the Indonesian Environment Ministry at the urging of environmental NGOs.[75] The allegations against Newport focused on the disposal of toxic tailings into Buyat Bay, allegedly causing death and illness by direct exposure to mercury and cyanide, and pollution of drinking water and fisheries, as well as loss of livelihood from damage to fisheries. Those allegations amount to violations of the rights to life, health and a decent standard of living, among others, although the case was not framed in human rights terms, as is usual in ordinary tort cases. The case was settled in February 2006 for US$30 million over ten years 'to fund environmental monitoring and community development.'[76]

Another example involves a United States mining firm, Freeport McMoRan, conducting gold mining operations in Irian Jaya.[77] In 1995, the Indonesian Human Rights Commission determined that human rights abuses committed near the mine were directly related to activities conducted by the armed forces to safeguard the operations of Freeport McMoRan from disturbances by local opposition.

73 Simply put, a home state is the state in which a corporation is registered. As recognised by the International Court of Justice ('ICJ') in *Barcelona Traction, Light and Power Company Limited (Belgium v Spain); Second Phase (Judgment)* [1970] ICJ Rep 3 ('*Barcelona Traction Case*'), this is the corporation's nationality at law. The 'host state' refers to the place of operations of a corporation. In the context of the present discussion, it specifically refers to the place in which the relevant harm occurred

74 See the discussion on jurisdiction in P Muchlinski, 'Corporations in International Litigation: Problems of Jurisdiction and the United Kingdom Asbestos Cases' (2001) 50 *International and Comparative Law Quarterly* 1.

75 J Rose, 'Indonesian Mining—All That Glitters', *Ethical Corporation Magazine* (London), 4 January 2006, 30.

76 'Mine Giant Settles Pollution Case', *BBC News* (online), 16 February 2006 <http://news.bbc.co.uk/2/hi/asia-pacific/4718672.stm>.

77 ELSHAM (Institute for Human Rights Study and Advocacy), *What's Wrong With Freeport's Security Policy? Summary Report: Results of Investigation into the Attack on Freeport Employees in Timika, Papua, Finds Corporation Allows Impunity of Criminal Acts by Indonesian Armed Force* (21 October 2002).

SNAPSHOT: ECUADOR[78]

In 1993, a group of Ecuadorian citizens of the Oriente region filed a class action lawsuit in US Federal Court against Texaco (*Aguinda v Texaco*[79]), and in 1994 a group of Peruvian citizens living downstream from the Oriente region also filed a class action lawsuit against Texaco in US Federal Court (*Jota v Texaco*[80]). Both complaints alleged that between 1964 and 1992 Texaco's oil operations polluted the rainforests and rivers in Ecuador and Peru, resulting in environmental damage and damage to the health of those who live in the region. Both lawsuits were dismissed by the US Federal Court in 2002 on forum *non conveniens* grounds (ie, the court stated that Ecuador was a more appropriate venue for litigating these claims). In connection with the dismissal, Texaco agreed that courts in Ecuador and/or Peru would have jurisdiction over the plaintiffs' claims.

In 2003, a class action lawsuit was brought against Texaco (acquired by Chevron in 2001) in Ecuador alleging severe environmental contamination of the land where Texaco conducted its oil operation activities. The claimants alleged that this contamination has led to increased rates of cancer as well as other serious health problems for the residents of the region ... On 14 February 2011, [an] Ecuadorian judge issued a ruling against Chevron in the lawsuit. The ruling ordered Chevron to pay $8.6 billion in damages and clean up costs, with the damages increasing to $18 billion if Chevron does not issue a public apology. Chevron has indicated that it believes the ruling is 'illegitimate' and 'unenforceable', and it intends to appeal the judgment.

Litigation Conducted in 'Home' States

An alternative and more controversial approach to litigating in a host state is to sue in the home state of a multinational enterprise for harm inflicted in countries where litigation by victims may prove fruitless. Transnational cases based on harm caused to communities in developing countries by multinational mining and chemical companies have been litigated in several home states.[81] Although framed in tort, these cases involved significant human rights issues, including the right to health, the right to compensation for land and a vast range of other rights.

Obstacles to such litigation will vary from jurisdiction to jurisdiction but will likely include legal costs, limits on personal and subject matter jurisdiction, constitutional limitations and discretionary doctrines (including *forum non conveniens*, act of state, international comity and the political question doctrine). Practical considerations include the availability of judicial experience, judicial biases, relevant political interests, the ability of victims' advocates to generate publicity or public sympathy, evidentiary limitations, asset tracing and statutes of limitations.[82] In addition, in most cases, there

78 Extract from Business and Human Rights Resource Centre, *Case Profile: Texaco/Chevron Lawsuits (re Ecuador)* <http://www.business-humanrights.org/Categories/Lawlawsuits/Lawsuitsregulatoryaction/LawsuitsSelectedcases/TexacoChevronlawsuitsreEcuador>.

79 303 F.3d 470 (2nd Cir, 2002)

80 157 F.3d 153, 159 (2nd Cir, 1998)

81 S Joseph, see above, n 58, 113–28.

82 M Ratner, 'Factors Impacting the Selection and Positioning of Human Rights Class Actions in United States Courts: A Practical Overview' (2003) 58 *New York University Annual Survey of American Law* 623.

will be significant obstacles to exercising jurisdiction in a case involving transnational corporations, particularly if the enterprise comprises multiple, separately incorporated companies and where the harm was suffered in a state other than the one where the case is being brought.[83] The extra-territorial application of national law is a particular concern for national courts. Those obstacles can potentially be overcome in certain cases if the wrongful act is characterised as a decision taken or order given at the corporate headquarters, or as a failure to properly supervise the operations overseas, if the plaintiff can establish a legal duty to do so.

In Australia, the Supreme Court of Victoria held in *Dagi v BHP*[84] that there was a serious issue to be tried in respect of the foreign plaintiffs' claims concerning the Australian mining company's operations at Ok Tedi in Papua New Guinea. Settlement was reached between the parties before going to trial.

Companies based in the United States have also been subjected to tort litigation for alleged violations of human rights in other countries. One example is the case of *Martinez v Dow Chemicals*,[85] in which workers from banana plantations in Costa Rica, Honduras and the Philippines sued the American chemical company for producing and exporting chemicals that it allegedly knew would cause serious health problems and had been withdrawn from use in the United States. The case eventually settled after the US District Court denied the company's application to dismiss the claim on the basis of *forum non conveniens*.

SNAPSHOT: UNITED KINGDOM

A series of cases in England focused on decisions made in the head offices of multinational enterprises (the 'home' state) that led to harm suffered in developing countries (the 'host' state).[86] In *Lubbe v Cape PLC*, for instance, the English parent company was sued for its failure to reduce the exposure to asbestos of workers employed by its foreign subsidiaries. After the House of Lords held that the English courts had proper jurisdiction to hear the case, rejecting an application by the defendant company to the contrary,[87] the case settled out of court. It is important to note, however, that none of these cases led to a merits decision, negating their value as formal precedents.

83 See above, n 74.

84 *Dagi v BHP* [1995] 1 VR 428; subsequent litigation of the issue in *Gagarimabu v BHP* [2001] VSC 517 (27 August 2001).

85 *Martinez v Dow Chemicals*, 219 F Supp 2d 719 (ED La, 2002). That case eventually settled after the District Court denied the defendants' application to dismiss the claim on the basis of *forum non conveniens*.

86 *Connelly v RTZ* [1998] AC 854; *Sithole v Thor Chemical Holdings* [1999] EWCA Civ 706 (3 February 1999); *Lubbe v Cape PLC* [2000] 4 All ER 268. The facts behind each of these cases and the early stages of the litigation are described by the principal solicitor in each case: R Meeran, 'The Unveiling of Transnational Corporations—A Direct Approach' in M Addo (ed), *Human Rights Standards and the Responsibility of Transnational Corporations*, Kluwer Law International, The Hague, 1999) 164–9.

87 The defendant applied for a stay on the ground of *forum non conveniens*, asserting that the proper forum for the case was South Africa, where the asbestos exposure occurred and the damage was suffered. The House of Lords rejected the application.

19.6 HUMAN RIGHTS ENFORCEMENT THROUGH INTERNATIONAL CRIMINAL PROCEEDINGS[88]

The International Criminal Court ('ICC') provides, in certain circumstances, the opportunity to hold individuals within companies accountable for egregious human rights abuses. The ICC has jurisdiction only over natural persons,[89] as a proposal for jurisdiction over corporations was rejected at the conference that drafted the Court's statute. However, as individuals, officials of corporations could be held accountable before the ICC for directly or indirectly facilitating conduct that leads to violations of international law. For example, if a company that trades natural resources pays money to a government that then uses the money to fund soldiers who commit war crimes, such a company may have facilitated a war crime and its relevant officers could be prosecuted.

The ICC has jurisdiction to try cases of genocide, crimes against humanity and war crimes, where the state with domestic criminal jurisdiction is unable or unwilling to carry out a criminal investigation. If the operations of a multinational corporation reach the level of these international crimes, or aid and abet the perpetration of such crimes by others, international criminal law can be used to prosecute the individuals involved if there is unwillingness or practical obstacles at the municipal level standing in the way of prosecution.

In legislating to give domestic effect to the crimes covered by the ICC, many states have created extra-territorial jurisdiction for the prosecution of their nationals for those crimes. For example, in Australia's *Criminal Code Act 1995* (Cth), Division 268, inserted in 2002, gives effect to Australia's ratification of the ICC statute.[90]

Other international criminal tribunals have prosecuted and convicted individuals for commercial operations that amounted to international crimes, although the corporations themselves have not been prosecuted as independent legal persons. In the *I G Farben case*, 12 out of the 23 accused were officers of a corporation that procured and used slave labour from Auschwitz concentration camps and were convicted by the US Military Tribunal at Nuremberg.[91] More recently, in *Prosecutor v Musema*,[92] the International Criminal Tribunal for Rwanda held Alfred Musema, the director of a tea factory, accountable for the acts of his employees in massacring Tutsis. He was convicted of genocide, and of the crime against humanity of extermination on the basis of command responsibility, and also on the basis of ordering and aiding and abetting. He was convicted as well of direct perpetration of other crimes arising from the same events.

---

88 See Chapter 11.

89 *Rome Statute of the International Criminal Court*, opened for signature 17 July 1998, 2187 UNTS 90 (entered into force 1 July 2002) art 25(1).

90 Ibid. See the discussion in A McBeth, 'Crushed by an Anvil: A Case Study on Responsibility for Human Rights in the Extractive Sector', (2008) 11 *Yale Human Rights and Development Law Journal* 127, 136–41

91 *In re Krauch and Others* (I G Farben Trial) (1948)15 ILR 668.

92 *Prosecutor v Alfred Musema (Judgment and Sentence)* (International Criminal Tribunal for Rwanda, Trial Chamber, Case No ICTR-96-13-T, 27 January 2000).

19.7 CONCLUSION AND ISSUES

Human rights are intrinsically connected to individuals but in a world economy with tens of thousands of TNCs and millions of smaller businesses, the relevance of human rights to the activities of corporations is no longer academic. The ultimate goal of establishing measures to deal with human rights infringements by corporations might logically be the prevention of harmful behaviour in the first place. How to achieve this? With power does indeed come responsibility but the rise and rise of the TNC as a powerful non-state actor might be said to have left human rights and international law in its wake without either body of law proposing any real sustainable mechanisms for holding business accountable for human rights abuses.[93] One of the continuing obstacles to establishing such accountability via the mechanism of international human rights law is residual concern about the imposition of positive obligations on corporations and the usurpation of the role of the state in upholding (and protecting) human rights.

Suites of voluntary codes, guidelines and reporting measures have been drawn up to encourage socially, ethically and environmentally responsible behaviour and highlight breaches of accepted standards when they occur. Some argue that the proliferation of such 'soft' standards may have indirectly closed the door on the development of any 'hard' international law on this topic. The question remains whether an international treaty in this area is appropriate, feasible or even necessary. If states can be relied on to fulfil their duties of protection of human rights, including monitoring the impact of non-state actors such as corporations including TNCs, then some might accept that there is little need to more formally adopt international mechanism to protect human rights from these juggernauts of the global economy. One of the many outstanding issues in this field is the degree to which such reliance on states is warranted.

93 J Nolan & D Kinley, see above, n 4, 376.

20 THE EXPANDING SCOPE OF INTERNATIONAL HUMAN RIGHTS LAW

CONTENTS

20.1 INTRODUCTION

The scope of international human rights law is not fixed. The traditional focus has been on the rights set out in the International Bill of Rights, with a corresponding focus on states as the obligation-holders. Given that state-centric focus, international human rights law has traditionally been concerned with the actions of governments within their own territory. However, none of those parameters is immutable.

The scope of a state's obligations today, or indeed in the future, may be broader than the traditional focus. Clearly a state has obligations to respect, protect and promote human rights within its own territory, where the sovereignty of the state and its ability to take action and regulate affairs is strongest. However, as states increasingly exert influence beyond their own borders, the question arises as to whether states have extra-territorial human rights obligations and, if so, what shape they take and in which circumstances they arise.

Acceptance of extra-territorial obligations then begs the question of when, if ever, states are obliged to intervene in the affairs of another state to prevent or halt atrocities or to secure the protection of human rights.

A related question of concurrent obligations is whether the obligations to respect, protect and promote human rights may apply not only to governments, but to others as well.

This chapter looks briefly at each of these areas of expanding scope. In each case, there is considerable debate about the precise current parameters of the law and the likely direction of future change. The intention in this chapter is not to cover each of those debates exhaustively, but merely to flag some of the most likely future areas of movement.

20.2 EXPANDING JURISDICTION: EXTRA-TERRITORIAL OBLIGATIONS

20.2.1 Responsibility for State Actions Outside Territory

'According to common perceptions of human rights obligations, whether a state can in any way be held responsible for human rights violations depends not only on the state's actions, but also where those actions took place, and/or the nationality of the victims of the violations'.[1]

The original focus of international human rights law was to place certain constraints on a state's treatment of its own people, pursuant to the demands of human dignity. Consistent with the principle of sovereignty, a state can only be expected to exercise the control demanded by human rights law within its own jurisdiction; it would be unreasonable to hold states responsible for situations over which they are unable to exert any control.

The scope of state obligations in the ICCPR is expressed in the following terms:

> Each State Party to the present Covenant undertakes to respect and to ensure to all individuals within its territory and subject to its jurisdiction the rights recognized in the present Covenant ...[2]

A narrow reading of that provision would require an individual to be both within a state's territory and within its jurisdiction before a state owed him or her any obligations under international human rights law. Under that interpretation, a state's human rights obligations stop at its own borders and it cannot be held accountable for any actions outside its own territory, but such a narrow interpretation has been repudiated by the Human Rights Committee. For example, in the case of *Lopez Burgos v Uruguay*, in which Uruguayan officials were accused of kidnapping a Uruguayan trade union activist in Argentina, the Committee held that 'it would be unconscionable to so interpret the responsibility under article 2 of the Covenant as to permit a State party to perpetrate violations of the Covenant on the territory of another State, which violations it could not perpetrate on its own territory'.[3]

In its *General Comment 31*, the Committee said:

> States Parties are required by article 2, paragraph 1, to respect and to ensure the Covenant rights to all persons who may be within their territory and to all persons subject to their jurisdiction. This means that a State party must respect and ensure the rights laid down in the Covenant to anyone within the power or effective control of that State Party, even if not situated within the territory of the State Party. ... the

1 S Skogly, 'Extraterritoriality: Universal Human Rights Without Universal Obligations?' in S Joseph & A McBeth (eds), *Research Handbook on International Human Rights Law*, Edward Elgar, Cheltenham, UK, 2010, 71.

2 ICCPR, article 2(1).

3 *Lopez Burgos v Uruguay*, Human Rights Committee, Communication No 052/1979, 29 July 1981, para 12.3.

> enjoyment of Covenant rights is not limited to citizens of States Parties but must also be available to all individuals, regardless of nationality or statelessness, such as asylum seekers, refugees, migrant workers and other persons, who may find themselves in the territory or subject to the jurisdiction of the State Party. This principle also applies to those within the power or effective control of the forces of a State Party acting outside its territory, regardless of the circumstances in which such power or effective control was obtained, such as forces constituting a national contingent of a State Party assigned to an international peace-keeping or peace-enforcement operation.[4]

The International Court of Justice has followed the same approach as the Human Rights Committee, concluding that a state's human rights obligations will therefore apply to all 'acts done by a State in the exercise of its jurisdiction outside its own territory.'[5]

The European Court of Human Rights has taken a narrower view of the scope of a state's extra-territorial obligations under the *European Convention on Human Rights* (ECHR), most notably in the case of *Bankovic v Belgium*.[6] In that case, which sought to hold the NATO states responsible for alleged human rights violations committed in the course of NATO's bombing of Kosovo in 1999, the court held that the NATO states had no responsibility under the ECHR for acts committed in Serbia and Kosovo, which were then outside of the Council of Europe and the coverage of the ECHR, and therefore held the case to be inadmissible.[7] The *Bankovic* decision has been heavily criticised, and has been called 'the most egregious decision in the history of the European Court of Human Rights'.[8]

European case law does acknowledge extra-territorial obligations in limited circumstances, when a state's authorities produce effects outside their own territory.[9] But more generally it can be distinguished from international human rights law on the basis that the ECHR is a geographically limited treaty, while general international human rights law operates globally. The clear trend in other international human rights forums has been an expansive one. There appears to be an emerging consensus, *Bankovic* notwithstanding, that a state has extra-territorial obligations in relation to foreign territory that it controls, such as occupied territory, and in relation to individuals under its control.[10] Beyond those situations, a state's extra-territorial obligations are currently unclear, and depend on the nature of the situation and the right in question. States are, for example, likely to have more onerous

4 Human Rights Committee General Comment 31, *The Nature of the General Legal Obligation Imposed on States Parties to the Covenant*, CCPR/C/21/Rev.1/Add. 13, 29 May 2004, para 10.

5 *Legal Consequences of the Construction of a Wall in the Occupied Palestinian Territory, ICJ Advisory Opinion* (9 July 2004) para 111.

6 *Bankovic et al v Belgium and 16 other states (Admissibility)* (2001) Eur Court HR (GC), Application No 52207/99 (12 December 2001). (*'Bankovic v Belgium'*)

7 *Bankovic v Belgium*, paras 59–82.

8 E Roxstrom, M Gibney & T Einarsen, 'The NATO Bombing Case (*Bankovic et al v Belgium et al*) and the Limits of Western Human Rights Protection' (2005) 23 *Boston University International Law Journal* 55 at 56. See also O De Schutter, 'The Accountability of Multinationals for Human Rights Violations in European Law', in P Alston (ed), *Non-State Actors and Human Rights* (2005) 247.

9 *Drozd and Janousek v France and Spain* (1992) 14 EHRR 745 at para 91.

10 F Coomans & M Kamminga, 'Comparative Introductory Comments on the Extraterritorial Application of Human Rights Treaties' in F Coomans & M Kamminga (eds), *Extraterritorial Application of Human Rights Treaties*, Intersentia, Antwerp, 2004, 4–5.

obligations in terms of refraining from harmful activity (respecting human rights) than in relation to taking positive measures (fulfilling human rights).[11]

20.2.2 Responsibility to Provide Aid and Assistance

Treaties addressing economic, social and cultural rights, unlike civil and political rights instruments, 'specifically envisaged extraterritorial obligations'.[12] The ICESCR makes no mention of a territorial limit to states parties' obligations, instead requiring each state party to 'take steps, individually and through international assistance and co-operation, especially economic and technical, to the maximum of its available resources, with a view to achieving progressively the full realization of the rights recognized in the present Covenant by all appropriate means, including particularly the adoption of legislative measures'.[13] The necessary implication is that all states parties are expected to provide assistance and cooperation to other states to help them achieve the realisation of economic, social and cultural rights that, by definition, would be extra-territorial in nature. However, the expectation to provide assistance is underdeveloped, and it could not yet be described as an obligation in the sense that failure to offer such assistance would be a breach of the ICESCR.

Another source of a responsibility to assist are the Millennium Development Goals. Agreed in 2000, they aim to make a measurable impact on global poverty by 2015 by setting eight clear goals for the international community.[14] The eight goals are: end poverty and hunger; universal education; gender equality; child health; maternal health; combat HIV/AIDS; environmental sustainability; and global partnership. Each of those contains measurable targets (for example, to halve between 1990 and 2015 the number of people whose income is less than $1 per day), most of which require significant international assistance or aid to be realised. One of the targets in goal 8 (global partnership) is for developed countries to meet the official UN goal of 0.7 per cent of gross national income on official development aid. In 2010, only five donors met that target.[15]

Despite the clarity of the targets in the Millennium Development Goals and the fact that governments agreed to them at the original Millennium Development Summit and have subsequently agreed to their revision, they are not in treaty form and do not constitute direct legal obligations. Overseas development aid can therefore be considered a strong moral obligation, but not yet a clear legal obligation. However, given the consensus on the moral imperative to deliver aid, the purposes for which it is to be given and even the precise quantity that ought to be given, it is conceivable that the obligation might attain customary legal status at some stage in the future.

11 S Skogly & M Gibney, 'Transnational Human Rights Obligations' (2002) 24 *Human Rights Quarterly* 781, 788.

12 See above, n 10, 2. See Chapter 4.3 for a detailed discussion of the nature of obligations under the ICESCR.

13 ICESCR, art 2(1) (emphasis added).

14 The Millennium Development Goals are available at <http://www.un.org/millenniumgoals/>.

15 United Nations, *The Millennium Development Goals Report 2011*, New York, June 2011. The five states were Denmark, Luxembourg, the Netherlands, Norway and Sweden.

20.2.3 Conclusions on Extra-territoriality

While the traditional focus of international human rights law has been on the obligations of states within their own borders, the more that states' own activity extends beyond those borders, the more their human rights obligations will expand. There is already recognition of the state's obligation to refrain from harm whenever it operates outside its borders, and when it exercises special jurisdiction over land (such as occupation) or individuals (such as offshore detention); those obligations clearly extend beyond 'do no harm' to encompass clear obligations to protect and fulfil human rights.

What is currently lacking is a positive obligation on states to act for the betterment of people outside their borders and over whom they exercise no particular control. The provision of international assistance is mandated in the ICESCR, while there is moral consensus on the need to devote substantial amounts to development aid. However, those imperatives currently fall short of constituting enforceable legal obligations. Indeed, the collective nature of obligations to provide assistance, in the sense that all states (or at least all developed states) would be under an equal obligation to provide assistance, would make it difficult to hold a recalcitrant state responsible for the non-fulfilment of human rights abroad.

20.3 EXPANDING MANDATE: THE RESPONSIBILITY TO PROTECT

20.3.1 Humanitarian Intervention

For many years, the question of whether states are permitted under international law to intervene through military force to stop mass atrocities in another country has been hotly debated. The core of the controversy is the cardinal prohibition in international law on the unilateral use of armed force:

> All Members shall refrain in their international relations from the threat or use of force against the territorial integrity or political independence of any state, or in any other manner inconsistent with the Purposes of the United Nations.[16]

Only two exceptions are permitted to the use of force: self-defence[17] and the authorisation of collective action by the UN Security Council.[18]

Despite the prohibition of the unilateral use of force, military action has on occasion been defended as 'humanitarian intervention'. The justification of humanitarian intervention is that the use of armed force for the protection of populations in another state, such as to stop ethnic cleansing, is not 'against the territorial integrity or political independence of any state', nor is it 'inconsistent with the Purposes of the United Nations'; on the contrary, it is said to be in pursuit of the purposes of the United Nations and therefore, it is argued, does not violate the prohibition in article 2 of the Charter.

16 *Charter of the United Nations* (1945), art 2(4).

17 Ibid art 51.

18 Ibid Chapter VII, particularly art 42.

The difficulty with humanitarian intervention is that virtually any armed incursion can be said to be for humanitarian purposes, or at least to have a humanitarian component. For example, ahead of the invasion of Iraq by the United States and its allies in 2003, politicians turned to humanitarian rhetoric once it became clear that UN Security Council authorisation for the invasion would not be forthcoming, and reprised it after the occupation had commenced and weapons of mass destruction were not found, retrospectively offering humanitarian justifications for the invasion when the primary justification was disproved.[19]

On the other hand, the failure of states to intervene in atrocities in other states is clearly problematic from a human rights perspective, as it prioritises state sovereignty over human rights and human suffering. The example most often cited to demonstrate the disaster of inaction is the international community's failure to intervene to stop genocide in Rwanda.[20] Failures such as this pointed to a need to resolve the tensions between state sovereignty, the primary obligation on states to protect human rights within their own territory, and the obligations of other states to protect the human rights of those outside their territories.

20.3.2 Emergence of the Responsibility to Protect

The challenge to balance the issues of sovereignty on the one hand, and the responsibility of the international community to intervene to protect human rights in the face of atrocities on the other, was laid down by then UN Secretary-General, Kofi Annan, in his Millennium Report to the UN General Assembly in 2000, when he asked: 'if humanitarian intervention is, indeed, an unacceptable assault on sovereignty, how should we respond to a Rwanda, to a Srebrenica—to gross and systematic violations of human rights that offend every precept of our common humanity?'[21]

The response was the development of a principle known as the 'responsibility to protect'. The principle was first outlined by the International Commission on Intervention and State Sovereignty,[22] established by the Canadian government in 2000, although it drew on existing principles regarding the norm of non-intervention and the notion of extra-territorial responsibility for human rights and obligations *erga omnes*.[23] At the 2005 World Summit, which was a follow-up to the Millennium Summit of 2000, states accepted the existence of a 'responsibility to protect populations from genocide, war crimes, ethnic cleansing and crimes against humanity'.[24]

19 See further K Roth, 'War in Iraq: Not a Humanitarian Intervention', in Human Rights Watch, *Human Rights and Armed Conflict*, 2004, available at <http://www.hrw.org/legacy/wr2k4/index.htm>.

20 See for example International Commission on Intervention and State Sovereignty, *The Responsibility to Protect*, December 2001, para 1.1. See also discussion of the Rwanda situation and the response of the international community in Chapter 11.4.2.

21 United Nations Secretary-General, *We the Peoples: The Role of the United Nations in the 21st Century*, March 2000, available at <http://www.un.org/millennium/sg/report/index.html>, para 217.

22 International Commission on Intervention and State Sovereignty, above, n 20.

23 Obligations *erga omnes* are obligations that are owed to the world at large, as opposed to obligations owed to specific individuals, groups or states.

24 *2005 World Summit Outcome*, 15 September 2005, UN document no A/60/L.1, paras 138–9.

2005 WORLD SUMMIT OUTCOME[25]

RESPONSIBILITY TO PROTECT POPULATIONS FROM GENOCIDE, WAR CRIMES, ETHNIC CLEANSING AND CRIMES AGAINST HUMANITY

138 Each individual State has the responsibility to protect its populations from genocide, war crimes, ethnic cleansing and crimes against humanity. This responsibility entails the prevention of such crimes, including their incitement, through appropriate and necessary means. We accept that responsibility and will act in accordance with it. The international community should, as appropriate, encourage and help States to exercise this responsibility and support the United Nations in establishing an early warning capability.

139 The international community, through the United Nations, also has the responsibility to use appropriate diplomatic, humanitarian and other peaceful means, in accordance with Chapters VI and VIII of the Charter, to help protect populations from genocide, war crimes, ethnic cleansing and crimes against humanity. In this context, we are prepared to take collective action, in a timely and decisive manner, through the Security Council, in accordance with the Charter, including Chapter VII, on a case-by-case basis and in cooperation with relevant regional organizations as appropriate, should peaceful means be inadequate and national authorities manifestly fail to protect their populations from genocide, war crimes, ethnic cleansing and crimes against humanity. We stress the need for the General Assembly to continue consideration of the responsibility to protect populations from genocide, war crimes, ethnic cleansing and crimes against humanity and its implications, bearing in mind the principles of the Charter and international law. We also intend to commit ourselves, as necessary and appropriate, to helping States build capacity to protect their populations from genocide, war crimes, ethnic cleansing and crimes against humanity and to assisting those which are under stress before crises and conflicts break out.

The terms of the responsibility to protect as expressed in paragraphs 138 and 139 of the 2005 World Summit Report were expressly endorsed by the UN Security Council in 2006.[26]

The main features of the responsibility to protect are that states have the primary responsibility to protect their own populations from atrocities, while the international community has a concurrent responsibility to act to prevent such atrocities, primarily through peaceful means, but extending to the use of force through the UN Security Council if necessary. The doctrine therefore emphasises a preventative duty on the part of the international community, as well as a responsibility to react quickly once gross violence occurs.

20.3.3 Conclusions on the Responsibility to Protect

From a human rights point of view, the confirmation of extra-territorial obligations that exist concurrently with the primary obligations of the state where the violence is occurring is noteworthy.

25 Ibid.

26 Security Council Res 1674 (2006), UN doc no S/RES/1674, 28 April 2006, especially para 4.

As far as the use of force is concerned, which is the element of the right to protect that has attracted most attention, nothing has changed in terms of the law. It remains unlawful for a state to use armed force unilaterally, even for humanitarian purposes or to intervene to prevent atrocities in another state, without UN Security Council approval, unless the use of force constitutes self-defence. The main shift is one of emphasis and priorities, in that the protection of civilian populations from mass atrocities is now clearly expressed as a legitimate concern of the international community, sufficient to trigger a threat to international peace and security for the UN Security Council to act under Chapter VII of the Charter.[27]

When it authorised the use of force in the form of a no-fly zone in Libya in March 2011, the UN Security Council used language reminiscent of the responsibility to protect, although did not expressly refer to the doctrine:[28]

THE SITUATION IN LIBYA, SECURITY COUNCIL RESOLUTION 1973 (2011)[29]

The Security Council ...

Expressing its determination to ensure the protection of civilians and civilian populated areas and the rapid and unimpeded passage of humanitarian assistance and the safety of humanitarian personnel,

...

3 Demands that the Libyan authorities comply with their obligations under international law, including international humanitarian law, human rights and refugee law and take all measures to protect civilians and meet their basic needs, and to ensure the rapid and unimpeded passage of humanitarian assistance;

4 Authorizes ... all necessary measures ... to protect civilians and civilian populated areas under threat of attack in the Libyan Arab Jamahiriya, including Benghazi, while excluding a foreign occupation force of any form on any part of Libyan territory...

...

6 Decides to establish a ban on all flights in the airspace of the Libyan Arab Jamahiriya in order to help protect civilians ...

The responsibility to protect is better understood as a re-expression and reorganisation of existing principles rather than a dramatic change in substantive international law. However, the reorganisation may ultimately have a significant impact if it influences the thinking and actions of states, including states taking responsibility to prevent or halt atrocities in their own territory, states on the Security

27 Chapter VII of the *United Nations Charter* empowers the UN Security Council to take 'action with respect to threats to the peace, breaches of the peace and acts of aggression'. The threshold for action under Ch VII is a determination of 'the existence of any threat to the peace, breach of the peace, or act of aggression', enabling the UN Security Council to take measures 'to maintain or restore international peace and security': *Charter of the United Nations* (1945), art 39.

28 Security Council Res 1973 (2011), UN doc no S/RES/1973, 17 March 2011.

29 Ibid.

Council becoming more willing to authorise intervention for humanitarian purposes, and other states applying pressure to ensure that that happens.

20.4 EXPANDING COVERAGE: APPLICATION TO NON-STATE ACTORS

20.4.1 The Traditional Approach

The origins of human rights as a concept were explored in Chapters 1 and 2. In essence, human rights are said to derive from inherent human dignity, in that the very nature of being human demands certain levels of respect (such as respect for life, physical integrity and liberty) and certain sustenance (food, shelter, health care) to live a dignified life. Historically, it was primarily the state that had the power to infringe human rights (for instance by detaining people arbitrarily), to protect rights (for instance, by prohibiting arbitrary killing, and prosecuting offenders) and to fulfil economic and social entitlements (for instance, by establishing a school system). When obligations to respect, protect and fulfil human rights were set out in legal instruments, it made sense to address those obligations to states.

Viewed as a body of positive law, it can therefore be said that only states have direct obligations under international human rights law. While entities other than states—so-called 'non-state actors'—are certainly capable of infringing an individual's rights, they cannot breach international human rights *law* under an orthodox interpretation:

> International human rights law, for all its diversity and size, places direct legal obligations only on states. The international human rights law system is a state-based system, a system in which the law operates in only one area: state action. It ignores actions by nonstate actors, such as the United Nations and other intergovernmental organizations, transnational corporations, armed opposition groups, and terrorists (however defined). Nonstate actors are treated as if their actions could not violate human rights, or it is pretended that states can and do control their activities.
>
> International human rights law privileges the state and is silent in relation to the nonstate. International human rights law simply does not hear the voices of those who are being violated by nonstate actors.[30]

In this traditional approach, if the actions of a non-state actor, such as an individual or a corporation or an armed group, can be attributed to a state, the state will be responsible for the breach. Similarly, if a non-state actor infringes human rights within a state's territory or jurisdiction, the state will be responsible if it can be shown that the state failed to take appropriate action to protect the victims' human rights. However, in an era of globalisation, there are many instances where a particular non-state actor cannot be considered to be entirely within the control of any one state. Accordingly, it is ineffective simply to rely on a state's duty to protect human rights from the actions of that entity.

30 R McCorquodale, 'Overlegalizing Silences: Human Rights and Nonstate Actors', (2002) 96 *American Society of International Law Proceedings* 384.

20.4.2 Corporations

The clearest example of a situation where state obligations alone cannot be relied on is the conduct of a transnational corporation. An entity that is based in one state and operates in another, often through a complex web of subsidiaries and related entities separately incorporated in different states, is typically beyond the regulatory reach of any one state. In some cases, the corporation might even be more wealthy and more powerful than the state where it is operating, particularly if the host country is a developing country that is reliant on the investment of the corporation. When human rights are infringed by a corporation in those circumstances, it can be difficult to identify which one or more states have a duty to protect human rights and, even then, the state may be unable or unwilling to regulate or to intervene.

For these reasons, the question of the human rights responsibilities of transnational corporations has been a hot topic in international human rights law in recent years, discussed separately in Chapter 19. The framework developed by the UN Secretary-General's Special Representative, Professor Ruggie, of 'Protect, Respect and Remedy'[31] is an example of the effort to combine the traditional focus on the state's obligation to protect human rights from infringement by private actors with a separate focus on the responsibility of the corporation itself.

20.4.3 International Institutions

Corporations are not the only kind of non-state actor capable of violating human rights. Institutions that are comprised of states but have their own legal personality, such as the International Monetary Fund, the Asian Development Bank, the various agencies of the World Bank[32] and the World Trade Organization (WTO), can have a significant impact on human rights in the course of their operations.

Some of those institutions engage directly with communities, such as the World Bank and the various regional development banks in their development projects. In that process, it is possible for the institution's actions to violate the human rights of individuals quite directly. For example, a large infrastructure project might force the eviction of local people to make way for the project without the appropriate safeguards or resettlement processes required by international human rights law.[33]

The impact of such institutions on human rights is not always negative. To the contrary, programs ostensibly aimed at poverty reduction and development may promote human rights for at least part

31 J Ruggie, *Report of the Special Representative of the Secretary-General on the Issue of Human Rights and Transnational Corporations and Other Business Enterprises, 'Protect, Respect and Remedy: A Framework for Business and Human Rights'*, UN Doc A/HRC/8/5 (7 April 2008). See the detailed discussion of Ruggie's mandate in Chapter 19.3.

32 The World Bank Group is comprised of five separate agencies: the International Bank for Reconstruction and Development, the International Development Association, the International Finance Corporation, the Multilateral Investment Guarantee Agency and the International Centre for the Settlement of Investment Disputes.

33 Some of the safeguards for forced evictions are set out in Committee on Economic, Social and Cultural Rights, *General Comment 7: The Right to Adequate Housing: Forced Evictions*, contained in UN Doc E/1998/22, annex IV (20 May 1997).

of the population, perhaps in a very significant way. The questions for international human rights law are to what extent international human rights standards should guide that activity, and whether there is any legal accountability for violating human rights standards. The World Bank has historically rebuffed responsibility, on the grounds that human rights are political rather than economic in nature and therefore outside the Bank's scope of responsibility. More recently, however, the Bank has begun to embrace the relevance of human rights to its work, while still stopping short of accepting legal accountability.

ROBERTO DAÑINO *LEGAL OPINION ON HUMAN RIGHTS AND THE WORK OF THE WORLD BANK*[34]

I INTRODUCTION

1 The World Bank's objectives and activities are deeply supportive of the substantive realization of human rights. This was affirmed by the Bank in 1998, and reiterated by its President in 2005:

> The Bank has long recognized that sustainable development requires both economic growth and social equity. There is, moreover, widespread recognition of the strong link between human rights and development. The connections between human rights and the attainment of the Millennium Development Goals are also significant. The Bank's work substantially contributes to the realization of rights of people in a number of areas, such as health, education, gender, participation, accountability, environment, and institutional reform activities and, above all, the fight against poverty itself as a fundamental denial of human rights. Other Bank activities also contribute to the realization of human rights: these include fighting corruption, increasing transparency and accountability in governance.

2 As the concept of development has evolved, human rights and international human rights law have become increasingly relevant to helping the Bank achieve its mission and fulfill its purposes by supporting better development practices and more sustainable, equitable outcomes. Human rights offer a standard by which to assess progress and the efforts of those with obligations to achieve development targets and the Millennium Development Goals. ... Human rights foster accountability of all actors involved in development by locating duty for particular development outcomes in duty-bearers (usually States). This advances accountability to the poor and a consequent empowerment of the poor. In short, human rights improve the processes through which development occurs for those it is designed to benefit.

3 However, there has not yet been a corresponding evolution in the Bank's legal views on the link between human rights and the Bank's work ...

III HUMAN RIGHTS CONSIDERATIONS IN THE BANK'S WORK

18 ... there are instances in which the Bank may take human rights into account, and others in which it should. Indeed, there are some activities which the Bank cannot properly undertake without considering human rights.

19 Where member countries have human rights law obligations that they wish to fulfill, the Bank may play a supportive role in assisting them. ...

20 Where violations or non-fulfillment of obligations are at issue, and where these have an economic impact, the Bank should take these into consideration. Furthermore, if a human rights violation leads to a breach of

34 Senior Vice President and General Counsel of the World Bank, 27 January 2006.

international obligations relevant to the Bank, such as those created under binding decisions of the UN Security Council, the Bank should also take those violations into account.

21 In some other areas human rights are directly relevant to the Bank's work. One example relates to the public participation and consultation requirements contained in several Bank policies. For instance, the recently revised Bank policy on Indigenous Peoples provides for the free prior and informed consultation of Indigenous Peoples leading to broad community support, and its preamble makes explicit reference to human rights.

22 The approach outlined here requires balance, moderation and engagement. Furthermore, as a development institution, the Bank should avoid imposing a 'double punishment' on the people of its member countries by withholding development assistance from those already disadvantaged by their countries' poor human rights records. It is easier for a private company to walk away from a particular investment than for the Bank to do the same with respect to an investment program affecting a whole country. If the Bank were to do so, it could inflict additional hardship on those who may already be suffering as a result of the government's failure to respect or protect human rights ...

23 Finally, it should be clear that the Bank's role is not that of an enforcer of human rights obligations. Enforcement is primarily the responsibility of member countries, and of other, non-financial entities such as the United Nations treaty monitoring bodies and regional human rights organizations. Rather, the Bank's role remains one of supportive cooperation with its members in the realization of human rights.

IV CONCLUSION

24 As the foregoing analysis demonstrates, the Bank has a significant role in helping member countries in the substantive realization of their human rights obligations in areas that fall within the remit of its mandate and where development activities and human rights are deeply interrelated. This is particularly important in cases where countries request such assistance, or where they frame questions or strategies related to poverty reduction or development in human rights terms. It is therefore legitimate for the Bank to take human rights into consideration as part of its economic decision-making process.

25 In conclusion, the Articles of Agreement permit, and in some cases require, the Bank to recognize the human rights dimensions of its development policies and activities since it is now evident that human rights are an intrinsic part of the Bank's mission.

Other institutions, such as the WTO, do not engage directly with communities the way development institutions do, but can still have a profound impact on human rights through the adoption of rules and policies and their interpretation. In the case of the WTO, the impact of its intellectual property rules on access to essential medicines has been singled out as an infringement of the right to health,[35] while its dispute settlement system has been criticised for the failure to take account of human rights principles when interpreting trade rules.[36] It has been argued that intergovernmental institutions such as the WTO are already bound by international human rights law, because the states that comprise

35 For more detailed examination of this issue, see A McBeth, 'When Nobody Comes to the Party: Why Have No States Used the WTO Scheme for the Compulsory Licensing of Essential Medicines?' (2006) 3 *New Zealand Yearbook of International Law* 69.

36 See discussion in S Joseph, *Blame it on the WTO? A Human Rights Critique*, Oxford University Press, Oxford, 2011, 50–5; A McBeth, *International Economic Actors and Human Rights*, Routledge, London, 2010, 101–13.

those institutions have human rights obligations which do not disappear just because the states are cooperating in an international forum rather than acting independently.[37]

While the position varies from one institution to another, international institutions generally acknowledge, to varying degrees, the relevance of human rights standards to their operations, but baulk at the idea of legal accountability for human rights. The member states that comprise the institutions are undoubtedly already bound by international human rights law in all of their actions, but when acting through the instrumentality of a multilateral institution, it is practically impossible to ascribe particular conduct to any given state or group of states, given the collective nature of decision-making in such institutions. In some institutions, the arm's-length nature of decision-making between states and the secretariat means that the relevant actions are really actions of the institution rather than collective actions of the member states, making a state responsibility approach quite artificial.

20.4.4 Armed Groups and Individuals

In a situation of non-international armed conflict between a state and a non-state group, such as an insurgency or a civil war, rules of international humanitarian law will apply to both sides,[38] even though only one side is an organ of a state or is able to be controlled by a state. The non-state forces will therefore be required to abide by rules protecting civilians from being targeted or cruelly treated, requiring the humane treatment of prisoners, and a wide range of other rules. Many of those international humanitarian law rules correspond with the protection of human rights of the vulnerable people concerned. Failure by individuals and commanders of the non-state forces to abide by international humanitarian law can lead to charges of war crimes, just as it can for their counterparts in the state's armed force.

Outside of armed conflict, individuals are generally the least problematic type of non-state actor for the traditional approach to international human rights law, because an individual can only be physically present in one state at a time, making it more straightforward to invoke the responsibility of the relevant state to protect human rights. Nevertheless, international criminal law—a body of law separate to international human rights law but effectively imposing accountability for gross violations of human rights in a particular context—imposes direct liability on individuals without going via the mechanism of the state. The objection that is sometimes raised against obligations for non-state actors—that they cannot consent to the obligations in the way that states can because they cannot be parties to a treaty[39]—has not prevented the direct liability of individuals under international criminal law.

From the international military tribunals at Nuremberg and Tokyo following the Second World War, through ad hoc criminal tribunals set up following the conflicts in the Former Yugoslavia and Rwanda, international law has held individuals directly responsible for the most egregious crimes arising from each conflict.

---

37 See, for example, A Clapham, *Human Rights Obligations of Non-State Actors*, Oxford University Press, Oxford 2006, 161–77; A McBeth, *International Economic Actors and Human Rights*, Routledge, London, 2010, 328–9.

38 In particular, common article 3 of the *Geneva Conventions and Additional Protocol II to the Geneva Conventions*.

39 This is what Clapham calls 'the legal impossibility argument'. See A Clapham, above, n 37, 35–41 for an explanation of the argument, which he ultimately dismisses as unconvincing.

> Since 2002, the International Criminal Court has provided a standing forum for the trial of individuals for international crimes.
>
> Given that individuals cannot conclude treaties and can neither consent nor object to the development of a norm of customary international law, since customary norms are based upon the practice and *opinio juris* of states, individuals prosecuted on this basis are being held to legal obligations to which they did not consent and from which they could not opt out. Indeed, in the case of the ad hoc tribunals, individual defendants were prosecuted for crimes that were not codified by tribunals that did not exist at the time the crimes were committed. In those cases, despite arguments about the legitimacy of the process at the time, customary international law was deemed capable of imposing obligations upon non-state actors, and the existence of a customary norm at the relevant time in the absence of a mechanism to enforce the corresponding obligation was not considered to preclude prosecutions for violating those obligations once an enforcement mechanism was established.
>
> Extrapolating from the example of international criminal law, it is clear that non-state actors can plausibly be said to be bound directly by norms of international law, even if such obligations are not set out in a written instrument. It is also clear that the absence of a mechanism for the enforcement of such a norm today does not preclude the existence of an obligation, nor the enforcement of that obligation if and when an enforcement mechanism is established.[40]

However, in international human rights law, as opposed to international criminal law, individuals and groups are not currently considered to hold direct obligations. Because the state-based system for the protection of human rights works reasonably well in relation to individuals, as individuals generally cannot operate beyond the control of a given state the way corporations and institutions sometimes can, the call for direct human rights obligations is not as strong for individuals as it is for those other categories of non-state actor.

20.4.5 Conclusions on Non-State Actors

Entities other than states clearly can and do affect human rights in profound ways, both for good and bad. Positive international human rights law is currently deficient in imposing direct obligations on non-state actors, even if such obligations can be inferred in some situations. Perhaps more crucially, international law currently lacks accountability mechanisms for non-state actors in relation to human rights, making enforcement all but impossible except through states, even if obligations can be identified. However, the focus on the responsibility of entities other than states for human rights is undoubtedly a growth area for the near future. The acceptance of the relevance of human rights to the World Bank, and the recognition, in the course of Professor Ruggie's work, of a duty of corporations to respect human rights are two developments that would have been unthinkable at the turn of the 21st century. The next step to direct, enforceable legal obligation has not yet been taken, but is at least foreseeable.

40 A McBeth, 'Every Organ of Society: The Responsibility of Non-State Actors for the Realization of Human Rights' (2008) 30 *Hamline Journal of Public Law and Policy* 33 at 69.

APPENDIX 1

UN DOCUMENT SYMBOLS[1]

A symbol serves as a unique identifier for a United Nations document. Each symbol is composed of numbers and letters which do not give any significant indication of the subject of a document. All language versions of a document carry the same symbol.

FIRST COMPONENT

Usually, the first component indicates the organ to which the document is being submitted or the organ that is issuing the document:

A/-	General Assembly
S/-	Security Council
E/-	Economic and Social Council
ST/-	Secretariat

Some bodies have a special series symbol that does not reflect the parent organ. For example:

CRC/C/-	Committee on the Rights of the Child
DP/-	United Nations Development Programme
TD/-	United Nations Conference on Trade and Development
UNEP/-	United Nations Environment Programme

SECOND COMPONENT

Secondary and tertiary components indicate subsidiary bodies:

-/AC. .../-	Ad hoc committee
-/C. .../-	Standing, permanent, or main committee
-/CN. .../-	Commission

1 <http://www.un.org/Depts/dhl/resguide/symbol.htm>

-/CONF. .../-	Conference
-/GC. .../-	Governing council
-/PC/. .../-	Preparatory committee
-/SC. .../-	Subcommittee
-/Sub. .../-	Subcommission
-/WG. .../-	Working group

SPECIAL COMPONENTS

Special components reflect the nature of the document:

-/CRP. ...	Conference room paper
-/INF/-	Information series (e.g., lists of participants)
-/L. ...	Limited distribution (i.e., generally draft documents)
-/NGO/-	Statements by non-governmental organizations
-/PET/-	Petitions
-/PRST/-	Statements by the President of the Security Council
-/PV. ...	Verbatim records of meetings (i.e., proces-verbaux)
-/R. ...	Restricted distribution; restricted access (unless subsequently derestricted)
-/RES/-	Resolutions
-/SR. ...	Summary records of meetings
-/WP. ...	Working papers

FINAL COMPONENT

The final component, appearing as a suffix to a symbol, reflects modifications to the original text:

-/Add. ...	Addendum
-/Amend. ...	Alteration, by decision of a competent authority, of a portion of an adopted formal text
-/Corr. ...	Corrigendum (which may not apply to all language versions)
-/Rev. ...	Revision (replacing texts previously issued)
-/Summary	Summarized version
-/-*	Reissuance of a document for technical reasons

SESSION OR YEAR COMPONENT

Many document symbols now include sessional or year elements, usually following the components that indicate the body. This was not the case prior to 1976 when the General Assembly began this practice. Other organs adopted similar practices. Subsidiary bodies generally follow the practice of the parent organ.

The General Assembly began to incorporate the session number into the symbols of its documents in 1976, at its 31st session (eg, A/31/99).

In 1978, the Economic and Social Council began incorporating the year into the symbols of its documents (eg, E/1978/99).

The Security Council began doing the same in 1994 (eg, S/1994/99), with the exception of resolutions and meeting records.

EXAMPLES

A/64/1	General Assembly, 64th session, document no. 1
A/CONF.157/PC/63/Add.4	General Assembly, World Conference on Human Rights, Preparatory Committee, document no. 63, addendum no. 4
E/CN.4/Sub.2/2003/38/Rev.2	Economic and Social Council, Commission on Human Rights, Subcommission on the Promotion and Protection of Human Rights, year: 2003, document no. 38, revision no. 2

INDEX